AF615403

LIBRARY
NETWORK

Proceedings

SUPERCOMPUTING '88

November 14-18, 1988
Orlando, Florida

Sponsored by
IEEE Computer Society and ACM SIGARCH 

IEEE Computer Society Order Number 882
Library of Congress Number 88-70918
IEEE Catalog Number 88CH2617-9
ACM Order Number 415883
ISBN 0-8186-0882-X

THE INSTITUTE OF ELECTRICAL AND ELECTRONICS ENGINEERS, INC.

The papers in this book comprise the proceedings of the meeting mentioned on the cover and title page. They reflect the authors' opinions and are published as presented and without change, in the interests of timely dissemination. Their inclusion in this publication does not necessarily constitute endorsement by the editors, the IEEE Computer Society Press, or The Institute of Electrical and Electronics Engineers, Inc.

Published by IEEE Computer Society Press
1720 Massachussetts Avenue, NW
Washington, DC 20036-1903

Cover designed by Jack I. Ballestero

IEEE Computer Society Order Number 882
Library of Congress Number 88-70918
IEEE Catalog Number 88CH2617-9
ISBN 0-8186-0882-X (paper)
ISBN 0-8186-4882-1 (microfiche)
ISBN 0-8186-8882-3 (case)
ACM Order Number 415883

Order from:

IEEE Computer Society
Terminal Annex
PO Box 4699
Los Angeles, CA 90080

IEEE Computer Society
13, avenue de l'Aquilon
B-1200 Brussels
BELGIUM

IEEE Computer Society
Ooshima Building
2-19-1 Minami-Aoyama, Minato-ku
Tokyo 107, JAPAN

IEEE Service Center
445 Hoes Lane
PO Box 1331
Piscataway, NJ 08855-1331

Association for Computing Machinery
Order Department
PO Box 64145
Baltimore, MD 21264

These organizations should be contacted before placing an order to determine availability of past Proceedings.

Foreword

Supercomputing '88 is the first of a new series of technical meetings for all those connected with supercomputers: manufacturers, suppliers, and users from a wide variety of disciplines. Sponsored by the ACM SIGARCH and the IEEE Computer Society, with the cooperation of SIAM and a number of national laboratories and federal agencies, this conference is the result of the creative collaboration of everyone on the committees. Ideas came from everybody and, by working together, we have built something we believe all of you will like. Our goal is to make this conference series a real clearinghouse for state-of-the-art technical activities and research in supercomputing.

Since this is a new series, we are trying a lot of new things. The North American Computer Chess Championship matches will be held in conjunction with the event. We have arranged many things so that the attendees may have the opportunity for hands-on interactions with the hardware and for meeting with other participants. Certainly, there will be the usual sessions with speakers to listen to, but we don't expect things to stop there.

We're delighted that approximately thirty companies will show their products in the vendor exhibits area.. Some of the vendors plan to install high-speed communications links to their home facilities, thereby allowing live, full-scale demonstrations of their state-of-the-art capabilities, products, and services.

The poster sessions will include snacks and cash bar, giving you another opportunity to interact with your colleagues. Researchers from universities and government labs have agreed to transport portions of their equipment to the conference where they will demonstrate their work and, in some cases, let attendees try hands-on experiments.

Today, the use of supercomputers has transformed practically all the natural sciences and engineering disciplines. But, it's not all grind, grind. Interspersed with the serious work are flashes of neat insights, humor, and fun. We have arranged some activities that demonstrate some of these novel ideas. There will be a presentation about some of the great hacks from MIT and Cal Tech. In addition, we have arranged for the first winners of the "Great Parallel Computing Race" – the Bell Prize – to discuss, informally, high performance computing and competitions. We have some of the most articulate spokesmen from the Free Software Institute coming to discuss the question of how to distribute software without having to hire an army of lawyers. There is a session on some of the more unusual applications of supercomputing and, finally, the Visualization Theatre will show some exciting pictures produced by supercomputers.

During the conference, (real) users will discuss the calculations they wish/need to make. (Real) technologists will talk about what's possible. (Real) manufacturers will outline what they can build. All this activity is aimed at you, the (real) attendees. Our aim is to create an aura of excitement and exuberance, so that you'll want to join in the discussions.

The program committee received a number of excellent papers. We could accept only about 40% of the submissions, but it would be wrong to say the rest were rejected. Of course, some were, but so many were of good enough quality that the committee took the unprecedented step of recommending those papers to various professional journals. In addition, the committee invited papers to cover topics that were not covered adequately by the submitted papers.

We expect that you will find the invited keynote speakers to be very interesting. Our first one will be Seymour Cray of Cray Research. Our banquet speaker will be Carl Conti of IBM Enterprise Systems. And later in the week, our third speaker will be Carl Ledbetter of ETA Systems.

All in all, this conference looks like a whizz-bang; excellent technical material and time to consider it all! We have built it with you in mind; if you are involved in supercomputing, this is your conference.

Obviously, there may be some things we didn't get right this time. Please use the opinion questionnaires to tell us what was wrong and (perhaps) how to fix it. If you have a pet idea, or just want to volunteer to help at the next conference, please tell us that, too.

Finally, plans are already well under way for our 1989 conference. We invite you all to join us next year, and in future years, to share the latest progress in supercomputing with your peers.

George A. Michael
General Chairman

Stephen F. Lundstrom
Program Chairman

Supercomputing '88

Executive Committee

General Chairman
George A. Michael
Lawrence Livermore National Laboratory

Program Chairman
Stephen F. Lundstrom
Consultant

Deputy Chairman
Robert G. Voigt
NASA Langley Research Center

Exhibits Chairman
Roger Anderson
Lawrence Livermore National Laboratory

Finance Chairman
Sidney Fernbach
Control Data Corporation

Arrangements Chairman
Dennis Duke
Florida State University

Publication Chairman
Harlow Freitag
Supercomputing Research Center

Publicity Chairman
George B. Adams III
Purdue University

Advisory Committee

F. Ron Bailey, *NASA Ames Research Center*
Robert Borchers, *Lawrence Livermore National Laboratory*
Bill Buzbee, *National Center for Atmospheric Research*
Melvin Ciment, *National Science Foundation*
Doug DeGroot, *ACM SIGARCH*
Jack Dongarra, *SIAM*
Joanne Martin, *IEEE Computer Society*
Norman R. Morse, *Los Alamos National Laboratory*
Paul Schneck, *Supercomputing Research Center*
Daniel Sorenson, *Argonne National Laboratory*

Supercomputing '88

Program Committee

Chairman
Stephen F. Lundstrom, *Consultant*

Duane Adams, *Carnegie Mellon University*
Robert G. Babb II, *Oregon Graduate Center (Poster Session Chair)*
Tor Bloch, *Unité Scientifique UESR*
Jean-Marie Cadious, *ESPRIT (Chair, European Subcommittee)*
David A. Carlson, *Supercomputing Research Center*
Ron Deiss, NINasa Ames Research Center
Jeffrey Deutsch, *Deutsch Research*
Jack Dongarra, *Argonne National Laboratory*
Iain Duff, *Harwell Laboratory*
Raymond Elliot, *Los Alamos National Laboratory*
Michael Flynn, *Stanford University*
Robert Flynn, *Polytechnic Institute*
Myron Ginsbert, *General Motors Research Laboratories*
Roger Hockney, *University of Reading*
Leah Jamieson, *Purdue University*
Howard L. Johnson, *Information Intelligence Sciences (Tutorial Chair)*
Hiroshi Kashiwagi, *Electrotechnical Laboratory (Chair, Japanese Subcommittee)*
Janusz S. Kowalik, *Boeing Computer Services*
John Levesque, *Pacific-Sierra Research*
Alain Lichnewsky, *INRIA*
Joanne Martin, *IBM (Science & Application Track Organizer)*
Edward McCluskey, *Stanford University*
Raul Mendez, *Institute for Supercomputing Research*
Hans Werner Meuer, *University of Mannheim*
Nenichi Miura, *Fujitsu America*
Eugene Miya, *NASA Ames Research Center*
Cleve Moler, *Ardent Computer*
Carl Moser, *University of Paris*
Bernie O'Lear, *National Center for Atmospheric Research*
Rodney R. Oldehoeft, *Colorado State University*
Constantine Polychronopoulos, *University of Illinois*
John E. Ranelletti, *Lawrence Livermore National Laboratory (Managers' Workshop Organizer)*
Pat Savage, *Shell Development*

REVIEWERS

Stuart Adams
Ramesh Agarwal
Roger Anderson
A. Auguskyn
Robert G. Babb II
David H. Bailey
Eric Barczcz
John Barton
Brace Baylor
Richard M. Beam
Boonsieng Benjauthrit
Philip Bitar
Tor Bloch
Ralph G. Brickner
Edward C. Bronson
Ingrid Bucher
Richard Buehrer
Duncan A. Buell
David A. Carlson
Robert Carpenter
Glenn L. Carter
Thomas Casavant
Albert Cazes
Tony Chan
Melvin Ciment
David Cohen
Neil B. Coletti
M. William Collins
John M. Conroy
Harvey Cragon
Edward Davidson
Doug DeGroot
Ron Deiss
Jeffrey Deutsch
Sudarshan Dhall
Robert J. Diersing
Henry Dietz
David C. DiNucci
Jack Dongarra
Jesse M. Draper
Daniel Drobnis
Michel Dubois
Iain Duff
Raymond Elliott
Perry Emrath
Paraskevas Evripidou
Antony Faustini
John Feo
Charlotte F. Fischer
Robert Flynn
Mike Flynn
Christian Fraboul
Paul O. Frederickson
John Gary
Jean Gaudiot
Myron Ginsberg
Milind Girkar
Raymond R. Glenn
Joseph Goodman
Vincent A. Guarna, Jr.
Adolfo Guzman
A. Hadjidimos
Lynda L. Haines
John Hanne
Ann Hayes
Mohammad Reza Hayhighat
Robert Hiromoto
Richard S. Hirsh
Roger Hockney
William Holmes
William C. Hopkins
Mark Horowitz
Elias Houstis
Wen-Jing Hsu
Ken Iobst
Mary Jane Irwin
Daniel Jablonski
William Jalby
Leah Jamieson
Greg Jaxon
Dennis Jespersen
Gary M. Johnson
Howard L. Johnson
Kirk E. Jordan
Sidney Karin
Lih-Hsing Ke
Rebecca Koskel
Suraj Kothari
Janusz S. Kowalik
Steven Kratzer
James T. Kuehn
Thomas A. Lasinski
Robert H. Leary
Ernst L. Leiss
John Levesque
Creon Levit
Z.N. Li
Alain Lichnewsky
Gary Lindstrom
Robert N. Linebarger
W.S. Luk
G. E. Lyon
Fred McClain
James Patrick McGee
Jim McGraw
Donald J. McMillan
Chris Mechels
Stephen Melvin
Phillip R. Merkey
Hans Werner Meuer
E. P. Meyer
George Michael
Randy Michelson
Alan Mink
Kenichi Miura
Eugene Miya
Cleve Moler
Reagan W. Moore
W.D. Moorhead
James Mundstock
Majid M. Naini
James Nechvatal
Dave Nelson
Tin-Fook Ngai
David M. Nicol
Bernie O'Lear
Eddy A. M. Odijk
Rodney R. Oldehoeft
Yakup Paker
Ian Parberry
Yale Patt
Vic Peterson
Ron Pfaff
Wayne Pfeiffer
Timothy M. Pinkston

REVIEWERS (continued)

Constantine Polychronopoulos
Jerry Potter
G.M. Prabhu
Dan Pryor
Arthur Ramer
John Ranelletti
Gregory Riccardi
John Riganatti
Pat Savage
Judith D. Schlesinger
Wayne Schroeder
Catherine Schulbach
Eugene P. Schumacher
Herb Schwetman
Mark Seager

Sanjay Sharma
Mark E. Sheddon
Yuan Shi
F. Sijsteumans
Margaret Simmons
Horst Simon
Joseph C. Slone
Marcelline C. Smith
Kim Smith
David Smitley
Thomas L. Sterling
Rick Stevens
Ken Stevens
Quentin Stout
Julie Swisshelm

Ping Tak Peter Tang
Josep Torrellas
Remi Triolet
E. A. Vavalis
Robert G. Voigt
Ken Wallgren
Tony T. Warnoch
Richard Warren
Harvey J. Wasserman
Yi-Hsiu Wei
Elizabeth Williams
Alan Wray
Chuan-lin Wu
Jerry Yan
Bonnie Yantis

Supercomputing '88

Table of Contents

Compiler Evaluation

Visualization

Compiler Technology

Operating Systems for Supercomputing

Mass Storage System - I

Supercomputer Performance

Algorithms - II

Supercomputing Center Management

Paper not received on time for publication.

Program Development

Chair: Jeffrey Deutsch
Deutsch Research

CFT-PREFINE: A Software Tool for Hand-Parallelizing Sequential Code

D. Klappholz and X. Kong

Paper not received in time for publication.

FAUST: AN ENVIRONMENT FOR PROGRAMMING PARALLEL SCIENTIFIC APPLICATIONS

Vincent A. Guarna, Jr., Dennis Gannon*, Yogesh Gaur, David Jablonowski

Center for Supercomputing Research and Development
University of Illinois at Urbana-Champaign
Urbana, Illinois 61801

Abstract

The subject of integrated programming environments for scientific computing has become very popular over the last few years. Environments such as R^n [3] are being constructed to help coordinate the disjoint activities of editing, debugging, and performance tuning typically seen in the development cycle for software for complex parallel architectures [13]. This paper overviews the Faust project at the Center for Supercomputing Research and Development at the University of Illinois. Faust is targeted at providing an integrated setting for the development of scientific applications. The overall structure of the Faust environment is presented, along with a discussion of some specific tools used to aid the applications programmer in the development of codes.

INTRODUCTION

Faust is a workstation-based programming environment for scientific applications currently being developed at the Center for Supercomputing Research and Development at the University of Illinois at Urbana-Champaign. The primary focus of Faust is to provide supercomputer users with a set of tools that makes the task of programming parallel machines easier. However, many of the problems encountered in the construction of such an environment are not specific to parallel programming. In particular, issues such as functional tool integration and uniformity of user interface are very basic problems which any computing environment must solve in order to be effective.

Faust Goals

The Faust project is directed toward several goals. The first goal is the design of a consistent user interface that can be used throughout all aspects of the program development cycle. This includes the development of a program abstraction mechanism that is useful during program editing, debugging, and performance tuning phases. The chosen model is a combination of graphical and textual representations for application programs. The textual source code presentation serves as the user's detailed view of an application, whereas hierarchical graphs serve as higher-level views that can be automatically generated to show inter-subroutine and inter-task relationships.

A second goal is portability. The Faust environment assumes the existence of a bitmapped workstation running the Unix** operating system and the X Windows System developed at MIT [8, 14]. X Windows is a general windowing environment enjoying increasing popularity in the graphic workstation market. By relying on X for primitive interactive I/O support, the Faust environment can migrate to additional machines as X implementations become available.

A third goal to be accomplished is non-intrusiveness of the environment. Faust is intended to be compatible with "conventional" Unix operations. The environment is not considered to be a "sealed" system -- users may wish to do some operations within the context of Faust while doing other operations with traditional shell commands. One main objective of the Faust project is the development of a user interface strategy that allows both modes of operation to coexist.

Architecture

The organization of the Faust environment is shown in Figure 1. The lines between boxes indicate paths of communications between system elements. As can be seen, program development tools such as compilers and editors can directly access the Unix file system. However, additional paths to the Faust support libraries have been created in order to facilitate the addition of a unified user interface that can be supported by all applications. The user interface functions comprise a library of routines for handling low-level functions such as displaying graphic and text primitives. However, it also contains the mechanics for the maintenance of a hierarchical program abstraction. This abstraction allows the user to view application programs in varying levels of detail, from a textual view of source code to a high-level graphical view of function and task relationships. The following sections describe the details of the user interface library and the hierarchical program abstraction as well as some examples of development tools which use them.

USER INTERFACE

The Faust user interface library comprises several components, including libraries for managing windows, user input,

*Department of Computer Science, Indiana University

**Unix is a trademark of AT&T Bell Laboratories.

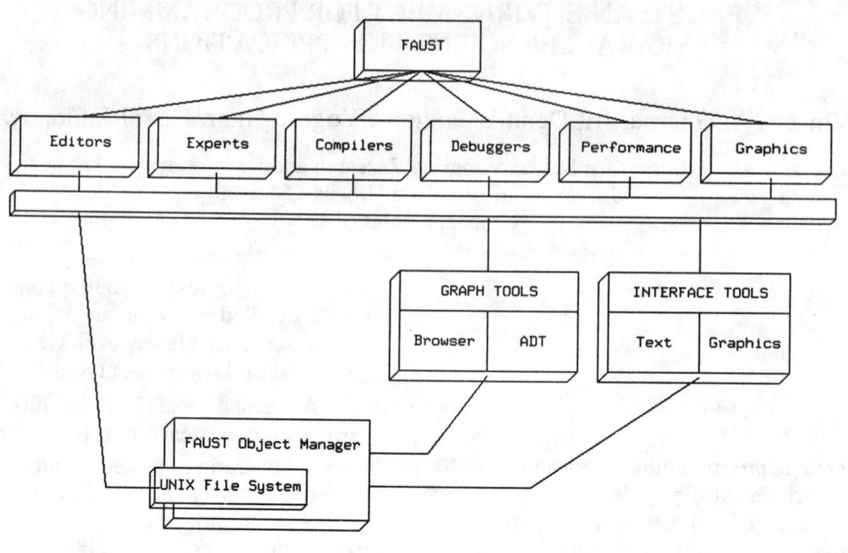

Figure 1. Architecture of the Faust environment

text objects, graphic objects, and application program objects. These libraries are collectively referred to as the Interface Manager (IM), and are described in the following sections.

Window Management

In any windowing environment, a user expects to have complete control of the images on his workstation screen. Faust makes minimal assumptions regarding the size and location of existing windows when new windows are created. Additionally, for simplicity, Faust windows can be manipulated by the window managers supplied with X Windows so that users who have familiarity with X realize a smoother transition to the Faust environment.

It is sometimes desirable to treat a series of windows as one collective unit. For example, Faust supports a performance analysis tool which shows the dynamic execution of eight processors in ten individual Faust windows [5] (see Figure 2). Since these windows represent a single user application, it is convenient for the user to treat them as a single entity. When one window is raised or brought up, all windows are raised. When one window is moved, others are also moved. To solve this problem, Faust allows applications to specify a group of windows that are to be treated as a single group for the purpose of window movement, raising, and lowering.

Text and Graph Operations

The Interface Manager contains a collection of routines for maintaining text objects in the system. The text handling subsystem provides an abstract data type for textual objects, including edit, search, and display functions. The rationale for including such a package in the Faust library is to promote reusability of basic functions to reduce development time of higher-level tools.

The Interface Manager also contains a collection of routines for maintaining graphic objects in the system. In addition to supporting a set of graphic primitives for drawing simple figures such as lines, circles, and boxes, the IM provides an extensive set of utilities for operating specific structures called *program graphs*. Program graphs and associated operations are described in detail in later sections.

The Sigma Editor

Sigma [6] is a Faust programming tool designed to help users of parallel supercomputers retarget and optimize application codes. In a sense, the system can be viewed as a tool to help users ''fine-tune'' the output of an automatic system or, if he or she has been so inspired, optimize the design of a new parallel algorithm.

Each program that enters the Sigma editor is completely parsed and all data dependences are recorded. The user then works with the system to restructure his code to a form suitable

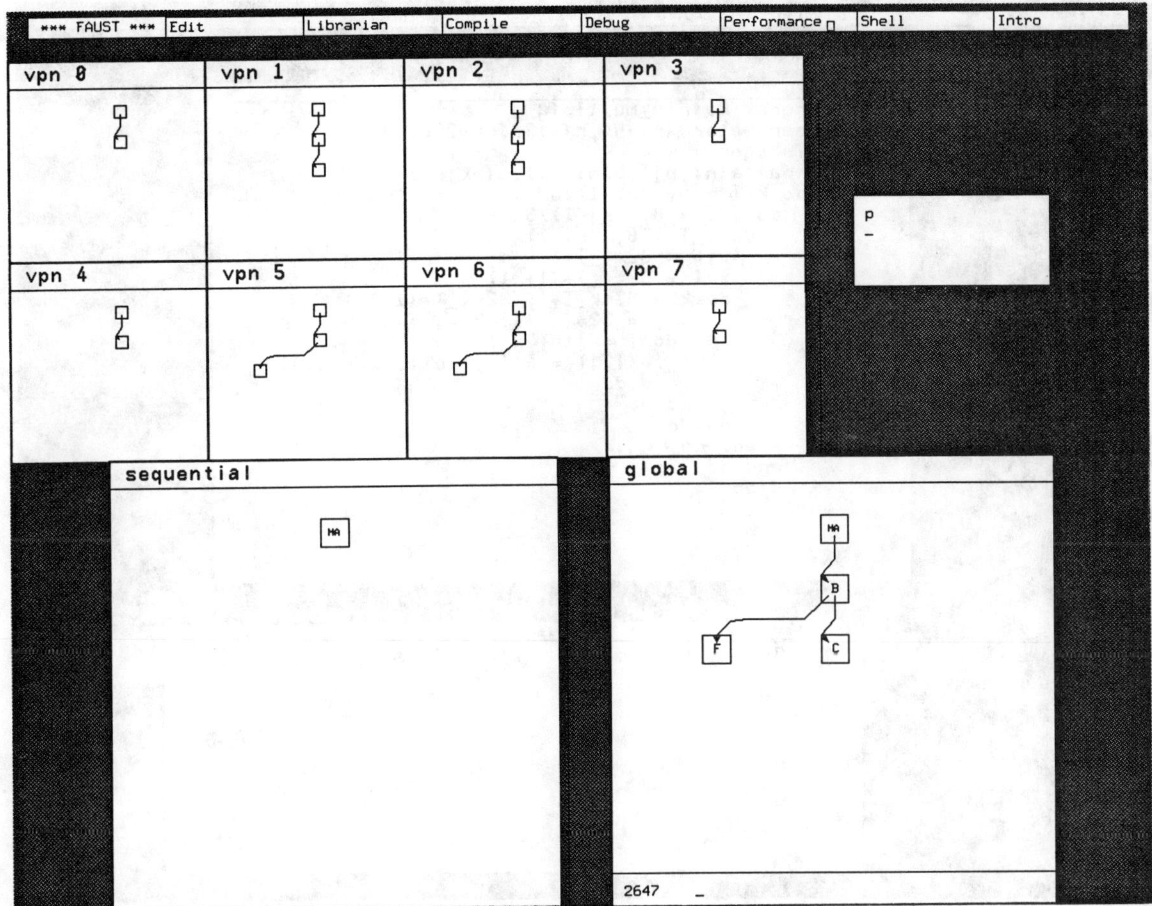

Figure 2. Dynamic Call Graph Monitoring Tool

for a given target architecture. If the target is known to the system, it monitors the user's transformations to the code. If the user attempts to transform the program in violation of the original semantics of the code he is warned that a change in the meaning of his program has taken place. At any time the user can ask the system to tell him what legal parallelizing transformation can be applied to a segment of selected code. More important, he can ask the system to make the program modifications the user desires. In this mode, the user is assured of the correctness of the changes in his code.

In its current form, Sigma can support FORTRAN (with Cedar and Alliant 8x [1] extensions), Blaze (a Pascal based functional language designed by Mehrotra and Van Rosendale [11]), and C with object-oriented extensions similar to C++ and Cedar Parallel C [9]. The target machines supported currently include the BBN Butterfly, the Alliant FX/8 and the Cedar System.

A Sample User Scenario. Sigma is designed to aid users in porting large applications to parallel machines such as the Illinois Cedar Multiprocessor. The first step in any such porting effort is to try any automatic restructuring optimization tools that are available for the target machine. For large applications, these will sometimes provide the needed performance without much effort on the part of the programmer. Unfortunately, for large, parallel MIMD machines like Cedar, these tools often fail to extract the parallelism that exists at a high level in the program structure that is often called "medium grain" or "coarse grain" concurrency. It is also often the case that this is exactly the type of parallelism that is best supported by the machine's parallel organization.

Once the application program has been compiled and tested the Faust system will have compiled a large amount of information that becomes part of the application program data base. This includes three primary components :

(1) Performance statistics, including static performance prediction information and binary code analysis.

(2) Data dependence analysis information used for global flow analysis and program transformation verification.

(3) Version control information about optimized and unoptimized copies of the source files.

After the code has been compiled and the performance information loaded into the data base, the programmer may

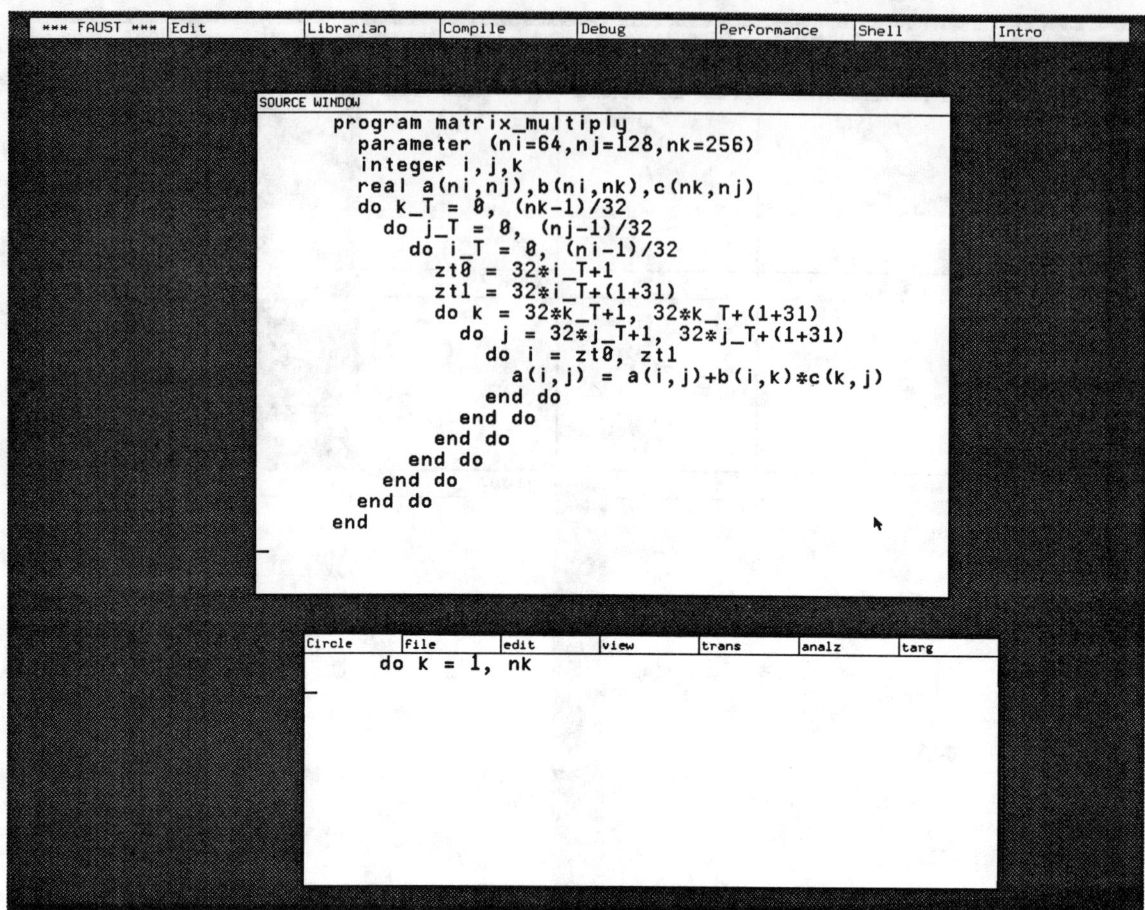

Figure 3. Multidimensional block transformation applied to a nested loop

have some idea how the program may be parallelized. The next step is to start the process of restructuring the program by transforming various segments of the code to express more parallelism. A simple example is presented to illustrate how a user would interact with the restructuring part of the system. Figure 3 shows a Sigma session in which the programmer is investigating a simple matrix multiplication subroutine.

The first thing the programmer may wish to do is tell the system which machine is the intended target of this optimization. Currently this menu lists three choices: the BBN butterfly, the Alliant FX/8, and the Illinois Cedar. In the case at hand, an optimization for the Alliant FX/8 is considered.

The reason for having the programmer tell the system about the choice of target is threefold. First, selecting the target machine enables the system to generate code for the given target. Second, selecting the target allows the system to disable program transformations that are inappropriate for the target machine. Third, selecting the target allows the system to enable the appropriate performance estimators which give the programmer immediate feed-back about the suitability of various transformations to the code. Currently, the system supports a cache use estimator (see [7]) and is being extended to provide an estimator for predicting vector instruction use efficiency.

For the example loop nest in Figure 3, the Alliant automatic vectorizing/parallelizing compiler would choose to parallelize the middle loop and either vectorize the inner loop or, if the loops are properly ordered, substitute a vector dot product instruction. This works very well for small matrices, but degrades by an order of magnitude for larger problems. To understand why this is the case, one needs to understand the Alliant memory system. In the FX/8, all processors share a common cache of 512K bytes. When data resides in cache, vector operations work at full speed on each processor; but, when the problem size grows, the algorithm sweeps over rows of the matrix and the cache is quickly filled. The next time the row is accessed the data is no longer in cache, so it must be refetched from memory. To avoid this problem, it is best to partition the iteration space into small blocks so that the computation takes the form of a matrix multiply where the elements are themselves matrices. This has the advantage that the data needed to multiply two of the submatrices will remain in cache until the submatrix multiply is complete.

Among the basic transformations supported by Sigma is a transformation (called multidimensional block) that will block

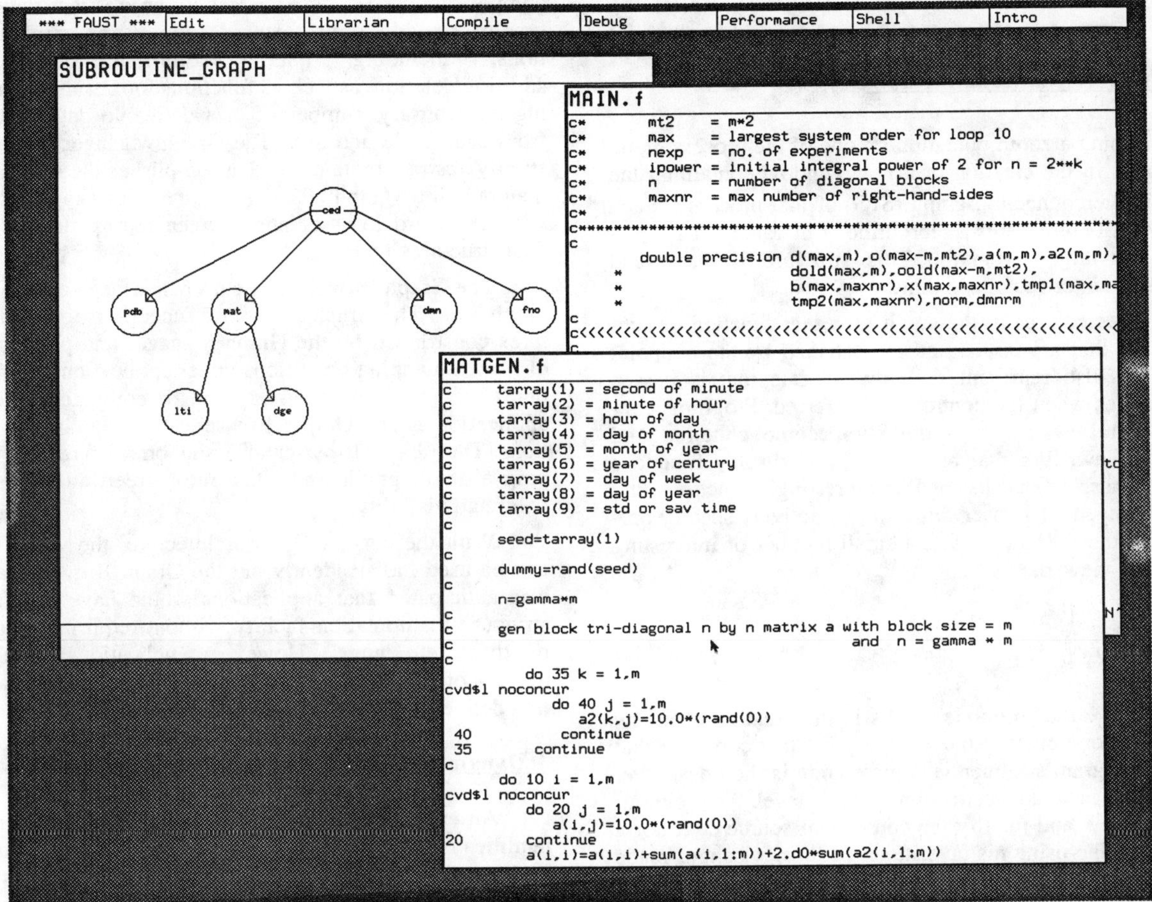

Figure 4. Fortran source code and associate SIG

any suitably nested loop into the form described above. In Figure 3, the user has selected the outermost loop with the mouse, and next invoked the transformation by selecting the correct menu entry. Sigma then checks to make sure no data dependences prohibit this operation and then makes the transformation. The resulting loop is also shown in Figure 3. The next step in this optimization is to vectorize the innermost loop and apply concurrency to one of the other loops. The result is a program that outperforms the original code by a factor of 6 on large matrices.

HIERARCHICAL PROGRAM ABSTRACTIONS

The Faust environment supports a representation for programs that is graphical as well as textual. Although the conventional source text model is still available to the programmer, higher level abstractions such as static subroutine call graphs and task/process graphs are useful in understanding overall program structure more readily. Just as graphic images can be used to render a concise representation of large volumes of output data, graphic program structures can be a useful tool for the programmers wishing to elide much of the source-level implementation details in favor of perusing a terse representation of an application's architecture.

The Faust program abstraction supports three levels of detail. These are the process graph, the subroutine interconnection graph, and the program source code. The Faust Interface Manager provides the facility to traverse levels of the hierarchy with the "zoom" and "unzoom" commands. Zoom and unzoom are reserved input events trapped by the input handler in program application windows. These operations are initiated by the user and the response is handled by the IM, transparent to the client application program. Each level of the abstraction is described in more detail in the next three sections.

Process Graphs

The highest level of the program abstraction is the process graph. Each node in the process graph represents an individual process or task - a parallel running entity. Nodes are created by issuing a "fork" style call in the target program. Directed arcs that connect these nodes represent the direction in which the fork was initiated and the data that was passed to the spawned task at creation.

Subroutine Interconnection Graphs

Performing a zoom operation on one of the process graph nodes results in the creation of a new window containing the subroutine interconnection graph (SIG) of that process*. Each node in the SIG represents a subroutine or hierarchy of subroutines in the target program. This structure is static and represents the inter-module binding.

The directed arcs in the graph represent function or subroutine calls that are issued and are satisfied by the endpoint nodes. They also represent the flow of data that is passed between nodes when the control is transferred. Programs containing several system calls quickly become cluttered and difficult to view. For that reason, the SIG display functions reference a user-defined list of ''uninteresting'' functions that are not displayed. The user can also interactively specify portions of the tree to hide so that a small number of interesting nodes can be viewed.

Source Windows

Zooming on a SIG node results in the creation of a new window that contains the source statements that comprise that node. The program's sequential source code is the finest level of detail in the program abstraction. At this level, the programmer may review and modify the constituent source code for a single subroutine using his favorite text editor. Changes made to the source which result in changes to the associated subroutine interconnection graph are ''remembered'' by the Interface Manager, and cause the regeneration of the SIG the next time the graph is to be displayed. Figure 4 shows some example Fortran source code and the associated subroutine interconnection graph.

The ''unzoom'' function works exactly in reverse to zoom. Unzoom operations from a particular level of detail result in the creation of a new window containing the next higher level of detail. In order to support the zoom and unzoom functions, the Interface Manager maintains a list of associations between source files and graph structures. Consistency checks are made when zoom and unzoom operations are requested by the user in order to guarantee the display of consistent information. New graph structures are rebuilt only when time-stamp information indicates that it is necessary.

SOME GRAPH-BASED PROGRAMMING TOOLS

Many techniques for the graphic visualization of the programming process are being explored in Faust through the use of a generalized Graph Manager/Browser tool that is built into the user interface [10]. The Graph Manager/Browser (GMB) comprises two major components (see Figure 1). The first component, the Graph Manager, is an abstract data type for graphs, providing full-featured support for graph manipulations, including node addition/deletion and arc addition/deletion, as well as functions for attaching and retrieving an arbitrary number of user-definable data fields to and from each node and arc. The Graph Manager is meant to be strictly abstract in nature and accomplishes the sole function of manipulating graph data structures for application tasks without regard to associating screen representations with the data structures.

The Graph Browser is the user-interface component of the graph tool. The Graph Browser's function is to use data structures constructed by the Graph Manager and perform a series of screen-mapping operations under application control. Attributes such as graph geometry can be computed by either the application or the Graph Browser, at the application's discretion. The Graph Browser also supports the facility for mapping abstract graph node data into screen attributes such as color and visibility.

With the current GMB architecture, the Graph Manager can be used independently but the Graph Browser can not. It was anticipated that applications would have use for a data structure manipulation facility without requiring visualization of those structures. However, applications requiring the display of graphical entities through the Graph Browser must first define those graphical entities to the Graph Manager.

A Dynamic Parallel Program Monitoring Tool

An example of a development tool which uses the GMB facilities is the dynamic call graph tool that is supported by the Faust performance evaluation system [5]. This tool is intended to provided an ''animated'' view of a program's execution to aid the user in understanding its operation*. The dynamic call graph tool displays the dynamic execution of a parallel program in the context of the original subroutine interconnection graph generated by the GMB. Dynamic execution is shown in **n** + 2 Graph Browser windows, where **n** is the number of processors allocated to the program (see Figure 2). In the example shown in Figure 2, the target machine is an Alliant FX/8 and **n** is 8. The first n windows each show the state of one processor's execution. One window shows the state of the program's call graph when it transitioned from a sequential execution mode to a parallel execution mode, and one window displays the union of all of the other views. By using the Graph Browser's multiple view facilities, the dynamic call graph tool is able to generate all of these windows from the single subroutine interconnection graph associated with an application.

A Graphical Makefile Tool

One program development tool that is easily constructed with the Interface Manager is a graphical version of the Unix ''Make'' utility [4]. The graphical makefile editor allows the user to specify program dependences by graphically creating a

*The words ''process'' and ''task'' are used somewhat interchangeably in this section. They are meant to represent a single thread of processor execution, not necessarily the traditional Unix process.

*Similar display and animation techniques are described in [12] and [2].

tree. At the root of the tree is the executable object that is to be created through local or remote compilations. The next level of the tree consists of all of the object files required to generate the executable. Each object file serves as the root of a subtree which defines all files necessary to generate it.

The graphical makefile editor highlights those executable files which are out of date or inconsistent to remind the user which recompilations need to be performed. The user may specify specific subtrees to be recompiled or allow the system to perform all necessary build operations.

The rationale for developing the graphical makefile editor is twofold. First, it serves as a nice demonstration of the Interface Manager tools with relatively little development effort. Second, the nature of traditional makefiles was seen as tedious, making the investigation of a graphical approach attractive. Although building makefiles through the graphical editing tool requires as much (if not more) effort than standard makefiles, the final product appears to be more intuitive, giving users a better understanding of the relationships in the program. Additionally, the graphical representation provides a convenient method for inspecting the state of the application with respect to object file consistencies. The graphical representation also gives the application writer a convenient platform on which to specify changes to the application building procedure for localized changes such as algorithm replacement and automatic instrumentation insertion.

SUMMARY

Five years ago the subject of Parallel Computation was an exotic sub-field of computer science that consisted largely of theoretical studies of potential parallel algorithm performance, a few university hardware projects, even fewer software design efforts, and (with the exception of Denelcor) no industrial products. Five years later, we now find that all U.S. supercomputers, and over one dozen mini-supercomputer vendors have entered the market with some form of general purpose parallel processing system.

Unfortunately, very few of these systems provide a software environment for building parallel programs that goes beyond a standard sequential language compiler and a microtasking library to support parallelism. None of our most widely used programming languages (C, Fortran, Lisp) have been given official extensions to support concurrency and no two vendors agree on any of the unofficial extensions. The task of porting parallel codes from one machine to another now involves large amounts of recoding to make a program work, and large amounts of restructuring of the algorithm organization to make it work well.

This paper has presented a brief sketch of the Faust programming environment and illustrated several of its development tools. Not covered in this paper are several other tools such as the Faust Parallel Program Debugger, an expert system librarian and full performance analysis package for the Cedar system. Faust is far from being a finished product; in fact, revisions and additions of tools are expected to continue for a long time. The current status of the project is that a first ''alpha'' version will be in the hands of the CSRD applications group by the Fall of 1988. A public distribution will follow in the next year.

ACKNOWLEDGEMENTS

Several people are responsible for the progress and existence of the Faust project. The authors wish to acknowledge James Krause, David Kuck, Duncan Lawrie, Paul Lewis, Allen Malony, and Dan Reed for the efforts already expended as well as the continuing support being provided on behalf of Faust.

The Faust Project is supported in part by the National Science Foundation under Grants No. US NSF MIP-8410110, the U. S. Department of Energy under Grant No. US DOE-DE-FG02-85ER25001, the U.S. Air Force Office of Scientific Research Grant No. AFOSR-F49620-86-C-0136, and the IBM Donation.

REFERENCES

[1] Alliant Computer Systems Corporation. *FX/Fortran Language Manual, Volumes 1 and 2.*, Littleton, Massachusetts, 1987.

[2] M. H. Brown. ''Techniques for Algorithm Animation,'' *IEEE Software* (Jan., 1985), Vol. 2, No. 1, pp. 28-39.

[3] A. Carle, K. D. Cooper, R. T. Hood, K. Kennedy, L. Torczon and S. K. Warren. ''A Practical Environment for Scientific Programming,'' *IEEE Computer* (Nov., 1987), Vol. 20, No. 11, pp. 75-89.

[4] S. I. Feldman. ''Make - A Program for Maintaining Computer Programs,'' *UNIX Programmer's Manual, Reference Guide--4.2 Berkeley Software Distribution* (March, 1984).

[5] K. A. Gallivan, W. Jalby, A. D. Malony and P. C. Yew. ''Performance Analysis on the CEDAR System,'' In: *Performance Evaluation of Supercomputers*, J.L. Martin, ed. Elsevier Science Publ. (North-Hollan), Amsterdam, The Netherlands, 1987.

[6] D. Gannon, D. Atapattu, M. H. Lee and B. Shei. ''A Software Tool For Building Supercomputing Applications,'' *Parallel Computations and Their Impact on Mechanics* (December, 1987), Vol. 86, pp. 81-92.

[7] D. Gannon, W. Jalby and K. Gallivan. ''Strategies for Cache and Local Memory Management by Global Program Transformation,'' *Proceedings 1987 International Conference on Supercomputing* (1987).

[8] J. Gettys, R. Newman and T. D. Fera. ''Xlib - C Language X Interface Protocol Version 11,'' *Programming With the X Window System* (September, 1987).

[9] V. A. Guarna Jr. ''VPC - A Proposal For a Vector Parallel C Programming Language'', CSRD Report No. 666, Univ. Of Illinois, Center for Supercomputer Research and Development, June, 1987.

[10] D. Jablonowski and V. A. Guarna Jr. ''A Dynamic Graph Tool and Its Use in an Integrated Programming Environment'', CSRD Report No. 746, February, 1988.

[11] P. Mehrotra and J. R. V. Rosendale. ''The BLAZE Language: A Parallel Language for Scientific Programming'', NASA Langley Research Center, Hampton, Va., May, 1985.

[12] B. A. Meyers. ''Incense: A System for Displaying Data Structures,'' *Computer Graphics* (Jul., 1983), Vol. 17, No. 3, pp. 115-125.

[13] D. Padua, V. A. Guarna Jr. and D. Lawrie. ''Supercomputer Programming Environments,'' *Parallel Computations and Their Impact on Mechanics* (December, 1987), Vol. 86, pp. 55-79.

[14] R. W. Scheifler and J. Gettys. ''The X Window System,'' *Programming With the X Window System* (November, 1986).

PARALLEL ALGORITHM DEVELOPMENT WORKBENCH

Siamak Arya and Blaine Gaither

Gould Inc.,
Computer Systems Division
15378 Avenue of Science
San Diego, California 92128

ABSTRACT

This paper proposes an approach, and a resulting tool, for developing algorithms for parallel processors. The problems in developing efficient algorithms for parallel systems are discussed. The objectives of this approach are to support the evaluation of the expected efficiency of algorithms on various interconnection network architectures before detailed code is written, optimization of interconnection network facility usage, and efficient evaluation of and tuning of codes (both systems and applications) to the CPU hardware. This proposed approach can be extended for the evaluation of alternative processor architectures as well.

This approach and associated tool will take information about computation and communication times and provide information about elapsed time, idle spots, conflicts,and deadlocks. This is achieved by modeling various aspects of the system in different levels of detail. The Communications Network is modeled by a discrete event simulation with stochastic service assumptions. These stochastic service assumptions can be refined by the invocation of a cluster model which takes into account more details of resource contention and delays within a group of processors. Finally, a trace driven model of internal CPU timing can be used to replace statistical assumptions and represent precise timing of application code such as information on the extent to which chaining occurs and the utilization of functional units. These components work together to achieve the objectives discussed above.

The proposed tool uses hierarchical simulation and provides a workbench environment for algorithm development. Transfer of data is represented via a high level notation which is independent of Interconnection Network architecture. The types of instrumentation and statistics required are discussed, as well as techniques under investigation for graphical representation of results. The structure of the simulator hierarchy, methods for extending the use of the model to evaluate real code, and the role of the modeling tool when used as part of a debugging environment are discussed. The processor model and the interpreter have currently been implemented. The remaining portions of the workbench are under incremental implementation.

INTRODUCTION

Efficient programming of parallel processing systems is a sophisticated task and requires powerful algorithm development tools. Most of the existing algorithms designed for uniprocessor environments must be modified or redesigned to efficiently execute on parallel systems. Any modification to an algorithm will require a reevaluation of its performance. A modification to the algorithm to speed up the computation in a processor may result in a less efficient algorithm due to increased cost of synchronization or increased ratio of communication to computation. Evaluation of algorithms on parallel processor is a complicated task due to the number of resources involved. Therefore, a tool that can assist in such development through automatic and rapid evaluation of parallel processing algorithms on pre-specified systems is greatly desired and necessary.

A parallel processing algorithm is considered efficient if the reduction in computation time due to parallelization far exceeds the synchronization and communication overheads. These overheads are dependent on the application, algorithm, Interconnection network (topology, bandwidth, connectivity, etc.), overlap of computation and communication, and so on. Consider a sort and merge operation. If the data is partitioned into multiple portions to be sorted in parallel, these portions must at once or in stages be transferred to logically neighboring processors for the merge operation. The efficiency of this approach is dependent on the data transfer overhead, the overlap between computation and communication, and the overlap between communication and communication. The latter overlap can range from complete overlap of data transfer between processors to overlap of the communication initiation overhead.

As another example, consider a parallel summation algorithm. The result of the computation in each processor will be a partial sum consisting of one word of data that must be transferred in one or multiple stages between processors to create the final sum. Depending on the communication overhead and the size of the data, a single processor approach may be superior to a parallel processing one. Thus, with all of the variables that are involved in the evaluation of a parallel processing algorithm, a tool that can assist in development of efficient algorithms on parallel processing systems is necessary.

In this paper, we propose a Parallel Algorithm Development Workbench (PADWB) to facilitate:

- o the evaluation of the expected efficiency of algorithms and associated communication overhead on specified architectures,
- o the evaluation of the fitness of various interconnection network architectures to a given algorithm,
- o the efficient use of the interconnection network,
- o the evaluation and tuning of parallel processing codes, and
- o the development and debugging of application and system code.

Note that the PADWB is not an automatic parallelizer. PADWB is a tool to facilitate the evaluation of a proposed algorithm. The result of the use of the tool may be statistics or timing charts to help in evaluation of the efficiency of the algorithm or in identifying the idle times and bottlenecks. Ultimately, graphical input and output will simplify the interaction with the workbench and will allow visual inspection of the operation of the algorithms. Portions of the workbench have been implemented. Section 4 describes the implementation status of the workbench at the time of submission of this paper.

PADWB will be composed of multiple layers of Network Model, Cluster Model, Processor Model, and processor interpreter; Section 3 will discuss the models in detail. Each layer of the model can be individually modified to adjust to its corresponding architecture. The network, cluster, and processor models are either stochastic or trace-driven models, [1] [2]. For test of correctness of an algorithm, the statistics or traces can be generated by the processor-interpreter by executing the actual code. Then, the data can be passed through the models to other processors to generate correct results. Statistics and traces can also be drawn from a library of previously used algorithms. Judicious use of these libraries will allow the rapid modeling of the compute intensive phases of new algorithms. Obviously, more complicated models result in slower response time. Therefore, the algorithm or code optimization and performance evaluation can be started with simple statistical models. As the high level modifications are done, details can be added to the model for more complex evaluation.

The following provides some scenarios for the use of the tool (PADWB) when multiple levels of complexity and detail are used.

- o An algorithm developer or a programmer can quickly evaluate the interaction between a proposed algorithm and the interconnection network. Therefore, rapidly identify areas of conflict, and experiment with different communication mechanisms to find the optimal match between the interconnection scheme and the algorithm.
- o A programmer can test his code for functionality and also performance using profiling and timers; use debugging facilities on a processor to obtain an instruction trace of a critical code segment. Measure the CPU execution time, as well as detailed information on resource utilization and conflicts.
- o Eventually software for a full configuration can be tested for both quality and performance, on a much smaller configuration of Prototype hardware. The Simulator subsystem will simulate both Interconnection Network performance and functionality.

The need for a tool like PADWB to measure the performance of a parallel machine in the presence of various algorithms can be felt from workshops such as [3] and [4]. The evidence of the amount of attention that is recently paid to such a need and demand is [6], [7], [8], and [9] all appearing in the 1987 International Conference on Parallel Processing. Such an attention to specifying the need and approaches to satisfy it is likely to intensify soon as availability of parallel machines increases. In the decade that software and ease of use have become the most important parts of the system development, lack of tools to aid in the design and use of parallel systems and algorithms will not be tolerated.

The tools that have currently been proposed or are under development cover a range from allowing parallel processing code portability [5], to modeling parallel communication environments [6], to analyzing parallel processing potential in a code [7], to writing code in parallel and experimenting with it [8] [9. Though, these environments are very valuable in development and analysis of parallel codes, an environment to allow algorithm analysis independent of a sequential language has not been proposed. The tool proposed in this paper is intended as a multi-level tool by which the parallel system can be modeled using a high level language and the algorithm can be described by its computational and communication complexity and requirements. Then, the algorithm can be gradually refined using the flow model, and eventually developed into a detailed code. PADWB will make development of parallel algorithms and the study of parallel systems one step easier.

In the following sections, we will present a description of the tool, Section 2, and some details of the implementation of the model, Section 3. In section 4, we will provide and update on the implementation status of the project. Section 5 concludes this paper.

THE TOOL (PADWB)

In order to efficiently develop algorithms in a parallel processing environment or to evaluate the performance of a parallel processing system, a means to estimate communication overhead and the total elapsed time given the computational and communication complexities and dependencies of the algorithm must be developed. The tool proposed here(PADWB) is intended to provide such a facility without requiring a long term coding or emulation for the preliminary evaluation. PADWB will provide a facility to receive a formulations for computation and communication complexities from the user by which it can estimate computation and communication times. It will also receive information on transfers of data between processors such as destination(s), size of data, and frequency of communication and will create a dependency relationship between computation and communication to predict elapsed time. The tool will provide a chart of the parallel computation and communication blocks for the whole computation to allow the visual detection of the bottlenecks and idle times.

To set up the model, the user must provide information on the communication protocol and topology. This information will be transformed into a network model that will be used to route data and to control communication dependencies. Such a model will determine the order and length of communication for each algorithm. Then, given the computation times between communications and the communication overhead, the model will provide an execution block diagram that will display the overlapped computations, the overlapped communications, the overlap between computation and the communication, and the CPU idle time due to communication delay or bottle neck. Such information, then, must be used to modify the algorithm or the architecture for improved performance.

PADWB will allow multiple levels of modeling from very abstract parallel processing model, to network model driven by statistics, to trace-driven CPU models producing statistics for the network model. Ultimately, the model will be extended to allow the simulation of the processors to run actual code in order to provide the real traces to the CPU model, and to produce the correct data. This data will be transferred to the destination processor model through the network model allowing the real execution of the algorithm in a parallel processing environment for verification of results of the computation. Obviously, the more detailed the model becomes, the slower the response time will become.

The following is an example of how the tool can be used for algorithm development or performance evaluation:

- Provide modeling information to generate the network model.
- Provide data on the amount of computation (e.g.: compute 300 clocks, communicate, compute 400 clocks) or a formulation to compute it.
- Provide data on the amount and destination of data communication and the transfer time.

At this point, given the network model, amount and destination of the data transfers, the communication overhead can be computed. However, this information must be combined with the computation data and be applied to the network model to determine the communication conflicts and their effect on the elapsed time. At this point the design can:

- Modify the algorithm to reduce the required communication. Reevaluate the algorithm.
- Generate a processor model by providing statistical data about the algorithm and the processor. Repeat the above steps more accurately by accumulating network statistics through modeling the execution of the code in the processors.
- Use an interpreter for the processor that will create an accurate code-execution trace to be used by the processor model to generate an accurate CPU model for use by the network model.

Thus, the interactive process of creating an efficient parallel algorithm can be accomplished in multiple levels of detail. In each level of detail, a reevaluation of the algorithm will provide sufficient data to proceed to the next level of detail or reexamine the algorithm for more efficient design.

To facilitate the identification of the bottle necks and idle times, the tool will provide a graphical representation of the execution, communication, and idle times of the processors. Figure 1 is a sample output that presents the chronological order of execution and overlap of the operations in a hypothetical sort-and-merge operation. The vertical axis is the time axis increasing from top to bottom, and the horizontal axis is the parallelization axis which specifies the number of processors that have been involved in the computation at each time interval. The computational and communication blocks are appropriately marked. It can be easily seen that the communication speed and imbalance of the algorithm are defeating he advantage of use of multiple processors for this algorithm. Thus, from Figure 1, it can be observed that to efficiently use the system, either the communication speed must be increased or a more balanced algorithm must be used, or both.

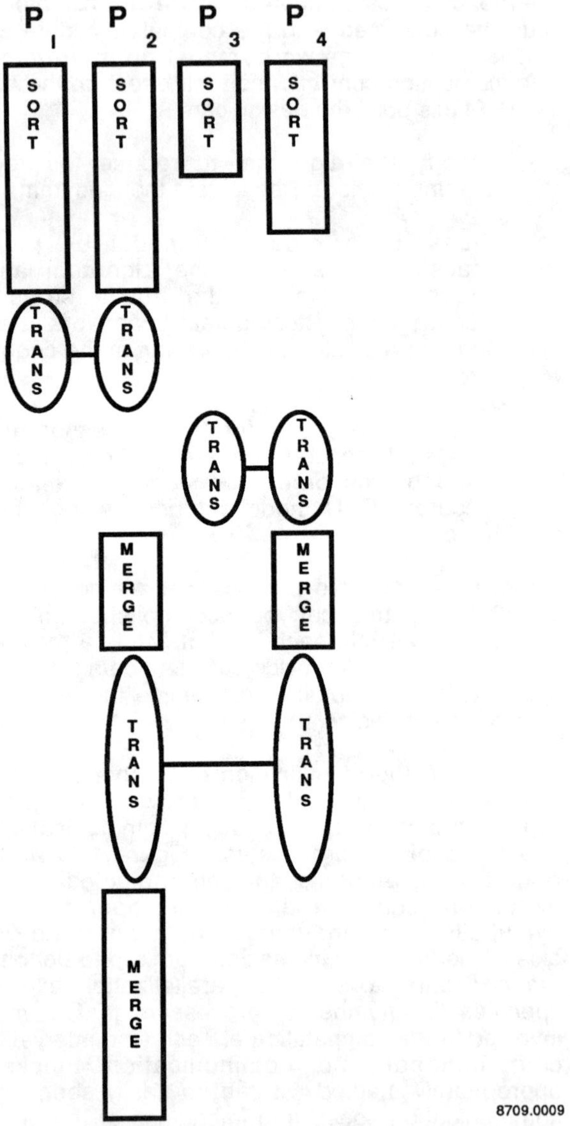

8709.0009

Figure 1- A Sample Sort-and-Merge Algorithm on A Loosely Coupled System of 4 Processors

MODEL ARCHITECTURE

The simulation system consists of several components which interact to meet the above stated goals. Figure 2 depicts the relationships between the components of the simulation and prototyping system.

The Interconnection Network model addresses interconnection network timing issues. It is capable of representing variety of interconnection methods for the system allowing the user to determine the best communication tradeoffs for a particular algorithm. It has provisions for high level specification of algorithm code characteristics, thus eliminating the need for a detailed design before evaluating the suitability of an algorithm/network configuration pair.

The Cluster Model provides a detailed model of the resource contention for a specific group of processors. If the system architecture does not include processor clusters, this level can be skipped. It will be used to assure that the resources of a cluster are not over committed, to provide statistics for realistic assumptions in the network model, and as an environment for the Processor Flow Model.

The Processor Flow Model replaces statistical Stubs in the Cluster model. It provides a detailed clock-by-clock model of CPU instruction execution timing. It models all resources of the processor hardware which are subject to contention. It models the applications codes use of these resources in great detail. It produces accurate information on the time actual code will take to run on the system, as well as information about resource utilization and contention useful in code optimization.

The Software Interpreter accepts assembly or machine code, and provides a functional simulation of the execution of that code. The Software Interpreter also produces instruction traces for use by the Processor Flow Model.

The Interconnection Network, Cluster, and Processor Flow Models concentrate on ever increasing levels of modeling detail in the temporal domain, while the Software Interpreter provides functional simulation and debugging facilities. The workbench can be used to analyze most interconnection networks and processors architectures.

The Processor Flow Model, Cluster Model, and Network Model are expected to be used even after actual hardware is selected. They will provide a level of visibility into the hardware which will allow for the optimum utilization of the systems power. This level of visibility can not be approached by software or hardware instrumentation.

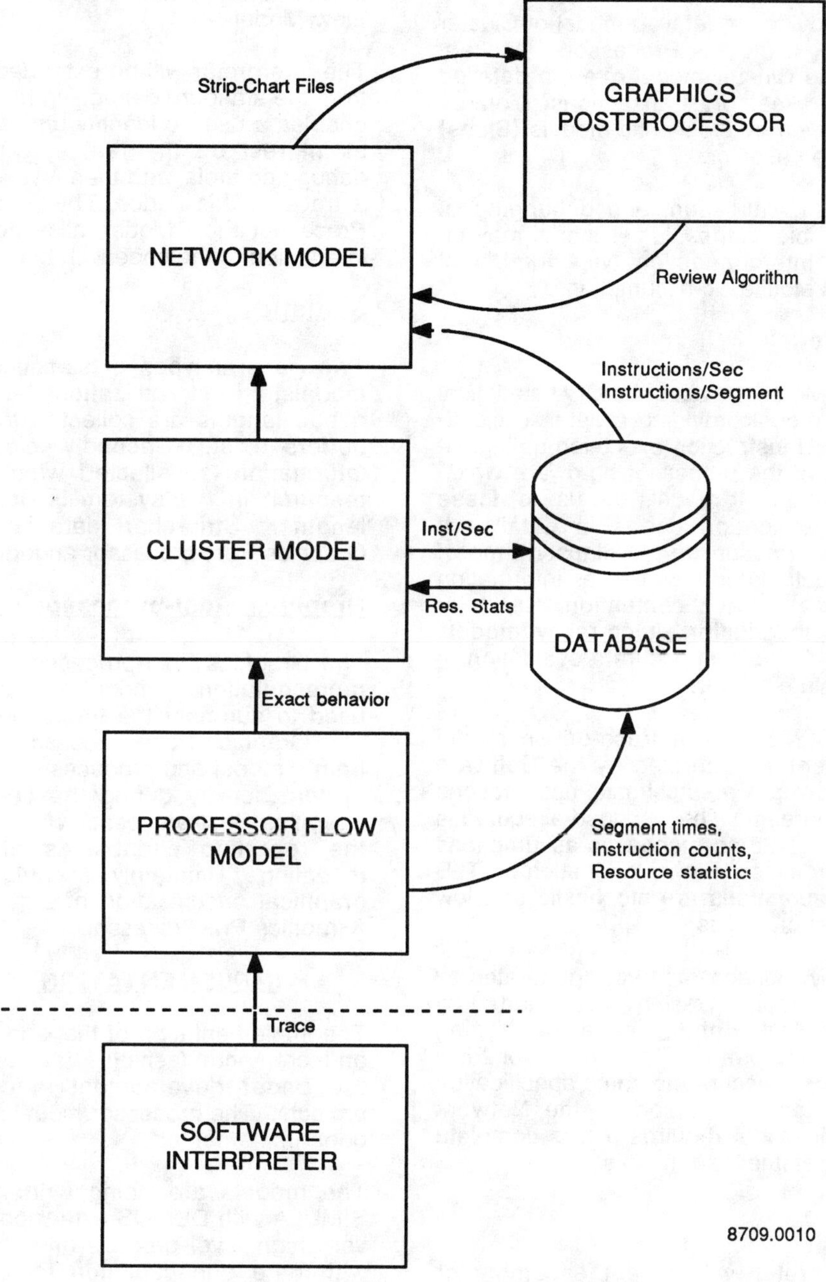

Figure 2- PADWB Architecture

Network Model

The principal interface for specification of algorithm behavior occurs in the Network Model. The Network Model requires three types of information. First it requires information about Cluster configuration, secondly it requires information about the configuration for the interconnection network. Finally, a specification of the algorithm is required.

An algorithm may be modeled at several levels. The highest level specifies the algorithm in terms of a very high level general purpose language (a SIMULA based package). This language provides basic synchronization primitives, along with standard data types and control structures. The algorithm expression is kept independent of the Physical allocation of processes to nodes by use of symbolic names for destinations.

Cluster Model

The Cluster Model provides a detailed model of Cluster resource contention. It models Processors, Caches, Busses, and I/O. The Cluster model offers a detailed model of the bus and memory transactions. Memory and bus activity is driven by stochastic models (Stubs) of CPU and I/O device behavior.

For detailed modeling, validation, and debugging of parallelism related problems the Cluster model may be embedded into the Interconnection Network Model replacing that models stochastic assumptions.

Processor Flow Model

The Processor Flow Model replaces the CPU statistical Stubs in the Cluster model providing a detailed clock-by-clock model of CPU instruction execution timing. It models all resources of the processor hardware which are subject to contention. It models the use of these resources by the application codes in detail. It produces accurate information on the elapsed time of the execution of the actual code, as well as information about resource utilization and contention useful for code optimization. In addition, it correctly models reference patterns which allows accurate evaluation of memory conflicts within a cluster.

The Processor Flow Model is a trace-driven model whose workload model is generated by the Software Interpreter. Thus there are no stochastic assumptions about the instruction stream. The workload executed is correct in all respects. Some stochastic assumptions may remain in the Processor Flow Model such as TLB hit rates. These assumptions are stochastic to allow realistic modeling of short traces.

The Processor Flow Model accepts traces generated by the the Software Interpreter. Tracing will be started by either a command line option, or a debugging command within the interpreter. The Processor Flow and Cluster models both accept the same specification of system configuration as is used by the Network Model. The Network Model requires a less complete description than do the other two models.

Software Interpreter

The Software Interpreter will accept assembly or machine code and provide a functional simulation of the execution of that code. In addition to providing exact simulation of the instruction set semantics, it also provides a simulated operating system environment which allows programs to open files and make standard UNIX systems calls in advance of the delivery of an operating system. This allows simulation of "Complete" programs.

In addition, the Software Interpreter provides a debugging environment, and in conjunction with the Processor Flow Model, accurate timing of application code execution. Performance tuning features include timers and profiling. The Software Interpreter also produces instruction traces for use by the Processor Flow Model.

The Interpreter will be extended to allow its invocation from the standard debugging tools: ADB and DBX. This enables a user to identify and isolate a section of code of interest on the real system using the standard debugging tools, and then invoke the interpreter to take a trace of this code. The trace is processed by the Processor Flow Model, allowing high visibility into the interaction of the code with the hardware.

Statistics

Two general types of statistics are provided by the models. First, utilizations and queuing times and queue lengths are collected for all resources; where buffers exist. Secondly, clock-by-clock strip-chart information is collected which identifies what each resource in the system is doing, as well as queue lengths. Strip-chart data is used as input to the Graphics Post-processor and for validation.

Graphics Post-processor

The Graphics Post-processor provides for a graphical representation of model results and is targeted to be used to augment the Interconnection Network Model. The Graphics Post-processor accepts strip-chart data from a model and produces a graphical depiction of the system activity during the observation period. The Graphics Post-processor will be extended to enhance the reporting capabilities of the other levels of modeling. Ultimately, it could be extended to allow graphical specification of algorithm structure as well (Graphics Pre-Processor).

IMPLEMENTATION AND RESULTS

The implementation of the workbench is in progress in an incremental fashion. Various pieces of the package are under development in conjunction with other projects. The processor model and the interpreter have been implemented.

The models are being written in a combination of SIMULA with DEMOS extensions, and C. SIMULA is a very high level process oriented simulation language with data encapsulation facilities. All models are process oriented next event simulations.

The Processor Flow Model is Trace-Driven. All other models have stochastic models of exogenous events (unless used in conjunction with the flow model). The coordination of multiple tasks on prototype systems by the Interconnection Network model will make use of distributed simulation techniques.

The Software Interpreter has been implemented in C and runs under UTX (Gould Unix). The interpreter can be used for interactive execution or debugging or for trace generation. Both of these functions will be used with workbench.

Several simple parallel processing algorithms, such as matrix multiply, have been modeled using the processor model. The results so far indicate that the model is effective in identifying resource contentions and bottlenecks. For example, one experiment resulted in identification of problems with fixed bus-priority scheme when executing a 2 cpu version of a parallelized matrix multiply algorithm.

CONCLUSION

We have discussed the need for rapid prototyping during algorithm and system development. We have proposed a workbench environment to support an analysts effort to optimize algorithms, communications schemes, and CPU designs for parallel processing applications. This environment allows these facets of a parallel system to be investigated and optimized either singly, or jointly.

We have described how an algorithm may be evaluated at various levels of abstraction, and how the environment can support the design decomposition down to real code. This environment should allow algorithm and system designers with minimal modeling experience to experiment and optimize applications expending minimal effort.

The implementation of the workbench is in currently in progress. The processor model and the interpreter have been implemented. The model has been successfully used in tuning algorithms and identifying resource conflicts and bottlenecks that has led to improvements in the design of the system under study.

After development of the proposed tool is complete, we will characterize the user/tool interaction and the performance critical features of the workbench. In addition, we will profile the speed of the tool as a function of the level of detail in order to analyze the efficiency of the workbench.

REFERENCES

[1] M. H. Mac Dougall, "Instruction Level Program and Processor Modeling," IEEE Computer, July, 1984, pp. 14-24

[2] A. J. Smith, " Two Methods for Efficient Analysis of Memory Address Data," IEEE Transactions on Software Engineering, Vol. SE-3, No. 1, January, 1977, pp. 97-101

[3] S. K. Tripathi, S. Kaisler, S. Chandran, A. K. Agrawala, " Report on the Workshop on Design & Performance Issues in Parallel Architectures," Performance Evaluation Review, ACM Sigmetrics, Vol. 14, No. 3 and 4, January, 1987, pp.16-31

[4] Edited by Z. Segall and L. Snyder, " Report of the NSF/CMU Workshop on Performance Efficient Parallel Programming," Performance Evaluation Review, ACM Sigmetrics, Vol. 15, No. 2, August, 1987, pp.16-31

[5] J. Dongarra and D. Sorensen, "Schedule: Tools for Developing and Analyzing Parallel Fortran Programs," Technical Memo 86, Argonne National Laboratory, November, 1986

[6] J. Purtilo, D. A. Reed, and D. C. Grunwald, "Environments for Prototyping Parallel Algorithms," Proceedings of the 1987 International Conference on Parallel Processing, pp.431-438

[7] K. So, A. S. Bolmarcich, F. Darema and V. A. Norton, "A Speedup Analyzer for Parallel Programs," Proceedings of the 1987 International Conference on Parallel Processing, pp. 653-661

[8] T. W. Pratt, "The PISCES 2 Parallel Programming Environment," Proceedings of the 1987 International Conference on Parallel Processing, pp. 439-445

[9] B. P. Lester and G. R. Guthrie," A System for Investigating Parallel Algorithm and Architecture Interaction," Proceedings of the 1987 International Conference on Parallel Processing, pp. 667-670

GROWING DISCORD: PROGRAMMING PHILOSOPHY AND HARDWARE DESIGN

Kenneth W. Neves

Boeing Computer Services
PO Box 34346 MS 7L-20
Seattle, WA 98124

ABSTRACT

Generally, vector compiler technology has been successful in achieving reasonable peak efficiency on "good" code. Moreover, the community's ability to generate "good" vector code has improved dramatically. As we move into the era of parallelism, particularly in supercomputing, we can observe certain trends among the leaders in compiler technology. The basic techniques are extensions of strategies for vector machines, but have limited effectiveness in a parallel environment.

In this paper, current techniques are examined with respect to choices or trends in hardware design. The ability for parallel compilers to be as effective on parallel machines, as they have been on vector machines is not likely. Technical reasons for this are presented. The human intervention to achieve peak optimization seems to be inevitable. The nature of automatic and non-automatic code optimization is explored.

INTRODUCTION

"What happens when an irresistible force is applied to an immovable object?" Whatever the outcome, harmony is an unlikely end. Yet, with tongue in cheek, one may relate this age old question to a conflict raging in the field of scientific computing. The analogy one could envision is to liken the current trend of parallelism in hardware design to that of an irresistible force. Almost every class of computing engine from workstation to supercomputer is employing an ever increasing amount of parallelism to improve price-performance. What better to liken to the "immovable object" than the vast body of existing application software. Large ponderous codes, old (yet tried and true) algorithm technology, and an unswerving bond to Fortran have made important application programs seem like immovable objects when attempting to migrate them to increasingly parallel systems. The thought of redeveloping software is an obvious alternative. Even if this were not cost prohibitive, redevelopment often is resisted for other more subtle reasons. Production software is only trusted, validated, or accepted through years of use; consequently, replacing production software with new software, however good, is almost always resisted -- if attempted at all.

To prevent total chaos, there has been but one intermediary between the software application and the hardware design, the compiler. [For scientific applications, the compiler of the masses has been Fortran. While the discussion will apply to other languages, Fortran is the language of primary focus in what follows.] Compiler technology has had to accommodate the ever increasing pressure from the "force" of parallelism. Through improved compilation strategy, extensions to the language, and diagnostic/debugging tools, compiler writers have tried to achieve a reasonable amount of reconciliation between software and hardware.

Yet, if one examines the near-term trends in compiler technology and hardware architecture, one can observe that the disparate philosophies of compiler writers and hardware architects is likely to create a greater discord in scientific computing. Either computer architects will have to rethink the forms of parallelism used, or programming methodology will have to attack parallelism in software design at a much higher level than afforded to the compiler. The grudging success of automatic vectorizers for pipelined architectures is not likely to be easily repeated for parallel architectures, particularly in mid-range parallelism (i.e., 8-200+ CPUs).

In this paper parallel processes (pipelining, MIMD parallelism, SIMD parallelism) are examined as applied to various aspects of software technology.

PARALLELISM IN COMPUTING

Long detailed taxonomies of computing architectures often contribute little to help assess the software implications of various machine designs. As computer architects use more (and often recurring) tricks to push performance beyond what component technology alone can offer, a greater obligation is placed on the users to accommodate these changes. The basic tool the architect uses to achieve "super" performance is parallelism. Parallelism has been with us from the very early days of computing. For example, the overlap of computation and I/O is a form of parallelism. In modern supercomputers, parallelism has invaded the very heart of computation -- the floating point operation itself. This latter phenomenon pervades modern supercomputing and is at the heart of the "MachoFLOP" wars raging in the "low price per MFLOP" marketplace.

<u>**Forms of Parallel Processing:**</u> In order to use vector or parallel hardware, one must address the instruction process and data flow. Perhaps the simplest terminology in this area is due to Flynn [1]. The terms are defined as follows:

SISD (single instruction stream/single data stream) - this is the conventional computing process, today often called scalar computing. The concept is that instructions are processed sequentially and result in a flow of data from memory to functional units and back to memory (perhaps through caches or registers). The data flow is equally sequential. This does not exclude the use of pipelining in the hardware, but does exclude manipulation of vector data types explicitly. The key is that operands are scalar objects and their manipulation is paced by the instruction processing rate.

SIMD (single instruction stream/multiple data stream) - the processing of instructions remains the same, but the data manipulated (i.e., the operands of the operations) can be explicitly "vectors" or arrays of data. In parallel machines, the data could come from separate memories simultaneously, but all CPUs perform the same set of instructions simultaneously. In either case, the floating point operations are "paced" by functional unit throughput as opposed to instruction processing rates. [Thus, it is no longer considered meaningful to rate vector/parallel computers in MIPs, millions of instructions per second.]

MIMD (multiple instruction stream/multiple data stream) - this process implies the ability to simultaneously process instructions. These instructions are then free to process independent data streams. [Note: each instruction stream may be allowed to issue SIMD instructions to vector units or synchronous subprocessors.]

<u>**Forms of Parallelism in Hardware:**</u> While the above are distinct processes, the architectures that they are employed in can be quite varied and, in some cases, support more than one of the above processes. Three techniques of parallelism in hardware design seem to be most common:

1. Simple replication --
identical and multiple operation of hardware functional units and/or CPUs.

2. Multiple non-identical functional units. (Overlapped functional units.)

3. Pipelining -- the segmentation of a single functional unit or process to achieve assembly line type operation leading to the simultaneous overlap of independent operations.

It is interesting to note, that it is rather difficult to categorize machines by the above definitions, and even if one could, the implications of each class is not always clear in terms of its impact on software. In order to see this, it is necessary to describe these forms of parallelism further.

Replication: The simplest form parallelism is replication. Yet, its simplicity becomes obscure when considering the variations of its use. For example, consider employing replication in floating point computation. One can design the CPU to include more than one functional unit, such as several floating point adders. This of course has fundamental software implications beginning with the compiler (usually Fortran) which does not have any concrete way to restructure software to insure that two or more adders can be kept busy. Furthermore, there is an issue related to "hardware balance." Increasing computational power without a corresponding increase in bandwidth to data memory can create a serious bottleneck that could easily nullify the value of increased functional units. Another way to use replication to improve floating point performance is to simply add more CPUs. This not only increases the number of floating point units, but increases the number of instruction processors. This creates further decisions to be made about data flow and instruction processing [e.g. SIMD vs. MIMD]. Both the operating system and compiler must be extended to handle parallel constructs and/or provide tools for direct user intervention. In this setting, questions arise related to resource contention and synchronization, such as memory, registers, cache, and peripherals.

Multiple (non-identical) Functional Units: Another form of parallelism is the use of additional functional units that are independent, and perhaps different. This technique has been used in computing since the earliest days (e.g. independent I/O processing). The overlap of instruction address computation with the floating point units is a common instance of this type of parallelism. More recent examples are the use of floating point accelerators or array/matrix multipliers appended to traditional floating point units in various designs. The "parallelism" comes from the concurrent operation of these units. Perhaps the most successful use of this technique is in the Floating Point Systems array processor line. The computer is composed of 10 to 15 functional units including various types of data storage and registers (data pads). The instruction word is wide enough so that a single instruction word can have as many as 13 simultaneous sub-instructions which can direct the various functional units. (Viewed in this manner one could classify the whole FPS line as MIMD. In fact, most computer taxonomies have difficulty classifying the FPS architecture.) This is, in fact, the same hardware approach employed by "very-large-instruction-word" machines, such as Multiflow.

Pipelining: Pipelining is currently the most used form of parallelism in modern scientific computers. The analogy of the automobile assembly line is often applied to this process. It is assumed the reader is familiar with this concept, and further elaboration is omitted. It is worthy to note that pipelining can be applied to all types of functional units, not just floating point units. Pipelined instruction processors have led to interesting designs of MIMD and SIMD machines. A notable machine of this type was the Denelcor HEP which supported 8 independent instruction streams by pipelining the instruction processor and functional units. The resulting processing element (called a PEM) was one CPU physically, but through the time-slice of the instructions, appeared as 8 logical CPUs.

It is quite likely that computers of the future will increase the use of these parallel techniques in all three areas of computer design: computation (functional units), instruction processing (instruction or control units), and data movement and handling (memory and I/O). This trend is illustrated by a recent addition to the "super" workstation market, by Stellar Computer Company. Their initial product design employs a separate vector floating point processor and graphics processor. In addition, the instruction processor is time-sliced through a four stage pipelining process (similar to the HEP mentioned above) allowing four independent instruction streams resulting in a design with multiple instruction streams, multiple functional units, a vector floating point unit, and hierarchical memory. All this in a device for a domain once solely occupied by "dumb" terminals.

VECTOR COMPUTERS: DATA AND INSTRUCTIONS

Today's parallelizing compilers and technological trends in parallelization are rooted in the past. Major advances in automatic parallelization come from "vector" technology. A brief review of vector computing is necessary to explain these new compiler philosophies.

Vector storage has become a critical aspect of computing. This is true on all vector/parallel machines. In fact, vector storage on multiple CPU machines with distributed memories or layered caches is a major programming consideration. A review of vector storage on today's supercomputers reveals a number of issues that impact software.

To a mathematician or scientist, a vector is simply an ordered array of numbers. For a computer this array doesn't exist until it is designated by the memory location of its ordered components. Various supercomputers have limitations as to the flexibility allowed for the specification of vectors. There are three common complexities found in manipulating vectors stored in computer memories, as illustrated by Figure 1. The figure displays the storage of a vector,

$$A = (A_1, A_2, \ldots, A_n)$$

in three different memory configurations.

Each vector type in Figure 1 is a subcase of its successor. Each successor requires "more" hardware support to implement as operands in vector instructions.

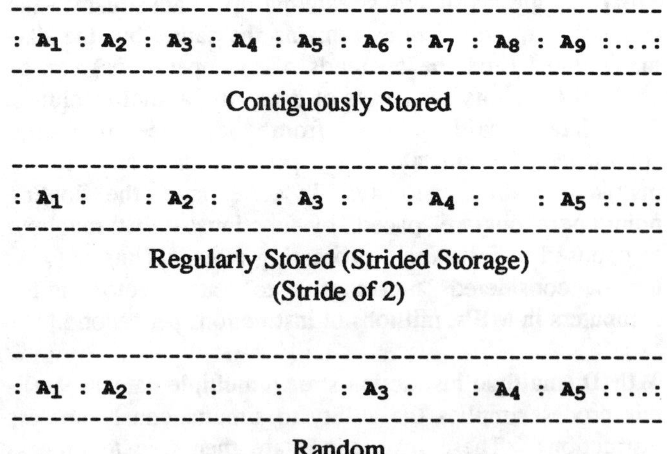

Figure 1
Types of Vector Storage

The hardware descriptors for each case are as follows:

- o Contiguous: first word location; vector length.
- o Regular: first word location; vector length; stride.

- o Random: first word location; vector length; index vector providing indirect address from first word location.

Regardless of type, the key feature of all vector operations is that the input vectors (operands) must be independent of the output vector (result). Thus, algorithms that employ recursive data references are prevented from performing in vector mode.

The following table lists the categories of operations supported by various computers. An "X" indicates the category is supported at maximum vector rate. An "R" indicates the feature is supported in vector mode and hence faster than scalar, but at a vector rate significantly slower than the peak vector rate for a dense operation (Reduced rate). Thus, not all vector operations are created equal (in performance), adding to compiler complexity. A "-" indicates the operation is not supported.

Vector Instructions by Category

1. DYADS (WITH STRIDE)
2. TRIADS (WITH STRIDE)
3. MASKED VECTOR
4. VECTOR TO SCALAR
5. LOAD/STORE (WITH STRIDE)
6. GATHER/SCATTER (RANDOM)
7. BIT/SHIFT
8. 1st RECURRENCE

COMPUTER Single CPU	1	2	3	4	5	6	7	8
CRAY-1	X	-	X	R	X	-	-	-
CRAY X-MP	X	X	X	-	X	-	-	-
new X-MPs	X	X	X	-	X	X	-	-
CRAY-2	X	-	X	-	X	R	-	-
CYBER 205	R	R	X	R	X	R	-	-
ETA-10	X	X	X	R	R	R	R	-
FUJ. VP 200	X	X	X	X	X	X	X	-
FUJ. VP 400	X	X	X	X	X	X	X	-
HIT. S-820	X	X	X	X	X	X	X	-
IBM 3090/VF	X	X	X	X	X	R	X	-
NEC SX-2	X	X	X	X	X	X	X	R

TABLE 2

When a computer doesn't have a certain type of vector operation in its instruction set, it can degrade a compiler's or preprocessor's ability to *vectorize*. As the various types of instructions become popular, compilers on various machines get "smarter" in being able to "map" program computations onto the available and appropriate instructions. The goal is to map all processing onto *vector*, as opposed to *scalar*, instructions achieving 100% "vectorization." Quite often a complicated do-loop will pass the vector operand dependency checks and vectorization is a potential. However, there are sometimes several possible vector instructions to map onto with varying efficiency ramifications depending on both problem characteristics, data storage, and hardware design. Many sophisticated compilers still make very poor decisions in this regard. The reader is referred to Gentzsch and Neves [2] for specific examples.

Dependency analysis is the basic tool of vector/parallel compiler optimizers, and some are extremely sophisticated. Unfortunately, compilers are often deprived of information that could determine more liberal dependency restrictions. The deprivation comes from the fact that often critical data values are not known until run time. An example is given later. Despite their obvious deficiencies, vectorizing compilers have done quite well on many scientific applications written with certain principles of vectorization in mind. It is not clear parallelizers will be so successful.

PARALLELISM IN SUPERCOMPUTER DESIGN

The trend to increase the computational power of supercomputers through replication of CPUs, is well established. While many industrial research projects, commercial companies, and academic research projects are heavily involved with distributed memory architectures, supercomputer vendors are currently exploiting a modest amount of parallelism. Their purpose is to achieve the greatest power, and their approach is to first use the most powerful single CPUs and minimize the number of CPUs. One might argue that this is not the best approach, but it is the most "evolutionary" and therefore has the least impact on the large body of applications software so important to users and vendors alike. This approach appears to be the trend well into the 1990s. Cray Research, IBM, HITACHI, NEC and ETA Systems offer multiple CPU supercomputers. The latter system notably is the only one, so far, to use large local (hence distributed) memories while still sharing a large main (global memory).

The initial foray into this arena has been largely motivated by job stream throughput considerations. In optimizing a single job, two or four CPUs, at best, can only increase performance by a factor of two or four, respectively. This can only be accomplished through some modifications to the application at hand, usually by the user. This requires time and effort. On the other hand, providing two CPUs, in proper coordination through the operating system, can easily, and without user intervention, nearly double the throughput of a system. For this purpose, IBM and its plug compatible competitors have been offering multiple CPU mainframes for some time in scalar computers. The multiple CPUs of Cray X-MPs, the most successful supercomputers in terms of sales, are largely used in this fashion at most user sites today. Cray Research will be offering 8 and 16 CPU machines on the X-MP, the Y-MP, and/or the CRAY-3 in 1988 and 1989. Several trade journals have predicted 8 CPU 3090s in the future as well. When the number of CPUs exceeds 4, the gains from improving job stream throughput begin to wane. Eight job streams would tend to randomly compete for critical resources such as memory and I/O ports to the detriment of performance.

To effectively use higher degrees of parallelism, the power of multiple CPUs have to be brought to bear on a single job. In order for this to take place the application program must be redesigned, and the operating system has to provide the mechanisms for higher level languages (such as Fortran) to create and coordinate tasks within a single job. Through this coordination (synchronization) the programmer can perhaps eliminate random contention and create much greater "job" efficiency. Ideally, if N processors are brought to bear on a single job, a performance improvement of a factor of N in real time is attained. Invariably, not all the contention for resources can be eliminated. In addition, the CPU coordination itself introduces overhead that can degrade potential performance.

It is instructive to observe how commercially available machines have implemented the same degree of parallelism differently -- the Cray X-MP/4-CPU, the ETA-10 (the 4-CPU version), and the NEC SX-2 (single CPU). All three of these machines have the same amount of computational parallelism in the following sense: they each have 4-add pipelines and 4-multiply pipelines which yield their respective peak performance rates by allowing simultaneous operation to produce one result per pipe per cycle when performing 64-bit arithmetic. We make the following observations:

- o The Cray has 4-CPUs that must contend for main memory. Each CPU is independently programmable.
- o The ETA-10 has 4-CPUs each endowed with its own memory sharing a secondary memory. Each CPU is independently programmable.
- o The NEC SX-2 has a single CPU with 4 pairs of pipelines and no contention for memory among CPUs. This is an entirely vector technology with respect to floating point operations.

At this point, there is no reason to suggest that any of the three designs is superior. ETA has substituted the memory contention problems of the X-MP with communication overheads for its distributed memory processors. The NEC design avoids resource contention altogether, but requires very long vector operations to ameliorate the startup times of 4-pipes. The ramifications of the three approaches on compiler design is significant. It is not at all clear that one single application program could run well on all three designs. In the next section compiler considerations will be explored.

NEAR-TERM COMPILER AND SOFTWARE CONSIDERATIONS

With the introduction of single CPU vector computers, it was discovered that by altering algorithms and inner-loop sequencing, better performance could be achieved, through more efficient usage of pipelining. Now, in dealing with parallel computers, the issues of efficiency go well beyond the confines of the compiler. The highest stages of the modeling process are often filled with parallelism. Many applications dealing with physical models have obvious parallel decompositions related to the geometry of the model itself. This "model" parallelism cannot generally be exploited from the inner do-loop level. Moving to a new computer can have, and has had, an impact in all stages of software design. Even if the physical model isn't changed, the algorithms used, the mathematical models, and range of the physical model parameters are often impacted.

It is useful to examine the ways in which a relatively small number of CPUs can be used to improve performance. There are three levels in which parallelism can be exploited to improve system performance.

1. The job stream level: Given the fact that supercomputers and general purpose computers often are used in a multi-user environment, system throughput can be improved by allowing different jobs to run concurrently and independently in the available CPUs. With only two (or perhaps four) CPUs, overall throughput can be improved relatively easily (without user intervention) by the operating system. Of course, this assumes that the individual jobs are not competing for shared resources such as memory or peripheral devices. It is not likely, however, that 16 or 32 CPUs could be utilized productively in this fashion.

2. The job step level: A common throughput performance improvement technique in scalar computers is to divide the

job into subtasks (typically I/O, CPU, compile etc.). This can be equally useful in a parallel environment. This technique can be distinguished from user influenced actions (below) in that it can be automated at the operating system level with perhaps help from the compiler.

3. Program level: At this level performance improvement is obtained by decomposing a single program into subtasks that perhaps require cooperation (synchronization and data exchange) among the subtasks. This type of job decomposition seems to be an inexorable requirement in the effective use of multiple CPU systems from 8 to several hundred CPUs. There have been two approaches to this decomposition.

1. Top-down decomposition requiring extensions to Fortran and user intervention. [This is often called **macrotasking** after CRI software.]

2. Bottom-up parallelization of inner or lower level do-loops across multiple CPUs. This can be automated through compiler or preprocessor technology using the multiple CPUs synchronously in a SIMD fashion. [This has been called **microtasking** after CRI software.]

Interaction between the various levels of parallelism is bound to occur. For example, recently, there has been interesting experimental evidence that shows that multitasking of individual jobs (both micro and macro) can have a positive effect on job stream throughput. Bieterman [3] shows that on a 4-CPU X-MP even poorly multitasked jobs (i.e. improved performance of a factor of only 2 or 3 on an 4-CPU system) can create and improvement in throughput greater than their cumulative individual improvement. Multitasked jobs decompose into smaller puzzle pieces which the job stream manager can fit (schedule) more tightly to achieve a more efficient job stream. This performance bonus is likely to extend to higher numbers of CPUs where the "program level" of parallelism will be virtually required to achieve the best performance.

To examine this further, consider Figure 2. This represents the process of a vectorizing compiler. The compiler recognizes independent array operations through dependency checking and maps various constructs, such as do-loops, onto the expanded vector instruction set. The goal is to achieve 100% vector instruction issue. The hope is that the vectors will be long to overcome the pipe overheads yielding a performance speed-up over scalar processing. This technology is well understood and is being refined by a number of compiler efforts. Vector dependency analysis is necessarily conservative. User diagnostics, and even, interactive queries are being built into some compiler environments.

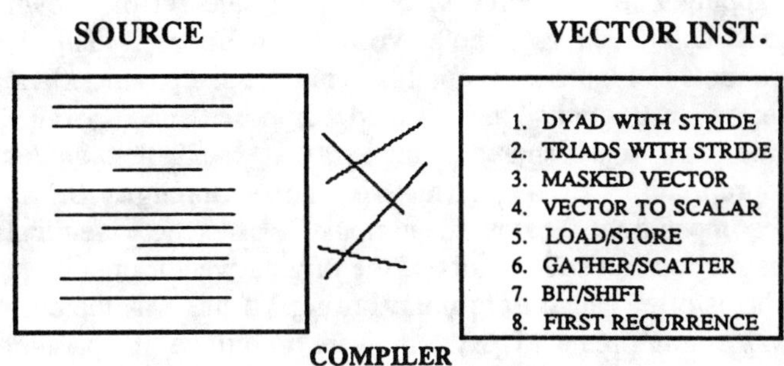

Figure 2
Vector Compilers Map to Vector Instruction Set

To address parallel architectures compiler developers are attempting to extend current vector techniques into the new domain of parallelism. Figure 3 illustrates the approach.

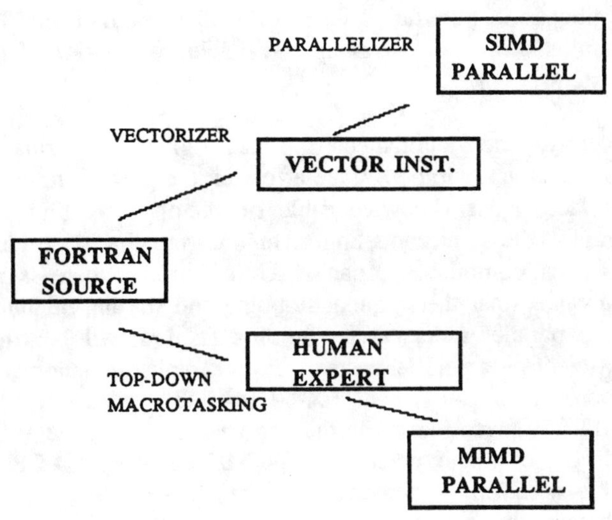

Figure 3
Automatic Parallelism vs. Human Intervention

The same dependency analysis is used to determine independent vector operands. Often loop sequencing is examined and altered with some eye toward creating parallel vector processes, but the basic approach is the same. In fact, one can view the process as being one of mapping Fortran source to an intermediate set of known constructs (such as popular vector instructions). This is identical to Figure 2 except this is not the end product. The vector instructions are then decomposed into parallel processes and shared among the available and/or appropriate CPUs. This is done through SIMD decomposition. That is, the various CPUs execute identical instructions on sub-vectors of the original vector operation. This is often called **data partitioning**. If this was the only way a multiple CPU system were to utilize its parallel capability, then in would probably be better to imbed the parallelism within a single CPU! Refer to the comparison of the NEC SX-2 and its 4-CPU competitors earlier. It would be reasonable to assume the vector computer would out perform the parallel-CPU SIMD computer given the same amount of internal computational parallelism and hardware circuit speeds.

Figure 3 indicates that there is another approach available to multiple CPU systems not afforded to single vector CPUs. By using the extensions provided by some manufacturers to create and synchronize independent tasks, the user can decompose the Fortran source into multiple processes that are "control-flow" oriented. The potential payoff of the two approaches vary from application to application, but the ability to utilize both forms of parallelism is an advantage available to multiple CPU systems.

Clearly, the automated approach gives performance improvement without undue effort on the part of the user. In fact, a user knowledgeable of vector computing can employ the same modeling techniques creating code ideal for this compiler approach. Unfortunately, there is no guarantee that the frequent stopping and starting of inner-loop parallel tasks created in this fashion will be truly efficient on a parallel system. For example, the automated approach of the Alliant FX-80 (4-CPU) yields only 5.8 MFLOPs performance on the Argonne Linpack benchmark [4], out of a peak potential of 94 MFLOPs for all 4 CPUs. This is 6.2% of peak. Using the same reference, we observe that vector machines such as the Cray X-MP, Convex C-2, and the SCS-40, achieve 20% of peak on this small problem. On a larger problem using Fortran more amenable to optimization (Table 5 of reference [4]), one can observe that the vector machines all exceed 80% of peak, while no parallel machine exceeds 20% of peak. One could argue that the solution of dense linear equations should offer as rich an opportunity to exploit bottom-up parallelization as one is likely to find in most scientific programs, with the possible exception of large iterative solutions found in partial differential equations.

Some programs simply do not offer an abundance of parallelizable do-loops, or the overhead for synchronization may be too great on some machines for the fine granularity of this bottom-up approach. In addition, if the target vehicle is a parallel system with vector CPUs, the vector length of the sub-vectors (partitioned data) needs to be large to ameliorate the overhead of the startup times of multiple vector pipelines.

The two techniques, discussed above, are not mutually exclusive and could be combined to achieve greater performance in multiple CPU machines. As a hypothetical example, imagine a 16-CPU machine, with each CPU, itself, a vector architecture (e.g., a CRAY-3). One could employ a top-down strategy of decomposition of an algorithm into four main synchronized subtasks. Quite often it is not too difficult (for the human) to recognized three or four relatively independent (and equally complex) tasks high in the program structure. Assume each subtask is repeatedly utilizing long vector operations. One could dedicate 4-CPUs to support each major task. A bottom-up approach, relying on automatic compiler technology, could be employed within each cluster. The vector lengths would be one quarter the original length, and hopefully not too severely shortened to achieve vector efficiency. This hypothetical situation is probably quite likely to be utilized on the CRAY line. In fact, CRAY users are already experimenting with macrotasking (top-down multitasking) and microtasking (bottom-up multitasking) interaction.

As simple as the above scenario is, several complex decisions must be considered. The fundamental penalty for parallelism is overhead for synchronization due to resource contention. When these overheads are large, it becomes hard to capitalize on performance improvement unless the "granularity" is also large. The term granularity refers to the "size" (measured in time) of the subtasks. We have previously alluded to the importance of the overhead of startup time of vector operations versus vector length. Vector length is analogous to granularity. The longer the vector, in a sense, the greater the vector task's granularity; consequently, the more productive the vector operation, since the overhead time is amortized over a larger time slice. In a parallel environment, the overhead for task starts is constant. Therefore, if a computation is being performed by N tasks, the overhead is N times a single task start. Thus, one would strive to have the computational task large enough to absorb this overhead. With these overhead concerns in mind, consider the following Fortran loop:

```
        DO 10 I = 1, N
        DO 10 J = 1, M
              A(I,J) =  A(I,J) + B(I,J)
10      CONTINUE
```

In a parallel vector environment, a number of options exist. First, the loop could be executed as follows:

```
        DO 10 I = 1, N*M
              A(I,1) =  A(I,1) + B(I,1)
10      CONTINUE
```

In fact, a good vector compiler will make this optimization. The parallelization of the original loop could be accomplished by spreading the outer-loop to the available processors each of which would have the inner-loop available for vectorization. Several questions come to mind:

> What if the overhead for so many processes is too great?
>
> What if both microtasking and macrotasking are available? Which should be used? Or should both be used?
>
> What if M is very small and N is very large?

Some of the answers are fairly obvious once overhead characteristics are known for both vector, macro-, and micro- processing. The approach to take also depends on the values of M and N, **which may not be known at compile time,** and could vary greatly through various passes through the loop nest during execution. It is clear that automatic parallelizers cannot overcome such problems.

Much is being learned from mid-range parallel processors such as Alliant, ELXSI, Sequent and others. However, CRAY machines are running the most ambitious large-scale application programs. Chen [5] offers the following statistics on top-down multitasking on real production programs.

Application Performance

(4-CPU X-MP)

APPLICATION	PERCENT PARALLELIZABLE	THEORETICAL SPEEDUP	ACTUAL SPEEDUP
PARTICLE-IN-CELL	97%	3.67	3.48
WEATHER FORECAST	98%	3.77	3.55
SEISMIC MIGRATION	98%	3.85	3.45
MONTE CARLO	99%	3.85	3.75
LATTICE GAUGE	100%	4.00	3.77
SEISMIC	98%	3.80	3.50
AERODYNAMICS	99%	3.86	3.60

TABLE 3

These figures hold promise for the efficacy of parallelism, but suggest alarming overhead due to non-parallel portions of programs or unbalanced task decomposition. Only four CPUs are used, and yet the degradation is already apparent in several cases (notably in the oil and aerospace applications).. What can be expected from 8 or 16 CPUs? To what extent can existing code really be migrated to a parallel environment and achieve effective results?

CONCLUSIONS

Compiler technology is seriously lagging behind changes in architecture. Current efforts in compiler technology seem to be concentrated on bottom-up inner-loop parallelism. This approach is important, but suffers from

- o not exploiting multiple CPUs at the highest levels of granularity;
- o being dependent on data not always available at compile time;
- o being better suited to hardware using pipelining and/or multiple function units as opposed to multiple CPUs.

In contrast, hardware technology is definitely moving toward parallel CPU architectures. The complacency of users and software tool developers to generate approaches to parallel programs could stand as a national research priority.

No commercial products are available today that will automatically decompose Fortran applications (from the top) into balanced multitasked processes. This will probably be the domain of human expert intervention for some time to come. Program analysis tools are sorely needed. Standardized Fortran extensions to provide task creation and synchronization are also imperative if portable and distributed processing is to be supported. Currently, *de facto* standards seem to be evolving based on the large community of Cray users exposed to tools which that company has provided. Several *ad hoc* committees have been formed among parallel CPU architecture vendors. Software tools that can perform static analysis of program flow exist, but are not being integrated into vendor supplied Fortran development environments, and no vendor is seriously investigating expert systems technology which may be an aid in this area. Modern workstations permit the visualization of program structure and offer the possibility of a much different form of interactive compilation process. Through these techniques Fortran could, perhaps, evolve to be an after-thought behind the person-machine interface, and in time, replaced by the interface itself as a software development language.

As a matter of observation, it seems likely that the gap between compiler technology and hardware architecture is enlarging. The ability to use new technology computers to achieve performance near their potential is diminishing. While some researchers may claim that 8-CPU shared memory systems are old hat, it is probably more accurate to say that the practical usage of such machines on large-scale scientific applications is a first rate technological problem yet to be addressed.

REFERENCES

1. M. Flynn, "Some Computer Organizations and their Effectiveness," IEEE Transactions on Computation, Vol. C-21, pp 948-60.

2. W. Gentzsch and K. Neves, Computational Fluid Dynamics: Algorithms and Supercomputers, NATO AGARDograph No. 311, March 1988, 150 pages.

3. M. Bieterman, "Impact of Multitasking on Job Stream Throughput," Proceedings of the Cray User Group, October, 1987, Bologna.

4. J. Dongarra, "Performance of Various Computers Using Standard Linear Equations Software in a Fortran Environment," TM-23, Argonne National Labs, April 18, 1988.

5. S. Chen, "Overview of the CRAY X-MP," Cray Research, 1984.

Horizon: A New Supercomputer Development

Chair: Burton J. Smith
Tera Computer Company

THE HORIZON SUPERCOMPUTING SYSTEM: ARCHITECTURE AND SOFTWARE

James T. Kuehn

Supercomputing Research Center
4380 Forbes Boulevard
Lanham, Maryland 20706

Burton J. Smith†

Tera Computer Company
P.O. Box 25418
Washington, D.C. 20007

Abstract

Horizon is the name currently being used to refer to a shared-memory *Multiple Instruction stream - Multiple Data stream (MIMD)* computer architecture under study by independent groups at the Supercomputing Research Center and at Tera Computer Company. Its performance target is a sustained rate of 100 giga (10^{11}) *Floating Point Operations Per Second (FLOPS).* Horizon achieves this speed with a few hundred identical scalar processors. Each processor has a horizontal instruction set that allows the production of one or more floating point results per cycle without resorting to vector operations. Memory latency is hidden, assuming enough parallelism is available, by allowing processors to switch context on each machine cycle.

In this overview, the Horizon architecture is introduced and its performance is estimated. The processor instruction set and a simple programming example are given. Additional details on the processor architecture, interconnection network design, performance analyses, machine simulator, compiler development, and application studies can be found in companion papers.

I. Design Philosophy

Shared-memory MIMD computers that can be utilized effectively are difficult to implement. The principal difficulty is the latency associated with memory access and its consequences for processor performance. If many processors are sharing memory, propagation delays in the interconnection network through either logic circuitry or wiring will limit the minimum latency attainable. There are at least two ways of lowering the effective latency, each of which should be employed to approach a minimum: latency reduction and latency hiding. *Latency reduction* is accomplished by arranging a processor's memory accesses so that most of them are to locations that are both spatially and temporally nearby. Caches, such as those used in Cedar and the IBM RP3 [1, 2], are a very popular and effective device for latency reduction. *Latency hiding* is brought about by introducing virtual processors and additional parallelism. While a virtual processor waits for a memory request, the physical processor switches to another task and continues to compute, as in HEP [3]. Memory requests en route from a processor to a memory or vice-versa in a shared-memory system will be referred to as *messages.*

The time needed to switch between tasks is important to the programmer because it determines the maximum message rate that the system will support. If a decomposition of a problem into parallel parts results in too few instructions executed per message sent, then the performance of each physical processor in the system will be limited by the peak message rate. In such cases, the system overhead of a virtual processor implementation is too great for the proposed problem decomposition, and another decomposition should be sought that requires less virtual processor switching. In other words, systems with *lightweight* (easily switched) virtual processors are more generally applicable than are systems with *heavyweight* (slow to switch) virtual processors.

The virtual processor idea is at least as old as multiprogramming, but it is especially relevant to parallel computing because it is only the presence of parallelism that makes virtual processors possible. One of the great strengths of the idea is that the precise reason a physical processor is waiting need not matter. If the virtual processors are lightweight enough, a single mechanism can handle waiting due to function unit latency, memory latency, interconnection network latency, and memory interference. (In shared-memory systems, a processor perceives interconnection network latency and memory interference as memory latency.) The important properties of a virtual processor implementation are its flexibility in handling these different causes of delay in parallel computations and the interaction of the virtual processor implementation with the architecture and the programming of the rest of the system.

The current generation of MIMD computer systems uses fairly conventional processors rather than processors specifically designed for the purpose. Although this approach is feasible, particularly for non-shared-memory systems, it is important to take a fresh look at processor architectures for shared-memory MIMD computers because both the problems and the opportunities are new. In the architecture to be described, the same ideas that let systems with many processors share memory efficiently also permit a "horizontal" instruction set that should be easy to generate good code for, uses most of the functional units most of the time, and thereby produces one or more floating point results per cycle without resorting to vector operations. This processor architecture is far more "general purpose" than the vector processor designs now in vogue and can support supercomputer-class clock rates given comparable logic technology. A fast implementation should easily outrun its vector contemporaries in sustained performance.

Vector instructions use hardware well because they overlap address generation, memory access, and operand computations. In contrast, a conventional scalar processor will use one instruction to generate a new address, a second instruction to load an operand, and a third to combine the operand just obtained with another, perhaps gotten earlier by similar means. The operand combination rate (e.g., mega-flops) of a conventional processor is consequently limited in practice to about one-third of its actual instruction issue rate. Although this is respectable performance, it does not compare favorably with that of vector processors, which can execute one operation per cycle. This performance is all the more remarkable when one remembers that even the fastest conventional processors are unable to issue instructions more often than once every three to five cycles. Therefore, the speed attainable with vector instructions is potentially ten to fifteen times greater.

†Work described here was performed at the Supercomputing Research Center.

Unfortunately, there are two distinct problems with using vector instructions to increase processor effectiveness in shared-memory MIMD computer systems. The first is well-known but not fatal; it is simply that many desired processor computations do not vectorize. This is not fatal precisely because many other computations *do* vectorize and because the familiar, scalar instructions are still available for those that do not. In marked contrast, the second problem is so serious that it might prevent shared-memory MIMD systems with many vector processors.

In the usual shared-memory MIMD system, a processor is not influenced by the others except when interaction occurs at the memory or in the interconnection network. Some interaction is intentional and some is not, but a processor cannot predict an interaction more quickly than the speed of light permits. If all interactions are to be predicted (presumably to allow intervention and scheduling when some undesirable conflict is predicted), the machine's cycle time must be slowed to somewhat greater than the light-diameter of the machine. This would be a serious restriction to the scalability of the machine. Therefore, unpredictable interactions must be allowed. In this setting, moving a vector between memory and a processor presents a problem because the stream of values may be interrupted, or worse yet, rearranged by memory conflict. The solution that has been adopted to date in vector multiprocessor systems has been to pre-assign memory cycles to processors. While this solution can work for small systems, it will not do for large ones: the vector gather/scatter rates and the start-up time for all vector operations become proportional to the number of processors.

Another possible way to achieve greater processor effectiveness and flexibility is by using "horizontal" instructions, instructions in which every processor function unit is controlled independently by its own operation field. Like vector processors, horizontal processors overlap address generation, memory access, and operand computations. Unlike vector processors, though, a horizontal processor architecture can execute nonvectorizable as well as vectorizable algorithms; the address computations can be arbitrary and there is no requirement for a stream of identical operations. Since each function unit can be invoked by each instruction, the possibility of high function unit utilization is present. Finally, no obvious problems are caused by delay or derangement of memory operands, at least none that is not shared by other processor architectures.

A commonly-heard complaint about horizontal processors is that they are hard to program. Some of this difficulty has been ameliorated recently by sophisticated compilers, but it is still unusual to obtain full performance from these processors, even under ideal conditions. In other words, the potentially high function unit utilization is not often achieved in practice. In addition, there is a particular problem surrounding the use of horizontal processors in shared-memory MIMD systems.

Traditionally, instruction lookahead has been used to exploit parallelism at the basic block level while preserving the program counter as the basic method of instruction scheduling. It is always important to overlap instruction execution to obtain good processor performance, even in a horizontal processor that already overlaps operations within each instruction. For non-horizontal processors, the most common implementation method for controlling instruction lookahead has been register reservation: the registers that will be modified by an instruction are all locked at instruction issue and unlocked as each new value is written. The alternative used in both horizontal and non-horizontal processors is "exposed pipeline" overlap. This type of overlap requires a detailed foreknowledge of operation timing to generate correct code. The programmer or compiler uses this knowledge to schedule the operations into the instructions, inserting no-operations when nothing else will work. Unfortunately, in a shared-memory MIMD computer system, the register timing for the memory operations cannot reasonably be known *a priori* and this method breaks down completely. An alternative overlap method using explicit dependency pointers will be described in the next section.

II. Architecture

Global Machine Model

Horizon is a shared-memory MIMD computer in which cooperating processors share a single address space for writable data. Instruction and read-only data spaces need not be shared. Noncooperating programs do not share memory; instead, they are protected from each other. There may be a variety of memory technology within the same system to allow for different uses. Memory and processors in the machine are spatially distributed and intermixed resulting in a structure that allows processors to have some nearby (but not private) storage for stacks and the like.

The Horizon machine to be described consists of 256 processors that share a memory with an address space of 2^{48} bits. The implemented memory space is divided among approximately 512 memory modules and may be considerably smaller than the address space. Virtual addressing is not planned, but hardware support is provided for it.

Address pointers are 64-bit quantities, of which the lower 48 bits represent a bit address. However, memory is organized in 64-bit words so memory operations fetch or store the full 64-bit word that contains the bit that was addressed. The alignment of the value returned/stored is unaffected by addressing a bit that is not on a word boundary. Because the least-significant six bits of the address are effectively ignored in memory operations, some language implementations may be able to use them as tag bits.

Associated with each memory word is a six-bit *access state* consisting of a *full/empty* bit, an *indirect* bit, and four *trap* bits numbered 0 to 3. These *access state bits* can modify the behavior of memory references to the associated location. The options available will be described later.

The interconnection network is a toroidally-connected 3-dimensional mesh of dimension 16×16×6. A 7-ported node is located at each mesh point [4]. Six of the seven bi-directional ports of a node connect it with its neighbors in the ±X, ±Y, and ±Z directions. The remaining port is connected to a processor, memory module, or itself (by looping its output back to the input). On every machine cycle, a node is capable of accepting a message on each of its input ports and routing them all. Hence, from the point of view of a processor, the network can accept a memory request and can deliver a memory response each cycle. Similarly, from the point of view of a memory module, the network can supply a memory request and can accept a memory response each cycle. Network routing strategies, topological considerations, performance, and other issues are discussed in [4].

Processor Model

At each cycle, each Horizon processor is capable of issuing an instruction chosen from an internal hardware pool of processes just as in the HEP architecture [3]. To reduce confusion with the operating system concept of a process, these very lightweight streams of instructions are called *instruction streams (i-streams).* Cooperating i-streams that are a part of a single program are referred to as a *task.* I-streams within a given task share memory but that memory is private to that task. A task may include i-streams on one or more processors.

Instructions are issued from different i-streams in turn based on a selection policy that takes into account such factors as the availability of the i-stream's registers and the completion of previous instructions from the same i-stream on which there is a dependence. The maximum number of i-streams per processor is 128.

The Horizon processor has a horizontal architecture with three major units: the *Memory unit (M-unit), Arithmetic unit (A-unit),* and the *Control unit (C-unit).* The actions of each unit are specified in independent fields in each 64-bit instruction. Hence, each instruction has three independent fields that control the units: the *M-field, A-field,* and *C-field.* There is also a *lookahead field* that is used to control instruction overlap. Each of the M-, A-, and C- fields consists of an *operation code (opcode)* (e.g., load, integer_add, compress) and the register operands to be used. Load and store, for example, are the only two operations that the M-unit can perform; hence, they are referred to as *M-operations* or *M-ops* for short. Other operations are found in either the A-unit or C-unit or in some cases, both.

State Model

The programmer-accessible state includes the registers and miscellaneous state of all of the i-streams in each of the processors and the memory address space of 2^{42} words. Some state is made unavailable when an i-stream is operating in the unprivileged user mode.

There are 32 64-bit general-purpose registers per i-stream, numbered r0-r31. A register set is private to an i-stream; hence, i-streams communicate only through memory. Register r0 is permanently set to the value zero; using it as a destination register has no effect on its value. In all other respects, general-purpose registers are identical: they can each hold integers, floating-point numbers, or pointers. Conventionally, r31 has been set aside as a stack pointer while r30 has been used to point to a *procedure constant table* (a per-procedure table of addresses and constant values too large to be loaded as "immediates") but hardware neither suggests nor enforces this convention in any way.

A 1024-word *processor constant table* (not to be confused with the procedure constant table) is a read-only table for commonly-used constants such as the floating point coefficients used by the math library, complex roots of unity for FFT's, and bit masks. This table is shared among all i-streams in the processor and is not writable in user mode. However, an operating system service in supervisor mode may write it on behalf of a user.

Also part of the programmer's visible state are four 64-bit *target* registers and the *Instruction-stream Status Word (ISW).* Target registers are numbered t0-t3 and are used to specify potential branch target addresses. The ISW specifies the current *Program Counter (PC)* rather than a branch target. Actually, branch targets can be thought of as "future" PCs. Thus targets and the ISW have the same format and consist of a 42-bit instruction address, a 12-bit condition vector, and a 6-bit trap mask. The *condition vector* consists of four three-bit *condition codes* numbered c0-c3. In the ISW, c0 is the most-recently-calculated condition code, c1 is the next-most-recently-calculated, and so on. Whenever a new condition code is calculated, it is placed in c0 of the ISW; the old c0 becomes c1 and so on and the former c3 is lost. The trap mask controls which classes of traps are to be ignored.

There are also some miscellaneous registers that control and summarize trap behavior. Other miscellaneous state includes performance monitors and information on pending memory references. These are more fully described in [5].

Data Formats

Integers are signed, 64-bit two's complement values.

Floating point numbers are also 64-bit quantities composed of a 48-bit binary fraction with a hidden bit just to the left of the implied binary point, a 15-bit binary excess 2^{14} exponent, and a sign bit [6]. The word format is conventional: the sign (s) is in the most-significant bit, the exponent field (E) is in bits 62-47, and the fraction (f) occupies the least-significant 48 bits. The values of positive floating point numbers (s=0) in this representation are given by:

$$2^e * 1.f, \ where \ e = E - 2^{14}$$

A zero value has a representation of all zeroes. Negative values have a sign bit equal to one and are obtained by two's complementing the entire 64-bit word representing the positive floating point value. Giving the integer and floating point formats the same numerical ordering allows testing, maximum, and minimum operations to serve for both signed integers and floating point numbers.

Table 1 summarizes the ranges of true exponents and fractions for valid, underflowed, and overflowed values.

Table 1. Numeric ranges of Horizon floating point numbers.

type	true exponent	fraction
zero	$e = 0$	$f = 0$
valid, non-zero	$-2^{13} \le e < 2^{13}$	$0 \le f < 1$
underflowed	$-2^{14} \le e < -2^{13}$	$0 \le f < 1^{(1)}$
overflowed	$2^{13} \le e < 2^{14}$	$0 \le f < 1^{(2)}$

(1) s=0, E=00...0, f=00...0 is reserved for zero
(2) s=0, E=11...1, f=11...1 is reserved for infinity

The exponent range for normal numbers was chosen so that the result of any single operation on normal numbers — even an overflowed or underflowed result — continues to be representable in the 64-bit format. The specification of floating point underflow and overflow ranges provide headroom for trap handlers to recover the offending number without having to rescale and re-issue the instruction. If the number is used in a subsequent operation, an unrepresentable number may result. Overflow and underflow may be detected by examining the exponent and fraction bits of the floating point value. The rules for floating point addition, multiplication, and other operations are given in [6].

Pointers consist of two parts: the leftmost 16 bits (bits 63-48) are the *access control* field; the rightmost 48 bits (bits 47-0) are the *base* field. The base field points to a specific bit location in the shared memory space. A pointer's access control field in combination with the memory access state bits of the addressed word (i.e., full/empty, indirect, and four trap bits) is used to control the synchronization, indirect addressing, and trapping properties of the memory reference. This will be explained in detail later.

III. Instruction Set Highlights

Introduction

In the syntactic descriptions below, a Roman letter or special symbol represents itself, *q, r, s, t, u, v, w, x, y,* and *z* represent one of the 64-bit general-purpose registers (r0-r31), *cn* represents one of the three-bit condition codes (c0-c3), and *tn* represents one of the 64-bit target registers (t0-t3). Other italicized strings are meta-variables representing some other form such as a condition name or a constant. A sample fragment of Horizon assembly language is given later.

Operation names ending in "_TEST" cause the 12-bit condition code vector to be updated. For most such operations, there is another operation identical in all respects except that it does not produce a new 3-bit condition code. Condition code c0 receives the newly-calculated 3-bit condition code, c1 contains the 3-bit condition code from the next-most-recently-executed "_TEST" instruction, and so on. The oldest 3-bit condition code in the vector, formerly c3, is lost.

The eight possible condition code values and their meanings are given in Table 2. 0, p, and n stand for zero, a positive integer, and a negative integer respectively.

Table 2. Condition code values.

Code value	Meaning	Integer examples
0	Zero, no carry	0 = 0 + 0
1	Negative, no carry	n = p + n, n = p − p
2	Positive, no carry	p = p + p, p = p − n
3	Overflow, no carry	n = p + p, n = p − n
4	Zero, carry	0 = n + p, 0 = n − n
5	Negative, carry	n = n + n, n = n − p
6	Positive, carry	p = n + p, p = n − n
7	Overflow, carry	p = n + n, p = n − p

The condition name *cond* in the BRANCH and related instructions describes a set of condition code values that would make the condition true. For example, the condition name "IF_E" (if equal) is true if the condition code has value 0 or 4. Similarly, the condition name "IF_L(ess)" is true if the condition code has value 1, 5, or 7. Sixteen distinct condition code name classes are defined, providing tests for integer and unsigned results and the presence/absence of carry.

A Horizon assembly language program looks like a sequence of Lisp expressions. Each expression is either an instruction having the format

(INST *lookahead M-operation A-operation C-operation*)

or is a pseudo-operation such as

(LABEL *symbol*)

The *lookahead* field is used to control instruction overlap. It is a positive integer guaranteed (by the code generator) to be less than or equal to the minimum distance to the next instruction that depends on the current one. The minimum is to be taken over all branch paths for which lookahead is enabled. In other words, the *lookahead* field supplies an upper bound on the number of additional instructions that may begin execution before the current instruction is finished. For example, if *lookahead* is 0 throughout a program, the hardware will finish each instruction before starting the next. The maximum possible *lookahead* value is currently assumed to be seven. This lookahead allows up to eight memory operations per i-stream to be outstanding at any instant.

For the purpose of lookahead calculation, there are two bases that could be used for determining dependences between instructions. The first assumes a dependence exists if there is a register flow dependence or a memory reference dependence. The second determines dependences solely on the memory references and assumes that the hardware prevents two instructions from the same i-stream from being in the A and C functional units simultaneously (thus preserving the register flow dependences). Lookaheads calculated on the second basis can usually be made larger than with the first basis. Also, the number of available registers appears larger using the second basis. However, use of the second basis can slow the execution progress of an i-stream.

The other fields, *vide infra*, describe the operations of the instruction. All registers used as source operands in the various fields of an instruction are assumed to be read before any part of the instruction is executed. Registers used as destination operands are assumed to be written after all parts of the instruction have completed. This allows the same register to be used as a source in one field of an instruction and as a destination in another will no ill effect. There are no restrictions on the number of times a single register can be named as a source operand in an instruction. If a single register is named as a destination more than once in an instruction, its value is undefined. The exception is r0, which when used as a destination, causes the result to be discarded.

M-Operations

(LOAD q r s)	$q \leftarrow$ memory at $(r + s)$
(STORE q r s)	memory at $(r + s) \leftarrow q$

The memory reference operations use a *pointer* in register r and an integer *offset* in register s to compute the address of the word in memory to be loaded to, or stored from, register q. The 42-bit memory address is computed by adding the pointer *base* field from r to the *offset* from s modulo 2^{48} and ignoring the least-significant six bits.

The six *access state* bits associated with every Horizon memory location, unless disabled by corresponding bits in the pointer's *access control* field, modify the behavior of the memory reference. The *access control* field contains an *indirect disable* bit, two *full/empty (F/E) control* bits, and eight *trap disable bits* (independently set-able for the LOAD and STORE operations for each of the four trap "color" bits in the *memory access state*). *Full/empty control* bits define one of the four behaviors given in Table 3.

Table 3. Pointer full/empty control.

F/E Control	LOAD behavior	STORE behavior
00	Wait for FULL	Wait for FULL
01	Wait for FULL, set EMPTY	Wait for EMPTY, set FULL
10	Get *value*	Set FULL
11	Get *access state*	Set EMPTY

When the *F/E control* bit pattern is "00" or "01," the memory cell's *access state* and the rest of the *access control* field determine the behavior of the LOAD or STORE. These operations do not modify the *trap* or *indirect* state bits in the memory location, only the *full/empty* state bit and the *value*. First, a trap occurs if a *trap* bit is set in the location and the appropriate *trap disable* bit in r is not set. Next, if the *indirect* bit is set in the location and the *indirect disable* bit is not set in r, the *value* in the cell is interpreted as a new *pointer* to be used for another memory access (with no *offset*). Register r is not modified in this process. Further trap processing is performed as before, using the *trap disable* bits from the new *pointer* and the *trap* bit from the new word it addresses.

Finally, the *full/empty* bit is tested. If its state is the one waited for, based on the *full/empty control* bits of the original *pointer* (before indirect addressing), then the LOAD or STORE of the *value* occurs (and the *full/empty* bit is changed for *F/E control* bit pattern "01"); otherwise, the operation is re-tried later. When an operation is re-tried, no issue cycle is consumed. The hardware determines when re-tries are to be submitted in lieu of new memory requests governed by variables such as the number of previous unsuccessful tries and the type of memory reference being attempted. Re-tries of indirections use only the "final" pointer: the chain of indirections is not re-traversed for each retry.

No memory trapping, indirect addressing, or *full/empty* bit testing occurs for the *F/E control* bit patterns "10" and "11." LOAD operations for these patterns fetch either the 64-bit *value* or the 6-bit *access state* of the addressed memory cell into register *q*. In STORE operations for these patterns, the *value* of the addressed memory cell is written from register *q* and the *access state* from the *access control* field of register *r*. The *full/empty* bit setting is initialized according to the table.

A Operations

The operations of the *A-operation* field use any or all of the four register fields *t*, *u*, *v*, and *w*.

(INTEGER_ADD_MUL *t u v w*)	$t \leftarrow u + v{*}w$, integer
(INTEGER_SUB_MUL *t u v w*)	$t \leftarrow u - v{*}w$, integer
(INTEGER_ADD *t u v*)	$t \leftarrow u + v$, integer
(INTEGER_SUB *t u v*)	$t \leftarrow u - v$, integer
(FLOAT_ADD_MUL *t u v w*)	$t \leftarrow u + v{*}w$, floating point
(FLOAT_SUB_MUL *t u v w*)	$t \leftarrow u - v{*}w$, floating point
(FLOAT_ADD *t u v*)	$t \leftarrow u + v$, floating point
(FLOAT_SUB *t u v*)	$t \leftarrow u - v$, floating point
(SELECT *t u v w*)	$t \leftarrow$ if $w \neq 0$ then u else v
(SELECT_COND *cond cn t u v*)	$t \leftarrow$ if $cond_{cn}$ then u else v
(SELECT_BITS *t u v w*)	$t_i \leftarrow$ if w_i then u_i else v_i for each i
(ANY_BITS_*fn t u v*)	$t \leftarrow$ if u_i *fn* v_i for any i then –1 else 0
(ALL_BITS_*fn t u v*)	$t \leftarrow$ if u_i *fn* v_i for all i then –1 else 0
(ODD_BITS_*fn t u v*)	$t \leftarrow$ if u_i *fn* v_i for oddly many i then –1 else 0
(TALLY_BITS_*fn t u v*)	$t \leftarrow$ the number of i with u_i *fn* v_i
(*fn t u v*)	$t \leftarrow u$ *fn* v

The operation suffix *fn* in these bit operations may be any of AND, NAND, OR, NOR, XOR, XNOR, IMP (not *u* or *v*) or NIMP (*u* and not *v*).

(COMPRESS *t u v w*)	$t_i \leftarrow w_j$ if v_j is the ith one in v else u_i
(EXPAND *t u v w*)	$t_j \leftarrow w_i$ if v_j is the jth one in v else u_i

These operations are used for manipulating bit-fields. The bits are both numbered and counted from right to left. COMPRESS "compresses" those bits from *w* that match the "one" bits in *v* into the rightmost bit positions of the destination register *t*; vacant places to the left of the compressed *w* are copied from *u*. In reverse fashion, EXPAND "expands" the rightmost bits from *w* into those bit positions corresponding to "one" bits in *v*; vacant places amid the expanded *w* bits are copied from *u*.

(IMMEDIATE *t value*)	$t \leftarrow value$
(PLUS_OFFSET *t value*)	$t \leftarrow 64{*}value$
(MINUS_OFFSET *t value*)	$t \leftarrow -64{*}value$

The signed IMMEDIATE *value* must satisfy $-2^{14} \leq value < 2^{14}$. The unsigned _OFFSET *values* must satisfy $0 \leq value < 2^{15}$.

(TARGET *tn offset*)	$target_{tn} \leftarrow pc + offset$
(TARGET_REG *tn w*)	$target_{tn} \leftarrow pc + w$
(TARGET_SAVE *t tn*)	$t \leftarrow target_{tn}$
(TARGET_RESTORE *tn w*)	$target_{tn} \leftarrow w$

A TARGET operation establishes target values for the trap mask (tm), condition vector (cv), and future program counter (pc) to be used by a subsequent control transfer, i.e., one of the *C-operations* CREATE, CALL, RESUME, RETURN, BRANCH, LOOP, EXIT, or JUMP. This approach separates the address-specifying function from both the decision-making function and the transfer itself. The separation of functions facilitates pre-caching the instructions at a branch target. Moreover, the loop address specification becomes an invariant and may be moved outside the loop.

The TARGET and TARGET_REG operations set the addressed target's tm, cv, and pc using the values from the ISW. The *offset* field must satisfy $-2^{17} \leq offset < 2^{17}$. TARGET_SAVE and TARGET_RESTORE transfer a target register's contents to/from a general-purpose register. The current condition codes and trap behavior are thus easily saved and restored in connection with a trap or procedure call.

Other A-operations not fully described here include UNSIGNED_ADD_MUL (calculates the upper 64 bits of the 64-by-64 multiply-add operation), modular add/subtract, field add/subtract (allows several bit fields packed into a word to be independently added/subtracted), double-word shifts, pattern-search (search for a 64-bit pattern in a 128-bit register pair), truth table look-up (function of four variables), and iterative reciprocal and square root approximations. These are discussed in [5].

C operations

The *C-operations* use register fields *x*, *y*, and *z*.

(INTEGER_ADD *x y z*)	$x \leftarrow y + z$, integer
(INTEGER_SUB *x y z*)	$x \leftarrow y - z$, integer
(INTEGER_ADD_TEST *x y z*)	$x \leftarrow y + z$, integer
(INTEGER_SUB_TEST *x y z*)	$x \leftarrow y - z$, integer
(FLOAT_ADD *x y z*)	$x \leftarrow y + z$, floating point
(FLOAT_SUB *x y z*)	$x \leftarrow y - z$, floating point

Because both the integer and floating point formats are two's complement, integer tests may also be used to test floating point values. Ordinarily, the result register *x* contains nothing of interest after a floating point test.

(CONSTANT *x cnum*)	$x \leftarrow constant_{cnum}$

One of the 1024 constants in the processor constant table is accessed.

(CREATE *tn z*)	start new i-stream using $target_{tn}$; deliver *z*
(QUIT)	cease executing the current i-stream

The CREATE operation starts a new i-stream on the same processor as the i-stream that executes it. The value in *z* is placed in r31 in the newly-created i-stream. An attempt to CREATE more than 128 i-streams on a processor results in a create fault trap.

(CALL *tn*)	save tm and cv and swap pc using $target_{tn}$
(RESUME *tn*)	swap tm, cv and pc using $target_{tn}$
(RETURN *tn*)	restore tm, cv, and pc using $target_{tn}$

Lookahead stops at a CALL, RESUME, or RETURN.

(BRANCH *tn cond cn*)	if $cond_{cn}$ then $pc \leftarrow pc_{tn}$
(LOOP *tn cond cn*)	if $cond_{cn}$ then $pc \leftarrow pc_{tn}$ else stop lookahead
(EXIT *tn cond cn*)	if $cond_{cn}$ then $pc \leftarrow pc_{tn}$ and stop lookahead
(JUMP *tn cond cn*)	stop lookahead; if $cond_{cn}$ then $pc \leftarrow pc_{tn}$

In place of *cond* and *cn* in these instructions, the words "always" and "never" can be given to force a true or false condition regardless of the condition codes.

Other C-operations not fully described here are for bit-pointer arithmetic (recall that pointers cannot be treated like integers because of the access control field), multiprecise integer add/subtract, maximum, minimum, and absolute value tests (the same instructions serve for both signed integers and floating point because the floating point representation is two's complement), boolean and, or, xor, and nimp, shifts and rotates, leftmost/rightmost zero/one finding, table-lookup approximations for reciprocal and square root, and various integer to floating point conversions. Also omitted from this summary are the privileged instructions and those involved with supervisor calls and trap handling. Details of these operations are given in [5].

Traps and Exceptions

Traps can result from floating point exceptions (overflow, underflow, indefinite, and loss of significance), invalid memory operations (attempts to access unimplemented or protected memory), memory operations on words having trap bits set in the memory access state, attempted execution of privileged instructions, or the creation of too many i-streams on a processor. The trap mask of the ISW controls which classes of traps are taken.

The trap mechanism in the Horizon processor is designed to be as lightweight as possible. In particular, when a trap is taken, the processor mode is unchanged (i.e., there is no automatic switch into supervisor mode). Because the lookahead feature allows up to eight memory references from the same i-stream to be simultaneously pending, the same type of trap may be caught all eight times (once on each memory reference). Similarly, if the hardware allows more than one instruction from the same i-stream in the pipelined functional units at the same time, the same type of trap may be caught several times before the pipes are drained and trap processing begins. In addition, a trap might not be the result of the most recent operation performed. These complexities demand that sufficient information be available about the machine state at the time of the trap to allow identification of the cause. The miscellaneous processor state available in user mode for this purpose includes a number of auxiliary registers used in trap diagnosis and handling, tables listing the outstanding memory references for the i-stream, trap vectors, and the like.

A more complete discussion of traps and trap handing appears in [7] and [5].

IV. Performance Estimates and Scheduling Philosophy

A plausible cycle time for the processors is 5 nanoseconds. Assuming that there are 256 processors and that at each cycle, an instruction containing two floating point operations is issued (e.g., FLOAT_ADD_MUL), the overall performance will be approximately 100 giga-FLOPS. This rate can be sustained because the horizontal instruction can include a memory operation and an additional integer operation (to index the next operand) in other instruction fields. Integer performance is comparable. Of course, not all applications will be able to use two-FLOP instructions each cycle. Concrete examples of performance for two applications are given in [8].

Network simulations indicate that average memory latencies of 60-80 cycles (assuming random addressing patterns and a memory access time of 20 cycles) are expected for systems having 256 processors and 512 memory modules [4]. Under the conditions of random addressing, i-streams issuing memory references on every cycle, and no use of lookahead, at least 60-80 i-streams per processor are required to ensure that an instruction is ready to issue on each cycle in order to achieve full utilization. Note that full utilization of the machine *does not* imply use of all 128 i-streams on each processor: for example, if only 64 i-streams are needed to hide the average latency but 128 are used, each stream will be serviced only half as often as it could if the i-streams were divided among two processors.

There are two factors that reduce the number of i-streams per processor required for full utilization. The use of i-stream lookahead increases the number of outstanding memory references, reducing the effective latency and therefore, the number of i-streams per processor required. For example, an average lookahead value of one (allowing two outstanding memory references) will halve the effective latency. Also, latency-reduction techniques such as the placement of locally-used values (such as stacks) in nearby memory modules reduce the i-streams per processor requirement. With a very pessimistic 80%-20% mix of global and local references, the effective latency would be reduced by somewhat less than 20%. However, the serendipitous effect of decreased network loading may result in much more significant reductions in effective latencies [4]. Offsetting factors that drive the number of i-streams per processor up are: (1) synchronizing (full/empty) memory references that increase effective latencies and reduce the number of ready-to-run i-streams, (2) hot-spots (that increase effective latencies), and (3) register bank scheduling conflicts that reduce the number of ready-to-run i-streams [7].

As just seen, Horizon tolerates increases in memory and other types of latencies at the cost of requiring more parallelism. When an application is expected to use a large fraction of the available memory and the access patterns cannot be predicted by the user or compiler, it matters little where (on what processor) the computations (i-streams) are scheduled. Enough parallelism either in the form of i-streams or lookahead will have to be present to hide the latency. As discussed earlier, if something is known about the access patterns, scheduling the i-streams on processors near the memory locations to be accessed reduces the average latency. This has the desirable effect of reducing the execution time, reducing the amount of parallelism required to hide the latency (reducing as well the software overheads of managing that parallelism), or both.

When a problem has a data set and an amount of parallelism that are small compared to the total available memory and i-streams, its i-streams and data are localized to a few processors and their nearby memories. Localization of small problems is important not only for reducing latency but for minimizing interactions with other tasks. The intra-task statistical behavior of i-streams is often known and can be carefully orchestrated by a compiler; however, the effects of interactions with other tasks are unknown and should be minimized. Therefore, a compiler should strive to estimate the minimum number of i-streams needed per processor to keep the processors fully utilized. Also, the scheduler should allow a processor to be shared by more than one task only when there are no other free (or under-utilized) processors available.

Additional performance considerations are given in [9].

V. Programming Example

The inner product calculation:

$$c = \sum_i a_i * b_i$$

is used to demonstrate Horizon programming. It is assumed that registers symbolically referred to as *aptr* and *bptr* hold pointers to the vectors *a* and *b* in memory. Registers *ai, bi,* and *c* contain the data values, *i* is a loop index holding a word offset, and *step* is the stride of both vectors (measured in bits). This fragment assumes that the registers *aptr, bptr, i,* and *step* have all been initialized. The loop index is run in reverse (descending) order.

```
(INST 1   (LOAD ai aptr i)
          (TARGET t1 again)
          (FLOAT_ADD c r0 r0))    // c = 0
(LABEL    again)
(INST 0   (LOAD bi bptr i)
          ()
          (INTEGER_SUB_TEST i i step)
(INST 1   (LOAD ai aptr i)        // ai for next iteration
          (FLOAT_ADD_MUL c c ai bi)
          (LOOP t1 IF_L c0))
```

Loop unrolling techniques could be used to obtain larger lookahead values but at the possible expense of reducing the number of instruction streams applicable to such a loop. In practice, the extent of unrolling is limited by the number of registers.

VI. Software

A software development system consisting of a (sequential) C compiler, assembler, linker, and simulator has been implemented at the Supercomputing Research Center. The C compiler is based on the GNU C implementation and produces "non-horizontal" (one operation per instruction) assembly language. A post-processing "packager" then constructs horizontal instructions by analyzing register and memory dependences, packing operations into the M, A, and C fields of Horizon instructions, and calculating the lookahead values. Another Horizon compiler effort is described in [10]. The simulator is overviewed in [11].

Both compiler projects are currently oriented toward understanding the complexities of packing instructions, optimizing the lookahead values, and effectively using the multiple target and condition code registers. One immediate goal is to determine if the relative utilization of the functional units is balanced and if not, to refine the instruction set accordingly. Currently, neither compiler automatically unrolls loops to increase lookahead nor "CREATE"s other i-streams to gain performance; explicit unrolling or calls to hand-coded assembly language stream-spawning routines are used. Parallelism detection and packaging are high on our list of development goals.

At the time of this writing, about two dozen kernels and small applications programs have been hand-coded in Horizon assembly language. Two of these are discussed in [8].

VII. Summary and Evaluation

The design philosophy and the resulting machine design of Horizon have been described. "Magic numbers" in the design are the number of processors (P), the number of memory modules (M), the interleaving factor of the memory modules (IF), the number of lightweight instruction streams per processor (S), the number of registers per instruction stream (R), and the maximum instruction lookahead (L). Evaluating the scalability of the machine requires an understanding of how they are related and how they were derived.

The relationship between P, M, and the number of network nodes is considered first. M must be at least as large as P because at each cycle, the network must be able accept a new memory request from each processor and the memories must be able to service them. M=2P relaxes the memory speed requirements somewhat and allows for the inevitable effects of hot spots, bank contention, and the like. Simulation studies in which M is varied from 1.0P to 2.0P are in progress.

To ensure that memory latencies can be hidden in a P-processor machine, the number of messages "in flight" must be on the order of P times the memory latency, requiring a proportional number of network nodes. (The lower bound on the number of network nodes is P+M.) Given the 7-ported nodes discussed for the 3-D mesh network, the number of wires available to hold messages en route is seven times the number of nodes. If a single message buffer is provided at each port of a node (as was assumed in the simulations), this message capacity doubles. Through simulation, a good compromise between capacity and cost for P=256 and M=512 was found to be approximately 6P nodes for a random reference pattern [4]. This number of nodes provided a message capacity of 84P which is somewhat larger than the number of new messages P processors would be expected to generate given the average network latency in the range 40-60 cycles (excluding memory access time).

Assuming P=256 and mesh-interconnected networks with 6P nodes, average memory access times (including memory access times) can be assumed to be 60-80 cycles. This influences S because it must be at least as large as the average latency (if the latency is to be hidden even when latency-reduction techniques are ineffectual). Hence, S was set to be 128. The interleaving factor, IF, depends on the memory access time and has not been determined as yet.

Lookahead and the number of registers per i-stream are also related. To achieve the maximum lookahead in an i-stream, L independent memory references must be able to be done. This implies use of L registers for the memory address pointers (if lookahead dependences are based on both register and memory references) and up to L registers to be used as destinations (sources) for the loads (stores). So 2L must be less than R if lookahead is to be useful. Generally, several registers are dedicated to other uses; hence, for a maximum lookahead involving eight outstanding memory references, R=32 registers is a reasonable choice. Note that L and R are not directly related to S. However, the amount of register state per processor is proportional to R×S and the amount of state for monitoring outstanding memory references is proportional to L×S. For much larger L and R, the latency incurred in accessing this internal processor state becomes significant, requiring a decrease in the clock rate or additional pipelining, each increasing the amount of parallelism required. Both R and L can likely be increased by a factor of two (to R=64 and L=15) with little effect on the clock rate. However, doing so would force instructions to be encoded in somewhat more than 64 bits.

It appears that P can be increased by at least a factor of four (to P=1024) while holding S constant before S is no longer sufficient to hide the increased interconnection network latency. Doubling R and L might allow P to be increased by another factor of two. Together, nearly an order of magnitude increase in capability over that proposed here seems possible without a change in the basic architecture of the machine.

References

[1] D. Gajski, D. Kuck, D. Lawrie, and A. Sameh, "CEDAR - A Large Scale Multiprocessor," *1983 International Conference on Parallel Processing,* 1983, pp. 524-529.

[2] G. F. Pfister, W. C. Brantley, D. A. George, S. L. Harvey, W. J. Kleinfelder, K. P. McAuliffe, E. A. Melton, V. A. Norton, and J. Weiss, "The IBM Research Parallel Processor Prototype (RP3): introduction and architecture," *1985 International Conference on Parallel Processing,* August 1985, pp. 764-771.

[3] B. J. Smith, "A Pipelined, Shared Resource MIMD Computer," *1978 International Conference on Parallel Processing,* 1978, pp. 6-8.

[4] F. M. Pittelli and D. L. Smitley, "Analysis of a 3-D toroidal network for a shared memory architecture," *Supercomputing '88,* 1988.

[5] *The Horizon Supercomputing System: Project Status Report (Version 1.1),* J. T. Kuehn, ed., Technical Note SYS-88-015, Institute for Defense Analyses -- Supercomputing Research Center, 1988.

[6] M. Thistle, *Floating Point Arithmetic on Horizon,* Technical Note APP-88-002, Supercomputing Research Center, 1988.

[7] M. R. Thistle and B. J. Smith, "A processor architecture for Horizon," *Supercomputing '88,* 1988.

[8] D. A. Carlson and J. M. Conroy, "The Fast Fourier Transform and sparse matrix computations: a study of two applications for the Horizon supercomputer," *Supercomputing '88,* 1988.

[9] R. R. Glenn, "Horizon performance projections," *Supercomputing '88,* 1988.

[10] J. M. Draper, "Compiling on Horizon," *Supercomputing '88,* 1988.

[11] D. J. Kopetzky, "Horse: a simulation of the Horizon supercomputer," *Supercomputing '88,* 1988.

A PROCESSOR ARCHITECTURE FOR HORIZON

Mark R. Thistle
Institute for Defense Analyses
Supercomputing Research Center
Lanham, Maryland 20706
thistle@super.org

Burton J. Smith †
Tera Computer Company
P. O. Box 25418
Washington, DC 20007-8418
burton@lll-crg.llul.gov

ABSTRACT

Horizon is a scalable shared-memory Multiple Instruction stream - Multiple Data stream (MIMD) computer architecture independently under study at the Supercomputing Research Center (SRC) and Tera Computer Company. It is composed of a few hundred identical scalar processors and a comparable number of memories, sparsely embedded in a three-dimensional nearest-neighbor network. Each processor has a horizontal instruction set that can issue up to three floating point operations per cycle without resorting to vector operations. Processors will each be capable of performing several hundred Million Floating Point Operations Per Second (FLOPS) in order to achieve an overall system performance target of 100 Billion (10^{11}) FLOPS.

This paper describes the architecture of the processor in the Horizon system. In the fashion of the Denelcor HEP, the processor maintains a variable number of Single Instruction stream - Single Data stream (SISD) processes, which are called instruction streams. Memory latency introduced by the large shared memory is hidden by switching context (instruction stream) each machine cycle. The processor functional units are pipelined to achieve high computational throughput rates; however, pipeline dependences are hidden from user code. Hardware mechanisms manage the resources to guarantee anonymity and independence of instruction streams.

1. Introduction

Over the last decade, supercomputer performance has risen by an order of magnitude. Machine cycle times of under 10 nanoseconds have become commonplace. However, this performances comes with a cost. Maximum performance can only be achieved with heavily vectorized codes. In addition, these codes must be tuned precisely to the machine on which they will run in order to achieve this maximum performance, thereby thwarting any effort to generate portable programs. Although non-vectorizable problems may benefit from the scalar performance of supercomputers over that of the more general purpose minisupercomputers, they still do not utilize the full potential of the machine. Consequently, scalar speed is low. A fundamental limit for scalar performance is memory latency for large memories. The problem is exacerbated in multiple processor systems by the physical and logical nonlocality of memory with respect to a processor. Cacheing techniques have been developed to reduce effective memory latency; however, in shared memory systems, cache coherence is a significant problem [1].

The Horizon supercomputer is a shared memory, Multiple Instruction stream, Multiple Data stream (MIMD) system that bridges the gap between scalar and vector performance. Each processor in the multiple processor system uses internal multistream parallelism to compensate for the latencies introduced by the large shared memory and the pipeline. The architecture of the processor in Horizon bears a strong resemblance to that of its predecessor: the Denelcor HEP. At the time of this writing, the SRC is completing a one-year study to demonstrate the feasibility of the Horizon architecture, its implementation, and its software approach. This paper describes the architecture of the Horizon processor and highlights many of the features which support the high performance targeted for the machine. Section 2 introduces the programmer's model of the Horizon system and of the individual processors. The details of the architecture are discussed in Section 3, with some of the major unresolved issues in Section 4.

2. Programmer Model

2.1 Global Machine Model

A Horizon machine consists of P processors, where P is currently defined in the range 256 to 1024, that share a memory with an address space of 2^{48} bits. Memory is organized into 64-bits words and is addressed through 48-bit virtual bit addresses, the most significant 42 bits of which form the word address. Loads and stores fetch or store the 64-bit word that contains the bit that was addressed. Associated with each memory word is a six-bit access state composed of a full/empty bit, an indirect bit, and four trap bits numbered 0 to 3. These access state bits can modify the behavior of memory references to the associated location. All communication among processes in the machine is through the shared memory [2]. describes the options available for memory access.

Processors and memory modules are spatially and logically distributed throughout a multidimensional, nearest-neighbor, packet-switched interconnection network. Each processor is individually connected to one node in the network and sends data to or receives data from a memory module by via this node. The current design calls for a ratio of the number of processors to memory modules from 1:1 to 1:2. The response time of the memory request is a function of the addressed module's distance from the processor and the traffic in the network. Simulation indicates that average response times of 50-80 cycles are attainable in a system containing 256 processors and 512 memory modules, with nearly all responses available within 128 cycles. Each machine cycle, the network is capable of receiving a message from every processor and memory module, and delivering a message to every processor and memory module. [3] describes the interconnection network for Horizon.

2.2 Processor Model

The Horizon processor manages a variable number of processes, as in the HEP architecture [4], called instruction streams (i-streams), each of which is an autonomous virtual processor with its own register set, program counter, and associated processor state. Each cycle, the processor issues the next instruction from an i-stream chosen from the set of active i-streams. Instructions from any single i-stream are executed in sequential order. Pipelining of instruction

† Work performed at the Supercomputing Research Center.

CH2617-9/88/0000/0035$01.00 © 1988 IEEE

execution is hidden from the user to avoid the complexity of managing exposed pipelines. The maximum number of i-streams per processor is 128. There is no sharing of registers or other processor state between i-streams; the processor manages each i-stream's state independently.

The processor has three major execution units: the Memory unit (M-unit), Arithmetic unit (A-unit), and the Control unit (C-unit). The architecture is horizontal; a 64-bit instruction can initiate three operations, an M-unit operation (M-op), an A-unit operation (A-op), and a C-unit operation (C-op), through three independent fields in the instruction. Also part of each instruction is a lookahead field that is used to control instruction overlap. The user-specified lookahead value in an instruction indicates the number of subsequent instructions that may be issued without waiting for the completion of that instruction.

M-ops include loads and stores. A load/store architecture was selected to maximize performance with high-bandwidth register operations. Shorter instructions, less hardware complexity, and better reuse of values are additional benefits of a load/store architecture. Arithmetic, logical, control, test, and miscellaneous operations are performed in the A-unit, C-unit, or both. [5] specifies the complete Horizon Instruction Set.

Synchronization between instruction streams is performed through memory operations that use the full/empty bit in each memory cell. An instruction stream can suspend its execution or can be placed into execution by a single instruction. The allocation of instruction streams to processors is handled jointly by user code and the operating system. The operating system allocates instruction streams in response to a system call. Such a system call requires a significant amount of operating system code to be executed and is therefore used relatively infrequently. Thereafter, the user program activates the allocated instruction streams as they are needed. The activation of an i-stream is accomplished by a single instruction.

Each of the M-, A-, and C- fields consists of an operation code (opcode) and the register operands to be used. An instruction may specify up to 7 register sources and 3 register destinations, or 8 sources and 2 destinations for the execution unit operations. These registers are referred to symbolically as q, r, s, (M unit operation), t, u, v, w, (A unit operation), x, y, z, (C unit operation). Register q is either a source or a destination register for the M-unit operation, t is the destination register for the A-unit operation, and x is the destination register for the C-unit operation. The other registers are sources. The number of register accesses for each instruction is an important parameter in the design and will be discussed later. The several dozen program fragments that have been written for Horizon confirm that the horizontal aspect of the instruction set is well balanced and not overly aggressive. From 1-1/2 to 3 floating point operations per instruction have been achieved for the various test programs. A compiler for a small FORTRAN-like language was written to provide data on the suitability of the Horizon instruction set for code generation; this compiler has been successful in achieving high utilization of all three operation fields [6].

The data formats supported include integer, floating point, bit vector, target, and pointer. Integers are signed, 64-bit two's complement values. Floating point numbers are also 64-bit quantities with a non-standard format, chosen for its dynamic range, compatibility with the integer format for common test and compare operations, and recoverability of results from operations that produce overflowed or underflowed results. The definition of the floating point format and the rules for floating point addition, multiplication, and other operations are given in [7]. Pointers are 64-bit values containing a base address and several bits that control the synchronization, indirect addressing, and trapping properties of memory references.

For each of the 128 possible i-streams in the processor, there are 32 64-bit general-purpose registers. The general-purpose registers can each hold integers, floating-point numbers, portions of bit vectors, targets, or pointers. There are four 64-bit target registers and one Instruction-stream Status Word (ISW). Target registers are used to specify potential branch target addresses. The ISW specifies the current Program Counter (PC) as well as the trap mask and condition vector. There is also a 1024-word processor constant table, a read-only table for commonly-used constants such as pi, e, and bit masks, that is shared among all i-streams in the processor.

3. Processor Architecture

3.1 Introduction

Each Horizon processor has a pipelined architecture capable of sustaining a performance of 400 MFLOPS. The target machine cycle time is 4 nanoseconds. To achieve the targeted performance, Horizon embodies four levels of parallelism. At the top level is the MIMD model with several hundred processors. The next three levels are supported within the processor and include: pipelined MIMD instruction execution, that is concurrent execution of multiple instruction streams in a round-robin fashion; overlapped and pipelined execution of instructions within each stream; and horizontal instructions each performing multiple functions. Compilers have traditionally assumed the burden of managing the last two levels of parallelism. The targeted high performance is, in general, accomplished by effectively managing the parallelism, i.e. rapidly switching context in order to hide the memory latencies introduced by a large shared memory, including distance as well as contention and synchronization delays.

The remainder of this paper describes the architecture of the Horizon processor and examines how the various levels of parallelism are implemented. An overview of the functional block level design will be presented, followed by detailed examinations of the important components of the processor architecture, namely, the register organization, instruction issue sequence, i-stream selection policy and mechanism, and memory interface.

3.2 Functional Unit Model

Each processor has seven main functional components: the three execution units - M, A, and C units; the Instruction Fetch and Issue unit, the I-stream Selection unit, the Instruction Cache and Prefetch unit, and the register set. Figure 1 shows the internal organization of a Horizon processor. The instruction execution logic is completely pipelined so that it can begin executing a new instruction every cycle. Each of the function units is pipelined and requires multiple cycles to complete each instruction. Pipeline lengths will be fixed and will appear identical for all instructions, regardless of their complexity. Fixed-length pipelines allow a simple scheme to be used for register scheduling. A variable pipeline length that depends on the complexity of the instruction being performed is also possible. This scheme adds complexity to i-stream scheduling and creates register bandwidth problems for simultaneous completion of instructions but reduces the number of i-streams needed to keep the machine busy. Implications of these alternatives will be discussed later.

Every cycle, the i-stream selection logic selects an i-stream from which to issue the next instruction. The processor hardware and the compiler together must guarantee that an i-stream is eligible for selection only when all the flow and output dependences on previously issued instructions have been satisfied (there are no control or antidependence problems with previously issued instructions), and the instruction has been prefetched into the instruction buffer. To simplify the instruction issue decision, it is convenient to arrange

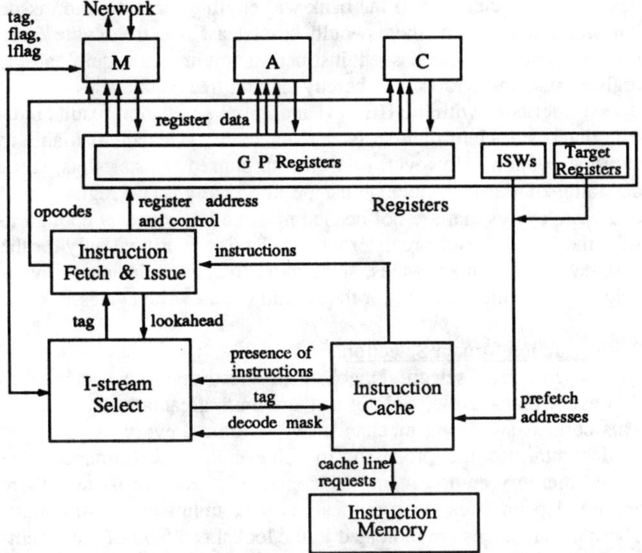

Figure 1. Horizon Processor Functional Architecture

pipeline lengths so that the earliest possible memory response (to the M-unit) is guaranteed to be later than responses from the other function units (A- and C-units). The completion of an instruction is thus made equivalent to the receipt of a response from memory. If no memory operation is specified in the instruction, instruction completion is signaled after the A- and C-units have completed.

After an i-stream has been selected for issue, its next instruction is issued to the execution units. Register operands are delivered to the execution units and execution begins. After a fixed delay, results from the A- and C- units are written back to the registers. Memory responses are essentially asynchronous events. Writing these results back to the registers will be discussed in the next section.

Every cycle the machine context is switched to another i-stream. This technique hides latencies due to memory and network response times and full/empty synchronization delays. As long as there are enough i-streams in the system to fill the pipeline in each processor, the system utilization will approach unity. The result is that the pipeline becomes totally invisible to the programmer. Instructions in a single i-stream seem to complete prior to the issue of the next instruction. The programmer need not be concerned with the number of pipeline segments in each function unit. Thus, pipelined MIMD instruction execution uses parallelism to compensate for lack of locality, and improves the programmability of horizontal (as well as conventional) processors by concealing the pipeline.

With 32 general-purpose registers, 4 target registers, 4 condition codes, the i-stream status word, and other miscellaneous state, the amount of state associated with each i-stream is large. Rather than saving and restoring the state at each instruction cycle, the processor switches context to the appropriate i-stream state. This context switching technique, taken directly from the Denelcor HEP, first appeared in the Control Data 6600 Peripheral Processor unit as the "barrel" and also in the Texas Instruments ASC I/O processor. One set of control logic is time-multiplexed among multiple i-streams. Each i-stream is served at a rate commensurate with its memory latency (or some other limiting function) while the control circuitry and arithmetic pipelines operate at a much higher rate. The maximum number of i-streams per processor 128. Technology considerations prevent it from being more than twice as large as this and 64 is too few to ensure that enough i-streams are ready to execute, given the expected network latency.

Because of the large number of i-streams in a processor, memory traffic generated by instruction fetch is considerable. Therefore access to instruction memory is made separate from data memory which is accessed by the processor through the interconnection network. Distinct processor ports for data and instruction memory operations are provided. An additional benefit of a separate instruction memory, aside from the increased bandwidth available, is that instruction security (ability to execute but not read or write instructions) may be enhanced. Depending on the speed of instruction access, an instruction cache may or may not be needed. Instruction cache issues are addressed in Section 4.

3.3 Register Organization

Each processor has one set of 32 general-purpose registers allocated to each of its i-streams. Because the number of registers per i-stream multiplied by the number of i-streams is large, it is impractical to implement the registers with individual latches or flip-flops. Instead, memory circuits must be used, thereby limiting the cycle time of the processor to some integral multiple of the register memory cycle time. This multiple depends on the number of register accesses in an instruction. Although it is possible to exchange space for time to some extent by implementing several copies of the registers behind the scenes, this approach is costly for horizontal instructions with many register references in each instruction.

The processor can achieve one instruction issue per register memory cycle while allowing a large number of register accesses per instruction by partitioning the register memory into banks. All of the registers for a subset of the processor's i-streams are resident in a single bank. In this scheme, an instruction reads and writes its registers one after another, using several cycles of the register memory bank. Other instructions that were started in the immediate past are meanwhile reading and writing their own registers which are located in other register memory banks. An i-stream becomes a candidate for execution of its next instruction based not only on whether prior instructions have finished but also on whether its register bank is available.

This register banking idea permits the implementation of a single register address space for each instruction rather than the fragmented register address spaces found in conventional horizontal processor designs. In conjunction with pipelined MIMD instruction execution register banking thus solves a problem traditionally associated with code generation for horizontal processors, namely the problem of deciding which registers should hold which values. This problem, together with the difficulty of managing an exposed pipeline with mixed function unit latencies, is largely responsible for much of the bad reputation horizontal machines have as targets for compilers.

The number of registers is a compromise stemming from the number of functional units, the number of source and destination registers needed by each function unit, the length of the instruction, and the register read/write bandwidth available. Each instruction contains up to ten references to registers requiring 50 bits of the 64-bit instruction to specify register names. The remaining 14 bits are used for the M-, A-, and C-unit opcodes and for the lookahead specification. Fewer registers, 16 for example, is not well-balanced with the number used in each instruction and would have led to under-utilized function units or worse -- register spills to memory. More registers, 64 for example, would have required too many bits (assuming fixed size instructions). Given a larger instruction width, 64 registers might be desirable.

Because every Horizon instruction requires either eight register reads and two register writes or seven register reads and three register writes, the sequential register read/write schedule would cause a long instruction cycle. To ease this problem, an identical copy of each register bank is maintained. This allows simultaneous reads to each copy, resulting in two register reads per cycle. A register write places identical data in both bank copies in one cycle. Trading space for time in this way reduces the requirement from eight to four cycles of register reads per instruction. Up to three cycles of register writes for each instruction are required.

With at most seven register cycles used by an instruction, at most seven register banks will be busy every cycle. There should be enough banks compared to the number of register references in an instruction so that there are always i-streams available to execute. If there were on the average only one or two free register banks at any cycle, the number of i-streams needed to keep the processor busy would have to be fairly large compared to the number of banks. To ensure there will always be enough free banks with ready i-streams, the number of register banks currently being considered is 16. Each bank contains the general-purpose registers for 8 i-streams.

This register organization requires a connection-intensive multiplexing scheme to route register accesses from the execution units to the correct register banks. A good implementation of this scheme is critical in order to achieve reasonably short register access latency.

3.4 Instruction Issue

The instruction issue sequence in the Horizon processor requires register bank schedule management similar to the pipeline reservation tables described by [8]. Future register bank cycles are reserved by issuing instructions for reading and writing operands, thereby affecting issue eligibility of other i-streams with registers in the same register bank. This section describes how this scheduling is performed.

When an instruction issues, four consecutive bank access cycles will be consumed reading up to eight source registers. During this time, no other instruction may issue from any i-stream whose registers are resident in that same bank. As the execution units receive their operands, their processing begins. There will be a fixed pipeline delay due to the processing time of the A- and C-units. As the results from each of the A- and C-units emerge from the pipe, they are written to the destination registers. Every cycle one instruction will issue from an i-stream in a different register bank . Instruction issue from a bank is allowed if the next four consecutive bank cycles are free (not previously reserved for register reads or writes). The pipeline schedule for a single instruction issue and execution sequence is illustrated in Figure 2.

The successful completion of a memory reference, unlike operations in the A- and C-units, is an asynchronous event. Memory references must traverse the interconnection network to reach the target address and then return to the source processor. In addition, some memory references may not be satisfied by the first access. For example, in a "wait-for-full-and-set-empty" load, unsuccessful attempts to read a full memory location require that the operation to be retried. Consequently, the register write resulting from a memory load cannot be scheduled at instruction issue time as are those for the results of the A- and C-units.

As memory references are completed, the information about that memory reference (i-stream number, destination register, 64-bit datum, etc.) is enqueued in the M-unit. The M-unit must then steal a cycle from the appropriate register bank to write the datum to the destination register. A bank is considered free for an M-unit result register write if there is no activity scheduled for that cycle. Free bank cycles arise in one of two ways: (1) Future reserved cycles could have prohibited instruction issue from the bank leaving the next several cycles free. If the bank was eligible for instruction issue but was not selected, there would be at least one free cycle for a register write; (2) An issued instruction might not require all its register read and write slots, thereby leaving free bank cycles.

Experience with the HEP [4] and initial simulation results indicate that a sufficient number of register write cycles are available to avoid starvation. However, to utilize all unused register slots, some decoding of the instruction must be done early. The register read and write cycles that are not needed must be known early enough to steal the free cycles for register writes. Timing is critical only for the first few register read cycles, since more than enough time is available to determine the need for the A- and C-unit write cycles.

3.5 Instruction Stream Selection

The i-stream selection mechanism selects and issues an instruction every clock cycle, as long as there are i-streams ready to issue. This context switching mechanism is performed every cycle and is fundamental for the processor to achieve high performance in a shared memory environment. An i-stream is ready to issue if there are no dependences on previously-issued, unfinished instructions. These dependences are indicated in the lookahead field of the assembly language instruction. The other factors which determine an i-stream's issue eligibility are (1) whether the i-stream's register bank is free for an instruction issue (described in the previous section), and (2) whether the next instruction is available. Every clock cycle, the selection mechanism chooses from among the instruction streams that are candidates for issue. A "fair" selection algorithm will help to ensure that issue starvation does not occur. Other selection mechanisms are being considered that impose issue priorities on streams; however, as yet, none have been formally defined.

The mechanism that manages a stream's dependence information is the lookahead logic. The lookahead value associated with an instruction indicates the number of subsequent instructions that may be issued before it must complete. Instruction completion is defined to be the completion of the memory operation; an instruction with no memory operation completes after the fixed delay of the pipeline. The lookahead logic allows instructions to overlap. Consider an instruction (i) containing a memory reference and a lookahead value of (L). Before instruction (i)'s memory reference is complete, instructions (i+1) through (i+L) may issue. The lookahead field in an instruction is 3 bits wide; therefore, the maximum lookahead value is 7. Hence an i-stream may have a maximum of 8 instructions simultaneously executing.

The maximum lookahead value is related to the instruction word size, the number of destination register references in an instruction and to the size of an i-stream's register set. With 32 registers and 3 destination registers per instruction, 24 registers would be reserved for 8 outstanding memory references (maximum lookahead value of 7). Since a nominal number of registers, say 8, will be live and unusable, a maximum lookahead of 7 seems reasonable. A maximum lookahead of 15, however, would allow all registers to be reserved for memory reference returns. This change would have a

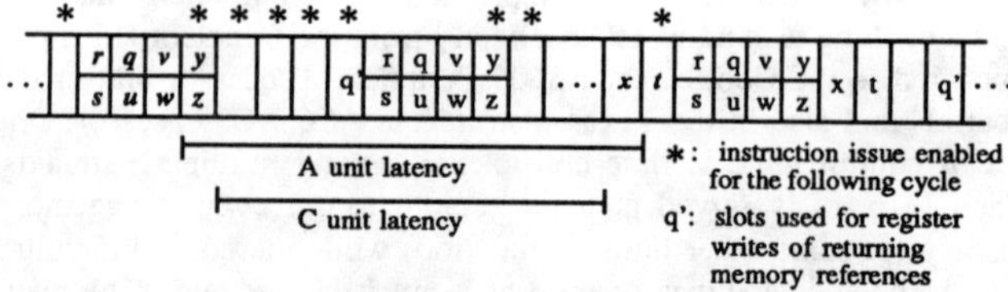

Figure 2. Instruction Execution Sequence

positive effect of reducing the number of i-streams required to keep the processor busy, since a greater memory latency could be tolerated by each i-stream. However, it has the negative effect of doubling the amount of state that must be kept by the M-unit for outstanding memory references, as well as increasing the amount of logic required to manage the additional lookahead and increasing the instruction width. Perhaps more importantly, a greater maximum lookahead also tends to increase the statically scheduled parallelism needed within each instruction stream. Experience with simulation of application codes has not yet provided insight into the realizable benefit from an extended lookahead.

The determination of whether an i-stream is a candidate for issue is performed by the lookahead logic. A functional block diagram of the lookahead mechanism and ready logic is shown in Figure 3. There are 8 locks per i-stream, each corresponding to one of 8 possible instructions awaiting completion. Since there are 128 i-streams per processor, there are a total of 1024 locks in the processor. This defines the maximum number of outstanding memory references allowed from the processor. The value of lock i indicates for how many previous instructions instruction i is waiting. An instruction may not issue until its lock is zero. The current instruction flag counter, flag, points to the lock of the instruction to issue next.

When an instruction issues, the lock associated with the future dependent instruction is incremented. The lock number, lflag, is stored in the M-unit along with the rest of the state describing the memory reference (M-unit) part of that instruction. Lflag indicates which lock is to be decremented when the memory reference completes. Each time an instruction is issued from an i-stream, flag is incremented mod 8. The i-stream is "ready" to issue if the lock addressed by flag is zero.

The inputs to the i-stream selection mechanism are the bank-free signals, the i-stream ready signals described above, and the instruction-present signals. With its current definition, the selection mechanism can be implemented entirely in combinatorial logic, as a two-level, inverted binary tree. On one side, a register bank from among the 16 possible banks is selected to issue an instruction. A register bank is "ready", i.e., is a candidate for this selection, only if there is at least one i-stream in the bank that is ready to issue an instruction and the bank is free. The bank-free bits for each register bank are generated in parallel from the bank schedules. Similarly, the ready bits for all the i-streams are produced in parallel by the lookahead logic. Bank readiness is determined for all free banks in parallel by OR-ing the i-stream ready bits in each bank. Bank selection is based on a "roving" round-robin algorithm, in which the highest priority rotates among the banks. The round robin selector determines the bank with the highest priority for issue each cycle. With this scheme, the maximum possible delay between instruction issues from a bank with ready i-streams is 16 cycles.

The other side of the tree is the selection of an i-stream from a bank. The same round-robin mechanism as in bank selection is used. The choice of which i-stream will be issued next from each bank is generated in parallel for each bank. The worst-case delay between issues from a particular i-stream (assuming it is ready) is 8 bank issue cycles; that is, 8 cycles in which some i-stream is selected from the particular i-stream's bank. The two sides of the tree are joined by multiplexing down the tag of the chosen i-stream in the chosen bank. This selection algorithm guarantees uniform treatment of banks and of i-streams within a bank. Given the register banking constraints, i-streams in lightly loaded banks will be favored for execution over those in heavily loaded banks. This natural priority may be useful for run time scheduling of multiple priority tasks within a processor.

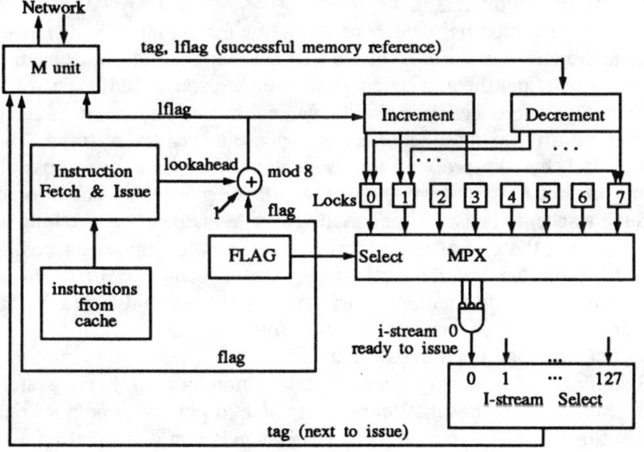

Figure 3. I-stream Lookahead Logic

3.6 Memory Interface

The M-unit directs all memory references from the processor into and out of the interconnection network. Memory requests are generated from instructions, processed after returning successfully from the network, reissued if unsuccessful, and rerouted if destined for another node. (Instruction cache lines are not fetched through the M-unit, since instructions do not travel through the network.) When a load or store instruction is issued, the M-unit receives the tag and flag (Figure 1) of the instruction from the I-stream Selection unit. This information is saved in the M-unit state table, along with the information about the request from the instruction.

The M-unit state table holds the following information: the operation to be performed (opcode), the virtual memory address, the tag and flag of instruction, destination register number, the 64-bit datum, a timestamp, and a retry value. The flag of the instruction is the address of the lock to decrement when the instruction completes. Because the arrival of a successful response from memory is an asynchronous event, some of the responses must be retained until the datum can be written to the registers during a free register bank cycle. Figure 4 shows a functional block diagram of the M-unit components. The 16 queues, one per register bank, are used to buffer completed memory requests until a register write can be performed. When the register write occurs, the datum is written to the destination register of the appropriate i-stream register set (in the case of a load). For either a load or a store, the lock addressed by lflag is decremented, indicating completion of the instruction. Assuming

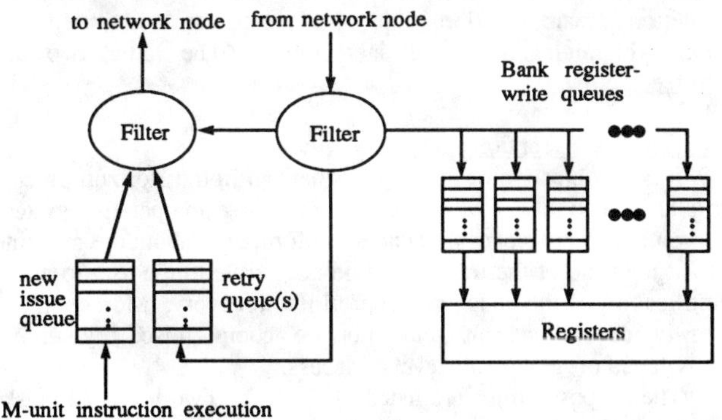

Figure 4. Memory Unit Network Interface

that each M-unit result register write queue is provided a unique data path to the registers and the i-stream selection logic can support parallel access to the locks, up to 16 M-unit result register writes could be performed in any cycle.

If the instruction contains a synchronizing load or store (e.g. wait-for-full), the M-unit must schedule a retry in the event of an unsuccessful request. Simply re-trying every unsuccessful request immediately might quickly flood the interconnection network with requests that would likely be unsuccessful again. (Flow control would limit the extent to which flooding will occur [3].) In addition retries would cause interference with issue of newly-generated requests from issued instructions since there is only a single port to the network. Hence, some back-off policy will be adopted for retry scheduling. Each successive unsuccessful attempt at a memory access will result in a greater delay before another re-try is issued. The back-off policy is further complicated by the possibility that a message may be returned without ever having gained access to its destination memory cell. Such is the case at "hot-spots" where bank conflicts overflow queues at the memory banks. Randomization policies reduce the probability of memory bank conflicts; however, hot spots will inevitably occur, whether because of poor programming practices, algorithmic constraints, or "bad" statistical epochs. Consequently, several classes of retry messages may be required.

The last responsibility of the M-unit is re-routing messages that are not addressed to it. A message may be delivered to a processor it is not intended for if there are no other links available for that message at the node [3]. Such a message is called a misrouted message. The M-unit must then turn the message around and re-issue it to the network. The filters in Figure 4 perform this function.

As indicated in Figure 4, there are essentially two queues from which messages are inserted into the network. One queue contains messages generated by newly issued instructions and the other contains messages to be retried. An alternating scheduling mechanism of memory references delivered into the network prevents starvation of either queue. Misrouted messages must have priority over either queue for injection into the network, since the processor has no knowledge about nor any reserved storage for such messages. The size of the issue queue is 1024, the maximum number of outstanding memory references allowed from the processor. To avoid deadlock, the retry queue must also be length 1024.

4. Unresolved Issues

4.1 Introduction

As the processor architecture evolves, many new (not yet resolved) issues are identified. Some of these issues are implementation details which become more important in later stages of development. However, there are important architectural topics which have not been addressed in this paper but are noteworthy, nonetheless. Instruction stream creation, traps and exceptions, and instruction memory hierarchy are three such topics. The latter two are addressed below.

4.2 Traps and Exceptions

It is an objective of the trap mechanism in the Horizon processor is to be as lightweight as possible, requiring no operating system intervention. This means that enough information about the machine state at the time of the trap should be accessible to the user to allow identification of the cause and appropriate recovery. Moreover, the integrity of the system must not be compromised by giving unprivileged programs this level of access.

The proposed traps are listed in Table 1. Two levels of masking are provided to the user for maskable traps. Summary trap mask bits are provided in the ISW for the countdown trap, branch trap, all the floating point traps and access state violation traps so that they

Table 1. Traps

CLASS[(1)]	TRAP	DETECTING UNIT[(2)]
m	Countdown	Iselect
u	Hardware Error	All
m	Single Memory Error	IF, M
u	Double Memory Error	IF, M
u	Memory Protection Violation	IF, M
u	Unimplemented Me.nory Address	IF, M
m	Access State Violation	M
m	Floating Point Overflow	A, C
m	Floating Point Underflow	A, C
m	Floating Point Indefinite	A, C
m	Floating Point Loss of Significance	A, C
m	Branch	C
u	Privileged Instruction Trap	IF, C
u	Unimplemented Instruction Trap	IF, A, C, M
u	Create Fault Trap	M

(1) m : a user-maskable trap
u : an unmaskable trap

(2) A : A-unit
C : C-unit
M : M-unit
IF: Instruction Fetch unit

can be manipulated easily inside target registers. For masking individual types of floating point traps, access state violations, and other traps listed in Table 1, separate mask registers are accessible as part of the processor state.

Because of the pipelined nature of the machine, all instructions, once issued, flow completely through the functional units. When a trap occurs, further instructions from the same i-stream may be prevented from being issued. Some traps are detected very early, even before the offending instruction enters the pipeline. In this case, the instruction(s) already in the pipeline may be completed correctly. However, some traps are not detected until the offending instruction has nearly completed and hence not in time to prevent one or more a subsequent instruction(s) from being issued (if allowed by lookahead). Depending on the nature of the trap, the later instruction(s) are either completed correctly or else their side-effects are inhibited.

Two scenarios were considered for generating traps: trap on generate and trap on use. In the latter scenario, if an error occurred in an operation, the associated destination register would be poisoned for future references, i.e., given a value that when encountered as an operand in a subsequent instruction would cause a trap. This approach has the property that traps are put off as long as possible and in fact may never occur if the offending value is not re-used. Such a scheme is useful for handling unsafe loads, where fetching an operand at the end of a loop for the next iteration causes an invalid address for the last iteration of the loop. Such an error could be ignored if the destination register is not subsequently read before being written again with valid data. However, this mechanism is not sufficient for operations that have no destination register. Specifically, a memory protection violation occurring on a store operation has no destination register value to poison. Another argument in favor of a trap on generate scheme is that a "fatal" trap may not be evidenced until much more (wasted) computation has been done. The potentially large "distance" from the condition which caused the trap to its detection makes debugging more difficult. Consequently, the trap on generate scenario was chosen.

4.3 Instruction Cache

One possible design for an instruction cache for the Horizon processor is simply an instruction prefetch buffer. The buffer should keep at least 6 lines for each active i-stream: one for the PC, one for the PC incremented, and one for each of the 4 targets. When the PC increments or a branch instruction is processed, the next instruction is always ready in the buffer. When an event occurs that changes the set of lines needed for a particular i-stream, the relevant lock is incremented in the lookahead logic for that i-stream. The lock is then decremented when the line is brought into the instruction buffer. With this instruction prefetch mechanism, instruction issue latency is only affected if the instruction prefetch time exceeds the minimum time between successive issues from a single i-stream, which is determined by the dependence on previous instructions and the number of i-streams contending for issue slots.

5. Conclusions

The processor architecture described in this paper combines three levels of parallelism, multiple instruction streams, instruction lookahead, and horizontal instructions to achieve vector-like performance on scalar code. The processor removes the burden of managing resources, hiding the pipeline and register read/write timing, from the compiler, thereby greatly simplifying code generation. Latencies caused by contention or synchronization through the shared memory, creating serious performance degradation in most machines, are effectively hidden by the processor. Each instruction stream is served at at rate commensurate with average operation latency, while the processor sustains a utilization (instructions issued per cycle) approaching unity. There are, however, many unresolved issues to be addressed. From early simulation studies and programming experience on the Horizon simulator, it appears that the underlying processor architecture is well balanced and is capable of achieving the targeted performance.

6. Acknowledgements

The authors gratefully acknowledge the contributions of the architecture team at the Supercomputing Research Center, all of whom share primary roles in the conceptual development and design of Horizon: Paul B. Schneck, Chief Architect of Horizon at the SRC, and James T. Kuehn, both of whom contributed to and provided consultation for this writing, William E. Holmes, Daniel J. Kopetzky, Fred A. More, and David L. Smitley. Steven Melvin is recognized for the origination of the register banking scheme developed originally for the HEP-3. The authors also recognize all those in industry and academia who contributed in no small part to the genesis and evolution of the Horizon processor architecture.

7. References

[1] M. Dubois, C. Scheurich, and F. A. Briggs, "Synchronization, Coherence, and Event Ordering in Multiprocessors," *IEEE Computer*, Vol. 21, No. 2, February 1988, pp 9-21.

[2] J. T. Kuehn and B. J. Smith, "The Horizon Supercomputing System: Architecture and Software," *Supercomputing '88*, submitted for publication, 1988.

[3] F. M. Pittelli and D. L. Smitley, "Analysis of a 3-D Toroidal Network for a Shared Memory Architecture," *Supercomputing '88*, submitted for publication, 1988.

[4] B. J. Smith, "A Pipelined Shared Resource MIMD Computer," *1978 International Conference on Parallel Processing*, 1978.

[5] B. J. Smith, "The Horizon Instruction Set," unpublished note, Supercomputing Research Center, 1987.

[6] J. Draper, "Compiling on Horizon," *Supercomputing '88*, submitted for publication, 1988.

[7] M. R. Thistle, "Floating Point Arithmetic on Horizon," Internal Research Note, Supercomputing Research Center, 1988.

[8] P. M. Kogge, *The Architecture of Pipelined Computers*, McGraw-Hill, NY, 1981.

Analysis of a 3D Toroidal Network for a Shared Memory Architecture

Frank Pittelli
David Smitley

Supercomputing Research Center
4380 Forbes Blvd.
Lanham, MD 20706

ABSTRACT

This paper describes a synchronized network model suitable for the Horizon architecture. The model is defined in terms of a topology and routing policy. A three dimensional toroidal topology is investigated for its multiple redundant paths, memory locality and simplicity in both routing and construction. The routing policy is based on a *desperation* routing scheme in which it is not guaranteed that a message will make progress on a given network cycle. This scheme requires no complex deadlock avoidance algorithms or node to node flow control, allowing a very simple and efficient implementation. Design considerations and preliminary performance results are discussed.

1. Introduction

The Horizon system makes use of an interconnection network to provide a shared memory address space across all processors. The interconnection network provides logical paths between any processor and memory module in the system (no processor-to-processor communication exists). A typical Horizon will consist of 256 processors together with 512 memory modules.

There exist four principal requirements that the network must meet. First, the network must allow each processor or memory module to initiate a new message every tick. Second, the average round trip delay (i.e., the number of ticks taken to reach a memory and return) should be as small as possible. Third, in the absence of hardware failures, the network must insure message delivery. No processor mechanism is planned to reissue lost messages. Finally, there must exist a technological and economical means of network implementation. This requirement places a limitation on the number of wires, connectors and logic gates that are used to implement the network.

In addition to these primary requirements, a network design should also take into account fault tolerance and scalability. A fault-tolerant network is one which allows one or more components to fail and yet still maintains logical connections between every processor and memory module. In the ideal case, the network should be able to reconfigure "on the fly" when an error occurs. Scalability with respect to a network concerns both design and performance. An increase in the size of the network should not require a complete redesign of the components used in the smaller network. In addition, average and maximum message delay should grow slowly with the number of processors.

Given these requirements, a network model is presented in Section 2. This model represents a class of networks that could be used to meet the Horizon interconnection requirements. We discuss the design and implementation tradeoffs within this class of networks in Section 3. Then, Sections 4 and 5 present preliminary results taken from a simulation of the basic network. Finally, we summarize our preliminary results and discuss ongoing and future work in Section 6.

2. Network Model

One class of networks suitable for Horizon can be modeled as a collection of tightly synchronized switch nodes. That is, all nodes perform the same function at the same time, routing messages from one node to the next. Each node supports a number of message ports. A port on a switch node is connected to another port by a bidirectional link. With regards to the model, there is no limitation on the way these links are assigned other than there may be only one link per port. In particular, some ports may have no links assigned to them and ports may be linked to themselves. Furthermore, we assume that there are *no* queues associated with the message ports. If two or more messages attempt to use the same port at the same time only one is granted access. The other messages must be routed elsewhere. This assumption may seem unrealistic but it is made to clarify the discussion of the network model. In general, adding queues to a network increases its overall capacity, which may decrease the severity of some problems, but it never eliminates them. (In Section 3, we introduce link queues as a network design issue, showing their performance benefits in Section 5.)

In addition to the inter-node ports on each switch node an additional port may be connected to either a processor, a memory module or an I/O channel. A LOAD or STORE request message from a processor is first injected into the network through the associated processor's port. The message is then routed from one switch node to the next until it arrives at the switch node associated with the desired memory module. The request then leaves the network to be serviced by the memory module. After service is complete, the process is reversed to return the memory response to the processor. (Similar processing is performed for I/O requests.)

Using the network model described above, the following design considerations must be examined.

2.1. Topology

The network topology is defined by the number of switch nodes, the number of ports per node and the assignment of links between the ports on each node. The network topology defines the basic connection between processors and memories without regard to how messages travel over those connections. The chosen topology has major ramifications for both the performance and buildability (feasibility and cost) of the network. Choosing the correct topology, however, is difficult since many tradeoffs must be examined. Ideally, a high performance network has:

- Small diameter - The average distance between any pair of nodes is small.
- Redundant paths - Redundant optimal paths between pairs of nodes decrease the probability of message collision and re-routing. Redundant paths also provide fault tolerance.
- Simple routing algorithm - If the time needed by a node to process a message is large, the time needed to traverse the network may likewise be large, even if the diameter is small.
- Short wires - As with complex routing algorithms, if the distance between neighboring switch nodes is large, the propagation time will adversely affect total message delay.

In addition to providing low latency, high bandwidth communication between nodes, the network must be buildable. Towards this goal a topology should have:

- Fixed degree, uniform nodes - Each node in the network should be identical in terms of logic and number of ports.

- Achievable Packaging - There should exist a compact layout for the network in two or three dimensions. Furthermore, this layout should be expandable to accommodate larger networks without a node redesign (i.e., it should be modular).
- Minimum wire count - The total number of wires and connectors in the network should be minimized to reduce cost and increase reliability.

Given this wide range of design criteria, a topology must be chosen. This problem is compounded by the fact that there are often complex interactions between many of the design criteria. For instance, a network with a compact layout and short wires often has large diameter due to the absence of *global* interconnections. These interactions have led to a wide variety of topologies such as crossbars, hypercubes, meshes and indirect binary *n*-cubes [Feng81, Witt81].

2.2. Placement

The network placement is defined by the number of processors, memory modules and I/O channels and their assignment to particular switch nodes. For example, in the indirect binary n-cube topology it may specify that all processors are placed on one "side" of the network, while the memories are placed on the other side.

Two issues in placement are buildability and congestion reduction. Any buildable placement will probably be regular in structure. For instance, processors may be placed on every fourth node with two memory modules connected to adjacent switch nodes. Processor and memory placements should also be chosen to reduce congestion. In the proposed model, those switch nodes connected to processors or memory modules are sources of congestion since they are the source and destination of all messages. Thus, one goal is to place them as far apart from one another as possible. Furthermore, if a particular memory access pattern is expected then the relative placement of processors and memory modules can be adjusted accordingly. This reduces congestion hot spots and hence the average message delay.

2.3. Routing Policy

Once the network topology and placement have been selected, a routing policy can be designed to route messages from one switch node to the next. That is, in a given network cycle every switch node executes the same routing policy, transferring messages from incoming to outgoing links. (Recall, we are considering a synchronous network.) The routing policy may depend on the node state, message state, both or neither.

A routing algorithm performs two principal functions. First, it examines the destination address of each incoming message and selects the output port that leads to the fastest delivery. The second function is that of conflict resolution. In many situations it will be the case that two (or more) incoming messages will need to exit the same output port. The routing algorithm must decide which message gets the desired output port and where the other message is re-routed. Since the re-routed message may not necessarily advance towards its destination, the routing algorithm must also provide a mechanism to insure that it is eventually delivered. (The same situation occurs with link queues after a link becomes full.)

When choosing a routing policy, the complexity of the logic implementation must also be considered. It is possible that additional complexity in the routing decision results in the negation of any performance gains due to this change, since more time is spent traversing a node. Making a decision as to whether one routing policy is superior to another often requires gate level knowledge of the implementation. Thus, the decision as to what constitutes an *optimum* routing policy is difficult to make. In the design of Horizon, we are looking at a variety of relatively simple routing policies. Those that appear to provide adequate performance are then further investigated in terms of implementation complexity and speed.

Other routing algorithm considerations include adaptability and fault tolerance. In a heavily-loaded network, there may be regions where switch nodes are heavily or lightly congested. Given complete global knowledge (i.e., the location and destination of all messages in the system) the routing algorithm may be able to determine the absolute shortest path (with regard to time) to its goal. Unfortunately, hardware considerations limit the size of an individual message and the distance that information can be transmitted in a given time. In other words, messages can only remember so much of their own state, and each node can only have so much timely information about the state of other nodes.

Some amount of global analysis, either static or dynamic, may also be performed to select message paths. Specifically, the expected message traffic patterns can be analyzed to determine the areas of congestion for given applications, or each node could maintain information concerning the load on neighboring nodes at run-time. In either case, the criterion used for choosing the shortest path could include the expected load in a given region, thereby decreasing the chance that a message is re-routed away from its destination.

Another routing policy decision concerns fault tolerance. In the event of a switch node failure, the routing algorithm should be able to re-route messages around the failed node. Thus, unless a large number of switch nodes have failed, full system capabilities should be maintained. The ease with which such reconfiguration occurs is also an issue.

3. Network Design

Given the network model as described there are a large number of design variations and optimizations. At this point, we present the design being considered for use as the Horizon interconnection network, proceeding in two steps. First, we specify the base design, discussing its operating characteristics. Then, we introduce a number of variations intended to optimize some aspect of the network. Naturally, not all of these variations are mutually beneficial, nor completely understood; they serve as the basis for current research.

3.1. Toroidal Grid Topology

The basic network topology has a total of 1536 switch nodes arranged in a 16x16x6 toroidal grid, with 256 processors and 512 memory modules. For placement purposes, the grid is logically divided into 6 levels, each containing 256 switch nodes. Currently, four of the levels (1, 3, 4 and 6) contain 64 processors each, uniformly separated on a given level. The remaining two levels are densely packed with 256 memory modules each. This placement strategy was chosen because of its uniform characteristics, not because of any expected performance benefits. (We will discuss the performance impact of various placement strategies in a future paper.)

To analyze the impact of link queues, the current design allows fixed-size message queues for all outgoing links. These link queues allow multiple messages to select the same outgoing port in the same network cycle. Specifically, one message proceeds over the link while the others are added to the queue. This ability to grant more messages their best choice may decrease the overall delay seen by those messages. However, if the queues grow too large (2 or 3) it may be advantageous for a message to take a secondary choice, rather than being added to the queue. That is, by traveling in another direction, the message might avoid a congested area where all link queues are full. Once a link queue is full messages are re-routed to other links as specified by the routing algorithm.

We have chosen a 3D toroid topology because it provides a large number of redundant paths to a given destination and because it has many features that reduce the difficulty of implementation. We feel that the abundance of redundant paths compensates for the lack of extensive queuing at each node. That is, we are trading extra links for queue space. To understand the tradeoff, consider the entire network of switch nodes as a single FIFO queue. Messages enter the queue at one end and proceed, in lock step, to the other end. However, paths in the network allow messages to "tunnel" their way from one stage of the queue (i.e., node) to another, provided no other message is attempting to enter that stage. In short, messages that cannot access a given link at a given time are "queued" by sending them to another part of the network. Provided the network has a sufficient number of redundant paths and the routing algorithm can handle starvation, we believe that such a network is superior to one with extensive link queues and no redundant paths because all nodes share one large queue. This eliminates under-utilized hardware together with flow control and deadlock avoidance problems.

3.2. Desperation Routing Scheme

Desperation routing represents a broad category of routing algorithms that *do not* always make the best routing decision, with regard to individual messages. That is, a given message may not always advance towards its destination. In fact, in some cases it may actually be sent away from its destination. Naturally, in some types of networks such routing algorithms could cause additional problems, such as deadlocks or livelocks. However, we believe that in networks with a sufficient number of redundant paths desperation routing provides adequate performance (both in terms of round-trip delay and throughput), while being relatively easy to implement.

Stating the problem more formally, we assume that each message has a fixed number of bits of information representing its state. We divide those bits into three fields, namely the source address, destination address and the message timestamp. (The source address allows Horizon memory modules to return values to the sender.) Furthermore, each switch node contains a fixed number of bits in which to store information about other nodes or messages in the system, called the node state. The routing algorithm is responsible for choosing a path through the network for each message based on the message state and the node state.

We divide desperation algorithms into two classes, negotiated and priority-based. In negotiated algorithms, each incoming message is assigned a default outgoing direction. Then, messages are allowed to swap their assignments provided the swap is mutually beneficial. For example, consider a switch node with two input ports, I1 and I2, and two output ports, O1 and O2. By default, messages arriving on port I1 are given O1, with messages on port I2 going to O2. Now, suppose that the message at port I1 would benefit more by using port O2. If a similar situation exists for the other message, they would swap output port assignments, benefiting both messages. Otherwise, the message on I1 would be forced to use port O1, even if it is disadvantageous. (Presumably, the overall strategy for assigning default ports would guarantee that all messages eventually reach their destination, as in the case of an Euler circuit, which defines a path that traverses every link and visits every node in the network.) This approach is somewhat complex but can lead to optimal direction assignments regardless of the default assignment. This entire class of algorithms has its strengths and weaknesses, but for the remainder of this paper we concentrate on the second approach, leaving negotiated algorithms for another paper.

In priority-based algorithms all the messages arriving at a given node are ranked according to their priority. Then, in rank order, each message is allowed to choose the "best" outgoing direction that is available. By using message timestamps as the priority mechanism, the routing algorithm can be designed to reduce the possibility that a message never gets its best choice. This approach is relatively easy to implement in hardware and is expected to provide good probabilistic performance for uniform workloads (as is shown in Section 5). However, given a priority-based algorithm, the following questions must be considered:

1) How does each message generate its own list of choice directions? That is, if all directions are available, which one is the best, the second best, and so on?
2) How should the timestamp be updated so as to minimize the round-trip delay for each message?
3) How is livelock prevented? That is, what prevents a message from being routed away from its destination most of the time?
4) What type of information should be maintained by each node to assist in routing decisions?

Now, we discuss the problems in more detail, including descriptions of the specific routing algorithms to be analyzed.

One of the advantages of a 3D toroidal network is the abundance of optimal paths to a given destination. That is, there are times when a message may travel in any of 2 or 3 directions and still decrease the distance to its goal. This is contrasted to more conventional interconnection networks, such as a butterfly switch network, that provide only a single path from source to destination. Essentially, the 3D toroidal network wastes links in order to provide better run-time performance. However, the abundance of paths to a given destination requires every message to make a decision at every node along the way, possibly increasing the complexity of each switch node.

The routing policy being considered is based on the Manhattan distance between the source and destination nodes. Each message maintains its current distance to the destination as a 3-tuple, known as the distance vector. Each entry in the distance vector represents the number of steps in a given direction that is required to reach the destination. The goal is to reduce the distance vector to zero for all entries. For example, the distance vector may contain a -2 value in the East-West entry that means the message should travel in the negative direction (west) for two steps. That is, at every node, each message should choose the outgoing port that will decrease the absolute value of one of the distance vector components. Regarding implementation, the distance vector can be carried as part of the message itself or may be computed dynamically using the current node and destination node locations.

The number of advantageous directions at every step is equal to the number of non-zero entries in the distance vector. For example, if the distance vector is $(2, -1, 0)$, then the message will be going towards its destination if it travels in either the positive X direction (decreasing 2 to 1) or in the negative Y direction (increasing -1 to 0). The choice of a single best direction depends primarily on the overall strategy for zeroing the distance vector. For instance, the message may choose between the alternatives randomly, in a pre-defined order, or by reducing the largest entry first. The current routing strategy attempts to reduce the largest entry first because this maximizes the message's degrees of freedom. For example, consider a distance vector of (3, 2, 1). If it is reduced to (3, 2, 0) the message has only two advantageous directions remaining. On the other hand, if it is reduced to (2, 2, 1) the message still has three advantageous directions to travel. In general, the goal is to increase the probability that a message stays on an optimal path by maximizing the number of choices at every step. Remember, in desperation routing, a message may not always get its best choice. Therefore, it is better to have a long list of equivalent choices.

Given the optimal paths for each message in the system, it remains a problem to select a priority assignment that guarantees that all messages reach their destination with minimal delay. Any solution must prevent messages from wandering around the network without reaching its destination (i.e., livelock). The probability of a livelock situation decreases rapidly as the number of bits in the priority timestamp increases. However, the complexity of the hardware increases as the size of the message increases due to the number of wires needed to transfer messages and the number of logic gates needed to perform the routing decision, so a compromise value must be selected. That is, the number of bits in the priority timestamp must be large enough to prevent livelock within a known probability, yet small enough to be implementable.

In the experiments presented in this paper we make use of timestamps based on pure aging. Pure aging increments the timestamp of every message, every network cycle. Accordingly, the longer a message stays in the network, the greater its probability of getting its best choice at every switch node. Although this priority mechanism potentially requires a large number of timestamp bits, we have chosen it as a basis for comparison. (A different method for timestamp maintenance is presented in Section 3.4 and is currently being examined through experimentation.)

3.3. Hardware Implementation

One advantage of a 3D toroid is the relative ease of implementation. For the routing decision, only the sign of the relative X, Y and Z fields need to be examined. For instance, if the remaining X distance is greater than 0, the message should exit the X port going in the positive direction. Such a decision can be made with a single *and* gate. In addition, the relative address itself must be updated and this is accomplished using a simple increment/decrement circuit.

In addition to a simple routing algorithm, the 3D toroid also has a compact, modular layout. The 3D toroid can be *folded* in such a way that all wires have the same length and no wire has to traverse a distance greater than the width of a switch node. Figure 1 gives a layout for a 4x4, 2D toroid (the 3D layout is a direct extension). This layout also has the advantage that larger networks are constructed simply by adding more switch nodes to the periphery of the original network. These added nodes are identical in structure to the nodes already in the network. Hence, networks of any size can be built using one basic module. The physical size of a switch node is estimated to be approximately 3 inches. Therefore, the longest wire in the network would also be 3 inches. One potential disadvantage of the 3D toroid is the number of wires. Assuming that the Z dimension is implemented as one unit, the number of connections between units is 150 (bits/link) * 2 (bidirectional

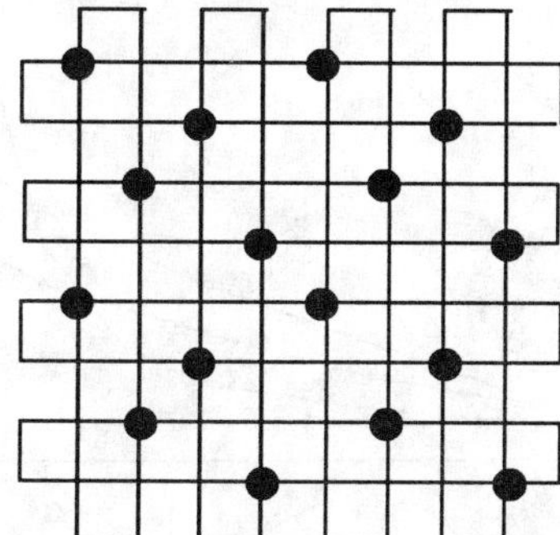

Figure 1. Wire layout for a 4x4, 2D Toroidal Grid

links) * 4 (X/Y dimensions) * 6 (Z depth) = 7200 connections. Implementing the node as a 3D unit with connectors on each side results in a requirement of 1800 connections per side, which should be achievable with current connector technology.

Another implementation consideration is the logic complexity for the desperation routing algorithm. In conventional packet switched interconnection networks, each node has a limited queuing capability together with flow control to prevent queue overflow. However, node-to-node flow control introduces the possibility of deadlock, requiring a hardware deadlock avoidance algorithm [Dall87]. These algorithms are often complex and hence difficult to execute quickly in hardware. For the proposed desperation routing policy, no complex deadlock avoidance is needed. However, the logic must be capable of assigning messages to output ports in a timestamp order. This implies sorting and hence a certain level of hardware complexity. See [Smit88] for a more detailed analysis of the implementation issues for the routing algorithm currently being investigated.

3.4. Variations and Optimizations

Having discussed the basic operation of the network we present an incomplete list of design variations and optimizations. For each, we describe the design areas affected and the expected benefits and/or disadvantages.

Battle Scars -

Unlike pure aging which increments a message timestamp every network cycle, battle scars are incremented only when a message fails to travel in a beneficial direction (i.e., is sent in the wrong direction because of a higher priority message). It is hoped that such a technique would reduce the number of timestamp bits needed within a message. However, it is unclear whether this approach yields the same average round-trip delay per message as pure aging. For example, when using battle scars, a message may travel quite a distance before losing a battle. At that point, it might run into a large number of veterans, thereby losing many battles (and wasting many cycles) before it wins. On the other hand, pure aging gives equal weighting to all messages, regardless of their previous life style.

Processor Placement -

The basic network design places processors throughout the network to maximize the distance between them. Given the other design variations such a "maximal" distance may not always be completely defined, or desirable. A reduction in network congestion may be achieved by randomly placing processors or placing them away from "switch highways". That is, given a particular topology, routing policy and class of applications (i.e., message load), sets of switches may be designated to process messages expected to go in a given direction, with processors placed strategically along those highways.

Flow Control -

A serious problem for any network design results when any processor attempts to overload the network's capacity. One way to limit the effects of such a situation is to limit the total number of outstanding messages transmitted by a given processor or memory module. That is, each processor is allowed to inject a fixed number of messages before it must wait for a reply.

Euler Last Resort -

In practice, the pure aging and battle scar priority mechanisms are expected to provide probabilistic message delays with a realistic distribution. That is, most messages experience a delay statistically close to the mean for the entire network. However, such priority mechanisms do not **guarantee** that every message will be delivered eventually. Such a problem exists whenever two or more messages exist with maximum age or battle scars and one of them is always re-routed because of the other. To guarantee delivery, such messages can be routed along an Euler Circuit defined across all switch nodes and links. That is, any message with a maximum delay count (age or battle scar) is given the highest priority during routing decisions and is sent directly along the Euler Circuit. It can be shown that all such messages will reach their destination within a bounded number of network ticks. Furthermore, deterministic local rules can be applied to shorten such a journey by "jumping" from one part of the Euler Circuit to another, without loss of generality. (See [Smit81] for a brief discussion on the use of Euler circuits in the HEP computer architecture.)

Link Removal -

This variation reduces the number of ports per switch node by selectively deleting certain links, re-connecting others and possibly adding more switch nodes. For example, the number of links can be reduced at every node by alternately deleting all links in a given direction. Specifically, in a 3D grid, the bottom level might have only EAST-WEST links, while the next level has only NORTH-SOUTH, etc. By reducing the total number of ports and links, this variation should ease many implementation problems associated with toroidal grids primarily because the switch node has simpler logic and can be implemented in a smaller area. However, this variation may introduce problems concerning physical link length, overall message delay, network capacity, and fault-tolerance capabilities.

4. Experimental Approach

The analysis of the network design described in Section 3 is being conducted through the use of a custom simulator written in C, under UNIX. The simulator runs on a number of different computers, including SUN workstations, the Convex C-1 and the Cray-2 supercomputer. Consequently, we are able to develop experiments quickly and can generate statistically valid runs for large networks (between 1200 and 2400 nodes). In this section, we describe the assumptions made concerning the use of the simulator and the basic measurements collected.

For all experiments the following definitions or assumptions apply. First, we define a single network tick to be the total time for each switch node to route messages between their input and output ports **and** the time to transfer messages across the corresponding link to the destination node. In reality such network operations will be implemented using a larger number of minor ticks, pipelined as necessary.

We also assume that memory modules process messages instantly. That is, if a memory request is received at time T by the memory module, the response is submitted to the network at time T+1. In reality, such memory operations require a substantial number of network ticks (approximately 10 to 20 on average) and are completely pipelined. Given that the throughput of memory modules is identical with or without our assumption, the overall impact on the network's throughput is unchanged. Furthermore, the extra delay caused by the memory operation is independent of the network delay to and from that memory.

Finally, we assume that processors submit messages to the network in a probabilistic manner, with parameters WORK and LOCAL.

The WORK parameter represents the probability that a given processor attempts to submit a message to the switch node attached to it. This desire to submit a message is independent of the network load or any previous messages submitted. However, if the switch node connected to a processor is heavily congested, it may block the processor from injecting a message. (Such an event is considered a negative part of network performance and is discussed in detail in our analysis of the results.) By varying the WORK parameter we vary the amount of work imposed on the system overall. The LOCAL parameter represents the probability that a given processor accesses the closest memory. That is, each processor is assigned a unique memory module that is relatively close to it in the network (e.g., one hop away). With probability 1–LOCAL each processor accesses all memories with uniform probability. By varying the LOCAL parameter we vary the memory reference patterns imposed on the network.

Throughout our analysis, we make use of the following performance metrics:

Message Delay
: The number of ticks for a given message to travel from a processor to a memory module and back.

Processor Utilization
: The number of times that a processor successfully submits a message to the network divided by the total number of times it attempted such an operation.

Based on these metrics, the overall goal of the Horizon network is to provide an average message delay less than 64 ticks while maintaining 100 percent processor utilization, for the message loads expected from various applications. In the next section we present the results of preliminary experiments intended to show the basic performance of the network described in the previous sections. The results provide a basis for the analysis of the network itself, allowing comparison with other interconnection networks. Furthermore, they can be used to compare the tradeoffs associated with the numerous optimizations and variations which stem from 3D toroidal grids and desperation routing strategies. (Such experiments are currently underway and will be discussed in a future paper.)

5. Experimental Results

In this section we present preliminary results taken from the Horizon network simulator. The analysis serves to verify that the network is working within expected limits and to point out those performance issues that need to be pursued in more detail. A more detailed analysis of the network's performance, including comparisons of the variations suggested in previous sections will be presented in the future.

Initially, a series of experimental runs were conducted to determine the number of network cycles required to reach steady-state behavior. Since we are interested primarily in the performance of the network during periods of sustained message traffic, we had to factor out measurements taken in the initial transient phase. This was accomplished by setting WORK to 1.0 and measuring the network utilization for various LOCAL values. Based on those results, all experiments were run for an initial 1000 ticks before collecting measurements, and then run for 10000 ticks to gather the statistics.

We begin our analysis by considering the effects of link queue size. Figure 2 shows the average round-trip message delay for link queue sizes of 0, 1, and 2, plotted as a function of the desired processor load, WORK. In this case, processors access all memory modules with uniform probability (i.e., LOCAL = 0).

At low workload levels (i.e., WORK < 0.7) the smaller the queue size, the lower the average message delay, which can be explained as follows. Consider a message that wants to use a given output port, but loses out to a higher-priority message. In general, the loser will have one or two other ports that are equally beneficial. Now, assuming the network load is relatively small, the loser will have fewer messages to compete with and, as such, has a greater chance of getting a beneficial port. Therefore, even without link queues the message will progress towards its destination. Given link queues, however, the message will simply join the queue. That is, it will elect to delay itself for one or more ticks in order to proceed along that particular path. In short, given a larger queue each message will probably get its first choice, but will suffer a delay accordingly.

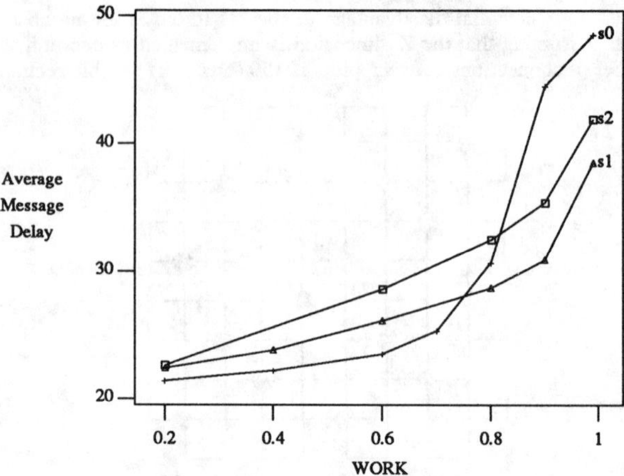

Figure 2. Impact of Link Queue Size on Average Round-Trip Delay

Although messages see a greater overall delay when the link queue size is increased in a lightly-loaded network, the network is actually working more efficiently with regard to the number of links used. This can be shown by examining the total number of ticks that each message spent traversing links, vice waiting on link queues. When WORK equals 0.6, the average message travels over 23.6, 21.2, and 21.0 links for link queue sizes of 0, 1, and 2, respectively. In short, for increased link queue sizes, messages travel over less links, but spend more time on them. In other words, link queues allow messages to remain on a chosen path, for which they pay an extra delay. The alternative is to force the message onto another path which may or may not be beneficial. The latter is preferred in lightly-loaded networks.

At higher workloads (i.e., WORK > 0.7), the link queue size determines whether or not the network becomes saturated. This is demonstrated clearly in Figure 2 by the sharp increase in the curve for queue size 0. Alternately, Figure 3 shows the processor utilization achieved for each link queue size.

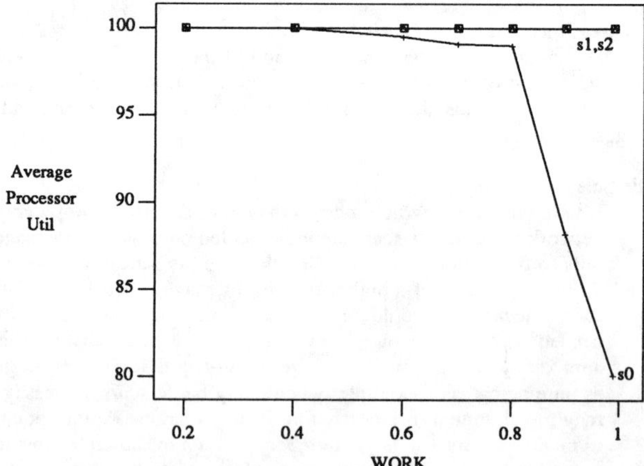

Figure 3. Impact of Link Queue Size on Processor Utilization

Queue sizes 1 and 2 allow 100 percent processor utilization for all workloads, while a link queue size of 0 shows a drop in utilization as the workload increases. Once again, this situation can be explained in terms of the number of links traversed for a given queue size. Specifically, when WORK equals 1.0, the average message travels over 48.0, 25.0, and 22.8 links for queue sizes 0, 1, and 2, respectively. For a link queue size of 0 the network is congested to the point that it cannot keep messages on their optimal routes all the time. This not only increases the round-trip delay of each message, but it decreases the total number of messages that can be initiated by the processors every tick (i.e., processor utilization). That is, since messages take longer to reach their goal and there are only a fixed number of links in the system, the throughput of the network must decrease. By increasing the link queue size the network allows more messages to stay on their optimal path. Clearly, this adds a queuing delay, but the increase is offset by a larger reduction in the number of links traversed. Specifically, when WORK equals 1.0, the average message experiences a queue delay of 0, 13.6, and 19.2 ticks for link queue sizes 0, 1, and 2, respectively. That is, a link queue size of 1 adds 19.2 ticks because of queuing, while reducing the number of links traversed by 23.4, as compared to a link queue size of 0. Across the range of WORK, the link queue size choice provides a performance tradeoff between the number of links traversed and the time spent on each link, which can be exploited to decrease the message delay and increase processor utilization.

It is important to note that beyond a certain size link queues are counter-productive. That is, the queue size should be chosen to guarantee that the network doesn't saturate and no larger. Otherwise, the tradeoff between queue delays and the number of links traversed will not be effective.

Although the average message delay is a good indicator of performance, we need to examine the distribution of delays seen by all messages. Accordingly, Figure 4 shows the distribution of message delays for a lightly-loaded (WORK = 0.6) and heavily-loaded (WORK = 1.0) network, given a link queue size of 1.

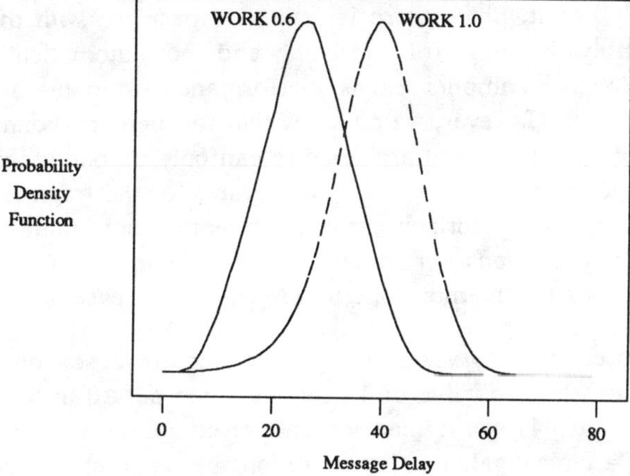

Figure 4. Distribution of Message Delay for Different Workloads

Both curves show a relatively normal distribution. Specifically, most messages experience a delay close to the average, with a small number of fast and slow responses. Keep in mind, in the experiments discussed up to this point processors access all memory modules with uniform probability. The primary concept shown in Figure 4 is that the routing algorithm provides a good average message delay, without unexpected variations.

Finally, Figure 5 shows the impact of local memory references. Specifically, it plots the average message delay based on the probability that each processor accesses neighboring memories (LOCAL), given WORK equal to 1.0 and a link queue size of 1.

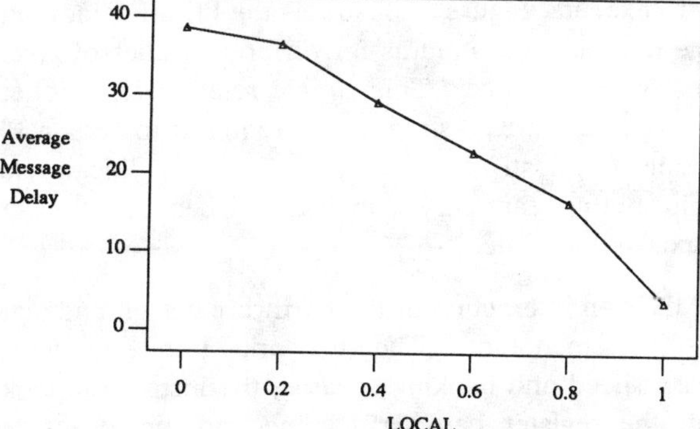

Figure 5. Impact of Memory Reference Locality

The results are not dramatic, but they serve to establish a worthwhile property of toroidal grids. In particular, memory access locality can be exploited to significantly decrease the average message delay. This property allows applications to allocate global data for maximum performance during periods when multiple processors are working independently. Although not shown in Figure 5, reference locality also affects the point at which a network becomes saturated. In particular, for a link queue size of 0, the network allows 100 percent processor utilization provided LOCAL is greater than 20 percent. Otherwise, as shown in Figure 3, the processor utilization is limited to 80 percent. Viewed another way, even without link queues, the 3D toroidal network provides full processor utilization if the application accesses global memory less than 80 percent of the time.

6. Summary and Future Work

In this paper we have described a 3D toroidal interconnection network which is being examined for use as part of the Horizon architecture. Such a network is intended to provide adequate message delays and sustained processor utilization over a wide range of network loads. Given that the 3D toroid provides a large number of redundant paths between switch nodes, desperation routing strategies can be used. Desperation routing algorithms have no need for flow control or deadlock avoidance algorithms because messages are always routed somewhere, not particularly in a beneficial direction. Any number of priority mechanisms can be used to guarantee that messages eventually reach their destination. Such strategies are quite simple to implement, providing fast switch nodes.

We have presented a number of variations and optimizations that can be made to the basic network to possibly increase its performance. Preliminary results showed the impact of link queue size and memory reference locality. In short, small link queues (i.e., size 0) cause the smallest message delay when the network is lightly-loaded, while larger queues (i.e., size 1) are more efficient at other times. The difference in performance can be explained by considering the number of links traversed and the time spent on each link.

The preliminary results also confirmed that memory reference locality has a major affect on the overall message delay and processor utilization; an increase in locality produces a decrease in the average message delay. This result is due to the decrease in message congestion throughout the network. Other experiments are currently being conducted to determine the exact characteristics of such network congestion with regard to various memory reference patterns.

One future goal is to provide a comprehensive description of the various tradeoffs that can be made in both routing and placement. It is hoped that mathematical analysis in addition to simulation will be available to provide a coherent node design theory. Furthermore, we hope to develop a network taxonomy in which the network model presented in this paper can be compared to other network models that have been proposed in the literature.

References

[Dall87] Dally, W. and Seitz, C., "Deadlock-Free Message Routing in Multiprocessor Interconnection Networks," *IEEE Transactions on Computers*, Vol. C-36, No. 5, May 1987, pg. 547-553.

[Feng81] Feng, T., "A Survey of Interconnection Networks," *Computer*, December 1981, pg. 12-27.

[Smit81] Smith, B., "Architecture and Applications of the HEP Multiprocessor Computer System," *Proceedings of SPIE*, Vol. 298, August 1981, pg. 241-248.

[Smit88] Smitley, D., "The Anatomy of a Network Node," Technical Report, Supercomputing Research Center, May 1988.

[Witt81] Wittie, L., "Communication Structures for Large Networks of Microcomputers," *IEEE Transactions on Computers*, Vol. C-30, No. 4, April 1981, pg. 264-273.

Performance Prediction for the Horizon Super Computer

Ray R. Glenn

Institute for Defense Analysis
Supercomputing Research Center
Lanham, MD. 20776

Abstract

The performance of one Horizon processing element can be quantified by user operations per instruction, the instructions per tick, and the basic clock rate. Assuming there is sufficient parallelism within a problem, the performance of one PE can be multiplied by the number of PEs contained in the Horizon system. For a 256–PE Horizon the expected sustained performance is in the order of 50 giga user operations per second for problems with sustained parallelism of 8,000 to 12,000 instruction streams.

1.0 Introduction

The Horizon performance for a users program is predicted by

$$\frac{User\ Operations}{Sec} = \frac{User\ Operations}{Instruction}\ \frac{Instructions}{Tick}\ \frac{Ticks}{Sec} \quad (1)$$

Each of the three factors on the right side of Equation (1) will be analyzed and predictions made on the range of expected values.

2.0 User Operations per Instruction

The value of the number of user operations per Horizon instruction is a function of the definition of a user operation, the algorithm being implemented, and the machine's instruction set design.

2.1 Definition of User Operation

User operations are the explicit operators on the right hand side of an assignment statement. It does not include indexing operations required to fetch or store operands. For example, there is one user operation per loop iteration in the following fragment:

```
Do I = start,end
    C(I) = A(I)*B(I+5)
End do.
```

2.2 Range of User Operations per Instruction

The Horizon instruction set permits at most three user operations per instruction, two in the "A" unit and one in the "C" unit. Since there is limited experience with the assembly language of Horizon, and no automatically parallelizing compiler exists, performance estimates are guesswork. However, we do know that for memory–bound problems the Horizon architecture can only do one memory operation per instruction. Therefore, for the fragment above, the best Horizon can achieve is the same number of user operations per instruction as the number of user operations per memory operation (1/3 in this case).

The prediction curves to be shown later are based on a most pessimistic value of 1 user operation per 10 instructions which is worse than we believe compilers will produce, a typical value of 1.5 operations per instruction, and a asymptotic value of 3 user operations per instruction as discussed above.

3.0 Instructions per Tick per PE

The number of instructions per clock tick per PE is primarily a function of the number of Instruction streams(I–streams) ready to execute. The best case is that some stream executes every clock tick. The Average Instruction Latency (AIL) of each I–stream determines when it is ready to execute. Figure 1 illustrates the PE efficiency versus the number of I–streams for different values of Average Instruction Latency. This simple relationship applies: for a given AIL, AIL I–streams are required to keep a PE executing at 1 instruction per tick. This is a linear relationship, but appears curved in Figure 1 because the vertical axis is log scale.

The AIL is an interaction of the hardware design and algorithm implementation. The network architecture, the memory speed and banking scheme, the instruction look-ahead, the register banking scheme and the locality of memory addresses all affect the AIL. At this time the in-

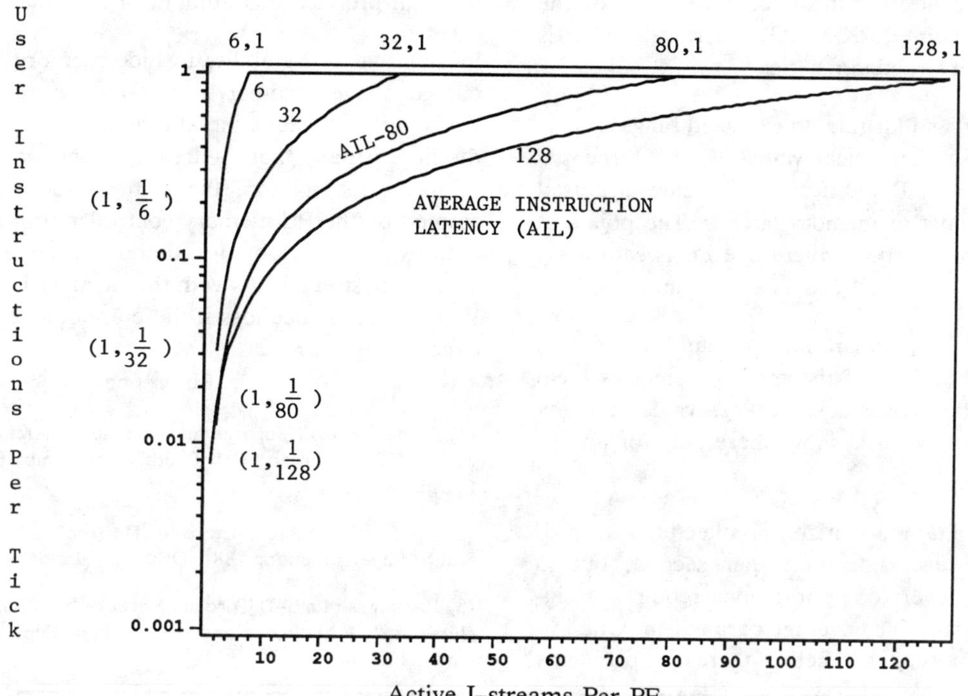

Figure 1 - Horizon PE Utilization

teractions between these factors are not known exactly. However some bounds can be put on the problem. The most optimistic instruction issue rate is 1 instruction every 6 ticks long term. This is based on an instruction latency of 24 ticks and a lookahead of 4. A lookahead of 8 would allow an instruction issue every 3 ticks (24/8) but the register logic will not allow access to registers more often than once every 6 ticks. Moreover, this is not a sustainable value, but only an upper bound because some instructions are memory references. We estimate the latency will be 24 ticks for register-to-register operations(AIL=24). The current memory architecture has a fast local memory. Instructions that fetch or store to those locations should take about 30 ticks(AIL=30), assuming there are no memory bank conflicts. Instructions that use the network to access remote memory modules will experience latencies between 32 and 128 ticks, again assuming no memory bank conflicts(AIL=80). The distribution of instructions into these classes and the access patterns on the network are unknown but most researchers believe that AIL values of 60 to 100 ticks without lookahead are to be expected.

In addition to the distribution of instructions into these groups is the lookahead issue. By judicious use of lookahead the AIL fjor memory operations can be reduced significantly by the overlap of instruction execution. For the code fragment shown above as many as three instructions can be execution simultaneously (both loads and the store). This has the effect of reducing the AIL to approximately the memory latency divided by 3. As discussed above, as least as many I-streams as the AIL will be required to keep a PE running at 1 instruction per tick.

One of the major attributes of Horizon is the ability to hide memory and network latencies. If the latency becomes large due to hot spots in the network or bank conflicts, it can be hidden if there are other streams ready to execute. This assumes that there is sufficient parallelism in the problem during the conflict time and there were enough streams allocated to each processor.

4.0 Tick Rate (clock frequency)

The clock rate for Horizon will be a function of the fabrication technology and the amount of funds available at the time the hardware is designed. Supercomputers today typically use a 5 to 10 ns. clock, so it seems reasonable to expect clock speeds to be in that range or better in the future. The following curves use a 4 ns. optimistic value, a best guess of 6 ns., and a pessimistic value of 7.5 ns. The reader can use his own value and scale the predictions accordingly.

5.0 Predicted Performance

Figure 2 illustrates the performance possible for a 256-PE Horizon. The vertical axis is the effective user rate in operations per second. The horizontal axis is the number of I-streams actively computing on the user's task. The lowest curve illustrates the performance for the worst of the three parameters in Equation (1). The point at 128 I-streams and 13.3 mega operations is where one PE is busy at 1 instruction per tick. At the maximum value of the same curve is the point (32K,3.41G) where all 256 PEs are operating at 1 instruction per tick.

The middle two curves illustrate an expected range of performance. They use the typical values of the three parameters in equation 1. Two different AIL values are used to illustrate the impact of memory latency. The points at 32 and 48 I-streams illustrate where one PE is saturated. The end points are where all 256 PEs are saturated.

The upper curve is a performance asymptote. It represents the most optimistic values of the three parameters: No application would be able to sustain these values for any extended period of time. It is shown here only for an upper bound.

As shown in Figure 2, the Horizon architecture can produce tens of giga user operations per second, but to achieve these high levels of performance requires a significant amount of sustained average parallelism. One important research question is whether there are problems that can produce this amount of sustained parallelism.

In addition to the ability to hide memory latency, as discussed above, another important feature affecting Horizon's performance is the ability of the architecture to hide the time penalty that I-streams spend waiting on barriers or locks. In Horizon, the spin on lock function is performed by the PE memory controller (in hardware, rather than by software looping); therefore, the PE is free to execute other streams. As with the memory latency, there will be no performance loss if there are other streams ready to execute.

References

(1) "The Horizon Supercomputer System: Architecture and Software", J.T. Kuehn and B.J. Smith, Supercomputing 88 , Orlando, Florida.

(2) "A Processor Architecture for Horizon", M.R. Thistle and B.J. Smith, Supercomputing 88 , Orlando, Florida.

(3) "Analysis of a 3-D Toroidal Network for a Shared-Memory Architecture", F.M. Pittelli and D.L. Smitley, Supercomputing 88, Orlando, Florida.

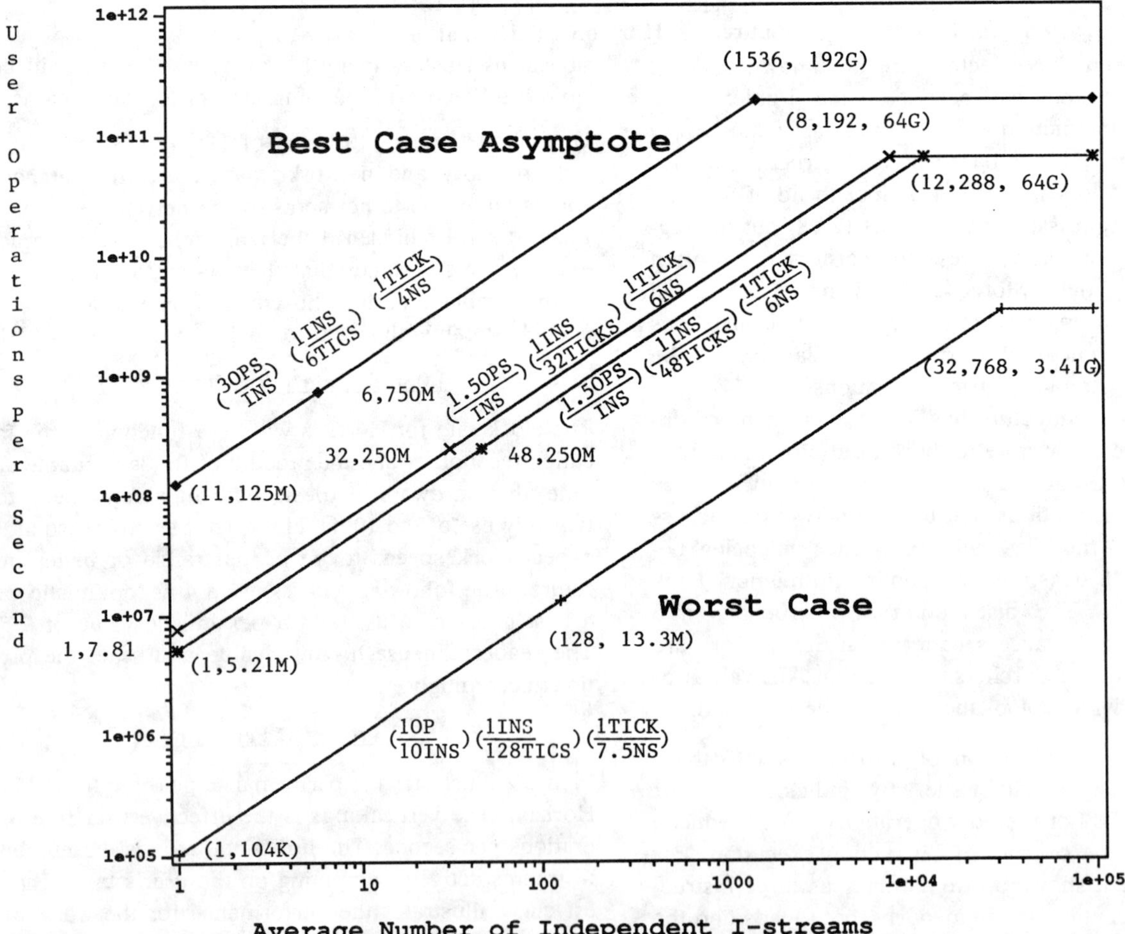

Figure 2 - Horizon Performance Projection

Compiling on Horizon

Jesse M. Draper

Supercomputing Research Center
4380 Forbes Blvd.
Lanham, MD 20706

ABSTRACT

Compiler research to test several hardware features of the Horizon supercomputer design has yielded some preliminary results based solely on code generation and local optimization. Correctly packing operations into the moderately wide instruction word seems relatively straightforward, and there is nothing to suggest that it will be impossible to discover a good heuristic for instruction scheduling. Lookahead values are easy to compute within basic blocks, but they have not yet been tested across block boundaries, and the overall efficacy of this hardware feature has not been proved. Static analysis shows that the arithmetic unit is noticeably busier than the control unit, but this apparent imbalance may disappear once global optimization permits reasonable dynamic analysis of compiler output. Similarly, it is too early to determine either the adequacy of 32 registers or the usefulness of multiple target registers and condition codes.

INTRODUCTION

We are currently building a prototype compiler to determine the appropriateness of the Horizon instruction set as a target for a compiler and to test several of Horizon's special hardware features.[1] While there are a number of critical issues involved in the effort, this paper first reports some early results that have affected the instruction set and then focuses on two aspects of the instruction set architecture: the moderately wide instruction word and the lookahead hardware.

EARLY RESULTS

One of the first results of the compiler research was to discover that Horizon's lack of memory operations with encoded "immediate" addresses posed a problem for register spills. Spilling a register requires putting the offset for the temporary into a register, which in turn could require spilling another register, and so forth in an endless loop. There are at least three solutions to this problem: (1) reserving a register for spills; (2) making sure at all times that at least one register contains a constant that does not have to be spilled and can be reloaded without using a register, and (3) changing the format of memory operations to allow the encoding of an offset value into an instruction. In its current form the compiler uses solution (1); number (3) is being considered.

A second early result of the compiler research was to add floating-point and integer add and subtract instructions to the A-unit. It was possible to perform these operations with the combined multiply and add, but doing so required that a register contain the value "1" in the correct format. Since it seemed important to keep registers as free as possible, and since op-code space was readily available in the A-unit, we added floating-point and integer add and subtract. Each of these four is identical in format and name to an instruction available in the C-unit.

No changes have yet occurred in the C-unit because of the compiler work, but a couple are being considered. Since one of the major uses for a condition code is to test for array bounds when stepping through an array, it could be useful to have either an instruction that adds (or subtracts) 64 and tests the result against 0, or an instruction that multiplies one value by 64 and adds the result to a second value. Either of these instructions might reduce the number of registers needed to calculate array addresses in inner loops.

INSTRUCTION PACKING

Packing operations into Horizon instructions is analogous in many respects to packing microprogramming operations into microinstructions.[2] Such work has led to a sophisticated trace-scheduling compiler for a very-long-instruction-word (VLIW) architecture.[3] On Horizon the task is simplified. Because each instruction controls only three functional units, it is possible to pack instruction words effectively without unrolling loops. Furthermore, registers are not only general purpose, but also uniformly addressed: any register can appear as an operand to any operation, no matter which unit performs the operation. Thirdly, all A-unit and C-unit instructions, no matter how complex, complete in exactly the same amount of time. Memory operations can vary widely in the time required for completion, but in applications with enough parallelism Horizon can hide the memory latency using a fast context-switching scheme similar to that implemented in the Denelcor Heterogeneous Element Processor (HEP).[4] As a result, the compiler can pack available operations into instructions without trying to fill "gaps" caused by varying execution times.

At the end of local optimization each block consists of a sequence of assignment statements possibly preceded by a label and possibly followed by a target and branch. All the leaves within a block are constants, either values needed in computations or offsets for live variables. These nodes and the dependence arcs of their ancestors determine all the constraints on instruction scheduling. To handle instruction packing and scheduling, the compiler maintains four lists in each basic block: M-ops, A-ops, C-ops, and AorC-ops. Each of the first three contains nodes from the DAG that are ready for that particular unit to compute. The fourth list has nodes representing operations that can be computed by either the A or the C unit. During code generation the compiler selects an operation (if available) for each unit to perform, updates the DAG and the ready lists, and records in an instruction array both the instruction and the nodes that it computes. Each node contains the index of the instruction and the register in which the computed value is stored. A separate array of registers records the node whose value is stored in each register.

In the first assembly language that the compiler produced for a locally optimized source program, the A-unit and M-unit were considerably busier than the C-unit. Much of this difference resulted directly from the overhead of loads and stores at the beginnings and ends of basic blocks. Each variable that had to be loaded required an A-unit

CH2617-9/88/0000/0051$01.00

operation to load an offset followed by an M-unit operation to load the variable. Because a number of the required values are identical in successive blocks, global optimization will eliminate many of the instructions in which the C-unit was idle. An architectural change that would allow the M-unit to use all 20 bits from the C-unit field might also be helpful, but it is still too early to be sure.

This initial observation about the relative idleness of the C-unit has made it seem attractive to give it more instructions (see the previous section on early results), but so far we have analyzed only the static output of the compiler. Its dynamic behavior could be considerably different, particularly since the C-unit contains the common control instructions that will be necessary in even the tightest inner loops. If the relative utilization of the two computational units is considerably different inside and outside loops, then it will be useful to make simple architectural changes that increase the compiler's flexibility in assigning operations to functional units. Moreover, optimizations like strength reduction will become especially important. On more conventional uniprocessors, strength reduction (e.g., from multiplication to addition) reduces the execution time of individual computations; on Horizon it provides flexibility since additions can be computed in the C-unit as well as the A-unit.

INSTRUCTION SCHEDULING

Although the four lists mentioned above essentially solve the problem of instruction *packing*, they do not solve the problem of instruction *scheduling*. Future research will attempt to discover a good heuristic for scheduling Horizon instructions using variations of known techniques.[5] For now, however, we are using a simple greedy algorithm. In the current version of the compiler, all four lists are sorted according to the critical paths of listed nodes. Each node has a maximum depth representing the longest path to the node from the root of any "tree" in the DAG. For example, the compiler will select from M-ops the load or store operation that is "deepest" in the DAG so that operations that use the loaded value can be scheduled as soon as possible. Store operations usually come late in the block since they are shallow. This simplistic approach to scheduling has the disadvantage of essentially trying to "lift" the entire DAG at once and therefore increasing the likelihood of register spills, although no such spills have occurred in the simple test cases tried so far. The primary advantage of using critical paths for scheduling is simplicity.

Selecting a memory operation to schedule is as simple as popping a node off the M-ops list, but selecting operations for the A and C units requires some comparisons of nodes from A-ops, C-ops, and AorC-ops. In its first version the compiler simply selected for each unit the operation whose depth was greater than or equal to that of any other operation that the unit could compute. Ties were decided in favor of the more restrictive list (A-ops or C-ops rather than AorC-ops). Because static analysis of compiler output showed that the A-unit was busier than the C-unit, the selection policy was changed to take some load off the A-unit. As long as A-ops is not empty, the A-unit takes the first operation from that list. The C-unit takes the operation with the longest critical path from C-ops or AorC-ops, but in the case of ties operations that can be performed on either unit (AorC) have precedence over those that can be performed only on C. This policy will remain in effect until global optimization provides more information about the probable dynamic loads of the two units.

LOOKAHEAD

The lookahead field encodes the shortest distance along any possible execution path to the next instruction that depends on the results of the current one. A lookahead of zero represents sequential code, with each instruction finishing before the next one is issued. A value of seven, the maximum in the current architecture, allows eight instructions from the same stream to be executing concurrently. Producing the right lookahead value for an instruction is primarily a matter of maintaining dependence information even after instructions have been generated. When the code generator produces an instruction, it looks at each node depended on by the nodes computed in the instruction; if necessary, it reduces the lookahead value of the instruction corresponding to that node. Initially set to seven, the lookahead value is reduced each time the code generator produces a dependent instruction less than "lookahead" instructions away. For example, if the current instruction is numbered 25 and depends on the results of instruction 22, the code generator will set the lookahead value of instruction 22 to the minimum of its current value and $[(25 - 22) - 1] = 2$. The extra "1" is necessary because sequential code has a lookahead of zero rather than one. If no subsequent instructions depend on the value of a given instruction, then its lookahead value will remain at the maximum of seven. This technique works well within basic blocks, but it has not been tested across block boundaries. The current implementation does not allow lookahead values greater than the distance to the end of the basic block. Once global optimization has been performed, it will be possible to reexamine not only lookahead calculations, but also the effect of instruction scheduling policies on lookahead values. It seems quite possible that selecting instructions by critical path and thus "lifting" the entire DAG will result in maximal lookahead values.

SUMMARY

The compiler research has revealed some useful information about the Horizon architecture. One of the general-purpose registers must be available to hold the offset for register spills, and add and subtract instructions have been added to the A-unit to reduce the need for constants in registers. Instruction packing seems relatively straightforward with the chosen data structures, and there is nothing to suggest that it will be impossible to discover a good heuristic for instruction scheduling. Lookahead values are easy to compute within basic blocks, but the overall efficacy of the feature has not been proved. Static analysis shows that the A-unit is noticeably busier than the C-unit, but changing the instruction set to compensate for this imbalance will have to wait until global optimization permits reasonable dynamic analysis of compiler output. A similar wait is necessary before deciding on the adequacy of 32 registers and the usefulness of multiple target registers and condition codes.

REFERENCES

[1] Kuehn, James T., and Burton J. Smith, "The Horizon supercomputing system: architecture and software," Supercomputing '88 Conference Proceedings, Kissimee, FL (1988).

[2] Landskov, David, Scott Davidson, Bruce Shriver, and Patrick W. Mallett, "Local microcode compaction techniques," *ACM Computing Surveys*, Vol. 12, No. 3 (September 1980), pp. 261-294.

[3] Ellis, John R., *Bulldog: A Compiler for VLIW Architectures*, MIT Press, Cambridge, MA (1986).

[4] Smith, Burton, "The architecture of HEP," in *Parallel MIMD Computation: The HEP Supercomputer and Its Applications*, ed. J. S. Kowalik, MIT Press, Cambridge, MA (1985), pp. 41-55.

[5] Aiken, Alexander, and Alexandru Nicolau, "Optimal loop parallelization," in *Proceedings of the SIGPLAN '88 Conference on Programming Language Design and Implementation* (June 1988), pp. 308-317.

HORSE: A SIMULATION OF THE HORIZON SUPERCOMPUTER

Daniel J. Kopetzky

Supercomputing Research Center
4380 Forbes Boulevard
Lanham, Maryland 20706

ABSTRACT

HORSE is a program that combines the simulation of the HORIZON multiprocessor architecture with an interactive debugging environment. The models for processing elements, interconnection network, and memory modules include enough detail to allow execution time to be estimated. Debugging commands, invoked by either the user or the program, can inspect the state of computation without perturbing the sequence of future events. A program's operating system requests are processed by the debugger. HORSE currently runs on a variety of UNIX machines including the Cray-2, Convex, and Sun.

INTRODUCTION

The HORIZON Supercomputer is a design for a shared-memory MIMD machine with a potential for a sustained 100 Giga-FLOP performance. Several hundred processing elements (PEs) each execute multiple instruction streams. The PE can switch active streams at every clock cycle to hide both memory latency and pipeline delay. A full description of the HORIZON architecture can be found in [1]. A concise description is contained elsewhere in this proceedings [2].

We have built a simulation environment that allows architecture experiments to be made. Potential applications are being designed and coded. Therefore, the simulator is also being used in debugging both hand-built assembly code and the output of experimental compilers. End users want quick execution. The two goals of simulation generality and speed of execution presented an interesting challenge for the simulator's implementors.

A second HORIZON simulator was concurrently developed in the Endot hardware description language. The Endot version is intended to be an executable specification for the architecture. Both simulations were derived from a user-level description of the HORIZON instruction set [3] augmented by working papers that document particular strategies for implementing those instructions.

ARCHITECTURE OF THE SIMULATOR

The simulator requires a minimum of two input files. One specifies the contents of memory. The other establishes design parameters for the machine model.

The memory image is established from a binary file that is produced by a cross-assembler. The first version of HORSE uses a file format derived from the Berkeley 4.2 UNIX a.out file format. Extensions have been made to convey the value of a small set of state bits that are attached to each 64-bit HORIZON memory word, and trivial modifications were made to increase symbol table addresses and relocation commands to 64 bits of precision. A second assembler system is under development with a file format derived from System V's Common Object File Format (COFF)[4]. The assignment of data structures to HORIZON's shared memory modules can be more easily specified with the new format files. Some segments in a COFF format file are not loaded into memory but will convey processor allocation preferences to an operating system and record compiler generated debugging information.

The program file may be paired with another command script file that is used to set the machine state to something other than a pristine power-up configuration. For example, multiple instruction streams may be enabled, appropriate breakpoints established, and measurement options enabled prior to the simulation of the first time step.

The other required configuration file defines specific implementation details of the HORIZON model that is to execute the program. Major architectural variations are implemented by recoding key modules. All versions of each module are loaded into the HORSE program and the configuration file chooses the modules that will be used. Generally it is possible to trade off execution speed for measurement collection or timing fidelity. Most parallel programmers would be advised to run their code under a machine configuration that has unrealistic timing (e.g. memories that respond instantaneously) but improved execution speed until the application is moderately bug-free.

Another use of the configuration file is to set some boundary on the consumption of host machine resources. The storage that records the internal state of a single HORIZON PE currently exceeds 512K bytes. Applications that do not activate every instruction stream can be simulated with arbitrary, lower limits to conserve host machine resources.

Finally, the configuration file specifies the placement of processors and memories within the node space of a network. While this placement is potentially under the user's control several off-the-shelf configuration files are available. Different versions of network simulation have been developed. They range from fixed uniform delay models to a model that has completely programmable topologies. The latter module has also been used in offline simulation studies. Some of the results of these studies are presented in this proceedings [5].

HORIZON program files and HORSE configuration files have headers that are recognized by the host UNIX operating system. Users can treat a HORIZON program as a standard UNIX executable program. Command line arguments can be used to vary the machine configuration or set initial parameters. Arguments that are unused by the simulation system are made available to both the HORIZON program and debugger command scripts.

CH2617-9/88/0000/0053$01.00 © 1988 IEEE

IMPLEMENTATION

The simulator is written entirely in the C programming language. Assembly language was avoided because of its inherent machine dependence and difficulty of use when combined with optimizing compilers.

The HORIZON machine model processes data in 64-bit registers and memory words. We wrote inline macro commands for all of the ALU's operations (with the exception of a 128-bit multiply subroutine call). The macros contend with C compiler implementations ranging from having native 64-bit integers (CRAY2), special non-standard types (Convex uses *long long* as a 64-bit data type), and machines with no support for 64-bit calculation. Curiously enough, the C code for a 64-bit add on a 68020 based machine is faster than using a subroutine call to an assembly language subroutine that can utilize instruction sequences designed specifically for multi-word addition.

Simulation speed is gained by attempting to do as much computation as possible at compile time and by table lookup. A block of code is reused by placing it in a separate file. Simulation modules use the C language `#include` directive to access those instructions. High performance modules simply place the code inline. Each module has an associated pre-processor control variable which can collapse the inserted code to a subroutine call. Furthermore, a global control variable can specify that all such module references be done by subroutine calls. The subroutine implementation is preferred during debugging and has been occasionally required when a fully inlined version of the code fails to compile or optimize correctly.

USER DEBUGGING INTERFACE

The debugging language in HORSE uses a style similar to that of a UNIX shell. A command verb is followed by optional arguments. The debugger language can access or modify any program visible values, most of the internal state of the simulated machine, and some of the HORSE control variables. A private variable space is also implemented. Expressions in command scripts can perform all of the primitive operations of the HORIZON processor. Procedures, selection, and iteration constructs are used to sequence debugger commands. The actual commands that are offered to the user depends on the selected machine configuration. Each simulation module can add its own commands coded in either C or the debugger language itself.

HORSE interprets a single, otherwise unused, opcode as an escape that allows arbitrary debugger commands to be executed. These instructions do not advance the simulation clock and are carefully isolated to avoid influencing any measurements being taken. The sequence of calculations will be insensitive to the presence of these extra instructions when the user restricts the commands to those that generate output.

Output is done by a command patterned after the UNIX `printf` library routine. A control string specifies the pattern of output with a flag character (%) identifying the position where a variable is to be interpolated. Characters after the flag character indicate the format of an individual datum. The standard output conversions of `printf` were extended to include new formats (symbolic addresses, un-assembled instructions, enumeration names, and bit fields), adding a variety of non-memory data sources (CPU registers, instrumentation, program invisible HORIZON machine state, and debugger variables), structured array processing, and access to operands in a non-linear order.

Breakpoints splice a string of debugger commands into the normal instruction sequence. The breakpoints are detected between simulated time ticks. The user can also stop the advance of the clock and interactively inspect the state of the computation.

RESULTS

The first HORIZON simulation was running solidly in February, 1988. In early June a version capable of simulating a full size HORIZON system (with the exception of physical memory capacity) was placed in service.

A Sun 3/280 processor typically can run 9,000 instructions of a single PE per second. That rate drops to 5,000 when inline code expansion is disabled. New versions are generated from identical source code that is generally accessed by a networked file system. An instruction set test suite is used for regression testing. Speeds on the Cray-2 are higher (20,000 instructions/sec) and much larger models can be accommodated.

The presence of a second simulation in Endot has allowed some cross checks to be made. However, the speed of that simulation (a few instructions per second) tends to discourage extensive comparisons.

FUTURE WORK

The current simulation produces only character output, relying on windowing systems or programmable editors for scrolling and command retry. A graphical interface is desirable in some sections of the simulator.

As languages are adapted or designed anew for HORIZON the debugging environment must be able to follow the location of language variables and provide execution breakpoints tied to the original source.

Finally, some of the internal services provided to support parallel process debugging are not implementable on a real machine. For example instantaneous communication may be required. We plan to work on evolving debugging and measurement constructs so that most features will be feasible on the real HORIZON system.

REFERENCES

[1] J. Kuehn, *ed.*, "The Horizon Supercomputing System: Project Status Report (Version 1.1)", *Internal Report*, Supercomputing Research Center, Lanham MD., 1988.

[2] J. Kuehn and B. Smith, "The Horizon supercomputing system: architecture and software", *Supercomputing '88*, 1988.

[3] B. Smith, "The Horizon Instruction Set", *Unpublished Note*, Supercomputing Research Center c Lanham, MD, 1987.

[4] –, "a.out manual pages", *UNIX System V Programmer Reference Manual*, AT&T Technologies, 1984.

[5] F. Pittelli and D. Smitley, "Analysis of a 3-D toroidal network for a shared memory architecture", *Supercomputing '88*, 1988.

The Fast Fourier Transform and Sparse Matrix Computations: a Study of Two Applications on the HORIZON Supercomputer

David A. Carlson, John M. Conroy

Supercomputing Research Center
Institute for Defense Analyses
4380 Forbes Boulevard
Lanham, MD 20706

ABSTRACT

As part of the HORIZON project currently underway at the Supercomputing Research Center, a set of application programs are being written and their performance is being evaluated. This paper discusses two of these applications: the fast Fourier transform and sparse matrix computations. For both problems, we develop efficient implementations that take advantage of HORIZON's many unique features, including fined-grained synchronization, multiple instruction streams, and a horizontal instruction set. Our results indicate that HORIZON will offer very high performance, sometimes in excess of a sustained rate of one floating point operation per tick.

1. Introduction

The HORIZON supercomputer is a 256 processor shared memory MIMD machine that is currently being designed and evaluated at the Supercomputing Research Center. As part of the evaluation of HORIZON, a set of application programs are being written and simulated to determine their potential performance. These application programs have been chosen to represent a variety of computationally intensive tasks that normally demand supercomputer performance.

In this paper, we give a flavor of these application studies by discussing work that has been done to date on the fast Fourier transform and sparse matrix computations. Our results indicate that HORIZON will indeed be a high performance machine capable of outperforming existing supercomputers by at least two, possibly even three orders of magnitude.

For both problems, we show how to map efficient algorithms effectively onto HORIZON in order to obtain high performance. A key part of this mapping process is the creation of multiple I-streams for each HORIZON processor, which allows the delay in accessing memory to be hidden in the algorithms. We also discuss how to take advantage of some of the novel aspects of the HORIZON instruction set in the code for our algorithms.

For the fast Fourier transform, we have implemented an algorithm based on the radix-4 Stockham variant that promises excellent performance. At each stage of the algorithm, multiple I-streams perform independent radix-4 computations. Each I-stream has enough registers to support a radix-4 computation without spilling to memory in the middle, which increases performance significantly. Even better performance results from the ability to perform floating point operations in parallel on two functional units contained in a HORIZON processor. By overlapping floating point operations with other floating point operations and with memory operations, extremely efficient code can be written for each of the many radix-4 computations that need to be done. Timing studies based on the code developed so far indicate that about 1.2 floating point operations per instruction (or tick) can be maintained for the Fourier transform.

The second application is a sparse matrix computation. We compute:

$$x_t = Ax_{t-1} + g \quad \text{until} \quad ||x_t - x_{t-1}|| < \varepsilon.$$

The matrix A is assumed to be large and sparse. Our results show that even when the sparsity structure of A is random, nearly 0.7 floating point operations per tick is achievable. If A is highly structured, as is the case in many finite element and finite difference problems, then even greater performance is possible.

2. Overview of HORIZON

HORIZON is a shared memory, MIMD multiprocessor, where each processor is capable of high performance in its own right. As such, HORIZON processors are able to execute a versatile and diverse set of horizontal (long word) instructions. Some of these instructions will be highlighted here; a more complete description can be found in [5].

Each HORIZON instruction takes scalar rather than vector arguments. An instruction consists of four fields: lookahead, M, A, and C. The lookahead field contains an integer, i, between 0 and 7, which indicates that the results of the current instruction are not needed until $i+1$ instructions beyond the current instruction. The M, A, and C fields roughly correspond to memory references, arithmetic operations, and program control. HORIZON has a globally addressable memory which can be accessed by any of the processors. Memory references can set or wait on a full/empty bit of the location that is being accessed. In this way, every memory location can be used for synchronization. The A field operations include a combined multiply and add (subtract) for integers as well as floating point numbers. Instructions such as double precision shifting and other bit operations are also included as A ops. One of the major functions of the C field operations is process (I-stream) creation and management. Other functions of the C field are: loop control, some logical operations, and a floating point add. The latter will be seen to be extremely beneficial for the FFT, which has more floating point adds than multiplies. All instructions are fed through a heterogeneous pipeline, which is described in further detail in [13].

The HORIZON network topology [9] is a 3-dimensional array of processors, memory, and network nodes, but allows any processor to load from any memory module. HORIZON is expected to have $O(N^3)$ memory modules and $O(N^2)$ processors, for $N=16$. The average latency to memory is expected to be a small constant times N, the diameter of the network. However, this latency can be hidden by the use of the lookahead facility

CH2617-9/88/0000/0055$01.00 © 1988 IEEE

and/or multiple I-streams on a single processor. In both cases, a processor is kept busy with work while memory requests are being handled by the network (see [5,9,13] for further details).

3. The Fast Fourier Transform on HORIZON

Computing the discrete Fourier transform of a vector is a problem that arises in a wide range of scientific applications, including signal and image processing. The development of the fast Fourier transform algorithm by Cooley and Tukey [4] made this computation tractable for medium to large sized vectors. Due to its importance, a significant amount of research has been devoted to the fast Fourier transform algorithm, including different formulations and implementations on modern supercomputers [1,2,7,10-12]. In this section, we develop an efficient implementation of the FFT algorithm for the HORIZON supercomputer.

The problem of computing a discrete Fourier transform can be stated formally as follows. Let A be a 2^m long array of complex numbers. The Fourier transform of A is the array B, where $B(j) = \sum_{k=0}^{2^m-1} A(k)e^{-(2\pi i/2^m)kj}$. The fast Fourier transform algorithm can be thought of as recursively computing the Fourier transforms of the odd and even components of the vector, and then composing together the results. The resulting algorithm runs in time proportional to $m \cdot 2^m$, versus the 2^{2m} operations implied by the above definition.

The FFT algorithm implemented on HORIZON is a radix 4 self-sorting (Stockham) FFT [12]. Working radix 4 allows us to achieve both fewer memory references and a minimum of complex multiplications. The self-sorting property eliminates the cost of reordering outputs at the end of the computation (other FFT algorithms produce their outputs in a bit reversal ordering). At a high level, the algorithm can be described as follows:

> Initialize the array B_{m+2} to the inputs of the FFT.
> Let $\omega = e^{-2\pi i/2^m}$.
> for ($s=m$; $s \geq 2$; s -=2){
> $\gamma_s = \omega^{2^{s-2}}$
>   for (j=0; $j<2^{m-s}$; j++){
>   for (k=0; $k<2^{s-2}$; k++){
> $t0 = B_{s+2}(j \cdot 2^s + k)$
> $t1 = \gamma_s^j \cdot B_{s+2}(j \cdot 2^s + k + 2^{s-2})$
> $t2 = \gamma_s^{2j} \cdot B_{s+2}(j \cdot 2^s + k + 2^{s-1})$
> $t3 = \gamma_s^{3j} \cdot B_{s+2}(j \cdot 2^s + k + 3 \cdot 2^{s-2})$
> $t4 = t0 + t2$
> $t5 = t1 + t3$
> $t6 = t0 - t2$
> $t7 = i \cdot (t1 - t3)$
> $B_s(j \cdot 2^{s-2} + k) = t4 + t5$
> $B_s(j \cdot 2^{s-2} + k + 2^{m-2}) = t6 + t7$
> $B_s(j \cdot 2^{s-2} + k + 2^{m-1}) = t4 - t5$
> $B_s(j \cdot 2^{s-2} + k + 3 \cdot 2^{m-2}) = t6 - t7$
>   }
>   }
> }

Only three complex multiplications are required in the radix 4 "kernel" (to form t1, t2, t3) since multiplication by i is done by switching real and imaginary parts with appropriate sign changes and the γ's can be precomputed and then simply fetched from memory. In practice, only two arrays are used, and their roles switch between input and output from stage to stage.

The salient features of the HORIZON architecture with respect to the FFT are that there are 256 processors, and each processor supports up to 128 independent I-streams. Each stage of an FFT can be broken up into $2^m/r$ independent radix-r computations, so if m is large enough, all processors can be saturated with I-streams, one per radix-r computation. We have chosen r=4, so that if $m \geq 17$, then there will be at least 128 separate radix-4 computations for each of the 256 processors. Having multiple I-streams allows one to hide memory latency in HORIZON, so that execution time is simply the number of instructions in the I-stream multiplied by the number of I-streams. Thus, for this parallel decomposition of an FFT algorithm, the major effort shifts to implementing efficiently an I-stream for the radix-4 kernel of the algorithm.

The arithmetic operations in the radix-4 kernel of the FFT algorithm are floating point multiplies, adds, and subtracts. A unique feature of HORIZON is that both the A and C units can perform floating point operations. This allows the radix-4 kernel to be written using fewer instructions by properly overlapping the A and C units. Loads and stores to memory are also overlapped with floating point operations wherever possible. Offsets into the array are fixed for a radix-4 kernel, thus we ignore the way addresses are computed in the following code. Each I-stream has 32 registers available for use, which is enough to hold all of the temporary variables arising in the radix-4 kernel (note that complex numbers are being represented) without having to spill to memory in the middle. Pseudo HORIZON assembly code for a radix 4 kernel is now given.

M-unit	A-unit	C-unit
(LOAD γ1r)	()	()
(LOAD x1r)	()	()
(LOAD γ1i)	(t1r=γ1r*x1r)	()
(LOAD x1i)	(t1i=γ1i*x1r)	()
(LOAD γ3r)	(t1r=t1r-γ1i*x1i)	()
(LOAD x3r)	(t1i=t1i+γ1r*x1i)	()
(LOAD γ3i)	(t3r=γ3r*x3r)	()
(LOAD x3i)	(t3i=γ3i*x3r)	()
(LOAD γ2r)	(t3r=t3r-γ3i*x3i)	()
(LOAD x2r)	(t3i=t3i+γ3r*x3i)	(t5r=t1r+t3r)
(LOAD γ2i)	(t2r=γ2r*x2r)	(t5i=t1i+t3i)
(LOAD x2i)	(t2i=γ2i*x2r)	(t7r=t3i-t1i)
(LOAD t0r)	(t2r=t2r-γ2i*x2i)	(t7i=t1r-t3r)
(LOAD t0i)	(t2i=t2i+γ2r*x2i)	(t4r=t0r+t2r)
()	(t8r=t4r+t5r)	(t4i=t0i+t2i)
(STORE t8r)	(t8i=t4i+t5i)	(t6r=t0r-t2r)
(STORE t8i)	(t9r=t6r+t7r)	(t6i=t0i-t2i)
(STORE t9r)	(t9i=t6i+t7i)	()
(STORE t9i)	(t10r=t4r-t5r)	()
(STORE t10r)	(t10i=t4i-t5i)	()
(STORE t10i)	(t11r=t6r-t7r)	()
(STORE t11r)	(t11i=t6i-t7i)	()
(STORE t11i)	()	()

To run even faster, an independent radix 4 computation in the first stage of the FFT can be coded so as to eliminate all complex multiplications (the j loop is null so the γ_s^js are not required). HORIZON code for this is simpler than that given above due to the elimination of the complex multiplications, and requires only 16 instructions to complete an I-stream. This is a minimum number of instructions due to the number of loads and stores that must be performed.

```
(LOAD t0r)      ()                ()
(LOAD t2r)      ()                ()
(LOAD t0i)      (t4r=t0r+t2r)     ()
(LOAD t2i)      (t6r=t0r-t2r)     ()
(LOAD t1r)      (t4i=t0i+t2i)     ()
(LOAD t3r)      (t6i=t0i-t2i)     ()
(LOAD t1i)      (t5r=t1r+t3r)     ()
(LOAD t3i)      (t7i=t1r-t3r)     (t8r=t4r+t5r)
(STORE t8r)     (t5i=t1i+t3i)     (t9i=t6i+t7i)
(STORE t9i)     (t7r=t3i-t1i)     (t8i=t4i+t5i)
(STORE t8i)     (t10r=t4r-t5r)    ()
(STORE t10r)    (t10i=t4i-t5i)    ()
(STORE t10i)    (t9r=t6r+t7r)     ()
(STORE t9r)     (t11r=t6r-t7r)    ()
(STORE t11r)    (t11i=t6i-t7i)    ()
(STORE t11i)    ()                ()
```

We are now in a position to analyze the performance of computing a medium to large sized fast Fourier transform using HORIZON. First of all, both versions of the radix-4 kernel require a minimum or near minimum number of instructions based on the number of loads and stores that must be performed. The kernel written for stages requiring complex multiplications achieves a floating point operation per instruction ratio of 28/23=1.217 (noteworthy since it is greater than one). Noting that nearly every instruction requires a memory reference, run time can be estimated based on expected memory latency, which exceeds arithmetic latency in HORIZON. Memory requests in our radix-4 kernel take 80 ticks to satisfy on average [9]. With this assumption, the estimated run time of a stage (2^{m-2} radix-4 kernels) is

$$(\#\text{instr. in I-stream})\cdot\max(\#\text{I-streams},80)$$

As discussed earlier, when $m \geq 17$, the number of available I-streams per processor is ≥ 128, so time becomes $23 \cdot 2^{m-2}/P$ for all but the first stage. There are $m/2$ radix-4 stages, so total run time on HORIZON is bounded by $T \leq (23/8) \cdot m \cdot 2^m/P$. This represents essentially a full speedup over a serial version of the algorithm, which on one HORIZON processor would require $T \cong (23/8) \cdot m \cdot 2^m$.

4. Sparse Matrix Computation on HORIZON

Solving sparse linear systems of equations is fundamental to many scientific computing applications. The problem is to solve the system $Kx=b$, where K is an n by n sparse matrix. When the system is very large, an iterative method is often employed. An important class of these methods is the stationary iterative method, which takes the following form:

$$x_t = Ax_{t-1} + g \quad \text{until} \quad ||x_t - x_{t-1}|| < \varepsilon \quad \text{or} \quad t > \text{tmax}.$$

The matrix A and the vector g are chosen such that x_t will converge to x.

In this paper we will consider one instance of this problem. We assume that A has l non-zeroes per row which are randomly distributed. Random sparsity often arises in modeling of electrical power grids and in the simulation of large scale integrated circuits [3,6,8,14]. In other applications, such as structural design problems, the matrices exhibit much more structure. This structure can often be exploited to produce efficient parallel algorithms. Here, we will demonstrate that even with random sparsity we can achieve nearly 2 floating point operations in 3 ticks.

The sparse matrix is represented by an n by l floating point matrix, a and an integer array, j, of the same size, which holds the the column indices for each row. We let is_id be the I-stream identifier, I be the number of I-streams per processor, P be the number of processors, and $p=IP$ be the total number of I-streams. Each I-stream will compute $m=n/p$ components of x_t. For ease of exposition, we assume that p, P, and n are all powers of 2. The above iteration can be achieved by the following algorithm:

```
    Code for I-stream is-id.
error=1.0; t = 0;
while (error > ε) and (t < tmax) {
   error = 0.0;
   for (i=m*(is_id+1)-1; i>=m*is_id; i--) {
      temp = g[i];
      for (off=l-1; off=>0; off--) temp += a[i][off]*x[j[i]];
      diff = abs(temp - x[i]);
      error = max(error, diff);
      y[i] = temp;
   } /* end for */
   t = t + 1;
   max(error);  /* Find maximum error across all I-streams. */
   swap(x,y);
} /* end while */
```

The above algorithm consists of two major parts. The first is computing the l long sparse inner product, given by the innermost *for* loop above. This stage can be computed with a loop consisting of three HORIZON assembly instructions. We pre-load the initial values of x, y, j, and a, so that full advantage of the horizontal nature of the instruction set can be exploited.

```
                  Initialize:
                  aptr = a[is_id*m]
                  jptr = j[is_id*m]
                  off  = m*(i+1)-1
Label    Lookahead      M-unit                A-unit        C-unit
n_j:         1          (load j jptr off)     (y=y+a*x)     ()
             1          (load a aptr off)     ()            (decrement off)
             0          (load x xptr j)       ()            (if off>0 go to n_j)
```

The second phase is checking for convergence. For definiteness, we use the infinity (supremum) norm. The norm is first computed within the I-stream for its m-long portion of the vector. This value is then compared with all other I-streams to determine if the convergence criterion has been met. Each processor must also receive the norm value, the maximum absolute difference between x_t and x_{t-1}. This inter-I-stream operation is accomplished through a recursive doubling algorithm (note that the data flow diagram for this stage is isomorphic to that of a radix 2 FFT). In the following code fragment, we assume that the maximum absolute difference between each I-stream's m-long portion of x_t and x_{t-1} is in the register labeled "error." Upon completion, this same register will contain the "global" infinity norm of $|x_t - x_{t-1}|$. A $p \log p$ long auxiliary array, labeled "d," is used for communication between the I-streams.

Initialize: dim = $p = 2^k$

Label	Lookahead	M-unit	A-unit	C-unit
		set full on store		
	0	(store error dptr is_id)	(off=dim .xor. is_id)	()
n_level:		wait full on load		
	0	(load error_1 dptr off)	(dim=dim>>1)	()
	0	()	(off=dim .xor. is_id)	(error=max(error,error1))
		set full on store		
	0	(store error dptr off)	(dptr=dptr+p*64)	(if dim>0 go to n_level)

We now estimate the total run time for this algorithm. When the full problem is coded, nearly every instruction requires a memory reference. For this reason, our timing is based on expected memory latency, which exceeds the arithmetic latency of any instruction in HORIZON. We assume that each memory operation that requires access of the status bits (full/empty) takes 120 ticks. Memory requests, which do not use the full/empty bits, are assumed to take 80 ticks [9]. Under these assumptions, the approximate run time for one iteration is given by:

$$t(I,P) = \left(\frac{3nl+3n}{IP} + 7\right) \max(80,I) + 3\log(IP) \max(120,I) \text{ ticks.}$$

If $I=128$, i.e each processor is given 128 I-streams, then the expected run time is approximately

$$t_1(P) = \frac{3nl+3n}{P} + 384\log P + 3584 \text{ ticks.}$$

When $nl+n$ is large relative to $128P\log P \leq 2^{18}$ then the above analysis indicates that this algorithm is quite efficient. We perform $2nl+2n$ floating point operations (nl multiplies, $nl+n$ adds, and n maximums) in roughly $3nl+3n$ ticks, or about 2 flops in 3 ticks. Alternatively, we can ask what is the optimal number of processors to use for fixed values of l and n? By simple calculus, we can show that t_1 is minimal for $P=(nl+n)/128$. This value of P corresponds to a speed up of order $P/\log P$. However, for large sparse matrix applications $nl>100{,}000$, while for HORIZON, $P \leq 256$; so, it is unlikely that we would use $O(nl)$ processors. On the other hand, this optimization does clearly indicate this application has far more parallelism than we are exploiting.

5. Conclusions

In this paper, we have examined implementations of two major applications, the fast Fourier transform and sparse matrix computations, on the HORIZON supercomputer. We found both applications to be supported well by the HORIZON instruction set, and that there is enough parallelism in the applications to create multiple HORIZON I-streams, which allows memory latency to be hidden. Thus, HORIZON should be able to execute code for these applications at a very high rate of performance.

References

[1] D. Bailey, "A High-Performance Fast Fourier Transform Algorithm for the Cray-2," *Journal of Supercomputing,* Vol. 1, pp. 43-60, 1987.

[2] E.O. Brigham, *The Fast Fourier Transform,* Prentice-Hall, Englewood Cliffs, NJ, 1974.

[3] D. A. Calahan "Randomly Sparse Equation Solution by Loopless Code Generated on the CRAY-1," *Technical Report* 162, System Engineering Laboratory, University of Machigan, May 1982.

[4] J.W. Cooley and J. Tukey, "An Algorithm for the Machine Calculation of Complex Fourier Series," *Mathematics of Computation,* Vol. 19, pp. 297-301, 1965.

[5] J. T. Kuehn and B. J. Smith "The HORIZON Supercomputing System: Architecture and Software," *Supercomputing 88,* Orlando, Florida, 1988.

[6] J. G. Lewis and W. G. Poole, Jr., "Ordering Algorithms Applied to Sparse Matrices in Electrical Power Problems," *Electrical Power Problems: The Mathematical Challenge,* A. M. Erisman, K. W. Neeves, and M. H. Dwarakanath (eds.), SIAM Publications, Philadelphia, 1980.

[7] M.C. Pease, "An Adaptation of the Fast Fourier Transform for Parallel Processing," *Journal of the ACM* Vol. 15, pp. 252-264, 1968.

[8] D. A. Reed and M. L. Patrick, "A Model of Asynchronous Iterative Algorithms for Solving Larger, Sparse, Linear Systems," *Proceedings of the 1984 International Conference on Parallel Processing,* Bellaire, Michigan, pp. 402-409.

[9] F. Pittelli and D. Smitley , "Analysis of a 3-D Toroidal Network for a Shared Memory Architecture," *Supercomputing 88,* Orlando, Florida, 1988.

[10] P.N. Swarztrauber, "FFT Algorithms for Vector Computers," *Parallel Computing,* Vol. 1, pp. 45-63, 1984.

[11] P.N. Swarztrauber, "Multiprocessor FFTs," *Parallel Computing,* Vol. 5, pp. 197-210, 1987.

[12] C. Temperton, "Self-Sorting Mixed Radix Fast Fourier Transforms," *Journal of Computational Physics,* Vol. 52, pp. 1-23, 1983.

[13] M. Thistle and B. J. Smith "A Processor Architecture for HORIZON," *Supercomputing 88,* Orlando, Florida, 1988.

[14] R. A. Wagner, "Parallel Solution of Arbitrarily Sparse Linear Systems," *Technical Report* CS-1984-13, Department of Computer Science, Duke University.

Dataflow Systems

Chair: Rod Oldehoeft
Colorado State University

Assessing the Benefits of Fine-grain Parallelism in Dataflow Programs[1]

Arvind
David E. Culler
Gino K. Maa
Laboratory for Computer Science
Massachusetts Institute of Technology
Cambridge, MA 02139

Abstract

A method for assessing the benefits of fine-grain parallelism in "real" programs is presented. The method is based on *parallelism profiles* and *speedup curves* derived by executing dataflow graphs on an interpreter under progressively more realistic assumptions about processor resources and communication costs. It is shown that programs, even using traditional algorithms, exhibit ample parallelism when parallelism is exposed at all levels, *i.e.,* within expressions, across nested loops and function calls, and in producer-consumer relationships on individual elements of data structures. Since only dataflow graphs compiled from the high-level language Id are considered, the bias introduced by the language and the compiler is examined. A method of estimating speedup through analysis of the ideal parallelism profile is developed, avoiding repeated execution of programs. It is shown that fine-grain parallelism can be used to mask large, unpredictable memory latency and synchronization waits in architectures employing dataflow instruction execution mechanisms. Finally, the effects of grouping portions of dataflow programs, such as function invocations or loop iterations, and requiring that the operators in a group execute on a single processor, are explored.

1 Introduction

The high-performance computing community has engaged in a long-standing debate on the proper "granularity of parallelism" for multiprocessors [22]. Coming from a mind-set of migrating sequential programs to complexes of sequential machines, one tends to view sequential execution as fast compared to the time required for communication and synchronization. It is observed that as the logical partitions of a program are made smaller the amount of external communication increases and this can offset the advantage of parallel execution. While this view is basically correct, the mind-set encourages one to consider only the sorts of parallelism these machines can exploit, and this can lead to the dubious conclusion that the "useful" parallelism in programs is small. We come into the debate with the opposite bias — a dataflow model where *any* two operators can execute in parallel, unless one actually provides data directly or indirectly to the other, and where no fundamental distinction is made between inter- and intra-processor communication. From this view point, it makes sense to ask how much parallelism is inherent in a program; can machines be built to exploit this kind of parallelism; and what advantages may such machines hold over currently available machines. If, indeed, a large class of programs have substantial fine-grain parallelism and the machines that exploit this parallelism are cost-effective, we can expect tremendous performance improvements in general-purpose computing.

In this paper, we focus on the first question and develop a methodology for studying inherent parallelism in programs. Though our methodology is developed in the context of dataflow, we believe it is applicable to other environments as well. Dataflow program graphs provide a precise description of parallel computation[11]. Arcs indicate data dependence between operations, and operators not connected by paths in the graph represent opportunities for parallel execution. In Section 2, we define an ideal execution model for dataflow graphs, which executes all operators in parallel except as constrained by data dependencies. Based on this model, programs can be characterized by their *parallelism profile*, from which critical-path length, average parallelism, and potential speedup can be deduced.[2]

Program graphs are generated by compiling Id, a high-level declarative language [19]. In Section 3 we examine the bias that this introduces and restrict our attention to problems which are comfortably expressed both in Id and in traditional languages. In Section 4, we offer experimental evidence for our primary claim: *parallelism is pervasive, even in programs employing traditional algorithms*, provided that parallelism is exposed at all levels, not only in loops and function calls but even in producer/consumer relationships which may require synchronization on individual elements of data structures.

In Section 5, we consider the behavior of programs under the constraint that at most a certain number of operations can be performed simultaneously. We then consider the impact of communication latency, showing that as the latency increases more parallelism is required to achieve a given speedup. Another inter-

[1]This research was done at the MIT Laboratory for Computer Science. Funding for this project is provided in part by the Advanced Research Projects Agency of the Department of Defense under the Office of Naval Research contract N00014-84-K-0099. An expanded version of this paper appears in the *International Journal of Supercomputing Applications*, vol. 2, no. 3, reprinted by permission of MIT Press.

[2]Elsewhere [1] we have presented a detailed account of the fraction of operators that represent the overhead or the cost of parallel execution. Resource requirements of parallel programs are discussed in [10]. Taken together, these papers provide a better characterization of the "useful" parallelism in dataflow programs than this paper alone does.

pretation of this data is that fine-grain parallelism can be used to mask large, unpredictable communication latency and synchronization waits, which will occur in any parallel architecture. A method for *estimating* the speedup from a single parallelism profile is also given.

Finally, we introduce program partitioning at various levels of granularity into the execution model. Since the operators in a partition are not allowed to execute in parallel, the available parallelism is reduced; Section 6 examines the effect of this restriction on potential speedup. We also consider the more realistic scenario in which external communication is expensive, and examine the trade-offs between the granularity and the speedup.

Throughout this paper we assume that the reader has some familiarity with dataflow; a good introduction to the MIT Tagged-Token Dataflow Architecture may be found in the references [5].

2 Parallelism Profiles under Ideal Execution

Dataflow is an asynchronous, time-independent model of computation; nonetheless, in order to characterize the parallelism in dataflow programs, we consider a synchronous execution model with unit time per operation. Timing assumptions are purely for quantification; we do not exploit any aspect of synchronous execution in dataflow program graphs.

The *parallelism profile* for a dataflow graph on a given input is a function $pp(t)$ which gives the number of operators executed at each step t on an ideal machine. The *ideal machine* has the following characteristics:

1. All operators take unit time,
2. Any number of operations can be performed in a step,
3. Communication is instantaneous, and
4. Each operator executes as early as possible, *i.e.*, as soon as *all* its input data are available.

This model assumes unbounded processor, storage, and communication resources.

We illustrate the method for generating parallelism profiles through an example. Figure 1 shows a simplified program graph which computes the inner products of two vectors, A and B, of size n. Initially, a token for sum, with value zero, is sent to the left switch, and tokens for i, with value one, are sent to the right switch and the $\leq$ predicate. The value n and the descriptors for the two vectors are *loop invariants*[5], and thus can be considered to be embedded in the graph. Assume that the value of n is 3. In step 1, instruction 1 (*i.e.*, the operator $\leq$) fires, producing tokens with value TRUE that are instantly available at the control inputs of the two switches. Instructions 2 and 3 fire in step 2 and produce tokens carrying the value of sum for instruction 8 and i for instructions 4, 5, and 6. In step 3, instructions 4, 5, and 6 execute while the token for sum waits for the other input to instruction 8. The firing of instruction 6 provides input to the predicate and the right switch. In step 4, the value of sum that has been waiting is added to the result of instruction 7, while the new value of i passes through the switch. Note that, in step 5 of the parallelism profile, the second iteration has begun while the first is still active. Execution continues in this manner until step 14 when a token on the FALSE side of the switch in instruction 2 is produced. The pattern in steps 4 to 6 covers all 8 instructions and repeats for every iteration. Note, an operator is executed at the step corresponding to the later of the arrival

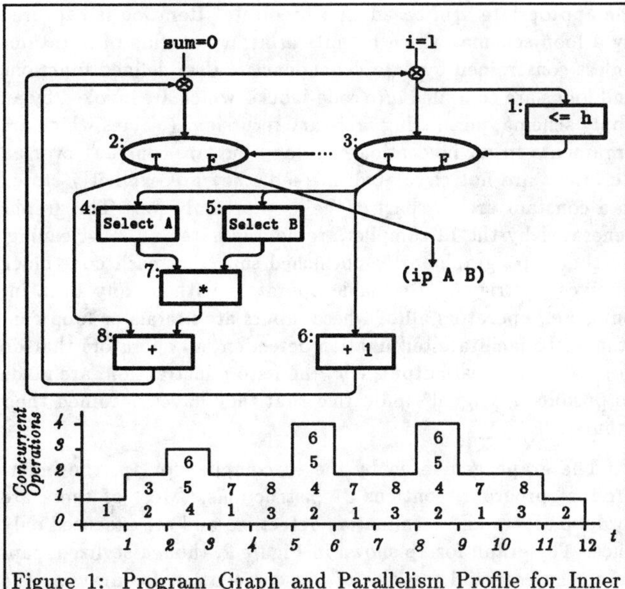

Figure 1: Program Graph and Parallelism Profile for Inner Product, n=3

times of its input tokens.

The step beyond which $pp(t)$ is uniformly zero is called the *critical path length*, and is denoted by T_∞. Thus, T_∞ is the length of the longest chain of data-dependencies in a program. The area under the curve $pp(t)$ gives the total number of operations executed, and is denoted by T_1. The ratio of these is the *average parallelism*, $\overline{P} = T_1/T_\infty$. The parallelism profile of the inner product of length 3 appearing in Figure 1 shows that the critical path length is 12, and the total number of operations is 27. Note, this describes the parallelism for this particular method of computing the inner product; it may be possible to achieve greater parallelism with a better algorithm, but that would be described by a different graph.

3 Generating Dataflow Graphs

Although dataflow graphs provide a precise representation of parallel execution, the utility of the model is limited by our ability to generate the graphs themselves. We will consider only graphs generated by a reasonably sophisticated compiler for the language Id[23]. Id is a functional language, extended with I-structures[6] to provide efficient array manipulation. A broad class of algorithms are easily expressed in Id, although we recognize that it is difficult, perhaps impossible, to express efficient algorithms for certain types of problems in the current version of Id. This section explores the implications of the language and the compiler on parallelism profiles.

3.1 Compiler generated graphs

The dataflow graphs produced by the Id compiler are based on a fixed set of schemas and rules of composition, described elsewhere [5, 23]. Very briefly, arithmetic expressions are translated into acyclic graphs. Blocks, which give names to expressions, are treated as "wiring diagrams" to compose graphs. Conditional expressions are constructed using switch operators to steer values to the appropriate arm based on a predicate. Iteration is captured by a loop schema, which permits arbitrary overlap of iterations unless constrained by data dependencies. User defined functions and loops are compiled into code-blocks, which are invoked by an apply schema, permitting arbitrary recursion. (Values which are arguments to an invocation of a loop but are constant over all iterations are not circulated; instead, they are explicitly stored in a constant area as part of the loop preamble[5].) The graphs generated by the Id compiler are determinate and self-cleaning. Furthermore, graphs are embellished such that each code-block receives a "trigger" to enable operators without any data inputs, *i.e.*, operators all of whose inputs are literals or loop constants. To facilitate termination detection, all operators that do not have a natural output, *e.g.*, the I-store instruction, are made to produce a "signal" indicating that they have consumed their inputs[23].

The graph generated by the Id compiler for ip, the inner-product program, contains 31 instructions. Most of these are for loop set-up and termination detection, and are executed only once. The graph for ip shown in Figure 2, though stylized, captures the essential features of the compilation for drawing the parallelism profile. The output of the Id compiler can be executed on GITA [18], the Graph Interpreter for the Tagged-Token Architecture, which generates parallelism profile graphs as a part of its runtime statistics report. As can be seen in the profile in Figure 2, the compiler-generated graph executes 5 more instructions per iteration than the graph in Figure 1. These additional instructions are for tag manipulation and control of loop unfolding, discussed further in [10]. Graphs generated by the current Id compiler incur roughly 150% overhead in terms of the number of instructions executed beyond the essential computation, in order to allow maximal parallelism[1] while preserving determinacy.

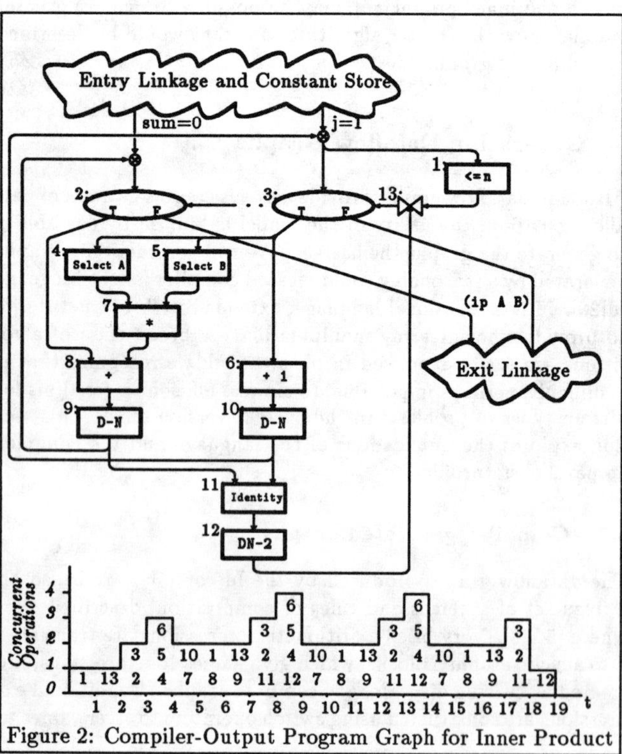

Figure 2: Compiler-Output Program Graph for Inner Product

3.2 Compiler Optimizations

The Id compiler performs most of the traditional optimizations, including constant propagation, common subexpression elimination, and code hoisting, plus optimizations which are particular to functional languages, such as tuple elision and arity analysis. A powerful function *inlining* capability is provided to reduce the overhead of function application. The traditional optimizations are very effective on dataflow program graphs, because of the clean semantics and structure of dataflow graphs. Optimizations such as loop fusion and unrolling, and incorporation of algebraic identities are planned for the future.

Note that in the inner-product example, the multiplications could execute in any arbitrary order and the sum would still be formed in sequence. In particular, if the `select` operators incur a delay in providing data to the multiply because of communication latency, the loop will unfold and multiple outstanding fetches will be issued, masking the latency. The critical path can be shortened if the compiler can recognize associative operations, reassociating them into balanced trees. For this problem, the programmer could also have used a recursive formulation to do a binary tree summation to achieve the same effect. It is also possible to describe dataflow graphs which combine arbitrary partial products, in whatever order they happened to be produced, but this will require a non-deterministic operator. Intentionally, Id has no means for expressing non-determinism; assuring determinacy under parallel execution is critical in developing correct applications. Still there are important application areas where non-determinism is essential and extensions to the language are being considered.

4 Fine-grain Parallelism in Programs

Generally, a given machine can exploit only certain kinds of parallelism. Most machines exploit parallelism within the instruction cycle through instruction prefetch. Many machines exploit local parallelism in an instruction sequence by using pipelined execution units. Vector processors [21] exploit parallelism in simple, inner-most loops. Long-instruction-word machines [7, 12] exploit fine-grain parallelism within many kinds of loops and possibly in instruction sequences, but generally do not consider executing completely unrelated loops together. Multicomputers generally exploit parallelism between large tasks, but little within a task. Only a few machines, the Sigma-1 [14] and HEP [16] being the most notable examples, have the capability to support parallelism between producers and consumers of data structures. The dataflow model does not draw a distinction between different kinds of parallelism; independent operators within an expression are treated in the same way as the operators within a vectorizable loop or those in large unrelated tasks. In this section we show how this results in ample available parallelism.

4.1 Non-strict Data structures

Generally, imperative languages compromise parallelism in manipulation of data structures by requiring a barrier between the producer of a structure and its consumers. Functional languages with "strict" semantics exhibit a similar shortcoming because data structures are treated as a single value, and operations which access particular elements of the structure cannot execute until the entire structure is defined [11]. This prevents asynchronous production and consumption of structures, much as does barrier synchronization. Our model avoids this limitation through I-structures, a form of non-strict array which is explicitly allocated and filled, with synchronization on an element-by-element basis. An attempt to read an element that is not present is deferred until the element is written, and processed immediately thereafter. To ensure determinacy, an element can only be written once. Approaches which detect parallelism in sequential programs are severely restricted by the difficulty of compile time analysis of subscript expressions; with I-structures no such analysis is required, as dependencies are resolved dynamically. With the help of the following example, we show concurrent production and consumption of an array which is produced by summing two vectors and then "consumed" by the inner-product program.

```
DEF ip_vsum A B = ip (vsum A A) (vsum B B) ;

DEF vsum A B = {l,h = bounds a;
               C = ARRAY (l,h) ;
               {FOR j FROM l TO h DO
                  C[j] = A[j] + B[j]}
               IN C } ;
```

The vsum program implies no restrictions on the order in which the elements of array C are filled. Furthermore, the iterations of the loop are independent and can proceed in parallel. In most conventional languages, the best one could hope for is that the critical path length for ip_vsum would be the sum of the critical path lengths of ip and vsum. In Id, however, vsum can return the descriptor of C, its result vector, *as soon as it is allocated, even before its loop has completed filling it.* ip gets these descriptors and can begin work immediately. Because arrays in Id have "I-structure" semantics, vsum and ip are automatically *pipelined*, working in tandem as producer and consumer respectively. I-structure operations introduce a minor complication in computing parallelism profiles. The operator which receives the result of a select operation does so one unit after either the time of the select or the time of the corresponding store, whichever comes later.

Figure 3 shows parallelism profiles for vsum, ip and ip_vsum respectively with $n = 10$. The critical path is 64 for vsum and the total operations 158. For ip they are 60 and 153, respectively. In ip_vsum, the individual profiles of vsum and ip are superimposed, rather than strung out in sequence. The critical path, instead of being 64+60, is only 77, even though the instruction count is 500. The last number is greater than 469 ($= 153 + 2 \times 158$) because of the three procedure calls. Figure 3 also introduces our notation for ideal profiles: $p = \infty$, unbounded operations per step, and $l = 0$, zero latency. More realistic models, to be introduced later, are indicated by the particular values of p and l.

Certainly, loops as simple as these could be made to work in tandem under synchronous execution, or by loop fusion transformations. However, such approaches break down when the producer and consumer are large, complex processes with irregular accessing patterns and varying computational requirements, operating asynchronously under the influence of unpredictable communication latency due to network contention and other factors. I-structures are still effective in this general setting.

4.2 Parallelism in Nested Loops

Composition of control structures does not inhibit parallelism in dataflow programs. In contrast, some approaches exploit parallelism only in outer-most or inner-most loops, or only within a procedure, or only in spawning a procedure. Id allows loops to unfold and functions to be spawned, irrespective of the nesting of control structures, constrained only by data-dependencies.

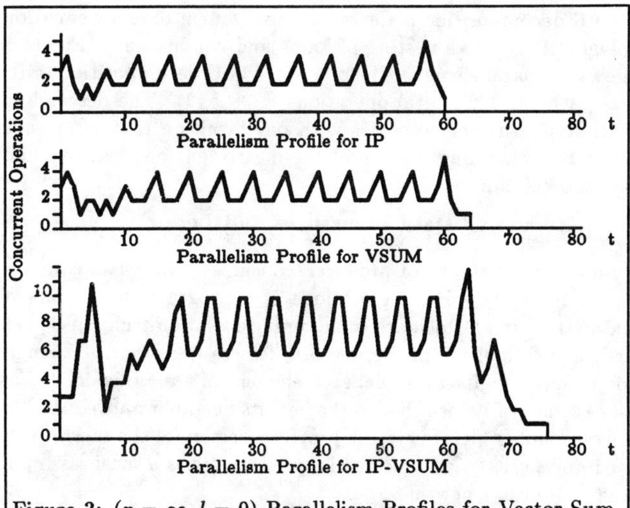

Figure 3: ($p = \infty, l = 0$) Parallelism Profiles for Vector Sum, Inner Product and their composition (size 10).

Figure 4 gives the parallelism profile for matrix multiplication of two 16×16 matrices by the traditional algorithm, showing unfolding of nested loops. The upper profile counts *all* operations, and the lower profile counts only the floating point operations. The outer loop spawns 16 concurrent instances of the middle loop, each of which spawns 16 instances of the inner product. Unfolding of the inner product depends on the availability of elements of the input matrices. The critical path length is 291 and the total number of operations is 72,344, out of which 8,192 are floating point operations. The average parallelism is 249 operations per step. The bell-shape of the profile arises because loop unfolding causes inner loops to be staggered slightly, and the summation in the inner-most loop is done sequentially. The rapid oscillations reflect the cumulative effect of the variations in parallelism in the inner-most loop. We could spawn the inner loops in a tree, and perform the summations as a binary tree to reduce the length of the critical path further, but it is evident that substantial parallelism is present even in the traditional algorithm.

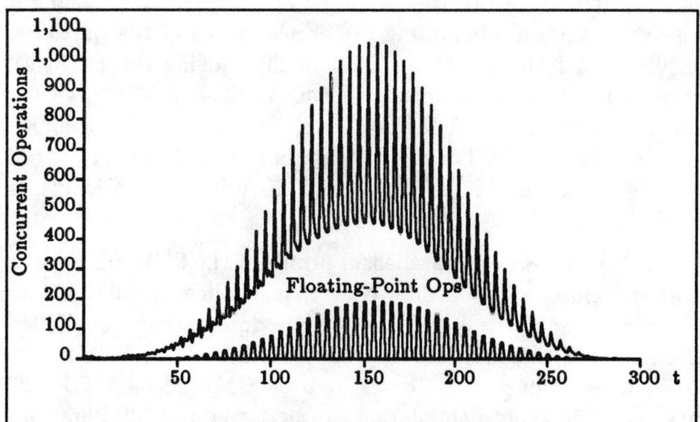

Figure 4: ($p = \infty, l = 0$) Parallelism Profile for Matrix Multiply (16×16)

LU decomposition is the central component of many equation solvers. It involves nesting of loops and conditionals. Figure 5 shows the parallelism profile for a 16×16 LU decomposition (critical path = 1312 , total operations = 35,552). The descending stair-step behavior coincides with our intuition that after each pivot the remaining portion of the matrix has one less row and one less column.

4.3 Recursive Data Structures and Loops

One normally thinks of producer/consumer relationships as being between two distinct portions of a program, but recursive data structures, which are common in relaxation techniques, can create such a situation between successive iterations of a single loop. Suppose, for example, each element of a mesh is defined as the average of its neghbor to the left, its neighbor above, and the corresponding element in the previous version of the mesh. This is simply written as a nested loop which takes a mesh as input and produces a new mesh.

Although, the loop body indicates a linear recurrence in both loop indices, computations along the diagonal of the mesh can be executed in parallel, so the parallelism profile increases linearly as the diagonal grows to $\mathcal{O}(n)$ and then decreases as the diagonal shrinks. Repeated applications of this relaxation step generates a plane of parallel activity, giving the profile with a single peak shown in Figure 6. The other profile in Figure 6 shows the behavior when parallelism is exposed within one relaxation step, but barriers are placed between the steps, excluding producer/consumer parallelism. To achieve even this level of parallelism under more traditional approaches, it is necessary to transform the relaxation loops so that the outer loop traverses the diagonal of the matrix sequentially and a parallel inner loop computes the elements on the perpendicular diagonal [17], resulting in a much more complicated and costly control structure.

4.4 Large Application Kernels: PIC and SIMPLE

We now discuss the parallelism profiles of the kernels of two large applications. These kernel codes are of the order of 1000 lines of Id, and are complex enough to make static analysis of parallelism a very difficult task. However, it is often possible to explain even complex parallelism profiles after they have been generated, provided one has a good understanding of the application.

Figure 7 shows the parallelism profile for an electrodynamics application (PIC) using a particle-in-cell approach. The idea is to model the movement of charged particles under the field they induce. This involves solving Laplace's equation, using a multigrid method, computing the accelerations of the particles, deriving a suitable time step, and finally moving the particles. This example shows 4 steps with 640 particles in 64 cells (8×8 mesh); realistic problems use 1 million particles and 100,000 cells, approximately. For the problem in Figure 7, the number of operations executed is 1,573,733 and the critical path length is 3,399.

Figure 8 shows the parallelism profile of the SIMPLE code, a hydrodynamics and heat flow code that has been studied extensively, both analytically [8] and by experimentation. A detailed discussion of the program appears elsewhere [3]. This profile shows 3 iterations of the outer loop of SIMPLE on a 20×20 mesh, while a typical simulation run performs 100,000 iterations on 100×100 mesh. The critical path is 1976 and the instruction count is 1,471,374. As can be seen from iterations 2 and 3,

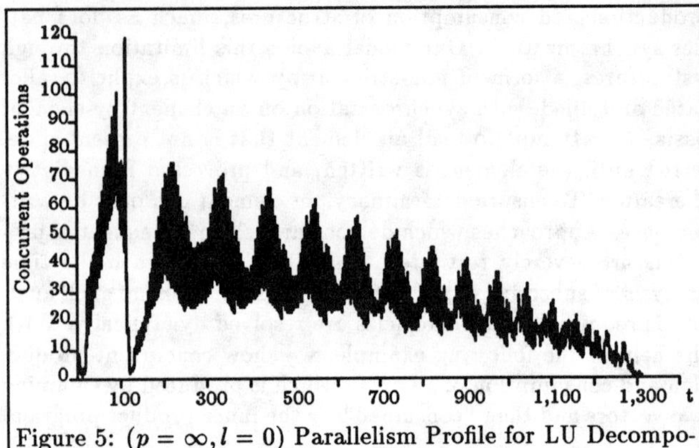

Figure 5: ($p = \infty, l = 0$) Parallelism Profile for LU Decomposition with Partial Pivoting (16×16)

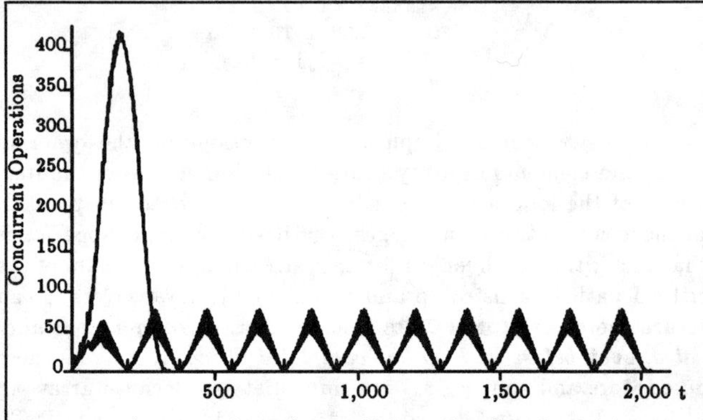

Figure 6: ($p = \infty, l = 0$) Parallelism Profiles for Multiwave, 10 iterations on a 16×16 mesh

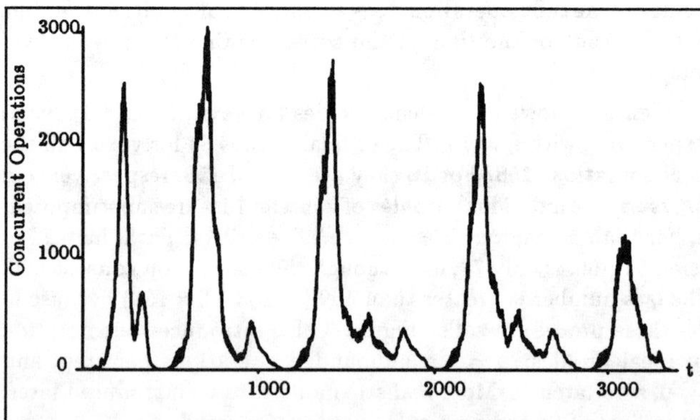

Figure 7: ($p = \infty, l = 0$) Parallelism Profile for Particle-In-Cell (4 steps, 8×8 cells, 640 particles)

there is no significant parallelism *between* the outer loop iterations of SIMPLE; the profile for N iterations can be obtained by repetition of a single iteration's profile. To see how the behavior changes with problem size, we observe that on a 32×32 mesh, the parallelism profile peaks at 6536, with critical path = 1082 and instruction count = 1,446,478.

Hidden in this profile is substantial producer/consumer parallelism, possible only with element by element synchronization. A total of thirteen matrices are created during each iteration, in eight distinct phases of the computation. If barriers are in-

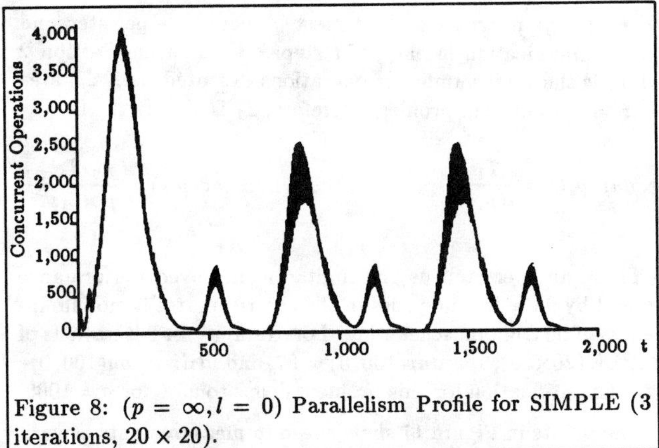

Figure 8: ($p = \infty, l = 0$) Parallelism Profile for SIMPLE (3 iterations, 20 × 20).

troduced between producers and consumers, the critical path increases by more than a factor of three.

Parallelism profiles accurately capture the inherent parallelism in programs, given the specific algorithms employed and the compilation technology. Factors which place additional constraints in any realistic implementation, such as multiple simultaneous reads to an array component, communication latency, locality, contention, and distribution of work are abstracted away and do not affect the parallelism profile. Profiles shown thus far provide an upper bound on the parallelism. Though this bound is not achievable, it still provides insight into the application. For example, it is noteworthy that the potential parallelism varies tremendously during execution, a behavior which in our experience is typical of even the most highly parallel programs. But more importantly, we have come to believe that any large program that runs for a long time on current supercomputers has sufficient fine-grain parallelism to keep hundreds of processors utilized.

5 Parallelism Profiles on a Finite Number of Processors

Characterizing the inherent parallelism in programs is important insofar as it allows us to infer the behavior of the program on a realistic machine, *i.e.*, a machine with finite number of processors and non-zero communication latency. We are unlikely to be interested in the maximum number of processors potentially active at one time, or the length of the critical path. Even average parallelism can be a misleading indicator of performance. In this section, we focus on the question of whether a given program has *sufficient parallelism* for a p processor machine with latency l. A related question is what speedup is to be expected as more machine resources are provided.

We present two approaches to characterizing the behavior of programs on a finite number of processors. The first modifies the ideal machine, *i.e.*, the graph interpreter, to constrain the program to execute a finite number of operations in each step, and the second *estimates* potential speedup from the parallelism profile itself.

5.1 The "Finite-Processor" Execution Model

As the first step towards a realistic execution model, we impose a limit of p operations to be executed during each step. This represents p processors only in a very abstract sense. We do not assign activities to processors, but rather choose up to p enabled activities in each step. One can view it as representing a dataflow system where the mapping of activities onto processors is perfect, in that there can never be a situation where p operations are enabled, but not all p can be processed because some are on the same processor. In addition, we introduce communication latency by assuming that the output of every operator takes l steps to be delivered to its destination.

In our abstract model, we assume that the communication system is highly pipelined, and has as much bandwidth as is needed. Thus, if an operator can produce a token at every step, the communication system can deliver the result tokens to their destinations at every step after incurring an initial delay of l. Modeling I-structure operations requires care, since a `select` is a split-phase transaction; the token produced by the `select` operator is sent to the I-structure and, once the data is available, another token carrying the value is sent back to the operator waiting for the result. Thus, the result of a `select` is available at the destination operator $2l + 1$ units after the later of the `select` and the store for the particular element.

Modeling latency in this manner avoids the issues of network congestion and topology. For realistic architectures, the latency a token may experience is determined by the number of stages in the processor and storage-controller pipelines, as well as the number of stages in the communications network, which is expected to grow as the log of the number of processors. Thus, l and p are really not independent parameters. However, we think it is better to estimate l for a real machine by taking a weighted average of latencies experienced by tokens taking different paths.

In summary, the (p,l) or the *finite-processor non-zero latency* machine has the following characteristics:

1. All operations take unit time,
2. At most p operations can be performed in a step,
3. Communication takes l steps, and
4. Enabled instructions are selected through "fair" scheduling.

Ignoring latency for the moment, the finite processor restriction will not alter behavior of a program whose parallelism profile is less than p throughout. When the parallelism exceeds p, the excess enabled instructions are thrown into a pool with the newly enabled instructions, and the instructions for the next step are chosen from this pool. In general, the choice of instructions from the pool at each step affects the finite-processor parallelism profile. However, the variation is negligible, provided the scheduling policy is *fair*, defined as follows.

Let S_i and S_{i+1} be the set of operators that execute in the ith and $i+1^{th}$ steps, respectively, on the infinite-processor machine. A *fair schedule* for the finite-processor model is one in which all operators in S_i are scheduled before any operators in S_{i+1}. In the profiles shown below, the particular fair schedule used by GITA, our graph interpreter, is determined by the way the compiler numbers destination arcs. It does not, for example, favor operators on the critical path. Figure 9 shows the profile for SIMPLE generated under this model with $p = 1000$, slightly greater than the average parallelism. The length of the critical path is increased from 1,976 to 2,763.

The effect of latency in the infinite processor model is uninteresting because the profiles are unchanged, except for gaps of l steps between each of the steps in the zero-latency profile. The critical path length is simply dilated to $(1 + l) \times T_\infty$, where T_∞ is the critical path length on the ideal machine.

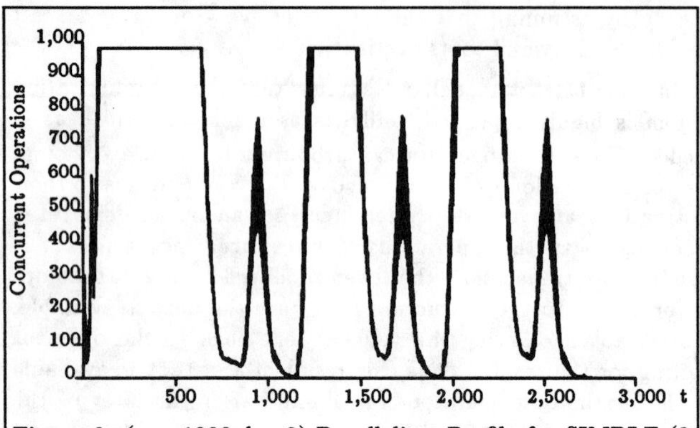

Figure 9: ($p = 1000, l = 0$) Parallelism Profile for SIMPLE (3 iterations, 20 × 20).

When there are a finite number of processors, "excess" parallelism, *i.e.*, $pp(\tau) > p$, can be used to mask delays due to latency, assuming dataflow instruction scheduling. Figure 10 shows two parallelism profiles for 3 iterations of SIMPLE on a 20×20 mesh, with at most 100 operations per step. The top profile has latency $l = 0$, while the bottom has latency $l = 10$. Note that in this example, *the length of the critical path is increased only by a factor of 2 when latency is increased from 0 to 10*. These profiles suggest that the program has enough parallelism to absorb significant latency on 100 processors, if the processors are designed to take advantage of fine-grain parallelism.

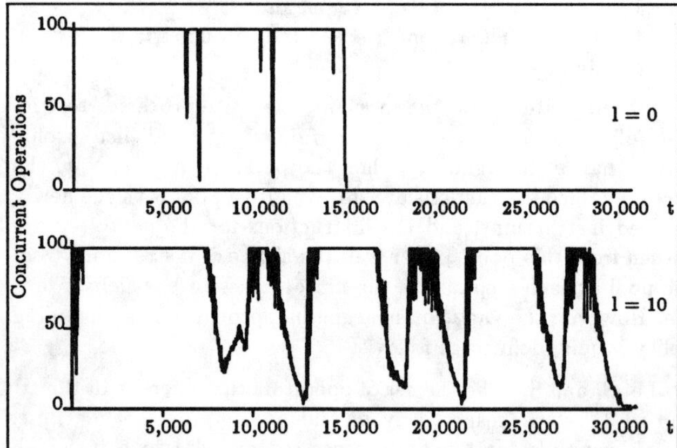

Figure 10: Effect of Latency on Parallelism Profile for Simple (100 processors, 3 iterations, 20 × 20).

5.2 Speedup and Utilization

The effective parallelism available in a program under the finite-processor model can be expressed in terms of *speedup* and *utilization*, as follows. Let $t(p, l)$ be the number of steps required to execute the program with at most p operations per step and fixed communication latency of l steps. Recall from Section 2 that T_1 is the total number of operations executed, *i.e.*, the area under the parallelism profile. Therefore, T_1 is simply $t(1, 0)$.

$$speedup(p,l) = \frac{T_1}{t(p,l)} \qquad utilization(p,l) = \frac{T_1}{p \times t(p,l)}$$

These numbers tell us the limits on improved performance imposed by data dependencies in the algorithm itself, modulo influences of instruction scheduling. For example, for 3 iterations of SIMPLE (20×20), $speedup(100, 0) = 97$, and $utilization(100, 0) = 97\%$. The utilization for this problem drops to 53% for $p = 1000$.

The points in Figure 11 show speedup measurements at various settings of p and l for OLD-SIMPLE, which is the same program as SIMPLE, but coded in a previous version of Id. (Since procedure calls were strict in the previous version, the potential parallelism in the program was significantly less. A direct comparison is difficult because the compiler for the previous version performed fewer optimizations.)

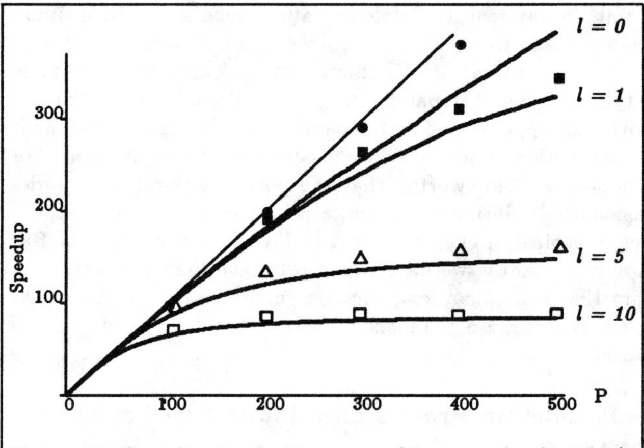

Figure 11: Speedup in the Presence of Latency for Simple (1 iteration, 32 × 32).

It is possible to derive asymptotes of the speedup curves, by observing that a machine with latency l cannot execute the program in less steps than $t(\infty, l)$, *i.e.*, $(1 + l) \times T_\infty$. Thus,

$$speedup(p,l) = \frac{T_1}{t(p,l)} \leq \frac{T_1}{(1+l) \times T_\infty} = \frac{\overline{P}}{1+l}$$

This shows the trade-off between average parallelism and latency, *i.e.*, we need more parallelism in a program to achieve the same speedup, if the latency is increased.

The curves in Figure 11 show speedup derived using the following formula, based on an estimate of how a finite processor machine would perform the operations comprising the parallelism profile.

$$t(p,l) \approx \sum_{\tau=1}^{T_\infty} \max\left(1 + l, \left\lceil \frac{pp(\tau)}{p} \right\rceil\right). \tag{1}$$

6 Parallelism and Speedup With Program Partitioning

In characterizing and analyzing the inherent parallelism in programs, we have taken the view that all operations are treated equally. In effect, this models a scenario where any operation can execute on any processor. In practice, there are numerous reasons to require that a collection of operations should execute on the same processor. Advocates of pure dataflow have suggested that this can reduce communication requirements, simplify resource management, tag manipulation, and handling of loop invariants[2]. Advocates of hybrid von Neumann/dataflow approaches suggest that collections of operators executing on a single processor should be collapsed into a sequential program serving as a kind of "macro" operator [13, 15].

Let us call a collection of operations which are constrained to execute on one processor a *task*. A task denotes the unit of work to be distributed. We allow an unbounded number of concurrent tasks, and tasks do not compete for processing resources. Within a task, instructions are *not statically ordered* by the compiler. Instead, they become enabled based on availability of data, and are scheduled fairly, as in the finite processor model. The scheduling of operations within different tasks is entirely independent, except as dictated by data dependencies. In a single step one operation is performed from each task that has any enabled operations. In this way, we isolate the effects of intra-task scheduling constraints without introducing additional effects due to the mapping of tasks onto a fixed set of processors. The parallelism available under this model can be viewed as an upper bound on that available under hybrid von Neumann/Dataflow approaches.

6.1 Parallelism Under Different Task Granularities

Program syntax suggests two natural places to partition programs: code-blocks, *i.e.*, instances of a loop or user-defined function, and, for a finer grain, iterations. Although we do not consider it here, one could imagine partitioning the program to minimize the number of arcs crossing the cut, ignoring the syntactic structure of the program.

We can characterize the inherent parallelism of the program under each task granularity through parallelism profiles generated on an unbounded-processor, *task-oriented* machine with the following characteristics:

1. All operators take unit time,
2a. At most one operation is performed per task per step,
2b. Operations from any number of distinct tasks may be performed in one step,
3. Communication is instantaneous, and
4. Fair scheduling within each task.

On such a machine, it makes sense to talk of task parallelism profiles, from which critical path, average parallelism, and peak parallelism can be computed. The following table shows the average parallelism for one iteration of OLD-SIMPLE with various mesh sizes under the three granularities.

Mode	16 × 16	32 × 32	50 × 50	64 × 64
Instruction $\overline{P}$	361	922	1584	2108
Iteration $\overline{P}$	40	110	199	270
Code-block $\overline{P}$	14	29	46	59

We see that with code-block level partitioning the average parallelism is roughly 1/35 of the unconstrained, *i.e.*, instruction level, execution, and with iteration level it is 1/8. These factors represent the loss in *potential parallelism* arising from the intra-task scheduling constraints. Within a task, the benefits of dynamic instruction scheduling are still realized, so these numbers represent the "best-case" using coarse-grain parallelism.

6.2 Speedup under different task granularities

In estimating speedup in a finite-processor, task-oriented model we place a bound on the number of operations per step, but not on the number of tasks. Since the task parallelism profiles show the number of concurrently enabled operations in each step (subject to intra-task scheduling constraints, in addition to data dependencies), speedup can be estimated from these profiles using Formula (1), taking $l = 0$. It is difficult to estimate the effect of latency from the parallelism profile, because different amounts of latency should be charged for inter-task and intra-task communication. To this end, we develop a *finite-processor task-oriented* machine model with the following characteristics:

1. All operators take unit time,
2a. At most one operation is performed per task per step,
2b. Operations from no more than p tasks may be performed in one step,
3a. Communication is instantaneous within a task,
3b. Communication requires l steps otherwise,
4a. Fair scheduling within each task, and
4b. Round-robin scheduling amongst tasks with enabled operations.

Under this finite-processor task-oriented model, we observe the speedups shown in Figure 12 on OLD-SIMPLE 32×32 for the three levels of granularity and latency of 0, 10, 20, and 40 units for non-local tokens. The instruction level versions experience this latency on every token. Code-block level versions experience it only in transfer of arguments and results, and in I-structure requests. Still, since I-structure operations constitute roughly 25% of the instruction mix[1], the latency is significant. Iteration level versions experience additional latency on values circulated across iterations. Therefore, we expect that for sufficiently high latency, the reduction in speedup due to latency may be greater than that due to intra-task scheduling constraints. Indeed, with

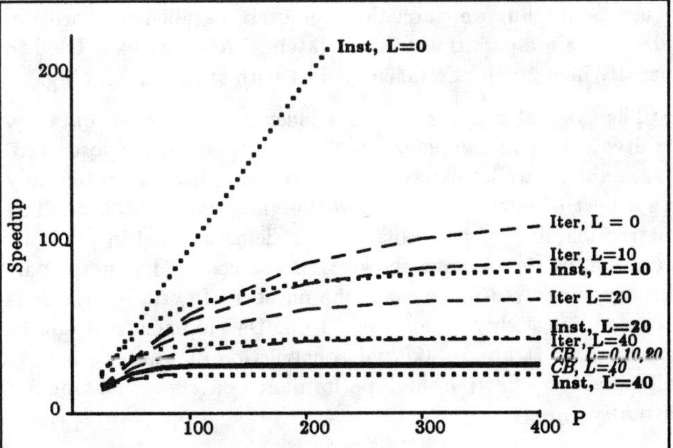

Figure 12: Speedup under various task granularities and latencies for OLD-SIMPLE 32 × 32.

$l = 10$ instruction- and iteration-level versions cross at roughly 200 processors. At $l = 40$ instruction-level falls below code-block level. However, we must note that the crossovers observed here occur at high latency relative to the number of processors and at a large number of processors given the problem size.

7 Conclusion

We have presented a method for quantifying the parallelism in real programs developed in the context of a dataflow model, but the method should be useful in providing insights into other systems as well. It allows programs to be studied in full detail, without biasing their behavior by implementation constraints. This allows us to draw a clear distinction between the parallelism inherent in a program and the speedup achieved under any specific implementation. We have presented two methods for deriving upper-bounds on potential speedup, and presented data on how speedup is affected by latency and intra-task scheduling constraints. This work brings us closer to answering questions of the form, "Does this program have sufficient parallelism for a machine of p processors?", considering the characteristics of the program and the characteristics of the machine. Studies using the techniques presented here have substantiated our belief that large dataflow programs, even employing traditional algorithms, have "sufficient" fine-grain parallelism for machines of reasonable size. We have examined the speedup on a detailed simulation of the MIT Tagged-Token Dataflow Architecture. However, these experiments have necessarily been limited, due to the enormous space required for even small problem sizes. We run out of space on a stand-alone IBM 4381 on a 10×10 run of OLD-SIMPLE! To gain further insight, it is essential to conduct experiments on real dataflow machines, such as Sigma-1 [14] and Monsoon [20], which is now under construction at MIT.

Elsewhere [4] we have argued that efficient synchronization and dynamic instruction scheduling are fundamental to general-purpose parallel architectures. Efficient synchronization is clearly essential to exploit producer-consumer parallelism. Here, we have shown the benefits of such an approach— by exploiting all forms of parallelism, ample parallelism is made available in most programs. Further, we have shown that a portion of this parallelism can be "invested" in masking communication latency, again relying on efficient low-level synchronization. Coarse-grain partitioning of programs may be advantageous to reduce communication requirements, but we claim that fine-grain parallelism is still required within a partition to mask latency. Also, we have tried to quantify how much parallelism is lost with such partitioning.

The goal of our research has been to show that dataflow architectures and languages can lead to general-purpose, programmable, parallel computers. This paper has presented only one aspect of our efforts to show the viability of dataflow. The programmability of these machines is demonstrated in [3]. Furthermore, in [1] we have shown that the cost of fine-grain parallelism, measured in terms of the number of extra instructions executed, is roughly a factor of 2 to 3. Development of resource management strategies [9] and construction of what we believe will be a cost-effective, high-performance dataflow machine are currently underway [20].

Acknowledgements: We are greatly indebted to Rishiyur S. Nikhil, whose thoughtful comments and advice, not to mention LaTeXpertise, were invaluable in producing this paper. Thanks also to Bhaskar Guharoy and Stephen Brobst for comments on earlier drafts, and to the members of the Computation Structures Group at the Laboratory for Computer Science.

References

[1] Arvind, D. E. Culler, and K. Ekanadham. The Price of Asynchronous Parallelism: An Analysis of Dataflow Architectures. Technical Report Computation Structures Group Memo 278, MIT Laboratory for Computer Science, 545 Technology Square, Cambridge, MA, Dec. 1987. (To appear in the *Proceedings of CONPAR 88*, Manchester, U.K., Sept., 1988).

[2] Arvind, D. E. Culler, R. A. Iannucci, V. Kathail, K. Pingali, and R. E. Thomas. The Tagged Token Dataflow Architecture. Technical Report FLA, MIT Laboratory for Computer Science, 545 Technology Square, Cambridge, MA, August 1983. Revised October, 1984.

[3] Arvind and K. Ekanadham. Future Scientific Programming on Parallel Machines. In *Proceedings of the International Conference on Supercomputing (ICS), Athens, Greece*, June 8-12 1987. (To appear in the *Journal of Parallel and Distributed Computing*).

[4] Arvind and R. A. Iannucci. Two Fundamental Issues in Multiprocessing. In *Proceedings of DFVLR - Conference 1987 on Parallel Processing in Science and Engineering, Bonn-Bad Godesberg, W. Germany*, June 25-29 1987.

[5] Arvind and R. S. Nikhil. Executing a Program on the MIT Tagged-Token Dataflow Architecture. In *Proceedings of the PARLE Conference, Eindhoven, The Netherlands. (LNCS Volume 259).* Springer-Verlag, June 15-19 1987.

[6] Arvind, R. S. Nikhil, and K. K. Pingali. I-Structures: Data Structures for Parallel Computing. Technical Report Computation Structures Group Memo 269, MIT Laboratory for Computer Science, 545 Technology Square, Cambridge, MA, February 1987. (Also appears in the *Proceedings of the Graph Reduction Workshop*, Santa Fe, NM. October 1986.).

[7] A. E. Charlesworth. An Approach to Scientific Array Processing: The Architectural Design of the AP-120B/FPS-164 Family. *IEEE Computer*, 14(9):18–27, Sept. 1981.

[8] W. P. Crowley, C. P. Hendrickson, and T. E. Rudy. The SIMPLE Code. Technical Report UCID 17715, Lawrence Livermore Laboratory, February 1978.

[9] D. E. Culler. *Effective Dataflow Execution of Scientific Programs.* PhD thesis, Dept. of Electrical Engineering and Computer Science, Massachusetts Institute of Technology, Cambridge, MA, Sept. 1988 (expected).

[10] D. E. Culler and Arvind. Resource Requirements of Dataflow Programs. In *Proceedings of the Fifteenth Annual International Symposium on Computer Architecture, Honolulu, Hawaii*, May 30 – June 2 1988.

[11] J. B. Dennis. First Version of a Data Flow Procedure Language. In G. Goos and J. Hartmanis, editors, *Proc. Programming Symposium, Paris 1974 (Lecture Notes in Computer Science 19)*, New York, 1974. Springer-Verlag. (Revised: MAC TM61, May 1975, MIT Laboratory for Computer Science, 545 Technology Square, Cambridge, MA).

[12] J. A. Fisher. Very Long Instruction Word Architectures and the ELI-512. Technical Report YALEU/DCS/RR-253, Yale University, Department of Computer Science, Apr. 1983.

[13] J. L. Gaudiot and M. D. Ercegovac. Performance Evaluation of a Simulated Dataflow Computer with Low Resolution Actors. In *Journal of Parallel and Distributed Computing*. Academic Press, Dec. 1987.

[14] K. Hiraki, S. Sekiguchi, and T. Shimada. System architecture of a dataflow supercomputer. Technical report, Computer Systems Division, Electrotechnical Laboratory, 1-1-4 Umezono, Sakura-mura, Niihari-gun, Ibaraki, 305, Japan, 1987.

[15] R. A. Iannucci. *A Dataflow/von Neumann Hybrid Architecture*. PhD thesis, Dept. of Electrical Engineering and Computer Science, Massachusetts Institute of Technology, Cambridge, MA, May 1988.

[16] H. F. Jordan. Performance Measurement on HEP - A Pipelined MIMD Computer. In *Proceedings of the 10th Annual International Symposium on Computer Architecture, Stockholm, Sweden*. North-Holland Publishing Company, June 1983.

[17] L. Lamport. The Parallel Execution of DO Loops. *Communications of the Association for Computing Machinery*, 17(2):83–93, Feb. 1974.

[18] R. S. Nikhil. Id World Reference Manual. Technical report, MIT Laboratory for Computer Science, 545 Technology Square, Cambridge, MA, April 1987.

[19] R. S. Nikhil. ID (Version 88.0) Reference Manual. Technical Report CSG Memo 284, MIT Laboratory for Computer Science, 545 Technology Square, Cambridge, MA, Mar. 1988.

[20] G. M. Papadopoulos. *Implementation of a General Purpose Dataflow Multiprocessor*. PhD thesis, Dept. of Electrical Engineering and Computer Science, Massachusetts Institute of Technology, Cambridge, MA, July 1988 (expected).

[21] R. M. Russell. The CRAY-1 Computer System. *Communications of the Association for Computing Machinery*, 21(1):63–72, January 1978.

[22] V. Sarkar and J. Hennessy. Partitioning Parallel Programs for Macro-Dataflow. In *Proceedings of the 1986 ACM Conference on Lisp and Functional Programming, Cambridge, MA*, pages 202–211, August 4-6 1986.

[23] K. R. Traub. A Compiler for the MIT Tagged-Token Dataflow Architecture. Technical Report LCS TR-370, MIT Laboratory for Computer Science, 545 Technology Square, Cambridge, MA, August 1986.

Tokenless Static Data Flow Using Associative Templates

Thomas L. Sterling
Harris Corporation

D. Scott Wills
MIT Laboratory for Computer Science

Ellery Y. Chan
Harris Corporation

Government Systems Sector
Harris Corporation

Abstract

The static data flow model of computation promises high performance from fine grained parallelism, but conventional token-driven static data flow architectures are inefficient in terms of memory bandwidth and microcycles required per operation. The associative template mechanism, a new application of associative techniques, employs specially configured content-addressable memories to provide efficient flow control for static data flow program execution. It supports static data flow semantics while exhibiting memory bandwidth and microcycle demands comparable to those of conventional uniprocessors. Associative diffusion, a second application of associative methods, provides communication between adjacent nodes of a mesh-connected network of associative-template-based processors. This mechanism achieves nearest-neighbor communication at speeds comparable to intra-node transactions by overlapping domains of associativity across boundaries between neighboring nodes. Together, associative templates and associative diffusion provide a token-free approach to static data flow computation.

1. Introduction

The static data flow computing model [1, 2, 3] has historically been bound to the token-driven mechanism [4, 5, 6]. Most static data flow architectures rely on result tokens and acknowledge tokens to transfer data values to recipient actors, and to manage the scheduling of actor activation. So convenient is the token mechanism for visualizing data flow concepts that the distinction between the semantics of the model and this particular method of implementation is often obscured or lost altogether in presentation.

Despite its appeal, however, token-based static data flow has several shortcomings. The overhead of performing a single operation with tokens is substantially greater than the total time required to perform the same operation on a conventional uniprocessor of equivalent technology: the memory bandwidth required for token-driven data flow computation can be an order of magnitude greater, and additional token queueing hardware may be necessary. These weaknesses severely detract from the potential efficiency of the static data flow model, making it less attractive as a method of parallel computation.

Yet, the deficiencies of the token-based mechanism need not eliminate the static data flow model as a viable strategy for parallel computing. Only the token approach itself is flawed. An alternate mechanism that fully supports the semantics of static data flow without the burdensome costs and limitations of using tokens can provide an effective static data flow computer architecture. This paper describes one such mechanism and demonstrates that it satisfies the semantic policies of the static data flow model.

Associative memories [7] are presently used for parallel searching of caches [8, 9] and translation lookaside buffers [10], for general sorting and searching in data base applications, and for performing simple logical operations on many data elements simultaneously. The *associative template* architecture, which is described in [11], applies associative processing to the control of static data flow program execution. The reduced operation overhead and memory bandwidth requirements of this new architecture provide increased execution speed and efficient resource utilization. As an added benefit of this approach, nearest neighbor interactions can be performed with no time penalty.

It can be demonstrated that the new architecture adheres to static data flow semantics. The token-based architecture, with its higher communication costs and increased memory bandwidth required for queueing tokens, less effectively supports the same model. Technical considerations of associative template implementation still present a challenge, however, and uninvestigated concerns may yet limit the effectiveness of the associative template architecture.

This paper gives a brief overview of static data flow semantics, then describes the typical token-based approach to static data flow computing. Following that, a simple single node associative-template-based architecture is presented and its operation is described and shown to support the requirements of static data flow. Finally, the issues of communication within a multiple node system and the feasibility of system implementation are each examined briefly.

2. The Static Data Flow Computing Model

Some terminology must be defined for the following discussion of static data flow semantics. An *actor* is the conceptual entity represented by an operation symbol, which appears at each junction in a data flow graph. The actor performs an operation on its input *arguments* and produces a *result*. The result becomes an input argument for *recipient* actors, and the actor that produced the result is its *source*.

CH2617-9/88/0000/0070$01.00

An actor is represented in a data flow machine by a template. An actor specifies, either explicitly or implicitly by context:

- ❑ an operation to be performed,
- ❑ the source actors for its input arguments,
- ❑ the recipient actors for its output results, and
- ❑ its intermediate state during execution.

An actor performs its operation, or fires, when a set of criteria are satisfied. These are:

- ❑ its source actors have fired and its argument values are available,
- ❑ its recipient actors have fired and are prepared to accept new result values, and
- ❑ enabling hardware resources are available and have been allocated to the actor.

An actor may fire more than once during the course of program execution, but each criterion must be satisfied anew before the actor can fire again.

The data flow paradigm is value oriented, or functional, with respect to program data: there are no global side-effects. Values are accepted from source actors and made available to destination actors. Internal state is inaccessible to all other parts of the program. All operation types are history insensitive: a specified actor with a given set of argument values will always produce the same result value, regardless of its past behavior.

Synchronization of actors is data driven, which permits eager evaluation. Assuming available destinations and resources, an actor may be executed as soon as its argument values arrive. Demand driven (lazy evaluation), in contrast, would also require that its results be needed by one or more other operations. Two other models, parallel control flow and communicating sequential processes, employ explicit commands for the creation and synchronization of parallel tasks. Data flow parallelism is completely defined by data precedence constraints.

Conditional flow control in the data flow model is provided by special purpose actors. The switch actor makes its first argument value available to one of two sets of destination actors depending on the Boolean value of its second argument. The select actor makes one of its first two argument values available to its destination actors depending on the Boolean value of its third argument. Other conditional actors are also possible, but these two can support all required conditional flow control relationships.

The firing constraint that requires all destination actors to be ready to receive new argument values distinguishes the static data flow model from the more general dynamic data flow model. A static data flow actor can have at most one active instance of an operation, and one set of pending argument values. While limiting in some ways, the constraints of the static data flow model make it more conducive to effective implementation.

3. The Token Mechanism

A brief examination of the token-driven static data flow architecture will reveal the sources and degree of the inefficiencies of the token-based approach. *A token* is a typed message that carries computation values and synchronization information between templates. All template activity is in response to incident tokens.

A static data flow actor is represented by a data structure called a *template.* A template contains all the information about the actor, which includes compile time information defining the function of the actor and its relationship to other actors in the data flow program, and runtime information indicating the current state of the actor's execution cycle. An example of a typical template is shown in Figure 1. This discussion focuses on actors supporting dyadic operations, and a result fanout of two is considered sufficient.

The *template status word* contains information about the actor's current execution state. Specifically, it indicates whether each of the argument value tokens have arrived, whether the acknowledge tokens have arrived, and the value of the Boolean argument for conditional actors. The template status word also contains compile time information defining the operation to be performed, the number of acknowledge tokens to be received, and whether each input argument is an immediate constant or a value computed by another actor.

The *A* and *B argument value* entries of the template temporarily hold copies of the actor's operand values provided by incoming tokens for the time when the actor fires and the operation is performed. Each of the two *acknowledge token address* fields holds the address of an actor that produces one of the input arguments. Upon completion of this actor's execution, the acknowledge tokens are sent, indicating that the argument values are no longer needed. Each of the two *result token address* entries indicates an actor that receives the result value produced by this actor.

The inefficiency of the token-based mechanism results from the complexity and number of token operations that must occur for an actor to be performed. For a typical actor,

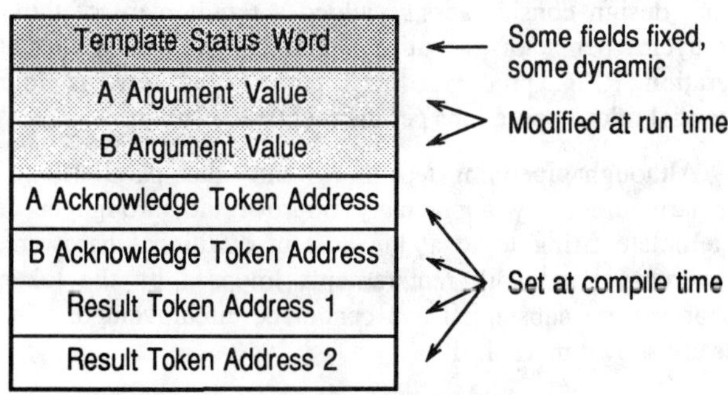

Figure 1. A typical static data flow template

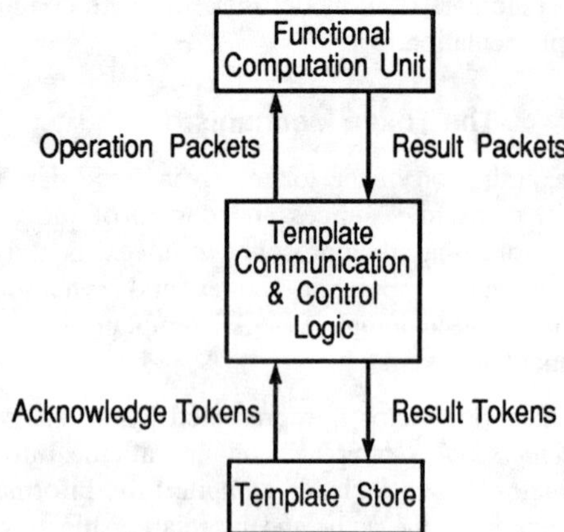

Figure 2. A simple static data flow implementation

two result value tokens must be received prior to execution. Further, if the actor has sent any result tokens, acknowledgment that the result has been consumed must be received. Once activated, the actor produces an operation data set or packet, which is sent to the functional computation unit. The result value is calculated and returned by the functional computation unit to the actor. After execution, the typical actor produces two result value tokens and two acknowledge tokens.

A generic static data flow architecture is shown in Figure 2. Operation and result packets are communicated, via some medium, between the template store and the functional computation unit. The *template communication and control logic* modifies the state of the actors in the template store, using result and acknowledge tokens to track the execution of the data flow graph.

Because the template store is connected to the rest of the data flow computer by its single communication interface, token transfers are serialized, each consuming at least a single microcycle. Additionally, the template status word is updated as each token is received, and examined to determine when the necessary conditions for firing have been satisfied. Each update is a read-modify-write operation costing at least two microcycles per token. Thus, a minimum of sixteen micro-operations must be performed serially for each actor activation. (In one implementation [12], practical engineering design considerations yielded a requirement of thirty microcycles per actor execution.) For comparison, a current generation RISC processor may perform as few as four sequential micro-operations per instruction execution.

Although pipelining techniques and other parallel hardware structures may appreciably improve the throughput of the template firing logic at the cost of additional hardware, the memory bandwidth requirements imposed by the token mechanism are substantial and cannot be circumvented. The costs are shown in Table 1.

Sixteen memory word accesses are performed during one actor firing. Since the template status word is updated for each incoming token, acknowledge tokens cost two memory cycles, and argument tokens cost four. After the actor fires, it takes two more memory cycles to send the acknowledges, two more to send the result values, and one to reset the template status word. Here, too, the token data flow architecture compares unfavorably to the current generation RISC microprocessor, which may perform only one or two memory accesses per instruction execution.

From this casual analysis it is apparent that the token-based mechanism for static data flow is considerably more expensive than the conventional alternative. It requires roughly five times the work and ten times the memory bandwidth as the uniprocessor per instruction execution, which does not include the extra work and extra bandwidth required to manage the token queueing buffer unique to token-based data flow architectures.

4. The Associative Template Mechanism

The *associative template* mechanism is an alternative to the token mechanism for efficient support of the semantics of static data flow. It applies associative processing to execution flow control of static data flow programs. An explanation of the basic associative template mechanism illustrates how it satisfies the semantics of the static data flow computing model.

4.1 Advantages of the Associative Template Method

Static data flow architectures incorporating the associative template mechanism avoid much of the burdensome overhead in time and space imposed by the token mechanism. Advantages of the associative template approach are:

- **Reduced memory bandwidth**
  Result values are not duplicated in multiple tokens and are written only once to memory.
- **Higher throughput**
  The associative template mechanism performs a more powerful primitive operation, doing in one cycle the work that would take the token mechanism several cycles to achieve.

Table 1. The execution cost of a token-based template

	Number of Tokens	Memory Cycles	Minimum Serial Microcycles
Acknowledge tokens in	2	4	2
Data tokens in	2	6	2
Operation	–	2	2
Acknowledge tokens out	2	2	2
Data tokens out	2	2	2
Total	8	16	10

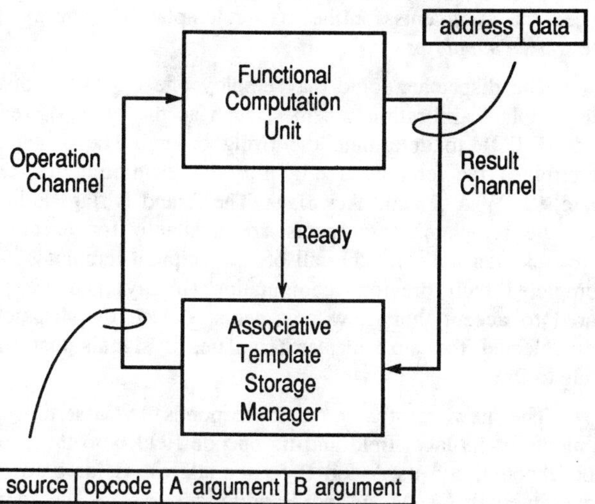

Figure 3. An associative-template-based static data flow architecture

- ❑ **Free acknowledgments**
  Acknowledgments can be delivered in parallel with each other and with other operations.
- ❑ **Smaller memory**
  Copies of result values and storage for token destination addresses are eliminated.
- ❑ **Queue elimination**
  All data accesses are demand driven, preventing the accumulation of communication packets before they can be used.

4.2 A Simple Single Node System

A simple data flow architecture, shown in Figure 3, is used to demonstrate how the associative template mechanism supports the semantics of the static data flow model. The *functional computation unit* (FCU) acquires operation packets via its *operation channel,* performs the specified operation and returns the result value via the *result channel.* The operation packet includes the values of the two arguments, a code indicating the operation, and the identifier of the template that created the request. The result channel returns the data value produced by the operation, and the address of the template that initiated it.

Template Label
Template Status Word
A Source Address
B Source Address
Result Value

Figure 4. An associative template.

The *associative template storage manager* (ATSM) is a smart memory that holds all the templates of the data flow program and updates the state of each template in response to the result values provided by the FCU. The purpose of the ATSM is to provide operation packets to the FCU via the operation channel at a rate that will keep the FCU fully utilized. The *Ready* signal from the FCU solicits operation packets from the ATSM at the rate the FCU can consume them.

The structure of an associative template differs from that of a token-based template. A simplified version of an ATSM template is shown in Figure 4. A *template label* entry uniquely identifies each template in the data flow program. The *template status word* entry serves the same purpose as the corresponding token-based template entry, although the internal fields are slightly different. The *A* and *B source address* entries replace the A and B argument values. Rather than retain a copy of the actual argument value when it is produced, each source address entry contains the identifier of the template that is responsible for computing that argument value. When the argument is an immediate constant, the value is directly stored in the source address entry. The *result value* entry is used to hold the value computed by the FCU when this template is fired.

Unlike the conventional memory in which token-based templates are stored, associative template memory incorporates some simple logic for each template. Much of this additional logic is dedicated to bit-level compare operations to determine whether the contents of one of several busses matches the value of the template label or either of the source address fields. Other logic detects the occurrence of specific states within the template, such as its readiness to fire.

The associative template storage manager comprises the elements shown in Figure 5. The *template store* holds the program templates and updates their state, based on the operation and result packets being exchanged with the FCU. The *dispatcher,* upon demand from the FCU, selects one template from among those ready to fire and directs that template to generate the next operation packet.

Together these elements provide the necessary mechanisms to support the semantic requirements of the static data flow computing model. Specifically, they:

- ❑ Define the computation to be performed,
- ❑ Determine when input argument values are available
- ❑ Determine when recipient actors are ready to receive new arguments,
- ❑ Generate operation packets for the FCU to process,
- ❑ Detect when templates are ready to be executed, and
- ❑ Select templates for execution.

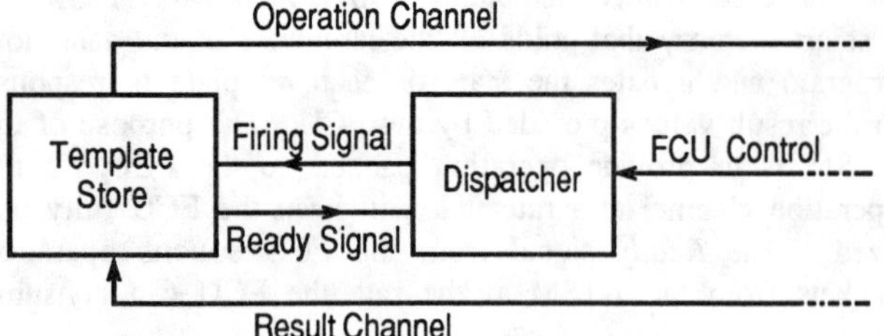

Figure 5. The associative template storage manager (ATSM).

The following subsections describe how associative techniques perform these functions while providing the performance advantages alluded to earlier.

4.3 Data Driven Synchronization

The result channel carries packets, each containing a computed value and a source template address, from the FCU to the associative template store. All templates monitor the address field of each packet. When a result packet address matches a template's label, A source address, or B source address, the template modifies its state accordingly. The match is performed by simple bitwise compare logic associated with the template's label and source address entries. This configuration is depicted in Figure 6.

A template modifies its state when the operation producing the result was initiated by it, or when the result is an argument it needs. The first of these conditions occurs when the result packet address field matches the template label. Since each template has a unique label, only one template will respond by copying the result packet value field into the template's result value. The second condition occurs when the result packet address matches one of a template's source address fields, which causes the corresponding TSW flag (A flag or B flag) to be set, indicating that that argument is available. Both arguments may come from the same template, in which case both flags will be set during the same TSW update cycle.

During a single result channel cycle, all templates that use the result value as an argument will act simultaneously. When the fanout is greater than one, multiple templates update themselves simultaneously, saving both bandwidth and time in delivering the result value to recipient templates.

4.4 Creating Operation Packets

When an associative template fires, it sends a packet via the operation channel to the FCU. The packet fully specifies the operation to perform, the argument values to be used, and the destination address of the result (the firing template's label), as shown in Figure 3.

The firing is initiated by the FCU when it becomes ready to accept more work. Multiple templates may be ready to fire; the *dispatcher logic* determines which one of the eligible templates will fire next and begins the firing sequence, which is illustrated in Figure 7. The template being fired is referred to as the *master template*. The templates that produced the arguments for the master template's operation are the *source templates*.

The dispatcher logic may employ one of several possible template arbitration schemes, such as the order of readiness (FIFO), to determine the firing order. The dispatcher determines the template's eligibility by examining the template's TSW A, B, and Ack flags. The A and B flags indicate that the template's arguments are available for execution. The Ack flag indicates that all of the recipient templates have completed their previous computation (if any) and are prepared to accept their new arguments. Once the dispatcher has selected the next master template, it signals that template to fire.

The new master template responds by asserting the contents of its label field and its opcode field onto the operation channel, and its A and B source address fields onto separate internal ATSM A and B address busses. The master template does not store its own operand values: its A and B source address entries specify the identities of the templates holding the required values. Compare logic associated with the label entry of each template watches both address busses to determine whether the contents of either bus matches its own label. Because the template labels are unique, each address bus will find only one matching source template. Upon detecting its address, each source template will assert the contents of its result value field onto the operation channel, thus completing the operation packet for the FCU.

The master template modifies its own internal state after having been fired. The A, B, and Ack flags of its TSW are cleared, indicating that it is prepared to start a new execution cycle. At this point, it ceases being the master template and resumes its normal behavior of watching the various busses for matching addresses.

4.5 Acknowledging

The value held in the result field of a template is used by one or more recipients as an argument. The template must retain that result value until all its recipients have fired, since it must produce the value each time a recipient executes. A token-based static data flow template relies on acknowledge tokens sent to it from the current master template to indicate that an operation no longer needs its result value as an argument.

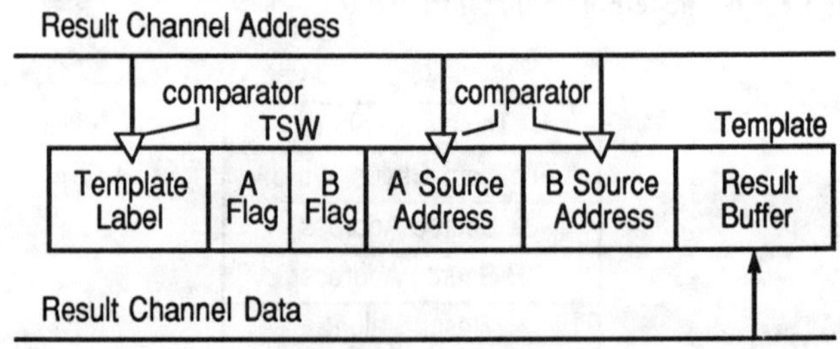

Figure 6. Associative template monitoring the result channel

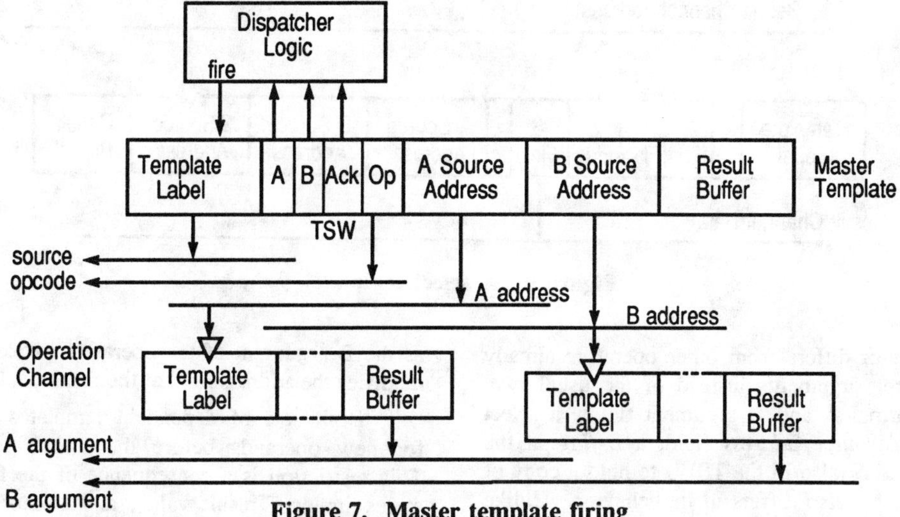

Figure 7. Master template firing

An associative template handles acknowledgment in a different manner. Whenever an argument source template detects its label on the A or B address bus and emits its result value for the operation packet being assembled, it also updates the Ack flag in its TSW based on the Boolean value of the *A* and *B acknowledge* signals, as shown in Figure 8. Each acknowledge signal is an open collector line, which can be driven true by any one of multiple outputs (only the A acknowledge is shown in the figure). Any other recipient of this argument value waiting to fire matches the source address. Since its corresponding argument flag (A flag or B flag) is also set, it asserts the (A or B) acknowledge signal, indicating that the source template's result value is still needed. Potentially, many acknowledging templates are simultaneously asserting their signals onto the acknowledge lines. Only when the last of the recipient templates is firing will the acknowledge lines be inactive.

Since the acknowledge signals are generated during the same interval that the argument values are being produced by the source templates, no time penalty is incurred: acknowledgment is essentially free. In practice, however, electrical loading on the open collector signal lines may slow the overall operation channel cycle.

4.6 Conditional Operators

Conditional operators require some slightly different behavior from the associative template mechanism. There are many possible choices of sets of conditional operators that fulfill the semantic requirements of data flow computation: one acceptable set is the *switch* and *select* (or *merge)* operators. These operators have the same semantics as the conditional operators described in Section 2 for token-based static data flow. The architectural problems that arise from the need for conditional flow control are solvable. Minor extensions to the associative template mechanism already described successfully support the switch and select operators.

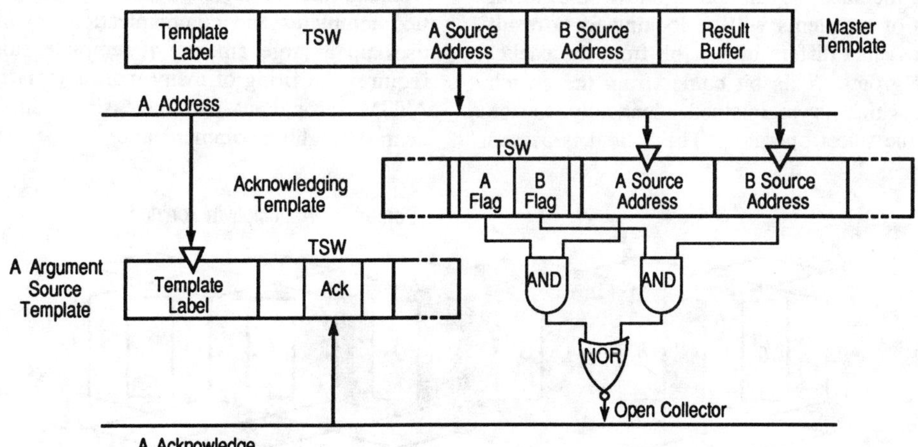

Figure 8. An A argument being acknowledged

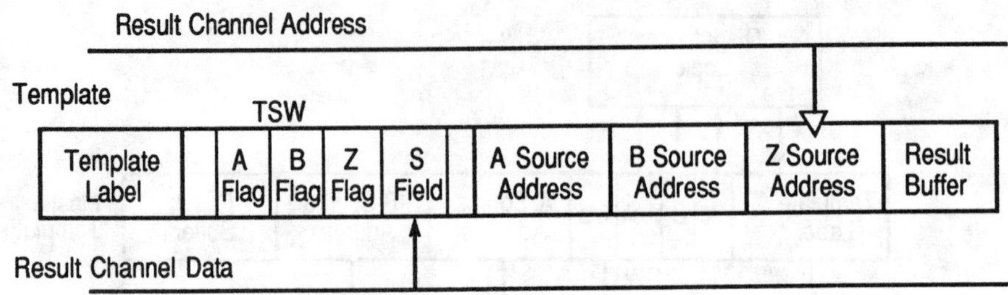

Figure 9. A select template

The select operator differs from other operators already presented: it has three arguments instead of the usual two. In addition to the normal A and B argument fields, a select template requires a Z *source address* field, a Z *flag* in the TSW, and a field called *S* (also in the TSW) to hold a copy of the Z argument value. It also differs in its behavior. Unlike the other operations, the select operator does not require all its input arguments to be available before firing. Only the Boolean argument (called the *Z argument*) and the argument selected by its Boolean value must be present.

The dispatching logic normally determines the next template to fire without knowing the value of any of the template's arguments, merely their availability. An exception is made for the Z argument. The value of the Z argument is copied by the select template into the S field of the TSW (it is always Boolean, so only a single bit is needed for storage), and is used by the dispatcher to determine firing eligibility. This is shown in Figure 9. When the template fires and its TSW is reinitialized for its next invocation, only the flag of the selected argument (A or B) is reset; the other argument is left pending. Acknowledgments are handled exactly as described earlier.

The switch template imposes a different problem on the associative template mechanism. Its result value will be used by one of two groups of potential recipients. Since each recipient individually detects the result as it returns on the result channel from the FCU, the Boolean value of the second switch argument is included as an extra bit of the result address. One group of recipients will be looking for a result packet with an address that differs by one bit from the packet needed by the other group. This bit comes from the switch template's S field, which is maintained identically to the Boolean S value of the select operator. The S field is passed as the B argument of the operation packet to the FCU, which modifies the address field of the result packet accordingly.

Both sets of dependent templates must become ready for new operands before the switch template again fires. This restriction is a consequence of the fact that the template stores its own result value, and cannot preserve one value while computing another. If it is necessary to be able to permit one path of the switch to be used while the other path retains a result value for its dependent templates, buffer templates can be employed between the outputs of the switch template and its two sets of dependent templates. A feature of the associative template's acknowledge mechanism is that the two sets of dependent templates may comprise different numbers of templates without the need of some special logic such as dual acknowledge counters or separate acknowledge acquisition flag fields.

5. Communication between Multiple ATSMs

The substantial performance gains achievable from data flow can only be fully realized through the use of multiple FCUs and ATSMs operating in parallel, cooperating to execute a single application program. A method of communication between associative templates in separate ATSMs is necessary to support this level of distributed processing.

Tokens could be used to transfer values between ATSMs that use associative mechanisms internally, but this is unsatisfactory for the reasons discussed in Section 3. Demand driven message passing using special communication templates and communication channels is practical, but uses up a large amount of template storage space. It also requires the firing of many more templates, reducing effective ATSM throughput and increasing transfer latency for even nearest neighbor communications.

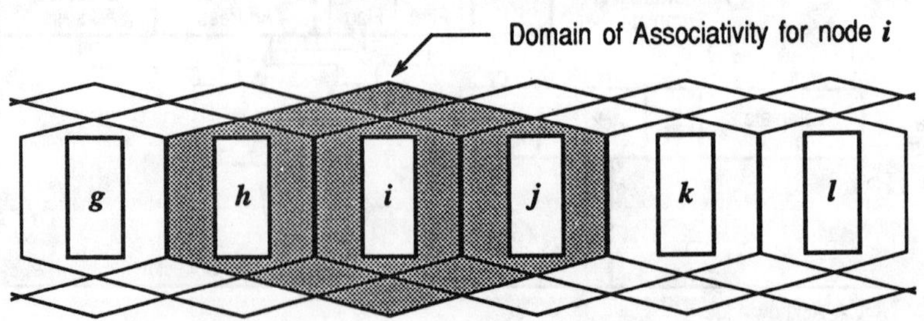

Figure 10. Ring interconnection showing domains of associativity.

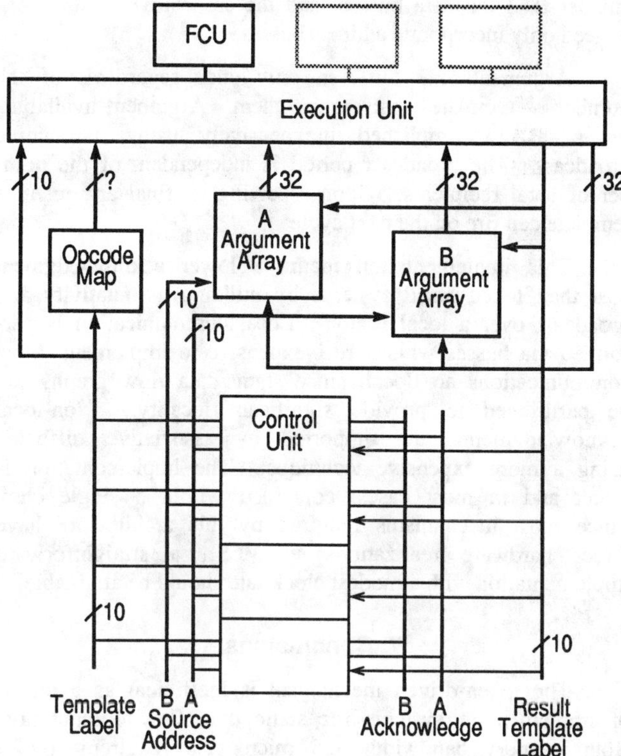

Figure 11. A more practical associative-template-based architecture

An alternate approach proposed here, called *associative diffusion,* overlaps the associative domains of neighboring ATSMs. This allows nearest neighbors access to template result values internally and directly from each other.

A restricted class of system topologies is considered here: topologies requiring nearest neighbor point-to-point connections to only a few nodes; namely, those with a degree of two or three, forming ring and quasi-toroidal structures, respectively. Here, a *node* refers to an ATSM coupled with an FCU and communication channels to its neighbors. These organizations place reasonable limits on the amount of interface logic required per ATSM.

There are two reasons why it is expected that such interconnection schemes are adequate for implementing useful data flow computers. First, many important applications may be mapped onto these topologies so that almost all communication is between nearest neighbors. Systolic algorithms [13] have this property. Second, the data flow computing model is particularly tolerant of extended message latency times. Messages that must travel across several nodes will not degrade system performance from processor waiting as long as the communication network capacity is sufficient to handle the total system traffic load. Nonetheless, this class of systems does impose some constraints on the general utility of application. The method is described for the ring topology. It may be extended to nodes of higher degree, but at correspondingly greater cost.

Associative diffusion allows communication between adjacent nodes of an associative template data flow computer without slowing internal ATSM communications. Thus, for applications distributed so all communications are between nearest neighbors, inter-template communication requires no extra time. For such applications, a sequence of operations in the directed flow graph tends to drift from one ATSM to the next using this associative mechanism; hence the name, *associative diffusion.*

The domain of associativity for a node comprising an ATSM and an FCU extends to the templates of its neighboring nodes: an ATSM watches the operation of templates in adjacent nodes as well as its own. A segment of a ring interconnected system is shown in Figure 10. In the diagram, each node is a box representing the collection of templates and its two channels. The domain of associativity for node ***i*** includes ***i***'s own templates, and those of ***h*** and ***j***. Only templates residing in ***i*** will be fired by ***i***'s dispatching logic and provide work to ***i***'s FCU. Also, results from ***i***'s FCU will only be stored by templates within ***i***.

Templates in ***h*** and ***j***, however, directly monitor ***i***'s result address as they do their own (and ***i*** similarly monitors the result addresses from ***h*** and ***j***), and can determine the availability of arguments produced by neighboring FCUs. The result value portion of ***i***'s result channel is available only to templates in ***i***, the one important exception being the Boolean value used by conditional operators, which is made available throughout the domain, since the templates that use the Boolean value must copy it into the TSW S field.

When a template becomes master and asserts the source addresses of its argument templates, extensions of the operation channel to both of the neighboring nodes permit templates of the entire domain to monitor the address busses. This makes possible the acquisition of arguments for its FCU from anywhere within the domain. Acknowledgments are handled similarly.

When data transfers of greater distance than one hop are required, the associative diffusion method must rely on intermediate value buffer templates, with all the costs of latency, performance, and memory this implies. Thus, this approach is best suited to those programs with the coupling properties described above. Even for these topologies, the hardware cost may be significant. The amount of comparator logic per node is triple that of the simple system discussed in Section 4. Another problem is the pin count implied by the channel extensions. If a direct translation from these concepts to VLSI implementation were attempted, the real estate and pin count would be prohibitive.

6. Implementation Issues

The principal design goal of the associative template model is to facilitate the implementation of a practical, high performance static data flow machine. It has been shown here that the associative template organization satisfies the semantics of static data flow. This section considers the technological feasibility of an innovative associative-template-based architecture (shown in Figure 11) which is more practical than the idealized one described in Section 4.

6.1 A Partitioned Implementation

Data and control have been separated in this architecture. Identical copies of result values are stored in two memory arrays for enhanced memory bandwidth, one for *A arguments* and one for *B arguments*. Each array is indexed by the template label. This eliminates the unnecessary use of associativity for accessing argument values in the earlier architecture. On each cycle, each array presents a selected argument to the FCU and receives a new result value back from it.

Argument synchronization and acknowledgment synchronization are provided by the *control unit*, which contains the associative matching logic for each template. This requires a custom VLSI implementation. However, each cell for storing template control information contains (in the case of dyadic operations) six ten-bit comparators (assuming ten-bit addresses), two ten bit registers, three bits of availability storage, and some combinational logic. Busses onto the control units account for 40 pins.

When a template has both argument bits set and its current value is no longer required, it awaits the template firing arbitration mechanism. This can be implemented as modified Manchester carry chain [14]. This circuit is anticipated to be the critical path of the architecture until a more clever scheme is devised. Each template propagates the activation signal when it is unable to fire and kills the activation when it fires. On the following cycle, the firing template generates the new activation signal for the chain.

The *operation map* translates template labels to operation codes for the execution unit. This reduces the storage and pin requirements on the control unit. The operation map can be implemented as a standard memory device.

The execution unit receives an operation packet on every cycle (unless no templates can fire). The packet can be sent to a pipelined FCU, an array of parallel FCUs, or an array of special purpose functional units (by dispatching on the operation). Sufficient buffering and control is required so that results are returned one at a time to the system. An uncomplicated implementation might include a standard floating point chip, an integer arithmetic unit, and a simple controller.

6.2 Analysis

Two factors about the system structure permit a decomposition into separately identifiable sub-units. One is that the data storage can be separated from the control logic. This greatly reduces the pin count for a given chip. The other is that the number of address bits required is relatively small, in the range of 10 to 14, and is insensitive to the number of nodes in the system. This fixed address size is a consequence of the fact that addresses are not global but only need to select among those templates in the node's domain of associativity. Therefore, the address busses are much smaller than the data busses, and the associative control logic need only incorporate address busses.

Arguments are buffered only once regardless of the number of templates that require them. Argument availability is also accomplished inexpensively using associative broadcast. The broadcast period is independent of the number of local recipients. Upon receiving its final argument, a template can fire on the next cycle.

This implementation incurs a lower acknowledgment cost than token-based systems by utilizing associativity and broadcast over a local region. Local communication is performed via busses which are inexpensive to implement. Most communications are local, since static data flow graphs can be partitioned to provide significant locality. Non-local acknowledgments are supported by associative diffusion using a more expensive technique. The implementation is direct and in most cases, contained within a single chip. Since most mechanisms required by this architecture have direct hardware realizations in VLSI, a straightforward implementation with a modest clock rate should be attainable.

7. Conclusions

The token-driven mechanism is inefficient as a means of implementing systems for static data flow computation. Both memory bandwidth and microcycle requirements for token-based operation execution exceed equivalent current generation uniprocessor costs per operation by amounts approaching an order of magnitude. The *associative template* mechanism is an alternate method of performing static data flow computation that does not exhibit the deleterious properties of the more conventional token approach. The associative template architecture employs associative processing methods to manage flow control of executing data flow programs, distinguishing it from conventional applications of content addressable memories. The associative template mechanism fully satisfies the semantic requirements of the static data flow model of computation. Memory bandwidth requirements (traffic across the memory I/O pins) and microcycles per operation of the associative template architecture approached that of uniprocessor performance.

Initially, the associative template mechanism was considered for a system consisting of a single node. For this simple case, computational parallelism made available by the data flow programming paradigm was exploited to keep the FCU's functional pipeline full. Then a second use of associative processing was applied to the problem of communication among multiple cooperating processing ensembles for additional performance gain through this second level of parallelism. Associative diffusion extends the domain of associativity beyond that of the local node to include the templates of the adjacent nodes, enabling data produced by adjacent nodes to be used for operands of local templates. By extending the search domain across node boundaries, result values can be accessed from neighbor nodes as efficiently as local data, providing nearest neighbor communication for free.

While the associative template and associative diffusion mechanisms are interesting alternatives to the token mechanism in an idealized context, many questions about the feasibility of implementation remain. One possible implementation indicates that the required functions could be divided so they would fit on current technology chips. This possibility was explored. Automated methods of static program distribution have yet to be developed for this particular architecture but can benefit from other work related to distributing programs on mesh connected parallel processors. Finally, questions regarding practical circuit design issues, including bus loading, number of devices per template, and power consumption and heat generation, have yet to be addressed at a quantitative level. This is a subject for future research. Only when this work is complete will the performance and cost benefits of the associative template mechanism be fully understood.

References

[1] Karp, R.M., and Miller, R.E., "Properties of a Model for Parallel Computations: Determinacy, Termination, Queueing", SIAM Journal of Applied Mathematics, Vol. 14, No. 6, Nov. 1966, pp. 1390-1411.

[2] Dennis, J.B., "Programming Generality, Parallelism and Computer Architecture," Information Processing 68, North-Holland, Amsterdam, 1969, pp. 484-492.

[3] Ackerman, W.B., "Data Flow Languages," AFIPS Conference Proceedings, Vol. 48: Proceedings of the 1979 National Computer Conference, pp. 1087-1095.

[4] Dennis, J.B. and Misunas, D.P., "A Preliminary Architecture for a Basic Data-Flow Processor," Proceedings of the Second Annual Symposium on Computer Architecture, Dec. 1974, pp. 126-132.

[5] Gurd, J.R., Kirkham, C.C., Watson, I., "The Manchester Prototype Dataflow Computer," Communications of the ACM, January 1985, pp. 34-52.

[6] Hiraki, K., Shimada, T., Nishida, K., "A Hardware Design of the Sigma-1, a Data Flow Computer for Scientific Computations," Proceedings of the 1984 International Conference on Parallel Processing, Aug. 1984, pp. 524-531.

[7] Foster, C.C., *Content Addressable Parallel Processors*, New York, Van Nostrand Reinhold Co., 1976.

[8] Smith, A.J., "Cache Memories," ACM Computing Surveys, Vol. 12, No. 3, Sept. 1982, pp. 473-530.

[9] Archibald, J., Baer, J.-L., "Cache Coherence Protocols: Evaluation Using a Multiprocessor Simulation Model," ACM Transactions on Computer Systems, Vol. 4, No. 4, Nov. 1986, pp. 273-298.

[10] Stone, H.S., *High-Performance Computer Architecture*, Reading, Mass.: Addison-Wesley, 1987.

[11] Sterling, T.L., "Intuitive Templates: A Static Data-Flow Architecture without Tokens," White Paper, Harris Government Systems Sector, May 25, 1987.

[12] Sterling, T.L., "The YARC Static Data-Flow Supercomputer," Yarc Note 5, Harris Government Systems Sector, Oct. 15, 1985.

[13] Kung, H.T., "Why Systolic Architectures?" Computer, Vol. 15, No. 1, Jan. 1982, pp. 37-46.

[14] Mead, C., Conway, L., *Introduction to VLSI Systems*, Reading, Mass.: Addison-Wesley, 1980.

ELIMINATION OF BOTTLENECKS IN DYNAMIC DATAFLOW PROCESSORS

Keki B. Irani & Khai-Quang Luc

Division of Computer Science and Engineering
Department of Electrical Engineering and Computer Science
The University of Michigan
Ann Arbor, MI 48109-2122

ABSTRACT

A key component of a dynamic dataflow processor, the matching unit, has been identified as a major bottleneck. An alternate implementation for the matching unit is presented. This implementation increases the operating bandwidth of the unit by allowing token matching operations to be done concurrently. The adoption of the proposed implementation also reveals throughput limitations of other units within the processor. As a result, a new configuration for a dynamic dataflow processor is proposed. We believe that the proposed processor is cost-effective, gives high performance, and is capable of incremental performance improvement.

Key Words: Dataflow, Dynamic Dataflow Processor, Matching Unit, Instance-Based Matching Unit, Parallel processing, Dataflow Multiprocessor System.

1. INTRODUCTION

Parallel processing is believed to be a useful way of achieving increased computing power. However, as the number of processors increases, a conventional von Neumann multiprocessor system either suffers from the problems of synchronization and memory latency [1], or becomes too unwieldly to be used effectively. For a multiprocessor system which uses dataflow processors, such problems either do not exist or are taken care of automatically.

Among the contemporary dataflow systems [2,3,4], those with a dynamic implementation allow a higher degree of parallelism to be exploited in the application programs. However, the performance of these systems is affected by the throughput of a key component, called a matching unit, or a waiting-matching store, within each component processor [5,6]. The function of a matching unit is to detect the executability of instructions in application programs. An obvious reason for its low throughput is the inherent memory reference operations performed within the unit. There are also less apparent reasons why the throughput of the unit is limited.

Throughput limitation of matching units not only degrades the performance of dataflow processors, but also reduces the degree of parallelism offered by the abstract model. To enhance the throughput of the unit, the approach we propose here is to extend the idea of parallel processing to a matching unit. This can boost the throughput of the matching unit as well as enhance the power of the processor itself. In Section 2, we briefly discuss the implementation, characteristics, and problems of contemporary matching units. The discussion leads us to the proposal of a new matching unit, called Instance-Based Matching Unit, in Section 3. Section 4 presents the simulation results on the performance of the proposed unit. These results reveal the possibility of further improvement of the performance of a dataflow processor by re-defining its configuration. A new configuration for dataflow processors is presented in Section 5. Section 6 concludes the paper.

2. CONTEMPORARY MATCHING UNITS

2.1. Overview

Programs executed in dataflow systems are usually expressed in the form of dataflow graphs [7] in which nodes represent instructions, and arcs indicate the relative ordering among nodes. Data is carried by tokens which move along arcs. In a dynamic implementation of the abstract dataflow model, more than one token is allowed to exist in any arc simultaneously [5]. This simultaneous existence of tokens occurs when more than one invocation of any re-entrant code segment, such as a sub-routine, a procedure, or a loop, is executed concurrently. Apparently, this feature of dynamic dataflow systems provides better exploitation of parallelism of application programs.

Only executable nodes are scheduled for functional units for execution in a dataflow system. A node in a dataflow graph is executable whenever all the required input tokens to it are available. For the sake of simplicity, instructions are restricted to two operands at the most, and hence, the maximum number of input tokens to a node is limited to two [5]. For a node which requires two input tokens, the tokens are called partner tokens. In a dynamic dataflow system, two tokens are called partner tokens if and only if they are destined for the same invocation of a node. The job of identifying partner tokens is performed in the matching unit of a dataflow processor. If the partner of a token is not available, the token, then called an unmatched token, is temporarily stored in the unit where it awaits its partner. The major concern regarding the implementation of a matching unit is how to store unmatched tokens in the unit efficiently so that the tokens can be easily retrieved.

It is estimated [5] that 10K to 100K of storage space is needed for tokens. For this size range, a completely associative memory for matching units is ruled out. Other implementation suggestions [5] include (1) the use of virtual memory for unmatched token storage and (2) allocation of token storage at the time of invocation of a re-entrant code segment. The latter needs the knowledge of storage requirement of a re-entrant code segment prior to invoking it. The former needs at least 40-bit addresses for the virtual memory. The feasibility of these suggestions for the implementation of a matching unit remains to be seen.

2.2. Hash-Table Approach

The hash table approach is adopted for implementing matching units in both the Manchester prototype processor [6] and the MIT Tagged-Token processor [2]. In this approach, the storage for unmatched tokens is equipped with a hash table [8]. Since a token in a dynamic dataflow processor carries the corresponding information on invocation number and instruction address, this information is then used to generate an address through the hash function when the token enters the matching unit. The generated address is used either to check the availability of the associated partner token or to store the incoming token which then awaits its partner token. In the Manchester prototype processor, the hash table is equipped with multiple memory banks so that multiple tokens can be stored at the same hash address. This is to reduce the collision effect caused by the hash function. In case all token slots of the same address are occupied, unmatched tokens are stored in an overflow area. Accessing the overflow area is a sequential process.

The disadvantages of adopting the hash table approach for the matching unit pertain to its high token storage requirement and low throughput. The former is contributed by two factors. Firstly, all the information carried by a token needs to be stored when the partner of the token is not available. This includes the information on the corresponding invocation number and the instruction address of the token. Secondly, the table has to be large if a good hash table performance is expected. As a result, the unit is identified as the location of a major resource waste [9]. As for the low throughput, in addition to the need of at least four memory references to match a partner token, token matching has to be done on per token basis.

3. INSTANCE-BASED MATCHING UNIT

3.1. Token partitioning

Token matching is sequential in nature. Throughput of a matching unit can be increased substantially only if multiple token matchings can be done concurrently. Concurrent matchings require partitioning of tokens into disjoint subsets in such a way that the partner tokens always belong to the same subset. Patnaik *et al* [10] implement this idea of partitioning tokens by the use of a hash function. The hash table approach is also used to perform token matching within each group. Consequently, inherent problems associated with the hash table approach still exist.

In the approach that we propose, tokens are grouped on an instance basis [11], where instances are defined as follows. Recall that in a dynamic dataflow environment, each token carries with it information regarding the associated invocation and instruction address. According to [5], the instruction address consists of the ID of the code block, called Code Block ID, to which the instruction belongs, and the relative address of the instruction, called Instruction Number, within the code block. The invocation information is contained in the Invocation ID and the Iteration ID. While the Iteration ID distinguishes different iterations of a particular invocation of the code block, the Invocation ID distinguishes different invocations. An instance here is then defined as a 3-tuple

Instance ID = <Invocation ID, Code Block ID, Iteration ID>

Rules to generate new instance ID's are taken from [12]. As mentioned earlier, one necessary condition for two tokens to be partner tokens is that they have the same instance ID. This guarantees that the resulting token subsets are disjoint.

3.2. Instance-Based Matching Unit

Based on the above method of partitioning, token matching can be performed in a proposed matching unit called Instance-Based Matching Unit (IBMU) shown in Figure 1 [11]. The Unit consists of a set of sub-units called Sub-Matching Units (SMU's). A SMU consists of a register, called Tag Register, a counter, called SMU counter, and a token storage, called Token Memory (TM). At any given time, each SMU provides a unique matching environment only for tokens carrying the same instance ID.

The function of each block within a SMU is now described: (1) The content of the Tag Register of a SMU is the ID of the instance currently assigned to the SMU. Only tokens which have the instance ID which is the same as that stored in the Register are allowed to enter the SMU for matching tokens. (2) Unmatched tokens are stored in the Token Memory of the SMU. Each incoming token uses the instruction number carried by the token itself to access these unmatched tokens. Consequently, neither the instance ID nor the instruction number of an unmatched token is needed to be stored in the Token Memory. Moreover, the number of tokens stored in a TM is just the number of instructions within a re-entrant code segment. Therefore, the size required for a TM is small. (3) The SMU counter is used to monitor the termination of matching process for the currently assigned instance. It is loaded, at the beginning, with a number indicating the number of Instance Output (INO) instructions within the assigned instance, and it counts down at the execution of each INO instruction. An INO instruction is an instruction which, when executed, assigns to the generated outgoing tokens different instance ID's than those carried by the incoming tokens used in the execution of the instruction. When the content of the SMU counter reaches zero, it indicates that the token matching operations for the current assigned instance are completed. The SMU is then ready for assignment of a new instance.

The principle of operation of the Instance-Based Matching Unit is as follow [13]: When an instance is assigned to an SMU, both the Tag Register and the SMU Counter of the SMU are properly loaded. Meanwhile, all the presence bits in the Token Memory of the SMU are reset. The SMU is now ready for token matching. When an incoming token is forwarded to the IBMU, it is stored in the input buffer of the SMU with the same instance ID and awaits token matching. When a SMU finishes the processing of a previous token, the first incoming token from the input buffer of the SMU initiates a memory fetch to the Token Memory for its partner token. If the fetched presence bit is reset, the fetched location is considered empty, and the search for the partner token fails. The incoming token is then stored into the location, and the corresponding presence bit is set. On the other hand, if the presence bit is set when it is

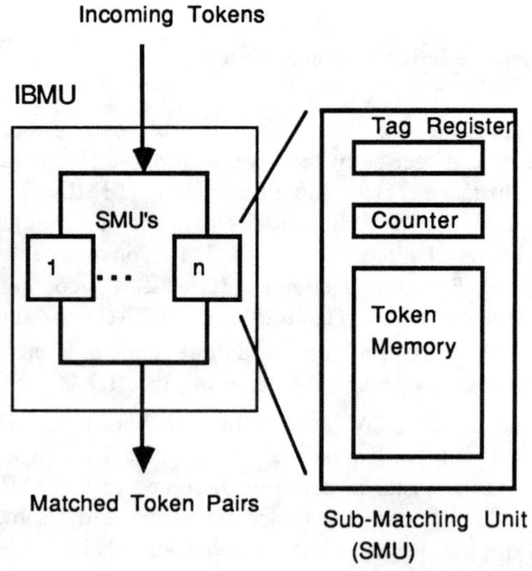

Fig.1 An Instance-Based Matching Unit

fetched, it indicates that the partner token is present, and the search is a success. The matched token pair is then forwarded to the next unit for further execution. There is no need to reset the presence bit of the location where the partner token was stored. Later, all the presence bits within the Token Memory are reset simultaneously when a new instance is assigned to the SMU. This shortens the time to match a token pair to three memory access cycles instead of at least four as in the hash table approach.

4. PERFORMANCE ANALYSIS OF IBMU

4.1. Simulation Models

The characteristics of the proposed Instance-Based Matching Unit are analyzed by simulation. The simulated processor model, similar to the Manchester prototype processor [6], consists of four stages: a Token Queue, the proposed IBMU, a set of Instruction Stores and a set of Functional Units. The object of using multiple copies of Instruction Store and Functional Unit is to highlight the performance of the proposed matching unit. I-Structures [14] are provided to handle structured data although the structures of simple forms are simulated. Scheduling assignment of instances to Sub-Matching Units is done manually.

To compare the throughput of the IBMU with that of the conventional matching unit, another simulator has also been constructed. The only difference between the two simulating models is in the matching unit block. The latter is equipped with a hash table of sixteen banks [6]. Memory reference time is assumed to be 4 clock cycles for both models. Speedup is defined as the ratio of the execution time obtained from the second simulator (with a hash table) and that from the first simulator (with an IBMU). Throughput of a matching unit is defined as the number of tokens processed per unit time within the unit. Performance comparison is done on the premise that both processors use approximately the same amount of memory storage for token matching.

The two simulators are driven by dataflow graphs of various application problems. Graphs are well-behaved and developed based on the constructs proposed in [15]. A well-behaved graph is self-cleaning, i.e., when the execution of an instance of the graph is terminated, there are no more tokens of the instance still waiting for their partner tokens. The well-behaved property of dataflow graphs is necessary because then a SMU can be recovered for the next instance assignment after the termination of the currently assigned instance.

The first dataflow graph is of matrix multiplication [16]. The second is of Fast Fourier Transform [17]. Each of these applications has a multiply-nested loop structure [18] and we are using them to create problems of large enough sizes. We do not taken into consideration other properties of this structure such as vectorizability. Furthermore, neither graph is optimized.

4.2. Performance Analysis

Various matrix sizes as well as vector sizes for the application graphs above are simulated. Figure 2 shows the execution times against the number of Sub-Matching Units for matrix multiplication with matrices of sizes ((7x5), (5x3)) and ((4x5), (5x3)), respectively. Figure 3 shows the execution time for Fast Fourier Transform with vector length 8. The execution times obtained from the processor equipped with a hash table remain the same even when different hash table sizes are used. This is because no overflow occurs during the processing. On the other hand, for the processor with an IBMU, the execution times decrease as the number of SMU's within the processor increases. Figure 4 shows the speedups for all three cases above. The speedups increase linearly up to a certain number of SMU's although the proportional constants differ from one.

While the hash table is busy for more than 98% of the execution time, the average utilization of individual SMU's is low. For the matrix multiplication, for instance, with the number of SMU's between 3 and 20, the utilization lies in the range of between 25% and 40% of the execution time. About 30% of the time, an individual SMU is not assigned to any instance at all. This implies that the application program has lack of parallelism *at the instance level* to keep all SMU's assigned. The situation can be improved if graphs

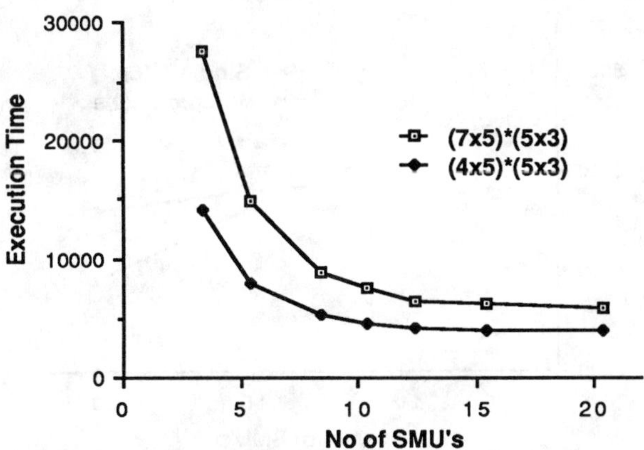

Fig.2 Execution Time v.s. No. of SMU's
(Matrix Multiplication)

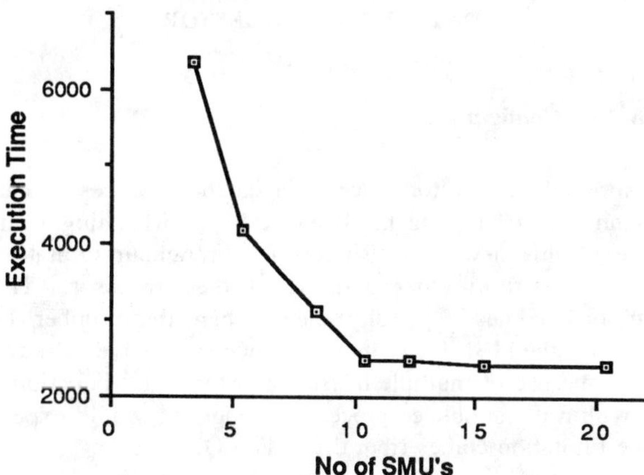

Fig.3 Execution Time v.s. No. of SMU's
(Fast Fourier Transform, Vector length = 8)

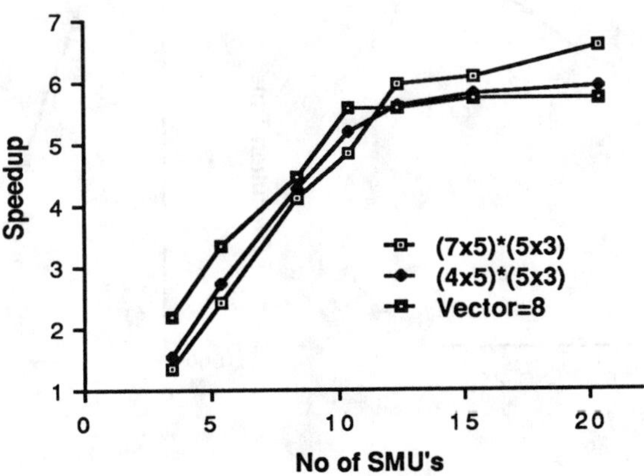

Fig.4 Speedup v.s. No. of SMU's

are optimized [19]. Meanwhile, another 30% of the execution time individual SMU's of the matching unit are idle due to the lack of incoming tokens. This may be the result of either the low degree of parallelism of application programs *at the instruction level*, or of potential bottlenecks that may exist in other portions of the simulation model. If all SMU's within the IBMU can be kept busy throughout the execution period, the throughput gain of the proposed IBMU with respect to the hash table is considerable. Figure 5a shows the maximum throughput gain of the unit. The curve is linear with a proportional constant greater than one. The value of the constant is the result of a shorter token matching time per token pair provided by the IBMU. Figure 5b shows the actual throughput gain for comparison.

5. NEW CONFIGURATION FOR DYNAMIC DATAFLOW PROCESSOR

5.1. A New Configuration

Although the performance of a dataflow processor can be enhanced by adopting the Instance-Based Matching Unit, the use of this new unit also reveals throughput limitation which results from other portions of the processor. The limitation becomes especially clear when the number of SMU's in the IBMU is high. Since we have already assumed the use of multiple Instruction Stores and Functional Units within the simulated processor model, we would expect that the limitation comes from the Token Queue unit.

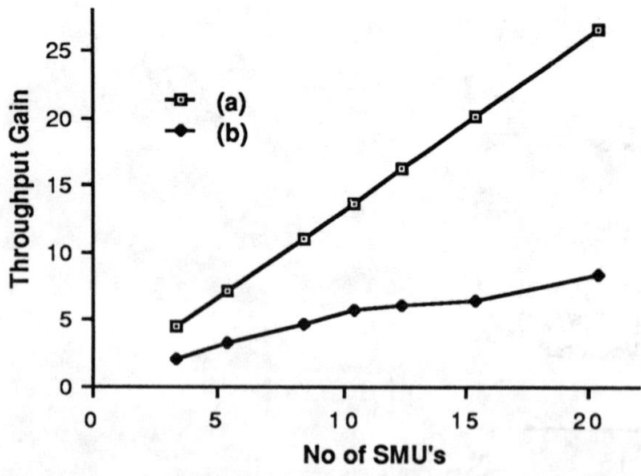

Fig.5 Throughput Gain v.s. No. of SMU's
(Matrix Multiplication: 4x5*5x3)

The object of providing the Queue unit in the processor is to smooth out uneven rates of generation and consumption of tokens [6]. The unit is expected to function as a buffer. However, for the sake of simplicity, it has been implemented in a FIFO manner and, within the simulated model, it can only dispatch one token per system clock. As the number of SMU's within the matching unit is high, token demand on the Queue unit will surpass the throughput of the Queue unit itself. This situation is confirmed by measuring the performance of a similar processor which is equipped with multiple Token Queues such that each SMU has its own dedicated Queue unit. The simulation results of this processor are shown in Figures 6 and 7. Compared with the one with single Token Queue, the processor with multiple Token Queues provides an average performance improvement

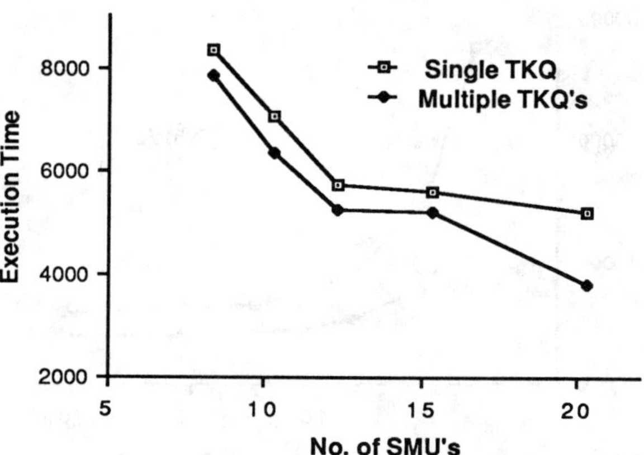

Fig.6 Execution Time v.s. No. of SMU's
(Matrix Multiplication: 7x5*5x3)

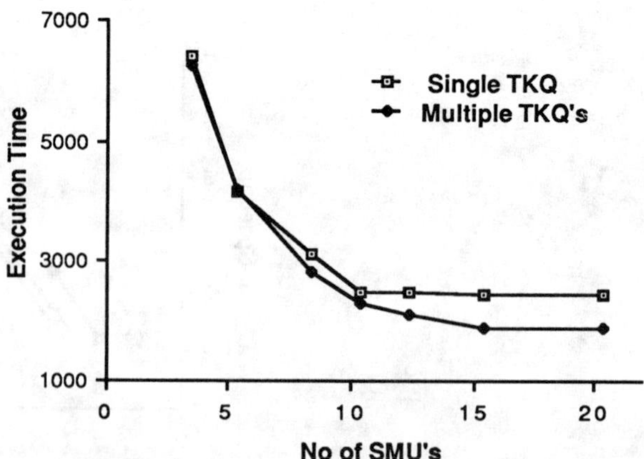

Fig.7 Execution Time v.s. No. of SMU's
(FFT of Vector Length = 8)

of 25% when 20 SMU's are used. This improvement is observed for both the matrix multiplication and Fast Fourier Transform problems.

The identification of this bottleneck within the processor leads us to propose a new configuration for dataflow processor which we believe gives high performance, and is capable of incremental expansion. The proposed processor is shown in Figure 8a. Basically, it consists of a set of Sub-Processors (SP's), I-Structures, an Arbitrator, and a Token I/O Switch. The Switch distributes tokens to Sub-Processors and is responsible for the interface between the processor and other processors. The Arbitrator unit collects outcoming tokens from Sub-Processors. I-Structures are storage for structured data. For Sub-Processors, as shown in Figure 8b, each of them is equipped with a single Token Queue, a small number of Sub-Matching Units, the same number of Instruction Stores, a number of two output-port Functional Units, and a Local Token Bus. The functions of the blocks within a Sub-Processor are the same as those described in the previous section except that Functional Units may direct output tokens through different ports depending on the tokens themselves. If a token is the result of an INO instruction, it is directed, through port B of a Functional Unit, to the outlet of a current SP. Otherwise, the token takes port A and is forwarded to the Token Queue of the current SP through the Local Token Bus.

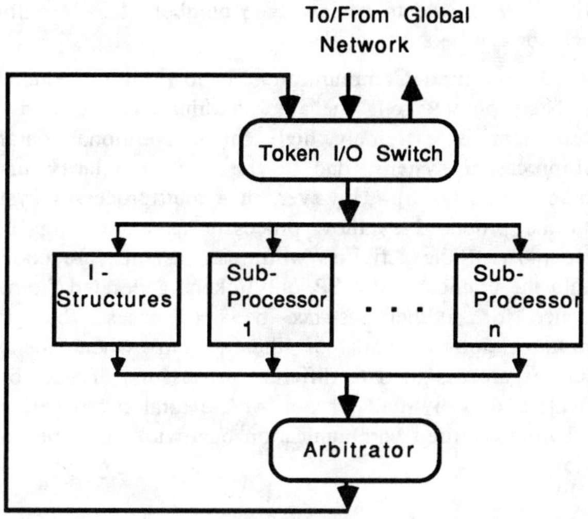

Fig. 8a A Proposed Dataflow Processor

5.2. Qualitative Analysis

Based on the results obtained from the proposed IBMU and the description of the proposed processor above, the following advantages of the new processor can be foreseen:

(a) Hardware utilization is high: Since the number of SMU's and the number of Functional Units within a SP are designed so that the average throughputs at different stages of a SP are close to others, the token stream flowing through these pipelined stages is expected to be smooth. Bubbles within the pipeline are then reduced. Therefore, hardware utilization of the proposed processor is expected to be high.

(b) Performance of Sub-Processors is high: The structure of each Sub-Processor is exactly the same as the structure of the simulated processor which we have evaluated in Section 4. As we have shown in Section 4 that the performance of the simulated processor is high. Thus each SP contributes a substantial amount of performance to the proposed new processor.

(c) Performance of the processor is expandable: The performance of the proposed processor can be raised incrementally by gradually increasing the number of SP's within the processor. This differs from von Neumann type processors which rely either on increasing the number of pipelined stages or on improving the technology in order to improve their performance. The possible limitation on the maximum number of SP's within the proposed processor may come from the Token I/O Switch. The Switch is responsible for the transfer of tokens among SP's within the processor, or

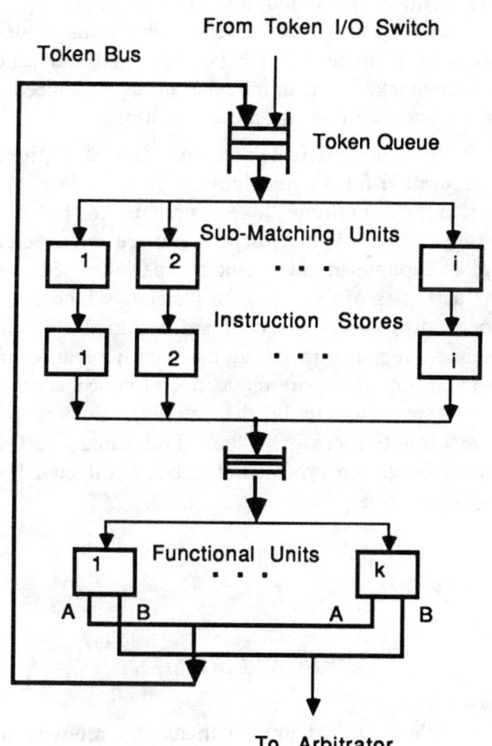

Fig. 8b A Sub-Processor

the transfer of tokens from the current processor to the other processors, and therefore, the frequency of access to the Switch is expected to be low. The number of SP's within a processor can be substantial.

(d) Required Communication bandwidth is reduced: It has been pointed out that the communication bandwidth requirement is extremely high for conventional dataflow multiprocessor systems due to the fine granularity of the dataflow model [20]. However, in a multiprocessor system, with the proposed dataflow processor as a building block, since most of the activities within an instance are confined within the boundary of a SP, only tokens generated from one instance for another instance need to access the global communication network of the system when the two instances are assigned to different processors. These tokens constitute only a small fraction of the total token set. As a result, the required communication bandwidth is expected to be low.

6. CONCLUSION

We have proposed a new way to implement a matching unit, a key component but also an identified bottleneck in a dynamic dataflow processor. The proposed Instance-Based Matching Unit allows multiple token matchings to be performed concurrently. As a result, the throughput of the matching unit is increased substantially and the unit is no more a bottleneck. In addition, the storage required for the unit is much smaller than for the conventional unit.

With the proposed matching unit, we have presented a new configuration for a dynamic dataflow processor. The new processor allows multiple token streams to be processed concurrently. Consequently, its performance is expected to be high and is capable of incremental expansion. Furthermore, since the activities of executing an instance which is assigned to a proposed processor are confined within the boundary of the processor, requests to the global communication network by individual processors are reduced, and hence, the proposed processor is expected to be the building block for a high performance multiprocessor system. Preliminary performance result of the proposed processor has been collected [19], and further evaluation is proceeding.

ACKNOWLEDGEMENT

The authors would like to thank the referees for their helpful comments and constructive suggestions.

REFERENCES

[1] Arvind & R.A. Iannucci, ''Two Fundamental Issues in Multiprocessing,'' Computation Structure Group Memo 226-6, Lab. for Computer Science, MIT, May 5, 1987.

[2] Arvind, D.E. Culler, R.A. Iannucci, V. Kathail, K. Pingali, & R.E. Thomas, ''The Tagged-Token Dataflow Architecture,'' Technical Report, Preliminary Version for Distribution in Subject 6.83s, Lab. for Computer Science, MIT, Aug.8, 1983.

[3] Barahona, P.M.C.C., & J.R. Gurd, ''Processor Allocation in a Multi-Ring Dataflow Machine,'' *Jour. of Parallel and Distributed Computing,* Vol. 3, 1986, pp.305-327.

[4] Dennis, J.B., ''Dataflow Ideas for Supercomputers,'' *Proc. 12th Ann. Symp. on Computer Architecture,* 1985, pp.15-19.

[5] Arvind & D.E. Culler, ''Dataflow Architectures,'' Technical Report, MIT/LCS/TM-294, Feb.12, 1986.

[6] Gurd, J.R., C.C. Kirkham, & I. Watson, ''The Manchester Prototype Dataflow Computer,'' *Communications of the ACM,* Vol.28, Jan. 1985, pp.34-52.

[7] Davis, A.L. & R.M. Keller, ''Data Flow Program Graphs,'' *IEEE Computer,* Vol.15, Feb.1982, pp.26-41.

[8] Da Silva, J.G.D. & I. Watson, ''Pseudo-Associate Store with Hardware Hashing,'' *IEE Proc.,* Vol.130, Pt. E, No.1, Jan. 1983, pp.19-24.

[9] Veen, A.H., ''Dataflow Machine Architecture,'' *ACM Computing Surveys,* Vol.18, No.4, Dec. 1986, pp.366-396.

[10] Patnaik, L.M., R. Govindarajan, & N.S. Ramadoss, ''Design and Performance Evaluation of EXMAN: An Extended MANchester Data Flow Computer,'' *IEEE Trans. on Comput.,* Vol. C-35, March 1986, pp.229-244.

[11] Luc, K.Q., "A Matching Unit for Dynamic Dataflow Processors,'' Proposal for Ph.D. Preliminary Examination, EECS Dept., University of Michigan, Ann Arbor, Sept., 1986.

[12] Arvind & K.P. Gostelow, ''The U-Interpreter,'' *IEEE Computer,* Feb. 1982, pp.42-49.

[13] Irani, K.B. & K.Q. Luc, ''An Instance-Based Matching Unit for Dynamic Dataflow Processors,'' *Proc. IFIP on Parallel Processing,* Pisa, Italy, April 25-27, 1988.

[14] Arvind, R.S. Nikhil, & K.K. Pingali, ''I-Structures: Data Structures for Parallel Computing,'' Computation Structures Group Memo 269, Lab. for Computer Science, MIT, Feb. 1987.

[15] Arvind & K.P. Gostelow, ''The U-Interpreter,'' *IEEE Computer*, 1982, pp.42-49.

[16] Gostelow, K.P. & R.E. Thomas, ''Performance of a Simulated Dataflow Computer,'' *IEEE Trans. on Computer*, Vol.C-29, No.10, Oct.1980,

[17] Aho, A.V., Hopcroft, J.E., & Ullman, J.D., *Data Structures and Algorithms*, Addison-Welsey, 1983.

[18] Tang, P., Yew, P.C., Fang, Z., & Zhu, C.Q., ''Deadlock Prevention in Processor Self-Scheduling for Parallel Nested Loops,'' *Proc. of 1987 Int. Conf. on Parallel Processing*, pp.11-18, 1987.

[19] Luc, K.Q. & K.B. Irani, ''A High Performance Dataflow Processor For Multiprocessor Systems,'' *Proc. Workshop on Future Trends of Dist. Comput. Syst. in the 90's*, Sept. 14-16, 1988, Hong Kong.

[20] Kaplan, I., ''The LDF 100: A Large Grain Dataflow Parallel Processor,'' *ACM Computer Architecture News*, Vol. 15, No. 3, June 1987, pp.5-12.

I-NET Mechanism for Issuing Multiple Instructions

Lingtao Wang, Motorola Inc., Austin, Texas

Chuan-lin Wu, The University of Texas at Austin

Abstract -- Conventional instruction issuing methods use hardware control mechanism to issue instructions in multiple-functional-unit systems. They reach physical limitations due to the complexity of issuing logic when they intend to issue multiple instructions per cycle. A new method, I-NET, is presented in this paper to overcome this shortcoming. I-NET uses a post-compiler to detect the data dependencies among instructions. The detected data dependence is then attached to the instruction code to form an instruction unit which can be executed independently with one another. These "pre-decoded" instruction units are fetched from the memory and sent to functional units directly. It achieve a maximal instruction issuing rate by avoiding a lengthy decoding procedure in the hardware. The performance study has shown I-NET to be a very promising method in exploring massive parallelism of a program in a multiple-functional-unit system.

Keywords -- Instruction network, forward routing, backward sorting, early bounding, post-compiler.

Introduction

To issue and execute multiple instructions is the bottom line in any parallel processing supercomputing scheme. Many issuing algorithms and methods have been investigated [1, 2, 3, 4, 5, 6, 7] and some have been implemented in real systems [1, 2, 3, 8]. The instruction issuing normally requires three steps: 1) detect data dependence of the operands in the instruction; 2) detect status of the functional units in the system; 3)issue the instruction. In most cases, these three steps are done sequentially. For example, in the Cray-1 pipelined system [1], an instruction is first decoded to check the operand. If the operand is currently used by another functional unit, the instruction is not "issuable" and is held until the operand becomes free. When the operand is free, the issuing logic then checks the status of the functional unit. If the unit is busy, the instruction is held again. The instruction is sent to the unit for execution only when the unit becomes free. This is the easiest but slowest way to issue an instruction. We classify it as a (1, 1, 1) issuing method.

Thornton's Scoreboard method implemented in the CDC6600 [2] uses multiple functional units for instruction execution. This gives the system a potential to execute multiple instructions simultaneously. The method checks one instruction at a time and stops the issuing when a data conflict occurs. It is classified as a (1, n, 1) issuing method. Tomasulo's Reservation Station [3] improves Thornton's method by removing the data interlock constraint. Instructions are issued regardless of the operand status which is coordinated through a common data bus and data buffers. It is a (n, n, 1) issuing method. Torng's Dispatch Stack [4] is a table-driven issuing method. The issuing rate is limited by the speed of the table-updating and the index-searching. Though the paper does not mention a method to send n "executable" instructions to n functional units, we classify it as an (n, n, n) issuing method.

The (n, n, n) issuing method has shown its superiority to (1, n, 1) or (n, n, 1) method to explore the parallelism of a program in a multiple-functional-unit system. It decodes and issues n instructions per cycle. However, it does not achieve an optimal issuing rate. Since its hardware decoding scheme depends on a large table for index searching and updating, it is expensive and time consuming. Also, the issuing logic uses a handshaking signal to detect the status of a functional unit before it sends an instruction to it. This further slows down the issuing rate. These implementation constraints lead us to investigate a new issuing method. In this paper, we propose to use software and the interconnection network to improve our instruction issuing rate. We call this new issuing method "Instruction Network Issuing Mechanism", or I-NET as short.

I-NET uses software to detect the data dependencies among instructions. It packs data dependence information as a data tag and attaches it to the instruction. The issuing logic fetches and sends an instruction to a functional unit directly. It does not need to decode the instruction to check the data dependency before it issues the instruction. It is the responsibility of each functional unit to check the data tag before it executes the instruction. By doing this, we eliminate the first step in the conventional issuing method. We further eliminate the second step by inventing a multistage interconnection network to transfer multiple instructions between functional units and the issuing logic. The transmission protocol is to ask the issuing logic to send each functional unit one instruction per cycle, regardless of unit's status. If the functional unit is kept busy by the previous instruction, it rejects the instruction. The network will automatically route rejected instructions back to the issuing logic for the next attempt. There is no need for the issuing logic to know the status of each functional unit before it sends an instruction. The combination of these two ideas, software data detection and hardware transmission network, enables the I-NET mechanism to achieve one step, n instructions per cycle, stream line issuing rate. It gives a great potential to explore the massive parallelism in a program at the instruction set level.

In this paper, we first propose a simple multiple-functions-system model which uses the I-NET mechanism for the instruction issuing. In the third section, we describe the idea of software data detection. In the fourth section, we present an instruction transmission network which is a multistage n*n interconnection network. In the fifth section, we evaluate the I-NET and compare it with other methods in a quantitative way. Finally, we outline the future research directions.

A Multiple Functional Unit System Model

We describe a multiple-functional-unit system which uses I-NET for instruction issuing with three indices, (c, n, m). c is the number of execution cycle per instruction, n is the number of functional units in the system, m indicates whether the system has a register-based (R) or memory-based (M) instruction execution model. A (c, n, m) system with n = 8 is shown in Figure 1. It has an instruction dispatcher (ID) to prefetch instructions from an instruction cache. ID has n channels to send n instructions to the instruction network. The instruction network (INET) is a multistage, circuit switching, n by n interconnection network. It routes n instructions to n functional units at the every transmission cycle. The routing follows a "two-phase" routing scheme. In the first phase of a transmission cycle, the INET detects the status of each functional unit to pre-set the routing path. It then routes n instructions from the ID to functional units. In the second phase of the cycle, it sends "unaccepted" instructions back to the ID. A functional unit (FU) is a complete ALU with some control logic. It receives a new instruction from the INET at the every cycle. If the instruction is "executable", it proceeds with execution. Otherwise, the FU holds the instruction and waits until the instruction become executable. It then proceeds with the execution.

The control flow diagram for this system is shown in Figure 2. The system starts the processing cycle with the ID to fetch multiple instructions from the system instruction cache. It then cooperates the instruction issuing with the INET to send n instructions to n FUs every cycle. A free FU accepts a new instruction and checks the packed data tag. If the tag shows the operand is not ready at the present, the FU updates the tag and holds the instruction for one cycle. Meanwhile, the INET will route the rejected instructions back to the ID. In the next transmission cycle, the FU rejects a new coming instruction from the INET and checks the tag again. It repeats the same sequence until the operand is ready. It then executes the instruction, and becomes available to accept a new instruction in the next transmission cycle.

The model is basically a multiple-instruction-multiple-data system. We use a simple and large register file in the model. The register file is assumed to support multiple read and single write per cycle.

Post-compiling Technique in Detecting Data dependence

The idea of I-NET is to use a software which we call post-compiler to detect the data dependencies in an instruction. There are three kinds of instructions that need to be considered: 1) static instruction with a fixed execution time; 2) dynamic instruction with a variable execution time; 3) exception or interrupt. For static instructions, the post-compiler can detect and determine the data dependence alone. For the dynamic instruction, the post-compiler scheme depends on the run-time information to complete the execution. Since there is no way to detect a run-time exception or interrupt, the scheme leaves the exception or interrupt to the hardware.

For a static instruction, Kuck [9] has classified three kinds of register dependence among instructions: flow, anti, and output dependence. The anti dependence is a write-after-read relation. The output dependence is a write-after-write relation. Both can be eliminated with a proper renaming mechanism and register buffers. The flow dependence is a read-after-write relation which requires a

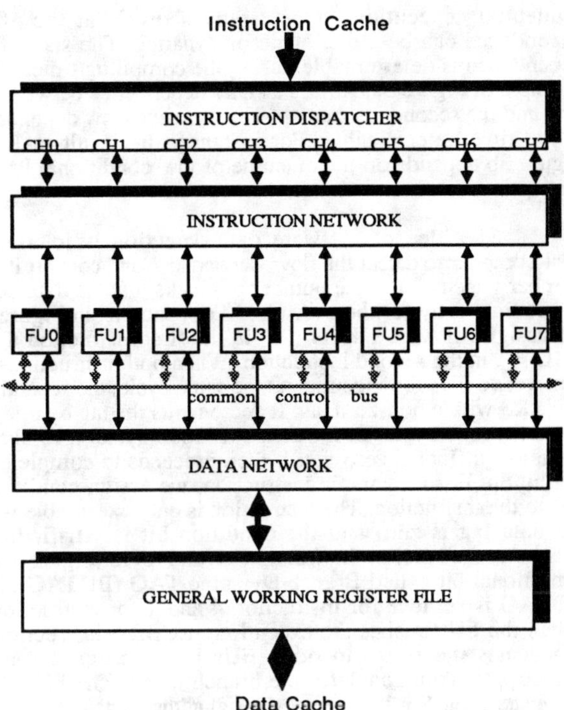

Figure 1: A Multiple-functional-unit System Organization

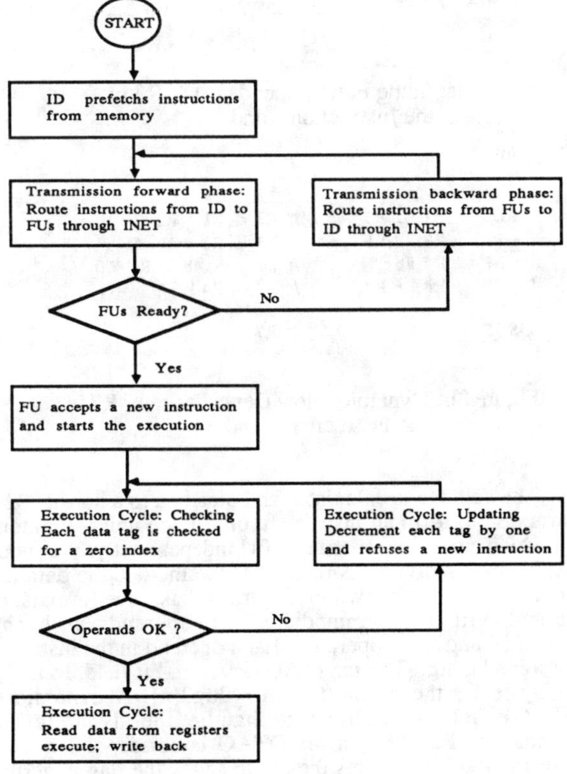

Figure 2: The I-NET Mechanism Control Flow Diagram

sequential execution. Our study shows that the flow dependence can be either static or dynamic. The static flow dependence is determinable during the compiling time. As an example in Figure 3a, R3 has a static dependence between the first and the second instruction. The dynamic flow dependence is run-time determinable. For instance, the result in R7 in Figure 3b depends on the outcome of the conditional branch instruction.

The idea of software data detection is to use the post-compiler to detect the flow dependence and convert it to a number which shows the number of clocks that the data needs to become ready for the execution. For example, in Figure 3a, we assign R3 with a TAG = 0 in the first instruction and a TAG = 1 in the second instruction. When both instructions are sent to two FUs for execution at the same cycle, the second FU finds R3 with a non-zero tag. It decrements the tag by one and waits for one cycle. In the next execution cycle, it re-checks the tag and finds a zero tag. It then proceeds to complete the execution. For a dynamic instruction, we assign conditional bits to the instruction. The instruction is only executable when the data tag is zero and the condition bit is satisfied. For example, we assign instruction 4 and b in Figure 3b a conditional bit called Branch Dynamic TAG (BDTAG). The BDTAG is set to 2 for instruction 4 and 1 for instruction b. When the FU finishes the execution of CBRA instruction, it broadcasts the result to other FUs by sending 2 for the branch-not-taken and 1 for the branch-taken. The FU which has instruction 4 or b receives the signal then acts accordingly. If 1 is broadcasted, instruction b will be executed and instruction 4 will be nullified as a no-operation instruction.

```
1. ADD    R1,R2,R3     /* R3 <- R1 + R2 */
2. OR     R3,R4,R5     /* R5 <- R3 or R4 */
3. CBRA   R5,#b        /* jump to #b, if R5 = 0 */
:
```

Figure 3a: Static Flow Dependence of R3 in the Instruction 1 and 2

```
1. ADD    R1,R2,R3     /* R3 <- R1 + R2 */
2. OR     R3,R4,R5     /* R5 <- R3 or R4 */
3. CBRA   R5,#b        /* jump to #b, if R5 = 0 */
4. SUB    R4,R6,R7     /* R7 <- R4-R6 */
:
b. SUB    R1,R2,R7     /* R7 <- R1-R2 */
:
```

Figure 3b: Dynamic Flow Dependence of R7 in the Instruction 4 and b

The data tag is calculated and attached to a normal 32-bit instruction to form an instruction unit. Each unit is an atomic unit which can be executed in a FU independently. We modify a 32-bit instruction set format to accommodate the data tags. The instruction, as shown in Figure 4, has three formats: one operand with long immediate, two operands with short immediate and three operands. Each operand in the instruction is assigned a tag. The tag (TAG) is an m-bit field. In a (1, n, R) system, the relation is m = log2(n). A dynamic tag (DTAG) field is defined to handle the dynamic flow information. Each bit in the DTAG is correspondent to an condition flag. It requires the FU to check the flag in addition to all the TAG fields.

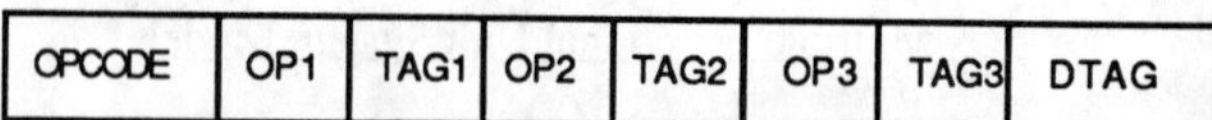

Figure 4a: 3-operand Tagged Instruction Format

OPCODE	OP1	TAG1	OP2	TAG2	IMMEDIATE	DTAG

Figure 4b: 2-operand Tagged Instruction Format

OPCODE	OP1	TAG1	IMMEDIATE	DTAG

Figure 4c: 1-operand Tagged Instruction Format

In the following section, we first describe the data tag calculation scheme for static instructions, then the method for dynamic instructions, the branch instruction and the memory instruction with a cache miss.

Tag Assignment Algorithm for Static Instructions

The post-compiler scans a "window" of the program at a time to calculate the data tag for each instruction. A window is defined in Definition 1. The post-compiler chooses the first n instructions in the program for the first window. It calculates the data tag for each instruction in the first window by following Algorithm 2. It then chooses the instructions for the next window by following Algorithm 3. It repeats the previous two steps until it finishes the whole program. The post-compiler procedure is shown in Algorithm 1. In Algorithm 2, we need four pieces of information to calculate the data tag for a register:

1. The number of execution cycles for an instruction: A register-to-register ALU instruction takes one cycle, and a memory load or store instruction takes two cycles with a cache hit.
2. The status of the register: Each register is assigned with a status of Read (R), Write (W), Load (L), or Store (S). For instance, R3 in the second instruction in Figure 3a is assigned a R status. A load register is associated with a L status and a store register is associated with a S status.
3. The data tag of the same register that appeared previously in the same window.
4. The window number difference between two appearances of the same register: Each instruction is assigned with a window number as its first entry into a window. In Figure 3a, the window difference is the window number of R3 in the second instruction and the window number of R3 in the first instruction.

Definition 1: Window

A window is a group of instructions which has a possibility to be executed at the same cycle. Its size, or the number of instructions in the window, depends on the number of FUs and the execution cycles per instruction.

Algorithm 1: Post-compiling Scheme

1. Choose the first n instructions as the first window.
2. Calculate the data tag for each instruction in the first window by following Algorithm 2.
3. Choose the instructions for the next window by following Algorithm 3.
4. Repeat steps 2 and 3 until the program is completed.

Algorithm 2: Data Dependency Calculation

OD: Old data tag (OD) is the data tag for the previous appearance of the same register in the same window.

WD: Window difference (WD) is the difference between the window number of current register and the window number of the same register which appears previously in the same window.

If the register in the new instruction has a R status,
- If the previous appearance of the same register has R status, TAG = OD - WD.
- If the previous appearance of the same register has W status, TAG = OD - WD + 1.
- If the previous appearance of the same register has L status, TAG = OD - WD + 1.
- If the previous appearance of the same register has S status, TAG = OD - WD.
- else TAG = 0.

If the register in the new instruction has a W status,
- If the previous appearance of the same register has R status, TAG = max(tag1, tag2, OD - WD).
- If the previous appearance of the same register has W status, TAG = max(tag1, tag2, OD - WD+1).
- If the previous appearance of the same register has L status, This situation will no occur.
- If the previous appearance of the same register has S status, TAG = max(tag1, tag2, OD - WD+1).
- else TAG = max(tag1, tag2).

If the register in the new instruction has a L status,
- If the previous appearance of the same register has R status, TAG= max(tag1+1, tag2+1, OD- WD+1).
- If the previous appearance of the same register has W status, This situation will not occur.
- If the previous appearance of the same register has L status, TAG=max(tag1+1, tag2+1, OD - WD+2).
- If the previous appearance of the same register has S status, The situation will not occur.
- else TAG = max(tag1+1, tag2+1).

If the register in the new instruction has a S status,
- If the previous appearance of the same register has R status, TAG = max(tag1+1, tag2+1, OD - WD).
- If the previous appearance of the same register has W status, TAG=max(tag1+1, tag2+1, OD - WD+1).
- If the previous appearance of the same register has L status, This situation will not occur.
- If the previous appearance of the same register has S status, TAG = max(tag1+1, tag2+1, OD-WD+1)
- else TAG = max(tag1+1, tag2+1).

Algorithm 3: Window Number Calculation

1. The first window has instruction 1 to n, n is the number of FUs in the system.
2. The i-th window has the instructions in the (i-1)-th window which has a tag greater than 0. Where, the data tag in each instruction is decremented by 1 and put into the i-th window.
3. Add new instructions to the i-th window up to a total of n instructions.

A matrix program is used to demonstrate the post-compiling scheme. The program written in C language is shown in Figure 5a. The program is hand-compiled to a generic 32-bit instruction set. The program assembly code is shown in Figure 5b. Following Algorithm 1,2 and 3, we hand post-compile the assembly code for a multiple-functional-unit system with four FU. The instructions in each window during the post-compiling is shown with its data tag in Table 1. Totally, there are 11 windows examined. It implies that the logic needs to issue instructions 11 times for one loop.

```
main()
{
    int a[100], b[100], c[100], i, j;
    for (i = 0; i < 100; i++){
            c[i] = a[i] + b[i];
            j = a[i] - b[i];
            b[i] = 2 * a[i] + 4*b[i];
            a[i] = j; }
}
```

Figure 5a: Matrix Program in C language

```
define abase 0;                              /* base address for array a */
define bbase 100;                            /* base address for array b */
1:  MOVE1      %100, R10      /* R10 <- 100 */
2:  MOVE1      %0,R1          /* R1 <- 0 */
3:  READ2      R1,abase,R24   /* R24<- memory<R1+abase > */
4:  ADD2       R24, %0,R11    /* R11 <- R24 + 0 */
5:  READ2      R1,bbase,R24   /* R24<- memory<R1+bbase > */
6:  ADD2       R24, %0,R12    /* R12 <- R24 + 0 */
7:  ADD3       R11,R12,R25    /* R25 <- R11 + R12 */
8:  STORE2     R1,cbase,R25   /* memory<R1+cbase> <- R25 */
9:  SUB3       R11,R12,R25    /* R25 <- R11 - R12 */
10: STORE2     R1,abase,R25   /* memory<R1+abase> <- R25 */
11: SHLL2      R11, %1,R13    /*R13<-left_shift_1_bit of R11*/
12: SHLL2      R12, %2,R14    /*R14<-left_shift_2_bit of R12*/
13: ADD3       R13,R14,R25    /* R25 <- R13 + R14 */
14: STORE2     R1,bbase,R25   /* memory<R1+bbase> <-R25 */
15: ADD2       R1, %1, R1     /* R1 <- R1 + 1 */
16. CBRA2,>    R10,%-13,R1    /* jump to 3 if R10 > R1 */
17. STP                       /* stop */
```

Figure 5b: Matrix Program in a Generic 32-bit Instruction Set

Table 1: Snapshot of Each Window in Post-compiling the Matrix Program

Window 1		
1. MOVE1	%100,R10	0,0,0
2. MOVE1	%0,R1	0,0,0
3. READ2	R1,abase,R24	1,0,2
4. ADD2	R24,%0,R11	3,0,3

Window 2		
3. READ2	R1,abase,R24	0,0,1
4. ADD2	R24,%0,R11	2,0,2
5. READ2	R1,bbase,R24	0,0,3
6. ADD2	R24,%0,R12	4,0,4

Window 3		
3. READ2	R1,abase,R24	0,0,0
4. ADD2	R24,%0,R11	1,0,1
5. READ2	R1,bbase,R24	0,0,2
6. ADD2	R24,%0,R12	3,0,3

Window 4		
4. ADD2	R24,%0,R11	0,0,0
5. READ2	R1,bbase,R24	0,0,1
6. ADD2	R24,%0,R12	2,0,2
7. ADD3	R11,R12,R25	1,3,3

Window 5		
5. READ2	R1,bbase,R24	0,0,0
6. ADD2	R24,%0,R12	1,0,1
7. ADD3	R11,R12,R25	0,2,2
8. STORE2	R1,cbase,R25	0,0,3

Window 6		
6. ADD2	R24,%0,R12	0,0,0
7. ADD3	R11,R12,R25	0,1,1
8. STORE2	R1,cbase,R25	0,0,2
9. SUB3	R11,R12,R25	0,1,3

Window 7		
7. ADD3	R11,R12,R25	0,0,0
8. STORE2	R1,cbase,R25	0,0,1
9. SUB3	R11,R12,R25	0,0,2
10. STORE2	R1,abase,R25	0,0,3

Window 8		
8. STORE2	R1,cbase,R25	0,0,0
9. SUB3	R11,R12,R25	0,0,1
10. STORE2	R1,abase,R25	0,0,2
11. SHLL2	R11,%1,R13	0,0,0

Window 9		
9. SUB3	R11,R12,R25	0,0,0
10. STORE2	R1,abase,R25	0,0,1
12. SHLL2	R12,%2,R14	0,0,0
13. ADD3	R13,R14,R25	0,1,2

Window 10		
10. STORE2	R1,abase,R25	0,0,0
13. ADD3	R13,R14,R25	0,0,1
14. STORE2	R1,bbase,R25	0,0,2
15. ADD2	R1, %1, R1	0,0,0

Window 11		
13. ADD3	R13,R14,R25	0,0,0
14. STORE2	R1,bbase,R25	0,0,1
16. CBRA2,>	R10,%-13,R1	0,0,0
17. STP		0,0,0

Tag Assignment Scheme for Dynamic Instructions

The dynamic instruction, such as branch or memory instruction with cache miss, has an unknown execution status during compiling time. The I-NET approach to these instructions is to use a hardware handshaking signal to assist the data tag to insure a correct execution sequence. We first discuss the branch instruction, then memory instruction.

The branch prediction (BP) scheme is used in I-NET to minimize the performance degradation due to the branch interrupt. According to the complexity of BP control mechanism, there are different levels of branch prediction. The 0-level BP is to stop issuing instruction whenever the ID has issued a branch instruction. The ID simply awaits the result to come back from the FU to continue the issuing. The 1-level BP is to issue the instructions together with the branch instruction and stops the issuing when it sees a second branch instruction in the same active window. This method requires hardware assistance as compared with the 0-level BP. The multiple level branch prediction is to issue multiple branch instructions within one active window. It requires maximum hardware assistance. In our current research, we adopt the 1-level BP on the post-compiler scheme. Since our research is to prove the idea of post-compiler, it will be unwise to bury ourselves in designing a complexed multiple-level BP.

Each instruction is assigned with a two-bit branch dynamic tag (BDTAG) to meet three branch conditions, TRUE, FALSE, DON'T CARE. For a structured branch, in Figure 6, we assign the instructions in the true portion with BDTAG = 01, the instructions in the false portion BDTAG = 10 and the rest of the instructions with BDTAG = 00. When an FU receives the branch instruction, it will raise two bits in the common control bus (Figure 1) high. When it finishes the execution, it puts 01 on the bus for a true condition and 10 for a false condition. Every other FU that has an instruction with BDTAG not equal to 00 needs to hold the execution. It checks the common control bus every cycle to determine the branch status. If the signal matches the BDTAG, it starts to execute the instruction. Otherwise, it nullifies the instruction. An example with 8 functional units is shown in Figure 7.

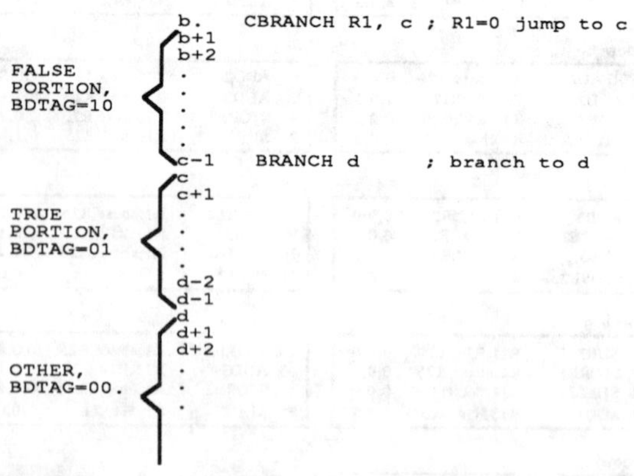

Figure 6: Dynamic Data Tag for Branch Instructions

```
1.  ADD   R1,R2,R3     /* R3 <- R1 + R2 */
2.  OR    R3,R4,R5     /* R5 <- R3. or. R4 */
3.  AND   R6,R7,R8     /* R8 <- R6 .and. R7 */
4.  SUB   R4,R5,R7     /* R7 <- R4 - R5 */
5.  CBRA  R7,R4        /* jump to 11, if R7 = 0 */
6.  AND   R1,R8,R9     /* R9 <- R1 .and. R8 */
7.  OR    R11,R9,R9    /* R9 <- R11. or. R9 */
8.  SUB   R9,R10,R12   /* R12 <- R9 - R10 */
9.  ADD   R12,R5,R9    /* R9 <- R12 + R5 */
10. BRA   R5           /* jump to PC + R5 = 14 */
11. OR    R4,R5,R4     /* R4 <- R4 .or. R5 */
12. SUB   R1,R2,R7     /* R7 <- R1 - R2 */
13. LSH   R4,R7        /* Shift R7 with R4 bits */
13. STP                /* stop */
```

Figure 7a: Program Example with Branch Instructions

	OPCODE	OP1	T1	OP2	T2	OP3	T3	DTAG Branch	WINDOW
1	ADD	R1	0	R2	0	R3	0	00	1
2.	OR	R3	1	R4	0	R5	1	00	1
3.	AND	R6	0	R7	0	R8	0	00	1
4.	SUB	R4	0	R5	2	R7	2	00	1
5.	CBRA	R7	3	R4	0	-	-	00	1
6.	AND	R1	0	R8	1	R9	1	10	1
7.	OR	R11	0	R9	2	R9	2	10	1
8.	SUB	R9	3	R10	0	R12	3	10	1
9.	ADD	R12	3	R5	1	R9	3	10	2
10.	BRA	-	-	R5	0	-	-	10	2
11.	OR	R4	0	R5	0	R4	0	01	3
12.	SUB	R1	0	R2	0	R7	0	01	4
13.	LSH	R4	0	-	-	R7	0	01	5

Figure 7b: Post-compiled Program With Dynamic Branch TAG

The impact of a branch instruction on our post-compiling scheme is definitely more complex than the above description. For a forward jump, the data tag scheme is interrupted. Though our tag scheme will recover itself to insure a correct execution, it suffer several idle cycles. Our current solution is to use no-operation (NOOP) instructions to insure that each potential branch-targeted instruction always starts as the first instruction in the window calculation. This avoids any performance penalty for a successful branch. However, we still pay the penalty for an unsuccessful branch. Another situation that requires special attention is when a branch instruction jumps to an instruction which follows another branch instruction. The targeted instruction which inherits a BDTAG from the second branch instruction during the post-compiling time will fail to point to the current situation. We use a hardware flag to solve this problem. The FU which executes the first branch instruction will set a Branch Flag (BFLAG) to 1 if branch is taken, otherwise it will be set it to 0. When a FU sees BFLAG = 1, it will ignore the BDTAG. If the target instruction is another branch instruction, the FU that executes the target instruction needs to set BFLAG = 0. Then, every following instruction is considered to have an adequate

BDTAG. These techniques fail in an indirect branch, since we do not know the target address during the post-compiling. In this case, a FU will idle for few cycles before it starts to execute a new instruction.

The memory instruction with a cache miss has an unknown execution time during the compiling. Our approach is to use a dedicated read/write register with a READY bit, and assign each instruction with a memory tag (MDTAG). When a memory module receives a load request from a FU, it sends a signal through the common control bus to notify each FU whether there is a cache hit or not. If a FU executes an instruction which depends on that memory data, it will not execute the instruction until it is notified with the cache hit. If there is a cache miss, the ID will stop issuing new instructions to FUs immediately. All the instructions in the FUs which need data from that cache-miss data will be frozen and the rest will be completed. As the data is brought from the main memory, the memory module notifies the ID and FUs to resume the normal operation.

We treat a TLB miss as an external interrupt, since we need FUs to process the memory mapping and table updating. Our current thinking about the interrupt and exception is the same as a conventional method. We will not discuss it here since it is beyond the scope of instruction issuing mechanism.

Instruction Issuing Network

The post-compiling technique has eliminated the first step in the conventional issuing methods. Our next goal is to eliminate the second step to achieve a one-step, (n), issuing method. Our approach is to design a multistage network which automatically transmits multiple instructions between the ID and FUs. The network is named instruction network, INET. INET routes instructions by itself with a built-in routing mechanism. It means that the ID does not need to know the status of each FU. It simply sends instructions to the INET which will route instructions to each FU. A FU can accept or reject an incoming instruction. The rejected instructions are routed back to the ID through the INET. They will be re-tried in the next transmission cycle.The basic philosophy used in our automatic routing is to keep sending instructions and ask each FU "Accept it if you can, otherwise return it".

During the routing, the INET needs to maintain the sequential order in the program. Otherwise, a system dead lock will be generated. A system deadlock is generated when the (i+1)-th instruction is routed earlier than the i-th instruction. If the (i+1)-th instruction is routed first, there is a possibility that all FUs are busy and become unable to accept new instructions since they are awaiting the data from the i-th instruction. However, there is no available FU to execute the i-th instruction. This is a subtle point. Though the instructions can be executed out of their sequential order, the issuing needs to follow their sequential order strictly.

Network Topology

The INET is a multistage n by n, circuit-switching, synchronous-controlled network. Each 2*2 switch element has a third control port to the elements above and below it. A built-in logic enables the upper output has a higher priority than the lower one. The switch element always tries to send an input instruction to the upper output port if it is available. The switch element in the last row has an internal buffer to hold blocked instruction. The INET with n = 8 is shown in Figure 8.

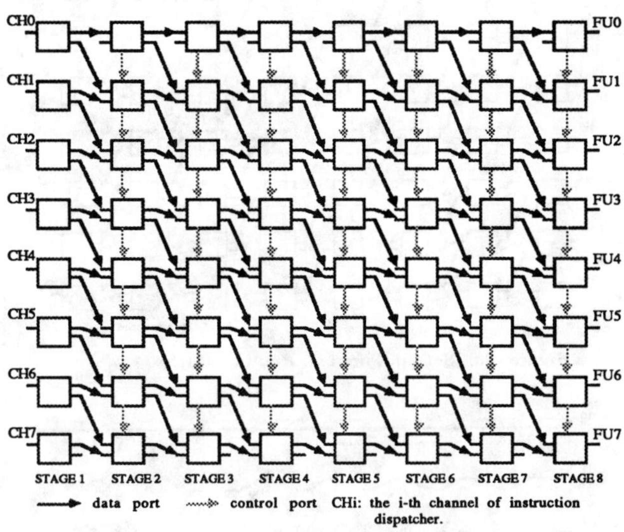

Figure 8: INET with 8 FUs

Network Routing

There are three stages in routing instructions from the ID to FUs. The first stage is to detect the status of FU and set up the forward routing paths for each channel. The second stage is to route the instructions from the ID to FUs. The third stage is to route those un-accepted instructions back to the ID.

In the first stage of a transmission cycle, a FU raises its input port to low or high to indicate that it is able or unable to accept a new instruction in this cycle. The switch element next to it raises both input ports and control output to high if it senses an "disable" FU. Then, each switch element detects the status of its previous elements and the element above it to set up its switch pattern. If both its outputs are high, it raises both input ports and control output to high. It only raises the lower input port and control output to high, if its control input port is high. A high port indicates the path is blocked. A switch element with both its outputs high is unable to receive and transmit any instruction. At the end of the first stage, there is a physical path set-up between a channel and a free FU pair. One example with five busy FUs, b = 5, is shown in Figure 9a. In the second stage, n instructions are routed simultaneously in the INET. There is no switch conflict. Each instruction is either sent to a free FU or blocked in the switch element of the last row, Figure 9b. In the last stage, the blocked instructions are sent one stage forward then routed backward to the ID through the upper port of each elements, Figure 9c.

The functionality of INET can be synthesized as a forward priority tree network and backward sorting tree network. We have investigated INET functionality on other multistage interconnection network [10, 11, 12]. It is verified that we could accomplish the forward routing function by controlling each switch element in any non-blocking interconnection network. However, the complexity of the control logic makes them impractical when n is greater than 8.

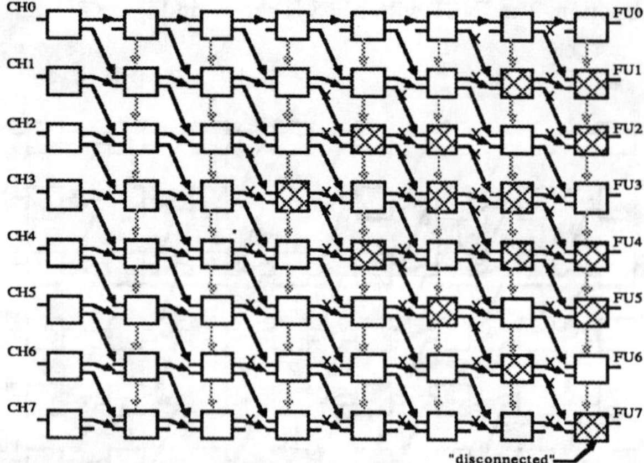

Figure 9a: Set-up Forward Routing Paths

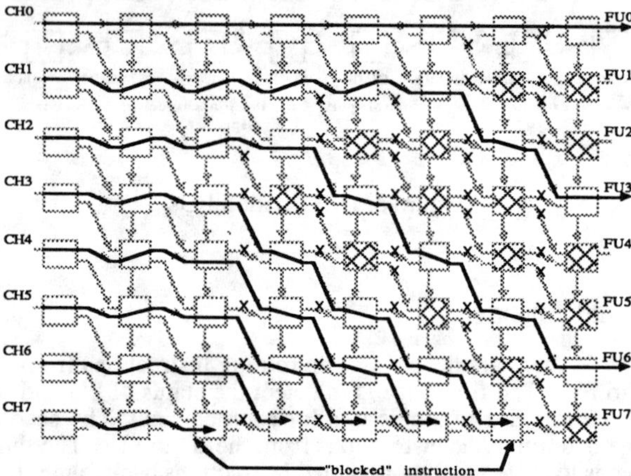

Figure 9b: INET Forward Routing

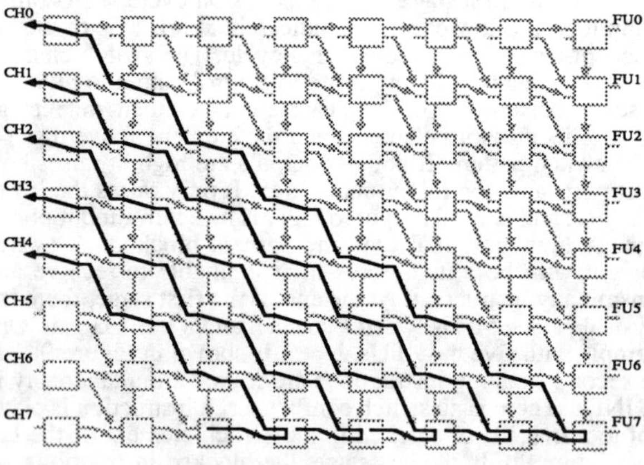

Figure 9c: INET Backward Sorting

FU1, FU2, FU4, FU5, and FU7 are busy and unable to accept new instructions

⊠ : BLOCKED SWITCH ELEMENT

One disadvantage of the INET is its lengthy transmission cycle time. In the first stage of routing, it needs to ripple the status of FUs b-1 stages from FUs toward ID, if there are b busy FUs. It takes n stages for the forward routing phase and n+1 stages for backward sorting. This gives a total 2n+b stages propagation for one transmission cycle. Fortunately, we can overlap the set-up stage with the backward sorting stage and the transmission cycle with the execution cycle. It results in a n+b stage cycle time. With the current CMOS technology, we need about 40ns to accomplish one execution cycle. By assuming a 2ns delay per stage, we feel comfortable in designing the INET for a system with 8 FUs.

Evaluation and Comparison

The I-NET mechanism is evaluated with the matrix program. The result is listed in Table 2. Table 2 shows the instruction in each FU at every cycle. The active instruction is marked with a * sign. For instance, in the 9-th cycle, three instructions, 9, 10 and 12 are executed simultaneously in FU0, FU1 and FU2. The stop instruction, STP, in the 11-th cycle has the BDTAG = 2. If the loop is repeated, the instruction is nullified in the 12-th cycle. Otherwise, the whole execution is terminated when STP is executed in the 12-th cycle. Since each load or store instruction takes two cycles to complete, we modify our data scheme to allow a FU to start executing a load or store instruction when it sees TAG3 = 1. This allows each FU to hold a memory instruction for two cycles. By including the first cycle to fetch instructions from the instruction cache to the ID and the last cycle to write data into the cache, the system takes 13 cycles to complete a loop. It takes 23 cycles in a system with a single CPU with equivalent 3-staged pipeline. We see a 77% performance improvement.

Table 2: The Snapshot of Each FU in Executing the Matrix Program

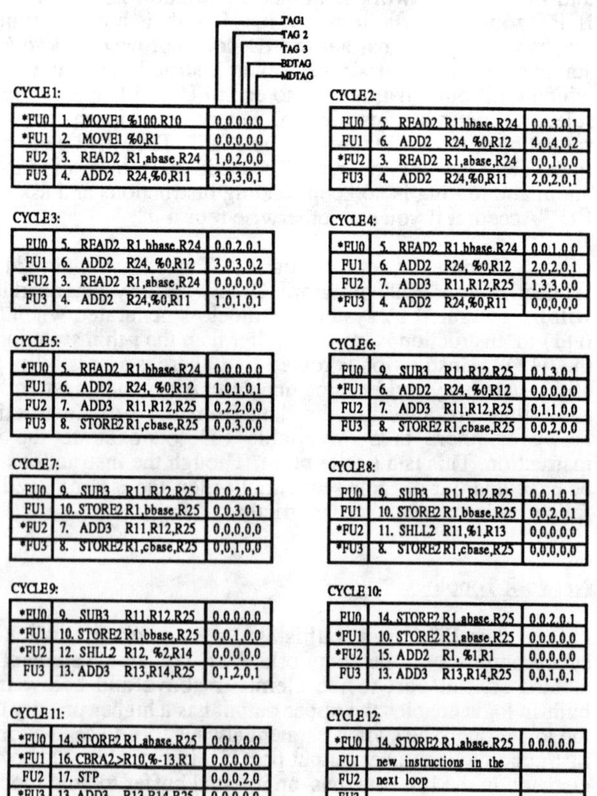

CYCLE 1:

FU	Instruction	Tags
*FU0	1. MOVE1 %100,R10	0,0,0,0,0
*FU1	2. MOVE1 %0,R1	0,0,0,0,0
FU2	3. READ2 R1,abase,R24	1,0,2,0,0
FU3	4. ADD2 R24,%0,R11	3,0,3,0,1

CYCLE 2:

FU	Instruction	Tags
FU0	5. READ2 R1,bbase,R24	0,0,3,0,1
FU1	6. ADD2 R24, %0,R12	4,0,4,0,2
*FU2	3. READ2 R1,abase,R24	0,0,1,0,0
FU3	4. ADD2 R24,%0,R11	2,0,2,0,1

CYCLE 3:

FU	Instruction	Tags
FU0	5. READ2 R1,bbase,R24	0,0,2,0,1
FU1	6. ADD2 R24, %0,R12	3,0,3,0,2
*FU2	3. READ2 R1,abase,R24	0,0,0,0,0
FU3	4. ADD2 R24,%0,R11	1,0,1,0,1

CYCLE 4:

FU	Instruction	Tags
*FU0	5. READ2 R1,bbase,R24	0,0,1,0,0
FU1	6. ADD2 R24, %0,R12	2,0,2,0,1
FU2	7. ADD3 R11,R12,R25	1,3,3,0,0
*FU3	4. ADD2 R24,%0,R11	0,0,0,0,0

CYCLE 5:

FU	Instruction	Tags
*FU0	5. READ2 R1,bbase,R24	0,0,0,0,0
FU1	6. ADD2 R24, %0,R12	1,0,1,0,1
FU2	7. ADD3 R11,R12,R25	0,2,2,0,0
FU3	8. STORE2 R1,cbase,R25	0,0,3,0,0

CYCLE 6:

FU	Instruction	Tags
FU0	9. SUB3 R11,R12,R25	0,1,3,0,1
*FU1	6. ADD2 R24, %0,R12	0,0,0,0,0
FU2	7. ADD3 R11,R12,R25	0,1,1,0,0
FU3	8. STORE2 R1,cbase,R25	0,0,2,0,0

CYCLE 7:

FU	Instruction	Tags
FU0	9. SUB3 R11,R12,R25	0,0,2,0,1
FU1	10. STORE2 R1,bbase,R25	0,0,3,0,1
*FU2	7. ADD3 R11,R12,R25	0,0,0,0,0
*FU3	8. STORE2 R1,cbase,R25	0,0,1,0,0

CYCLE 8:

FU	Instruction	Tags
FU0	9. SUB3 R11,R12,R25	0,0,1,0,1
FU1	10. STORE2 R1,bbase,R25	0,0,2,0,1
*FU2	11. SHLL2 R11,%1,R13	0,0,0,0,0
*FU3	8. STORE2 R1,cbase,R25	0,0,0,0,0

CYCLE 9:

FU	Instruction	Tags
*FU0	9. SUB3 R11,R12,R25	0,0,0,0,0
*FU1	10. STORE2 R1,bbase,R25	0,0,1,0,0
*FU2	12. SHLL2 R12, %2,R14	0,0,0,0,0
FU3	13. ADD3 R13,R14,R25	0,1,2,0,1

CYCLE 10:

FU	Instruction	Tags
FU0	14. STORE2 R1,abase,R25	0,0,2,0,1
*FU1	10. STORE2 R1,abase,R25	0,0,0,0,0
*FU2	15. ADD2 R1, %1,R1	0,0,0,0,0
FU3	13. ADD3 R13,R14,R25	0,0,1,0,1

CYCLE 11:

FU	Instruction	Tags
*FU0	14. STORE2 R1,abase,R25	0,0,1,0,0
*FU1	16. CBRA2,>R10,%-13,R1	0,0,0,0,0
FU2	17. STP	0,0,0,2,0
*FU3	13. ADD3 R13,R14,R25	0,0,0,0,0

CYCLE 12:

FU	Instruction	Tags
*FU0	14. STORE2 R1,abase,R25	0,0,0,0,0
FU1	new instructions in the	
FU2	next loop	
FU3		

An interesting question is how the I-NET mechanism compares with other instruction issuing methods. In order to answer this question, we need to consider many factors, such as issuing rate, cost of issuing, overall performance gain. Instead of pursuing a lengthy and detailed comparison work, we did a very high level comparison from the standpoint of issuing step. We estimated the number of cycles in each step for each method to finish issuing one loop of the matrix program. The result is listed in Table 3. Table 3 shows that a conventional pipeline (1, 1, 1) issuing method needs 21 cycles in each step. This is because there are 5 memory instructions and each memory instruction takes 2 cycles. For Torng's Dispatch Stack, we assume the table has all the instructions before the issuing and the hardware supports multiple table entry search, index updating and instruction issuing. It needs 11 cycles in each step. The improvement over 21 cycles in a (1, 1, 1) is due to multiple functional units. Table 3 shows the I-NET mechanism has the least number of steps among the five issuing methods. It proves the concept of I-NET to move part of issuing work into software is a valid and promising approach in a multiple-functional-unit-system.

Table 3: Number of Steps Need in Different Issuing Mechanisms.

algorithm / issuing stages	Pipeline	Thornton's Scoreboard	Tomasulo's Researvation Station	Torng's Dispatch Stack	I-NET
First Stage	21 steps	16 steps	11 steps	11 steps	0 steps
Second Stage	21 steps	11 steps	11 steps	11 steps	0 steps
Third Stage	21 steps	16 steps	16 steps	11 steps	11 steps
Total	63 steps	43 steps	38 steps	33 steps	11 steps

Conclusion

We have shown that the one-step, (n), I-NET mechanism is a very promising issuing method in exploiting the instruction level parallelism in a multiple-functional-unit system. One argument about the I-NET mechanism is its low logic utilization on functional units. This is true since some of the FUs will be held idle due to data dependence. We are investigating some compiling techniques, such as re-ordering [13], register allocation [14], to improve the logic utilization. We are currently constructing a system [15] based on the I-NET mechanism to study the performance improvement. Also, a great amount of the research effort is devoted to develop a complete post-compiler program [16].

References

[1] R. M .Russell, "The Cray-1 computer system", Commun. ACM, vol. 21, no. 1, pp. 63-72 Jan. 1978.

[2] J. E. Thornton, Design of a Computer System: the Control Data 6600; Scott, Foresman and Company, 1970.

[3] R. M. Tomasulo, "An efficient algorithm for exploiting multiple arithmetic units", IBM Journal, vol. 11, pp. 25-33, Jan. 1967.

[4] R. D. Acosta, J. Kjelstrup, and H. C. Torng, "An instruction issuing approach to enhancing performance in multiple functional unit processors", IEEE Trans. Comput., vol. C-35, no. 9, pp. 815-828, Sep. 1986.

[5] S. Weiss and J. E. Smith, "Instruction issue logic in pipelined supercomputers", IEEE Tran. Comput., vol. C-33, no. 11, pp. 110-118, Nov. 1984.

[6] G. S. Tjaden and M. J. Flynn, "Detection and parallel execution of independent instructions", IEEE Trans. Comput., vol. C-19, no. 10, pp. 889-895, Oct. 1970.

[7] R. M. Keller, "Look-ahead processors", Comput. Surv., vol. 7, no. 4, pp. 63-72, Dec. 1975.

[8] Y. N. Patt, W. M. Hwu and M. Shebanow, "HPS, A new microarchitecture: rationale and introduction", Proceedings of the 18th Microprogramming Workshop, pp.103-108, Dec. 1985.

[9] D. Kuck, et al, "Dependency graphs and compiler optimizations," Proceeding of the 8th POPL, Jan. 1981.

[10] C. Wu and T. Feng, "On a class of multistage interconnection networks", IEEE Trans. Comput., pp. 125-133, Aug. 1980.

[11] L.R. Goke and G. J. Lipovski, "Banyan networks for partitioning multiprocessor systems", IEEE the 1-th Ann. Symp. on Comput. Arch., pp. 21-28, Dec. 1973.

[12] D. H. Lawrie,"Access and alignment of data in an array processor", IEEE Tran. on Computer, vol.C-24, No.12, pp. 1145-1154, Dec. 1975.

[13] J. Hennessy and T. Gross, "Postpass code optimization of pipeline constraints," ACM Trans. on Pro. Lan. Sys., pp. 248-274, Jul. 1983.

[14] G. J. Chaitin, et al, "Register allocation via coloring," Computer Languages, vol. 6, no. 1, pp .47-57, 1981.

[15] L. Wang and C. L. Wu," Distributed instruction set computer", in Proc. 88 Int. Conf. Parallel Processing, St. Charles, Illinois, Aug. 1988.

[16] L. Wang, D. Z. Ju, J. M. Chai, and C. L. Wu, "An early bounding algorithm for fine-grain parallel processing", the 3nd Int. Conf. on Arch. Support for Prog. Lang. and Opert. Sys., Apr. 1989 (submission).

Compiler Evaluation

Chair: John Levesque
Pacific Sierra Research

Vectorizing Compilers: A Test Suite and Results

David Callahan

Computer Science Department
Rice University
Houston, Texas 77251

Jack Dongarra* and David Levine*

Mathematics and Computer Science Division
Argonne National Laboratory
Argonne, Illinois 60439-4801

ABSTRACT

This report describes a collection of 100 Fortran loops used to test the effectiveness of an automatic vectorizing compiler. We present the results of compiling these loops using commercially available, vectorizing Fortran compilers on a variety of supercomputers, mini-supercomputers, and mainframes.

1. Introduction

This report describes a collection of 100 Fortran loops used to test the effectiveness of an automatic vectorizing compiler. An automatic vectorizing compiler is one that takes code written in a serial language (usually Fortran) and translates it into vector instructions. The vector instructions may be machine specific or in a source form such as the proposed Fortran-8x array extensions or as subroutine calls to a vector library.

The loops in the test suite were written by people involved in the development of vectorizing compilers. Several of the loops we wrote ourselves. All of the loops test a compiler for a specific feature. These loops reflect constructs whose vectorization ranges from easy to challenging to extremely difficult. We have collected the results from compiling these loops using commercially available, vectorizing Fortran compilers on a variety of supercomputers, mini-supercomputers, and mainframes.

This paper is organized into seven sections. Section 2 categorizes the collection of loops used in the test. Section 3 describes the methodology used to perform the test. Section 4 explains how the results were scored. Section 5 presents the results of our testing, and Section 6 analyzes the results. Section 7 contains a discussion of the test suite. In Section 8 we make a few concluding remarks.

2. The Test Suite

The objective of the test suite is to test four broad areas of a vectorizing compiler: dependence analysis, vectorization, idiom recognition, and language completeness. For each of these areas, we have identified a number of subcategories. All of the loops in this test are classified into one of these categories**. A complete listing of the source code for the loops used in this test may be found in [3].

* Work supported in part by the Applied Mathematical Sciences subprogram of the Office of Energy Research, U. S. Department of Energy, under Contract W-31-109-Eng-38.

We define all terms and transformation names but discuss dependence analysis and program transformation only briefly. Recent discussions of these topics can be found in [1] and [4].

2.1 Dependence Analysis

Dependence analysis comprises two areas: global data flow analysis and dependence testing. Global data flow analysis refers to the process of collecting information about array subscripts. Dependence testing refers to the process of testing for memory overlaps between pairs of variables in the context of the global data flow information.

Dependence analysis is the heart of vectorization, but it can be done with very different levels of sophistication ranging from simple pattern matching to complicated procedures that solve systems of linear equations. Many of the loops in this section test the aggressiveness of the compiler in normalizing subscript expressions into linear form for the purpose of enhanced dependence testing.

1. *Linear Dependence Testing.* Given a pair of array references whose subscripts are linear functions of the loop control variables that enclose the references (e.g., the statement A(I)=A(I-1)+A(I) is vectorizable inside a DO I=1,N,2 loop but not a DO I=1,N,1 loop) decide whether the two references ever access the same memory location. When the references do interact, additional information can be derived to establish the safety of loop restructuring transformations.
2. *Induction Variable Recognition.* Recognize auxiliary induction variables (e.g., variables defined by statements such as I=I+1 inside the loop). Once recognized, occurrences of the induction variable can be replaced with expressions involving loop control variables and loop invariant expressions.
3. *Global Data Flow Analysis.* Collect global (entire subroutine) data flow information, such as constant propagation or linear relationships among variables, to improve the precision of dependence testing.
4. *Nonlinear Dependence Testing.* Given a pair of array references whose subscripts are not linear functions, test for the existence of data dependencies and other information.
5. *Interprocedural Data Flow Analysis.* Use the context of a subroutine in a particular program to improve vectorization. Possibilities include in-line expansion, summary information

** Not all the subcategories listed are represented in this report. Missing are subcategories 1.4, 2.6, 2.10, 4.3, 4.9, and 4.12. Over time we plan to add tests for these categories to complete the current set.

(e.g., which variables may or must be modified by an external routine), and interprocedural constant propagation.

6. *Control Flow*. Test to see whether certain vectorization hazards exist and whether there are implied dependencies of a statement on statements that control its execution.

7. *Symbolics*. Test to see whether subscripts are linear after certain symbolic information is factored out or whether the results of dependence testing do not, in fact, depend on the value of symbolic variables.

2.2 Vectorization

A simple vectorizer would recognize single-statement Fortran DO loops that are equivalent to hardware vector instructions. When this strict syntactic requirement is not satisfied, more sophisticated vectorizers can restructure programs so that it is. Here, program restructuring is divided into two categories: transformations to enhance vectorization and idiom recognition. The first is described here, and the other in the next section.

1. *Statement Reordering*. Reorder statements in a loop body to allow vectorization.
2. *Loop Distribution*. Split a loop into two or more loops to allow partial vectorization or more effective vectorization.
3. *Loop Interchange*. Change the order of loops in a loop nest to allow or improve vectorization. In particular, make a vectorizable outer loop the innermost in the loop nest.
4. *Node Splitting*. Break up a statement within a loop to allow (partial) vectorization.
5. *Scalar and Array Expansion*. Expand a scalar into an array or an array into a higher dimensional array to allow vectorization and loop distribution.
6. *Scalar Renaming*. Rename instances of a scalar variable. Scalar renaming eliminates some interactions that exist only because of reuse of a temporary variable and allows more effective scalar expansion and loop distribution.
7. *Control Flow*. Convert forward branching in a loop into masked vector operations; recognize loop invariant IF's (loop unswitching).
8. *Crossing Thresholds (Index Set Splitting)*. Allow vectorization by blocking into two sets. For example, vectorize the statement A(I) = A(N-I) by splitting iterations of the I loop into iterations with I less than N/2 and iterations with I greater than N/2.
9. *Loop Peeling*. Unroll the first or last iteration of a loop to eliminate anomalies in control flow or attributes of scalar variables.
10. *Diagonals*. Vectorize diagonal accesses (e.g., A(I,I)).

2.3 Idiom Recognition

Idiom recognition refers to the identification of particular program forms that have (presumably faster) special implementations.

1. *Reductions*. Computation of a scalar value or values from a vector, such as sum reductions, min/max reductions, dot products, and product reductions.
2. *Recurrences*. Special first- and second-order recurrences that have logarithmically faster solutions or hardware support.
3. *Search Loops*. Searching for the first or last instance of a condition, possibly saving index value(s).
4. *Packing*. Scatter or Gather a sparse vector from or into a dense vector under the control of a bit-mask or an indirection vector.

2.4 Language Completeness

This section tests how effectively the compilers understand the complete Fortran language. Simple vectorizers might limit analysis to DO loops containing only floating point and integer assignments. More sophisticated compilers will analyze all loops and vectorize wherever possible.

1. *Loop Recognition*. Recognition and vectorization of loops formed by backward GO TO's.
2. *Storage Classes and Equivalencing*. Understanding of the scope of local vs. common storage; correct handling of equivalencing.
3. *Parameters*. Analysis of symbolic named constants and vectorization of statements that refer to them.
4. *Non-logical IF's*. Vectorization of loops containing computed GO TO's, assigned GO TO's, arithmetic GO TO's, alternative returns from CALL statements, and END= clauses on I/O statements.
5. *Intrinsic Functions*. Vectorization of or around functions that have elemental (vector) versions such as SIN and COS or known side effects.
6. *I/O Statements*. Vectorization of statements in loops that contain I/O statements.
7. *Call Statements*. Vectorization of statements in loops that contain CALL statements or external function invocations.
8. *Non-local GO TO's*. Branches out of loops and RETURN or STOP statements inside loops.
9. *Vector Semantics*. Load before store and preservation of order of stores.
10. *Data Types*. Vectorization of COMPLEX and INTEGER as well as REAL.
11. *Indirect Addressing*. Vectorization of subscripted subscript references (e.g, A(INDEX(I))) as Gather/Scatter.
12. *Statement Functions*. Vectorization of statements that refer to Fortran statement functions.

3. Testing Methodology

Vendors were mailed a magnetic tape containing all the loops we had collected. They were asked to compile the loops without making any changes* using only the compiler options for automatic vectorization. Thus, the use of compiler directives or interactive compilation features to gain additional vectorizations was not tested. Further, many runtime details of vectorization and what Arnold [2] and Wolfe [5] refer to as "vector optimization" are not tested.

After compiling the loops, the vendors sent back the compiler's output listing (source echo, diagnostics, and messages). We then examined these listings to see which loops had been vectorized. No attempt was made to execute the loops to verify the

* Separate compilation of the subroutines used for interprocedural analysis testing was permitted.

correctness of the compiler-generated code or to measure the efficiency of the code when run.

We mailed a total of approximately 240 loops to each vendor. These consisted of all the different loops we had collected over the past several years. From this set we selected the 100 whose results are presented in this paper. This was done by eliminating loops that tested the same or similar features, tested vector optimization, or contained errors of some sort. The selection of which loops to include was made previous to, and independent of, receiving the results from the vendors.

4. Loop Scoring

We define a statement as vectorizable if one or more of the expressions in the statement involve array references or may be converted to that form. All loops in the test suite consist of one or more such statements.

We define three possible results for a compiler attempting to vectorize a loop. A loop is *vectorized* if the compiler generates vector instructions for all vectorizable statements in the loop. A loop is *partially vectorized* if the compiler generates vector instructions for some, but not all, vectorizable statements in the loop. No threshold is defined for what percentage of a loop needs to be vectorized to be listed in this category, only that some expression in a statement in the loop is vectorized. A loop is *not vectorized* if the compiler does not generate vector instructions for any vectorizable statements within the loop.

For a few loops the IBM and Amdahl compilers generated scalar code even though the compiler indicated vector code was possible. This was because for those loops, scalar code was more efficient for their machines. These loops have been scored as *vectorized* and *partially vectorized*, as appropriate.

The Cray CF77 and CFT77 compiler's conditionally vectorized certain loops. This means that for loops with ambiguous subscripts, a runtime test was compiled that selected a safe vector length†. These loops have been scored as either *vectorized* or *not vectorized* according to whether or not vectorized code would actually be executed at runtime.

For some loops the Cray CFT compiler generated a runtime IF-THEN-ELSE test which executed either a scalar loop or a vectorized loop. These loops have been scored as either *vectorized* or *not vectorized* according to whether or not vectorized code would actually be executed at runtime.

The Alliant, Ardent, Convex, and Stellar compilers support the generation of both parallel and vector code. For some loops the Alliant, Ardent, and Convex compilers generated parallel code but not vector code. This may be because the loop was difficult to vectorize but simple to parallelize, or because parallel execution was the most efficient on these machines. These loops have been scored as *not vectorized.*

Some of the loops are really tests of the underlying hardware and may not accurately reflect the ability of the compiler itself. For example, in the statement A(I)=B(INDEX(I)) a compiler may detect the indirect addressing of array B but not generate vector instructions because the computer does not have hardware support for array references of this form. In this and similar cases, the loop is still scored as *not vectorized.*

† A safe vector length is one which allows the compiler to execute vector instructions and still produce the correct result. E.g., the statement A(I)=A(I-7) with loop increment one may be executed in vector mode with any vector length less than or equal to 7.

5. Results

Tables 1-6 list the results of compiling this set of loops on different computers. Table 1 summarizes the results for all 100 loops. Table 2 is also a summary of all the loops; here, however, the column P/V gives a count of loops that were either fully or partially vectorized. Tables 3-6 contain results by category as defined in Section 2.

Table 1. Summary of Test Suite (100 loops)

Machine	Compiler	V	P	N
Alliant FX/8	FX/Fortran V4.0	68	5	27
Amdahl VP-E Series	Fortran 77/VP V10L30	62	11	27
Ardent Titan-1	Fortran V1.0	62	6	32
CDC Cyber 205	VAST-2 V2.21	62	5	33
CDC Cyber 990E/995E	VFTN V2.1	25	11	64
Convex C Series	FC5.0	69	5	26
Cray Series	CF77 V3.0	69	3	28
CRAY X-MP	CFT V1.15	50	1	49
Cray Series	CFT77 V3.0	50	1	49
CRAY-2	CFT2 V3.1a	27	1	72
ETA-10	FTN 77 V1.0	62	7	31
Gould NP1	GCF 2.0	60	7	33
Hitachi S-810/820	FORT77/HAP V20-2B	67	4	29
IBM 3090/VF	VS Fortran V2.4	52	4	44
Intel iPSC/2-VX	VAST-2 V2.23	56	8	36
NEC SX/2	FORTRAN77/SX V.040	66	5	29
SCS-40	CFT x13g	24	1	75
Stellar GS 1000	F77 prerelease	48	11	41
Unisys ISP	UFTN 4.1.2	67	13	20

Key to symbols for Tables 1-6

V	--	vectorized
P	--	partially vectorized
N	--	not vectorized
V/P	--	fully or partially vectorized

Table 2. Full and Partial Vectorization (100 loops)

Machine	Compiler	V/P	N
Alliant FX/8	FX/Fortran V4.0	73	27
Amdahl VP-E Series	Fortran 77/VP V10L30	73	27
Ardent Titan-1	Fortran V1.0	68	32
CDC Cyber 205	VAST-2 V2.21	67	33
CDC Cyber 990E/995E	VFTN V2.1	36	64
Convex C Series	FC5.0	74	26
Cray Series	CF77 V3.0	72	28
CRAY X-MP	CFT V1.15	51	49
Cray Series	CFT77 V3.0	51	49
CRAY-2	CFT2 V3.1a	28	72
ETA-10	FTN 77 V1.0	69	31
Gould NP1	GCF 2.0	67	33
Hitachi S-810/820	FORT77/HAP V20-2B	71	29
IBM 3090/VF	VS Fortran V2.4	56	44
Intel iPSC/2-VX	VAST-2 V2.23	64	36
NEC SX/2	FORTRAN77/SX V.040	71	29
SCS-40	CFT x13g	25	75
Stellar GS 1000	F77 prerelease	59	41
Unisys ISP	UFTN 4.1.2	80	20

Table 4. Vectorization (34 loops)

Machine	Compiler	V	P	N
Alliant FX/8	FX/Fortran V4.0	20	5	9
Amdahl VP-E Series	Fortran 77/VP V10L30	21	8	5
Ardent Titan-1	Fortran V1.0	19	5	10
CDC Cyber 205	VAST-2 V2.21	20	5	9
CDC Cyber 990E/995E	VFTN V2.1	6	8	20
Convex C Series	FC5.0	25	4	5
Cray Series	CF77 V3.0	18	3	13
CRAY X-MP	CFT V1.15	12	1	21
Cray Series	CFT77 V3.0	8	1	25
CRAY-2	CFT2 V3.1a	3	1	30
ETA-10	FTN 77 V1.0	18	7	9
Gould NP1	GCF 2.0	19	7	8
Hitachi S-810/820	FORT77/HAP V20-2B	24	4	6
IBM 3090/VF	VS Fortran V2.4	19	3	12
Intel iPSC/2-VX	VAST-2 V2.23	17	8	9
NEC SX/2	FORTRAN77/SX V.040	21	5	8
SCS-40	CFT x13g	6	1	27
Stellar GS 1000	F77 prerelease	20	9	5
Unisys ISP	UFTN 4.1.2	19	8	7

Table 3. Dependence Analysis (24 loops)

Machine	Compiler	V	P	N
Alliant FX/8	FX/Fortran V4.0	19	0	5
Amdahl VP-E Series	Fortran 77/VP V10L30	16	1	7
Ardent Titan-1	Fortran V1.0	18	0	6
CDC Cyber 205	VAST-2 V2.21	16	0	8
CDC Cyber 990E/995E	VFTN V2.1	8	0	16
Convex C Series	FC5.0	17	0	7
Cray Series	CF77 V3.0	20	0	4
CRAY X-MP	CFT V1.15	16	0	8
Cray Series	CFT77 V3.0	17	0	7
CRAY-2	CFT2 V3.1a	5	0	19
ETA-10	FTN 77 V1.0	18	0	6
Gould NP1	GCF 2.0	14	0	10
Hitachi S-810/820	FORT77/HAP V20-2B	14	0	10
IBM 3090/VF	VS Fortran V2.4	12	0	12
Intel iPSC/2-VX	VAST-2 V2.23	15	0	9
NEC SX/2	FORTRAN77/SX V.040	17	0	7
SCS-40	CFT x13g	7	0	17
Stellar GS 1000	F77 prerelease	14	0	10
Unisys ISP	UFTN 4.1.2	21	3	0

Table 5. Idiom Recognition (15 loops)

Machine	Compiler	V	P	N
Alliant FX/8	FX/Fortran V4.0	10	0	5
Amdahl VP-E Series	Fortran 77/VP V10L30	11	1	3
Ardent Titan-1	Fortran V1.0	9	0	6
CDC Cyber 205	VAST-2 V2.21	7	0	8
CDC Cyber 990E/995E	VFTN V2.1	3	1	11
Convex C Series	FC5.0	11	0	4
Cray Series	CF77 V3.0	9	0	6
CRAY X-MP	CFT V1.15	10	0	5
Cray Series	CFT77 V3.0	7	0	8
CRAY-2	CFT2 V3.1a	8	0	7
ETA-10	FTN 77 V1.0	7	0	8
Gould NP1	GCF 2.0	8	0	7
Hitachi S-810/820	FORT77/HAP V20-2B	14	0	1
IBM 3090/VF	VS Fortran V2.4	5	1	9
Intel iPSC/2-VX	VAST-2 V2.23	6	0	9
NEC SX/2	FORTRAN77/SX V.040	12	0	3
SCS-40	CFT x13g	5	0	10
Stellar GS 1000	F77 prerelease	4	1	10
Unisys ISP	UFTN 4.1.2	10	2	3

Table 6. Language Completeness (27 loops)

Machine	Compiler	V	P	N
Alliant FX/8	FX/Fortran V4.0	19	0	8
Amdahl VP-E Series	Fortran 77/VP V10L30	14	1	12
Ardent Titan-1	Fortran V1.0	16	1	10
CDC Cyber 205	VAST-2 V2.21	19	0	8
CDC Cyber 990E/995E	VFTN V2.1	8	2	17
Convex C Series	FC5.0	16	1	10
Cray Series	CF77 V3.0	22	0	5
CRAY X-MP	CFT V1.15	12	0	15
Cray Series	CFT77 V3.0	18	0	9
CRAY-2	CFT2 V3.1a	11	0	16
ETA-10	FTN 77 V1.0	19	0	8
Gould NP1	GCF 2.0	19	0	8
Hitachi S-810/820	FORT77/HAP V20-2B	15	0	12
IBM 3090/VF	VS Fortran V2.4	16	0	11
Intel iPSC/2-VX	VAST-2 V2.23	18	0	9
NEC SX/2	FORTRAN77/SX V.040	16	0	11
SCS-40	CFT x13g	6	0	21
Stellar GS 1000	F77 prerelease	10	1	16
Unisys ISP	UFTN 4.1.2	17	0	10

6. Analysis of Results

The average number of loops vectorized (Table 1) was 55%, and vectorized or partially vectorized (Table 2) was 61%. The best results were 69% and 80%, respectively. Of the 100 loops, only 4 were not vectorized or partially vectorized by any of the compilers. All 4 loops can be vectorized by a knowledgeable programmer. There is probably no significant difference between vendors within a few percent of each other. Slight differences may be due to different hardware, the availability of special software libraries, the architecture of a machine being better suited to executing scalar or parallel code for certain constructs, or the makeup of the loops used in our test.

Comparing Table 1 to Table 2, we see that the inclusion of partially vectorized loops in the totals places the Amdahl and Unisys compilers among the top performers. Similarly the CDC Cyber 990E/995E and Stellar compilers, which also did a significant amount of partial vectorization, moved up in the list.

Tables 3-6 show that some compilers did particularly well in certain categories. In the Dependence Analysis category, Unisys vectorized or partially vectorized all 24 loops. Convex had the best result in the Vectorization category, vectorizing 25 and partially vectorizing 4 of the 34 loops. Hitachi did very well in the section on Idiom Recognition, vectorizing 14 of the 15 loops. Cray's CF77 compiler had the best result in the Language Completeness category, vectorizing 22 of the 27 loops.

In analyzing the results we found that some vendors, with approximately equal results, did much better in one category than another. Interprocedural analysis, recognizing loops formed by IF and GOTO statements, and vectorizing loops containing COMMON or EQUIVALENCE statements are examples of such categories. We conclude that the compiler vendors have focused their efforts on particular subsets of the features tested by the suite. Possible reasons might include hardware differences or (self-imposed) limits on compilation time, compilation memory use, or the size of the generated code.

The results reported in this paper were collected over a period of approximately a year. Many of the results are from compilers in production use. Some compilers were in beta test (Alliant FX/Fortran V4.0, Convex FC V5.0, Cray CFT77 V3.0, NEC FORTRAN77/SX V.040), some were in various stages of development of the next release (Gould V2.0, IBM V2.4, Unisys V4.1.2), and some were prerelease systems (Stellar F77, Cray CF77).

In the following subsections, we discuss the results in more detail using the categories defined in Section 2. Results, on a loop-by-loop basis, for all vendors may be found in [3].

6.1 Dependence Analysis

Most compilers vectorized a majority of the linear dependence tests, which analyze subscript expressions and loop control variables to detect access to the same memory location. In the induction variable recognition tests the Unisys compiler did the best job; it vectorized or partially vectorized all the loops. Ardent, Cray CF77, Hitachi and the VAST systems* also did a good job, missing only the loops with an induction variable under an IF.

Alliant, Amdahl, Ardent, Convex, Cray CF77, ETA, and Unisys vectorized both interprocedural analysis tests, and the CFT77 compiler vectorized one, all via a procedure integration capability. The Cray CFT compiler also vectorized one of these loops using a runtime test.

Most compilers did very well in the symbolics section, where the information necessary to recognize dependencies is contained in the loop bounds. Many were also able to do the global analysis necessary to vectorize statements like A(I) = A(I+M) where the value of M was supplied outside the loop block.

6.2 Vectorization

The Vectorization category contained the largest amount of partial vectorization. Most compilers were able to vectorize the tests that required reordering statements within a loop. In loop distribution testing we found most compilers able to do partial vectorization; Alliant, Amdahl, CDC Cyber 205, Hitachi, NEC, and Unisys with their capabilities for vectorizing recurrences completely vectorized at least one of the loops.

Loop interchange was a challenging section: all vendors missed at least 2 of the 4 loops. There were a variety of results in the node-splitting tests. Some vendors, particularly those that could vectorize recurrences, did quite well vectorizing or partially vectorizing most or all of the loops. The scalar expansion tests also showed varied results. All vendors were able to vectorize at least one of the loops. Ardent, Convex, and Hitachi vectorized all 5 loops.

Many vendors did very well in vectorizing loops containing IF tests. Unisys vectorized all 12 loops. Amdahl, Convex, IBM, and Stellar each vectorized 11. Cray CF77, Hitachi, NEC, and the VAST systems vectorized 10.

The tests for crossing thresholds and loop peeling were among the most difficult. These tests require breaking up the loop or peeling off some iterations. Hitachi and NEC were the most successful, followed by Ardent and Convex.

* We use the term VAST systems to refer to the Alliant FX/8, CDC Cyber 205, ETA-10, Gould NP1, and Intel iPSC-VX compilers, all of which were using Pacific Sierra's VAST product as a front-end.

6.3 Idiom Recognition

Idiom recognition, more than the other categories, relies on special-purpose hardware or software to enable the compiler to vectorize some of the loops. All systems vectorized sum and dot product reductions. Most also vectorized product reduction, loops to find the maximum or minimum element in an array, and an unrolled dot product loop. First-order recurrences were vectorized by Alliant, Amdahl, Cray CFT2, Hitachi, NEC, and Unisys. Only Alliant vectorized a second-order recurrence. Only Hitachi vectorized a coupled recurrence.

Many systems had trouble vectorizing search loops and loops that packed or unpacked an array. Both types of loops require an element-by-element search through an array, under the control of an IF test, to look for a certain condition. Amdahl and Hitachi vectorized all 4 loops. Convex, Cray CFT, and NEC vectorized 3 of the loops.

6.4 Language Completeness

Cray CF77 and the VAST systems were the only compilers to vectorize loops formed by IF and GOTO statements. Vectorization of loops containing COMMON and EQUIVALENCE statements showed interesting results. All vendors vectorized either most (5-7) of the 7 loops, or else just 1 or 2. CDC Cyber 205, Cray CF77, and Cray CFT77 vectorized all 7 loops.

There were mixed results in vectorizing loops containing various Fortran constructs. Some of the difficult loops that were vectorized contained an arithmetic IF statement, a WRITE statement, a CALL statement, and a STOP statement. Doing well in these tests were Amdahl, Convex, Cray CF77, CDC Cyber 990E/995E, and Hitachi. Most systems vectorized a loop containing the SIN and COS intrinsic functions.

Almost all of the compilers vectorized Gather/Scatter loops. We believe those compilers that did not vectorize these loops currently lack the hardware necessary to support this type of addressing.

7. Discussion

How good is this test suite? The question can be answered in several ways, but we will address three specific areas: coverage, stress, and accuracy.

7.1 Coverage

By "coverage" we refer to how well the test suite represents typical, common, or important Fortran programming practices. We would like to assert that high effectiveness on the test suite will correspond to high effectiveness in general. Unfortunately, there is no accepted suite of Fortran programs that can be called representative, and so we have no quantitative way of determining the coverage of our suite. We believe, however, that the method used to select the tests has yielded reasonable coverage. This method consisted of two phases.

In the first phase, a large number of loops were collected from several vendors and interested parties. This gave a diverse set of viewpoints, each with a different machine architecture and hence somewhat different priorities. In a few cases the loops represented "real" code from programs that had been benchmarked. The majority, however, were specifically written to test a vectorizing compiler for a particular feature. Independently, the categorization scheme used in Section 2 was developed based on experience and published literature on vectorization.

In the second phase, the test suite was culled from the collected loops by classifying each loop into one or more categories and then selecting a few representative loops from each category. Our interest was in coverage, and since "representative" is not well defined, we made no attempt to weight some of the subcategories more than others by changing the number of loops. Where we felt that testing a subcategory required a range of situations, we included several loops; in other cases we felt that one or two loops sufficed. There is significant weighting between major categories. For example, the test suite places greater emphasis on basic vectorization (34 loops) than on idiom recognition (15 loops). This weighting was an artifact of the selected categories and was reflected in the original collection of samples. We felt that this weighting was reasonable and made no attempt to adjust it.

7.2 Stress

By "stress" we refer to how effectively the test suite tests the limits of the compilers. We want the test to be difficult but not impossible. Again there is no absolute metric against which we can measure the test suite, but we can use the performance of the compilers as a measure. Table 7 lists the results for the various compilers. In this table, each row corresponds to a particular compiler. Rows are sorted in order of decreasing full and partial vectorization (see Table 2). Each column corresponds to a particular loop, and the columns are sorted in order of increasing difficulty.

The loop scores at the bottom of Table 7 are based on the number of compilers that vectorized or partially vectorized the loop. Many of the loops are inherently only partially vectorizable and so we have not attempted to weight full versus partial vectorization. Only in a few cases were loops vectorized by some vendors and only partially vectorized by others. We interpret a low score as an indication of a difficult test. From the table we observe a good distribution of test difficulties from "easy" (everyone vectorizes) to "difficult" (no one even partially vectorizes).

This method of judging difficulty will be skewed if many of the compilers are similar. Using the performance of the compilers to measure the difficulty of the loops assumes that each compiler is an independent measure. When there are significant relationships between compilers, loops may seem artificially easy or difficult depending on whether the related compilers all vectorize or all fail to vectorize. As an example, in our suite, 6 of the 19 compilers vectorize implicit loops constructed from backward GOTO's. Five of these are based on Pacific Sierra Research's's VAST system. The effect on the scoring is that these loops seem easier than some others. On the other hand, in a few cases the VAST systems did comparatively poorly on some loops. Here, the effect on the scoring is that these loops appear more difficult than is perhaps true. Similar relationships exist among some of the other compilers reported on in this paper.

Table 8 contains a matrix of linear correlations between the performance of the systems. Since a large number of loops were vectorized by most of the systems, all of the correlations shown in Table 8 are positive. The correlations between Alliant, CDC Cyber 205, ETA, Gould, and Intel (the VAST systems) are all between 0.81 and 0.91, significantly higher than all other correlations. If we ignore the easy and the difficult tests, more variation appears. Table 9 is the correlation matrix restricted to tests that were vectorized or

Table 7. Loops Sorted by Difficulty

```
Unisys ISP        VVVVVVVVVVVVVVVVVVVVVVVVVVVVVVVVVVVVVVVVVVVVVVVVVVVVVVVVVVVVVV.VVVVVV.VV.VVVVVVVV.VV.......VV..VVVVV.......
Convex C Series   VVVVVVVVVVVVVVVVVVVVVVVVVVVVVVVVVVVVVVVVVVVVVVVVVVVVVVVVVVVVVV.VVVVVVVVVVVV.V.VV.VV.VV....V.V...V............
CRAY CF77 V3.0    VVVVVVVVVVVVVVVVVVVVVVVVVVVVVVVVVVVVVVVVVVVVVVVVVVVV.VVVVVVVVV.V.VVVV..VVV.V.VV..V..VVV.V.VV..V............
Alliant FX/8      VVVVVVVVVVVVVVVVVVVVVVVVVVVVVVVVVVVVVVVVVVVVVVVVVVVVVVVVVVVVVVVVV.VV.V.VV..V..VVVV.............V...
Hitachi S-810/8   VVVVVVVVV.VVVVVVVVVVVVVVVVVVVVVVVVVVVVVVVVVVVVVVVV.V.VVVVV..VVVV..VV...VV.V.V...VVVV.V..V.......V...
NEC SX/2          VVVVVVVVVVVVVVVVVVVVVVVVVVVVVVVVVVVVVVVVVVVVVVVVVV..VVVVVVVV..V..VVV.VVVV..V...V....V.......V......
Amdahl VP-E Ser   VVVVVVVVVVVVVVVVVVVVVVVVVVVVV.VVVVVV.VVVVVVVVVVVV.V.VVVVV..VVV.V.V.VVVVV.VVV...VVVV..V..V..........
ETA-10            VVVVVVVVVVVVVVVVVVVVVVVVVVVVVVVVVVVVVVVVVVVVVVVVVVVVVVVVVVVV.VVVVV.VV.V.V.......VVV.......................
Ardent Titan-1    VVVVVVVVVVVVVVVVVVVVVVVVVVVVVVVVVVVVVVV.VVV.VVVVVVVV.VVVVVVV..VVVV.VVV....V.....VVV.......................
CDC Cyber 205     VVVVVVVVVVVVVVVVVVVVVVVVVVVVVVVVVVVVV.VVVVVVVVVVVVVVVVVVVVVV.VVVVV..V.V.........VVV....V..................
Gould NP1         VVVVVVVVVVVVVVVVVVV.VVVVVVVVVVVVVVVVVVVVVVVVVVV.VVVVVVVVVVVVVVVVVVVVVV..V........V.V.VVV.................
Intel iPSC/2-VX   VVVVVVVVVVVVVVVVVV.VVVVVVVVVVVVVVVVVVVVVVVVVVVVVVV..VVVVVVVVVVVVVV..V...........VVV.....................
IBM 3090/VF       VVVVVVVVVVVVVVVVVVVVV.VVVVVVVVVV.VVVVVVVV.VVVVVVVV.VV..V.V.....VVVV...V..V.VVV..V......................
Stellar GS 1000   VVVVVVVVVVVVVVV..VVVVVVVVVVVVVVVVVVVVVVVVVVVVVVVVVVVVV.V..VVV.V...VV...V.V.....VV......V.....V..........
CRAY CFT V1.15    VVVVVVVVVVVVVVVVVVVVVVVVVVVVVVV.VVVVVV.VVVV..V.V.V..VV..V..........VV.V..VVV...........V...V..........
CRAY CFT77 V3.0   VVVVVVVVVVVV.VVVVVVVVV.VVV.VVVVVVVVV.VVVVV...V.......VVV....VVV...VVV....V..V.......V.VV..V..........
CDC Cyber 990E/   VVVVVVVVV.VV..VVVV.VVVVV....VV.V.VV....VV...V..........V...V....V.....V...V.....VV....V...........
CRAY CFT2 V3.1A   VVVVVVVV.VVVVVVVVVVVV....VVVV.........V...........VV...............V...............V...................
SCS-40            VVVVVVVVVVVVVVVVVV.VVV...V...................V...V......................V..V...........................

                  111111111111111111111111111111111111111111111111111111111111111
                  99999998888888888777777777766666666665555544444333222222222222211099888777766666666665543333211111110000
```

Table 8. Correlation of Compiler Performance

Unisys ISP	1.00																		
Convex C Series	0.50	1.00																	
Alliant FX/8	0.43	0.51	1.00																
Amdahl VP-E	0.37	0.72	0.34	1.00															
CRAY CF77 V3.0	0.36	0.34	0.67	0.22	1.00														
Hitachi S-810/8	0.34	0.58	0.36	0.60	0.24	1.00													
NEC SX/2	0.62	0.63	0.50	0.46	0.44	0.56	1.00												
ETA-10	0.42	0.59	0.91	0.37	0.69	0.38	0.48	1.00											
Ardent Titan-1	0.35	0.67	0.60	0.45	0.53	0.46	0.51	0.65	1.00										
CDC Cyber 205	0.39	0.51	0.82	0.29	0.65	0.40	0.49	0.91	0.57	1.00									
Gould NP1	0.39	0.55	0.82	0.34	0.60	0.35	0.49	0.82	0.52	0.82	1.00								
Intel iPSC/2-VX	0.35	0.55	0.81	0.34	0.60	0.39	0.48	0.85	0.56	0.85	0.85	1.00							
Stellar GS 1000	0.40	0.66	0.45	0.55	0.30	0.54	0.50	0.50	0.52	0.50	0.54	0.60	1.00						
IBM 3090/VF	0.51	0.53	0.46	0.37	0.43	0.32	0.54	0.54	0.47	0.53	0.53	0.59	0.53	1.00					
CRAY CFT V1.15	0.41	0.42	0.31	0.40	0.50	0.39	0.48	0.38	0.36	0.33	0.29	0.31	0.36	0.46	1.00				
CRAY CFT77 V3.0	0.31	0.24	0.35	0.12	0.64	0.12	0.30	0.34	0.49	0.33	0.38	0.39	0.24	0.42	0.52	1.00			
CDC Cyber 990E	0.11	0.35	0.22	0.36	0.14	0.25	0.25	0.28	0.47	0.30	0.30	0.30	0.33	0.33	0.24	0.24	1.00		
CRAY CFT2 V3.1A	0.31	0.32	0.33	0.33	0.34	0.30	0.40	0.32	0.38	0.30	0.30	0.24	0.25	0.33	0.57	0.39	0.23	1.00	
SCS-40	0.29	0.34	0.25	0.30	0.31	0.27	0.37	0.29	0.25	0.31	0.26	0.29	0.34	0.33	0.57	0.57	0.29	0.34	0.67

Table 9. Correlation of Selected Compiler Performance

Unisys ISP	1.00																	
Convex C Series	0.12	1.00																
Alliant FX/8	0.30	-0.02	1.00															
Amdahl VP-E	-0.14	0.44	-0.42	1.00														
CRAY CF77 V3.0	0.05	-0.43	0.42	-0.49	1.00													
Hitachi S-810/8	-0.31	0.19	-0.14	0.52	-0.39	1.00												
NEC SX/2	0.41	0.09	0.04	-0.10	-0.08	0.11	1.00											
ETA-10	0.20	0.20	0.86	-0.31	0.43	-0.10	-0.08	1.00										
Ardent Titan-1	-0.35	0.14	0.25	-0.24	0.13	-0.14	-0.25	0.42	1.00									
CDC Cyber 205	0.11	0.11	0.75	-0.39	0.29	0.10	0.08	0.87	0.31	1.00								
Gould NP1	0.16	0.16	0.66	-0.35	0.21	-0.15	0.00	0.64	0.07	0.79	1.00							
Intel iPSC/2-VX	0.07	0.23	0.70	-0.25	0.23	0.04	0.02	0.81	0.25	0.93	0.87	1.00						
Stellar GS 1000	-0.19	0.47	-0.16	0.39	-0.50	0.24	-0.11	-0.05	-0.01	0.05	0.15	0.11	1.00					
IBM 3090/VF	0.35	0.02	-0.10	-0.29	0.02	-0.47	0.11	0.02	-0.25	0.13	0.22	0.19	-0.14	1.00				
CRAY CFT V1.15	0.18	-0.18	-0.38	0.10	0.04	-0.09	0.00	-0.29	-0.38	-0.37	-0.41	-0.33	-0.26	0.21	1.00			
CRAY CFT77 V3.0	-0.02	-0.52	0.14	-0.52	0.69	-0.53	-0.26	0.10	0.14	0.05	0.15	0.11	-0.56	0.16	0.26	1.00		
CDC Cyber 990E	-0.37	0.00	-0.21	0.10	-0.29	0.09	-0.17	-0.12	0.46	-0.04	-0.08	0.00	0.09	-0.13	-0.14	-0.09	1.00	
CRAY CFT2 V3.1A	0.12	-0.30	0.15	0.10	-0.21	0.14	0.17	-0.21	-0.24	-0.18	-0.19	-0.17	-0.14	-0.15	-0.11	-0.14	-0.11	1.00
SCS-40	0.12	0.12	-0.24	0.10	-0.21	0.14	0.17	-0.21	-0.24	-0.18	-0.19	-0.17	0.26	-0.15	0.33	-0.14	-0.11	-0.04

partially vectorized by no more than half the highest score nor less than one fourth of the maximum score. Scores were computed with only one VAST system represented. This table still shows high positive correlations between the VAST systems but also shows some high negative correlations, such as -0.49 between Cray CF77 V3.0 and Amdahl. We assume these negative correlations are the effects of different machine architectures and different decisions by the vendors about what is important or worthwhile.

7.3 Accuracy

By "accuracy" we refer to how well the test can measure the quality of a vectorizing compiler. Since the difficulty of the tests was determined by the performance of the compilers, it would be circular now to judge the absolute quality of the compilers by their performance on this suite. What about relative performance? It is tempting to distill the results for each compiler into a single number and use that to compare the systems. Such an approach, however, is clearly incorrect, since these compilers cannot be compared in isolation from the machine environment and target application area for which they were designed. The negative correlations in Table 9 support the view that multiple distinct, but correlated factors are involved.

We conclude that the suite represents reasonable coverage and adequate stress, but that we cannot determine the accuracy of the suite.

8. Conclusion

Our initial goal has been twofold: (1) to compare the ability of different Fortran compilers to automatically vectorize various loops, and (2) to try to understand their capabilities and limitations. The real test of a vectorizing compiler can be determined only by actually comparing the execution time of the vectorized and non-vectorized code. We caution that the information presented here tests only one aspect of a compiler and should in no way be used to judge the overall performance of a vectorizing compiler or computer system. The results reflect only a limited spectrum of Fortran constructs. Also, subsequent compiler and hardware changes may affect which loops can be vectorized.

We intend to update and expand the results presented here. In particular, we plan to develop a check to verify the correctness of the compiler-generated code and a measure of its efficiency. A copy of the source code used in the test is available from netlib at Argonne National Laboratory. To receive a copy of the code, send electronic mail to netlib@anl-mcs.arpa. In the mail message, type:

send vector from benchmark

Acknowledgments

We thank all the people who have helped us put together this collection of loops and results. Particular thanks are given to people at IBM in Kingston, N.Y., Steve Wallach of Convex Computer Corporation, and Michael Wolfe of Kuck & Associates who provided an initial set of loops used as the basis of this test.

REFERENCES

[1] J. R. Allen and K. Kennedy, "Automatic translation of FORTRAN programs to vector form," *TOPLAS*, vol. 9, no. 4, pp. 491-542, October 1987.

[2] C. Arnold, "Vector optimization on the Cyber 205," Proc. of the International Conf. for Parallel Processing, pp. 530-536, August 1983.

[3] D. Callahan, J. Dongarra, and D. Levine, "Vectorizing compilers: A test suite and results," Argonne National Laboratory MCS-TM-109, March 1988.

[4] D. Padua and M. Wolfe, "Advanced compiler optimizations for supercomputers," *CACM*, vol. 29, no. 12, pp. 1184-1201, December 1986.

[5] M. Wolfe, "Vector optimization vs. vectorization," Proc. of the 1987 Conf. on Supercomputing, Athens, Greece, June 1987.

AN EVALUATION OF VECTOR FORTRAN 200 GENERATED BY CYBER 205 AND ETA-10 PRE-COMPILATION TOOLS

Robert N. Braswell and Malcolm S. Keech

Florida State University Computing Center
Tallahassee, FL 32306-3042

ABSTRACT

Vectorizing pre-compilers such as KAP/205 and VAST-2 complement the efficient use of FORTRAN on the CDC Cyber 205. With the advent of the ETA-10 and its EOS/VSOS environment, the performance of these FORTRAN 200 pre-processors has come under closer scrutiny. The extent or quantity of vectorization that can be achieved has been examined elsewhere with reference to a test set of FORTRAN DO-loops. The quality of the translated code is another issue which deserves attention of course. KAP/205 and VAST-2 will be contrasted in this respect to reveal differences in the vectorized FORTRAN.

1. Introduction

This paper follows up on an earlier investigation [1,2] of vectorization by FORTRAN 200 [3] pre-processors for the CDC Cyber 205 and ETA-10. The pre-compilation tools under consideration are VAST-2 [4] from Pacific-Sierra Research Corporation and KAP/205 [5] from Kuck and Associates, Inc. An up-to-date version of VAST-2 is available in a different guise on the ETA-10 as ETA VAST-2 [6]. The discussion here will focus on the relative merits of these products on program execution with regard to a test set of FORTRAN DO-loops [7].

The distinction is drawn between the quantity and quality of vectorization achieved by the compiler and pre-compilers. Of primary importance is whether or not 'prominent' loops are vectorized in the first place. Accepting that this is a requirement, whenever possible, the question becomes one of what will happen at run-time? (We do not address the issue of code restructuring here.) An assessment is made of the vector FORTRAN 200 generated and compared with actual performance on the Cyber 205 and ETA-10.

2. Vectorizers

As a matter of convenience, we choose to distinguish four vectorization tools namely the FORTRAN 200 automatic vectorizer, VAST-2, KAP/205 and ETA VAST-2. Of course, ETA VAST-2 merely represents a further development by Pacific-Sierra of the VAST-2 product line, but there are several differences in its structure and use.

The ability of FORTRAN 200 to automatically vectorize DO-loops has been much-maligned over the years. This is because certain loop constructs (e.g. conditional statements) inhibit vectorization and others are not recognized as vectorizable due to the limited scope of code inspection. The effectiveness of FORTRAN 200 when succeeding in translating loops has been the subject of less criticism. In fact, exception case apart, one philosophy that can be adopted in practice is to allow full compiler optimization and hand-select important (but neglected) loop vectorization with the pre-compiler of choice.

The original Vector and Array Syntax Translator, VAST, became available early and provided an alternative method of achieving 'portable' vectorization. There has been significant improvement with VAST-2 which emerged along with the Kuck Analyzer Program, KAP/205, last year. These two pre-compilers cover similar ground but may go about realizing vectorization in rather different ways. This can have a significant bearing on the run-time

CH2617-9/88/0000/0106$01.00 © 1988 IEEE

efficiency of a program.

3. Test Loops

Although the 'acid test' is to compare the performance of vectorizers when working with real live codes, it is instructive to create and test model DO-loops encompassing a broader range of FORTRAN constructs. A test set of seventy-two FORTRAN loop cases has been constituted [7], there being ninety loops in total. It must be pointed out that some of the loops may appear pathological, but this serves to reflect the customary balance in a typical large program.

The test set by no means represents a comprehensive collection, but includes examples from the following five categories :

- Index Expressions (14 cases)
- Reduction Functions (12)
- Conditionals (14)
- Data Dependency (17)
- Nested Loops (15 cases, 33 loops)

Notable omissions include subroutine/function handling and IF loops.

The 'index expressions' category covers various non-sequential methods of array addressing including the use of constant increment integers, non-linear indexing and non-unit loop incrementation. Recognition of 'reduction functions' is tested by the usual dot product, maximum/minimum and position of elements strategy. 'Conditionals' includes an assortment of loops containing conditional statements, e.g. logical, arithmetic and block IFs. 'Data dependency' brings together loops that are potentially recursive in various different ways, although they may be safe to vectorize in practice. Finally, the 'nested loops' category exhibits multiple loops that can be collapsed (into one), interchanged or exploited in other ways to achieve better vectorization.

A detailed breakdown of loops vectorized appears elsewhere [2] and a summary table is given in the Appendix. It turns out that the success rate quoted by any given product does require some interpretation. Moreover, it is not always clear which of the vector versions generated is going to perform best on execution, if indeed any advantage has been gained at all over scalar. Eighteen of the loop cases were of particular interest in this respect. They have been selected from the original seventy-two to highlight differences in the vectorizers that might not otherwise have been obvious.

4. Subjective Performance Evaluation

The first thing that is apparent on inspection of the vectorized code is that KAP/205 employs the FORTRAN 200 descriptor notation, while VAST-2 deals directly with explicit vectors. (No impact on performance of course.) The subset of eighteen loop cases is treated in some detail below, there being twenty-two loops in all. A degree of familiarity with certain non-standard, vector features of FORTRAN 200 is assumed.

(a)
```
C     Gather Counter (1,3,6,10,...)
      J=0
      DO 150 I=1,N
      J=J+I
150   A(I)=B(J)
```

VAST-2 sets up an index vector for J in a scalar loop and partially vectorizes to the extent of invoking Q8VGATHR. KAP/205 leaves entirely scalar, but this might not affect run-time efficiency much.

(b)
```
C     Non-Unit Increment 2
      DO 210 1=1,N,2
210   A(I)=B(I)+C(I)
```

VAST-2 gathers up the right-hand side vectors via Q8VGATHP, performs the vector summation and scatters back via Q8VSCATP. KAP/205 does the same. ETA VAST-2 employs the Q8VMKO function to create an alternating bit mask within a WHERE statement and performs the vector summation for all I, storing only alternate values. The last method ought to be superior.

(c)
```
C     Negative Increment
      DO 230 I=N,1,-1
230   A(I)=B(I)+C(I)
```

VAST-2 gathers up the right-hand side vectors again, performs the vector summation and scatters back. KAP/205 reverses the vectors via the Q8VREV function, performs the summation and reverses back. The latter approach is likely to be more efficient (although neither pre-compiler has taken the opportunity to run the loop forwards).

```
(d) C     Position of Maximum
          J=1
          S=A(1)
          DO 300 I=2,N
          IF(A(I).GT.S) THEN
             S=A(I)
             J=I
          ENDIF
      300 CONTINUE
```

VAST-2 employs the Q8SMAXI function while KAP/205 invokes the Q8MAX special call statement. Q8 special calls directly generate machine language instructions on the Cyber 205 and sometimes have the ability to perform certain operations 'on-the-fly', achieving increased efficiency.

```
(e) C     Position of Last Positive
          DO 330 I=1,N
      330 IF(A(I).GT.0.0) J=I
```

VAST-2 leaves scalar while KAP/205 sets up a bit vector for the IF condition, uses Q8VINTL to count forwards and appeals to the Q8MAX special call under the control of the bit vector. Even though it seems like a lot of effort to expend to achieve vectorization here, it may be of value.

```
(f) C     Arithmetic IF (3-Way)
          DO 380 I=1,N
          IF(IA(I)) 20,30,40
       20 A(I)=B(I)
          GO TO 380
       30 B(I)=C(I)
          GO TO 380
       40 C(I)=D(I)
      380 CONTINUE
```

VAST-2 uses a WHERE statement three times to vectorize the loop, hence performing three times the amount of work, while KAP/205 leaves scalar. This effort may well be worthwhile.

```
(g) C     Redundant IF
          DO 420 I=1,N
      420 IF(B(I).NE.0.0)A(I)=A(I)+B(I)*(C(I)+D(I))
```

VAST-2 uses WHERE, whereas KAP/205 detects the redundancy and performs a straight vector assignment. There should be some advantage in the latter approach.

```
(h) C     Special/Cut-Off Points
          DO 440 I=1,N
          A(I)=SQRT(B(I)+C(I))
          IF(I.EQ.J) A(I)=-A(I)
          IF(I.LE.K) THEN
             A(I)=A(I)*D(I)
             D(I)=B(I)*C(I)
          ENDIF
      440 CONTINUE
```

VAST-2 employs the VSQRT function and then Q8VINTL twice within respective WHEREs, while KAP/205 does the same but saves one of the Q8VINTLs. It is clear that there should be some small benefit here.

```
(i) C     Last Value OK
          DO 470 I=1,N
          S=0.0
          IF(A(I).GT.0.0) GO TO 470
          S=B(I)+C(I)
      470 D(I)=S**2
```

VAST-2 promotes S to a vector and forms a WHERE block around the (now) two vector assignments. KAP/205 essentially does the same thing but uses two WHERE statements and the Q8LOD special call (twice) to load the last value(s) from the promoted vector into S. The latter method seems a little more cumbersome.

```
(j) C     Scalar Feedback
          DO 570 I=1,N
          C(I)=1.0/S
      570 S=A(I)+B(I)
```

VAST-2 vectorizes the numeric operations involved but fails to grasp the full opportunity available, leaving behind copy-overs from/to S in a scalar loop. KAP/205 leaves the loop entirely scalar. The former approach ought to reap some benefit.

(k) C Irrelevant Recursion

```
      DO 590 I=1,N
590   A(I)=A(N/2)
```

VAST-2 fails to vectorize this loop unless directed, while KAP/205 gathers up the right-hand side (repeatedly) into a vector. This method is successful but once VAST-2 is directed it performs a straight vector assignment, with the obvious conclusion.

(l) C Non-Existent Recursion

```
      DO 600 I=1,N
600   A(I)=B(I)-A(N*N)
```

VAST-2 fails again to vectorize this loop unless directed, while KAP/205 goes ahead with the vector assignment.

(m) C Single Statement Recursion

```
      DO 640 I=1,N-1
      S=A(I)*B(I)+C(I)
      D(I+1)=E(I)/D(I)+S
640   F(I)=E(I)+F(I)*S
```

VAST-2 promotes S to a vector and translates both non-recursive statements, while KAP/205 leaves the loop entirely scalar. This partial vectorization should be useful.

(n) C Partial Expression Recursion

```
      DO 650 I=1,N-1
650   A(I+1)=B(I)+S*C(I)+T*D(I)+E(I)*F(I)/A(I)
```

VAST-2 vectorizes all operations bar the recursive divide and final summation, while KAP/205 leaves the loop entirely scalar. Again, this partial vectorization should be useful.

(o) C Statement in Outer Loop

```
      DO 700 J=1,M
      G(J)=H(J)
      DO 700 I=1,N
700   A2(I,J)=B2(I,J)+C2(I,J)
```

VAST-2 only vectorizes the inner loop here, while KAP/205 collapses the nested pair. This case has been selected primarily because FORTRAN 200 vectorizes both loops also!

(p) C Single Dimension Receiver

```
      K=0
      DO 730 J=1,M
      DO 730 I=1,N
      K=K+1
730   A(K)=B2(I,J)+C2(I,J)
```

VAST-2 and KAP/205 both vectorize the inner loop only, while FORTRAN 200 claims to vectorize the pair. Performance on execution will confirm the effectiveness (or otherwise) of the latter approach.

(q) C Inner Loop Falls Shorter

```
      DO 750 J=1,M
      DO 750 I=3,N-2
750   A2(I,J)=B2(I,J)+C2(I,J)
```

Both VAST-2 and KAP/205 only vectorize the inner loop again. However, when appropriate, VAST-2 can be directed to 'picture-frame' collapse the pair under the control of a WHERE statement. The value of N would be expected to determine run-time efficiency.

(r) C Inner Loops Recursive

```
      DO 820 I=1,N
      DO 800 J=1,M-1
800   A2(I,J+1)=A2(I,J)+C2(I,J)
      DO 810 J=1,L-1
810   B2(I,J+1)=B2(I,J)=C2(I,J)
820   CONTINUE
```

VAST-2 fails to vectorize any loop at all. KAP/205 performs the required interchange vectorizing along the outer I loop. ETA VAST-2 is able to achieve this translation also.

5. Actual Performance Information

Tables of results are given below for loop execution on the Cyber 205 using code generated by the following products (and options):

FTN200 Level 678B (OPT=V)
VAST-2 Version 2.21K8 (OPT=2)
KAP/205 Version 4.24.01 (O=4)
ETA VAST-2 Version 2.23C26 (V=D)

	FTN200	VAST-2	KAP/205	ETA VAST-2
(a)	0.00650	0.00356	0.00502	0.00352
(b)	0.00093	0.00077	0.00078	0.00062
(c)	0.00138	0.00124	0.00085	0.00121
(d)	0.00870	0.00071	0.00066	0.00072
(e)	0.00806	0.00703	0.00254	0.00703
(f)	0.01504	0.00127	0.01562	0.00141
(g)	0.01573	0.00082	0.00060	0.00084
(h)	0.03038	0.00257	0.00228	0.00257
(i)	0.01262	0.00099	0.00095	0.00098
(j)	0.01946	0.01100	0.01719	0.00819
(k)	0.00602	0.00603 (1)	0.00116	0.00522
(l)	0.00883	0.00883 (2)	0.00028	0.00705
(m)	0.03925	0.02029	0.03607	0.01970
(n)	0.03728	0.01849	0.03376	0.01845
(o)	0.00165	0.00346	0.00126	0.00347
(p)	0.00892	0.00196	0.00198	0.00197
(q)	0.00223	0.00197 (3)	0.00197	0.00197
(r)	0.19405	0.16505	0.00360	0.00360

Table 1: CPU Times for Cyber 205 with N=100, M=10

(1) VAST-2+directive timing is 0.00026
(2) " " 0.00027
(3) " " 0.00159

	FTN200	VAST-2	KAP/205	ETA VAST-2
(a)	0.16096	0.12817	0.14395	0.12835
(b)	0.00539	0.00520	0.00518	0.00346
(c)	0.00939	0.00918	0.00555	0.00943
(d)	0.08142	0.00539	0.00534	0.00538
(e)	0.08007	0.07006	0.02148	0.07005
(f)	0.15011	0.00603	0.15012	0.00602
(g)	0.15716	0.00442	0.00330	0.00442
(h)	0.23932	0.01719	0.01509	0.01717
(i)	0.12221	0.00455	0.00458	0.00454
(j)	0.19422	0.10781	0.17225	0.11362
(k)	0.06008	0.05206 (1)	0.00961	0.05207
(l)	0.08808	0.08406 (2)	0.00118	0.08017
(m)	0.39595	0.19265	0.36449	0.19269
(n)	0.37623	0.18151	0.34089	0.18150
(o)	0.06876	0.07869	0.06650	0.07876
(p)	0.39143	0.07142	0.07120	0.07162
(q)	0.07089	0.07003 (3)	0.07001	0.07109
(r)	15.07476	14.78657	0.07420	0.07440

Table 2: CPU Times for Cyber 205 with N=1000, M=50

(1) VAST-2+directive timing is 0.00117
(2) " " 0.00119
(3) " " 0.07878

VAST-2 partial vectorization employed. This is counter-balanced to some extent by the (scalar) loop-unrolling performed by KAP/205 here. In the second case, (b), ETA VAST-2 does adopt a more effective technique, especially for longer vector lengths.

It turns out that the use by KAP/205 of a Q8 special call in case (d) does not deliver increased efficiency over the VAST-2 version, which is therefore considered more user friendly. The effort expended by KAP/205 in case (e) is indeed worthwhile - it is better to vectorize, albeit in a complicated fashion, than to not vectorize at all. By the same token, vectorization of case (f) by VAST-2 pays great dividends for this arithmetic IF construct.

The partial vectorization achieved by VAST-2 in the recursive cases (j), (m), and (n) is beneficial compared to the scalar KAP/205 approach. The two cases (k) and (l) where VAST-2 was concerned about data dependency highlight both the negative and positive side of user direction. VAST-2 performs much better than KAP/205 when directed in the former case, achieving parity in the latter. However, the pre-compiler should not really require direction for these loops in the first place.

Performance in the case (o), where FORTRAN 200 and KAP/205 both vectorize the nested pair, is interesting. VAST-2 translates only the inner loop and suffers at the shorter vector lengths, although this deficiency appears to diminish as N, M increase. Conversely, the FORTRAN 200 claim to vectorization of the nested pair in case (p) is not effective on execution. Both VAST-2 and KAP/205 do much better with just the inner loop.

The VAST-2 picture-frame collapse ability is demonstrated, under user direction, by case (q). This yields a positive outcome for the shorter vector lengths, but begins to go the other way as N, M increase. Finally, case (r) illustrates the dramatic improvement that can be made by a pre-compiler. FORTRAN 200 and VAST-2 are unable to perform any translation here, but both KAP/205 and ETA VAST-2 vectorize along the outer loop giving a speed-up of roughly 200 times over pure scalar.

It has been shown that genuine run-time performance differences sometimes arise from translations of FORTRAN DO-loops for the Cyber 205 and ETA-10. Moreover, remaining scalar is not usually a good idea if something constructive can be done instead. The picture presented is not uniform across the products but does serve to emphasise the respective merits of KAP/205 and VAST-2.

Appendix

NUMBER OF LOOPS TRANSLATED BY VECTORIZERS

	FTN200	VAST-2	VAST2+dir	KAP/205	ETAVAST-2	ETAVST2+dir
Index Expns	11	11+2		11	11+2	
Reduction Fns	3	9		10	9	
Conditionals	0	11		9	11	
D. Dependency	3(!)	7+3	9+3	8+1	6+3	8+3
Nested Loops	19	19	21	22+1	20	22
TOTAL	36(!)	57+5	61+5	60+2	57+5	61+5

+n denotes extra loops partially (or conditionally) vectorized

All FORTRAN 200 scalar optimization has been suppressed in the runs, but maximum vector optimization has been selected. Full details of the test program will be available in reference [8].

The timing for an individual loop/vectorizer combination is given in seconds and corresponds to 100 trips round each case in question. This is done in an attempt to minimize discrepancy, but there have been minor fluctuations from run to run. Note that when user directives are allowed, VAST-2 can achieve improved timings in Tables 1 and 2.

Table 3 has been drawn up to illuminate the relative performance of the products. An asterisk (*) denotes superior performance of a particular vectorizer, while a hyphen (-) denotes tied situations. The effect of user directives is highlighted by annotation in three cases and ETA VAST-2 shown as an extra column when appropriate. Information in the table is biased in favor of the longer vector length and, hence, the more general case on the Cyber 205/ETA-10.

The ETA VAST-2 column in Table 3 should be interpreted as an indication of some further benefit that can be realized over and above (205) VAST-2. It is worth recording the ETA VAST-2 timings on the ETA-10 for the two active entries:

N=100, M=10	(b) 0.00034
	(r) 0.00135
N=1000, M=50	(b) 0.00185
	(r) 0.03614

The clock cycle time on the Cyber 205 is 20 nanoseconds, whereas on the ETA-10 it is 10.5 nanoseconds currently.

6. Final Analysis

Some concluding remarks are made relating the evaluation in section 4 to the information in section 5. The first loop case, (a), demonstrates that some advantage can be gained by the

	FTN200	VAST-2	KAP/205	ETA VAST-2
(a) Gather Counter		*		
(b) Non-Unit Increment 2	-	-	-	*
(c) Negative Increment			*	
(d) Position of Maximum		-	-	
(e) Position of Last Positive			*	
(f) Arithmetic IF (3-Way)		*		
(g) Redundant IF			*	
(h) Special/Cut-Off Points			*	
(i) Last Value OK		-	-	
(j) Scalar Feedback		*		
(k) Irrelevant Recursion			* (1)	
(l) Non-Existent Recursion			* (2)	
(m) Single Statement Recn.		*		
(n) Partial Expression Recn.		*		
(o) Statement in Outer Loop	-		-	
(p) Single Dimension Receiver		-	-	
(q) Inner Loop Falls Shorter	-	- (3)	-	
(r) Inner Loops Recursive			*	*

Table 3: Evaluation of Run-Time Performance

(1) VAST-2 performs much better than KAP/205 when directed
(2) VAST-2 performs the same as KAP/205 when directed
(3) VAST-2 performs differently when directed

Acknowledgements

This research was supported in part by the Florida State University through time granted on its Cyber 205 supercomputer. We are grateful to ETA Systems and FSU for access to the ETA-10 (Model E) located at FSU Computing Center. The views and opinions expressed in this paper do not imply endorsement by CDC, ETA Systems, FSU or any other agency referred to herein.

References

[1] R. N. Braswell and M. S. Keech, "Extent of Vectorization achieved by FORTRAN 200 Pre-Processors for the Cyber 205 and ETA-10 Supercomputers", Proceedings of the Third International Conference on Supercomputing, Vol. III, pp. 441-4, 1988.

[2] M. S. Keech, "Performance of FORTRAN 200 Pre-Processors on a DO-Loops Benchmark: I - Quantity of Vectorization", Technical Report #3, FSU Computing Center, Tallahassee, May 1988.

[3] FORTRAN 200 Version 1 Reference Manual, Revision J, CDC, October 1987.

[4] VAST-2 Version 2 User's Guide, Revision A, ETA Systems, Inc., June 1987.

[5] KAP/205 User's Guide, Version 4, Kuck and Associates, Inc., 1987.

[6] ETA VAST-2 Release 1 User's Guide and Reference, Revision A, ETA Systems, Inc., November 1987.

[7] M. S. Keech, "Test Loops for FORTRAN 200 Vectorizers", Technical Report #2, FSU Computing Center, Tallahassee, April 1988.

[8] M. S. Keech, "Performance of FORTRAN 200 Pre-Processors on a DO-Loops Benchmark: II - Quality of Vectorization", Technical Report, FSU Computing Center, Tallahassee, to appear.

Cedar Fortran* and Other Vector and Parallel Fortran Dialects

Mark D. Guzzi, David A. Padua, Jay P. Hoeflinger, Duncan H. Lawrie**

University of Illinois at Urbana-Champaign
Center for Supercomputing Research and Development
305 Talbot Laboratory / 104 S. Wright Street
Urbana, Illinois 61801

ABSTRACT

The introduction of vector processors and multiprocessors punctuate the most dramatic changes in Fortran and its dialects. The emerging generation of supercomputers utilize both vector processing and multiprocessing simultaneously. The challenge is to provide language constructs and software tools that will allow the programmer to easily exploit the capabilities of the machine.

This paper will outline the development of vector and multiprocessor language constructs in Fortran. The significant architectures, their languages, and optimizers will be described. The paper concludes with a description of Cedar Fortran, the language for the Cedar Multiprocessor under development at the University of Illinois, Urbana-Champaign. Cedar is a hierarchical, shared-memory, vector multiprocessor. As such, its language, Cedar Fortran, contains many of the language features that will be described for vector processors and multiprocessors.

1. Introduction

The study of supercomputers and their languages is very much a study in evolution. It is a study of gradual development punctuated with an occasional dramatic change. The machines and languages that prosper are those most suited to the current environment rather than those with the most aestheticly pleasing characteristics. Through this development, Fortran has proven to be a hearty species that refuses to become extinct. As A. Perlis writes, "Fortran is not a flower, but a weed. It is hardy, occasionally blooms, and grows in every computer." It adapts to changes in the landscape, and it survives attempts to be supplanted with more attractive languages. This paper will describe vector and parallel machines and their corresponding Fortran dialects. The relationship between language features and machine architecture will be explored.

Let us examine the history and development of the Fortran family tree. Fortran was designed to be simple and efficient for executing numeric programs on a uniprocessor system. It was developed in 1958 by an IBM software team headed by John Backus [1]. This early programming language bore some resemblance to the assembly language that it was intended to replace. Possessing limited control structures and cumbersome I/O statements, Fortran programs were sometimes difficult to write and read, but Fortran compilers produced fast and efficient code. The Fortran 66 standard did little to alleviate the coarseness of the original Fortran. It was not until the Fortran 77 standard that Fortran became somewhat more palatable to the users of more modern programming languages.

The introduction of vector processors and multiprocessors punctuate the most dramatic changes in Fortran and its dialects. Vector statements have been standardized to the extent that they will be part of the next Fortran standard. No consensus has yet been reached with regard to language extensions for multiprocessing. Some proposals for parallel extensions to Fortran will be presented later in this paper. The emerging generation of supercomputers utilize both vector processing and multiprocessing simultaneously. The challenge is to provide language constructs and software tools that will allow the programmer to easily exploit the capabilities of the machine.

*This work was supported in part by the **National Science Foundation** under Grant No. US NSF MIP-8410110, the **US Department of Energy** under Grant No. US DOE DE-FG02-85ER25001, and by a donation from the IBM Corporation.

**This Author may be reached at:
Encore Computer Corporation
257 Cedar Hill Street
Marlborough, MA 01752-3004

This paper will outline the development of vector and multiprocessor language constructs in Fortran. The significant architectures, their languages, and optimizers will be described. The paper concludes with a description of Cedar Fortran [2] [3], the language for the Cedar Multiprocessor [4] under development at the University of Illinois, Urbana-Champaign. Cedar is a hierarchical, shared-memory, vector multiprocessor. As such, its language, Cedar Fortran, contains many of the language features that will be described for vector processors and multiprocessors.

2. Vector Processing

With the advent of vector supercomputers in the early 70's, a new branch began to form in the Fortran Family tree, a branch that would later be spliced back into the main development by the Fortran 8x standard. The vector/array processor system was the general model for most early supercomputers. In order to utilize the power of these new vector machines, statements were added to Fortran to specify vector operations. The first such machine was the Illiac IV [5] completed in 1971. Several different Fortran compilers were developed for this machine. The first was the Burroughs Illiac IV Fortran [6] which used *control vectors* as array subscripts. The elements of a control vector took on values of `.true.` and `.false.` A value of `.true.` indicated that the operation should be performed for the corresponding array element. A * denoted a control vector of any length with all elements set to `.true.` Thus, the code fragment

```
        Real A(100), B(100), C(100)
        do 10 i = 1, 100, 2
              M (i) = .true.
              M (i+1) = .false.
10      continue
        A(*) = B(*) + A(*)
        C(M(*)) = B(M(*)) + A(M(*))
```

adds corresponding elements of arrays A and B and assigns the result to array A. While only the odd elements of A and B are added and assigned to the odd elements of C.

Control vectors were somewhat cumbersome to use for complicated vector expressions. The next compiler for the Illiac IV, the IVTRAN Compiler [7] of 1973, took another approach to expressing vector operations. All assignment statements were written in standard Fortran, using array subscripts. To indicate vector operations, this language used a generic vector loop statement `do for all` to indicate that a loop should be compiled as vector instructions. IVTRAN even allowed subroutine and function calls within the body of the `do for all` which were recursively expanded in line to verify the correctness of the loop. This verification consisted of range checking and insuring that all statements could be vectorized.

Unlike the serial Fortran do loop statement, the `do for all` loop statement used an index set instead of a single index variable to specify the execution range. The index set consisted of an n-tuple of index variables and an n-dimensional range expression indicating the range of each variable in the index set. `Do for all` loops could not be nested and only limited conditional statements could be used within the body of the loop. The following code shows a simple, properly formed `do for all` statement:

```
        Real A(10,20), B(10,20)
        do 10 for all (i,j) / [1...10].C.[1...20]
              A(i,j) = B(i,j) + A(i,j)
10      continue
```

The `[1...10].C.[1...20]` specifies the range of the index variable `i`, 1 through 10, and the index variable `j`, 1 through 20. The `.C.` stands for *cross*, the cartesian cross product. Thus, a grid of values is specified

CH2617-9/88/0000/0114$01.00 © 1988 IEEE

that encompasses all elements of A and B. Complementing IVTRAN, the IVTRAN Paralyzer[8] was the first source-to-source restructuring parallel optimizer. Starting with standard Fortran, the paralyzer transformed do loops and perfect loop nests into IVTRAN do for all loops. This optimizer was significant because it utilized dependence analysis to determine if loops could be safely parallelized.

Pipelined vector processors also emerged in the early 1970's: the Texas Instruments Advanced Scientific Computer (ASC) [9] in 1972 and the Control Data Corporation Star-100 [10] in 1973. The TI-ASC NX Fortran[11] Compiler was one of the first vectorizing compilers developed. This compiler could take standard Fortran 66 and produce vectorized code. The language did have a few minor vector extensions, such as triplets (see below), but the use of these extensions was not required for vector code to be generated.

Lawrence Livermore Labs developed an extented Fortran language, Vector LRLTRAN [12] for the CDC Star-100. Starting with LRLTRAN (a Fortran dialect also developed at Lawrence Livermore Labs), vector extensions were added specifically targeting the Star-100 architecture. All vectors were restricted to one-dimensional arrays. Vector assignments, vector expressions, vector functions, and control vectors were all implemented, but all vector operations required contiguous access of stride one.

Vector LRLTRAN also provided a facility for dynamically equivalencing vectors and subvectors. Given an array A(100), a subvector B of 10 elements could be dynamically defined using the statement:

```
vector (B, A((11, 20)))
```

B(1) now refers to element A(11), B(2) refers to A(12), etc. Since vectors are one dimensional and double sets of parentheses are used to specify vector ranges, no syntactic ambiguity exists between vector statements and two dimensional arrays, but the programs can be confusing to the programmer if he does not pay careful attention to the syntax.

The stride and dimensionality restrictions of Vector LRLTRAN made working with matrices cumbersome. These restrictions stem from the desire to translate vector operations in LRLTRAN directly into the vector machine instructions of the Star-100. Additionally, the use of commas to specify ranges of vectors was confusing and ensured that the current notation could never be generalized to express operations on multi-dimensional arrays as vector operations.

New vector statements, operators, and notations were introduced in 1973 by the IBM Vectran [13] and the BSP Fortran [14] compilers. Triplet expressions, identify statements, and where statements replaced control vectors and other vector notations. These vector statements are part of the proposed 8x standard. The triplet notation consists of three expressions separated by colons. These expressions indicate the range of execution of this statement and correspond to the beginning, end, and stride – as in a Fortran do loop. If the beginning of the triplet is omitted, it is assumed to be the beginning of the array; if the end is omitted, it is assumed to be the end of the array. Unless otherwise specified, the stride is assumed to be 1, and it may be omitted along with its separating colon. This notation makes it possible to assign a section of one array to a section of another array or array section expression. For example, the following instructions first assign all of A to be the values of B (a full array assignment). The next statement assigns A(1) the value 6 and A(2) the value 8 leaving the other elements unchanged:

```
integer A(4), B(4), C(8)
data B/2,4,6,8/, C/1,2,3,4,5,6,7,8/
A = B
A(1:2) = B(3:4)
```

A stride may also be used, so the following statement

```
A(1:3:2) = B(2:4:2) * C(3:8:4)
```

is equivalent to

```
A(1) = B(2) * C(3)        A(3) = B(4) * C(7)
```

Array sections can also be specified for multidimensional arrays with one triplet for each dimension of the array, and triplet notation may be mixed with the normal array index notation. The only restriction is that any two sections appearing together in the same statement must be conformable, ie. both sections must have an equal number of elements in each corresponding dimension. For example:

```
integer A(4,4,4), B(4,8), C(4,6,4,4)
A(1:3:2,2:4:2,1)=B(1:2,2:4:2)*C(3:4,5,2:4:2,1)
```

All the array sections in the above example are 2 x 2 sections. Expanded, they are:

```
A(1,2,1) = B(1,2) * C(3,5,2,1)
A(3,2,1) = B(2,2) * C(4,5,2,1)
A(1,4,1) = B(1,4) * C(3,5,4,1)
A(3,4,1) = B(2,4) * C(4,5,4,1)
```

Triplets are not sufficient to express all vector operations. Specifically, conditional operations that were possible with control vectors cannot be performed with triplets. The where statement, another Vectran construct, is a conditional vector assignment that allows more flexibility than control vectors. The syntax of the where statement is shown in Figure 1. The where statement first evaluates a logical array expression. The statements in the body of the where are executed for each index value for which the logical array expression evaluated .true. The body of the where statement, either a single statement or a block, contains only array assignments. The right hand side of every array expression in the body must be conformable to the logical array expression. This is a vector statement, so the logical array expression and all right hand side (rhs) expressions in the body are evaluated before the assignments are performed. If the otherwise block is present, the array assignment statements of the otherwise block will be performed for every corresponding element of the logical array expression of the where statement whose value is .false.

```
where (<logical_array_expr>)
        <array_assignment_statements>
[otherwise
        <array_assignment_statements>]
end where
```

Figure 1. Where Statement Specification

A simple example of the use of the where statement would be to zero all array elements that are negative. In this example only the elements of a that have values less than zero will be set to zero. All the other elements will remain unchanged.

```
integer A (100)
where (A(1:100) .LT. 0)
      A(1:100) = 0
end where
```

The combination of triplets and where statements is still not adequate to express all vector operations. Particularly, it is not possible to express operations that have a regular stride in physical memory but an irregular stride in array indices. Assigning to the diagonal elements of a two-dimensional array is a simple example. Given an array, a(10,10); it is not possible to assign just the diagonal elements using triplets and where statements without control vectors even though the distance between all the referenced elements is the same (stride = 11 in this case). The identify statement of Vectran and Fortran 8x [15] allows aliasing to a part of an array so that such operations can be performed. To access the diagonal of array A, the following code would be used:

```
real A(10,10)
identify (Diag(I) = A(I,I), I = 1, 10)
Diag(:) = 1
```

Although sufficient, the identify statement introduces aliasing into the program. The forall statement, which has been removed from the proposed 8x standard, provides the same functionality as identify without the additional aliasing. The forall looks very much like an identify statement, except that it performs operations within the statement instead of just aliasing. The equivalent code using the forall statement is:

```
real A(10,10)
forall (I = 1:10) A(I,I) = 1
```

The forall also allows conditional assignment making it possible to express complicated vector operations with a single statement. In the following example, the diagonal elements of a matrix are tested, and any element that is negative is set to zero:

```
integer a(10,10) i
forall (i=1:10, a(i,i) .LT. 0) a(i,i) = 0
```

The forall syntax is shown in Figure 2 and is essentially the same as the the IVTRAN do for all statement.

```
forall ([<loop_spec>]+...[,<log_array_exp>])
    <array_section_expr> = <array_section_expr>
where
    <loop_spec> -> <integer_variable> = <triplet>
    <log_array_exp>->same as in Where statement.
```

Figure 2. `Forall` Statement Specification

Most compilers for vector machines from the late 1970's and early 1980's accept standard Fortran as input, and vectorization is done by the compiler. The Cray CFT compiler [16] (the Cray 1 Fortran compiler) accepts standard Fortran and directives from the programmer. The compilers for the Cyber 205 (Cyber 205 Fortran [17]) and the Fujitsu VP-200 (Fujitsu Fortran 77 [18]) are also full vectorizing compilers, but the Cyber 205 Fortran also supports the Vectran-style vector extensions. Recently, many vectorizing compilers have been developed for various architectures: IBM VS Fortran [19], Alliant FX/8 Fortran [20], NEC SX Fortran [21], and others.

Also during the 1970's, software tools that perform program restructuring for vectorization and then report back to the user were introduced; tools such as Parafrase [22] [23] [24], developed at the University of Illinois, and PFC [25], developed later at Rice University. The goals of such tools were to provide very powerful system-independent vectorizers, to evaluate the effectiveness of new optimizations, and to involve the user in the optimization process with the ultimate goal to educate the programmer to enable him to write better programs.

3. Multiprocessing

The introduction of multiprocessor systems has also had a dramatic affect on Fortran dialects, but no standardization of multiprocessor constructs has been attained. Multiprocessor systems offer greater flexibility than vector processors, but they also offer a greater challenge in programming and compiling. Unlike compiling and programming for vector machines, which involve localized decisions, compiling and programming for multiprocessors often involve global consideration of the program. Additionally, utilization of a multiprocessor often requires consideration of both the operating system environment and the machine architecture making standardization difficult.

From the large number of multiprocessor systems that have been designed or proposed, two basic multitasking methods have emerged to increase the performance of a single program: macrotasking and microtasking. Macrotasking involves breaking the problem into large chunks, called *tasks* that can execute more or less independently on the multiple processors. Macrotasking is usually realized with the familiar `fork/join` constructs of [26]. The `fork` construct creates a new task that will be scheduled for execution by the operating system. Creating a new task is generally a very expensive operation. The useful work performed by the task must be sufficiently large to compensate for this startup overhead if macrotasking is to be efficient.

A very interesting system was the Denelcor HEP [27] developed in the late 1970s. A single HEP cpu executed multiple instruction streams in parallel. The cpu was time-multiplexed between the instructions streams. Multiple pipelines and register sets allowed the HEP to switch rapidly between processes without saving process state information. A minimum of eight processes was required to keep the cpu fully utilized. Therefore, even on a uniprocessor system, the HEP relied on macrotasking to increase performance.

The HEP Fortran contained extensions to utilize the multitasking capabilities of the machine. Two new statements, `create` and `resume`, were added to the Fortran 77 base language. The `create` statement allowed the parent process to invoke a subroutine as a new process; the `resume` statement allowed a called routine to force its parent to continue while the called routine executed in parallel. The following two code segments in HEP Fortran would both result in subroutine `subr` executing in parallel with its parent process.

```
create subr (x,y,x)        call subr (x,y,z)

subroutine subr (x,y,z)    subroutine subr (x,y,z)
<some computation>         resume
return                     <some computation>
                           return
```

Many current supercomputers consist of a relatively small number of very high performance vector processors. They rely on multiprocessing to provide higher performance than single-processor vector systems. Both the Cray-XM/P [28] and the ETA-10 [29] provide macrotasking library routines in their Fortran languages. These systems require the programmer to divide the work of his program into tasks that may execute in parallel. No automatic task generation is done by the compiler. The library routines instantiate new tasks at the subroutine level. For example, the following piece of Cray-XM/P Fortran code results in two tasks executing the same subroutine with different parameters:

```
external subr
integer task1(3), data(1000)
call tskstart (task1, subr, data, 1, 500)
call subr (data, 501, 1000)
```

The first call creates a new task executing `subr` with `data` elements from 1 to 500. The second call invokes `subr` directly with `data` elements from 501 to 1000. The `task1` array is a control array used by the macrotasking library.

Along with the ability to create multiple instruction streams, effective multitasking also requires some method of controlling (synchronizing) the executing tasks. For the purpose of this paper we distinguish between *critical section* synchronization and *event-waiting* synchronization. A critical section implies that entrance to a particular section of code must be restricted so that only one processor may execute it at a time. This is done to prevent processors from interfering with one another. *Event-waiting* synchronization imposes an ordering upon asynchronous events. The *producer-consumer* problem is a good example of event-waiting synchronization. Critical section synchronization is usually handled with a semaphore [30] mechanism. Event waiting synchronization may be handled in a variety of ways: a processor may wait until the value of a particular variable becomes zero or explicit event posting and waiting mechanisms may be used.

The HEP provided synchronization using *asynchronous variables*. An asynchronous variable was any variable whose name began with a dollar sign ($). These variables had a `full/empty` synchronization bit associated with them. An asynchronous variable could only be read if its synchronization bit was `full`; it could only be written if its bit was `empty`. A read automatically set the bit to `empty`, and a write automatically set the bit to `full`. An instruction stream wanting to read or write a such variable would wait until the synchronization bit was in the proper state. A section of code bounded by a read and a write of an asynchronous variable therefore became a critical section. These variables could also be used for event-waiting synchronization.

Synchronization in Cray-XM/P Fortran is done with calls to the runtime system. Routines are provided for locking (critical section) and event-waiting synchronization. Figure 3 compares the HEP and the Cray-XM/P synchronization methods for a simple producer-consumer synchronization problem and a simple critical section problem.

Another consideration in macrotasking is the nature of the program data. Multiple tasks executing a single program require that multiple data spaces also exist. Cray Fortran uses stacks to allocate data local to subroutines and functions. This departs from the more common static allocation of local data in typical Fortran implementations, but this change is necessary to accommodate macrotasking. In both Cray and HEP, a local variable allocated on the stack can be passed by reference to newly spawned tasks. Care has to be taken, however, that variables are not deallocated from the stack before all tasks finish using those variables.

`Common` blocks also require some consideration. `Common` blocks are used in Fortran to share data across subroutine calls. In a macrotasking environment, is there one `common` block for the entire program or one per task? In the HEP only one `common` block exists per program and is shared by all tasks. In the Cray two types of common are allowed. Plain `common` blocks are shared by all tasks in the program. `Task common` blocks are allocated one copy per task. The variables within a `task common` could be passed by reference to newly spawned tasks.

Microtasking exploits parallelism at a more local level than macrotasking. Microtasking is often used to execute iterations of a loop in parallel. In addition to loop parallelism, speedups can be achieved by overlapping segments of sequential code. This operation is called low-level spreading if the spreading is done on a statement-by-statement basis; it is called high-level spreading if the spreading is performed upon large instruc-

	HEP	Cray-XM/P
Producer-Consumer		

Initialization	`integer $emp`
	`integer $fll`
	`purge $emp,$fll`
		`integer emp, fll`
		`call evasgn (emp)`
		`call evasgn(fll)`
		`call evpost(emp)`

Producer	`e = $emp`
	`<produce>`
	`$fll = 1`
		`call evwait(emp)`
		`<produce>`
		`call evpost(fll)`

Consumer	`f = $fll`
	`<consume>`
	`$emp = 1`
		`call evwait(fll)`
		`<consume>`
		`call evpost(emp)`

Critical Section		
Initialization	`integer $lkvar` `purge $lkvar`	`integer lkvar` `call lockasgn(lkvar)`

Section	`l = $lkvar`
	`<Crit. Sect.>`
	`$lkvar = 1`
		`call lockon(lkvar)`
		`<Crit. Sect.>`
		`call lockoff(lkvar)`

Figure 3. HEP vs. Cray Synchronization

tion streams [31]. This optimization adds to the overall speedup of the program because it overlaps instructions that are not vectorizable. Microtasking is efficient on such small execution units because it does not incur the large task creation overhead of macrotasking. Instead of creating new tasks for each new parallel execution stream, a fixed number of computational resources, either "helping" tasks or real processors, are allocated at the beginning of the program. These resources remain idle until parallel code is encountered by an active task. At this point, the "helping" resources join in the parallel execution. Once a resource joins in the execution, it is committed until the parallel execution completes. The overhead for starting this parallel execution is much lower than in macrotasking.

In 1979, Burroughs proposed the FMP multiprocessor and a companion extended Fortran (called FMP Fortran) [32]. The FMP was never built, but its design foreshadowed the development of future multiprocessor systems. The machine was comprised of 512 processing elements with local memory. All processors could also access a much slower shared extended memory. Additionally, a processor could broadcast to the other processors for quick distribution of information. The early strategy of FMP Fortran was to allocate all variables in the local memory of the processor unless instructed to do otherwise. FMP Fortran introduced a new concurrent construct called the `doall`, one of the first uses of a microtasking construct. The `doall` allowed the specification of multiple index variables or n-tuples of indexes, called *domains*. All iterations of the `doall` were considered discrete and independent. The FMP `doall` format is shown in Figure 4. This `doall` required the user to specify the intended use of variables. The `using` clause identified input variables, and the `giving` clause identified output variables.

Any variable that does not appear in the `using` or `giving` clause is allocated locally to each processor. The `using` and `giving` clauses in the FMP `doall` statement force the user to provide the FMP Fortran compiler the dependence information necessary to make proper allocations, and thus relieves the compiler of this task. Another important feature of this `doall` is that no information is passed between the iterations of the loop. At the beginning of the loop, the state of the extended memory is "frozen." All modifications are local until the end of the `doall`, then the variables listed in the `giving` clause are written back. This value/restore form of execution eliminates the possibility of asynchronous side-effects (loop executions are determinant), but it also limits the types of loops that can be converted into a `doall`. Later versions of the FMP `doall` allowed data sharing and asynchronous operation.

```
doall <domain>; using <variable list>
        <loop body>
enddo [<domain>]; giving <variable list>
```

Figure 4. FMP `Doall` Specification

Microtasking has also been used in a number of current multiprocessor systems. In some of these systems, the processors execute in a more independent fashion than in the FMP. In all of these systems, data may be shared between the iterations of the loop. With data sharing, nondeterminacy may be introduced into the execution of the loop. In loops where the iterations are completely independent (or require some critical section synchronization), a more general `doall` loop statement may be used. The iterations are executed by multiple processors and no guarantee is made about the order of execution of the iterations of the loop.

Many loops, however, have some serial component. The natural ordering of the loop must be preserved for the loop to execute correctly. The `doacross` loop is a parallel loop that assumes synchronization from left to right [33] [34] [35], meaning that dependences may exist between iteration `I` and some previous iteration(s). The iterations of the loop are scheduled "horizontally" – meaning that no processor will begin execution of iteration `I` until iteration `I-1` has been started. (Horizontal scheduling is also called cascading execution.) Additionally, an iteration may have to wait during its execution for a previous iteration in order to satisfy dependences. In other words, a producer-consumer relationship exists between the iterations of the `doacross` loop.

Among the microtasking libraries of current multiprocessor systems, a great variety of routines exists with varying levels of sophistication. The Cray-XM/P supports a `doall` style loop in its microtasking system as well as high-level spreading. Sequent Fortran [36] provides a `doacross` style loop and microtasking `fork/join` style constructs. The microtasking constructs of both are supported in software. The Alliant FX/8 multiprocessor [37] and the IBM RP3 multiprocessor [38] support microtasking `doacross` loops at the hardware level. Special hardware that schedules the iterations of concurrent loops is incorporated into their architectures. In some systems (Cray, Sequent), the user must insert statements or compiler directives to use the microtasking. In the Alliant, the compiler automatically converts serial `do` loops into microtasking loops. One of the major advantages of loop parallelism and high level spreading is that the block-structure of the program is maintained while parallelism is exploited. Macrotasking usually requires a complete rewriting of the program to break it into asynchronous tasks.

It may initially seem that microtasking is superior to macrotasking for exploiting concurrency, but each method has advantages and disadvantages. In the development of multiprocessor systems, both microtasking and macrotasking have been used, and they both continue to be used. The appropriate method of execution depends both on the underlying architecture and the nature of the application.

Microtasking has the advantage of reducing overhead and exploiting parallelism at a finer grain. Microtasking also has two major disadvantages. First, the number of helping resources is usually fixed at compile time or at program startup time (this is done to reduce runtime overhead). Thus, the system does not adapt well to data size or system load. Second, the combination of resource commitment with the non-determinacy of the number of helping tasks that will actually participate in the execution of the parallel code restricts the synchronization that may be used safely. Non-cascading synchronization in microtasking may be disastrous because a task performing a waiting synchronization may be the only task in the execution. Since the resource is committed to its instruction stream, it cannot switch execution streams to satisfy the wait condition. Deadlock is the result. Both of these problems can be remedied with operating system intervention, but then much of the efficiency advantage is lost.

Macrotasking, on the other hand, suffers from higher overhead and thus necessitates a coarser granularity of tasks, but it does not have the above problems of microtasking. Since macrotasking relies on operating system task management, dynamic adaptation to system load and problem size can be incorporated into the runtime system. Additionally, macrotasking does not have the deadlock problem of microtasking. When synchronization is required, a single resource can perform the synchronization and then context switch to another instruction stream. At some later time, the wait condition may be satisfied by the execution of another task, thus releasing the original task.

Many multiprocessor systems, such as the Encore Multimax[39], the Sequent Balance, and IBM Parallel Fortran 3090 [40], now have or are developing Fortran systems that incorporate both macrotasking and microtasking. Table 1 compares the capabilities of many multiprocessor systems.

This great variety of macrotasking/microtasking libraries/routines has caused some cries of despair among the user community: "Parallel programs are not portable!", "Parallel programs are more difficult to write!", etc. In response to these cries. two approaches have been taken. The first approach is to provide an automatic parallelizer – an optimizer that takes a standard sequential program and converts it into a parallel program. This is the approach taken with IBM VS Fortran and Alliant Fortran.

The other approach is to provide a generic parallel environment in which to produce parallel code. Software systems such as Linda [41] have been created which present a uniform parallel programming language that can be implemented on a variety of multiprocessor and distributed systems. In Linda, shared memory is represented as a tuple space. A tuple consists of a variable and one (scalar) or more (array) values. Variables are not written and read as in most languages. Instead, a tuple acts like a mailbox. Values are output to (received by) the tuple, read from the tuple, or removed (input) from the tuple. A value cannot be overwritten; it must be consumed as input before a new value can be output. Data items are not referenced by address, but by name. Accessing a shared variable is similar to searching a distributed database. This shared data feature coupled with elegant methods for handling multitasking make Linda a pleasant programming environment.

4. The Cedar Multiprocessor and Cedar Fortran

The Cedar multiprocessor is a hierarchical shared-memory supercomputer under development at the University of Illinois, Urbana-Champaign. The processors are grouped into clusters that share access to a cluster memory. Processors in one cluster may not access the cluster memory of another cluster. All processors in the machine share access to a large global memory through an interconnection network. The Cedar-1 machine comprises four clusters of eight processors for a total of 32 processors, but this hierarchical architecture may be extended to hundreds of processors. The clusters in Cedar-1 are Alliant FX/8 multiprocessor systems. Each processor is capable of performing vector operations, and the Alliant concurrency hardware allows the processors in each cluster to share the execution of concurrent loops.

The Cedar Fortran Language is based on Fortran 77 [42] and has remained mostly consistent with that standard, but many extensions have been added to provide for optimized concurrent execution. In trying to adapt Fortran to a multiprocessor, multitasking system such as Cedar, many serious problems arose because of the simplicity of the language. The Cedar extensions mostly take the form of new statements and "intrinsic" functions: vector statements, statements for expressing concurrent loops, statements and functions for synchronization, and functions for multitasking. The concurrent loop extensions mentioned above necessitated another extension to standard Fortran, block structured data scoping. Data allocation and scoping presented the greatest problem in adapting Fortran to the multiprocessor/multitasking environment. The data scoping issues are more easily understood with knowledge of the parallel control structures that have been implemented. For this reason, discussion of data scoping will be postponed until after the introduction of the control structures.

4.1 Array/vector Extensions

The vector extensions of Cedar Fortran provide powerful constructs for manipulating data in a vector fashion. Cedar Fortran implements three vector statement types, triplet notation assignments, `forall` statements, and `where` statements. The triplet notation and `where` statements are compatible with the proposed Fortran 8x standard. Their derivation from Vectran was described in a previous section. The `forall` statement has been included in Cedar Fortran because it provides the same functionality as the 8x `identify` statement without introducing more aliasing. The `identify` statement has been omitted in favor of the `forall` statement.

Conceptually, the triplet is a vector assignment statement, the `forall` is a vector loop statement, and the `where` statement is a vector `if` statement. These vector statements are essential to the Cedar Fortran optimizer because they allow all vectorizable instructions to be represented. Once statements have been expressed in vector form, it is much easier for the back end compiler to generate efficient code.

4.2 Concurrent Loops

Vector operations provide one avenue for increasing program performance, but not all code is vectorizable. Concurrent execution with the use of multiple processing resources provides another avenue of optimization. Just as vector operations can be substituted for many Fortran `do` loops, concurrent loops can also be substituted for `do` loops. Additionally, high-level spreading makes it possible to parallelize code that is not in `do` loops. Concurrent constructs can easily be integrated with vector statements to provide multiple levels of parallelism.

The language constructs used to define concurrent execution in Cedar Fortran are derived from the `doall` and `doacross` statements described in the previous section. Each of these loop types is further divided into three groups: cluster statements (`cdoall` and `cdoacross`), spread statements (`sdoall` and `sdoacross`), and cross cluster statements (`xdoall` and `xdoacross`). The distinctions between the groups will be explained below.

The syntax of the `doacross` loop in Cedar Fortran (subsequently to be referred to as CF) is similar tc the standard Fortran do loop; its form is shown in Figure 5. Provision has been made for statements that are to be executed once for each processor participating in the loop using the optional `loop` statement. Those statements that appear before the `loop` will be executed once per processor. Those statements that appear after the `loop` will be executed on every iteration. If the `loop` statement is not present, all statements will be executed once per iteration. Type statements may appear immediately after the `doacross` statement. The function of these type statements is to declare `doacross`-internal variables and arrays which may be referenced only inside that `doacross` loop. Each iteration of the loop allocates a local, private copy of these internal variables and arrays. Each variable and array that is to be internal to a `doacross` loop must be declared explicitly. Any previous declarations are superceded for the duration of the loop.

```
          doacross   [label[,]] i = e1, e2 [, e3]
               [<type_statements>]
               [<statements>]
          [loop]
               [<statements>]
     {label    <next_statement>}   |   {end doacross}
```

where

`i` is the name of an integer variable, called the `doacross`-variable.

e_1, e_2, and e_3 are each integer expressions.

Figure 5. `Doacross` Loop Specification

If data or control dependences exist between the iterations of the loop, the programmer must insert proper synchronization instructions to insure the correct execution of the loop. Two routines, `advance` and `await`, are provided for `doacross` synchronization. An iteration of the `doacross` uses `await` to wait for a previous iteration. An `advance` releases the `await` of a future iteration. (These routines are very efficient because they interface directly to the Alliant concurrency bus.) If no data dependences exist between the iterations of the loop, then the programmer should use the `doall` statement instead of `doacross`. The `doall` loop is very similar to the `doacross` loop; The syntax is identical except for replacing the "doacross" with "doall". While the iterations of a `doacross` are scheduled horizontally, no order is implied in the execution of the iterations of a `doall`. This distinction is important because CF will not override the programmer's declaration of independent parallel execution. The CF compiler may, however, take advantage of this declaration and restructure the loop to achieve greater speedup. If a specific execution order is necessary for the loop to execute correctly, a `doacross` should be used.

It is sometimes desirable to exit a loop before all the iterations of the loop have been completed. A `goto` statement cannot be used to exit from a parallel loop because a `goto` would only affect a single processor. The result would be that one processor would leave the concurrent loop while the other processors continued to execute within the loop. Instead, the following two statements, `quit` and `qquit` have been provided.

```
quit [label]
qquit [label]
```

The `quit` statement causes the parallel loop to be terminated cleanly. It waits for all iterations with a loop index less than the current loop index to finish before it actually quits the loop. Without the `label`, execution resumes at the first statement after the end of the innermost loop containing the `quit`. With the `label`, execution resumes at that label, terminating all loops out to that level.

If multiple iterations of a loop perform a `quit` operation, then the iteration with the smallest iteration number (if the stride is positive) will control the exit of the loop reguardless of which iteration actually issued the `quit` first in real time. The `qquit` statement is similar to the `quit` statement, except that it terminates the loop immediately. (It does not wait for all previous iterations to finish.) It is a "quick `quit`." Caution must be taken when using `qquit` because previous iterations may be only partially complete when the loop terminates.

4.3 Macrotasking

In addition to the microtasking of concurrent loops, CF provides macrotasking via the macrotasking library (similar to the Cray macrotasking routines). The macrotasking routines are the interface between the CF language and the Xylem operating system [43]. This library provides routines for creating and controlling "tasks." (An entity of concurrent execution in Xylem is called a "cluster task" or just a "task" for convenience.) A task begins execution at the specified routine and continues independently until the end of the subroutine is reached. When the `return` statement is reached, the task is terminated rather than returning to the parent task. The macrotasking library provides routines for the creation and monitoring of these user defined tasks. These routines are described in Figure 6.

4.4 Cluster, Spread, and Cross Cluster Loops

The format of the `ctskstart` call may initially appear strange to the reader because it specifies a number of processors to be allocated to the new task. This number of processors is significant in the execution of concurrent loops. As was mentioned earlier, there are three forms for each concurrent loop: `cdoall`, `sdoall`, and `xdoall`, and `cdoacross`, `sdoacross`, and `xdoacross`. The "`c`" loops are cluster or "confined" loops, meaning that the processing resources used for the execution of the loop are confined to processors allocated to the current cluster task. For example, a cluster task with five processors is started with:

```
taskid = ctskstart (5, subr, x, y, z)
```

This creates a task for subroutine `subr` with arguments `x`, `y`, and `z`. Within `subr`, a program segment

```
      cdoall i=1, 100
            <statements>
      end cdoall
```

executes a concurrent loop using only the five processors allocated to the task at the task's creation. The execution of the loop is confined to the processor resources of the cluster task.

Also within `subr`, a very similar program segment

```
      sdoall i=1, 100
            <statements>
      end sdoall
```

has a very different meaning. In this loop, the execution is being spread to processing resources outside the current cluster task. A concurrent loop statement that begins with an "`s`" indicates that this is a "spread" loop. In the loop above, each iteration of the loop may be assigned to a different cluster task. If the CF user specifies his own concurrent loops, then he is responsible for proper declaration and allocation of variables. However, the compiler will provide warnings of improper user declarations. Any concurrent loops generated by the CF optimizer will have the variable declaration done automatically to match those loops.

In order to make effective use of the computational resources on Cedar, a `sdoall` loop should have a nested `cdoall` loop to bring all the processors within each task into execution. It may initially seem strange that the `sdoall` allocates whole cluster tasks to the iterations of the loop instead of just processors, but one must remember the hierarchical structure of Cedar. In order to reach the processors within a cluster, one must go through the cluster control hardware (Alliant concurrency bus). The `sdoall/cdoall` loop combination provides the programmer maximum flexibility in controlling the parallel execution of loops.

If the programmer desires to run one loop across all processors of the machine and s/he does not want to deal with the precise details of loop blocking and processor scheduling, the `xdoall` or `xdoacross` statements may be used. These "cross cluster" parallel loops take the confined processors of the given cluster task and combine them with the processors of other tasks to create a single loop with processors from different clusters taking iterations of the loop. The `x` concurrent loops are functionally equivalent to a `s` loop with an inner nested `c` loop, except the loop blocking and processor utilization is managed by the compiler instead of the programmer. (These `x` concurrent loops are currently unimplemented in CF.)

- `int = ctskstart (num_proc, sub [,arg]...)`

  `Ctskstart` spawns a new task, and returns an integer that identifies it. The first argument, num_proc, specifies the number of processors to be allocated to the new task for execution of any `cdoall` or `cdoacross` loops. If the value is zero, then the system is free to allocate any number of processors to the cluster task.

  The second argument, `sub`, is the subroutine or entry point at which execution will begin in the new task. The remaining arguments are those passed to the subroutine. These arguments may be of any type (scalar or array), but they should match the formal parameters of `sub`. Expressions are allowed as arguments and enclosing an argument in parentheses indicates that the argument is to be passed by value. The value returned by `ctskstart` will either be a positive integer corresponding to the id number of the newly spawned task, or -1 if `ctskstart` fails.

- `logical = ctskdone (int)`

  `Ctskdone` reports the state of a task created by `ctskstart`. The value of the argument identifies a task and must have been obtained from `ctskstart`. Returns `.false.` if the specified task has been created and has not terminated. Returns `.true.` otherwise.

- `call ctskwait (int)`

  `Ctskwait` suspends the task referencing it until the task whose identification is the argument completes execution. The value of the argument must have been obtained from `ctskstart`.

Figure 6. Macrotasking Library Routines

4.5 Synchronization

With the addition of concurrent loops and macrotasking, a mechanism for controlling the execution streams is required. New statements and intrinsic functions were added to CF to provide for varying granularities of synchronization. Fine grain synchronization is used between processors within concurrent loops, larger grain synchronization is used between tasks.

Cedar Fortran provides mechanisms for both critical section and producer-consumer synchronization, adopting the full set of Cray lock and event synchronization routines. These routines are classified as medium grain synchronization, appropriate for synchronization between cluster tasks, but too expensive for general use between the processors in a single task.

```
with <resource> when|if <expression>
      <statements>
end with
```

Figure 7. The `With` Statement

Besides these synchronization primitives, we find the `with` statement described by Hoare [44] to be useful in expressing critical section synchronization. The general form of the `with` block is shown in Figure 7. This construct means that the `<statements>` are in a critical section for the `<resource>`. In CF the `<resource>` is a variable or array element declared as `sync`. In the `with/when` form, these `<statements>` will not be executed until exclusive access can be granted to the `<resource>` and the `<expression>` is true. (Note that the `with` statement does not hold the `<resource>` while it is waiting for the `<expression>` to become true.) In the `with/if` form, exclusive access to the `<resource>` is granted and the `<expression>` is evaluated; if the `<expression>` is true, the `<statements>` are executed, otherwise execution continues immediately after the `end with`. Exclusive access is always released at the termination of each `with` statement.

The `sync` type statement declares a variable or array element, `X`, to have a data field, a tag field, and a hidden lock field. When referring to the data elements, one simply uses the variable name, `X`. The tag field is referenced as `X.tag`. Figure 8 shows a `do` loop with a subscripted-subscript transformed to run in parallel. This requires both event-waiting and critical-section synchronization. Using `b(i)` as the index variable causes the order of storing the array `a` to be unpredictable. The tag field is used to maintain the order of the accesses to the elements of `a`. More examples of the use of this synchronization method can be found in [45].

Although any statements may be contained in the body of a `with` statement, the Cedar hardware provides synchronization primitives that can be used to implement some `with` statements as single instructions. The `with` statement in the above loop, for example, can be implemented as a single instruction in Cedar. If the operations in the body of the with are limited to only one operation each on tag and data, then the entire body of the `with` may be executed as a single instruction. If the body contains more operations, then additional software synchronization must be used.

The loop:

```
          do i = 1, N
                    a(b(i)) = c(i) + 1
          end do
```

The equivalent parallel versions using the `with` statement:

```
          doall i = 1, N
                    with a(b(i)) if (a(b(i)).tag < i)
                              a(b(i)) = c(i) + 1
                              a(b(i)).tag = i
                    end with
          end doall
```

Figure 8. `With` Statement Example

4.6 Data Declarations, Scoping, and Nested Concurrent Loops

The Cedar architecture physically distinguishes two types of memory: global memory which is accessible to all processors and cluster memory which is only accessible to the processors in that cluster. Specification of location attributes for data in CF are supported by extending the standard Fortran declaration statements with two new attribute statements, `global` and `cluster`. While the architectural classifications of global and cluster are very distinct, Cedar Fortran, with the help of the Xylem virtual memory system, presents a more homogeneous virtual address space. All data that is declared locally in a subprogram and passed outside that subprogram is heap-allocated and sharable with other tasks. The `cluster` and `global` attributes define only initial locations of data. Data will be demand-paged to the physical location necessary to meet the access demands of the program. Data that is read and written by multiple tasks must be moved to the global memory. Read-only data, program code, and unshared data may move to cluster memory. The programmer must be somewhat aware of the underlying architecture to avoid excessive paging activity. Data to be shared by several cluster tasks or that is shared among the iterations of an `sdoall` loop should be declared `global`. Library routines are provided to the programmer for changing location attributes of data.

`Common` blocks are used in Fortran to share data across subroutine calls. In CF, there are two types of common, plain `common` and `process common`. In plain `common`, one copy of the common is (potentially) created for each task within the program. In `process common`, one copy of the common is shared by all tasks within the program. Unlike the `task common` of Cray Fortran, plain `common` of CF cannot be passed by reference to newly spawned tasks. Unlike local data which can be shared, the data within a plain `common` is strictly private to the task. This undesirable restriction is forced by the back-end compiler. In future implementations, it is hoped that this restriction will be lifted so that the programmer is presented with uniform data behavior where data sharing is completely dictated by visibility and scoping.

`Common` names may appear in the CF memory attribute type statements. This means that the `common` defined by this name and all of the identifiers located within it are of the indicated type. Any plain `common` that is not specifically given attributes will be given the `cluster` attribute. Any `process common` that is not specifically given attributes will be given the `global` attribute. All identifiers in a `common` take on the initial location attribute of the `common` block. The actual location may be changed by demand paging or by library routine calls.

The open scoping of identifiers in Fortran proved to be unmanageable for concurrent loops. A C-like block-structured scoping system was added to CF in order to isolate variables in a single instruction stream. Specifically, variables and arrays may be declared inside any concurrent construct. The newly declared variables will be allocated one copy per iteration of the concurrent construct, and these declarations will supersede any variable of the same name declared outside the construct. These declarations remain in effect until the construct terminates or until new declarations of a more nested construct supersede the older declarations. When a construct terminates, the declarations as they existed before the construct began are restored.

The scoping levels have similar implications for `goto` statements. CF allows `goto`s to be performed only to statements at the same scope. This essentially means that CF will not allow `goto`s to be performed into or out of `doall` or `doacross` constructs. Of course, this rule applies to any type of `goto`, either explicit, or by result of an arithmetic if or any other Fortran branching construct. Recall that `quit` or `qquit` must be used to terminate a parallel loop before all iterations have been completed.

Nested concurrent loops should allow greater exploitation of parallelism within a program. Multi-level loop parallelism can be supported under the current implementation of CF using a combination of `sdoall` and `cdoall` or `cdoacross` loops. The Alliant hardware controlling the cluster loop execution permits only the outermost cluster loop to execute concurrently; all inner cluster concurrent loops will execute sequentially.

When using an `sdoall` loop, all input and output data from the loop must be accessible outside the initiating cluster task. All such data should therefore be declared `global` to avoid excessive data movement (and that data cannot appear in plain common blocks). Below is a properly constructed nesting of spread and cluster loops.

```
     dimension a(10,20)
     global a, i
     sdoall i = 1, 10
          integer j
     loop
          cdoall j = 1, 20
               a(i,j) = i+j
          end cdoall
     end sdoall
```

5. Conclusion

In this paper, we have traced the development of vector extensions to Fortran from their diverse beginnings to the current general consensus. The continuing variety of multiprocessing extensions has also been presented. Most current multiprocessor extensions are still deeply intertwined with their corresponding architectures and operating systems. Cedar Fortran is no exception. Our primary goals in designing and implementing the language were:

(1) to provide a language that easily allowed direct access to all the power of the Cedar system, both for the programmer and for source-to-source optimization.

(2) to provide a Fortran dialect in which users could easily adapt their existing Fortran applications.

In these two goals, we feel we have been reasonably successful. Our secondary goals were:

(1) to adapt the language to the needs and desires of programmers as they gain experience with parallel programming.

(2) to add to the overall knowledge and experience of parallel programming and parallel languages.

We are confident that time will provide a general consensus on multiprocessor Fortran constructs, just as it has with vector constructs. The diversity of multiprocessors is much greater than that of vector processors, and the problem is compounded by the interrelated issues of concurrent execution and proper data allocation. The convergence of ideas and attitudes may, therefore, take more time and effort.

REFERENCES

[1] J. Backus, "The History of FORTRAN I, II, and III," *Annual History of Computers*, vol. 1,1, July, 1979, pp. 21-37.

[2] M. Guzzi, "Cedar Fortran Programmer's Manual," CSRD doc. no. 601, U of I Center for Supercomputing R and D, Jan. 1987.

[3] D. Padua and D. Lawrie, "Proposed Cedar Fortran Extensions," CSRD doc. no. 509, U of I Center for Supercomputing R and D, Sept. 1985.

[4] D. Kuck, E. Davidson, D. Lawrie, and A. Sameh, "Parallel Supercomputing Today and the Cedar Approach," *Science*, Vol. 231 (28 Feb. 1986), pp. 967-974.

[5] G. Barnes, R. Brown, M.Kato, D. Kuck, D. Slotnick, and R. Stokes, "The Illiac IV Comuputer," *IEEE Transactions on Computers*, Vol C-17 No. 8 (Aug. 1968), pp. 746-757.

[6] *Array Processing System Fortran IV Reference Manual*, Defense, Space, and Special Systems Group, Burroughs Corporation, Paoli, Penn., Change No.3, August 31, 1971.

[7] R. Millstein and C. Muntz, "The Illiac IV Fortran Compiler," *ACM Sigplan Notices*, Vol. 10 No. 3 (March 1975), pp. 1-8.

[8] D. Presberg and N. Johnson, "The Paralyzer: IVTRAN's Parallelism Analyzer and Synthesizer", *ACM Sigplan Notices*, Vol. 10 No. 3 (March 1975), pp. 9-16.

[9] L. Higbie, "Supercomputer Architectures," *IEEE Computer*, Vol. 6 (Dec 1973), pp. 48-58.

[10] *Control Data Star-100 Computer System – Hardware Reference Manual*, Control Data Corporation Technical Publications Department, Arden Hills, Minn., 1971.

[11] D. Wedel, "Fortran for the Texas Instruments ACS System", *ACM Sigplan Notices*, Vol. 10 No. 3 (March 1975), pp. 119-132.

[12] R. G. Zwakenberg, "Vector Extensions to LRLTRAN", *Sigplan Notices*, Vol. 10, No. 3 (March 1975), pp. 77-86.

[13] G. Paul and M. Wilson, "An Introduction to VECTRAN and Its Use in Scientific Computing," *Proceedings of the 1978 LASL Workshop on Vector and Parallel Processors*, 1978, pp. 176-204.

[14] *Burroughs Scientific Processor Vector Fortran Specification* Defense, Space, and Special Systems Group, Burroughs Corporation, Paoli, Penn., 1978.

[15] *Fortran 8x, X3J3/S8 (X3.9-198x)*, American National Standards Institute, 1986.

[16] *Cray-1 Fortran (CFT) Reference Manual*, Pub. no. SR-0009, Cray Research, Inc., Mendota Heights, Minn., 1979.

[17] *Fortran 200 Version 1 Reference Manual*, Control Data Corporation Technical Publications Department, Arden Hills, Minn., 1982.

[18] K. Miura and K. Uchida, "FACOM Vector Processor VP-100/VP-200," *Proc. NATO Advanced Research Workshop on High-speed Computing*, Julich, W. Germany, Springer-Verlag, June 20-22, 1983.

[19] R. Scarborough and H. Kolsky, "A Vectorizing Fortran Compiler," *IBM Journal of R and D*, 30(2), March 1986, pp. 163-171.

[20] *FX/Fortran Language Manual*, Alliant Computer Systems Corporation, Acton, Mass., April, 1985.

[21] T. Watanabe, "Architecture and Performance of NEC supercomputer SX system," *Parallel Computing*, Vol. 5 (1987), pp. 247-255.

[22] D. Kuck, Y. Muraoka, and S. Chen, "On the Number of Operations Simultaneously Executable in Fortran-like Programs and their Resulting Speedup," *IEE Transactions on Computers*, Vol. C-21 no. 12 (Dec. 1972).

[23] D. Kuck, P. Budnick, S. Chen, E. Davis, Jr., J. Han, P. Kraska, D. Lawrie, Y. Muraoka, R. Strebendt, and R. Towe, "Measurements of Parallelism in Ordinary Fortran Programs," *IEEE Computer*, Vol. 7 no. 1 (Jan. 1974).

[24] D. Kuck, R. Kuhn, B. Leasure, and M. Wolfe, "The Structure of an Advanced Vectorizer for Pipelined Processors," *Fourth International Computer Software and Applications Conference*, October 1980.

[25] R. Allen and K. Kennedy, "PFC: A Program to convert Fortran to Parallel Form," Tech. report MASC-TR 82-6, Department of Mathematical Sciences, Rice University, March 1982.

[26] J. Dennis and E. Van Horn, "Programming Semantics for Multiprogrammed Computations," *Communications of the ACM*, Vol. 9 No. 3 (March 1966), pp. 143-155.

[27] *HEP Fortran 77 User's Guide*, Pub. no. 9000006, Delelcor, Inc., Aurora, Co. 1982.

[28] *Cray Computer Systems Technical Note: Multitasking User Guide*, Pub. no. SR-0222, Cray Research, Inc., Mendota Heights, Minn., Jan. 1985.

[29] "Notes from ETA Presentation," Second International Conference on Supercomputing, Santa Clara, CA., May 1987.

[30] E. Dijkstra, "Cooperating Sequential Processes," *Technical Report EWD-123*, Techological University, Eindhoven, The Netherlands, 1965, reprinted in [Genu86], pp. 43-112.

[31] A. Veidenbaum, "Compiler Optimizations and Architecture Design Issues for Multiprocessors," CSRD doc. no. 520, U of I Center for Supercomputing R and D, 1985.

[32] *Final Report – Numerical Aerodynamic Simulation Facility Feasibility Study*, Defense, Space, and Special Systems Group, Burroughs Corporation, Paoli, Penn., March 1979.

[33] D. Padua, "Multiprocessors: Discussion of Some Theoretical and Practical Problems", Ph.D. Thesis, report 79-9990, Dept. of Computer Science, Univ. of Illinois Urbana-Champaign, Oct. 1979.

[34] R. Cytron, "Doacross: Beyond vectorization for multiprocessors." *Proceedings 1986 International Conference on Parallel Processing*, Aug. 1986, pp. 836-844.

[35] C. Polychronopoulos, *On Program Restructuring, Scheduling, and Communication For Parallel Processor Systems*, CSRD doc. no. 595, U of I Center for Supercomputing R and D, August 1986.

[36] A. Osterhaug, *Guide to Parallel Programming on Sequent Computer Systems*, Sequent Computer Systems, Inc., Beaverton, Oregon, 1986.

[37] *FX/Series Architecture Manual*, Alliant Computer Systems Corporation, Acton, Mass., April, 1985.

[38] G. Pfister, W. Brantley, D. George, S. Harvey, W. Kleinfelder, K. McAuliffe, E. Melton, V. Norton, and J. Weiss, "The IBM Research Parallel Processor Prototype (RP3): Introduction and Architecture," *Proceedings 1985 International Conference on Parallel Processing*, Aug. 1985, pp. 764-771.

[39] *Encore Parallel Processing Guide*, Encore Computer Corporation, Marlborough, Mass., 1988.

[40] *Notes from the Argonne National Labs Parallel Computing Forum*, Argonne National Labs, Nov. 1987.

[41] S. Ahuja, N. Carriero, and D. Gelernter, "Linda and Friends," *IEEE Computer*, Vol, 19 no. 8 (Aug. 1986), pp. 26-34.

[42] *Programming Language Fortran ANSI x3.9-1978*, American National Standards Institute, 1978.

[43] Perry Emrath, "Xylem: An Operating System for the Cedar Multiprocessor", *IEEE Software*, Vol. 3 No. 4 (July 1985), pp. 30-37.

[44] C. Hoare, "Towards a Theory of Parallel Programming," *Operating System Techniques*, C. Hoare and R. Perrott (Eds.), Academic Press, London, 1972, pp. 61-71.

[45] C. Zhu and P. Yew, *A Scheme to Enforce Data Dependence on Large Multiprocessor Systems*, CSRD doc. no. 40, U of I Center for Supercomputing R and D, July 1984.

System	Microtasking				Data	Macrotasking			
	doall	doacross	high-level spreading	automatic parallelization	shared/private common	spawn	wait	locks	events
Alliant	no	yes	no	yes	no	no	no	no	no
BBN Butterfly – future plans	Doparallel,unlocked Do ... Continue	Doparallel,locked Do ... Begin Ordered End Ordered	Begin Parallel End Section	no	Shared Common Common	no	no	yes	no
Cray	yes	no	yes	no	Common Task Common	yes	yes	yes	yes
Encore Parallel Fortran	yes	doall send/wait end doall	Parallel End Parallel	yes	Shared Private Volitile	no	wait and barrier	yes	yes
IBM Parallel Fortran PRPQ – future plans	Parallel loop Continue	no	Parallel Case End Case	yes	yes	yes	yes	unknown	unknown
Sequent	no	yes	no	yes	shared by compiler option	yes	yes	yes	no

Table 1. Comparison of Multiprocessor Tasking Systems

Polycyclic Vector Scheduling vs. Chaining on 1-Port Vector Supercomputers

Ju-ho Tang and Edward S. Davidson

Department of Electrical Engineering
and Computer Science
University of Michigan
Ann Arbor, MI 48109-2122

Johau Tong

The Center for Advanced Computer Studies
University of Southwestern Louisiana
Lafayette, Louisiana 70504

ABSTRACT

This paper studies the impact of chaining and several instruction scheduling schemes on one-memory-port vector supercomputers, illustrated by the Cray-1 and Cray-2. The lack of instruction chaining in the Cray-2 vector processor requires a different instruction scheduling scheme from that of the Cray-1. Situations are characterized in which *simple vector scheduling* can generate optimal code, which fully utilizes at least one functional unit for machines with chaining. With enough registers *polycyclic scheduling*, even without chaining, guarantees full utilization of one functional unit, after an initial transient, for loops with acyclic dependence graphs. Workloads are represented by vectorizable Livermore Fortran Kernels (LFKs). The effectiveness of applying polycyclic scheduling to the Cray-2 is compared with optimal simple vector scheduling on the Cray-1. The speedup of polycyclic vector scheduling on the Cray-2 over the schedule achieved by the current CFT77 compiler on several vectorizable LFKs is also presented.

1. Introduction

The Cray-2 [1] is a descendent of the Cray-1 [2] with clock period reduced from 12.5 nsec to 4.1 nsec. Several data sets on the performance of 24 Livermore Fortran Kernels (LFKs) on the Cray-1 and Cray-2 have been reported [3]. With the clock speed improved 3 times, the single processor peak performance of Cray-2 is about 3 times that of the Cray-1. But the reported Cray-2 speedup over Cray-1 for the vectorizable LFKs is always less than 3. In order to achieve the clock speedup, the Cray-2 has deeper pipelines which aggravates performance degradation due to dependence. The Cray-2 processor contains a local memory in addition to vector registers in an attempt to reduce the traffic demand, and hence the performance bottleneck, at its single port to common memory. Finally, the Cray-2 does not support chaining between functional units. Therefore two vector operations can be executed concurrently only if they have no vector registers in common, whereas with chaining on the Cray-1 an operand register of the second could be the result register of the first.

This research was supported by the University of Michigan.

The purpose of this paper is to study the impact of chaining on the instruction scheduling and performance of the Cray-1 and Cray-2. *Simple vector scheduling* (SVS) is the most commonly used scheduling scheme that the Cray Fortran compilers (CFT) apply to generate vector code for the Cray-1. In some situations, for a machine with chaining, SVS can generate code that achieves optimal performance by fully utilizing one of the functional units. Some of these situations are characterized here. In other situations, some alternative scheduling strategy might be preferred.

Polycyclic scheduling has been proposed [4] to solve the scheduling problem for horizontal architectures. Horizontal architecture, like Multiflow's Trace/7 or Cydrome's Cydra 5, are scalar machines with multiple functional units that rely on their compilers to locate and explicitly schedule parallel functional unit operations. Polycyclic scheduling can guarantee full utilization of one functional unit, after an initial transient, for loops with acyclic dependence graphs provided that the processor has a sufficient number of registers. Polycyclic scheduling is now commercially implemented as Directed Dataflow in Cydrome's Cydra 5 computer [5]. Polycyclic vector scheduling (PVS) is an extension of polycyclic scheduling for vector machines. The effectiveness and difficulties of applying PVS to the Cray-2 to achieve full utilization of one functional unit are studied.

The LFKs 1, 2, 7, 8, 9, 10, 12, 18, and 21, which are vectorized by CFT77.20, have been chosen as the set of benchmarks in our study. Four other vectorized LFKs 3, 4, 6, and 22 are not considered because LFKs 3, 4, 6 do not have acyclic dependence graphs and LFK22 contains a function call. The speedup of polycyclic vector scheduling on the dynamic-memory Cray-2 over the current CFT77.20 compiled code on these LFKs is presented.

2. Time Bound

If the data dependence graph of a loop contains no cycles then every iteration of the loop is independent of every other iteration and the loop is vectorizable. Patel [6] has shown that for such acyclic dependence graphs there always exists a schedule that fully utilizes at least one functional unit. This fully utilized unit is the *most frequently used (MFU)* unit and its usage determines a lower

CH2617-9/88/0000/0122$01.00

bound on the time to execute that loop. The Cray-1 and Cray-2 each have one floating point unit for addition, one for multiplication, and one memory port for load and store. The Cray-2, unlike Cray-1, does not have a reciprocal approximation unit as the Cray-1 and this operation is performed by the multiplication unit. The Cray-2 has an additional port for load and store to its local memory. In the following paragraph, these memory ports are considered as functional units.

A *simple (lower) bound* on run time, in clock periods (CP), can be computed by counting the number of instructions for each functional unit in each iteration. A floating point division is executed as one reciprocal approximation operation followed by three multiplication operations.

$$T_{Cray-1} \geq max \left\{ \#+,\ \#*,\ \#r,\ L+S \right\} \bullet LL$$

$$T_{Cray-2} \geq max \left\{ \#+,\ \#* + \#r,\ L+S \right\} \bullet LL$$

MFU unit = name of term selected from *max* expression

where *LL* is the loop limit, i.e. the total number of loop iterations in the LFK source code,
#+ is the number of floating addition instructions,
#* is the number of floating multiplication instructions (plus 3 per divide instruction),
#r is the number of floating reciprocal approximations (i.e. one per divide instruction),
L is the number of memory loads and *S* is the number of memory stores in each iteration.

Table 1. Simple Bound for Vectorizable LFKs on Cray-1 and Cray-2.

LFK	#+	#*	#r	L/S	CP ≥
1	2	3	0	3/1	4LL
2	2	2	0	5/1	6LL
7	8	8	0	9/1	10LL
8	21	12	0	15/6	21LL
9	9	8	0	10/1	11LL
10	9	0	0	10/10	20LL
12	1	0	0	2/1	3LL
18-1	10	8	2	12/2	14LL
18-2	16	10	0	16/2	18LL
18-3	2	2	0	4/2	6LL
21	1	1	0	2/1	3LL

3. Cray-1 and Cray-2 Architectures and Timing Models

3.1. Overview of the Cray-2

The Cray-2 computer contains four identical background processors. Each background processor contains vector registers, scalar registers, local memory, and functional units to perform both vector and scalar operations. The foreground processor supervises the four background processors [1]. Only a single background processor is discussed in this paper.

The B and T registers used as auxiliary storage for the A and S registers in the Cray-1 are replaced by local memory in the Cray-2. The local memory can also be used as auxiliary storage for vector register spilling. With a size of 16,384 64-bit words, it can store the images of up to 256 vector registers. Only read and write instructions between local memory and A, S, and V registers can access local memory.

3.2. Cray-1 and Cray-2 Instruction Issuing

The Cray-1 scalar instruction issuing scheme is described in [7]; vector instruction issuing is described in [8]. Except for the set vector length (VL) instruction, each one-parcel instruction issue in the Cray-2 takes two clock periods, whereas in the Cray-1 one-parcel instructions can be issued on successive clocks. The Cray-2 instruction issuing process contains conflict checking of functional unit and register reservations as in the Cray-1, except that when a vector instruction uses an operand register that is reserved as the result register of a previous instruction, the instruction cannot be issued until the register is free, i.e. there is no chaining in the Cray-2. The Cray-1 can issue that instruction at the chain slot time which occurs well before the register is free; however, if the chain slot time has been missed, the instruction must then wait until the register is free. With flexible chaining, as in the Cray X-MP, there is no specific chain slot time and the instruction issue is not delayed if any one of the vector register operands is reserved as a result register. The functional units and vector registers of the Cray-1 and the Cray-2 are reserved similarly. Local memory in the Cray-2 is reserved each time a vector register is spilled or restored.

3.3. Timing Model

Like the Cray-1, the Cray-2 has a register-register architecture, i.e. its functional unit operands come only from registers and its results go only to registers. To perform a memory-memory operation, explicit load and store instructions are required to move data between registers and memory. Each vector register can hold a maximum of 64 floating point numbers. Vector operations with vector lengths greater than 64 elements are cut into vector *strips* of 64 elements [9]. The short strip, if any, is executed first. Each floating point vector instruction initiates one floating point operation per cycle for *VL* times, where *VL* is the vector length of the strip. Scalar instructions generate addresses for vector loads and stores, update the loop index and control the vector loop turning. Most of these scalar instructions execute concurrently with the vector instructions and do not increase the loop execution time.

For each compiled kernel, accurate execution timing can be calculated from the instruction issuing conditions and the instruction execution and resource reservation times. Memory conflicts are the only element of unpredictability. A timing model is developed to express the execution time of each LFK code in clock periods. We ignore memory conflicts, .e.g. due to I/O activity and multiple processors. We also assume sufficiently large vector length in each vector strip and ignore instruction access time and all the effects caused by limited instruction buffer size. Reser-

Table 2. Timing Parameters of the Cray-1 and Cray-2

Group	Name	Definition	Cray-1	Cray-2
1	LCST	vector load chain slot time	√	
	MCST	vector floating point multiplication chain slot time	√	
	ACST	vector floating point addition chain slot time	√	
2	LPD	vector load extra port delay	√	√
	SPD	vector store extra port delay	√	√
	LMPD	local memory extra port delay		√
	MFD	vector floating point multiplication unit extra delay	√	√
	AFD	vector floating point addition unit extra delay	√	√
3	LD	result register extra delay at vector load	√	√
	LMLD	result register extra delay at local memory vector load		√
	MD	result register extra delay at vector floating point multiplication	√	√
	AD	result register extra delay at vector floating point addition	√	√
	RAD	result register extra delay at vector floating point reciprocal approx.	√	√
4	SOD	operand register extra delay at vector store		√
	LMSOD	operand register extra delay at local memory vector store		√
	MOD	operand register extra delay at vector floating point multiplication		√
	AOD	operand register extra delay at vector floating point addition		√

vations of functional units, vector registers and local memory are the main things to check at instruction issue time in our model. The model has proved to be an accurate predictor of run time for the Cray-1. The long instruction access delay and some scalar instructions that do not execute concurrently with vector instructions make this model less accurate for the Cray-2. Timing parameters of the vector instructions are defined in Table 2. The Cray-2 timing values, in number of clocks, are typically double the Cray-1 values [10].

In general, the execution time for the first vector strip is different from the others. The difference is not significant for simple vector scheduling. To simplify the timing expression, for simple vector scheduling we use the execution time of the middle strips, $T_{strip}(VL)$, and for polycyclic vector scheduling we concentrate on the steady state iterations of the vector loops, after the initial transient. The complete loop execution time for a simple vector schedule is:

$$T_{total} = \left\lfloor \frac{LL}{64} \right\rfloor \bullet T_{strip}(64) + T_{strip}(LL\,(mod\ 64))$$

where $T_{strip}(0) = 0$.

4. Simple Vector Scheduling

Each vector loop iteration in a simple vector schedule contains exactly the instructions for a single vector strip. In particular, during one iteration of a loop there can be no load instruction to preload operands for the next iterations, or store instructions to store results of previous iterations. CFT77.20 applies simple vector scheduling to most of the LFKs that it can vectorize for the Cray-1, but for LFKs 3, 6, and 12 it applies a vector loop unrolling technique, which executes two vector strips in each vector loop. The lack of chaining in the Cray-2 makes simple vector scheduling perform poorly for the Cray-2. Look ahead beyond one strip in the scheduler is often required in order to find instructions that can execute concurrently without chaining.

4.1. Simple Vector Scheduling for Processors with Chaining

Without considering hardware implementation limitations, some properties of simple vector scheduling can be developed for vector processors with chaining. To analyze an expression, it is first transformed to *reduced form* by removing excess parentheses that are used to group some, but not all, terms when three or more terms are added or when three or more terms (factors) are multiplied. For example, y(i)=(((a*b(i))*c(i)+d(i))+e(i)+f)*w(i)+x is transformed to y(i)=(a*b(i)*c(i)+d(i)+e(i)+f)*w(i)+x. The mathematical integrity of the expression is preserved by the associativity of addition and multiplication. Parentheses in a reduced expression are used only to surround an index expression or to surround an addition expression that is used as an operand of a multiplication. According to the ANSI Fortran standard, the commutativity of addition and multiplication can be used to change the order of execution of operations within a pair of parentheses [11]. Only expressions in reduced form are considered here. The sum of n terms is counted as n-1 additions and one of these additions is considered ready to start if *any* pair of terms has been computed. The product of n terms is treated similarly.

For simplicity of analysis, we assume a machine that has the same floating point functional units as the Cray-1, but flexible chaining between functional units, a sufficient number of processor registers to keep all the temporary results, and sufficient memory bandwidth so that fetching the needed operands and storing the results does not limit performance. Also, we assume that a floating point addition and a floating point multiplication can be issued at the same clock period. Flexible chaining is assumed so that one operation does not have to try hitting two different chain slot times. In fact, most chain slot times can be met for these LFKs by a code generator with a good timing model [8].

Consider an expression with no common subexpressions and an acyclic dependence graph that contains only addition (+) and multiplication (*) operators. Such an expression has a simple vector schedule that makes the utilization of at least one functional unit equal to 1, provided that $VL \geq AD + MD$. Full utilization of a functional unit means that once that functional unit starts, (i) its execution is continuous without any idle gap until the completion of a strip, and (ii) no idle gap occurs between successive strips.

A *level-one* expression is an expression whose only common subexpressions are of the form *a op b* where *a* and *b* are simple variables or constants and *op* is an operator [12]. For a level-one expression that contains only one common subexpression, if that subexpression has an addition operator and #+ > #*, then there is a simple vector schedule that fully utilizes the addition unit; when #+ < #*, then there exists a simple vector schedule that fully utilizes the multiplication unit if and only if at least one * can start immediately.

For loops that contain several expressions, even if for each expression there is a functional unit that can be fully utilized, there may not be a functional unit that can be fully utilized for the complete loop. When the fully utilized functional unit is the same for each expression, as in LFK8 and 18-2, this unit is fully utilized for the complete loop. When these fully utilized functional units are not the same, then more complicated analysis is needed to decide whether simple vector scheduling can fully utilize one functional unit. All the loops in Table 1 contain either a single expression or multiple expressions with the same fully utilized functional unit.

Although sufficient memory bandwidth was assumed above, the bandwidth of one-port machines is inadequate for some LFKs. Kernels 8 and 18-2 need more than one vector operand before some floating point computation can be started and in this situation simple vector scheduling for a machine with only one memory port cannot generate code to overlap the operations of floating point functional units with memory accessing; therefore, it cannot achieve full utilization of the memory port although it is the MFU unit.

A vector loop unrolling technique that overlaps the memory loads of the next strip with the floating point computations of the current strip can, however, solve this problem. Similarly, an unrolling technique that not only overlaps the memory loads of next strip with the floating point computations of the current strip but also overlaps the memory store with the floating point computation of the next strip can eliminate delay caused by the nonchainability of vector store. After adapting these *improved operand fetching techniques*, the simple bound can be achieved for LFK8 and 18-2 after an initial transient.

4.2. Simple Vector Scheduling for the Cray-1

For some kernels in Table 1, simple vector scheduling does not generate a schedule that fully utilizes one of the Cray-1 functional units. The reasons are limited memory access bandwidth and the nonchainability of vector store. Eight vector registers are sufficient for simple vector scheduling (enhanced with the improved operand fetching) to generate code without spilling for all the vectorized LFKs.

The optimal run time of a single vector strip of the vectorizable LFKs on the Cray-1 with simple vector scheduling is shown in Table 3. In Table 3, the nonchainability of vector store has contributed an extra 1VL for LFKs 7, 8, and 18-2. If the loop unrolling technique described in section 4.1 were used, the run time for each strip of LFKs 7, 8, and 18-2 would be reduced by 1VL, 3VL, and 3VL, respectively. These reduced times meet the simple bounds shown in Table 1 (plus a constant term).

5. Polycyclic Scheduling for the Cray-2

The lack of chaining in the Cray-2 makes simple vector scheduling perform poorly for the Cray-2. A chain that contains memory load, floating point addition and multiplication takes $\approx 1VL + LCST + ACST + MD$ on the Cray-1, but takes $\approx 3VL + LD + AD + MD$ on the Cray-2. For the Cray-2, CFT77.20 unrolls a vector loop a fixed number of times so that it can overlap operations between that many successive strips, but no further overlapping is done. In contrast, polycyclic scheduling systematically unrolls loops until it achieves maximum overlapping and generates an optimal throughput schedule, provided that there is sufficient temporary storage in the processor. Polycyclic scheduling is proposed in [4] for loops with acyclic data dependence

Table 3. Optimal Cray-1 Strip Run Time with Simple Vector Scheduling(SVS)

Kernel	*Timing Equation (in CPs)*	*Time (in CPs)*
1	*4VL+LPD+SPD+2LCST+2MCST+AD+1*	*4VL+54*
2	*6VL+3LPD+SPD+2LCST+MCST+AD+1*	*6VL+53*
7	*11VL+6LPD+SPD+2LCSt+ACST+3MD+AD+3*	*11VL+92*
8	*24VL+7LCST+4ACST+5LPD+4SPD+2AFD+5MD+4AD+1*	*24VL+221*
9	*11VL+2LPD+SPD+8LCST+ACST+7MCST+AD+7(1)*	*11VL+171*
10	*20VL+10LPD+9SPD+1*	*20VL+86*
12	*3VL+LPD+SPD+LCST+AD*	*3VL+26*
18-1	*14VL+5LPD+SPD+5LCST+3ACST+AFD+2MD+RAD+4(1)*	*14VL+136*
18-2	*21VL+2LPD+2SPD+2AFD+9LCST+4ACST+3MCST+4AD+4MD+6(1)*	*21VL+240*
18-3	*6VL+2LCST+1+2LPD+2SPD+AD*	*6VL+45*
21	*3VL+1+2LCST+AD+SPD*	*3VL+32*

graphs and has been generalized in [13] for loops even with data dependence cycles. Polycyclic vector scheduling is used in [14] and in this paper to generate code for the Cray-2.

5.1. Background on Polycyclic Scheduling for Acyclic Dependence Graphs

This section briefly illustrates the work done by Hsu [13]. The problem of optimal throughput scheduling is to find a valid schedule that achieves the *minimum initiation interval (MII)* between successive loop iterations. Consider a pipelined horizontal scalar machine with the same number of functional units (including the single memory port) as well as the same number of pipeline stages in each functional unit as the Cray-2. Assume that the polycyclic architecture has a wide enough instruction word to initiate two floating point operations (one + and one * or reciprocal) and one memory access request per clock period. Instead of 8 vector registers, the polycyclic architecture can use delay elements as proposed in [4] or a scalar register file with sufficiently high throughput to support the concurrency of two floating point operations and one memory access. For loops with acyclic dependence graphs, since there exists an optimal schedule that can fully utilize at least one functional unit, *MII* is given by

$$MII = \max\left\{\#+,\ \#* + \#r,\ L+S\right\}$$

$$= \textit{number of operations in the MFU unit}$$

Once *MII* has been found, a valid schedule with that initiation interval can be constructed by either of the two algorithms in [13]. Assume that the acyclic dependence graph is sorted into a linear sequence of N nodes in which every node depends only on nodes preceding it in the sequence. Here we describe algorithm A, which generates schedules with shorter transients than algorithm B.

```
1   p ← MII
2   for j ← 1 to N do
3       t_j ← 0
4       for each i ∈ K_j,
            where K_j is the set of nodes on which j depends
            do t_j ← max{ t_j, t_i + delay of i's functional unit}
5       while j's functional unit is busy at (t_j mod p)
            do t_j ← t_j + 1
```

When computing the earliest issue time, t_j, for node j, the data dependence requirement is met in step 4 by examining all the predecessor nodes that j depends on. If issuing node j at t_j does not cause a resource conflict, then node j is assigned to that time. Otherwise, the starting time of node j is incremented in step 5 until there is no conflict. Among the p choices, there is always a conflict-free time to use since p ≥ the number of operations in any (fully pipelined) functional unit. With this schedule, a new (independent) scalar iteration can start every p clocks. Register conflicts are not checked in the algorithm, i.e. it is assumed that there is an adequate number of registers.

Polycyclic schedules achieve optimal performance only after several loop iterations; the first few iterations are not optimal because resources reserved for nonexistent previous iterations are unused. The number of suboptimal iterations is

$$\left\lceil \frac{\textit{last issuing time of the 1st iteration}}{MII} \right\rceil$$

Similarly, the same number of final iterations are suboptimal. The startup penalty is amortized over the total number of loop iterations. The steady state schedule is optimal, in the sense that at least one functional unit is fully utilized. Furthermore, there is no loop turning penalty in a polycyclic schedule.

For a simple loop with a single expression like C(J)=(B(J)/A(J)+X))+Y, simple vector schedules cannot generate code that fully utilizes any of the functional units. For loops with several expressions where some expressions have distinct fully utilized functional units, it is either more complicated or impossible for simple vector scheduling to generate code that fully utilizes one functional unit. But polycyclic scheduling can always construct code that fully utilizes one functional unit. When the dependence graph has cycles, representing dependence between iterations, polycyclic scheduling can be adapted by increasing MII. When a loop iteration has internal conditional branches, polycyclic scheduling has further difficulties, since it is based on deterministic optimization at compile time; however, some heuristics are proposed in [13].

5.2. Polycyclic Vector Scheduling

Instead of issuing one operation at a time, polycyclic scheduling for acyclic dependence graphs can be used to issue vectors of operations. This is called *polycyclic vector scheduling (PVS)* and the vector length is called the *polycyclic vector length (PVL)*. Each time slot in algorithm A now represents PVL successive clocks.

If $PVL \geq \max\left\{LD,\ AD,\ MD,\ RAD\right\}$ *(seeTable 2)*, then all data dependence can be satisfied by issuing a node at least one time slot after the last predecessor node that it depends on. Such a schedule still fully utilizes the MFU unit after an initial transient.

The above properties are true only for scalar or vector machines with flexible chaining. For the Cray-2, the result vector register can be used only after *VL+result register extra delay*. The result register extra delay at vector load is approximately VL for the dynamic memory Cray-2 [10]. Algorithm A can be adapted to approximate the Cray-2 by letting each time slot be VL clock periods, the delay of each addition and multiplication vector operation be one time slot, and the delay of memory load and reciprocal approximation be two time slots. The approximation arises from the fact that two operations in the same time slot may in fact be skewed by a small constant number of clocks.

Table 4: Modulo Reservation Table of LFK1

time slot	load/store	*	+
0	l_1^0		a_1^{-1}
1	l_2^0	m_3^{-1}	
2	l_3^0	m_1^0	a_2^{-1}
3	s^{-1}	m_2^0	

l_1 denotes load Z(K+11), l_2 denotes load Z(K+10), l_3 denotes load Y(K), s denotes store X(K), m_1 denotes the multiplication of T with Z(K+11), m_2 denotes the multiplication of R with Z(K+10), m_3 denotes the multiplication of Y(K) with (R*Z(K+10)+T*Z(K+11)), a_1 denotes the addition of R*Z(K+10) with T*Z(K+11), and a_2 denotes the addition of Q with Y(K)*(R*Z(K+10)+T*Z(K+11)).

Superscripts denote the strip number, where 0 is this strip and -1 is the previous strip. $MII = 4$.

For LFK1, algorithm A generates a modulo reservation table [13] as in Table 4, where LFK1 is

```
      DO 1 K=1,990
1     X(K) = Q + Y(K) * (R * Z(K+10) + T * Z(K+11))
```

Each operation except vector store requires a result vector register. Hence,

$$\#\ of\ Virtual\ Registers = \#+ + \#* + \#r + L$$

In LFK1, only 8 virtual vector registers are required and these can easily be allocated to the 8 physical vector registers of the Cray-2.

For loops that require a large number of virtual registers, local memory can be used to spill registers so as to reduce the required number of physical registers to 8 without increasing the traffic at the common memory port, which is often a bottleneck. Only one vector register can be spilled into local memory each VL, and a spill and the following eventual reload takes 2VL clocks. Each spilled virtual register requires a physical register for at least $4 \bullet VL + result\ register\ extra\ delay$ clocks, corresponding to using the register $1 \bullet VL + result\ register\ extra\ delay$ for a result, and 1VL each for a spill, a restore, and an operand. The *result register extra delay* of vector load and reciprocal approximation is approximated by 1VL. The *result register extra delay* of addition and multiplication is approximated by 0. Therefore, a virtual result register with lifetime $l \bullet VL + result\ register\ extra\ delay \geq 4VL$ clock periods can be spilled into local memory to reduce the register requirement by 1 for $(l-4) \bullet VL$ clock periods without increasing run time, provided that there are no local memory access conflicts.

The number of vector registers required to achieve the simple bound after spilling into local memory and the number of virtual registers for the code generated by PVS are listed in Table 5. The number of physical vector registers required to achieve the simple bound depends on the linear node list of algorithm A. For particular situations where more than 8 registers are required, further evaluation is needed to decide which one of the following methods will work and will increase run time the least: (1) increasing the initiation interval by some amount and completely rescheduling, (2) spilling into common memory, or (3) breaking a time slot into several sequential time slots and spreading its operations so that an operand of one operation can share a register with the result of another. The third method is used in the next section.

Table 5. Register Requirement for Polycyclic Vector Scheduling

LFK	No. of Virtual Regs	No. of Required Regs
1	8	< 8
2	9	< 8
7	25	9
8	51	11
9	27	8
10	19	< 8
12	3	< 8
18-1	32	11
18-2	42	10
18-3	8	<8
21	4	< 8

6. Performance Results of Polycyclic Vector Scheduling

6.1. Polycyclic Vector Scheduling vs. Chaining

The run time per steady state vector loop strip of the LFKs in Table 1 on the Cray-2 with PVS, as derived from the timing model with evidence from Cray-2 runs, is shown in Table 6. Except for LFK10, which has no initial transient, each of the the vectorized LFKs in Table 1 has an initial transient of one vector loop with PVS. The total loop run time for such a schedule is

$$T_{total} \approx \left(\left\lceil \frac{LL}{64} \right\rceil - 1 \right) \bullet T_{steady\ state} + T_{final\ transient} + T_{initial\ transient}$$

When PVS generates code that requires no more than 8 vector registers, it can achieve the time bound of Table 1 without chaining, if given enough iterations to amortize the initial transient. The Cray-2 speedup over Cray-1 in this case can approximate the three times clock speed improvement ratio. But, PVS makes temporary data remain live longer than with SVS. Even after spilling vector registers into local memory, LFKs 7, 8, 18-1, and 18-2 require more than 8 vector registers in order to execute each vector loop in *MII* time slots. Spilling registers into local memory reduces the number of required registers, but when the register requirement in each time slot frequently exceeds 8 as in LFK8, the local memory access path is jammed with register spilling and restoring. Considering that today's trends in application codes show an increasing number of variables in their vector loops, the vector register limitation can become an increasingly serious bottleneck of the Cray-2.

An operand register cannot be repeated as the result register in a single Cray-2 vector instruction, although it can be repeated in scalar instructions. When two floating point instructions are executed in the same time slot, the vector register requirement could be reduced by 2 if each

Table 6. Cray-2 Steady State Strip Run Time with Polycyclic Vector Scheduling (PVS)

Kernel	Timing Equation (in CPs)	Time (in CPs)
1	4VL+SPD+2AD+MD+8	4VL+70
2	6VL+5LPD+SPD	6VL+48
7	10VL+LD+3LPD+SPD+2MD+AD+MFD+AOD	10VL+151
8	28VL+3MD+7AD+3AFD+8LMPD+LMLD+3AOD+LMSOD+2LMLD	28VL+272
9	11VL+2MD+6AD+AOD+MFD+AFD	11VL+155
10	20VL+10LPD+9SPD+AOD+2	20VL+157
12	3VL+2LPD+SPD	3VL+24
18-1	15VL+2LD+MD+4AD+MFD+AFD+MOD+5AOD+10	15VL+242
18-2	26VL+7AD+4MD+4AFD+LMLD+LPD+SPD+LMPD+2LMSOD+2MOD+3AOD+14	26VL+279
18-3	6VL+4LPD+2SPD	6VL+48
21	3VL+2LPD+SPD	3VL+24

instruction could reuse an operand register as its result register. For LFKs 7, 8, 18-1 and 18-2, this change in the instruction set architecture, as found in the Cray X-MP, could reduce the vector loop run times. Increasing the local memory bandwidth to enable two concurrent accesses, would also reduce the run time for LFKs 8, 18-1, and 18-2, which require frequent register spilling. Increasing common memory bandwidth to enable two concurrent accesses, would make the common memory port no longer the MFU unit for LFKs 8, 18-1, and 18-2; this would also be useful for spilling.

6.2 Polycyclic Vector Scheduling vs. CFT77

CFT77.20 unrolls LFKs 1, 2, 12, 18-3, 21 and does not unroll the other LFKs in Table 1. Each of these unrolled LFKs requires fewer than 8 physical vector registers. The speedup of polycyclic vector scheduling over the schedule achieved by CFT77.20 on the LFKs of Table 1 is shown in Table 7. CFT77 overlaps 9 floating point subtractions with the 20 memory accesses of LFK10; therefore, not much speedup is achieved by PVS. For LFK12, CFT77.20 unrolls 4 strips in a single loop iteration to gain performance. Since the inner loop iteration lengths of LFKs 2 and 21 are less than 64, the full effect of polycyclic vector scheduling is not seen. The increased code size due to either loop unrolling or PVS increases the instruction buffer loading, which affects the run time. Larger inner loop limits help to amortize this increase in run time

Table 7. PVS vs. CFT77.20

kernel no.	loop limits	CFT77.20 Time (in CPs)	PVS Time (in CPs)	speedup
1	990	7556	5434	1.39
2	50	4540	4131	1.10
7	995	17174	13305	1.29
8	100x2	8878	8626	1.03
9	101	2237	2033	1.12
10	101	2515	2486	1.01
12	1000	4289	4250	1.01
18-1	100x5	15184	12564	1.21
18-2	100x5	20836	18926	1.10
18-3	100x5	4516	4256	1.12
21	25x25x25	197156	192553	1.02

and other transients, as reflected in the higher speedup seen in Table 8.

Table 8. PVS vs. CFT77.20 with extended loop limit

kernel no.	loop limits	CFT77.20 Time (in CPs)	PVS Time (in CPs)	speedup
2	501	13805	12172	1.13
8	1000x2	81292	72498	1.12
9	1001	19170	14800	1.29
18-1	1000x5	137701	100607	1.37
18-2	1000x5	192540	156240	1.23
21	1000x25x1	372320	316480	1.18

7. Summary and Conclusion

The impact of chaining on the performance of the Cray-1 and Cray-2 can be studied by comparing each processor's scheduling scheme. In some situations, simple vector scheduling can generate code that fully utilizes one of the functional units of a vector machine with chaining. Some of these situations have been characterized in this paper. In particular, simple vector scheduling with the vector unrolling techniques described in section 4.1 can fully utilize one of the functional units for each of the vectorizable LFKs in Table 1. Polycyclic vector scheduling can fully utilize one of the functional units, after an initial transient, for all loops with acyclic dependence graphs. When polycyclic vector scheduling generates code that requires no more than 8 vector registers, which includes LFKs 1, 2, 9, 10, 12, 18-3, and 21, it can achieve the time bound of Table 1 plus a constant without chaining, if given enough iterations to amortize the initial transient.

The unrolling required for polycyclic vector scheduling makes temporary data remain live longer, thus increasing the number of registers needed relative to simple vector scheduling for machines with chaining. While 8 vector registers are enough for simple vector scheduling to generate Cray-1 code without spilling for all the vectorizable LFKs in Table 1, a polycyclic vector schedule requires 11 vector registers to execute LFK8 in order to achieve full utilization of one functional unit, even with frequent spilling to the Cray-2 local memory.

Polycyclic vector scheduling by maximizing execution overlap gains speedup over CFT77.20. The advantage of polycyclic vector scheduling decreases when the register requirement frequently exceeds 8 and the local memory port is jammed with register spilling and restoring. To apply polycyclic vector scheduling to the Cray-2, further evaluation is needed to learn how to minimize the run time when more than 8 vector registers are required in order to fully utilize one functional unit. Some hardware modifications would increase the effectiveness of applying polycyclic vector scheduling to the Cray-2.

Acknowledgement

The authors would like to thank N. Pang and J. E. Smith for the use of their Cray-1 simulators to verify our timing model. We also thank Cray Research, Inc., for the use of the Cray-2 at Mendota Heights.

REFERENCES

[1] Cray Research Inc., "*The CRAY 2 Computer System Functional Description,*" HR-2000, Cray Research Inc., Chippewa Falls, WI, July 1987.

[2] R. M. Russell, "The Cray-1 Computer System," *Communications of the ACM,* Vol. 21, No. 1, pp. 63-72, January 1978.

[3] F. H. McMahon, "The Livermore Fortran Kernels: A Computer Test of the Numerical Performance Range," UCRL-53745, Lawrence Livermore National Laboratory, Livermore, Calif., December 1986.

[4] B. R. Rau, C. D. Glaeser and R. L. Picard, "Efficient Code Generation for Horizontal Architectures: Compiler Techniques and Architectural Support," *Proceedings of 9th Annual International Symposium on Computer Architecture,* pp. 131-139, 1982.

[5] B. R. Rau, "Cydra 5 Directed Dataflow Architecture," *Spring Compcon '88,* pp. 106-113, Feb. 29-March 4, 1988.

[6] J. H. Patel and E. S. Davidson, "Improving the Throughput of a Pipeline by Insertion of Delays," *Proceedings of 3rd Annual International Symposium on Computer Architecture,* pp. 159-164, 1976.

[7] S. Weiss and J. E. Smith, "Instruction Issue Logic in Pipelined Supercomputers," *IEEE Trans. on Computers,* Vol. C-33, No. 11, pp.1013-1022, November, 1984.

[8] J. Tang and E. S. Davidson, "An Evaluation of Cray-1 and Cray X-MP Performance on Vectorizable Livermore Fortran Kernels," *Proceedings of 1988 International Conference on Supercomputing,* pp. 510-518, July, 1988.

[9] I. Y. Bucher and M. L. Simmons, "A Close Look At Vector Performance of Register-To-Register Vector Computers And A New Model," *Proceedings of ACM Sigmetrics Conference on Measurement and Modeling of Computer Systems,* pp. 39-45, May, 1987.

[10] J. A. Swensen, "High-Bandwidth/Low Latency Temporary Storage for Supercomputers," Technical Report No. UCB/CSD 87/383, Computer Science Division(EECS), Univ. of California, Berkeley, CA, December 1987.

[11] *American National Standard FORTRAN (ANSI X3.9-1978),* American National Standards Institute, New York, 1978.

[12] E. Horowitz and S. Sahni, *Fundamentals of Computer Algorithms,* Computer Science Press, Maryland, 1978.

[13] P. Y. Hsu, "Highly Concurrent Scalar Processing," Technical Report CSG-49, Coordinated Science Lab., Univ. of Illinois, Urbana, IL, January 1986.

[14] C. Eisenbeis, W. Jalby, A. Linchnewsky, "Squeezing More CPU Performance out of a Cray-2 by Vector Block Scheduling," *Proceedings of Supercomputing '88,* November, 1988.

Visualization

Chair: Raymond Elliott
Los Alamos National Laboratory

Interactive Scientific Visualization and Parallel Display Techniques

J.A. Sethian
Department of Mathematics
University of California, Berkeley
Berkeley, California 94720

James B. Salem
Thinking Machines Corporation
245 First Street
Cambridge, Massachusetts 02142

A.F. Ghoniem
Department of Mechanical Engineering
Massachusetts Institute of Technology
Cambridge, Massachusetts 01236

Abstract

In this paper, we describe a new graphics environment for essentially real-time interactive visualization of computational fluid mechanics. Within this environment, the researcher may interactively examine fluid data on a framebuffer with animated flow visualization diagnostics which mimic those in the experimental laboratory. This provides an effective and interactive way to analyze the underlying physical mechanisms, and to compare results with laboratory experiment.

The system is implemented on a data parallel supercomputer attached to a framebuffer. Since most fluid visualization techniques are highly parallel in nature, this allows rapid animation of fluid motion. The fluid diagnostic tools include display of moving color contours for scalar fields, smoke/dye injection of passive particles to identify coherent flow structures, and bubble wire tracers for velocity profiles.

We demonstrate our interactive graphics fluid flow system by analyzing data generated from a numerical simulation of laminar and turbulent flow over a backwards-facing step. Input parameters are menu-driven, and images are updated at nine frames updates per second.

I. INTRODUCTION

In this paper, we present a new graphics environment for essentially real-time visualization of the results of numerical simulations of fluid mechanics. Starting from a pre-computed discrete set of time-dependent flow quantities, such as velocity and density, the user may interactively examine the data on a framebuffer with animated flow visualization diagnostics which mimic those in the experimental laboratory. Images are updated at nine frames per second, providing an effective way to study the validity of the solution, analyze fluid flow mechanisms, and compare numerical results with experiment.

The goal of this project is to provide interactive flow visualization tools together with rapid animation to allow feedback between display information, input parameters, the algorithm chosen and, ultimately, the underlying model. Much as in a laboratory experiment, our graphics environment allows the researcher to study fluid velocity by injecting color-coded dye which is passively advected as the animation sequence unfolds. Because the animation is both interactive and in real-time, as moving eddy structures form they can be tagged and tracked with dye mid-animation. Different colored dyes can be used to watch regions merge or diffuse, and mixing mechanisms may be studied. Time-dependent scalar fields, such as temperature and density, can be displayed as color-tagged moving regions, and the range of displayed values may be changed mid-animation. Within this environment, the researcher typically performs dozens of realistic flow visualization experiments in rapid succession.

The system is implemented on a data parallel supercomputer with parallel input/output to a framebuffer. Rapid display results from the fact that fluid visualization techniques are highly parallel. The key components of this interactive graphics environment are a Connection Machine CM-2 data parallel supercomputer, a CM-2 framebuffer, and a front end Symbolics Lisp Machine.

The environment assumes a stored data field, obtained either through numerical simulation or physical experiment. The data is preprocessed so that the relevant physical quantities, such as velocity, vorticity, density, pressure, temperature, etc., are given at each time step on a fixed discrete grid in the computational domain. The full set of data is then loaded into the memory of the front end machine. At each time step, the next data field is downloaded into the CM-2's memory, the appropriate numerical calculations are performed in parallel on the CM-2, and the images are displayed on the framebuffer. The key visualization tools are summarized below.

Vector Quantities

For vector quantities, such as velocity, the tools are

- Injection of passively advected tracer particles.
- Mouse-driven location of injection points.
- Menu-specified frequency and number of injections.
- Menu-driven color-tagging according to location, frequency, time, and number of injections.
- Menu-driven type of injection of tracer particles, either
  - along a line ("hydrogen bubble" tracers).
  - concentrated in a disk ("smoke/dye" injection).
  - on a ring.
  - continuous injection at a point.
- Zoom and pan, interactively controlled during display.

Scalar Quantities

For scalar quantities, such as temperature, density, and pressure, the tools are

- Motion of regions of selected contoured scalar values, generated by appropriate coloring of all points in selected range.
- Mouse or menu-driven selection of range of scalar values and color map to be displayed.
- Zoom and pan, interactively controlled during display.

Images are updated on the framebuffer at nine frames per second, producing essentially real-time motion.

As a demonstration, we analyze data produced from a numerical simulation of two-dimensional viscous, incompressible flow. In [20], a detailed convergence study of flow over a backwards-facing step was performed for a wide range of flow conditions using the random vortex method, showing excellent agreement with experimental measurements. Using our graphics environment, we isolate and identify a variety of physical flow phenomena, such as eddy formation, merger, propagation and

CH2617-9/88/0000/0132$01.00

decay, mixing and intertwining of fluid structures, and pairing of counteroscillatory vortical structures.

II. PHYSICAL AND NUMERICAL FLOW VISUALIZATION

A. Physical

Flow visualization has a long and rich history as a technique for analyzing fluid mechanics in laboratory apparatus. Starting with the experiments of Reynolds and Prandtl, flow visualization techniques can be divided into three main categories, as described in [7,13,26]. The first involves the addition of foreign materials (either fluid or solid) into the flow. The added substance is visible, and the flow is indirectly viewed through the motion of the foreign substance. In such techniques, it is important to minimize the effect of the added substance on the original flow. The second category of visualization techniques rely on the determination of physical qualities of the flow itself. An example is variation in fluid density, which relates to the refractive index of the fluid. Measurement of optical changes in the refracted light shows density variations in the flowing fluid. The third category involves the introduction of physical changes into the flow. Examples are the release of luminescent particles and the introduction of localized energy at specific points. Using these techniques, photographs illustrating a variety of fluid phenomena may be found in [2,11,13,15,24,25,26].

The type of technique chosen depends on what one wants to see. In the first category, namely the addition of foreign objects, one might wish to examine three different objects: (1) a *streamline,* which is a curve in the domain that is tangent to the instantaneous (time-frozen) velocity field, (2) a *pathline,* which is the path in the domain a particle takes as it moves through the flow as a function of time, and (3) a *streakline,* which is the position of all particles in the flow that have passed through a fixed point in the domain during a given time interval. For stationary flow, (1), (2) and (3) are equivalent. We illustrate the distinction between (2) and (3) for time-dependent flow by imagining a foreign object which drops anchors as it is advected. The set of all dropped anchors is a pathline. Conversely, suppose dye is injected in time-dependent flow through a fixed point over a finite time interval. The positions of the dyed fluid particles at a later time gives a streakline.

One way to illuminate these flow structures is to inject dye in fluids and smoke into gases (see [7,13]). Injection is either through small holes or slots in the sides of the apparatus, or externally into the body of the flow, by means of a hypodermic needle (for dye) or wires/tubes (for smoke). The exposure time and the number and frequency of injection points determine the type of curve obtained. Sprinkling a large number of particles throughout a domain (such as aluminum dust, see [11]), and photographing a short-length time exposure shows streamlines. A long-time exposure of a single particle shows a pathline, whereas continuous injection of dye through a fixed point shows a collection of streaklines passing through the same point.

Smoke/dye injection is particularly effective for visualizing the development of large coherent flow structures, such as vortices (see [13]). In the roll-up of these large structures, smoke/dye can concentrate within the structures connected by thin wisps of dye. To illustrate velocity profiles, one common technique is a hydrogen bubble wire placed in the physical domain. Relying on the electrolysis of water [13], a voltage is applied through the wire, and hydrogen bubbles are emitted (as well as smaller oxygen bubbles). If the wire is placed normal to the flow, the bubbles are carried away from the wire, showing the velocity profile.

The second category of fluid visualization relys on optical effects due to the density variations in the flow. As outlined in [13], this can be used to illustrate such mechanisms as (1) shock formation in compressible flow, (2) mixing of fluids of differing densities, and (3) combustion. The most straightforward technique is a shadowgraph, which is simply a photograph of the image of the shadow from a point-shaped light source, yielding qualitative information about density variations. A more involved, but highly effective, technique results from schlieren methods which use optical devices to qualitatively measure the diffraction of light and hence fluid density variation.

Photographs produced from the above are often enhanced through image-processing. The image is digitized, and streaklines and streamlines may be identified. Mathematical techniques such as splines and Fourier filtering are used to extract quantitative flow data (see a series of articles in [2,25]). A particularly intriguing application of image-processing is in the identification of large coherent structures in turbulent flow. Such structures are often masked by small-scale noise; in [5] a filtering technique is used to bleed out high wave numbers and identify large, coherent, low wave fluid structures. The application of some of these techniques to numerical flow data will be discussed in [17].

B. Numerical

Extracting flow properties from numerical data is equally challenging. In numerical simulations, immense amounts of data are produced, far more than can be understood as raw data. For example, Winkler et. al. [27] have calculated that their two-dimensional code with 250,000 computational zones yielding 5 flow variables every 4 time steps gives a sustained data generation rate of 3.47 megabits per second, where a megabit is defined to be 1024x1024 bits. As an alternative, the researcher tries to extract the "right" quantities from the data to verify conjectures and generate new ones. A natural way of performing such extraction is through visualization; as pointed out in [27,28], the human brain deals with the complexity of raw data through images [22]. Another role of visualization, as discussed in [22], is to avoid the prohibitively high cost of central mass storage; it may be more cost-effective to store computed images, rather than all the intermediate results. For further discussion of scientific visualization, see [12].

Flow visualization in numerical experiments performs a role similar to that in physical experiment, namely to isolate particular variables or fluid quantities, such as wave interactions, surface instabilities and vortex generation (see [27]). Large aggregate structures, such as moving fluid eddies, are difficult to quantify, but easy to compare with experiment and other simulations. Motion (animation) provides history, which allows one to see dynamic changes in the flow, both on the small-scale (sharp gradients) and the large-scale (topological changes). Such mechanisms may be very hard to extract from raw data or vector velocity plots. As pointed out by Zabusky in [28], visualization also provides an avenue for discovering new phenomena, such as the strong supersonic vortex ring behind a shock shown in [27]. Using computer versions of the flow visualization techniques described above, images of a variety of flow phenomena have been generated in recent years [15,16,21,22,27,28].

III. PAST WORK

There are several different approaches underway to visualize numerical flow simulations. A major difference in the approaches lies in the division of computer resources between the algorithms that approximate the equation of motion and the algorithms that generate the image.

A sophisticated graphics environment has been developed by Winkler, et. al. [27] at Los Alamos National Laboratory, and duplicated at other institutions [22,27]. The basic arrangement, referred to as a "numerical laboratory", is that the algorithms that approximate the equations of motion in terms of key variables run on a large supercomputer, while a secondary machine accepts intermediate values as they are computed and generates auxiliary variables, along with visual images which are turned into movies. An important issue is to maximize communication rates between the various components. Some spectacular movies have been made with this facility [27], and the ability to generate a movie of virtually every numerical simulation provides a record of variations in computed results and images as the model and numerical parameters are changed. In this arrangement, the researcher must reside at the facility to produce both the numerical solution and the images. At the other extreme, the user is located far from the supercomputer facility. A low-cost environment for producing local images from data generated at a remote site is described in [10].

In the above arrangements, the generation of images is non-interactive. A different approach with some interactive features was developed at the Numerical Aerodynamic Simulation program at NASA Ames Research Center [16]. Here, the full set of results of a numerical simulation are stored before images are made. Images are then produced from the stored data using a distributed interactive graphics environment.

Working from a graphics workstation, the user can display arrows to represent velocity vectors and contours and surfaces for scalar variables. To display particle trajectories, the coordinates of the injected particles are entered into the workstation. The trajectories are then computed on a remote supercomputer, shipped back to workstation, and then displayed. Images computed in this manner are shown in [16].

In this paper, we present a third approach, namely that of using a data parallel supercomputer with parallel I/O to a framebuffer to analyze precomputed data. Since most flow visualization algorithms are highly parallel, this allows rapid animation of flow visualization. The suitability of a massively parallel processer to scientific visualization was mentioned in [28], and the Connection Machine in particular in [27].

IV. THE CONNECTION MACHINE CM-2 SYSTEM

The Connection Machine CM-2 data-parallel computer contains up to 65,536 1 bit processors, each with 8K bytes of local memory. The communications network is essentially a hypercube, however, a general purpose communications system called the "router" allows messages to be sent from any processor to any other while the exact patterns are hidden from the user. Nearest neighbor routing patterns for n-dimensional grids are preprogrammed for efficiency. Each processor is also directly connected to one of eight possible 75 Mbyte/sec I/O channels.

The CM-2 is a single-instruction multiple-data (SIMD) computer. It is programmed in a data-parallel fashion: one assigns a processor to each data element in the problem. The user writes and debugs CM programs using high level languages which are parallel extensions of FORTRAN 8X, C or LISP on a front end computer such as a SUN or a VAX. The serial portions of the program are executed on the front end, and the parallel instructions, including communications, I/O and indirect addressing, are broadcast to all the processors via a sequencer. The sequencer's microcode library translates the front-end's parallel instruction set to the processors' very simple RISC instruction set. Each group of 32 processors, hereafter called a "node", shares an optional floating point accelerator and indirect addressing hardware. A table may be stored at each node and, using the indirect addressing hardware, each processor in the node may access a different value in the table.

The flexibility of the machine is greatly enhanced by the notion of "virtual processors". Each physical processor simulates a number of virtual processors by segmenting its memory and time multiplexing the processor hardware. Its implementation is transparent, in that the user simply declares the number of virtual processors needed. The number of virtual processors may be changed dynamically and tuned to fit the problem's data set.

The Connection Machine system's I/O devices include a framebuffer, a high-speed parallel disk, and a VME interface. The framebuffer display is a high-resolution 1280 x 1024 display with up to 24 bits per pixel. The Connection Machine system can update a television quality (NTSC) image in real time (30 frames per second.) The programs used in this paper are written in *LISP (pronounced star-lisp) a set of parallel extensions to the Common Lisp language. More information on the Connection Machine system and *LISP may be found in [9,23].

V. DISPLAY OF TIME-DEPENDENT SCALAR FIELDS

For scalar variables Ψ, such as stream function, temperature, density, energy or pressure, moving color-coded contours are displayed. Here, $\Psi = \Psi(x,y,t)$ is a function of space variables (x,y) and time t. Display of only a limited range of Ψ is permitted, allowing the user to isolate particular phenomena, such as the merger of vortex structures.

A standard technique is to display contour lines. However, the calculation of contour lines is time-consuming, and, ultimately, not necessary. Instead, each pixel lying in the interior of the fluid flow geometry is colored according to the current magnitude of the variable under examination at each time step. The algorithm works as follows. We configure the CM-2 with enough virtual processors to assign one per pixel. Let C_i be the value of the color of the pixel corresponding to processor i. At the beginning of the run, the full data set of scalar variables is loaded in memory of the CM-2. Since there are more pixels than discrete grid values for Ψ, bilinear interpolation is used to go from the coarse data grid to the fine processor pixel grid. The user then specifies Ψ_{min} and Ψ_{max}, which are minimum and maximum display values for Ψ. Every time step, each processor i sets C_i to Ψ if $\Psi_{min} < \Psi(x,y,t) < \Psi_{max}$ (otherwise, C_i equals the background color), and displays its value of C_i at the appropriate place on the CM-2 framebuffer display. The region of values in the selected range moves as the flow evolves. The image may be panned zoomed, and the number of interpolations between one time step and the next may be changed.

VI. DISPLAY OF TIME-DEPENDENT VELOCITY FIELDS

Velocity fields are displayed by injecting tracer particles into the flow. A processor is assigned to each injected particle. Since the particles are passively advected, each may be moved in parallel.

The algorithm works as follows. We set the initial positions of the injected particles (possible injection layouts are described below). Each injected particle is assigned to a processor, whose memory contains the position and color of the injected particle. During each time step, first a new grid velocity field is retrieved from the front-end machine and spread in parallel in the Connection Machine to each node's memory. Second, to advance the location of the injected particles, each processor, using indirect addressing, retrieves from its nodal memory the velocity components located on the corners of the grid cell containing its particular particle. The velocity at the particle's position is obtained by using bilinear interpolation in space and time between neighboring grid points and the two velocity fields (current and next). The position of each particle is then updated using a first-order Euler scheme. Finally, the positions and colors of the particles are displayed by accessing in parallel the pixels on the attached CM-2 framebuffer.

The size and number of time steps used between displays for the Euler integration are user-defined parameters. Too big a time step results in jerky, disjointed motion, similarly, too small a time step results in a slowed motion of the injected particles. Similar effects occur with poor choices for the number of time steps. Zoom and pan are provided, and the number of interpolations between one time step and the next may be changed.

Several different injection layouts are possible, depending on the phenomenon under study.

A. Smoke/Dye Injection

Smoke/dye injection is used in the laboratory to visualize the evolution of flow. As mentioned earlier, this technique is useful in isolating and identifying coherent fluid structures [13]. The user specifies the number of particles injected, injection point (or points), injection radius R_{inj}, frequency of injection (number of time steps between injections), and color-tagging scheme. Particles are then injected inside a circle of radius R_{inj} around each injection point. To give the appearance of dye, the distribution of injected particles is a truncated Gaussian with mean at the injection point. A large number of particles are released to give a dense concentration similar to dye. The injected particles are then advected by the underlying velocity field.

B. Bubble Wire Injection

In this technique, used to illustrate velocity profiles [13], fewer particles are released along a thin, straight line in the flow. We typically release between 20 and 100 particles evenly along the wire. This tool is used to illustrate velocity gradients, and mimics the creation of a thin line of gas bubbles in the flow. The user specifies the beginning and end of the wire, as well as the number and frequency of released particles.

C. Ring Injection

In an incompressible flow, one may wish to follow the evolution of a patch of constant area. Here, we might examine the change in the length of the boundary in an attempt to understand what happens to a free surface. Since the boundary of the region is passively advected in an incompressible flow, there is no flow through the boundary and the area inside remains constant, even though the boundary becomes wildly distorted. In this technique, we place an extremely large number of particles in a ring around a specified center. We use enough particles so that even with large stretch and distortion, the boundary of the region is discernible. Other initial boundary configurations can be easily programmed.

D. Continuous Injection

In this technique, we inject a stream of particles continuously at a point in the flow. This gives a collection of streaklines and can provide a good way to gauge unsteadiness in a flow [13].

VII. TIMINGS

One measure of the system is the total number of frame updates per second. Each frame update requires

- downloading of the data from the front-end machine to the CM-2's memory
- advancement of the particles positions through Euler's method
- display of particles, which consists of
  - assignment of particles to display grid
  - setting processors to background colors
  - displaying colors

The total number of frame updates depends on many variables, such as the physical size of the machine (and the corresponding ratio of virtual to physical processors), the number of particles injected, the number of bits used to store the fluid data in memory, and number of time steps used in the Euler integration between displays, as well as the manner in which data is stored in the CM-2's memory. A full investigation of the various effects of these parameters will be discussed elsewhere [19].

The fluid calculation discussed in the next section yields 2200 floating point numbers (two velocity components on a 11x100 grid) every time step, as well as data for the stream function. The visualization is displayed on a 1280x128 grid of pixels. To inject as many particles as processors, it takes 34 milliseconds to download the data, and 41 milliseconds to update 8000 injected particles for one Euler time step. The time for display depends on the ratio of virtual processors to physical processors, since there is one virtual processor per pixel. On a 8K processor machine, with a virtual processor (VP) ratio of 20, display takes 55 milliseconds; on a 16*K* machine (VP ratio 10), display takes about 38 milliseconds. The total image update time on a 16K machine is .113 seconds, and we typically clock a sustained, running frame update speed of about 9 frames a second.

One of the current limitations of the environment is the amount of data that can be loaded into the memory of the Connection Machine at each time step. The current memory available allows us to fill each node's memory with at least 50,000 floating point numbers, after allowing memory for temporary software and particle positions. Thus, for example, we can load velocity components u and v on at least a 200x200 grid into each node. If we are given more data points (either a finer two-dimensional grid calculation or a three-dimensional calculation with an additional velocity component). we can employ other options. First, one can increase the amount of data that can be put into each node's memory by truncating the floating point numbers of the numerical data, since there is little need to carry more significant digits than the accuracy of the time integration in Euler's method, or more than the capabilities of the output device. Beyond this, a subset of the data can be spread to each node, which can slow down the response time. Another option is to increase the memory per node. Finally, one could download the data from the high speed parallel disk. These issues will be discussed in [19].

VIII. NUMERICAL SIMULATION OF FLOW OVER A BACKWARDS-FACING STEP

A. Experimental Results

The data under study comes from a numerical simulation of fluid flow using a particle-particle type algorithm known as the random vortex method [3,4,18,20]. In [20] an extremely detailed convergence study of flow over a backwards-facing step for a wide range of flow conditions was performed using a version of the random vortex method presented in [8]. The velocity field and stream function data on a fixed grid serves as the input to the graphics environment described here.

The domain geometry consists of a narrow inlet on the left through which flow enters. A sudden step expansion then occurs, and the flow exits 20 step heights downstream on the right. The critical parameter is the *Reynolds number R*, which describes the balance between inertial and viscous forces. The results of numerous laboratory experiments [1,6,11,14] are described in [20], and summarized below.

At low Reynolds number ($R < 250$), the flow can be characterized as smooth, or "laminar". In this range, the flow portrait consists of a single recirculation zone in the lower-left hand corner. This recirculation bubble is steady and stable; flow is essentially trapped while the majority of the fluid rides over it. Experimental studies report that if the apparatus is tapped, the flow rapidly returns to the steady elliptical profile. Fluid mixing is limited: smoke injection near the inlet stays confined to a narrow path through the chamber. As the Reynolds number is increased through the laminar regime, the scaled portrait remains essentially unchanged, with the length of the recirculation eddy increasing linearly with increasing R.

The beginning of the transition regime ($R \approx 500$) is marked by a clear change in the flow portrait. The downstream edge of the recirculation bubble tears off and moves downstream as a distinct eddy structure. This eddy diffuses rapidly as it moves, and is almost completely dissipated as it exits the channel. When the eddy tears off, the shortened recirculation bubble begins to entrain more fluid, growing in size until another downstream eddy is shed. This periodic growth and shedding mechanism persists as the Reynolds number is increased through the transition regime. As the Reynolds number is increased, stronger and stronger eddies are shed as distinct structures which last for longer times. Significant mixing occurs: photographs of smoke injection into experimental flow in the transition regime show convoluted corkscrew-type paths with fairly wide dispersal.

As the Reynolds number is increased still further, experiments show that the flow becomes fully turbulent for R greater than a few thousand. Here, while eddies continue to shed from the recirculation bubble near the step, boundary layer flow along the top wall separates, and rolls up into counterrotating eddies. These counterrotating eddies intersperse with those shed from the step, trapping a thin narrow band of rapidly moving fluid. Fluid mixing is most pronounced in the turbulent regime.

B. Numerical Algorithm

Many traditional numerical algorithms rely on finite difference approximations to the key fluid quantities, such as velocity, and density (so-called "primitive" variables). Discrete values of these quantities are calculated on logically rectangular grids by approximating derivatives in the equations of motion by appropriate algebraic operations involving neighboring grid points. The accuracy of such a calculation is increased by decreasing the mesh size (increasing the number of mesh points). While such techniques work well in the laminar regime, prohibitively many mesh points may be needed in the turbulent regime to capture the flow characteristics described above.

An alternative is offered by the random vortex method [3,4], which is a Lagrangian particle method that relies on a discretization of the vorticity field of the flow. Vorticity, which is the curl of the velocity, describes the amount of rotation in the flow, and is a particularly appropriate approximation variable for flow which exhibits large global rotating structures. In the random vortex method, the velocity is approximated by a set of discrete vortex elements, or "blobs", whose relative positions and strengths determine the over-all velocity field. The motion of the fluid is approximated by updating the position of the individual vortex elements according to the influence of the aggregate velocity field, plus a random step to model diffusion processes. Boundary conditions are met through the addition of potential flow to satisfy the normal boundary condition and a vorticity creation algorithm to satisfy the tangential no-slip condition on solid walls. For details, see [3,4,18,20].

We performed a two-dimensional calculation, which is a somewhat limiting simplification of real three-dimensional flow. While the laminar and turbulent flow are observed as essentially two-dimensional mechanisms, three-dimensional mechanisms (vortex stretching, etc.) in the transition stage influence the flow portrait. However, in general, the experimental flow picture described above holds.

IX. RESULTS

In this section, we describe the results of our graphics analysis of data computed for laminar ($R = 125$), transitional ($R = 500$), and turbulent ($R = 5000$) flow over a backwards-facing step. The data was generated as follows. We placed a uniform mesh (11x100) on the computational domain, and calculate at each grid point the velocity and stream function from the positions and strengths of the vortex elements. This was done every ten time steps, and the results were written onto tape. Note that this grid plays no role in the numerical simulation: it just provides discrete temporal and spatial sampling of the flow.

Our results illustrate the fluid phenomenon described in [20]. We display the results of smoke/dye injection, bubble wires, and rings of tracer particles at various points in the domain. In addition, we display the scalar stream function Ψ, where $\vec{u}$ is the velocity field and $\vec{u} = (u,v) = (\Psi_y, -\Psi_x)$. Thus, the boundaries between constant colors of Ψ are parallel to the flow. In the display of the scalar variable Ψ, the incoming inlet channel on the left is ignored.

A. Laminar Flow

In this regime the flow is smooth, steady, and stable, and is characterized by a single, stationary recirculation zone wedged in the lower left corner. In Figure 1, we show the time evolution of multi-colored smoke particles injected into the flow using smoke/dye injection. We periodically inject yellow particles in the inlet and purple particles along the bottom wall (see attached slides for color displays; in the below figures, the background is black and all injected particles are white, regardless of position). The moving particles trace out the flow in good agreement with the experimental results described earlier. The parabolic shape of the profile is formed by the advected yellow particles. At the same time, the purple particles are caught up in the recirculation zone, and clearly outline the elliptical bubble near the base of the step.

FIGURE 1:
Dye Injection into Laminar Flow

Next, in Figure 2, we illustrate what happens to a ring of particles placed near the inlet. We begin with a yellow ring, followed by a purple and then blue ring. The rings always contain the same "amount" of fluid, even as they distort and move downstream. One can easily see how some part of each ring moves downstream in the parabolic profile, and some part is caught up in the recirculation zone.

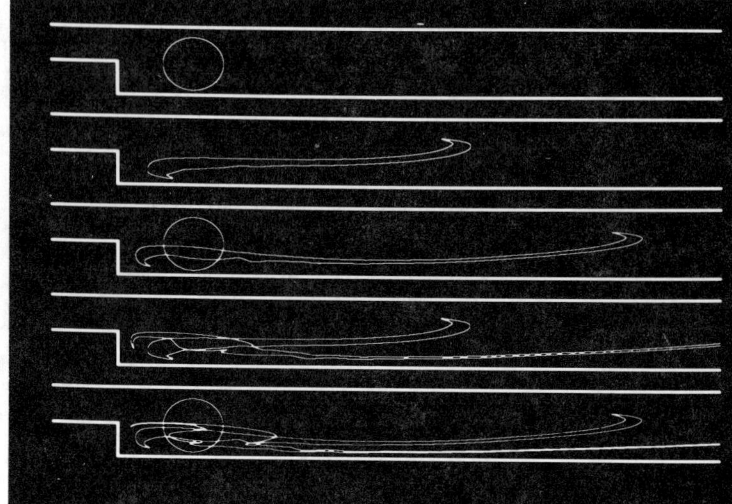

FIGURE 2:
Ring Injection into Laminar Flow

B. Transitional Flow

In this regime, the large recirculation eddy continually breaks off and sheds eddies which move downstream. In Figure 3, we show the time evolution of the scalar field Ψ with color map corresponding to values of Ψ. Here, we have truncated values so only those values of Ψ between 0.0 and .35 are displayed. This isolates the rolled up eddies as they move downstream. Note that the eddies seem to form in pairs: one can clearly see two eddies merge as they start to form a single eddy that moves downstream. This paired merging is difficult to discern from raw data and only becomes evident through the animation of the flow. Other examples of phenomenon revealed through graphics are discussed in [27].

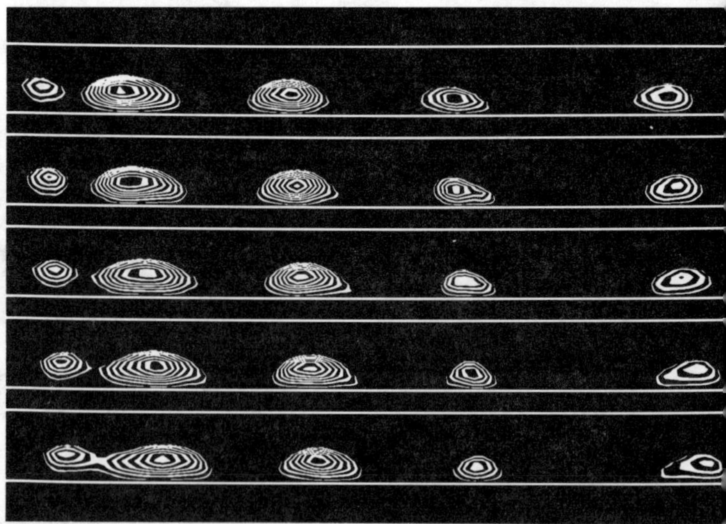

FIGURE 3:
Instantaneous Streamlines for Transitional Flow

In Figure 4, we show the time evolution of particles injected into the transitional flow using smoke/dye injection. The displayed re^ults clearly resemble smoke injection in laboratory apparatus, see [11]. We inject purple particles near the inlet, and blue particles in near the base of the bottom wall. One can easily see the injected particles caught up in the large, clockwise rotating eddies as they move downstream.

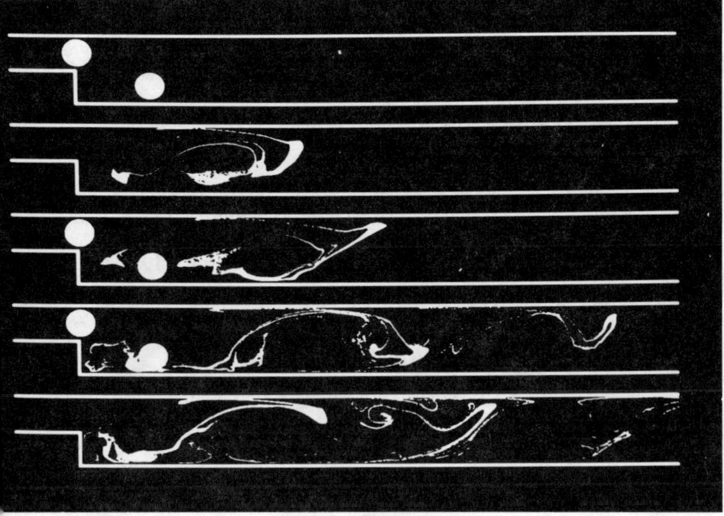

FIGURE 4:
Dye Injection into Transitional Flow

In Figure 5, we use the bubble wire technique along a vertical line just past the inlet. This shows the development of the velocity profile of the evolving flow. We inject 200 particles in repeating sequence of red, blue and yellow, illustrating the evolution of various lines and velocity gradients in the flow.

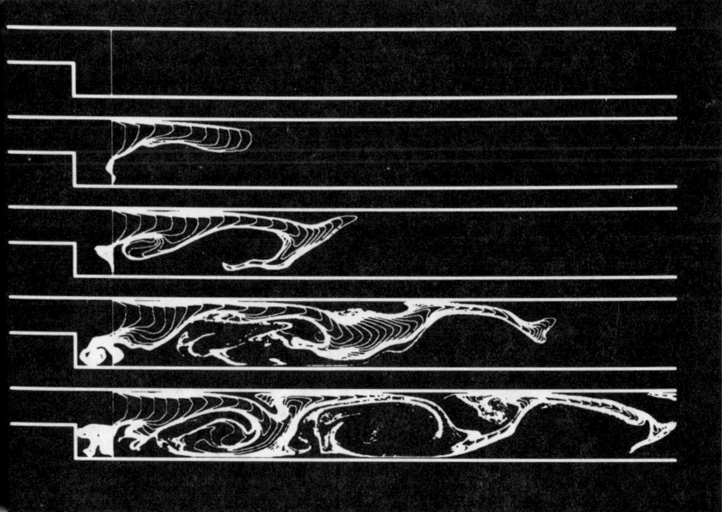

FIGURE 5:
Bubble Wire Injection into Transitional Flow

In Figure 6 we perform a single ring injection of 256,000 yellow particles along a ring near the inlet. Although it is difficult to believe, the collection of yellow particles in each portrait actually represents a single, closed curve that has been distorted by the flow. It is a remarkable indication of the mixing power of transitory large-scale fluid structures that the evolving ring of yellow particles forms such a wildly contorted boundary. For further discussion of this phenomena, see [17,20].

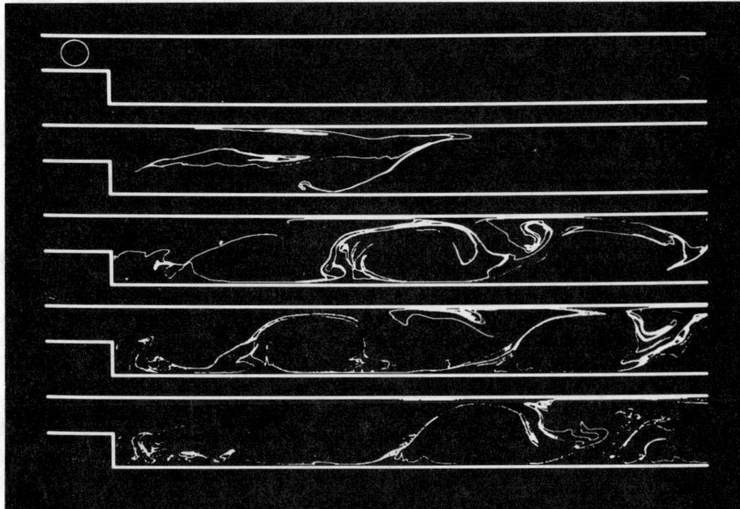

FIGURE 6:
Ring Injection into Transitional Flow

In Figure 7 we blow-up Figure 4 near the lower-left corner near the base, providing further detail about the growth and shedding of large eddy structures.

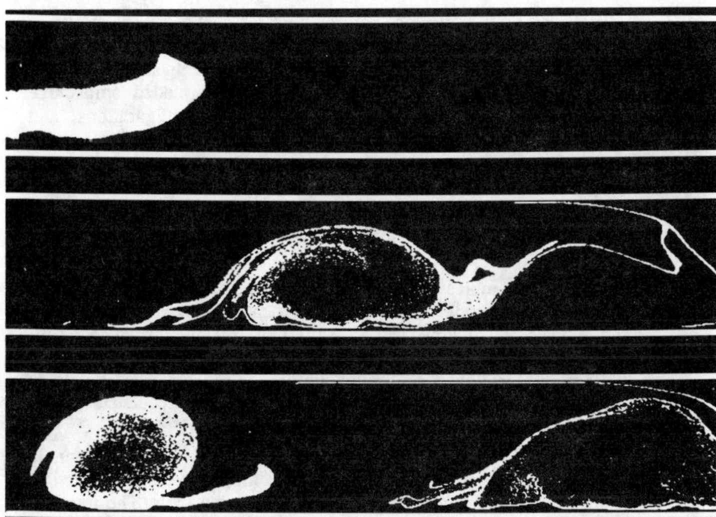

FIGURE 7:
Blow-up of Corner for
Dye Injection into Transitional Flow

C. Turbulent Flow

In this flow regime, eddies are shed off the top wall as well off the step. In Figure 8, we show the time evolution of two sets of smoke particles injected into the flow. Blue particles are injected near the bottom towards the corner, and yellow particles are injected near the middle of the top wall. The blue particles near the step are first dragged backwards by the recirculation zone, and then outline a large, clockwise rotating eddy that moves downstream. Conversely, the yellow particles are sent into a large eddy that rotates in the opposite direction as it moves downstream. The two streams are caught up in different eddy structures as they move downstream and intertwine. For further discussion of this phenomena, see [20].

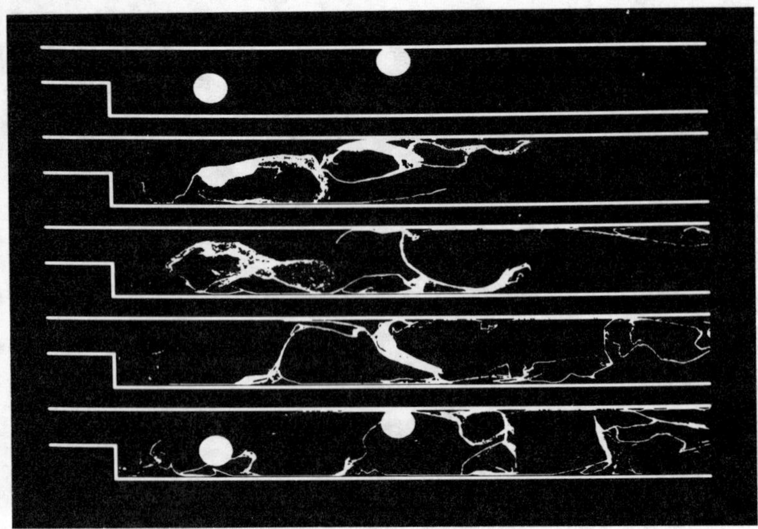

FIGURE 8:
Dye Injection into Turbulent Flow

X. CONCLUSION

We have built a graphics environment for analyzing the results of numerical simulations of fluid mechanics. The purpose of this environment is to provide visualization tools which mimic those in physical experiment. For velocity fields, tools include color-coded smoke/dye injection in user-defined intervals, locations, and configurations, and "hydrogen" bubble-wire tracers for determining velocity profiles. For scalar quantities, color-coded contour maps within user-selected ranges are available. The tools were used to analyze data from a numerical simulation of two-dimensional viscous flow over a backwards-facing step. Further applications to two- and three-dimensional flow can be found in [19].

This project represents a step towards the goal of using interactive visualization as real tool in designing numerical flow experiments. Given a pre-computed set of flow data on a discrete grid, the current environment allows the user to interactively execute computationally intensive calculations as the flow visualization unfolds. Thus, the user is able to perform dozens of experiments with various injection frequencies, locations, and configurations in rapid succession.

The next development might be a true interactive environment, in which the simulation of the underlying fluid mechanics is calculated in real-time and examined using the above visualization tools. The immediate goal would not be the most accurate and refined calculation, but a coarse enough simulation to proceed in close to real-time while observing significant fluid mechanics. Optimally, one could experiment interactively with different design parameters, such as confinement geometries and inlet parameters. If a rough picture of the flow dynamics could be obtained, the user could quickly compare a large number of possible configurations, and select some subset for more refined, detailed calculation. Preliminary work on such an environment has begun, and will be reported elsewhere.

Acknowledgements: We wish to acknowledge the contributions of Jill P. Mesirov and Washington Taylor IV. The velocity field used for display was computed at the Lawrence Berkeley Laboratory, University of California, Berkeley, California. The first author is partially supported by the Applied Mathematics Subprogram of the Office of Energy Research under Contract DE-ACO3-76SF00098. The images were computed at Thinking Machines Corporation, Cambridge, Massachusetts.

REFERENCES

1) Armaly, B.F., Durst, F., Pereira, J.C.F., Schonung, B., *J. Fluid Mech.*, **127,** 473, (1983).

2) Billet, M.L., Kim, J.H., Heidrick, T.R., Eds., *International Symposium on Physical and Numerical Flow Visualization,* Fluid Engineering Division, ASME, **223,** (1985)

3) Chorin, A.J., *J. Fluid Mech.*, **57** 785, (1973).

4) Chorin, A.J., *J. Comput. Phys.*, **27** 428, (1978).

5) Corke, T.C., *AIAA J.* **22,** 1124, (1984).

6) Denham, M.K., and Patrick, M.A., *Trans. Instn. Chem. Engrs.*, **52,** 361, (1974).

7) Gad-el-Hak, M., *Review of Flow Visualization Techniques for Unsteady Flow,* in Flow Visualization IV, Proceedings of the Fourth International Symposium on Flow Visualization, Veret, C., Ed. Hemisphere Publishing Company, Harper and Row, (1987).

8) Ghoniem, A.F., Chorin, A.J., Oppenheim, A.K., Philos. Trans. Roy. Soc. London Ser. A., **304,** (1982), 303-325.

9) Hillis, D., *The Connection Machine,* MIT Press, 1985.

10) Johnston, W.E., Hall, D., Huang, J., Rible, M., Robertston, D., *Distributed Scientific Video Moving Making,* to be presented, Supercomputing88, 1988.

11) Honji, H., *J. Fluid Mech.*, **69,** 229, (1975).

12) McCormick B., DeFanti, T., Brown, M., *Visualization in Scientific Computing,* Report to the National Science Foundation by the Panel on Graphics, Image Processing, and Workstations, 1987.

13) Merzkirch, W., Flow Visualization, 2nd Edition, Academic Press, New York, 1987.

14) Periaux, J., Pironneau, O., Thomasset, F., *Fifth International GAMM Conference on Numerical Methods in Fluid Mechanics,* Springer-Verlag, 1983. **9,** 75, (1976).

15) Reed, H.L., Phys. Fluids, **30,** 2597, (1987).

16) Rogers, S., Buning, P., Merritt, F., Inter. Jour. SuperComput. Appl., **1** No.4, (1987).

17) Sethian, J.A., *Identifying and tracking coherent structures in turbulent flow,* in progress.

18) Sethian, J.A., J. Comput. Phys., **55,** 425, (1984).

19) Sethian, J.A., Salem, J.B., *Interactive Flow Visualization on a Massively Parallel Processor,* to be submitted, Int. Jour. Super-Comput. Appls.,

20) Sethian J.A., Ghoniem, A.F., J. Comput. Phys., **74** 283, (1988).

21) Sethian, J.A., "*Visualization of Data from Numerical Simulations: Moving Surfaces and Fluid Flow*", Video Tape, Lawrence Berkeley Laboratory, 1987

22) Smarr, L., *The Computational Science Revolution: Technology, Methodology and Sociology,* in High-Speed Computing: Scientific Applications and Algorithm Design, Wilhelmson, Ed., Univ. of Illinois Press, (1987).

23) Steele, G., *Connection Machine Model CM-2 Technical Summary,* Thinking Machines Corporation, 1987.

24) Van Dyke, M., An Album of Fluid Motion, Parabolic Press, Stanford, Ca., (1982).

25) Veret, C., Ed. Flow Visualization, IV, Proceedings of the Fourth International Symposium on Flow Visualization, Hemisphere Pub-

lishing Company, Harper and Row, (1987).

26) Werle, H., *Hydrodynamic Flow Visualization*, in Annual Review of Fluid Mechanics, Van Dyke, M., Vincenti, W.G., Wehausen, J.V., Eds., Annual Reviews, Palo Alto, Ca., **5**, 361, (1973).

27) Winkler, K.H.A., Chalmers, J.W., Hodson, S.W., Woodward, P.R., Zabusky, N.J., Phys. Today, Oct., 1987.

28) Zabusky, N.J., Phys. Today, Oct., 1987.

Design and Implementation of a Supercomputer Frame Buffer System

John D. Fowler, Jr. Michael McGowen

Computational Physics Group Computer Network Engineering Group
Los Alamos National Laboratory
Los Alamos, NM 87545

ABSTRACT

A 512 by 512 pixel by 8 bits per pixel frame buffer has been designed, constructed, and installed on a 48 Mbit/s I/O channel of a Cray X-MP 4/16 supercomputer. This project was undertaken to test whether such a system would be useful and, if so, how it would be used. Supporting software provides the ability to convert vector graphics description files into raster format, to show raster movies interactively, and to show vector files by real-time conversion from vector to raster formats. We have shown that real-time animations in an interactive supercomputer environment are feasible and useful with this system.

Keywords: Supercomputer, Graphics, Frame buffer, Rasterization, Animation, User Interface, Scientific Visualization

Introduction

Frame buffers came into use in the mid-seventies as an integral part of raster display systems.[1][2] The frame buffer, also called refresh buffer, is the link between the raster processor and video hardware. It is a memory array that holds a digital representation of the current picture to be displayed on the viewing device. Typically, this display memory corresponds directly to pixels on the screen, with the requisite number of bits per pixel stored sequentially in display memory or in separate physical planes, one plane for each bit per pixel. The key to frame buffer viability is fast, cheap memory, and a relatively fast bus for accessing it.

In practice, frame buffers, being near the end of the graphics chain, have been located in the end-user graphics terminal or workstation, far away from the main computer which was the source of the graphical data. With the introduction and increasing popularity of local area networks and graphics workstations, this distance from the source has both decreased and lengthened: the former for calculations for which the workstation has sufficient power, and the latter for applications which still require supercomputer power, but the results of which are viewed on the user's workstation.

For supercomputer applications we have attempted the approach of putting the frame buffer as close as possible to the application itself, for a number of reasons:

1. We are interested in real-time user control of data while the program is running on the supercomputer. The closer the graphics gets to the main application, the easier it is to build a system to do this in a highly interactive fashion. The data are already there, so putting the graphics on the supercomputer eliminates the burden of shipping huge amounts of data through the network.
2. Suitable bandwidths between supercomputers and frame buffers are becoming available. All Cray supercomputers have a 48 Mbit/s channel, and X-MP models allow the use of an 800 Mbit/s HSX channel. Updating a 512 by 512 pixel by eight bits per pixel frame buffer at 24 frames per second requires a channel bandwidth of 50 Mbit/s. 1000 by 1000 by 24 bits at the same rate requires 625 Mbit/s.
3. Given the existence of a supercomputer with an available channel and interface, such a system is inexpensive. The only hardware expense is for the frame buffer itself.
4. Our users show a certain reluctance to learn a new system of interaction, as would be required with a workstation. They are already familiar with the operating system on the supercomputer, Cray Time Sharing System (CTSS), and appear willing to learn a few simple utilities on this system in order to get the graphics to the frame buffer.
5. As higher speed channels and switchers become available, along with more and faster CPUs per mainframe, the simple concept of frame buffers becomes supportable for many users simultaneously at many locations from a given supercomputer.

In order to accomplish our objectives, we had to answer satisfactorily several questions:

1. Can a time-shared machine in a demanding, multiuser environment support real-time graphics? There are at least two issues here: a) Will the operating system allow enough sequential time-slots to show continuous motion? b) Can graphics algorithms, which are mainly integer and sequential in nature, be programmed to run efficiently on a supercomputer optimized for vectorized floating-point operations?

2. Will the computing cost of such graphics swamp the system and/or bankrupt the user?

3. Will users have a use for such a system if it can be developed?

4. What are the required spatial and color resolutions for typical applications? In particular, what are the tradeoffs between resolution and frame rate? How well does temporal antialiasing overcome the effects of jaggies in animations?

5. What sort of real-time control do users need? Is interaction over a serial network using a dumb terminal sufficient?

In order to answer these questions, we built and wrote supporting software for a simple 512 by 512 by eight bits per pixel frame buffer and attached it to a 48 Mbit/s Cray channel.

The User Environment

The user environment at Los Alamos National Laboratory includes about 30 Cray-1 equivalents, in the form of Cray-1s and Cray X-MPs, tied to a common file system and a common user interface through keyboard control concentrators (kcc's). The network allows serial communications at up to 38 kbaud from the supercomputer to the user, and a few hundred baud in the other direction. In addition, we have a number of Tektronix 4125 terminals supported through the Tektronix DMA interface at effective rates of about 225 kbit/s. Most of our serious users have this capability, and this is the standard by which we are judged. Additionally, a growing number of local area networks and workstations (mostly Sun 3's) is supported by Ethernet communication links at peak sustained rates of about 100 kbit/s.

The supercomputers run the Cray Time-Sharing System (CTSS) in a highly interactive user environment. Most of our users' graphics are created by programs running on the Crays. Some of the graphical output is intended to be viewed interactively as the data are being created, but most of the graphics is written to files or drawn on film for later viewing.

Most of the graphics consists of vector descriptions containing frames with 5,000 to 50,000 vectors per frame, but we see an increasing number of raster images, mainly solid modeler-based frames and animations from calculations that lend themselves to raster display, such as fluid flow instabilities.[3] The advent of a significant amount of 3-dimensional calculations is starting to have an impact on our graphics systems, due to the increased amounts of data in 3-D descriptions and the need to manipulate (rotate) and illuminate images in order to perceive them properly. Nevertheless, our current environment is predominantly 2-D vector in nature.

Hardware

In order to demonstrate that our approach was viable in a larger context than direct Cray connections, the frame buffer was designed to connect to a High Speed Parallel Interface (HSPI) device, which is our standard network connection. Each host in the Central Computing Facility has such a device, which converts its unique I/O interface to a common format. The connection to the HSPI was done to demonstrate two things: first, that full access to all the bandwidth available in existing equipment would enable extreme simplification of the hardware architecture, which in turn allows enormous gains over current solution methods; and second, that the hardware architecture used in image capture systems could be employed in network processor design, enabling the devices to sustain full bandwidth transfers of real-time digital video across a network. This second issue is detailed in another publication.[4]

The HSPI definition was developed when Los Alamos installed its first Cray supercomputer and is similar to the I/O channel definitions of the Cray (the DN/DO and DA/DB channels).

These channels share a fundamental feature: They transmit exactly that data which is of interest, with no command structure or format specification embedded in the data stream. We use this feature to make the frame buffer system simple and efficient. The host maintains an array in memory which represents the image to be displayed. When a frame is complete, the whole array is output to the frame buffer. By continuously outputting data, the display achieves animation.

The frame buffer display is organized as an array of 512 by 512 pixels. This corresponds to the memory organization of the device, which is an array of 512 by 512 bytes. Each byte is an index to one of 256 colors from a palette of 262,144. The Cray channels run at 48 Mbits per second, which allows the transmission of 24 complete image frames per second.

The frame buffer consists of four main sections: The HSPI front-end, video refresh memory, a micro-program engine, and a video interface. Figure 1 contains a block diagram of the frame buffer. Its architecture addresses the primary function, which is the movement of data into and out of memory.

HSPI Front End

The HSPI front end manages the flow control on input from the HSPI channel and notifies the micro-program engine when the input shift register buffers are full. The front end is also responsible for delineating the data in a fashion that is acceptable by the memory array. The memory buffers provide a depth of 256 words that can be strobed in without any other action being taken. The front end counts

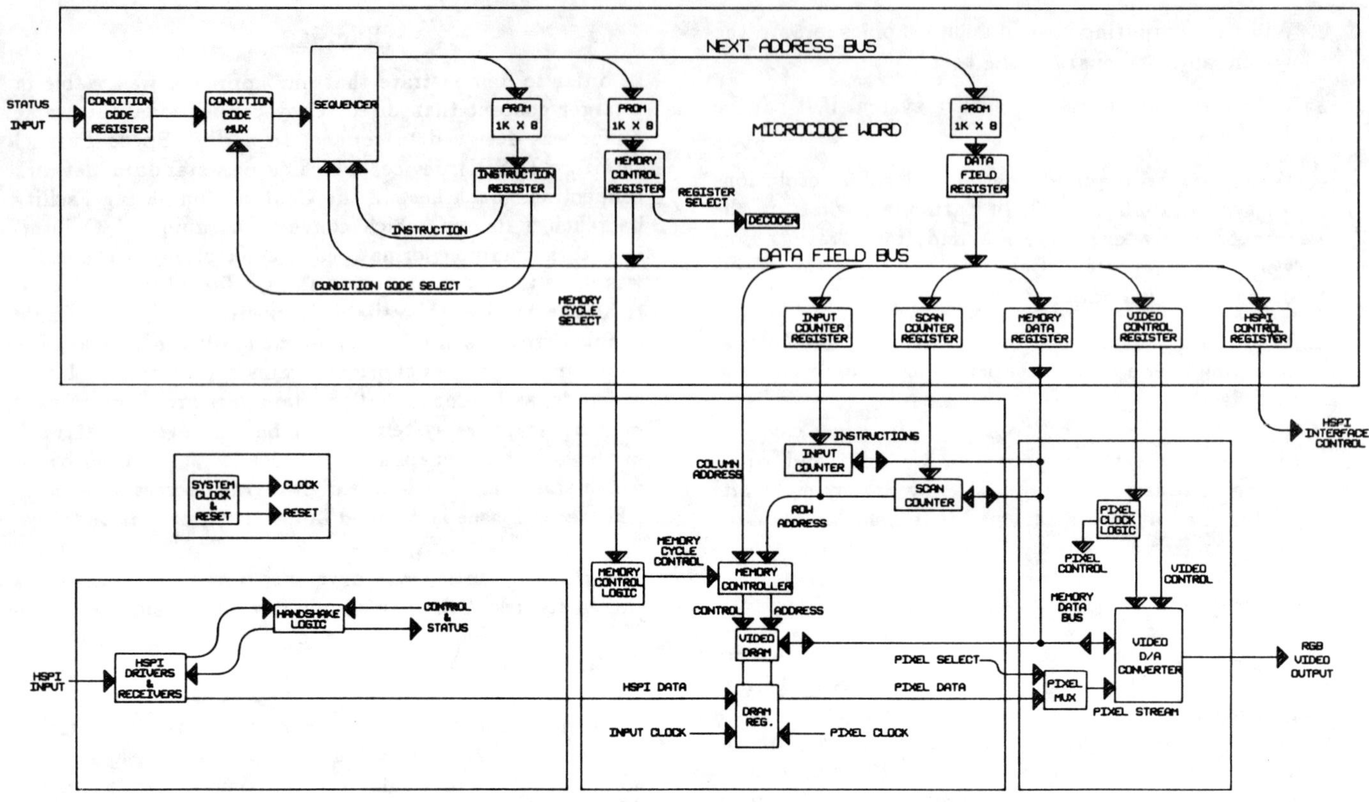

Fig. 1. Block Diagram of Frame Buffer

256 strobes and asserts a signal to the micro-controller notifying it that the buffer is full. This memory is double buffered so that input can immediately proceed with data being directed to a second buffer while the first is being processed. The HSPI channel also contains a RESET line, asserted by the transmitter, which is used to signal an abnormal termination or to provide a resynchronizing event. On RESET, the frame buffer reads the color table.

Video Refresh Memory

Video refresh memory consists of 64k video DRAMs which provide an independent shift register for the input and output of sequential data. The shift registers are 256 locations deep. After they are full, the 256 data values can be moved in parallel into the memory array with one random access memory cycle. High-speed output is accomplished by loading the shift register with the 256 memory locations in parallel and then sequentially shifting the data out. Display memory is single-buffered. Two separate and independent shift registers with separate clocks allow reading and writing without sparkles of random data being displayed on the screen.

Video Interface

The video interface converts the sequential stream of digital data from refresh memory into analog red, green and blue (RGB) signals which drive the display monitor. The display is treated as a 1024 by 1024 image that is updated at 60 frames per second. Each pixel and each row are displayed twice to convert the 512 by 512 memory organization into display format. The video signal is RS-343A compatible.

Micro-Program Engine

The micro-program engine is responsible for maintaining the proper sequencing of events such as video timing and generation of addresses for the next destination of input or the source of the video output. All timing parameters are programmable so that adjustments can be made for different display formats. Input is a completely asynchronous event, yet the output timing must be synchronous and the same every time. The micro-program engine code coordinates all activities and in fact generates the control signals of every function. It is this micro-code that actually defines the behavior of the frame buffer.

Connection to Supercomputer

The frame buffer at Los Alamos is connected to a Cray X-MP 4/16 supercomputer having four processors, 16 million 64-bit words of memory, and a 512 million word solid-state storage device (SSD). A switch on the frame buffer output directs the video signals to either a nearby monitor or to a fiber-optic modem for transmission to a monitor in a user's office about 150 meters away. The picture quality in the user's office is actually better than that from the local monitor because of the amount of radio-frequency interference in the central computing facility. Normally output from the frame buffer is directed to the user's office.

Users access the frame buffer software by logging onto the Cray X-MP 4/16 in the usual manner through our standard network, using any terminal.

Software

The purpose for writing the software was dual: to find answers to the questions posed and, if the answers were sufficiently encouraging, to provide a basic set of programs for our users. Therefore, we tried to make the programs useful both for testing the system and for showing graphics under realistic situations.

We wrote three programs and one utility. The software was written using the FORTRAN 77 compiler provided by Cray Research, Inc., CFT77. Although we have multitasking support on our machines, we have not used it. We have also used traditional graphics algorithms (See below for descriptions). We are confident that by programming in Cray Assembly Language, using multitasking, and/or using more advanced algorithms, we could substantially better the performance reported here.

Software support for the frame buffer consists of three programs and one library of subroutines. These programs are concerned with converting vector descriptions to raster and showing the results. The Common Graphics System (CGS), supported at Los Alamos, uses a vector graphics description embedded in a system-independent graphics metafile.[5] Consequently, our raster programs were written to read graphics files created with this system.

Brief descriptions follow of the programs we have written for this project.

MR (Metafile-to-Raster)

The program MR accepts as input a CGS metafile and creates a raster movie file, with a minimum of user interaction. The program prompts the user first for the name of the metafile, then for the name of the raster file. The program then processes the metafile, frame-by-frame, into raster frames, placing each frame sequentially in the raster movie file. At the end of the program, the first frame of the movie file is created, containing the color lookup table definition and the number of frames in the file. This information is needed by VCR, the program that reads and displays the raster movie file.

The number of different colors in the CGS metafile determines the color lookup table, which is not known until the metafile has been processed. Each time a unique color is requested, it is added to the lookup table. If the maximum of 255 colors is reached, subsequent colors are drawn in white. The first color index, index zero, is reserved for the background color, usually black, and the next index is always defined as white. The color lookup table is packed into the rightmost word of each of the first 256 scan lines. The contents of these words are not displayed.

MR supports the following CGS metafile codes:[6] move, draw, draw marker, set rgb color, hardware text string, set aspect ratio, new page, and end of data.

VCR (Video Cassette Recorder)

This program reads raster movie files generated by MR or any other program that creates a raster file with the proper format, and sends the output to the frame buffer. Its name comes from its ability to emulate many of the functions of a video cassette recorder.

VCR lets the user interactively show a movie in forward or reverse directions, at normal, fast, or slow speeds, and pause on any given frame. The movie can also be shown as an endless loop.

PZIP

PZIP reads a CGS metafile, converting it to raster and showing it under interactive user control. It converts the same CGS opcodes and transforms at the same vector rates as the program MR, above. Interactively, it acts much the same as VCR, except for the fast and reverse commands, with additional commands described below.

PZIP lets the user zoom and/or pan while in single-frame (pause) mode or while in slow-motion or forward mode. At any time, the user can write raster frames from PZIP into a file for subsequent showing with VCR. Whatever the user sees on the screen goes into the raster file. One reason for writing a movie file from PZIP is that VCR is less CPU-intensive than PZIP and has additional commands.

FBLIB

FBLIB is a library that lets the CGS user create a CGS view surface which is the frame buffer. Any CGS program can initialize this view surface at graphics initialization time with a single subroutine call. Subsequently, CGS commands can go to any CGS-supported device and/or to the frame buffer. This is accomplished by using the CGS GON and GOFF view-surface commands and by writing the frame-buffer driver as a so-called CGS "XX" driver.

FBLIB uses run-time memory management to run-time allocate the 262,144-word raster array. Thus, this library adds very little to the executing program's field length until FBINIT is actually called.

Data Structures

The important data structures used by the software reported here are:

the raster array
the packed raster array
the color index array

The Raster Array

The raster for the frame buffer contains 512 lines of 512 pixels, of which 475 lines of 495 pixels are viewable on the screen. Each pixel is defined by a six-bit color index.

A time-efficient but space-consuming method of retaining the raster data is to dedicate a 64-bit Cray word for each pixel, using a 512-by-512 word array (262,144 words) to hold the raster. This affords quick access by the program to any pixel, since each pixel is just a pair of indices into the array.

A more space-efficient approach would involve packing the raster into a smaller-sized array. A natural size would be a 32,768-word array containing the pixels packed into bytes, since this is the form of the packed raster array required by the hardware. This approach would require expending shifts, masking, and logical operations to add a pixel to the array. This was tried and found to be too time consuming. The temporal overhead to such an approach varies with the complexity of the picture, but typically a 20 percent run-time overhead was imposed by this approach. Thus it was dropped in favor of the more space-consuming method, which requires vectorizable packing only at the end of each frame.

The Packed Raster Array

This array contains 32,768 64-bit words for a 512-by-512 pixel raster, allowing eight bits per pixel.

At the end of each frame, the raster array is packed into the packed raster array, an eight-into-one packing. Swapping of adjacent even and odd bytes is necessary to undo what the network does to the data between leaving the Cray and arriving at the frame buffer.

The Color Index Array

This array contains the color index to red, green, and blue intensity definitions. Each color has a range of 64 shades and takes six bits of data. Each index, starting with zero and going to 255, is packed into word 64*(index + 1) of the packed raster array. This information is read by the frame buffer only when a channel reset occurs, which is sent by VCR on the first frame, and by PZIP whenever a new index has been added since the previous frame.

Algorithms

MR, PZIP, and the library FBLIB use Bresenham's line algorithm[1] for vector-to-raster conversions and the Cohen-Sutherland clipping algorithm[1] for clipping.

Rasterization

Converting vector information to raster typically takes about half of the time in MR and PZIP. Because most of the vectors are short in the CGS metafiles we have used (typically, 90 to 99 percent of the vectors in a given file will be fewer than 10 pixels long), vectorizing approaches to rasterization such as the incremental slope method[1] have not been very successful. We have found that Bresenham's algorithm, although it is not vectorizable, converts typical frames faster.

Clipping

The Cohen-Sutherland clipping algorithm was chosen because it provides for trivial acceptance or rejection of most vectors without further testing, when vectors are short. The required testing and further clipping when necessary uses about ten percent of the time in PZIP.

Hardware Characters

We provide hardware character emulation by inserting five-by-seven bit-map representations of characters directly into the raster array. Characters at this size are larger than users expect, based on experience with their terminals, but they are legible. Most CGS metafiles contain at most only a few dozen hardware characters per frame. We have not attempted to evaluate the efficiency of this technique.

Results and Discussion

Because the showing of raster movies consists of simply reading a frame, writing a frame, and checking for user input, it places very little demand on the CPU resources of the supercomputer. Showing a movie from a vector description file, on the other hand, can be quite CPU intensive. The operations for showing a vector frame include reading from the CGS metafile, unpacking and decoding op codes and data, performing the indicated operations (such as setting color index, hardware text, accumulating vectors and rasterizing), packing the output array, and sending it. Because of these differences, we consider the two processes separately.

Two other timing issues arise. We found using the SSD for file storage to be much more satisfactory than using a physical disk unit. In the timings below, we give results for files which were on a "real" disk and for files on the SSD. The SSD on our machine is large enough to hold about 15 minutes of raster information at one time. The other timing issue is the number of users competing for the four CPUs on a Cray X-MP 4/16. We considered three environments: Single-user, where we were the only ones on the machine, Moderate interactivity, involving about 15 users in the execution queue (ready for a CPU), and Heavy, with about 30 users in the execution queue.

In the tests that follow, our timings indicate throughput as measured by timing actions on the display with a stopwatch. Data obtained in this manner are more indicative of usefulness than are data obtained by calculating theoretical performance, by using system timings, or by timing individual loops in the code. The data we measured indicate throughput from reading a file to showing the image on a monitor.

Raster Movies

Showing raster movies with VCR uses about four percent of a single CPU, or about two and a half minutes of CPU time per wallclock hour of movie. Because of this low rate of CPU usage and the presence of four CPUs on an X-MP 4/16, fairly continuous movie rates are perceived in all but the Heavy environment, where pauses of about a second occasionally occur. Table I shows the frame rates we observed in our tests.

Table I. Frame rates (frames/second) for raster movies shown with VCR under various circumstances.

Environment	Disk Real	Disk SSD
Single-User	19.3	23.3
Moderate (15 Users)	13.1	20.2
Ratio (Single/Moderate)	1.47	1.15

We have found that in a heavy environment, the ratios shown above would approximately double.

For SSD files, the performance in a moderate environment is perceived to be quite satisfactory. Even in a heavy environment, useful animations can occur. The performance using a real disk is much more sporadic, depending on who else is using the disk unit on which the file resides. The average frame rates quoted above are far from uniform, and long pauses can occur in an interactive environment using a real disk. Our measurements in the single-user environment indicate that the disks themselves are capable of supplying data fast enough for animations. We believe that if we had a dedicated physical disk unit, performance from it would be satisfactory even in an interactive environment. Operating system constraints prevent us from testing this hypothesis.

Vector Movies

Performance issues concerning vector movies are more complicated because of nonuniformity in frame sizes and in the information to be converted and displayed. Considerations such as the number and length distribution of vectors, number of color changes, and hardware characters complicate the issue.

We have tested the system for a range of vector files covering most of the spectrum our users typically encounter. The results for Single-user tests are shown in Fig. 2. For a moderately loaded system, the data in Fig. 2 will shift to the left by about 30 percent. For a heavily loaded system, the shift will be about 60 percent.

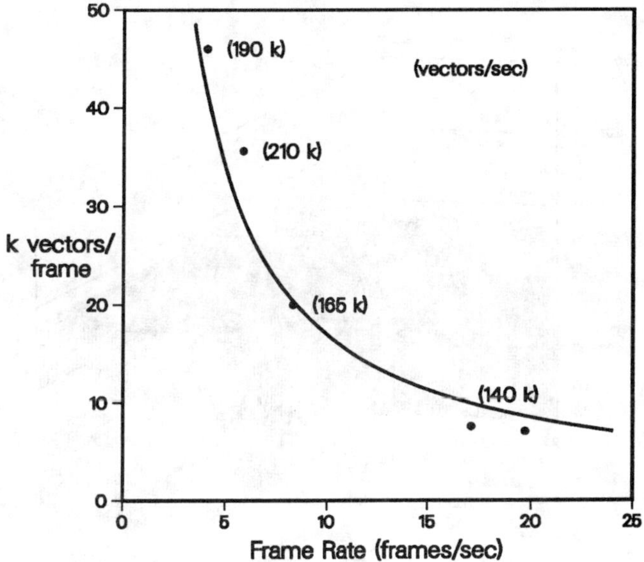

Fig. 2. Frame rates for five CGS metafiles using PZIP in a single-user environment. Numbers in parentheses are average vector rates per frame for the indicated metafiles. Solid line represents the equation: vectors/frame = 170,000/(frames/sec). In a moderately interactive environment, frame rates would be reduced by about 30 percent.

One would expect that the simplest predictor of performance might use an inverse relationship between number of vectors per frame and frame rate. The constant of proportionality is the vector conversion rate (vectors per second). The solid line in Fig. 2 is such a curve with the constant equal to 170,000 vectors per second. This appears to fit our observations fairly well over a wide range of files. It is reasonable that, if the curve is normalized near the middle of the range, frames with few vectors would fall to the left of the curve due to the frame-constant overhead of packing arrays, sending data, and waiting for I/O completion. For the same reason, large frames, which have low frame rates, should exceed the curve and have higher than average vector conversion rates.

All other considerations being equal, the average vector throughput should increase with frame size. This is true for the data in Fig. 2, except for the file with the most data per frame. This file contained unusually large vectors and also a larger than average number of color changes.

Figure 3 shows a typical frame from the file that had a frame rate of 17 frames per second in Fig. 2. This file has about 7,500 vectors and a few dozen hardware characters per frame.

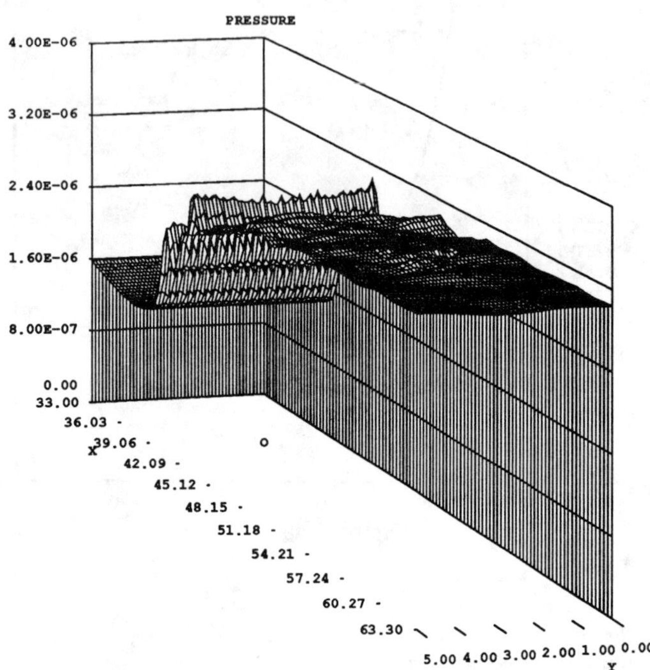

Fig. 3. A frame from an animation sequence containing about 7,5000 vectors and 80 hardware characters.

Qualitatively, users find the current performance in a moderate environment to be adequate over the range of frame sizes considered here. Obviously, performance improvements for frames with more than about 20,000 vectors would be welcomed. Many of the large-data frames are zoomed on, to examine details. When most of the vectors are removed by clipping, some performance is restored.

Resolution and Color Capability

Our observations on resolution are that 512 by 512 pixels is satisfactory in animations because of temporal antialiasing. Jaggies can be seen but are not obtrusive. For viewing still frames, this resolution is marginal, especially for users who are accustomed to seeing images at about twice this linear resolution. The ability to zoom and pan interactively to magnify fine detail in vector images partially alleviates this problem.

Most of our users' vector description files contain just a few colors, so limitations on color selection are not an issue. For purely raster images, however, 256 colors is often not enough. Sometimes useful information can be conveyed within these color limitations, but realistic image rendering is difficult or impossible.

Cost of Use

Our user accounts are sufficient that no one has trouble paying for time to show raster movies with VCR. Running PZIP, on the other hand, can be costly. A wallclock minute with PZIP typically is almost a full CPU minute. Nevertheless, we do show frames from CGS metafiles about fifteen times more efficiently (in CPU utilization) than does CGS itself when sending the same frames to a Tektronix 4115 terminal. Users with limited accounts can limit their charges by running MR or PZIP only once to create a raster file for subsequent extended viewing with VCR.

The question of using a vector supercomputer for tasks which are largely scalar or I/O bound requires further justification. We already use our Crays for many scalar applications, including graphics. The software we described in this paper draws a given frame from a vector description file more than ten times faster in CPU speed than our traditional graphics libraries. Data transfer rates from DD49 disks are faster than those generally available on more-specialized graphics workstations. And some of the software is vectorized. As we go to higher resolutions, it will become feasible to vectorize more of the rasterization algorithm. The final justification is that this system is inexpensive, easy to use, and shows complex animations in time from disk faster than any other system we have seen.

Conclusions

Based on over six months' experience using the system described here, we offer the following conclusions:

1. A Cray X-MP 4/16 running CTSS in moderate to heavy interactive environment can support real-time animation from raster graphics files. Animations using interactive zoom and pan from vector description files are useful, but the graphics algorithms and coding we currently use for rasterization and clipping need to be improved in order to make rendering of large vector frames more interactive and less costly.

2. The computing costs of such graphics are not beyond the means of most of our users, nor does the CPU load in driving a single frame buffer overtax the supercomputer. We believe that future supercomputers, with more processors and power, will be able to support many such users simultaneously.

3. Users will be quick to take advantage of the animation capabilities of the system described here, if it is located sufficiently nearby. We have found that most of

our users work on the same hallway where the frame buffer's output monitor is located. Some users who generate raster animations and have no viewing alternative except film come from large distances (up to several miles) to use the frame buffer. The key to user support is getting the capability into, or near, their offices.

4. Spatial and color limitations in the current system restrict its use to animations of wire-frame images, line drawings, and raster images with fewer than 256 colors. Almost all of our users' graphics fall within these limits.

5. User interaction with the frame buffer system over a 9600 baud line is sufficient. Although network limitations prevent use of a mouse or other locator device, we find that interactive features such as zoom and pan can be accomplished by having the user initiate the action with a single keystroke, and having the action continue until another keystroke is issued. A more natural interface should be developed when the network allows it.

6. Although enthusiasm has been high for the current system, users would like higher resolution, support for eight bits of red, green, and blue, higher speed, and more interactivity. We also believe that three-dimensional polygon rendering support would be found useful by those involved in three-dimensional calculations.

We view this system as a step closer to the goal of scientific visualization, which is to provide the user with real-time visualization and control of his or her calculations.

Acknowledgements

The authors wish to thank Joseph Rieken, of Los Alamos National Laboratory, for providing the CTSS channel driver, Steve Poole, of the Center for Scientific Computer Visualization, Houston, TX, for supplying an efficient packing subroutine, and Digital Equipment Corporation for providing hardware support for the prototype frame buffer board.

References

[1] J. D. Foley and A. Van Dam, *Fundamentals of interactive computer graphics*, Addison-Wesley, Reading, Mass., 1983.

[2] W. M. Newman and R. F. Sproull, *Principles of interactive computer graphics*, McGraw-Hill, New York, 1973.

[3] K-H. A. Winkler, J. W. Chalmers, S. W. Hodson, P. R. Woodward, and N. J. Zabusky, "A numerical laboratory," *Physics Today* 40(10), October 1987, pp. 28-37.

[4] K-H. A. Winkler, S. W. Hodson, J. W. Chalmers, M. McGowen, and D. E. Tolmie, "Ultra-speed graphics for computational science," *Cray Channels* 9(2), Summer 1987, pp. 4-9.

[5] T. N. Reed, "Experiences in the design and support of a graphics device driver interface," Eurographics'81 Proceedings, September 1981, pp. 281-289.

[6] T. N. Reed, "A metafile for efficient sequential and random display of graphics," *Computer Graphics* 16(3), July 1982, pp. 39-43.

A Scientific Visualization Workbench

Richard L. Phillips[1]
Los Alamos National Laboratory
P. O. Box 1663, MS B-272
Los Alamos, NM 87545
505-665-1343
rlp@lanl.gov

ABSTRACT

A system for visualization of data from supercomputer simulations has been developed for use by scientists and engineers at Los Alamos National Laboratory. The *scientific visualization workbench*, as the system is called, is based on an industry standard workstation (a Sun 3/160C), the NeWS window system, and a video/graphics add-in card, which is supported by NeWS. Also involved is a frame buffer attached to a 48-Mbit/s Cray channel and a video link from the frame buffer to the Sun workstation. Computation and graphics preparation are performed on the Cray under the control of a NeWS client program. Images are rasterized and sent to the workstation at the rate of 25 frames/s. The workbench permits the scientist to converse with applications running on a Cray but still retain the convenience and flexibility of a personal workstation environment. Moreover, the video link allows animated graphics images to be displayed on the workstation at a much higher rate than would be possible with a conventional network connection, i.e., Ethernet. Also, NeWS affords the convenience of a modern window system. Live video can be displayed in a window anywhere on the screen, while other windows may contain conventional text or graphics.

Keywords: workstation, supercomputer, video, window system, visualization

INTRODUCTION

There has long been an interest in providing researchers with a method for viewing data derived from large-scale scientific computations. The sheer volume of data emitted by today's supercomputers demands a way of representing it compactly; graphics is the solution. Several approaches to visualization exist; they can all be classified as either *interactive* or *non-interactive*.

The *non-interactive* approach involves running a scientific simulation as a batch job and processing the data at a later time. One method of viewing, which has been used by large scientific installations for years, is to produce a film or microfiche on a film recorder. This usually takes the form of a two-dimensional graphical representation of isolines or finite difference meshes. Often an animated film sequence is produced showing the temporal evolution of a simulation. Another approach to offline visualization is the TMDS [1] system, developed at Lawrence Livermore National Laboratory. In TMDS several hundred centralized frame buffers service over 1800 remote video displays located throughout the Laboratory. Graphical information is rasterized on the supercomputers and distributed to a user's display. Under some conditions animation rates as high as 15 frames/s can be achieved, but mostly a series of static images is displayed. TMDS is also used for conversational monitoring and suspension of the progress of a simulation, but this is by no means considered interactive.

More recent approaches to non-interactive visualization involve using modern computer graphics techniques to produce synthesized, realistic images from the simulation data. Here models of lighting, reflectance, and transparency can be applied to render data to an easily perceivable form. Methods such as ray tracing and radiosity, which in themselves consume large amounts of supercomputer time, can produce images of striking reality. Sometimes these tools are used directly by the scientists who produced the original data, [2] but the "service bureau" approach is also widely used. Here experts in graphic design and animation consult with scientists and produce slides, videotape, or film that depict the desired phenomena [3].

The *interactive* approach to visualization actually represents a spectrum of interactivity. In general it means having some degree of capability to view and control a simulation while it is being performed. One extreme would be the ability to periodically interrupt the computation and view intermediate results. The other extreme would be a dedicated supercomputer tightly coupled to a dedicated high-performance display system.[2] Even then, the degree of interactivity would depend on the complexity of the simulation being performed. Moreover, this is not a cost-effective approach to visualization. Recently, a new class of computer has been announced by several companies.[3] Called graphics supercomputers, they have mini-supercomputer (Alliant and Convex class) computing power with tightly coupled, high-performance graphics displays. These machines, however, are in the $100,000 price range and may not be cost-justifiable in situations where many scientists require visualization capability.

A common situation in many large scientific organizations is where hundreds of workstations are connected over a local area network to one another and to one or more supercomputers. This situation not only provides the user with the wealth of software and graphics utilities that today's workstations offer, it also gives him a degree of control over simulations running on a supercomputer from a system conveniently located in his office.

1 This work was performed under the auspices of the U.S. Department of Energy.

2 Apple Computer often uses their CRAY X-MP/48 with attached Ultra frame buffer as a single user system.

3 Ardent Computer, Stellar Computer, and Apollo Computer all offer machines in this class.

Computing tasks can be distributed to machines where the job can be done best and, with modern window systems like X-Window and NeWS, a program running on a supercomputer can control the display in a window on the workstation [4]. Best of all, since workstations are relatively inexpensive, organizations can afford to provide them in quantity for all who need them. The workstation approach to visualization is explored in the remainder of the paper.

WORKSTATION-BASED SYSTEMS

Object Data Approach

The most common local area network used for workstations is Ethernet, a baseband 10-Mbit/s contention-based network. The most often-used protocol is TCP/IP,[4] which because of its overhead, seldom yields an actual throughput greater than a few hundred kilobits per second. This limitation strongly affects how one uses a workstation for visualization of supercomputer data. For example, one can transmit graphical data in object form[5] from supercomputer to workstation and use the local graphics hardware to display it. For complex images, however, or where animation is desired, the limitation of the Ethernet, coupled with the relatively low performance of standard workstation graphics hardware, yields a drawing speed that is just too slow. On standard workstations, even with careful tuning of hardware and software, one can achieve animation rates of only a few frames per second for images containing a few hundred vectors. For proper animation, one would like about 20 frames/s, preferably 30 frames/s.

One can partly overcome the speed limitation by turning to graphics accelerators, specialized boards that significantly speed up graphical operations. Workstation manufacturers provide these as do third-party hardware suppliers. Recently, Raster Technologies and Trancept Systems (now a subsidiary of Sun Microsystems) introduced accelerators that promise to have a strong impact on visualization efforts. Raster Technologies offers the GX4000, a board set that plugs in to a standard Sun Microsystems workstation. This board implements the proposed PHIGS+ standard in microcode and thus provides a three-dimensional graphics capability for the host workstation. This means that full three-dimensional data can be sent from a supercomputer and transformed locally. Thus, an object can be animated just by transforming it and re-displaying it in a new orientation. Depending on the complexity of the object, good to excellent animation rates can be achieved.

The Trancept board is called the TAAC-1, which is an acronym for **T**rancept **A**pplication **A**ccelerator. As the name suggests, this board can be used to speed up all kinds of local computing tasks. When used for graphics applications, it can perform sophisticated rendering operations at very high speed. While the board is an add-on to a Sun Microsystems workstation, it has its own frame buffer and is capable of producing high-resolution 32-bit/pixel images. The board also has the the potential of accepting data directly (bypassing the Sun processor) at 800 Mbyte/s, but further development work is required before this feature can be used.

While the graphics performance of both of these accelerators outstrips conventional workstation hardware, the rate at which data can reach them is, in general, still limited by Ethernet throughput. This may not be a problem for investigations where a relatively small amount of object data is sent from the supercomputer and is expanded locally to produce high-quality images, animated sequences, or both.

There is a large class of problems, however, where this is not an especially useful approach. These are typically simulations involving finite difference calculations where complex meshes are used to describe the spatial aspects of the problem. An example of such a mesh is shown in Figure 1. This represents one instant in time in a sequence of many thousands of such images. As the problem evolves, some part of the mesh changes from one time step to another. Each image comprises several thousand data points and, because of Ethernet limitations, one cannot expect to achieve very good graphics display rates. The accelerator boards are no help here because there is no local algorithmic processing they can usefully perform. An exception would be the case where only those parts of the image that change in a time interval are sent to the workstation; the accelerator would maintain the graphics database and apply the changes locally. This is not a simple task, however, and has not been done in practice.

Image Data Approach

Another approach to remote data visualization is to perform some, if not all, of the graphics processing on the supercomputer and send the complete representation to the workstation as an image, i.e., pixels. But, if the image resolution is say, 1024 x 1024 x 8, a megabyte of data must be sent for each data display. Thus, there is no speed advantage to this approach unless a transmission medium other than Ethernet is used. Providing a second data transmission path, one that has a much higher bandwidth than Ethernet, is the thrust of this paper. Of course, there must be a device in the workstation that can handle that data. This device is another type of accelerator, a board that accepts an image directly and displays it on the

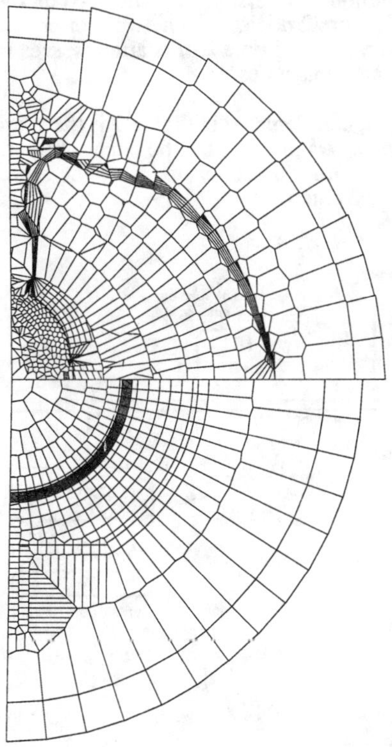

Figure 1.

4 Transmission Control Program/Internet Protocol.

5 The term, object data, refers to the numerical representation of the graphical data as calculated by the simulation.

workstation screen. Parallax Graphics, Inc., makes such a board. It can digitize an NTSC[6] video signal in real time, i.e., 30 frames/s. The *scientific visualization workbench*, the subject of this paper, makes use of the Parallax board capabilities, in conjunction with an already-developed supercomputer frame buffer system and the NeWS window system. This image-based approach to visualization overcomes the speed limitations of the object-based approach, but at a price. Image quality is lost by NTSC encoding of a video signal. Thus, one is trading image fidelity for bandwidth. On the other hand, the user sees images as fast as they can be produced by the supercomputer, and temporal fidelity is often more important than image quality. There is another advantage to be gained from processing graphics data on a supercomputer--the flexibility to experiment with new visualization algorithms, rather than rely solely on rendering methods provided by the workstation vendor.

NETWORK WINDOW SYSTEMS AND NeWS

A key element of the *scientific visualization workbench* is a workstation window system that permits distribution of computing tasks in a network environment, in this case Sun Microsystems' NeWS. The acronym NeWS, derived from **N**etwork-extensible **W**indow **S**ystem, suggests the network orientation of this window system. As such, it allows the computing resources in a heterogeneous computing environment to be effectively used. NeWS runs on a machine with one or more bit-mapped displays. It acts as a window server, managing input and output on its host machine. Application programs--called clients--send messages causing NeWS to render images on the display. The clients may reside anywhere on the network. Server-based window systems are often called distributed window systems, because the server and its clients may be distributed over the network. This concept is not unique to NeWS. It appears in Andrew [5], a system developed at Carnegie-Mellon University, and the X-Window System [6] from MIT. Figure 2 depicts this network orientation, where the NeWS server, running on a workstation, serves remote clients running on other machines.

The supercomputer depicted in Figure 2 is the source of data for the *workbench*. As the host for the client program, it provides graphical data, either object or image, to the server running on the user's workstation.

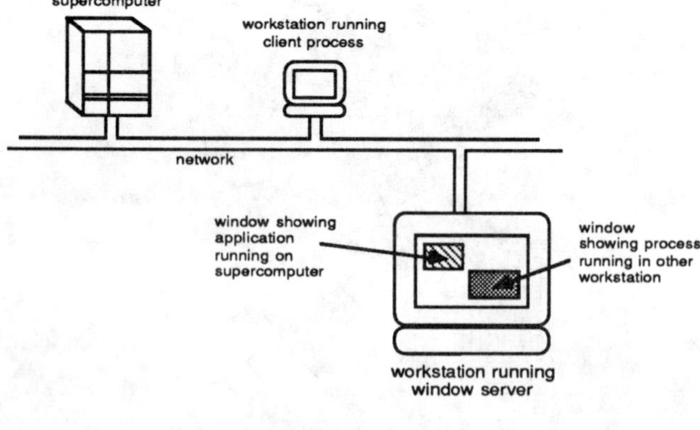

Figure 2.

6 NTSC stands for National Television Standard Committee. Often referred to as composite video.

One of the key features of NeWS is the use of a programming language for communication between the server and its clients. Instead of sending messages consisting of commands and parameters in a fixed format, clients send programs that the server interprets. The language used by NeWS is POSTSCRIPT [7], which was originally developed as a language to drive printers. Sun has extended POSTSCRIPT to include features necessary for operation in an interactive workstation environment. These features are described in detail elsewhere [8]. It is important to note here that the presence of POSTSCRIPT provides an extremely powerful window system extension facility, making it possible to rapidly develop new tools.

THE SCIENTIFIC VISUALIZATION WORKBENCH

System Overview

The structure of the scientific visualization workbench is depicted in Figure 3.

Each component of the workbench will be described in detail, but briefly, it comprises a Sun Microsystems 3/160C workstation equipped with a Parallax 1280 Series Videographics Processor, a high-resolution color monitor, a Cray Research, Inc., supercomputer equipped with a Solid-state Storage Device (SSD), and a 512h x 512v x 8 bits/pixel frame buffer attached to the Cray by a 48-Mbit/s channel. Communication between the Sun and the Cray is via Ethernet using TCP/IP protocol. The Cray runs the UNICOS 3.0 (System V-based UNIX), and a special Parallax version of the NeWS 1.1 window system runs on the Sun. A NeWS client program on the Cray controls the transmission of rasterized data to the frame buffer and ultimately to the workstation over an NTSC video link. The magnified workstation screen in the lower left of the diagram suggests the presence of several types of windows, in which independent processes are running simultaneously.

The Supercomputer Subsystem

The supercomputer side of the workbench is based upon work previously reported by Fowler and McGowen [9]. They describe the development of a 512h x 512v x 8 bit/pixel frame buffer installed on a 48-Mbit/s I/O channel of a CRAY X-MP/416. Output from the frame buffer is separate red, green, and blue (RGB) non-interlaced video signals with a refresh rate of 60 Hz. The output signal is viewed on a color monitor attached directly to the frame buffer or is transmitted over a fiber optic link to a remote location. Output to the frame buffer is controlled by a highly tuned program that takes advantage of the vectorization capabilities of the Cray. Under certain loading conditions (the Cray is not dedicated to this task) users can achieve animation rates of almost 25 frames/s. The Cray operating system is CTSS, the Cray Timesharing System, and users access the frame buffer control program by logging in on high-speed serial lines. The control process and the display process are disjoint, i.e., they are associated with two different devices.

The workbench uses the supercomputer facilities somewhat differently. The operating system is UNICOS (a UNIX-like operating system developed by Cray Research), and the control and display functions are both incorporated into the workstation. From the workstation end, the user controls Cray activity over an Ethernet link through a NeWS process. This process communicates with a Cray-based NeWS client program, which in turn directs the frame buffer display software described above. There is a separate video link that transmits the frame buffer video signal to the Parallax processor. This is currently an NTSC video signal, derived by encoding the RGB output of

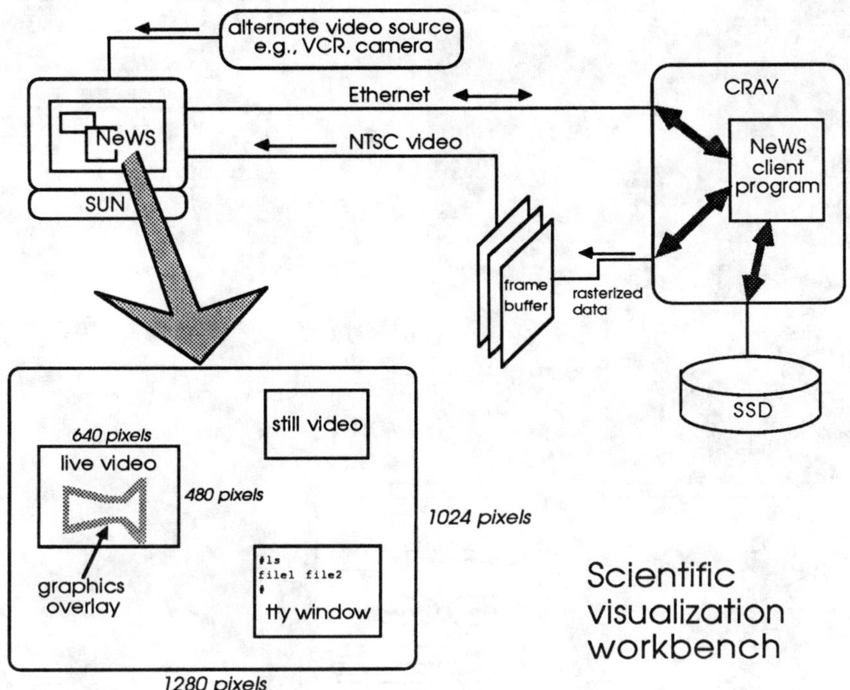

Figure 3.

the frame buffer. The signal is channelized onto a (ubiquitous) cable video network and decoded with a tuner at the user's location. The trade-off of image quality for bandwidth extracted by NTSC encoding was mentioned earlier; a later generation of the system will hopefully involve direct transmission of RGB video to the workstation.

The Workstation Subsystem

The workstation is a Sun 3/160C, but any Sun model with a VME bus interface can be used. This bus accommodates the Parallax 1280-V-8VN videographics card set. Other workstations, supporting different bus protocols, could also be used. For example, Parallax has a Q-Bus version of the videographics card set that can be accommodated by the Digital Equipment Corporation's line of MicroVAX workstations. Naturally, a different set of software would be required. The video display can be either the standard Sun color monitor (1152h x 900v resolution) or any number of third-party monitors. The Parallax board normally produces a 1280h x 1024v signal but it can be programmed to provide a wide range of video formats. The monitor used for the development project is a 19-inch Sony GDM 1950 with 1280 x 1024 resolution.

The Parallax Videographics processor is a complete graphics controller and frame buffer, with a size of 2048 x 2048 x 8. Of this, only 1280 x 1024 is viewable. The graphics hardware of the parent workstation is not used at all; indeed, the Parallax standard graphics performance generally exceeds that provided by the workstation. What makes the board set unique, however, is its ability to digitize and display an NTSC video image anywhere in its graphical address space. Video digitization is performed at 30 frames/s and produces an image size of 640h x 480v, consistent with NTSC bandwidth. Because of a proprietary dithering technique, which uses a 14-bit YUV (luminance and chrominance) color space, the resulting image quality is extraordinary. The board outputs RGB video directly into the color monitor. More details on the Parallax product can be found in the user manual [10].

PNeWS, NeWS Enhanced for Video

Parallax Graphics has ported the NeWS 1.1 system to its videographics card and extended it to support video features. The resulting system, called PNeWS [11], is the foundation for the scientific visualization workbench. PNeWS preserves the purity of the original NeWS product. Only five new operators have been added: four to support video and one to provide general access to all features of the Parallax hardware. One extension, for example, defines a new type of window, a video window. There is a corresponding operator that specifies the source of data to be displayed in the window, i.e., a live video signal. Video windows can contain still as well as live video. Moreover, conventional graphics can be overlaid on any video window. One can selectively digitize live video frames, each in a separate window, and resize them at will. The workbench builds on these capabilities by allowing the user to produce hard copy, film, or printed output of any such video image. PNeWS also supports the Parallax board capability of switching between two separate video signals, a feature that is useful for recording and accessing images on a laser disk recorder. Details of the tools available to the workbench user follow.

System Operation and Capabilities

Launching the workbench is simple. Once in the NeWS environment, the user opens an authorized session on the Cray through a terminal emulator window on the workstation. By pressing a (software) button on the workstation screen, the user begins the client process, which in turn establishes the client/server path on the network. At this point NeWS is in control of the entire distributed environment. The user issues commands via software sliders, buttons, and text fill-in dialogs. Figure 4 shows a typical screen layout for the workbench. In the upper right, for example, there is a partly visible control panel for setting video parameters such as contrast and brightness. The image in the lower right shows a video image annotator and its associated controls. Other controls are used for

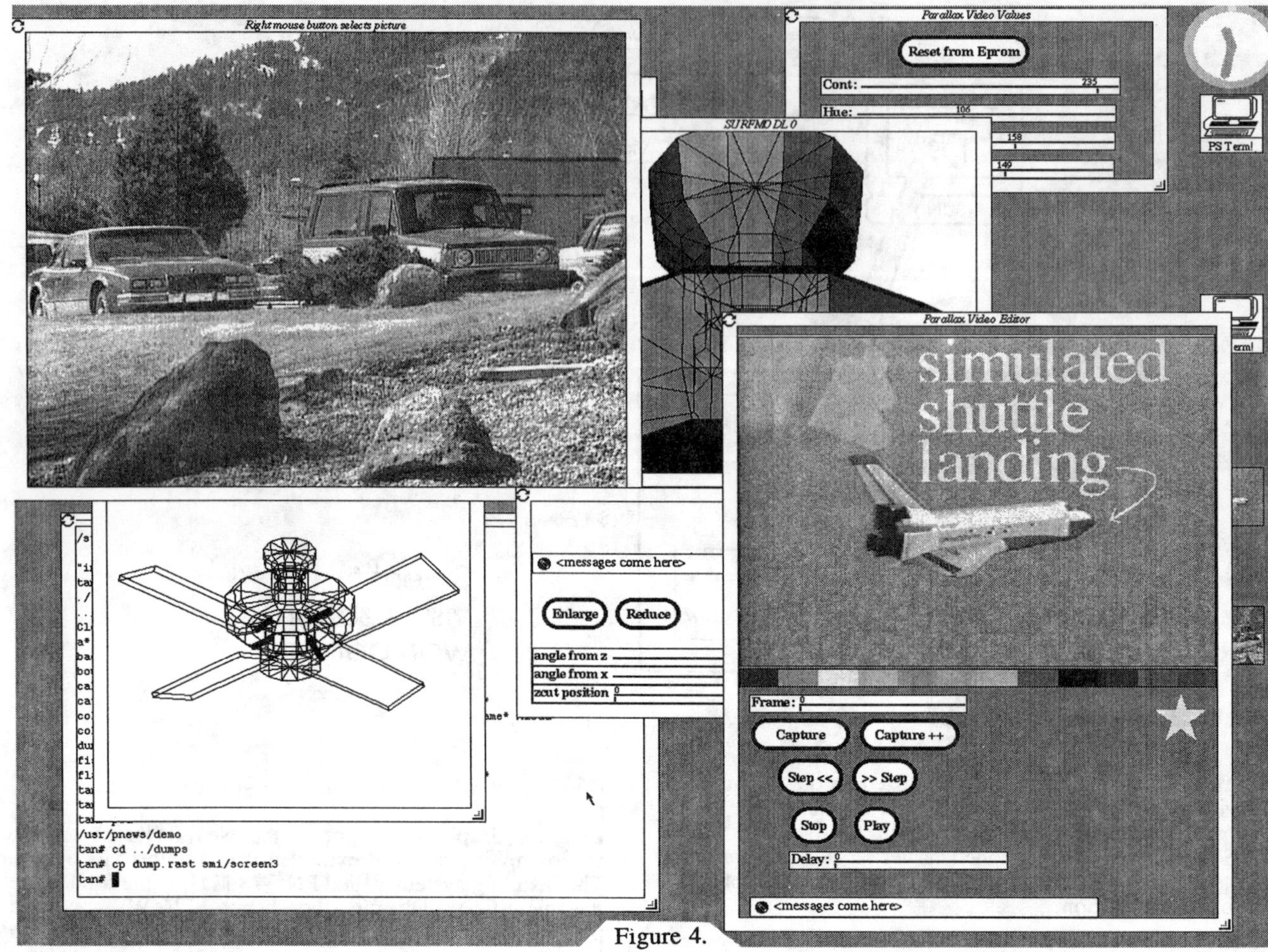

Figure 4.

such operations as video image sequencing and speed, video frame capture, graphics overlay, etc.

The user has control over many aspects of the workbench user interface. Naturally, all windows, video or conventional, can be sized and located as the user wishes. In addition, the default color look-up table can be modified to suit the image being viewed. For example, there is often more insight to be gained by viewing an image in shades of gray rather than color; the workbench provides that flexibility. Also, an alternate source of video images can be selected; Figure 5 shows a situation where the image in the lower right was produced by a video camera viewing an outdoor scene while that in the upper left is a frame from a supercomputer simulation of supersonic jet flow [12]. Yet another tool is the capability of capturing many video images in sequence and playing them back in a rapid loop, or one frame at a time. While there can be only one live video window active at a time, many loop sequences can be captured and, if one wishes, played back simultaneously. Finally, one can apply a 2X zoom to a live video window, causing it to fill the entire screen. Hardware pixel magnification is used to accomplish this but the quality of the image suffers little.

Visualization Tools for Scientific Analysis

In addition to the user interface controls described above, there is a set of higher level tools available to the workbench user. One of these tools has already been mentioned and appears in Figure 4. This is a video image annotator, which also has a database function. Images can be captured from any source and can be annotated with a variety of textual and graphical features. Thus, the user can produce sets of images, all cataloged with appropriate annotations, and recall them for later viewing and hard copy production. The ability to easily produce hard copy should be emphasized. It is due in large part to the fact that PostScript is the language underlying NeWS, the window system used for the workbench.

Often the workbench user wishes to view images in a fixed spatial relationship, i.e., in the form of a mosaic or montage. The display could show several images that bear a temporal relationship to one another, or they could be drawn from different parameter spaces. In fact, one might wish to combine video images from different sources into a single mosaic, e.g., from a videodisk and an online database. The workbench provides this tool, and an example of its use is shown in Figure 6, which shows the temporal evolution of a supersonic jet. Time begins in the lower left corner and progresses from bottom to top, left to right. The user can select any order of presentation and any size and number of images. Another capability, not shown here, is automatic textual annotation of each image in the sequence with an appropriate parameter value.

Another tool allows the user to superimpose arbitrary graphical data on a live or still video image. Plotting isolines, e.g., temperature or pressure contours, is a common use for this tool. The isoline data is sent from the supercomputer (over Ethernet) and is transformed and drawn in the specified window. If the

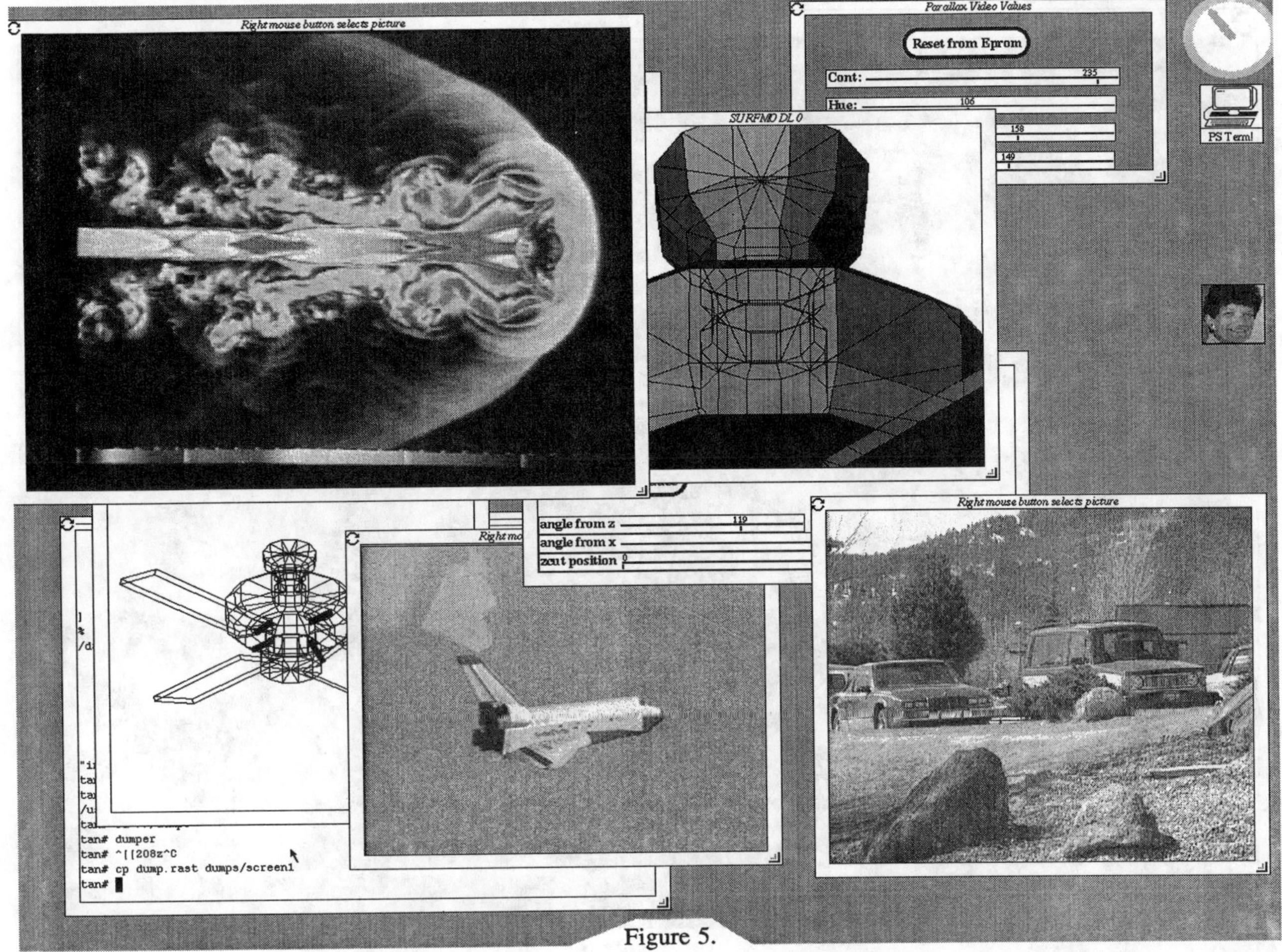

Figure 5.

data in the overlay do not change, the display can be converted to an image for subsequent immediate overlay. This is useful if the window is often closed and re-opened.

USING THE WORKBENCH

Because the workbench is still a development system, it is not widely accessible by potential users. Still, there is some indication how a typical user will interact with the system. When a scientist runs a large simulation on a supercomputer, he generally saves the graphical output in the form of a CGS metafile [13]. The NeWS client program, which is running on the supercomputer, processes those metafiles to produce rasterized output suitable for display on the channel-attached frame buffer. From a control panel displayed on the workstation screen, the user manipulates the display of these rasterized images as live or still video windows. The scientist can control the speed of animation and can browse forward and backward through the graphical data. Interesting, short sequences of data can be captured locally on the workstation and displayed either animated or a frame at a time. Typically, a user looks for features in the data that suggest a further investigation or highlight an error. Selective color table modification is often used in this process.

The video annotation tool described earlier is used as sort of a scientist's logbook. Up to 25 images can be saved in a named folio (file), along with appropriate textual and graphical markup. Any number of folios can be created and later retrieved by a rudimentary keyword search facility. Selected images from the folios can be printed or saved for incorporation into any documentation system that accepts a POSTSCRIPT representation.

SYSTEM PORTABILITY

While the workbench was developed for use in the Los Alamos computing environment, every aspect of the system technology can be transferred to another setting. While a direct connection to a Cray computer is considered an important attribute of the workbench, there are elements of it that will be useful even when this is not available. For those many Cray sites throughout the world, however, all elements should be applicable. All Cray computers are equipped with 48-Mbit/s channels. The frame buffer, which was developed at Los Alamos, is now available as a product.[7] It can be used on either of the Cray DA/DB or DI/DO channels. While the frame buffer produces RGB video signals, there are many NTSC video encoders on the market. The resulting signal can be sent to the workstation via either cable video or a fiber optic link.

As noted earlier, the workstation used in the system need not be a Sun. The Parallax board is available for several bus architectures other than VME, in particular for the Q-Bus, AT Bus, and the bus for the IBM RT/PC. Apollo Computer, for example, uses the AT Bus in their DN-3000 and DN-4000

7 Available from Sivco Engineering, Albuquerque, NM.

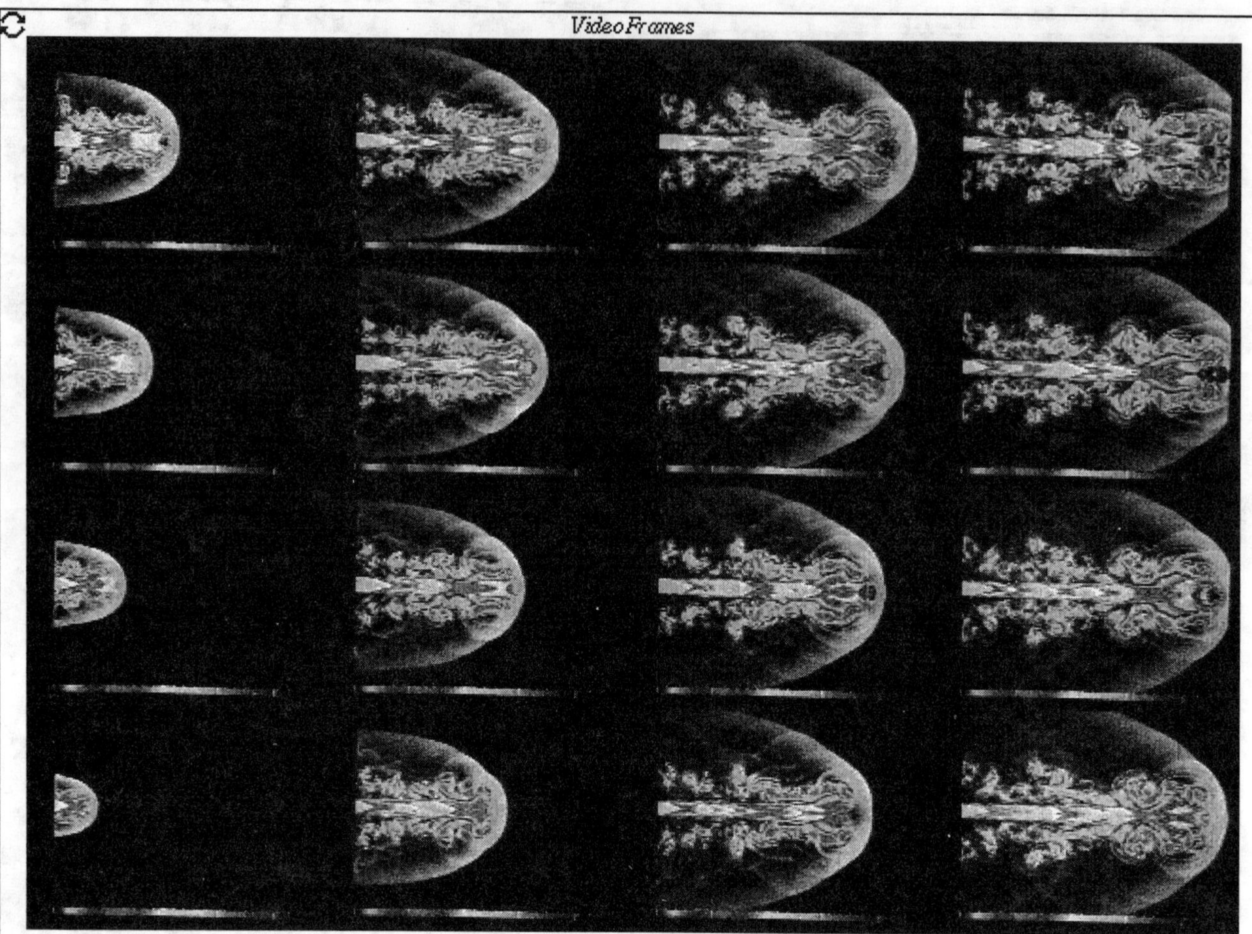

Figure 6.

series workstations and Digital Equipment Corporation uses the Q-Bus in their MicroVAX workstations. UNIX is available for both companies' workstations, and ports of NeWS exist for them as well. Of course, it would be possible to develop the equivalent capabilities of the scientific visualization workbench using the X-Window System; Parallax has software to support it as well as NeWS. But the higher level tools described here are NeWS-specific and would have to be rewritten for X-Window.

FUTURE DIRECTIONS AND ENHANCEMENTS

While the *scientific visualization workbench* is very useful in its current state, there are several features that remain to be added. Among these is a rudimentary page layout and report building facility. This will permit the user to assemble pages of figures and images into a form suitable for direct hard copy production on, for example, the new color POSTSCRIPT printer from QMS.

There are several host-based facilities that must be provided. Most important of these is a programmatic interface to simulation programs that run on the supercomputer. Currently, the workbench client program only processes metafiles that were previously produced by a simulation. Coupling the workbench to the simulation will provide more user control and interactivity. Finally, an image database facility should be provided, complete with run ID and parameter specification. This will allow the workbench to quickly and selectively retrieve images from an archive for display as single images or as part of a mosaic. Other enhancements, not envisioned now, will no doubt be requested by users of the workbench.

REFERENCES

[1] J. Fletcher, *The TMDS Manual*, Lawrence Livermore National Laboratory, UCID 30118, Feb. 9, 1976.

[2] M. L. Prueitt, "A Window on Science," IEEE Computer Graphics & Applications, Sept. 1987

[3] C. Upson, "Issues in Visualization," JPL Workshop on Scientific Visualization, Pasadena, CA, Jan. 1988

[4] R. L. Phillips and D. W. Forslund, "Using the NeWS Window System in a Cray Environment," Cray Users' Group Meeting, New York, NY, May 1987.

[5] J. Morris et al., "Andrew: A Distributed Personal Computing Environment," Communications of the ACM, Vol. 29, No. 3 (March 1986).

[6] R. W. Scheifler and J. Gettys, "The X Window System," ACM Transactions on Graphics, Vol. 5, No. 2, April 1986, pp. 79-109.

[7] Adobe Systems Inc., *PostScript Language Reference Manual*, Addison-Wesley, 1985.

[8] Sun Microsystems, Inc., *NeWS Technical Overview*, March 1987, Part No. 800-1498-05.

[9] John D. Fowler, Jr., and Michael McGowen, "Design and Implementation of a Supercomputer Frame Buffer System," LA-UR-88-890, Los Alamos National Laboratory, March 1988.

[10] Parallax Graphics, Inc., *User's Manual for 1280 Series Videographics Processor*, January 27, 1987.

[11] M. Picco, "Live Digital Video in a Windowing Environment," National Computer Graphics Association, Anaheim, CA, March 1988.

[12] K. A. Winkler, J. W. Chalmers, S. W. Hodson, P. R. Woodward, N. J. Zabusky, "A Numerical Laboratory," Physics Today, October 1987.

[13] T. N. Reed, "A Metafile for Efficient Sequential and Random Display of Graphics," Computer Graphics, Vol. 16, No. 3, July 1982.

Distributed Scientific Video Movie Making

W. E. Johnston, D. E. Hall, J. Huang, M. Rible, and D. Robertson*

Advanced Development Group
Lawrence Berkeley Laboratory
University of California
Berkeley, California, 94720

ABSTRACT

We describe a versatile, low cost, video movie making system for generating and displaying scientific graphics from remote supercomputers. The system makes video movies by single frame animation from the output of time dependent, numerical simulations typically done on supercomputers. The system uses extensive data compression to permit its use over wide area, as well as local area networks. The system demonstrates an easily used, elementary visualization capability for time dependent data in a heterogeneous, distributed computing environment.

1. Introduction

Most scientists access supercomputers remotely.** Supercomputing will probably always be a scarce and oversubscribed resource for the general scientific community. Usage is characterized by slow turn around, large quantities of data, and remote locations connected by wide area networks.

Supercomputer output may often be displayed as animated sequences that we will refer to as "scientific movies". These movies provide an insightful way to view time dependent results, such as flow fields and moving surfaces, and complex 3D structures that can be animated by rotation and translation.

We have developed a scientific movie system that is both easily used in the environment of remote supercomputing, and relatively low cost ($10K - $15K). The distributed graphics system has modules that are distributed among the supercomputer, a local workstation for some of the intermediate steps (optional), and a video animation controller workstation. The modules use Berkeley Sockets [1 and 2] and Sun Microsystem's Remote Procedure Call package (RPC) and External Data Representation language (XDR) [3], to effect interprocess communication (IPC). Using these, the movie system operates over the many networks that make up the TCP/IP Internet. This internet provides supercomputer access for a substantial fraction of the U.S. scientific community.

The system is written mostly in C, and has been demonstrated to run in a variety of environments including VAX VMS™, Sun OS™, 4.3 BSD Unix, Cray Unicos™ and CTSS.

2. Scientific Video Movies

Video graphics are different from pen plotter, terminal and film graphics. The spatial resolution of the NTSC video signal used for video recording is low compared to the more traditional media [4,5], while the color resolution is relatively high. These factors must be taken into account when designing a graphics representation for video tape. One does not count on producing the fine line drawings that are displayed, for instance, on laserprinters, but rather uses smoothly shaded areas that are easily reproduced on video tape. However, even with the relatively low spatial resolution of NTSC video, line and point drawings can still be useful if special care is taken in their design. Figure 1 shows sample frames from four movies made by using this system and supercomputer generated data. Each movie illustrates different data transfer and compression characteristics. (The original color movie frames are reproduced in black and white in Figure 1).

The system provides interfaces at several levels, including the compression and transfer of a frame buffer, 2D and 3D graphics primitives, and visualization modules such as 3D surface tessellation and particle advection.

The design goal of the system is to provide scientific visualization using state of the art graphics algorithms. A certain degree of "realism" is necessary, for instance, when presenting 3D geometric shapes to resolve any viewing hypothesis ambiguities. For example, the front of the torus in Figure 1d is clipped away so that the inside is visible. A reasonable level of sophistication in the rendering is needed to produce the realism necessary to be able to recognize that we are looking at the concave inner surface of the object, rather than the convex outside surface. The use of simple "flat" shading frequently produces an image in which the

---

*All of the authors can be reached via USMail at: Lawrence Berkeley Laboratory, Bldg. 50B, Rm. 3238, Berkeley, CA 94720. Email addresses are: wejohnston@lbl.gov, ...ucbvax!lbl-csam.arpa!johnston; hall@lbl-csam.arpa, huang@lbl-csam.arpa, max@lbl-csam.arpa, davidr@lbl-csam.arpa. The work presented in this paper is supported by the U.S. Department of Energy under contract DE-AC03-76SF00098. Any conclusions or opinions, or implied approval or disapproval of a company or product name are solely those of the authors and not necessarily those of The Regents of the University of California, the Lawrence Berkeley Laboratory, or the U.S. Department of Energy. Trademarks are acknowledged by TM.

** Only a handful of sites in the U.S. supply supercomputing to the general scientific community: National Magnetic Fusion Energy Center (NMFECC), National Center for Atmospheric Research (NCAR), and the NSF supercomputer centers (SDSC, PSC, JvNC, NCSA). The primary access to all of these centers is via wide area networks.

CH2617-9/88/0000/0156$01.00 © 1988 IEEE

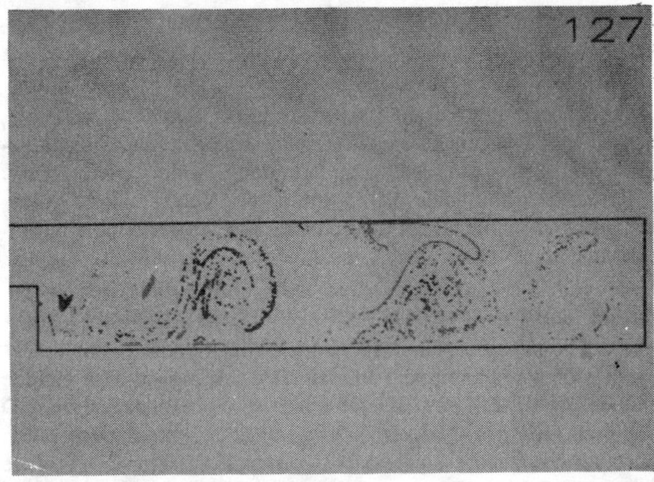

Figure 1a
Flow Over a Backward Facing Step - J. Sethian, UC Berkeley, A. Ghoniem, MIT

Figure 1c
Kummer Surface - E. Yeh, W. Johnston, D. Robertson and M. Rible, Lawrence Berkeley Laboratory

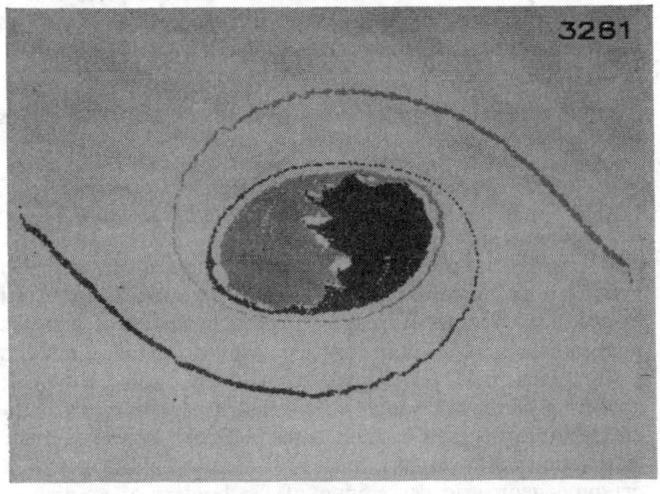

Figure 1b
Vortex Modeling - S. Baden, Lawrence Berkeley Laboratory

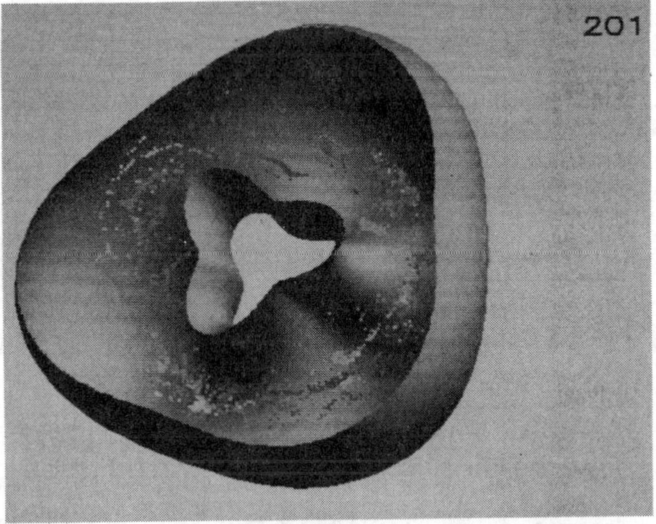

Figure 1d
3D Flow Through a Torus - C. Peskin and D. McQueen, Courant Institute, New York University, and D. Robertson, Lawrence Berkeley Laboratory

concave-convex distinction cannot be made. On the other hand, for the Kummer surface in Figure 1c, the function is defined on a 100×100×100 grid and the tessellated surface for one function value results in about 100,000 polygons. With this many polygons flat shading is generally used, as the interpolation of Gouraud shading [18] is both expensive and not needed to improve the visualization. Our approach is to use the minimal shading and lighting algorithms necessary to accomplish an unambiguous representation. This reduces CPU and network demands while keeping the software volume manageable. See [6] for more information.

3. The Distributed Movie System

The video movie system software is a distributed application with several modules. The optimal distribution strategy for wide area networks is usually to select the partitioning that minimizes the data transported over the wide area network. However, this may be tempered by the relative cost of computing on supercomputers as opposed to workstations.

The modules that make up the system are illustrated in Figure 2. There are four main groups of modules: generating a numerical representation of some mathematical model (the application); converting the numerical representation to a graphics representation; converting the graphics representation to a raster image representation; and finally the display and recording of the image. These steps are connected pro-

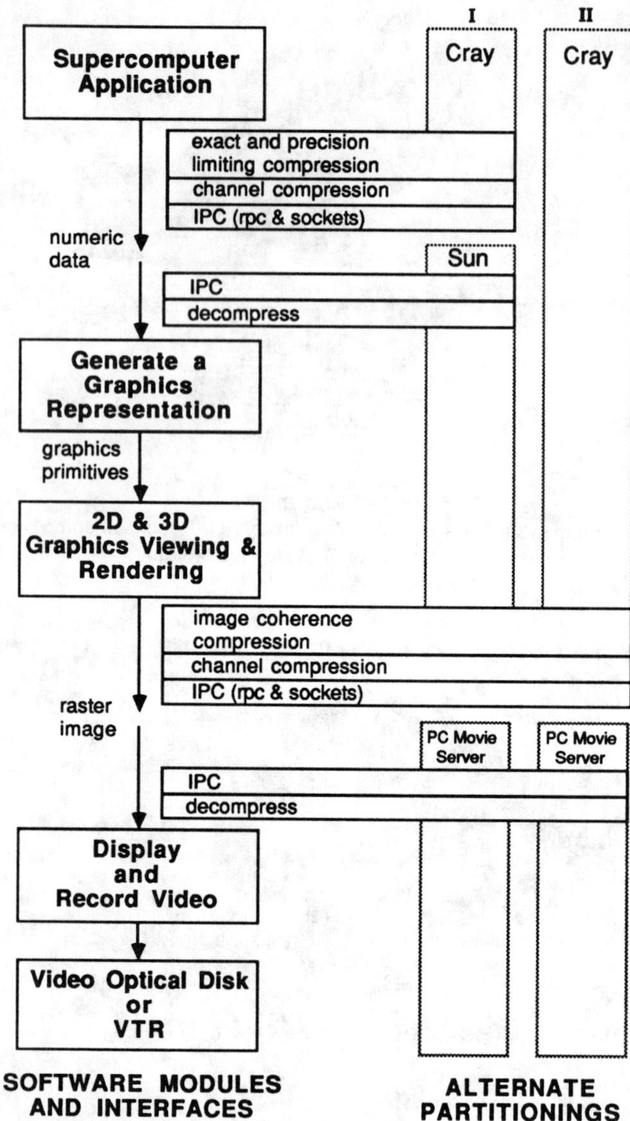

Figure 2
The Distributed Software Architecture

cedurally on a local system, or by data compression and transport to remote systems, depending on the distribution of the modules.

Though not formal "objects" in the Smalltalk sense [7], these modules are designed to have many of the characteristics found in an object oriented programming environment. We feel that this view of distributed computing aids in implementing distributed applications in a heterogeneous environment.

3.1 The Numerical Representation: Generating the Data

The supercomputer application is a numerical implementation of a mathematical model. Typical applications include modeling of 2D and 3D flow fields, wave propagation, 3D surface topology studies, and various simulations (e.g. accelerator design studies) that produce 2D and 3D particle position fields. These models produce a numeric representation that is converted to a graphics representation (either on the local system or on a remote workstation after the numeric data is sent over a network). If the data is sent over a network, it is compressed by limiting its precision and removing redundancy as described in section 7. Table 1 gives typical *per frame* volumes of data for several applications at various points in the pipeline illustrated in Figure 2 (partitioning II).

3.2 The Graphics Representation: Conversion to Graphics Primitives

A graphics representation algorithm converts a numeric representation of the model output into the graphics primitives (points, lines, polygons and text) that describe an image. The process is not graphics *per se*, but algorithms that transform the numeric representation to a geometric form that can be displayed as an image. Typical examples of graphics representations algorithms are: level curve following through a 2D scalar field ($z=f(x,y)$) to produce "contour plots"; advecting particles through a flow field to obtain tracer particle positions that can be plotted (as in Figure 1a and 1b); and tessellating the level surface of a 3D scalar field (Figure 1c), or some geometric description of the borders of an area of flow, to get a polygonal representation that can be rendered as a shaded surface (Figure 1d).

Table 1
Data Volumes per Frame for Typical Applications

Figure number and data type	Numeric representation of the data	Graphics representation type, and data volumes of the resulting graphics primitives	Compressed raster image size (uncompressed image size is 410KB)
1a; 2D flow field (u, v) on 100×11 grid	17KB	5000 tracer particles + 5000 attributes = 90KB	2.5KB (164:1)
1b; 2D flow field on 13,000 grid points	310KB	13000 tracer particles + 13000 attributes = 230KB	6.2KB (66:1)
1c; 3D scalar field on 100×100×100 grid	4000KB	Tessellated level surface: 110,000 polygons = 1800KB	7.8KB (52:1)
1d; 3D flow field on 100×100×100 grid	24000KB	2000 tracer particles + 4500 polygons = 100KB	19KB (21:1)

The volume of data associated with an op-code and coordinate form of the graphics primitives depends on the graphics representation algorithm. For example, particle advection converts a flow field description to positions of a set of tracer particles. The number of particles is independent of the flow field size. When tessellating a sequence of surfaces that evolve in time, the number of polygons in a surface at each time step is frequently roughly proportional to the number of points on the outer surface of the grid. Table 1 gives some examples of data volumes generated by graphics representation algorithms.

The graphics primitives produced by this step are usually sent by a procedural interface to a rendering module on the same system, though they are sometimes sent over the network.

3.3 Graphics Rendering: Conversion to a Raster Image Representation

The graphics rendering process converts the primitives generated by the graphics representation into a raster image. In the distributed movie system, graphics primitives are rendered by scan conversion into a software frame buffer located in main memory. For 3D primitives the hidden surface, or visibility problem, is solved by using a "z" or "depth" buffer approach. This results in the final image having visual priority that corresponds to the geometric priority of the scene and eye point. The rendering of polygons additionally entails shading (varying the pixel color across the polygon surface to present the appearance of a curved surface) according to some interpolation model, and assignment of color according to some lighting model (calculating the color of a pixel based on the position of the light source and glossiness of the surface).

The size of the software frame buffer is fixed according to the targeted output device. In the case of the current hardware of the distributed movie system [4] this is $400 \times 512 \times 3 \times 5$ bits $\cong$ 400K bytes. This software frame buffer is compressed and sent over the network to the video animation controller workstation.

3.4 Compressing the Raster Representation

The utility of compression is obvious in wide area networks. Sending 400KB/frame is currently out of the question. What is less obvious is that compression is also advantageous in local area networks. Typical 4 MIP workstations can send about 200 packets, or 300K bytes, per second among themselves on an Ethernet. This is well below the Ethernet bandwidth and packet rate limits. The limiting factor is the CPU time spent in the "protocol stack". For a slower processor, like the PC used for the animation workstation in our system, the maximum packet rate is substantially lower than 200 per second (more like 30 packets/second). Therefore, compression that reduces the number of packets per graphics frame will result in a net increase in the throughput, provided that the PC processor does less work decompressing the data than it would do to handle the packets of uncompressed data. Variations of the Block Truncation Coding (BTC) compression algorithms [8 and 10] provide this tradeoff. For BTC most of the work is in the encoding. The decoding process is just a table lookup to reconstruct the compressed image into the hardware frame buffer. This technique reduces the number of packets to be processed by the PC animation controller workstation without adding any significant overhead on the PC. The result is noticeably higher throughput, even on an Ethernet.

Over a wide area network, bandwidth dependence is the limiting factor. When using wide area networks, further compression of the image is obtained by processing the BTC compressed image through an adaptive Huffman compression algorithm [9]. This algorithm is much more symmetric than BTC, and takes as much CPU time to decode as it does to encode. Therefore, there is a network bandwidth break-even point above which the PC CPU time to decode is greater than the time to send an uncompressed BTC image over the network. We believe that the break-even point is a few hundred Kbits/second of network bandwidth for an IBM PC/AT™. However, this break even point is pushed to above 10 Mbits/second by using a 68020 co-processor in the PC to decode the Huffman coding. Therefore, compression pays off even in high speed local area networks where both BTC and Huffman coding are used to advantage.

3.5 The Video Animation Controller Workstation

The animation controller workstation accepts raster data from the network, and generates and records a video signal one frame at a time. The hardware consists of an IBM PC/AT™ (or clone), an Ethernet controller used for TCP/IP based IPC, a video frame buffer for reconstructing the raster image and generating the video signal, a single frame animation controller and a video tape recorder (VTR) (or alternatively a video-optical disk) for recording, and optionally a 68020™ co-processor board for doing the Huffman decompression. The hardware configuration is discussed in more detail in [4].

The PC runs as a remote procedure call server whose only task is to receive compressed images from the graphics workstation or remote supercomputer and record them on video tape or video disk. There is no user interaction with the PC server. It is just a peripheral hardware controller serving the system that generates and sends the compressed images. The PC server looks like any other RPC server, except that it will only accept one connection at a time, and there is no portmapper function [3]. This implies that the user must know both the Internet address of the video animation controller workstation, and the (fixed) port that the RPC server responds to. Given the role that it plays (running video recorders that record frame-at-a-time movies) the "single client" PC server is a useful paradigm.

In the case where a video-optical disk is used instead of the VTR, the PC also serves as a simple, but useful and convenient, video editing system. The movie clips from the supercomputer are recorded frame-at-a-time onto the optical disk, and title frames are usually added later, anywhere on the disk. (Titling may be generated from a front end system, with a paint program on the PC, or simply by aiming a video camera at laserprinter output and recording a single analog frame on the optical disk.) The optical disk has a simple set of commands that allow a sequence of frames to be played at any speed, forward or backward, and separate sequences of frames to be played in any order. The movie making scenario is to: generate the graphics movie clip; put a titling frame on the video-optical disk; and write a script on the PC to compose the movie. A typical script contains instructions to: play the title frame for a certain number of seconds; seek to the graphics clip; hold the first frame for 10 seconds; play the remaining frames at 1/3 speed (10 frames/second animation); and hold the last frame for a few seconds. To achieve smooth animation, the graphics frames must be recorded in sequence on the video-optical disk, since the disk cannot seek to "out of sequence" frames fast enough to generate smooth video. When the user has constructed a script that produces a satisfactory movie, a VHS recorder is connected to the output of the optical disk, the script is loaded and executed, and the resulting video is recorded to produce a scientific animation that can be viewed on a home VHS player.

4. Partitioning a Distributed Application

We had several design goals related to the distributed aspects of the system. First the modules had to be easy to distribute. This meant we had to design the primary interfaces to be implementable on a variety of systems, and minimize our use of non-standard operating system functions. Second, whenever possible we wanted to take advantage of the coarse grained parallelism afforded by pipelines. Therefore, our algorithms were implemented to perform local operations on data streams rather than to read an entire data set before beginning processing. Third, we hoped eventually to compare our data stream design to an object oriented design. Therefore, all modules were instrumented for performance monitoring.

The movie making process is typically distributed across three different systems (partition I in Figure 2). The supercomputer application generates data (e.g. flow field vectors) that are compressed and sent to a graphics workstation. The graphics workstation environment is used to design and debug the graphics representation for a movie. The graphics workstation then produces the frames of the movie. These raster images are compressed and sent to the animation controller workstation. The modules are all tied together by remote procedure call based collections of servers and clients.

Partition II of Figure 2 has all the modules executing on the Cray up to, and including, the generation and compression of the software frame buffer. This partition is used when it is impractical to move the application data off the Cray. For instance, in making a movie of a 3D flow field, the vector field data may easily amount to 30 to 50 Mbytes per frame. Even the advected particles can be more than 100K bytes per frame. The compressed movie frame is usually less than 20K bytes (see Table 1), an amount that is practical to send over current wide area networks.

5. Internetworking

The established TCP/IP networking infrastructure is a versatile and powerful tool for distributed applications geographically dispersed around the country.

An internet is a network of networks. It accommodates multiple, diverse underlying hardware technologies, network technologies, and operating systems while providing a uniform set of conventions for usage. The distributed movie system takes advantage of the extensive internet technology of the TCP/IP Internet. The success of internetworking is that our application sees and uses only one, uniform interface: The Internet protocols and Berkeley sockets [2].

6. Numeric and Image Data Compression

Data compression is an important aspect of wide area network based distributed applications. Compression can be divided into two types: entropy reduction, an irreversible compression since some (maybe insignificant) information is lost; and redundancy reduction, a reversible compression technique that tries to identify redundant information and encode it more efficiently. We use both types of compression, frequently together, in the movie system.

Synthetic raster images generated by computer graphics have an enormous amount of redundancy. There is typically high spatial coherence in the image, and high temporal (frame to frame) coherence. To compress these images, the system first applies entropy reduction techniques. Block truncation coding (BTC) [8,10] reduces the total number of colors needed to represent an image by reducing the colors in a block of pixels to two "best" representatives. A further compression is achieved by limiting the choice of possible representative colors to those of a short table whose index is then used to represent the colors in the blocks. Heckbert's median cut algorithm is used to populate the table with a set of colors that best reproduces the image. See [11]. One effect of this encoding is that areas of an image that appear different may result in the same block code, thus increasing the redundancy. This entropy reduced form is then encoded with a redundancy reduction algorithm such as Lemple-Ziv coding [9]. Using these techniques in combination, the overall compression of synthetic raster images can be substantial. Averaged over the length of a movie we typically see 20:1 - 60:1 compression for complex, shaded 3D images that fill most of the frame (e.g. Figure 1c-d), and 100:1 - 200:1 for simpler 2D images (e.g. Figure 1a-b).

The traditional wisdom is that floating point numbers from numerical simulations do not compress. Indeed, this can be seen to be true by applying an adaptive Huffman coding to a collection of floating point numbers, where one seldom sees greater than 1.3:1 - 1.5:1 compression. However, if we accept a limiting of precision then we can compress floating point numbers. To compress these numbers we use what amounts to a sequential quantization entropy reduction technique similar in principle to differential pulse code modulation [12]. We quantize the floating point numbers, limit their dynamic range and reduce them to integers. We then take differences between adjacent integers to further reduce the size requirement. In addition to reducing the word size, these techniques tend to generate repeated patterns that are then encoded by redundancy reduction techniques. The amount of information lost by this scheme is controlled primarily by specifying the quantization. It has been our experience that quantization to five digits, and limiting dynamic range to five orders of magnitude, is adequate for the graphics representation algorithms that we use. Using these techniques we typically achieve 12:1 - 15:1 compression of numeric data. (See [13] for more information.)

In Figure 2 "channel compression" is a term that we use to describe a type of redundancy reduction algorithm that compresses an unstructured byte stream. Channel compression is frequently used as the last step of a multistep compression process before that data is handed off to the network transport (or disk storage) functions.

7. The Structure of the User Interface

The typical user of the movie system is a physicist/programmer who needs to produce a movie of the output of a mathematical model. The basic user interface to the distributed movie system is the rendering module. This module implements a low level, GKS like interface for 2D viewing and graphics [14], and a SIGGRAPH Core like interface for 3D viewing and graphics [15]. To the 3D interface we have added a more intuitive set of 3D viewing controls [16]. This interface also has a polygon primitive with the necessary provisions for shading and lighting. To the basic depth buffer we have added a mechanism that allows clipping of a fixed portion of the object, as opposed to the usual view volume clipping. This is illustrated by the clipped torus of Figure 1d. The display of complex 3D objects, such as those illustrated in Figure 1c and 1d, is facilitated by the use of a routine that varies the view position from frame to frame in a way that results in a smooth yaw and pitch rotation. This provides a slow, continuously changing view of the 3D object [6].

Layered on top of this interface are two graphics representation algorithms that are general enough to be considered part of the system. The first is an algorithm to advect particles through a rectangular region of 2D flow. The user interface to this algorithm is where, and how many particles, to inject into the flow field, and the specification of (u,v,x,y) defining the flow. No provision is made for at the interface to change the boundary conditions of laminar flow. This algorithm was used to make the movie illustrated in figure 1a.

The other representation algorithm is Lorensen's Marching Cubes [17]. This algorithm provide a mechanism for displaying the level surfaces of a 3D scalar field of arbitrary complexity. We have used this to explore mathematical functions by displaying a sequence of surfaces $f(x,y,z)=c_1,c_2,c_3, \cdots$ as a movie, as well as showing a single level surface evolving in time for applications such as flame front propagation studies. The user interface to this algorithm entails specification of a 3D grid of function values, and the function value to be displayed (as well as the color, light source position, viewing position, etc.). The Kummer surface in Figure 1c was produced using this algorithm.

In addition to the graphics, there is a user interface for numeric data compression. We have attempted to identify a few prototypical "types" of data, and to provide user callable functions to compress this data. We have, for example, routines that accept 2D particles and attributes, 2D flow fields (u,v,x,y), and 3D scalar fields (function values on a 3D grid). In each case the user supplies the data, and the precision that needs to be recovered after decompression. The compressed data stream is written to a network stream or disk file.

8. Conclusions

From the success of this system we conclude: 1) Distributed computing among remote supercomputers and local workstations is a viable technique even over wide area networks. 2) Sophisticated graphics techniques and displays can be made available to the general scientific community by leveraging on the low cost of home video equipment. 3) Compression is an essential part of distributed computing.

References

[1] S. Leffler, R. Fabry, W. Joy, P. Lapsley, S. Miller, C. Torek, "An Advanced 4.3BSD Interprocess Communication Tutorial," Computer Science Research Group, University of California, Berkeley, CA, 94720, 1986.

[2] D. Comer, *Internetworking With TCP/IP: Principles, Protocols, and Architecture,* Prentice Hall, 1988.

[3] Sun Microsystems, Inc., "Networking on the Sun Workstation," Report 800-1324-03, Mountain View, CA, 1986.

[4] W. Johnston, D. Hall, F. Renema, D. Robertson, "Principles and Techniques for Low Cost Computer Generated Video Movies," LBL-22330, University of California, Lawrence Berkeley Laboratory, Berkeley, CA, 1987.

[5] D. Fink, Editor, *Color Television Standards: Selected Papers and Records of the National Television System Committee,* McGraw-Hill, 1955.

[6] D. Robertson, "Use of a Distributed Movie Making System for Presentation of Fluid Flow Data," San Francisco State University, San Francisco, CA, (Masters Thesis - available as LBL-25036 from Lawrence Berkeley Laboratory), 1988.

[7] A. Goldberg, D. Robson, *Smalltalk-80: The Language and Its Implementation,* Addison Wesley, 1983.

[8] G. Campbell, T. DeFanti, J. Frederiksen, S. Joyce, L. Leske, J. Lindberg and D. Sandin, "Two Bit/Pixel Full Color Encoding," *Computer Graphics,* vol. 20, no. 4, 1986. (Proceedings ACM SIGGRAPH, 1986)

[9] T. Welch, "A Technique for High Performance Data Compression," *IEEE Computer,* vol. 17, no. 6, June, 1984.

[10] N. Texier, W. Johnston, D. Robertson, "Encoding Synthetic Animated Images," LBL-24236, University of California, Lawrence Berkeley Laboratory, Berkeley, CA, 1987.

[11] P. Heckbert, "Color Image Quantization for Frame Buffer Display," *Computer Graphics,* vol. 16, no. 3, 1982. (Proceedings ACM SIGGRAPH, 1982)

[12] T. Lynch, *Data Compression,* Van Nostrand Reinhold, 1985.

[13] J. Huang, "Numeric Data Compression for Graphics," San Francisco State University, San Francisco, CA, (Masters Thesis - available as LBL-25037 from Lawrence Berkeley Laboratory), 1988.

[14] G. Enderle, K. Kansy, G. Pfaff, *Computer Graphics Programming: GKS, 2ed.,* Springer-Verlag, 1987.

[15] Graphics Standards Planning Committee, "Status Report of the Graphics Standards Planning Committee," *Computer Graphics*, vol. 13, no. 3, 1979.

[16] BJ Wishinsky, W. Johnston, "A Simplified Interface for SIGGRAPH Core Viewing," LBL-25038, University of California, Lawrence Berkeley Laboratory, Berkeley, CA, 1987.

[17] W. Lorensen, H. Cline, "Marching Cubes: A High Resolution 3D Surface Construction Algorithm," *Computer Graphics*, vol. 21, no. 4, 1987. (Proceedings ACM SIGGRAPH, 1987)

[18] J. Foley, A. Van Dam, *Fundamentals of Interactive Computer Graphics*, Addison-Wesley, 1982.

Compiler Technology

Chair: John Levesque, Pacific-Sierra Research

Compiling Issues for Supercomputers *

Milind Girkar
Constantine Polychronopoulos

Center for Supercomputing Research and Development
University of Illinois at Urbana-Champaign
Urbana, IL 61801

Abstract

Accurate and fast methods for computing data dependences are vital to the efficiency of vectorizing and parallelizing compilers. Program transformations employed by these compilers are effective only if dependences are computed as accurately as possible. In this paper we consider two issues for supercomputer compilers. First, we discuss in detail exact and inexact tests for computing data dependences and focus on the linearization scheme. We then discuss a program transformation call loop spreading which allows us to execute in parallel adjacent loops with interloop dependences.

Keywords: Compilers, Data dependences, Program transformations.

1 Introduction

The recent advances in new supercomputer architectures in general, and parallel processor architectures in particular, have not been met with corresponding (and necessary) advances in software techniques. This is primarily true in the case of supercomputer compilers. For example, little is known on program restructuring and compiling for message-passing multiprocessors, most of the existing compilers use approaches which are direct analogs (or extensions) of schemes used by vectorizing compilers. Program vectorization is a well researched and well understood subject [AlCo72] [AlKe82] [AlKe87] [Kuck78] [KKLW80] [KKPL81] [Wolf82]. The same can not be said for program parallelization (or concurrentization) especially for hierarchical architectures [KDLS86]. Recent efforts (and long overdue) in this direction are currently underway in a few research centers including the Parafrase-2 project at University of Illinois, PTRAN at IBM, and PTOOL at Rice [Alle88] [BuCy86] [Cytr84] [MiPa86] [Nico84] [PaKL80] [Peir86] [Poly86] [PoKu87] [Poly87].

*This work was supported in part by the National Science Foundation under Grant No. US NSF MIP-8410110, the U. S. Department of Energy under Grant No. US DOE-DE-FG02-85ER25001, the IBM Donation, IBM Parafrase Contract No. 632613, and the Control Data Corporation.

The results presented in this paper touch upon two issues for parallelizing compilers. We compare and discuss existing schemes and present new algorithms for discovering parallelism in serial programs. The first issue we consider is exact and inexact tests for computing data dependences. We consider the general case of dependence calculation in nested loops and compare the effectiveness and efficiency of linearization versus the system of Diophantine equations approach.

The second subject of this paper is *loop spreading*, a new program transformation for parallelizing compilers. Loop spreading can extract parallelism out of serial loops in cascade. We consider pairs of adjacent serial loops with interloop dependences. Even though the asymptotic improvement in execution time obtained by loop spreading is only a factor of two, repeated application of the transformation in a chain of serial loops may result in higher speedup factors.

The rest of the material is organized as follows. Section 2 deals with data dependences. The necessary definitions are presented in Section 2.1. Section 2.2 discusses the two main methods of computing data dependences and their equivalence is shown in Section 2.2.1. In Section 2.3 we study methods to do exact data dependence calculations and an analysis of the complexity results is given in Section 2.4. Section 2.5 examines inexact tests for data dependences. In Section 3.1 we present loop spreading and its generalizations are considered in Section 3.2.

2 Data Dependence Analysis

Data dependence testing has been an extensively studied area [Bane76] [Bane79] [Wolf82] in the context of automatic parallelization of sequential programs. Data dependences give information about the flow of data in a program. This can be used to restructure the program and find blocks of code which can be executed in parallel. Optimizations are done with the constraint of retaining the correctness of the program (as the programmer intended it to be) and thus conservative estimates for dependences are the norm in compiler writing in the absence of accurate data dependence information.

Data dependences are normally defined with respect to the set of variables which are used and modified by a statement; denoted by the IN set and the OUT set respectively [AhSU86]. The next section gives a formal definition of data dependences and other associated terms which are used throughout the paper.

2.1 Background and Definitions

A *program* is a list of $k \in N$ statements. S_i denotes the i-th statement in a program (counting in lexicographic order). I_j denotes a DO loop index, and i_j a particular value of I_j. L_j and U_j denote the lower and upper bound of a loop index I_j, and $N_j = U_j - L_j + 1$ is the number of different values that I_j can assume. We have two types of statements, *scalar* and *indexed* statements. An indexed statement is one that appears inside a loop, or whose execution is explicitly or implicitly controlled by an index (e.g., vector statements). All other statements are scalar. The *degree* of a program statement is the number of distinct loops surrounding it, or the number of dimensions of its operands. $S_i(I_1, I_2, \ldots, I_k)$ denotes a statement of degree k, where I_j is the index of the j-th loop or dimension. An indexed statement $S_i(I_1, \ldots, I_k)$ has $\prod_{j=1}^{k} N_j$ different instances, one for each value of each of I_j, $(j = 1, \ldots, k)$. The first and last instance of a statement of degree k is $S_i(L_1, L_2, \ldots, L_k)$ and $S_i(U_1, U_2, \ldots, U_k)$ respectively. S_i will be used in place of $S_i(I_1, \ldots, I_k)$ whenever the set of indices is obvious. The *order of execution* is defined between pairs of statements instances S_i, S_j as follows. For (scalar) statements with degree 0 we say that S_i is executed before S_j and denoted by $S_i \leq_o S_j$ if $i \leq j$, i.e., if S_i lexically precedes S_j. For S_i, S_j with degree k (if they have different degrees then scalar order of execution applies as well), we have the following three cases. If S_i and S_j do not have common indices, then $S_i \leq_o S_j$ if $i \leq j$. If they have the same k indices, then $S_i(i_1, \ldots, i_k) \leq_o S_j(j_1, \ldots, j_k)$ if $i \leq j$ and there is an m such that $0 \leq m \leq k$, $i_l = j_l$, $(l = 1, \ldots, m)$, and $i_{m+1} < j_{m+1}$. We assume that $i_{k+1} < j_{k+1}$ trivially. If $i > j$, it is as above but with $m < k$. If S_i and S_j have $m < k$ common indices and $i_l = j_l$, $(l = 1, \ldots, m)$, then $S_i \leq_o S_j$ if and only if $i \leq j$. Otherwise the previous definition holds. We also need to extend the definition of the $IN(S)$ and $OUT(S)$ sets (i.e., the sets of variables read and written by statement S respectively). We denote by $OUT(S_i(i_1, \ldots, i_k))$ the set of *variable instances* (not necessarily different) defined by statement instance $S_i(i_1, \ldots, i_k)$. Similarly, $IN(S_i(i_1, \ldots, i_k))$ is the set of variable instances used by the same statement instance. Now we can proceed with the definition of data dependences. Two statements $S_i(I_1, \ldots, I_k)$ and $S_j(J_1, \ldots, J_k)$ are involved in a *flow* dependence $S_i \; \delta \; S_j$ if and only if there exist index values $(i_1, i_2, \ldots, i_k)$ and $(j_1, j_2, \ldots, j_k)$, such that

$$S_i(i_1, \ldots, i_k) \leq_o S_j(j_1, \ldots, j_k), \text{ and}$$

$$OUT(S_i(i_1, \ldots, i_k)) \cap IN(S_j(j_1, \ldots, j_k)) \neq \emptyset.$$

An *antidependence* from S_i to S_j is defined as the flow dependence above, except for the second condition which now is

$$IN(S_i(i_1, \ldots, i_k)) \cap OUT(S_j(j_1, \ldots, j_k)) \neq \emptyset.$$

It is denoted by $S_i \; \bar{\delta} \; S_j$. An *output* dependence is again defined as above but with

$$OUT(S_i(i_1, \ldots, i_k)) \cap OUT(S_j(j_1, \ldots, j_k)) \neq \emptyset,$$

and it is denoted by $S_i \; \delta^o \; S_j$.

The program *data dependence graph* or DDG, is a directed graph $G(V, E)$ with a set of nodes $V = \{S_1, S_2, \ldots, S_n\}$ corresponding to statements in a program, and a set of arcs $E = \{e_{ij} = (S_i, S_j) | S_i, S_j \in V\}$ representing data dependences between statements. Figure 1 shows the DDG of a set of scalar statements.

2.2 Testing for Data Dependences

Detecting scalar dependences among statements is comparatively easy. It just involves taking the intersection of the corresponding IN and OUT sets [AhSU86]. The same strategy works for arrays too, but gives coarse dependence results. For more accurate information, subscript analysis of array variables needs to be done. Testing for dependences then involves checking whether two subscript expressions would take an identical value during the execution of the program. There are various methods for doing this check when the subscript expressions are simple and straightforward.

The problem in the most general form involves index expressions of the type shown in the following loop.

$$
\begin{array}{l}
\texttt{DO } I_1 = L_1 \ldots U_1 \\
\quad \vdots \\
\quad \texttt{DO } I_n = L_n \ldots U_n \\
\qquad A(f_1(I_1, \ldots, I_n), \ldots, f_k(I_1, \ldots, I_n)) = \ldots \\
\qquad \quad \vdots \\
\qquad \ldots = A(g_1(I_1, \ldots, I_n), \ldots, g_k(I_1, \ldots, I_n)) \\
\quad \texttt{END DO} \\
\quad \vdots \\
\texttt{END DO}
\end{array}
$$

The question that needs to be answered is whether there are two different sets of values, $I = (i_1, i_2, \ldots, i_n)$ and $I' = (i'_1, i'_2, \ldots, i'_n)$ such that they satisfy the following k equations simultaneously.

$$
\begin{aligned}
f_1(i_1, \ldots, i_n) &= g_1(i'_1, \ldots, i'_n) \\
&\vdots \\
f_k(i_1, \ldots, i_n) &= g_k(i'_1, \ldots, i'_n)
\end{aligned}
\tag{1}
$$

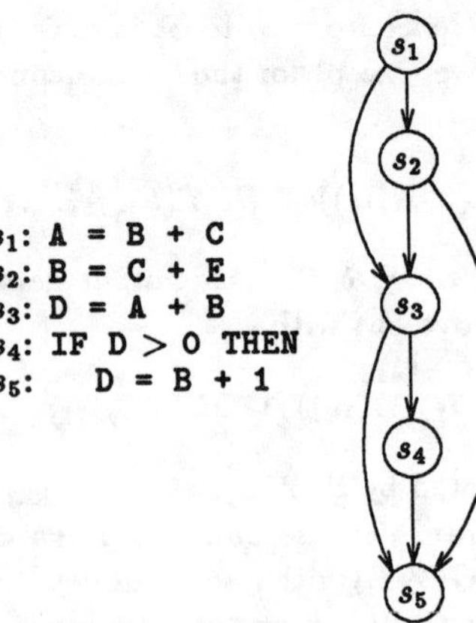

Figure 1: Example

If the answer is affirmative, then there may be a dependence between the two statements which, essentially, puts some restrictions on the order of execution of (instances of) these two statements. If $I \leq I'$ (lexicographic ordering) then the dependence is a flow dependence, otherwise it is an anti-dependence. However, one more condition needs to apply : the index vectors I and I' must lie within the iteration space defined by the loop. In other words, I and I' must satisfy the following n inequalities.

$$L_1 \leq i_1, i'_1 \leq U_1$$
$$\vdots \tag{2}$$
$$L_n \leq i_n, i'_n \leq U_n$$

If the do-loop nesting level is n, and the array is k dimensional, we get k simultaneous equations involving $2n$ variables. One can solve the system as it is, or reduce the k simultaneous equations into one equation with $2n$ variables using a method called *linearization* [Bane76] [BuCy86]. This involves mapping the array variable into a memory location and then checking if access to two memory locations can be overlapped. From elementary data structures we know that assuming row major storage, $A(f_1, \ldots, f_k)$ is mapped into location $\alpha + \sum_{j=1}^{k} (f_j - l_j) \prod_{m=j+1}^{k} N_m$ where α is the address of the first element, l_i, u_i, $(i = 1, 2, \ldots, k)$ are the lower and upper bounds on the dimensions of A, and $N_i = (u_i - l_i + 1)$, $(i = 1, 2, \ldots, k)$. Linearization then involves solving the following equation :

$$\alpha + \sum_{j=1}^{k} (f_j(i_1, \ldots, i_n) - l_j) \prod_{m=j+1}^{k} N_m =$$
$$\alpha + \sum_{j=1}^{k} (g_j(i'_1, \ldots, i'_n) - l_j) \prod_{m=j+1}^{k} N_m \tag{3}$$

which simplifies to

$$\sum_{j=1}^{k} f_j(i_1, \ldots, i_n) \prod_{m=j+1}^{k} N_m =$$
$$\sum_{j=1}^{k} g_j(i'_1, \ldots, i'_n) \prod_{m=j+1}^{k} N_m \tag{4}$$

where $(i_1, \ldots, i_n)$, $(i'_1, \ldots, i'_n)$ should also satisfy (2). The advantages and disadvantages of each method are discussed in the following sections.

2.2.1 Equivalence of the two methods

The following three lemmas compare the nature of solutions from linearization and non-linearization.

Lemma 1: If a solution satisfies (1) then it also satisfies (4).

Proof: Obvious, because (4) is obtained by taking a linear combination of the equations in (1). □

Lemma 2: If a solution satisfies (4) then it need not satisfy (1).

Proof: By counterexample. Consider the following loop.

```
DIMENSION A(5,5)
DO I = 1,5
     A(2,3I) = ...
     ... = A(3,I+3)
END DO
```

The system of equations without linearization is :

$$2 = 3 \tag{5}$$

$$3i = i' + 3 \tag{6}$$

which obviously does not have any solution because (5) can never be true. The linearized equation is

$$(2-1)5 + 3i - 1 = (3-1)5 + i' + 3 - 1$$

which after some simplification yields

$$3i = i' + 8. \tag{7}$$

Equation (7) can be seen to have a solution $i = 3, i' = 1$. □

The following lemma tells when such cases will not occur.

Lemma 3: If a solution satisfies (4) and it is guaranteed that the subscript expressions of arrays stay within bounds set by the dimensions of the array i.e. $l_j \leq f_j$, $g_j \leq u_j$ for $1 \leq j \leq k$ in all iterations, then the solution also satisfies (1).

Proof: Let the solutions be $I = (i_1, \ldots, i_n)$ and $I' = (i'_1, \ldots, i'_n)$. Then the linearized equation gives us

$$\sum_{j=1}^{k} f_j(i_1, \ldots, i_n) \prod_{m=j+1}^{k} N_m =$$
$$\sum_{j=1}^{k} g_j(i'_1, \ldots, i'_n) \prod_{m=j+1}^{k} N_m. \tag{8}$$

Rewriting (8) with the first term on the left hand side gives

$$(f_1 - g_1) \prod_{m=2}^{k} N_m = \sum_{j=2}^{k} (f_j - g_j) \prod_{m=j+1}^{k} N_m \qquad (9)$$

where we have dropped the variables $I = (i_1, \ldots, i_n)$ and $I' = (i'_1, \ldots, i'_n)$ for clarity.

If the subscript expressions of arrays stays within the bounds set by dimensions of arrays i.e. $l_j \leq f_j,\ g_j \leq u_j$ for all j, the value of $f_j - g_j$ is at most $N_j - 1$, and at least $-(N_j - 1)$, for $1 \leq j \leq k$. (Recall that $N_j = u_j - l_j + 1$.) Hence the maximum value of the expression on the right hand side of (9) is $\sum_{j=2}^{k}(N_j - 1)\prod_{m=j+1}^{k} N_m$ which simplifies to $(\prod_{m=2}^{k} N_m) - 1$, and similarly its minimum value is $-(\prod_{m=2}^{k} N_m)+1$. If f_1 is not equal to g_1 then the value of the left hand side is either greater than or equal to $\prod_{m=2}^{k} N_m$, or less than or equal to $-(\prod_{m=2}^{k} N_m)$. Therefore the two sides could never be equal. Thus $f_1 = g_1$. We can now cancel out the first term from both sides of the equation and repeat the process. Continuing in this vein, one can prove that $f_j = g_j$ for $1 \leq j \leq k$. This implies that the solution also satisfies (1). □

Since we expect that the subscripts will remain within the bounds of the corresponding dimension of an array, Lemma 3 indicates that there is no loss in correctness of the solutions due to linearization.

Methods to solve (1) or (4) are known only for the case when $f_j, g_j, 1 \leq j \leq k$ are linear functions of $I_1, \ldots, I_n$. In the next section we consider such cases and present specific examples that show how the two approaches can be used to compute precise dependences.

2.3 Exact Tests

When $f_j, g_j,\ 1 \leq j \leq k$ are linear functions of $I_1, \ldots, I_n$, (1) is a system of linear Diophantine equations and (4) is a single linear Diophantine equation. We illustrate the method of solving such equations by an example.

Consider the following loop.

```
DIMENSION X(10,15)

DO I1 = 1...2
      DO I2 = 1...5
            X(2I1 + 3, I2 + 1) = ...
            ... = X(I1 + I2 + 3, 2I2 + 1)
      END DO
END DO
```

To check whether the two statements are dependent on one another one needs to solve the following system of Diophantine equations for $I = (i_1, i_2)$ and $I' = (i'_1, i'_2)$.

$$2i_1 + 3 = i'_1 + i'_2 + 3 \qquad (10)$$

$$i_2 + 1 = 2i'_2 + 1$$

The general solution of (10) is given by

$$\begin{aligned} i_1 &= s \\ i_2 &= 2t \\ i'_1 &= 2s - t \\ i'_2 &= t \end{aligned}$$

where s and t can range over all integers. Since we also need $1 \leq i_1, i'_1 \leq 2$ and $1 \leq i_2, i'_2 \leq 4$ the only solutions possible are $i_1 = 1, i_2 = 2, i'_1 = 1, i'_2 = 1$ (which occurs at $s = 1, t = 1$) and $i_1 = 2, i_2 = 4, i'_1 = 2, i'_2 = 2$ (which occurs at $s = 2, t = 2$).

Using the linearization approach we will try to solve the single equation

$$(2i_1 + 3)15 + i_2 + 1 = (i'_1 + i'_2 + 3)15 + 2i'_2 + 1$$

which simplifies to

$$30i_1 + i_2 - 15i'_1 - 17i_2 = 0 \qquad (11)$$

The general solution of (11) is given by

$$\begin{aligned} i_1 &= r \\ i_2 &= -s - 30r \\ i'_1 &= -8s - 17t \\ i'_2 &= 7s + 15t \end{aligned}$$

where r, s and t can vary over all integer values. Again, using the fact that $1 \leq i_1, i'_1 \leq 2$ and $1 \leq i_2, i'_2 \leq 4$ we see that the only solutions are $i_1 = 1, i_2 = 2, i'_1 = 1, i'_2 = 1$ (which occurs at $r = 1, s = -32, t = 15$) and $i_1 = 2, i_2 = 4, i'_1 = 2, i'_2 = 2$ (which occurs at $r = 2, s = -64, t = 30$).

The example illustrates the general method for computing exact dependences. One finds the general solution using methods to solve Diophantine equations and then tries to get the solutions within the specified loop bounds. There are some factors of interest here.

1. In the first approach we had to solve a system of Diophantine equations. With linearization we had to solve only a single Diophantine equation.

2. The solution from the first approach was expressed in terms of only two free variables (s and t) where as the one from linearization was in terms of three free variables (r, s and t).

3. The constants in (11) were somewhat larger than those in (10).

We now turn to consider the complexity of finding the solution in both cases.

2.4 Complexity of the two approaches

As observed before, finding exact data dependences involves solving Diophantine equations. We now summarize the methods to find the solutions in both approaches (which we choose to call Banerjee's method and the Linearization method) and examine the tradeoffs involved.

Banerjee's Method

1. Find the general solution for the system of k equations. The solution is in terms of $2n - k$ free variables.

2. Find the solutions within loop bounds by suitably constraining the free variables.

Linearization Method

1. Find the general solution of the linearized equation. The general solution is in terms of $2n - 1$ free variables.

2. Find the solutions within loop bounds by suitably constraining the free variables.

Steps 1 of both methods are explained in many elementary number theory textbooks (e.g. [Malm80]) or in [Bane79]. It can be seen from the methods in [Malm80] that Step 1 of Banerjee's method takes k times the time required for the corresponding part in the Linearization method because it involves solving k Diophantine equations in sequence.

Steps 2 of both approaches are ad hoc in nature and the only known methods for constraining the free variables (so that the solutions lie within loop bounds) use brute force enumeration of free variables. The solutions formed by Banerjee's method have $k - 1$ less free variables than those formed through the Linearization method and thus the problem of constraining the free variables is considerably simpler in Banerjee's method. Therefore Step 2 of Banerjee's method is much faster than that of the Linearization method.

In many practical cases, $k = n$ and the functions f_j (g_j) have the nice property of being dependent on only I_j. Then each of the j equations in (1) is a Diophantine equation in two variables (i_j and i'_j) and can be solved independently of the other equations. In this case the Linearization method is clearly inferior to the first approach because Step 1 in Banerjee's method takes about half the time as Step 1 of Linearization [Malm80]. Step 2 of Banerjee's method is also much faster than its counterpart.

Another factor which also affects complexity measurements is the following. Since the dimensions of arrays (N_j) can be very large, the magnitude of the coefficients in the linearized equation is much larger than those in the original equations. Computation of the greatest common divisor (g.c.d.) is a common occurrence in steps 1 of both approaches, and finding the greatest common divisor of two numbers a, b requires $O(\log_\phi \sqrt{5} \max(a, b))$ divisions (in the worst case) where $\phi = \sqrt{5}+1/2$ [Knut69] [Bane79]. If there is an increase of three orders of magnitude (array sizes of about 1000 are fairly common) the computation of each g.c.d. in the Linearization method could take about ten more divisions.

If the functions f or g are non-linear in any one dimension of the array, (4) would result in a single non-linear equation which is of no help. In the system of equations without linearization, however, only one equation is non-linear and one could still attempt to solve the rest of the system to check for dependence. Another disadvantage of linearization is that if the dimensions of the array are not known at compile time then the linearized equation cannot be constructed at all.

Linearization with all its defects has, however, one advantage in some practical cases. Many FORTRAN programs contain the EQUIVALENCE statement which permits the programmer to alias memory locations. For example, the following FORTRAN program aliases the arrays A and B.

```
DIMENSION A(10,10), B(100)
EQUIVALENCE (A(1,1), B(1))
```

In this case to check for a dependence when one statement makes a reference to A and another to B one needs to linearize the references to array A.

2.5 Inexact Tests

Often, exact tests are avoided in compilers because of their complexity. In such cases, inexact tests can be used to obtain some information regarding dependences. Inexact tests need to be conservative in approach, i.e. due to the lack of adequate information or the high cost of detailed analysis they may assume dependences that do not exist. Two such inexact tests are the

1. The g.c.d. test and

2. The bounds test.

In this section we will compare the performance of the g.c.d. test when applied to the linearized equation as opposed to the original system of equations. We say that the g.c.d. test is in error if it answers "yes" and there is no actual dependence. For example consider the following loop.

```
DO I = 1...N
    A(2I + 1) = ...
    ... = A(4I + 4)
END DO
```

In order to test for dependence we have to solve the equation

$$2i + 1 = 4i' + 4$$

which can be written as

$$2i - 4i' = 3$$

The g.c.d. test involves computing the g.c.d. of the coefficients of i and i' and checking whether it divides the constant term on the right hand side. If it does, the test answers "yes", else it answers "no". In this case the g.c.d. is 2 which does not divide 3 and this tells us that the two references can never access a common memory location. In general the g.c.d. test tells us whether the Diophantine equation has any solution in integers, but it ignores the fact that the solution may not lie within loop bounds. We will say that the g.c.d. test is in error if it answers "yes" and there is no solution within loop bounds.

The following two examples (the first is from [BuCy86]) show that neither Banerjee's approach nor the Linearization approach have any advantage over the other when it comes to inexact tests. Consider the following loop.

```
DIMENSION A(10,M)
DO I = 1...N
    A(2I,2I+1) = ...
    ... = A(I,I)
END DO
```

By Banerjee's method we get the system of equations

$$2i = i'$$

$$2i + 1 = i'$$

each of which is known to have a solution (independently) by the g.c.d. test. In reality there is no dependence since the subscripts of the first array reference are always of the type even-odd, while the subscripts of the second array element are always of the same type. Therefore the test is in error here. The corresponding linearized equation is

$$2iM + 2i + 1 = Mi' + i'$$

which simplifies to

$$2(M+1)i - (M+1)i' = -1$$

The g.c.d. of the coefficients of i and i' is seen to be $M+1$ which does not divide -1 for positive M, and hence the g.c.d. test answers "no".

Now consider the second example.

```
DIMENSION A(1000,1001)
DO I = 0...5
    A(2I+1,2I+2) = ...
    ... = A(2I+2,-2I+13)
END DO
```

By Banerjee's method we get the system of equations

$$2i - 2i' = 1$$

$$2i + 2i' = 11$$

none of which has a solution by the g.c.d. test and hence there is no dependence. The linearized equation (after simplification) is

$$2004i - 2000i' = 1012$$

The g.c.d. of the coefficients of i and i' is seen to be 4 which divides 1012 and hence the test is in error here because actually there is no dependence.

In one case, which occurs often in practice, it can be shown that if the g.c.d. test using Banerjee's method is in error, then the g.c.d. test by the Linearization method is also in error. Lemma 4 illustrates this case.

Lemma 4: Given that each of the index variables, $I_1, \ldots, I_n$ appears in at most one of the f_j (g_j) functions, if the g.c.d. test is in error in Banerjee's method then it is in error in the Linearization method also.

Proof: If the g.c.d. test is in error in Banerjee's method then it must have answered "yes" to all the equations in (1). It is well known [Hard79] that the g.c.d. test answers "yes" to any equation if and only if there is a solution (maybe not within loop bounds) to that equation. Since the g.c.d. test answered "yes" we know that there is a solution to each equation (independent of others). However, we also know that an index variable appears in at most one equation. Hence it is clear that by just putting the solutions of all equations together will yield a solution ($I = (i_1, \ldots, i_n), I' = (i'_1, \ldots, i'_n)$) which satisfies all the equations simultaneously. By Lemma 1, this is also a solution to the linearized equation. Hence the g.c.d. test for the linearized equation must answer "yes" and must be in error also.

3 Loop Spreading

In this section we consider a new transformation called *loop spreading*. Loop spreading can be used to extract limited parallelism out of loops in sequence (which individually may have to be executed sequentially) by obtaining a partial overlap of their iterations. In addition, we assume dependences across loops. This inhibits independent and concurrent execution of the individual loops. Our presentation is based on the case of two loops. However, loop spreading can be applied iteratively to a chain of several loops in the same manner. This and other generalizations are handled similarly and are considered later in this section.

3.1 The transformation for chains of loops

We will consider the body of a loop as a block. Let us denote the body of the kth loop in a program by $\beta_k(*)$ and let $\beta_k(i)$ denote the loop body of the ith iteration of that loop. We will assume for convenience that the index variable of the kth loop varies from 1 to N_k. Obviously, $\beta_k(*) = \cup_{i=1}^{N_k} \beta_k(i)$. We will first consider the transformation for two loops in sequence. Let B_1 and B_2 be two serial loops in sequence and let $\beta_i(j)$ denote the jth iteration of B_i. The transformation will produce a new serial loop such that each iteration of the new loop will execute one iteration of B_1 (say $\beta_1(i)$) and one iteration of B_2 (say $\beta_2(i-k)$) in parallel. Thus the two following loops

```
DO I = 1...N1
    β1(I)
END DO
```

```
DO I = 1...N2
    β2(I)
END DO
```

will be transformed to

```
DO I = 1...N1
    COBEGIN
        β1(I);
        IF I > K THEN β2(I − K);
    COEND
END DO

DO I = N1 − K + 1...N2
    β2(I)
END DO
```

Since the original iterations of $B_1(B_2)$ are still executed in sequence, violations may arise from loop across dependences only. Thus if iterations $\beta_1(i)$ and $\beta_2(i-k)$ are to be executed in parallel we must verify that no flow, anti, or output dependences exist for all i such that $1 \le i \le N_1$ [Bern66]. This translates to

$$\cup_{p=i}^{N_1} OUT(\beta_1(p)) \cap IN(\beta_2(i-k)) = \emptyset \tag{12}$$

$$\cup_{p=i}^{N_1} OUT(\beta_1(p)) \cap OUT(\beta_2(i-k)) = \emptyset \tag{13}$$

$$\cup_{p=i}^{N_1} IN(\beta_1(p)) \cap OUT(\beta_2(i-k)) = \emptyset \tag{14}$$

We will try to choose a value of k such that the above equations are satisfied. It is clear that for maximum parallelism we must choose the minimum value of k.

The IN/OUT set for the iteration i will typically consist of scalars and arrays indexed by subscript expressions. Determining scalar intersection is quite easy and obvious methods will suffice. For arrays, to get a better idea of the intersection set we need to study the functions of loop variables which appear in their subscript expressions. When these functions are non-linear little can be done except taking a conservative approach and assuming dependence. Hence we assume that the functions are linear which is the most common case in real programs. Let $f_1, \ldots, f_n(g_1, \ldots, g_m)$ be the functions appearing in the subscript expressions for an array, say X, in iterations $\beta_1(i)(\beta_2(j))$ respectively. We will first consider the case when $n = m = 1$. In this case let $f(g)$ be the only functions in the subscript expression. Hence, we have simplified the problem to finding when we can do the following conversion:

```
DO I = 1...N1
    X(f(I)) = ...
END DO

DO I = 1...N2
    ... = X((g(I))
END DO
```

to

```
DO I = 1...N1
    COBEGIN
        X(f(I)) = ...;
        IF (I > K) THEN ... = X(g(I − K));
    COEND
END DO

DO I = N1 − K + 1...N2
    ... = X(g(I − K))
END DO
```

Let $f(i) = ai + b$ and let $g(j) = cj + d$. Then the problem reduces to checking whether there are values i_0 and j_0 within loop bounds such that $f(i_0) = g(j_0)$. If there are no such values or if $i_0 < j_0$ then the dependence is not hard to satisfy, indeed, any non-negative value of k will satisfy it. If $i_0 > j_0$ then the value of k chosen must be greater than $i_0 - j_0$. If either a or c is equal to zero then the process of checking dependence and computing the value of k is trivial. In what follows, we assume that neither a nor c is zero. First, we can check the existence of i_0, j_0 (maybe not within loop bounds) by the g.c.d. test. If that is passed then we can do the following to obtain the value of k.

The problem has been reduced to choosing the value of k such that

for all $i, 1 \le i \le N_1$, if $f(i) = g(i-k+l)$ then $l > 0$.

Substituting we get $f(i) = g(i-k+l)$, or $ai + b = ci - ck + cl + d$, or finally

$$l = \frac{(a-c)i + (b-d)}{c} + k. \tag{15}$$

Since we must have $l > 0$, we get

$$k > \frac{(c-a)i + (d-b)}{c}. \tag{16}$$

Also, since $1 \le i \le N_1$, we know that the maximum value of $\frac{(c-a)i+(d-b)}{c}$ must occur at $i = 1$ or $i = N_1$ depending on the sign of $\frac{c-a}{c}$. In either case we see that the following must hold.

$$k > \left(\frac{c-a}{c}\right)^+ (N_1 - 1) + \frac{c-a+d-b}{c} \tag{17}$$

where x^+ is defined [Bane76] as

$$x^+ = \begin{cases} x & \text{if } x > 0 \\ 0 & \text{otherwise} \end{cases}$$

Notice that a, b, c, and d are (in practice) compiler constants. The loop bound N_1 must also be known. This may not necessarily be the case. When N_1 is unknown, only the cases where $\frac{a}{c} < 1$ are affected and (for these cases) a conservative estimate of N_1 can be used.

3.2 Generalizations

In this section we consider the application of loop spreading to more general cases, including multidimensioned arrays, chains of loops, and multiple interloop dependences. The principle is always the same as indicated above, the main difference is the calculation of the best value of k. Let us consider each of these cases.

1. The example above cites only flow dependences. The case of anti and output dependences can be handled similarly. If k_1, k_2, k_3 are the minimum values of k such that equations (12), (13) and (14) are satisfied respectively, then choosing $k = \max(k_1, k_2, k_3)$ will satisfy all three equations.

2. The example above cites just a single array. The case of many arrays can be handled by a repetition of the method for all arrays and choosing the maximum value of k over all arrays.

3. In the example the array X is one-dimensional. If it was multidimensional we would apply the above method in each dimension and then choose the minimum value of k as the appropriate value. This is because if two references to a multidimensional array X are to reference the same memory location, the subscript functions must agree on all dimensions.

4. There is only one reference to X in each loop body. When there are many references this method must be applied to each pair of such references, and then the appropriate value of k must be chosen to be the maximum over all such pairs of references.

5. In the example there are only two loops in sequence. When there are n loops in sequence the following method can be applied to compute k_j for the jth loop, $2 \leq j \leq n$.

   $k_1 = 0$
   for $j = 2$ **to** n **do**
       for $i = 1$ **to** $j - 1$ **do**
           Compute k'_{ij} with respect to the loops B_i and B_j using the above method.
       end for
       $k_j = \max\{k'_{ij} + k_i | 1 \leq i \leq j - 1\}$
   end for

Let us now look at an example. Consider the two loops:

```
DO I = 1...10
      X(3I + 4) = A(I - 1) + 1
      A(I) = Y(-2I + 25)
END DO
DO I = 1...10
      D(I) = X(4I + 2)
      X(I + 1) = D(I) ** 2 + D(I - 1)
      E(I) = Y(-2I + 23)
END DO
```

There are possible dependences from the first statement of the first loop to the first and second statement of the second loop because both could conceivably reference the same locations of the array X. Similarly, there could be dependences from the second statement of the first loop to the last statement of the second loop because of the array Y.

Then for the array X we have the following pairs of functions $(3i+4, 4i+2)$ and $(3i+4, i+1)$. For array Y we have $(-2i+25, -2i+23)$. In the pair $(3i+4, 4i+2), a = 3, b = 4, c = 4, d = 2$. Since $N = 10$, we get

$$\begin{aligned} k &> \left(\frac{4-3}{4}\right)^{+}(10-1) + \frac{4-3+2-4}{4} \\ &> \left(\frac{1}{4}\right)9 + \frac{-1}{4} \\ &> 2. \end{aligned}$$

Similarly, from the other two pairs we get $k > -5$ and $k > 1$. Choosing the minimum value of k satisfying the above inequalities, we get $k = 3$. Hence the parallel version of the above loop is

```
DO I = 1...10
      COBEGIN
            β1(I);
            IF (I > K) THEN β2(I - 3);
      COEND
END DO
DO I = 8...10
      β2(I)
END DO
```

Assuming $\beta_1(I)$ and $\beta_2(I)$ take the same time, τ, to execute, the total execution time of the original loops is 20τ, while that of the transformed loop is 13τ. This is the best possible overlap for the above example.

4 Conclusion

Program concurrentization is still a largely unexplored research area (unlike vectorization). In this paper we discussed issues in dependence analysis and program transformations for concurrentization.

More specifically, we considered two approaches for computing data dependences inside loops. The first well-known approach derives a system of Diophantine equations whose solutions give precise dependence information within predefined bounds. The second approach constructs a single equation through linearization. We showed that for all practical cases the two schemes are equivalent although different in complexity.

Subsequently we considered the application of these two schemes for exact and inexact tests through specific examples. In the inexact case both methods can succeed (or fail) exclusively depending on the particular example. However, in many practical cases, the linearization approach is inferior.

Finally we presented loop spreading for extorting parallelism out of a sequence of serial loops with inter dependences. Loop spreading works by executing in parallel successive iterations of the serial loops. For the case of two adjacent loops we described a formula which can be used to compute the maximum degree of overlap.

References

[AhSU86] Aho A. V., R. Sethi, J. D. Ullman. *Compilers: Principles, Techniques, and Tools*, Addison-Wesley, Reading, Massachusetts, 1986.

[AlCo72] Allen F. E., J. Cocke. *A Catalogue of Optimizing Transformations* in **Design and Optimization of Compilers**, R. Rustin, Ed. Prentice-Hall, Englewood Cliffs, New Jersey, 1972, pp. 1-30.

[Alle88] Allen F. E. et. al. *An overview of the PTRAN analysis system*, **Proceedings of the 1987 International Conference on Supercomputing**, Springer-Verlag, LNCS, February 1988.

[AlKe82] Allen J. R., K. Kennedy. *PFC: A Program to Convert Fortran to Parallel Form*, Tech. Rept. MASC-TR82-6, Rice University, Houston, Texas, March 1982.

[AlKe87] Allen R., K. Kennedy. *Automatic Translation of FORTRAN Programs to Vector Form*, **ACM Transactions on Programming Languages and Systems**, Vol. 9, No. 4, October 1987.

[Bane76] Banerjee U. *Data Dependence in Ordinary Programs*, M.S. Thesis, University of Illinois, DCS Report No. UIUCDCS-R-76-837, November 1976.

[Bane79] Banerjee U. *Speedup of Ordinary Programs*, Ph.D. Thesis, University of Illinois at Urbana-Champaign, DCS Report No. UIUCDCS-R-79-989, October 1979.

[Bern66] Bernstein A. J. *Analysis of Programs for Parallel Processing*, **IEEE Trans. on Electronic Computers**, Vol. EC-15, No. 5, October 1966, pp. 757-763.

[BuCy86] Burke M., Cytron R. *Interprocedural Dependence Analysis and Parallelization*, **Proceedings of the SIGPLAN 86 Symposium on Compiler Construction**, 21(7), July 1986 pp. 162-175.

[Cytr84] Cytron R. G. *Doacross: Beyond Vectorization for Multiprocessors (Extended Abstract)*, **Proceedings of the 1986 International Conference on Parallel Processing**, St. Charles, IL, August, 1986, pp. 836-844.

[Hard79] Hardy C. H., E. M. Wright *An Introduction to the Theory of Numbers*, Oxford, 1979.

[Knut69] Knuth D. E. *The Art of Computer Programming, Vol. 2 / Seminumerical Algorithms*, Addison-Wesley, Reading, Mass., 1969.

[Kuck78] Kuck D. J. *The Structure of Computers and Computations*, Volume 1, John Wiley and Sons, New York, 1978.

[KDLS86] Kuck D. J., E. S. Davidson, D. H. Lawrie, A. H. Sameh. *Parallel Supercomputing Today and the Cedar Approach*, **Science**, Vol. 231, 4740, February 28, 1986, pp. 967-974.

[KKLW80] Kuck D. J., R. H. Kuhn, B. Leasure, M. Wolfe. *The Structure of an Advanced Vectorizer for Pipelined Processors*, **Fourth International Computer Software and Applications Conference**, October, 1980.

[KKPL81] Kuck D. J., R. Kuhn, D. Padua, B. Leasure, M. Wolfe. *Dependence Graphs and Compiler Optimizations*, **Proceedings of the 8-th ACM Symposium on Principles of Programming Languages**, January 1981, pp. 207-218.

[Malm80] Malm D. G. *A Computer Laboratory Manual for Number Theory*, COMPress, Inc., Wentworth, New Hampshire, 1980.

[MiPa86] Midkiff S. P., D. A. Padua. *Compiler Generated Synchronization for DO Loops*, **Proc. of the 1986 International Conference on Parallel Processing**, St. Charles, IL, August, 1986, pp. 544-551.

[Nico84] Nicolau A., *Parallelism, Memory Anti-Aliasing and Correctness for Trace Scheduling Compilers*, Ph.D. Thesis, Yale University, June 1984.

[PaKL80] Padua D. A., D. J. Kuck, D. H. Lawrie. *High-Speed Multiprocessors and Compilation Techniques*, **IEEE Transactions on Computers**, Vol. C-29, No. 9, September 1980.

[Peir86] Peir J. K. *Program Partitioning and Synchronization on Multiprocessor Systems*, Department of Computer Science, University of Illinois at Urbana-Champaign, DCS Report No. UIUCCDCS-R-86-1259, March 1986.

[Poly87] Polychronopoulos C. D. *More on Advanced Loop Optimizations*, CSRD Technical Report No. 667, Center for Supercomputing Research and Development, University of Illinois, 1987.

[Poly86] Polychronopoulos C. D. *On Program Restructuring, Scheduling, and Communication for Parallel Processor Systems*, Ph.D. Thesis, CSRD Technical Report No. 595, Center for Supercomputing Research and Development, University of Illinois, August, 1986.

[PoKu87] Polychronopoulos C. D., D. J. Kuck *Guided Self-Scheduling: A Practical Scheduling Scheme for Parallel Supercomputers*, **IEEE Trans. on Computers**, Vol. 36, No. 12, December 1987.

[Wolf82] Wolfe M. J. *Optimizing Supercompilers for Supercomputers*, Ph.D. Thesis, University of Illinois at Urbana-Champaign, DCS Report No. UIUCCDCS-R-82-1105, 1982.

Compiling Techniques for First-Order Linear Recurrences on a Vector Computer

Yoshikazu Tanaka *Kyouko Iwasawa* *S. Gotoo** *Yukio Umetani*

Central Research Laboratory, Hitachi, Ltd.
Higashikoigakubo, Kokubunji-shi,
Tokyo, Japan

*Software Works, Hitachi, Ltd.,
Shinanomachi, Totsuka-ku,
Yokohama-shi,Kanagawa, Japan

Abstract

Linear recurrences are the most important class of non-vectorizable problems in typical scientific/engineering calculations. This work discusses high performance methods for solving first-order linear recurrences on a vector computer, investigates automatic transformations, and develops the compiling techniques for first-order linear recurrence problems.

These results show that the improved vector code generated by the vectorizing compiler run at the rate of 150 MFLOPS (million floating operations per second), in the case of the moderate loop lengths (>1000), and at the rate of over 200 MFLOPS, in the case of the long loop lengths (>10000), on the HITAC S-820 supercomputer. Also, overall performance improvements of 69% in the 14 Lawrence Livermore Loops and 25% in the 24 Lawrence Livermore Loops, as measured by the harmonic mean, are attained.

1. Introduction

Supercomputers have been providing increased computational power to users in many scientific and engineering fields. Many compiling techniques have been developed such as in Refs. [3,4,5,6,7] that provide powerful automatic vectorizing functions necessary for high supercomputer performance. Because vectorization is so successful, fast algorithms for non-vectorizable problems have become the key to overall performance improvements.

This paper investigates an important class of non-vectorizable problems: first-order linear recurrence. This algorithm is often seen in numerical calculations such as classical Gaussian elimination in bi-diagonal and tri-diagonal simultaneous equations, and iterative methods (ICCG, SLOR, SOR methods) in simultaneous equations. The following FORTRAN program in Fig. 1 denotes a first-order linear recurrence relation.

```
         A(1) = C(1)
         DO 10 J = 2, N
10       A(J) = B(J)*A(J-1) + C(J)
```

Fig.1 Simple linear recurrence program

The most obvious characteristic in this DO loop is that the right-hand side of this statement uses a result computed on the immediately preceding iteration. Therefore, programs with recurrences are not easily run in parallel. To illustrate the importance of linear recurrences to overall performance, consider the 14 Lawrence Livermore Loops and the 24 Lawrence Livermore Loops. Of these FORTRAN kernels, seven loops (5, 6, 11 in the 14 Loops, 5, 11, 19, 23 in the 24 Loops) have first-order linear recurrence relations. The performance of the HITAC S-820 supercomputer for these benchmarks with the recurrences run in scalar mode (unrolling technique used) is shown in Table 1. Doubling the speed of these loops would result in an overall performance improvement of 34% in the 14 Loops and 15% in the 24 Loops, as measured by the harmonic mean.

This shows that the attainment of high performance in ordinary FORTRAN programs is dependent on the development of program transformation techniques for first-order linear recurrences in an automatic vectorizing compiler.

2. Previous Research

Two parallel algorithms, the recursive doubling method [1] and the cyclic reduction method [2], are well known for dealing with this problem. The first algorithm, however, is not appropriate for a vector computer, because it takes $N\log N$ steps in ordinary FORTRAN programs (where N is the problem size). The second algorithm, which is effective for vector supercomputers, can be written in FORTRAN as shown in Fig. 2.

In this coding, all inner DO loops are vectorized, but the asymptotic performance rate is approached only when R and S (nearly proportional to the square root of N) are quite large. The line (R) in Fig. 3 represents the performance of this method by the HITAC S-820 supercomputer. Where R and S are small, the vector code performance is lower than that of scalar code. In this figure the DO 20 and DO 30 loops are excluded because they are initialization steps. Also, it is assumed that the orders of R and S are nearly equal and not a multiple of the power of 2 to prevent memory bank conflicts.

On the other hand, some vector computers such as the HITAC M-180 IAP (Integrated Array Processor, 1978), S-810 (1983), and S-820 (1987) are equipped with macro vector instructions for first-order linear recurrence(from now on referred to as the VITR

CH2617-9/88/0000/0174$01.00 © 1988 IEEE

```
      DIMENSION  AA(R,S), BB(R,S), C(R,S), TT(R,S)
      EQUIVALENCE  (AA(1,1),A(1)), (BB(1,1),B(1)),
                   (CC(1,1),C(1))

      DO 20  K = 1, S         where N = R*S
      DO 20  J = 1, R
20    AA(J,K) = CC(J,K)

      DO 30  K = 1, S
30    TT(1,K) = BB(1,K)

      DO 40  J = 2, R
      DO 40  K = 1, S
      AA(J,K) = AA(J,K) + BB(J,K)*AA(J-1,K)
40    TT(J,K) = TT(J-1,K)*BB(J,K)

      DO 50  K = 2, S
      DO 50  J = 1, R
50    AA(J,K) = AA(J,K) + AA(R,K-1)*TT(J,K)
```

Fig. 2 R-cyclic reduction method for loop in Fig. 1

instruction). Also, the HITACHI FORTRAN compiler generated vector code directly for loop in Fig. 1 by making a pattern match of FORTRAN sources. But this macro vector instruction (not an elementwise vector instruction) executes much slower than other elementwise vector instructions. In Fig. 3, line (V) denotes the performance of the VITR instruction, line (S1) the scalar code, and line (S5) the scalar code improved by 5-times loop unrolling. The VITR code runs only 3.3 times faster than the optimized scalar code, where the value calculated at the previous iteration is maintained in a scalar register. Moreover, the difference between the VITR code and the scalar loop unrolling code becomes shorter.

This shows that a new method which exploits the vector performance of the supercomputer is desirable.

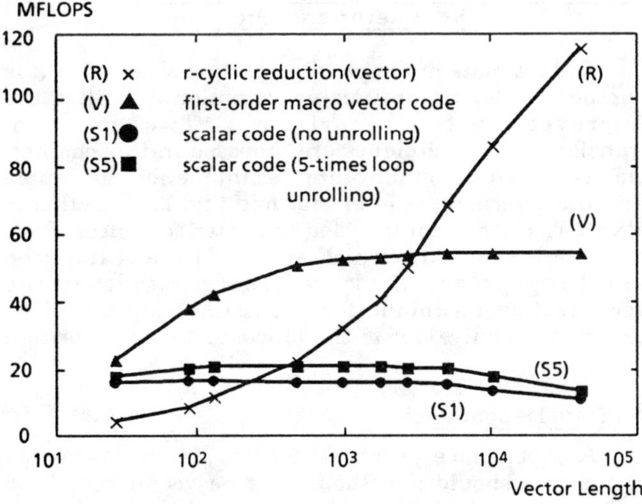

Fig. 3 Performance of first-order linear recurrence with conventional methods on the HITAC S-820

3. New Fast Algorithm for the Vector Computer

A fast algorithm for vector computers equipped with the VITR instruction is written in Fig. 4.

```
      DO 60 J = 2,N,m
        E = B(J + m-1)*B(J + m-2)* --- *B(J + 1)*B(J)          Sc1
        F = B(J + m-1)*B(J + m-2)* --- *B(J + 1)*C(J)          Sc2
#           + B(J + m-1)*B(J + m-2)* --- *C(J + 1)
                          ¦
#           + B(J + m-1)*C(J + m-2)
#           + C(J + m-1)
      A(J + m-1) = E*A(J-1) + F                                Sitr
      A(J) = B(J)*A(J-1) + C(J)                                S1
      A(J + 1) = B(J + 1)*A(J) + C(J + 1)                      S2
                          ¦
      A(J + m-2) = B(J + m-2)*A(J + m-3) + C(J + m-2)          Sm-1
60  CONTINUE
```

Fig. 4 New fast algorithm for the vector computer

In this program, statement Sitr can be vectorized by the VITR instruction, and the other statements can be vectorized by the ordinary elementwise vector instructions. The intention of this algorithm is to reduce the number of iterative calculations. It increases the total calculations, but these operations can be run in vector mode. Let us examine this algorithm on an virtual vector computer to estimate the performance of this program. Suppose the computer has two load/store pipes, one adder pipe, one multiplier pipe and one VITR pipe, all of which can be chained to each other. Also, suppose it has the following virtual vector instructions in Fig. 5. In this figure, *ri* denotes a vector/scalar register and M denotes the memory address.

VL	r,M	Load from memory to vector register r ← M
VST	r,M	Store from vector register to memory r → M
VADD	r3,r1,r2	Vector elementwise addition r3 ← r1 + r2
VMUL	r3,r1,r2	Vector elementwise multiplication r3 ← r1*r2
VITR	r3,r1,r2	Vector linear recurrence operation r3(j) ← r3(j-1)*r1 + r2

Fig. 5 Vector instructions in the virtual machine

For simplicity, assume that VITR instruction can produce one result per 20 cycles, and other instructions can produce one result per one cycle. Let us estimate the performance of the program in Fig. 4. The program needs 2m + 1 load pipes, m store pipes, 1 VITR pipe, 3m-3 multiplier pipes and 2m-2 adder pipes; these pipes run in parallel. The concept of *chime* is used for an examination of the performance. A *chime* is defined as the number of cycles needed to perform a vector operation, not including the start-up time. This program takes total (3m + 18) chimes, as shown in Fig. 6.

```
                                                cumulative no.
                                                of chimes taken
(Sc1)
VL       VR0,       B(J + m-1)                 ¦
VL       VR1,       B(J + m-2)                 ¦
VMUL     VR2,       VR0,        VR1            ¦ 1 chime
VL       VR3,       B(J + m-3)                 ¦
VMUL     VR4,       VR3,        VR2            ¦ 2 chimes
                    ¦                          ¦
VL       VR2m-3,    B(J)                       ¦
VMUL     VR2m-2,    VR2m-3,     VR2m-4         ¦ m-1 chimes
                                               ¦
(Sc2)
VL       VR2m-1,    C(J)                       ¦
VMUL     VR2m,      VR2m-1,     VR2m-4         ¦
VL       VR2m + 1,  C(J + 1)                   ¦ m chimes
VMUL     VR2m + 2,  VR2m + 1,   VR2m-6         ¦
VADD     VR2m + 3,  VR2m + 2,   VR2m           ¦
                    ¦
VL       VR5m-5,    C(J + m-1)                 ¦ 2m-2 chimes
VADD     VR5m-4,    VR5m-5,     VR5m-6         ¦ 2m-1 chimes
                                               ¦
(Sitr)
VITR     VR5m-3,    VR2m-2,     VR5m-4         ¦
VST      VR5m-3,    A(J + m-1)                 ¦2m + 19 chimes

(S1)
VL       VR5m-2,    A(J-1)                     ¦
VMUL     VR5m-1,    VR5m-2,     VR2m-3         ¦
VADD     VR5m,      VR5m-1,     VR2m-1         ¦
VST      VR5m,      A(J)                       ¦2m + 20 chimes

(S2)
                    ¦                          ¦
(Sm-1)
VL       VR8m-8,    A(J + m-3)                 ¦
VMUL     VR8m-7,    VR8m-8,     VR2m-5         ¦
VADD     VR8m-6,    VR8m-7,     VR5m-8         ¦
VST      VR8m-6,    A(J + m-2)                 ¦3m + 18 chimes
```

Fig. 6 Vector object codes for the program in Fig. 4

The asymptotic cpu time (for very large vector length N) can be estimated by

$$Tm = (3m + 18)N/m \qquad (1)$$

If the effect of m is defined to be $Eu = T1(m = 1)/Tm$, then $Eu = 21m/(3m + 12)$. For m = 3, 5, and 9, Eu = 3.0, 3.8, and 4.8, respectively. Since VITR instruction can run approximately 3.3 times faster than scalar instructions, this improved code is estimated to run 9.9 times (for m = 3), 12.5 times (for m = 5), 15.8 times (for m = 9) faster than the scalar code. If program in Fig. 1 is assumed to run without recurrence, it requires 2 chimes; therefore it takes $2N$ cpu time. This shows that the improved method for first-order linear recurrences yields approximately two-thirds of the speed of ordinary elementwise vector instructions, when m is sufficiently large.

The performance of the program in Fig. 4 on the HITAC S-820 supercomputer was measured. The relation between the vector length and the first-order linear recurrence performance is shown in Fig. 7. Lines (V3, V5, V9) denote m = 3, 5, and 9 respectively. The trend shown by Fig. 7 is in fairly good agreement with our estimate. This figure shows that our improved vector algorithm performed better than the r-cyclic reduction method in common vector length.

Next, the asymptotic cpu time ratio between these methods is estimated. The asymptotic cpu time of the r-cyclic reduction method for program in Fig. 2 (excluding DO 20 and DO 30) can be estimated with

$$Tr = 5N$$

The performance ratio of Tm/Tr is from 4.2(m = 1) to 1.0(m = 9). So, for very large vector length, the r-cyclic reduction method will be slightly superior. But, since this difference is small when m is large, this improved vector first-order method surpasses it overall.

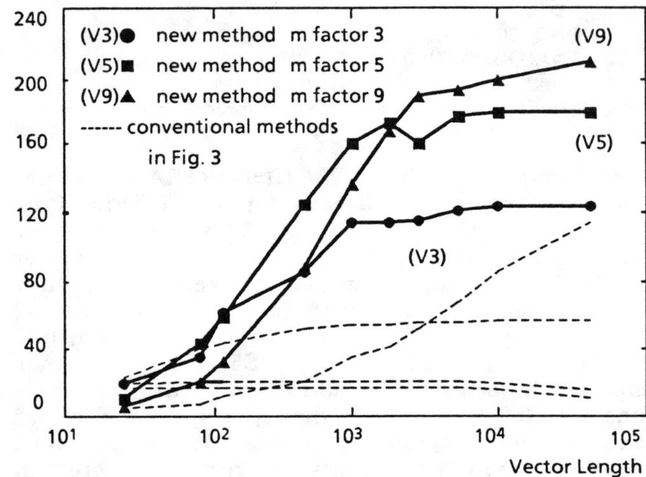

Fig. 7 Improved Performance of first-order linear recurrence with the new method on the HITAC S-820

4. Program Transformation Techniques in the First-Order Recurrence Problem

The estimate in the previous section shows that it is appropriate for an optimizing compiler to utilize the improved vector algorithm. Two program transformation techniques are proposed in this chapter. One is a vector loop unrolling technique for the simple first-order recurrence form shown in Fig. 1. The other is a vectorization technique for the inter-sentences first-order recursion codes which appear in the scalar loop unrolling program. It will be shown that the vectorization technique for the scalar loop unrolling program is equivalent to the proposed vector algorithm in Fig. 4.

4.1 Data Dependences

A dependence graph is used to determine which statements should and should not be vectorized. The new dependence analysis method needed to construct the dependence graph is described in Refs. [5, 7]. Therefore, this chapter explains only the concept of data dependence used here.

4.1.1 Kinds of Data Dependences

A variable (R1) is data-dependent to a variable (R2) if any of three well-known types of dependences exist between them. They are flow dependence, anti-dependence, and output dependence [3].

[def 1] Flow Dependence

If the value of a variable defined at a definition *d* may be used at a use *u*, a flow dependence from *d* to *u* exists.

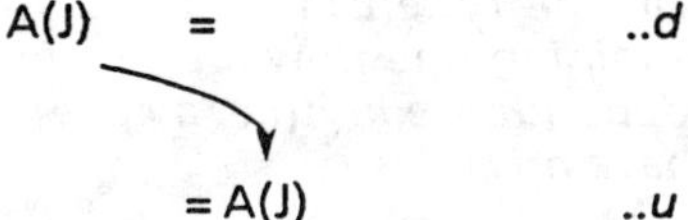

[def 2] Anti-Dependence

If a value used at a use *u* may be redefined at a definition *d*, anti-dependence from *u* to *d* exists.

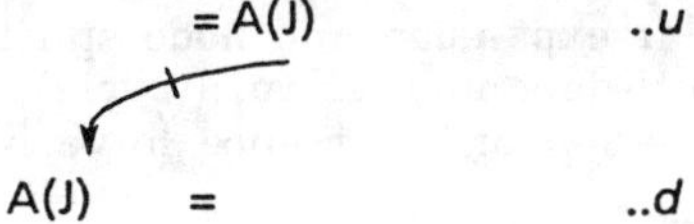

[def 3] Output Dependence

If a value defined at a definition *d1* may be redefined at a definition *d2*, an output dependence from *d1* to *d2* exists.

```
A(J)  =          ..d1
A(J)  =          ..d2
```

Each of the above data dependences can be classified as follows with regard to the loop iteration[6].

[def 4] Loop-Independent Data Dependence

Dependences that may occur on the same loop iteration are called loop-independent dependences.

```
    DO 70 J = 1, N
       A(J) =             ..S1

           = A(J)         ..S2
70  CONTINUE
```

Statement *S1* defines A(1) when J equals 1. Statement *S2* uses A(1) when J equals 1. There is a flow dependence on the same loop iteration. This definition, however, is not generally convenient for optimization. The following section defines loop-complete independent data dependence.

[def 4.1] Loop-Complete Independent Data Dependence

If two array references indicate the same subscript expressions, the loop-independent data dependence is called loop-complete independent data dependence (hereafter abbreviated as LCI data dependence). Loop-independent data dependence in a simple variable always means LCI data dependence.

```
      DO 80 J = 1, 10
         A(J)  =
         K = J + 1
                 = A(K-1)
80    CONTINUE
```

[def 5] Loop-Carried Data Dependence

Dependences that may occur between different loop iterations are called loop-carried data dependence[6].

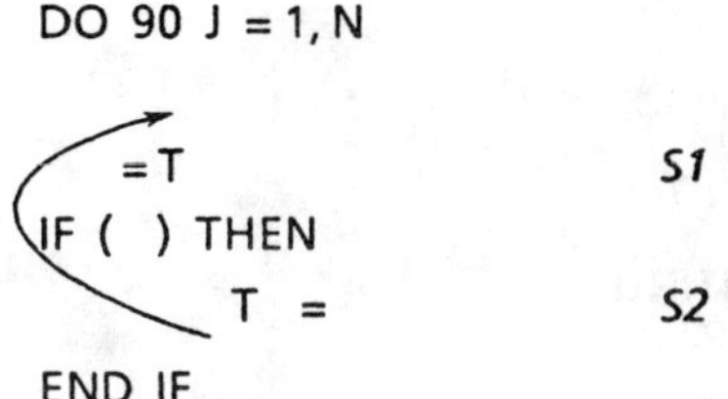


```
   S1
   S2
90    CONTINUE
```

The value of simple variable T used at *S1* when J equals 3 may be defined at *S2* when J equals 1 or 2 or may be defined before entering the loop in DO 90. There is a flow-loop carried data dependence from *S2* to *S1*.

Because this definition is also not convenient for our first-order recurrence optimization, it is enhanced so that loop-carried data dependence can be classified in more detail.

[def 5.1] Loop-Complete Next-Iteration-Carried Data Dependence

If a value referred at the j-th iteration of a loop may be referred to at the next (j+1)-th iteration, the data dependence is called loop next-iteration-carried data dependence. If, for all j, an array element at an array reference *r1* referred to in the j-th iteration of loop is always referred to at another array reference *r2* in the (j+1)-th iteration, this dependence is called loop-complete next-iteration-carried data dependence (hereafter abbreviated as LCNIC data dependence). If a simple variable has loop next-iteration-carried data dependence whose graph starts from uncontrolled statements, it is said to have LCNIC data dependence. Obviously this dependence denotes a first-order linear recurrence relation.

Below are some examples of LCNIC data dependences:

```
      DO 100 J = 1, 10
```

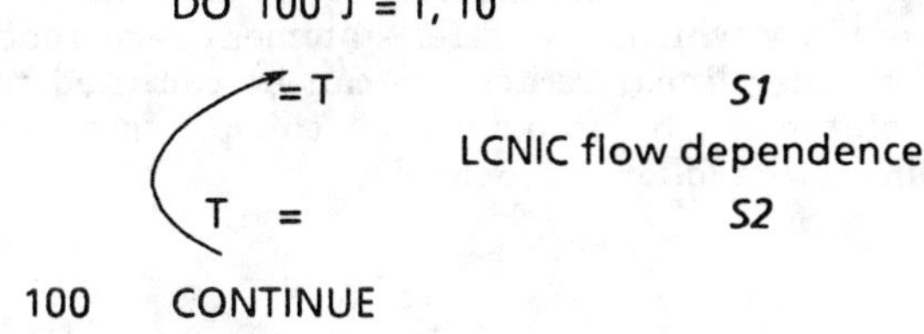


```
100   CONTINUE
```

```
      DO 110 J = 1, 10
            = A(J + 1)                S1
          LCNIC anti- dependence
      A(J)   =                        S2
110   CONTINUE
```

Examples below denote only loop next-iteration-carried data dependence or loop-carried data dependence

```
      DO 120 J = 1, 10
         IF ( )THEN
                 = T                  S1
             T   =                    S2
         END IF
120   CONTINUE
```

```
      DO 130 J = 1, 10
         IF ( )THEN
                       = A(J)         S1
            A(J + 1)   =              S2
         END IF
130   CONTINUE
```

4.2 Vector Loop Unrolling in First-Order Recurrence

If first-order linear recurrence appears in a simple FORTRAN statement like Fig. 1, the compiler recognizes certain forms of first-order linear recurrences, generates vector code, and does loop unrolling if necessary. The method of recognition is provided as a special case of 4.3. The vector unrolling code becomes the same as program in Fig. 4

4.3 Vectorization for Inter-Statement Recurrence

The #5 and #6 kernels in the 14 Lawrence Livermore Loops were examined. They contain first-order linear recurrences, which have been unrolled in the original code for improved performance in scalar mode .

In Fig. 7(a), a first-order recurrence exists between statements *S1* and *S3*. Since conventional compiler cannot generate a VITR instruction, a method was developed to apply this macro vector instruction to program parts which have inter-statement recurrence . The first-order linear recurrence can be confined to a single statement by transforming the program part according to the following lemma 1.

Lemma 1:
If a cycle of dependences (i.e. flow, anti- or output dependence) exists between statements, and:
If only one flow loop-complete next-iteration-carried (LCNIC) data dependence in the cycle always exists, and:
If flow loop-complete independent (LCI) data dependences always exist between adjacent statements in the cycle, and:
If no other loop dependences between statements in the cycle exist,
Then the statements in the cycle can be transformed into one statement containing one flow loop-complete next-iteration-carried dependence in it(i.e. a cycle), and other statements that have no cycles. □

The proof of Lemma 1 follows quite easily from the definition of data dependences. Based on this lemma we have developed a transformation algorithm named "Procedure Intermacro", which is presented in Fig. 8. This procedure is called after reduction of dependence (scalar renaming, scalar expansion and node splitting which removes all anti-dependences in a cycle) and minimization of the region of recurrence have been attempted.

```
Procedure Intermacro(R,D);
  /* R is the intermediate texts  of statements*/
  /*  that constitute dependence cycles.*/
  /* D is the dependence graph in R.*/
  begin;
  (A) Save R
  (B) Node-splitting
       split variables that have only the start edge
       of the anti-dependence graph out of cycle.
  (C) Check the data-dependence condition
       based on the above lemma 1.
  If condition satisfied then
     begin;
     (D) Reduce a cycle to one statement
          by substituting each statement into the next
          until only one statement has a cycle.
     (E) Reorder statements according to the directed
          graph.
     (G) Transform the statement that has a cycle
          to use the VITR instruction form
          ( solve Bi,Ci in Ai = Ai-1*Bi + Ci ).
      If not transformable then
          begin;
          (H) Restore R
          end;
     end;
  else
     begin;
     (I) Restore R
     end;
  end Intermacro
```

Fig.8 Inter-statement recurrence vectorization procedure

This procedure establishes the validity of some powerful vectorized transformations for recurrence problems. Here, "Restore R" means that if this vectorization method cannot be applied, the scalar code based on the original intermediate texts is generated in place of the transformed redundant intermediate ones. Here, only the simple recurrence that is implemented by a macro vector instruction is considered, but if the fast algorithm of other recurrences such as

$$A(J)=B(J)/A(J-1)+C(J)$$

can be found, they can be efficiently processed by library call codes that use a fast algorithm at step (G) in this procedure *Intermacro*.

The transformation processes for program in Fig. 7(a) will be shown in Fig. 7(b)-(d). The transformed program in Fig. 7(d) can be fully vectorized.

Next other examples of the effective application of this lemma are shown. Consider the program in Fig. 9(a) selected from a two-dimensional hydrodynamics calculation code for updating pressure and velocity[8]. Because this is an implicit relaxation scheme that contains first-order linear recurrence in both J and K directions, it cannot be vectorized by simple techniques. But, in our proposed method, after minimizing the recurrence region and applying this procedure intermacro to the recurrence part *S1* and *S2* in Fig. 9(b), VITR vector instruction can be used for this recurrence. Therefore, program in Fig. 9(a) can be fully vectorized despite its first-order linear recurrence

Lastly, the application to the sum operations of multiple statements is shown in Fig. 10(a). This is a special case--only the final value of loop iteration is needed in the first-order linear recurrence. In Fig. 10(a) *S1* and *S2* constitute a cycle, and the conventional compiler cannot recognize the the semantics of the sum reduction operation because of the limited pattern-matching used. In our method, this program is vectorized as follows. First of all, in order to reduce the number of arcs, using well known techniques such as renaming and variable expansion [3], reduction program is derived in Fig. 10(b). Next, applying procedure *Intermacro* to it, transformed program is obtained in Fig. 10(c). After the dead code elimination for *S3* (general optimization for vector texts) , and the application of the following lemma 2 to it, the vectorizable sum program is obtained in Fig.10(d).

Lemma 2:
If a VITR instruction has a temporary vector introduced by the compiler as a cycle operand, and:
If this temporary vector is not used in other statements, and:
If multiplication is not available in the VITR instruction,
Then the temporary vector reduces to a temporary scalar variable, and a macro sum reduction instruction can be applied.
If addition is not available in the VITR instruction,
Then the temporary vector reduces to a temporary scalar variable, and a macro product reduction instruction can be applied. □

5. Performance in the Lawrence Livermore Loops

The Lawrence Livermore Loops have been widely used as a benchmark job to measure the performance of many supercomputers. For this type of measurement,

```
      DO 140 J = 1, N, 3
                                        LCNIC flow dependence
         A(J) = B(J)*A(J-1) + C(J)                            S1
                                        LCI flow dependence
         A(J + 1) = B(J + 1)*A(J) + C(J + 1)                  S2
                                        LCI flow dependence
         A(J + 2) = B(J + 2)*A(J + 1) + C(J + 2)              S3
140   CONTINUE
```

(a) Original program

```
      DO 140 J = 1, N, 3
                                        LCNIC flow dependence
         A(J) = B(J)*A(J-1) + C(J)
                                        LCI flow dependence
         A(J + 1) = B(J + 1)*A(J) + C(J + 1)
                                        LCNIC flow dependence
         A(J + 2) = B(J + 2)*(B(J + 1)*(B(J)*A(J-1) + C(J))
#                    + C(J + 1)) + C(J + 2)
140   CONTINUE
```

(b) After steps (A),(B),(C) and(D) in the procedure

```
      DO 140 J = 1, N, 3
                                        LCNIC flow dependence
         A(J + 2) = B(J + 2)*(B(J + 1)*(B(J)*A(J-1) + C(J))
#                    + C(J + 1)) + C(J + 2)
                                        LCNIC flow dependence
         A(J) = B(J)*A(J-1) + C(J)
                                        LCI flow dependence
         A(J + 1) = B(J + 1)*A(J) + C(J + 1)
140   CONTINUE
```

(c) After step (E) in the procedure

```
      DO 140 J = 1, N, 3
         E = B(J + 2)*B(J + 1)*B(J)
         F = B(J + 2)*B(J + 1)*C(J)
#          + B(J + 2)*C(J + 1)
#          + C(J + 2)
                                        LCNIC flow dependence
         A(J + 2) = E*A(J-1) + F            VITR instruction
                                        LCNIC flow dependence
         A(J) = B(J)*A(J-1) + C(J)
                                        LCI flow dependence
         A(J + 1) = B(J + 1)*A(J) + C(J + 1)
140   CONTINUE
```

(d) Vectorizable program

Fig. 7 Successive application of transforms to the unrolling program

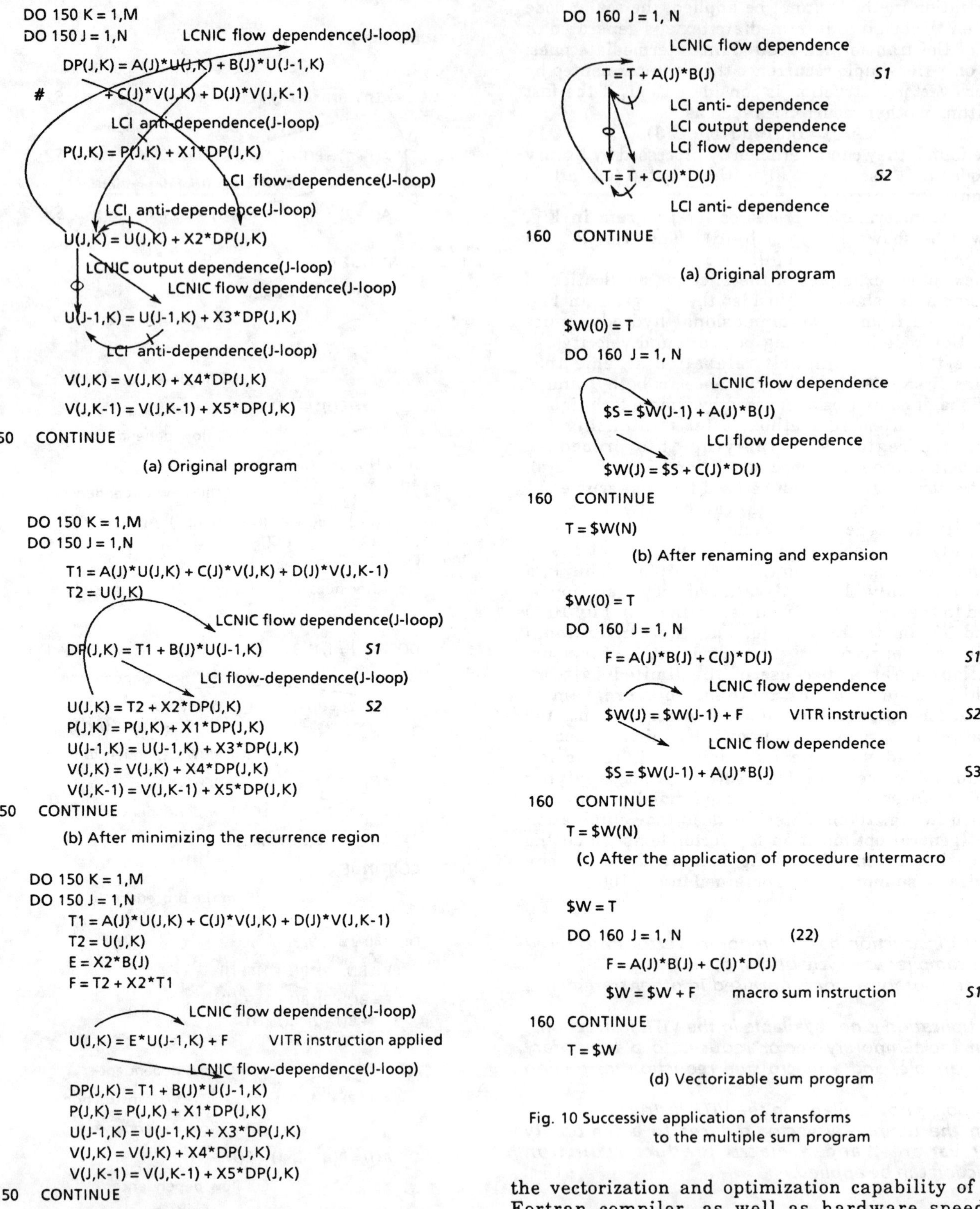

Fig. 9 Successive application of transforms to the hydrodynamics program

Fig. 10 Successive application of transforms to the multiple sum program

the vectorization and optimization capability of the Fortran compiler, as well as hardware speed is important. The speed in MFLOPS for the 14 Livermore Loops and the 24 Livermore Loops on the HITAC S-820 supercomputer are shown in Table 2. The results were measured by the authors. Comparing Table 2. with

Table 1 showed that overall performance as measured by the harmonic mean was greatly improved from 49.4 MFLOPS to 83.7 MFLOPS (69% improvement) in the 14 kernels, and from 35.9 MFLOPS to 44.7 MFLOPS (25% improvement) in the 24 kernels.

6. Conclusion

Efficient compiling algorithms for the first-order linear recurrence problem were described. The following two vector algorithms were proposed: (1)Vector unrolling for the VITR instruction and (2)Vectorization of inter-statement recurrence. Recently, the authors have implemented these algorithms in their vectorizing compiler eliminating many of the restrictions that prevented the vector computer from reaching its full potential.

References

[1] H. Stone: "An Efficient Parallel Algorithm for the Solution of Tridiagonal Linear System of Equations", JACM, Vol. 20, No. 1, pp. 27-38, 1973.

[2] D. Heller: "Some Aspects of the Cyclic Reduction Algorithm for Block Tridiagonal Linear Systems", SIAM J.Numr.Anal., Vol. 13, No. 4, pp. 484-496, 1976.

[3] D. J. Kuck, R. H. Kuhn, D. A. Pauda, B. R. Leause and M. J. Wolfe: "Dependence Graphs and Compiler Optimizations", Conf. Record of the 8th ACM Symposium on Principles of Programming Languages, pp. 207-218, 1981.

[4] M. Yasumura, Y. Tanaka, Y. Kanada and A. Aoyama: "Compiling Algorithms and Techniques for the S810 Vector Processor", Proc. of the 1984 International Conference on Parallel Processing, IEEE Press, New York, pp. 285-290, 1984.

[5] S. Gotoo, Y. Tanaka, K. Iwasawa, Y. Kanada and A. Aoyama: "Advanced Vectorization Techniques for Supercomputers", Journal of Information Processing, Vol. 11, No. 1, pp. 22-31, 1987

[6] J. R. Allen and K. Kennedy: "Automatic Loop Interchange, ACM SIGPLAN 1984 Symposium on Compiler Constructions", SIGPLAN Notices, Vol. 19, No.6, pp.233-246, 1984.

[7] Y. Kanada, K. Ishida and E. Nunohiro: "A method of Global Dataflow Analysis for arrays", Transactions of Informations Processing Society of Japan, Vol.28, No. 6, pp.567-576, 1987(in Japanese).

[8] C. Rodrigue(editor): "Parallel Computations", Academic press, 1982.

Table 1 Performance of the Livermore Loops without vectorization of first-order linear recurrences on the HITAC S-820

	14 Kernels (64bits)	24 kernels (DO SPAN=471) (64bits)
Loop1	989.7	1347.6
Loop2	857.1	31.5
Loop3	786.9	838.7
Loop4	199.8	258.5
Loop5	18.4*	17.5*
Loop6	19.8*	36.9
Loop7	930.9	1494.4
Loop8	240.0	813.8
Loop9	832.6	1093.2
Loop10	231.0	203.5
Loop11	25.4*	20.1*
Loop12	489.8	509.1
Loop13	12.7	16.8
Loop14	25.4	24.4
Loop15	/	108.1
Loop16	/	6.6
Loop17	/	13.4
Loop18	/	525.5
Loop19	/	19.3*
Loop20	/	19.4
Loop21	/	453.5
Loop22	/	184.3
Loop23	/	27.8*
Loop24	/	422.3
Average mean	404.3	353.6
Harmonic mean	49.4	35.9

(in MFLOPS)
*forced to scalar mode

Table 2 Performance of the Livermore Loops with onthe HITAC S-820 with application of these improved techniques
(Compiler FORT77/HAP V21-00)

	14 Kernels (64bits)	24 kernels (DO SPAN=471) (64bits)
Loop1	989.7	1347.6
Loop2	857.1	31.5
Loop3	786.9	838.7
Loop4	199.8	258.5
Loop5	112.4**	51.1**
Loop6	113.3**	36.9
Loop7	930.9	1494.4
Loop8	240.0	813.8
Loop9	832.6	1093.2
Loop10	231.0	203.5
Loop11	96.2***	55.7**
Loop12	489.8	509.1
Loop13	12.7	16.8
Loop14	25.4	24.4
Loop15	/	108.1
Loop16	/	6.6
Loop17	/	13.4
Loop18	/	525.5
Loop19	/	52.7**
Loop20	/	19.4
Loop21	/	453.5
Loop22	/	184.3
Loop23	/	145.1**
Loop24	/	422.3
Average mean	422.7	362.8
Harmonic mean	83.7	44.7

(in MFLOPS)
**techniques described in 4.3
***techniques described in 4.2 (2-times loop unrolling)

V-Pascal: an Automatic Vectorizing Compiler for Pascal with No Language Extensions

Takao Tsuda and Yoshitoshi Kunieda

Department of Information Science
Kyoto University, Kyoto, Japan

Abstract

Detailed anatomy of automatic vectorizing compiler V-Pascal (Version 1, now operational) is given. With no language extensions, V-Pascal efficiently vectorizes the whole of arbitrarily given multiply nested **for** loops using the mechanism of vector indirect addressing. Higher functions of V-Pascal, such as (a) vectorization of **while-do** and recursive calls, (b) vectorization of relational operations on relational database defined by record-type data structures, and (c) automatic parallel decomposition for multiprocessor environments, are considered for Version 2 and are now in the process of design and implementation.

I. Introduction

The present paper is the sequel of our IFIP86 paper [1] where we showed basic ideas on the mechanical vectorization of multiply nested DO loops as a whole. In what follows, we give a detailed description of the compiler we have designed and implemented; its main novel feature is such that the range of automatic vectorization is expanded by reducing the whole of multiply nested loops to equivalent single loops by vector indirect addressing. The effect of such ideas was verified by actually constructing a Fortran preprocessor as was discussed in [1]; the result was so encouraging that, as shown in this paper, we have developed a full-fledged compiler where our sophisticated techniques are exercised on the lower level of operations rather than the statement level.

The target language is the standard Pascal; there are no language extensions used for vectorization *per se*. Language extensions are nothing but the exposure of the compiler's weakness to be removed by human intervention. The language Pascal is more abundant and flexible in data types than Fortran, thereby allowing for various nonnumeric applications such as vector-mode high-speed manipulation of relational database defined by record-type data structures.

Our compiler called V-Pascal is written in Pascal; the size of V-Pascal (Version 1) now operational is about 60,000 lines of Pascal code. The Version-1 V-Pascal covers the vectorization by equivalent transformation of multiple **for** loops to single loops and the vectorization of **if** statements as well.

The Version-2 V-Pascal is now being developed with the intention of introducing higher functions: (a) the vectorization of **while-do** statements and recursive calls, (b) vector-mode execution of nonnumeric operations such as relational database operations and (c) automatic parallel decomposition for the forthcoming Japanese multi-vector-processors.

Vector indirect addressing, namely, vector indirect load/store (or vector load/store by list vector) can in principle be executed at the same speed as vector direct addressing, aside from the effects of memory bank and port conflicts. This is actually the case with Hitachi's S-810 and S-820 systems. The target machine of V-Pascal is S-820/80 installed at the Tokyo University Computation Center. This machine has 8 data paths, each with 8-byte width, between vector registers and the main memory. More exactly, there are (4 data parallel) × 2 load pipes; one of the two pipes also serves for a store pipe. "4 data parallel" means that requests for referencing 4 array elements are issued simultaneously. What is important is that each of the 8 data paths is equipped independently with an address-calculation circuit. Owing to this hardware arrangement, vector indirect load can be done at the same speed as vector (direct) load. As for vector indirect store, two kinds of machine instructions are provided: Vector Store Indexing (Double) VSTX(D) and Vector Indirect Store (Double) VIST(D). VSTX(D) serializes the store actions between the simultaneous stores of 4 data parallel. VIST(D), however, does not do such serialization, so that, by use of this instruction, vector indirect store acquires the same speed as vector direct store. When we reduce multiply nested loops to the equivalent single loops, the main-memory destinations of vector indirect stores are non-overlapping; one can use the VIST(D) instruction.

Compiler V-Pascal consists of 5 phases. By rewriting Phase 5, we can have different target machines; by recoding Phase 1, programming languages other than Pascal can be handled.

II. Organization of V-Pascal (Version 1)

The flow of processing with V-Pascal (Version 1) is shown in Fig. 1.

Intermediate code generation is done in Phase 1 where the Pascal source code is read, and converted to scalar-mode intermediate code after syntactic and semantic analyses. The intermediate code is an assembly of operation-level instructions including load/store that are represented as

CH2617-9/88/0000/0182$01.00 © 1988 IEEE

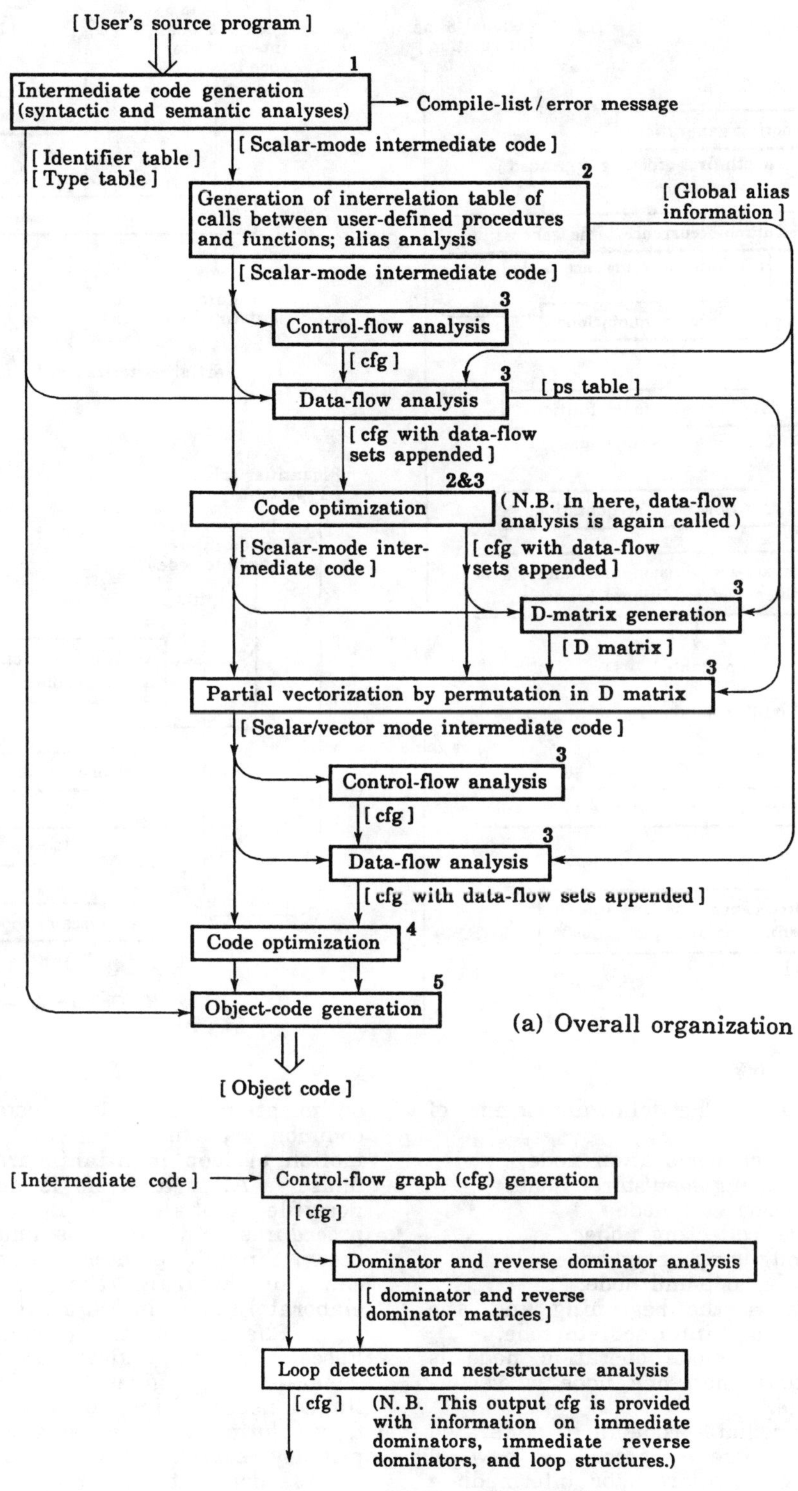

(a) Overall organization

(b) Control-flow analysis

Fig. 1 Processing with V-Pascal.

Those enclosed by square brackets are information passed on. cfg and ps stand for control-flow graph and primary set, respectively. The number at the right top corner of each box in (a) indicates the phase number. (b) – (f) give datails of relevant parts appearing in (a).

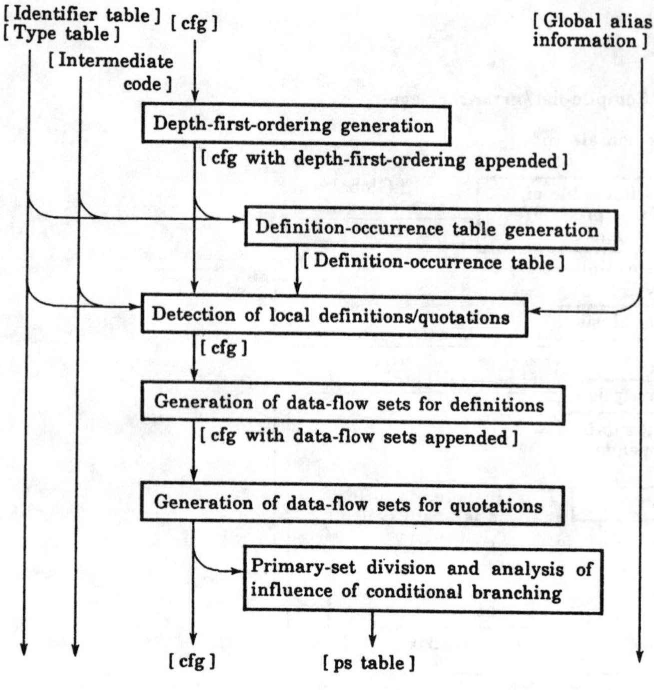

(c) Data-flow analysis

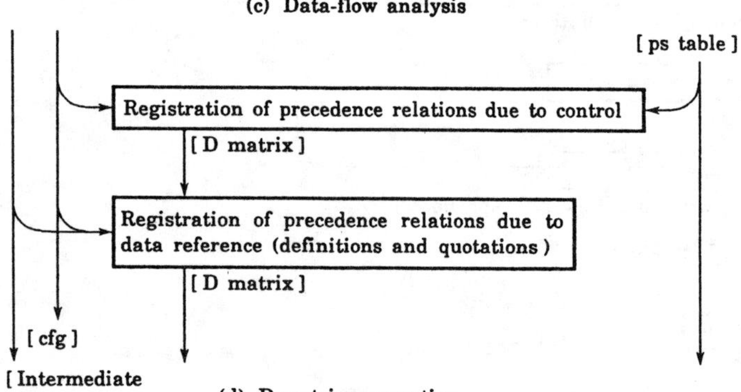

(d) D-matrix generation

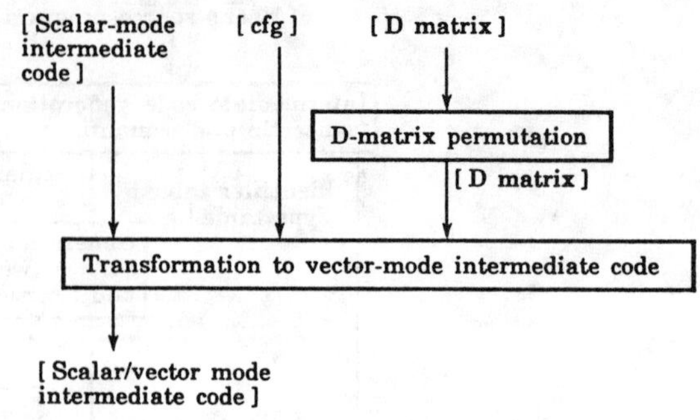

(e) Partial vectorization by permutation on D matrix

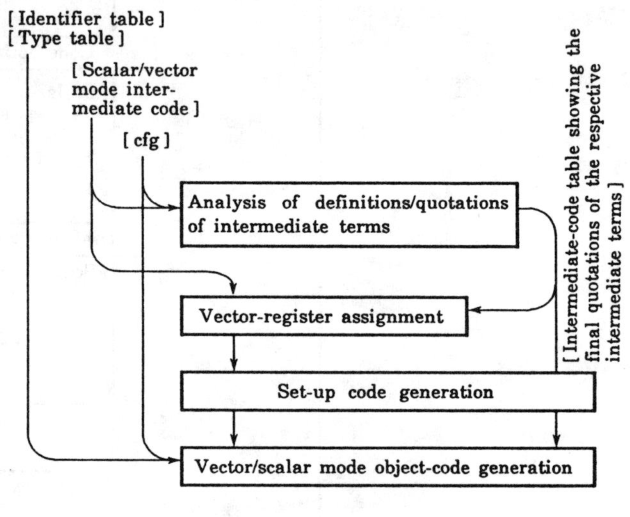

(f) Object-code generation

mutually linked nodes. The following kinds of nodes are provided:

procedure/function declaration node,
operation (including load/store) node,
procedure/function call node,
predicate node, collecting node,
go-to node, long-jump entry node,
loop-begin node, loop-end node,
nodes that mark the beginning and the end of vector-mode intermediate code.

When vectorized, a scalar-mode operation node is replaced by one or more than one node of vector-mode intermediate code.

Nodes of intermediate code are generated dynamically at compile time by procedure 'new' of Pascal. In the nodes of scalar/vector intermediate code, the temporary data resulting from the respective operations are numbered; these data are called intermediate terms or temporaries. An intermediate term thus numbered can only be generated in one node of intermediate code. Using a hash table, one can identify the node of intermediate code at which a given numbered intermediate term is generated.

Phase 2 performs intermediate-code level optimization. Namely, constant folding, removal of common subexpressions and dead code, and code motion of loop invariants are done as part of this phase. Alias analysis is also carried out for the possible global aliasing between user-defined procedures and functions and also for aliases that occur through pointer-type variables. Unlike the case of Fortran, the analysis of aliases is elaborately done in V-Pascal.

Phase 3 is the central part of compiler V-Pascal. Control flow graphs (cfg for short) are generated; cfg gives an abstraction of mutually linked nodes of intermediate code by which control-flow information is more aptly treated. Division to primary sets follows the dominator matrix and reverse dominator matrix analysis. A primary set (denoted by ps for short) is defined to be a set of those intermediate-code nodes that are collectively affected in the same common way by control-flow branching. Loop detection and nest-structure analysis is done with the use of cfg. The data-flow analysis is then performed using cfg and the ps table together with identifier and type tables. Processing with the D matrix proceeds as follows.

The D matrix (D for dependence) is a matrix

where precedence relations between a pair of intermediate-code nodes are registered. Such a precedence relationship in scalar-mode execution must be preserved even in vector-mode execution. A nonzero element of the D matrix, D(i,j) ≠ 0, indicates that there is the restriction that the execution of the ith node precede that of the jth node. Precedence relations originate from data dependence and control dependence. If D(i,j) = 0, then there is no dependence between the ith and the jth nodes, these two nodes being executed in an arbitrary order. If nonzeros reside only in the upper triangle with the diagonal inclusive, then every node partaking in defining the D matrix can be vectorized. When the presence of a directed closed path (i.e., strongly connected component) is detected by following nodes one after another, those nodes assisting in the formation of the closed path cannot be vectorize by any permutation whatever, thus resulting in the appearance of some nonzeros in the lower triangle of the D matrix. We therefore *degenerate* all those nodes of the closed path to a single scalar-mode node of intermediate code. In this way we have nonzero elements of the D matrix only in its upper triangle plus the diagonal. Of the scalar nodes of the D matrix thus processed, those resulting from the above degeneration procedure can only be executed in scalar mode, while remaining other nodes that have not been degenerated are the objects of vectorization.

When one is interested in vectorizing a **for** loop, the D matrix associated with the loop suffices. We, however, consider precedence relations due to data and control dependences across and beyond the loop boundaries; what we call the *global* D matrix must therefore be maintained for the entire objective program. The global D matrix is useful for the automatic parallel decomposition of given user programs.

Phase 3 also reduces multiply nested **for** loops to equivalent single loops in the way shown in [1], and this will be again a subject of discussion in the section that follows. If the objective loop is a single loop, then redefining the control variable as an integer array does not take place. The loop is vectorized by the conventional direct method.

In Phase 4, redundant intermediate code that has resulted from the Phase 3 transformation is removed and those loops that should be executed in scalar mode are further optimized.

Phase 5 performs object code generation. Conferring with the information gathered in the previous phases, the compiler yields the object code of the target machine.

The above is an overview of the flow of processing in compiler V-Pascal (Version 1).

III. Special features of V-Pascal (Version 1)

(a) *Reduction of multiple loops to equivalent single loops*

As was stated in our IFIP86 paper [1], our technique vectorizes a multiply nested **for** loop as a whole by redefining the control variables of all the constituent loops to be each a one-dimensional array (called a "basic" vector), which then can be accessed by a single variable called the "basic" control variable. In this way any array element appearing in the objective multiple loop can be accessed by vector indirect addressing. We thus compute a multiply nested **for** loop as a single loop in vector mode with a sufficiently long vector-length.

Now let us return to the D matrix discussed in the preceding section. Suppose that in the D matrix associated with a multiply nested **for** loop the strongly connected components of nodes have been degenerated. We thus have a D matrix whose upper triangle plus diagonal hold nonzeros and whose lower triangle does not. The nodes of the D matrix are scanned in order and checked on the vectorizability with the compiler referring to the loop information of cfg. Once found vectorizable, each node of scalar-mode intermediate code is replaced by one or more than one node of vector-mode intermediate code. As already mentioned, those scalar nodes generated by procedure of degeneration cannot be vectorized.

Those scalar mode nodes that have not originated from degeneracy and yet cannot be vectorized are examined to see what iterative loop of the objective multiply nested loop gives the dependence that hinders vectorization. Such information is recorded in the D matrix and is used in the *loop selection* of vector-mode execution, namely, when the compiler determines up to which loop of a multiple loop can be vectorized from inside out.

Consider the individual scalar mode nodes of intermediate code that initially define the relevant D matrix, including those nodes controlling the flow of computation. Each of the scalar mode nodes generally assumes the following form with the loop information appended:

$$\left.\begin{array}{l} \textbf{for } i_1 := 1 \textbf{ to } f_1 \textbf{ do} \\ \quad \textbf{for } i_2 := 1 \textbf{ to } f_2(i_1) \textbf{ do} \\ \qquad \cdots \qquad \cdots \\ \qquad\quad \textbf{for } i_n := 1 \textbf{ to } f_n(i_1, \cdots, i_{n-1}) \textbf{ do} \\ \qquad\qquad a[h_1(i_1, \cdots, i_n), \cdots] := \cdots \end{array}\right\} \quad (1)$$

The first n lines are the loop information held by cfg. These lines may be missing for some nodes. Call lines (1) an *elementary multiple loop*. The permutation of nodes based on the D matrix is the permutation of elementary multiple loops. This is the novel feature of V-Pascal, because we do not know to date of a commercially available compiler that moves statements either from outside in or from inside out across the boundaries of the inner loops of the source text. V-Pascal can do it.

For $n \geqq 2$ (see n of (1)), Version 1 of V-Pascal either reduces a given multiply nested **for** loop to a single loop by vector indirect addressing to execute it at a sufficiently long vector length or, when the gain is judged to be marginal, vectorizes only the innermost loop by usual direct addressing. For $n = 1$, V-Pascal vectorizes the objective loop by direct addressing.

Those vector machines capable of vector indirect addressing with the same speed as vector direct addressing yield a substantial gain by the above transformation.

In the previous feasibility study [1], there was the restriction that the upper and lower bounds of the outermost-loop control variable of the objective multiply nested DO loop be constants. This was to facilitate the compile-time analysis of dependences. To get around this restriction our V-Pascal uses the following two methods. One is to extract relevant pieces of information from the interprocedural data-flow analysis which was originally meant for acquiring global aliasing information. What counts in the present context is the information only on those variables which may appear as bounds of the outermost-loop control variables. These loop bounds designated by a variable may define a multiple loop within a *called* procedure. Usually the loop-bound variables of this kind are formals of the called procedure to be replaced by actuals that are passed by the *calling* procedure. In much the same way as, or rather more easily than, recognizing aliases, therefore, loop-bound variables are tracked out; the bindings to those constants defined by the presiding main program are thus done at compile time. The other of the two methods handles the case where the objective multiple loop is enclosed in a comparatively small procedure. In-line expansion then takes place like macros, so that the bindings of loop-bound variables, if they are variables at all, can be done directly. In this way the upper and lower bounds of the outermost loop of a multiple loop are reduced to constants.

The above V-Pascal policy takes advantage of an idiosyncrasy of language Pascal. In the case of Fortran the solution is found, but becomes more involved, because the program units that constitute a whole Fortran program are separately compiled.

Even at the final stage of D-matrix processing, there is still an arbitrariness for permuting nodes. V-Pascal therefore shortens the intervals of definitions and associated quotations of the same intermediate term so that vector registers can better be utilized. Referring to some rules, V-Pascal also performs further optimization in such a way that vector load instructions are not concentrated at the beginning of a vectorizable loop.

Buried definitions [1] are degenerated to scalar-mode nodes in Version 1 of V-Pascal.

(b) *Analysis of data dependences*

As we stated in the concluding remarks of IFIP86 paper [1], a pair of references to an array element is examined whether there is a collision of references to that array element. If, first, by applying symbolic manipulation techniques to the subscripts of the objective array variable the absence of collisions is positively demonstrated, then there is no data dependence. Should it turn out to be the reverse case, there may be a data dependence. Compiler V-Pascal then takes the second step where over the narrowed-down domain of search the sort-merge technique detects the presence or absence of a collision of references infallibly. The results are registered in the D matrix.

(c) *Analysis of control dependences*

In the source text, **if-then-else**, for example, causes the flow of computation to branch into two ways depending on the decision of the conditional clause. In the intermediate code level, similar branching occurs. As already mentioned, compiler V-Pascal divide the intermediate code nodes into primary sets. In vector-mode execution, operations in the **if** part must precede those in the **else** and **then** parts. The **if-then-else** statement is cut apart in pieces to yield the intermediate-code counterparts, which are then the objects of mechanical vectorization with the D matrix. Generally, global permutation of nodes over and beyond the primary sets can take place. Compiler V-Pascal must therefore recognize and preserve all the precedence relations between nodes that arise from control dependences in vector-mode execution. For this purpose, cfg is used, and the information on control dependences is registered in the D matrix. A special technique has been devised so that the abstraction of control dependences can be done simultaneously with the data-flow analysis. This will be discussed as a separate paper in more detail.

(d) *Vectorization of* **if** *statements*

After its relevant conditional expression has been computed with the result assigned to an intermediate term, a predicate node quotes or uses the intermediate term. In the same way as with definitions and quotations of ordinary intermediate terms, a data dependence is considered to exist between the intermediate code node that defines the intermediate term and the predicate node that subsequently uses the term. This data dependence is registered in the D matrix.

Predicate nodes are permuted indiscriminately with other kinds of nodes and can be degenerated when necessary. Scalar-mode nodes of intermediate code, other than those which have resulted from the degenerating procedure, are vectorized in principle, and therefore replaced by vector-mode nodes. Those nodes that carry control-flow information, such as loop-begin and loop-end nodes, predicate nodes and collecting nodes, are once removed.

A scalar process node of intermediate code, when occupying a new position after permutation, is replaced by a vector-mode code if vectorizable, or remains linked as it is if not vectorizable. If the process node belongs to a primary set distinct from the one immediately preceding in the link, then the node is enclosed by relevant loop-begin and loop-end nodes in such a way that the node can identify the correct primary set it belongs to. A process node of intermediate code may be under the influence of some predicate node. This process node on being vectorized must then use the mask vector generated by the same intermediate term of the conditional expression that has been quoted by the predicate node. The compiler can thus generate vector-mode object code with mask operations corresponding to the intermediate code using a mask vector.

In this way the presence of **if-then-else** and nested **if-then-else** statements in a **for** loop does not hinder vectorization in the absence of harmful dependences.

If statements combined with **go to** statement (not directed backward in the text) in some cases yield control flow graphs with 'mesh' structures. Such **if** statements that give program structures other than standard **if-then-else** structures are also analyzed for possible vectorization.

IV. Performance evaluation of V-Pascal (Version 1)

We now show the results obtained by our compiler V-Pascal on Hitachi's vector computer S-820/80. The execution times for 64-node FFT butterfly operations are shown in Table 1. The program given in Fig. 5.14 (p. 311) of [4] has been used without any alteration except that, since Pascal cannot declare a complex variable, the real and imaginary parts are separated so that the whole computation reduces to real-number arithmetic. V-Pascal transforms the inner double loop of the program to an equivalent single loop which can be executed in vector mode.

Table 2 shows the results of similar computation by Fortran (OPT(3)) on the same machine. The same program given in Fig. 5.14 (p. 311) of [4] has been used without any alteration. Interestingly, Pascal (see V(1) of Table 1) is about 4 times faster than Fortran (see V(2) of Table 2), even though the scalar execution in Pascal code is inferior to that of Fortran. The usefulness of our approach is thus clearly verified.

Table 1
64-node FFT computation by V-Pascal. 16 bytes per node. S (micro seconds) is the scalar execution time; V (micro seconds) is the time by vector-mode execution.

V(1)	S(1)	S(1)/V(1)
23.48	891.4	38.0

Table 2
64-node FFT computation by Fortran. 16 bytes per node (complex). S and V are the same as Table 1.

V(2)	S(2)	S(2)/V(2)
81.02	163.2	2.01

Similarly the timing measurement on S-820/80 was done concerning the following Program 1 (Pascal) compiled by V-Pascal and its direct Fortran counterpart. Note that Fortran's two-dimensional array is stored column-major so that the two subscripts of each array element of A are interchanged. The results are shown in Table 3.

Program 1 (Pascal)

```
FOR I := 1 TO NMAX DO BEGIN
  FOR J := I TO NMAX DO BEGIN
    A(.I,J.) := 1;
  END;
  FOR J := 1 TO I-1 DO BEGIN
    A(.I,J.) := 0;
  END;
  A(.I,I.) := 2;
  A(.I,I+1.) := 3;
  FOR J := 1 TO I DO BEGIN
    A(.I,J.) := A(.J,I.);
  END;
END;
```

Program 1 (Fortran)

```
      DO 300 I=1,NMAX
        DO 100 J=1,I-1
          A(J,I) = 0
100     CONTINUE
        DO 200 J=I,NMAX
          A(J,I) = 1
200     CONTINUE
        A(I,I) = 2
        A(I+1,I) = 3
        DO 110 J=1,I
          A(J,I) = A(I,J)
110     CONTINUE
300   CONTINUE
```

Again V-Pascal results in the gain of 3 or 4 times over vectorized Fortran.

Program 2 below is an example that contains an if statement.

Program 2

```
FOR I := 1 TO NMAX DO BEGIN
  FOR J := I TO NMAX DO BEGIN
    IF A(.I,J.)>0 THEN
      A(.I,J.) := -1;
  END;
  FOR J := 1 TO I-1 DO BEGIN
    A(.I,J.) := 0;
  END;
  A(.I,I.) := 2;
  A(.I,I+1.) := 3;
  FOR J := 1 TO I DO BEGIN
    A(.I,J.) := A(.J,I.);
  END;
END;
```

Initialization was separately done by

```
FOR I := 0 TO NMAX+1 DO BEGIN
  FOR J := 0 TO (NMAX+1) DIV 2 DO
    A(.I,2*J.) := 0;
  FOR J := 0 TO (NMAX+1) DIV 2 DO
    A(.I,2*J+1.) := 1;
END;
```

Table 4 gives the timing results. We do not show the obvious Fortran counterpart, where again the pair of subscripts of array variable A were interchanged to equalize the array-accessing condition between the two languages.

V. Higher functions of V-Pascal (Version 2, now being developed)

Compiler V-Pascal (Version 1) is presently operational. The language Pascal is as ubiquitous as Fortran, and yet has the strengths of its own in numeric as well as nonnumeric computations. To exploit the favorable language features, some higher functions are now being added to Version 1.

(a) *Mechanical vectorization of* **while-do** *loops*

If what is defined in the **do** part is quoted in the conditional expression of the **while** part, then there is difficulty vectorizing the whole of such a **while-do** loop. In this context the following are of interest.

1. Mechanical vectorization of value-assignments and operations over a partial set of array elements in the **do** part

There are two cases. The first case is such that the vector length can be known at run time separately from the **do** part. Vectorization is similar in this case to that of **for** loops. The second case is one in which the vector length cannot be determined unless **while-do** loops are actually executed. A **while-do** loop in this latter case reduces to scalar statements that count the number of iterations, followed by a separate group of those statements which can be executed in vector mode with the vector length just known. In both cases there is difficulty in the minute analysis of data dependence for a pair of references to the

Table 3
Execution times of Program 1. For symbols S and V, see the legend of Table 1.

NMAX	Pascal V(3)	Pascal S(3)	Pascal S(3)/V(3)	Fortran V(4)	Fortran S(4)	Fortran S(4)/V(4)	Gain V(4)/V(3)
20	10.46	270.4	25.9	38.17	70.39	1.84	3.7
50	31.44	1579.	50.2	100.9	375.9	3.73	3.2

Table 4
Execution times of Program 2. For symbols S and V, see the legend of Table 1.

NMAX	Pascal V(5)	Pascal S(5)	Pascal S(5)/V(5)	Fortran V(6)	Fortran S(6)	Fortran S(6)/V(6)	Gain V(6)/V(5)
20	10.69	291.5	27.3	44.01	80.08	1.82	4.1
50	33.58	1666.	49.6	117.1	441.7	3.77	3.5

same array variable. This is because of the indefinite nature of the **while-do** loops.

2. Mechanical vectorization of processing over data linked by pointers

By vector indirect addressing the data are loaded to vector registered, but if the number of data is not known, then the loading is done by a **while-do** loop. Binary-tree search and database manipulation can therefore be amenable to automatic vectorization.

(b) *Mechanical vectorization of operations on non-numeric data*

Vector-mode manipulation of a set of character strings is now becoming possible. Consider a character string which should be compared against a given set of character strings. Because this set of character strings can be represented by a two-dimensional array of integers, the comparison can be efficiently done in vector mode either rowwise or columnwise, whichever preferable. Direct assignment of record-type data, each holding several fields, to record-type variables is done in vector mode.

One may define a relational database by help of record-type data structures of Pascal. Pascal's records can have variant fields. Once the compiler is designed to have workspace vast enough for numerous record-type data, then a practically useful database can be constructed. Otherwise time-consuming operations, such as join and others, can be executed in vector mode. Record-type data are generated by procedure 'new'.

(c) *Mechanical vectorization of recursive calls*

Any recursion can be reduced to iterations by simulating stack operations in the source level [2]. Mechanical transformation of recursive calls to iterations is done in the intermediate-code level by V-Pascal.

(d) *Automatic parallel decomposition*

The next-generation Japanese supercomputers will be vector multiprocessors made up of a few (8 to 16 most probably) vector processors. Each constituent processor is as capable as the uniprocessor currently used with units for vector and scalar processings. In light of this situation it is worthwhile to prepare algorithms for compiler V-Pascal to automatically decompose a sequential Pascal program and assign a share to each processor.

A comment is given to the Alliant FX system before proceeding further. Alliant's *outer-scalar inner-vector* scheme computes a multiply nested loops as follows. Each processor executes the innermost loop in vector mode, while the outer loops are executed in scalar mode with different values of control variables for different processors. In this scheme, however, if there is a loop-carry data dependence involving a control variable of outer loops, then the parallel execution is not feasible. Alliant's *vector-concurrent* scheme interleaves the value sequence of a control variable associated with a vector instruction, and explicitly performs parallel execution with multiple processors. This low-level parallelism is, however, already covered in the present-day supercomputers by the multiplicity of pipelines provided for one and the same type of operation. For example, Hitachi's S-820 has pipelines for operations each with four data in parallel.

We want to propose, and describe briefly, an entirely new vein of approach for automatic parallel decomposition. The idea has been conceived as a natural consequence of V-Pascal's D-matrix processing. ① Dissection of the vector/scalar instruction sequence and ② dissection of the vector length will be given below. A full account of the present method of decomposition will appear elsewhere [3].

① Dissection of the vector/scalar instruction sequence

Consider the global D matrix, optimized for a single processor, which has been just finalized as an input to the part of object-code generation. More than one kind of dependences are registered as nonzero elements in the matrix with * (an asterisk) showing such a nonzero collectively. After the procedure of degeneration previously mentioned has been called to reduce the D matrix, nonzeros can reside only in its upper triangle including its diagonal. At this point, further permutation of the nodes is allowed with the restriction that any nonzero never move to the lower triangle of the matrix. By thus rearranging columns and the corresponding rows as well, have all the * as close as possible to the diagonal, so the result will be as shown in Fig. 2 (a). Carry out dissection of the matrix into smaller upper triangular submatrices, each differing in size, as indicated in (b) of Fig. 2. If these submatrices are mutually non-intersecting,

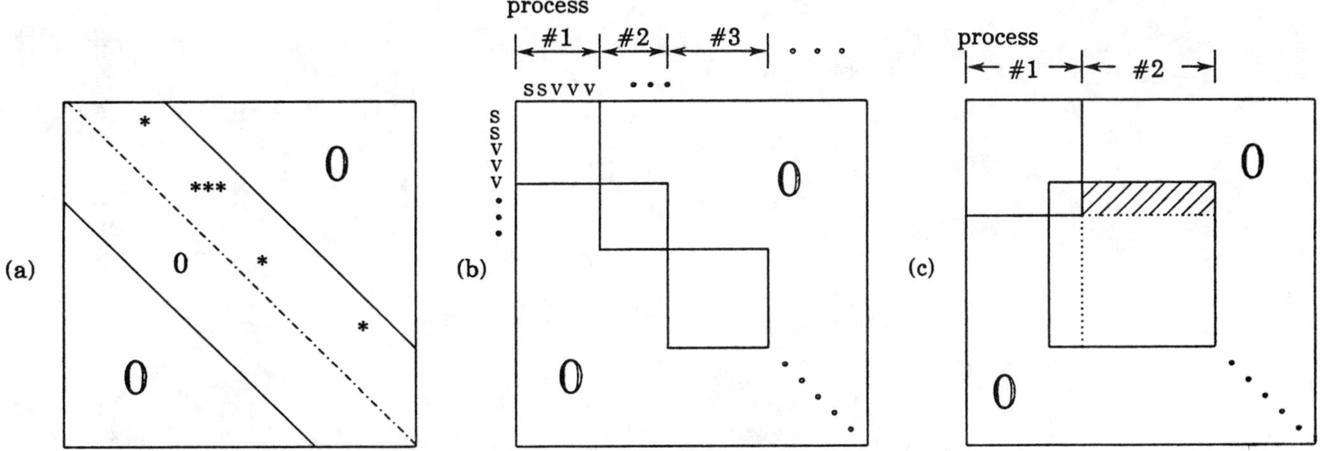

Fig. 2 Dissection of D matrix in submatrices. (a) Nonzeros gatherd toward the diagonal by node permutation; (b) Disjoint submatrices; (c) Overlapping submatrices. S and V of (b) represent a scalar-mode node and a vector-mode node, respectively.

then the subsequence of scalar/vector instructions corresponding to a submatrix can be executed independently of other subsequences thus cut apart. Generally the adjacent submatrices are not non-intersecting, so that the case may be as shown in (c) of the same figure. In this case then the execution of process #1 and #2 must be synchronized at the instructions associated with * appearing in the shaded portion of (c). It may however be added that not all the * in the shaded portion need be considered, because synchronization at one point can preserve precedence relations at other points of the shaded portion. There is the algorithm that handles this situation.

The sizes of the submatrices may differ, one from the other; it can be approximately equilibrated among processes to be assigned to processors if the average computational cost of scalar/vector instruction is known. In this way each process with the subsequence of instructions can be allotted to each processor, from left to right of the D matrix, process #*n* being assigned to processor #*n* mod (the number of processors).

② Dissection of the vector length

By reducing to the equivalent single loop, the vector length of a vector instruction can be extremely long. This long vector length can be cut apart in pieces, each piece being assigned to a processor. Dissections ① and ② can be combined.

(e) *Demonstration of portability*

As stated in the Introduction of this paper, we can have different target machines by rewriting Phase 5 of compiler V-Pascal. To demonstrate the portability of V-Pascal, therefore, Phase 5 is now actually being rewritten in such a way that V-Pascal will yield vectorized object code for NEC's SX-2A.

VI. Concluding remarks

V-Pascal (Version 1) is a full-fledged Pascal compiler whose details have been shown in this paper. By constructing this compiler the primary objective of our work has been attained. Namely, as expressly stated in our previous IFIP86 paper [1], a breakthrough in the as yet difficult automatic vectorization of complex multiple loops has been found by an extensive, as well as intensive, use of vector indirect addressing. Hardware designers of vector supercomputers seem to consider this important mechanism of vector indirect addressing to be of minor importance. In principle the vector indirect addressing can be designed to be as fast as the vector direct addressing.

In the latter half of this paper, higher functions considered for Version 2 of V-Pascal were briefly described.

Acknowledgments

Compiler construction is a difficult and exacting job. If it were not for the efforts and labor by the following people, which are therefore gratefully acknowledged here, this work would never have been accomplished: Kenji Yabuuchi, Satoru Hayama, Tatsuya Ohnishi, Hideo Nataka, Piyaporn Atipas, and Kenji Sato. Thanks are also due to Dr. Eiji Okubo for his constructive comment. Demonstration of the V-Pascal portability is now being done by Yasuo Okabe, Kenji Suehiro and Takashi Saito.

References

[1] T. Tsuda and Y. Kunieda, Mechanical Vectorization of Multiply Nested DO Loops by Vector Indirect Addressing, *Information Processing 86* (ed. H.-J. Kugler), Elsevier Science Publishers, North Holland, 1986, 785 – 790.

[2] J. L. Wagener, *Fortran 77 Principles of Programming*, John Wiley & Sons, Inc., 1980, Chap. 11.

[3] T. Tsuda, Asynchronous Parallel Execution of a Multiply Nested DO Loop by Vector Indirect Addressing, to be presented in IFIP Working Conference on 'Aspects of Computation on Asynchronous Parallel Processors,' Stanford, California, August 1988.

[4] R. W. Hockney and C. R. Jesshope, *Parallel Computers*, Adam Hilger Ltd., Bristol, 1981.

Operating Systems for Supercomputing

Chair: Robert Flynn
Polytechnic Institute

Using Linda for Supercomputing On a Local Area Network

Robert A. Whiteside
Scientific Computing Division, Sandia National Laboratories, Livermore, California, 94551.
whiteside@sandia-2.arpa
Jerrold S. Leichter
Department of Computer Science, Yale University P.O. Box 2158 Yale Station New Haven, CT 06510.
leichter-jerry@cs.yale.edu

Abstract

A distributed parallel processing system based on the LINDA programming constructs has been implemented on a local area network of computers. This system allows a single application program to utilize many machines on the network simultaneously. Several applications have been implemented on the network at Sandia National Laboratories and have achieved performances considerably faster than that of a Cray-1S. Several collections of machines have been used including up to eleven DEC VAXes, three Sun/3 workstations, and a PC.

1 Introduction.

Many organizations have extensive networks of time-shared computers. Although these machines may be quite heavily loaded during the day with various interactive computations, it is not uncommon for them to sit idle overnight. The reason for this idle time is that any one of these machines is too slow to be useful for many interesting large scientific and engineering applications. These applications are allocated to supercomputers on the network instead. Collectively, however, the smaller machines can represent a considerable computational resource. Sandia National Laboratories (SNL), for instance, has an NSU equivalent of twenty-five Cray-1S's in such machines. (NSU is a metric used by the U. S. Department of Energy to measure computer performance.) Of course, many of these machines are dedicated to specific tasks and are not attached to the network. Nonetheless, the collective computational power of the machines on the SNL network is substantial. In this paper, we demonstrate that distributed parallel processing can permit some applications to achieve supercomputer performance from such a local area network.

The parallel applications described here utilize a VAX VMS Ethernet implementation of the Linda [1,2,3] programming constructs for communication and synchronization. The current implementation is restricted to a single physical Ethernet. That is, machines on the other side of a gateway cannot be fully integrated into the parallel system. However, some simple extensions permit a subset of the Linda operations to take place over DECnet (giving access to distant VAX/VMS systems) and TCP/IP (giving access to SUN workstations and some PC's).

In the following section we describe Linda and its VMS Ethernet implementation. Section 3 describes and gives performance results for three applications that have been implemented on our network: a charged particle transport program, a parameter sensitivity analysis, and a finite element equation solver. Finally, section 4 provides some concluding remarks.

2 The Linda language

The Linda language was first defined by Gelernter in [1]. As it has evolved, however [2,3], Linda is not a complete language. Rather, it is a set of objects and operations on those objects that are intended to be *injected* into an existing language, thus producing a new language intended for distributed programming.

In the following sections we present a simple, language-independent description of Linda.

2.1 Fundamental objects

Linda is based on two fundamental objects: *tuples* and *tuple spaces.*

2.1.1 Tuples

Tuples are collections of *fields.* Fields have fixed types associated with them; the types are drawn from the underlying language. A field can be a *formal* or an *actual.* A formal field is a place-holder — it has a type, but no value. An actual field carries a value drawn from the set of possible values allowed for that type by the underlying language.

For example, suppose that the underlying language has types **int** (integer) and **float** (floating-point number). Then

$$\langle 1_{\mathbf{int}}, 1.5_{\mathbf{float}}, 2_{\mathbf{int}} \rangle$$

is a tuple with three fields: Two integers, 1 and 2, and a floating point value, 1.5. It is essential to distinguish it from the tuple:

$$\langle 1_{\mathbf{int}}, 1.5_{\mathbf{float}}, 2_{\mathbf{float}} \rangle$$

which differs in the type of its third field.

The previous two tuples contain only actual fields. The tuple

$$\left\langle 1_{\mathbf{int}}, \square_{\mathbf{float}} \right\rangle$$

contains an integer actual, and a float formal.

The definition of the Linda language places no *a priori* restrictions on what types are allowed. *Any* types from the underlying language are allowed, including records, arrays, and pointers. Similarly, tuples may have any number of fields.

2.1.2 Tuple space

Tuples live in tuple space which is simply a collection of tuples. It may contain any number of copies of the same tuple; it is a *bag*, not a set.

Tuple space is the fundamental medium of communication in Linda. Linda processes communicate through tuple space. All Linda communication is a three-party operation — Sender interacts with tuple space, tuple space interacts with Receiver — rather than a two-party operation as in traditional models.

Tuple space is a *global*, *shared* object — all Linda processes that are part of the same Linda program have access to the same (logical) tuple space. In a strong sense, it is access to this shared object that *defines* what processes constitute a single Linda program.

2.2 The operators

The **out** operator inserts a tuple into tuple space; for example, if f is a variable of type **float** with the value 1.5, and i is an **int** with the value 2, then

$$\mathbf{out}(1,f,i)$$

would insert into tuple space the tuple we saw earlier,

$$\langle 1_{\mathbf{int}}, 1.5_{\mathbf{float}}, 2_{\mathbf{int}}. \rangle$$

The **in** operator extracts tuples from tuple space. It finds tuples that *match* its arguments, in a sense we will describe shortly. However, equal tuples match. The tuple of the previous paragraph could be extracted by the operation:

$$\mathbf{in}(1,1.5,2)$$

Formal fields are created by adding a question mark prefix. What should follow a question mark is language-dependent; the intent is that it should be "anything that can be on the left hand side of an assignment statement."

When a formal is used in an **in**, any actual in the tuple will match. The operation

$$\mathbf{in}(1,?f,2)$$

might extract the same tuple as in the previous example without a formal. In addition to removing the tuple, it would assign 1.5 to f. Note that the type of f is significant — for this match to be possible, f must have type **float**. If f has any other type, even double precision floating point, the match will not succeed.

After an **in** operation, the tuple matched is removed from tuple space. The **rd** operator is similar to **in**, but leaves the matched tuple in tuple space unchanged. It is used for its side effects — bindings and synchronization.

The "?" prefix may be used with **out** as well. The tuple

$$\langle 1_{\mathbf{int}}, \square_{\mathbf{float}} \rangle$$

could be produced by **out**$(1,?f)$. An "**out**" of this form is unusual, and its utility is described in the next section on "tuple matching".

2.3 Tuple matching

The **in** and **rd** operators are defined in terms of *matching*. Call the tuple defined by the fields in an **in** or **rd** a *template*. A template $\mathcal{M}$ matchs a tuple $\mathcal{T}$ in tuple space if:

- $\mathcal{M}$ and $\mathcal{T}$ have the same number of fields;
- Corresponding fields have the same types;
- Each pair of corresponding fields $F_{\mathcal{M}}$ and $F_{\mathcal{T}}$ match as follows:
  - If both $F_{\mathcal{M}}$ and $F_{\mathcal{T}}$ are actuals, they match if and only if their respective values are equal, where equality is defined by the base language for objects of this type;
  - If $F_{\mathcal{M}}$ is a formal and $F_{\mathcal{T}}$ is an actual, they match; the value of $F_{\mathcal{T}}$ may eventually be assigned to some variable. No assignment takes place unless *all* the fields match, however.
  - If $F_{\mathcal{M}}$ is an actual and $F_{\mathcal{T}}$ is a formal, they match unconditionally. The value of $F_{\mathcal{M}}$ is discarded.
  - If both $F_{\mathcal{M}}$ and $F_{\mathcal{T}}$ are formals, they never match.

If no matching tuple can be found in tuple space, **in** and **rd** block, and the process waits for a tuple to appear. If there is more than one matching tuple, **in** and **rd** choose one non-deterministically.

2.4 Linda implementations

The first implementation of Linda, due to Nicholas Carriero, ran on an experimental machine developed at Bell Labs, the S/Net. Carriero has also produced implementations for the Encore and Sequent shared memory multiprocessors [4]. Robert Bjornson at Yale produced an implementation for the Intel iPSC, and another hypercube implementation is reported in [5]. All of these implementations inject Linda into the C programming language. Carriero [6] reports progress on a "Linda in FORTRAN" implementation. Another current project [7] is developing hardware that directly supports the Linda operations.

The particular incarnation of Linda used in the experiments reported in this paper is known as VAX LINDA-C. As the name indicates, it is an embedding of Linda into VAX C. VAX LINDA-C extends the C type system to make it more appropriate for use with the (type-driven) Linda tuple-matching operations. In addition, the extensions allow the programmer to provide the LINDA-C compiler with information it needs to determine the sizes of objects to be placed in tuples. It is possible, for example, to **out** an array whose size is determined at run-time. A full description of the language appears in [8].

VAX LINDA-C was designed to support parallel Linda programs at two levels of coupling simultaneously: multiple processes running on a single "node", and multiple nodes communicating across an Ethernet. A "node" may contain more than one processor, but only a single shared memory. A great deal of flexibility is required to make effective use of hardware ranging from shared memory multiprocessors to independent computers communicating over an Ethernet. We believe Linda can provide that flexibility, although the set of machines available to us does not include any multi-processor VAXes. Nonetheless, the ability to run multiple processes on a single node is useful. For example, the implementation of TACO3D discussed in Section 3.3 was developed for a hypercube and assumes that the number of worker nodes is a power of two. We were able to run the program on three VAXes, for instance, by starting multiple processes on one of them. This is also useful for programs structured as a master with multiple workers. While the workers in such a program are busy, the master is often idle. Letting the master share its node with a worker avoids wasting a processor.

The current implementation of LINDA-C is limited to a single physical Ethernet. Communication among the nodes uses a private Ethernet protocol, so no gateways can intervene. LINDA-C was designed that way since the designer (Leichter) felt that the performance using a direct Ethernet connection would be about as slow as anyone would find useful. However, it has become clear from our experiments that this assessment was wrong: some applications can utilize a large number of machines, even with very high communications costs. The network we used for these experiments has several physical Ethernets interconnected *via* gateways. We have therefore used DECnet task-to-task communication to extend a subset of Linda operations to more remote VMS machines and TCP/IP tools to access UNIX machines. A high-priority item for future work is to merge these extensions, modified to support all the Linda operations, back into the base system.

The tuple space in LINDA-C is distributed — each of the VAXes participating may hold some subset of the tuples. This is desirable for performance reasons, since each machine may be able to satisfy an **in** or **rd** from its local set of tuples without accessing the network. However, this distribution of tuples also means that a loss of any machine in the network can cause part of the tuple space to be lost, and perhaps to cause the entire computation to fail. Thus, this possible performance/robustness tradeoff is a topic for further investigations.

2.5 Specialized communication using Linda

The Linda operators and tuple space provide a very general and powerful communication facility. Most programs need only a fraction of this potential power, though exactly *which* fraction varies from program to program. The codes we discuss were all developed using much simpler communications regimes. One, TACO3D (Section 3.3) was originally developed for an Intel iPSC Hypercube [9]. Simulating the iPSC's message-passing functions takes a couple of lines of Linda code, and each hypercube node is implemented by a separate Linda process. Messages are implemented as tuples whose fields correspond to the parameters of the iPSC **send** routine: the name of the recipient (the node number within the cube), the message type (an integer), the number of bytes in the message, and the message itself. One difficulty arose from the need to provide explicitly for the sequencing of messages, since tuple space communication is not guaranteed to be order-preserving.

Note that even when simulating message passing, the power of the Linda communication model is helpful. We may *think* of messages as being sent from one particular process on a particular node to another, but in fact, how the processes are assigned to nodes is completely invisible to the program.

2.6 An example

To provide a flavor of what VAX LINDA-C programs look like, we include a brief example. Figure 1 is a matrix multiplication worker for square matrices. It waits for the arrival of tuples of the form:

$$\langle \Lambda_{REQUEST}, rownum_{\mathbf{int}}, dimension_{\mathbf{int}} \rangle$$

The first field in the tuple contains "$\Lambda_{REQUEST}$". This denotes a null value of type *REQUEST* and serves to identify the tuple as input to the matrix multiplier. The second and third fields define a row number r within a square product matrix with side *dimension*. The worker proceeds to **in** row r of the left multiplier matrix and **rd** the columns of the right multiplicand. The left multiplier is available in tuple space by rows, and the multiplicand is available by columns. The rows and columns do not need markers since they contain vectors of distinct types, *ROW* and *COLUMN*. The worker calculates inner products and builds a row of the result matrix, which it finally **out**'s, marking it with a null value of type *RESULT*. Notice that the worker **in**'s the row vector — no other worker will need it. However, it

```
/*
 * Matrix multiply worker process.
 */
#include "matrix.h"

LindaMain()
{       int r, c, dim;
        $MAKE_ARRAY(row,ROW,rowData,double,MAXDIM);
        $MAKE_ARRAY(col,COL,colData,double,MAXDIM);
        $MAKE_ARRAY(result,ROW,resultData,double,MAXDIM);

        for (;;)
        {       in(REQUEST,?r,?dim);
                $SET_DIM(row,dim);
                $SET_DIM(col,dim);
                $SET_DIM(result,dim);
                in(r,?row);

                for (c = 0; c < dim; c++)
                {       rd(c,?col);
                        resultData[c] =
                                innerProd(rowData,colData,dim);
                }
                out(RESULT,r,result);
        }
}

static double
innerProd(rdata,cdata,dim)
{       /* Compute inner product */         }
```

Figure 1: Matrix multiplication worker

rd's the columns, since they are needed by other workers computing other rows. The right multiplicand is a *distributed data structure* [10].

Figure 2 illustrates code that makes use of the matrix multiply worker. Figure 3 is the include file referred to in the other two figures.

3 Applications and results.

It is generally true in parallel processing that the performance is best when a large amount of computation is performed for each communication or synchronization operation. Because of the high overhead involved in network operations, this effect is particularly severe in computations on local area networks as compared to more tightly coupled multiprocessors. Thus, applications that run best in this environment will have a large granularity, dividing into large, autonomous pieces.

So far, three applications have been implemented in this environment. Two of these divide into large, independent pieces in a straightforward manner, and give quite good performance results. In the third application, a finite element equation solver, the parallel computations have a much smaller granularity, and the resulting poorer performance shows a limitation of the current implementation.

3.1 The BOHR program.

The BOHR computer program[11] is used at Sandia for studying early events in radiation damage of semiconductors. These computations examine the interactions between a high-energy incoming projectile and a target system. For example, one computation studied an argon projectile scattering from a silicon target. This Monte Carlo technique uses a few random numbers to initialize the projectile direction and velocity. It then follows the trajectory by numerically integrating the classical equations of motion until the collision is completed. Results of the collision are then assessed. Electrons in the target, for instance, may have been ejected, excited, or transferred to the projectile. The recoil energy of the target is computed. After this, another trajectory is set up and followed. One run of BOHR consists of following thousands of trajectories for which various possible outcome results are averaged, counted, and tabulated.

The parallel implementation of Bohr is straightforward, since each trajectory is completely independent of

```
#include "matrix.h"

LindaMain()
{       double  A[DIM][DIM], B[DIM][DIM], C[DIM][DIM];
        int     r, c;
        $ARRAY(rowTemp,ROW,A[0]);
        $MAKE_ARRAY(col,COL,colData,double,DIM);

        /* Drop the rows of A and the columns of B into tuple space, along
         * with a "request" tuple for each result row. C stores arrays
         * row-wise, so out the rows of the A matrix in place. But the
         * non-contiguous elements of B are copied into COL.
         */
        for (r = 0; r < DIM; r++)
        {       out(REQUEST,r,DIM);
                rowTemp.data = A[r]; out(r,rowTemp);
                for (c = 0; c < DIM; c++)
                        colData[c] = B[c][r];
                out(r,col);
        }
        /* Extract the results; re-use rowTemp                  */
        for (r = 0; r < DIM; r++)
        {       rowTemp.data = C[r];
                in(RESULT,r,?rowTemp);
        }
        /* Clean up all the junk                                */
        for (r = 0; r < DIM; r++)
                in(r,?COL);
}
```

Figure 2: Matrix multiplication master

```
/*
 * Matrix multiplier standard include file
 */
#ttcontext matrix
#include "LINDA_LIBRARY:lindadefs.h"
#define MAXDIM 100
#define NULL 0

$ARRAY_TYPE(ROW,double);
$ARRAY_TYPE(COL,double);

newtype void REQUEST;
newtype void RESULT;
```

Figure 3: Matrix multiplication include file

the next. We employ a single master process and many worker processes—one on each machine participating in the computation. Each slave process repeatedly follows one trajectory, and sends the results back to the master process. We used the technique proposed by Percus and Kalos[12] to provide each slave processor with its own independent sequence of random numbers. The master process receives and tabulates trajectory results until the required number has been received, and writes the output file.

One useful aspect of this implementation is its robustness in the face of inevitable difficulties with machines on the network. If a machine running a slave process crashes, or runs very slowly because it is heavily loaded, the computation as a whole still proceeds with only a degradation in performance. Although the master process receives no results from that one slave, eventually enough trajectories are received from other machines to complete the job. Load-balancing occurs quite naturally and easily: each machine computes as fast as it can, and the job completes when the master has received and processed the required number of trajectories.

We have run the network version of BOHR on several configurations of machines on our network, and performance results are summarized in Table 1. Although a

Configuration	*Time (min)*	*Cray Eq*
Cray-1S	7.4	1.0
VAX 8700	152	.05
SNL-L[a]	42	.18
SNL[b]	15	.49

[a]The SNL-L set consisted of: 2 VAX 8700's, 1 VAX 8650, 3 VAX 780's, and 3 MicroVAX II's

[b]The SNL set consisted of 4 VAX 8700's and 7 VAX 8650's

Table 1: Summary of performance results for the BOHR application. The "*Cray Eq*" column gives the fraction of Cray-1S performance delivered by the configuration.

production run for the program often requires over 2000 trajectories, in generating these results we stopped the run at only 200. Production runs would be at least ten times longer than those in our timing runs.

Comparison of the times in Table 1 for the Cray-1S and the VAX 8700 shows that the BOHR program vectorizes rather well on the Cray. The Cray-1S runs BOHR about 20 times faster than the 8700, and our experience is that for strictly scalar computations, the Cray-1S runs only about five times faster than the VAX 8700. Thus, BOHR is rather well suited to the Cray.

The configuration labeled "SNL-L" in Table 1 consists of a set of machines on our network located at Sandia National Laboratories in Livermore (SNLL). There were nine machines in all, with three 8000 class VAXes, three MicroVAXes and three 780's. An accurate estimate of the "ideal" performance of this collection of machines would be difficult. However, a rough estimate can be obtained by considering the three 8000 class machines as equivalent, and the six smaller machines collectively as about an 8700, giving a total of four VAX 8700 equivalents. The Cray therefore should run about 5 times faster than the SNL-L set. Instead, from Table 1, we see that the Cray is 5.7 times faster than the SNL-L set, indicating some degradation from the ideal performance in the SNL-L set.

The SNL set consisted of eleven VAX 8700, 8650, and 8550 machines in Livermore, CA and Albuquerque, NM. The two sites are networked together *via* a 56 Kbit link. Since a single VAX 8700 requires 152 minutes to perform the computation, this ensemble of eleven similar machines should take about 14 minutes. Table 1 shows the time required to be 15 minutes, once again indicating some small source of performance degradation which we have not yet characterized. It can also be seen that the "SNL" set runs at about half the speed of the Cray-1S.

Although performance results for this are not reported in Table 1, we were able to run this application on a (more) heterogeneous collection of machines. In one such set, the parallel BOHR program utilized five VAX (VMS) systems, three Sun/3 (Unix) workstations, and an Intel 310 (XENIX) personal computer.

3.2 Rocket plume sensitivity analysis.

CHARM is a computer program for modeling high-altitude rocket plumes. The model has a number of parameters, and a study underway at Sandia seeks to determine the sensitivity of plume simulation results to the values of these parameters. A sophisticated technique is used to select parameter values for scanning the space, but the computationally intensive portion of the study reduces to running CHARM many times with different input values. Each CHARM run requires from 15 minutes to 2 hours of execution time on a VAX 8700, and a full sensitivity analysis may require hundreds of such runs.

The parallel implementation is once again straightforward. Three types of processes are employed: one master, one post-processor, and a slave process on each worker VAX. Each slave participating in the computation posts a Linda tuple indicating that it is idle, then waits for a response from the master. The master process waits for such "Idle VAX" tuples to appear, and sends each such process the index of the next simulation run to be performed. When the run is completed, the slave posts a message to the post-processor indicating that the output from the CHARM run is available for analysis. It then requests more work from the master.

This application, too, can be made robust in the face of difficulties with a remote slave processor. The master assigns simulation runs to slaves until all have been assigned. At this point, although all of the simulation runs have been assigned to slaves, not all of them have completed. When another slave process requests more work, it is assigned one of these not yet completed simulations. Thus, if one slave process never completes its task, either because of a machine failure or because the machine is heavily loaded, it will simply never report back to the master. Its task, however, will eventually be re-assigned to another slave process and the job as a whole will still complete.

The timing data for the parallel implementation are presented in Table 2. These are for a sensitivity analysis that required 99 runs of the CHARM program. The analysis required about 1500 minutes on the VAX, or about 15 minutes per simulation. CHARM runs mostly in single precision on the VAX, and vectorizes very poorly on the Cray. Thus, the Cray-1S runs only a factor of 4.4 faster than a VAX 8700 for this application, and a collection of fourteen 8000-class machines runs over twice as fast as the Cray. Thus, for this application at least, the network delivers true supercomputer performance.

There are five different types of VAXes in our collection of fourteen "8000-class" machines, and each type has different performance characteristics. Because of this heterogeneity, the computation of parallel efficiency, or some relative speedup is difficult. Nonetheless, based upon our estimates of the performances of each machine in the ensemble, we estimate that in the ideal case the job should have completed in 121 minutes, rather than

Configuration	*Time (min)*	*Cray Eq*
Cray-1S	343	1.0
VAX 8700	1516	.23
14×VAX 8000	143	2.40

Table 2: Timing results for CHARM. The "*Cray Eq*" column gives the fraction of Cray-1S performance delivered by the configuration.

the 143 minutes reported in Table 2. This loss of performance may be due to communication overheads on the network. However, we did not have exclusive access to the machines during the timing runs, and the loss of performance may be simply due to other jobs competing with CHARM on some of the machines. Since the performance degradation is small, we have not performed the experiments necessary to pinpoint its source.

3.3 Finite element thermal analysis.

A number of applications have been developed both at Sandia and at Yale for the Intel iPSC hypercube[9]. The system calls used for communication and synchronization on the hypercube[13] (send, recv, *etc*) can be implemented on our network with appropriate Linda constructs. We have done this, and hope in this way to run a number of programs developed for the hypercube on our network. The hypercube programs were developed, of course, with some assumptions about the relative speeds of computation and communication operations. These assumptions are invalid for our network: the computation is faster and the communication slower. However, if we use only tens of processors, rather than the hundreds that the hypercube algorithms targeted, it is possible that acceptable performance will be achieved for some of these algorithms. Furthermore, this hypercube work represents a source of parallel programs that can be run on the network with little development effort, and that will stress the communication network. By studying the performance of these we will understand more clearly the limitations of this type of network parallel processing.

The first of these parallel hypercube applications that we have studied on the network is an equation solver for TACO3D, a finite element thermal analysis computer program[14] in use at Sandia. The iterative algorithm employed is a modified version of an SOR solver. The matrix and vectors are distributed in a block-wise fashion between the participating machines. Within a block, each processor performs the usual SOR computations, but the inter-block computations are modified to permit parallelization. A constraint on the current implementation, due to its origins as a hypercube program, is that the number processors participating must be a power of two.

There are two sources of performance degradation in the parallel equation solver as the number of participating processors in increased. The first arises from communication costs which increase with the number of processors. The second is that the number of iterations required to achieve convergence also increases with the number of processors. We modified the usual SOR procedure to permit parallelization of the computation. However, these modifications slow the rate of convergence when multiple processors are used. For instance, our sample problem required 19 iterations for convergence when a single procesor was used, but required 21 iterations when using two processors.

Configuration		*Times in seconds (speedup)*		
8700's	780's	Total	# Iter	Time/Iter
1	0	32.5 (1.0)	19	1.71 (1.0)
2	0	24.9 (1.3)	21	1.19 (1.4)
0	1	174.9 (1.0)	19	9.21 (1.0)
0	2	106.1 (1.6)	21	5.05 (1.8)
1	3	69.7 (2.5)	24	2.90 (3.2)

Table 3: Execution times for the TACO3D equation solver.

Timing results for solution of a sample TACO3D matrix are presented in Table 3. The matrix is of size 1000 with a bandwidth of 258. As shown in Table 3, we ran the solver on several combinations of Vaxes, including one and two 8700's, and one and two 780's. Unfortunately, we had access to neither four 8700's nor four 780's for these runs, but we did run the problem on a set of three 780's and one 8700. In the current implementation, the work is divided into pieces of equal sizes and no load-balancing is done, so we expect that the performance of this last set will be very similar to that for four 780's.

For each set of machines, we report several values. The column labeled "Total" gives the total execution time in seconds required to solve the matrix, and in parenthesis the speedup is given. The *speedup* s_n of an n processor parallel program is given by:

$$s_n = \frac{t_{serial}}{t_n}$$

where t_{serial} is the execution time for the serial version of the program, and t_n is the execution time for the parallel program running on n processors. In this particular program the serial version of the solver is identical to the parallel version running on only one processor, so $t_{serial} = t_1$. Thus we see that two 8700's runs the solver 1.3 times faster than only one. Although the execution times for the 780's are of course larger, the speedup results for these machines are better. This is because the time spent doing the numeric computations in these slower machines increases by a factor of over five, while the increase in communication overhead is much smaller. Thus, our estimated speedup for four VAX 780 computers on this application is 2.5.

As described earlier, in addition to the communication overhead there is an algorithmic source of performance degradation in the parallel solver. This can be seen in the column in Table 3 labeled "# Iter" showing the number of iterations necessary to produce the solution, which increases as the number of processors increases. The final column labeled "Time/Iter" isolates the communication overhead by presenting the execution time for one iteration, and the corresponding speedup values in parenthesis.

4 Conclusion and summary.

We have successfully implemented several application programs on a local area network of VMS VAX computers using Linda. Two of the applications, BOHR and CHARM, decouple nicely into parallel pieces, and the network of VAXes runs these at a substantial fraction of the speed a Cray-1S supercomputer. For BOHR, which vectorizes on the Cray, this was achieved with a collection of eleven 8000 class VAXes. For CHARM, which vectorizes poorly on the Cray, only three of these VAXes provides over half of the performance of the Cray-1S.

The TACO3D equation solver provides a more stressing test of the performance of the Linda implementation. The parallel processes in this application are much more tightly coupled than in the other examples, and there is frequent interprocess communication. The resulting performance on the network is certainly worse than for the other two applications, but we find even these results encouraging. While TACO3D running on four machines is not twice as fast as on only two, it does run faster, and we have not reached the point where adding more machines actually slows the computations down. Thus, we may find the network Linda implementation useful for even fairly tightly coupled computations. Even if *efficiency* of the use of the computers is poor in some relative sense, the absolute performance may nonetheless be acceptable, and we can make productive use of a computer resource that might otherwise be unused.

5 Acknowledgements.

Work at Sandia was supported by the United States Department of Energy. Jerrold Leichter's work is supported by a grant from the Digital Equipment Corporation's Graduate Engineering Education Program, and by National Science Foundation grants CCR-8601920 and CCR-8657615, and ONR N00014-86-K-0310. We are grateful to Ray Cline for providing the parallel random number generator for the BOHR application.

References

[1] D. Gelernter. *Generative Communication in Linda.* Technical Report YALEU/DCS/RR-294, Yale University Department of Computer Science, November 1983.

[2] S. Ahuja, N. Carriero, and D. Gelernter. Linda and friends. *IEEE Computer*, 26–34, August 1986.

[3] R. Bjornson, N. Carriero, D. Gelernter, and J. Leichter. *Linda, the Portable Parallel.* Technical Report YALEU/DCS/TR-615, Yale University Department of Computer Science, February 1987.

[4] N. J. Carriero. *Implementation of Tuple Space Machines.* Technical Report YALEU/DCS/RR-567, Yale University Department of Computer Science, December 1987.

[5] S. Lucco. A heuristic Linda kernel for hypercube multiprocessors. In *Proceedings of the SIAM Conference on Hypercube Multiprocessors*, September 1986.

[6] N. J. Carriero. Private communication.

[7] S. Ahuja, N. Carriero, D. Gelernter, and V. Krishnaswamy. Matching language and hardware for parallel computation in the Linda machine. *IEEE Trans. on Computers*, to appear.

[8] J. S. Leichter. *The VAX Linda-C User's Guide.* Technical Report YALEU/DCS/TR-520, Yale University Department of Computer Science, March 1988.

[9] R. Asbury, S. Frison, and T. Roth. Concurrent computers ideal for inherently parallel problems. *Computer Design*, 24(11):99–107, September 1985.

[10] N. Carriero, D. Gelernter, and J. Leichter. *Distributed Data Structures in Linda.* Technical Report YALEU/DCS/TR-438, Yale University Department of Computer Science, November 1985.

[11] R. E. Olson and A. Salop. Charge-transfer and impact-ionization cross sections for fully and partially stripped positive ions colliding with atomic hydrogen. *Phys. Rev. A*, 16(2):531–541, August 1977.

[12] O. E. Percus and M. H. Kalos. *Random Number Generators for Ultracomputers.* Ultracomputer note 114, New York University, Division of Computer Science, 251 Mercer Street, New York, NY 10012, February 1987.

[13] *iPSC Programmer's Reference Guide.* Intel Scientific Computers, Beaverton, OR, 1987.

[14] W. E. Mason. TACO3D—*A Three-Dimensional Finite Element Heat Transfer Code.* Technical Report SAND83-8212, Sandia National Laboratories, Livermore, CA, 94550, April 1983.

Development of Job-Job Step Scheduler for NAL Numerical Simulator

S. Hatayama M. Tsuchiya

National Aerospace Laboratory
7-44-1 Jindaijihigashi-machi, Chofu-shi, Tokyo

Y. Shinkai H. Morishige

Fujitsu Limited
3-3-1 Shinyokohama, Kohoku-ku, Yokohama-shi, Tokyo

Abstract

In this paper we present the concepts and functions of the job-job step scheduler which is the kernel of the software packages developed for the management of the NAL Numerical Simulator (NS). This scheduler is partially responsible for the high operating ratio of supercomputers in NS, while there is some guarantee of job turnaround.

Introduction

The word "supercomputer" is generally understood to mean computers with very high peak hardware performance. However, to use the potential of supercomputers, management systems must be developed, and vectorization of application programs must be improved. In this paper, we deal with NAL supercomputer management systems.

For 10 years, schedulers have been developed for managing supercomputers in NAL. The FACOM 230-75 APU, which was the first Japanese supercomputer, was developed jointly by NAL and Fujitsu Limited and was introduced to NAL in August 1977 [1-3]. We made every effort to utilize this machine effectively, but the improvements that could be made in its operating ratio were limited, and there was no guarantee of job turnaround.

The main reason, as determined by system simulation [4-7] was:

A job input to the FACOM 230-75 APU system queues up a job class. Each job class has different limits and controls. Started jobs are controlled by the CPU and memory priorities. However, no matter how these limits and controls are adjusted, CPU and memory conflicts and a statistical fluctuation of workloads in the job stream occur, and hence there is a limit to the improvements in the operating ratio that can be made.
On the other hand, as long as different CPU priority is assigned for each job class, there is no guarantee of turnaround for low priority jobs.

Eight years ago, we designed a new job control method called the job-job step scheduler to solve the above problems [8]. The scheduler was first developed for the FACOM M380 + M180 Ⅱ AD×2 system, which began operation in February 1982 [9-11]. In this system, however, we could not implement several functions of the job-job step scheduler because the operating system was not adequate. The original functions of this scheduler are implemented in the present FACOM VP400 + VP200 + M780 system (called the Numerical Simulator (NS)) which has been operating since February 1987. In this paper, we would like to explain the role this scheduler plays in NS.

CH2617-9/88/0000/0200$01.00 © 1988 IEEE

NS Hardware

The most important role of the job-job step scheduler is load distribution of the jobs input to NS. The supercomputer can execute only highly vectorized programs at a high speed. Therefore, if we use the supercomputer to process programs with a low vectorization ratio, we are not utilizing the supercomputer's full potential.

The hardware configuration of the NS kernel is shown in Fig. 1. It operates as a loosely coupled multiprocessor (LCMP) with two supercomputers (VP400: SHP1 and VP200: SHP2) as the local processors and with a general-purpose computer (M780: FEP) as the global processor. Some data transfer between the FEP and SHP is done by the CTC, but most is done through the shared disks or the SSD. This LCMP is the best environment for implementing the job-job step scheduler functions.

Steps must be taken to prevent I/O processing competition in this system, because it is inevitable that I/O demands from the FEP, SHP1, and SHP2 will conflict. The NS disks were configured to make the SHP1 as efficient as possible. Each disk file is either on the SHP1 private disk, on the SHP1-FEP shared disk, or on the FEP-SHP2 shared disk. The SHP1 private disk has four channel paths and contains large disk files used when the SHP1 processes numerical simulation programs. The FEP-SHP2 shared disk contains permanent disk files. The SHP1-FEP shared disk contains temporary disk files to avoid I/O competition between the FEP or SHP2 and the SHP1.

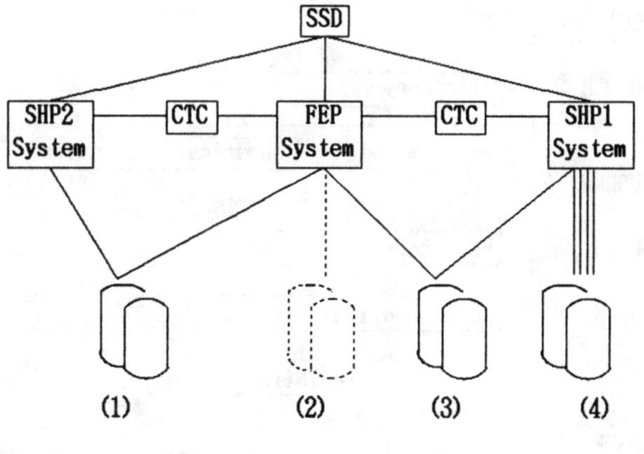

(1) FEP-SHP2 shared disk for permanent files
(2) FEP private magnet-optical disk for mass storage
(3) SHP1-FEP shared disk for temporary files
(4) SHP1 private disk for high-speed files
SHP1: FACOM VP400 SSD: Solid-state disk
SHP2: FACOM VP200 CTC: Channel-to-channel adapter
FEP : FACOM M780

Fig. 1 Hardware configuration of the NS kernel

Job Processing Concept

The processing scheme of the job-job step is diagrammed in Fig. 2. A job submitted to NS, if the job definition is clear, is entered into one of the input job queues, and waits to be started by the scheduler. At the input and termination of a job, the scheduler checksif the number of jobs already run is smaller than the run limit of its job class. If it is, the next job of its job class is started.

Jobs are processed sequentially from the first job step by the FEP, until an SHP job step appears. The scheduler then puts it in an SHP job step queue. At the input and termination of an SHP job step, the scheduler checks if an SHP job step of its job class has already run. If not, the next SHP job step of its job class is started.

After an SHP job step terminates:

(1) If the job step is the last one, the job is terminated.

(2) If the next job step is an SHP job step, the scheduler reenters it into an SHP job step queue.

(3) If the next job step is an FEP job step, it is started immediately.

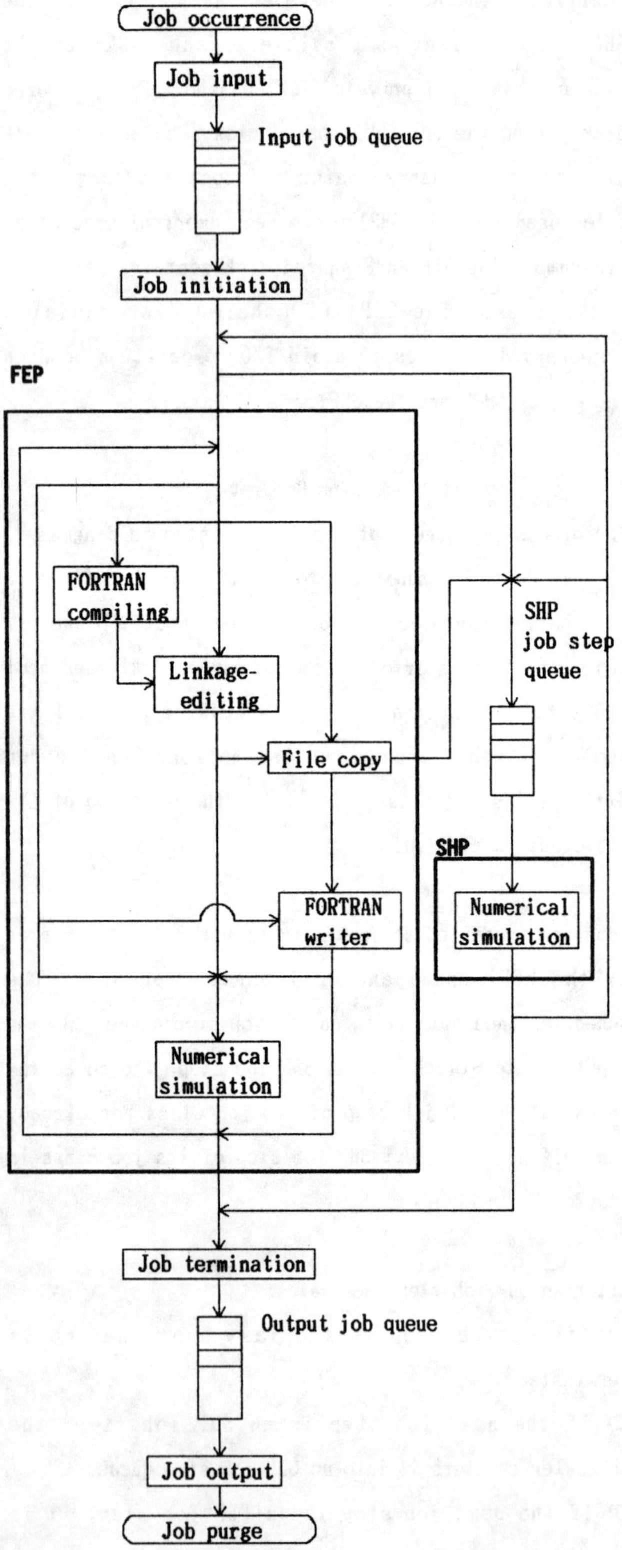

Job occurrence

Job input

Input job queue

Job initiation

FEP

FORTRAN compiling

Linkage-editing

File copy

SHP job step queue

SHP

Numerical simulation

FORTRAN writer

Numerical simulation

Job termination

Output job queue

Job output

Job purge

Fig. 2 Job-job step processing scheme

Functions of Job Step Scheduler

An example of the job step scheduling for the execution of a numerical simulation program on the SHP1 is shown in Fig. 3. The job step scheduling for the execution of numerical simulation programs on the SHP2 or the FEP is similar but simpler, since it does not require the scheduler to add file copy job steps to user job steps.

```
①//X01PASS JOB SMAL
②//     EXEC    FORTC1,SF= 'SOURCE.CFD'
③//     EXEC    LIED1,ALIB= 'ULIB.CFD'
④//*/   EXEC    GO1
⑤//*/   EXPAND  USDKR,RNO=01,FILE= 'DATA.A'
⑥//*/   EXPAND  USDKW,RNO=02,FILE= 'DATA.B'
⑦//*/   EXPAND  USDK,RNO=03,FILE= 'DATA.C'
⑧//*/   GOEND
⑨//     EXEC    GO,EF= 'CFD.LOAD',EMEM=WING
⑩//     EXPAND  USDK,RNO=02,FILE= 'DATA.B'
⑪//     EXPAND  XY
⑫//
```

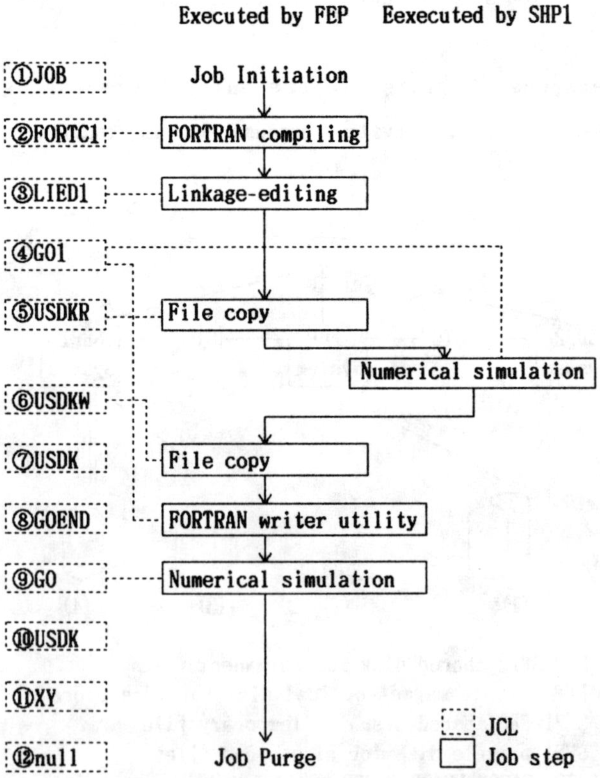

Executed by FEP   Eexecuted by SHP1

①JOB — Job Initiation

②FORTC1 — FORTRAN compiling

③LIED1 — Linkage-editing

④GO1

⑤USDKR — File copy

Numerical simulation

⑥USDKW

⑦USDK — File copy

⑧GOEND — FORTRAN writer utility

⑨GO — Numerical simulation

⑩USDK

⑪XY

⑫null — Job Purge

JCL

Job step

Fig. 3 Job step scheduling for the SHP1 execution of a numerical simulation program

In NS, the job procedure is defined between the JOB statement ① and the null statement ⑫.

① The beginning of the job is indicated by the JOB statement. When the JOB statement is read, the center routine confirms and sets up parameters such as the user name, the password, the job class etc., and notifies the scheduler of this information.

② The FORTC1 statement instructs the FEP to execute the compile job step. An object module is output to the FEP-SHP2 shared disk.

③ The LIED1 statement instructs the FEP to execute the linkage-editing job step. A load module is output to the SHP1-FEP shared disk.

④ The G01 statement instructs the SHP1 to execute a numerical simulation job step. The SHP1 executes the load module output by ③. The list is output to the SHP1-FEP shared disk as an internal code. The FEP executes the FORTRAN writer transform utility after the G01 job step ends.

⑤ The USDKR statement instructs the G01 job step to read the file on the FEP-SHP2 shared disk. The FEP copies the file from the FEP-SHP2 shared disk to the SHP1-FEP shared disk, before beginning the G01 job step.

⑥ The USDKW statement instructs the G01 job step to write the file to the FEP-SHP2 shared disk. The FEP copies the file from the SHP1-FEP shared disk to the FEP-SHP2 shared disk after the G01 job step ends.

⑦ The USDK statement instructs the G01 job step to use the file on the SHP1 private disk.

⑧ The GOEND statement indicates the end of control statements for the G01 job step.

⑨ The GO statement instructs the FEP to execute a numerical simulation job step.

⑩ The USDK statement instructs the GO job step to use the file on the FEP-SHP2 shared disk.

⑪ The XY statement instructs the GO job step to use the XY plotter file on the FEP-SHP2 shared disk.

It should be mentioned that users can define an execution system (the FEP, SHP1, or SHP2) only for the numerical simulation job steps.

Requirements for Job Scheduler

To develop a job scheduler, it is necessary to divide jobs into job classes based on their system resource requirements such as CPU and memory.

There are three things that must be kept in mind when designing a job scheduler.

(1) A high operating ratio for all systems, especially the SHP, must be maintained.

(2) Turnaround for jobs in each job class must be guaranteed.

(3) A variety of functions for flexible operation must be included.

These three requirements are not compatible with each other. Our policy is to place the most stress on the requirement (1) on condition that the requirement (2) would be satisfied to some extent.

Job Scheduler Functions

The current job classes of NS are summarized in Table 1. NS can execute very large numerical simulation programs for hours, if a LARG or HUGE job class is used.

The job scheduler has the following functions, labeled (A) to (H) :

Functions (A) and (B) increase the operating ratio of the SHP, (C) and (D) guarantee turnaround, and (E) to (H) are operation functions.

(A) Reserve and control executable SHP job steps

To maintain a high SHP operating ratio, the next SHP job step must be started, as soon as the current SHP job step terminates. Therefore, all the FEP job steps prior to the next SHP job step must be completed. Several executable SHP job steps must be constantly reserved in case SHP job steps end quickly. We designed the SHP job step queue (Fig. 2) to solve this problem [8].

Table 1 NS job classes

(1)SHP1 (VP400)

Job class	Run limit			CPU limit (MIN)			Memory limit (MB)	
	JOB	FEP	SHP	JOB	FEP	SHP	FEP	SHP
SMAL	4	4	1	60	5	60	5	50
LARG								
Short-time	4	4	1	3	2	3	5	968
Long-time	4	4	1	100	5	100	5	968
HUGE								
Short-time*	4	4	1	3	2	3	5	968**
Long-time	1	1	1	300	5	300	5	968**
VSRV***	1	1	1	1	1	1	1	1

* Not operating at present

** Possible to enlarge to 1,018 MB

*** Job class for utility processing

(2)SHP2 (VP200)

Job class	Run limit			CPU limit (MIN)			Memory limit (MB)	
	JOB	FEP	SHP	JOB	FEP	SHP	FEP	SHP
SHRT	4	4	1	3	2	3	5	16
MIDL	4	4	1	30	5	30	5	32
LONG	4	4	1	100	5	100	5	74
HJOB*	4	4	1	300	5	300	5	122

* Not operating at present

(3)FEP (M780)

Job class	Run limit			CPU limit (MIN)			Logical memory limit(MB)	
	JOB	FEP	SHP	JOB	FEP	SHP	SS*	GO step
SERV	2	2	0	3	3	0	5	6
HANJ	1	1	0	30	30	0	5	16
DATA	1	1	0	5	5	0	5	8
FJOB	1	1	0	60	60	0	5	50

* Service step

(4)Operating time

System		Operating time	
		9:00-22:00	22:00-9:00
SHP1	Preference class	LARG*	HUGE**
	Nonpreference class	SMAL LARG**	SMAL LARG* LARG**
SHP2	Preference class	SHRT MIDL LONG	SHRT MIDL LONG
	Nonpreference class	———	———

* Short-time

** Long-time

(B) Set the preference and nonpreference classes

The goal of NS is to enable the execution of large numerical simulation programs with the overhead reduced. Since main memory control of the SHP is the real storage method, it is impossible to allocate more main memory to SHP job steps than the mounting main storage capacity.

As a result, a Short-time LARG job step and a Long-time LARG job step, or an LARG job step and an HUGE job step can never be executed at the same time. This is the same for an HJOB job step and other SHP2 job steps.

To solve the problem, we operate such job classes as LARG, HUGE, and HJOB by using a function to set the

Tabel 2 Example of the operating time setup

Operating time (setup time)		First 9:00- 12:00	Second 12:00- 16:00	Third 16:00- 22:00	Fourth 22:00- 9:00
SHP1 class	Preference	LARG* SMAL	HUGE* SMAL	LARG* SMAL	HUGE SMAL
	Nonpreference	LARG**	LARG	LARG**	HUGE
SHP2 class	Preference	SHRT MIDL LONG	SHRT MIDL LONG	SHRT MIDL LONG	HJOB
	Nonpreference	——	——	——	SHRT MIDL LONG
FEP class	Preference	SERV DATA HANJ FJOB	SERV DATA HANJ FJOB	SERV DATA HANJ FJOB	FJOB
	Nonpreference	——	——	——	SERV DATA HANJ

* Short-time

** Long-time

preference and nonpreference classes in the operating time as shown in Table 2. This function makes either multihour operation or the debugging of large numerical simulation programs possible during a certain operating time, without the excessive overhead.

(C) Set subclasses for the SHP1

The subclass reduces the time required to debug large numerical simulation programs. If the user specifies the CPU time in the procedure of a LARG or HUGE job, the scheduler will recognize it as a Short- or Long-time job and define a subclass of these job classes based on the specified value. At present, NS's basis value is set as three minutes (Table 1).

(D) Set and control CPU contribution ratio for each job class

There are two methods of throughput control. The first controls throughput with different CPU priorities. In this method, there is no guarantee of turnaround of low priority jobs. The second adjusts each run limit under the same CPU priority. This method is not compatible with the real memory method, unless the memory limit value of each job class is small.

We designed a new method which solves these problems [8 ,11] . In NS, we can allocate a different time slice value for every job class in the SHP. Therefore, the CPU contribution ratio of each job class, the percentage of a CPU time used by each job class per unit time, can be adjusted under the same CPU priority without increasing the run limit.

(E) Schedule urgent jobs

NS jobs are controlled as FIFO. However, often there are urgent jobs. In NS, jobs can be scheduled as privilaged jobs which are executed at the highest priority. Jobs can also be scheduled as semiprivileged jobs which are started at the highest input job queue priority.

(F) Set user time and priority

This is a function that gives specific users higher priority during a certain operating time. The scheduler forces the FEP or SHP to preferencially process the job. The operating ratio of NS, however, does not fall because other jobs are processed as described above, whenever no job of specific users exists.

(G) Prohibit processing of the same user's jobs

This function prevents one user from occupying a job class for a long time. Its current algorithm is that the scheduler does not start the next job in a job class successively if it belongs to the same user. It conducts a FIFO search for another user's job instead.

(H) Limit the number of jobs for the same user

This function prevents one user from stacking an excessive number of jobs in NS. This limits the total number of the same user's jobs, and limits the number of jobs in each job class a user can have.

Conclusion

This paper has detailed the job-job step scheduler for NS which enables effective load distribution of jobs. The first design goal was to fully utilize the high processing performance of the SHP, the second was to provide a good debugging environment for large numerical simulation programs, and the third was flexible operation. More than one year has elapsed since NS operation began, and the functions described in this paper have been confirmed by actual operation.

The features confirmed were:

(1) A high SHP operating ratio can be maintained because the next SHP job step can be started immediately after

termination of the present one.

(2) The throughput of each job class can be flexibly controlled by controlling the CPU contribution ratio of each job class. This throughput control is extremely effective because it does not require an increase in memory.

(3) Since preference and nonpreference classes in the operating time can be set, flexible operation can be done automatically.

(4) The debugging environment of large numerical simulation programs is good despite some increased overhead.

(5) It is possible to deal with urgent jobs flexibly by assigning them a privilage level.

(6) In the conventional environment it is very difficult to assign user time. However, since NS is able to set up any user time and specific users, not only do users not have to do system operation, but the operating ratio never falls.

Since the beginning of operation, this scheduler has been refined, and has grown even closer to our original hopes. However, we are striving for further improvements in the following areas:

(1) Speeding up the swapping processing further.

(2) Enabling the file copy between the SHP1 private disk and the FEP-SHP2 shared disk without using the SHP1-FEP shared disk.

(3) Outputting numerical simulation data from the SHP1 private disk directly to graphic displays.

References

[1] H. Miyoshi et al., "On the FACOM 230-75 APU(I)," NAL TM-325, 1977.

[2] H. Miyoshi et al., "On the FACOM 230-75 APU(II)," NAL TM-369, 1978.

[3] T. Nakamura et al., "Design of the Center-Routine for the FACOM 230-75 APU System," NAL TM-344, 1977.

[4] H. Miyoshi et al., "Job Processing Simulator for the FACOM 230-75 APU System," NAL TM-384, 1979.

[5] K. Nakamura et al., "Statistics of the NAL Computer System's Jobs," NAL TM-382, 1979.

[6] H. Miyoshi et al., "System Simulation for the FACOM 230-75 APU System," NAL TR-590, 1979.

[7] S. Hatayama et al., "Several Methods for Effective Utilization of Main Memory and Study to Apply to the NAL System," NAL TM-419, 1980.

[8] S. Hatayama et al., "New Scheduler for Job Processing in Computer Systems," NAL TR-659, 1981.

[9] S. Hatayama et al., "Operation Scheme for the Next NAL Computer System," NAL TR-659, 1981.

[10] S. Hatayama et al., "Design of JCL Macros for the Next NAL Computer System," NAL TM-444, 1981.

[11] S. Hatayama et al., "Transaction Processing Simulator for the NAL Computer System," NAL TM-543, 1985.

The Symbolic Hyperplane Transformation for Recursively Defined Arrays

Maya B. Gokhale   Todd C. Torgersen

Department of Computer and Information Sciences
University of Delaware*

Abstract

This paper describes a restructuring transformation which can be used to parallelize recurrence relations. The transformation is based on the hyperplane (or wavefront) method, but extends the applicability of the method to irregularly-structured recurrences.

We assume that the time of computation of an array element is a linear combination of its indices, and we use a variation of the simplex method to seek a succession of hyperplanes along which array elements can be computed concurrently. Portions of the work reported here have been implemented in the PS automatic program generation system.

Key Words and Concepts: parallel scheduling, automatic program generation, program transformation, hyperplane, wavefront, linear programming, equational specifications, applicative programming

1 Introduction

The hyperplane method is a well-known program transformation which is used to generate concurrent DO loops from recurrence relations. [3] introduces hyperplane scheduling, in which the nested loop indices of an iterative program are viewed as defining a single multidimensional $M_1 \times M_2 \ldots \times M_n$ array of events. For some common kinds of computation, we can schedule large numbers of events in parallel by selecting a time axis. At any time t, those events will be scheduled which lie on the hyperplane normal to the time axis at t. When this method is successful, the time required is reduced from the volume of the multidimensional array down to the length of some line through it, provided that enough processors are available. The concurrency generated is suitable for a shared-memory multiprocessor and is amenable to either self-scheduling or pre-scheduling.

The hyperplane (wavefront) concept has also been used to aid in the design of VLSI array processors and much has been written in this context ([11], [8], [10], [9], and [12]). Recently, [8] and [9] use the hyperplane method and other transformations for automatic mapping of algorithms onto VLSI array processors. The "standard" hyperplane method as it appears in [3], [11], [8], [10], [9], and [12] is applicable only in the case of regularly structured recurrences, i.e. those recurrences described by constant values in the associated dependency vectors.** The goal of this paper is to extend the class of algorithms to which the hyperplane method applies. The methods we have developed can be used to identify the set of feasible hyperplanes in the presence of certain forms of symbolic entries in the dependency vectors†. In particular, the dependency vectors may contain references to the index sets over which the recurrence is defined. A heuristic method for determining the set of feasible hyperplanes under these conditions is given in [4]. Our current work has been to develop a technique which is exact rather than heuristic ([5]). The technique has been prototyped under MACSYMA and PASCAL and is being incorporated into the PS automatic program generation system ([1], [2]).

Once the set of feasible schedules have been found, a number of techniques may be used to select a desirable schedule. [9] give an exact method for finding a truly optimal schedule provided certain restrictions on the index sets hold. [4] gives a computationally less costly method for finding a good, but not necessarily optimal schedule. Other methods for selecting a desired schedule are discussed in [3], [8] and [5].

Regular and Irregularly-Structured Recurrences

The PS system deals primarily with specifications which describe how the values of array elements are to be computed. A specification consists of a set of equations whose form is restricted enough that simple, efficient loop programs can be generated from it. In the examples below we structure the conditional equations conventionally rather than introduce the formal syntax of the PS language. We write a sequence of rules, with each rule in the form "item=value, if condition". Each item is a scalar, usually an array compo-

*Supported in part by NSF grant 3-1-21-2586-09 and in part by UDRF Grant LTR860114.

**For a recurrence defined by the equation $A[I, J] = f(A[I + k, J + l])$, the dependency vector is $(-k, -l)$. For the standard hyperplane method to be applicable, k and l must be manifest integer constants.

†Symbolic inequalities are also discussed in the context of dependency analysis in [14].

nent. Each value is an expression whose value is to be that of the item, provided the corresponding condition is true. The rules are tried in order, so that each presupposes the complement of the conditions of previous rules. Normally there is a default equation at the end of the rule set defining one item, which is labeled with the trivial "otherwise" condition which is assumed always to be true.

For example,

$$\begin{aligned} P[i,j] &= 1, \text{ if } i = 0 \vee j = 0 \\ &= P[i-1,j] + P[i,j-1], \text{ otherwise} \end{aligned} \quad (1)$$

defines a function (Pascal's Triangle) on the ranges of index sets of i ($\{i : 1 \leq i \leq M\}$) and j ($\{j : 1 \leq j \leq N\}$); the equations specify values and dependencies, but not scheduling. Thus, we are given the equations which define each point $P[i,j]$, possibly as depending on points $P[i',j']$. Let $t(P[i,j])$ denote "the time at which $P[i,j]$ is computed". We want to find the time t in such a way that:

1. Dependencies are respected, i.e., $t(P[i,j])$ is greater than each $t(P[i',j'])$.
2. The maximal time (i.e., the last time involved in the computation) is minimal.

To make the problem more tractable, we assume that the time-function $t(P[i,j])$ for an array P will always be a linear combination of the subscripts i and j, i.e., the time at which $P[i,j]$ is computed is given by the *time equation*

$$t(P[i,j]) = ai + bj \quad . \quad (2)$$

This "hyperplane" assumption enables us to adapt linear programming techniques to solve a variety of subproblems.

Note that Pascal's Triangle involves dependencies similar to the more computationally relevant grid relaxation computation, in which a new value for each point on a grid is computed as the weighted average of neighboring points.

If we apply the assumption given by (2), to the example given in specification (1) then we obtain

$$\begin{aligned} ai + bj &> a(i-1) + bj & (3) \\ ai + bj &> ai + b(j-1) & (4) \end{aligned}$$

which simplify to $a > 0$ and $b > 0$ respectively*. The scheduling problem for this specification reduces to choosing an a and b such that these inequalities hold and the desired output values may be computed in as few time steps as possible. [4] closely approximate the latter goal by choosing the least integers a and b for which these dependence inequalities will hold. In this example, these are $a = 1$ and $b = 1$**. With $t(P[i,j]) = ai + bj$, $a = 1$ and $b = 1$, we get $t(P[i,j]) = i + j$. All array elements $P[i,j]$ such that $i + j = t$ will be defined at time t. For given t, these entries comprise a "hyperplane", at right angles to the vector $(1,1)$. As t is increased from 0 to $t_{Max} = i_{Max} + j_{Max}$ we find a sequence of such hyperplanes which cover every point in the array.

Consider, however, the following "twisted" rule set, which also computes Pascal's Triangle:

$$\begin{aligned} P[i,j] &= 1, \text{ if } i = 0 \vee j = 0 \\ &= P[j,i-1] + P[j-1,i], \text{ otherwise} \end{aligned} \quad (5)$$

Applying the same technique to this formulation (5) of Pascal's Triangle, we find:

$$\begin{aligned} ai + bj &> aj + b(i-1) & (6) \\ ai + bj &> a(j-1) + bi & (7) \end{aligned}$$

which "simplify" to

$$\begin{aligned} a(i-j) + b(j-i+1) &> 0 & (8) \\ a(i-j+1) + b(j-i) &> 0\,. & (9) \end{aligned}$$

Our problem is that since the i and j do not cancel as in the first formulation, we are left with a set of inequalities in 4 unknowns, the coefficients a and b, and also the index variables i and j. Theoretically the problem could be solved by replacing the two inequalities in four unknowns by $i_{Max} \times j_{Max}$ inequalities in two unknowns (assuming that i_{Max} and j_{Max} are known at compile time).

Our technique is instead to replace the set of inequalities in 4 unknowns by a small number of inequalities with numeric values substituted for the index variables i and j. The collection of representative values for the index sets has the property that the feasible region for new set of inequalities is identical to the feasible region for the original symbolic inequalities. Since the new system of linear inequalities involves only numeric coefficients and the scheduling variables a and b, the desired schedule may be chosen as in the standard hyperplane method (see [3], [4], [5], [8], and [9]). Further, it is not necessary that upper bounds for the index sets are known at schedule-time.

An overview of our approach is given below. The reader is referred to [5], from which this presentation is adapted, for the full algorithm, sub-algorithms, and correctness proof.

2 Symbolic Linear Inequalities

In section 3, a method is given for solving a restricted class of symbolic inequalities which may arise from scheduling considerations. Before presenting the general algorithm, we consider an example which illustrates the basic idea. Suppose we are given a symbolic inequality

$$ix - y > 0 \quad (10)$$

which must hold for all $i \geq 1$. In the context of hyperplane

*Commonly, this information is expressed in terms of dependency vectors. For this discussion, however, we choose to use inequalities.

**Our overall objective is to minimize the number of hyperplanes required to reach $t = i_{Max} + j_{Max}$. It is not necessarily true that minimizing the coefficients a and b (or even their absolute value) will give us that objective.

scheduling, inequalities of this type must hold for all *integer* values of the index variable(s) involved in the computation (specification). In the interest of working over a continuous domain, we require that these inequalities hold for all rational values in the desired set.

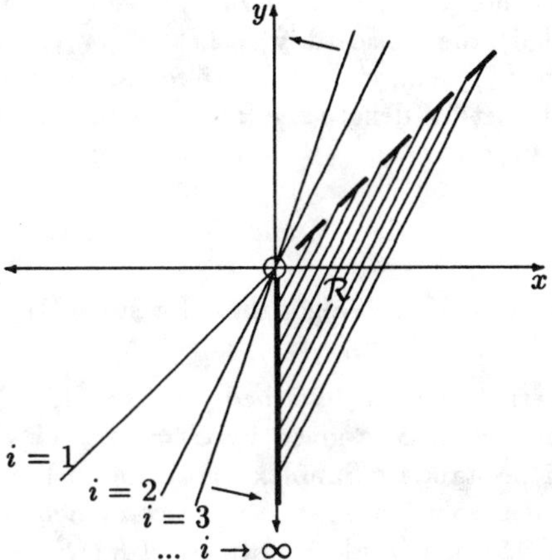

Figure 1: Symbolic Inequality $ix - y > 0$ as $i \to \infty$.

Figure 1 illustrates the region $\mathcal{R}$ which is the intersection of all half planes described by inequality (10) for $i = 1, i = 2, \ldots$ etc. When $i = 1$, the region $\mathcal{R}$ is bounded by the open half plane given by the strict inequality $x - y > 0$. As $i \to \infty$ the line $ix - y = 0$ asymptotically approaches the vertical line $x = 0$. Similarly, as $i \to \infty$ the open half plane $ix - y > 0$ approaches a half plane bounded by the line $x = 0$. The resulting region $\mathcal{R} = \bigcap_{i \geq 1} \{(x, y) : ix + y > 0\}$ which is the intersection of infinitely many open half planes, has an open boundary $x - y > 0$ (dashed, bold line in figure 1) and a closed boundary $x \geq 0$ (solid, bold line in figure 1). Thus two inequalities (with numeric coefficients) in the variables x and y describe the same region as (10). Formally,

$$(x - y > 0 \ \& \ x \geq 0) \Leftrightarrow (\forall i)_{\geq 1}(ix - y > 0) \ . \qquad (11)$$

Figure 2 illustrates the region of those i of interest for this example. Note that this region is a one dimensional convex polyhedron which is completely characterized by a vertex ($i = 1$) and the unbounded edge emanating from that vertex. Note also that the vertex of this region gives rise to a strict inequality and the unbounded edge gives rise to a non-strict inequality in the resulting numeric system. This is not a coincidence. Algorithm 3.1 is a generalization of the ideas illustrated by this example ; the vertices and unbounded edges of a convex polyhedron are used to construct the desired strict and non-strict inequalities.

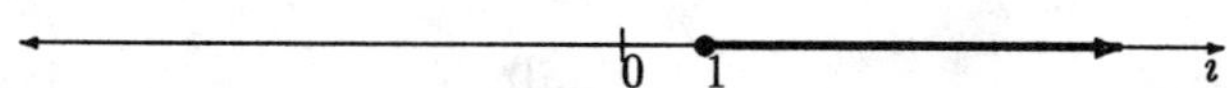

Figure 2: Region of those i for which the symbolic inequality $ix - y > 0$ holds.

Algorithm 3.1 is applicable to sets of linear inequalities in the variables $\mathbf{a} = (a_1, a_2, \ldots a_k)$ with symbolic coefficients which are affine (linear plus a constant) expressions in $\mathbf{i} = (i_1, i_2, \ldots i_k)$ where $\mathbf{i}$ is restricted to a convex set with linear boundaries $\mathcal{S} \subset Q^k$, (i.e. $\mathcal{S}$ is a k dimensional convex polyhedron over the rationals). This method finds a description of those $\mathbf{a}$ for which the symbolic inequality holds for all $\mathbf{i} \in \mathcal{S}$. The purpose of algorithm 3.1 is to replace a symbolic inequality in the original scheduling problem by a set of linear inequalities with numeric coefficients. Once all symbolic inequalities are removed from the scheduling problem, standard techniques for handling sets of linear inequalities may be used.

Fortunately, most program specifications which arise in practice conform to the requirement that the set of all $\mathbf{i}$ of interest is a convex polyhedron. Many specifications also conform to the additional requirement that the subscript expressions involved in the specification are affine in the index variables $i_1, i_2, \ldots i_k$.

For clarity of explanation, the ideas in this section are presented in the case of a single symbolic inequality. In the case where the scheduling problem gives rise to several symbolic inequalities, algorithm 3.1 may be applied to each inequality individually and the resulting numeric systems combined. A more efficient approach is obtained by a modification which is beyond the scope of this paper.

3 An Algorithm for Eliminating Symbolic Linear Inequalities

Algorithm 3.1 is based on a characterization of the region $\mathcal{S}$. Two important cases arise depending on whether $\mathcal{S}$ is bounded or not. If $\mathcal{S}$ is bounded, then $\mathcal{S}$ is a convex polytope and is completely characterized by its vertices. Otherwise, if $\mathcal{S}$ is unbounded, then $\mathcal{S}$ is characterized by its vertices together with all unbounded edges. An unbounded edge is represented by an ordered pair $u = (x, d)$ where x is the vertex from which an extremal direction of unboundedness* d emanates. Similar to the example given above ($ix - y > 0$, $i \geq 1$), the vertices of $\mathcal{S}$ give rise to a small number of strict inequalities. Further, the directions of unboundedness of $\mathcal{S}$ give rise to a small number of non-strict inequalities. The combined mixed system of strict and non-strict inequalities has identically the same solution set as the original symbolic inequality.

The following algorithm finds a small number of inequalities with the desired properties.

Algorithm 3.1 :

Input:

1. A symbolic inequality in the indeterminate vectors of length k, $\mathbf{a}$ and $\mathbf{i}$ of the form:

*See [6] for a formal definition and further discussion of directions of unboundedness.

$$\mathbf{a} \cdot (\mathbf{Di} + \mathbf{e}) > \mathbf{0} \quad (12)$$

where $\mathbf{e} \in \mathcal{Q}^k$, and $\mathbf{D} \in \mathcal{Q}^{k \times k}$. Finally, let $L{:}\mathcal{Q}^k \rightarrow \mathcal{Q}^k$ denote the affine mapping defined by $\mathbf{D}$ and $\mathbf{e}$.

2. A convex set with linear boundaries $\mathcal{S} \subset \mathcal{Q}^k$ described by r linear inequalities in $\mathbf{i} = (i_1, i_2, ..., i_k)$. Let $\mathbf{T}$ be the $r \times k$ matrix with rational entries and $\mathbf{u}$ be the $r \times 1$ column vector of rationals such that $\mathcal{S}$ is described by the inequality: $\mathbf{Ti} + \mathbf{u} \geq \mathbf{0}$.

Output:

1. A $k \times n$ matrix $\mathbf{V}$ whose columns represent the desired strict inequalities.
2. A $k \times q$ matrix $\mathbf{W}$ whose columns represent the desired non-strict inequalities.

$\mathbf{V}$ and $\mathbf{W}$ are such that:

$$(\mathbf{aV} > \mathbf{0} \;\&\; \mathbf{aW} \geq \mathbf{0}) \Leftrightarrow (\forall \mathbf{i})_{\in \mathcal{S}} (\mathbf{a} \cdot (\mathbf{Di} + \mathbf{e}) > 0) \quad (13)$$

Method:

[1] Let K denote the kernel of L. If $K \cap \mathcal{S} \neq \phi$ then terminate with failure, i.e., "unschedulable".

[2] Find the desired characterization of the region $\mathcal{S}$. Let $s_1, s_2, ..., s_m$ denote the vertices of $\mathcal{S}$. Let $\mathbf{S}$ denote the $k \times m$ matrix whose columns are the coordinates of the m vertices of the region $\mathcal{S}$ and let $\mathbf{s}_1, \mathbf{s}_2, ..., \mathbf{s}_m$ denote the columns of the matrix $\mathbf{S}$. Similarly, let $u_1, u_2, ..., u_p$ denote all the unbounded edges of the region $\mathcal{S}$ and let $y_1, y_2, ..., y_p$ denote all the extremal directions of unboundedness of the region $\mathcal{S}$ corresponding to the unbounded edges $u_1, u_2, ..., u_p$. Finally, let $\mathbf{Y}$ denote the $k \times p$ matrix whose columns are the coordinates of the p extremal directions of unboundedness of $\mathcal{S}$ and let $\mathbf{y}_1, \mathbf{y}_2, ..., \mathbf{y}_p$ denote the columns of the matrix $\mathbf{Y}$.

[3] Compute the images of $s_1, s_2, ..., s_m$ under L, i.e., compute $\mathbf{S}' = L(\mathbf{S}) = \mathbf{DS} + \mathbf{E}$ where $\mathbf{E}$ is the $k \times m$ matrix whose columns are repetitions of the vector $\mathbf{e}$. Let $\mathbf{s}'_j = \mathbf{Ds}_j + \mathbf{e}$ denote the columns of $\mathbf{S}'$ for $1 \leq j \leq m$.

[4] Compute the images of the directions of unboundedness $y_1, y_2, ..., y_p$ under L, i.e., compute $\mathbf{Y}' = L(\mathbf{Y}) = \mathbf{DY}$ (note that mapping a direction under the affine mapping L is somewhat different than mapping a vertex). Similar to step [3], let $\mathbf{y}'_j = \mathbf{Dy}_j$ denote the columns of $\mathbf{Y}'$ for $1 \leq j \leq p$.

[5] Eliminate redundant inequalities in the system $\mathbf{aS}' > \mathbf{0}$. Any column $\mathbf{s}'_j$ of $\mathbf{S}'$ which is a multiple of a convex combination of other columns of $\mathbf{S}'$ is redundant with respect to those other columns and may be discarded*. Let $\mathbf{V}$ denote the $k \times n$ matrix derived from $\mathbf{S}'$ by eliminating redundant columns and let $\mathbf{v}_1, \mathbf{v}_2, ..., \mathbf{v}_n$ denote the columns of the matrix $\mathbf{V}$.

[6] Similarly, eliminate redundancy in the columns of $\mathbf{Y}'$. Consider each $\mathbf{y}'_j$ in sequence for $1 \leq j \leq p$. If $\mathbf{y}'_j$ is a multiple of a convex combination of $\mathbf{v}_1, \mathbf{v}_2, ..., \mathbf{v}_n$ and other $\mathbf{y}'_1, \mathbf{y}'_2, ..., \mathbf{y}'_m$ (which have not yet been discarded) then discard $\mathbf{y}'_j$. Let $\mathbf{w}_1, \mathbf{w}_2, ..., \mathbf{w}_q$ denote those $\mathbf{y}'_1, \mathbf{y}'_2, ..., \mathbf{y}'_m$ which are found to be not redundant. Let $\mathbf{W}$ denote the $k \times q$ matrix whose columns are $\mathbf{w}_1, \mathbf{w}_2, ..., \mathbf{w}_q$.

[7] Return the matrices $\mathbf{V}$ and $\mathbf{W}$.

*See [5] p. 19 for a proof of this statement.

A sketch of the sub-algorithms for steps [1] – [6] of algorithm 3.1 is as follows.

The kernel of L is described by $K = \{\mathbf{i} : \mathbf{Di} + \mathbf{e} = \mathbf{0}\}$ and the region $\mathcal{S}$ is given by $\mathcal{S} = \{\mathbf{i} : \mathbf{Ti} + \mathbf{u} \geq \mathbf{0}\}$. Phase 1 of the standard Simplex algorithm ([6]) may be used to decide if a solution exists to the combined constraints defining $K \cap \mathcal{S}$; this decides emptiness of $K \cap \mathcal{S}$. Alternately, the Fourier-Motzkin method given in [13] may be used for deciding systems of inequalities of this type.

In step [2], a modified graph traversal is used to find the desired characterization of $\mathcal{S}$. The vertices and edges of the convex polyhedron $\mathcal{S}$ are viewed as the nodes and edges of an undirected graph. Phase 1 of the Simplex algorithm finds some vertex (basic feasible solution)* to start the traversal. A modification of the pivot operation of the Simplex algorithm is then used to recursively find adjacent vertices or detect extremal directions of unboundedness. The usual node marking technique which prevents infinite looping in cycles of the graph is not applicable and its function is replaced by maintaining (and checking for membership in) the set of vertices encountered as the traversal progresses.

Steps [3] and [4] involve only standard matrix operations.

In steps [5] and [6], the following idea is used. A vector $\mathbf{b}$ is a multiple of a convex combination of the columns of a matrix $\mathbf{A}$ if and only if there exists a solution $\mathbf{x}$ to the system $\mathbf{Ax} = \mathbf{b}$ where $\mathbf{x} \geq \mathbf{0}$. Such systems may be decided by either phase 1 of the Simplex algorithm ([6]) or the Fourier-Motzkin method ([13]).

4 Examples

Example 1

The following example, although somewhat contrived, illustrates the steps of the algorithm presented in section 3.

$$A[5i + j + 5, -2i + 5j + 10] = 0.0, \text{ if } i = 0 \vee j = 0$$
$$= f(A[i, j]), \text{ otherwise} \quad (14)$$

*See [6] for the definition of a basic feasible solution and detailed discussion of the Simplex algorithm.

where f is some function. Assume also for this specification that the ranges of the index sets for i and j are given by $\{i : 0 \leq i \leq 120\}$ and $\{j : 0 \leq j \leq 100\}$ respectively*. Applying the hyperplane assumption from equation (2) to the subscript expressions of A in the assertion above yields:

$$a(5i + j + 5) + b(-2i + 5j + 10) > ai + bj \qquad (15)$$

which can be re-written as:

$$(4i + j + 5)a + (-2i + 4j + 10)b > 0 \qquad (16)$$

Inequality (16) can be considered as a linear inequality in the variables a and b with coefficients $(4i+j+5)$ and $(-2i+4j+10)$ which are affine symbolic expressions in i and j.

In matrix notation, the affine mapping L defined by the symbolic expressions in i and j is given by:

$$L\left(\begin{bmatrix} i \\ j \end{bmatrix}\right) = \mathbf{D}\begin{bmatrix} i \\ j \end{bmatrix} + \mathbf{e} = \begin{bmatrix} 4 & 1 \\ -2 & 4 \end{bmatrix}\begin{bmatrix} i \\ j \end{bmatrix} + \begin{bmatrix} 5 \\ 10 \end{bmatrix}$$

Further, i and j are bounded within a rectangle $\mathcal{S} = \{(i,j) : 0 \leq i \leq 120, 0 \leq j \leq 100\}$ because of available information about the index sets of i and j. The situation is illustrated in figure 3.

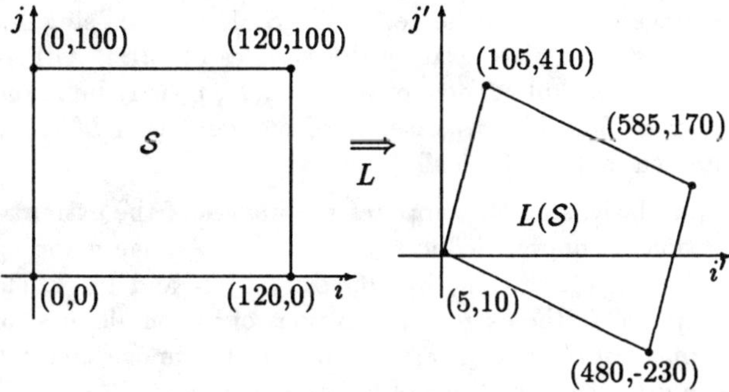

Figure 3: Regions $\mathcal{S}$ and $L(\mathcal{S})$

The steps of algorithm 3.1 applied to this example are outlined below.

Step 1: It is clear that $K \cap \mathcal{S} = \phi$ since equivalently, $\mathbf{0} \notin L(\mathcal{S})$. Therefore continue.

Step 2: The vertices of $\mathcal{S}$ are (0,0), (0,100), (120,0), and (120,100). Form the matrix $\mathbf{S}$ whose columns are the vertices of $\mathcal{S}$.

$$\mathbf{S} = \begin{bmatrix} 0 & 0 & 120 & 120 \\ 0 & 100 & 100 & 0 \end{bmatrix}$$

There are no directions of unboundedness for this example, thus $\mathbf{Y}$ is empty.

Step 3: Compute $\mathbf{S}' = L(\mathbf{S}) = \mathbf{DS} + \mathbf{E} =$

$$\begin{bmatrix} 4 & 1 \\ -2 & 4 \end{bmatrix}\begin{bmatrix} 0 & 0 & 120 & 120 \\ 0 & 100 & 100 & 0 \end{bmatrix} + \begin{bmatrix} 5 & 5 & 5 & 5 \\ 10 & 10 & 10 & 10 \end{bmatrix} =$$

$$\begin{bmatrix} 5 & 105 & 585 & 485 \\ 10 & 410 & 170 & -230 \end{bmatrix}$$

Step 4: Since $\mathbf{Y}$ is empty in this example, so is $\mathbf{Y}'$.

Step 5: The points (105,410) and (485,-230) are extremal points, each of which is not a multiple of a convex combination of the other points in $L(\mathcal{S})$. Therefore, the matrix $\mathbf{V}$ is given by:

$$\mathbf{V} = \begin{bmatrix} 105 & 485 \\ 410 & -230 \end{bmatrix}.$$

Step 6: Since $\mathbf{Y}'$ is empty in this example, so is $\mathbf{W}$.

Step 7: Return $\mathbf{V}$ and $\mathbf{W}$.

The output $\mathbf{V}$ corresponds to the inequalities:

$$105a + 410b > 0 \qquad (17)$$
$$485a - 230b > 0 \qquad (18)$$

Divide out the greatest common divisors of the coefficients of each inequality to obtain:

$$21a + 82b > 0 \qquad (19)$$
$$97a - 46b > 0 \qquad (20)$$

which describe a feasible region $\mathcal{A}$ for a and b as shown in figure 4.

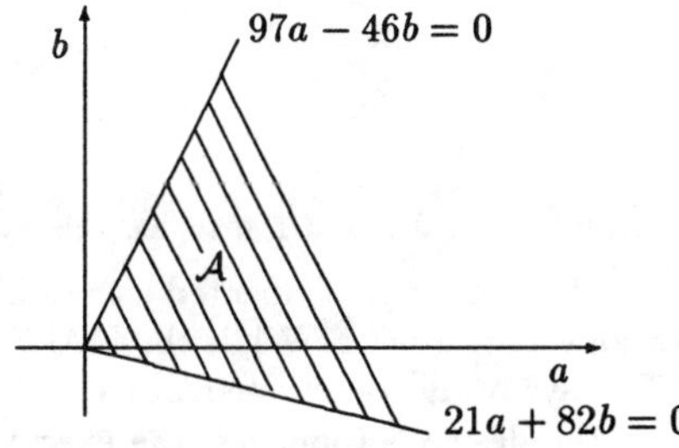

Figure 4: Feasible region $\mathcal{A}$

Example 2

Recall the specification of the Pascal's Triangle example given in equation (5) and the two symbolic inequalities (8) and (9) which arose from the data dependencies for this specification. Algorithm 3.1 is applied independently to each of these inequalities as follows.

Inequality (8) is expressed in matrix form as $\mathbf{a} \cdot (\mathbf{Di} + \mathbf{e}) > 0$ where $\mathbf{a} = [a, b]$,

$$\mathbf{D} = \begin{bmatrix} 1 & -1 \\ -1 & 1 \end{bmatrix}, \ \mathbf{i} = \begin{bmatrix} i \\ j \end{bmatrix}, \text{ and } \mathbf{e} = \begin{bmatrix} 0 \\ 1 \end{bmatrix}.$$

The only assumptions which we can make about the range of i and j is that $i \geq 1$ and $j \geq 1$, thus i and j are bounded within the region $\mathcal{S} = \{(i,j) : 1 \leq i, 1 \leq j\}$. In the interest of space, we omit a detailed trace of algorithm 3.1. Algorithm 3.1 produces the outputs:

*In the high level specification language PS, bounds on the index variables are declared by the user.

$$\mathbf{V} = \begin{bmatrix} 0 \\ 1 \end{bmatrix} \text{ and } \mathbf{W} = \begin{bmatrix} -1 & 1 \\ 1 & -1 \end{bmatrix},$$

which should be interpreted as a mixed system of strict and non-strict inequalities:

$$\begin{bmatrix} a & b \end{bmatrix} \begin{bmatrix} 0 \\ 1 \end{bmatrix} > 0 \tag{21}$$

and

$$\begin{bmatrix} a & b \end{bmatrix} \begin{bmatrix} -1 & 1 \\ 1 & -1 \end{bmatrix} \geq 0 \,. \tag{22}$$

This procedure is repeated for the second symbolic symbolic inequality (9) which arose in the Pascal's Triangle example. In this case, algorithm 3.1 produces the system of inequalities:

$$\begin{bmatrix} a & b \end{bmatrix} \begin{bmatrix} 1 \\ 0 \end{bmatrix} > 0 \tag{23}$$

and

$$\begin{bmatrix} a & b \end{bmatrix} \begin{bmatrix} -1 & 1 \\ 1 & -1 \end{bmatrix} \geq 0 \tag{24}$$

The system given by (23) and (24) above may be re-written and combined with the previous result in system (21) – (22) to obtain:

$$\begin{aligned} a &> 0 & (25) \\ b &> 0 & (26) \\ a - b &\geq 0 & (27) \\ -a + b &\geq 0 \,. & (28) \end{aligned}$$

Note the schedule $a = 1$ and $b = 1$ satisfies this system.

Algorithm 3.1 has been implemented using MACSYMA and exact (rational) arithmetic. While the MACSYMA implementation always produces a system of inequalities guaranteed to have the desired properties, the execution times for typical examples are much too long for use in a compiler. For this reason, algorithm 3.1 was also implemented using PASCAL and floating point arithmetic*. Table 1 gives average** execution times in milliseconds for symbolic inequalities (16) and (8) on a variety of machines. These times are well within acceptable limits for practical use in a compiler.

Table 1: Execution Times (Milliseconds) for Sample Problems.

Example	Vax 780	Vax 8500	Sun 3/180
Inequality (16)	79.4	25.1	129.4
Inequality (8)	24.9	7.1	31.2

*The extent to which rounding errors could cause an incorrect system of inequalities to be produced remains to be investigated.

**Averages were taken over 100 trials with identical inputs. Input and output times are excluded from these measurements. These times represent averages of the user time as returned by the standard UNIX "getrusage" function.

5 Correctness of Algorithm 3.1

The following lemmas and discussion sketches a correctness proof of algorithm 3.1. See [5] for a more detailed discussion.

In step [1], if $K \cap \mathcal{S} \neq \phi$, then there can be no $\mathbf{a}$ satisfying inequality (12) for all values $\mathbf{i} \in \mathcal{S}$ (no schedule satisfying the data dependencies). A proof is as follows.

Suppose $K \cap \mathcal{S} \neq \phi$. Let $\bar{\imath} \in \mathbf{K} \cap \mathcal{S}$. Since $\bar{\imath} \in \mathcal{S}$, $\bar{\imath}$ satsifies $\mathbf{a} \cdot (\mathbf{D}\bar{\imath} + \mathbf{e}) > 0$. But since $\bar{\imath} \in K$, $\bar{\imath}$ also satsifies $\mathbf{D}\bar{\imath} + \mathbf{e} = \mathbf{0}$. By substitution, we then have $\mathbf{a} \cdot \mathbf{0} > 0$; clearly there can be no such $\mathbf{a}$.

The condition $K \cap \mathcal{S} = \phi$ is also *sufficient* for the existence of a valid schedule. The reader is referred to [5] for a proof.

In step [2], the vertices $s_1, s_2, ..., s_m$ and the unbounded edges $u_1, u_2, ..., u_p$ form a characterization of the region $\mathcal{S}$ which allows us to easily find the image of $\mathcal{S}$ under L. For the purposes of algorithm 3.1, only the directions of unboundedness corresponding to $u_1, u_2, ..., u_p$ are essential.

Step [3] computes the images of the vertices of $\mathcal{S}$ under the affine mapping L, $s'_1, s'_2, ..., s'_m$. by straightforward matrix operations. By convexity of $\mathcal{S}$ and the affine property of L, the vertices of the image of $\mathcal{S}$ under L are a subset of the image under L of the vertices of $\mathcal{S}$. If L is non-singular then $s'_1, s'_2, ..., s'_m$ are exactly the vertices of $L(\mathcal{S})$. Otherwise, if L is singular, some of the $s'_1, s'_2, ..., s'_m$ may be in the interior of $L(\mathcal{S})$. In any case, all of the vertices of $L(\mathcal{S})$ are contained in $\{ s'_1, s'_2, ..., s'_m \}$.

Similarly, step [4] computes the images of the extremal directions of unboundedness of $\mathcal{S}$ under the affine mapping L, $y'_1, y'_2, ..., y'_p$. Again, by convexity of $\mathcal{S}$ and the affine property of L, the extremal directions of unboundedness of the image of $\mathcal{S}$ under L are a subset of the image under L of the extremal directions of unboundedness of $\mathcal{S}$.

The characterization of $L(\mathcal{S})$ computed by step [3] and step [4] is formally justified in lemmas 5.1 and 5.2.

Steps [5] and [6] serve only to reduce the size of the output system of inequalities. The claimed properties of the outputs $\mathbf{V}$ and $\mathbf{W}$ also apply to $\mathbf{S}'$ and $\mathbf{Y}'$ after step [4].

Finally, lemmas 5.1 – 5.3 establish the claimed property of the output $\mathbf{V}$ and $\mathbf{W}$.

Lemma 5.1 *Let $\mathcal{S}$ be a convex set with linear boundaries (i.e., a convex polyhedron) and let $L{:}\mathcal{Q}^k \to \mathcal{Q}^k$ be an affine mapping. Let $s_1, s_2, ..., s_m$ denote the vertices of $\mathcal{S}$, then the vertices of $L(\mathcal{S})$ are contained in $\{L(s_1), L(s_2), ..., L(s_m)\}$.*

proof: See [5] p. 15.

Lemma 5.1 establishes that in the context of step [5], the set $\{s'_1, s'_2, ..., s'_m\}$ contains the vertices of $L(\mathcal{S})$. The next lemma gives a similar result for the unbounded edges of $L(\mathcal{S})$.

Lemma 5.2 *Let $L{:}\mathcal{Q}^k \rightarrow \mathcal{Q}^k$ be an affine mapping given by $L(\mathbf{x}) = \mathbf{D}\mathbf{x} + \mathbf{e}$. Further, let $y_1, y_2, ..., y_p$ denote the extremal directions of unboundedness of a convex set with linear boundaries $\mathcal{S}$, and for $1 \le j \le p$ let $y'_j = \mathbf{D}y_j$ denote the images of $y_1, y_2, ..., y_p$ under L, then the extremal directions of unboundedness of $L(\mathcal{S})$ are contained in $\{y'_1, y'_2, ..., y'_m\}$.*

proof: See [5] p. 16.

Lemmas 5.1 and 5.2 show that $s'_1, s'_2, ..., s'_m$ in step [3] and $y'_1, y'_2, ..., y'_p$ in step [4] form an appropriate characterization of $L(\mathcal{S})$. The next lemma is the main result of this section and encapsulates the essential idea in algorithm 3.1.

Lemma 5.3 *Let $\mathcal{S} \subset \mathcal{Q}^k$ be a convex region with linear boundaries and let $L : \mathcal{Q}^k \rightarrow \mathcal{Q}^k$ be an affine mapping. Let $\mathbf{D} \in \mathcal{Q}^{k \times k}$ and $\mathbf{e} \in \mathcal{Q}^k$ define L as in algorithm 3.1, i.e., $L(\mathbf{x}) = \mathbf{D}\mathbf{x} + \mathbf{e}$. Suppose further that $0 \notin L(\mathcal{S})$. Let $\mathbf{a} = (a_1, a_2, ..., a_k)$ be an indeterminate vector of length k. Let $\mathbf{S}'$ be the $k \times m$ matrix and $\mathbf{Y}'$ be the $k \times p$ matrix constructed by steps [2] through [4] of algorithm 3.1, then*

$$(\mathbf{aS}' > \mathbf{0} \ \& \ \mathbf{aY}' \ge \mathbf{0}) \Leftrightarrow (\forall \mathbf{x})_{\in L(\mathcal{S})}(\mathbf{a} \cdot \mathbf{x} > 0) \tag{29}$$

proof: ("$\Rightarrow$"). Suppose $\mathbf{aS}' > \mathbf{0}$ and $\mathbf{aY}' \ge \mathbf{0}$. Let $\tilde{\mathbf{x}} \in L(\mathcal{S})$ be an arbitrary fixed point. Note that $\tilde{\mathbf{x}} \ne \mathbf{0}$ since $\mathbf{0} \notin L(\mathcal{S})$. Since convexity is preseved under an affine mapping, $L(\mathcal{S})$ is a convex region with linear boundaries. Every point in $L(\mathcal{S})$ can be written as a non-trivial convex combination of the vertices of $L(\mathcal{S})$ and points on the unbounded edges of $L(\mathcal{S})$. Let $\mathbf{x}_1, \mathbf{x}_2, ..., \mathbf{x}_l$ denote the vertices of $L(\mathcal{S})$ and let $u_1 = (\mathbf{x}_{e_1}, \mathbf{d}_1), u_2 = (\mathbf{x}_{e_2}, \mathbf{d}_2), ..., u_r = (\mathbf{x}_{e_r}, \mathbf{d}_r)$ denote the unbounded edges of $L(\mathcal{S})$. Note that every point $\mathbf{z}$ on the unbounded edge $u = (\mathbf{x}, \mathbf{d})$ is of the form $\mathbf{z} = \mathbf{x} + t\mathbf{d}$ where $t \ge 0$. Thus $\tilde{\mathbf{x}}$ can be written as the convex combination

$$\tilde{\mathbf{x}} = c_1\mathbf{x}_1 + ... + c_l\mathbf{x}_l + c_{l+1}(\mathbf{x}_{e_1} + t_1\mathbf{d}_1) + ... + c_{l+r}(\mathbf{x}_{e_r} + t_r\mathbf{d}_r) \tag{30}$$

where

1. For $1 \le i \le l + r$, $c_i \ge 0$,
2. There exists some $1 \le j \le l + r$ such that $c_j > 0$,
3. For $1 \le j \le r$, $t_j \ge 0$,
4. $\sum_{i=1}^{l+r} c_i = 1$.

Distributing and collecting terms, equation (30) can be re-written as

$$\tilde{\mathbf{x}} = c'_1\mathbf{x}_1 + ... + c'_l\mathbf{x}_l + c'_{l+1}\mathbf{d}_1 + ... + c'_{l+r}\mathbf{d}_r \tag{31}$$

where

1. For all $1 \le i \le l + r$, $c'_i \ge 0$,
2. There exists some $1 \le j \le l$ such that $c'_j > 0$,
3. $\sum_{i=1}^{l+r} c'_i = 1$.

It is important to note here that one of the coefficients of the vertices $\mathbf{x}_1, \mathbf{x}_2, ..., \mathbf{x}_l$ is strictly positive in equation (31).

Let $\mathbf{s}'_1, \mathbf{s}'_2, ..., \mathbf{s}'_m$ denote the (points represented by) the columns of $\mathbf{S}'$. Similarly, let $\mathbf{y}'_1, \mathbf{y}'_2, ..., \mathbf{y}'_p$ denote the (directions represented by) the columns of $\mathbf{Y}'$. By lemma 5.1 and lemma 5.2, $\{\mathbf{x}_1, \mathbf{x}_2, ..., \mathbf{x}_l\} \subseteq \{\mathbf{s}'_1, \mathbf{s}'_2, ..., \mathbf{s}'_m\}$ and $\{\mathbf{d}_1, \mathbf{d}_2, ..., \mathbf{d}_r\} \subseteq \{\mathbf{y}'_1, \mathbf{y}'_2, ..., \mathbf{y}'_p\}$. Thus for some suitable indices $f_1, f_2, ..., f_l$ and $g_1, g_2, ..., g_r$, equation (31) can be re-written as

$$\tilde{\mathbf{x}} = c'_1\mathbf{s}'_{f_1} + ... + c'_l\mathbf{s}'_{f_l} + c'_{l+1}\mathbf{y}'_{g_1} + ... + c'_{l+r}\mathbf{y}'_{g_r} \ . \tag{32}$$

Now compute $\mathbf{a} \cdot \tilde{\mathbf{x}}$ using equation (32).

$$\mathbf{a} \cdot \tilde{\mathbf{x}} = \mathbf{a} \cdot (c'_1\mathbf{s}'_{f_1} + ... + c'_l\mathbf{s}'_{f_l} + c'_{l+1}\mathbf{y}'_{g_1} + ... + c'_{l+r}\mathbf{y}'_{g_r}) \tag{33}$$

$$= \underbrace{c'_1\mathbf{a} \cdot \mathbf{s}'_{f_1} + ... + c'_l\mathbf{a} \cdot \mathbf{s}'_{f_l}}_{} + \underbrace{c'_{l+1}\mathbf{a} \cdot \mathbf{y}'_{g_1} + ... + c'_{l+r}\mathbf{a} \cdot \mathbf{y}'_{g_r})}_{} \tag{34}$$

$$= \text{terms, one of which is } > 0 \ + \ \text{terms which are} \ge 0$$

Since $\mathbf{aS}' > \mathbf{0}$ (by hypothesis), then $\mathbf{a} \cdot \mathbf{s}'_{f_1} > 0, \mathbf{a} \cdot \mathbf{s}'_{f_2} > 0, ...,$ and $\mathbf{a} \cdot \mathbf{s}'_{f_l} > 0$. Since $c'_j > 0$ for some $1 \le j \le l$, we conclude that one of the terms $c'_1\mathbf{a} \cdot \mathbf{s}'_{f_1}, c'_1\mathbf{a} \cdot \mathbf{s}'_{f_2}, ..., c'_1\mathbf{a} \cdot \mathbf{s}'_{f_l}$ in equation (34) is strictly positive. Facts already established (including the hypothesis that $\mathbf{aY}' \ge \mathbf{0}$) guarantee that all the other terms in the sum (34) are non-negative. Thus the sum given by (34) is strictly positive and therefore $\mathbf{a} \cdot \tilde{\mathbf{x}} > 0$.

("$\Leftarrow$"). We now consider the implication (29) in the reverse direction. Suppose,

$$(\forall \mathbf{x})_{\in L(\mathcal{S})}(\mathbf{a} \cdot \mathbf{x} > 0) \ . \tag{35}$$

In particular, $\mathbf{s}'_1, \mathbf{s}'_2, ..., \mathbf{s}'_m$ belong to $L(\mathcal{S})$. Thus,

$$\begin{aligned} \mathbf{a} \cdot \mathbf{s}'_1 &> 0 \\ \mathbf{a} \cdot \mathbf{s}'_2 &> 0 \\ &\vdots \\ \mathbf{a} \cdot \mathbf{s}'_m &> 0 \end{aligned} \tag{36}$$

In matrix notation, the above system (36) is given by $\mathbf{aS}' > \mathbf{0}$. To show $\mathbf{aY}' \ge \mathbf{0}$, let $\mathbf{y}'_j$ be an arbitrary, fixed column of $\mathbf{Y}'$. It suffices to show $\mathbf{a} \cdot \mathbf{y}'_j \ge 0$. Let $\mathbf{y}_j$ denote the corresponding column of $\mathbf{Y}$ in step [2] of algorithm 3.1. Note that $\mathbf{y}_j$ is a direction of unboundedness of $\mathcal{S}$. Let $\mathbf{s}_i$ be the vertex (column i of $\mathbf{S}$ in step [2] of algorithm 3.1) from which direction $\mathbf{y}_j$ emanates. Let $u = (\mathbf{s}_i, \mathbf{y}_j)$ denote the unbounded edge in $\mathcal{S}$ corresponding to $\mathbf{s}_i$ and $\mathbf{y}_j$. For all $t \ge 0$, $\mathbf{z} = \mathbf{s}_i + t\mathbf{y}_j$ is on the unbounded edge u and is therefore in $\mathcal{S}$. Now consider the image of $\mathbf{z}$ under L.

$$\begin{aligned} L(\mathbf{z}) &= L(\mathbf{s}_i + t\mathbf{y}_j) &&= \mathbf{D}(\mathbf{s}_i + t\mathbf{y}_j) + \mathbf{e} \\ &= (\mathbf{D}\mathbf{s}_i + \mathbf{e}) + t\mathbf{D}\mathbf{y}_j &&= \mathbf{s}'_i + t\mathbf{y}'_j \end{aligned}$$

Thus, $(\forall t)_{\geq 0}(\mathbf{s}'_i + t\mathbf{y}'_j \in L(\mathcal{S}))$ and by hypothesis (35),

$$(\forall t)_{\geq 0}(\mathbf{a} \cdot (\mathbf{s}'_i + t\mathbf{y}'_j) > 0)\ . \tag{37}$$

Distributing, we have

$$(\forall t)_{\geq 0}(\mathbf{a} \cdot \mathbf{s}'_i + t\mathbf{a} \cdot \mathbf{y}'_j > 0)\ . \tag{38}$$

From inequality (38) we may conclude that $\mathbf{a} \cdot \mathbf{y}'_j \geq 0$ as follows. Suppose $\mathbf{a} \cdot \mathbf{y}'_j < 0$. Then for $t^* = -(\mathbf{a} \cdot \mathbf{s}'_i)/(\mathbf{a} \cdot \mathbf{y}'_j)$, (note $t^* > 0$), we have

$$0 > \mathbf{a} \cdot \mathbf{s}'_i + t^*\mathbf{a} \cdot \mathbf{y}'_j = \mathbf{a} \cdot \mathbf{s}'_i - \frac{\mathbf{a} \cdot \mathbf{s}'_i}{\mathbf{a} \cdot \mathbf{y}'_j}\mathbf{a} \cdot \mathbf{y}'_j = 0 \tag{39}$$

which is a contradiction. ∎

6 Summary

In summary, we present an algorithm to find the region of feasible hyperplane schedules (from which an optimal one may be selected) in the presence of certain types of symbolic entries in the dependency vectors. Algorithm 3.1 finds a small number of numeric inequalities which may be used in place of the original symbolic system. Once this numeric system is found, standard techniques appearing in [3], [4], [5], [8], and [9] for choosing an optimal schedule may be used. The algorithm has been implemented in MACSYMA and PASCAL. Performance results for two examples are presented.

References

[1] Maya B. Gokhale. "Algorithm Specification in a Very High Level Language". *Fall Joint Computer Conference*, 1987.

[2] Maya B. Gokhale. "Exploiting Loop Level Parallelism in a Nonprocedural Dataflow Program". *International Conference on Parallel Processing*, 1987.

[3] Leslie Lamport. "Parallel Execution of DO Loops". *Communications of the ACM*, February 1974.

[4] Thomas J. Myers and Maya B. Gokhale. "Parallel Scheduling of Recursively Defined Arrays". *Journal of Symbolic Computing*, to appear.

[5] Todd C. Torgersen. "Algebraic Techniques for Automatic Detection of Parallelism". *University of Delaware CIS Technical Report*, January 1988.

[6] Daniel Solow. Linear Programming: An Introduction to Finite Improvement Algorithms. North Holland, 1984.

[7] Tyrrell R. Rockafeller. Convex Analysis. Princeton University Press, 1970.

[8] Dan I. Moldovan and Jose A. B. Fortes. "Partitioning and Mapping Algorithms into Fixed Size Systolic Arrays". *IEEE Transactions on Computers*, Vol. C-35, No. 1, January 1986.

[9] Jose A. B. Fortes and F. Parisi-Presicce. "Optimal Linear Schedules for the Parallel Execution of Algorithms". *Proceedings of the 1984 International Conference on Parallel Processing*, August 1984, pp. 322-329.

[10] D. I. Moldovan, C. I. Wu, and Jose A. B. Fortes. "Mapping an Arbitrarily Large QR Algorithm into a Fixed Size VLSI Array". *Proceedings of the 1984 International Conference on Parallel Processing*, August 1984, pp. 365-373.

[11] Sun-Yuan Kung, K. S. Arun, Ron J. Gal-ezer, and D. V. Bhaskar Rao. "Wavefront Array Processor: Language, Architecture, and Applications". *IEEE Transactions on Computers*, Vol. C-31, No. 11, November 1982.

[12] Dan I. Moldovan. "On the Analysis and Synthesis of VLSI Algorithms". *IEEE Transactions on Computers*, Vol. C-31, No. 11, November 1982.

[13] R. J. Duffin. "On Fourier's Analysis of Linear Inequality Systems". *Mathematical Programming Study 1*, North Holland, 1974.

[14] Remi Triolet. "Direct Parallelization of CALL Statements". *Proceedings of the ACM SIGPLAN '86 Symposium on Compiler Construction, SIGPLAN Notices*, Vol. 21, No. 7, July 1986.

Mass Storage Systems - I

Chair: B.T. O'Lear
National Center for Atmospheric Research

NASA's Requirements for a Massive Space Science Data Bank

M. Halem and J. Green

Paper not received in time for publication.

Mass Storage Support for Supercomputing

Robert F. Bedoll

Boeing Computer Services

Mass Storage support for supercomputing at Boeing Computer Services is satisfied by a locally developed storage system known as FMS, the File Management System. The product of a joint development project between CDC and Boeing, it runs on a dedicated back-end system and communicates with multiple processor types through several different local area networks. FMS follows the proposed IEEE mass storage reference model. This paper discusses many of the problems and benefits which arise when implementing a file system which addresses supercomputing as a component of a large data center.

INTRODUCTION

Boeing Computer Services (BCS) is a division of the Boeing Company which provides a wide range of computing services to both The Boeing Company and to outside government and commercial entities. Within BCS, the Commercial/Engineering Services Group operates a data center consisting of large scale mainframes from Cray Research, Control Data, and IBM. The data-center provides engineering and scientific computing services to both the Boeing Company and to commercial customers throughout the world.

FMS, the File Management System, provides a common permanent-file storage system for the entire data center. As shown in the figure, FMS runs on a back end file storage node, which is a CDC Cyber 730 and Cyber 825. It is connected over multiple high-speed local-area networks to a Cray X-MP, 2 Cyber 760's, a Cyber 875, and an IBM 3091.

HISTORY

The FMS project began in 1979 with a joint study team consisting of representatives of the data-center and our Boeing Company users. Out of this effort came an initial requirements document which reflected several key concepts: a central file repository which would serve multiple machines, from multiple vendors, and support multiple storage media featuring a range of price and performance.

During 1980 and 1981, various options were analyzed and vendors were surveyed. An RFP was issued to vendors in August, 1982, specifying the requirements and the project ground rules. In early 1983, Control Data was selected for a joint-development project with Boeing. A joint Boeing-CDC design team was formed, and work began on the architecture and external design of FMS. The software was designed following early ideas on the mass storage reference model -- this allowed each team to develop major pieces of software separately, performing testing by simulating the interface and the other team's software. Production use began in August, 1985. The design and development of FMS required about 16 man years.

EXTERNAL DESIGN.

FMS is a centralized file repository for all the mainframes in our data center. It employs a common user interface across multiple mainframes, multiple vendors, and multiple storage media.

CH2617-9/88/0000/0217$01.00

FMS deals with complete copies of a file. It supports a hierarchical directory structure, with any number of subdirectories nested up to 7 levels deep. File and directory names may be up to 31 characters, and file titles and a number of other file attributes are provided to help the user identify and track his files. A complete set of access permissions may be set at the user, group, or company level.

The FMS command language was patterned after CDC's NOS/VE command language. The commands are identical on all systems, and for all storage levels. Commands fall into 5 categories: file, directory, display, backup, and session.

File commands deal with files, regardless of their storage media. Examples are:

STORE,FILE FETCH,file
DELETE-FILE
SET-FILE-PERMISSION
SET-FILE-DESCRIPTOR

Directory oriented commands:

CREATE-DIRECTORY
DELETE-DIRECTORY
SET-DIRECTORY-DESCRIPTOR
SET-WORKING-DIRECTORY

Display commands:

DISPLAY-FILE
DISPLAY-DIRECTORY
DISPLAY-FILE-PERMISSION

Session Control

SET-SESSION-ENVIRONMENT

Backup commands

DISPLAY-FILE-BACKUP
RELOAD-FILE-BACKUP

Multiple Machines and Vendors.

FMS deals with a multi-vendor environment by supporting 2 classes of files, native mode and shared mode. By default, a file is stored in native mode; such files cannot be reliably interchanged between different systems, but the retrieval on the same system is bit-for-bit identical with what was stored. By contrast, shared mode files are usually stored in an interchange format; such files may be shared between systems and automatic conversion will occur.

Multiple Storage Media.

FMS was designed to support many different types of storage, on multiple storage nodes. Currently, 2 levels are supported, disk and tape. Other than retrieval time, the distinction between these two storage media is invisible to the user.

The philosophy of tape storage on FMS is price driven, rather than space driven. In space driven systems, disk space is viewed as finite and managed by the data

BOEING WESTERN SERVICE CENTER CONFIGURATION

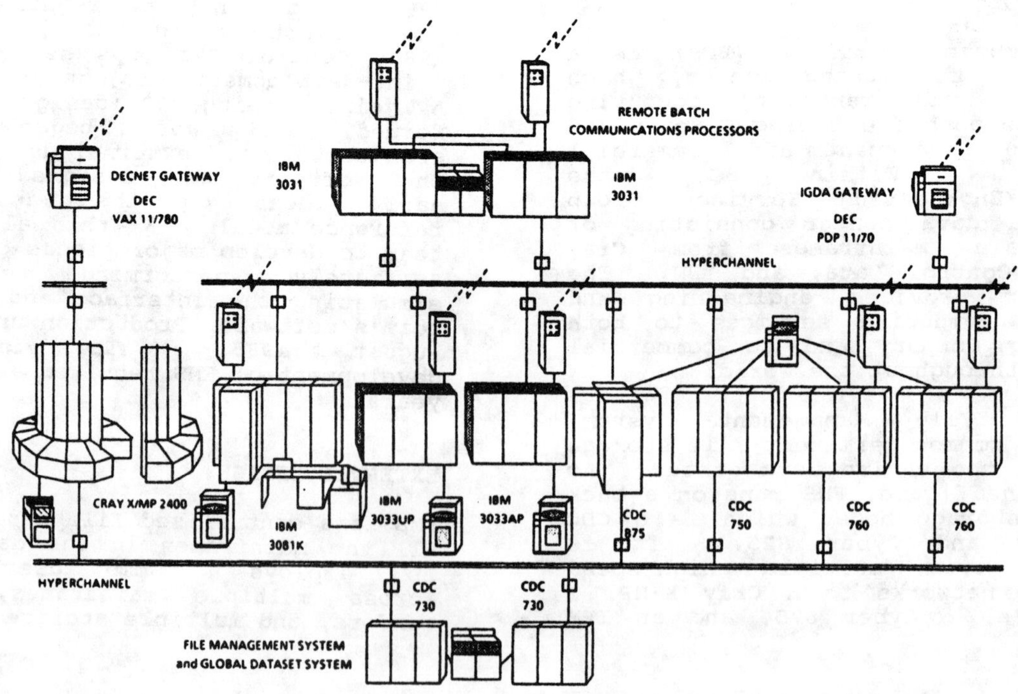

center on an as needed basis, with no user control. Tape becomes a disk overflow mechanism. FMS was designed to be price driven - disk space is viewed as infinite, and users are given a large price incentive to request that their files be made tape resident. In addition, FMS employs a simple space-time working set model for moving files to tape if they are larger than 200K characters and have not been accessed in 14 days. Hence, FMS allows the user to manage his storage cost by selecting his storage level (media).

To guarantee that tape-resident files can be read, FMS makes three tape copies: two are held locally, and one is sent to a vault for backup. All tapes are recycled and compacted on a 180 day cycle by copying active files onto a new set of tapes, and erasing the old set.

ARCHITECTURE.

FMS follows the design outlined in the proposed IEEE mass storage reference model, and consists of the following major components:

Communications Server.

FMS supports two different local area networks, but both are based on the Network Systems Corporation HYPERchannel product. Each network supplies both interprocess communication and file transfer. A locally developed network executive, known as HAM, is used to support our Cyber and Cray systems. HAM has been in use since 1981. To support our IBM VM systems, and for new systems such as SUNs and CRAY UNICOS, we use NETEX, which is a software package provided by Network Systems Corporation. To address the problems of two different network interfaces, we developed a common set of interfaces, known as the GNI - Generic Network Interface. This allows us to make identical network calls in all the FMS software, and to confine the network difference to the GNI routines.

Application Client.

The FMS client process is what we generally refer to as the User Interface (UI). The UI is a Fortran program - Fortran was chosen as the implementation language to ensure portability to multiple systems. At the time, neither the Cybers nor the Cray had a reasonable C implementation. The UI is called directly when the user enters an FMS command; it runs in the user's address space on the user's local machine. It accepts user commands, parses them, and converts them into an FMS protocol message, which is sent over the network to the directory manager.

Bitfile Server.

The FMS implementation of the bitfile server combines the concepts of a name server, request processor, and directory manager. A single server program, the Directory Manager (DM), performs all three functions. These concepts were combined for the purposes of implementation convenience and simplicity. The DM is a large Fortran program which processes almost all FMS commands. It uses CDCS, a data-base management system, to actually manage the FMS directory. The DM is a single threaded program which processes FMS requests in a sequential manner. Hence, several DMs run at the same time. The DM translates the user's FMS file name into a 'bitfile' name - thus acting as a name server.

Storage Manager.

Rather than multiple bitfile servers, FMS keeps a single directory manager, but supports multiple storage managers. As in the MSS reference model, the storage manager uses a bitfile ID and other retrieval information to locate the physical file. Currently, FMS uses the NOS indirect access file system as the disk storage manager. It uses a locally developed tape storage systems as the tape storage manager.

Migration Server.

As in the MSS reference model, the FMS migration server moves bitfiles within the storage hierarchy to optimize the performance of the MSS. Our migration server is actually implemented as a utility which runs on a daily basis.

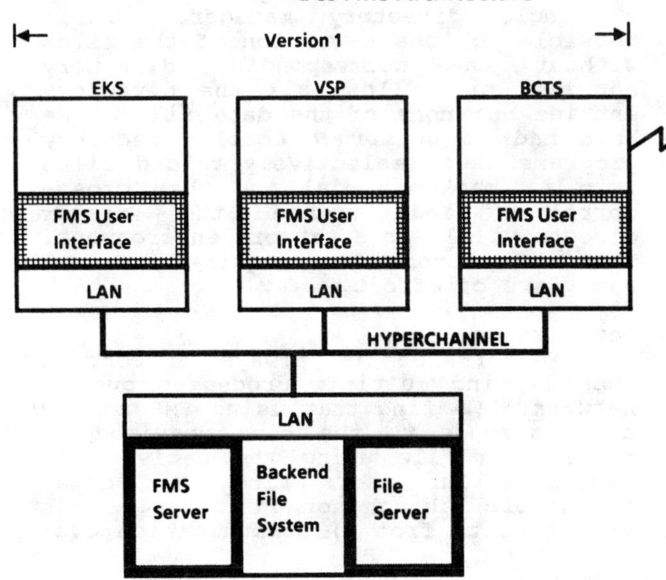

Site Manager Client.

The site manager client encompasses most of the FMS operator interface. This includes a set of utilities to do accounting, backup and recovery, space management, user account changes, operator visibility, and reporting. This aspect of an MSS is often neglected in preliminary designs, but we have found it to be one of the most complex and time consuming aspects of the entire FMS project.

UNIQUE PROBLEMS OF THE MSS APPROACH.

The concepts behind the mass-storage reference model allowed us to develop a modular and expandable system. However, such a system, particularly when distributed across multiple machines, possesses a number of unique problems.

Large Windows of Vulnerability.

All MSS systems have windows of exposure, for example, when a directory entry has been made, but before the data is actually saved. In a networked system, these windows are greatly enlarged because a) the interprocess communication between hosts takes longer than within a host, b) the probability of one machine failing while another keeps running is much greater. We have addressed these by a) on store operations, making directory entries both before and after the file is stored, b) accepting potential minor errors in last access information.

Very complex backup and recovery Schemes.

With multiple storage managers and a single directory manager, it is possible to lose a portion of the files without the corresponding directory entries, or to lose all the directory entries but none of the data files. We have had to construct complex recovery programs which selectively reload files from a backup medial and then cross-correlate and update the master directory, all in a network environment. This development has required several man-years of effort.

Performance.

Performance is always a concern when linking multiple processes over a network. We find that using FMS adds 2 to 3 seconds to the time required to retrieve a file using the native file system. Our users find this delay acceptable, though not desirable. This time results from a) communication over the network b) bringing into memory the directory and storage management processes, c) transferring data over the network.

Daily operational functions.

Daily functions such as accounting, backup dumps, migration, etc. are generally time consuming even on a single system. In a complex, networked environment, the time to do such activities increases greatly, and the complexity of the operations and the restart procedures can impose a major burden on operations and systems personnel.

Validation.

Users wish files to be stored under their own user name. When multiple systems are storing into the same file base, procedures must exist to ensure that user names are unique across the systems, and that identical user names on different systems are indeed identical users. We have taken steps to make FMS viable in this environment a) we have manual procedures to ensure that user names uniquely identify users, b) we operate all our machines as trusted hosts, c) when the user name on the originating host does not match an FMS user name, the user must supply an FMS user name and password.

File Structure and Character Sets.

Like file services such as FTP, FMS provides automatic conversion of file structure and character sets, but it places the burden on the user to identify that a file is binary or coded. Coded files are stored in a neutral data format and converted to proper format when retrieved. Reaching agreement on what file formats to support and how to map between formats on different machines was one of the most time consuming aspects of the FMS development.

System Checkout and Change Control.

Developing and testing new versions of FMS software is complicated by having processes on multiple machines. The thorough testing and quality assurance of such systems means dedicated test time on every system simultaneously - a costly investment.

Maintenance on Multiple Machines.

We maintain all code for all systems on a single source library, with conditional compilation directives. This eases the propagation of global changes into multiple operating systems, but it makes simple operating-system dependent changes more difficult.

FMS PRODUCTION EXPERIENCE.

FMS was introduced as an alternative to our NOS, COS, and VM permanent file systems. To use it, a user must convert his JCL; user conversion is strictly voluntary. To sell FMS to our users, we stress two themes: cost reduction and productivity.

Cost reduction has proven to be the most attractive aspect of FMS; we emphasize the trade-off of access-speed for storage cost when files are tape resident. Productivity is viewed by our users as a side benefit of FMS, rather than a primary motivation for using it.

User Acceptance.

FMS has been in production for 3 years, experiencing extremely steady growth. It currently controls about 100 gigabytes of data. This prompts several observations. First, users are slow to change, unless the change is invisible or forced upon them. Second, even clear cut cost savings, in a company with a high-profile cost saving campaign, does not guarantee acceptance. The reasons for this include: a) user inertia, especially for FMS where JCL changes are necessary, b) home grown capabilities have evolved over the years to solve the same problems FMS solves, c)there is always a cheaper way. FMS is more expensive than simply using magnetic tape for everything, and cost pressures often force users into less attractive but also less costly alternatives.

User Profile.

Somewhat to our surprise, FMS is being used in a manner different than the native file systems.

a. Users keep larger files on FMS than on the native on-line systems; the average file is about 10 times larger on FMS.

b. 1/4 of the FMS files are kept on disk, and 3/4 on tape, but 95% off all storage space is on tape. This has kept FMS on-line disk requirements relatively low.

c. FMS tape mounts average about 0.1% of the FMS files per day.

d. About 2/3 of the tape resident files are put on tape through explicit user request; the remainder migrate to tape based on the default migration algorithm.

e. A user settable migration algorithm, introduced at user request, is hardly used.

UNIX.

Like many sites, we are moving to a UNIX environment, and are attempting to fit FMS into the UNIX world. Our initial approach is to simply port the FMS user interface to UNIX; this will give our UNIX users complete access to FMS. We would like to merge FMS into the UNIX world, so that the FMS system appears as an extension of the user's native UNIX file system. We would also like to provide an NFS interface to FMS. As yet, we have no clean solutions for these requirements.

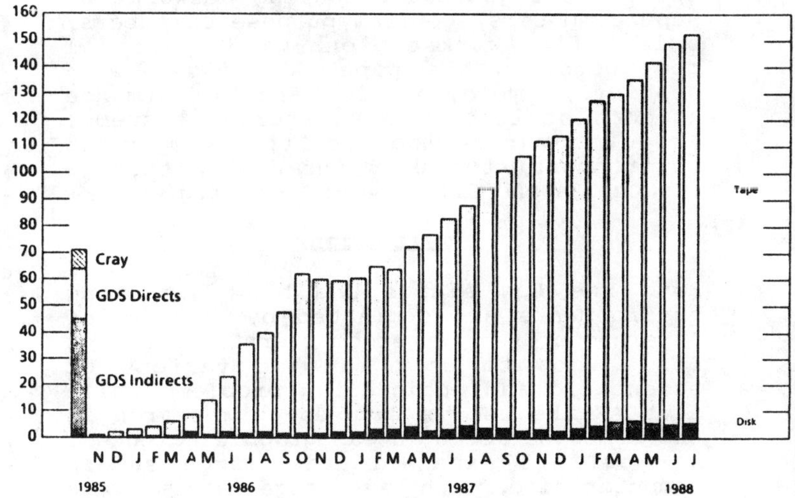

Profiles in Mass Storage: A Tale of Two Systems

Bill Collins
Marjorie Devaney

Computing and Communications Division
Los Alamos National Laboratory
Los Alamos, NM 87545

David Kitts

Scientific Computing Division
National Center for Atmospheric Research
P. O. Box 3000
Boulder, CO 80307

Abstract

The Los Alamos Common File System (CFS) and the NCAR Mass Storage System (MSS) are file storage and file management systems that serve heterogeneous computing networks of supercomputers, general purpose computers, scientific workstations and personal computers. This paper details philosophical, implementation and performance aspects of the two mass storage systems. Areas covered include the computing environment, the user interface, storage strategies and file movement strategies.

Environment

Both the Los Alamos and NCAR computing environments are dominated by the use of supercomputers. Supercomputers are used at Los Alamos to solve a wide variety of scientific and engineering problems while at NCAR the use is focused on research in the atmospheric and oceanographic sciences. As would be expected of a large supercomputer site, both have large data storage and data retrieval requirements. Both systems currently store over seven terabytes of data, are growing at the rate of over two terabytes per year and transfer over 50 gigabytes of data each day. Although Los Alamos has significantly more computational power and users, the NCAR data storage requirements are equivalent due to their more data intensive applications and large data bases.

The major uses of a centralized file storage system at Los Alamos and NCAR are:

• Archival Storage. Large quantities of infrequently accessed data are saved for long periods of time.

• Inactive Files. Files are off-loaded from the expensive supercomputer disk during periods of time when they are not being used.

• File Backup. Users, operating systems, and servers throughout the network have a reliable place to back up their permanent files.

• File sharing. Files may be conveniently shared between users and machines in a heterogeneous network.

The CFS Environment

The Los Alamos Integrated Computing Network (ICN) is a large scientific computing network that provides services for over 8,400 users. The ICN is a network of many different machines running eight different operating systems (CTSS, UNICOS, UNIX, VMS, NOS, MVS, VM/CMS and MS-DOS). The machines include supercomputers, general purpose computers, scientific workstations and personal computers. These resources are summarized in Figure 1. Network support servers are provided for such functions as file storage, output processing, data import/export, access control, accounting, and batch job submittal/control. The ICN is partitioned to allow classified computing, privacy computing and unclassified computing. The Common File System (CFS) provides a centralized file storage and file access capability for all machines and servers in all partitions [1]. The success of centralized mass storage systems has resulted in the CFS software being installed by seventeen other computing sites.

Worker Machines	QTY
CRAY X-MP/416	2
CRAY X-MP/48	2
CRAY X-MP/24	1
CRAY 1	4
IBM 3090-200	1
CDC CYBER	4
DEC Distributed Processors	160
SUN Workstations	400
IBM Workstations	100
Other Workstations	75
CRAY Y-MP/832 (4th Qtr. 1988)	2

Los Alamos Computing Network Resources

Figure 1

At Los Alamos, the supercomputers are primarily used interactively during the day, and for the running of batch production jobs during the night. The interactive use includes program development, job setup, running short jobs, and output analysis. Users submit production jobs to a job control server which selects where and when to run each job, using job and input files stored on CFS. The production jobs generate restart files and graphics files which are stored on CFS as they are generated. During the day, users analyze these graphics files using supercomputers and high performance graphics terminals.

Distributed processors have been used for a number of years to provide a general purpose computing capability at remote sites and to provide special computing services for the entire network. More recently, scientific workstations and personal computers have been connected to the network to provide stand-alone computing capabilities and pre/post processing for supercomputer applications. The distributed processors, scientific workstations and personal computers have the same access to the CFS capabilities as do the supercomputers. Each machine has a user-level utility for request/response communication with CFS, and has implemented the file transport protocol to transmit files with CFS and any other machine or server in the network.

The NCAR MSS Environment

The NCAR Scientific Computing Division provides supercomputing resources and services that support research in the atmospheric, oceanographic and related sciences. These functions are supported by computers and operating systems from various manufacturers that include COS, MVS, VM/CMS and VMS, and in the future, the UNICOS operating system will also be supported. These operating systems are run on supercomputers, general purpose computers, and workstations. Their resources are serviced by the NCAR Mainframe and Server network (MASnet) and TCP/IP networks. These networks supply communications for file storage, import/export of data, access control, and batch job submission. These resources are listed in Figure 2. The NCAR MSS provides centralized file storage and access capability for all machines and servers in this network and a high-speed data path that is a unique feature of this system.

At NCAR, supercomputers are currently operated in a batch job mode. Interactive use is available but lightly used. Future plans to support UNICOS as the operating system for supercomputers will facilitate user interactive access. Currently, a user selects the supercomputer to be used for execution of a job and submits a batch job control program via the MASnet system. Input files stored on the MSS are accessed as needed by the program. Using this facility, large production jobs are restarted and massive amounts of data acquired and disposed to the MSS. Supercomputers at NCAR have limited local storage in relation to the amount of data processed in some sessions. This limitation forces users to save data and restart-images on the MSS, because space allocation mechanisms used at NCAR will delete files on the supercomputer that are not in use, in order to make room for current space demands.

Worker Machines	QTY
CRAY X-MP/48	1
CRAY-1A	1
IBM 4381-P14	1
SUN Workstations	20
Other Workstations	50

NCAR Computing Resources

Figure 2

Implementation

Both the NCAR MSS and CFS software have been implemented to run as application programs under the IBM MVS operating system without any changes to MVS. MVS and the System 370 architecture provide software and hardware interfaces for high performance commercial storage systems, efficient I/O processing, large memory addressing, a rich software environment upon which to base a file storage system, and a wide range of processors to run the software. PL/1 was chosen as the implementation language by both sites since it provides a good multitasking environment and requires only a minimum of assembler code. The software of each system has elements providing the functions of the IEEE Mass Storage Reference Model [2]. These elements include the Name Server, Bitfile Server, Storage Server, Physical Volume Repository, and Bitfile Mover.

Implementation of the NCAR MSS

The selection of MVS/XA was done after examining operating systems of several manufacturers and was totally independent of the Los Alamos selection. Each of the processes that comprise the MSS constitute a separate MVS batch job. These batch jobs run independently of each other and communicate using the NCAR Inter Process Communication Subsystem (IPCS). The IPCS is an independent process which passes "messages" between other processes. The processes may be separate MVS batch jobs or separate tasks within the same batch job. IPCS is not a protocol. The protocol is defined by the two unrelated communicating processes. IPCS is only a message passer. An important feature of IPCS is the ability to add new processes to the MSS system without modifying all of the MSS software and, in many cases, without modifying any of the MSS software. New processes can be easily integrated into the MSS system and test processes can be executed concurrently with the production system.

Utilizing individual batch jobs enhances the MSS system availability and reliability. The use of the IPCS has isolated software failure. Modules that generate a problem can be automatically restarted avoiding failure in associated processes. If the MSS were run as a single batch job, a software failure could interrupt the entire system. Enhanced and maintenance versions of processes can be installed while the system is running by simply restarting the appropriate batch job.

IBM channels allow device independence that NCAR was unable to obtain using other products. This flexibility is demonstrated by the multiporting of the IBM storage devices between the IBM 4381 control processor and supercomputers. This access of storage devices is a unique implementation method which allows a supercomputer direct communication to IBM 3380 disk and IBM 3480 tape cartridges. This data link was discussed in another paper [3], and in this paper it is referred to as the Local Data Network (LDN).

IBM access methods were not used as an interface to the 3380 disk farm and the 3480 archive storage devices. Common and individual problems were encountered on each device which prevented the use of vendor access methods. A large physical record size (40 KB) facilitated data transfer over the LDN. However, physical records of this size are not supported under MVS/XA.

Implementation of CFS

CFS has progressed, with minimal changes, from the original use of 3350 disk, the 3850 Mass Storage System and a 370/148 processor to the current use of 3380 disk, 3480 tape, a 3090 primary processor and a 4381 backup processor. In large part, this was due to the extensive use made of the MVS software. This use includes the access methods for storage system input/output, standard IBM tape labeling, and the use of VSAM data sets for the CFS directory system. However, key areas of CFS such as file cataloging, space management, volume management, volume mounting and tape drive selection are done with CFS software to satisfy the CFS performance, reliability and security requirements, and so that changes and enhancements can be quickly made to deal with new performance, operational and user requirements. The CFS software is very robust, and is able to intercept and recover from most hardware errors without impacting system availability.

The CFS software consists of the Production Program which provides the File Server, Name Server, Storage Server and File Mover functions of the Reference Model, the File Migration Program which decides where in the storage hierarchy each file should reside, and support programs that perform system management functions such as directory backup, directory recovery, volume labeling, tape analysis, performance measurement, etc. The implementation of the Production Program is based upon the primary or driving functions being the user requests (get a file, store a file, etc.). Network input is done by a single router task which allocates a request task for each new user request and then directs subsequent input for the request to that task. Except for network input, the request task performs all processing of the request including storage system input/output, directory read/writes and network output. All the program modules are reentrant so they can be used simultaneously by multiple tasks. This architecture has resulted in a very efficient and easy-to-modify system. The use of external servers such as a storage system on another machine is not precluded.

User Interface

CFS and the NCAR MSS are complete file management systems which provide file storage, file access and file management capabilities to a diversity of users that include interactive humans, batch programs, operating systems and other network servers. The file management includes a human oriented naming capability as contrasted with the machine oriented "bitfile ID" of the Reference Model and a tree structured directory system that allows users to organize the storage of files in a manner that facilitates the file access and file management. Users have a device independent interface to CFS and MSS where the systems determine where files will reside based on file size and file activity. CFS and MSS do not support or recognize any data structure. Files are stored as bit strings. When the user wishes to access data in a file, the complete file is transmitted to the machine. If a user changes the file, the complete file must be transmitted back to the storage system. CFS and MSS provide the capability for users to group files on tape volumes so the files may be efficiently retrieved as a "family."

Both systems have kept the user interface at a very simple level by keeping most of the decision process at the user level. The user must take explicit action to store, retrieve, delete, convert and backup files. This requires the user to be more knowledgeable and to do more work, but gives more control and flexibility.

CFS User Interface

The CFS user interface provides requests to create, delete, modify, move, merge and list directory structures and directory information, and to save, replace, get, delete, move and copy files. An application level utility, called the CFS Interface, is available on all network machines to pass text string requests from the user to CFS. CFS will parse and execute the request, and send a text response back to the Interface utility which will pass the response back to the user. The Interface utility is easy to implement and easy to maintain since existing CFS requests can be modified and new CFS requests added without affecting the Interface utility. The Interface utility presents the same interface to users on all of the many operating systems for which it has been implemented. Other utilities that use the Interface utility provide higher level interfaces that are often tailored to specific operating systems and environments. Examples are a graphics window interface for UNIX based workstations, a menu driven interface for MVS, program callable interfaces for different languages and various utilities that provide wildcard capabilities.

The NCAR MSS User Interface

The user interface is determined by the operating system used for communicating with the NCAR MSS. Almost every computer at NCAR has existing software to transfer data between itself and others via the MASnet. Many of the operating systems have built-in facilities to do this, such as the COS ACQUIRE/DISPOSE mechanism [4]. The NCAR MSS uses native operating system interfaces, thereby reducing the need for users to learn a new interface to read and write files on the MSS.

When a user generates a new file which has a tree structure of undefined directories it is not necessary, and no capability is provided, to create empty directories. All necessary directory structures are created when a file is created. When the last entry in a directory is removed, the directory is deleted from the tree structure. In addition, if any directory parent becomes empty it is also removed. Separate utilities are provided to modify directory and file names, touch a file to reset retention time for archival purposes, delete files, and to request status and all attributes of a file or directory.

Storage Stragegies

Storage strategies used by the NCAR MSS and CFS are very similar. They both use IBM 3380 disk for active file storage and group the disk files by size to minimize fragmentation problems. Migration algorithms move inactive files from disk to IBM 3480 archival tape cartridges based on idle time and file size, and archival files are migrated back to disk when they become active.

Neither system allows a file to span multiple volumes and thus restrict the maximum file size to about 200 megabytes. Each system has its own unique format for files. Therefore, both NCAR and Los Alamos have special systems to "import/export" external files. Special utilities are responsible for purging files whose release dates have passed, and for clearing volumes and reclaiming fragmented space.

Strategies of the NCAR MSS

In most cases data written to the MSS is routed to disk. This data is duplicated onto archive tape within five days. This results in a form of temporary backup until the file migration program deletes the disk copy.

Cartridge volume space allocation and formats are handled by the MSS. All cartridge volumes in the MSS are preformatted with non-MVS volume labels which allow the cartridges to be mounted on nonspecific drives. Each volume has a header block with a copy of the Master File Directory (MFD) entry for that volume. Each file on a volume has a header and trailer block with a copy of the MFD entry for that file (before and after write). The MSS uses standard MVS space allocation for disk volumes. Disk volumes and disk files do not have the specal MSS header blocks.

Each file has a checksum stored as its last block. MSS includes a utility to verify the data on randomly selected archive volumes using this checksum. Historically, this utility has enabled NCAR to predict deteriorating media and to detect unreadable data before a client discovers the problem.

Strategies of CFS

Besides the 3380 disks and the 3480 archive tape systems, CFS has a 3480 active tape system where very large files are written directly from the network to tape cartridges. These active tapes are stored near the tape drives for faster mounting and would be candidates for automation. CFS also supports a variety of other storage systems, including various disk systems, round tapes, the IBM 3850 MSS, the Automated Tape Library for round tape and the MASSTOR M860. Standard MVS access methods are used.

CFS uses bitmaps to handle the space allocation for all volumes. The size of the allocation unit can be varied for different disk volumes to give storage efficiency. A disk file on CFS can be stored in five non-contiguous extents. All tape volumes within CFS use standard MVS labels.

All files within CFS consist of one or more data blocks. Each block is labeled with information that identifies the file to which the data belongs and the classification of the data. The label is verified before the data block is transmitted over the network. The label may also contain a checksum for each block, for error detection and recovery at the data block level.

File Movement Strategies

It is with file movement that CFS and the NCAR MSS differ most significantly. The NCAR MSS allows the supercomputers to directly read and write the storage systems. This approach gives higher data transfer rates and allows a smaller control processor to be used. CFS requires all storage system access to be through the control processor which provides better integrity and security.

File Movement in CFS

The CFS file movement strategy is to simultaneously transmit many files using multiple direct connections to the Los Alamos File Transport System. All supercomputers and some of the other network servers are also directly connected to the File Transport System. Other machines and servers are connected through gateways. The File Transport System is a number of Gould computers connected in a ring to provide a high performance store and forward network. This File Transport System offers the advantages of having large memory to buffer transmissions, and the intelligence to restrict communications and thus enforce security partitioning in the network. Burst rates of 50 Mb/sec are supported. Los Alamos developed protocols and networking software provide message passing, process-to-process communication, end-to-end file transmission, and remote procedure calls. Implementation of the networking software allows any machine to communicate with any other machine within the security rules, and to use the services of all network servers including CFS. DECNET networks of VAX distributed processors and TCP/IP networks of scientific workstations and personal computers are connected through gateways to the File Transport System.

The CFS software also supports the Network Systems HYPERchannel™ network which is used by most CFS sites either with NETEX™ or with direct drivers. The CDC Loosely Coupled Network and the Cray Superlink are used by one CFS site, and another CFS site uses the MASSTOR MASSNET™ protocol.

File Movement in the NCAR MSS

There are two strategies used to move files within the NCAR MSS. The first services supercomputers via the LDN, the second services network nodes with small file requirements on the MASnet. The LDN allows up to six parallel data streams to be moving data. Each stream can move data at a 3 MB/sec. burst rate for a total system bandwidth of 18 MB.

The file movement through the MSS to a supercomputer starts with a request being presented to the COS MSS control kernel via the COS ACQUIRE/DISPOSE mechanism. This kernel makes certain low-level parameter checks and forms a message packet which is sent to the mass storage control processor via a Network Systems HYPERchannel™ adapter connection. The processor accepts the message, makes further validity checks and queues the request for processing. When resources are available the medium is mounted and positioned, if necessary, and the data path to be used in the LDN is assigned. A message is returned to the supercomputer requesting data be moved via the LDN between a specified device and CPU local disk. When finished, control is returned to the requesting client. If, during a read request, the second access has occurred during a two-day period the data will be migrated from archive storage to the disk farm thereby increasing the chance of the data being read from an online device the third time it is needed.

A file moving through MASnet follows a similar procedure to the LDN path. A request is made from a node on MASnet and received by the MSS. Next, all parameters are verified and a data path prepared. A write to the MSS requires space be allocated on the disk farm. A read from the MSS requires that the data be resident on the disk farm. Once a path has been prepared, data is moved between the disk farm and MASnet. When finished, the MFD is updated and the request is acknowledged complete.

Performance

Both the NCAR MSS and CFS provide a high level of performance, reliability and availability. The MSS uses fast, dedicated paths with the supercomputers while CFS relies on being able to transmit many files in parallel. Both systems have had very good experiences with IBM 3380 disk and 3480 tape. Neither site has lost a file due to 3380 hardware or media problems and only a few files have been lost from 3480 hardware and media problems. Both systems use multiple controllers and multiple paths to provide a high degree of redundancy. Failing equipment is automatically or manually removed from operation without affecting system availability.

NCAR MSS Performance

At the time the MSS was planned and designed, several studies indicated a need for a high bandwidth data path [5]. As compute power, memory, and local disk storage increased, the requirement for high-bandwidth also increased. A relatively small number of large files occupy most of the MSS. Moving these data between a CPU and a device becomes significant. The LDN has provided these transmission rates. We see a maximum data rate of 20 Mb/sec. with an average data rate of 10 Mb/sec. When data is moved over the MASnet the maximum data rate is about 3.5 Mb/sec. with an average rate of less than 1 Mb/sec. The above rates are measured from the time the bitfile mover is granted permission to move data until the request is satisfied.

CFS Performance

The most important CFS performance requirement is to satisfy requests from interactive users in a timely manner. Currently, 97 percent of the 24,000 file transfer requests that typically occur each day are satisfied from disk, where, for machines connected to the File Transport System, the average response is five seconds from the time of the request until the file has been transmitted. The response time depends on the file size and the transmission rate which can vary from 10 Mb/sec for supercomputers to 10 kilobits/sec for personal computers. For the supercomputers, file transmission rates of 5 Mb/sec for disk and 8 Mb/sec for tape are typical.

The most demanding performance requirement is when a large number of graphics files are retrieved from CFS for analysis on the supercomputers. For instance, it is common for a designer to transfer a gigabyte of data which at 5 megabits/sec would take almost 30 minutes. Users improve their response time by sending multiple requests to CFS and transmitting three or four files in parallel.

To keep pace with increasing supercomputer capacity and problem requirements, a goal is to double the CFS file transmission rate in the coming year. The IBM 3990 cache controller will mask most of the disk rotational delay and increase the burst data transfer to 36 Mb/sec. Also, changes will be made to more easily allow users to transmit multiple files simultaneously. The current CFS throughput of about 100 megabits/sec can be increased to provide as much parallelism as is needed.

Future Directions

The future of mass storage systems such as CFS and the NCAR MSS will be to provide storage for extremely large amounts of data and increase the bandwidth at which large amounts of data can be moved. New storage media such as optical disk, optical tape, VHS tape, 8mm tape and any exotic technology yet to be developed will be considered. The media must have capacities on the order of hundreds of gigabytes. Files this large will be generated by future supercomputers. Data transfer rates will have to be over 100 MB/sec in order to move the large files. As file sizes grow, the current top-level error rates of 10^{-14} will have to be improved. Storage system interfaces must be made standard to allow their easy use and interchange by mass storage systems. Current magnetic devices will have to be improved in the near future in order to process the immediate needs of the mass storage community. Robotics for archival storage devices are needed in order to process the large number of mounts across a randomly accessed, large capacity storage.

Future Directions for CFS

The future directions of CFS are being driven by the future directions of the Los Alamos Computing Network. As part of the movement toward the use of standard network protocols and the use of UNIX as a standard operating system, the TCP/IP suite will be implemented in CFS and new CFS interfaces will be developed based on UNIX syntax and conventions. As the use of workstations grows, better CFS interfaces that exploit the graphics capabilities of workstations will be developed, and implementations will be done to provide better storage solutions for an environment of integrated supercomputers and workstations. For instance, a CFS front-end could be developed to provide a Sun Network File System interface to CFS. Ways to provide file transparency throughout the user's environment will be investigated.

The acquisition of more powerful supercomputers, the availability of higher performance graphics and the implementation of a very high-speed network based on the Los Alamos proposed High-Speed Channel (HSC) [6] will greatly increase the CFS file access and file storage requirements. To meet these requirements, high-performance storage systems such as disk arrays and VHS tape systems will have to be acquired. It is likely that these storage systems will be managed by CFS but the data will be accessed directly by the supercomputers. This would have to be done in such a manner that the stringent CFS security and integrity requirements are not compromised. A planned first step is to give supercomputers direct access to the CFS 3480 tape drives.

Future Directions in the NCAR MSS

There are plans to provide an interface for the TCP/IP which would allow the File Transfer Protocol (FTP) access to the NCAR MSS. Plans are also under consideration to provide a process to allow devices compatible with the Small Computer System Interface (SCSI) standards. These devices will not be attached to the MSS LDN. A separate access will be provided by attaching an IBM RT to the IBM 4381 and using its SCSI compatible port. This will allow access to many forms of media including tapes such as 8mm and VHS tapes. In addition to these media, there are slow speed optical disks currently available on the market that are interfaced on SCSI channels. An RT access to SCSI ports promises to provide a flexible and speedy path for clients to introduce data into the MSS.

Future media storage systems will be increasing in capacity and reliability. New disks are already available for replacing the 120 GB disk farm which will increase storage capacity to 240 GBs and increase the bandwidth to 4.5 MB/sec. These devices are available from IBM and other manufacturers and are compatible to current IBM channel specifications.

References

[1] B. Collins and C. Mexal, "The Los Alamos common file system," Tutorial Notes, Ninth IEEE Symposium on Mass Storage Systems, October, 1988.

[2] S. Miller, "IEEE reference model for mass storage systems, version 2.0," SRI Project 4211, Technical Report, 4211-87-TR208, October 1987.

[3] M. Nelson, D. Kitts, J. Merrill, and E. Harano, "The NCAR mass storage system," Digest of Papers, Eighth IEEE Symposium on Mass Storage Systems, pp. 12-20, May 11-14, 1987.

[4] COS Version 1, Reference Manual, SR-0011, Cray Research, Inc., Mendota Heights, Minnesota, 1986.

[5] P. Rotar and R. Jenne, "Mass storage system requirements and projections," Proceedings, Third Annual Computer Users Conference, NCAR Technical Note (NCAR-TN/219+PROC), pp. 90-107, November, 1983.

[6] D. Tolmie, "High speed channel (HSC)," ANSI Draft X3T9.3/88-023, June 29, 1988.

Supercomputer Performance

Chair: Raul Mendez
Institute for Supercomputing Research

Vector and Parallel Processing of the Nuclear Reactor Transient Analysis Code RELAP5

Misako ISHIGURO
Japan Atomic Energy Research Institute
Tokai, Ibaraki, Japan

Mitsuhiro MAKINO and Naohisa SHINOZAWA
FUJITSU Ltd.
Shinkamata, Ota, Tokyo, Japan

An experiment of vector processing and multi-tasking of nuclear reactor transient analysis code RELAP5 has been made at Japan Atomic Energy Research Institute. Vector processing and multi-tasking of the RELAP5 were achieved by using the independency of the spatial meshes. The vectorization ratio is 83%. The performance ratio in the vector mode to that in the scalar mode is about 3 on the FACOM VP-100. For multi-tasking, the spatial meshes are halfed and each group of meshes is processed on different processor. The effect of multi-tasking was estimated from the CPU time on the FACOM VP-100, which is single processor system. The improvement of wall clock time will be about 1.6 for parallelized subroutines. The total improvement of wall clock time will be about 1.2 because of parallelization ratio 45%.

1. Introduction

A demand for high speed computation in the field of nuclear energy research has been increased for analyzing complex physical phenomena. An effort of vector processing of nuclear codes has started at Japan Atomic Energy Research Institute (JAERI) since 1976. First step of the effort is the feasibility study of vector processing for various nuclear codes. The distribution of the execution time consuming parts in the nuclear codes was analyzed. The possibility of vector processing of these parts was investigated. Some nuclear codes were executed on a FACOM 230-75 APU which is a pipelined array processor and an ancester of FACOM VP. These investigations showed that most of nuclear codes could not achieve significantly higher performance on a vector processor by using the automatic vectorization, but restructuring of the nuclear codes was required to provide the vectorization ratio necessary for sizable performance gains.

After the installation of the two FACOM VP-100s at JAERI in 1984 and 1986, the vectorization, that is, changing the program structure, replacing kernel algorithms and tuning the DO-loop structure of subroutines, has been done for more than 40 nuclear codes [1]. These codes have been selected out among the codes used frequently at JAERI computing center. The research area in which the vectorized codes are used covers reactor safety analysis, design of tokamak fusion system, and reactor engineering.

The system configuration of computing center at JAERI in 1988 is shown in Fig. 1.1. Two VP-100 systems and three general purpose computer FACOM M-780 systems are installed.

Although nuclear codes are successfully processed on the vector processor, some codes require still higher computational speed. An example of such codes is the thermohydraulic reactor codes which simulate the transient behavior of nuclear reactor at its accident. In order to predict the anticipated danger of the reactor accident, the codes should run faster than the transient of reactor. The RELAP5 code [2] is the typical code used for the reactor transient analysis. The code has been developed at Idaho National Engineering Laboratory (INEL) for analyzing transient behavior of reactor including Loss of Coolant flow Accident (LOCA). The code has been heavily used at JAERI to analyze the experimental results.

The vectorization of RELAP5/MOD2 code has been done at JAERI. It runs in the vector mode on the FACOM VP-100 about 3 times as fast as that in the scalar mode. Another approach for speedup of code is the parallel processing attempted at INEL [3]. The attempt for multi-tasking of RELAP5/ MOD1 has made and they reported that the execution speed increases 1.7 times on the four processors in

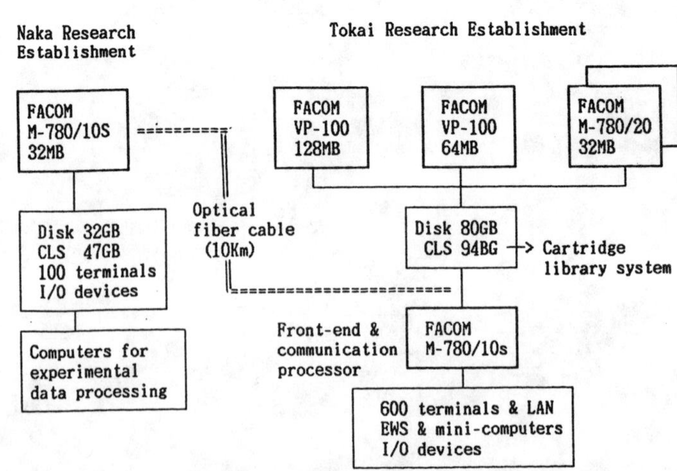

Fig. 1.1 Configuration of JAERI computer systems in 1988

comparison with the uniprocessor on the CRAY X-MP, where the code did not vectorized.

At JAERI, a preliminary research of multi-tasking has been done. We evaluated the improvement of performance by parallel processing of the vectorized DO-loop of the RELAP5.

The plan of this paper is as follows: In Chapter 2, the performance of vectorized nuclear codes at JAERI including the current problems on the vectorization of neutron transport Monte Carlo codes are briefly summarized. Chapter 3 describes the vector and parallel processing of the RELAP5 code. Chapter 4 is devoted to the discussions and concluding remarks for the vector and parallel processing of the RELAP5 code.

2. Summary of the Performance of JAERI Vectorized Nuclear Codes

In this Chapter, the performance of 40 vectorized nuclear codes at JAERI is summarized. It is well known that the performance ratio P of a program in the vector mode to in the scalar mode is expressed by the following formula:

$$P = \frac{1}{(1-V) + V/\alpha}$$

where V is the vectorization ratio and α is the vector to scalar performance improvement ratio of the vectorized parts of a program.

In Fig. 2.1 the performance ratio P versus the vectorization ratio V is shown. The solid and hatched lines indicate the performance ratio derived from above equation with respect to the vector to scalar speed ratios α=7.6 and α=30.0, respectively. The value of α averaged over 40 nuclear codes at JAERI is 7.6, and the theoretical maximum of α is 30 when addition and multiplication pipelines operate concurrently on the FACOM VP-100 with the infinite vector length. The average value of P is 5.0 and the average vectorization ratio V is 83%.

The vectorization ratio of the original codes prior to modification was less than 50% by automatic vectorization by compiler, because the codes have only a few DO-loops that are effective on the vector processor. The vectorization ratio is considerably increased by the vectorization effort.

Forty vectorized nuclear codes are divided into three groups according to overall performance. The group H is the high-performance group with a performance ratio greater than 6. The number of codes in group H is 12. The group M is the medium-performance group with a performance ratio from 3 to 6. The number of codes in group M is 11. Group L is the low-performance group with a performance ratio less than 3. The number of codes in group L is 17.

Group H codes are characterized by a high vectorization ratio and a high ratio of vector to scalar speed. The values of vectorization ratio of these codes are greater than 95%. The ratio of vector speed to scalar speed α is more than 9, because of both long vector length and suitable memory access method for the FACOM VP series. These feature come from the following characteristics of codes: The system of basic equations that governs these calculations is theoretically determined. The geometry treated by these codes is not too complicated. The typical restructuring effort of these codes for vectorization is the replacement of kernel algorithms and rearrangement of the nested DO-loops, so that the vector length becomes large. In such a code the occurrence of IF statements is infrequent. As a consequence, the vector is kept long and advantageous memory strides can be applied using direct memory access.

Group M is characterized by a high vectorization ratio but a low ratio of vector speed to scalar speed. The vectorization ratio is comparable with that of group H, but the ratio of vector speed to scalar speed is low. The value of V is more than 90%, but the value of α is from 3 to 7, and averaged value is 4.9, because the vector length of group M is shorter than that of group H. The short vector length is resulted from the following factors: First, the parallelism provided for the physical model is not large, such as the number of fuel blocks in a reactor. Second, some codes need not deal with an extensive number of meshes. Third, the codes calculate time-dependent phenomena, where the spatial mesh number tends to decrease with an increase in the number of time steps.

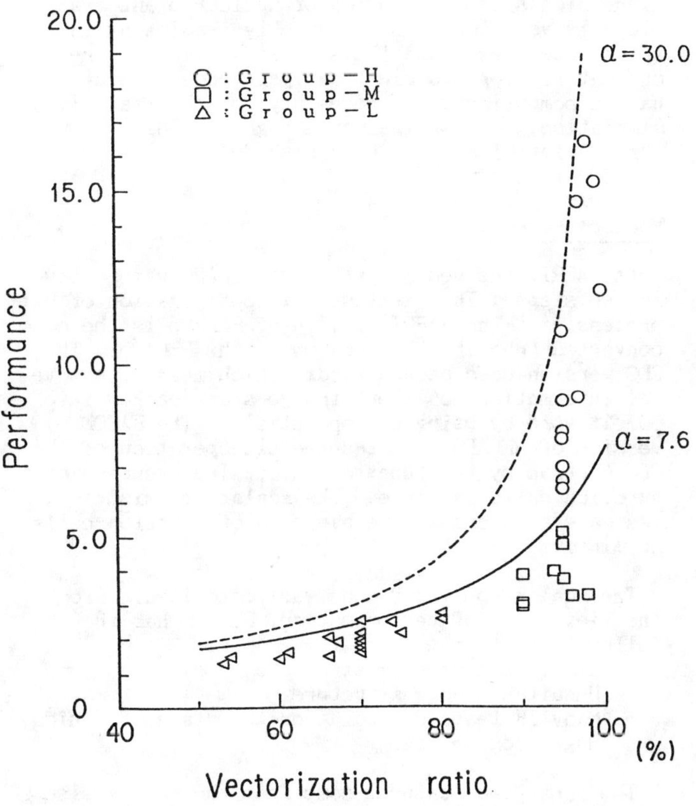

Fig. 2.1 Plot of the performance of each of the 40 nuclear codes

Group L is characterized by both a low vectorization ratio and a low ratio of vector speed to scalar speed. The two application fields are included in this group, that is, the thermohydraulic reactor transient analysis codes and the Monte Carlo codes for neutron transport.

The characteristics of the reactor transient analysis codes will be written in the following Chapters on RELAP5 as an example. The difficulties in vectorizing Monte Carlo codes are discussed here. The first reason is short vector length, since the vector length is determined by the number of particles calculated in parallel and the number of particles decreases physically with the random walk by absorption and leakage from the calculated geometry, etc. The density of arithmetic operations in the DO-loop is low and the indirect memory addressing is used frequently. The recurrent calculation appears in the DO-loop for accumulating the statistical values at the spatial meshes over the neutrons. Since the original codes are highly optimized on the scalar computer, any change of codes for vectorizat- ion brings into overhead and the overhead is fairly large compared with the total computing time [4]. Finally, the program and data structures of the conventional scalar-oriented Monte Carlo codes are inadequate to vector processing.

3. Experience of Vector and Parallel Processing of RELAP5 Code

The high speed simulation of nuclear plant transient is very important in quickly predicting the anticipated danger at the accidents. Few of the current reactor transient analysis codes, however, have a computing speed necessary for the real time simulation, even on the world highest speed computer. A lot of efforts have been done for reducing the CPU time of RELAP5.

Vector processing

At JAERI, the vectorization of RELAP5 was achieved in two steps. The first step is optimization of bit processing. The JAERI version of RELAP5 is the code converted from the CDC version of the RELAP5. The CDC version uses packed words, which means the several informations of short integers are packed into 60-bit word by using bit-operations. The FACOM version of RELAP5 emulates the bit-operation of the CDC Fortran by the function call. The overhead of function calls is large. The scalar optimization was made to decrease the overhead of function calls to minimum.

The scalar optimized code was vectorized. From the view point of vectorization, RELAP5 has the following features:

. Unsuitable program structure
. Unsuitable data structure
. Many IF tests depending on the state of fluid
. Huge program size

The first two features come from the memory size of computer on which the RELAP5 code was developed. RELAP5 was designed to reduce the memory size. The data are transferred to the small but fast core memory SCM from the large but slow core memory LCM. The subroutine at the top level has DO-loop and many subroutines are called in the DO-loop in order to keep the data on the SCM as long time as possible.

An example of program structure of RELAP5 is shown in Fig. 3.1. Fig. 3.1(a) illustrates the program structure of the subroutine STATE and its invoked subroutines in the original code. The STATE subroutine calculates the state relationship of water. The DO-loop for volumes, which are discretized elements of reactor component such as pipe, pump, and reactor vessel, is in the STATE subroutine. However, this DO-loop can not be vectorized because a subroutine STATEP is called in the DO-loop. The subroutine STATEP, in turn, calls the subroutines VISCOL, VISCOG, and THCON. These-bottom level subroutines calculate the state quantities and their derivatives. The STATEP subroutine, called from STATE, can not be vectorized too, since these subroutines do not have DO-loops. This type of program structure appears in RELAP5 frequently, because of the efficient use of the SCM.

```
SUBROUTINE STATE                SUBROUTINE STATEP

┌ DO-loop for volumes           CALL VISCOL
│    .
│    .                          CALL VISCOG
│ CALL STATEP
│    .                          CALL THCON
│    .
│    .                          CALL THCON
└ CONTINUE                           .
     .                               .
     .                          RETURN
  RETURN                        END
  END
```

(a) Original program structure

```
SUBROUTINE STATE                SUBROUTINE STATEP
     .
CALL STATEP                     CALL VISCOL
     .
     .                          CALL VISCOG
RETURN
END                             CALL THCON

                                CALL THCON
                                     .
SUBROUTINE VISCOL               RETURN
                                END
┌ DO-loop for volumes
│    .
│ (vectorized)
│    .
│    .
└ CONTINUE
     .
  RETURN
  END
```

(b) Vectorized program structure

Fig. 3.1 DO-loop transfer in STATE subroutine

The vectorization of these subroutines can be achieved by the transfer of DO-loop from STATE to STATEP and to its slave subroutines as shown in Fig. 3.1(b).

The data structure of RELAP5 is also affected by the memory size of computer. An example of data structure in RELAP5 is shown in Fig. 3.2. The data, which belong to the same volume or junction, are grouped by using EQUIVALENCE statements. Here the junction is another typical spatial node used in RELAP5 and it stands for a connection of two volumes. In each group of volumes or junctions, physical quantities are ordered as indicated in EQUIVALENCE statements. As shown in the DO-loops of Fig. 3.2, when the same physical quantities such as HV are referred over the total volumes, the memory is accessed by every IVSKP*8 byte.

This memory access method has no problem on the CDC small memory computer, because only the data belonging to one volume or junction would be stored on the SCM. For the vector processor, however, some distanced memory access causes a memory conflict.

```
      COMMON / FAST / FA( 100000 )
      INTEGER  LFA(1)
      EQUIVALENCE ( FA(1) , LFA(1) )
C
      INTEGER  FILNDX(40)
      COMMON /CONTRL/ FILNDX(40)
C
      INTEGER NVOL(1),NVSKP(1)
      REAL    HV(1),PV(1),UV(1),VV(1)
      EQUIVALENCE  ( NVOL(1)  , LFA(1) )
     &             ,( NVSKP(1) , LFA(2) )
     &             ,(    HV(1) ,  FA(3) )
     &             ,(    PV(1) ,  FA(4) )
     &             ,(    UV(1) ,  FA(5) )
     &             ,(    VV(1) ,  FA(6) )
C
      INTEGER NJUN(1),NJSKP(1)
      REAL    GJ(1),RJ(1),VJ(1)
      EQUIVALENCE  ( NJUN(1)  , LFA(1) )
     &             ,( NJSKP(1) , LFA(2) )
     &             ,(    GJ(1) ,  FA(3) )
     &             ,(    RJ(1) ,  FA(4) )
     &             ,(    VJ(1) ,  FA(5) )
C
      IVB    = FILNDX(1)
      IVSKP  = NVSKP(IVB)
      IVE    = IVB + ( NVOL(IVB) - 1 )*IVSKP
      IJB    = FILNDX(2)
      IJSKP  = NJSKP(IJB)
      IJE    = IJB + ( NJUN(IJB) - 1 )*IJSKP
C
      DO 10 I = IVB , IVE , IVSKP
        HV( I ) = PV( I ) + UV( I )*VV( I )
   10 CONTINUE
C
      DO 20 J = IJB , IJE , IJSKP
        GJ( J ) = RJ( J )*VJ( J )
   20 CONTINUE
```

Fig. 3.2 Data structure of RELAP5/MOD2

We could not change this data structure for vectorization, since the whole program would be rewritten.

The code contains many IF statements depending on the fluid state. The IF tests were replaced into a list vector in order to process efficiently in the vector mode. Fig. 3.3(a) shows the program of DO-loop transferred from the top-level subroutine. The same IF statement on the fluid state appears several times in different subroutines. These IF statements were modified as shown in Fig. 3.3(b). At the top-level subroutine, the list vectors LIST1 and LIST2 are generated once. The list vector keeps the volume numbers or junction numbers which should be calculated. At the bottom-level subroutines, the list vectors are used instead of IF statements. By using the list vectors, the redundant IF statements in the program are removed.

Another problem of IF statements is the short vector length. Typical number of volumes or junctions is about 100. The number of volumes or junctions which are calculated at the same time in the vectorized DO-loop is decreased by the IF branches.

One of the vectorization techniques used to the heat calculation of the RELAP5 are shown in Fig. 3.4. This vectorized method is applied to solve the one-dimensional heat conduction equations. In the original code, the program is coded as doubly nested DO-loops. The inner loop index m is for heat meshes, and the outer loop index i is for heat structures as shown in Fig. 3.4(a). The maximum numbers of heat meshes and heat structures are indi- cated as ¥MNN and ¥NN, respectively. This nested DO-loops solve tri-diagonal system of equations by using a scalar Gaussian elimination algorithm for the heat meshes.

```
DO *** I=IVB, IVE, IVSKP
  IF(ISTATE(I).EQ.1) THEN
       .
       .
  ELSE
       .
       .
  ENDIF
CONTINUE
```

(a) Original coding

Top-level subroutine

```
L1=0
L2=0
DO *** I=IVB,IVE,IVSKP
  IF(ISTATE(I).EQ.0) THEN
     L1=L1+1
     LIST1(L1)=I
  ELSE
     L2=L2+1
     LIST2(L2)=I
  ENDIF
CONTINUE
```

Bottom-level subroutines

```
DO **  II=1,L1
  I=LIST1(II)
     .
     .
```

```
DO **  II=1,L2
  I=LIST2(II)
     .
     .
```

(b) Vectorized coding

Fig. 3.3 List vector method

For the vectorization, the DO-loop indices are inverted because the DO-loop for heat mesh is recursive and the heat structure can be calculated in parallel.

In addition to the inversion of DO-loops, the indices of heat structure i' are changed in ascending order of mesh numbers as shown in Fig. 3.4(b). A list is provided to keep the maximum heat mesh number corresponding to each mesh index. By using this list, we could avoid the IF tests in the inner loop when the number of meshes is different between heat structures.

Finally, the thermohydraulic reactor transient analysis code such as RELAP5 is very large, since the real large scale complicated physical models are treated. For example, the number of subroutines in RELAP5/MOD2 is 283, and the number of Fortran statements is 100,000. This program size is the problem on vectorization. The 49 subroutines about 20,000 statements were rewritten for vectorization and for optimization of bit-processing. The manpower required for vectorization of RELAP5/MOD2 was 17 menmonths by the well-trained engineers. Noted that at the first time of vectorization of RELAP5/MOD1 [5], which is a previous version of RELAP5, 40 menmonths were required.

By these efforts, the vectorization rate 83% was achieved. The vectorized RELAP5 runs in the vector mode 3 times faster than that in the scalar mode on the FACOM VP-100 and 4.6 times faster than the version converted from CDC in the scalar mode. Fig. 3.5 shows the program flow of the vectorized RELAP5, the CPU time ratio in the scalar mode, and its performance ratio of vector mode to scalar mode when

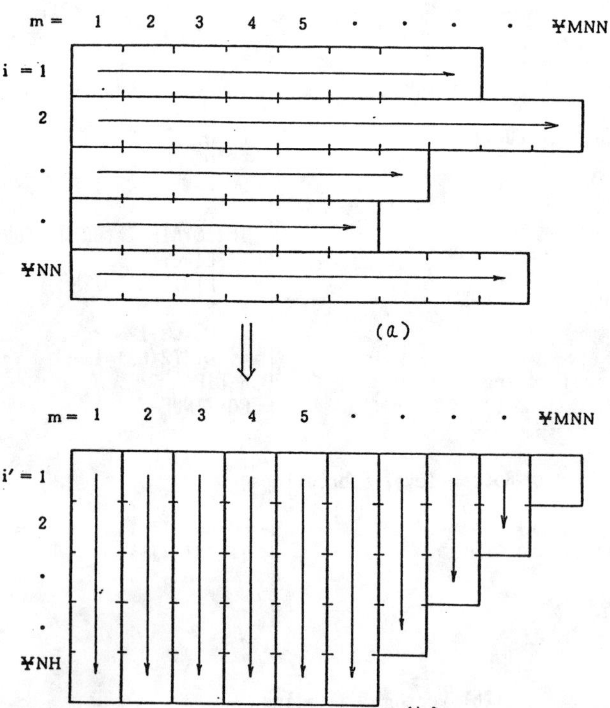

Fig. 3.4 Method for DO-loop interchange

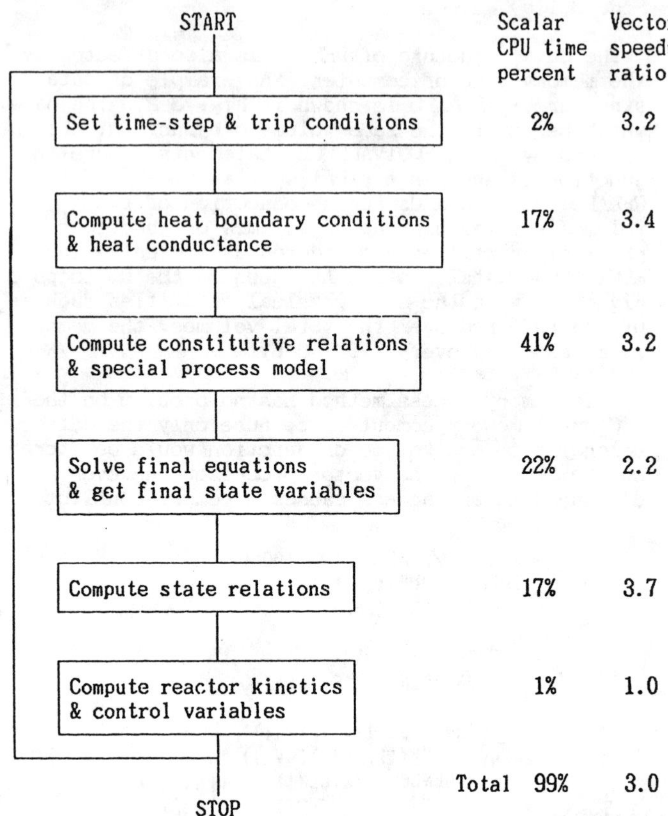

Fig. 3.5 Program flow, CPU time ratio in scalar mode, and performance ratio of vector mode to scalar mode in RELAP5

Table 3.1 Timing comparison of vectorized code in RELAP5/MOD2/C36.05

Version	Time-steps	CPU time (sec.) Heat	Hydro	State	Others	Total
Original version Scalar	16513	600.5 (1.0) (0.88)	3285.7 (1.0) (0.59)	616.4 (1.0) (0.88)	266.7 (1.0) (0.23)	4769.4 (1.0) (0.65)
Vector version Scalar	16513	530.5 (1.1) (1.0)	1944.2 (1.7) (1.0)	542.2 (1.1) (1.0)	60.9 (4.3) (1.0)	3077.8 (1.5) (1.0)
Vector version Vector	16227	154.8 (3.9) (3.4)	706.8 (4.6) (2.8)	149.2 (4.1) (3.6)	31.6 (8.4) (1.9)	1042.5 (4.6) (3.0)

Calculated parallelism: 196 junctions, 192 volumes, 43 heat structures, 662 heat meshes

calculated for a 1000 seconds loss of coolant flow accident on a nuclear plant. Table 3.1 is the summary of CPU time for the original version and the vector version. The discrepancy of time steps between vector and scalar modes is caused from the difference of the order of operation between vector operation and scalar operation, such as summation. Timing data for each component of the program will be referred later.

Multi-tasking

In order to get further performance gains, a preliminary trial of multi-tasking was made. The consideration was based on the vectorized RELAP5. The target computer of multi-tasking assummed is the multi-processors of FACOM VP-100s. Since the VP-100 does not have multi-processor feature, the estimation of multi-tasking was made.

The code was modified for multi-tasking. Then the modified code was run on the VP-100, and the effect of multi-tasking was evaluated from the measured CPU time. Idea of the method for multi-tasking is that the vectorized DO-loop is separated into two DO-loops and each DO-loop is processed on the different processor.

The multi-tasking structure used at JAERI for RELAP5/MOD2 is shown in Fig. 3.6. Two tasks are attached once at subroutine TRAN which controls the time advancement of the RELAP5 calculation. At each time step, synchronization between tasks is made by POST/WAIT operations at the subroutines indicated in Fig. 3.6.

In order to divide the spatial meshes into two tasks, the method used here is that the indices are separated into first half and last half indices instead of odd and even indices which is usually used. By this method, the reconstructions of list vectors introduced in the vectorization are avoided and only the initial and final numbers of the DO-loop are changed. COMMON data were shared between tasks to preserve the original data structure.

Generally speaking, the overhead of multi-tasking is greater than that of vector processing. The balance between overhead and granularity is important for considering the performance of multi-tasking. When RELAP5 analyze the transient of nuclear plant, one time-step calculation takes about 60 milli-seconds in the vectorized code. At least 16 times task synchronizations are necessary during one time-step. The granularity of a task is about 4 milli-seconds.

Table 3.2 shows the granularity of the major subroutines HTCOND, HTADV, PHAINT and STATE. The first row of the table is CPU time of each subroutine, the second row is the number required for task synchronizations in each time-step. The third row is the number of time-steps. The fourth row is the granularity of each subroutine. The overhead of task switch or task synchronization for the typical computer such as CRAY-XMP is several ten micro-seconds [6]. We chose the parts whose granularity is greater than several milli-seconds. Only 45% of the computing time of vectorized code was parallelized, which consists of heat calculation including heat advancement (HTADV) and heat conduction (HTCOND) (15%), heat transfer coefficients and interface drag (PHAINT) (14%) and state relationship calculation (STATE) (16%). These parts will be effective in the multi-tasking mode.

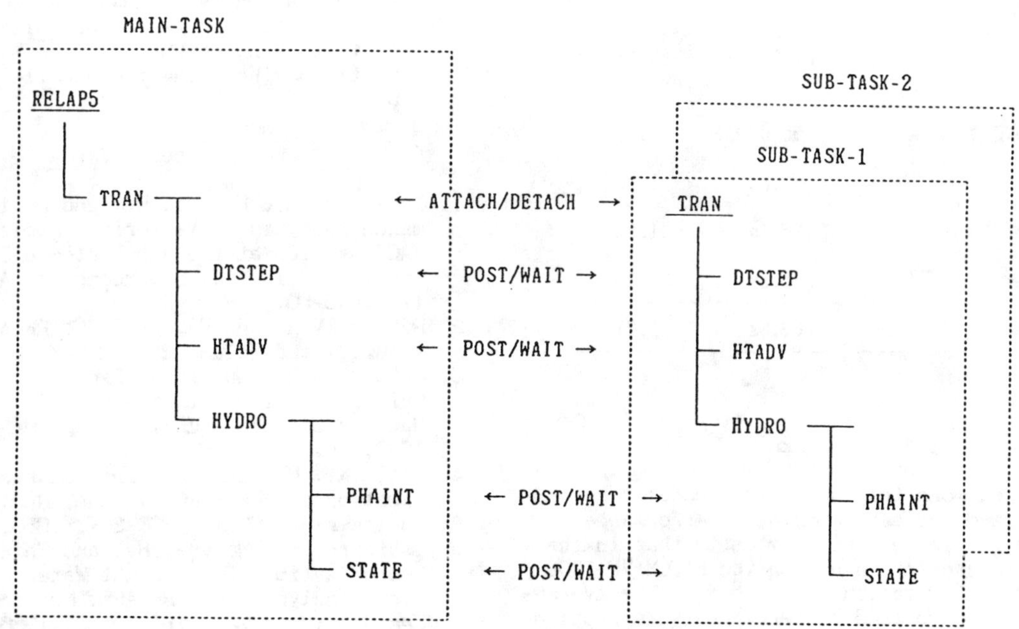

Fig. 3.6 Multi-tasking structure of RELAP5/MOD2

In Table 3.3, the performance of multi-tasking is summarized. The first column is the subroutine name. Second and third columns are the elapsed time for single-task and the estimated elapsed time for multi-task, respectively. The fourth column is the performance ratio of multi-tasking to single-tasking. In this estimation, the overhead for task switch and task synchronization is neglected, since the granularity is far greater than the overhead time. The value of performance is about 1.6 for processing on two CPUs. However, total performance is limited to 1.2, because only 45% of total program is parallelized. The parts which run in parallel can be increased, if the small granularity parts can improve the performance effectively.

Table 3.2 Granularity of the parallelized subroutines

	HTADV HTCOND	PHAINT	STATE
CPU time	295.7s	181.2s	185.2s
Task synchronizations	1	2	1
Time steps	14482	14482	14482
Granularity	20.4ms	6.3ms	12.7ms

Table 3.3 Summary of the performance of multi-tasking for 1000 sec. loss of coolant flow accident analysis

Subroutines	Single-task	Multi-task	Parallel performance
HTADV,HTCOND	154.8s	95.0s	1.63
STATE	149.0s	95.5s	1.56
PHAINT	162.5s	96.1s	1.69
Others	576.2s	576.2s	1.00
Total time	1042.5s	862.8s	1.21

4. Concluding Remarks

We vectorized more than 40 nuclear codes. For 23 of 40 vectorized nuclear codes, the performance ratio of program in the vector mode to that in the scalar mode is greater than 3 on the FACOM VP-100. The averaged vectorization ratio is 83%. The averaged performance ratio is 5. There are two exceptional area which prevent the performance improvement by vectorization, that is, thermohydraulic reactor transient analysis codes and neutron transport Monte Carlo codes. These codes have the conventional scalar-oriented program and data structures which are not suitable for vector processing.

RELAP5, typical thermohydraulic reactor code, was successfully vectorized. The performance ratio of vectorized RELAP5 in the vector mode to that in the scalar mode is 3. This performance is limited by the data structure and frequent appearance of IF tests in RELAP5. The data structure of RELAP5 causes some distanced memory access, which is inefficient because of memory conflict. Frequent appearance of IF tests in the program causes the short vector length and the indirect memory addressing by the list vectors which are introduced to vectorize IF tests.

Multi-tasking of RELAP5 was also considered. Vectorized DO-loops were separated into the two DO-loops and each DO-loop was processed in different processor. The estimated performance improvement of the vectorized multi-task program to single-task one is 1.2. We considered only the DO-loop whose granularity is greater than several milli-seconds, and the overhead of task switch or task synchronization is assumed to be several ten micro-seconds. It is very difficult to find the parallelism in the RELAP5 code except for DO-loop, without modifying the numerical models which have been established for several years.

The computing time of the vectorized RELAP5 code is comparable with the real reactor transient time on VP-100. It would achieve faster than real time if processed by two VP-100s concurrently.

Finally, our recommended approach to increase the computational speed such as RELAP5, real large scaled code, by using the parallelism is presented as follows:

(1) Vectorization by automatic vectorizing compiler
(2) Vectorization or vector optimization by hand
(3) Multi-tasking of DO-loops
(4) Multi-tasking using the parallelism except for DO-loops.

References

1. Ishiguro, M., Harada, H., and Makino, M.: Performance Analysis of Vectorized Nuclear Codes on a FACOM VP-100 at the Japan Atomic Energy Research Institute, Int. J. Supercomputer Applications, 1-3, p45-56, 1987.
2. Ranson, V.H. and Wagner R.J.: RELAP5/DOD2 Manual, Volume 1 and Volume 2, EGG-SAMM-6377, INEL,1984
3. Makowitz, H.: Numerical Experiments in Concurrent Multiprocessing with the RELAP5 Nuclear Codes, Nuclear Science & Engineering, 92-1, p136-143 1986.
4. Asai, K., Higuchi, K., and Katakura, J.: Vectorization of the KENO-IV Code, Nuclear Science & Engineering, 92-1, p298-307, 1986.
5. Ishiguro, M., Harada, H., and Shinozawa, N.: Vectorization of the Light Water Reactor Transient Analysis Code RELAP5, Nuclear Science & Engineering , 92-1, p126-135, 1986.
6. Seager, M.K.: Parallelizing Conjugate Gradient for the CRAY X-MP, Parallel Computing, 3-1, p35-47 1986.

SQUEEZING MORE CPU PERFORMANCE OUT OF A CRAY-2 BY VECTOR BLOCK SCHEDULING

C.Eisenbeis, W. Jalby, A. Lichnewsky*

I.N.R.I.A. Domaine de Voluceau 78153 Le Chesnay CEDEX

Abstract

Compile time scheduling of vector activities on the CRAY 2[1] is studied using a simplified model of the vector instruction stream. Due to several of the hardware characteristics of the machine, an approach using much know-how obtained on Array-Processor micro-code scheduling by the authors is shown practical. It calls for a pass of loop scheduling followed by a pass of resource allocation. Actual benchmarks of the resulting code are shown, exhibiting speed-ups as large as 50% over the current CFT77 compiler. Our results also give a new perspective in the comparison of vector chaining and non-chaining processor architectures.

INTRODUCTION

In the race towards peak performance, all the forms of parallelism present in the code have to be exploited. In fact, the challenge is double: parallelism must first be detected and then matched with the architecture. Moreover, it has to be determined if these problems have to be solved by hardware, software or a subtle cooperation of the two.

A low level of parallelism exists in most modern architectures, permitting the simultaneous operation of independent units for computation, memory access, control. This means that parallel activities must be scheduled and synchronized, in order to maintain the code semantics while enhancing the overall performance. The memory units often have an asynchronous behaviour that must be matched to a general synchronous organization.

The hardware conflict resolution approach is embodied in the Tomasulo algorithm, the Scoreboard of the CDC - 7600 and Cray "issue" strategy. (cf.[15]).

The other extreme relies on the software to solve these problems, and is exhibited by some RISC and horizontally micro coded - VLIW - architectures. Going from the first set to the second, the requirements for the software increase: good scheduling is an optimization feature in the first case which presents no interlock detection need, the second assumes a very good conflict resolution and scheduling capability.

The purpose of this paper is to describe code scheduling techniques well adapted for the Cray 2 making a very efficient use of the hardware resources for vector loops. An amazing corollary of our proposed techniques, is that we show that our code scheduling algorithm overcomes the absence of chaining on the Cray 2. More precisely, we achieve similar performance as for an extended architecture incorporating full chaining mechanism, with the same memory bandwidth.

In section 1, we describe how the Cray 2 is modeled in our study. We consider vector instructions as atomic blocks, whose interaction is very simple, due to the absence of chaining. The latency of the memory access pipeline, which is a well known characteristic of this machine, is adequately rendered using a two stage block level pipe. Moreover, our model can be treated without the complex linear programming methods of Aryia [1] taking into account potential chaining in the Cray 1.

In section 2, we describe the software scheduling of the arithmetic units and memory access units. The technique used is cyclic scheduling which is basically local scheduling of the body of the loop taking into account the cyclic nature of the loop. This technique was developed for optimizing code for horizontally microcoded architectures such as the ST100, by one of the authors. The asymptotic speed obtained is very similar to the one obtained by trace scheduling; moreover due to the use of cyclic nature of a loop, the peak performance is reached

*On leave from Université de Paris Sud.

[1]Computations performed on the Cray 2 at CCVR, Palaiseau (France)

for relatively small number of iterations (relatively small $N_{\frac{1}{2}}$).

In section 3, we describe the register allocation strategy. In fact, the scheduling algorithm of the section 2 allows us to overcome the lack of chaining, the price to pay is a higher register usage (increased residence time of data in registers): it is the classical well known space time tradeoffs. This problem is not adapted for the classical graph coloring algorithm due to cyclity. However, the strong cyclic regularity of the graphs stemming from vector loops allows us to devise an optimal polynomial register allocation algorithm. In this phase, spilling is also introduced, using the fact that spilling can be done in local CRAY 2 memory in complete overlap with other operations, i.e. spilling can be free when scheduling allows.

In section 4, we present systematic benchmarking of our proposed algorithms. We describe experimental results on a CRAY 2 obtained using code generated according to our techniques. These results are compared against those obtained using the current CRAY 2 compilers. Our techniques is clearly superior even compared with the CFT77 compiler which is using some sort of trace scheduling technique: as an example, we get 50% performance improvement on simple loops such as the multiplication of 2 complex vectors. In many cases, we obtain optimal speeds saturating one of the hardware resources, which is often the global memory path.

1 Machine Model

In the first part of this section we describe the general structure of the target architecture and how its behavior is modeled for the code optimization procedure. Then, we explain how we imbedd the Cray 2 architecture in this model. The key point here is to abstract the architecture in order to apply efficiently optimization tools, while preserving the essence of the machine run-time behaviour. As we will see in section 5, the pertinence of the model is clearly validated by the experimental results obtained.

1.1 Description of the generic architecture

In our architecture model, we distinguish two kinds of hardware resources:
- Functional Units: floating point and integer arithmetic, memory access, data paths subject to reservations.
- Storage Units: registers, local memory, main memory.

To operate on the run time behaviour of these resources, the concept of reservation tables permits to describe the use of resources for a series of discrete time steps. The time steps, also called granules, are not necessarily cycles. The table explicits, for each of these time steps, the occupancy of the resources subject to reservation. These resources are defined in terms of the above hardware elements, and of their organization with respect of the flow of data. Thus, when functional units are pipelined, their different stages are considered as different reservation entities.

Following this correspondence, instructions, which control the run time activity of physical resources, are associated with elementary reservation tables – also called templates – which describe the impact of the instruction execution on the reservation table. Each template may specify reservations of several resources spanning several time granules. Scheduling the basic operations and checking for interlocks now amounts to placing the templates onto the reservation table. The role of the scheduler is to compact the reservation table templates without violating dependence and resource constraints thus minimizing the actual execution time.

1.2 Modeling the Cray 2

Since we are primarily interested in vector loop optimization, we choose a time granularity (macrocycle) corresponding to a 64 elements long vector elementary operation, or a reservation implied by it. The practical size of a granule, or macrocycle, is thus between 64 and 82 cycles. During our optimization process, all the vector instructions will be supposed to be 64 elements long: this assumption is not too constraining because vector lengths less than 64 occurs only once per loop after the classical strip mining loop optimization. The complete code optimization process has become hierarchical, and a second pass is necessary to emit and schedule the scalar instructions. It also performs local – within time granule – vector code fine tuning, working with a time granularity of a single cycle, which is more than one order of magnitude smaller. This second pass can be made quite easily because the most crucial vector block scheduling is known, and because many reservation table slots remain free to schedule the scalar operations.

The resources which must be considered in the reservation table are the functional units which are

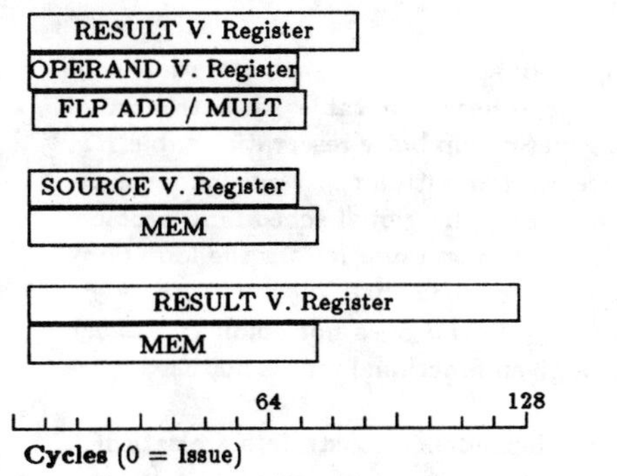

Figure 1: Instructions and Resource Reservations

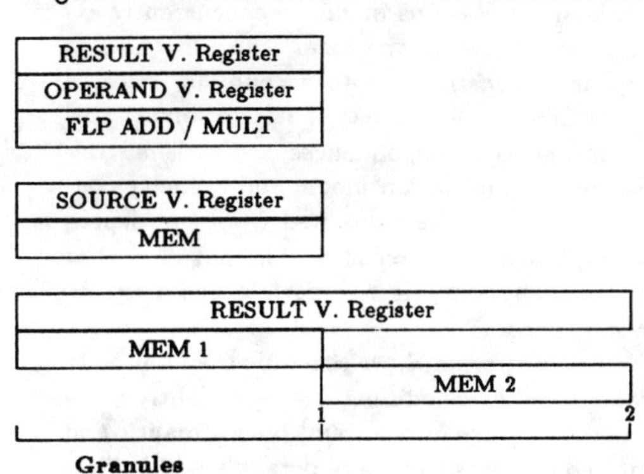

Figure 2: Templates

all considered single stage, except the main memory access path, which is considered a 2 stage pipeline. Thus, in the case of a main memory store or load the access is split in 2 macrocycles and main memory accesses might be partially overlapped. The local memory access path is single stage. The vector registers should have entries in the reservation table, but we take them into account only in a separate phase, following the basic loop scheduling of the previous resources, which uses virtual registers.

The templates are derived straightforwardly from the description of the instructions, by marking the resources occupied during each time granule. The busy times are simply rounded up to the next granule. For example, figure 2 gives the templates with a macrocycle of 82 clock periods. The number 82 corresponds to longest reservation time, in processor cycles, which occurs for the result register in a floating point add. (Cf. Figure 1).

As described elsewhere [6], the choice of the macrocycle and the reservation tables can be changed for different optimization purposes.

For example, a macrocycle of 72 cycles can be adopted. This choice will give a better usage of the functional units, because the approximation is more accurate for their reservation time, at the cost of a more expensive allocation for the result register. This might be worthwhile for vector loops without scalar operations. Moreover, the reservation tables can be used to force the code scheduler to increase the distance between 2 dependent instructions. This might be extremely useful for damping the variations of the main memory latency and throughput. Our model offers a large degree of flexibility which can be adjusted for various optimization purposes making them applicable to a large class of vector architectures.

2 Scheduling of the Functional units

Our code optimization strategy distinguishes between vector operations and scalar operations: in a first coarse granularity pass, we schedule vector operations, then, in a subsequent pass, we schedule scalar operations working at the machine cycle granularity.

The optimization of vector operations, itself is decomposed in two consecutive phases:
- scheduling of the functional units assuming an unbounded amount of storage resources (infinite number of registers). This means that the physical registers entries in the reservation table can be ignored. However, the life span of virtual registers is computed and used in the allocation phase.
- management of the storage units: register allocation, spilling in local memory

Assigning real registers too early during the scheduling phase is unnecessary due to the interchangeable character of the registers. Furthermore, such an allocation would require to add several lines to the reservation table, making the scheduling more complex and less efficient.

2.1 Preprocessing

We are working on a vector loop which has been already detected and processed by a vectorizer (in our case VATIL [11]). The dependence graph [9] is available at this stage and several optimizations including strip mining have been performed. The dependence information – intra- and inter-iterations – is used during the scheduling process to preserve the semantics of the program. The strip mining operation consists in breaking - blocking - all the vectorized loops into blocks of 64 iterations. For a loop of N iterations, the result is an outermost loop of $\left\lceil \frac{N}{64} \right\rceil$ and an innermost loop of 64 iterations.

Since vector operations are considered as atomic blocks, the term iteration (resp. loop) will denote exclusively outer iteration (resp. outer loop).

2.2 Code Generation of the Loop Body

In this phase, we generate an intermediate vector code for the loop body, which is used as basic pattern for the cyclic scheduling of the iterations.

The registers are handled in a virtual manner according to a single assignment rule: the number of registers is supposed unbounded, at each time a register is needed to hold a value resulting from a load or an operation, a new register is allocated. In the cyclic scheduling, each iteration of the loop body will be represented by a similar copy of the generated intermediate code. The virtual register defined in the generic loop body are named R_k. The copy corresponding to iteration i will create the registers numbered $R_1(i)$ through $R_k(i)$. The virtual registers which are either live on loop entry or invariant, are named $R_l(0)$. Globally, as a consequence of the single assignment rule, each virtual register is written once but may be read several times. The main advantage of such a technique is to avoid introduction of artificial dependencies due to a bad allocation [4].

The intermediate code is represented by a graph whose vertices are the instructions. The edges are of two kinds: first those representing the intra-loop data flow which are labeled by the corresponding virtual register name and second those representing the inter-iteration dependence information (distance vector and dependence type). Classical optimization procedures such as finding common subexpressions, redundant and deadcode elimination are performed on it.

2.3 Scheduling

The scheduling of the whole loop involves two intimately related subproblems: scheduling of the generic loop body code, and then scheduling of the successive iterations. Our strategy will be to use the cyclic scheduling technique which was developed for array processor microcode compaction [12], and which tackles the two issues simultaneously.

In this method, all the iterations are scheduled exactly following the same pattern derived from the generic loop body. Therefore each iteration contributes to the reservation table by a translated copy of the generic loop body reservation table RT. Iterations are started with a constant unknown period of d granules. The global scheduling problem is to build a reservation table RT for the loop body and find a period d, such that:

- the sequence $RT + kd$ does not conflict: at each macrocycle, a given functional unit is not used more than once.
- the semantic dependence constraints are satisfied.
- the total execution time is minimized.

The execution of one iteration may span over more than d granules and therefore at a given cycle several successive iterations might be concurrently executing. Consequently the local scheduling has to take ***cyclicity constraints*** into account in order to avoid resource conflicts between iterations. This simply means that dependences are satisfied under the periodic initiation mode, and cyclicity constraints can readily be computed from the dependence graph as a function of d. The payoff of that additional complexity is the perfect chaining between iterations.

For a given period d, we schedule the loop body according to a list scheduling strategy slightly modified in order to take into account both semantic and cyclicity constraints (for more details see [6]). Taking into account cyclic constraints while scheduling the generic loop body allows to optimize globally the execution time, by permitting a small value of the period d. In fact, this is equivalent to the insertion of delays suggested in [5], but we have more flexibility in the process because much semantic information is available. However, since at that stage, we are not considering physical register assignment, our introduction of delays will not add complexity to the reservation table describing functional units.

The period d is simply determined by computing for each functional unit t, the number of macrocycles n_t where t used is during one iteration. In our current implementation, d is chosen starting at the maximum value of n_t; this value of d corresponds to the saturation of one of the functional unit. Further work is required to investigate this choice.

The success of such a strategy of scheduling is mainly due to the fact that the templates are extremely simple: most FUs is not used more than one macrocycle.

2.4 Global Register Usage

We call the birth date of a virtual register the cycle where it is assigned a value. Correspondingly, the death date is the cycle where its content is used for the last time. Between its birth and death, the virtual register is said live. At each cycle, the total number of live registers is determined and the maximum number of live registers over the whole execution is called the critical register quantity (CRQ). This number clearly corresponds to the minimum number of physical registers needed to execute the loop without spilling.

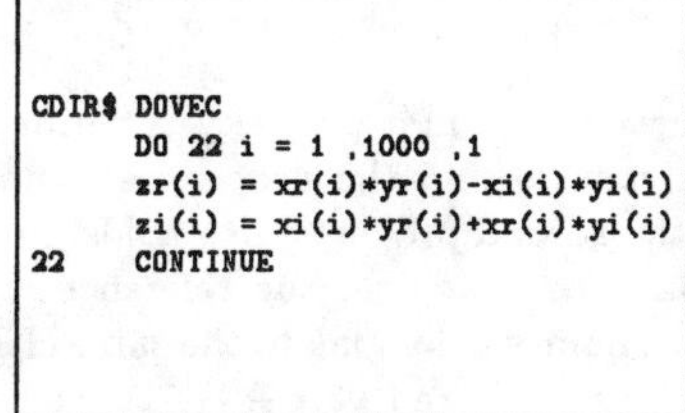

```
CDIR$ DOVEC
      DO 22 i = 1 ,1000 ,1
      zr(i) = xr(i)*yr(i)-xi(i)*yi(i)
      zi(i) = xi(i)*yr(i)+xr(i)*yi(i)
22    CONTINUE
```

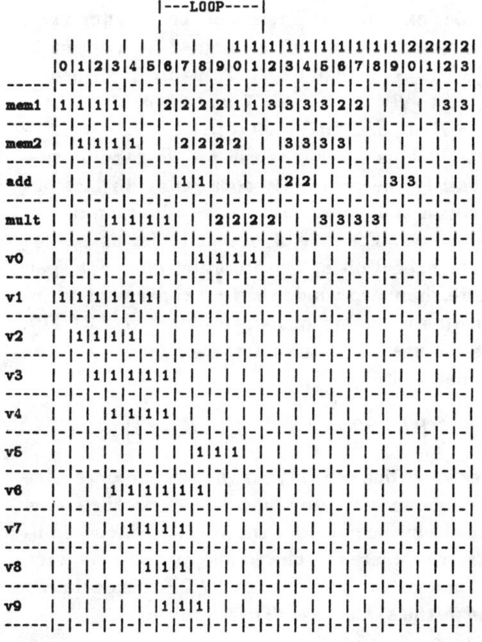

	0	1	2	3	4	5	6	7	8	9	10	11	12	13	14	15	16	17	18	19	20	21	22	23
							LOOP																	
mem1	1	1	1	1			2	2	2	2	1	1	3	3	3	3	2	2					3	3
mem2		1	1	1	1			2	2	2	2			3	3	3	3							
add								1	1					2	2					3	3			
mult				1	1	1	1			2	2	2	2			3	3	3	3					
v0									1	1	1	1												
v1	1	1	1	1	1	1																		
v2		1	1	1	1																			
v3			1	1	1	1	1																	
v4				1	1	1	1																	
v5									1	1	1													
v6				1	1	1	1	1	1															
v7					1	1	1	1																
v8						1	1	1																
v9							1	1	1															

Figure 3: Source Code and Reservation Table after Pass 1

A register class C is said critical if suppressing the reservations associated with elements of C reduces CRQ. For example, register classes whose elements have a life span of d granules are critical (for example the registers v1 and v6 in figure 3). This notion helps to select good candidates for the allocation of a physical register or for spilling.

In the scheduling procedure described above, there is no direct attempt to minimize that quantity. However, as we observed in practice, the resulting CRQ is generally not far from the optimal due to the fact that we are scheduling as early as possible, the executable templates, which in fact, directly reduces the lifespan of virtual register names and therefore CRQ. To refine our approach, we are currently testing a level scheduling strategy which instead linearly ordering the templates, allows to choose for execution between several templates. The criteria used for selection is the local minimization of the number of simultaneously live registers.

```
         ENTRY      |---UNROLLED  LOOP------ |   EXIT
                    |          ..            |
      | | | | | | || | | | |1|1||1|1|1|1|1|1||1|1|2|2|2|2|
VIRT. |0|1|2|3|4|5||6|7|8|9|0|1||2|3|4|5|6|7||8|9|0|1|2|3|
------|-|-|-|-|-|-||-|-|-|-|-|-||-|-|-|-|-|-||-|-|-|-|-|-|
v0    | | | | | | || | :6|6|6|6:: | :3|3|3|3:: | :6|6|6|6:
------|-|-|-|-|-|-||-|-|-|-|-|-||-|-|-|-|-|-||-|-|-|-|-|-|
v1    |0|0|0|0|0|0::0|0|0|0|0|0::0|0|0|0|0|0:: | | | | | |
------|-|-|-|-|-|-||-|-|-|-|-|-||-|-|-|-|-|-||-|-|-|-|-|-|
v2    | :2|2|2|2: || :5|5|5|5: || :2|2|2|2: || | | | | | |
------|-|-|-|-|-|-||-|-|-|-|-|-||-|-|-|-|-|-||-|-|-|-|-|-|
v3    | | :5|5|5|5||5: :2|2|2|2||2: :5|5|5|5||5: | | | | |
------|-|-|-|-|-|-||-|-|-|-|-|-||-|-|-|-|-|-||-|-|-|-|-|-|
v4    | | | :6|6|6||6: | :3|3|3||3: | :6|6|6||6: | | | | |
------|-|-|-|-|-|-||-|-|-|-|-|-||-|-|-|-|-|-||-|-|-|-|-|-|
v5    | | | | | | || | :7|7|7: || | :4|4|4: || | :7|7|7: |
------|-|-|-|-|-|-||-|-|-|-|-|-||-|-|-|-|-|-||-|-|-|-|-|-|
v6    | | | |1|1|1||1|1|1:1|1|1||1|1|1:1|1|1||1|1|1: | | |
------|-|-|-|-|-|-||-|-|-|-|-|-||-|-|-|-|-|-||-|-|-|-|-|-|
v7    | | | | :7|7||7|7: | :4|4||4|4: | :7|7||7|7: | | | |
------|-|-|-|-|-|-||-|-|-|-|-|-||-|-|-|-|-|-||-|-|-|-|-|-|
v8    | | | | | :2||2|2: | | :5||5|5: | | :2||2|2: | | | |
------|-|-|-|-|-|-||-|-|-|-|-|-||-|-|-|-|-|-||-|-|-|-|-|-|
v9    | | | | | | ::3|3|3: | | ::6|6|6: | | ::3|3|3: | | |
------|-|-|-|-|-|-||-|-|-|-|-|-||-|-|-|-|-|-||-|-|-|-|-|-|
      |            ||            ||            ||           |
      |   WINDOW   ||   WINDOW   ||   WINDOW   ||  WINDOW   |
      |      1     ||      2     ..      3     ||    4      |
```

Figure 4: Allocation of Real to Virtual Registers

3 Register Allocation and Spilling

In this section, the mapping of the virtual registers onto the physical ones is described. First we present an allocation strategy using exactly CRQ physical registers (3.1). Therefore, if CRQ is less than the number of physical registers available (NPR), we just apply this allocation scheme. Otherwise, we study the life of the virtual registers to determine the ones to be spilled, in order to reduce CRQ, (cf. 3.2). This process is iteratively repeated up to the point where CRQ is less than than NPR which is relevant of the previous case. During that phase, spilling code is introduced and scheduled. In many practical cases, the spill will take place in parallel with other operations, without delaying any arithmetic or main memory operation.

3.1 Register Allocation Strategy

In that section we show how to produce a physical register assignment requiring CRQ physical registers at most. The register assignment will be described by a function ϕ associating to each virtual register a physical one in $RV[1..NPR]$.

As justified in [6], we look for periodic allocation functions of integer period t :

$$\exists t \in \mathcal{N} \quad \phi(R_l(i) = \phi(R_l(i+t)).$$

When such a couple (ϕ, t) is found, we just unroll the loop t times, and we generate the code for the block of t iterations, spanning td granules, according to the mapping defined by ϕ.

As a preliminary step, the critical names are allocated. On the example of figures 3 and 4, v1 is assigned to RV0 and v6 to RV1, leaving 6 critical registers. This reduces the complexity of the problems without any loss. Now we can focus on the allocation of the remaining names.

In the sequel, the term window will denote d consecutive granules, and the loop execution is decomposed in a sequence of windows. On the example, the first window consists of granules 0 up to to 5, the second from 6 to 11,... Except for the startup and pipeline flush windows, the execution pattern on these windows is exactly identical. One of them is arbitrarily selected as a reference window, (window 2 in the example).

We will construction a window by window basis, a function ϕ satisfying the following constraints:

- first over each window considered separately the function ϕ is an admissible allocation: any pair of virtual registers simultaneously alive in a cycle of the window will be assigned through ϕ different register names
- between two consecutive windows, the function ϕ preserves the continuity of the assignment: a register name whose life span several windows, is assigned across all the windows the same number

It can be readily checked that such a function, constitutes an admissible assignment for the whole loop.

To satisfy the first constraint, we start the construction by building an assignment ϕ_r over the reference window. This is a problem which can be solved in polynomial time using exactly CRQ registers. The assignment over the other windows is now defined by a permutation σ of the physical register number:

$$\text{over any window:} \quad \phi = \sigma \circ \phi_r.$$

By construction, the first property is verified. The problem is now to find the proper permutation σ such that the second property also holds.

Let us notice that over the reference window, two different names belonging to the same class may appear such as $v3(i)$ and $v3(i+1)$. During the allocation phase, these names may be allocated to different physical registers.

In our example, as a result of the assignment on the reference window, $v0$ is assigned to $RV6$, $v2$ to $RV5$, $v3$ to $RV5$ then to $RV[2]$, $v4$ to $RV6$ then to $RV3$, $v5$ to $RV7$, $v7$ to $RV7$ and $RV4$, $v8$ to $RV2$ then to $RV5$, and finally $v9$ to $RV3$.

Now, let us determine the proper permutation σ to satisfy the continuity constraint. In fact our problems is that some names have a lifespan of several windows. For sake of simplicity, let us assume that the execution of one iteration does not span on more than two windows. It is convenient to introduce here the set of names (denoted RIGHT), whose life span over the reference window and the next one:

$$RIGHT = \{R_{i_1}(j_1), ...R_{i_s}(j_s)\}$$

Similarly, we define LEFT as the set of names alive in the reference window and in the previous one. Due to the cyclic nature of the loop and our scheduling strategy, there is a one to one mapping between the elements of $LEFT$ and $RIGHT$ associating names in the same class. Therefore:

$$LEFT = \{R_{i_1}(k_1), ...R_{i_s}(k_s)\}$$

In our example:

$$\begin{aligned} RIGHT &= \{v3(2), v4(2), v7(2), v8(2)\} \\ LEFT &= \{v3(1), v4(1), v7(1), v8(1)\} \end{aligned}$$

Looking closer at the physical registers allocated at the element of left and right, we define a partial mapping θ over the physical register numbers by:

$$\begin{aligned} \theta(R_{i_1}(k_1)) &= R_{i_1}(j_1) \\ &\cdots\cdots \\ \theta(R_{i_s}(k_s)) &= R_{i_s}(j_s) \end{aligned}$$

This an injective partial mapping which can be completed into a bijection σ. It is easily checked that such a permutation satisfies the continuity property by construction. The order t of σ will give the period t, recalling that σ^t = Identity In our example,

$$\begin{array}{lllllllll} \theta(v3(1)) & = & \theta(5) & = & 2 & \sigma(2) & = & 5 & \\ \theta(v4(1)) & = & \theta(6) & = & 3 & \sigma(3) & = & 6 & \\ \theta(v7(1)) & = & \theta(7) & = & 4 & \sigma(4) & = & 7 & \\ \theta(v4(1)) & = & \theta(2) & = & 5 & \sigma(5) & = & 2 & \\ & & & & & \sigma(6) & = & 3 & \\ & & & & & \sigma(7) & = & 4 & \end{array} \tag{1}$$

There are many ways to complete θ in order to get σ. For this purpose, we build the partial graph of θ and complete it to limit the length of the cycles. The reason is that the order of σ (and therefore the degree of unrolling) is the least common multiple of the length of the cycles. By the same token, for eight registers of the Cray, the maximal t is 15. In practice, this is a very large upper bound; for all the loops described in the benchmark section, the unrolling factor is not greater than 3 .

3.2 Spilling

We present here the simplest of our strategies for spilling, more elaborated ones are under development. Although fairly simple, this technique seems well adapted to the frequent case where CRQ is not too large compared to NPR. It can be assumed that the local memory is large enough to hold all the spilled data, the limit in the local memory of the Cray 2 being of 256 full vector registers. Several problems need to be solved:

- selecting a candidate for spilling
- scheduling of the transfers
- bookkeeping in the register data structures of the compiler

The registers are spilled one by one as long as CRQ is greater than NPR. The criteria to select the next register to spill is

- if a register being spilled reduces CRQ, select it immediately.
- otherwise, spill the register with the longuest life.

The move to or from local memory is simply inserted in the reservation table on the line corresponding to the local memory access unit. If there is a conflict on the local memory unit, we try to schedule later or earlier but while preserving the decrease in CRQ. If none of these costless solutions is feasible, a granule of delay is inserted. The bookkeeping amounts to mark as killed a register spilled at the first time after it has entered the local memory. When the data is needed again, a new name is created.

The other strategies under development for spilling incorporate spilling directly into the scheduling phase. This amounts to add constraints in the same spirit as "register pressure".

4 Experimental Results

We present here some benchmark results and compare our code generation techniques with the main FORTRAN compilers available on the Cray2. The machine used was a Cray2 using dynamic main memory implying a long latency. The experiments presented here were performed on dedicated time in order to get an accurate view of the performance; more extensive results are described elsewhere [6]. In our tables, CFT77 denotes the Fortran compiler CFT77 2.0, CFT2 denotes the Fortran compiler CFT2 3.0b and VASCO denotes the code generated according to our method. In our case (VASCO), the vector code was automatically generated using VATIL for the vectorization and dependence analysis and a version of the microcode compacter MIMOSA modified to perform as described in this paper. At the time of the experiments, the address generation, done in scalar, was not fully operationnal, so the address computations were inserted semi-manually. This does not affect the results due to their minor impact on the overall performance.

Our benchmarks (Cf. Figures 6,7,9, 8,10,12 and 11) contained vector loops – m mv mvf families – and two larger kernels (Cf. 5) – multiplication of two complex vectors: mulcomp and applying a Givens rotation: drot –. The goal of the m, mv and mvf families is to get a systematic evaluation of the behavior of the different code generators for various possible 2, 3 and 4 adic vector operations; we wanted to check that our method was not sensitive to some patterns of operations. All these loops are very good candidates for the use of chaining mechanism.

As a first conclusion, for our benchmark, CFT77 achieved better performance than CFT2, in particuliar for vector length greater than 256. This is due to the fact that CFT77 unrolls the loops by blocks of 256 iterations, then on block of 256 iterations, it reschedules the operations in fashion quite similar to trace scheduling 10. In both cases our method achieves better performance, and might be of interest for the evolution of commercial compilers, which obviously have to work under more stringent reliability requirements. On most cases, our methods permits to use fully the possible memory bandwidth.

m1	y(i) = (a * x(i)) + b
m2	y(i) = (a + x(i)) * b
mv1	z(i) = ((x(i) * y (i)) + a) * b
mv2	z(i) = ((x(i) * b + a) * y(i))
mv3	z(i) = (y(i) + (a * x(i))) + b
mv4	z(i) = (a * x(i)) + (y(i) + b)
mv5	z(i) = ((a * x(i)) + b) + y(i)
mv6	z(i) = ((x(i) + b) * a) + y(i)
mv7	z(i) = ((x(i) + y(i)) * a) + b
mv8	z(i) = ((x(i) + y(i)) + a) * b
mv9	z(i) = (((x(i) + a) + y(i))) * b
mvf1	t(i) = ((x(i) * a) + y(i)) * z(i)
mvf2	t(i) = ((x(i) + y(i)) * z(i)) + a
mvf3	t(i) = (x(i) + (y(i) * z(i))) * a
mvf4	t(i) = x(i) + ((y(i) + a) * z(i))
mvf5	t(i) = (x(i) + y(i)) + (a * z(i))
mvf6	t(i) = (x(i) + (y(i) * a)) + z(i)
mvf7	t(i) = ((x(i) * y(i)) + a) * z(i)
mvf8	t(i) = ((x(i) + a) * y(i)) * z(i)
mulcomp	zr(i) = xr(i) * yr(i) - xi(i) * yi(i) zi(i) = xr(i) * yi(i) + xi(i) * yr(i)
drot	x(i) = c * z(i) - s * t(i) y(i) = s * z(i) + c * t(i)

Figure 5: Program Kernels used in the Experiments

Conclusions

A new approach to vector code generation and vector code scheduling for the Cray-2 has been described. It is built upon ideas from micro-code compaction, program restructuring, and an original allocation strategy adapted to the periodicity of the loops. Our present implementation is based on the MIMOSA micro-code optimizer, and has permitted to validate the approach as well as test several strategies. The experimental results show the quality of the code produced, and the adequacy of the simple machine model used. The fact that speeds near the peak potential performance of the machines can be reached, also give some insights on the efficiency aspects of the non chaining Cray 2 Architecture. Directions for further research contain comparative studies of spilling strategies, and optimization of the use of local memories.

References

[1] ARYA,S., "Optimal Instruction Scheduling for a Class of Vector Processors: an Integer Programming Approach", *Report CRL-TR-19-83, University of Michigan*, 1983.

[2] BERGE, C., **"Graphes"**, *Gauthier Villars, Paris*, 1970.

[3] CHAITIN,G.J., "Register Allocation and Spilling via Graph Coloring", *Proc. ACM SIGPLAN Symp. on Compiler Construction*, Boston, 1982.

[4] CYTRON,R., FERRANTE,J., "What's in a name? The value of renaming for parallelism detection and storage allocation", *ICPP '87*, 1987.

[5] DAVIDSON,E.S., "The Design and Control of Pipelined Function Generators", *Proc. 1971 Int. IEEE Conf. on Syst., Networks, and Computers*, 1971.

[6] EISENBEIS,C, JALBY,W, LICHNEWSKY,A, "Squeezing more CPU performance out of a CRAY-2 by vector block scheduling", *INRIA Res. Rep. no 841*, 1988.

[7] FISHER,J.A., ELLIS,J.R., RUTTENBERG,J.C., NICOLAU,A., "Parallel processing:a smart compiler and a dumb machine", *Proceedings of the 1984 SIGPLAN Symposium on Compiler Construction*, 1984.

[8] KENNEDY, K., "Automatic Vectorization of Fortran Programs to Vector Form", *Technical Report, Rice University, Houston, TX, October 1980.*

[9] KUCK, D.J., KUHN, R., PADUA, D., LEASURE, B., WOLFE, M., "Dependence Graphs and Compiler Optimizations", *Proc. 8th ACM Symp. POPL, Williamsburgh, VA, 1981.*

[10] LICHNEWSKY, A., LOYER, M., "Un Module Vectoriel Flottant sur SPS7. Pourquoi?", *Bulletin de Liaison de Liaison INRIA, no 112, 1987.*

[11] LICHNEWSKY,A., THOMASSET, F., "Techniques de base pour l'exploitation automatique du parallelisme dans les programmes", *Rapport de Recherche INRIA, N 460, 1985.*

[12] LICHNEWSKY, A., THOMASSET, F., EISENBEIS, C., "Automatic Detection of Parallelism in Scientific Programs with Application to Array-Processors", *Proc.of IBM Institute, North Holland, 1986.*

[13] MACKE, T., HUSON, C., DAVIES, J., LEASURE, B., WOLFE, M., "The KAP/ST-100 : A Fortran Translator for the ST100 Attached Processor", *International Conference on Parallel Processing 1986.*

[14] SHAR, L.E., "Design and scheduling of statically configured pipelines", *Stanford Univ., Technical Report n 42, 1972.*

[15] WEISS,S., SMITH,J.E., "Instruction Issue Logic in Pipelined Supercomputers", *IEEE Tr. Comp., Vol. C-33, NO.11, Nov. 1984, pp 1013-1022*, 1984.

Performance for V. Length = 490				
Loop	CFT 2	CFT 77	VASCO	Speedup
m1	67.99	90.73	113.22	1.24
m2	66.62	93.03	108.89	1.17
mv1	70.87	89.99	123.25	1.37
mv2	84.64	106.93	137.90	1.29
mv3	78.95	111.57	146.94	1.32
mv4	78.36	99.43	145.51	1.46
mv5	85.57	106.98	149.32	1.39
mv6	82.34	103.86	135.86	1.31
mv7	72.86	84.05	115.36	1.37
mv8	72.30	87.45	127.86	1.46
mv9	81.33	104.82	133.08	1.27
mvf1	74.72	92.69	109.81	1.18
mvf2	68.01	83.29	117.40	1.41
mvf3	64.65	87.08	97.48	1.12
mvf4	79.78	88.05	92.74	1.05
mvf5	64.73	85.15	111.24	1.31
mvf6	78.69	89.40	120.23	1.34
mvf7	71.64	87.07	117.13	1.34
mvf8	72.75	90.79	119.03	1.31
mulcomp	104.71	111.37	152.12	1.36
drot	130.35	123.94	130.35	1.05

Figure 7: Performance in MFLOPS under Average Load

Performance for V. Length = 234				
Loop	CFT 2	CFT 77	VASCO	Speedup
m1	62.92	71.93	102.07	1.42
m2	62.11	57.23	100.12	1.61
mv1	67.39	70.81	109.54	1.55
mv2	78.54	80.84	122.47	1.51
mv3	79.06	87.21	116.79	1.34
mv4	75.68	82.88	121.34	1.46
mv5	82.39	81.82	122.04	1.48
mv6	79.04	80.26	119.06	1.48
mv7	67.79	71.50	88.160	1.23
mv8	67.87	73.03	106.08	1.45
mv9	75.85	82.71	117.67	1.42
mvf1	71.25	70.81	107.21	1.50
mvf2	67.02	72.10	99.250	1.38
mvf3	64.80	71.08	100.77	1.42
mvf4	72.80	74.27	103.08	1.39
mvf5	62.61	69.37	102.34	1.48
mvf6	70.27	80.37	109.33	1.36
mvf7	68.06	74.49	96.570	1.30
mvf8	70.61	75.39	113.39	1.50
mulcomp	98.52	108.5	128.44	1.18
drot	127.6	121.3	148.95	1.17

Figure 6: Performance in MFLOPS under Average Load

Performance for V. Length = 256			
Loop	CFT 77	VASCO	Speedup
m1	78.09	141.24	1.81
m2	75.87	129.40	1.70
mv1	83.41	119.61	1.43
mv2	100.48	143.75	1.43
mv3	96.82	144.75	1.49
mv4	96.96	145.20	1.50
mv5	95.32	144.75	1.52
mv6	86.74	143.75	1.66
mv7	80.14	105.11	1.31
mv8	80.74	130.80	1.62
mv9	95.80	144.87	1.51
mvf1	87.62	115.77	1.32
mvf2	84.67	111.36	1.32
mvf3	83.17	114.21	1.37
mvf4	77.50	115.69	1.49
mvf5	84.09	113.45	1.35
mvf6	98.26	110.32	1.12
mvf7	84.17	111.23	1.32
mvf8	93.34	123.56	1.32
mulcomp	128.84	163.66	1.27
drot	150.11	165.62	1.10

Figure 8: Performance in MFLOPS on a dedicated machine

Performance for V. Length = 960			
Loop	CFT 77	VASCO	Speedup
m1	131.787	180.202	1.38
m2	122.260	159.663	1.30
mv1	121.277	139.789	1.15
mv2	142.381	178.148	1.25
mv3	135.306	179.560	1.32
mv4	139.608	178.738	1.28
mv5	136.248	167.727	1.23
mv6	112.518	165.983	1.47
mv7	112.254	146.464	1.30
mv8	118.987	153.976	1.29
mv9	128.110	174.086	1.35
mvf1	107.678	125.998	1.17
mvf2	115.552	131.174	1.13
mvf3	118.210	138.521	1.17
mvf4	106.112	122.504	1.15
mvf5	111.679	132.461	1.18
mvf6	116.838	125.12	1.07
mvf7	115.461	131.101	1.13
mvf8	108.584	135.921	1.25
mulcomp	129.429	192.898	1.49
drot	151.892	250.655	1.65

Figure 9: Performance in MFLOPS on a dedicated machine

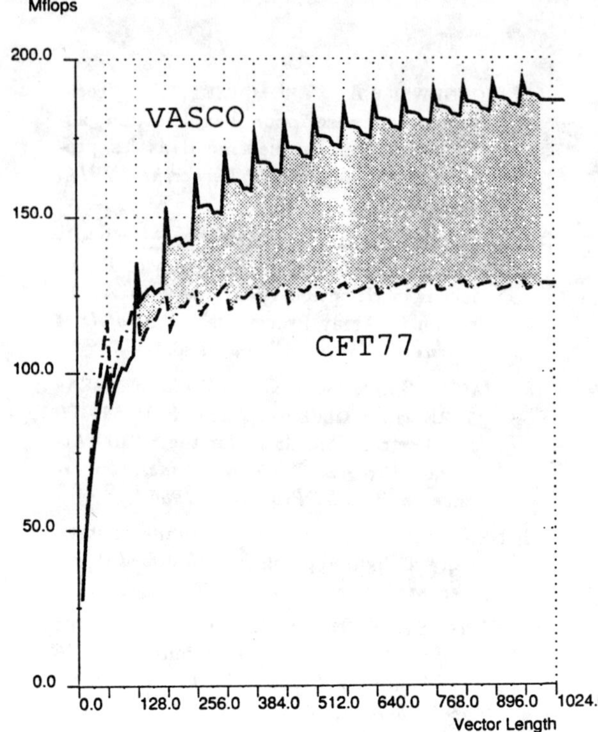

Figure 11: Performance in MFLOPS on a dedicated machine: mulcomp

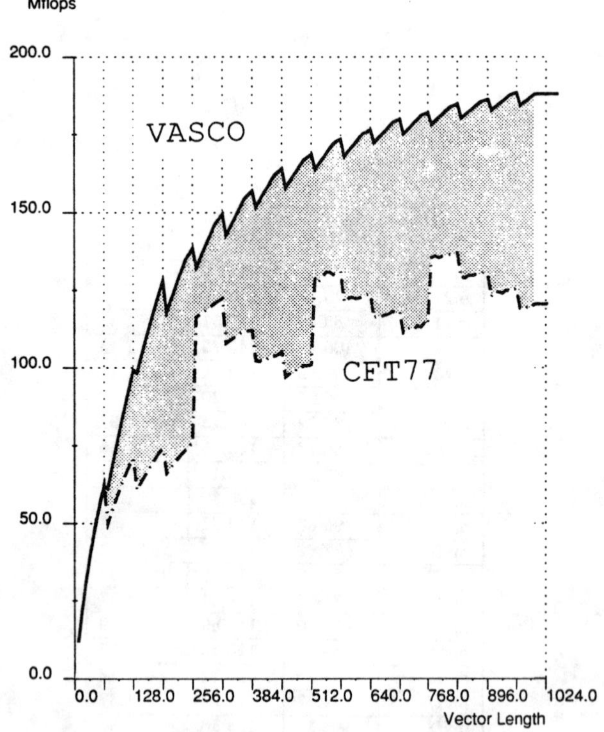

Figure 10: Performance in MFLOPS on a dedicated machine: m1

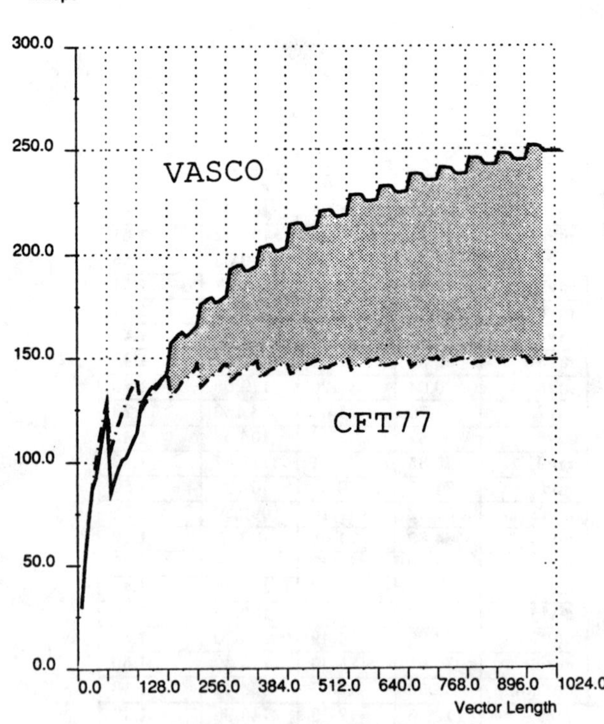

Figure 12: Performance in MFLOPS on a dedicated machine: drot

Parallel Processing on Supercomputers: A Set of Computational Experiments*

N. Balram C. Belo[†] J. M. F. Moura

Depart. Elect. and Comp. Eng., Carnegie Mellon University, Pittsburgh, PA, 15213.

Abstract

One of the trends in supercomputer evolution lies in the direction of multiprocessor systems with increasing numbers of powerful processors. The user who is interested in attaining the maximum achievable computation rates on these machines must understand the philosophy underlying the parallel processing mechanisms provided on them. This paper focuses on the three types of parallelism currently available on the Cray: vectorization, microtasking, and macrotasking. Experiences with all three constructs are presented with a view to exposing the improvements possible with each of them. While this paper deals with a particular machine, the Cray X-MP/48, many of the observations, comments, and conclusions derived can be generalized to other shared-memory multiprocessor systems.

1 Introduction

One of the trends in supercomputer evolution lies in the direction of multiprocessor systems with increasing numbers of powerful processors. Consider Cray as an example. The Cray-1 was introduced in 1976 as a uniprocessor system with orders of magnitude speedup over mainframes, because of its faster clock cycle, large and fast memory, and its ability to perform vector arithmetic. The Cray X-MP/2, introduced in 1982, has 2 CPUs, the Cray X-MP/4, introduced in 1984 has 4 as does the Cray-2, introduced in 1985. The trend in the next generation Cray machines is towards even larger numbers of processors: the Cray Y-MP with 8 CPUs, the Cray-3 with 16, and the Cray-4 with 64. While each of these machines will have improved computation rates for each CPU because of advances in technology (further decrease in clock cycle times, faster memories, etc.), the major speedup will result from the availability of larger numbers of CPUs to process work in parallel.

The different types of parallelism available on the Cray X-MP are *vectorization*, *microtasking*, and *macrotasking*, the last two often collectively referred to as *multitasking*. Vectorization is the process of replacing a block of sequential code by instructions that use vector functional units. The compiler analyzes the user program, identifies computations that can be overlapped, and produces object code to carry out these computations using the vector hardware available. On the Cray, this is presently done at the level of the innermost DO loop.

CRI[1] defines multitasking to be the process of dividing a program into segments which are then executed in parallel. This paper discusses our experiences with both forms of multitasking available on the Cray X-MP. Vectorization issues are dealt with only when they arise in connection with multitasking. This approach is adopted because vectorization is performed automatically by the compiler and therefore requires only a little insight and care on the part of the programmer. Furthermore, well written, general references on this subject are available (see [3]). Also, in [8] a pertinent detailed discussion on some vectorization issues, is presented. We concentrate on multitasking, instead. Section 2 deals with microtasking while section 3 discusses macrotasking, comparing and contrasting it with microtasking. Details of the actual implementation of these constructs are avoided. There is ample literature available on this (see [4], [5], [6]). The goal is to focus on the principles behind them and use experimental results to derive rules of thumb to guide other users in implementing multitasked programs. All programs discussed are coded in Fortran.

Even though this paper is primarily concerned with

*The work reported here was performed using the facilities of the Pittsburgh Supercomputing Center(PSC), and sponsored by NSF grant # ECS-8515801

†on leave from Instituto Superior Técnico and CAPS, Universidade Técnica de Lisboa, Portugal, on a fellowship from Junta Nacional de Investigação Científica e Tecnológica (JNICT).

[1] Cray Research Inc.

the Cray X-MP architecture and the parallel processing structures available on it, many of the principles incorporated are general enough to be applied to other systems such as the IBM 3090, and the Alliant FX/Series, which, like the X-MP, are shared-memory multiprocessor configurations. See [1] for a comprehensive architectural taxonomy of supercomputers.

The applications discussed in this paper were run on two Cray X-MP/48 machines, one at the Pittsburgh Supercomputing Center (PSC), the other at CRI in Mendota Heights. The Cray X-MP/48 consists of 4 independent enhanced Cray-1 processors, sharing a 32 or 64 way interleaved central memory of 8Mwords (64 bit words). Each CPU has a set of address computation units, two sets of integer functional units, and one set of floating point functional units comprising of add, multiply, and reciprocal approximation. In addition, each CPU has four ports to main memory, allowing two memory reads, one memory write, and I/O to proceed simultaneously. The Cray X-MP is a register-to-register architecture, with each processor having a set of 8 vector registers of 64 words (64 bits/word). The clock period of the X-MP/48 at the PSC is 9.5 nano seconds, corresponding to a peak rate of 210 MFLOP per CPU.

2 Microtasking

Microtasking is a simple mechanism for partitioning a task into independent segments that can be processed in parallel (see [4], [6]). Microtasking was designed to automatically do dynamic load partitioning, i.e., the work is assigned to the processors available at runtime. The idea is to stack up parallel work in independent pieces that are picked up by processors as and when they are available, instead of assigning it to specific CPUs. This eliminates time wasted when one CPU is waiting for another to return from other duties and finish processing its assigned work. Dynamic load partitioning makes efficient use of idle CPUs in a batch environment.

Microtasking does not involve programming individual processors. It is primarily a method of controlling access of available processors to segments of code and variables in the program. This is done by inserting directives in the code. A preprocessor, called PREMULT, is invoked prior to the running of the microtasked code. It interprets the directives and rewrites the program, making calls to the microtasking library where necessary. This is transparent to the user. Since these directives appear as comment lines (they always begin with a C), they do not reduce the portability of the program. Furthermore, since the successful execution of the program is independent of the actual number of processors, the code written for a particular machine, say the Cray X-MP/4, can be run efficiently on other machines with different numbers of CPUs (for example Cray X-MP/2 or Cray Y-MP).

Because of its low overhead, microtasking can be used to process tasks with small granularity as well as large. In [7], it is concluded that microtasking is useful for tasks with granularity greater than 1000 clock periods, which allows it to be used at the DO loop level and sometimes even at the statement level.

The fine-granularity possible makes a bottom-up approach to parallelizing a problem/program viable. Since multitasking a program is primarily a data access problem, one of the most important steps is the analysis of the scope of the variables. A bottom-up approach simplifies the data analysis, because it is easier to analyze scope at lower levels. Bottom-up is particularly convenient when, as is often the case, most of the computation is concentrated in a few subroutines. Microtasking allows the programmer to exploit any parallelism in these routines, without needing to bother about the rest of the program.

The first of our algorithms that was considered for microtasking was the two dimensional convolution. The bulk of the computational load, in many signal processing applications is concentrated in this operation. That along with the nested loop structure of the algorithm makes it ideal for microtasking. Figure 1 shows the two dimensional asymmetric convolution (see [8]). It has three loops nested one inside the other; often one of them is short. The optimized implementation, from the vectorization point of view, has the short loop unrolled (to minimize memory references) with the innermost loop being the largest one. The outer loop can be microtasked, because the iterations are independent of each other, and can therefore be performed by different processors in any order (see Figure 1).

The unmicrotasked routine ran at 159 MFLOPS while the microtasked one ran at 618 MFLOPS thus providing a speedup of 3.88 (the speedup due to multitasking is defined as the ratio of the wall clock time of the unmultitasked code to the wall clock time of the multitasked code with both being run on a dedicated system). The symmetric version of the two dimensional convolution has array B(*) identical to A(*). The asymmetric code is converted into the symmetric version by replacing the B(*) array by A(*) and then pulling out the A(I) common to each pair of operands, for example A(5)*XN1(I,J+5)+B(5)*XN1(I,J+15) becomes A(5)*(XN1(I,J+5)+XN1(I,J+15)) (see Fig-

```
CMIC$ MICRO
      SUBROUTINE conv2d
      COMMON /VECT/ A(500)
      COMMON /MATRIX/ XN(65,543),XN1(65,543)

CMIC$ DO GLOBAL
      DO 40 I=1,64
      DO 20 J=1,512
      XN(I,J)= A(5)*XN1(I,J+5)+B(5)*XN1(I,J+15)
     ,        +A(4)*XN1(I,J+6)+B(4)*XN1(I,J+14)
     ,        +A(3)*XN1(I,J+7)+B(3)*XN1(I,J+13)
     ,        +A(2)*XN1(I,J+8)+B(2)*XN1(I,J+12)
     ,        +A(1)*XN1(I,J+9)+B(1)*XN1(I,J+11)
     ,    +XN1(I,J+10)
20     CONTINUE
40     CONTINUE
      RETURN
      END
```

Figure 1: Two-dimensional asymmetric convolution

ure 1). The unmicrotasked two dimensional symmetric convolution ran at 145 MFLOPS while the microtasked one ran at 547 MFLOPS thereby providing a speedup of 3.78. The excellent computation rate obtained for both versions of the convolution confirms that the performance of this kind of operation is considerably enhanced by microtasking.

The one dimensional convolution is another worthwhile candidate for microtasking, for the same reasons mentioned in the context of the two dimensional convolution. The operation requires two DO loops, one nested inside the other. Often one of the DO loops is much smaller than the other. This is the case in a program which is discussed later in this section. The numbers used in the convolution correspond to the actual numbers in production runs of that program, making it a real example rather than a cookbook one. In such cases, optimum vectorization dictates that the shorter loop be unrolled to minimize memory references. Three possible implementations are shown in Figure 2: *conv1* (Figure 2(a)) has the smaller loop nested inside the larger one, *conv2* (Figure 2(b)) has the larger one inside the smaller, *conv3* (Figure 2(c)) is the same as *conv2* but has the outer loop unrolled to minimize memory references.

All three were microtasked and run on a dedicated machine (see Figure 3 and Table 1). As expected, *conv1* performed the worst in both cases (microtasked and unmicrotasked) because the inner loop is too small to provide good vector performance, and the gain in performance, as a result of microtasking is not enough to offset the loss in vectorization. The unmicrotasked version of *conv2* (*conv2-A*) ran at 135 MFLOPS because of the large inner loop length (1792). Since the outer loop iterations are not independent, this could not be microtasked the way the

```
      SUBROUTINE conv1-A
C
      DO 16 J=20,1812
      P(J)=F(J)
      DO 15 I=1,19
      P(J)=P(J)+A(I)*(F(J-I)+F(J+I))
15     CONTINUE
16     CONTINUE
      RETURN
      END
```

(a)

```
      SUBROUTINE conv2-A
C
      DO 1 J=20,1812
1      P(J)=F(J)
      DO 16 I=1,19
      DO 15 J=20,1812
      P(J)=P(J)+A(I)*(F(J-I)+F(J+I))
15     CONTINUE
16     CONTINUE
      RETURN
      END
```

(b)

```
      SUBROUTINE conv3-A
C
      DO 16 J=20,1812
      P(J)= A(19)*(F(J-19)+F(J+19))
     ,    +A(18)*(F(J-18)+F(J+18))
     ,    +A(17)*(F(J-17)+F(J+17))
     ,    +A(16)*(F(J-16)+F(J+16))
     ,    +A(15)*(F(J-15)+F(J+15))
     ,    +A(14)*(F(J-14)+F(J+14))
     ,    +A(13)*(F(J-13)+F(J+13))
     ,    +A(12)*(F(J-12)+F(J+12))
     ,    +A(11)*(F(J-11)+F(J+11))
     ,    +A(10)*(F(J-10)+F(J+10))
     ,    +A(9)*(F(J-9)+F(J+9))
     ,    +A(8)*(F(J-8)+F(J+8))
     ,    +A(7)*(F(J-7)+F(J+7))
     ,    +A(6)*(F(J-6)+F(J+6))
     ,    +A(5)*(F(J-5)+F(J+5))
     ,    +A(4)*(F(J-4)+F(J+4))
     ,    +A(3)*(F(J-3)+F(J+3))
     ,    +A(2)*(F(J-2)+F(J+2))
     ,    +A(1)*(F(J-1)+F(J+1))
     ,    +F(J)
16     CONTINUE
      RETURN
      END
```

(c)

Figure 2: Three different implementations of the one-dimensional convolution

Table 1: Wallclock times: unmicrotasked (version A) and microtasked (version B) one-dimensional convolution

routine	wall-clock time (ms)	MFLOPS	Speed Up (A/B)
conv1-A	163.2	12.5	
conv1-B	46.19	44.23	3.53
conv2-A	15.09	135.4	
conv2-B	7.305	279.66	2.065
conv3-A	14.11	144.8	
conv3-B	4.342	470.5	3.25

two dimensional convolution was. To microtask this we split the inner loop into 4 smaller loops, each of which could then be run in parallel (see *conv2-B*, Figure 3(b)).

The resulting task granularity was too small to provide good speedup (we define 3.0 or more as good on a 4 processor system). Therefore the microtasked code ran at 280 MFLOPS, corresponding to a speedup of 2.07 (see Table 1). As expected the unmicrotasked version of *conv3* (*conv3-A*) ran faster than either of the other two unmicrotasked versions, at a speed of 145 MFLOPS. It has no outer loop at all, so, as before, to microtask the routine, we broke the loop into 4 smaller loops (see *conv3-B*, Figure 3(c)). The task granularity was enough to allow a reasonable speedup (more than 3). The microtasked version A ran at 471 MFLOPS, a speedup of 3.25 . Increasing the loop length by an order of magnitude produced a rate of 557 MFLOPS for the microtasked code as opposed to 148 MFLOPS for the unmicrotasked, a speedup of 3.77.

The reason why the strategy of breaking up the inner loop into smaller loops to be run in parallel worked so well here is that the Cray is a register-to-register architecture. This makes it possible to run even short vectors at reasonable computation rates, i.e, the half performance length is fairly small. The half performance length, $l_{1/2}$, is defined as the length of a vector for which half of the maximum performance is obtained for that operation [3]. A vector typical of the kind generated by unrolling small outer loops was run with different loop lengths, on a dedicated machine (see Figure 4). The resulting performance is plotted in Figure 4 . From the plot, it is clear that for vector lengths greater than 48 the computation rate increases very gradually, approaching 148 MFLOPS asymptotically. Therefore, once past the knee of this curve, the best strategy is to break up the loop into smaller loops that can be run in par-

```
CMIC$ MICRO
      SUBROUTINE conv1-B
CMIC$ DO GLOBAL
      DO 16 J=20,1812
      P(J)=F(J)
      DO 15 I=1,19
      P(J)=P(J)+A(I)*(F(J-I)+F(J+I))
15      CONTINUE
16     CONTINUE
      RETURN
      END
```

(a)

```
CMIC$ MICRO
      SUBROUTINE conv2-B
      DO 1 J=20,1812
1       P(J)=F(J)
      L = 1812/4
      DO 16 I=1,19
CMIC$ PROCESS
      DO 15 J=20,L
      P(J)=P(J)+A(I)*(F(J-I)+F(J+I))
15      CONTINUE
CMIC$ ALSO PROCESS
      DO 17 J=L+1,2*L
      P(J)=P(J)+A(I)*(F(J-I)+F(J+I))
17      CONTINUE
CMIC$ ALSO PROCESS
      DO 18 J=2*L+1,3*L
      P(J)=P(J)+A(I)*(F(J-I)+F(J+I))
18      CONTINUE
CMIC$ ALSO PROCESS
      DO 19 J= 3*L+1, 1812
      P(J)=P(J)+A(I)*(F(J-I)+F(J+I))
19      CONTINUE
CMIC$ END PROCESS
16      CONTINUE
      RETURN
      END
```

(b)

```
CMIC$ MICRO
      SUBROUTINE conv3-B
      L = 1812/4
CMIC$ PROCESS
      DO 16 J=20,L
      P(J)= A(19)*(F(J-19)+F(J+19))
      . . .
     ,   +A(1)*(F(J-1)+F(J+1))
     ,   +F(J)
16      CONTINUE
CMIC$ ALSO PROCESS
      DO 17 J= L+1, 2*L
      . . .
17      CONTINUE
CMIC$ ALSO PROCESS
      DO 18 J= 2*L+1, 3*L
      . . .
18      CONTINUE
CMIC$ ALSO PROCESS
      DO 19 J= 3*L+1, 1812
      P(J)= A(19)*(F(J-19)+F(J+19))
      . . .
     ,   +A(1)*(F(J-1)+F(J+1))
     ,   +F(J)
19      CONTINUE
CMIC$ END PROCESS
      RETURN
      END
```

(c)

Figure 3: Microtasked versions of the 3 implementations of the one-dimensional convolution

allel.

The degradation in performance due to smaller loop length is very small in this region (see Figure 4) while the computation rate possible, with even 2 CPUs available, will exceed that of the single larger loop run on one CPU. For example (see the table in Figure 4) a loop of length 64, which runs at 106 MFLOPS on a single CPU, can be broken into 4 loops of size 16 each of which can now run on separate processors at 53 MFLOPS apiece giving a best case rate of 212 MFLOPS, an improvement of 100% . For larger loop lengths the improvements possible are even greater.

A simple formula[2] to compute the asymptotic computation rate for any vector involving only floating point additions and multiplications, and memory reads and writes is:

$$MFLOPS = \frac{64}{68} \times 105 \times \frac{n_a + n_m}{\max(n_a, n_m, m_r, m_w)} \quad (1)$$

where n_a is the number of floating point additions, n_m the number of floating point multiplications, m_w the number of memory writes, and m_r half the number of memory reads, performed per iteration of the loop. The composition of the formula is intuitive. The (64/68) factor comes from the fact that a floating point unit can perform a maximum of 64 operations in 68 clock periods. The (105) factor converts this to the number of floating point operations per second. A clock period of 9.5 nano seconds corresponds to 105 million periods per second. When using this formula for an X-MP with a different clock period, this factor will have to be changed accordingly. The remaining factor measures the overlap of the addition and multiplication functional units. For example, the two dimensional symmetric convolution has 10 adds and 5 multiplies in each iteration of the inner loop and so the overlap factor works out to be 1.5. The best case performance would be for an algorithm with an equal number of additions and multiplications thus leading to an overlap factor of 2, i.e., the add and multiply units overlap completely and in every 68 clock periods 64 adds and 64 multiplies are performed. The denominator of this factor reflects the constraints imposed by the limited number of paths between a CPU and main memory, allowing only 2 memory reads and 1 memory write to proceed simultaneously.

[2]This formula was communicated to the authors by David Slowinski of Carnegie Mellon University and the Pittsburgh Supercomputing Center(PSC).

```
      DO 20 J=11,N
        F(J)=B(10)*(C(J-10) + C(J+10))
     ,        +B(9)*(C(J-9) + C(J+9))
     ,        +B(8)*(C(J-8) + C(J+8))
     ,        +B(7)*(C(J-7) + C(J+7))
     ,        +B(6)*(C(J-6) + C(J+6))
     ,        +B(5)*(C(J-5) + C(J+5))
     ,        +B(4)*(C(J-4) + C(J+4))
     ,        +B(3)*(C(J-3) + C(J+3))
     ,        +B(2)*(C(J-2) + C(J+2))
     ,        +B(1)*(C(J-1) + C(J+1))
     ,        +C(J)
 20   CONTINUE
```

(a)

Loop Length	MFLOPS
8	31.15
16	53.4
32	80.97
48	96.24
64	106.54
96	113.71
150	125.00
200	126.06
512	139.18
1024	142.29
2048	143.97
4096	144.79
8192	144.82

(b)

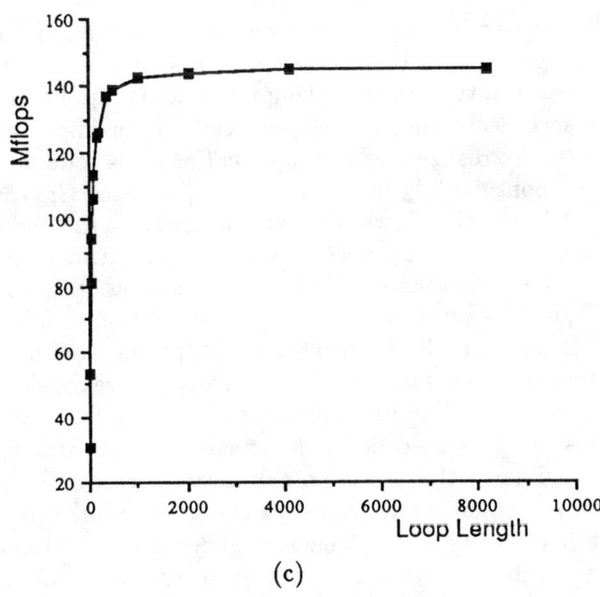

(c)

Figure 4: Vector performance of an example loop on a single CPU

Using this formula the sample loop, displayed in Figure 4, (as well as the loop in *conv3* of the convolution) is computed as having an asymptotic computation rate of 148 MFLOPS. This corresponds well with the experimental results obtained . The half performance length, $l_{1/2}$, for this example is between 16 and 32 (see table in Figure 4) reinforcing the assertion that even moderately long (64 and above) loops of this kind should be broken into smaller loops that can run in parallel.

Some general conclusions can be drawn from these experiences. We looked at one implementation of the one-dimensional convolution, in which microtasking was substituted in place of vectorization (in *conv1*, in which the innermost loop is the shortest one). Clearly this is not a good idea because vectorization currently provides a larger speedup than microtasking (an order of magnitude versus 4), though this could change in systems with more CPUs. The other two implementations of the one-dimensional convolution (*conv2* and *conv3*) allowed us a less drastic choice, namely to tradeoff some vectorization performance in exchange for microtasking. This was done by breaking up loops into smaller ones, which could then be run, albeit at lower vector rates, in parallel using multiple CPUs. High computation rates (up to 557 MFLOPS) were achieved in this manner, because of the small amount of degradation in vector rates for even moderate loop lengths (see Figure 4). This approach is viable in batch environments, because an increase in computation rate is possible with as few as two CPUs available.

Finally, an application program of considerable interest to the authors' research was considered for microtasking. It serves here the objective of testing the viability of microtasking in an actual application where decreasing the elapsed time is an important goal. To realize real-time applications this code must run considerably faster than a uniprocessor Cray X-MP presently allows. One way of achieving the higher computation rates needed is by using multitasking.

The computer program we are dealing with simulates the phase modulation/demodulation problem. See for example [9] for more on the physics and practical interest of the problem, and alternative considerations regarding its implementation in an array processor. The so-called point-masses filter, which approximates the optimum nonlinear filter with arbitrarily small error, computes the a posteriori probability density, $F_n(\mathbf{i})$, (conditional density of the signal given the observations) as a sequence of masses at discrete points, $\mathbf{i}$, of a grid.This density is propagated in time using the relations

$$\begin{aligned} P_{n+1} &= F_n * Q_n \\ F_{n+1} &= P_{n+1} \bullet O_{n+1} \end{aligned} \tag{2}$$

where P_{n+1} is the prediction density, Q_n is a function of the signal model, and O_{n+1} depends only on the observations at the current time, n. The symbols $*$ and $\bullet$ denote convolution and pointwise function multiplication respectively. All the quantities in (3) are computed in a discrete set of grid points, although the dependence on $\mathbf{i}$ has been omitted. The specific grid to use depends on problem parameters such as the signal-to-noise ratio.

Once the a posteriori density, F_n, is known for a particular time instant, n, signal estimates are computed according to the cost-function one wants to minimize. The algorithm (3) can be interpreted as a discretized version solution to a partial differential equation (PDE).

The performance of this filter, and in general the performance of a nonlinear filter, can only be assessed by Monte Carlo methods. Signal and observations are generated for a given time set I^N (e.g., $I^{1000} = [1, 2, \ldots, 1000]$), the estimate being the output of the filter routine. This procedure is repeated a large number of times. As long as one guarantees statistical independence between data at each repetition, meaningful statistical results can be obtained. Aside from the initialization procedures, the main program consists of a large outer (Monte Carlo) DO loop, each iteration computing a time sequence of signal estimates. The actual error for each time instant is computed as well as other parameters describing the behavior of the filter. This data is written to a file for processing.

Convolution is the most computationally intensive routine in the program. This routine, along with all the other routines that can be microtasked, account for at best 75% of the execution time. Amdahl's law predicts that this would provide a speedup of less than 2.3, even if the microtasked code ran at 100% efficiency, i.e., if all the microtasked segments ran 4 times faster than their unitasked versions. Instead of microtasking at the lower level, as is usually the case, a more productive (in terms of speedup obtainable) approach is to exploit the natural parallelism of the problem, namely the almost independent Monte Carlo iterations.

For the purpose of parallel execution, the main problem arises in the generation of independent paths for each Monte Carlo loop iteration. Actually, random number generators guarantee independence (more rigorously very small correlation) between numbers computed sequentially, but if a copy of the same generator is given to each task running in parallel the random numbers, and consequently the signal and the observations, would be the same for all tasks. To overcome this problem, the random generator routine can be defined as a protected region whose updates are known by every task. There are two reasons why this solution is not viable: i) the overhead due to tasks waiting to entering the critical region would be large (each observation requires 3 random numbers) in comparison with the computations; ii) the order in which microtasked loop iterations are processed is non-deterministic, varying from run to run, leading to results that are not reproducible.

An alternative solution, that avoids the two problems mentioned above is to precompute all the random numbers needed and store them in a matrix. Each Monte Carlo iteration accesses the numbers it needs, stored in different columns of the matrix. This makes the iterations independent. The only remaining issue is the handling of the critical regions in the loop, i.e, those places in which all the iterations make use of a shared resource. The original program was coded so as to output results during each Monte Carlo iteration. The I/O has to be monitored to ensure that no two tasks write to the same file at the same time. With these issues taken care of, the program was microtasked by placing the entire Monte Carlo loop inside a subroutine and then defining each iteration of the loop as a process (the smallest amount of work handled by a processor at a time).

Scaled down versions (with 48 Monte Carlo iterations) of both the unmicrotasked and the microtasked programs were run on a dedicated machine as well as in a batch environment. Program execution times (i.e., wallclock time) are consistent on a dedicated machine. In batch mode, however, the execution time depends on the load on the system and fluctuates widely from one run to another. In order to facilitate comparisons between the performance of the multitasked code and the unitasked (i.e., unmultitasked) code, with both run in batch mode, they were run in multiple sessions at different times of the day. Each session consisted of one unitasked run, one microtasked run, one macrotasked (using static partitioning), and one macrotasked (using dynamic partitioning). The programs comprising a session were run one after another, always ensuring that only one of them was running on the machine, at a time. Thus for example the 10 am session began with the unitasked program. As soon as it finished executing, the microtasked version was executed, then the two macrotasked versions one after another (they are discussed in the next section). The timing data compiled from these sessions is recorded in Table 2, with the batch runs distinguished by the time the session was conducted at.

The best speedup obtained was 3.06 (see results in Table 2). This was computed using the wall clock timings on the dedicated machine. As predicted by Amdahl's law the maximum speedup theoretically possible is limited by the sequential portion of the program, in this case mainly the random number generator. With the help of FLOWTRACE, an analysis tool, the percentage of execution time of the unitasked program spent in the random number generator was computed to be 5.67. The other sequential portions of the program contribute another 2.14% to this. Then Amdahl's law predicts that the maximum speedup possible is 3.24 $(100/(7.81 + 92.19/4) = 3.24)$, assuming the microtasking is 100% efficient, i.e., the microtasked segment runs 4 times faster than the original unitasked version. Note that Amdahl's law is applicable here because the serial portion of the problem grows along with the parallel portion when the number of Monte Carlo iterations is increased. Thus the ratio of serial to parallel portions remains constant with increasing problem size (i.e., increasing Monte Carlo iterations) unlike the kinds of problems dealt with in [2].

The actual speedup obtained (3.06) is close to this. Using Amdahl's law, the microtasked portion speedup works out to be about 3.7. The I/O in the Monte Carlo loop is responsible for restricting the microtasking segment speedup to 3.7 because it creates a critical region in the code (a critical region is one which can be accessed by only one processor at a time, see [4]). The program could be rewritten to avoid performing I/O in the Monte Carlo loop, but the modest gain in performance (an increase in total program speedup, from 3.06 to 3.24) makes the additional labor an unattractive proposition. There is an important philosophical difference between writing a multitasked program from scratch and converting existing sequential code into a multitasked form. When writing a multitasked program, the programmer can structure it so as to exploit all the natural parallelism in the problem. For most applications, however, working sequential code exists. It is more practical to multitask this, while retaining the basic structure, rather than rewriting it. Situations such as in the phase demodulation program discussed here often arise, i.e., some facet of the original program inhibits full multitasking. In such cases a tradeoff is evident here in terms of time spent versus speedup obtained. A judgement has to be made whether the increase in performance that results from the restructuring of the original program justifies the amount of time it takes to do it. The phase demodulation program could have been microtasked by simply microtasking the convolution and other amenable routines. This provided a maximum attainable speedup of 2.3, for the entire program. As discussed earlier, the restructuring of the program to precompute the random numbers before the Monte Carlo loop increased this to 3.06. The increase clearly justified the modest effort required. Further restructuring, of the I/O in the Monte Carlo loop, could bring this closer to 3.24, the theoretical maximum. At this stage, the marginal improvement in performance was considered too small to justify the additional effort.

The dedicated system timings show that microtasking can improve the performance of this program by a factor of 3. For practical reasons, the improvement achieved in the batch environment was considered more important. Since batch system timings vary from run to run, it is difficult to find a metric to quantify the speedup achieved through microtasking. It makes no sense to compare the microtasked code timings with the timings of the unitasked code with the latter run on a dedicated machine. Nor is it reasonable to compare any arbitrary microtasked timing with just any unitasked timing, with both being run in a batch environment. One reasonable way to gauge the speedups possible is by comparing the wall clock timings for the microtasked code with the timings for the unitasked code, run on a batch system, as close together as possible without having both jobs running on the system at the same time (i.e., the jobs run in the same session are compared). Thus for example, the microtasked program run in batch mode at 10 am took 57.48 seconds, while the unitasked program run in the same session took 114.10 seconds (see Table 2), thereby producing a speedup of 1.99. This procedure gives speedups ranging from 1.47 to 2.84 (see Table 2). These are conservative estimates since these jobs were run on a very heavily loaded machine at Mendota Heights. The price paid in terms of CPU overhead, i.e., the increase in the total CPU time of the program because of microtasking, is small (between 7 and 8%, see Table 2).

The results obtained from these experiments demonstrate that microtasking is useful in batch environments too in addition to dedicated ones. Recent studies [10] have shown that microtasking can boost total batch system throughput by 20 to 30%. This is

Table 2: Execution times for the phase demodulation program: Ded. = Dedicated, B = Batch, CPU = CPU time in seconds, WC = Wall-clock time in seconds

Version	Type	CPU (s)	WC (s)
Unitasked	Ded.	53.61	53.94
	Ded.	53.49	53.87
	Ded.	53.72	54.07
	B-10AM	57.11	114.10
	B-11AM	56.40	115.50
	B-Noon	56.82	135.30
	B-1PM	56.43	280.40
	B-2PM	56.91	128.30
	B-3PM	55.30	175.70
Macrotasked (Static)	Ded.	58.04	17.82
	Ded.	58.01	17.80
	Ded.	58.10	17.81
	B-10AM	58.22	53.26
	B-11AM	57.24	63.92
	B-Noon	57.56	67.37
	B-1PM	58.03	149.00
	B-2PM	56.97	90.79
	B-3PM	57.68	99.91
Macrotasked (Dynamic)	Ded.	58.14	17.86
	Ded.	58.02	17.86
	Ded.	58.09	17.79
	B-10AM	57.86	45.35
	B-11AM	57.39	66.68
	B-Noon	57.34	50.42
	B-1PM	57.45	125.20
	B-2PM	57.61	79.79
	B-3PM	58.01	126.00
Microtasked	Ded.	57.74	17.76
	Ded.	57.72	17.74
	Ded.	57.71	17.69
	B-10AM	57.67	57.48
	B-11AM	57.08	60.82
	B-Noon	58.49	70.77
	B-1PM	58.62	98.70
	B-2PM	57.23	87.26
	B-3PM	58.85	99.60

another good reason to use it whenever possible.

A major shortcoming apparent in microtasking is the absence of any mechanism to control the sequence of events. Because of this limitation, a DOPIPE cannot be microtasked. A DOPIPE is a software pipeline of segments within a loop that have dependencies among them that prevent the loop from having independent iterations. However if these dependencies are satisfied, the iterations can be executed in parallel. In the next section an older form of multitasking, known as macrotasking, is discussed. This does have the constructs needed to impose an ordering on the execution of segments of code.

3 Macrotasking

Macrotasking was the forerunner to microtasking. When first introduced by CRI it was known as multitasking, but with the introduction of microtasking CRI decided to rename it macrotasking. The term multitasking now refers to both microtasking and macrotasking. Macrotasking was designed to handle programs that could be divided into large segments which could be executed in parallel, once any critical regions were identified and protected and synchronization points were inserted where necessary (see [4], [5]). It is a sophisticated and sometimes cumbersome way of partitioning work among multiple CPUs. Unlike microtasking, the user has full freedom to assign packages of work to individual CPUs thereby giving him/her control over the partitioning of the tasks. The mechanism used to do the partitioning has a significant overhead associated with it, as compared to microtasked tasks. The effect of this is to force a lower bound on the granularity of the tasks created by the user. As a result, macrotasking cannot exploit parallelism at as low levels as microtasking can. Experiments performed in [7] suggest that a task granularity of at least 20,000 clock periods is needed before macrotasking provides any improvement in performance. The same experiments also indicate that for large grained tasks (1,000,000 clock periods and more) the speedups obtained using macrotasking are in the same range as those obtained with microtasking.

The need for larger grain partitioning naturally leads to a top-down approach in the search for parallelism in a problem/program. The first step to macrotasking a program involves an examination of the problem being coded. Any natural parallelism can be exploited with an aim to breaking the program into large chunks of code that can be executed in parallel once any dependencies are taken care. Unlike microtasking, the work to be done can be partitioned out to the CPUs before the program is run. This is known as static load balancing. Below, we comment on a different technique, dynamic load partitioning. When used with static load partitioning, macrotasking is recommended for use on dedicated systems only. In a batch environment, if there are dependencies between one or more of the user defined tasks, then one task may have to wait for another. In addition, at any synchronization point the master task will always have to wait for the slave tasks to complete their assigned duties before proceeding. The wait time can be minimized on a dedicated machine by intelligent balancing of the computational load among the CPUs. This is not possible in a batch environment because the availability of any processor at any particular instant is unpredictable. This makes the efficiency of static load balancing entirely dependent on the state of the machine at run time.

For this reason Microtasking was designed to automatically do dynamic load partitioning, i.e, the work is assigned to the processors available at runtime. Macrotasked programs can be designed to do this too. This is particularly simple in the case of partitioning iterations of a loop. Instead of assigning a fixed number of iterations (a fourth of the total, for a 4 processor machine) to each task (static load partitioning), a global counter can be used to keep track of unprocessed iterations. Each processor accesses and updates the counter and then processes a small number of iterations (the number depends on the granularity of each iteration, the total number done each time must be enough to make the macrotasking overhead worthwhile). The counter is protected to ensure that only one CPU can access it at a time. This method has two advantages over the more conventional assigning of work to each processor. Firstly, as explained before, its performance is usually better in a batch environment because situations when one or more processors are waiting for another one to return to complete its assigned piece of work are eliminated. Secondly, designing a macrotasked program to be independent of the actual number of processors in the system enables it to be run efficiently on any multiprocessor system in the Cray family. Statically balanced programs are explicitly designed to run using a fixed number of CPUs, so for example a program written to run on the Cray X-MP/2 would run inefficiently on the X-MP/4 because it would only use 2 of its 4 processors.

The phase demodulation program discussed in the previous section was macrotasked using the same approach as in the previous section. The data analysis and reordering of the program that was done for microtasking is applicable here too. Two macrotasked versions of the scaled down program (48 Monte Carlo iterations) were created. The first one used static partitioning, with the 4 tasks created being assigned 12 iterations each. In the second version, dynamic load partitioning was used, with the 4 tasks updating a shared counter one at a time and then performing one iteration per update. The iterations take slightly over one second each, to execute. This makes them of large enough grain to be set up as individual processes (as defined before, a process is the smallest amount of work assigned to a processor at a time, [4]). The results (see Table 2) show that both versions have speedups ranging between 3.02 and 3.04 on a dedicated machine. Once again, the performance in batch environment is of more interest for practical reasons. Using the same metric as in the microtasked section, i.e., comparing the times of unitasked and macrotasked versions that were run in the same session, we see that the speedups for the static version range from 1.41 to 2.14, while those for the dynamic version range from 1.39 to 2.68. The important thing to note here is that, even though the times obtained are rarely an improvement on the unitasked times on a dedicated machine, they often show a factor of two improvement over the times that a unitasked program would run in under the same system conditions. As stated in the previous section, the batch system speedups are conservative estimates of performance, because these programs were run on a very heavily loaded machine. On a machine with a more reasonable load, at the PSC, the same macrotasked code (dynamic version) has run in as little as 29 seconds. We conclude that a macrotasked program could be viable in a batch environment in addition to a dedicated one, particularly if dynamic load balancing is used.

As mentioned in the previous section, there are certain situations in which microtasking cannot be used but macrotasking can. This happens because unlike microtasking, macrotasking provides mechanisms (LOCKS, EVENTS, see [4]) to allow the programmer to enforce a particular ordering on the execution of pieces of code, according to the dependencies that may need to be satisfied between them. A simple example of such a case is considered (see Figure 5).

```
      DO 100 I=2,1000
        A(I)=A(I-1)*B(I)
        X(I)=A(I)+Y(I)
        Z(I)=A(I)*(B(I)+C(I))
          . . .
100   CONTINUE
```

(a)

```
      COMMON /count/ I
      I = 1
      CALL tskstart(task1ary,task)
      CALL task
      CALL tskwait(task1ary)

      SUBROUTINE task
      COMMON /count/ I
10     CALL lockon(lock1)
      J = I + 1
      I = J
      IF (J .GT. 1000) GO TO 100
      A(J) = A(J-1)*B(J)
      CALL lockoff(lock1)
      X(J) = A(J) + Y(J)
      Z(J) = A(J)*(B(J)+C(J))
          . . .
      GO TO 10
100    CALL lockoff(lock1)
```

(b)

Figure 5: (a) DO loop with dependency between iterations; (b) Macrotasked version of the DO loop.

It is a DO loop whose iterations are not independent but exhibit only a limited dependency. The dependency is due to a small portion of the loop, the rest of the computations in the loop being independent for each iteration. This can be macrotasked (see Figure 5). See [4] for a full explanation of the constructs used here. Figure 5 shows how the loop can be macrotasked to run on two processors, using locks to preserve the correct sequence of operations. It is also an example of dynamic load partitioning (see [4] for more examples). Static partitioning would not work here because of the dependencies between iterations. The same approach can be used to execute the program in parallel using 4 or more CPUs.

When microtasking is possible, why bother macrotasking when this obviously involves higher overhead than microtasking ? In most cases the answer to this is that one would prefer to microtask whenever possible. However, it is also possible to use both macrotasking and microtasking in the same program. A situation in which this is more useful than simply microtasking is when severe load imbalances exist. In such a case, macrotasking should be used at the highest level possible, while lower levels are microtasked. Macrotasked tasks have priority over microtasking, so, as long as all available CPUs are occupied, the microtasked code is processed by only a single processor. Whenever a CPU finishes its assigned task before the others do, instead of idling, it is used to process the microtasked code.

4 Conclusions

The paper has discussed the three types of parallelism presently available on the Cray: vectorization, microtasking, and macrotasking. By analyzing a specific family of applications which are important in Signal Processing and Communication problems, general conclusions were drawn in terms of how to structure algorithms to make best use of these constructs. Microtasking was used with small kernels such as the two dimensional convolution to attain computational rates of up to 618 MFLOPS. Speedups of up to 3.88 on a 4 CPU machine were obtained for these kernels.

The main advantages of microtasking are its simplicity, and its applicability at low levels thereby simplifying the data analysis problem. Because of its dynamic load partitioning, microtasking is viable in batch environments. A major limitation, but one which is seldom an issue in most applications, is its lack of a mechanism to control the sequencing of operations. When a specific ordering of events is necessary, only macrotasking can be used. Conversely, when the parallelism is of small granularity only microtasking may be viable because of the larger overhead associated with macrotasking. Whenever possible microtasking should be preferred over macrotasking because of the larger overhead associated with the latter. An exception to this is the case when large load imbalances exist, in which case both macrotasking and microtasking should be applied.

Macrotasking gives the programmer the option of static or dynamic load balancing. Dynamic load partitioning makes macrotasking more efficient, more portable, and also viable in batch environments as well as dedicated.

5 Acknowledgements

The authors thank the assistance provided by the following people: Ron Selva, Jeff Nicholson, and Lauren Radner at CRI; Steve Mittereder, David Slowinski, and Douglas Fox at the PSC.

References

[1] Kai Hwang, "Advanced Parallel Processing with Supercomputing Architectures," Proceedings of the IEEE, Vol.75, no.10, October 1987, pp.1348-1379.

[2] John L. Gustafson, "Reevaluating Amdahl's Law," Communications of the ACM, Vol.31, no.5, May 1988, pp.532-533.

[3] "Supercomputer Vectorization and Optimization Guide," Engineering Technology Applications Division, Boeing Computer Services, October 1984.

[4] "Cray X-MP Multitasking Programmer's Reference Manual," Cray Computer Systems, 1986.

[5] John L. Larsen, "Multitasking on the Cray X-MP-2 Multiprocessor," IEEE Computer Mag., Vol.17, no.7, July 1984, pp.62-69.

[6] Mike Booth, Kent Misegades, "Microtasking: a new way to harness multiprocessors," Cray Channels, Cray Research Inc.,Summer 1986, pp.24-27.

[7] Herbert U. Cornelius, "Some Timings for Synchronization on the Multiprocessor System Cray X-MP," Parallel Computing 85, eds. M.Feilmeier, G.Joubert and U.Schendel, Elsevier Science Publishers B.V.(North-Holand), 1986, pp.457-462.

[8] S.C. Perrenod, R.S. Bucy, "Supercomputer Performance for Convolution," Proceedings of 1st International Conference on Supercomputing, St. Petersburg Fla., December 1985, 16 pp.

[9] R.S. Bucy, F. Ghovanlou, J.M.F. Moura, K.D. Senne, "Nonlinear Filtering and Array Computation," IEEE Computer Mag., Vol.16, no.6, June 1983, pp.51-61.

[10] Michael Bieterman, "The Impact of Microtasked Applications in a Multiprogramming Environment," National Science Foundation study conducted at the Pittsburgh Supercomputing Center, as quoted by Mike Schneider in PSC News, Vol.3, No.3, March 1988.

Optimal Scheduling Policies for mixed Scalar-Vector Multiprocessor Supercomputers

Yiwei Liu
Ph.D. Candidate
Department of Computer Science
University of Houston

Olin Johnson
Professor of Computer Science
University of Houston
and
Director, CSARC
Houston Area Research Center

Abstract

A queueing network model is developed for multiprocessing supercomputer systems implemented on two heterogeneous processors which are thought of as a scalar unit and a vector unit which work concurrently on a single process. The model is analysed theoretically for a representative case of model job mixes. It is found that the utilization of one of the two central service stations in the model can only be maximized at the expense of minimizing the utilization of the other central service station. The method of analysis adopted is the technique of variable aggregation based on nearly complete decomposability.

1. Introduction

The performance of multiprogramming systems implemented on conventional single processor computer systems have been studied extensively. General queueing network models such as the finite-source queueing model [5], machine-repairman model [8], central-server model [2], etc. have been developed and studied by simulation [1, 13], numerical analysis [2, 3] and theoretical analysis [12, 5, 6, 7]. Some results concerning the performance of multiprogramming systems, in relation to resource scheduling policies, have been obtained by these studies.

In recent years, a number of new multiprocessing (i.e. multiple processors) systems have been developed. Some of these systems such as the Cyber 205 and the NEC SX-2 have co-operating scalar and vector processors. In these machine, a large scale scalar main-frame is coupled with a high performance arithmetic processor (AP) which performs both vector and scalar arithmetic in parallel. The main-frame is used as a control processor (CP) for time-sharing and I/O. In evaluating the performances of multiprogramming and time sharing systems implemented on computer systems of this kind, one should keep in mind that the processor for high speed numerical calculation is the key resource and usually the bottleneck of such systems. Because this processor is not considered in the finite-source model, that model is not suitable for the performance evaluations of these new multiprocessing and time sharing systems.

The Heterogeneous Processor Model (HPM) used here, as shown in Figure 1, is a queueing network model for these types of multiprocessing systems. The AP service station corresponds to the processor engaged in numerical calculation (the supercomputer); the CP service station corresponds to the conventional processor; the IO service station corresponds to IO devices. Generally, two classes of jobs run through the HPM. Jobs of the first class need service of the CP and the IO only while jobs of the second class need service of the CP, the IO and the AP. This model will be discussed in detail in section 2.

In this paper, the HPM is analysed theoretically for a simple and representative job mix (the set of jobs running through the model). Our main concerns are the utilizations of the AP server and the CP server in relation to the scheduling policies of the AP and the CP. Because the utilization of a server has the same variance as the throughput of that server[9], the result is also applicable to the throughputs of the CP and the AP. Only the two job classes mentioned above are considered for simplicity and generality. The scheduling policies which give the maximum utilizations of the CP and the AP have been found. The formulas for computing the maximum utilizations of the CP and the AP are also developed. It has also been found that the utilizations of the AP and the CP can not be maximized together, one of them has to be maximized at the expense of minimizing the other.

In section 2, the HPM and its job mix are discussed in detail. The theoretical assumptions about the HPM used in the analysis are also discussed.

The most general method for theoretical analysis of queueing models is the global flow balance method, which gives rise to a complicated symbolic system of equations which is unmanageable in our study. So, an approximate method for theoretical analysis of queueing models — the method of variable aggregation based on nearly complete decomposability is adopted. The results obtained by this method become increasingly exact as the error parameter (determined by the particular model) of this method approaches zero. In section 3, the process of this analysis and its analysing results are given.

In section 4, further research directions are discussed.

2. The Heterogeneous Processor Model (HPM)

The queueing network model to be studied is as shown in Figure 1. It consists of three service stations, named CP, AP and IO, respectively; and a group of jobs (job mix of the model) served by the servers in the stations. The CP and the AP are single-server stations where jobs may suffer queueing delays. The IO is an infinite service station where no delay occurs. The reason behind this supposition is that the IO contains enough servers that whenever a job needs IO service, there is a free IO server available.

This model has a finite memory capacity. It supports N_1 jobs of class 1 and N_2 jobs of class 2 running concurrently, of which the fixed job mix of this model consists. Jobs have no difference in their memory requirements. Jobs in the job mix are classified into the two job classes (class 1 and class 2) according to their routing patterns. The routing pattern of a class 1 job is the cycle consisting of CP and IO. That means that a job of class 1 only needs CP and IO services; it enters the IO (or CP) queue as soon as it leaves the CP (or IO) queue. A job of class 2 needs services of the CP, the IO and the AP. When a job of class 2 leaves the IO or the AP, it will join the jobs in the CP queue; when it leaves the CP, it will enter the AP queue with probability p and enter the IO queue with probability $q(= 1 - p)$.

In this study, it is supposed that jobs have exponential service time distributions at all servers with mean μ at the CP, mean λ at the IO and mean α at the AP. Let γ denote λ/μ. It is further assumed that jobs inside each class are indistinguishable to the scheduling policies of the CP and the AP. Theoretically, of course each of the two job classes may be further divided into subclasses in a variety of ways, for instance according to their mean service times at the CP or the AP. However, we leave such assumptions to further study.

Suppose that the model is a Markovian system and has only one equilibrium. Let $W = \{1, 2, \ldots, N_1 + N_2\}$ be the job mix of the model; which means that we name jobs by sequential integers without considering which class they belong to. Note that the job mix W can also be expressed as (N_1, N_2). Let $S_{(WC,WA)}$ express the system state in which the sets of jobs in the CP queue and the AP queue are WC and WA, respectively. Hence, the set of jobs being served at the IO service station is $W - WC - WA$ when the system is in state $S_{(WC,WA)}$. The state $S_{(WC,WA)}$ is an aggregate system state not concerned with the scheduling policies of the service stations. Denote $S^{(i,j)}_{(WC,WA)}$ as the system state in which job $i(\in WC)$ is being served by the CP server and job j ($\in WA$) is being served by the AP server, assuming that the system is in the aggregated state $S_{(WC,WA)}$. Denote the stationary probabilities of $S_{(WC,WA)}$ and $S^{(i,j)}_{(WC,WA)}$ by $V_{(WC,WA)}$ and $V^{(i,j)}_{(WC,WA)}$, respectively. It's obvious that

$$V_{(WC,WA)} = \Sigma_{i \in WC} \Sigma_{j \in WA} V^{(i,j)}_{(WC,WA)}. \qquad (2.1)$$

Because the model has Markovian properties and only one equilibrium, it has to satisfy the following two conditions.

Condition A. *The expected rate of the system leaving state $S_{(WC,WA)}$ due to job i leaving the CP is $\mu * \Sigma_{j \in WA} * V^{(i,j)}_{(WC,WA)}$; the expected rate of the system leaving state $S_{(WC,WA)}$ due to job j leaving the AP is $\alpha * \Sigma_{i \in WC} * V^{(i,j)}_{(WC,WA)}$; the expected rate of the system leaving state $S_{(WC,WA)}$ due to a job leaving the IO is $\lambda * V_{(WC,WA)}$.*

Condition B. *The scheduling policies of the CP and the AP must belong to a broad class of scheduling policies, a scheduling policy belonging to this class schedules jobs according to the information about past and current model processing states (current system states) only. This class includes first-come-first-served, preemptive and non-preemptive priority, shortest and longest expected remaining service time first, preemptive and nonpreemptive last-come-first-served, processor-sharing, generalized processor-sharing (i.e., the processing capability of a server is distributed to the jobs inside the queue of that server by specified ratios.), etc. This class excludes the shortest remaining service time first scheduling policy.*

Condition A is the theoretical basis to calculate the probability transition rates of our model. Condition B gives the range of scheduling policies that we can deal with in this model.

Remark The HPM may have more general application than multiprogramming systems of double processor computer systems. For example, we can take each IO server in the HPM as an interactive terminal; and there are $N_1 + N_2$ of them all together. The distributions of the thinking times of the terminal users are exponential and have the same mean λ. N_1 interactive transactions need services of the CP and the IO, but not the AP; while the other N_2 transactions need services of all the three service stations.

3. Analysis of the HPM

The most direct and most exact way to analyse the model is to use the global flow balance equation method [11]. In that method, the system states must first be enumerated. Then the probability flow rates into and out from each state are computed, remembering that they are supposed to be equal. So, a system of equations of stationary probabilities is obtained. If that system of equations can be solved, it will be possible to figure out the properties of the model from the stationary probabilities. However, the number of equations increase nearly exponentially with the number of servers or jobs inside the model. Usually, the number of equations is very large or even infinite, which makes the solving of that equation system prohibitive. Our model is one of these cases. Our analysis using this method thus comes to halt.

Due to the above difficulty, approximating methods were considered. The method of variable aggregation based on nearly complete decomposability [4] is such a method. It has been successfully used [6, 7] in analysing the finite-source queueing model. This method was tried successfully, but it should be kept in mind that this method is only an approximation method; its results are asymptotically correct in certain error parameters.

In section 3.1, the method of variable aggregation is summarized. It is slightly different from the one used by [6] in order to make the method fit our situation. Certain properties needed in the decomposition of HPM are listed in Section 3.2. These properties are obtained and proved by [6]. In section 3.3, the process and results of the analysis are demonstrated. The main results are expressed there by two theorems.

3.1 The Technique of Variable Aggregation Based on Nearly Complete Decomposability

Consider a stochastic system. Let us aggregate system states into separate groups, each of which is denoted by $G_I (I = 1, 2, \ldots, N)$. Denote each state in group G_I by $S_{i_I} (i = 1, 2, \ldots, n(I))$, where $n(I)$ is the number of states in G_I. Let v_{i_I} denote the stationary probability of state S_{i_I}; and $\mathbf{v}$ denote the vector $[v_{1_1}, v_{2_1}, \ldots, v_{i_I}, \ldots, v_{n(N)_N}]$. V_I $(I = 1, 2, \ldots, N)$ denotes the stationary probability of group G_I; and V denotes vector $[V_1, \ldots, V_N]$. It's obvious that $V_I = \Sigma_i v_{i_I}$, $(I = 1, \ldots, N)$. Let $\mathbf{Q}$ denote the transition rate matrix of the system. That means that the (i_I, j_J)-element of $\mathbf{Q}$, Q_{i_I, j_J} namely, is the direct transition rate to state S_{j_J} when the system is in state S_{i_I} and i_I is not equal to j_J; when i_I is equal to j_J, Q_{i_I, j_J} is the negative sum of all transition rates into (out from) S_{i_I}. The stationary probability vector $\mathbf{v}$ can be obtained from the following equation,

$$\mathbf{vQ} = \mathbf{0}. \tag{3.1.1}$$

We now compute an approximate value of $\mathbf{v}$. Let Q_{IJ} denote the submatrix of Q, which contains only and all the (i_I, j_J)-elements (i = 1, ..., $n(I)$, j = 1, ..., $n(J)$). Obviously, $\mathbf{Q}$ is arranged in such a way that the transitions within G_I are expressed by Q_{II} $(I = 1, \ldots, N)$, ignoring the diagonal elements.

1) Obtain a completely decomposable transition rate matrix $\mathbf{Q}^*$ such that

$$\mathbf{Q} = \mathbf{Q}^* + e\mathbf{C} \tag{3.1.2}$$

where

$$Q^*_{IJ} = \mathbf{0} \quad for \quad I \neq J \tag{3.1.3}$$

and

$$e = \max_{i,I} \left(\sum_{J \neq I} \sum_{j} Q_{i_I j_J} \right) \tag{3.1.4}$$

is small compared with most nonzero elements of Q_{II} (I = 1, ..., N); e can be interpreted as the maximum degree of coupling between groups, each of which is described by the submatrix Q_{II} ($I = 1, \ldots, N$) of transition rate matrix $\mathbf{Q}$; $\mathbf{C}$ has rowsum equal to zero, and

$$\max_{i,I} \left(\sum_{J \neq I} \sum_{j} C_{i_I j_J} \right) = 1. \tag{3.1.5}$$

Denote Q^*_{II} (defined in the same way as Q_{II}) as Q^*_I. Then $\mathbf{Q}^*$ can be expressed as

$$\begin{bmatrix} Q^*_1 & \mathbf{0} & \ldots & \mathbf{0} \\ \mathbf{0} & Q^*_2 & \ldots & \mathbf{0} \\ \vdots & \vdots & \ddots & \vdots \\ \mathbf{0} & \mathbf{0} & \ldots & Q^*_N \end{bmatrix}.$$

Each Q^*_I is a square submatrix of the order $n(I)$. Q_{II} is assigned to Q^*_I as an approximate value of Q^*_I.

2) Obtain the stationary probability vector $\mathbf{v}^*_I$ of Q^*_I such that

$$\mathbf{v}^*_I Q^*_I = \mathbf{0} \quad for \quad I = 1, \ldots, N. \tag{3.1.6}$$

Let $v^*_{i_I}$ denote the i-element of $\mathbf{v}^*_I$.

3) Obtain the N dimensional transition rate matrix $\mathbf{R}$ such that

$$R_{IJ} = \sum_i v^*_{i_I} \sum_j Q_{i_I j_J} \qquad for \quad I, J = 1, \ldots, N; \tag{3.1.7}$$

where R_{IJ}, the approximate direct transition rate from G_I to G_J, denotes the (I,J)-element of $\mathbf{R}$.

4) Obtain the stationary probability vector $\mathbf{X}$ of $\mathbf{R}$ such that

$$\mathbf{XR} = \mathbf{0}. \tag{3.1.8}$$

Let X_I denote the I-element of $\mathbf{X}$. Note that $\mathbf{X}$ is an approximation of the stationary probability vector $\mathbf{V}$.

5) Finally, x_{i_I} computed as following is used as an approximation of v_{i_I}:

$$x_{i_I} = X_I v^*_{i_I} \qquad for \quad i = 1, \ldots, n(I); \quad I = 1, \ldots, N. \tag{3.1.9}$$

The errors in this approximation (i.e., $x_{i_I} - v_{i_I}$ and $X_I - V_I$) are of the same order of magnitude as e. Therefore x_{i_I} and X_I become nearly exact approximates of v_{i_I} and V_I, respectively, as e becomes infinitely small (but remains nonzero).

3.2 Properties of the Finite-Source Queueing Model

The finite-source queueing model used here is given in Figure 2. Extensive research has been done for this model. From another viewpoint, it's the model resulting from deleting the AP service station from the HPM. The job mix of the finite-source model is defined as (N_1, i), where N_1 is a fixed integer and $0 \le i \le N_2$. This is a derivation of the job mix of the HPM by considering that $N_2 - i$ jobs are in the AP queue. Class 2 jobs have the same routing pattern as class 1 jobs in the finite-source model. In this section, two properties (which are derived from [6] directly) of the finite-source model, which will be used in analysing the HPM, are listed below. Denote the utilization of the CP server of the finite-source model with job mix (N_1, i) as $\rho^{(i)}$; and the utilization, for class j (j = 1,2) jobs, of the CP server is expressed by $\rho_j^{(i)}$.

A1. The CP utilization $(\rho^{(i)})$ depends on the job mix (N_1, i) only (is independent of the CP scheduling policy); and can be calculated by the following formula:

$$\rho^{(i)} = 1 - \left[\sum_{n_1=0}^{N_1} \sum_{n_2=0}^{i} (n_1 + n_2)! \binom{N_1}{n_1} \binom{i}{n_2} \gamma^{n_1+n_2} \right]^{-1}. \tag{3.2.1}$$

A2. $\rho_j^{(i)}$ is maximum if and only if all class j jobs are given, preemptive priority at the CP server over all other jobs in the job mix (N_1, i) for $j = 1, 2$. In that case, $\rho_j^{(i)}$ is independent of the relative scheduling priority or priority assignment within each class.

From property A1, we can further derive the following property.

A3.

$$\rho^{(i)} < \rho^{(i+1)}. \tag{3.2.2}$$

Proof. According to A1, we have

$$\rho^{(i+1)} = 1 - \left[\sum_{n_1=0}^{N_1} \sum_{n_2=0}^{i+1} (n_1 + n_2)! \binom{N_1}{n_1} \binom{i+1}{n_2} \gamma^{n_1+n_2} \right]^{-1}. \tag{3.2.3}$$

Note that

$$\binom{i+1}{n_2} = \binom{i}{n_2} + \binom{i}{n_2 - 1}. \tag{3.2.4}$$

Substitute eq.(3.2.4) into eq.(3.2.3), we get

$$\rho^{(i+1)} = 1 - \left[\sum_{n_1=0}^{N_1} \sum_{n_2=0}^{i} (n_1 + n_2)! \binom{N_1}{n_1} \binom{i}{n_2} \gamma^{n_1+n_2} + \sum_{n_1=0}^{N_1} \sum_{n_2=0}^{i} (n_1 + n_2 + 1)! \binom{N_1}{n_1} \binom{i}{n_2} \gamma^{n_1+n_2+1} \right]^{-1}. \tag{3.2.5}$$

Based on eq.(3.2.1) and eq.(3.2.5):

$$\left(1 - \rho^{(i+1)}\right)^{-1} - \left(1 - \rho^{(i)}\right)^{-1} = \left[\sum_{n_1=0}^{N_1} \sum_{n_2=0}^{i} (n_1 + n_2 + 1)! \binom{N_1}{n_1} \binom{i}{n_2} \gamma^{n_1+n_2+1} \right]^{-1}. \tag{3.2.6}$$

Because every item in the right hand side of eq.(3.2.6) is positive, we conclude

$$\rho^{(i+1)} - \rho^{(i)} > 0. \Updownarrow \tag{3.2.7}$$

3.3 The Analysis

In this section, the HPM is analysed by following the five steps in section 3.1. Here, **Q** is taken as defined specially for the HPM. And the system states that we consider are the basic states defined by $S^{(i,j)}_{(WC,WA)}$, given in Section 2.

1) We aggregate states, in which the number of class 2 jobs at the AP server are the same, into the same group. Let G_I (I = 1, ..., N_2 + 1) denote the group of states $S^{(i,j)}_{(WC,WA)}$, where $| WA | = N_2 - I + 1$. Remember, that **Q** is arranged in such a way that the internal transitions of G_I are expressed by Q_{II} (ignoring the diagonal elements). Hence, $S^{(i,j)}_{(WC,WA)}$ can also be expressed as S_{i_I} as defined in section 3.1. Because the number of jobs inside the AP queue can only change (increase or decrease) one by one, it's obvious that

$$Q_{IJ} = 0 \qquad for \quad | I - J | \ge 2. \tag{3.3.1}$$

What is more, from state $S^{(i,j)}_{(WC,WA)}$ ($\in G_I$), the system may only transfer to two states outside group G_I; namely $S^{(k,j)}_{(WC\setminus\{i\},WA\cup\{i\})}$ ($\in G_{I-1}$) and $S^{(i,k)}_{(WC\cup\{j\},WA\setminus\{j\})}$ ($\in G_{I+1}$). Hence, for the i_I row of **Q**, we only have two nonzero elements outside Q_{II},

$$Q_{i_I j_{J-1}} = p\mu\beta_{i_I,2} \qquad for \quad I = 2, \ldots, N_2 + 1; \tag{3.3.2}$$

$$Q_{i_I j_{I+1}} = \alpha \qquad for \quad I = 1, \ldots, N_2; \tag{3.3.3}$$

where $\beta_{i_I,j}$ ($i = 1, \ldots, n(I), 1 \le I \le N_2+1, j = 1, 2$) is the ratio by which the processing capacity of the CP is given to jobs of class j when the system is in state S_{i_I}. Therefore, the maximum degree of coupling between groups is

$$e \le \max(p\mu, \alpha). \tag{3.3.4}$$

2) Note that the system described by $Q_I^* = Q_{II}$ (I = 1, ..., $N_2 + 1$) is the system formed by the finite-source model with job mix $(N_1, I-1)$, which has been thoroughly studied by [6]. The properties needed of $\mathbf{v}^*$ are given in section 3.2.

3) According to the definition given in section 3.1, the transition rate matrix **R** is defined by

$$R_{II-1} = \sum_i v^*_{i_I} p\mu\beta_{i_I,2} = p\mu\rho_2^{(I-1)} \qquad for \quad I = 2, \ldots, N_2 + 1, \tag{3.3.5}$$

$$R_{II+1} = \sum_i v^*_{i_I} \alpha = \alpha \qquad for \quad I = 1, \dots, N_2, \qquad (3.3.6)$$

$$R_{IJ} = 0 \qquad for \quad |I - J| \geq 2, \qquad (3.3.7)$$

$$R_{II} = -(R_{II+1} + R_{II-1}) \qquad for \quad I = 1, \dots, N_2 + 1. \qquad (3.3.8)$$

In eq.(3.3.8), undefined R_{II-1} or R_{II+1} is taken as zero.

4) V_I ($I = 1, \dots, N_2 + 1$) is the stationary probability of group G_{I+1}. We estimate V_I by

$$V_I = X_I \qquad for \quad I = 1, \dots, N_2 + 1. \qquad (3.3.9)$$

where $\mathbf{X}$ is defined by eq.(3.1.8). So, we have

$$p\mu\rho_2^{(I)} V_{I+1} - \alpha V_I - p\mu\rho_2^{(I-1)} V_I + \alpha V_{I-1} = 0 \qquad (3.3.10)$$

for $I = 2, \dots, N_2$;

$$\alpha V_{N_2} - p\mu\rho_2^{(N_2+1)} V_{N_2+1} = 0 \qquad (3.3.11)$$

and

$$p\mu\rho_2^{(1)} V_2 - \alpha V_1 = 0. \qquad (3.3.12)$$

From eq.(3.3.10), eq.(3.3.11) and eq.(3.3.12), we can derive the following result:

$$\frac{V_I}{V_{I-1}} = \frac{\alpha}{p\mu\rho_2^{(I-1)}} \qquad I = 2, \dots, N_2 + 1. \qquad (3.3.13)$$

We now define

$$\alpha_I = \frac{\alpha}{p\mu\rho_2^{(I-1)}} \qquad for \quad I = 2, \dots, N_2 + 1; \qquad (3.3.14)$$

$$\alpha_1 = 1. \qquad (3.3.15)$$

Then we get

$$V_j = V_1 \prod_{i=1}^{j} \alpha_i \qquad for \quad j = 1, \dots, N_2 + 1. \qquad (3.3.16)$$

Summing both sides of eq.(3.3.16) over j, it is obtained that

$$\sum_{j=1}^{I} V_j = \frac{\sum_{j=1}^{I} \prod_{k=1}^{j} \alpha_k}{\sum_{j=1}^{N_2+1} \prod_{k=1}^{j} \alpha_k} \qquad for \quad I = 1, \dots, N_2 + 1. \qquad (3.3.17)$$

Reformulating eq.(3.3.17), we have

$$\left(\sum_{j=1}^{I} V_j \right)^{-1} = 1 + \frac{\sum_{j=I+1}^{N_2+1} \prod_{k=I+1}^{j} \alpha_k}{1 + \sum_{j=1}^{I-1} \prod_{k=j+1}^{I} \left(\frac{1}{\alpha_k} \right)} \qquad (3.3.18)$$

$$for \quad I = 1, \dots, N_2 + 1.$$

Note that the AP utilization is

$$U_{AP} = \sum_{j=1}^{N_2} V_j. \qquad (3.3.19)$$

From eq.(3.3.18) and eq.(3.3.19), we get the following lemma.

LEMMA 1. The AP utilization of the HPM with job mix (N_1, N_2) is maximum if α_k ($k = 1, \dots, N_2 + 1$) are minimum.

From Property A2 (section 3.2), eq.(3.3.14) and eq.(3.3.15), we obtain another lemma.

LEMMA 2. α_k ($k = 1, \dots, N_2 + 1$) are minimum if class 2 jobs have preemptive priority over class 1 jobs at the CP server.

According to *LEMMA 1* and *LEMMA 2*, we have our first result about the scheduling policies of the HPM.

***THEOREM 1.* The AP utilization of the HPM with job mix (N_1, N_2) is maximum if class 2 jobs have preemptive priority over class 1 jobs at the CP server; and is independent of the scheduling policy of the AP server.**

5) In this step, the estimates x_{i_I} of v_{i_I}, for $I = 1, \dots, N_2 + 1$, $i = 1, \dots, n(I)$ are calculated. But we only need x_{0_I} ($I = 1, \dots, N_2 + 1$), because we are only interested in the CP utilization U_{CP}. We have

$$x_{0_I} = V_I v^*_{0_I} \qquad for \quad I = 1, \dots, N_2 + 1. \qquad (3.3.20)$$

Remember that

$$\rho^{(I-1)} = 1 - v^*_{0_I} \qquad for \quad I = 1, \dots, N_2 + 1; \qquad (3.3.21)$$

and

$$U_{CP} = 1 - \sum_{I=1}^{N_2+1} v_{0_I} = 1 - \sum_{I=1}^{N_2+1} x_{0_I}. \qquad (3.3.22)$$

Hence, we have

$$U_{CP} = \sum_{I=1}^{N_2+1} \rho^{(I-1)} V_I. \qquad (3.3.23)$$

We define

$$g_I = \rho^{(I-1)} - \rho^{(I)} \qquad for \quad I = 1, \dots, N_2. \qquad (3.3.24)$$

Then, we have

$$U_{CP} = \sum_{I=1}^{N_2} g_I \sum_{j=1}^{I+1} V_j + \rho(N_2). \qquad (3.3.25)$$

Note that $\rho^{(I-1)} - \rho^{(I)}$ is independent of the CP scheduling policy and is negative according to property A1 and A3 in section 3.2. Considering eq.(3.3.18) and eq.(3.3.25), we have another lemma.

LEMMA 3. The CP utilization of the HPM with job mix (N_1, N_2) is maximum if α_k ($k = 1, \dots, N_2 + 1$) are maximum.

From property A2 (section 3.2), eq.(3.3.14) and eq.(3.3.15), we also have.

LEMMA 4. α_k $(k = 1, \ldots, N_2)$ *are maximum if class 1 jobs have preemptive priority over class 2 jobs at the CP server.*

Combining the above two lemmas, we get our second result about the scheduling policies.

THEOREM 2. **The CP utilization of the HPM with job mix (N_1, N_2) is maximum if class 1 jobs have preemptive priority over class 2 jobs at the CP server.**

Remark From *THEOREM 1* and *THEOREM 2*, we see that maximum utilizations of the CP and the AP cannot be achieved together. We can only achieve one of them at the expense of the other. The maximum utilization of the AP can be calculated by the combined use of eq.(3.3.19), eq.(3.3.16), eq.(3.3.15) and eq.(3.3.14). The maximum utilization of the CP can be calculated by the combined use of eq.(3.3.25), eq.(3.3.16), eq.(3.3.15) and eq.(3.3.14). Because the AP is much more powerful and expensive than the CP, the AP utilization should be maximized on the expense of the minimum utilization of the CP. It can be further seen that the utilizations of the CP and AP are independent of the scheduling policies inside each job class.

The two theorems we have obtained are based on the approximations of the stationary probability V_I $(I = 1, \ldots, N_2 + 1)$ and v_{i_I} $(i = 1, \ldots, n(I), I = 1, \ldots, N_2 + 1)$. The errors (i.e., $V_I - X_I$ and $v_{i_I} - x_{i_I}$) are of the same order of magnitude of $\max(p\mu, \alpha)$. When $max\,(p\mu, \alpha)$ gets infinite small (but remains nonzero), X_I and x_{i_I} are asymptotically exact.

4. Discussion

Because the HPM is a general performance model for the multiprogramming and time sharing systems implemented on double processor computer systems, the family of which is enlarging rapidly nowadays; it is worth more thorough and exhaustive studies. What is more, it may have more applications. The direct extension of this study should be the study of performance variation after dividing class 2 into several subclasses, each of them has a distinct mean (nonzero) of exponential service time distributions. That is the optimality of scheduling policies for more general cases of the job mix. The relationship between the performance and the change of the job mix, i.e. the effect on the system performance of the system job scheduling (loading jobs into the model for execution) policies, also deserves some research. Alter all, some simulation and numerical analysis of the HPM, practical measurement of some particular systems can supply more understandable results.

Reference

[1] R.M. Browne and J. Lean and F. Baskett, The Interaction of Multi-programming Job Scheduling and CPU Scheduling, Proc. FJCC(1972), 13-21.

[2] W.W. Chiu and D. Dumont and R. Wood, "Performance Analysis of Multiprogrammed Computer System," IBM J. of Research and Development 19, 3(May 1975) 263-271.

[3] W.W. Chiu and W-M. chow, A Performance Model of MVS," IBM System Journal 17, 4(1978)444-462.

[4] P.J. Courtois, Decomposability: Queueing and Computer System Applications. Academic Press, New York, 1977.

[5] H. Kameda, "A Finite-Source Queue with Different Customers," JACM 29, 2(april 1982), 478-491.

[6] H. Kameda, "Optimality of a Central Processor Scheduling Policy for Processing a Job Stream," ACM Trans. Compt. Syst. 2,1(Feb. 1984), 78-90.

[7] H. Kameda, "Effects of Job Loading Policies for Multiprogramming Systems in Processing a Job Stream," ACM Trans. Compt. Syst. 4, 1(Feb. 1986), 71-106.

[8] L.Kleinrock, Queueing Systems Volume 2: Computer Applications, Wiley, New York(1976).

[9] J.D.C. Little, A Proof of the Queueing Formular $L = \lambda W$, Operation Research, 9, 333-398 (1961).

[10] NEC Corporation, NEC Supercomputer SX-2/SX-1/SX-1E General Description, (1980).

[11] C.H.Sauer and K.M. Chandy, Computer Systems Performance Modeling, Prentice-Hall, Inc., Englewood Cliffs, New Jersey(1981).

[12] J.R. Spirn, "Multi-queue Scheduling of two tasks." Acta Inf. 7,2(1976), 217-226.

[13] H.D. Schwetman, Job Scheduling in Multiprogrammed Computer Systems. Softw. Pract. Exper., 8(1978), 241-255.

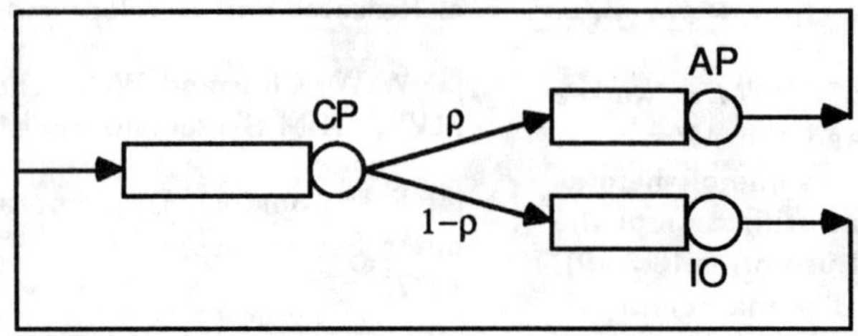

Figure 1. The Heterougeneous Processor Model (HPM)

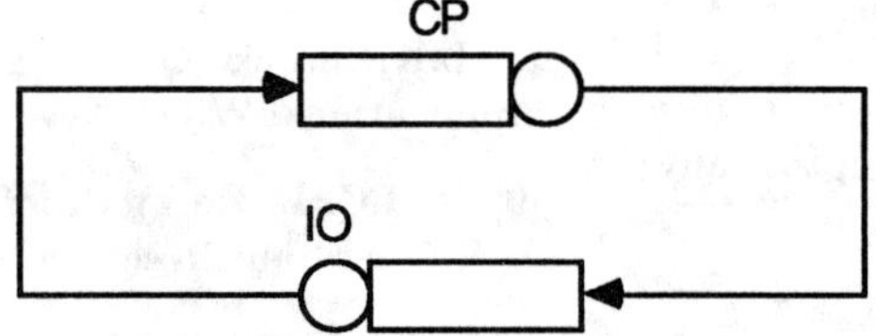

Figure 2. The Finite-Source Queueing Model

Mass Storage Systems - II

Chair: Pat Savage
Shell Development

FACOM 6443 Magneto-Optic Disk Sub-System

Yuji Inouye

FUJITSU LIMITED

Shigeki Hatayama

National Aerospace Laboratory

Abstract

There has always been a strong market requirement for rewritable optical disk drive as a follow-on product to read-only and write-once type optical disks. Fujitsu has been researching magneto-optic recording technologies for rewritabe optical disk , and has developed a disk sub-system with initiative of the National Aerospace Laboratory (NAL) in Tokyo.
The drive has a large storage capacity of 8.9 GB/spindle with a few seconds of access time. It can store data economically in a small floor space, and it can be used as a supplement or partial alternative to magnetic disk drives or tape library units. The sub-system will be used from the beginning of 1989. This paper explaines the drive technologies, support software as well as the application of this new sub-system at NAL.

1. Background for the Development

Today, magnetic disk drive is primarily used in computer systems to store large amounts of data because of its large storage capacity and relatively high performance. However, since the cost of magnetic disks accounts for a large share of total system cost, the steady increase in recording density, year by year, has helped to reduce bit-cost.

Optical disk has been expected to be a very inexpensive storage medium, because its recording density is about ten times higher than magetic disk. However, optical disk technology available today is ready-only and write-once, and rewritability is strongly required.

Fujitsu has been researching magneto-optic technology which enables data rewriting, and has developed a rewritable optical disk sub-system using this technology with initiative of NAL who has been investigating eligible external storage device for storing huge amount of aircraft design data .

2. Requirements from NAL

Many factors must be considered in designing aircraft : safety, low energy consumption, high performance and durability in a severe environment. It is no more possible to rely on experiments with scale models, but it is practical to use numerical simulation by super-computer. Such a super-computer system must have an exceptionally large data base of dimension data, wind tunnel data, test flight data, numerically simulated data, etc.. The data to be stored in NAL is rapidly increasing. In 1986, it was about 150 GB, but today, it is estimated to be doubled. So that, magnetic disk drives, despite their high performance, are not practical to store all of this data from the view-points of economics, floor space and power consumption, and alternative storage is urgently required.

3. Magneto-Optic Disk Technology

Fig.-1 shows the principle of the Magneto-Optic technology. Writing uses both thermal heating by a laser diode and an externally applied magnetic field on a media which is coated with a ferromagnetic recording layer. The laser raises the temperature at a small spot on the layer above the ferromagnetic material's Curie temperature so that the small applied magnetic field can flip the direction of electron spins. During a read, a polarized reflected beam from the recording layer is rotated depending on the electron spin's orientation (a phenomenon called the Kerr effect). A polarized analyzer in the optical head discriminates between the two polarization, which represent the binary information stored in the media

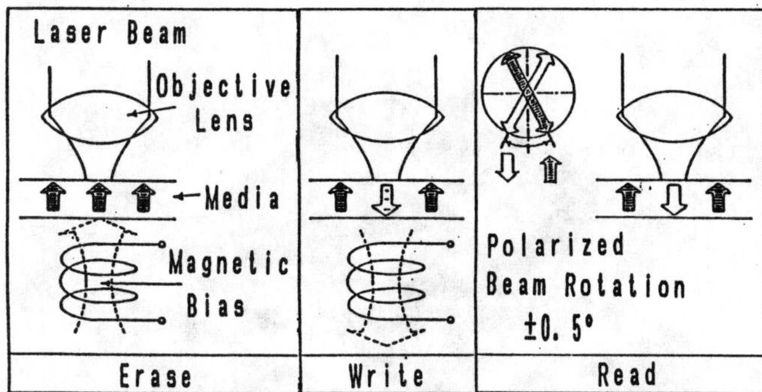

Fig.-1 Principle of the Megneto-Optic Recording

4. Drive Technology

4-1 Drive [1]

The mechanical design of the drive is shown in Fig. -2. Eight 8-inch two-sided media are stacked with a spindle shaft, and rotate at 1,8000 rpm. A couple of actuators are provided to the spindle. Each actuator has two optical heads, each of which is arranged to face the other. Each actuator with its own electronics can be used independently to provide higher throughput in normal operation. If an error occurs accidentally with one actuator, the job can be continued with another actuator, thus providing high system reliability and availability.

Head and media assembly is sealed to avoid contamination by environmental dust. Access to a specific track is done with two steps, i.e., media-to-media access followed by on-media access. The former access takes 3 seconds maximum, and the later, 200 ms on average. As a mass storage device, the access time is very much improved from such conventional mass storage devices as magnetic tape library or optical jukebox units whose access times are between 10 and 20 seconds. Table-1 shows the drive unit specifications.

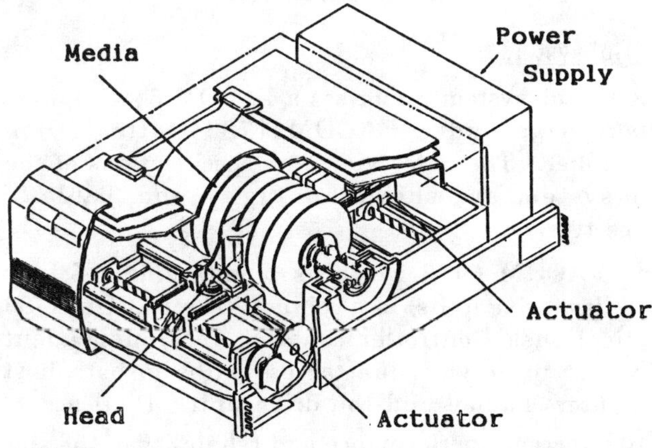

Fig. -2 Mechanical Design of the Drive Unit

Table-1 Drive Unit Specifications

Storage Capacity/Unit	8.89 GB (Formatted)
Media	Eight 8-Inch, Glass substrate
Recording Surface/Unit	16
Tracks/Surface	23,640
Sectors/Track	23
Capacity/Sector	1,024 Bytes (Formatted)
Recording Density	19,098 BPI, 15,875 TPI
Data Error Rate	<1E-12 (After Error Correction)
Rotatioanl Speed	1,800 rpm.
Data Transfer Rate	Reading---979 KB/s, Writing--326 KB/s
Access Time	200 ms (Average access time on a media) 3 s (Max. access time from media-to-medium)
Heads/Unit	4 (2 Actuators/Unit X 2 Heads/Acutuator)
Media Life	>10 years
Interface	M-SMD
Outer Dimension	450(W)×820(D)×260(H) mm
Power Supply	100/200 Va.c. (0.4 KVA)

Note that FACOM 6443 includes Max. 4 drive units in a standard 19-inch rack.

4-2 Media

Cross sectional view of the media is shown in Fig.-3. Glass substrates extend the media life by protecting the recording layer from oxidization caused by environmental humidity. The ferromagnetic recording layer, a Rare-Earth Transition-Metal alloy of Terbium, iron and Cobalt, is sputtered with a protective over-coat.

Fig.-4 shows results of accelerated life test and estimated life of media with various protective layers. At least ten years of media life can be expected with our proprietary protective layer, Tb SiO_2 [2].

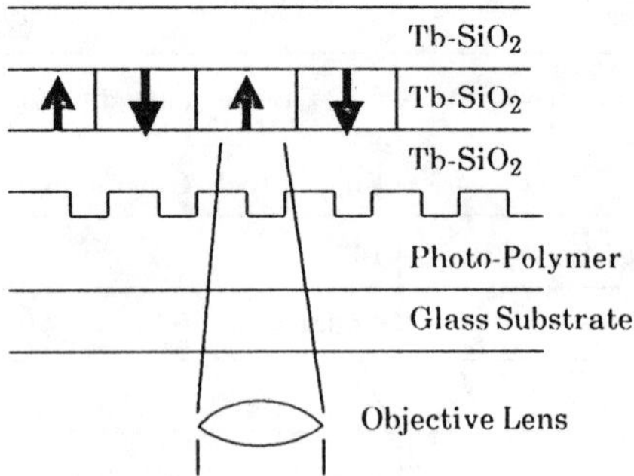

Fig.-3 Cross Sectional View of the Media

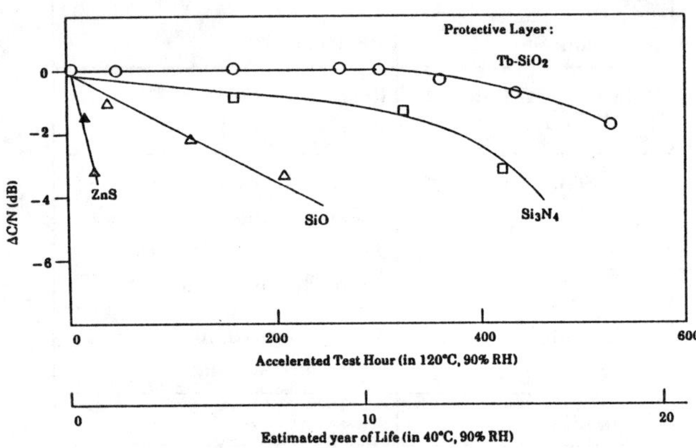

Fig.-4 Result of the Media Life Test

Direct over-write is not possible today. In order to update the data, three media rotations are required to "erase" the new data, and "verify" that the new data has been correctly written without errors caused by defects on the media. Therefore, though the data transfer rate during reading is 979 KB/s, total data transfer rate at updating is one third of the data transfer rate at reading.

4-3 Head

Fig.-5 and 6 show the outer view of the optical head and schematic diagram of optical system. The size of the head is 55×70×22mm, and 120gm. in weight [3].

A laser beam from a laser diode goes through a collimating lens and beam splitter. It is then reflected by a mirror, and focused on the recording layer by an objective lens. At writing, the laser power on the media is big enough to rise the recording layer above Currie temperature.

Fig.-5 Outer View of the Optical Head

At reading, the reflected polarized beam from the recording layer takes the same optical path back to the beam splitter. Then the beam goes through a half wavelength plate and is devided into two by a polarized beam splitter. Finally, magneto-optically recorded data is differentially detected by two photo-detectors.

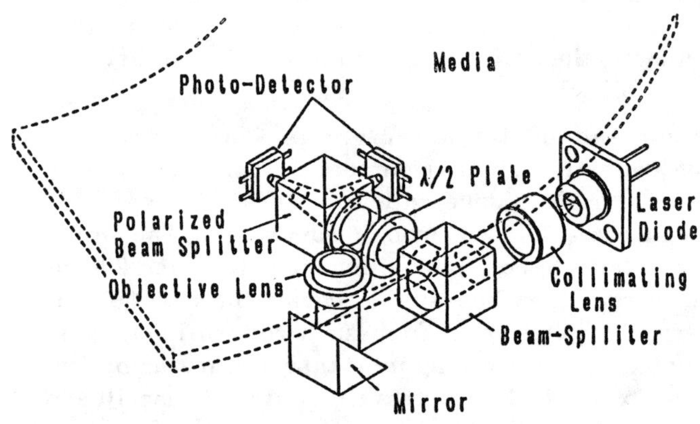

Fig.-6 Optical System

5. Subsystem

A disk sub-system comprises a FACOM 6443 Optical Disk Drive and a FACOM 1783 Optical Disk Controller. The outer view and specifications of the sub-system are shown in Fig.-7 and Table-2, respectively.

The FACOM 6443 contains a maximum of four spindles (drive units) in a cabinet. The FACOM 1783 Optical Disk Controller contains two independent directors to provide dual access paths to both host computer channel and the drive unit. Dual access paths increase performance and reliability of the sub-system.

Fig.-7 Outer View of the Sub-system

Table-2 The Sub-System Specifications

	FACOM 1783 Optical Disk Controler	FACOM 6443 Optical Disk Drive
Components	2 Directors	4 Drive Units
Cabinet Size (W × D × H)	645 × 880 × 1,400 mm	512 × 880 × 1,400 mm
Weight	250 kg	320 kg
Power Consumption	0.8 KVA	1.6 KVA
Input Power Supply	100/200 V a.c.	100/200 V a.c.
Environment Requirements	15~32°C, 20~80% RH	15~32°C, 20~80% RH

Floor space and power consumption for FACOM 6443 and IBM 3380AK4/BK4 magnetic disk sub-systems are compared below on the base of almost the same storage capacity of 35 GB.

Table-3 Comparisons to Magnetic Disk Sub-System

Sub-system Configuration :

FACOM : FACOM 1783 + FACOM 6443
IBM : IBM 3990-1 + IBM 3380AK4 + 3 × IBM 3380BK4

	FACOM	IBM	FACOM /IBM
Capacity/Sub-sytem (GB)	35.6	37.8	0.94
Space including maintenance area (Sq. meter/GB)	0.073	0.409	1/6
Space excluding maintenance area (Sq. meter/GB)	0.028	0.136	1/5
Power Consumption (KVA/GB)	0.067	0.238	1/4

The sub-system can be hooked to mainframe through a Block Multiplexer Channel as shown in Fig.-8.

Though the mechanical design of the drive unit is similar to fixed media magnetic disk drives, the storage management and formatting functions differ as follows.

(1) Emulation of library type drive

It is very important to prevent frequent media-to-media access, because this access takes up to three seconds. To minimize this long seeks, the controller and software see the drive as a library unit, and each medium is managed as a logical volume. By this emulation, it is possible to prevent the second job to start before the first job is completed.

(2) Fixed sector format

The recording density is so high that even a small defect on the recording layer may cause a data error.

However, the very powerful ECC, Inter-Leaved Reed Solomon Code, is used to decrease the bit error rate from 1E−05 to 1E−12. This bit error rate is good enough for storing coded data.

Because of this ECC algorithm, data length should be predetermined, causing the media format to be not variable, but a fixed sector format.

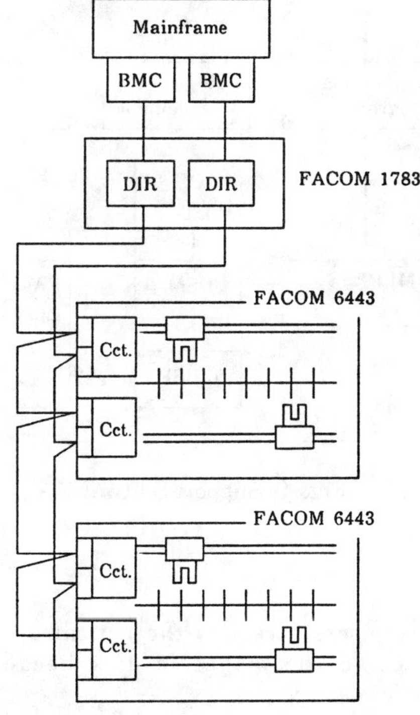

Fig.-8 Sub-System Configuration

6. Support Software

The basic softwares supporting the sub-system are schematically shown in Fig.-9.

- IMPRESS (Image Information Processor)

  Provides interface from/to OSM.
  Maximum 1 MB of data length can be handled.
- OSM (Optical Storage Manager)

  Controls data transfer between main-memory and the drive.
- LIBSP (Library-system Support Program)

  Controls the optical head access.
- RACF (Resource Access Control Facility)

  Provides File Name, and defines Read/Write authority.
- DSCF (DASD Space Control Facility)

  Manages space on the media.

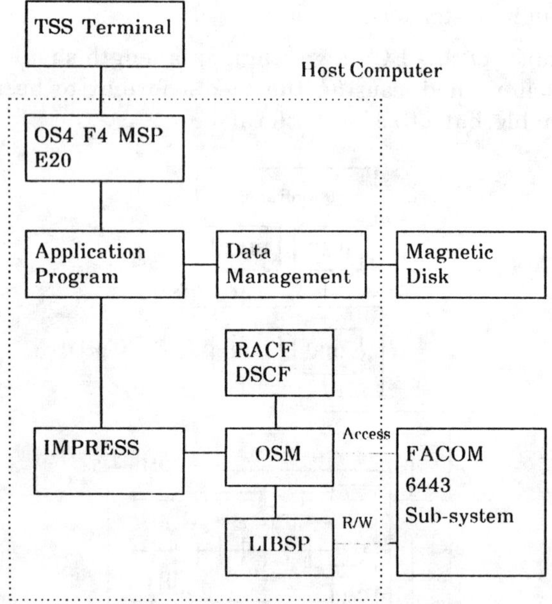

Fig. -9 Support Softwares

7. Operation at NAL

Normally, users access to the optical disk through work area in the magnetic disk because of the following reasons :

- Low performance of the drive unit.
- User data in variable format must be converted to fixed sector format to be stored in the optical disk. The format conversion is done by software at transferring data between magnetic and optical disks.

A data set is first generated in the magnetic disk, then transfered to the optical disk. At retrieving, the data set is transfered from the optical disk to the magnetic disk, then retrieved from the magnetic disk. In case of the operation at NAL, this staging/de-staging had better not be done automatically by LRU (Least Recently Used) algorithm but by an operation managing program, because the computer environment for the scientific calculation varies day by day.

For operators in the computer center, special features are prepared to allow them to directly access to the optical disk. This mode will be used for maintenance of the file, or at generating big data base.

Following softwares are prepared to enable the above mentioned operations.

- Staging/de-staging of the data set
- Delete of the data set
- Re-name of the data set
- Copy of the data set between magnetic and optical disks
- Indication of file attribute and usage information to the user
- Back-up/Restore of the data set

8. Future Enhancements

The FACOM 6443 is the first generation erasable optical disk to be used in mainframe computer environments. Its performance and storage capacity will be improved along with advancement of technologies. Examples of improvements are :

(1) Data transfer rate

The data transfer rate is mainly limited today by the laser diode power. Successful developments of higher power lasers are being announced. Introducing these new lasers in the drive, the transfer rate will be increased along with the rotational speed of media.

Besides the laser power, three rotations of media are required at updating data, reducing the total data transfer speed. In the futures, direct over-write will be possible, and read-after-write for data verification will be unnecessary, thanks to high reliability of the media and to defect mapping.

These improvements will enable write operation within one rotation, enabling read and write data transfer rate to be equally high.

(2) Access time

If a small and light-weight integrated optical head is available in the future, the access time will be greatly reduced by installing heads on every surface of the media, just like magnetic disk drives.

(3) Storage capacity

Storage capacity will be increased by higher recording density technology as well as increased number of media in the unit.

(4) Staging/de-staging in the sub-system

As described in Section-8, NAL is requiring staging/de-staging for quick response in a job and for conversion of data format. However, data transfer from/to the magnetic disk through the channel may cause degradation of total system throughput.

To solve this problem, a controller to which optical and magnetic disks can be connected is desirable for enabling staging/destaging and data format conversion within the sub-system.

9. Conclusions

A rewritable optical disk sub-system has been developed which has much larger storage capacity than magnetic disk drives and much shorter access time than library type storage devices. It is believed that super-computer applications may be expanded by the features of this optical disk sub-system, allowing for the economic storage of greater quantities of data on-line.

However, magneto-optic is a state-of-the-art but not yet matured technology, and the sub-system itself is a completely new type. Thus, there are many items to be advanced, but the underlying technologies are being improved day by day.

Fujitsu is commited to improve the specifications of the sub-system with these advanced technologies to serve customers needs for high performance access to increasing amounts of data.

References

1. FUJITSU

   R. Kudo, et. al. Vol. 39, No.3 (June, 1988)

2. A New Protective File for Magneto-Optical TbFeCo Media, J. of Appl. Physics

   M. Miyazaki, et. al Vol. 61, pp 3325-3328 (1987)

3. Interlinked Servo Tracking Technology, Processings SPIE

   S. Arai, et. al. Vol. 695, pp. 141-146 (1986)

A Scheme for Data Compression in Supercomputers

M. A. Bassiouni, N. Ranganathan, and Amar Mukherjee

Department of Computer Science
University of Central Florida, Orlando, Florida 32816

Abstract

There is a growing recognition of the importance of efficient coding and data compression schemes in supercomputing centers and in networks of high-speed computing machines. Recently, there has been a considerable interest in arithmetic coding as a promising technique for reducing the cost of data storage and transmission. In this paper, we present a compression algorithm that is tailored to utilize the enormous speed and memory size of supercomputers and which utilizes an enhanced arithmetic coding scheme. The paper also presents efficient VLSI designs for the enhanced scheme. These hardware designs are suitable for inclusion in disk and communication controllers of supercomputers and would provide a practical way to effectively increase thresholds of data transfer rates and communication bandwidth.

1. Introduction

Data compression is becoming increasingly important as a useful tool for the reduction of the cost of data transmission and storage. In [BASS87, MUKH88], we presented efficient encoding algorithms and VLSI chips for supercomputers based on the Huffman's encoding method [HUFF52]. Recently, arithmetic coding [WITT87] has received considerable interest as a promising technique for the reduction of the cost of data transmission and storage. In this paper, we present enhanced arithmetic coding scheme specially designed to utilize the high speed of supercomputers. VLSI chip designs suitable for implementation in device controllers, I/O channels, and communication controllers of supercomputing machines are also presented. As explained below, data compression is particularly important to the design of high-speed vector machines. Some supercomputers (e.g., Fujitsu VP-200 [RIGA84, LUBE85]) use a compress/ expand mode as one of the available vector instruction modes.

It has been typically noticed that vector rates (sustained rates) attained from high-level compiled source code are significantly lower than the announced machine peak rates. For example, the observed sustained rates (measured in Mflops) for Fortran code on the Cray-1S machine have been found to be less than 18% of the peak rate for that machine [HACK86]. There are several factors affecting the sustained rate, e.g., the degree of vectorization, average vector length, memory access patterns, I/O latency and I/O transfer rates, etc. As explained in [HACK86], I/O delays can severely degrade the net sustained performance because of low processor utilization in spite of the high vector processing speeds. Unless I/O transfer rates are proportionally improved, sustained performance figures (in terms of turnaround time) will continue to be orders of magnitude lower than peak rates. Attaining dramatic gains in the performance of I/O devices may therefore prove to be one of the most important challenges facing the design of future supercomputers. Efficient implementations of data compression (e.g, high speed VLSI chips for data compression/expansion) represent a viable solution that can effectively increase the speed of I/O and overcome the limitations of mechanical disk devices.

There is a growing recognition of the importance of data compression in reducing the cost of data transmission. This is particularly important for networks containing supercomputing machines. Data compression can be implemented in the transmitter logic of the communication/line controllers of these machines so that huge amounts of data and electronic mail can be compressed before they are transmitted over long distance communication links. The original data can be recovered by the expansion process in the receiver logic of the communication controllers at the receiving machines. Since communication devices represent a bottleneck similar to I/O devices, the improvement achieved by compression will contribute significantly to the enhancement of the performance of supercomputer networks.

Similarly, implementing compression in device controllers and I/O channels of supercomputers will reduce the storage requirements of large data sets, reduce the size of recovery tapes, and speed up the process of recovery [BASS85].

The organization of this paper is as follows. Section 2 presents an optional preliminary phase of the compression process. Sections 3 and 4 present an enhanced version of arithmetic coding suitable for supercomputers. VLSI designs of the proposed scheme are presented in Section 5.

2. An Optional Preprocessing Phase

Dictionary-based encoding is a popular method for the compression of text, alphanumeric records, and business databases. The basic idea is to use a dictionary of common words or phrases and to replace dictionary words in the input text by their address in the dictionary. The scheme is often augmented by tables of common word endings/prefixes in order to increase the effectiveness of the dictionary. In many systems (micro- and mini-computers), the dictionary cannot be stored in main memory and is therefore placed on disk storage. This increases considerably the overhead associated with compression and decompression. To alleviate this problem, core-resident Bloom filters are used to avoid searching the dictionary for some nondictionary words (each word in the input data is hashed to some bit in the filter; the value of the bit is zero if none of the words that hash to it is in the dictionary).

2.1. Effect of Supercomputers

With supercomputers, it is possible to store entire dictionaries of large sizes in main memory. This, together with the high speed of supercomputers, can make dictionary-based compression more practically affordable and can make possible the use of this technique as one of the stages in a multiple-phase compression scheme as will be explained shortly (the idea of multiple-phase compression has been motivated in [BASS86] which gives a preliminary scheme for text compression). Also, vectorization (pipelining) can have a major effect on data compression. Compression techniques like arithmetic coding and adaptive methods are inherently sequential in nature. In supercomputers, the whole operation of encoding as well as decoding can be implemented as pipeline stages for improving compression rates, as will be discussed later in this paper.

2.2. An Encoding Scheme for Supercomputers

It is possible to combine run-length encoding [GOLO66] with dictionary compression. A sequence of repeated character can be replaced by a count field and a single occurrence of that character. Thus the resulting encoding can be described as follows.

Let

$E(e)$ represent the encoding of entity e ,

$LOC(W)$ represent the binary representation of the address of word W in the dictionary,

X^i represent a run-length of character X repeated i times,

$BIN(i)$ indicate the binary representation of i ,

$FIRST(W)$ represent the first character of word W

$SUBSTR(W,2)$ represent the substring of W starting at position 2

$S1 \mid\mid S2$ represent the concatenation of $S1$ and $S2$

$ASCII(X)$ represents a byte with the 7-bit ASCII code of character X

Then

$$E(X^i) = B'10' \mid\mid BIN(i) \mid\mid ASCII(X)$$

where B'10' denotes the bit-string '10', and

For a word W in the dictionary, the encoding is given by

$$E(W) = B'11' \mid\mid LOC(W)$$

For a word V not found in the dictionary, the encoding is given by

$$ASCII(FIRST(V)) \mid\mid E(SUBSTR(V,2))$$

We assume that compression of entities will be aligned on byte boundaries (to enable applying other phases of compression as will be explained later). A good choice will be to use two bytes for the encoding of run-lengths and dictionary words, and one byte for each character in other entities (e.g., words not in the dictionary).

Notice that ASCII(X) is encoded in 8 bits; the leftmost bit is always zero. Thus in the compressed output of an entity, a "1" in the leftmost bit of the first byte indicates that the entity is either a run-length (second leftmost bit is 0) or a word in the dictionary (second leftmost bit is 1). A value of 0 in the leftmost bit indicates a normal uncompressed character (in 7-bit ASCII representation).

2.3. Properties of Compressed Output

If the previous encoding scheme uses lengths that are aligned on byte boundaries, e.g., if

$$length(\ B'10' \ \| \ BIN(i)) \ = \ 16 \quad bits$$

$$length(\ B'11' \ \| \ LOC(W)) \ = \ 16 \quad bits$$

$$length(\ ASCII(X)\ ) \ = \ 8 \quad bits$$

Then the following properties can be expected to hold in the compressed output:

(1) The skewness in the distribution of single (uncompressed) characters and their locality (sequentiality) pattern will be largely preserved. This is because these characters are expected to occur in groups (e.g., within letters of words not found in the dictionary or digits within a number), thus exhibiting a good locality behavior.

(2) Some byte patterns (other than single characters) are expected to occur more frequently than others. For example if W_m is the most frequently occurring dictionary word, then the pair of bytes representing $E(W_m)$ will occur quite often in the compressed output.

The above properties make the compressed output suitable for the implementation of a specially tailored arithmetic coding scheme. This will be explained next.

3. Arithmetic Coding

The basic principles of arithmetic coding were first described by Elias in early 1960s [ABRA63]. Later, Rissanen and Pasco have proposed several practical techniques ([RISS76], [PASC76], [RISS79]). In a recent paper by Ian Witten et all [WITT87], an implementation of arithmetic coding is discussed in detail.

In arithmetic coding, a message is represented by an interval of real numbers between 0 and 1. The consecutive symbols in a message are coded recursively using the frequency of occurrences of the symbols within the message. Data compression using arithmetic coding is viewed as two parts: modeling the statistics of the source message and the coding of the message using the statistics generated by the model. The model could be static or adaptive. When the model is static, fixed probabilities are used throughout the process of coding. In the adaptive model, the frequency counts are updated during the coding of each symbol and the model dynamically adapts to the varying statistics of the source message. The fixed model case is a two-pass version where the first pass is to gather statistics and the second pass is used to actually code the message. The adaptive model dynamically changes its model while coding the message in one pass. It has been found that the adaptive model is never significantly worse than a two-pass approach while it could be significantly better than the fixed model most of the time. One problem with the adaptive model is that during the initial phase of coding, it does not have enough information about the statistics. So using a reasonable initial model to begin with is an important consideration for the adaptive model.

The technique of arithmetic coding can be described as follows: initially, before any message is coded, the message is represented by the entire interval [0, 1). This interval is divided into subintervals such that each symbol is assigned a particular subinterval and the length of the subinterval for a symbol is proportional to its frequency count. As each symbol is processed, the interval representing the message is narrowed to that portion of it allocated to the symbol. Thus the interval length narrows down with the coding of each symbol. While encoding high probability symbols, the interval reduces at a slower rate than when coding low probability symbols, the interval length reduces more rapidly. Also, as the interval size reduces, more bits are needed to represent it without loss of precision.

In general, the codeword is an interval represented as (L, L+W) where L is the current low point and W is the width of the current interval. Say, for character i, p(i) is the symbol probability and P(i) is the cumulative probability. Then while encoding character i, the new L is calculated as L + W*P(i) and the new W is calculated as W*p(i). The new L and L+W will represent the interval soon after the encoding of character i. We will illustrate the technique with an example of the fixed model.

Let us assume a simplified alphabet set for our example, and that is { a, b, c, 0, 1, 2, * } with the probabilities being 0.1, 0.1, 0.1, 0.3, 0.1, 0.1 and 0.2, respectively. The symbol "*" is used to denote the end of the message. The character set and the corresponding symbol probabilities p(i) are listed in Table 1.

Table 1. Probabilities for the character set

Symbol	p(i)	P(i)
a	0.1	0
b	0.1	0.1
c	0.1	0.2
0	0.3	0.3
1	0.1	0.6
2	0.1	0.7
*	0.2	0.8

The table also shows the cumulative probabilities P(i) calculated using the symbol probability. The order of the symbols does not matter in calculating the cumulative probabilities. Suppose the message to be coded is "0001abb". The initial code is the range [0, 1). The first symbol is encoded by narrowing the interval to the range that corresponds to the symbol. After the symbol "0" is coded using the values in Table 1, the range narrows down to [0.3, 0.6), where L = 0.3 and H = 0.3 + 0.3 = 0.6. This process is repeated until the end of the message and the character "*" is encoded. The coding of the various symbols in the message string is illustrated in Table 2.

Table 2. Encoding of string 0001abb

Symbol	L	W	H = L+W
0	0.3	0.3	0.6
0	0.39	0.09	0.48
0	0.417	0.027	0.444
1	0.477	0.0027	0.4797
a	0.477	0.00027	0.47727
b	0.477027	0.000027	0.477054
b	0.4770297	0.0000027	0.47770324
*	0.47703186	0.00000054	0.47703240

The columns "L" and "H" give the low and high values of the range and "W" gives the width of the interval after the encoding of the symbol in the left-most column. Once the final range has been calculated after the encoding of the end-of-message symbol "*", any value within that range can be selected to represent the compressed codeword. The decoder on the other hand, recursively undoes what the encoder had done during the coding phase. The steps involved in decoding are:

(i) find the symbol for which the codeword lies within the allocated range for the symbol and include that symbol in the expanded message.

(ii) subtract the symbol's cumulative probability P(i) from the codeword.

(iii) divide the resultant value from (ii) by the symbol probability p(i) which gives the codeword after the decoding of symbol i.

4. Enhancement of Arithmetic Coding

It should be noted that in arithmetic coding, the interval reduces in size as more symbols are encoded and also more number of bits are required to represent the interval as its size decreases. The interval size decreases more rapidly when a less probable symbol is encoded. Thus the precision required to represent the encoded message may increase so much that it might not be possible to continue the encoding. At that point, the end-of-message character has to be encoded and then the rest of the message is coded starting with the initial interval [0, 1). More symbols can be encoded within a limited precision if the probabilities of the symbols being encoded are large. The arithmetic coding scheme uses only the distributional property of data. We present an enhancement to arithmetic coding scheme which utilizes the correlational properties of data, i.e., the property that consecutive characters tend to be of same type (alphabets, digits, blanks, successive zeros etc). The scheme is based on the observation that in many data files, data records exhibit a strong locality behavior of character reference. Again we will describe the scheme with the help of an example.

The simplified character set shown in Table 1 is split into two groups as alphabets and digits. The alphabet group will consist of {a, b, c, &, *} where the symbol "&" indicates a group switch and the symbol "*" is used to indicate the end of the message. The digit group will consist of {0, 1, 2, &, *}. The probabilities for the symbols in the two groups are given in Tables 3 and 4.

Table 3. Probabilities for Group-1

Symbol	p(i)	P(i)
a	0.3	0
b	0.3	0.3
c	0.2	0.6
&	0.1	0.8
*	0.1	0.9

Table 4. Probabilities for Group-2

Symbol	p(i)	P(i)
0	0.5	0
1	0.15	0.5
2	0.15	0.65
&	0.1	0.8
*	0.1	0.9

Suppose we have to encode the string "0001abb". The string will actually be coded as "0001&abb*", where "&" indicates the switch from digits to alphabet group while "*" indicates the end of message. The message is coded using the arithmetic coding scheme, but the probabilities are taken from the appropriate table depending on the group of the character being encoded. The encoding of the message and the code ranges are shown in Table 5.

In our example, since the character set is split into two groups and the probabilities are assigned with respect to the characters within a group, the symbols get higher probability values. Thus in this new scheme, the interval length reduces at a slower rate as the message is being encoded. For our example, the same string when encoded using the enhanced version of arithmetic coding scheme, the resultant interval length is 14.075 times larger than the interval length when coded using the original scheme.

Table 5. Encoding of string 0001abb with the modified scheme

Symbol	L	W	H = L+W
0	0.0	0.5	0.5
0	0.0	0.25	0.25
0	0.0	0.125	0.125
1	0.0625	0.01875	0.08125
&	0.0775	0.0028125	0.0803125
a	0.0775	0.0008445	0.0783445
b	0.07775335	0.00025335	0.07800665
b	0.077829355	0.000076005	0.0778369555
*	0.077905400	0.0000076005	0.0779130005

5. Hardware Implementation

In this section, we present a hardware design for the modified arithmetic coding scheme which is suitable for VLSI implementation in supercomputing systems. The basic hardware for the enhanced arithmetic coding scheme is shown in Figure 1.

For the enhanced arithmetic coding scheme, the probabilities are stored in the RAM by separating the characters in each group. Also, the probabilities corresponding to the group switch characters are stored. The RAM is addressed by the binary value of the ASCII symbol set. For each symbol i, the symbol probability p(i) and the cumulative probability P(i) are stored. We assume integer arithmetic since it has been shown in [WITT87] that arithmetic coding can be implemented using integer arithmetic. Since arithmetic coding consists of simple arithmetic operations like add and multiply, it can be easily implemented in hardware.

In order to encode a symbol i, during the first cycle P(i) is input to the multiplier and W*P(i) is calculated and during the second cycle, the product is input to the adder to be added to L. Also, during the second cycle, the product W*p(i) is computed to obtain the new width. A 2:1 multiplexer is used to multiplex between P(i) and p(i) as input for the multiplier. The boxes labeled New W, Cur W, New L and Cur L are registers to hold the new and current values of interval width W and and the low point of the interval, L.

The overall operation of the hardware is as follows: The next input symbol is loaded into a register from the buffer, which is used by the Group Switch Logic GSL to determine if there is a

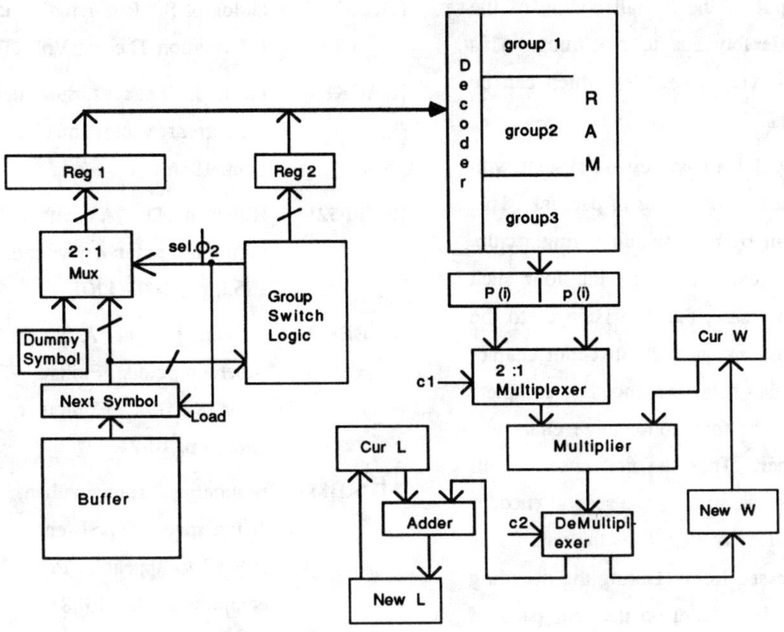

Figure 1. Hardware for Enhanced arithmetic coding

change of group. If there is no change in the group, then GSL activates the sel.phi2 signal which passes the symbol to the register Reg1 to be decoded. In this case, GSL loads the other register Reg2 with a fixed binary value. The bits in Reg2 are appended to those in Reg1 before they are input to the decoder in the RAM. These extra bits from Reg2 will be used in selecting the current group. Also sel.phi2 signal loads a new character into the next symbol register from the buffer. If there is a change in the group, the next symbol is made to wait and the sel.phi2 loads the dummy symbol into Reg1. Thus the sel.phi2 signal acts as a control input to the 2:1 Multiplexor which selects between the next symbol and the dummy symbol. Again this dummy symbol corresponds to the situation where no symbol from any group is selected. Simultaneously, GSL loads a value in Reg2 which will select the group switch character and the corresponding probabilities will be output from the RAM. The size of Reg1 will be 8 bits in order to hold the ASCII symbols, while the size of Reg2 will depend on the number of groups. If there are three groups, then Reg2 will need 3 bits in order to represent six possible group switches.

The decoding algorithm for the above compression schemes recursively do the reverse of the operation done by the compression algorithm. The algorithm is described in section 3 which can be modified to obtain the decompression algorithm for our modified scheme. The decoding hardware will require a content addressable memory (CAM) instead of a RAM for storing the symbols as well as their probabilities. The decompression of a symbol involves the arithmetic operations, subtraction and division as against addition and multiplication for compression.

The above hardware algorithms can be implemented in VLSI using CMOS technology and the clock period of the circuit depends on the time needed to perform multiplication. With the high packing density possible in VLSI chips today, the above encoding hardware can be easily built within a single chip. The details of layout designs are beyond the scope of this paper. The arithmetic coding scheme is very sequential in nature. The encoding of the next symbol cannot start until the current symbol has been encoded and the interval representing the codeword is available. In order to obtain speedup, there are two approaches possible and here, we just outline the approaches.

The first approach is to pipeline the whole operation of encoding and perform block coding. In this case, we will use a pipeline multiplier and the various stages of encoding like fetching the probabilities, multiplication, addition etc can be done in a pipeline fashion. Say the entire hardware consists of n stages. The entire data file can be split into n blocks and during the first n cycles, the coding of a new block is initiated during each cycle. The first symbol of the first block is coded at the end of the nth cycle and during the $n+1$th cycle, the encoding of the second symbol of the first block is initiated. During the following cycle, the encoding of the second symbol of the second block is initiated.

Thus the utilization and throughput of the overall coding of the data file can be improved considerably due to pipelining. This scheme will be effective only for very large files which can be broken into reasonably sized blocks.

The second approach is to build a compression system with several modules of the encoder circuit operating in parallel. This is possible since each encoder can be built within a single chip. We explain the scheme with the example of having four such chips operating in parallel. In this case, the data is input to the compression system in the following manner: the first four characters are input to the four encoders. After the encoders complete the entire coding operation, the next four consecutive characters are input to the encoders in order. Thus the first encoder will encode the 1st, 5th, 9th characters and so on. The second encoder will encode the 2nd, 6th, 10th characters etc. Thus the data file is stored in four parts in the compressed form. During the decoding phase, four decoders will operate in parallel on the four parts of the compressed file. The first four characters will be output by the decoders at the same time and they can be assembled in the same order as they were in the original file before being disassembled and compressed. The speed up we can obtain is a direct ratio of the number of encoder/decoder modules operating in parallel. With the decreasing cost of hardware due to the advancement in VLSI technology, it is not expensive to build such a compression system in an environment where compression could yield considerable improvement in the overall system performance.

References

[ABRA63] Abramson, N. *Information Theory and Coding.* McGraw-Hill, New York, 1963.

[BASS87] Bassiouni, M. and Mukherjee, A. "Supercomputer algorithms for data transmission and encoding" Proc. 2nd International Conf. on Supercomputing, May 1987.

[BASS86] Bassiouni, M. and Ok, B. "Double encoding- a technique for reducing storage requirement of text" J. Information Systems, Vol. 11, No. 2, 1986, pp. 177-184.

[BASS85] Bassiouni, M. "Data compression in scientific and statistical databases" IEEE Transactions on Software Engineering, Vol. SE-11, No. 10, October 1985, pp. 1047-1058.

[GOLO66] Golomb, S. "Run-length encodings" IEEE Trans. on Information Theory, Vol. IT-12, 1966, pp. 399-401.

[HACK86] Hack, J. "Peak vs. sustained performance in highly concurrent vector machines" Computer, Vol. 19, Sept. 1986.

[HUFF52] Huffman, D. "A method for the construction of minimum redundancy codes" Proc. IRE, Vol. 40, 1952, pp. 1098-1101.

[LUBE85] Lubeck, J. et al "A benchmark comparison of three supercomputers: Fujitsu VP-200, Hitachi S810/20, Cray X-MP/2" Computer, Vol. 18, No. 12, Dec. 1985, pp. 10-24.

[MUKH88] Mukherjee; Ranganathan, N. and Bassiouni, M. "High-speed VLSI encoding chips for supercomputers" to appear in Proc. 3rd Int. Conf. on Supercomputing, May 1988.

[MUKH86] Mukherjee, A. *Introduction to nMOS and CMOS VLSI Systems Design.* Prentice-Hall, Englewood Cliffs: N.J., 1986.

[PASC76] Pasco, R. Ph.D. thesis, Dept. of Electrical Engineering, Stanford University, Stanford, California, 1976.

[RIGA84] Riganati, J. and Schneck, P. "Supercomputing" Computer, Vol. 17, October, 1984.

[RISS76] Rissanen, J. J. "Generalized Kraft inequality and arithmetic coding." IBM J. Res. Dev. 20 (May 1976), pp. 198-203.

[RISS79] Rissanen, J. J. and Langdon, G. G. "Arithmetic Coding" IBM J. Res. Dev., 23, 2 (Mar 1979), pp. 149-162.

[WITT87] Witten, I.; Neal, R. and Cleary, J. "Arithmetic coding for data compression" Communications of ACM, Vol. 30, No. 6, June 1987, pp. 520-540.

A MASS STORAGE SYSTEM FOR SUPERCOMPUTERS BASED ON UNIX

J. Richards
NAS Systems Division
NASA Ames Research Center
Moffett Field, CA 94035

T. Kummell, D.G. Zarlengo
Sterling Software, Inc.
Palo Alto, CA. 94303

ABSTRACT

This paper presents the design, implementation and utilization of a large Mass Storage Subsystem (MSS) at the Numerical Aerodynamics Simulation (NAS) at NASA-Ames Research Center. The MSS supports a large networked, multi-vendor Unix-based supercomputing facility.

The MSS at Ames Research Center provides all processors on the Numerical Aerodynamics System Processing Network (NPSN), from workstations to supercomputers, the ability to store large amounts of data in a highly accessible, long-term repository. The MSS uses Unix System V and is capable of storing hundreds of thousands of files ranging from a few bytes to 2 Gigabytes in size. This utilization of Unix, to mask the underlying MVS system, reduces the training requirements for the end user and allows the use of existing Unix networking solutions such as RCP, REMSH, and TCP/IP with locally developed performance enhancements. The systems are currently networked via the NSC HYPERchannel and Ethernet. To assure data integrity and to accommodate spanned volume files the IBM MVS Operating System was implemented so that it is transparent to the Unix user.

Since the MSS was released for production at NAS in June of 1987, experience with the system has led to design improvements and enhancements which have resulted in more than an order of magnitude in performance improvement. The current production system is capable of data transfer rates in excess of 6,900 Kilobits per second end-to-end from the Cray 2 supercomputer disk to the MSS DASD. Future improvements include parallel data transmission across multiple NSC HYPERchannel adapters and data-striping on the Amdahl 6380 double density disk drives. Initial performance tests have demonstrated a further increase to 17,800 Kilobits per second when these improvements are placed into production.

This article is based upon a less extensive paper presented at the IEEE Symposium on Mass Storage Systems, October 1988 [1].

INTRODUCTION

Design and development of the Mass Storage Subsystem for NAS Systems Division began in 1981 [2]. The objective was to integrate a Mass Storage Subsystem into a network of heterogeneous computing systems intended to be one of the world's leading scientific supercomputing facilities which is available as a resource to government, industry and academic research programs. The requirements, design, specifications, and implementation [3], [4] were completed by NASA-Ames Research Center in 1987.

The primary design factor of the Mass Storage Subsystem (MSS) was the decision to implement Unix (in most cases the Unix implementation was based on the AT&T System V.2 with 4.3 bsd networking) with extensions RCP, REMSH, CSH, etc. across user-accessible computers as the single user interface in the NAS Processing System Network (NPSN). This was done to provide a common user interface across all systems. Consequently, the initial design concept of the MSS was to provide the end user with a single consistent interface that is both familiar and easy to use. Because of the wide usage of the Unix operating system here at NAS, it was decided to implement a system that would provide the Unix file structure and allow utilization of the existing networking software components. This decision facilitated the connection of a wide variety of processors to the MSS, minimized the training required, and reduced the impact of implementing a major software component in an existing environment.

The NPSN now includes multiple Cray 2 systems, Amdahl mainframes, assorted DEC VAXs, several mini-supercomputers, and numerous workstations networked with HYPERchannel, Ethernet, and long-haul communications. Shortly, a new Cray Y-MP will be added to the processing network. Even though there were great benefits in the common Unix interface for the NAS users, the inherent weaknesses of the Unix file system (the lack of file integrity, archiving, and spanned volume files) led the designers to include the IBM MVS operating system and Sterling Software's DMS/OS for DASD and tape cartridge hierarchical management.

CH2617-9/88/0000/0279$01.00 © 1988 IEEE

Other than the Unix user interface, the five original fundamental requirements set by NAS for the MSS were:

1. Data transfer rate of 25 Megabits/sec;
2. Unlimited number of files;
3. File size limit no less than 2 Gigabytes;
4. No single failure of media, hardware, or software would cause the loss of data; and
5. Tape library data Archival/Retrieval .

To provide all these capabilities, several commercially available software products and about thirty thousand lines of source code were necessary. All objectives were accomplished with the one exception that the data transfer rate was limited to 6.9 Megabits/sec due to systems software and hardware architecture impediments. Today the NAS Mass Storage Subsystem serves 900 system accounts under 311 research programs and contains more than 120,000 files totaling in excess of 0.5 Terabytes of user data.

The NAS Systems Division continues with its commitment to state of the art networked mass storage under Unix. Planned future research and development include enhancements to the current system described in the following sections plus the development of a Unix-only single operating system design to be implemented with a hardened Unix file system that satisfies the five requirements listed above.

Since the MSS was released for production at NAS in June of 1987, performance analysis and experience with the system has led to design improvements which resulted in performance enhancements greater than an order-of-magnitude. The current system is capable of data transfer rates in excess of 6,900 Kilobits per second end-to-end from the Cray 2 supercomputers disk to the MSS DASD.

FUNCTIONAL DESCRIPTION

Dual Operating Systems.

There are two basic components of the MSS. Each component is associated with a separate operating system and provides specific functionality for the MSS application. The first component called UTS-MSS, is Amdahl's version of UNIX System V. In the current release of the MSS, UTS-MSS runs in a virtual operating system mode provided by the Amdahl Multiple Domain Facility (MDF) and IBM's VM/370 operating system. The primary function UTS-MSS serves is to provide a UNIX interface to all of the remote processors. UTS-MSS is responsible for maintaining the UNIX directory structure and all of the pertinent inode information. The MSS is a true Unix file system as far as file naming, access control, and I/O operations. Modifications to the Unix kernel facilitate the expansion of the file system structures to include the concept of virtual disk devices described later.

The second component of the MSS is an application written under IBM's MVS operating system. The MVS-MSS component provides a reliable disk data store that is capable of supporting files spanning more than one volume. Standard MVS utilities are used to support MSS file system maintenance and catastrophic error recovery. In the current release, the MVS operating system runs in a virtual mode similar to UTS-MSS under MDF but without VM/370. The MVS-MSS is primarily concerned with storing and retrieving the data on disk, archiving older data to tape, and reorganizing the data for efficient utilization of disk space. The MVS operating system was chosen for this task because it supports files that are larger than one physical disk device and secondly because the MVS file system is very reliable.

Communications and Networking - SOURCE to UNIX.

In order to be as flexible as possible, the networking protocol in the UTS-MSS was designed as a true data communications protocol; it includes check sums, time outs, and re-transmissions, and will work over unreliable links. This is so the SOURCE (ie. source of data files) and Unix systems do not have to be physically adjacent, but instead may be connected by some high-speed network such as an NSC HYPERchannel.

Communications and Networking - UNIX to MVS.

Communications between the UTS and MVS systems is achieved using a communications protocol similar to the networking solution described in the paragraph above. However, the communications path is via Channel-to-Channel Adapters (CTCA) rather than HYPERchannel. The CTCAs may be real or they may be simulated under the VM/370 operating system. The basic packet of control information is called the Message Control Block (MCB). The MCB is always check-summed, and check summing of the associated data block is optional.

DASD Configuration.

The DASD pool associated with the MSS is theoretically limitless. A parameter table is developed during the MSS initialization phase that defines the number of volumes associated with the MSS. The system programming staff can manage the number of volumes in the DASD pool, and the three size classes (small, medium and large) by modifying entries in the MSS parameter table.

Software Configuration.

A logical diagram of the basic MSS configuration is presented in the Figure 1 which shows the flow of data and control from the SOURCE Unix system (from supercomputer to workstation) to the UTS-MSS process.

MSS commands invoked on the SOURCE system cause the UTS-MSS system to create UTS file inode directory on disk. Once this is created the MCB and the associated data are passed via the Channel-to-Channel link (CTCA) to the MVS-MSS. In MVS, the file is created and the associated data is passed to VSAM to be written on the appropriate disk drive.

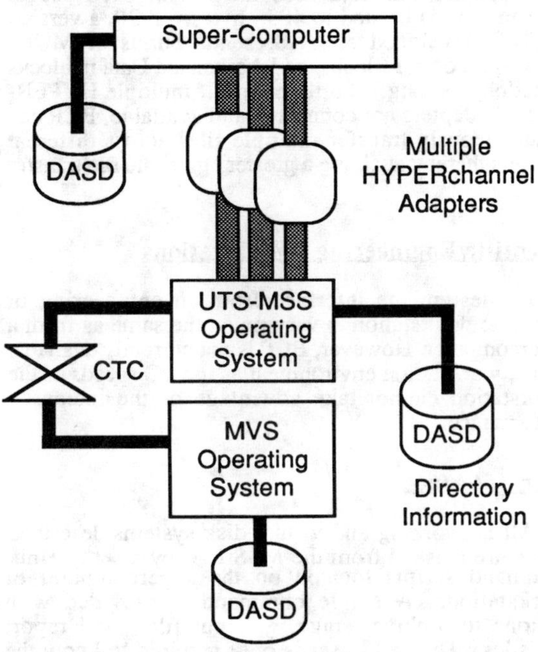

Figure 1 MSS Release 6 Logical Diagram

Hardware Configuration

Figure 2 shows a typical Supercomputer MSS facility configuration. The configuration shown is similar to the existing configuration at the AMES Research Center NAS facility.

Two Cray-2 supercomputers are attached to the NSC HYPERchannel via multiple NSC A-130 HYPERchannel adapters capable of data transmissions in the region of 50 million bits per second. The MSS is connected to the NSC HYPERchannel via NSC A-222 adapter pairs. Multiple adapters are used to increase the bandwidth between the SOURCE system and UTS-MSS.

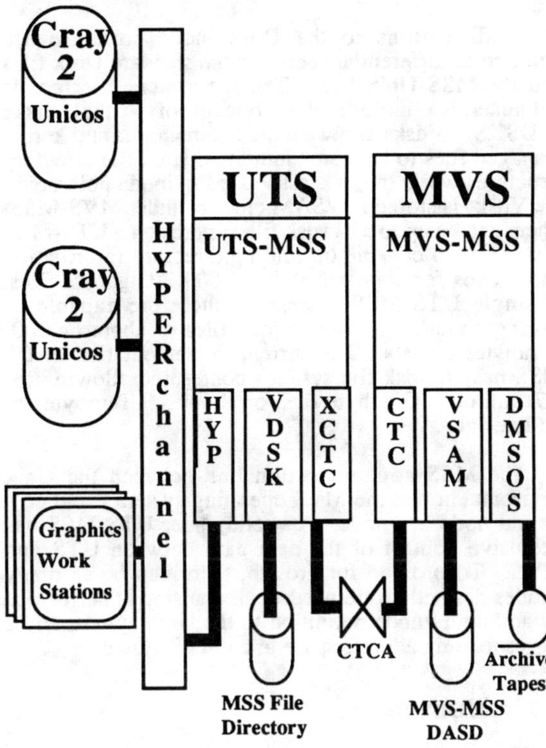

Figure 2 MSS Release 6 Logical Diagram (Detailed)

Referring to Figure 2, the data path between the Unix and MVS portions of the MSS is via the channel-to-channel adapters (CTCA). Normally, there are eight devices configured between the two operating systems. Each device passes only one kind of data in one direction to allow consistent buffer sizes and prevent bi-directional conflict. This gives a configuration as displayed in Table 1.

Table 1
CTCA Configuration

Dev	Type	Transfer Direction
1	MCB	from Unix to MVS
2	MCB	from Unix to MVS
3	MCB+DATA	from Unix to MVS
4	MCB+DATA	from Unix to MVS
5	MCB	from MVS to Unix
6	MCB	from MVS to Unix
7	MCB+DATA	from MVS to Unix
8	MCB+DATA	from MVS to Unix

Vdsks Structure

Modifications to the Unix inode structure are required to differentiate between the standard Unix files and the MSS Unix files. The file system interface is enhanced to include the concept of virtual disks (VDSKS). Vdsks allow the inode directories and kernel managed files to be stored in normal Unix file directory structures while the data associated to inode pointers in the Vdsks is stored in VSAM clusters under MVS-MSS. There can be up to 512 vdsk file systems on a UTS-MSS system, each capable of holding directory information and inodes for approximately 65,000 2-Gigabyte files. A single UTS-MSS system is, therefore capable of storing about 32 million unique files or about 64,000-Terabytes of data. The current implementation of the MSS has 26 vdsk file systems configured allowing for 1.7 million 2-Gigabyte files or about 3.3-Terabytes of on-line data .

The MSS communication link between the Unix environment and the MVS operating system is called a virtual node or vnode. A vnode under UTS-MSS has exclusive control of the data path between UTS and MVS. To provide for growth, there can be as many vnodes defined as are needed. Expansion is performed by adding a vnode definition to the Unix system and a corresponding address space to an MVS system.

Inode Structure

The implementation of the VDSK structure is accomplished by the addition of three fields in the Unix inode structure. They are as follows:

i_vsize: This field is used only at file creation time. It is used to log the estimated size of a VDSK file for eventual transmission to MVS. This is useful for pre-allocation on the MVS side.

i_vfile: This flag is set to 0 for non-vdsk files. It is set to 1 for files residing on a vdsk file system. This allows UTS-MSS to distinguish between devices.

i_conid: When a vdsk file has been opened by UTS-MSS for read or write, the MVS system returns a conid (Connection ID). This value is passed back to MVS on subsequent I/O operations to indicate that the request is for an open file.

Networks

The MSS is capable of networking with one or more SOURCE systems using the existing Unix networking support. Remote Copy (RCP) and a special high performance process called Bulk file Copy (BCP) are used on the SOURCE systems to transfer files across the network to and from the the Unix system component (UTS-MSS).

Supercomputers

The interface between the MSS and the various supercomputers consists of a number of separate processes. The user has the option of using RCP, FTP, BCP to accomplish the data transfer between the SOURCE system and the MSS. Although RCP is the easiest to use, it is the slowest method for transferring files because the data associated with each packet transmission is limited to 4096 bytes. BCP, a version of RCP developed at NAS, sends bursts of MCBs (Message Control Blocks) and Associated Data in blocks 56 Kilobytes long. Furthermore, if multiple HYPER-channel adapters are connected and available, BCP can simultaneously transfer multiple files across different adapters thereby attaining a greater aggregate file transfer rate.

Scientific/Engineering Workstations

By design, the interface from an engineering or scientific workstation is very much the same as from a supercomputer. However, BCP is not currently available for the workstation environment as the I/O speeds of the workstation cannot take advantage of the increased performance.

User Interface

All networking and virtual disk systems described above are masked from the MSS user by a set of Unix command scripts located on the supercomputer or workstation. A single command is provided with options to archive, stage, get, put files, and report statistics. The MSS user is only required to know the command script name, which will invoke the best protocol such as BCP.

DATA TRANSFER RATES

Aggregate and Single File Transfers

The performance characteristics of the MSS are measured under two different operating modes: single file and multiple file transfer. In single file mode, there is very little parallelism in the software or the I/O hardware. The software executes a transfer then issues a WAIT for the next event and I/O operations cannot be overlapped. Conversely, in multiple file mode overall bandwidth improves because other MSS tasks execute during the WAIT periods and I/O operations to different I/O devices can be overlapped. The effect of the parallelism is a much more efficient utilization of the entire MSS resource. To measure aggregate data transfer rate the elapsed time is calculated as the difference between the earliest start time and latest completion time for a set of file transfers. The total number of bits transferred is divided by the total elapsed time yielding the number of Kilobits per second.

The performance experienced by the end user is usually much different than either of these two measurements which indicate a range of best to worst performance. The actual data transfer rate is rarely as good as the aggregate rate but is usually better than a single file transfer.

Performance vs File Size

Since the MSS was placed in production, new releases have added features, improved reliability, and increased performance. Experience has shown that the best performance is achieved when transferring large files (in excess of 10 MB). Small files suffer an adverse performance penalty induced by the fixed overhead of file creation, open and close. Table 2 shows maximum observed aggregate data transfer rates for large (>100 MB) and small (<1MB) files on the various releases of the MSS during dedicated time.

The wide variation in the performance, particularly in releases 4 and 5, is due to the penalty imposed by the fixed overhead of creating many small files. The best performance is attained by transferring large files.

Table 2
Transfer Rates Supercomputer to DASD

		Transfer Rate (kb/s)	
Release	**Date**	**Large Files**	**Small Files**
4	03/87	30	30
5	10/87	600	30
6	07/88	6900	1500
7	01/89 *	17800	4500

*Targeted

IMPLEMENTATION REQUIREMENTS

Hardware

The MSS is capable of running in a wide variety of IBM 370 architecture configurations. The hardware necessary to support the MSS is variable depending on the software configuration and the performance goals desired. The MSS Release 7 General Overview [5] describes the hardware requirements for releases 5, 6, and 7. As an example of how performance is impacted by hardware configuration, the communication between the UTS-MSS and the MVS operating system is designed to utilize a Channel-to-Channel adapter (CTCA). This important function can be provided by a real CTCA such as a 3088 or by a virtual CTCA (requires the VM/370 operating system). The emulated CTCA is of course much slower as it uses the compiled 370 assembler instruction set instead of microcode. The performance discussed in this paper was attained with the following equipment configuration.

Table 3
Typical MSS Equipment Configuration

QTY	DESCRIPTION
2	CPUs (12+ MIPs each)
32	Channels
48 MB	RAM
1/or more	NSC HYPERchannel
8	3420 or 3480 Tape Drives
1	3088 CTC Adapter
**	3380 Disk Drives

** The number of disk drives is dependent upon floor space and the amount of on-line storage necessary for the application.

This configuration features two computing engines, each capable of driving the two operating systems; UTS-MSS and MVS-MSS, a multitude of channel pathing, extensive I/O buffering space in RAM, and a hardware path between the operating systems. The multiple channel pathing provides channel to channel overlapping for the DASD farm, as well as channel to processor overlap. The number of channels necessary is dependent upon the size of the DASD pool and the number of HYPERchannel adapters associated with each processor. The additional memory, that above the 16 MB line, is only useful for MVS/XA. The amount of memory utilized by the MSS for data buffering is a configurable parameter. MVS/XA allows buffers to be defined up to 2 Gigabytes where the MVS/SP maximum available is 7 Megabytes. The 3088 Channel-to-Channel adapter can have one or two internal channel paths. Of course higher performance is achieved with more CTCA paths between the operating systems.

Software

Unix and UTS-MSS Application Module. The design and implementation of the Unix side of the MSS system has few requirements outside of those already necessary for Unix to exist on the 370 architecture hardware. As already described, the UTS kernel has been modified in two areas. First, to support a new type of block device called a VDSK, and secondly to support the Channel-to-Channel Adapter (CTCA) devices. Application modules have been added outside the Unix kernel as separate and distinct processes. Included here is the general purpose interface used to manage the MSS.

MVS and MVS/MSS Application Module. The MVS operating system has not been modified in any manner for the implementation of the MVS/MSS function. However, servicing Channel-to-Channel adapter asynchronous interrupts requires the addition of a 370 instruction Supervisor Call (SVC) and placing the application in an authorized MVS operating system library. The MSS application consists of about 27,000 lines of assembler language code in 49 modules and more than 70 macros. The MSS runs under MVS/SP or MVS/XA (although different versions of the MSS programs are necessary).

DMS/OS In order to provide a storage hierarchy, i.e. a migration path for aged data, the MSS application requires the inclusion of DMS/OS or another data management product such as DFHSM. The DMS/OS program product has not been modified in any way.

ADMINISTRATION

System administration for the MSS includes activities associated with the customization of the MSS application. These tasks include allocating devices, classifications of DASD devices, allocating buffer space and selecting modes of operation such as enabling or disabling the logging and debugging facilities, asynchronous or synchronous open, close, and write operations, and enabling or disabling the reorganization facility.

Tuning

The MSS is an application system in the sense that the compiled source code resides in IBM executable load module libraries. Tuning the MSS application system consists of increasing or decreasing the amount of storage available for buffering on both the UNIX and MVS sides of the system, the number of DASD devices, the number of signalling paths between Unix and MVS, the number of paths between the SOURCE and the MSS, and the number of CPU cycles available to the MSS application system. In addition to system level tuning, the MSS was designed to include several parameters that may be modified by the systems programming staff to provide detailed data logging. This information is used to analyze MSS performance and for diagnostic purposes. The amount of data logging directly affects the performance of the MSS application.

DASD Allocation.

The size of the MSS DASD pool is not limited by the application. The system programming staff may add or delete DASD volumes in the MSS DASD pool by modifying the MSS parameter table data set in MVS.

In addition to controlling the number of devices, the system programming staff has the option of partitioning the DASD pool into three classes of DASD device; LARGE, MEDIUM, and SMALL thereby dividing the files in the MSS according to file size. This makes a large DASD pool more manageable. By altering entries in the MSS parameter table data set, the system programming staff may change the definition of LARGE, MEDIUM, and SMALL files. Each classification defines a file size in terms of 4096 byte blocks. The MSS places files on specific volumes depending on file size to facilitate the DASD pool maintenance and migration when necessary. The different size DASD pools may be controlled by different archival algorithms.

Archiving.

The MSS is a two tiered hierarchical storage system. Aged data are automatically selected for relocation from DASD to cartridge tape. This is accomplished by an ancillary task that is scheduled to run one or more times each day. The task, named VTOCSCAN, selects files to be archived and builds an entry in DMS/OS which periodically checks for archival candidate files and eventually moves them to tape. VTOCSCAN also insures that the oldest file on each volume is selected first. The number of files archived is based on a value in the VTOCSCAN parameter table. The parameter represents the percentage of free space desired on each volume in the DASD pool. DMS/OS was selected also for its Hierarchical Storage Manager (HSM) because it provided both a software interface and user friendly interface.

Unix-MSS System Administration.

Several new or modified commands are used to install and maintain the MSS under Unix. The mkvdsk command is used to modify a Unix file system making it useable by the MSS as a vdsk file system. The command mssclear can be used to pre-format entire physical disk volumes for use as one or more Unix file systems. This command also supports the partitioning concept of some Unix file systems. The MSS command along with various sub-command options are used to start, stop, enable, kill, synch, and query the status of the MSS. Additional options, archive and stage, are used to cause specific files to be archived to tape or staged to disk.[2]

MVS-MSS System Administration.

The administration of the MVS-MSS application is accomplished through standard IBM systems programming utilities.

Checkpoint and File Recovery.

Information associated with the files stored in the MSS are kept in two places. The inode and directory information reside on DASD attached to the UTS-MSS. The data associated with these directory entries is stored in files on the MVS operating system. The possibility for a catastrophic failure on either side of the MSS is very real. Therefore, steps must be taken to insure the integrity of the data stored in the MSS.

To protect against a failure under UTS-MSS, pertinent information relating to the directory and inode is kept in synchronization files which reside under MVS-MSS. In the event of the loss of a directory file the MSS can be reconstructed by issuing a re-synchronization command which will read the directory and inode information from the synchronization file and build the necessary directory entries under the UTS-MSS application.

HISTORY OF DEVELOPMENT PHASES

The original production release of the MSS relied heavily on an additional operating system (VM/370) to provide a level of isolation from the hardware. The VM operating system allowed both halves of the MSS to be active in a single processor in a virtual environment. VM further assisted the MSS by emulating the Channel-to-Channel Adapters that provide the data path between Unix and MVS. The isolation and emulation was not without cost. The performance of this release of the MSS was minimally acceptable. The role of the VM operating system has been reduced to the point where it is no longer required in the current implementation. Significant performance increases have been attained by installing MVS as a native rather than a VM guest operating system.

Upgrades to the existing Amdahl 6380 disk drives were recently completed doubling the storage capacity to approximately 240 Gigabytes.

PLANNED ENHANCEMENTS

MSS Release 7

Future improvements include parallel data transmission (striping) across multiple NSC HYPERchannel adapters and a stripped DASD access method for the AMDAHL 6380 disk drives. Preliminary performance tests have demonstrated data transfer rates as high as 17,800 Kilobits per second.

The performance of the MSS has been a key design issue since its inception. MSS Release 6.0 has improved performance by more than a factor of 12 over the first release to users of the MSS at Release 5.0.

With MSS Release 7, DASD striping under MVS, striping across HYPERchannel adapters and a direct HYPERchannel path between the supercomputer and MVS all contribute to substantially improve performance for file transfers. The current design of the MSS Release 6 relies heavily on Unix and MVS operating systems. Every block of information, and every request must traverse the same path as shown in Figure 3. Release 7 of the MSS is scheduled to be placed in production in January of 1989.

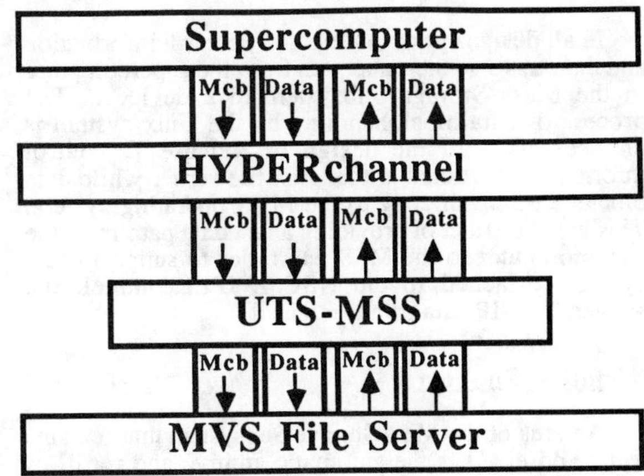

Figure 3 MSS Release 6 Data Paths

The data transfer rate to DASD for a single file is observed to be about 8 Megabits. The data transfer rate of a single A222 HYPERchannel adapter is also about 8 Megabits. The data transfer rate between Unix and MVS via the Channel-to-Channel-Adapter (CTCA) is 16 Megabits. The path from supercomputer memory to MVS DASD is a single thread with little parallelism. Therefore, increasing the size of the data block between the supercomputers and the MSS, and improvements in the Channel-to-Channel adapter driver greatly improved the end-to-end data transfer rates. However, further performance improvements are limited by the speed of the IBM channel architecture. For release 7, striping of the DASD and direct HYPERchannel to MVS connection improves performance by a factor close to 2 without additional hardware channels or stripping across HYPERchannel adapters. Further improvements in performance are possible by adding additional HYPERchannel and CTCA hardware to increase the number of parallel paths.

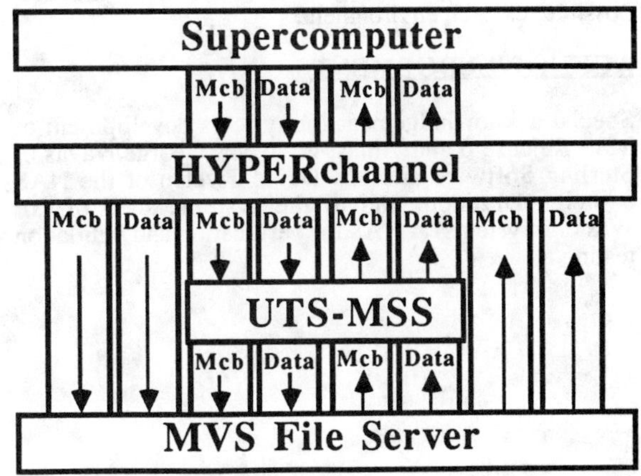

Figure 4 MSS Release 7 Data Paths

In all designs prior to Release 7, control information and data traverse the same path from the supercomputer to the Mass Storage Subsystem disk devices. The process of data block handling by the Unix system is unnecessary. In the design of Release 7, control information is routed to the Unix file server while data blocks are sent directly to the MVS operating system. This has the effect of providing a fast data path from the supercomputer to the MSS. In order to support other systems attached to the NSC HYPERchannel, the slower, TCP/IP data path is retained.

Robotics Support

An area of the Mass Storage Subsystem that remains to be addressed is the automatic archive and recall of subscriber data. The current automated process is hindered in that it requires operator intervention for the mounting of cartridge tapes. This area of the Mass Storage Subsystem can be improved with the addition of a tape cartridge robot/storage system. DMS/OS is currently limited to single-threaded tape-cartridge I/O, impeding throughput. A solution for this problem has not been found as the current version of DMS/OS code is not re-entrant. Possible plans include the addition of two tape robots which will provide storage for 12,000 tapes or about 2.4 Terabytes.

CONCLUSION

MSS Release 6 has made a significant contribution to the Unix-based Mass Storage solution for supercomputing environments. It has improved file transfer rates while providing the supercomputer and workstation Unix user with a large file system which can accommodate hundreds of thousands of files up to 2 Gigabytes each with complete backup and recovery. As part of the NAS mission to advance the state-of-the-art in supercomputing, continuous improvements will be implemented to enhance the NAS performance and functionality, providing NAS users with the best possible research environment.

ACKNOWLEDGEMENTS

Special acknowledgement for systems development of MSS Release 6 and 7 must go to Mr. George Navas of Sterling Software and Mr. David Tweten of the NAS Systems Division, and to the systems staff of GE Western Systems at NAS for verification and validation testing.

REFERENCES

[1] J. Richards, T. Kummell and D. Zarlengo, A UNIX-MVS based Mass Storage System for Supercomputers IEEE Symposium on Mass Storage Systems, October 1988

[2] Mass Storage Subsystem Specification, Numerical Aerodynamic Simulation Division, NASA Ames, 1982.

[3] MSS Design Study, Interim Report, CC-223-40.02F; NPS Software Subsystem Specification, PC-325-01.00; MSS Specification PC-326-01.00; J. Richards, NPSN Mass Storage Subsystem Evaluation Test Plan, NAS Division, NASA Ames, 1987.

[4] W. Hathaway and G. Lewis, The NPSN Mass Storage Subsystem, NAS Division, NASA Ames, 1986.

[5] G. Navas, T. Kummell, J. Richards, D. Zarlengo, MSS Release 7 General Overview, NAS Division internal document, NASA Ames Research Center, 1988.

Supercomputer Benchmarking

Chair: Hans W. Meuer
University of Manheim

PERFORMANCE COMPARISON OF THE CRAY-2 AND CRAY X-MP/416 SUPERCOMPUTERS

Margaret L. Simmons and Harvey J. Wasserman

Computing and Communications Division
Group C-3, MS B265
P. O. Box 1663
Los Alamos National Laboratory
Los Alamos, New Mexico 87545
mls@lanl.arpa (505) 667-1749
hjw@lanl.arpa (505) 667-2136

Abstract

The serial and parallel performance of one of the world's fastest general purpose computers, the CRAY-2, is analyzed using the standard Los Alamos Benchmark Set plus codes adopted for parallel processing. For comparison, architectural and performance data are also given for the CRAY X-MP/416. Factors affecting performance, such as memory bandwidth, size and access speed of memory, and software exploitation of hardware, are examined. The parallel processing environments of both machines are evaluated, and speed-up measurements for the parallel codes are given.

Keywords: performance, benchmark, supercomputer.

1. Introduction

In 1985, the first Cray Research Incorporated CRAY-2 supercomputer was installed at the National Magnetic Fusion Energy Computational Center (NMFECC). Since that time this series of machine has undergone many changes, both in hardware and software. This paper evaluates some of these changes by observing their effect on a series of computationally intensive benchmark codes. We measured the performance of three models of the CRAY-2 that differ in their common memory hardware. The first two models we measured had common memory implemented with dynamic random-access memory (DRAM) with chip access times of 120 and 80 nanoseconds (ns). These machines are Serial 2003, located at the University of Minnesota, and Serial 2011, located at the Air Force Weapons Laboratory in Albuquerque, New Mexico. The third model, Serial 2012, located at Cray Research, uses static random-access memory (SRAM) with a chip access time of 55 ns.

In Section 2, we present a brief outline of the architectural and functional features of the CRAY-2, with emphasis on those features that affect performance. For comparison, corresponding architectural features from another Cray Research product, the X-MP/416, are included. Later sections present benchmark data with single-processor and multiprocessor results discussed separately.

2. Comparison of Architectures

The CRAY-2 is a general-purpose parallel/vector supercomputer system. There are four central processing units (CPUs), each with vector and scalar capabilities. Up to 256 million words of dynamic CMOS memory gives the CRAY-2 one of the largest memory capacities of any supercomputer on the market today. For a schematic of the mainframe configuration, see Figure 1. For comparison, the X-MP is also a 4-CPU machine, each CPU having vector and scalar capabilities, but with a common memory of up to 16 million 64-bit words of static bi-polar memory.

2.1 CPUs

The CPU clock period on the CRAY-2 is 4.1 ns, while on the X-MP/416, the CPU clock period is 8.5 ns. The effect of this difference is not always as large as it at first seems. Instructions can issue from the instruction buffer on the X-MP every clock period (CP), while on the CRAY-2 the rate is one every other clock period. This gives the CRAY-2 an effective clock period of 8.2 ns with respect to instruction issue, nearly equal to that on the X-MP. After an appropriate start-up, however, arithmetic results are produced every CP on both machines.

The CPUs on both machines contain three sets of registers that serve as source and destination for computations in the functional units. These are address registers, scalar registers, and vector registers, referred to as A-, S-, and V-registers. In addition, the CRAY-2 has 16K words of local (or fast) memory that can be used by these registers as temporary storage. The access time between local memory and A and S registers is 5 and 4 CPs, respectively. The access time for V-registers is 8 CPs + length of the vector. Instead of local memory, the X-MP has an extra set of 72 temporary storage registers called B- and T-registers. Access times for these registers is 1 CP. The V-registers on the X-MP have no corresponding temporary registers. In addition to these registers, the CRAY-2 has eight semaphore flags to enable synchronization of common memory during multitasking. Only one of these semaphores can be assigned to a "job." In contrast, the X-MP has five sets of shared registers (shared among the four CPUs) including 32 semaphores. Arithmetic on both machines is done in fully seg-

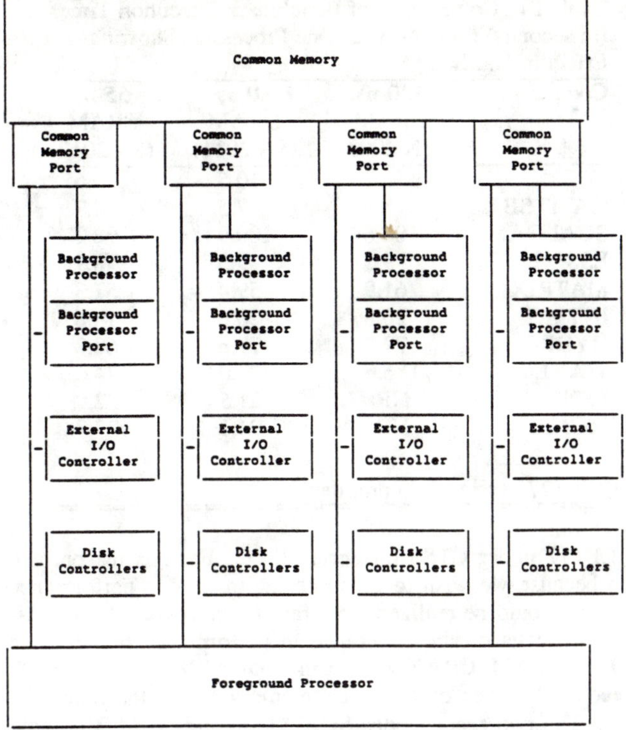

Figure 1. CRAY-2 mainframe configuration.

mented (pipelined) functional units. This pipelining allows the functional units, some of which can also operate in parallel, to deliver a result every clock period, after a suitable start-up time. Chaining, which allows the output of one arithmetic operation to serve as the immediate input to a subsequent operation, is not available on the CRAY-2. There are also different numbers of functional units on the two machines: the X-MP has 14 while the CRAY-2 has 9, including the reciprocal square root unit. Table I gives some representative times for arithmetic operations. For a more complete explanation of the CPU organization, see [1].

2.2 Memory

As mentioned previously, the CRAY-2 has up to 256 million 64-bit words of common, or shared, memory, interleaved up to 128 ways. The memory is organized into quadrants with 32 banks in each quadrant. Each quadrant has a data path to four common memory ports, one for each processor. The four quadrants are accessed by the four processors in "phase time." This means that each processor can access one particular quadrant every fourth clock period. The quadrants are accessed in a round robin fashion, that is, processor 1 can access quadrant 1 at cycle 1, quadrant 2 at cycle 2, and so on, back to quadrant 1 at cycle 5. This arrangement has important implications for strided memory references, as discussed below. With one port per processor, the CRAY-2 can do one load or one store at a time. The X-MP, with its four ports per processor, can do two vector loads, one vector store, and one IO memory reference simultaneously.

Table I. Scalar Floating Point Operation Times

Operation	CRAY-2	X-MP/416
Add	76 ns (19 CP)	51 ns (6 CP)
Multiply	76 ns (19 CP)	59.5 ns (7 CP)
Divide	88 ns (22 CP)	119 ns (14 CP)

While the large size of the memory on the CRAY-2 is an asset, the memory cycle time on the early CRAY-2 models of 234 ns (57 CPs) was slow enough to be a detriment. Cray's first solution to the memory speed problem was pseudobanking, a technique to allow access to a physical memory in less time than the memory chip cycle time. Cycle time is made up of two parts, access time and off-chip time. The logic chips are busy for a time equal to the access time, while the memory chips are busy for an additional time equal to the off-chip time. Pseudobanking uses the simple trick of addressing alternate planes of chips within the module. This can be done in a time equal to the access time, effectively reducing the cycle time by nearly half. Using this approach the effective cycle time on the 256-Mword DRAM decreased from 57 CPs to 33 CPs [2]. Pseudobanking is only needed on CRAY-2s with DRAM. Later solutions have involved the use of faster memory chips and static rather than dynamic memories. The X-MP uses chips with a scalar memory access time of 14 CPs (119 ns).

Several factors affect the rate of data transfer between common memory and the vector registers on the CRAY-2.

The first is the rate of instruction issue for vector reads and writes. With only one common memory port per processor, each read or write instruction must wait for the port to be free before it can issue. If one word transfers per clock period, then the next instruction can issue $VL + 8$ CPs later [2], where VL is the requested vector length. The minimum transfer time per word, $T(\min)$, is approximated by

$$T(\min) = (VL + 8)/VL \quad CPs. \tag{1}$$

For a vector length of 64, this time is 72/64 or 1.125 CP/word, giving a maximum transfer rate of 217 Mword/s (assuming a 4.1 ns clock). This rate is highly optimistic and assumes no quadrant or bank conflicts.

Memory conflicts also reduce the data transfer rate. Memory conflicts on the CRAY-2s occur at two levels: quadrant conflicts and bank conflicts. Quadrant conflicts are caused by the difference in the rate at which memory-request addresses arrive at the port and the rate at which the port can process these requests. Recall that each memory quadrant on the CRAY-2 can be addressed by each processor only once every 4 CPs. The time between memory requests to the same quadrant is called the quadrant period. Quadrant periods of four cause no conflicts to occur, while periods of two or one do cause conflicts. Vectors with odd strides, including strides of one, have a quadrant period of four, and thus cause no conflicts. Even strides, however, cause conflicts of varying severity. The worst case is a stride divisible by four; here the quadrant period is one. Even in the absence of other conflicts, memory quadrant conflicts can cause performance degradation.

Bank conflicts, like quadrant conflicts, are caused by attempts to access data in the same bank within too small a time period. The bank conflict effect is a function of bank cycle time and number of banks. See Table II for a list of cycle times for the machines we tested. When a bank conflict occurs, the address in the quadrant buffer requires more than the 4-CP quadrant access time to clear. Memory backup then occurs because these quadrant buffers remain full until the requested bank is free.

3. Description of Benchmark Programs

The Computing and Communications Division at Los Alamos National Laboratory maintains a set of portable benchmark programs representing characteristic tasks that a large supercomputer would be required to run at the Laboratory. This benchmark set has been run on a wide range of both scalar and vector machines [3-9]. A database is maintained containing results of past runs of these programs on a variety of computers. A report from the National Research Council has characterized supercomputer benchmarks in terms of a hierarchy [10]. Using their characterization, the Los Alamos benchmark set consists of tests at the levels of hardware demonstration programs, basic routines, and stripped down applications. A description of the codes can be found in Ref. [11]. The programs described there are coded in ANSI Fortran for portability and typically can be run on a new machine with little or no change. Execution rates will be indicative of the potential initial usefulness of a new machine.

4. Single-Processor Results

The benchmark of CRAY-2 Serial 2003 took place in July 1987, while Serial 2011 was measured in October 1987, and Serial 2012 was measured in January 1988. The X-MP results were obtained in November 1987. Two of the CRAY-2s, Serial 2003 and 2012, ran UNICOS, a UNIX-like operating system; Serial 2011 and the X-MP/416 ran the Cray Timesharing System (CTSS). All measurements were made during dedicated time on a single processor.

4.1 Comparison of Three Types of CRAY-2 Hardware

Table III shows the effect of the faster memory hardware on our benchmark codes. The results for the 80-ns DRAM CRAY-2 are not always consistent with results from the other two machines. That is, the times for some benchmarks increase in going from the 120-ns CRAY-2 to the 80-ns CRAY-2. We believe this is due to different implementations of the CFT77 compiler, and, in particular, the implementation

Table II. Memory Characteristics for Three Tested Models of the CRAY-2

Model	Chip Access Time (ns)	Memory Access Time (CP)	Memory Type	Memory Size (Mword)
2003	120	57	Dynamic	256
2011	80	48	Dynamic	256
2012	55	41	Static	128

Table III. Comparison of Benchmark Execution Times (in seconds) for CRAY-2 (One Processor) Showing Effect of Hardware*

Code	120-ns DRAM (SN 2003)	80-ns DRAM (SN 2011)	55-ns SRAM (SN 2012)
FFT	10.7	10.5	9.6
GAMTEB	5.3	7.5	4.7
SCALGAM	104.6	100.9	92.2
LSS	9.5	9.5	8.9
MATRIX	61.9	59.4	57.3
INTMC	20.8	20.6	18.6
HYDRO	79.7	79.6	68.8
WAVE	186.6	203.0	174.6
ESN	NR	21.5	22.9
MCNP	NR	94.1	77.8

*CFT77 version 1.3 compiler.

of CFT77 under CTSS on Serial 2011. For this reason, and also because we wish to illustrate the maximum performance gain that could be realized from faster memory, in this discussion we focus on the difference in performance between the 120-ns DRAM CRAY-2 and the 55-ns SRAM CRAY-2S. Speedups because of the static memory are in the range 7 - 16%. The two scalar codes SCALGAM and GAMTEB show identical speedups of 13%. HYDRO, which is nearly 100% vectorizable, shows the largest speedup. Note that a twofold change in memory chip access time should not yield anything close to a twofold speedup in the codes. The more pertinent hardware feature is the memory latency, which is the time to do loads from common memory. On the DRAM machine, the scalar access latency is 59 CPs, while on the SRAM machine, the latency for scalar loads is 43 CP. Thus, the maximum speedup we could observe here is about 37%. That the maximum observed speedup is still smaller than this may suggest that the compiler could hide some of the memory latency, perhaps by more use of the local memory.

4.2 Comparison of Compilers

Table IV shows a comparison of execution times on the fast memory CRAY-2S (Serial 2012) using the two CFT77 compilers (1.3) and (2.0). Version 2.0 yields a dramatic improvement on some of the codes. The FFT code speeds up by a factor of 2.3 relative to CFT77 1.3. All previous versions of CFT77 vectorized several loops in FFT *conditionally*; the repeated execution of the conditional code at run time caused much slower execution rates. In FFT the conditional code is generated because a loop bound is passed as an argument to a subroutine. These loops are now fully vectorized in version 2.0.

Using CFT77 2.0, HYDRO speeds up by 35%. HYDRO contains one minor loop that conditionally vectorized with CFT77 1.3 and now fully vectorizes with CFT77 2.0. HYDRO also has three loops, in the time-consuming subroutines VSETUV and VQTERM, that had not vectorized at all in version 1.3 and now vectorize in version 2.0. Each of these three loops did not vectorize with version 1.3 because of function references in conditional blocks. However, another loop in HYDRO that

Table IV. Comparison of Benchmark Execution Times (in seconds) for Serial 2012 CRAY-2S (55 ns Memory, One Processor) Showing Effect of Compiler

Code	CFT77 1.3	CFT77 2.0	Speed-Up
FFT	9.6	4.1	2.34
GAMTEB	4.7	4.4	1.04
SCALGAM	92.2	92.8	0
LSS	8.9	8.9	0
MATRIX	57.3	57.0	0
INTMC	18.6	18.2	1.02
HYDRO	68.8	51.1	1.35
WAVE	174.6	109.7	1.6
ESN	21.5	20.4	1.05
MCNP*	77.8	78.1	0

*Four thousand source particles.

consumes a considerable portion of the execution time does not vectorize with any Cray Research compiler, although we know of other compilers that are successful in vectorizing this loop.

The WAVE code also derives impressive gain from use of CFT77 2.0 on the CRAY-2S. The 60% decrease in execution time results from full vectorization of over 50 loops that had been conditionally vectorized in version 1.3. However, 16 loops in WAVE remain conditionally vectorized.

So far we have focused on CRAY-2 results obtained with the CFT77 compiler. A version of the Cray Research CFT compiler, called CFT2, is also available on the CRAY-2. A comparison of benchmark execution times for code produced using both compilers is given in Table V. The CFT77 2.0 compiler produces much better code in all cases.

4.3 Comparison of CRAY-2S with CRAY X-MP/416

In this section we examine the performance of only the CRAY-2S with that of the CRAY X-MP/416 results. We used a pre-release of CFT77 2.0 (BF185) on a CRAY X-MP/416 running the CTSS operating system at Los Alamos National Laboratory (LANL). (The version of CFT77 2.0 we used on the CRAY-2S was also a pre-release, BF184.)

Table V. Comparison of Benchmark Execution Times (in seconds) for CRAY-2 (One Processor) Using CFT2 and CFT77 Compilers on SN-2012

Code	CFT2	CFT77 2.0
FFT	4.9	4.1
GAMTEB	10.0	4.4
SCALGAM	144.7	92.8
LSS	12.4	8.9
MATRIX	*	57.0
INTMC	20.6	18.2
HYDRO	107.0	51.1
WAVE	*	109.7
ESN	27.0	20.4
MCNP	*	78.1

*Did not compile.

4.3.1 Primitive Vector Operations

First we examine performance of selected elementary vector operations, listed in Tables VI and VII. These tables contain rates, in MFLOPS, for various elementary vector operations as a function of vector length. All operations were carried out with unit stride except for the second and third operations in both tables. The X-MP/416 tests used bidirectional memory.

For the non-strided, non-scatter/gather operations in Tables VI and VII, the differences between the two machines at vector length 1000 can generally be reconciled with the rate at which each machine is capable of producing results. For example, on the first operation, V = V + S, we expect comparable rates, and we observe 83 MFLOPS for the CRAY-2S and 97 MFLOPS for the X-MP. As another example, on the fourth operation, V = V * V, we expect the asymptotic rate on the CRAY-2S to be less than that of the X-MP by about a factor of 1.5; at vector length 1000, the observed ratio is 1.76 (51 MFLOPS for the CRAY-2S and 90 MFLOPS for the X-MP). However, the CRAY-2S compiler has to unroll all these loops (to a depth of four) to achieve this performance. At shorter vector lengths the X-MP is faster than the CRAY-2 by about a factor of 2.

Comparison of the first and second operations in Table VI shows that, as expected, the CRAY-2S suffers no performance degradation with odd strides. However, with stride 8, performance on the CRAY-2S is about one-fourth of the non-strided rate. The minimum time for memory transfer on the CRAY-2S is slightly more than 1 CP/word. However, with stride 8 all words of data reside in the same quadrant. Therefore, the minimum transfer time, delayed by quadrant conflict only, is about 6.5 CP/word. With a stride of 8, there are no bank conflicts on the machine we used.

Scatter/gather operations, the last two rows in Tables VI and VII, are much more efficient on the X-MP than they are on the CRAY-2, over the entire range of vector lengths. The gather operation on the CRAY-2 is subject to a special hardware delay so that references are allowed roughly once every 4 CPs.

4.3.2 Benchmark Codes

A comparison of the current CRAY-2S results with the CRAY X-MP/416 for the rest of the benchmark codes is shown in Table VIII. Two sets of results are given for the X-MP: one from a pre-release of CFT77 2.0 and one from the production compiler, CFT 1.14. The first thing to notice in Table VIII (comparing columns two and three) is that on the X-MP, CFT77 2.0 now produces better code than CFT1.14 (with no compiler options) for all but one benchmark. The only (minor) exception is MATRIX, for which CFT 1.14 with the BTREG option (shown in parenthesis in Table VIII) is slightly faster than CFT77 2.0.

The X-MP has a significant performance advantage over the CRAY-2S on seven of the ten codes. Of the seven, four are highly vectorizable: HYDRO, LSS, MATRIX, and WAVE. In HYDRO, LSS, and MATRIX, the predominant loop length is about 100. The VECOPS data in Tables VI and VII showed

Table VI. Rates (MFLOPS) on the CRAY-2S for Selected Vector Operations as a Length (Single Processor; CFT77 2.0)

Operation	10	50	100	200	1000
a(i) = b(i) + s	10	37	44	47	83
a(i) = b(i) + s(i=1,n,23)	9	35	42	46	84
a(i) = b(i) + s(i=1,n,8)	8	16	16	16	18
a(i) = b(i)*c(i)	8	28	33	36	51
a(i) = b(i) + s * c(i)	15	54	65	72	113
a(i) = b(i)*c(i) + d(i)*e(i)	19	60	66	76	90
a(i) = b(j(i)) + s	7	19	21	22	29
a(j(i)) = b(i)*c(i)	8	28	29	34	35

Table VII. Rates (MFLOPS) on the CRAY X-MP/416 for Selected Vector Operations as a Function of Vector Length (Single Processor; CFT77 2.0; Bidirectional Memory)

Operation	10	50	100	200	1000
a(i) = b(i) + s	20	74	77	86	105
a(i) = b(i) + s(i=1,n,23)	19	86	87	86	99
a(i) = b(i) + s(i=1,n,8)	19	87	87	89	103
a(i) = b(i)*c(i)	14	68	70	71	90
a(i) = b(i) + s * c(i)	27	136	145	143	173
a(i) = b(i)*c(i) + d(i)*e(i)	32	114	126	126	143
a(i) = b(j(i)) + s	14	54	58	49	57
a(j(i)) = b(i)*c(i)	13	44	43	43	48

that the X-MP ran loops at vector length 100 nearly twice as fast as the CRAY-2S did. In WAVE, the predominant loop length is 256. WAVE also involves many gathers for which, as shown above, the X-MP is superior.

Interestingly, in contrast with the VECOPS data, the X-MP is only about 5% faster on the FFT code, a highly vectorized code with short vector lengths on which the X-MP should be fastest.

An important aspect of vectorization on the CRAY-2S concerns the way in which arrays are dimensioned. Because of quadrant conflicts that can have a noticeable effect on performance, arrays with even dimensions will suffer performance degradations relative to arrays with odd dimensions. This fact is highlighted in the performance of the codes LSS and MATRIX relative to the X-MP. Both codes spend most of their time in SAXPY, and both have loop lengths of 100. Yet MATRIX runs nearly 63% faster on the X-MP than it does on the CRAY-2S, whereas LSS runs about 45% faster on the X-MP. In MATRIX, two of three critical arrays have even dimensions, while in LSS, all critical arrays have odd dimensions. Thus, relative to the X-MP, one must be far more careful of program array dimensions on the CRAY-2S.

The relationship between the X-MP and the CRAY-2S on codes not overwhelmingly vector in nature is harder to explain. Of the two Monte Carlo photon transport codes, one, SCALGAM, runs about 28% faster on the X-MP, while the other, GAMTEB, runs about 18% faster on the CRAY-2S. ESN, a totally scalar code, runs about 28% faster on the X-MP. But on MCNP, the X-MP is only 7% faster than the CRAY-2. The reason for this is not clear.

Table VIII. Comparison of Benchmark Execution Times (in seconds) for CRAY-2S (Serial 2012) and CRAY X-MP/416 (Single Processor)

Code	CRAY-2 (CFT77 2.0)	X-MP/416 (CFT77 2.0)	X-MP/416 (CFT 1.14)	
FFT	4.1	3.9	4.3	
GAMTEB	4.4	5.2	7.6	
SCALGAM	92.8	72.5	88.4	
LSS	8.9	6.1	11.6	(6.7)*
MATRIX	57.0	34.9	54.7	(33.2)*
INTMC	18.2	12.1	40.2	
HYDRO	51.1	39.8	48.9	
WAVE	109.7	86.0	111.2	
ESN	20.4	15.9	18.2	
MCNP**	78.1	73.2	76.7	

*Time in parenthesis is with bidirectional memory and OPT = BTREG for the CFT 1.14 compiler.
**Four thousand source particles started.

4.3.3 X-MP/416 External Storage Performance

The larger central memory on the CRAY-2 is an important asset for this machine. However, the X-MP can be equipped with an external Solid-state Storage Device (SSD) that can also offer potential for large codes. An obvious question is: if a problem can be programmed with an "out-of-core" algorithm, how does the X-MP with SSD perform relative to the same problem run "in-memory" on the CRAY-2?

The WAVE code can be so programmed. We ran a job requiring about 20 Mwords of storage on the CRAY-2 (Serial 2011, 80-ns memory). We ran the same code on an X-MP/416 running CTSS and equipped with a 512-Mword SSD using one channel (1250 Mbyte/s). Both machines used the CFT77 version 2.0 compiler. The X-MP/416 version transferred to the SSD in block sizes of 204800 words. The CRAY-2 ran the job in 461 seconds, while the X-MP required 355 seconds CPU time and 360 seconds elapsed (wall-clock) time. Although we did not run this code on the 55-ns CRAY-2S, we can approximate what the performance will be. Using the CFT77 version 2.0 compiler, the standard WAVE benchmark runs about 12% faster on the 55-ns CRAY-2S than it does on the 80-ns CRAY-2, so the best CRAY-2S time for the 19-Mword job would be about 411 seconds. This value is still larger than the X-MP wall clock time. Note that although I/O to the SSD does not require particularly difficult coding (as might I/O to a disk) other than insuring a large block size, the CRAY-2 version requires no extra coding.

5. Multitasking Results

The four processors of the CRAY-2 can simultaneously be brought to bear on a single job through the multitasking environment. We ran our large Monte Carlo transport code, MCNP, in this environment on the Serial 2011 CRAY-2 at the Air Force Weapons Laboratory in February 1988. The compiler was CFT77 2.0, the operating system was CTSS, and the multitasking library was Multilib. We ran a problem size of 60000 source particles. For comparison, we ran the same problem on an X-MP/416 at Los Alamos using the CFT77 2.0 compiler, the CTSS operating system, and a multitasking library that is a local system. We used a parallelization method called macrotasking developed at Cray Research and adapted for CTSS on the CRAY-2 by the NMFECC. This method operates at the granularity level of the subroutine.* Multitasking runs on both machines were done during dedicated time. The times are given in Table IX. Note that the X-MP is about 40% faster than the CRAY-2 for one to four processors. The serial times differ by 34%, which is comparable to the differences observed for the other scalar serial codes.

Speedup is defined as

$$S = T_s / T_n \ , \qquad (2)$$

where T_s is the serial execution time and T_n is the execution time using n processors. The speedups for MCNP are plotted in Fig. 2. The CRAY-2 shows a speedup of 3.53 for four processors, while on the X-MP, speedup is 3.65. This difference might be attributed to several factors, one of which is the availability of only a single semaphore per job on the CRAY-2. The X-MP has 32 semaphores available to a job. Another factor affecting speedup is the implementation of synchronization primitives. The Los Alamos system has implemented spin-wait locks while the Cray Research/NMFECC implementation is somewhat less efficient. Since Monte Carlo algorithms are considered to be ideal candidates for parallel processing, one might expect a speedup for four processors that is somewhat closer to four. One reason that we do not see this for this set of runs is that the time spent in the serial sections, such as the setting up of the problem, is constant and independent of the

*Another approach, called microtasking, operates at the granularity of the DO loop and can be much more efficient. However, since MCNP does not contain many DO loops, a moderate amount of reprogramming would be required in order to take advantage of microtasking.

Table IX. Multitasking Execution Times (in Seconds) for MCNP on the CRAY-2 (Serial 2011) and the CRAY X-MP/416		
	CRAY-2 TOTAL	CRAY X-MP/416 TOTAL
1 Processor	1343.3	963.6
2 Processor	697.4	486.3
3 Processor	477.2	330.9
4 Processor	351.5	253.0
Serial	1240.9	923.8

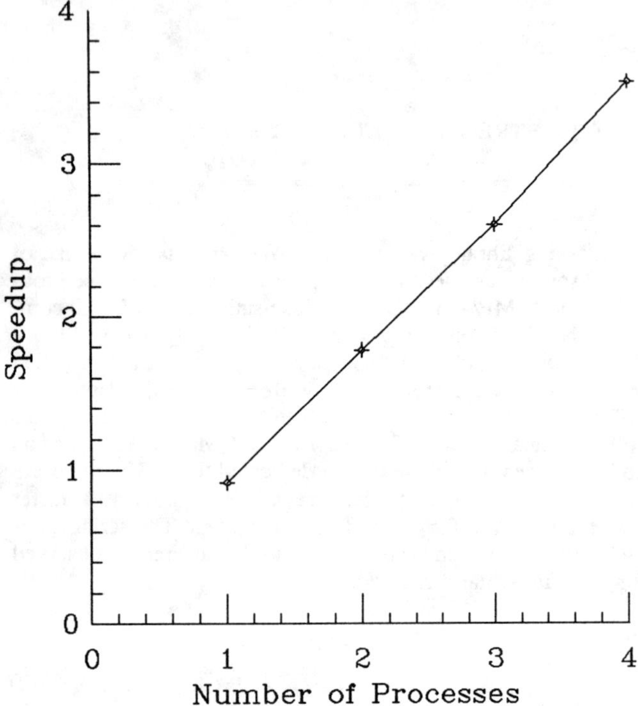

Figure 2. Speedup on a CRAY-2.

number of source particles. This means that as more and more processors are brought to bear on a problem of fixed size, the serial portion takes a larger percentage of the time. This is, of course, Amdahl's law [12].

If we interpret Ware's model [13] (of Amdahl's law) of vector performance as applying to multiprocessor performance, we can also define speedup as

$$S = [(1-f) + (f/p)]^{-1} , \quad (3)$$

where f is the fraction of the code that can be executed in parallel and p is the number of processors. For MCNP, which is about 98% parallel, we get a predicted speedup of 3.77 for four processors. This is quite a bit higher than our measured speedup of 3.53 on the CRAY-2S.

There are several reasons for the difference in these two speed-ups. One is the effect of multiprocessor synchronization overhead [14]. Another is the additional time required for system overhead in the multiple processor runs. The serial version of MCNP, for example, is not stack based and so incurs no overhead associated with stack management.

6. Conclusions

The faster memory chips on recent models of the CRAY-2 provide some improvement on our benchmarks, but do not, by themselves, allow the CRAY-2S to perform better than the X-MP/416 in single-processor mode. This is because too much of the memory bottleneck on the CRAY-2 is due to factors other than chip access time.

The biggest improvements we have observed during the evolution of the CRAY-2 are derived from compiler changes, not hardware changes. In particular, HYDRO and WAVE, two benchmark codes that closely resemble production codes at the Laboratory, benefit significantly from the combination of new hardware and a new version of CFT77 on the CRAY-2S.

The X-MP has a clear performance advantage over the CRAY-2S on our codes that are highly vectorized. However, the difference between these machines is less clear on codes that are not overwhelmingly vector. The significant factor here appears to be the longer memory latency on the CRAY-2. Although the CRAY-2 provides more central memory than the X-MP, we have shown that on one code that takes advantage of the X-MP SSD, the faster processor and high I/O rates can overcome the lack of X-MP memory.

In multitasking mode, the CRAY-2 performs about as well as the X-MP on the problem that we ran. While the overall times are not as fast as the X-MP, the speedups are comparable. The overhead observed for the problem we ran could be reduced either by running a larger problem or by the use of more efficient synchronization (microtasking).

Acknowledgments

This work was performed under the auspices of the United States Department of Energy. We are grateful to Dr. Larry Rapagnani of the Air Force Weapons Laboratory for a generous allocation of resources on the CRAY-2 (Serial 2011). Ann Hayes, Rebecca Koskela, Olaf Lubeck, and James Moore of Los Alamos National Laboratory helped collect some of the benchmark data. We thank Ken Lord of Cray Research for his assistance during all phases of the benchmark process.

References

1. Frank C. Kampe and Tung M Nguyen, "Performance Comparison of the CRAY-2 and CRAY X-MP on a Class of Seismic Data Processing Algorithms," *Parallel Computing* (1986) 559-570.

2. Robert Numrich, "CRAY-2 Memory," private communication, June, 1985.

3. R. G. Brickner, H. J. Wasserman, A. H. Hayes, and J. W. Moore, "Benchmarking the IBM 3090 with Vector Facility," *Los Alamos National Laboratory Unclassified Release LAUR-86-3300* (1986).

4. J. H. Griffin and M. L. Simmons, "Los Alamos National Laboratory Computer Benchmarking 1986," *Los Alamos National Laboratory Unclassified Report LA-10151-MS* (1984).

5. O. Lubeck, J. Moore, and R. Mendez, "A Benchmark Comparison of Three Supercomputers: Fujitsu VP-200, Hitachi S810/20, and CRAY X-MP/2," *IEEE Computer* **18** (1985), 10-29.

6. O. Lubeck, J. Moore, and R. Mendez, "The Performance of the NEC SX/2 and CRAY X-MP Supercomputers," *Los Alamos National Laboratory Unclassified Release LAUR-87-227* (1987).

7. M. L. Simmons and O. Lubeck, "Benchmark of the Convex C-1 Mini Supercomputer," *Los Alamos National Laboratory Unclassified Release LAUR-86-2890* (1986).

8. M. L. Simmons and H. J. Wasserman, "Los Alamos National Laboratory Computer Benchmarking 1986," *Los Alamos National Laboratory Report LA-10898-MS* (1987).

9. H. J. Wasserman, M. L. Simmons, and A. H. Hayes, "A Benchmark of the SCS-40 Computer: A Mini Supercomputer Compatible with the CRAY X-MP/24," *Los Alamos National Laboratory Unclassified Release LAUR-87-659* (1987).

10. "An Agenda for Improved Evaluation of Supercomputer Performance," National Research Council (National Academy Press, Washington D.C., 1986).

11. Harvey J. Wasserman, "Los Alamos National Laboratory Computer Benchmarking 1988," Los Alamos National Laboratory technical report to be published.

12. G. Amdahl, "The Validity of the Single Processor Approach to Achieving Large Scale Computing Capabilities," AFIPS Conf. Proc. 30, 1967.

13. W. Ware, "The Ultimate Computer," *IEEE Spectrum*, March 1972.

14. B. L. Buzbee, "The Efficiency of Parallel Processing," *Computer Design*, June 1984.

The Birth of the Second Generation: The Hitachi S-820/80

Christopher Eoyang* Raul H. Mendez* Olaf M. Lubeck**

*Institute for Supercomputing Research
8F Recruit Kachidoki Bldg.
2-11 Kachidoki, Chuo-ku
Tokyo, JAPAN

**Los Alamos National Laboratory
Los Alamos, NM
USA

Abstract

A performance evaluation and comparison of the new Hitachi S-820/80 supercomputer on a set of standard Fortran benchmark codes which range from simple kernels to fluid dynamics applications.

Keywords: Supercomputer Vector processor LFK Loops LANL Codes

Introduction

The entry of the Hitachi S-810/20 and Fujitsu VP-200 supercomputers in late 1983, followed by the NEC SX-2 in 1984, gave much credibility to the advanced technology of the Japanese manufacturers, and had a profound impact on the area of supercomputing, not only in Japan, but throughout the world. All single processor machines were capable of a peak speed in excess of 700 MFLOPS, and boasted very advanced compilers and vectorizing tools. Although the performance of the Fujitsu VP Series is, in general, slower than that of the SX-2 and faster than that of the S/810, the VP has taken the dominant share of the Japanese market (well over half), with about 50 systems currently installed.

A little more than four years later, all three manufacturers have introduced new machines, which could be said to constitute the "second generation" of Japanese supercomputers, even though the degree to which the new machines differ from their predecessors varies to a great extent. NEC and Fujitsu, having respectively introduced the SX A and VP-E Series supercomputers, have not departed significantly from the architecture and technology of their original machines: the new machines have additional pipelines, higher capacities, and/or improved features, but the basic hardware remains essentially unchanged.

On the other hand, Hitachi has introduced a true second generation machine, the S-820/80 (the other model, the S-820/60, has half the performance), which maintains the same architecture of its predecessor, while making tremendous technological improvements on the device level. This has resulted in a scalar clock speed of 8 ns (compare 28 ns on the S-810) and a vector clock of 4 ns (14 ns on the S-810), the fastest vector clock of any machine made today, closely edging that of the Cray-2 (4.1 ns). The theoretical peak performance of the S-820/80 is 2 GFLOPS, making the S-820 the fastest single processor vector machine in the world, for which scalar-vector speedups of 30 or more are not unusual.

In this article we shall evaluate the performance of the S-820 by using various benchmark codes (the LFK loops, the LANL benchmark set, and the Mendez fluid dynamics codes) not primarily to quote and compare the CPU times and MFLOPS rates, but to determine the strengths and weaknesses of this machine in comparison to other machines. We firmly believe that one cannot reduce supercomputer performance down to a single number on a single benchmark or set of benchmarks, any more than one can generalize the characteristics of supercomputer application codes. Conclusions regarding the performance of a supercomputer are perhaps best made after running a wide range of codes and then trying to correlate the observed performance with the various attributes and peculiarities of the machine.

Vector machines are best suited for completely vectorized applications, and it is well known that due to Amdahl's Law, performance will drop off drastically from the theoretical peak if the vector ratio of an application is not well into the 90th percentile. It has also been established that the average vectorization ratio of scientific applications being run on current supercomputers is much closer to the 70th, rather than the 100th, percentile [5], and in many cases scalar speed is the determining factor in a machine's overall performance.

CH2617-9/88/0000/0296$01.00 © 1988 IEEE

In Section 1 we will describe the basic features of the S-820, paying attention to the technology used on the device level. In Section 2 we will discuss the performance of the S-820 on the Livermore Fortran Kernels (LFK), and Section 3 will cover the LANL benchmark set. Section 4 deals with the Mendez fluid dynamics codes.

The S-820/80 was benchmarked at Hitachi's Kanagawa Works in January and February 1988, using the FORT77/HAP (V21-0b) compiler.

1. Architecture of the S-820

The computational processor of the S-820 has the same basic architecture as its predecessor, the S-810, consisting of separate vector and scalar units which can be run in parallel. The 8 ns scalar processor, based on the Hitachi M-series mainframes, is augmented with a very powerful vector processor with a cycle time of 4 ns. To increase the efficiency with which the scalar and vector units can be run in parallel, Hitachi has added "link" and "signal" functions to coordinate simultaneous operation between the units [1]. The basic architecture of the S-820 is shown in Appendix A.

The vector processor has 32 vector registers (each capable of containing 512 64-bit words) and 16 vector mask registers, supported by four vector load and four vector load/store pipes capable of concurrent operation (up to 8 load operations, or 4 loads and 4 store operations simultaneously). The vector register LSIs have 2500 gates, a capacity of 6912 bits, and an access time of 2.5 ns. Computation takes place in the four arithmetic units (add/logical, multiply-add, divide, mask). Each load and load/store pipe can transfer 8 bytes (1 word) to/from memory every 4 ns, for a total bandwidth of 16 GB/sec (2 Gwords/sec). The add/logical and multiply-add units each consist of 4 fully segmented pipelines; with an execution speed of 1 GFLOPS for the add/logical unit and 2 GFLOPS for the multiply-add unit, the theoretical maximum computational performance of the S-820 is 3 GFLOPS, when both units are running concurrently. This is limited, in many cases, by the 2 Gword main memory to vector register bandwidth. The divide and mask units both consist of one pipeline each. Buffer storage is 256 KB.

The scalar processor is also much improved over the S-810, with add operations requiring 16 or 24 ns (2 or 3 clock periods), and multiplication taking 24 or 32 ns (the slower times for each operation occur only when one of the operands has been used in the previous instruction). Division times have also been improved from 588 ns to 168 ns.

Maximum main memory on the S-820 is 512 MB, using bipolar CMOS (bi-CMOS) 256 Kbit static RAMs with access times of 20 ns. Up to 12 GB of extended storage (using 1 Mbit 120 ns DRAMs) can be added. The bandwidth between main memory and extended memory is 2 GB/sec. The input/output processor of the S-820 is the same as on the M-Series mainframes, and has a maximum capacity of 64 channels, with a total bandwidth of 288 MB/sec.

The FORT77/HAP (version V21-0b) compiler on the S-820 has been improved considerably, and appears to be comparable to those of the other Japanese manufacturers. For example, the compiler is capable of vectorizing loops containing IF-statements, intrinsic functions, loops with out-of-loop GOTO statements; it is also capable of handling a variety of special case combination functions (inner product, 1st order linear recurrences, summation, first maximum/minimum, gather/scatter operations). For nested loops, the compiler can perform loop splitting, loop unrolling, and loop interchanging, to maximize the vectorization ratio of a code.

2. The LFK Loops

The Livermore Fortran Kernels (LFK) are a widely used performance benchmark that serve as a general indication of both a machine's maximum and minimum performance [4]. The data in Figures 1 and 2 indicate the scalar and vector performance of the S-820 compared with the NEC SX-2 and Cray X-MP (single processor) on the revised set of 24 LFK loops (see Figure 7 for actual values).

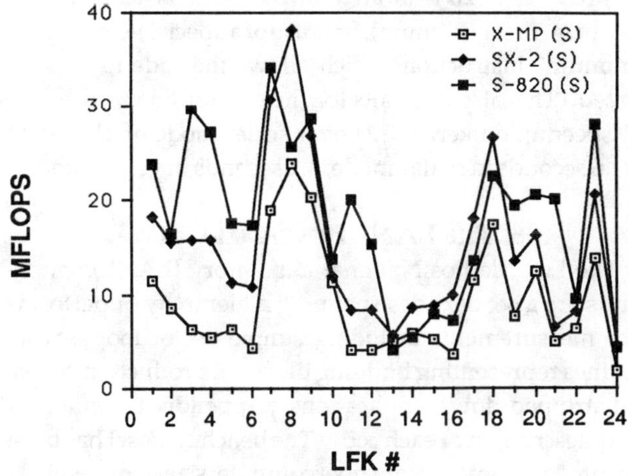

Of particular interest is the fact that kernels 5, 11, and 19 (all of which include first order linear recurrences which are not vectorized on any other machine) are vectorized by the Hitachi compiler: all of these kernels showed speedups of about 2.7 in vector mode, whereas scalar mode was generally faster on the other machines. As indicated in the scalar performance data, the S-820 scalar mode is faster than the other machines in most, but not all of the kernels (the NEC is faster in 6 of the 24 loops). Furthermore, the speedup over the NEC is only marginal.

Since the scalar clock of the S-820 is 8 ns (double the vector clock of 4 ns), slower than the 6 ns NEC clock, these results suggest a very efficient scalar code generation on the S-820, which was also characteristic of its predecessor on the S-810 [2, p. 22].

Figure 2. LFK (Vector) Performance

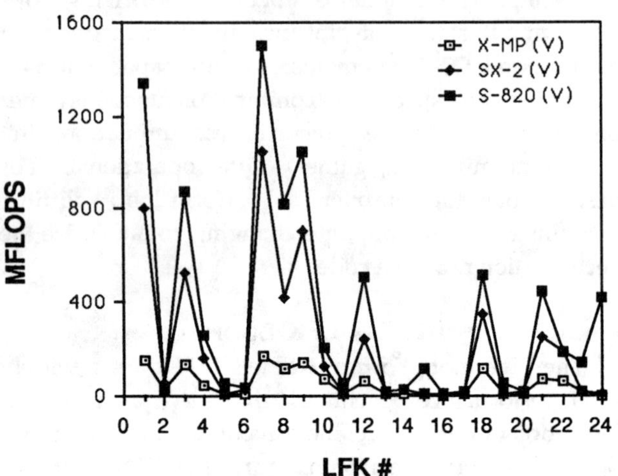

In vector mode, the performance of the S-820 is outstanding (Figure 2). On highly vectorizable code, it exhibits nearly twice the performance of the SX-2, and has about seven times the vector speed of a Cray X-MP/1. In the extreme, the S-820 is more than 200 times faster than the Cray (#24, first minimum), because of a special vector "find minimum" instruction, which allows the code to be vectorized. This also accounts for the extraordinary factor of 100 speedup on kernel #24 over scalar mode on the S-820 (421.6 seconds in scalar mode, 4.2 seconds in vector mode).

3. The LANL Benchmark Set

The Los Alamos National Laboratory (LANL) benchmarks are a set of codes spanning a hierarchy of performance measurements including simple vector loops, basic routines representing building blocks of production codes, and stripped-down applications. Appendix B contains a short description of each code. The benchmark set has been executed on most major supercomputers and mini-supercomputers [5]. In this section, we will compare the results of the S-820 with another Japanese supercomputer, the NEC SX-2, and the Cray X-MP/48 (single processor results).

Figures 3a, 3b, and 3c show the performance data from simple vector loops as a function of vector length on three supercomputers. Short vector performance on the S-820 has improved by a factor of 2.5 to 3 over the S-810 [5]. Comparing with X-MP data, we see that the new Hitachi machine is significantly better than the Cray at short vectors. Comparison with the SX-2, which had been the best short vector machine, shows that the new Hitachi is 30-40% faster. At long vector lengths, the S-820's 4ns cycle time and 4 sets of functional units are evident in the impressive rates achieved, clearly outperforming the single processor X-MP and SX-2. In vector mode across all vector lengths, the S-820 is consistently faster than any other supercomputer that we have measured.

Figure 3a NEC SX-2

Vector Length	10	50	100	200	1000
A(I)= B(I) + S	22	110	219	340	382
A(I)= B(I) + S, I=1,N,23	22	108	136	449	153
A(I)= B(I) + S, I=1,N,8	21	87	125	146	150
A(I)= B(I) * C(I)	20	97	181	265	275
A(I)= B(I)*C(I) + D(I)*E(I)	38	191	365	521	528
A(I)= B(J(I)) + S	11	33	44	50	52
A(J(I))= B(I)* C(I)	13	38	47	53	54

Figure 3b Cray X-MP/48 (single processor)

Vector Length	10	50	100	200	1000
A(I)= B(I) + S	14	50	58	61	67
A(I)= B(I) + S, I=1,N,23	10	35	47	52	64
A(I)= B(I) + S, I=1,N,8	10	36	45	53	66
A(I)= B(I) * C(I)	14	48	50	59	61
A(I)= B(I)*C(I) + D(I)*E(I)	33	87	92	97	100
A(I)= B(J(I)) + S	13	32	37	38	42
A(J(I))= B(I)* C(I)	12	29	31	32	36

Figure 3c HITACHI S-820

Vector Length	10	50	100	200	1000
A(I)= B(I) + S	26	122	237	382	736
A(I)= B(I) + S, I=1,N,23	26	113	185	270	419
A(I)= B(I) + S, I=1,N,8	25	113	191	237	247
A(I)= B(I) * C(I)	27	116	186	276	418
A(I)= B(I)*C(I) + D(I)*E(I)	50	212	393	617	982
A(I)= B(J(I)) + S	16	64	111	185	311
A(J(I))= B(I)* C(I)	15	57	83	105	137

Figure 3. Simple Vector Operations in MFLOPS
(as a function of vector length)

On strided vector operations, the Hitachi asymptotic rate is half of the contiguous vector performance, and can degrade further with memory conflicts (stride 8, for example). However, the performance of the S-820 with strided

	S-820/80	X-MP/48	SX-2
GAMTEB	4.2	5.2	3.8
SCALGAM	94.1	72.5	67.7
BMK21	1.8	2	1.6
PHOTON	116.1	120.3	
SIMPLE	4.4	5.8	2.4
FFT	2	3.9	3.7
LSS	5.5	6.1	3.7
MATRIX	25.6	34.9	24.7
INTMC	6.1	12.1	10.8

Figure 4. LANL Benchmark Results (CPU times)

vectors is still significantly better than the Cray or NEC machines.

The first four codes in Figure 4 show the scalar performance of the Hitachi S-820/80. These codes are scalar Monte Carlo simulations of neutral particle transport through a material. In two of the codes, (PHOTON and BMK21), the S-820 is comparable to the single processor X-MP and the SX-2. In the second code (SCALGAM), the Hitachi is 20-30% slower than both and in the third code, GAMTEB, the S-820 is 20% faster than the X-MP. Overall, the S-820 has comparable scalar speed to both the X-MP and SX-2.

On the remaining codes in Table 12, the S-820 compares favorably with both of the other supercomputers. Of note is its performance on FFTs and the integer Monte Carlo (INTMC), where it is roughly a factor of 2 faster than either the SX-2 or the X-MP. On the hydrodynamics code, SIMPLE, it is equivalent to the X-MP, but is significantly slower than the SX-2.

4. The Mendez Codes

The Mendez suite of fluid dynamics codes have been used in earlier studies to characterize the performance of vector and parallel machines on a class of applications [5][6][7]. Although the characteristics of these codes are very different and cover a range of fluid dynamics applications, performance on these codes is by no means meant to be strictly representative of the aptitude of any given machine to handle fluid dynamics codes in general. Of these five codes, three are highly vectorizable (VORTEX, MHD2D, and BARO are all over 95% vectorizable) and two have vectorization ratios of 73% and 89%. The codes are briefly described in Appendix B.

The results, shown below in Figures 5 and 6, are in line with what one would expect given the performance data on the LFK loops. In scalar mode, the S-820 is just a little slower than the SX-2 in four of the codes, and faster in one (BARO). With the exception of MHD-2D, the machines divide into two groups, with the S-820 and SX-2 on the faster side, and the X-MP and VP-200 running about equal.

	S-820	SX-2	X-MP/1
VORTEX	1.65	1.80	1.00
EULER	2.59	2.59	1.00
MHD2D	0.88	1.00	1.00
BARO	2.40	1.79	1.00
SHEAR3	1.96	2.62	1.00

Figure 5. Mendez Codes: Relative Scalar Performance

	S-820	SX-2	X-MP/1
VORTEX	3.77	1.93	1.00
EULER	1.15	1.53	1.00
MHD2D	5.52	2.31	1.00
BARO	5.16	3.63	1.00
SHEAR3	1.70	1.31	1.00

Figure 6. Mendez Codes: Relative Vector Performance

In vector mode, the type of application is the crucial factor in determining the performance of the S-820. In particular, the three highly vectorized codes are all 3 – 5 times faster than the X-MP, and quite a bit faster than the SX-2. In EULER, a scalar-dominated code where the memory accesses are powers of two, the Hitachi machines finishes second behind the SX-2. In SHEAR3, the S-820 is faster by a nose, but the differences between machines are minimal.

Conclusion

The Hitachi S-820 is a great deal faster in vector mode than any other supercomputer we have measured, with almost twice the performance on highly vectorized codes than the fastest machine we have seen up to now, the NEC SX-2. In scalar mode, however, the S-820 is roughly even with the X-MP and the SX-2, with a slight advantage going to the SX-2 in the applications we have tested.

We must emphasize that the applications we have tested are CPU intensive and not I/O bound, and that results obtained on other benchmark sets may lead to different conclusions. In any case, the S-820 is substantially faster than its predecessor, the S-810. Although improvements have been made in both the hardware and software of the machine, our results indicate that the compiler technology is roughly on par with those of the other supercomputer manufacturers, and that most of the major speedups have been realized through improvements in hardware and device technology.

ACKNOWLEDGEMENTS

We would like to thank the engineers and staff at Hitachi for their cooperation and generous assistance.

REFERENCES

[1] Shun Kawabe, *et al*, "The Single Processor S-820: Peak Speed 2 GFLOPS", Nikkei Electronics, No. 437, December 1988 (in Japanese).

[2] J. M. van Kats, R. Llurba, and A. J. van der Steen, "A Close look at the First Generation of Japanese Supercomputers," Technical Report TR-22, ACCU, Utrecht, 1986.

[3] Frank H. McMahon, "The Livermore Fortran Kernels: A Computer Test of the Numerical Performance Range," Lawrence Livermore National Laboratory document UCRL-53745, December 1986.

[4] Frank H. McMahon, personal communication, May 1988.

[5] Olaf M. Lubeck, "Supercomputer Performance: The Theory, Practice and Results," Los Alamos National Laboratory document LA-11204-MS, January 1988.

[6] Stephen C. Perrenod, "Automatic Parallel Processing for Science and Industry," Proceedings of the First Appi Workshop on Supercomputing.

[7] R. H. Mendez, "The Performance of the NEC SX-2 Supercomputer System Compared with that of the Cray X-MP/4 and Fujitsu VP-200," preprint.

Figure 7. LFK Comparison in Vector Mode
(in MFLOPS)

Loop	S-820	X-MP	SX-2
1	1337.1	152.26	800.05
2	31.6	27.53	49.94
3	873.4	135.27	528.67
4	262.4	41.98	164.18
5	51.1	6.18	11.26
6	38	11.84	29.3
7	1504.4	171.35	1042.33
8	820.1	115.41	415.68
9	1050	144.69	705.28
10	202.2	69.13	120.75
11	55.7	8.25	8.32
12	510.3	66.54	242.8
13	16.7	4.82	16.78
14	24.4	13.12	25.79
15	120	5.23	8.73
16	6.7	3.6	9.85
17	14.5	11.56	17.89
18	515.1	111.74	349.42
19	52.6	7.64	13.4
20	18.9	12.26	16.12
21	450.3	73.03	253.03
22	183.4	66.28	183.34
23	144	13.76	20.52
24	421.6	1.84	4.59
H. Mean	**45.4**	**8.75**	**22.32**

Appendix A. S-820 Architecture

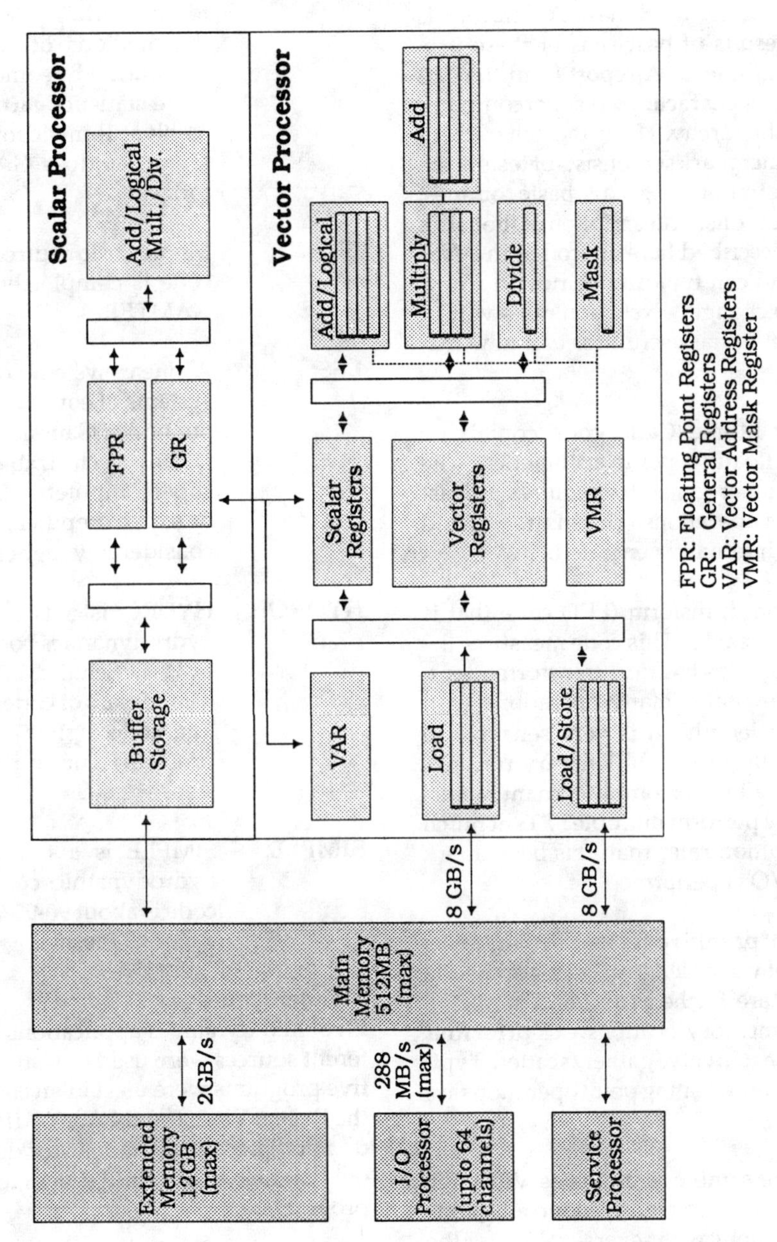

Appendix B: Description of Codes

Los Alamos National Laboratory Codes:
The Computing and Communications Division at Los Alamos National Laboratory maintains a set of portable benchmark programs representing characteristic tasks that a large supercomputer would be required to run at the Laboratory. This benchmark set has been run on a wide range of both scalar and vector machines. A database is maintained containing results of past runs of these programs on a variety of computers. A report from the National Research Council has characterized supercomputer benchmarks in terms of a hierarchy. Using their characterization, the Los Alamos benchmark set consists of tests at the level of hardware demonstration programs, basic routines, and stripped down applications. A description of the codes follows. The programs described here are coded in ANSI Fortran for portability and can typically be run on a new machine with little or no change. Execution rates will be indicative of the potential initial usefulness of a new machine.

INTMC: An integer Monte Carlo code containing almost no floating point arithmetic. The random number generator requires at least 32 bit integer operations. There is no I/O and all data are internally generated.

FFT: A fast Fourier transform (FFT) code that is highly vectorizable. This code measures the speed of single Fourier transformations. Because it executes many operations with short vector lengths, it is very sensitive to vector start-up times. FFT library routines supplied by all supercomputer manufacturers generally perform multiple FFTs at much higher execution rates than this benchmark code. No I/O is performed.

VECOPS: Tests rates of primitive vector calculations as a function of vector length. Vector operands and results are fetched from and stored to contiguous memory locations, except for four operations that involve gather/scatter. Typically one million floating point operations are timed.

VECSKIP: Performs the same operations as VECOPS. The vectors are accessed in noncontiguous memory locations with several values for the stride, which can be adjusted to test for performance during memory conflicts.

MATRIX: Basic matrix operations, including multiplication and transpose, on matrices of order 100. The code is highly vectorizable but not optimized for vector computers.

GAMTEB: A Monte Carlo photon transport code. This is a relatively small model code with a simple source and straightforward geometry. It is only slightly vectorizable.

PHOTON and SCALGAM: PHOTON and SCALGAM are very similar Monte Carlo photon transport codes that use the methods of GAMTEB, but with more complicated geometry, more materials, and more statistics gathered. Both codes require 64-bit arithmetic for its random number generator, as does GAMTEB, and neither vectorizes.

BMK21: Monte Carlo neutron transport algorithm. The code is completely scalar, and is similar to GAMTEB.

LSS: A linear system solver from LINPACK for systems of equations of order 100. It uses the method of Gaussian elimination. Although it is fully vectorizable, it is not optimized for supercomputers. Library routines supplied by supercomputer manufacturers will achieve considerably higher execution rates.

HYDRO: HYDRO is a two-dimensional Lagrangian hydrodynamics code based on an algorithm by W. D. Schultz. HYDRO is representative of a large class of codes in use at the Laboratory. The code is 100% vectorizable. A typical problem is run on a 100 x 100 mesh for 100 time steps.

SIMPLE: SIMPLE is a two-dimensional Lagrangian hydrodynamics code with heat diffusion. The code is about 90-95% vectorizable, and it uses a 63 x 63 mesh.

Mendez Codes
Five fluid dynamics applications codes gathered from different sources were used as testing instruments. The same five programs were used in an earlier comparison study of the Fujitsu VP-200 and Cray X-MP systems [2]. These codes do not represent any given workload and are characteristic only of the types of fluid dynamics modeling used in these programs.

BARO: BARO is a two-dimensional shallow water model of the atmosphere, which was developed on the CDC CYBER 205. The sixty-one loops of this code vectorized in all three systems amount to more than 99% of the total work. Memory accesses are contiguous and vector length moderately long at 300. Performance is dominated by vector speeds.

VORTEX: VORTEX is a particle code which simulates the dynamics of a 1-D vortex sheet by means of discrete vortices, developed on an IBM 3033 mainframe. In VORTEX as in BARO, memory accesses are contiguous and the vector ratio is quite high (99% vector operation ratio).

EULER: EULER is a one-dimensional spectral code used to model the shock tube problem, developed on TI's ASC system. Because of the type of FFT used in this code and because it is a one-dimensional code, EULER is perhaps, within the benchmark set, least representative of the codes used in large scale computing. The vectorization ratio is 73%.

MHD-2D and **SHEAR3:** These codes are two and three dimensional turbulence fluid dynamics simulation based on spectral techniques, which have been used extensively in turbulence simulations and were developed on Cray systems. The same FFT routine is used in both codes (different from the one in EULER), and accounts for most of the CPU time. The vector operation ratios of MHD2D and SHEAR3 are 99% and 89%, respectively.

Benchmarking the Connection Machine 2

Richard K. Sato Paul N. Swarztrauber

National Center for Atmospheric Research
1850 Table Mesa Drive
Boulder, CO 80307

ABSTRACT

The Connection Machine 2 (CM-2) made by Thinking Machines Corporation is a massively parallel, single instruction multiple data machine with potential for computational rates in the range of several billions of floating point operations per second. A two-dimensional shallow water equations model was run on a CM-2 to obtain an estimate of its performance on atmospheric and ocean sciences problems. C* and *LISP versions were developed and the performance of these codes on the CM-2 is compared with the performance of a FORTRAN version run on a Cray X-MP/48.

INTRODUCTION

Computers with potential for very high computational performance are of considerable interest to the atmospheric and ocean sciences research community. While traditional single processor, vector computers have been used extensively for the last decade, multiprocessor, parallel architecture machines are now being utilized to meet computational requirements [1]. Massively parallel machines are now available and, together with recent work in algorithm development for these architectures [2], offer potential for very high computational performance. However, peak rates are invariably quite different from rates that are realized on actual applications.

The Connection Machine 2 (CM-2) is made by Thinking Machines Corporation (TMC) in Cambridge, MA and it has a peak performance rate of 32 billion floating point operations per second (32 GFLOPS). To better assess the capabilities of the CM-2, arrangements were made with TMC to run a benchmark code on the machine. The benchmark code was a 2-dimensional, shallow water equations model. The code is highly vectorizable and parallelizable and executes very efficiently on most computer architectures [3], [4]. The performance level achieved on this code gives an indication of the high-end performance that is achievable on the system for more complex atmospheric models. C* and *LISP versions were coded from FORTRAN and C versions respectively, prior to our visit. During our visit, the codes were run and optimized to some extent. The optimized C* version attained a rate of 1.5 GFLOPS and the *LISP version attained a rate of 1.7 GFLOPS. Both results were for 32-bit floating point precision. The periodic boundary conditions were handled by a periodic array option of the mapping of the processors to the model grid rather than by explicit data moves. The FORTRAN version executes at a rate of 0.15 GFLOPS on one processor of a Cray X-MP/48 for 64-bit floating point precision.

ARCHITECTURE

Processors

The CM-2 is a massively parallel, single instruction multiple data (SIMD) machine [5]. A fully configured CM-2 has 64K (65,536) single-bit processors that are packaged 16 per chip. For every two chips (32 processors), there is a Weitek 3132 floating point chip. The CM-2 operates at an 8.0 MHz clock speed and the Weitek processors can produce an add and a multiply per cycle for a peak computational rate of 16 MFLOPS (millions of floating point operations per second). The 2048 Weitek processors therefore combine for a total peak floating point computational rate of 32 GFLOPS.

Memory

Each processor has 8K (8192) bytes of memory totalling 512 megabytes of memory for a 64K processor system. Each processor can access data from its memory at a rate of 5 megabits per second. The total memory bandwidth is therefore over 300 gigabits per second. A processor can only operate on data that is in its own memory but the processors are logically interconnected so that data can be transferred between processors.

CH2617-9/88/0000/0304$01.00 © 1988 IEEE

Communications

The 4096 CM-2 chips are connected in a 12-dimensional hypercube network. General communication between processors is handled by a router that can transmit messages of any length. The throughput of the router depends on the length of the messages and on the access patterns with typical values ranging from 80 - 250 million accesses per second.

A second, faster mechanism for communications between chips is a programmable *NEWS* grid that can be configured to support several multi-dimensional configurations. For a 64K CM-2 system, the following grid configurations are supported: 256 x 256, 1024 x 64, 8 x 8192, 64 x 32 x 32, 16 x 16 x 16 x 16, and 8 x 8 x 4 x 8 x 8 x 4. The *NEWS* grid allows processors to transmit data between processors according to a regular rectangular pattern. For example, in a 2-dimensional grid, each processor could simultaneously execute the same instruction to fetch data from its neighbor to the north or east or west or south. Use of the *NEWS* grid eliminates the overhead of the router.

Virtual Processors

The CM-2 is a data parallel computer. For variables that are declared to be ***parallel variables***, each processor will have a single element of that variable in its memory. When an operation is to be performed on a parallel variable, each processor performs the operation on its data value for that variable. For example, if A, B, and C are declared as parallel variables, then each processor will have a single element from each of the three arrays and a parallel operation such as C = A + B will be executed by each processor using its A, B, and C variables.

Through the concept of ***virtual processors***, the CM-2 can support applications that require more processors than are physically available. For example, parallel variables with 64K elements will have one value associated with each processor. If, however, parallel variables have 256K elements, then four virtual processors are created for each physical processor at the time the CM-2 is initialized for the application.

The physical memory is divided equally among the virtual processors so that the four virtual processors will each have 1/4 of the 8K bytes of memory or 2K bytes each. The ratio of the number of virtual processors to physical processors is referred to as the *VP ratio* which is four in this example. The execution of instructions by the virtual processors is performed by time-slicing the physical processor and therefore the execution rate of each virtual processor is approximately 1/(*VP ratio*) the rate of the physical processor. However, the overall performance is improved because of two factors: a) there is a slight speedup in overall MIPS rate because the instruction is only decoded once by the sequencer for *VP ratio* number of executions of the instruction and b) the overall communications costs are reduced with higher VP ratios since a larger fraction of the communication will be between processors that are on the same chip and the slower off-chip communications would not be required.

Front End

The front end system or host controls the execution on the CM-2. A CM-2 can support up to four front end systems that must currently be either a DEC VAX 8000 series or a Symbolics 3600 system. Programs are developed, stored, compiled, loaded, and executed on the front end. Program steps which are operations on parallel variables are passed over an interface to the CM-2 where they are broadcast for execution by all processors simultaneously. Program steps that do not involve operations on parallel variables are executed on the front end. The CM-2 parallel processing unit acts as an extension to the front end by providing computational power for operations on parallel variables.

The CM-2 does not support multi-programming in the traditional sense. That is, several jobs cannot share the same processors but rather a job must complete execution before another job can be allowed access to the processors. However, a CM-2 can be configured as several smaller subsystems and each of these subsystems can be simultaneously running independent jobs each from a separate front end machine. A block diagram of a CM-2 is given in Figure 1 which is from a TMC Technical Summary Document [6] where more details of the CM-2 can be found.

BENCHMARK PROGRAM

The benchmark code that was run on the CM-2 is a simple atmospheric dynamics model based on the shallow water equations [7]. The shallow water equations represent a primitive but useful model of the dynamics of the atmosphere. The computer code therefore provides a rough estimate of the performance of more complex atmospheric models on various computer systems. This estimate is generally of the higher performance capabilities of a system since more complex models have more physical parameterizations which result in 'scalar' code: that is, code that may have to run on the front end system or code that has conditional logic which, for the CM-2, would result in only a subset of the processors executing some of the instruction and therefore not making efficient use of all of the processors.

The shallow water equations consist of a system of three time dependent, partial differential equations [3].

$$\frac{\partial u}{\partial t} - \varsigma v + \frac{\partial H}{\partial x} = 0$$

$$\frac{\partial v}{\partial t} + \varsigma u + \frac{\partial H}{\partial y} = 0$$

$$\frac{\partial P}{\partial t} + \frac{\partial}{\partial x}(Pu) + \frac{\partial}{\partial y}(Pv) = 0$$

Where u and v are velocities in the x and y directions, respectively, P is the density or pressure; and ς is vorticity given by

$$\varsigma = \frac{\partial u}{\partial x} - \frac{\partial u}{\partial y}$$

The quantity H is related to the height field and is defined as

$$H = P + \frac{1}{2}(u^2 + v^2)$$

The solution of these equations is computed on a rectangular domain in Cartesian coordinates. Periodic boundary conditions are used in both directions. The leapfrog scheme is used for the time differencing and second order, centered finite difference approximations are used for spatial derivatives.

The model is an in-memory model with variables declared as two-dimensional arrays that are the size of the grid plus 1 (an extra row and column are defined for storage of periodic boundary values). For a grid of 256x256 points, the memory requirement on the Cray X-MP/48 is about one million words. There is no usage of secondary storage for model data and therefore no requirement for I/O to external devices. The computationally intensive portions of the code consist of three doubly-nested DO-loops in which various quantities are computed over the two-dimensional grid. Each of the loops is evaluated in a separate subroutine and the computations in the loops account for more than 90% of the floating point operations in the code. The inner loops are easily vectorized and for systems like the CM-2 which support parallel execution on multiple processors, the computations that correspond to both the inner and outer loops can be executed in parallel.

RESULTS

Overview

The original shallow water equations model was written in FORTRAN and has performed very efficiently on many computer systems [3]. The FORTRAN version was sent to TMC where it was recoded in C*. C* is a programming language consisting of the C programming language with extensions to support parallel variables and parallel operations on these variables. A standard C version was written from the FORTRAN version and in a separate effort, the C version was converted at TMC to a *LISP version. *LISP is a language which consists of common LISP plus extensions for parallel variables and parallel operations on these variables. The *LISP compiler is more mature than the C* compiler and generates code which is more highly optimized. A FORTRAN compiler is currently under development and is expected to be available in the third quarter of 1988. It will be based on FORTRAN 77 with FORTRAN 8X array extensions to support parallel variables and operations on these variables. The longer term goal of TMC is to provide compilers for each of the three languages which generate highly optimized code.

The benchmark results are presented in Table 1. All cases were run on an 8K processor system using 32-bit precision floating point arithmetic. The 8K system was the only system available for benchmarking during our visit, although fully configured 64K systems have been delivered by TMC. It is reasonable to assume that the performance results for an 8K system will scale up linearly to a larger system when the work per processor remains constant. That is, if on a larger system, the problem size is increased so that the VP ratio remains the same, then each processor will perform the same amount of work in both cases. Since there are more processors on the larger system, the amount of work performed per unit-time increases linearly with the number of processors and therefore the overall system performance increases linearly with the number of processors.

The CM-2 system that was benchmarked operated at a clock speed of 6.5 MHz rather than at 8 MHz which is the normal clock speed for systems shipped to customers. As of this writing, the reported performance rates for the C* version are considered tentative since the results did not agree with the results from the FORTRAN version. Because of time constraints during our visit, it was decided that the time would be better spent benchmarking the performance capabilities of the machine rather than debugging the C* version. We believe that the performance figures are representative since results from the C* version were approximately the same as the results from FORTRAN versions. Although the results from the *LISP version were also not correct during the visit, further debugging after the visit produced correct results with no change in performance values.

Unoptimized C* Version

The first three rows of Table 1 give the performance achieved by an unoptimized C* version of the model. Calls to a lower level language (PARIS) subroutine library were required to access data from neighboring processors. For example, the line

CM_get_from_west_always(&pW, &p, FLEN)

fetches the value of the variable "p" from the processor to the west and stores it in the local variable "pW". The grid size was specified as a power of two in order to map efficiently onto the CM-2 processors and to obtain the highest computational rates. For Case A, a model grid of 64x128 was specified to

TABLE 1.

MFLOPS for Shallow Water Code on Thinking Machine CM-2

Case	Language	CM Size	Model Grid	VP ratio	MFLOPS (measured)	MFLOPS (est. for 64K sys)
A	Unopt C*	8192	64 X 128	1	83	664
B	Unopt C*	8192	64 X 4096	32	110	880
C	Unopt C*	8192	256 X 256	8	110	880
D	Opt C*	8192	64 X 128	1	112	896
E	Opt C*	8192	64 X 4096	32	164	1312
F	Opt C*	8192	256 X 256	8	183	1464
G	*LISP	8192	512 X 512	32	215	1720

correspond to the 8K processors of the CM-2 and hence there was a physical processor for each point of the model grid giving a VP ratio of 1.

For Case B, the model grid was specified as 64x4096 which has 32 times more points than the number of physical processors giving a VP ratio of 32. Case C was a run with a 256x256 model grid. This again represents more points than the total number of physical processor, and in this configuration, each physical processor represents a 4x2 array of virtual processors for a VP ratio of eight. For both Case B and Case C, the performance achieved was 110 MFLOPS on the 8K system which would correspond to 880 MFLOPS on a full 64K system. Although the performance improved when the VP ratios increased from one to eight and from one to 32, performance did not improve when the VP ratio increased from eight to 32. This is evidently because the communications overhead is less efficient for the 64x4096 configuration than for the 256x256 configuration.

Optimized C* Version

The optimized C* version and the unoptimized C* version are compared in the next three entries of Table 1. In the optimized version, additional subroutines were added to the lower-level subroutines library and invoked in the C* program. These additional routines allowed more efficient use of the processors by overlapping communications with computations. For example, if a value was fetched from a neighboring processor and was to be added to another variable a "fetch and add" instruction was issued rather than a "fetch" instruction followed by an "add" instruction. The line

CM_get_from_west_with_f_add_always (&cu, &cu, FLOAT)

fetches the value of "cu" from the west neighbor and adds it to the local value of "cu". The optimized C* version resulted in MFLOPS rate improvements of 35%, 49%, and 66% over the unoptimized version for the three cases that were run with a top rate of 1464 MFLOPS for the 256x256 grid.

*LISP Version

The *LISP version resulted in the highest performance rates although the corresponding model configuration (512x512) was not run for the optimized C* version. The *LISP version produced 215 MFLOPS on the 8K processor system. Assuming a linear scale up in performance, a 64K system would execute at a rate of 1.7 GFLOPS if a VP ratio of 32 is maintained. The *LISP compiler is considered to be more highly optimized than the C* compiler.

Cray X-MP Version

The Cray X-MP version is a vectorized FORTRAN code. The 256x256 grid requires one million words of memory and executes at 148 MFLOPS on one processor of the X-MP. The 512x512 case requires 3.9 million words of memory and also executes at 148 MFLOPS. The Cray X-MP floating point operations use 64-bit precision.

Observations

As with all computational models of multidimensional phenomena, the benchmark included loops of lower dimension. For example, periodic boundary conditions are implemented in the FORTRAN version by one dimensional loops in which the left boundary is copied to the right as well as the top to the bottom. These loops are usually implemented on a serial or vector computer without much consideration since it is known that their contribution to the computing time is an order of magnitude below that of the doubly-nested loops. However, when implemented in this manner on the Connection Machine, the total computing time (for the *LISP version) was increased by a factor of 2.5 to 4 depending on the VP ratio. The largest increase corresponded to the highest VP ratios for which the least amount of interprocessor communications is required and hence the highest computational rates are achieved. Although the boundary computations are performed on a subset of processors, it requires the same amount of time as computations on the interior that uses all of the processors. In addition, the communications that were explicitly specified by the code are not directly supported by the NEWS communication.

These reduced rates were not representative of the rates that could be obtained via alternate algorithmic and coding efforts and therefore the periodic boundary conditions were implemented using the periodic communications that are available using NEWS communication. This was achieved by simply branching around the code that explicitly implemented the boundary conditions and increasing the number of grid points to the nearest power of two.

This modification in the computation is representative of the efforts that will be necessary to implement existing codes on a parallel processor. If time had permitted, the periodic boundary conditions could have been implemented as in the original code using more efficient communications methods such as the scan instruction or perhaps in microcode using the hypercube communications. These efforts are seen as typical with any significant change in computer architecture and not unlike the efforts that were required to adapt codes to early vector architectures.

CONCLUSIONS

The main purpose of the visit to Thinking Machines Corporation was to measure the performance capabilities of the CM-2. The shallow water equations model was selected as the benchmark code to be run for two reasons: (1) the effort to convert the code to C* and to *LISP would be reasonable; and (2) because the performance results would give an indication of the high-end performance from the system for problems found in the atmospheric and ocean sciences.

The MFLOPS rates which were measured for this code were impressive. Normalizing these rates for 64-bit operations (instead of 32), for a clock speed of 8 MHz (rather than 6.5), and including some explicit treatment for the periodic boundary conditions, the CM-2 performance for this benchmark was considered to be on the order of that of a Cray X-MP/48.

It is clear that existing codes will not run *as is* on the CM-2. Existing codes of the atmospheric and ocean sciences community are written almost exclusively in FORTRAN. Even when a FORTRAN compiler is available, significant modification to existing codes will be required. Initially, explicit subroutine calls, similar to those in the C* version of the model, to lower level subroutine libraries will be necessary to achieve satisfactory performance levels on the CM-2. In the longer term, the FORTRAN compiler will recognize FORTRAN 8X array extensions for parallel operations on parallel variables but this will also require modification of existing codes.

While significant coding efforts may be required to develop or convert models to run efficiently on a CM-2, the possibility of execution rates on the order of several GFLOPS would make this effort worthwhile. The potentials for applying a CM-2 to more complex problems is currently under investigation.

ACKNOWLEDGEMENTS

We would like to thank the Thinking Machines Corporation for allowing us to visit their organization and for allowing us to benchmark the CM-2. We are grateful to Dr. Lennart Johnsson of TMC for his assistance in arranging the visit and for his assistance during the visit. We would like to thank Dr. John Richards for developing the C* version of the model and particularly Dr. Oliver McBryan for his extensive support of this project and for developing the *LISP version. We are grateful to many TMC staff members for their assistance during our visit.

REFERENCES

[1] Hoffman, G.-R. and D.F. Snelling, eds, *Multiprocessing in Meteorological Models,* Springer-Verlag, New York, 1988.

[2] McBryan, O., and E. Van de Velde, "Hypercube Algorithms and Implementations," *SIAM J. Sci. Stat. Comput.,* 1987, Vol 8, pp s227-s287

[3] Hoffman, G.-R., P. N. Swarztrauber, and R. A. Sweet, "Aspects of Using Multiprocessors for Meteorological Modelling," in: *Multiprocessing in Meteorological Models,* G.-R. Hoffmann and D. F. Snelling, eds., Springer-Verlag, New York, 1988.

[4] Snelling, D.F., "A Solution to the Shallow Water Equations on the FPS T Series," presented at the Second International Conference on Vector and Parallel Computing, Issues in Applied Research and Development, Tromso, Norway, June 6–10, 1988.

[5] Hillis, D., *The Connection Machine,* MIT Press, Cambridge, MA., 1985.

[6] *Connection Machine Model CM-2 Technical Summary,* Thinking Machines Technical Report HA87-4, April, 1987.

[7] Sadourney, R., "The Dynamics of Finite-Difference Models of the Shallow-Water Equations," *Journal of Atmospheric Sciences,* 32, (1975), pp 680-689.

FIGURE 1. Connection Machine Model CM-2 System Organization

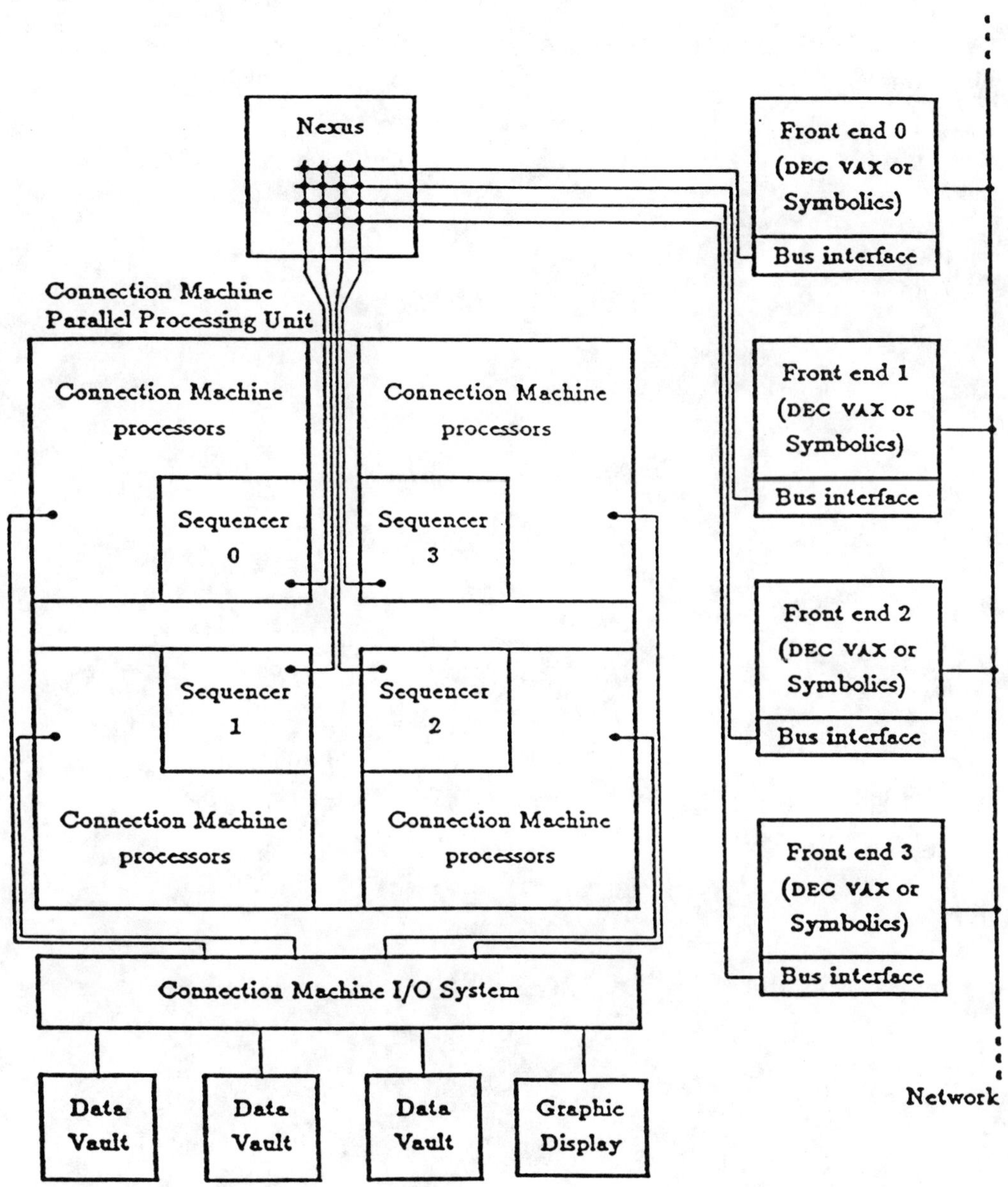

(Reproduced with the permission of Thinking Machines Corporation.)

Supercomputer Architecture - I

Chair: Jack Worlton
Worlton and Associates

SOME PATTERNS OF TECHNOLOGICAL CHANGE IN HIGH-PERFORMANCE COMPUTERS

Jack Worlton

Worlton & Associates
3089 Villa
Los Alamos, NM 87544

ABSTRACT

High-performance computer technology is undergoing a period of unusually rapid change, and this paper attempts to describe the patterns of these changes in a systematic way. Pattern recognition is the basis of technology forecasting, and it is through technology forecasting that we obtain the anticipatory information that allows us to avoid problems and create opportunities. We will first identify the stages in which technological changes occur, and then define "change" as the first derivative of an information function that describes the state of a technology. We then explore the driving forces that cause three generic patterns of technological change: incremental, exponential, and logistic. Some areas in high-performance computer technology that are following these patterns are then identified, and a forecast is developed. Finally, some limits of high-performance computing are discussed.

RATIONALE

It is inherent in the nature of the future that it contains both problems and opportunities. How well we manage these events depends to a great extent on how well we anticipate their occurrence. Anticipatory management is much to be preferred to reactive management: managers who are successful in solving problems after they occur are not as effective as those who anticipate and thereby avoid the occurrence of these problems altogether. Correcting problems after they occur is often vastly more costly—and sometimes impossible—compared to preventing their occurrence. For example, polluting the atmosphere with carbon dioxide and thereby causing a "greenhouse" effect that turns the worlds farmlands into giant dustbowls and then trying to correct this problem is obviously inferior to preventing the problem in the first place. Similarly with opportunities: opportunities are rarely simply found but have to be created, and creation of opportunities requires anticipatory information. This point is succinctly put in Alvin Toffler's dictum that "We can manage the future only to the extent that we can anticipate it" [1].

Anticipatory information can be obtained only through pattern recognition, and as far back in time as we have any record, humans have attempted to identify patterns that could be used to anticipate current and future events for decision making. These early patterns now seem somewhat naive: the flight of birds, the appearance of the entrails of sacrificial victims, the movement of the stars, and the inspiration of oracles. The earliest record of Chinese writing, for example, is on "oracle bones"; an oracle bone is a piece of bone that has been heated to produce a pattern of cracks that was interpreted to mean something about the future, and this forecast was then written on the bone itself [2]. Even the most sophisticated modern forecasts, including the predictions of science and technology, are based on pattern recognition, using empirical models, analytical models, theories, and laws.

The patterns of technological change provide a basis for anticipating future technological change and therefore altering and controlling future directions in technology. However, technology forecasting is more complex than the predictions of science and technology themselves, because it is driven not only by technical complexities, but also by political, economic, marketing, and social complexities as well. These additional difficulties and the frequent failures of forecasting often lead people to make decisions and undertake planning without the benefits of forecasting, but in fact, we cannot avoid forecasting: to make no forecast is to assume that the future will be exactly like the present, and while that may have been a reasonable forecast in, say, the tenth century, it is a completely unreasonable forecast in the twentieth century, especially in high-performance computing.

A TAXONOMY OF ANTICIPATORY METHODS

There is an extensive literature on the subject of technology forecasting, and brief but useful guides are found in [3], which reviews several dozen methods, and in [4], which provides a critique of forecasting methodologies. Figure 1 shows a "pruned" taxonomic tree of anticipatory methods.

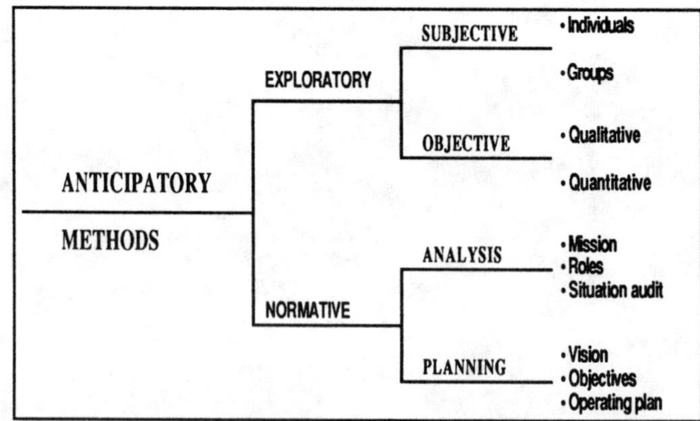

Figure 1. A partial taxonomy of anticipatory methods.

Anticipatory methods can be either exploratory (starting from the present and advancing step by step toward the future) or normative (inventing some future and identifying the actions needed to bring that future into existence). Strategic planning should always include both of these methods: exploratory methods to clarify the changes in the technical environment that will occur but which are not under our control, and normative methods that help us to invent the future. This essay is concerned largely with exploratory methods.

EXPERT FORECASTING

Exploratory methods can be either subjective (based on expert opinion) or objective (based on empirical or analytical models). Subjective methods are the easiest to use: merely hire some expert and have the expert prepare a forecast. However, all experts have blind spots and biases, and the limitations of expert forecasting in general are explored in [5]; Table 1 shows four examples of rather startlingly erroneous forecasts from prominent experts, taken from this source.

EXPERT	FORECAST
Lord Kelvin	*Heavier-than-air flying machines are impossible (1895).*
Albert Einstein	*There is not the slightest indication that [nuclear] energy will ever be obtainable (1932).*
Thomas J. Watson	*I think there is a world market for about five computers (1943).*
Kenneth Olsen	*There is no reason for an individual to have a computer in their home (1977).*

Table 1. Selected examples of expert forecasting.

Because of the limits of individual expert forecasting, it is often necessary to aggregate expert opinion in some way, either as committees or through what is called the "Delphi" technique—which is essentially an anonymous committee and the most accurate method of expert forecasting [6]. In this method, a group of experts is formed and questions circulated to them for their comments about future events, but the members of the group are unaware of the identity of the other members. The responses to the questions are then compiled and circulated to the members for comment, and this procedure is iterated until the opinions converge. In a study of six Delphi forecasts of computer technology [7], it was found that the accuracy of the Delphi technique falls exponentially with time, decreasing to less than 0.5 in four years; if we extrapolate this trend, the accuracy would fall to 0.3 in six years, to 0.2 in eight years, and ten-year forecasts would be accurate in only about one event in seven. Clearly, accurate expert forecasting is limited to relatively short periods—say, no more than three years—and must be augmented with objective methods.

STAGES OF TECHNOLOGICAL CHANGE

Technological change usually occurs in four stages: invention, innovation, diffusion, and change of scale [8, 9]. Invention of new technology can be based on either the creation of new knowledge (science-driven) or new tools and techniques (technology-driven). Historians of technology argue that most technological inventions are incremental improvements on existing technology rather than dramatic breakthroughs based on science. Inventions are rarely ready for immediate commercial exploitation, so a period of "innovation" is required, i.e., exploration of methods of using the invention for practical purposes. For a set of 44 inventions, the innovative period ranged from as short as one year to as long as 79 years, with an average of 13 years [10]. For example, it took about a decade between the invention of the transistor to its diffusion into the computer market place, and a similar period was required for vector architectures to be successful.

The innovative period is often characterized by false starts and failures, and it is only when a clearly superior product is created—a "guidepost" [11]—that successful diffusion can begin. For example, the period of innovation for electronic computers began in 1946 with the dedication of the ENIAC and continued through the mid-1950s when the IBM 704 became a guidepost product because it brought together core memory, floating-point operations, and index registers. All of these elements had been invented before, but it was their convergence into a single design that guided the way to further computer evolution. Similarly, in 1976 the CRAY-1, with its vector registers and improved balance in scalar-vector performance, provided a guidepost for further development of vector computers, after vector processors of the early 1970s had failed as commercial products. Parallel processing has been going through an innovation period for more than three decades and has yet to find its guidepost. Guideposts are often followed by imitators and this leads to a clustering effect in which many incremental improvements occur in a short period of time.

It is useful to distinguish between simple diffusion of products into the market and a radical change of scale in their use. Hamming points out that when some important parameter of a technology changes by an order of magnitude or more, this often creates qualitative change as well as quantitative change [9]. An automobile is only one order of magnitude faster than a horse, but this quantitative change created radical qualitative changes in modern society. Similarly, the orders of magnitude difference between VLSI and discrete transistors has led to qualitative effects in product development, such as the development of the microprocessor. In parallel processing, change of scale is being used to increase performance, with the number of processors ranging from as few as 2 up to more than 10,000.

MODELS OF TECHNOLOGICAL CHANGE

Description, Explanation, and Prediction

In a generic sense, the term "models" refers to abstract representations that help us describe, explain, or predict events in real or hypothetical environments. It is useful to bear in mind the distinction among description, explanation, and prediction. In his book *A Philosopher Looks at Science*, Kemeny argues that explanation and prediction are ultimately the same function because an explanation can be viewed as a prediction from a hypothetical time before an event in the past [12]. Gill, however, argues that there are explanations that do not predict and predictions that do not explain [13]. For example, Darwin's theory of evolution is a valid explanation of past evolutionary change, but it rarely allows us to predict future evolutionary changes because we lack information on the causative events that will drive the evolutionary model. On the other hand, primitive peoples were able to predict certain astronomical events such as the phases of the moon and the changes of the seasons without having an adequate explanation for them.

Description is empirical in nature, telling us *what* is true, whereas explanation is analytical in nature, telling us *why* things are true. Neither of these activities is time dependent: they can apply equally well to the past, present, or future. Predictions can take either of these forms: descriptive predictions which merely tell us what things may happen in the future, and explanatory predictions that tell why things may happen in the future. It is the need for explanatory predictions that leads us to search for patterns of change based on analytical models.

Defining "Change"

One of the difficulties in the systematic study of technological change is finding a metric of progress that is satisfactory. Suggested metrics include the number of patents issued, the number of papers printed, or the level of performance in a technology [11]. Patents are not entirely satisfactory because many important inventions are not patented at all, and many inventions that are patented do not represent significant technological progress. The same problem attends the use of published technical papers as a metric of progress. And the performance metrics of high-performance computing are notorious for their inability to accurately represent sustained performance.

However, doing the best we can with metrics of technological progress, we define the state of a technology at any time by the information function, I(t); change is then defined as the first derivative of this function, and its second derivative is also useful to determine whether change is constant, increasing, or decreasing. Once we have identified the causes (explanatory variables) for change, we can then solve the differential equation to obtain the function that identifies the pattern of development. We consider three basic patterns of change.

(1) $dI/dt = k$	Change is constant. This leads to a linear pattern of development.
(2) $dI/dt = k \cdot I$	Change is driven by the current information we have about a technology. This leads to an exponential pattern of development.
(3) $dI/dt = k \cdot I \cdot (1-I/L)$	Change is driven not only by current information, but also by how close a technology is to its limit, L. This leads to a logistic (S-shaped) pattern of development.

Linear Change

Solving the differential equation $dI/dt = k$ gives us $I_t = I_o + k \cdot t$ for the function that describes this linear pattern of change. Oddly enough, it is rather difficult to find linear patterns of change in high-performance computation, in part because so many of the trends are based on electronics where many changes are exponential. For example, in Osburn and Reisman's detailed review of semiconductor electronics for high-speed computation, they show only the gate-oxide depth of semiconductor devices as changing linearly in time, whereas all other parameters are changing exponentially [14]. The price-performance relationships in vendor's product lines often follow a linear pattern, being driven by both marketing and technical reasons. For example, the price-performance pattern of the high-end mainframes from Amdahl, IBM, and NAS are all linear, as illustrated in Figure 2 [15].

A special case of linear change occurs when k = 0, that is, when there is no change. In modern times it is difficult to conceive of such an environment, but histories of technology show no notable changes in any technologies in periods as recent as the tenth century. Why should the twentieth century experience

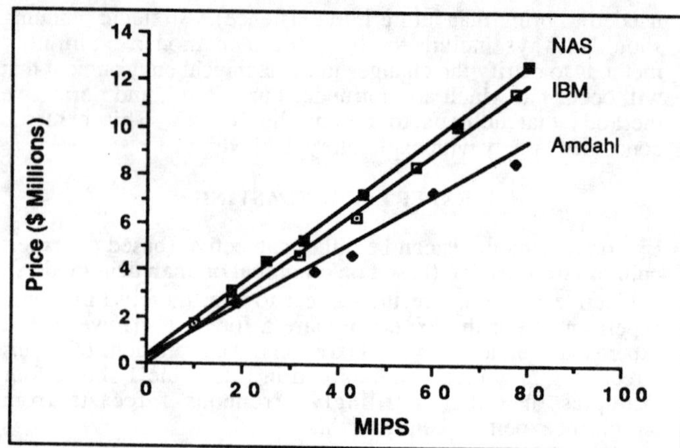

Figure 2. Price-performance for high-end mainframes.

almost daily technological advances when one thousand years earlier a whole century saw none at all? What happened in the last thousand years to accelerate technological change? The concept of "enabling" technologies is useful in understanding the rate of technological progress. An enabling technology is one that enables the development of not just a single tool or technique, but the development of many other technologies as well. For example, the Gutenberg printing press was an enabling technology of the fifteenth century that led to the spread of knowledge and hence to the rise of modern science and technology in the succeeding centuries. Similarly, the high-performance computer is one among many enabling technologies of the twentieth century that enable rapid advances in other technologies.

Exponential Change

If we assume that technological change is proportional to the knowledge we already have, then change will be slow when a technology is immature but will accelerate when the knowledge base grows. This situation is encoded in the differential equation $dI/dt = k \cdot I$, where I represents the information about the current state of the technology, and solving this equation gives us $I_t = I_o \cdot e^{kt}$. Much is hidden in the constant of proportionality, k, in this model, because this determines the *rate* of change. Magnetic core memories followed a pattern of exponential change in the 1950s and 1960s, with the outer diameter of the cores following the pattern $d_t = d_o \cdot 2^{-t/5}$ [16]. That is, the diameter of the cores was reduced by a factor of 2 every five years. This pattern was observed from the mid-1950s until the late 1960s when magnetic core memory was largely replaced by semiconductor memory.

Not all exponential patterns are driven by a time exponent; for example, the relationship between the access time and capacity of memory chips is described in [14] to be 0.6 decades of access time per decade of memory capacity, i.e., that the access time of a memory chip increases by a factor of $10^{0.6}$ (≈ 4) as the chip capacity increases by a factor of 10. This can be expressed by the exponential pattern $T = T_o \cdot 4^{\log M}$, so the change in access time is driven by M, the relative change in memory capacity.

Another non-time-dependent exponential pattern is found in what are called "learning curves" [17-21]. As the volume of production increases, efficiency rises and the cost per unit falls. This can be expressed by the pattern $C_2 = C_1 \cdot F^{\lg V}$, where C_2 = the cost per unit for a volume of production V_2, C_1 = the cost per unit for a volume of production V_1, $F < 1$ is the factor of cost decrease per doubling of production, and lg V is the binary logarithm of the increase in the volume of production, $V = V_2/V_1$. Thus, as the volume of production doubles, lg V increases by 1 and the cost per unit decreases by a factor of F. This pattern was shown to apply to 15 industries, including integrated circuits (F = 0.72), random-access memories (RAMs) (F = 0.68), and disk drives (F = 0.76), during the mid-1970s [17].

Time-dependent exponential change by its nature must be short term or it would eventually violate some limit of science, technology, or economics. However, when an exponential change slows down, it need not stop growing at all or become linear; rather, it typically becomes an exponential change with a smaller exponent, and the generalization of exponential change is toward "piecewise-exponential" change. This pattern is occurring in several of the technologies that support the evolution of supercomputers, including the number of components per chip, as illustrated in Figure 3.

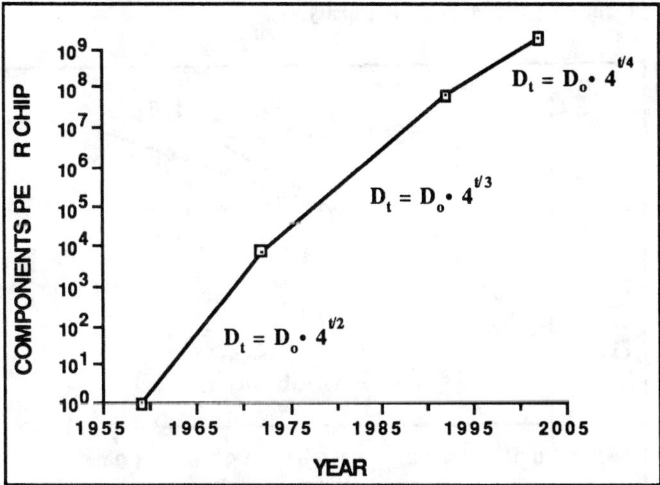

Figure 3. Trend in the density of components per chip.

It is useful to track the trend in component density in terms of its quadrupling period, that is, the time to develop a new generation of chips with four times the density of the previous generation. This is the pattern of change in the RAM industry, for example. The density of components per chip followed the pattern $D_t = D_o \cdot 4^{t/2}$ during the period 1959 to 1972 (quadrupling every two years); it has slowed down to $D_t = D_o \cdot 4^{t/3}$ since 1972 (quadrupling every three years); and it is expected to slow to a rate of $D_t = D_o \cdot 4^{t/4}$ sometime in the 1990s (quadrupling every four years) [22]. This trend is reflected directly in the capacity of RAM chips, as illustrated in Figure 4.

The dynamic RAM (DRAM) chips are typically one generation ahead of the static RAM (SRAM) chips in terms of capacity, and both follow the exponential growth pattern of a factor of 4 about every three years [23]. The trend in memory-chip capacity is equivalent to growth by a factor of 10 in five years, i.e., $M_t = M_o \cdot 10^{t/5}$. This pattern implies that both vendors and users should plan to have memory capacities about a factor of 10 larger than they are today in just five years. Some 1987 developments in RAM technology are summarized in Table 2 [24].

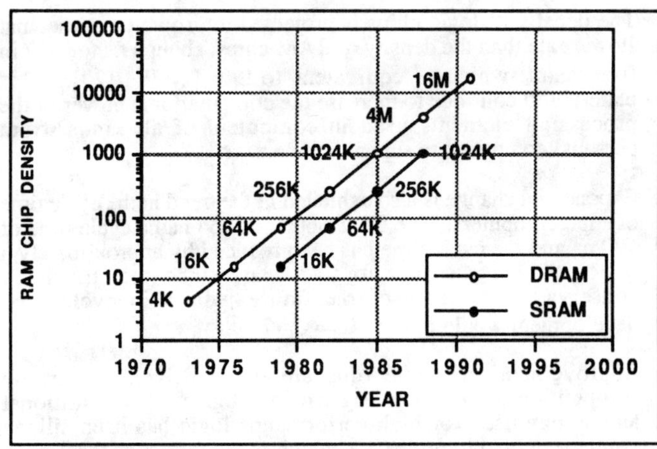

Figure 4. Trend in RAM chip capacity.

DEVELOPMENT	COMPANY
• 16 Mbit DRAM prototype, 80 ns	NTT
• 4 Mbit DRAM, 65 ns, CMOS	7 companies
• 1 Mbit SRAM, CMOS	IBM
• 64K SRAM, 7 ns	Hitachi
• 64K SRAM, 5 ns	Fujitsu

Table 2. Some developments in RAM technology in 1987.

Limits to the future development of technologies in general and RAM technology in particular include not only fundamental and technological limits but also economical limits, as illustrated in Figure 5 [25]. This data is from a report on the Intel decision to exit the RAM market. The cost of developing the memory chip with 2^{12} = 4096 = 4K bits was about \$1 million, but as the memory chip capacity has grown by a factor of 16, the cost of design has grown by a factor of 10. The competition in this market has been especially fierce and the profits marginal or non-existent. As the chip size grows it is clear that most single companies will be unable to afford the cost of design, and two options are available: (1) share the design costs among many companies as has been done in Japan through projects supported by the Ministry of International Trade and Industry (MITI), or (2) develop lower-cost methods of design.

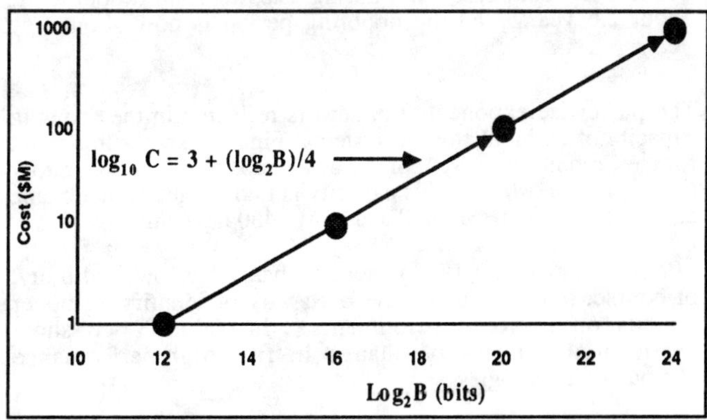

Figure 5. Trend in RAM chip design cost.

The density of logic chips is projected to grow at a somewhat slower rate than the density of RAM chips, about a factor of 7 in five years, which is equivalent to $L_t = L_o \cdot 7^{t/5}$ [23]. This pattern will continue to increase the computational power of the processing elements used in computers of all kinds, from personal computers to supercomputers.

Exponential change is also exhibited in the trend in the cycle time of supercomputers. The CDC 6600 of 1964 had a cycle time of 100 ns and the cycle time has been reduced by approximately a factor of 2 every four to five years since that time. A conservative estimate of the future pattern in cycle time development would thus be $C_t = C_o \cdot 2^{-t/5}$.

Improvements in cycle time are being driven in part by competition among new logic technologies. The traditional technology used for high-performance logic has been silicon emitter-coupled logic (ECL), which is the fastest of the silicon logic technologies and continues to be used in most supercomputers [14]. However, departures from this logic family are being incorporated into two new designs: gallium-arsenide (GaAs) in the CRAY-3 and complementary metal-oxide semiconductor (CMOS) in the ETA10. The GaAs technology has the advantage that it is faster than ECL and uses less power per logic gate. If the CRAY-3, which is scheduled for initial delivery in 1989 or 1990, is successful, it may provide a new technological guidepost for high-speed logic, and there will be many imitators. On the other hand, to use CMOS as a logic technology in a supercomputer seems odd because it is slower than ECL; however, its slower speed can be partially compensated for by cooling it with liquid nitrogen to a nominal temperature of 77°K. The CMOS technology has the advantage of low power and high component density, so more gates per chip and hence fewer chips per logic function than ECL are its main advantages. There have been some failures and delays experienced in meeting the design goals of the ETA10 and it is unclear whether this technology will be used in future supercomputers or not. Both the CRAY-3 and the ETA10 should be viewed as experiments, and their success monitored for their implications for future supercomputer logic technology.

The density of magnetic disk recording is another technology that is exhibiting piecewise exponential change, as illustrated in Figure 6 (based on data from [26]). A simple exponential fit to this data shows a doubling of density every two years, but the piecewise exponential pattern can be used to make this trend more precise. During the period 1956 through 1965, density doubled in about 1.3 years; during 1965 to 1980 it doubled in about 2.6 years; and the doubling period is now about four years.

The piecewise exponential pattern is reflected in the growing capacity of archival storage systems; Figure 7 shows this trend for the Common File System at Los Alamos National Laboratory (LANL) [27]. Most of this capacity is in off-line magnetic tape cartridges for the IBM 3850 and IBM 3480 tape units.

Long-term projection of exponential change has low credibility, of course, but it is instructive as a way of identifying upper bounds on future developments. In Table 3 we show exponential patterns of change in five high-performance computer technologies.

These trends are shown on a semi-log plot in Figure 8 for a 20-year period, assuming for purposes of illustration that no breakthroughs or limits will occur in this period, so current trends will continue. Note that the trend in execution rate crosses the line for a 1000-fold increase from current rates a few years after the year 2000; assuming the current *sustained* execution rate is on the order of 10^9 operations per second, this means that a general-purpose computer with a sustained execution rate of 10^{12} operations per second could be available around the year 2000. This assumes that the cycle time is improved by a factor of 2 every five years and that the number of processors per system is increased by a factor of 4 every four years. Note that Figure 8 is *not* a prediction, merely a naive projection of some exponential trends over a 20-year period assuming no changes from current trends.

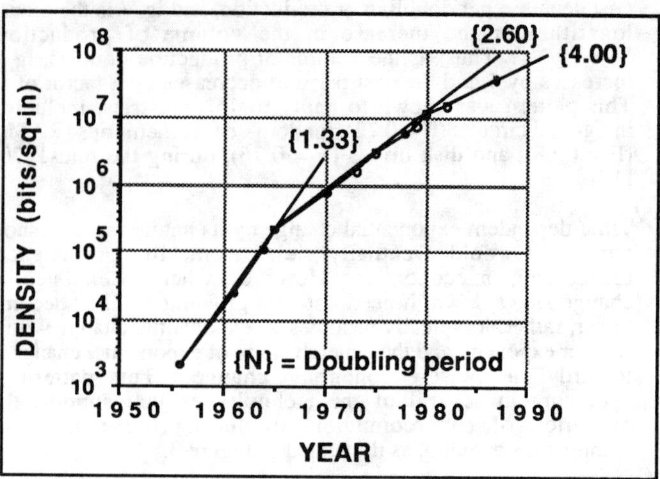

Figure 6. Trend in disk density.

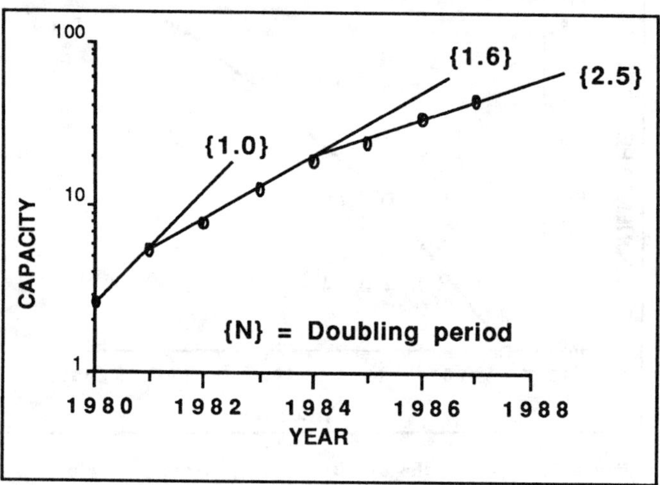

Figure 7. Trend in archival storage capacity at LANL.

TECHNOLOGY	TREND
• Cycle time	$C_t = C_o \cdot 2^{-t/5}$
• Processors per system	$P_t = P_o \cdot 4^{t/4}$
• Logic density	$L_t = L_o \cdot 7^{t/5}$
• Memory chip density	$M_t = M_o \cdot 10^{t/5}$
• Execution rate	$R_t = R_o \cdot 2^{7t/10}$

Table 3. Trend patterns in five technologies.

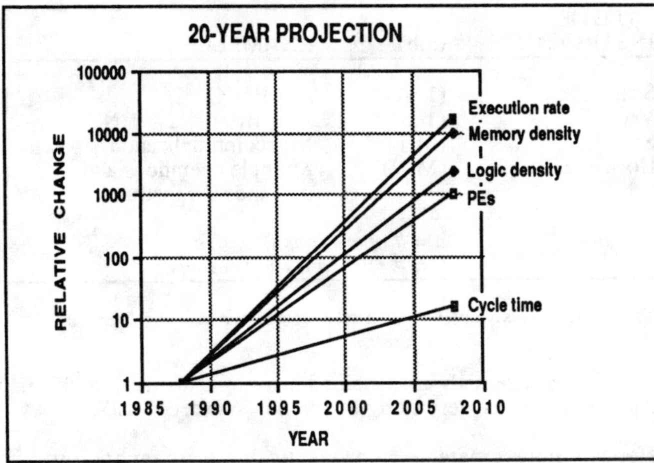

Figure 8. Projection of some current technology trends.

Logistic Change

Piecewise exponential change ultimately approaches some limit in its gradually decreasing exponential rates, beyond which the technology is increasingly expensive and time-consuming to improve, and this leads to a third generic pattern of technological change—logistic ("S-shaped") change. Here change is driven by both the current state of information (I) and the limit to further change (1-I/L), where L is the limit to progress. Encoding these explanatory variables into a differential equation yields $dI/dt = k \cdot I \cdot (1-I/L)$, and solving this equation gives us the logistic pattern, as illustrated in Figure 9. Here the parameters are set to unity for purposes of illustration.

Logistic change is characterized by an initial period of slow growth, followed by a period of exponential growth, then a point of inflection, and finally a period of asymptotic growth as the technology approaches a limit. This pattern of change was first observed in population studies [28], and it has since been found to be descriptive of change in a remarkably diverse set of circumstances, including technological evolution in general and the evolution of electronic and computer technologies in particular.

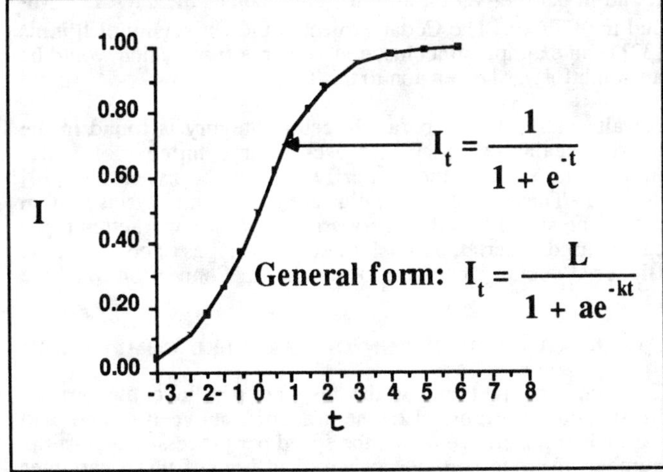

Figure 9. Logistic change.

The generalization of logistic change is found in patterns that are "piecewise logistic," i.e., one S-shaped curve is followed by another overlapping curve at a higher level, which is followed by another at a yet higher level, and so on. This is a very general pattern of technological change, as illustrated in Figure 10.

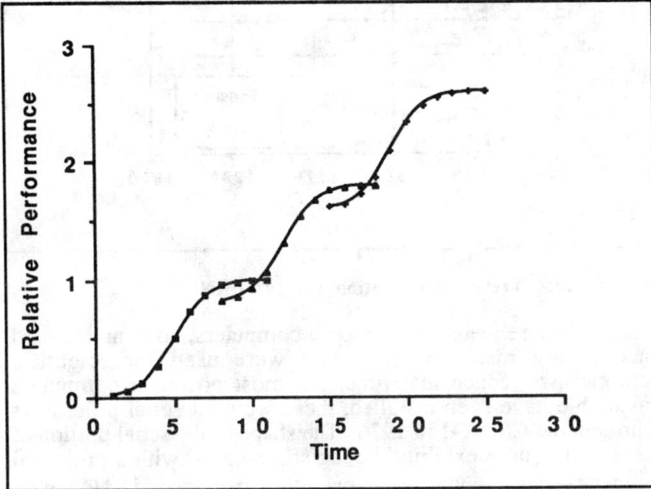

Figure 10. Piecewise-logistic patterns of change.

The transition from one curve to another represents a technological discontinuity, and the failure to manage discontinuities properly is a common source of management failure by both vendors and users. This is succinctly put in the dictum that "History proceeds by changing the subject" [29]. That is, today the subject is how to improve and effectively use the current technology, but tomorrow this technology will not even be a subject of interest. Examples include the transition from magnetic cores to semiconductor memory, the transition from vacuum tubes to transistors, the transition from scalar to vector architectures, and the transition from serial to parallel architectures. Richard Foster's study *Innovation* is based largely on this pattern [30]. He argues that defending an old technology too long is a strategy of failure, because the attackers are already developing a new technology; the new technology may not yet be as effective or economical as the old technology, but it is on a growth curve that will ultimately project it to heights that cannot be reached with the old technology. Both the users and the developers of high-performance computers must be concerned not only with using and defending their current technology, but also with developing and using new technologies. An example of combining defense and attack is found in the strategy of Cray Research, Inc., with its development of the CRAY Y-MP, a defensive product, and the CRAY-3, an attacking product.

An example of the piecewise-logistic pattern occurs in the execution rate of supercomputers installed at LANL from 1943 to the present, as shown in Figure 11 (the performance units are normalized to the CDC 7600 in millions of instructions per second for administrative purposes). This is a semilog plot that gives the logistic curve a somewhat different shape than the linear plots shown above. The circular points are serial (single-processor) designs and the square points are parallel (multiple-processor) designs.

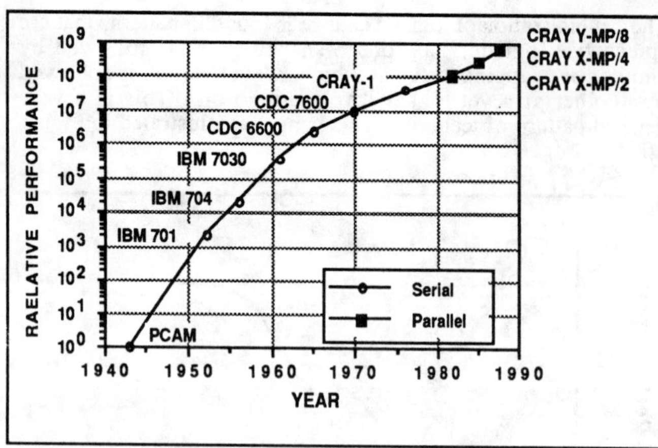

Figure 11. Trend in execution rate at LANL.

In 1943 there were no electronic computers, so punched-card accounting machines (PCAMs) were used for scientific computing. Since that time, the most powerful computers available have been installed; these were all serial processors through the CRAY-1 in 1976. The shape of the serial portion of this trend curve exhibits the logistic pattern, with a projected upper bound of about $3 \cdot 10^9$ operations per second. However, with the installation of parallel processors, beginning with the two-processor CRAY X-MP/2 in 1982 and continuing with the four-processor CRAY X-MP/4 in 1985 and the eight-processor CRAY Y-MP/8 in 1988, the trend line has started on a new pattern of growth, essentially a new logistic curve driven by a new technology—parallel processing.

EXTENDING THE FLYNN TAXONOMY OF COMPUTER ARCHITECTURES

The dominant trend in the architectural design of high-performance computers is the trend toward parallel computation, and to understand the patterns of change in parallel architectures it is useful to develop an intellectual road map—a taxonomy—of the possibilities. A rigorous taxonomy has two key characteristics: exclusion and exhaustion. The categories used must be exclusive to avoid ambiguity, and they must be exhaustive to avoid incompleteness. Thus, a rigorous taxonomy provides an unambiguous category for every instance presented to it.

The well-known taxonomy developed by Michael Flynn [31], that matched instruction streams vs data streams, met these criteria and this was one of the reasons for its success. However, that taxonomy was developed in the 1960s and it is an incomplete guide to current architectures. Flynn's classification of control concurrency (single and multiple instructions streams) needs to be augmented with clustering (clusters of multiple instruction streams). Also, this taxonomy covered only the scalar instruction type, and this needs to be systematically extended to cover several new instruction types, as illustrated in Table 4. Here "a" is the number of operations specified, and "b" is the number of operands or operand pairs specified.

A *scalar* instruction is defined as one in which there is a single operation specified and the operation is applied to only one pair of operands. A *vector* instruction is one in which a single operation is specified, but the operation is applied to many pairs of operands. A *systolic* instruction is one in which multiple operations are performed on each specified operand. Finally, a *horizontal* instruction is one in which both multiple operations

TYPE OF INSTRUCTION	(a,b)	EXAMPLES
Scalar	(1,1)	$A = B + C$
Vector	(1,N)	$A_i = B_i + C_i, i = 1,N$
Systolic	(M,1)	Matrix multiplication
Horizontal	(M,N)	Multiple operations and operands per instruction
Notation:	*a = # operations specified*	
	b = # operands (pairs) specified	

Table 4. Classification of instruction types.

and multiple operands are specified in a single instruction (this is also referred to as Very Long Instruction Word, or VLIW).

We can now create a rigorous twelve-way taxonomy of computer architectures to extend the four-way Flynn taxonomy, as illustrated in Table 5.

	<——Generic instruction types——>			
Concurrency	Scalar (1,1)	Vector (1,N)	Systolic (M,1)	Horizontal (M,N)
Serial				
Parallel				
Clustered				

Table 5. An extended taxonomy of computer architectures.

Each of the twelve categories is itself the root of a taxonomic tree; for example, the vector category can be further subdivided into register-to-register and memory-to-memory, and the parallel category can be further subdivided into shared-memory and distributed-memory. Thus, the parallel-vector category can be articulated into a four-way taxonomy. This same method could be used to systematically expand the twelve-way taxonomy in greater detail.

The historical trend in supercomputer architectures can now be readily described: most high-performance computers through the CDC 7600 and the IBM 360/95 in the late 1960s were serial-scalar designs; these were followed by serial-vector designs such as the CRAY-1 and CYBER 205 in the late 1970s and early 1980s; the current leading edge of supercomputer designs is found in parallel-vector architectures such as the CRAY Y-MP and the ETA^{10}. The Cedar Project at the University of Illinois [32] is an example of a clustered-vector design, which would be a straightforward extension to this trend.

An alternative to the parallel-vector category is found in the parallel-scalar category that uses a large number of scalar processors, such as the Butterfly [33] or the hypercube [34] designs. These, too, can be clustered, as in the Myrias system [35]. The systolic [36] and horizontal [37, 38] instruction types can be used in serial, parallel, or clustered types of concurrency. Bit-serial vector processing occurs in the Connection Machine [39].

TRENDS IN THE DESIGN OF PARALLEL COMPUTERS

Two fundamental trends in the design of parallel computers are illustrated in Figure 12: the tradeoff between speed and parallelism. Here we match the speed per processor against the number of processors per system, and *both* of these variables are increasing. The large-grain designs (such as the CRAY Y-MP and the ETA^{10}) use a small number of extremely fast processors, each of which is a supercomputer in its own right; the medium-grain designs (such as the Cedar Project at the University of Illinois and the Alliant on which it is based) use slower processors than the large-grain designs but more of them; and the fine-grain designs (such as the Connection Machine with its 2^{16} bit-serial processors) use even slower processors and even more of them. All three of these types of parallel computers are following the same dual-trend pattern: increasing the speed per processor and increasing the number of processors. The trend in speed per processor is driven largely by the advances in component technology noted above. It is rather early in the development of commercial parallel computers to be able to establish a trend in the increase in the number of processors from one generation to the next, but the trend in the CRAY X-MP and Y-MP product line is following a pattern of $P_t = P_0 \cdot 2^{t/3}$, i.e., the number of processors is being increased by a factor of 2 about every three years. On the other hand, the CRAY-2/CRAY-3 pattern (assuming the CRAY-3 plans are successful) would be $P_t = P_0 \cdot 4^{t/4}$, which is equivalent to a quadrupling every four years, and hence a somewhat faster rate of increase. It will take at least another generation of development of commercial parallel computers to determine an industry-wide trend in this pattern, however.

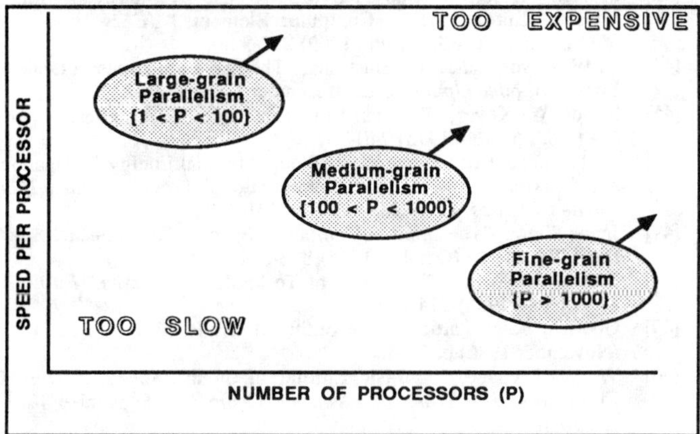

Figure 12. Trends in parallel computer design.

One way of viewing what is happening in high-performance computing is that the industry is going through a period of innovation, searching for the design of a definitive guidepost for parallel computers. Indeed, there may be more than one; for example, large-grain parallelism might be the guidepost for designs that are more general-purpose and fine-grain parallelism the guidepost for designs that are more special-purpose. The innovative period in the design of parallel computation began over 30 years ago, and the definitive guidepost has yet to be found, although there are dozens of competitors for this honor.

LONG-TERM PATTERNS OF CHANGE

In Table 6 we summarize some long-term trends in technologies in general and high-performance computing in particular.

Over the long term, all technologies increase in complexity, where complexity refers to the number of components in the system and their relationships. The first electronic computer, the ENIAC, had 18,000 active elements, whereas modern supercomputers have millions. However, "Technologies constantly strive towards the condition of transparency" [40], where transparency means the user can achieve the function of the technology without being concerned with the details of how the function is achieved—that is to say, its complexity. The user

CHARACTERISTICS	TRENDS
Complexity Transparency Efficiency	• *Increasing*
Cost Time Size	• *Decreasing for constant function* • *Constant for increasing function*
Discontinuities	• *History proceeds by changing the subject.*

Table 6. Long-term patterns of technological change.

interface of the Apple Macintosh is a well-known example of a transparent interface. Automatic vectorizing compilers increased the transparency of vectorization and compilers are being developed to do the same thing for parallel processing. Efficiency also tends to increase as a technology matures; the history of the steam engine is often presented in this way, and the history of computing can be similarly characterized. Architectural features that have increased the efficiency (measured in results generated per clock period) of high-performance computers have included lookahead, multiple functional units, pipelining, and vectorization.

Cost, time, and size share two long-term trends: they all decrease for constant functionality, and they remain constant for increasing functionality. For example, if we hold the problem size constant, then the run time decreases with new computer generations; if we hold the run time constant, then the problem complexity that can be solved in that time increases with new computer generations. Similar trends occur for system cost and size.

Finally, as noted earlier, in the long term it is necessary to be aware of discontinuities in technologies, for "History proceeds by changing the subject." [29].

LIMITS

All technologies have inherent limits to their improvement, so the study of limits is an important part of analyzing patterns of technological change, both in the short term as limits affect individual technologies and in the long term as limits might impose ultimate bounds on computational capabilities [22, 41-51]. A useful principle to keep in mind, however, is that fundamental limits of any given technology can often be dealt with successfully by changing to another technology. For example, it has been suggested that there is a fundamental limit in computer execution rate of about 10^{15} operations per second, beyond which computers would either implode down their own black hole or melt due to excessive heat generation [41]. However, given computers with that limit, a computational scientist would put P of them together, decompose problems so they could be executed more or less independently in P parallel streams, and thereby exceed the "limit" by a factor approaching P.

CONCLUSION

Because of space limitations, this essay on patterns of technological change has been limited to a brief discussion of hardware issues. A broader perspective would include not only further detail on trends in system hardware but also patterns of change in system software and applications, because the time required for solving problems is reduced by advances in all three of these information technologies. For example, it has been pointed out that in the period 1947 to 1984, progress in hardware contributed some five orders of magnitude to reduction in the solution time for the Poisson equation, but algorithmic improvements contributed an equal factor of improvement [52]. Ultimate limits to high-performance computation will not be reached until we can no longer improve any of the three generic high-performance computational technologies.

REFERENCES

[1] Alvin Toffler, *Future Shock*, Bantam Books, New York, 1970, p. 379.

[2] Kwang-chih Chang, *The Archeology of Ancient China*, 4th edition, Yale University Press, New Haven, 1986.

[3] H. W. Lanford, "A Penetration of the Technological Forecasting Jungle," *Technological Forecasting and Social Change*, **4** (1972) 207-225.

[4] Michel Godet, "Reducing the Blunders in Forecasting," *Futures*, **15**, 3 (June 1983) 181-192.

[5] Christopher Cerf and Victor Navasky, *The Experts Speak*, Pantheon Books, New York, 1984.

[6] Joseph P. Martino, *Technological Forecasting for Decision Making*, 2nd ed., North-Holland, New York, 1983, Chapter 2.

[7] Grabbe and Pyke, *Technological Forecasting and Social Change* **4**, (1972) 143-150.

[8] Donald A. Schon, "Forecasting and Technological Forecasting," *Daedalus*, Summer 1967, pp. 759-770.

[9] R. W. Hamming, "The Impact of Computers," *American Mathematical Monthly*, **72**, 2 (February 1965) 1-7.

[10] F. R. Bradbury, "The Economics of Technological Development," Chapter 3 in *A History of Technology*, Trevor I. Williams, ed.,Vol. VI, Part I, Clarendon Press, Oxford, 1978, pp. 48-76.

[11] Devendra Sahal, *Patterns of Technological Innovation*, Addison Wesley, Reading, MA, 1981.

[12] John Kemeny, *A Philosopher Looks at Science*, D. Van Nostrand, Princeton, 1959.

[13] Susan P. Gill, "The Paradox of Prediction," *Daedalus*, **115**, 3 (Summer 1986) 17-48.

[14] C. M. Osburn and Reisman, "Challenges in Advanced Semiconductor Technology for High-Performance Supercomputer Applications," *The Journal of Supercomputing*, **1**, 2 (1987) 149-189.

[15] Jeff Moad, *Datamation*, March 15, 1987, p. 22.

[16] E. W. Pugh, D. L. Critchlow, R. A. Henle, and L. A. Russell, "Solid-State Memory Development in IBM," *IBM Journal of Research and Development*, **25**, 5 (September 1981) 585-602.

[17] James A. Cunningham, "Using the Learning Curve as a Management Tool," *IEEE Spectrum*, June 1980, 45-48.

[18] Alan R. Fusfeld, "The Technological Progress Function: A New Technique for Forecasting," *Technological Forecasting*, **1** (1970) 301-312.

[19] Frank J. Andress, "The Learning Curve as a Production Tool," *Harvard Business Review*, Jan/Feb 1954, 87-97.

[20] Winfred B. Hirschmann, "Profit from the Learning Curve," *Harvard Business Review*, Jan/Feb 1964, 125-139.

[21] William J. Abernathy and Kenneth Wayne, "Limits of the Learning Curve," *Harvard Business Review*, Sept/Oct 1974, 109-119.

[22] James D. Meindl, "Chips for Advanced Computing," *Scientific American*, **257**, 4 (October 1987), 78-88.

[23] Mikio Itoh and Keiichiro Uchida, "Trends in Fujitsu Large-Scale Computer Technology," *Parallel Computing*, **5** (1987) 105-115.

[24] Katherine Wollard, "Solid State," *IEEE Spectrum*, **25**, 1 (January 1988) 44-45.

[25] (Anonymous), *IEEE Institute*, April 1985, p. 9.

[26] Geoffrey Bate, "The Limits of Magnetic Recording," *Digest of Papers, Compcon Spring 88*, February 29-March 4, 1988, 128-131.

[27] N. R. Morse, *C-Division Annual Review and Operating Plan*, Los Alamos National Laboratory Report LA-11216-MS, January 1988.

[28] Ralph Sanders, "Penetrating the Fog of Technology's Social Dimensions," *Technology in Society*, **9** (1987) 163-180.

[29] Ralf Dahrendorf, *The New Liberty*, pp. 13-14. Cited in Arnold Pacey, *The Culture of Technology*, MIT Press, Cambridge, MA, 1983, p. 33.

[30] Richard Foster, *Innovation: The Attacker's Advantage*, Summit Books, New York, 1986.

[31] Michael J. Flynn, "Some Computer Organizations and Their Effectiveness," *IEEE Trans. on Computers*, **C-21**, 9 (September 1972) 948-960.

[32] David J. Kuck, Edward S. Davidson, Duncan H. Lawrie, and Ahmed H. Sameh, "Parallel Supercomputing Today and the Cedar Approach," *Science*, **231** (28 February 1986) 967-974.

[33] Carl D. Howe, "An Overview of the Butterfly GP1000," *Proc. Third Int. Conf. on Supercomputing, 1988*, **2**, 134-131.

[34] Charles L. Seitz, "Concurrent VLSI Architectures," *IEEE Trans. on Computers*, **C-33**, 12 (December 1984) 1247-1265.

[35] Chris Thomson and Kent McPhee, "Experience Scaling the Myrias System to Hundreds of Processors," *Proc. Third Int. Conf. on Supercomputing, 1988*, **2**, 125-129.

[36] H. T. Kung, "Special-Purpose Supercomputers," *Proc. IFIP 1986 (Information Processing 86)*, H.-J. Kugler, ed., Elsevier, Amsterdam, 1986, pp. 565-570.

[37] B. R. Rau, "Cydra 5 Directed Dataflow Architecture" *Digest of Papers, IEEE Compcon 88*, February 29-March 4, 1988, 106-113.

[38] Joseph A. Fisher, "A New Architecture for Supercomputing," *Digest of Papers, IEEE Spring Compcon '87*, February 23-27, 1987, 177-180.

[39] W. D. Hillis, *The Connection Machine*, MIT Press, Cambridge, MA, 1985.

[40] Anthony Smith, "Technology, Identity, and the Infor-mation Machine," *Daedalus*, **115**, 3 (Summer 1986) 155-169.

[41] Jacob D. Bekenstein, "Energy Cost of Information Transfer," *Physical Review Letters*, **45**, 10 (9 March 1981), 623-626.

[42] Jan Davidse, "Characteristics of Growth and Limitations in Electronics," *Technological Forecasting and Social Change*, **24** (1983) 125-135.

[43] Marvin Freiser, Jr., and Paul M. Marcus, "A Survey of Some Physical Limitations on Computer Elements," *IEEE Trans. on Magnetics*, **MAG-5**, 2 (June 1969) 277-306.

[44] R. W. Keyes and J. A. Armstrong, "Thermal Limitations in Optical Logic," *Applied Optics*, **8**, 12 (December 1969) 2549-2552.

[45] Robert W. Keyes, "Physical Limits in Digital Electronics," *Proc. IEEE*, **63**, 5 (May 1975) 740-767.

[46] Rolf Landauer and James W. F. Woo, "Minimal Energy Dissipation and Maximal Error for the Computational Process, *Journal of Applied Physics*, **42, 6** (May 1971) 2301-2308.

[47] Janos Simon, "The Limit of Computing Speed," *Communications of the ACM*, **21**, 10 (October 1978) 876-877.

[48] Rias J. van Wyk, "The Notion of Technological Limits," *Futures*, **17**, 3 (June 1985) 214-223.

[49] Geoffrey Bate, "Particulate Recording Materials," *Proc. IEEE*, **74**, 11 (November 1986) p. 1524.

[50] W. W. Bledsoe, "A Basic Limitation on the Speed of Digital Computers," *IRE Trans. on Electronic Computers*, September 1961, p. 530.

[51] James D. Meindl, "Ultra-large Scale Integration," *IEEE Trans. Electron Devices*, **ED-31**, 11 (November 1984) 1555-1561.

[52] Jon Bentley, "Programming Pearls," *Communications of the ACM*, **27**, 11 (November 1984) 1087-1092.

THE CONVEX C240 ARCHITECTURE

- Mike Chastain, Gary Gostin, Jim Mankovich and Steve Wallach

CONVEX Computer Corporation
Richardson, Texas

ABSTRACT

The C240, a tightly coupled, shared memory, parallel/multi-processor, supports up to 4, 40-nanosecond ECL/CMOS Cray-like processors. Managed by a fully semaphored UNIX operating the C240, it can support up to 4 gigabytes of directly addressable physical memory. CONVEX proprietary compiler technology provides automatic vectorization and parallelization for FORTRAN, C, and ADA. Allocation of parallel threads to physical processors is managed by an innovation approach ASAP (Automatic Self-Allocating Processors). ASAP dynamically allocates and deallocates parallel threads to the processors.

In creating a second generation supercomputer, several factors were considered prior to commencing design. Among these factors are:

1) Performance - Scalar/Vector/Parallel.

2) Parallel processing efficiency.

3) Semiconductor technology.

4) Compiler optimization strategies.

With these factors in mind, the C240 system evolved. The salient features of the C240 are:

1) Tightly coupled, MIMD processor system. Where each processor, up to 4, is a general purpose scientific processor, with a 4 gigabyte virtual address space. Operands are addressed at the byte level.

2) Each processor is a 40 nanosecond, ECL/CMOS implementation of the CONVEX C1, Cray-like, instruction set architecture (see WALLACH 85). Additional instructions were added, in a super-set manner using pre-existing spare opcodes. These instructions provide vector conversions, vector shifts, vector square root, and fully pipelined operations under mask. Additional scalar instructions were added mainly in the area of intrinsics: Sin, Cos, etc.

A set of parallel processing instructions was also added and will be discussed in more detail later.

3) A very high bandwidth, 800 mbytes/sec, multiported memory system capable of supporting up to 4 gigabytes of directly addressable physical memory.

4) Revisions of CONVEX's proprietary compiler technology that support automatic parallelism for Fortran, C and ADA.

5) A fully semaphored UNIX kernel. The UNIX kernel was modified extensively to support multiple simultaneous system calls to different resources and the management of CONVEX's parallel processing paradigm.

6) Lastly, a new and innovative concept for the allocation and scheduling of parallel processes and threads is supported. This unique concept, ASAP, (Automatic Self-Allocating Processors), is a distributed mechanism that permits physical processors to dynamically associate and disassociate themselves from an executing process.

TIGHTLY COUPLED MIMD PROCESSOR SYSTEM

Figure 1 is a block system diagram of the C240 system. Up to 4 processors are supported. One processor is a minimum, with additional processors inserted into the mechanical cavities provided. The memory system supports a tightly coupled, shared processor structure. There are 5 physical ports to the memory system. Each port supports 64-bit data transfer (plus byte parity), every 40 nanoseconds. Each physical port interfaces to the memory system via a non-blocking crossbar mechanism.

The functionality and structure of the crossbar is as follows:

1) Simultaneous access by all 5 ports to different memory banks.

2) The crossbar is distributed across the memory modules. That is there is *no* functional unit called a crossbar. But, on each memory module, there are VLSI gate arrays that implement the crossbar function. Within each crossbar gate array there are two levels of

CH2617-9/88/0000/0321$01.00 © 1988 IEEE

pipelining per access port. This optimizes pipelined memory accesses should a bank conflict occur. That is, if two or more simultaneous references occur to the same memory bank, fifo buffering within the crossbar obviates the need for the requester to reissue the request (commonly referred to as a camp-on feature of digital PBX's).

This permits physical memory is to be kept as busy as possible under all circumstances of pipelined loads and stores for both scalar and vector operations.

The I/O bus is capable of sustaining up to 200 mbytes/sec of data transfer, read or write. Two separate adaptors from this bus generate the CONVEX C1's (CONVEX's original supercomputer) 80 mbytes/sec I/O bus. The 80 mbytes/sec bus, Input/Output processors support both VME and Multibus I/O busses.

Directly supporting multiprocessing and parallel processing are a set of shared, multiported communication registers (1024 x 64 bits wide). These registers, implemented in high speed static ECL rams, provide single cycle access to their contents. Additionally, atomic accesses to these registers are provided. These registers generally contain iteration values, address offsets and other parameters used to support automatic parallelization provided by the CONVEX compilers. They also contain process information necessary for automatic thread creation, deletion, and scheduling. A thread is a sequence of instructions that represents the smallest schedulable entity.

PROCESSOR DETAILS

Each processor implements the C240 (see figure 2) instruction set. The C240 instruction supports a general purpose scientific environment. There is a 4 gigabyte directly addressable, virtual address space. Hardware vector operations are provided for integer *1, *2, *4, *8, real *4, and real *8. Manipulations of these operands are supported by the CONVEX compilers (Fortran, C, and ADA) resulting in compiler support of integer *1, *2, *4, *8, logical *1, *2, *4, *8, real *4, real *8, complex *8, and complex *16.

Each processor is a 5 board implementation of the CONVEX architecture. The major cycle time is 40 nanoseconds, with many operations occurring in 20 nanoseconds. Two types of semiconductor technology are used.

The scalar portion of the processor is built using 100K ECL air-cooled logic. The scalar unit uses 3000, 4500, and 10,000 ECL gate arrays manufactured by Fujitsu. The scalar unit is microprogram controlled. The control store is built using static rams. Upon power up, the microcode is loaded from an integrated 5-1/4 inch winchester.

There are separate, highly pipelined scalar functional units for floating point add, multiply, divide/square root, load/store, as well as for address generation and integer arithmetic. A multiported register simultaneously permits up to 3 reads and 4 writes. Scalar floating point can execute concurrently with vector floating point.

There are three caches; instruction, scalar data, and virtual address (sometimes referred to as an address translation unit). Instructions are fetched and decoded from a 8 kbyte logical instruction cache. Scalar data is loaded from or stored into a 4 kbyte, write through logical cache. That is, the association is on logical addresses, permitting single cycle access. Due to the high performance of the main memory system, the scalar data cache is treated as a look-aside structure. Thus, if a cache miss occurs, there is no extra time needed to initiate access to main memory. The third and last cache is for addresses. The address translation unit (ATU) contains the last 1024 logical to physical address translations.

The vector unit is built using 20,000 gate CMOS arrays for arithmetic functions and a mix of 3000 and 4500 ECL gate arrays for bus arbitration and data multiplexing. There are three separate and unique vector units or pipes; load/store, add/subtract/logical, multiply/divide/square root. Each pipe has its own static ram microprogram control unit. There are 8 vector registers, each 64 bits wide by 128 elements deep. Sufficient data paths exist for the vector accumulators to sustain up to 2.4 gigabytes/sec of arithmetic processing.

Fully asynchronous chaining between functional units is supported. Loads and stores from one vector accumulator will chain with arithmetic processing with other vector accumulators. Loads and stores from one vector accumulator will execute concurrently with arithmetic processing referencing a separate set of vector accumulators (e.g., load V0 [Vector Register 0] executes concurrently with ADD V1 to V2 and store the result into V3). Vector dispatch hardware dynamically schedules these instructions as they are decoded.

All vector loads and stores directly reference main memory. There is *no* use of the scalar cache during vector operations. If during a vector store a previously encached scalar operand is referenced, its cache location is marked invalid. Thus, any subsequent scalar loads referencing this operand must first load the operand into the scalar cache.

Page faults during the execution of a vector load or store are fully supported. When a page fault is detected (as indicated by a bit in a page table entry), arithmetic processing continues until all outstanding memory references have been completed. Then the internal processor machine state is saved within a process control block allocated by the operating system. The internal processor state includes registers and flags that are *not* visible or accessible to the programmer. Programmer visible state is explicitly saved by the operating system. The operating system resolves the page fault and then resumes execution of the faulted process. This is accomplished by the operating system exiting the page fault handler by executing the *return from context block* instruction.

For example, if a page fault occurred while referencing the 53rd element of a 100 element vector load, after 52 elements are loaded into the destination vector accumulator, a page fault exception occurs. After its resolution, execution resumes by loading the 53rd element.

To enhance the support of 32 bit floating point computations, two 32-bit vector load instructions are executed in the same time as one 64-bit vector load. This generally increases the performance of 32-bit programs, by 20 - 30% over 64-bit applications.

To fully support the vectorization of DO loops with IF statements, the vector processing unit supports full speed operations under mask. This is done by modifying selective elements of the destination register according to the status of bits of the VM register. Chaining, with results produced every 40 ns, is supported for operations under mask. The VM register is 128 bits in length. A set of vector compare instructions load the value of this register.

Two strategies were analyzed as to the method by which operations under mask would be implemented. The first strategy was to always have all vector operations work under mask. The compiler would load a mask of all 1's for DO loops without IF statements. This strategy was not chosen. Extra instructions for DO loops without IF statements and the need for inverting the VM register for the complementary part of the IF...THEN...ELSE resulted in the choice the second strategy.

The second strategy and the one implemented was to extend the vector instruction set with operations executed under VM and the complemented value of VM (VM itself is not changed). This is in addition to vector instructions that ignore the VM Register. Thus, for the following simple loop:

```
DO i = 1,N
IF (A(i).EQ.B(i)) THEN
        Z(i) = X(i) + Y(i)
ELSE
        Z(i) — X(i) - Y(i)
ENDIF
ENDDO
```

The compiler generated code is as follows (without scalar and loop overhead instructions):

```
Load A,V0
Load B,V1
EQUAL V0,V1          ; Set VM Register
Load X,V0
Load Y,V1
ADD.T V0,V1,V2       ; THEN part
SUB.F V0,V1,V2       ; ELSE part merged with THEN part
Store V2,Z           ; Store Z away
```

The above sequence takes 5 chimes (a chime is the time to execute a chained operation) to execute. The subtract under complemented VM (SUB.F) chains into the store.

Due to the availability of 4 separate and unique control stores, as well as an independently controlled instruction processing unit for branches and coupled with pipelined scalar floating point units, the compiler adopts an instruction scheduling strategy that results in 6 to 10 assembly language instructions executing at any given time. This results in very high performance scalar and vector processing.

COMPILER TECHNOLOGY

The CONVEX compiler technology (see MERCER 88), is based on a common global optimizer supporting multiple front ends. Each front end produces a common intermediate language that is a global data flow representation of a program. This structure (figure 3) has proven to be very robust and easily extended to support additional languages.

When automatic vectorization and parallelization is requested by the user, a comprehensive dependency analysis is performed. Based on Banajee's inequality and supplemented by other mechanisms, this analysis has proven to achieve extremely high levels of automatic vectorization and parallelism. In a recent evaluation, the C240 series Fortran compiler achieved the highest level of automatic vectorization as compared to other vendors of vectorizing compilers (see CALLAHAN 88).

For automatic parallelization, this dependency analysis identifies loops with no loop carried dependencies, (see ALLEN 83). For these loops, parallel code can be generated with no synchronization between iterations. Loops, with loop carried dependencies, are transformed into DO ACROSS loops and then executed in parallel with synchronization between iterations. It is very important to recognize the tradeoffs between parallelization and vectorization. There are a class of loops that should be vectorized but not parallelized when synchronization is required. For example:

```
DO i — 1, N
A(i) = A(i + 1) + B(i)
END DO
```

The CONVEX compilers use sophisticated cost/benefit analysis to decide whether to vectorize, parallelize, or both, should the opportunity arise. When parallelization is automatically detected, several innovative code generation strategies are supported. These strategies are as follows:

Code is generated independent of the number of physical processors within a C240 system. Thus, only one executable parallel image is required. As physical processors are added, performance can increase without requiring recompilation.

An optimization, called variable strip-mining, is also implemented to reduce the number of synchronization points and communication register accesses. Thus, for the following nested loops:

```
DO j = 1,N
          DO i = 1,N
          A(i,j) = 0
          END DO
END DO
```

The code generated and executed for a 4 processor complex would behave as if these loops were structured as:

```
DO j = 1, N/4              DO j = N/4 + 1, N/2
   DO i = 1,N                 DO i = 1,N
   A(i,j) = 0                 A(i,j) = 0
   END DO                     END DO
END DO                     END DO
```

That is, sub-matrices (block partitioning) are constructed as opposed to column at a time scheduling. This allows more work to be performed per thread and minimizes parallelization overhead.

Another code generation strategy is called dynamic selection. In an attempt to maximize multi-user throughput and in support of the ASAP scheduling philosophy the compiler only generates parallel code when there is a performance to be gained. However, under some circumstances, parameters necessary for this decision are only known at execution time.

Consider the following trivial loop:

```
Read *,N
DO i = 1,N
   A(i) = B(i) + C(i)
END DO
```

Depending upon the value of N, either scalar (N being very small, less than 6), vector (N being between 7 and 32), or parallel (N being greater than 32) different code is executed. This feature optimizes both single user performance, as well as, multi-user. That is, if parallel is not necessary, the program does not go parallel and tie up processors that are not needed.

UNIX OPERATING SYSTEM

The CONVEX UNIX (see MANKOVICH 88) is an implementation of 4.2 BSD, with most of the 4.3 extensions and enhancements supported.

Major enhancements to the 4.2 distribution are implemented to maximize performance and provide easy access to the capability of the C240 architecture.

Currently, user transparent disk striping, dynamic disk buffer cache, and real-time capabilities are but some of the extensions provided.

In support of the symmetric multiprocessing capabilities of the C240, a substantial rewrite of the UNIX kernel was necessary. The major areas of modification were in the scheduler and semaphoring kernel tables that deal with resource sharing and file management.

Additional capabilities had to be added to support the parallel processing ASAP feature.

AUTOMATIC SELF-ALLOCATING PROCESSORS (ASAP)

As part of the design effort, several objectives were established for the parallel processing aspects of the design. These were:

1) Support of fine grain parallelism from the statement level up through the loop level.

2) Support of parallelism at the coarse level in a MIMD type of operation. Examination of programs like Gaussian (molecular electronic structure calculation) and Spice (circuit simulation) indicate opportunity for parallelism at the coarse level. Typically these programs have structures of the type.

```
DO i = 1,N
          Call Subroutine
END DO
```

Where the subroutine, in fact, represents several pages of FORTRAN and involves additional subroutine calls. In the above case, each iteration is executed on a different processor, with multiple subroutine calls and multiple regions of scalar and vector processing.

3) Generalize the abstraction of the tightly coupled processor complex, so that there is no distinction between parallel processing and multiprocessing.

4) Dynamically control the allocation of processors to processes and threads. That is, as a program runs, processors are allocated and deallocated as

a function of compiler and operating system strategies, much in the same manner as physical memory is dynamically allocated and deallocated to a virtual memory process. The compiler strategies deal with the number of iterations that are expected to run in parallel. The operating system strategies deal with the parallel regions (generated by the compiler). The operating system establishes the environment by which this can be accomplished. Part of this environment includes allocation of a stack for each parallel region, timing the execution of each parallel region, and handling page faults for each parallel region. Others (see KUCK 87) have proposed similar allocation strategies.

Consequently, CONVEX has developed an approach called ASAP, Automatic Self-Allocating Processors. The implementation of this approach follows.

Within the C240 Series architecture there are a special series of instructions, such as, spawn, join, get, put, increment, etc. These instructions access values kept in the shared communication register set.

When a parallel region is detected by the compiler, a thread is created. A thread is the series of instructions that represent the smallest schedulable entity. This results in all idle processors (the number responding is not fixed) responding to the spawn. Since all generated code is reentrant, all idle processors begin executing parallel threads. A thread initiates execution with its own values of the program counter and stack management registers. When a parallel region is exited, all threads, on all processors, asynchronously and independently execute join instructions. The last processor executing the join continues to execute the subsequent scalar part of the program.

When a join is finished executing on a processor, the processor becomes free to execute other threads or processes of different programs. When a join is executed by other than the last processor, the processor self-schedules itself through dispatch queues maintained in the communications registers.

The interaction of the ASAP mechanism, compiler, and architecture is now described in more detail. First a discussion of the communication register and virtual address translation mechanisms followed by an example of the instruction sequences executed for a sample parallelized loop.

Each processor is connected via a shared access bus to a set of shared communication registers. See Figure 1. These communication registers are accessed by special atomic instructions which treat the register set as a separate address space. Memory reference instructions and communication register instructions both develop an effective address through the addition of a general address register to an immediate offset. This effective address, produced by the address generator, is then modified as a function of two special registers, the Communication Index Register (CIR) and the Thread Identifier (TID), to produce either a physical communication register address or a physical memory address respectively.

The Communication Index Register (CIR) is an index to one of N identical partitions of the communication register set, each of which contains the current state of a single UNIX process. See Figure 6. Thus, the CIR is, in essence, a virtual process identifier which is managed by the CPU, either under the direction of UNIX or automatically via the ASAP mechanism. A process whose state is currently represented by a partition of the communication register set is said to "mounted" on the processing complex. Any CPU can execute any mounted process by simply switching its CIR register to the partition describing the process.

A user process views a single set of communication registers and performs atomic operations on this set to effect communication and synchronization between portions of the process which are allowed to execute in parallel on multiple CPUs. The CIR, which is not accessible to the user, defines the mapping from the communication register virtual addresses generated by the process to a particular physical register set. The operating system, and the hardware ASAP mechanism, may access the communication registers "virtually", i.e. under control of the current CIR, or physically. This permits multiple processes to simultaneously execute parallel threads. A thread never references a communication register by its physical address.

A CPU may exist in one of two states: Active or Idle. An active CPU is busy executing on behalf of the process selected by the CPU's CIR. In a conventional UNIX environment, an Idle CPU is actually executing the UNIX scheduling loop, waiting for some event to make a process ready to run. The CONVEX UNIX scheduler is only executed when there are processes ready to run and idle CPUs on which to run them or when processes are released from suspended states; there is no "idle loop". An Idle CPU is defined as a CPU which has no process context. These idle CPUs continually poll all partitions of the communication registers, searching for a process in need of compute power or a pending interrupt. If there are additional "unmounted" processes ready to run, the UNIX scheduler will be mounted as a process and will be requesting processor resources via the ASAP mechanism just as any other process. When a CPU resource becomes available, the scheduler will mount another process. The CPU complex is completely symmetrical and all CPU resources are dynamically scheduled by the ASAP mechanism to achieve very fine-grain load balancing without operating system intervention.

Mounted processes may request and relinquish CPU resources totally independent of the UNIX scheduler. CPUs may enter a process, execute on behalf of the process, and exit to the Idle state without ever entering or notifying the operating system. When a CPU enters a process, the ASAP mechanism creates a unique context consisting of the program counter, stack pointer, frame pointer and argument pointer passed by the process plus a unique identifier. This dynamically created context is called a Thread. The dynamic Thread Identifier, contained in the TID register, uniquely identifies the thread if the thread should enter the operating system for a system service, exception handling, or due to an interrupt. CONVEX UNIX handles such events on a thread basis, i.e. the remainder of the process may continue execution.

Memory addresses are a function of both the CIR, which identifies the process and its respective virtual to physical memory address translation, as well as the TID. The TID modifies the virtual to physical address translation for the thread to allow each thread of a process to have private physical storage for unshared variables. See Figure 7. Since threads are created and terminated by the ASAP mechanism, independent of the operating system, the hardware must perform the equivalent of dynamic memory allocation. At the time a parallelized process is mounted, the operating system defines a "pool" of available thread identifiers within the processes' communication registers. The operating system also marks the address translation descriptors (in physical memory) for all pages which are to be private, per thread of execution, and allocates a page of storage for each TID in the "pool" for each unshared page. The ASAP mechanism then allocates TIDs and corresponding unshared storage from this pool as CPUs enter and exit the process.

The communication register address space is illustrated in Figure 6. A given implementation of the C-Series architecture contains N sets of communication registers with $P+1<N<MAX$ where P is the number of processors in the complex and MAX is an architecturally defined upper limit. Each set maintains the context of a process. This allows one set to be allocated for interrupt context, one for the UNIX scheduler, and at least one per physical processor. Each set of communication registers is further divided into three expandable regions; one for the ASAP hardware mechanism and one each for UNIX and user process communication and synchronization. The UNIX and user areas consist of a set of general purpose 64-bit registers each of which has an associated lock/valid bit. Instructions are provided to manipulate the data portion and the lock/valid bit separately or as a mailbox with atomic lock. The data portion can be treated as either a word (32-bit) or longword (64-bit) operand.

The memory address space of the C240 is illustrated in Figure 7. The three MSB's of the logical address select one of the SDRs (Segment Descriptor Register) from the communication register set selected by the current CIR. The selected SDR provides the base address of the first level page table in main memory. Translation proceeds in a conventional manner with each page table entry providing the base address of the next page, unless the level 2 page table entry enables unshared thread memory for the respective page. In this case, the level 2 entry specifies the base address of the data page. The level T table is then indexed by the TID register to find the base address of the unshared data page. This translation sequence is somewhat involved. However, the processor encaches the most recent level 2 or level T entries allowing all but one translation for a page to proceed in a single clock cycle.

The following loop is now used to present how these mechanisms are used to support parallelism.

```
DO i = 1,N
    A(i) = B(i) + C(i)
ENDDO
```

The compiler generates the following instruction sequence:

```
Instruction
1.       ESTABLISH Parallel Stripmine Value
2.       SND NEG(S0), Com_Reg_1  ;Send and lock a comm. register.
3.       PUT S1, Com_Reg_2       ;vector length
4.       SPAWN L1,SP             ;Post parallel event.
5.  L1;  LD Com_Reg_2,S1         ;Establish address offset
6.            INC S1, Com_Reg_1  ;Next offset return value to S1. Atomic op.
7.            Use S1 for address calculations
8.            LD C, V0
9.            LD B, V1
10.           ADD V0,V1,V2
11.           ST V2, A
12.           Branch Back To L1 if stripmine is complete.
13.           JOIN
14.      UNLOCK Com_Reg_1        ;Unlock address offset synchronization register.
```

Instruction 1 is a sequence of instructions that establish the parallel stripmine factor to be used for this particular loop. This value is loaded into register S0. Instruction 2 sends the negated value to communication register 1 and locks this register. All further references to this register use atomic fetch and add type of instructions. The compiler establishes, globally, which register is used. Instruction 3 saves this block stripmine factor in Com_Reg_2. (This register need not be locked. Its contents are read only). Instruction 4 spawns (attempts) multiple threads. The branch address is to the next sequential instruction. The spawn instruction establishes a stack for the thread defined by instructions 5-13. Architecturally defined registers in the communication register set are accessed and modified. The spawn posts the desire for all idle processors (current or to be) to participate in the execution of this process. There is an architecturally defined communication register which keeps track of the number of processors participating. All references to unshared data in subsequent instructions use the thread ID created by this instruction. Instruction 5 loads the stripmine length into register S1. Instruction 6 atomically increments the parallel strip being used, and returns the incremented value. So if N were initially 1000, 4 parallel strip of length 250 are created. (Note: by initializing Com_Reg_1 to -250 the first execution of the increment instruction results in the value 0. On successive iterations the values: 0, 250, 500, and 750 are used as the base offsets for address calculations. In all cases the vector length is 250 and, in effect, the values of i are 1-250, 251-500, 501-750, and 751-1000. Instructions 7-11 implement the DO loop. Instruction sequence 12 branches back to instruction 5 if all the iterations are exhausted, otherwise the next instruction is executed. Instruction 13, the JOIN, decrements the thread count by 1. If the new count is 1, this processor executes the subsequent serial portion of the program. If the new count is not 1, then other processors are still working on threads. Thus, a search of the communication registers occurs by the processor just idled. This search looks for other processes that have events posted. If none exist, the search continues. Instruction 14 unlocks the communication register set in instruction 2. At this time only the processor executing the JOIN with a thread count of 1 is proceeding. Subsequent instructions execute the serial portion of the process.

When additional hardware processors respond to the spawn they begin executing at statement label L1. The initial instructions always obtain the current stripmine value and address offset. This permits addresses to be calculated for the next block partition. Additional processors or threads initiate execution asynchronously with respect to all other executing threads. Thus, one thread can page fault while other threads of the same process continue to execute.

These hardware and software attributes result in the following parallel/multi processing paradigm.

With a static allocation approach (i.e., the program always has a fixed number of processors attached to it), a multi-user profile could look as depicted in figure 4. With the ASAP approach the profile in figure 5 results. Looking at this profile, we observe that single-job performance is not sacrificed and multi-user performance is greatly enhanced. Also, two or more jobs can run in parallel at the same time. From an architectural viewpoint, there are no restrictions as to the number of processors or number of jobs that can run in parallel or supported by the system software.

Another benefit of this approach is that the operating system has a single, generalized, view of the processor resources. There is no notion of time spent behaving as a parallel processor or as a multiprocessor. Lastly, through the use of user priority levels, the operating system determines the amount of processor resources allocated to a given program. Thus, even though a processor may demand additional processors to participate in a parallel region, actual priorities may result in the process running serial. The number of processors attached to a parallel process can vary from run to run. Capabilities are provided, via priorities, for all processors to eventually associate themselves with a running parallel process (maximum parallelism).

CONCLUSION

The CONVEX C240 supercomputer represents a new generation of parallel processors. Through the use of high density VLSI, vectorizing and parallelizing compilers, and an innovative scheduling approach, ASAP, users are provided with a high throuhgput parallel and multi-user environment. Furthermore, all these system features are accessible in a very easy to use, highly interactive virtual memory UNIX implementation.

References

[ALLEN 83] Allen, J. R., "Dependence Analysis for Subscripted Variable and its Application to Program Transformations", Ph.D Dissertation, Rice University, Houston, Texas, April 1, 1983.

[CALLAHAN 88] Callahan, Dongarra, Levine, "Vectorizing Compilers: A Test Suite and Results", Argonne National Laboratories, Illinois, ANL-MCS-TM-109, March 1988.

[KUCK 87] Kuck, D. J., and Polychronopoulous, C. D., "Guided Self-Scheduling: A Practical Scheme for Parallel Supercomputers", IEEE Transaction on Computers, December 1987, Vol. C-36, Number 12, pages 1425-1439.

[MANKOVICH 88] Mankovich, J., "The CONVEX C200 UNIX", Third International Conference on Supercomputing, Boston, Mass. May 1988.

[MERCER 88] Mercer, Randall, "The CONVEX Fortran 5.0 Compiler", Third International Conference on Supercomputing", Boston, Mass. May, 1988.

[WALLACH 85] Wallach, Steven J., "The CONVEX C-1 64-bit Supercomputer", Spring CompCon '88, February 1985.

Figures

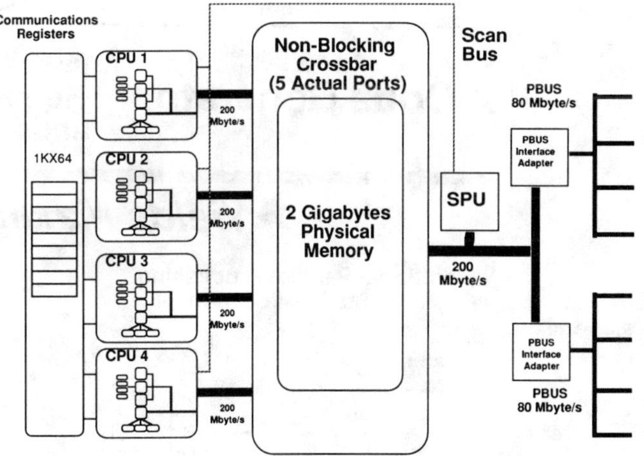

Figure 1

C210 - C240 Vector Processor

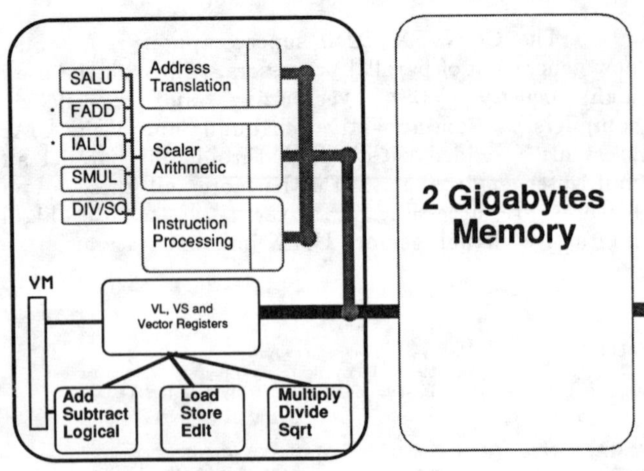

- *Multiple functional units*
- *Chaining of vector instructions*
- *Cache bypass*
- *Fully Pipelined Operations Under Mask*

Figure 2

Automatically Takes Advantage of Hardware

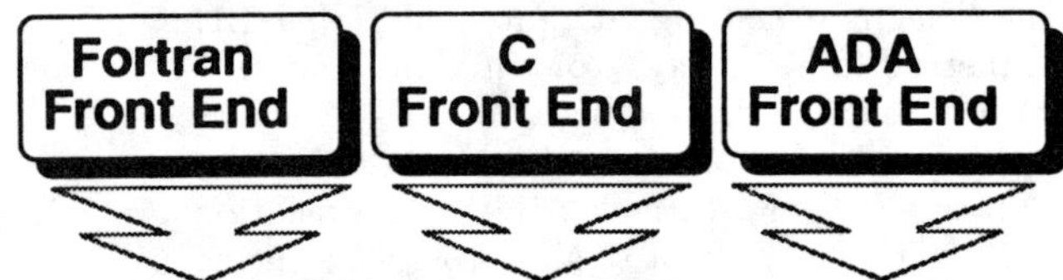

✓ Optimizer
- Performs In-line Subroutine Expansion
- Automatically Detects All Data Dependencies
- Computes Profit of Vectorization/Parallelization

✓ Code Generator
- Analyzes Timing of Instruction Sequences
- Runtime Selection between Scalar, Vector and Parallel Code

➤ Yields Maximum Performance

Figure 3

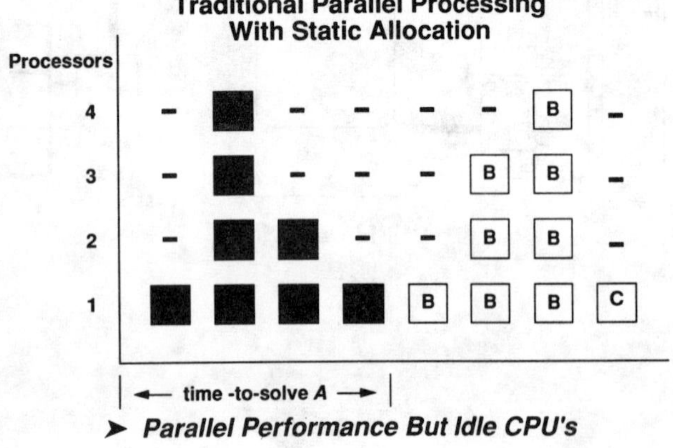

➤ Parallel Performance But Idle CPU's

Figure 4

CONVEX ASAP Scheduling

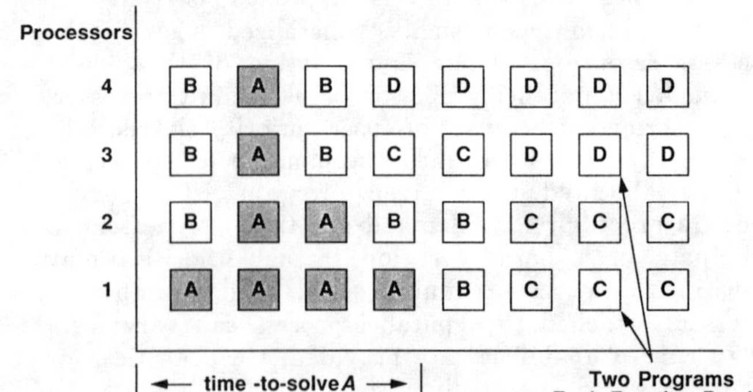

Figure 5

COMMUNICATION REGISTER STRUCTURE

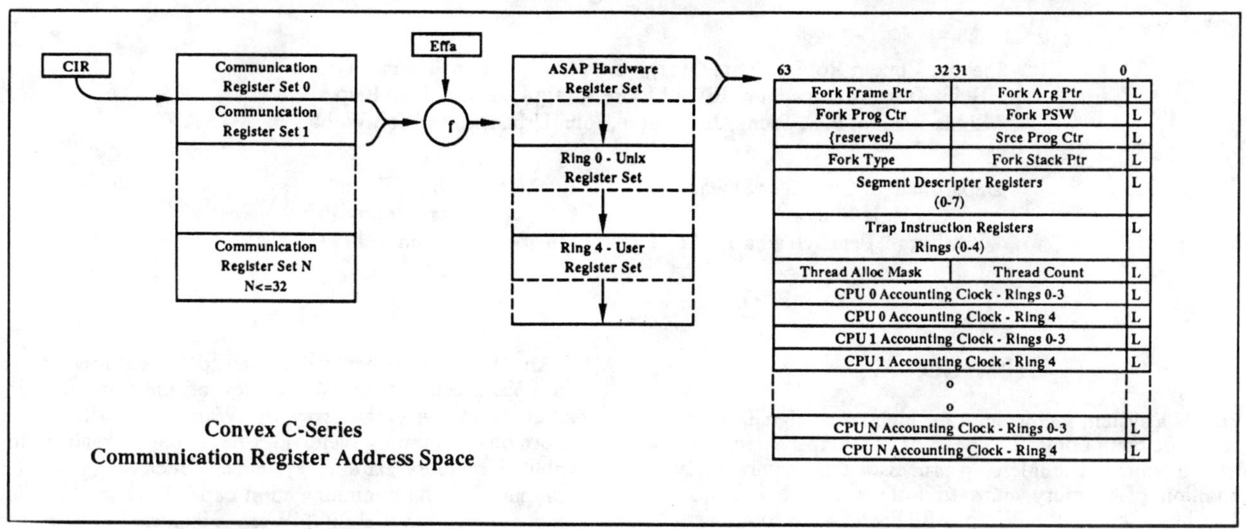

Figure 6

MANAGING STACKS AND MEMORY

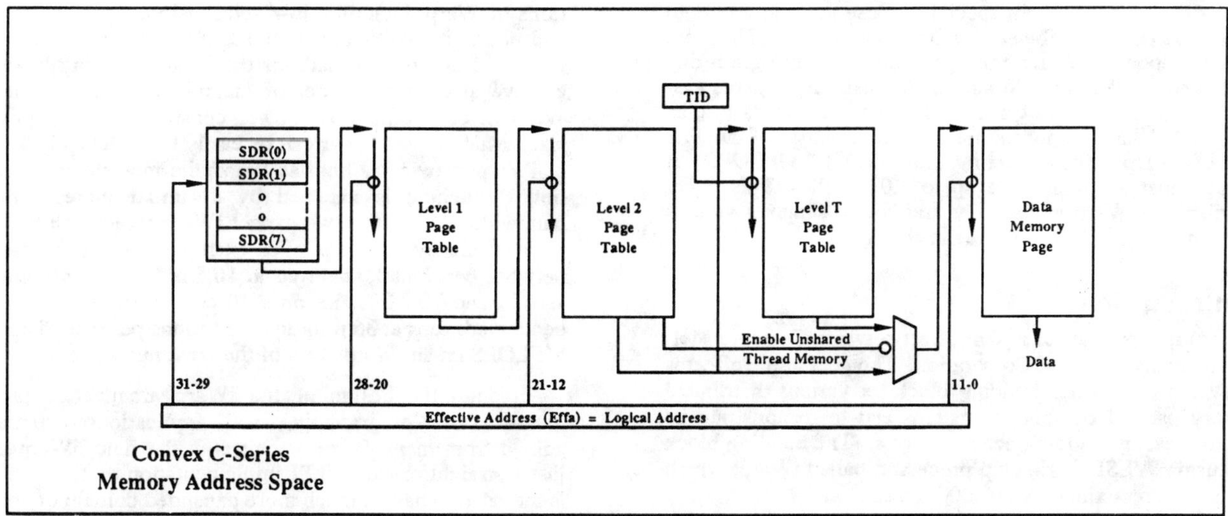

Figure 7

iWarp: An Integrated Solution to High-Speed Parallel Computing

Shekhar Borkar, Robert Cohn, George Cox, Sha Gleason, Thomas Gross,
H. T. Kung, Monica Lam, Brian Moore, Craig Peterson, John Pieper,
Linda Rankin, P. S. Tseng, Jim Sutton, John Urbanski, and Jon Webb

Department of Computer Science
Carnegie Mellon University
Pittsburgh, Pennsylvania 15213

Intel Corporation, JF1-60
5200 N.E. Elam Young Pkwy
Hillsboro, Oregon 97124

Abstract

iWarp is a system architecture for high speed signal, image and scientific computing. The heart of an iWarp system is the iWarp component: a single chip processor that requires only the addition of memory chips to form a complete system building block, called the iWarp cell. Each iWarp component contains both a powerful computation engine (20 MFLOPS) and a high throughput (320 MBytes/sec), low latency (100-150 ns) communication engine for interfacing with other iWarp cells. Because of its strong computation and communication capabilities, the iWarp component is a versatile building block for various high performance parallel systems. These systems range from special purpose systolic arrays to general purpose distributed memory computers. They are able to support both fine-grain parallel and coarse-grain distributed computation models simultaneously in the same system. An iWarp system can include a large number of cells; the initial iWarp demonstration system consists of an 8×8 torus of iWarp cells, delivering more than 1.2 GFLOPS. It can be expanded to include up to 1,024 cells. This paper describes the iWarp architecture and how it supports various communication models and system configurations.

1. Introduction

iWarp is a product of a joint effort between Carnegie Mellon University and Intel Corporation. The goal of the effort is to develop a powerful building block for various distributed memory parallel computing systems and to demonstrate its effectiveness by building actual systems. The building block is a custom VLSI single chip processor, called iWarp, which consists of approximately 600,000 transistors.

The iWarp component contains both a powerful computation processor (20 MFLOPS) and a high throughput (320 MBytes/sec), low latency (100-150 ns) communication engine. Using nonpipelined floating-point units, the computation processor will sustain high computation speed for vectorizable as well as non-vectorizable codes.

The research was supported in part by Defense Advanced Research Projects Agency (DOD) monitored by the Space and Naval Warfare Systems Command under Contract N00039-87-C-0251.

Authors' affiliations: S. Borkar, G. Cox, S. Gleason, B. Moore, C. Peterson, L. Rankin, J. Sutton, J. Urbanski: Intel Corporation; R. Cohn, T. Gross, H. T. Kung, M. Lam, J. Pieper, P. S. Tseng, J. Webb: Carnegie Mellon University

An iWarp component connected to a local memory forms an iWarp cell; up to 64 MBytes of memory are directly addressable. A large array of iWarp cells will deliver an enormous computing bandwidth never before realized in distributed memory parallel systems. Because of the strong computation and communication capabilities and because of its commercial availability, iWarp is expected to be an important building block for a diverse set of high performance parallel systems.

The iWarp architecture evolved from the Warp machine [1], a programmable systolic array developed at Carnegie Mellon and produced by General Electric. All applications of Warp, including low-level vision, signal processing, and neural network simulation [2, 18], can run efficiently on iWarp. But systems made of the iWarp building block can achieve at least one order of magnitude improvement over Warp in cost, reliability, power consumption, and physical size. Much larger arrays can be easily built. The clock speed of iWarp is twice as high as Warp; the increase in computation throughput is matched by a similar increase in I/O bandwidth. Therefore we expect iWarp to achieve the same high efficiency as Warp. For example, the NETtalk neural network benchmark [20] runs at 16.5 million connections per second and 70 MFLOPS on a 10 cell Warp array; the same benchmark runs at 36 million connections per second and 153 MFLOPS on an iWarp array of the same number of cells.

Although the design of the iWarp architecture profited greatly from programming and applications experiences gained from many Warp machines in the field, iWarp is not just a straightforward VLSI implementation of Warp. iWarp is intended to have a much more expanded domain of applications than Warp. The following summarizes the goals of iWarp as a system building block:

- iWarp is useful for the implementation of both special purpose arrays, which require high computation and I/O bandwidth, and general purpose arrays where programmability and programming support are essential.
- iWarp is useful for both high performance processors attached to general purpose hosts and autonomous processor arrays capable of performing all the computation and I/O by themselves. That is, iWarp can be used for both "host centric" and "array centric" processing.
- iWarp supports both tightly and loosely coupled parallel processing, and both systolic [12] and message passing models of communication.

- iWarp can implement a variety of processor interconnection topologies including 1-dimensional (1D) arrays, rings, 2-dimensional (2D) arrays, and tori.
- iWarp is intended for systems of various sizes ranging from several processors to thousands of processors.

This paper will explain how the iWarp architecture addresses these objectives.

Besides conventional high level languages such as C and FORTRAN, the programming of iWarp arrays will be supported by programming tools such as parallel program generators. Previous experience and current research on Warp indicates that parallel program generators are one of the most promising approaches to programming distributed memory parallel computers. In this approach, a specialized, machine independent language is created, which embodies a particular parallel computation model (for example, input partitioning, domain partitioning, or task-queuing [13]). The compiler for that language then maps the program onto a target parallel architecture. This approach can allow efficient parallel programs to be generated automatically for large processor arrays.

Automatic parallel program generators have been developed for iWarp in two applications areas: scientific computing and image processing. The scientific computing language, called AL (Array Language) [21], incorporates the domain partitioning model and allows programmers to transfer data between a common space and a partitioned space, perform computation in parallel in the partitioned space, and then transfer data back. For scientific routines such as those found in LINPACK [5], the AL compiler generates efficient code for iWarp and Warp, as well as for uniprocessors. The image processing language, called Apply [9], incorporates the input partitioning model: the input images are partitioned among the processors, each of which generates part of the corresponding output image. Apply compilers exist for iWarp, Warp, uniprocessors, and the Meiko Computing Surface, as well as several other computer architectures. Benchmark comparisons on Apply programs have validated the above claims [22].

As of July 1988, the architecture and logic designs for iWarp have been completed. In the software area, an optimizing compiler developed for Warp [8, 16] has been retargeted to generate code for iWarp. Using this compiler, the iWarp performance on real programs, including those generated by the parallel program generators mentioned above, have been evaluated on an iWarp architecture simulator. A prototype iWarp system is expected to be operational by the end of 1989. Three demonstration systems, each consisting of an 8×8 torus of iWarp cells, are scheduled to be operational in the middle of 1990.

The organization of this paper is as follows. In the next section, we give an overview of iWarp and how iWarp systems can be constructed from them. Some sample iWarp usages and system configurations are described in Section 3. Sections 4 and 5 deal with one of the most innovative features of the iWarp architecture—the iWarp intercell communication models and mechanism. The computation part of the iWarp component is discussed in Section 6, which also includes some preliminary iWarp performance figures on the Livermore Loops benchmark. Finally, a summary of the paper and some concluding remarks are given.

2. iWarp overview

An iWarp system is composed of a collection of iWarp cells, each of which consists of an iWarp component and its local memory. This section first gives an overview of the iWarp component and then summarizes how an iWarp cell physically interfaces with the external world so that various iWarp systems can be constructed.

2.1. iWarp component

The iWarp component has a *communication agent* and a *computation agent*, as depicted in Figure 1. The computation agent can carry out computations independently from the operations being performed at the communication agent. Therefore a cell may perform its computation while communication through the cell from and to other cells is taking place, and the cell program does not need to be involved with the communication. While separating the control of the two agents makes programming easy, having the two agents on the same chip allows them to cooperate in a tightly coupled manner. The tight coupling allows several communication models to be implemented efficiently, as to be discussed in Section 4. The major blocks in iWarp are shown in Figure 2.

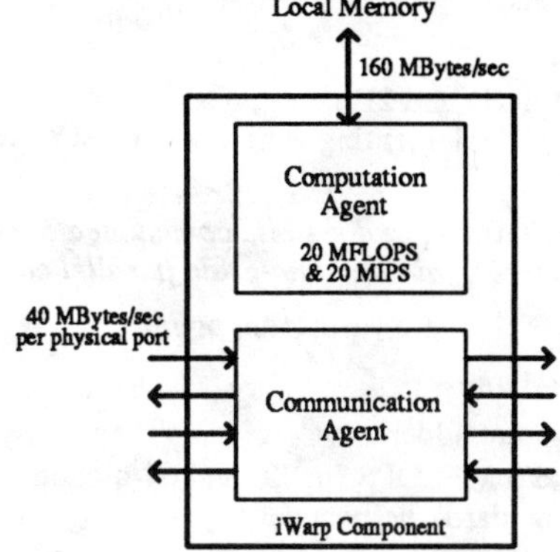

Figure 1. iWarp component overview

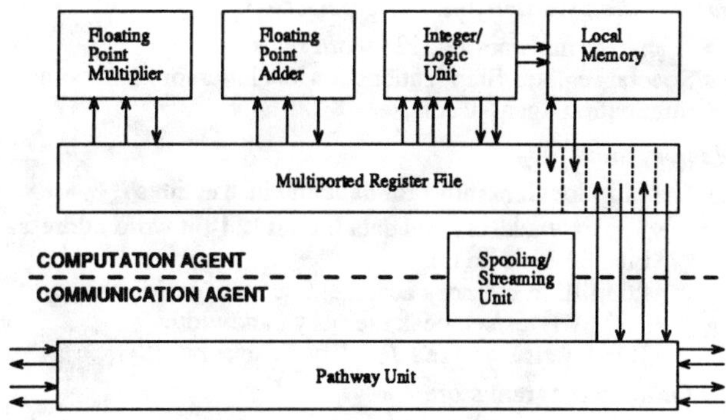

Figure 2. Major functional units in iWarp

In the following we summarize the major features in the two agents and their interface. The performance numbers are based on the expected clock speed of 20 MHz, i.e., a clock is 50 ns. Further discussions on iWarp communication and computation features are provided in Sections 5 and 6, respectively.

Communication agent

Four input and four output ports

- 40 MBytes/sec data bandwidth per port
- Word by word, hardware flow control at each port
- An output port can be connected to an input port of another iWarp cell via a point-to-point *physical bus.*

Multiple logical busses multiplexed on each physical bus.

- Maintaining up to 20 incoming pathways simultaneously in an iWarp component
- Idle logical busses do not consume any bandwidth of the physical bus.

Pathway unit

- Routing for 1D and 2D configurations
- Capable of implementing wormhole and streetsign routing schemes

Both message passing and systolic communication are supported for coarse-grain and fine-grain parallel computation.

Computation agent

Computational units

- Floating-point adder
  - 10 and 5 MFLOPS for 32- and 64-bit additions (IEEE 754 standard), respectively
  - Nonpipelined
- Floating-point multiplier
  - 10 and 5 MFLOPS for 32- and 64-bit multiplications (IEEE 754 standard), respectively
  - Nonpipelined
  - Full divide, remainder, and square root support
- Integer/logical unit
  - 20 MIPS peak performance on 8/16/32-bit integer/ordinal data
  - Arithmetic, logical, and bit operations

All the above three units may be scheduled to operate in parallel in one instruction, generating a peak computing rate of 20 MFLOPS plus 20 MIPS.

Internal data storage and interconnect

- A shared, multiported, 128 word register file
- Special register file locations for local memory and communication agent access

Memory units

- Off-chip local memory for data and instructions
  - Separate address and data busses (24-bit word address bus, 64-bit data bus)
  - 20 million memory accesses/sec peak performance
  - 160 MBytes/sec peak memory bandwidth
  - Read, write, and read/modify/write support
- On-chip program store
  - 256 word cache RAM
  - 2K word ROM (built-in functions)
  - 32- and 96-bit instructions

Communication and computation interface

Communication agent notifies computation agent on message arrival.

Dynamic flow control: Computation agent spins when reading from an empty queue or writing to a full queue in communication agent.

Hardware spools data between queues and local memory.

2.2. Forming iWarp systems

Various iWarp systems can be constructed with the iWarp cell. We describe how copies of the iWarp cell can be connected together, and how an iWarp cell can connect to peripherals to form these systems.

There are two ways that an iWarp cell, consisting of an iWarp component and its local memory, physically interfaces with the external world. Recall that the iWarp component has four input ports and four output ports. The first interface method is to use a physical *bus* to connect an output port of an iWarp to an input port of another. The former and latter port can write to and read from the bus, respectively. Thus this is a unidirectional bus between the two components, as represented by the arrowed edge in Figure 3 (a). Usually another unidirectional bus in opposite direction is also provided, so that bidirectional data communication between the two component is possible. This is illustrated in Figure 3 (b).

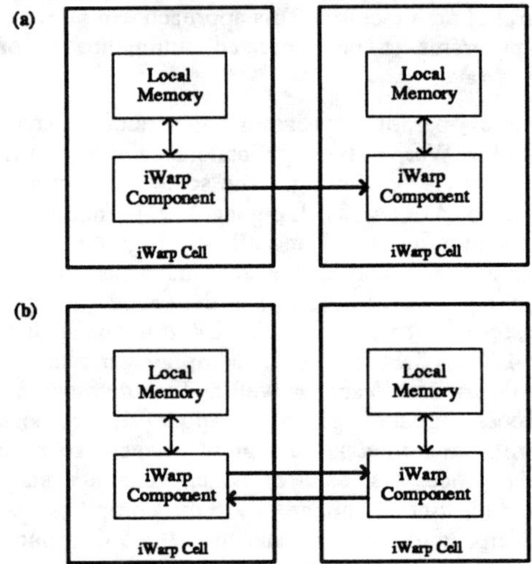

Figure 3. Intercell connection via ports of iWarp components: (a) unidirectional bus and (b) two unidirectional busses in opposite directions

The second interface method is via the local memory of the iWarp cell, as depicted by Figure 4. Using this interface the

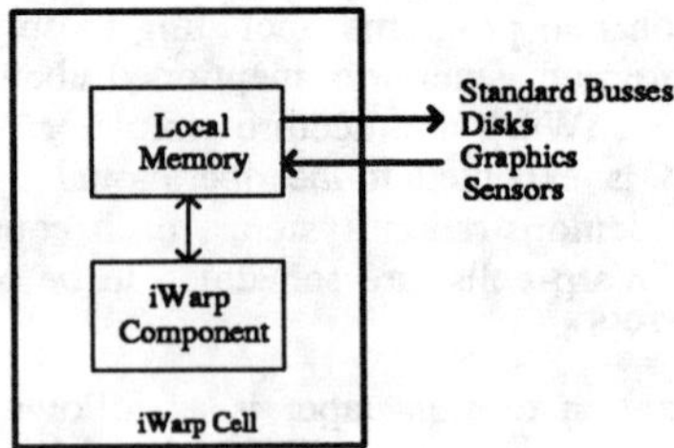

Figure 4. Connection with peripherals via local memory of an iWarp cell

iWarp cell can reach peripherals such as standard busses, disks, graphics devices and sensors. Therefore the iWarp cell's connection with peripherals uses the local memory, while its intercell connection uses ports of iWarp. Since these two functions use different physical resources of the iWarp cell, they can be implemented independently from each other. This implies, for example, that peripherals can be attached to any set of iWarp cells in an array of iWarp cells, independently from the array interconnection topology. With these two interface methods many system configurations can be implemented, as will be shown in Section 3.

3. iWarp usages and system configurations

The iWarp cell, consisting of the iWarp component and local memory, is a building block for a variety of system configurations. These systems can be used as general and special-purpose computing engines. This section describes some of these usages and system configurations.

3.1. General purpose arrays

With its four pairs of input and output ports, the iWarp cell is a convenient building block for a 2D array or torus. Figure 5 depicts a 3×3 torus. Peripherals can be attached to any of the iWarp cells via its local memory. The initial demonstration iWarp system in 1990 is an 8×8 torus, with a total of 32 MBytes SRAM. It has a peak performance of 1,280 MFLOPS. The memory of each cell can be expanded up to 1.5 MBytes, and with different memory components, a memory space of up to 64 MBytes per cell is possible. The same system design can be extended to a 32×32 torus, giving an aggregate peak performance of 20,480 MFLOPS.

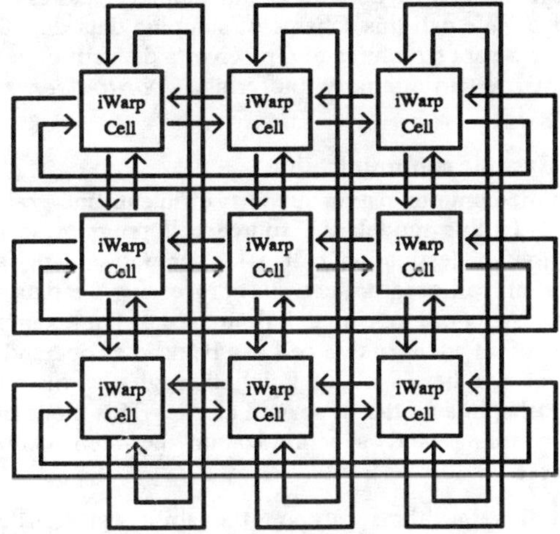

Figure 5. 3×3 torus

The iWarp cell is a building block for 1D arrays or rings as well. Figure 6 depicts a 6-cell ring. A 1D array or ring of a moderate number of iWarp cells, delivering on the order of hundreds of MFLOPS, can be an effective attached processor to a workstation. This has been demonstrated by the 10-cell Warp array. Using the same approach with iWarp, we will achieve an order of magnitude improvement in cost-performance over Warp. To meet the requirement of lower cost (and lower performance) applications, one or a few iWarp cells can also form a single-board accelerator for low-end workstations or PCs.

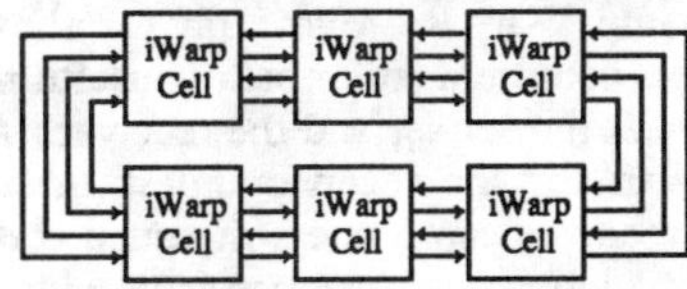

Figure 6. 6-cell ring

3.2. Special-purpose arrays

Many systolic algorithms can make effective use of large processors arrays for applications such as signal processing and graphics [10]. With the iWarp cell, various special-purpose arrays that execute only a predetermined set of these algorithms can easily be built. For example, a hexagonal array (as depicted in Figure 7) with unidirectional physical busses between cells can be built to execute some classical systolic algorithms for matrix operations [15]. For such an array, sensors and array output ports may be connected to the local memories of a number of cells, so that I/O can be carried out in parallel. In areas such as high-speed signal processing, special-purpose arrays can effectively use hundreds or even thousands of iWarp cells. In some systolic algorithms, cells on the array boundary may execute a different function from cells inside the array [7]. In this case, individual iWarp cells can be programmed to perform different functions according to their locations in the array.

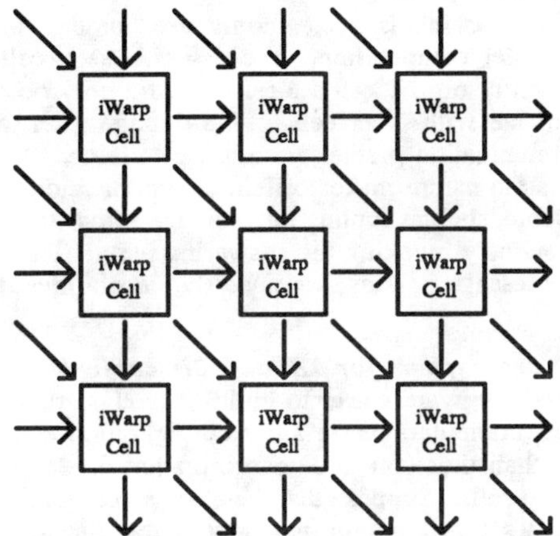

Figure 7. Hexagonal array with unidirectional physical busses between cells

In general, the performance of special-purpose arrays made of iWarp cells will be comparable to that of those arrays made of custom hardware using similar VLSI technology. Although the iWarp array will probably have a larger physical size, it can be readily programmed to implement the target algorithms and will incur a much shorter development time.

4. Communication models

Interprocessor communication is an integral part of parallel computing on a distributed memory processor array. To balance the high numerical processing capability on the processor, iWarp must be equally efficient in communication. The development of efficient parallel software is simplified if the communication cost is low and can be estimated reliably.

To motivate the communication agent design on iWarp, in this section we first describe two important communication models commonly used on distributed memory processor arrays: message passing and systolic communication. We will study the requirements to implement these models efficiently, from the data transport level all the way to the integration of communication with the data processing. We then describe a set of unifying programming abstractions to support these models. The next section shows how they are supported by the iWarp communication facility, while meeting the performance requirements of their usages.

4.1. Communication models

We have identified two communication models used for distributed memory parallel systems: *message passing* and *systolic*. They differ primarily in the granularity of communication and computation. In message passing mode, as in computer networks, the unit of processing is a complete message. That is, a message is accumulated in the source cell memory, transmitted (as a unit) to the destination cell, and only when the full message is available in the local memory of the destination cell is it ready to be operated upon. Conversely, in systolic mode [12], the unit of communication and processing can be as fine grained as a single word in a message.

4.1.1. Message passing

Message passing is a commonly used model for coarse-grain parallel computation. Processes at each cell operate independently on the cell's local data and only occasionally communicate with other cells. The timing, order, and even the communication partner are often determined at run time. The dynamic nature makes certain communication overheads unavoidable, such as routing the message across the array and asynchronously invoking the answering party. To efficiently support message passing, we need the capabilities described below.

Hardware support for 1D and 2D configurations. 1D arrays and rings are easier to build than 2D arrays and tori. However, computations on a 2D configuration can be more efficient than those on a 1D configuration for large systems with many cells. Suppose that there are n cells in the system. Using a 2D configuration, not only is the distance between cells reduced from $O(n)$ to $O(\sqrt{n})$ hops, but also is the effective bandwidth of the communication network increased since a transfer takes up fewer hops.

Spooling. Suppose a process wants to send a message to a destination cell. Since the communication network is shared, a process does not have guaranteed instantaneous access. Ideally, the sender process can simply specify the destination and message location, and continue with its processing regardless of the availability of the network, and a separate thread of control spools the data out of the memory. Similarly, another spooling process can take the data from the network and store it into the receiver's memory, with minimal interference with the computational process in progress.

Separate communication support hardware. In an iWarp array, a message may be routed through intermediate cells before reaching the final destination. The routing of data through a cell is logically unrelated to the process local to the cell. It can be supported in dedicated hardware to handle the high bandwidth of the array.

Word-level synchronization. Although the granularity of communication is a message, this does not mean that the intermediate hops should forward the data at the same grain size. In wormhole routing [3], the routing information in the header of the message can be used to set up the next leg of the communication path even before the rest of the data arrives. The contents of the message can be forwarded word by word, without having to be buffered in entirety on intermediate cells. Wormhole routing reduces the latency of communication and does not take up any of the memory bandwidth of the intermediate cells. Since the communication path is built link by link, a word-by-word handshake is necessary to throttle the data flow in case the next link is temporarily unavailable.

Multiplexing messages on a physical bus. Since wormhole routing may use up multiple links at the same time, prevention of deadlock is necessary in ring or torus architectures. One scheme to prevent deadlock is the virtual channel method, which uses another set of links when routing beyond a certain cell [4, 19]. If in each direction only one physical bus is available between two connecting cells, this deadlock prevention scheme requires that multiple communication paths be multiplexed on a physical bus. Multiplexing can also be used to keep a long message from monopolizing the physical bandwidth for an indefinitely long time.

Door-to-door message passing. When a message arrives at the destination cell, it is generally first buffered in a system memory space and then copied into the user's memory space. This extra copy can be eliminated if the data is stored directly into the desired memory location. Using the data throttling mechanism above, the receiving process can first examine the message header to determine the memory address for the message. We call this scheme of shipping data directly from a sender's data structures to a receiver's data structures, without any system memory buffering, *door-to-door* message passing.

4.1.2. Systolic communication

Systolic communication supports efficient, fine-grain parallelism. In this model, the source cell program sends data items to the destination cell as it generates them, and the destination cell program can start processing the data as soon as the first word of input has arrived. For example, the outputs of an adder in one cell can be used as operands to the adder of another, without going through the memories of either cells, in a matter of several clocks. This mode provides tight coupling and synchronization between cooperating processes.

Systolic algorithms rely on the ability to transfer long streams of intermediate data between processes at high throughput and with low latency. More importantly, the communication cost must be consistently small, because cost variations can greatly increase delays in the overall computation. This implies that dedicated communication paths are desirable, which may be neighboring or non-neighboring paths depending on communication topologies of the algorithm.

Raw data words are sent along a communication path, identified only by their ordering in the data stream. The sender appends data to the end of the data stream and the receiver must access the words in the order they arrive. Our experience with the Warp systolic array [1] shows that FIFO queuing along a communication path is useful in relaxing the coupling between the sender and the receiver. A sender does not need to wait for the receiver unless the queue is full; similarly, the receiver can process the queued data until they run out. Word-level synchronization is provided by stalling a process that tries to read from an empty queue or write to a full queue.

A special-purpose systolic array can be tailored to a specific algorithm by implementing the dedicated communication paths directly in hardware and providing long enough queues to ensure a steady flow of data. As a programmable array, iWarp processors should implement the common systolic algorithms well, but can also degrade gracefully to cover other algorithms. We have identified the following requirements for efficient support of systolic communication.

Hardware support for 1D and 2D configurations. Many systolic algorithms in signal and image processing and in scientific computing use 1D and 2D processor arrays [10]. iWarp can directly support such configurations in hardware.

Multiplexing communication paths on a physical bus. iWarp can also support other configurations, with degraded performance, if necessary. A systolic algorithm may call for more communication paths between a pair of connecting cells than those provided directly by hardware. It may require extra communication paths for configurations such as a hexagonal array, or to implement deadlock avoidance schemes [14]. Divide-and-conquer algorithms may require communication between powers of two distances away at different times of the algorithm. All these considerations motivate the need to multiplex multiple communication paths on a physical bus.

Coupling of computation and communication. The computation part of a cell needs to access the communication part directly without going through the cell's local memory. This extra source of data is a key to systolic algorithm's efficiency. For example, fine-grained systolic algorithms for important matrix operations can consume and produce up to four data words per clock. Memory bandwidth cannot match this high communication bandwidth.

Spooling. Regardless of the size of the hardware queue available on each cell, there is always some systolic algorithm that requires deeper queues. For example, a systolic algorithm for convolving a kernel with a 2D image requires some cells to store the entire row of the image [11]. Therefore, it is desirable to provide an automatic facility to overflow the data to the cell's local memory if necessary.

4.1.3. Reserving a communication subnetwork

In both message passing and systolic communication models, there is a need to multiplex multiple communication paths onto a physical bus. Efficient support of communication paths requires dedicated hardware resources, thus only a small number of paths can be provided. This resource limitation raises the issue of resource management.

The need for managing the communication resource is more pronounced in the systolic communication model. This is because the production and consumption rates of a data stream are tied directly to the computation rates of the cells. As the computation on a cell can stall and even deadlock while waiting for data, the lifetime of a communication path can be arbitrarily long. Although an idle communication path does not consume any communication bandwidth, if all the multiplexed paths on a physical bus are occupied, no other traffic can get through.

In message passing, an entire message is first prepared and buffered in the sender cell's local memory, and the message is stored into the destination cell's local memory directly. Once a communication path becomes available, the data can be spooled in and out of the memories. With a proper routing scheme to avoid deadlocks a message can always get through, although it may have to wait for a while if the network is backed up with long messages.

Both models can benefit from a mechanism to reserve a set of communication paths for a class of messages. For instance, we can reserve a set of communication paths for system messages for purposes such as synchronization, program debugging and code downloading. First of all, this guarantees that the system can reach all the cells even if the user uses up all other paths. Moreover, since the system has full control over all messages on the reserved network, the behavior of the network is more predictable, and attributes such as a guaranteed response time are possible.

4.2. Messages and pathways

Message passing and systolic communication are two very kinds of communication. The former supports coarse-grain parallelism where processes at different cells behave independently, and the latter supports fine-grain parallelism where processes at different cells cooperate synchronously. However, on examining the requirements to make message passing *efficient* and systolic communication *general*, they are not that dissimilar. For example, wormhole routing uses up multiple hardware links simultaneously, much like a communication path in systolic communication that connects two non-neighboring processes. On iWarp, both communication models can be unified and supported efficiently by the same programming abstractions of a *pathway* and a *message*, defined below.

A *pathway* is a direct connection from a cell (called the source cell) to another cell (called the destination cell). Each segment of the pathway that connects the communication agent of a cell to the computation agent of the same cell or to the communication agent of another cell is called a *pathway segment*. (See Figure 9 for examples of pathways.)

A *message* consists of a header, a sequence of data words, and a marker denoting the end of the message. Messages can be sent from the source cell to the destination cell over a pathway. The pathway is initiated and terminated by the source cell. It assembles a header containing a destination address and additional routing information and hands it to the communication agent. The source cell closes the pathway by sending a special marker to signal the end.

Normally, one pathway is set up for each individual message. The source cell opens a pathway to the destination cell, sends its message, and then closes the pathway. In the message passing model, the sending process dynamically creates a new pathway and message for each data transfer. Not all intermediate links of a pathway need to exist at the same time. In wormhole routing, the marker denoting the end of the pathway may have reached an intermediate cell even before the header and data reach the destination. In the systolic communication model, the cells typically set up required pathways for a longer duration. The sending program transmits individual data words along a pathway as they are generated without sending any additional headers or markers. On termination, the cell programs close the message and the pathway.

However, it is possible that a pathway is set up for multiple messages. That is, the sender cell does not take down the pathway immediately after the first message has passed through, so the sender can send further messages over the same pathway. The sender cell has reserved the pathway for its future use.

Reservation of multiple pathways is also possible on iWarp. Two pathways are said to be connected if the destination cell of one is the source of the other. The sender of the first pathway can send messages to the destination of the second using both pathways. In this way, a cell can send messages to multiple destinations through a set of reserved pathways.

5. iWarp communication

This section describes how the communication agent on iWarp implements the above programming abstractions and satisfies the performance requirements of both the message passing and systolic communication models. We break down the functionality of the communication agent into four categories. The categories and the requirements they fulfill are summarized as follows:

1. ***Physical communication network***: Hardware support for 1D and 2D configurations.
2. ***Logical communication network***: A mechanism to multiplex multiple pathway segments on a physical bus on a word level basis.
3. ***Pathway unit***: A mechanism to establish pathways.
4. ***Streaming and spooling unit***: Direct access of communication agent from the computation agent, and a spooling mechanism to transfer data from and to local memory.

5.1. Physical communication network

The communication network of iWarp is based on a set of high bandwidth point-to-point physical busses, linking the input and output ports of a pair of cells. Each cell has four input and four output ports, allowing cells to be connected in various topologies. Figure 8(a) illustrates the 2D array configuration where each cell is connected bidirectionally to four cells.

Each physical bus can transmit one 32-bit word data every 100 ns. The VLSI, custom chip implementation made it possible to have fine-grain, word level handshaking without any synchronization delay. Thus, each physical bus has a data bandwidth of 40 MBytes/sec, giving an aggregate data transfer rate of 320 MBytes/sec.

5.2. Logical communication network

Besides the four input and four output *external* busses described above for connecting to other cells, a communication agent is also connected to the computation agent in its cell through two input and two output *internal* busses. Each of these busses can be multiplexed on a word level basis to support a number of *logical busses* in the same direction, whereas each logical bus can implement one pathway segment of a pathway at a time.

To the communication agent on a cell, there are four kinds of logical busses:

1. incoming busses from communication agent of a neighboring cell,
2. incoming busses from computation agent of the same cell,
3. outgoing busses to communication agent of a neighboring cell, and
4. outgoing busses to computation agent of the same cell

The mapping of the logical busses to physical busses is performed statically, under software control. The hardware allows the total number of incoming logical busses in the communication agent of each cell to be as large as 20. For example, in a 2D array, the logical busses can be evenly distributed among the four neighbors and the computation agent, as shown in Figure 8(b). In this case, the heart of the communication agent is a 20×20 crossbar that links incoming logical busses to outgoing logical busses. Logical busses are managed by the source, i.e., the sending cell. The sender can initiate communication using any of its pre-allocated free logical busses without consulting the receiver. This design minimizes the time needed to set up a pathway between cells.

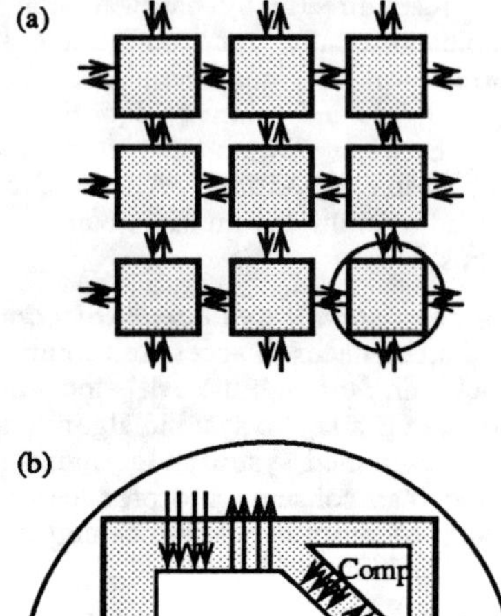

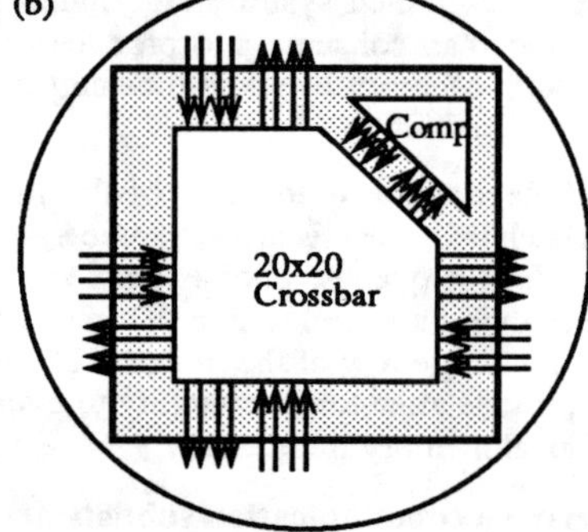

Figure 8. (a) Physical communication network
(b) logical busses of a cell

5.3. The pathway unit

A pathway is formed by connecting a sequence of pathway segments together. Figure 9 contains an example of three pathways through some cells in a 2D array. Pathway 1 connects the computation agent of B to that of A through a pathway segment between the communication agents of the two cells. Pathway 2 passes through cell A, turns a corner at cell C and finally reaches the destination D. Lastly, pathway 3 passes through both cells C and D. Two pathway segments are multiplexed on the physical bus from cell C to cell D.

A new pathway is established by the use of a special *open pathway marker*. As the communication agents pass the open pathway marker along from cell to cell, they allocate resources to form the pathway.

Open pathway markers carry *addresses* to tell how to route them from their source to their destination, using *streetsign* routing (e.g., "go to Jones and stop"). There are two components of such a streetsign: the *streetname* (e.g., Jones) and the associated *action* (e.g., stop). The controller provides special hardware support for address recognition with a multiple entry *Address Match CAM*. For example, a pathway route might consist of "go to Jones, turn right, go to Smith, turn left, go to Johnson, and stop". Each pathway unit is responsible for recognizing addresses of open pathway markers requiring service or attention at that cell. Given the sequential nature of streetsign routing interpretation, a given communication agent needs to deal with only the "next" streetname on passing open pathway markers.

Upon the arrival of an open pathway marker, the pathway unit interprets the address to see if it is addressed to this cell, and, if so, posts an event to the computation agent to invoke the appropriate routine. Otherwise, it finds a free outgoing logical bus along the route given by the header and connects it to the incoming logical bus. The pathway is dismantled, one link at a time, by the flow of a *close pathway marker* along the pathway, cell to cell, from the source to the destination.

The latency of communication through a cell is 100 ns normally, and 150 ns in the case of corner turning. The interpretation of addresses and the establishment of pathways are completely performed by hardware. Creating a new pathway segment does not incur any additional time delay.

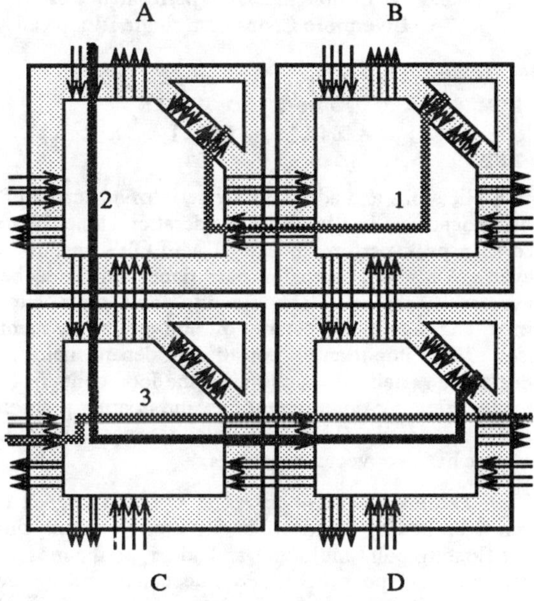

Figure 9. Pathways in a 2D array

5.4. The streaming and spooling unit

The computation agent can get access to the communication data by (1) directly accessing the communication agent a word at a time, or (2) spooling the data in and out of local memory using special hardware support.

Programs can read data from a message or write data to a message via the side effects of special register references. These special registers are called *streaming gates*, because they provide a "gating" or "windowing" function allowing a stream of data to pass, word by word, between the communication agent and the computation agent. There are two input gates and two output gates. These gates can be bound to different logical busses dynamically. A read from the gate will consume the next word of the associated input message; correspondingly, a write to an output gate will generate the next word of the associated output message. Data word-at-a-time synchronization is expressed in algorithms by the side effects of gate register references (e.g., a read of an input gate at which no data is available causes the instruction to spin until the data arrives).

iWarp also provides a transparent, low overhead mechanism for transferring data between the pathway unit and the local memory via *spooling gates*. Spooling has low overhead to avoid significant reduction of the efficiency of any ongoing or parallel computation. Spooling is transparent except for delays incurred due to either cycle stealing (i.e., for address computation) or local memory access interference from other memory references (i.e., due to concurrent cache or instruction activities).

6. iWarp computation

The iWarp processor is designed to execute numerical computations with a high sustained floating-point arithmetic rate. The iWarp cell has a high peak computation rate of 20 MFLOPS for single precision and 10 MFLOPS for double precision. More importantly, iWarp can attain a high computation rate consistently. This is because the multiple functional units in the computation agent are directly accessible through a long instruction word (LIW) instruction. By translating user's code directly into these long instructions using an optimizing compiler [16], a high computation rate can be achieved for all programs, vectorizable or not.

6.1. The computation agent

The computation agent has been optimized for LIW controlled, parallel operation of multiple functional units. Chief among these optimizations are:

- nonpipelined floating-point arithmetic units,
- inter-unit and intra-unit, output to input, operand bypassing,
- parallel, hardware supported, zero-overhead looping,
- large, shared, multi-ported register file,
- a high bandwidth, low latency (no striding penalty) memory,
- high bandwidth, low latency interface with the communication agent.

The LIW workhorse instruction of iWarp is called the *ComputeAndAccess* (C&A) instruction. As an example of the parallelism available, a loop with code

```
FOR i := 0 TO n-1 DO BEGIN
    f:=(A[i]*B[3*i])+f;
END;
```

is compiled into a loop that initiates one iteration every cycle surrounded by a loop prologue and epilogue to get the iterations started. Similarly, a loop body that reads a value **V1** from one message, **V2** from another message, computes **V1 * V2 + C[i]** and sends the result as well as **V2** on to the next processor is also translated into a single C&A instruction in the loop body. The single precision C&A instruction executes in two clocks, and the double precision C&A instruction executes in four clocks, so both loops execute at the peak computation rate of the processor.

A C&A instruction requires up to 8 operands and produces up to 4 results. Memory accesses may produce or consume up to two of those operands: either a read and a write or two reads. Each memory reference includes an address computation (e.g., an indexing operation with a non-unit stride). The C&A instruction employs a read-ahead/write-behind pipeline that makes memory read operands from one instruction available for use in the next. Conversely, computational results of one instruction are written to memory during the next.

Those operand references that are not satisfied by the memory read operation or read from a gate (see Section 5.4) must be to the register file. These operands may themselves be the results of previous operations (e.g., intermediate results held in the register file). To avoid any interinstruction latencies, the results of the integer unit or a floating-point unit may be "bypassed" directly back to that unit as an input operand, without waiting for the destination register file location to be updated. Also, the results of either floating-point unit may be "bypassed" directly to the other floating-point unit (e.g., to support multiply-accumulate sequences).

Thus, the execution of a single C&A instruction can include up to one floating-point multiplication, one floating-point addition, two memory accesses (including two integer operations for addressing), four gate accesses, several more register accesses (enough to provide the rest of the required operands), and branching back to the beginning of the loop.

Incremental to the single "long" C&A instruction, the iWarp computation agent provides a full complement of "short" instructions. They can be thought of as 2 and 3 address RISC-like instructions. These "short" instructions are provided to make iWarp a generally programmable processor. They usually control only a single functional unit.

6.2. Livermore Loops performance

The Livermore Loops [6], a set of computational kernels typically found in scientific computing, have been used since the 1960's as a benchmark for computer systems. The loops range from having no data dependence between iterations (easily vectorizable) to having only a single recurrence (strictly sequential). This combination of vector and scalar code provides a good measure on the performance of a machine across a spectrum of scientific computing requirements.

The Livermore loops were manually translated from FORTRAN to W2. (W2 is a Pascal-like language developed for the Warp machine. The retargeted W2 compiler [8, 16, 17] has been used as a tool in developing and evaluating the iWarp architecture.) The translation into W2 was straightforward, preserving loop structures and changing only syntax, except for kernels 15 and 16, which were translated from Feo's restructured loops [6].

The performance of Livermore Loops (double precision) on a single iWarp processor is presented in Table 6-1. The unweighted mean is 4.2 MFLOPS, the standard deviation is 2.6 MFLOPS and the harmonic mean is 2.7 MFLOPS. Since the machine's peak double-precision performance is 10 MFLOPS, these numbers demonstrate a highly effective use of the raw computation power of iWarp.

The iWarp cell is a scalar processor, and does not require that loops be vectorizable for full utilization of its floating-point units. This is why it does not exhibit the same tremendous disparity in MFLOPS rates for the different loops as do vector machines. Nonetheless, the variation between the MFLOPS rates obtained is still significant. Near peak performance can be achieved (using a high-level language and an optimizing compiler), as demonstrated by kernels 3 and 7. On the other hand, performance of near 1 MFLOPS is also observed. The factors that limit iWarp performance are data dependency and the critical resource bottleneck.

Kernel	MFLOPS	Kernel	MFLOPS
1	8.2	13	1.8
2	3.3	14	3.2
3	9.8	15	1.6
4	3.2	16	0.8
5	3.3	17	1.6
6	5.0	18	6.6
7	9.9	19	4.0
8	7.4	20	3.1
9	6.7	21	4.1
10	2.0	22	3.1
11	2.0	23	6.3
12	2.5	24	0.9

Table 6-1: Double precision performance of Livermore Loops on a single iWarp cell

Data dependency. Consider kernel 5:

```
FOR i := 0 TO n-1 DO BEGIN
    X[i] := Z[i] * (Y[i] - X[i-1]);
END;
```

The multiplications and additions are serialized because of the data dependencies. Just by this consideration alone, iWarp is limited to a peak performance of 5 MFLOPS on this loop. However, iWarp still executes data dependent code better than vector machines. The floating-point units are not pipelined, and there is no penalty on non-unit stride memory accesses. More importantly, not all data dependencies force the code to be serialized. As long as the loop contains other independent floating-point operations, the floating-point units can still be utilized. This is a unique advantage an LIW architecture has over vector machines.

Critical resource bottleneck. The execution speed of a program is limited by the most heavily used resource. Unless *both* the floating-point multiplier and adder are the most critical resources, the peak MFLOPS rate cannot be achieved. Programs containing no multiplications cannot run faster than 5 MFLOPS since the multiplier is idle all the time. For example, for kernel 13 since the integer unit is the most heavily used resource, the MFLOPS measure is naturally low.

7. Summary and conclusions

iWarp is the first of a new class of parallel computer architectures. iWarp integrates both the computation and communication functionalities into a single VLSI component. The communication models supported range from large-grain message passing to fine-grain systolic communication.

The computation agent of an iWarp component contains floating-point units with a peak performance of 20 and 10 MFLOPS for single and double precision operations, respectively, as well as an integer unit that performs 20 million integer or logical operations per second. The communication agent operates independently of the computation agent; since both are implemented on a single chip, tight coupling between communication and computation is possible. This permits efficient systolic communication, as well as low-overhead message passing.

iWarp is designed to be a building block for high performance parallel systems. Not only does iWarp have impressive computational capabilities, it also has exceptional communication capabilities, making iWarp suitable for both scientific computing and high speed signal processing. The first iWarp based systems will be 1D arrays, rings, 2D arrays or tori, but the iWarp component is flexible enough to be used in numerous other organizations.

We anticipate iWarp to have a significant impact on the practice of parallel computing. Arrays of thousands of cells are feasible, programmable, and much cheaper than many other supercomputers of comparable power. iWarp systems can have a variety of goals: they can be special or general purpose, and experimental or commercial. The support of well accepted languages for the cell like FORTRAN and C, together with parallel program generators to simplify the programming of the array, make it possible to program the diverse parallel machines that can be realized with iWarp components.

The iWarp component has to meet the diverse requirements of fine-grain and coarse-grain communication for various applications including scientific computing and signal processing. The design of the iWarp component has convinced us that these requirements are not incompatible and, in fact, do reinforce each other. The high bandwidth/low latency communication mechanism in iWarp implements both message passing and systolic communication efficiently. This synergy makes iWarp a suitable building block for the affordable supercomputing systems of the future.

References

1. Annaratone, M., Arnould, E., Gross, T., Kung, H. T., Lam, M., Menzilcioglu, O. and Webb, J. A. "The Warp Computer: Architecture, Implementation and Performance". *IEEE Transactions on Computers C-36*, 12 (December 1987), 1523-1538.

2. Annaratone, M., Bitz, F., Deutch, J., Hamey, L., Kung, H. T., Maulik, P., Ribas, H., Tseng, P. and Webb, J. Applications Experience on Warp. Proceedings of the 1987 National Computer Conference, AFIPS, 1987, pp. 149-158.

3. Dally, William J.. *A VLSI Architecture for Concurrent Data Structures*. Kluwer Academic Publishers, 1987.

4. Dally, W.J., Seitz, C.L. "Deadlock-Free Message Routing in Multiprocessor Interconnection Networks". *IEEE Transactions on Computers C-36*, 5 (May 1987), 547-553.

5. Dongarra, J.J., Bunch, J.R., Moler, C.B. and Stewart, G.W.. *LINPACK Users' Guide*. Society for Industrial and Applied Mathematics, Philadelphia, 1979.

6. Feo, J. T. "An Analysis of the Computational and Parallel Complexity of the Livermore Loops". *Parallel Computing 7*, 2 (June 1988), 163-186.

7. Gentleman, W.M. and Kung, H.T. Matrix Triangularization by Systolic Arrays. Proceedings of SPIE Symposium, Vol. 298, Real-Time Signal Processing IV, Society of Photo-Optical Instrumentation Engineers, August, 1981, pp. 19-26.

8. Gross, T. and Lam, M. Compilation for a High-performance Systolic Array. Proceedings of the SIGPLAN 86 Symposium on Compiler Construction, ACM SIGPLAN, June, 1986, pp. 27-38.

9. Hamey, L. G. C., Webb, J. A., and Wu, I. C. Low-level Vision on Warp and the Apply Programming Model. In *Parallel Computation and Computers for Artificial Intelligence*, Kluwer Academic Publishers, 1987, pp. 185-199. Edited by J. Kowalik.

10. Kung, H.T. "Why Systolic Architectures?". *Computer Magazine 15*, 1 (Jan. 1982), 37-46.

11. Kung, H.T., Ruane, L.M., and Yen, D.W.L. "Two-Level Pipelined Systolic Array for Multidimensional Convolution". *Image and Vision Computing 1*, 1 (February 1983), 30-36. An improved version appears as a CMU Computer Science Department technical report, November 1982..

12. Kung, H. T. Systolic Communication. Proceedings of the International Conference on Systolic Arrays, May, 1988, pp. 695-703.

13. Kung, H. T. "Computational Models for Parallel Computers". *Philosophical Transactions of the Royal Society* (1988).

14. Kung, H. T. Deadlock Avoidance for Systolic Communication. Conference Proceedings of the 15th Annual International Symposium on Computer Architecture, June, 1988, pp. 252-260.

15. Kung, H.T. and Leiserson, C.E. Systolic Arrays (for VLSI). Sparse Matrix Proceedings 1978, Society for Industrial and Applied Mathematics, 1979, pp. 256-282.

16. Lam, M. S. *A Systolic Array Optimizing Compiler*. Ph.D. Th., Carnegie Mellon University, May 1987.

17. Lam, M. Software Pipelining: An Effective Scheduling Technique for VLIW Machines. ACM Sigplan '88 Conference on Programming Language Design and Implementation., June, 1988.

18. Pomerleau, D. A., Gusciora, G. L., Touretzky, D. S. and Kung, H. T. Neural Network Simulation at Warp Speed: How We Got 17 Million Connections Per Second. Proceedings of 1988 IEEE International Conference on Neural Networks, July, 1988, pp. 143-150.

19. Raubold, E. and Haenle, J. A Method of Deadlock-Free Resource Allocation and Flow Control in Packet Networks. Proceedings of the Third International Conference on Computer Communication, International Council for Computer Communication, August, 1976.

20. Sejnowski, T. J., and Rosenberg, C. R. "Parallel Networks that Learn to Pronounce English Text". *Complex Systems 1*, 1 (1987), 145-168.

21. Tseng, P. S., Lam, M. and Kung, H. T. The Domain Parallel Computation Model on Warp. Proceedings of SPIE Symposium, Vol. 977, Real-Time Signal Processing XI, Society of Photo-Optical Instrumentation Engineers, August, 1988.

22. Wallace, R. S., Webb, J. A. and Wu, I-C. Architecture Independent Image Processing: Performance of Apply on Diverse Architectures. Third International Conference on Supercomputing, International Supercomputing Institute, Inc., Boston, MA, May, 1988, pp. 25-34.

Training & Education

Chair: Dan Sulzbach
University of California at San Diego

A Training Program for Scientific Supercomputing Users

Floyd Hanson*
Mathematics, Statistics, and Computer Science

Thomas Moher
Electrical Engineering and Computer Science

Nora Sabelli
Computer Center and Chemistry

University of Illinois at Chicago
Chicago, IL 60680-6998

Ann Solem**
Computing and Communications
Los Alamos National Laboratory
Los Alamos, NM 87545

ABSTRACT

There is need for a mechanism to transfer supercomputing technology into the hands of scientists and engineers in such a way that they will acquire a foundation of knowledge that will permit integration of supercomputing as a tool in their research. Most computing center training emphasizes computer-specific information about how to use a particular computer system; most academic programs teach concepts to computer scientists. Only a few brief courses and new programs are designed for computational scientists.

This paper describes an eleven-week training program aimed principally at graduate and postdoctoral students in computationally intensive fields. The program is designed to balance the specificity of computing center courses, the abstractness of computer science courses, and the personal contact of traditional apprentice approaches. It consists of seminars and clinics given by many visiting and local faculty and covers a variety of supercomputing concepts, issues, and practices related to architecture, operating systems, software design, numerical considerations, code optimization, graphics, communications, and networks. Its research component encourages understanding of scientific computing and supercomputer hardware issues. Flexibility in thinking about computing needs is emphasized by the use of several different supercomputer architectures, such as the CRAY X-MP/48, the IBM 3090 600E/VF, and the Alliant FX/8.

Keywords: Supercomputing, training program, remote supercomputing center, secondary supercomputing center, computational scientists, supercomputing support environment, supercomputing application environment, user experience.

INTRODUCTION

Increased Hardware Availability and Increased Supercomputing Education

In 1984 the National Science Foundation (NSF) launched a program designed to bring supercomputing to scientists and engineers engaged in basic research outside the national laboratories [1], [2]. The availability of supercomputers in the Phase I and Phase II NSF-supported national centers, plus the NSFnet communications backbone, has had a profound impact on the way computational science is conducted and, perhaps more importantly, on the expectations of the scientific community.

In addition to improvements in hardware, software, and communications, supercomputing training is an important component of any national effort to advance the use of supercomputers. This importance of training was emphasized by the Panel on Large Scale Computing in Science and Engineering, chaired by Peter Lax in 1982 [1], and was restated in the report on a National Supercomputing Initiative, chaired by H. Reveche, D. Lawrie, and A. Despain in 1987 [3].

Increased capability in modeling physical systems requires advances in scientific software, as well as in hardware and systems. Advances in scientific application software have been mostly the result of increased access to minicomputers and minisupercomputers and are probably not yet the result of the increase in supercomputing access [4]. Full potential for development of sophisticated supercomputer software has yet to be realized. Scientific software for supercomputers lags behind minicomputing software for several reasons, among them: (1) lack of pervasive guaranteed access conducive to uninhibited exploration; (2) consequent lack, except in a few instances, of direct familiarity with the characteristics that transform a "computer" into a "supercomputer"; and (3) the lengthy time for development of large-scale software.

Where do we find supercomputing applications expertise? Supercomputing centers are typically headed by physical scientists engaged in computational science, rather than by computer scientists engaged in software or hardware development. So, it is to the potentially large pool of physical scientists and engineers, whose practice pushes them toward increasingly sophisticated use of supercomputers, that we must pay attention and address our efforts if effective supercomputer use is to follow closely on the heels of innovative supercomputer architecture design. Yet, this is a group that has traditionally learned computing by word of mouth within its own applied field; and the word-of-mouth approach is terribly archaic given the huge investments in computer hardware that have been made and the pace at which they will continue to be made. The National Supercomputing Initiative report [3] urges that "universities receive incentives to develop both undergraduate and graduate curricula for large-scale computing in engineering and science. The curricula must be interdisciplinary and foster a deeper understanding of the underlying problems in large scale computer modeling."

The task that we proposed for ourselves is more in line with technology transfer programs than with either supercomputing center training or academic computer science programs [3], [5]: to provide scientists at secondary supercomputing centers with enough background and experience to understand the concepts and issues of supercomputing as they relate to their own discipline and to integrate supercomputing as a tool in their research. Bringing professionals to the forefront of technology is nothing new: industry has engaged in it for a long time, and professionals in academia often use sabbatical

*This work was partially funded by a Faculty Research Leave at Argonne National Laboratory, Argonne, IL 60439-4844.

**This work was performed while on a one-year sabbatical at the University of Illinois at Chicago and was supported by the U.S. Department of Energy.

leaves or their own research to fulfill the same need in an informal manner. What makes supercomputing unique now is the accelerated pace of supercomputer availability, the remote nature of supercomputer equipment (in most cases), and the lack of a sufficient body of experienced scientific programmers (outside of a few industrial and academic centers and the national laboratories, where supercomputer users are scientists who grew up with computers as computers were developed). Our program tries to provide an environment (utilizing remote access to supercomputers and providing comprehensive supercomputing support locally) where a group of experienced computational scientists can be built up much faster than it would grow otherwise.

Traditional computer science curricula do not, and cannot, provide the kinds of detailed background necessary to help non-computer scientists port their code to supercomputers. The typical computer science program rarely, if ever, offers a course in supercomputing, and such a course is more likely to be a generic course that considers a broad class of architectures than an in-depth investigation of programming techniques (for example, see [6]). Non-computer specialists may have little interest in the computer science aspects of these systems, and, realistically, the knowledge they need may require several months of detailed study at the intersection of their application and the capabilities of the target machine.

Most supercomputing center training emphasizes computer-specific information about specific tools for specific computer systems. It does not come to grips with several crucial aspects of the scientist's needs: (1) problems arise after the scientist returns to home base, (2) many problems are due to networks and remote connections, and (3) the scientist often does not have the conceptual framework that is necessary in order to fully absorb the computing information in a few weeks. These problems are, of course, compounded at institutions without local supercomputer equipment. The very natural expectations created by the rise of "user friendly" microcomputer software tools and by the use of packaged software in disciplines without a long tradition of software development further complicate the problem.

Supercomputing Education for Non-Computer Scientists

That "supercomputing" is a topic of study on its own is not as obvious as it should be. An introduction to supercomputing certainly involves learning some principles of computer science, which short-term training programs cannot cover. Moreover, non-specialists typically do not have the time (or interest) to sit through a series of specialized computer science courses containing material that is of only selective relevance. On the other hand, the usual computer science survey courses have little to offer in this respect, since they are oriented toward a different audience. Furthermore, supercomputing imposes certain constraints (and opens up new avenues) that are not traditionally covered in computer science, so it is unclear whether traditional courses would really be all that helpful. For example, in the area of programming languages, it is one thing to rail against Fortran as an inappropriate vehicle for expressing algorithms, but if that is what you have, then the topic of interest is how to make best use of the tool you have, not what is the best tool [7].

Our approach is to capitalize on pressing research needs and on the traditional role of graduate and postdoctoral students as harbingers of new techniques for their research groups. To engage their full cooperation, the participant and his or her group must feel that they are accomplishing something of direct relevance to their research, must remain in constant touch with each other, and must come to understand the problems and challenges of supercomputing as they relate to their professional future. This is not to say that there is no need for scientists to spend long periods at supercomputing centers, nor that supercomputing center training workshops are not needed; rather, our program addresses the specific issues of incorporating supercomputing expertise in the shortest possible time into research groups not ready for other approaches and of making this expertise readily available locally.

METHOD

We describe the structure and content of this workshop program to clarify how the structure of these workshops is different from others and to outline the breadth, depth, and balance of topics that are covered.

Goals

Today, computational scientists must be proficient in the use of a variety of supercomputers for their research. As national supercomputing centers become saturated, computer cycles will have to be used on whatever machines may be available. Developing technologies, such as parallelism, will likely worsen this situation for some time to come. Thus, the goals of our program are the following:

1. Prepare participants to become "educated consumers" of supercomputing technology.
2. Create adaptable people.
3. Bridge the gap between computer-specific training and computer science education.

Researchers need a training program that gives them the tools to adapt to multiple environments while focusing on their own research needs. We believe that participants must have significant time to view and re-view the same issues from different viewpoints, to learn more than simply how to use a particular supercomputer, and to learn more than abstract concepts. Direct presentations from different experts in a technical context and lack of emphasis on any single computer architecture broadens participants' views and helps prepare them to become "educated consumers" of this technology.

A difficult problem in developing supercomputer applications is the fine balance between portability across machines and optimization on a single machine. With such rapidly changing technology, it may be expedient to overtrain on a particular machine for a specific application, but this tends to subvert overriding educational goals. We are interested in training scientists and engineers about supercomputing concepts and issues, not about a particular supercomputer, because we know that over the course of their careers, technology will change, change, and change again. We want people who can adapt to rapid technological changes and avoid becoming obsolete.

The result is a training program that attempts to bridge the gap between computer-specific training and computer science education. It treats scientific supercomputing conceptually and pragmatically. We have combined some features of both types of programs and added an emphasis appropriate for our audience [8]. This training program gains its strength from our long experience in education and the support of a traditional computing center combined with our more recent experience in the support of a variety of remote supercomputing centers and their users. It can be seen as a step in the evolution of an integrated network of centers of supercomputing. This training program does not teach participants how to use particular supercomputer systems, although they do learn this. It helps them understand what concepts and issues are central to supercomputing. Thus, they will be better able to approach any supercomputer, evaluate its program development tools, adapt their application programs to the hardware, and evaluate the supercomputer's performance on application programs in their fields of research.

Computing Facilities: Critical to this robust approach has been access to not one, but several, advanced computing centers. Computers used in this program include: CRAY X-MP/48 running CTSS at the National Center for Supercomputing Applications (NCSA) at the University of Illinois at Urbana-Champaign, IBM 3090 600E/VF running CMS at the Cornell National Supercomputer Facility (CNSF), IBM 3081 plus FPS 164 running 1CAP at IBM Kingston, Alliant FX/8 running UNIX at the Advanced Computing Research Facility (ACRF) at Argonne National Laboratory, and Cyber 205 running VSOS (soon to be an ETA10) at the John von Neumann Center. Workstations used in this program include: IBM PC2/60, IBM PC/AT, Macintosh SE, and Sun.

Professional Level Audience: The program is designed for researchers in computationally intensive research areas. Typically, the program has included graduate-level science and engineering students who have completed their course work and are already engaged in computing as part of their research. The program is also appropriate for postdoctoral students and others who have recognized the need and who can devote a significant amount of time to research.

Prerequisite knowledge includes: (1) a working familiarity with Fortran programming and some mainframe operating system, and (2) a working application program. Because of the intensity of this workshop program, there is little time for significant code development, and participants are encouraged to have a working application program ready to explore, port, time, and debug. Appropriateness of the research code to supercomputers is a factor in selection of participants; if needed, we help students obtain code in their own field appropriate for the workshop. Participants work on the applications they know, and both students and advisors consider time spent in the training program to be part of their research experience.

Time Commitments and Program Size: Participants focus on this training program and their own research full-time for eleven weeks without distractions from teaching or other duties. Student participants receive a research assistantship from their department or from the program so that they may devote their full time to the program. It is this immersion that allows participants to develop a better understanding about what makes computing a bottleneck and a rate-limiting step in their research.

The number of participants is kept small (four to six) to promote master/apprentice relationships with experienced scientific programmers and to help develop a sense of "team work" that is emphasized by repeated participant presentations and by group debugging sessions with the staff.

Cross Fertilization of Research Areas: The training program is not limited to particular fields of research, but rather is open to any research area that needs the capabilities of supercomputers. Participants are selected from a balanced variety of disciplines so that they have the opportunity to learn from each other about a wider range of applications, problems, and solutions. This cross fertilization contributes to an understanding of the benefits to be gained from interdisciplinary interactions. Typically, the program has included two participants from applied fields and two from computer science, mathematics, or electrical engineering (see Table 1). It is our objective to maintain this balance for the foreseeable future; our experience with participants' interactions reinforces our expectations for the success of this approach.

All this is not to say that program participants do not need a background in computer science. The way to make the most significant improvements in the computing time of an application program lies more often in a better algorithm than in optimization or hardware improvements, and computer science knowledge often leads to these algorithm improvements. It is a secondary role of the computer science participants to help other participants gain an informal understanding of this value, while they themselves come to understand the application of supercomputers to scientific problem solving.

Table 1: Student Participants and Their Research Areas

Student	Field of Study	Research Area
	Fall 1987 Program	
Victor Dirda	Electrical Engineering and Computer Science, UIC	Natural language interface for the development of large-scale software systems
Vanessa Job	Mathematics, Statistics, and Computer Science, UIC	Error-correcting, duadic cyclic codes
Prasad Ravi	Chemical Engineering, UIC	Simulation of heat exchange and liquid propellants
Nazeer Shareef	Mechanical Engineering, UIC	Robotics and finite-element stress analysis
	Winter 1988 Program	
James Choi	Electrical Engineering and Computer Science, UIC; and Bioengineering, UIC	Image processing, analysis, and classification of diatoms
Matt Hettinger	Physiology and Biophysics, UIC	Time series modeling of electrical evoked potentials, as related to memory
Anil Manhapra	Mechanical Engineering, UIC	Computational fluid mechanics
Li Zhou	Mathematics, Statistics, and Computer Science, UIC	Parallel processing in sorting and searching of rule-based systems in artificial intelligence
	Spring 1988 Program	
Hui Cheng	Mechanical Engineering, UIC	Dynamic control of robotics by parallel computers
Sharon Fetzer	Chemistry, UIC	Biophysical chemistry
Devinder Singh	Chemical Engineering, UIC	Computer simulation of molecular dynamics
Xian Zhang	Mathematics, Statistics, and Computer Science, UIC	Hidden surfaces in computer graphics

Implementation

Rather than approach this training program from traditional points of view, such as hardware or software or algorithms or specific computers, we examined the nature of scientific supercomputing to reveal how it is different from other kinds of computing and, consequently, what knowledge and understanding is essential for computational scientists. As described by Lawson [9], many courses derive from the instructor's own background and educate people to have a similar outlook of relative importances. However, we felt that, having an application science orientation, a computational scientist should approach computing from neither hardware, software, nor algorithms, but from a blend and balance of all [10].

The program includes two components, seminars and research [11].

Seminar Component: Seminars cover many concepts and issues of current and future scientific supercomputing. These seminars are conducted roughly every other day by a variety of visiting lecturers—users, vendors, computer scientists, mathematicians, and engineers from academic departments, computing and research centers, and the computing industry—each an expert in his or her own field, and by students themselves and staff. The goal is to provide the breadth of topics that is necessary to understand scientific supercomputing in the practical environment of the participant's own application code running on a variety of supercomputers. Seminars emphasize general concepts of scientific supercomputing, supported by some specific technical details, so that participants are not completely overwhelmed and are able to retain enough of each topic to make sense out of the whole. We ask visitors to concentrate on similar concepts as related to their expertise so that participants are exposed to different points of view and learn, first hand, why there are many approaches to supercomputing and which ones suit their purposes. Seminar topics are described below, and the relative weights of each can be seen in Table 2.

What is scientific supercomputing? To establish a foundation of knowledge, participants inventory their breadth of experience in computing: in hardware, in the use of existing software, and in the building of new software. We discuss characteristics that distinguish scientific supercomputing from other types of computing, such as student classroom computing, business computing, system programming, and real-time computing. This helps participants identify areas that are familiar and those that are new. The rest of the training program elaborates these distinguishing characteristics.

Table 2: Seminar Topics

Topic	Number of Sessions
What is Scientific Supercomputing?	1
Introduction to Supercomputer Architectures and Operating Systems	2
Supercomputer Architectures: Cray, IBM, others, experimental	3-5
Operating Systems and Environments: CTSS, CMS/MVS, UNIX	3-5
Communications and Networks	2
Software Design and Maintenance	3
Code Optimization:	
Timing and Debugging	1
Vectorization	2-3
Parallelization	2-3
Numerical Considerations	2
Computer Graphics	2
Evaluation of Design and Implementation	2
The Science:	
Students	3-5
Advisors	1-2
Site Visits: NCSA, Argonne, other	2-4
Wrap-Up	1

Architecture of supercomputers. We introduce principles, concepts, and terminology of supercomputer architectures; discuss vector processing hardware and multiple processors for parallel processing; and learn how several computers (such as Cray, IBM, and Alliant) work, including CPU, registers, and memory. Lecturers emphasize knowledge of hardware and system architectures and how they affect efficient coding techniques.

Operating systems and environments, communications and networks. We discuss concepts upon which different operating systems are based and examine several (such as CTSS, CMS, and UNIX) to understand important differences between them and how this affects scientific supercomputing. The importance of local area communications at the University and wide area communications via NSFnet and other national networks, including definitions and protocols, is included.

Software design and maintenance. Because scientific application programs have a long lifetime and are in a perpetual state of evolution as research needs change, we encourage special understanding of the need for good software design and analysis techniques and for re-evaluation of software after it has been implemented in a new environment. Modularity—both small-grain modularity for subroutine libraries and large-grain modularity for problem setup, computing, and post-processing—enhances readability and modifiability, two concerns that are dealt with in the research component of the training program.

Code optimization. Before a program can be made more efficient, it must be analyzed and timed to discover the most fruitful regions for optimization. The effect of choice of data structures on execution time, space/time trade-offs, and the need to discover better algorithms are discussed, as is automatic compiler optimization and the effects of vectorization and parallelization on coding and algorithms.

Numerical considerations. Computational scientists need to learn about the nature of computer arithmetic, round-off errors, random number generators, the stability of algorithms, and the different nature of errors in vector and parallel processing. Evaluating and selecting algorithms from existing libraries is another topic that does not have a regular place in curricula and that is of practical importance to our audience.

Computer graphics. Because of limited graphics hardware availability and current performance problems of graphics in a networked environment, some participants have little experience with computer graphics. These sessions expose participants to a wide variety of graphics, set their future sights on the importance of graphical output in the analysis of results, and help them understand the use of graphics as a tool in thinking about science. It also helps them understand the difference between lower-cost scientific graphics for day-to-day research and higher-cost presentation graphics for final research results.

Evaluation of program design and implementation. We emphasize the need to assess a computer program as a separate step: to remember the scientific problem we are exploring, and to evaluate if this program is the best mapping of the problem onto the computer and if this computer is the best choice for this problem.

Research Component: Early in the program, each participant defines his or her own workshop research objectives and then pursues implementation of an application program on a variety of supercomputers and discovery of particular criteria for understanding. Participants present aspects of their research several times during the program as their application advances and receive suggestions from staff and other participants on the methods used. In this way, the team continues learning from each other's work. Advisors' presentations are an important part of this process and help emphasize the relationship of the workshop to the participant's career.

After adapting their codes to particular supercomputer architectures and operating systems, participants spend several days at a supercomputing/research center to work closely with researchers and experts in studying their application programs and the effects of supercomputing environments. The site visit provides participants with intensive experience working on their application programs with the close assistance of on-site experts.

To facilitate the participants' research, "toolkit" and "clinic" sessions are conducted by workshop staff and faculty sponsors; these are a more formal learning part of the research (or laboratory) component of the workshop.

Half-hour toolkit sessions assist participants in identifying useful computing tools and related documentation for particular computers. We want to emphasize that each toolkit covers a variety of operating systems and encourages a system-independent comparative attitude. Topics covered in toolkit sessions are given in Table 3.

Clinics provide an opportunity to discuss particular programming problems and issues in detail with experts and students together; these team discussion/debugging meetings cover students' actual problems. For example, we have guided tours of how to read and debug programs, including those written by others, a very important part of all our professional lives. Other successful clinics include design of testing procedures for each code and participants' presentations of several different approaches to a problem gathered from the literature. These clinics, together with student and staff presentations, serve a fundamental purpose: they provide a computing "apprenticeship" that is the counterpart of the apprenticeship provided by students' advisors in their scientific field. We have found, time and time again, that these sessions are where participants learn the limitations of their own approaches and start to develop wider perspectives. Topics covered in clinics are given in Table 4.

Facilities and Support: Each participant has exclusive use of a workstation connected to local and national networks; the proximity of participants throughout the program contributes to interchange of ideas and understanding. Participants also have easy access to local and remote consultants, online information systems, and a local library of materials, which includes books, journals, supercomputer manuals, articles on computer optimization, mathematical libraries, videotapes, and online pointers to this material. Into the existing online computer documentation system, we have incorporated an online bibliography of materials available in our local library and in the University library. This integration of mainframe and microcomputer documentation with the supercomputing bibliography has two objectives: (1) it makes clear to the student that supercomputing is not a cure-all but must be used only when it is effective, and (2) it introduces, to the rest of the computing community, the idea that supercomputing can be used to expand local computing capabilities.

Table 3: Toolkit Topics

Topic	Number of Sessions
Signing On and Off, and Shipping Files	1
Finding Information	1
Compiling, Loading, and Executing, and Their Listings	1
Editors	3
Debugging Tools	2
Timing and Analysis Tools	3
Vectorization	2
Parallelization	2
Controllers, Batch Processing, and Background	3
Checkpoint/Restart	1
Building User Libraries	1
Math Libraries	1
Computer Graphics	2

Table 4: Clinic Topics

Topic	Number of Sessions
Compiler and Loader Listings	1
Reading and Reviewing Programs	1
Testing	2
Timing and Debugging	1
Vectorization	1
Parallelization	1
Reading the Literature	1
Computer Graphics	1
Optimizing an Application Program and Comparing Supercomputers	1

RESULTS

When the program was designed, we recognized that its unique features should be continuously evaluated, since there was no previous experience to draw upon. The most useful feedback is that from the students themselves—we distributed detailed evaluation sheets after each seminar, toolkit, and clinic session; these sheets were reviewed by the program staff weekly. We also scheduled a post-mortem session with each group of students. The most important conclusions of this evaluation process are enumerated below and are then elaborated.

1. The "immersion workshop" approach was extremely successful in beginning to create robust, flexible supercomputer users. Immersion led to a qualitative change in the students' understanding of the process of computing and its relationship to their scientific aims.

2. Research assistantships give participants the time and support to immerse themselves in this program.

3. Access to different computer architectures and to supercomputing centers of expertise is fundamental; the program would not exist without them.

4. Direct exposure to vendors in a technical context was an important part of the learning experience; this analytical interaction with vendor experts is characteristic of the forefront of technology.

5. Repetition of presentations by the students as their work progressed was very useful to the students themselves and an effective method of sharing strategies.

6. Greater participation of students' research advisors should be encouraged.

7. Site visits are important to the sense of growth, understanding of research computing trends, and camaraderie among participants.

8. Most students were surprised to discover that they did not have the basic computing and debugging techniques that would have been useful in all kinds of software development.

Main Results of the Program

Workshop Approach Success: Immersion of a few students into concepts, issues, and practices of scientific supercomputing for a relatively long time was fundamental. Participants learned a great deal about supercomputing in general, adapted their application programs for several supercomputers, and compared performance. About the sixth week of each workshop, we started to see participant research develop with a better understanding of the nature of supercomputing. After completing three workshops, we also see that links are by no means cut at the end of one term, and alumni draw freely on our resources as needed.

A good way to show the success of the program is through its effects on participants and their research groups. Because of their new understanding of fundamental concepts and their newly perceived need for information, two engineering alumni will take computer science classes next fall in numerical algorithms and introduction to computer architecture. An alumnus was able to demonstrate, by careful benchmarking of a speeded up program, an error that cropped up after 4000 iterations and opened the way for making the group results more accurate. We have a second applicant from this same research group, which is already a heavy user of supercomputers at CNSF and Palo Alto IBM 3090 installations. An alumna who was not computer proficient before the program was able to expand the complexity of her thesis research in one quarter; and we have a second applicant from the same research area. An engineering alumnus was asked by his department head to make a presentation to the whole department on his timing benchmarks on finite-element program optimization; we have had an applicant from that department every time the program has been offered.

Changes in Point of View: Students who have participated in our model program have learned how to diminish the role of computing as a bottleneck in their research. They are able to assess the value of different computers; as one participant put it, "I am more relaxed at the terminal. I also am able to implement new programs more quickly than before and I 'dream bigger,' i.e., consider implementing programs that I would have considered to be too difficult before." We have also seen an increase in interdisciplinary questions among participants themselves and among participants and faculty engaged in the clinic sessions.

Direct Application on Own Codes: Perhaps the single most important factor in the success of the program is the requirement that participants bring to the training program a specific problem that they need to solve. The danger of such an approach is that participants may over-specialize on their specific applications; in fact, however, our experience has been quite the opposite. By providing a firm focus for their work, participants have a much stronger motivation for assimilating new information, and they treat the workshop as much more than just an intellectual exercise.

Education of Non-Programmers: Of wider implication is the realization that there is no mechanism in place for non-programmers to learn "good programming habits," since these are still passed on in an apprenticeship context and professional scientific programmers are not common in academia. The students discovered that they lacked basic skills that would have been useful in the program; it is very important that additional avenues be established so that non-programmers gain the background that is essential to their development and productivity.

Efficiency of the Educational Process and Resource Allocation: In evaluation sessions with current and past students, it has become obvious that there are two things students perceive as most useful: (1) the time available to go over their own programs again and again and the repeated presentation of their results, each time with more knowledge and understanding, learning something new as time and their background progress, and (2) sitting down with experts to deal with specific issues (such as what do you need to know in order to move from fully supported mainframe use to almost unsupported supercomputer use or how do you time and speed up difficult code). Participants have been very clear that they consider the program a success from their standpoint: they have advanced in their research at the same time that they have absorbed an enormous amount of background education. The fact that this knowledge makes participants more valuable to their present research groups and more employable in the future plays no small part in their dedication.

This program has been able to bring to campus professionals not otherwise accessible. Visitors come as seminar speakers, but the program has waiting for them, in addition to the usual interested audience, a small group of dedicated students with the time and knowledge to get more out of the visit. The program has increased communications between the graduate student cohort on campus and computing center staff in charge of research computing support; it has allowed us, as computer professionals, to pass on to participants much more than what we were able to before. Staff whose time commitment is substantial consists of one full-time equivalent person during the two initial quarters of program design, redefinition, and search for support; this was reduced to three-quarters of a person for the third quarter. But, we should not lose sight of the fact that a great part of this effort (for example, user contact and keeping abreast of developments in the field) would be expended by center staff in any case; in this sense, the program has provided an efficient and satisfying framework for furthering support of computer teaching and research on campus.

Unanticipated Findings: The best lecturers for this training program are experts who understand the concepts and issues and can interpret the significance of various practices. People with limited skill in teaching or narrow experience in the use of supercomputers were not suitable.

Although we give invited speakers an outline of the whole training program, including the seminars they are involved in, we cannot predict what will actually be covered in each seminar. Thus, it is important that the workshop coordinator attend all seminars, toolkit, and clinic sessions to maintain knowledge of what has been covered, to identify topics that need further elaboration, and to help participants relate material to what has been covered and what will be covered.

Technical presentations on computer architecture and program optimization by computing industry experts are invaluable for their thorough knowledge of their own machines. It exposes participants to a breadth of viewpoints that increases their analytical skills.

We were surprised how important site visits were. Site visits contributed significantly to the development of shared experience of participants from different research areas. They afforded an opportunity for participants to break from their absorption of the large quantity of new material and spend some less pressured time with each other. As participants acquired common experiences, their discussions and interactions grew.

Participants did not have realistic expectations; they did not anticipate how beneficial this program would actually be or how much they would want to accomplish during it. Thus, we emphasize the value of starting their research component as soon as possible.

Advisors, too, share the lack of clear expectations of the students; they are aware of the benefits expected but not of the work involved to achieve them. Students' advisors are a valuable resource of knowledge and experience from which participants can benefit. Involvement of advisors also increased their own understanding of the role of the program and its significance for their students. This involvement must be encouraged; it does not necessarily come by itself.

FUTURE DIRECTIONS

Program Content

The intellectual content of a training program of this nature is determined by its participants' needs; adaptability is one of its advantages. It is easy to imagine that in several years many topics covered now (vectorization and portability, for example) may have become part of the arsenal of tools of most computer-sophisticated research areas and will demand supercomputing center consulting rather than background educational programs. If our approach is successful, though, we will by then have evolved toward both the new needs in the current constituency (more parallelism, more visualization, and more workstation/supercomputer interface development) that are barely touched now and the new needs of an expanding new constituency, those social and medical scientists and humanists who now shy away from supercomputing. To fulfill the hopes for supercomputing, we have to seek these non-traditional users, adapt the program content to their research needs, and adjust the program size to accommodate them. In the same way that mathematicians and computer scientists in the program are important resources for the applied scientists in the team, we will use the expertise of applied scientists more comfortable with computing issues to expand the computing vocabulary of newer groups.

Adaptation for Other Scientific Computing Centers

The environment that we create for participants is, in terms of hardware and connectivity, the same one provided for their research by the University. In this sense, the program can be easily duplicated by any institution involved in computing support; in particular, any university affiliated with an NSF-supported supercomputing center is probably in a good position to duplicate the program with limited local effort. Discussions with colleagues at national laboratories (Argonne and Los Alamos, in particular) and with industry have made evident the appeal of this approach to other institutions engaged in transferring professional knowledge. As said in the introduction, this program owes much to an understanding of the way in which professionals keep abreast of new developments in technical fields.

For others seeking to emulate what we have done, we emphasize the importance of a broad-based pool of human resources and, particularly, communication and cooperation among all academic units that might be affected. Certainly, participation from computer science, mathematics, engineering, physical sciences, and computing centers is essential; ideally, social scientists, artists, and others would help round out the program and open the eyes of their colleagues to potential applications of supercomputers. Given the emphasis we place on team work and interactions, it is not enough just to advertise the training program. For the program to be successful, it is necessary to search for appropriate workshop participants and instructor expertise. This is another by-product of a multidisciplinary base, in that the more disciplines that are actively involved in the program, the broader the pool of potential participants. It is also important to remember that, in a fast moving field like this, no single entity can count on in-house expertise necessary to realize the full potential of this program. Vendors, supercomputing centers, national laboratories, and academia must be part of the human resource pool to be drawn upon. Technical presentations by vendors and students' own advisors are a rich source of information not otherwise available; the potential for expansion has been barely tapped.

SUMMARY

The UIC Workshop Program in Scientific Supercomputing is presented as a link between supercomputing centers and their users and as a link between computational scientists and computer scientists. As such, it cannot exist on its own but must be coordinated with all of these. Success with the program allows us to offer it with confidence as a viable program for other universities with limited local supercomputing support but with a strong computing research environment. Its dissemination benefits not only individual universities and their supercomputer users; it also benefits national supercomputing centers as well, by providing these centers with a larger pool of supercomputer-sophisticated users and relieving their consulting staff of some onerous and repetitive questions. It increases interaction between computer scientists and the scientists who benefit from their research and who are often unaware of how effective a tool computer science can be. Also, we should not forget that, in the last instance, integration of supercomputing into everyday science and engineering practice depends on a large pool of trained users; development of new algorithms and techniques depends on a large pool of sophisticated users. These users are being formed at universities, and the rate at which supercomputing expertise diffuses through a university has a fundamental importance in the formation of the next pool from which we all will draw.

ACKNOWLEDGMENTS

A workshop program such as this relies on the support of visiting lecturers, computing time on a variety of supercomputers, and fellowship money to support the students.

This workshop program was made possible through the generous support and contributions of many people. Joint sponsorship within the University (UIC) provided a breadth of support that gave this program necessary validity. George Yanos, from the Computer Center, UIC, contributed to the program development; Steve Roy, from the Supercomputing Support Office of the Computer Center, UIC, provided consulting support; and Maxine Brown, from the Electronic Visualization Laboratory, UIC, provided graphics coordination. Seed money from the University's Graduate College was essential in funding participants, and research assistantships from the Departments of Chemical Engineering and Mechanical Engineering demonstrated their confidence in this program. Office space, seminar space, and staff from the Computer Center were essential.

This workshop program could not exist without the technological base, supercomputing support, and computer time provided by the National Center for Supercomputing Applications, the Cornell National Supercomputer Facility, and the Advanced Computing Research Facility at Argonne National Laboratory. Support of the computing industry was vital in providing expert visiting lecturers and workstation equipment. We thank Kelly Altman of Cray Research and Kevin Quinn of IBM for their support in obtaining excellent speakers. And we thank IBM for their generous loan of equipment for participants and for supporting a Vectorization Fellowship for a student to act as class assistant and consultant. Site visits significantly affected the viewpoint of the participants and contributed to their growing understanding of scientific supercomputing. We thank Enrico Clementi and Douglas Logan of IBM Kingston, James Bottum and Alan Craig of NCSA, and Rick Stevens of Argonne National Laboratory for supporting and arranging visits to their sites.

Students made a significant commitment of their time based only on our promise to provide a worthwhile program for them; their names are listed in Table 1. The advisors generously supported their students in this opportunity to bring knowledge of supercomputing into their research group. Perhaps most importantly, we thank the many visiting lecturers for their time and effort in creating seminars of value to our students and for their long, fruitful discussions with the workshop staff; their names are listed in Table 5.

Table 5: Faculty

Associated Faculty

Kathy Barbieri - Cornell National Supercomputer Facility
Ingrid Bucher - Los Alamos National Laboratory
Duncan Buell - Supercomputing Research Center, Institute for Defense Analyses
Helen Doerr - Cornell National Supercomputer Facility
Dennis Duke - Florida State University Supercomputer Institute
Evelyn Goldfield - Cornell National Supercomputer Facility
Robert Haber - National Center for Supercomputing Applications
Moham Jayaram - IBM Kingston
John Lacher - Cray Research
Rick Lawrence - IBM Kingston
David Levine - Argonne National Laboratory
Douglas Logan - IBM Kingston
Michael Norman - National Center for Supercomputing Applications
David Soll - IBM Kingston
Craig Upson - National Center for Supercomputing Applications
Tony Warnock - Cray Research at Los Alamos National Laboratory

University (UIC) Faculty

Maxine Brown - Electrical Engineering and Computer Science, UIC
Earl Gose - Bioengineering, UIC
Krishna C. Gupta - Mechanical Engineering, UIC
Floyd Hanson - Mathematics and Computer Science Division, Argonne National Laboratory; and Mathematics, Statistics, and Computer Science, UIC
Pierre LeBreton - Chemistry, UIC
Tom Moher - Electrical Engineering and Computer Science, UIC
Sohail Murad - Chemical Engineering, UIC
Nora Sabelli - Computer Center, UIC; and Chemistry, UIC
Shin-Min Song - Mechanical Engineering, UIC
Jose Sousa - Electrical Engineering and Computer Science, UIC; and Borg Warner
George Yanos - Computer Center, UIC; and Mathematics, Statistics, and Computer Science, UIC
John Andrews - Computer Center, UIC
Peter Asick - Computer Center, UIC
Fred Damen - Computer Center, UIC
Robert Goldstein - Computer Center, UIC
Steve Roy - Computer Center, UIC
Ann Solem - Computer Center, UIC; and Computing and Communications Division, Los Alamos National Laboratory
Michael Sperberg-McQueen - Computer Center, UIC
Kathi Suchy - IBM Vectorization Fellowship

REFERENCES

[1] *Report of the Panel on Large Scale Computing in Science and Engineering,* Peter Lax, Chairman. Sponsored by the U.S. Department of Defense and the National Science Foundation, in cooperation with the Department of Energy and the National Aeronautics and Space Administration, Washington, D.C., December 26, 1982.

[2] *A National Computing Environment for Academic Research.* Marcel Bardon and Kent Curtis, NSF Working Group on Computers for Research, National Science Foundation, July 1983.

[3] *A National Computing Initiative: The Agenda for Leadership.* Chaired by Harold J. Raveche, Duncan H. Lawrie, and Alvin M. Despain. SIAM Workshop, Leesburg, Virginia, February 2-3, 1987. Society for Industrial and Applied Mathematics, Philadelphia, 1987.

[4] Saxe, Paul, Los Alamos National Laboratory. Unpublished report, presented to *Theory and Simulation in Chemistry: The Impact of Minisupercomputers and Supercomputers,* organized by Thom H. Dunning, Jr. and Ron L. Shepard, Argonne National Laboratory, and Lola Anacker, John von Neuman Center, 1987.

[5] Hyman, James M. "Future Directions of Large Scale Scientific Computing," in *Large Scale Scientific Computation,* edited by Seymour V. Parter, Academic Press, 1984, pp. 51-83.

[6] Berztiss, Alfs. "A Mathematically Focused Curriculum for Computer Science," *Communications of the ACM.* Vol. 30, No. 5, May 1987, pp. 356-365.

[7] Knuth, Donald E. "An Empirical Study of FORTRAN Programs," *Software--Practice and Experience,* Vol. 1, 1971, pp. 105-133.

[8] NCSA Summer Training Seminar course notes. National Center for Supercomputing Applications, University of Illinois at Urbana-Champaign, June 1986.

CNSF Smart Node training course notes. Cornell National Supercomputer Facility, Cornell University.

Anderson, Jess. "Local course near leading edge," *MACC News.* Academic Computer Center of the University of Wisconsin-Madison, Vol. 22, No. 7, August 24, 1987, pp. 4-5.

Hanson, Floyd B. Numerical methods for parallel and vector computers syllabus. Department of Mathematics, Statistics, and Computer Science, University of Illinois at Chicago.

Maisel, Merry. "Educating Rita," *Gather/Scatter.* San Diego Supercomputer Center, Vol. 3, No. 7, July 1987, pp. 1-3.

Moses, Greg. Private communication. University of Wisconsin, August 1987.

Moyer, Tom. Private communication. Department of Civil, Mechanical, and Environmental Engineering, George Washington University, August 1987.

Panoff, Robert M. Private communication, computational physics course notes, and NCSA Summer Institute course notes. Department of Physics, Kansas State University, August 1987.

[9] Lawson, Harold W., Jr. "Computer Architecture Education," in *New Computer Architectures,* edited by J. Tiberghien, Academic Press, 1984, pp. 225-286.

[10] *UIC Workshop Program on Scientific Supercomputing, Fall 1987 Quarter.* University of Illinois at Chicago, 1987.

UIC Workshop Program on Scientific Supercomputing, Winter 1988 Quarter. University of Illinois at Chicago, 1988.

UIC Workshop Program on Scientific Supercomputing, Spring 1988 Quarter. University of Illinois at Chicago, 1988.

[11] Dwyer, Thomas. "Discussant Remarks," *Computer Literacy: Issues and Directions for 1985,* National Goals for Computer Literacy in 1985 Conference, Reston, Virginia, December 18-20, 1980, edited by Robert J. Seidel, Ronald E. Anderson, and Beverly Hunter, Academic Press, 1982, pp. 193.

Architecture - II

Chair: Jack Worlton
Worlton and Associates

THE DESIGN OF A LOCKUP–FREE CACHE FOR HIGH–PERFORMANCE MULTIPROCESSORS*

C. Scheurich and M. Dubois
Department of Electrical Engineering
University of Southern California
Los Angeles, California, 90089–0781
(213) 743-8080, dubois@priam.usc.edu

Abstract—High-performance multiprocessors must incorporate a high-bandwidth, short-latency memory aggregate to support maximal processor utilization. Cache memories are often used to meet this requirement. The performance of cache-based, shared-memory multiprocessors can suffer greatly from moderate cache miss rates because of the usually high ratio between memory-access and cache-access times. In this paper we propose a lockup-free cache design in which the handling of one or several cache misses is overlapped with processor activity. In multiprocessors, lockup-free caches aggravate the memory coherence problem. Three different cache architectures relying on different compiler interventions are introduced. A performance model demonstrates the usefulness of lockup–free caches for high–performance processors. The merits and disadvantages of the three schemes are discussed and compiler techniques, to take advantage of the proposed designs, are illustrated at the end of the paper.

1 Introduction

Cache memories have been proven to be effective in reducing the memory access latency for most uniprocessors [1]. For fast processors, however, the difference between the cache access time and the memory access time tends to increase. The ratio between these two latencies severely affects the *miss penalty.* When the miss penalty is high, then even small cache miss rates result in low processor efficiency. This is due to the large number of wasted processor cycles while a processor waits for a cache miss to be resolved.

When private caches are used in multiprocessors then the *cache coherence* problem must be addressed [2]. Cache-based, shared-memory multiprocessors tend to exhibit large cache miss penalties since main memory access latencies are likely to be large and since coherence activities, such as invalidations, reduce the overall cache hit rates. Increased memory access latency and conflicts reduce the efficiency of each processor. Prefetching, which can reduce the apparent access latency visible to the processors, is also more difficult in multiprocessors because of the coherence problem.

Kroft [3] has described a *lockup-free* cache architecture for uniprocessors. In such a design the cache does not block the processor on an access miss. Several cache misses may be outstanding at the cache at any time, while being resolved by main memory. For multiprocessors, lockup-free caches must incorporate a coherence protocol; beyond coherence, the architecture must also preserve certain access orders which may otherwise be reversed by the lockup-free nature of the caches.

In this paper the problems which lockup-free caches pose in multiprocessor configurations are described. Three schemes are outlined which can be used to address these logical difficulties. A performance model is derived to demonstrate the utility of lockup-free caches in the context of processor utilization. Software support for lockup–free cache–based multiprocessors is discussed in Section 6. Conclusions are drawn in Section 7.

2 Multiprocessor Performance and Correctness

If we assume that a cache with a perfect hit rate can service processor requests as fast as they are issued, then the processor will be running at its peak speed. Any cache miss causes the processor to idle for the duration necessary to service the miss. The effect on overall processor utilization is an easily derived function depending on the ratio of memory access versus cache access times, the hit rate, and the average number of memory accesses issued per instruction. In a system, for example, for which the average number of memory accesses per instruction is 1.5, and the ratio of access times is 10, utilization drops to approximately 25%, 60%, and 78% of peak performance, for hit rates of 0.8, 0.95, and 0.98, respectively.

Cache hit rates can be improved by using larger caches and "good" replacement policies. However, the faster the processor, the larger the ratio between memory and cache access times tends to become. In multiprocessors, contention in the processor to memory interconnection, can increase the ratio further. Cache block invalidations caused by other processors wishing to modify a block can also depress the cache hit rates.

In a lockup-free cache architecture neither the processor nor the cache block if an access misses at the cache. The processor can continue to execute instructions and issue memory accesses to cache and the cache can continue to service processor requests. The outcome of any sequential execution in this type of architecture (uniprocessor) must be indistinguishable from the outcome of a similar architecture using a locking cache. This requirement dictates that a processor must block itself if a not yet resolved access (due to a miss) can affect the next to be executed instruction. Such *hazard* detection mechanisms are commonly used in pipelined processors [4] to preserve dependencies.

The cache controller, on the other hand, must maintain status information on misses currently being resolved, and on the action to be taken once the memory forwards a block which pre-

*This research is supported by an NSF Research Grant No. CCR–8709997.

CH2617-9/88/0000/0352$01.00 © 1988 IEEE

viously caused a miss. Since status information is maintained by the cache, the number of misses which can be kept pending is finite, and hence the cache must be able to block the processor from issuing more requests if the "status space" is exhausted. Kroft [3] gives a complete description of the necessary control actions of a uniprocessor lockup-free cache.

In uniprocessors, lockup-free cache architectures cause reversals in the order in which accesses are executed from the access order implied by the program. For example, for a code sequence (1) `Load [A]`, (2) `Load [B]`, an access to B may occur before the access to A, if access (1) misses at the cache and access (2) hits at the cache. If this reversal has no associated hazard, then the reversal is acceptable.

In multiprocessors the arbitrary reversal of memory accesses *within* a single instruction stream, and with no hazard within the stream, may or may not be allowable. Whether such reversals are allowable depends on the expected behavior of the multiprocessor. A *sequentially consistent* multiprocessor models the behavior of a uniprocessor in the manner in which it executes parallel programs. In such a multiprocessor synchronization can be implemented by shared memory accesses. Therefore memory accesses within a single instruction stream may never be reversed. It is difficult, if not impossible, to design a sequentially consistent multiprocessor with lockup-free caches.

Alternate models of behavior of multiprocessors do exist. In [5] one was described and referred to as a *weakly ordered* system. In a weakly ordered system all shared memory writes must be made from within critical sections. Within a critical section memory accesses may be made in any order which does not violate intra-process dependencies. Critical sections are "guarded" by special hardware recognizable memory accesses (synchronization accesses). Before a synchronization access may proceed all previous accesses must have been concluded. It is possible to incorporate lockup-free caches in weakly ordered multiprocessors. This paper introduces several such designs.

A weakly ordered system assumes three types of shared data:

1. Instructions[1], private data, and non-writable data can be accessed and cached by all processors in any possible order. Since non-writable data are never modified, the order in which they are read is irrelevant. Likewise, with private data which are only modified and read by one processor.

2. All other ordinary shared writable data can only be modified in *mutual exclusion.* These are data used to transfer information from one process to another.

3. Synchronization variables are data used to enforce mutual exclusion on write accesses to ordinary shared writable data. Synchronization variables are hardware recognizable as such.

The order of accesses to type (1) data are constrained by the usual single instruction stream hazard detection rules. Data of type (2) are user/compiler generated. Accesses to such data must be protected by critical sections or semi-critical sections [6]. In the first case data may only be read or written by one processor at a time the processor which has gained access to the appropriate critical section. In the second case, several processes are allowed to read the same data at the same time but updates must occur in a critical section.

[1] We assume separation of instructions and data so that instructions can never be modified.

Accesses to data of type (3) are synchronization primitives such as `test&set` operations. Since data modified within a critical section cannot be read by another processor, while the modifying processor is still executing the critical section, the order in which the data are modified within the critical section is immaterial. The only ordering constraint for correctness is that all updates have properly propagated when the critical section is exited. A processor need not keep track whether a synchronization access indicates the end of a previous or the beginning of a new critical section—it must simply ensure that all previous type (2) accesses have concluded before the synchronization access can proceed.

We summarize this section by defining four properties that must be maintained for a weakly ordered system to remain correct:

P1: Intra-process dependencies must be observed at all times. Such dependencies must be treated as in any conventional uniprocessor.

P2: Memory coherence must be maintained. This is true for all three data types. Any processor's read operation will always reflect the most recent write operation to the datum. (Memory coherence of type (2) data only has to be restored *before* the processor that modifies it exits the critical section. Whether this relaxation is useful depends on the unit of data (i.e., block size) on which coherence is maintained versus the modifiable unit of data (i.e., word size)).

P3: All modifications of type (2) data must be performed from within critical sections. The compiler or the programmer must ensure that no two or more processes can be in the same critical section at the same time.

P4: All pending misses must be resolved before an access to type (3) data can proceed.

3 Lockup-free Caches and Coherence

The previous section addressed correctness of execution in weakly ordered systems based on the allowable ordering of accesses with respect to word accesses. Multiprocessor cache coherence is however usually not enforced on words but rather on blocks, where one block contains several words. The manner in which coherence and concurrent miss resolutions affect each other depends on the block size and the allocation of data to blocks. Three different schemes are practical and possible:

Word-sized blocks: The easiest way to coordinate access ordering and coherence is to let the cache block size be equal to one word. A shared word fills exactly one block and therefore the entire content of a shared writable block is always modified by only *one* processor at a time. If partial word modifications are disallowed, then the scheme has the further advantage of never experiencing a write cache miss to type (2) data. Such a write can immediately proceed, whether or not the block (word) is present in cache, and only an invalidation needs to be broadcast informing all other caches that their copies of the block are invalid.

A one-word block size architecture does not take advantage of spatial locality which inevitably results in lowered hit rates. However, small block sizes take better advantage of available cache space, and improve execution speed [7]. A one-word block size, lockup-free cache multiprocessor architecture is described in [8].

Exclusive blocks: If cache blocks contain more than one word, then two or more different words belonging to the same block can conceivably be modified from within different critical sections. If the compiler ensures that *all* words belonging to a single block are *only* accessed from within *one* critical section, then the block is called exclusive. This scheme is logically similar to the one-word block size approach, except that cache write misses *can* occur. A write miss results in the buffering of the written word and a subsequent retrieval of the block the word belongs to. Data allocation in this type of scheme can be difficult and inefficient. Since private data are accessed by one processor only, a block can never contain either a mix of private data belonging to different processes or a mix of private and shared data.

Non-exclusive blocks: If the compiler does not ensure modification of block contents by one processor at a time only, then blocks can be concurrently accessed by different processors. Words modified in a block are still accessed in mutual exclusion, but *different* words in the same block can belong to different critical sections. Blocks can contain any mix of non-modifiable, private, and shared words. This approach can cause logical problems which must be solved by the hardware. If multiple processors write to a block concurrently then two rules must be upheld:

1. A read of a word by a processor either must reflect the value of the word valid *before* the most recent synchronization access by the processor, if the processor has not modified the word since then; or must reflect the most recent write of the word by the processor, if indeed the processor has modified the word since the last synchronization.
2. All words modified by a processor after a synchronization access S1 and before a synchronization access S2, must be correctly reflected by read accesses made by any processor after S2 has been performed. That is, the modifications must be "inserted" into their respective blocks, before access S2 may proceed.

4 Lockup-free Cache Architectures

In the following, three lockup-free cache architectures are described, using word–sized block, exclusive block, and non-exclusive block caches. The purpose of these descriptions is to outline how lockup-free caches can be used in weakly ordered multiprocessors. Many implementation details are not described. The architectures described will function correctly with most multiprocessor coherence protocols. Whether distributed or centralized, such schemes usually rely on a serialization of block state changes. This serialization can be enforced by means of a central controller, or by using broadcast buses and bus–snooping. For simplicity's sake, the following descriptions are based on the assumption of a single broadcast bus and a three–state invalidation protocol. The following assumptions hold for all three architectures:

1. Processors issue accesses to cache only if the access does not cause a hazard with respect to a not yet resolved miss.
2. Caches maintain records on pending misses, such as block address, operation type that missed, word that missed (if applicable), destination of word (in the case of a read), and some other information. These registers are called MSHR (miss information status/holding register) registers—using Kroft's terminology [3].
3. A cache blocks the processor from issuing more accesses when it has exhausted its storage capability to keep track of pending misses.
4. Blocks are either absent in cache, or present and tagged as RO (Read Only) or RW (Read Write). A RO block copy may be read but not modified. A RW block copy can be read and modified. Usually only one RW copy of a block is allowed to exist at any given time.
5. A block is fetched if there is a write miss (write allocate) (if applicable).
6. A synchronization access cannot proceed until all pending misses have been resolved.
7. All coherence traffic with respect to any one block is globally serialized, either by a broadcast bus, or by means of central directories.
8. A cache block frame is cleared and allocated to a pending miss at the time of the miss.
9. Block frames in state RO are overwritten, blocks in state RW are written back to main memory upon replacement.
10. The replacement policy is such that a block which has been allocated a block frame cannot be replaced before it has been copied into the frame. (it may be invalidated, though, in the case of non-exclusive blocks.)

In the following, we further assume that coherence is enforced by means of a snoopy cache protocol which uses a single bus (coherence bus) to serialize all coherence traffic. Multiple coherence buses, interleaved by address ranges could be used as well. The same explanations also hold for centralized table schemes to enforce coherence.

The following nomenclature applies:

A destination within a processor is the logical or physical intended destination of a resolved read access. A destination can be a register, a functional unit, or a processor assigned context ID.

A cache hit occurs if an accessed block is present either in state RO or RW in cache.

A primary miss occurs if an access is not a cache hit *and* no MSHR entry exists for the block (i.e., the block is not presently being fetched).

A secondary miss occurs if an access is not a cache hit and an MSHR entry for the block *does* exist.

A miss resolution occurs when a pending block is copied into cache and its MSHR entry is cleared.

An invalidation request causes an invalidation of all other cache's copies of a block. In a bus-based protocol, an *invalidation request* and an *invalidation* are one and the same signal. In a system using a central controller an invalidation request causes the controller to issue an invalidation of the block to other caches in response—in this case an *invalidation request* and an *invalidation* are different signals. If a central controller and table exist, then the sender of the invalidation request is marked as the *only* cache with a valid copy of the block (including main memory).

A block read request by a cache is answered with a copy of the block. Again a *block read request* is issued by the requester and a *block read* is issued to the requestee. In a bus-based system the signals are the same. If the block exists as a single RW copy in a cache, then that cache supplies the block copy and changes the state of its copy from RW to RO. If no cache copies or several RO copies of the block exist, then main memory supplies a copy of the block.

An RW block read request by a cache is answered with a copy of the block, and causes the invalidation of all other copies of the block. The requester cache issues the *RW block read request* and the requestee caches receive *RW block reads.* Again in the case of a bus-based system the signals are the same.

4.1 One–word block size

If the block size is equal to one word, only one processor can attempt to modify a block at any time, since only one processor has access to the relevant critical section at any time. Write accesses always appear to hit at the cache since a write to a word modifies the entire block it belongs to. MSHR registers must contain (1) block ID, (2) frame ID, and (3) destinations. The block ID is simply the word address. The frame ID is the cache block frame to which the block has already been allocated. The destinations field contains one bit for every possible destination of the word (see Figure 1). Multiple destinations of a word are possible if a second or third access to the same word misses at the cache before the first miss has been resolved.

A read hit is serviced as in any ordinary cache. MSHR registers need not be accessed. In case of a read miss, MSHR registers must be (associatively) searched to check whether the "missing" block is already in transit. If that is the case (secondary miss), then the additional destination of the word is added to the destinations field of the already existing MSHR entry. If return of the block is not pending (primary miss) then an MSHR register is "filled out" with the block ID, a vacant cache block frame is located or a block frame is freed and allocated to the block. The block frame ID is also entered into the MSHR register. Finally the destination of the to be returned block is entered in the MSHR and a block read request is placed on the interconnection port—indicating that a read–only (RO) copy of the block is requested.

A write access to a block in state RW can proceed immediately. If the block exists in state RO, then the write may proceed and an invalidation request of the block is placed on the interconnection port. The state of the block is changed from RO to RW. Similarly, a write to an absent block can proceed—once a block frame has been freed—and only an invalidation request

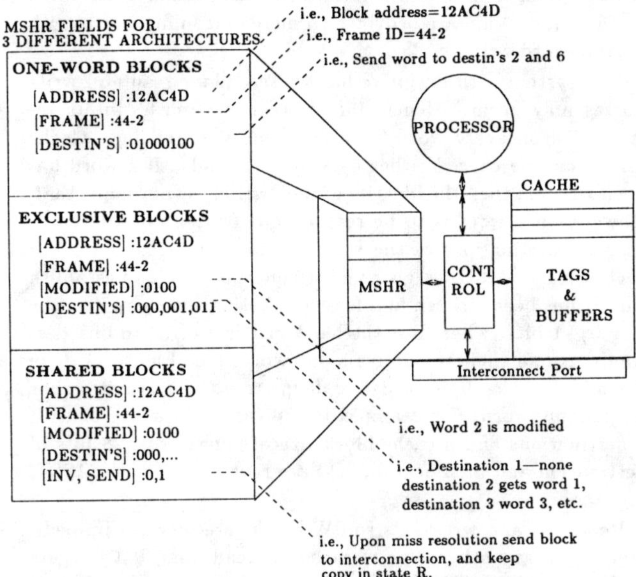

Figure 1: Cache organization and MSHR fields for the three different block types.

of the block must be placed on the interconnection port.

The architecture and lockup–free protocol are so simple because only one processor modifies a block at a time, and since hazards are avoided by the processor. For example, external invalidation requests for blocks with pending read misses cannot occur. Likewise, write accesses to blocks for which a read is still pending cannot occur.

If a snoopy–cache protocol is implemented, then each cache must continuously monitor the bus. The cache may have to supply blocks which it owns in state RW by interrupting the block read requests to memory and supplying the word itself. The state of the block is then changed from RW to RO. Since any block present in any cache in state RO must also be valid in memory, cache–interrupted bus reads also trigger main memory write–backs. The other bus requests which caches must react to are invalidations. Invalidations cause present blocks to be invalidated regardless of their state. Any block returned to the cache after a miss request is matched to its MSHR register which defines the word's destination(s) and its allocated block frame.

4.2 Exclusive blocks

An architecture relying on exclusive blocks retains the advantage of allowing only one processor at a time to access or modify any of the contents of a block. The architectural difference between one–word blocks and exclusive blocks (which contain more than one word) is that write accesses can miss at the cache and that the missing block must be fetched from main memory or another cache. If the write access can be buffered and later, when the missing block arrives, is incorporated into the missing block, then all write accesses are immediately performed with respect to the issuing processor at the time of the miss. We assume that write accesses are stored in the appropriate word offset of the block frame allocated to the block at the time of the primary miss. This strategy can be extended to allow byte or half-word modifications if additional control and status information are provided to merge incoming words with partial-word writes.

In a system with exclusive blocks, secondary read and write misses may occur. Hence, MSHR registers must contain information on every word for which a miss is pending. Cache misses can be caused either by writes or reads. If a word has been written, then the identity of the "writer" is not important. However, if a word is to be read by one or more destinations, then all destinations of the word must be known. Hence, for each word an MSHR register must contain one bit to establish that it has been written and for each destination there must be (log b)+1 bits (where b is the block size in words) to link destinations and their respective input words (see Figure 1). The extra bit over log b, is needed to define that the destination has *no* pending word. For example, in the case of a processor with 8 destinations and a cache block size of four words, 28 bits of destination and modification field are required for each MSHR register.

Read hits and write hits to RW blocks are serviced immediately as in any other type of cache. A read miss first triggers a check of the MSHR registers to determine whether it is a primary or a secondary miss. In the case of a secondary miss, the MSHR will indicate whether the word in question has been written due to a primary or a secondary miss and hence is already located at its block frame. If this is the case, then the word can be fetched from the block frame and be forwarded to its destination immediately. No further modification of the MSHR or outside communication are necessary. If the word is not marked as written in the MSHR, then its ID (i.e., block offset) is placed in the appropriate destination field of the MSHR, so that the word will be forwarded correctly upon miss resolution. In the case of a primary read miss, an MSHR register is allocated with the block ID, a block frame is freed and its ID is stored in the MSHR, and the word offset and its destination are linked. A block read request of the block is placed on the interconnection port.

A write access to a block in state RW can proceed immediately. If a write access hits on a block in state RO, then the write may proceed, the block state is changed from RO to RW, and an invalidation request of the block is placed on the interconnection port. If a write access misses, then MSHRs are checked first. If it is a secondary miss, then the write (of the word only) proceeds at the designated block frame, and the word is marked as written in the MSHR. If all access misses of the block since the primary miss have been reads then an invalidation of the block is placed on the interconnection port (since the block will be placed in state RW upon miss resolution due to at least one modified word).

If the write causes a primary miss, then an MSHR is allocated, a block frame is allocated and the modified word is written to the block frame. Furthermore, an RW block read request is placed on the interconnection port. In the MSHR the modified word is marked as written.

Upon miss resolution (when a block arrives via the interconnection) the incoming block is matched to the appropriate MSHR register, and all marked destinations are forwarded the pending word(s). The block is copied to its allocated block frame, except that words that are marked as already modified in the MSHR, are not overwritten in cache. The block is marked

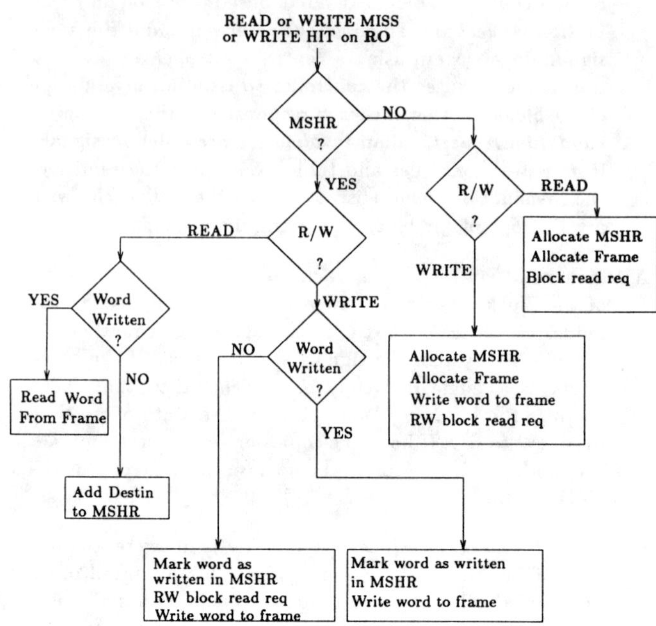

Figure 2: Cache miss management for non-exclusive block lockup-free caches.

as RO if no write flags are set in the MSHR, and is marked as state RW if words of the block had been written.

4.3 Non-exclusive blocks

In the case of non-exclusive cache blocks more than one processor can modify different words belonging to the *same* block concurrently. A block always has a single *global* state, determined by the most recent state change executed on or by the serializing device. If the "serializing device" is a shared bus, then every processor (cache) observes all coherence activity in the same order. If a central controller is used to which coherence requests are sent and which in turn sends coherence commands, grants, or acknowledgements, then it must be ensured that all signals sent by the controller, pertaining to the same block, are received in the same order by all processors (caches).

Two additional flags for each MSHR register are necessary for concurrent read and write operations of the same block by different processors. An *invalidation* flag is set if an external invalidation arrives at a cache while the referenced block is present in an MSHR register. A *send* flag is set if a request for the block (block read) arrives while the referenced block is present in an MSHR register. Both flags are set if an RW block read to the block occurs (see Figure 1). Furthermore, any write access on a block in state RO is handled as a miss. Similarly, secondary write misses on an otherwise unmodified block cause a RW block read request on the first occurrence (see Figure 2).

If the primary miss was a read miss and no further write misses occur, then miss resolution occurs when the block read request is answered. If a secondary write miss occurred, then miss resolution only occurs once the subsequently triggered RW block read request is answered—the response to the simple block read request is ignored. If the primary miss is a write miss, then miss resolution occurs upon the reply of the initial RW block read request.

Upon miss resolution all destinations receive their pending words. If both the *send* and the *invalidate* flags are set, then the block, including newly modified words from the assigned block frame, is written back to the interconnection and then invalidated at the cache. If only the *send* flag is set, then the block is copied to the assigned block frame without overwriting any words already in the frame which are marked as modified in the MSHR *modified* field. The block is marked to be in state RO and then written back to the interconnection port. If neither the *send* nor the *invalidate* flag are set, then the block is copied to its assigned block frame. If any words were modified during primary or secondary misses then the modified words are not overwritten and the block is retained in state RW. If no writes occurred, the block is kept in state RO.

Note that as in the case of one-word blocks, no secondary write miss on a word can occur on which a primary or a secondary read miss is still pending—this would violate a write-after-read hazard.

An alternative to using the additional *invalidate* and *send* flags is to permit processors to block incoming invalidations with a *busy* signal. In this case, the cache which sends the invalidation request cannot proceed until the busy signal has been terminated.

5 Analysis

A lockup-free cache performance model is presented here. The throughput of a processor using a lockup-free cache is compared with the performance of a processor using a blocking cache. Several approximations are made, but useful information can be derived. We assume that a sufficient number of MSHR registers exists at the cache so that the processor is never blocked due to unavailability of a vacant MSHR register. This assumption will be justified later by the results derived. We make the following additional assumptions in our model:

1. A processor makes d memory references per instruction.
2. The distance between references with dependencies in the reference string of a process is fixed and is equal to l. Hence, after a miss, up to l references can be made before the processor blocks and has to wait for the miss to be resolved.
3. For each access the probability of a hit is h and the probability of a miss is $(1-h)$. Successive accesses are independent. Therefore, the number of references between two consecutive misses is geometrically distributed with mean $1/(1-h)$.
4. The memory access time is constant and equal to T_m.
5. The time to execute an instruction if all accesses hit in the cache is constant and equal to $t_{i,0}$. We associate a time of $t_{i,0}/d$ with each reference.
6. Effects of synchronization are neglected.

The model does not focus on a single specific cache scheme. Under the assumptions given it holds true for one-word block sizes, and approximates the performance of exclusive and non-exclusive block schemes. Results for exclusive block architectures should be slightly better since the average miss resolution latency is reduced by the fact that secondary cache misses *appear* to be resolved faster than primary cache misses. The same holds true for non-exclusive block architectures. For non-exclusive block systems, the impact of invalidations caused by block-sharing is ignored. However, this effect is present whether the cache is lockup-free or not.

There are several approximations in the model. First of all, in a practical system the dependency distance is usually variable and the memory access time is random because of memory conflicts. These two approximations were made here to facilitate the solution of the model. Second, the successive accesses to the cache are correlated; however, the hypothesis of independent accesses is often made in cache models (see for example [9]) and is as good as any other hypotheses in the absence of real program traces. Overall, we feel that the models include the most important parameters affecting the performance of the lockup-free caches and should give indications as to system configurations for which the complexity of lockup-free caches is warranted.

Case 1: In this case we assume $t_{i,0}l/d < T_m$. After the first miss, at reference $1/(1-h)$, l references can be generated by the processor while the first miss is resolved by the memory system in time T_m. Therefore, a processing time of $t_{i,0}l/d$ can be overlapped with the first miss. If any one of these l references causes a miss, it can be serviced immediately because there are an infinite number of buffers. The misses occurring for the l references do not cause additional blocking due to dependencies because the processor has to wait until the first miss is resolved before initiating new references. When the first miss is completed, the processor can continue execution, and because of the geometric distribution assumption, the next miss occurs $1/(1-h)$ references later, on the average. The sequence of events after the first miss is repeated.

Therefore, in a time

$$\frac{t_{i,0}}{d}\frac{1}{1-h}+T_m$$

a number of $\frac{1}{1-h}+l$ references are performed, corresponding to

$$\left(\frac{1}{1-h}+l\right)\frac{1}{d}$$

instructions.

The average time per instruction is

$$\frac{t_{i,0}+T_m d(1-h)}{1+l(1-h)}$$

and the performance ratio of a lockup-free cache-based processor versus the same processor with ideal zero-latency memory is given by:

$$\frac{1+l(1-h)}{1+T_m^0 d(1-h)}$$

Case 2: In this case we assume that $t_{i,0}l/d \geq T_m$. When a reference has a dependency with a previous access that missed, the miss has had the time to complete and therefore, the dependencies do not block the processor. We have achieved total overlap of miss handling and the processor executes at its peak speed (the ratio described in the first case, becomes 1 here).

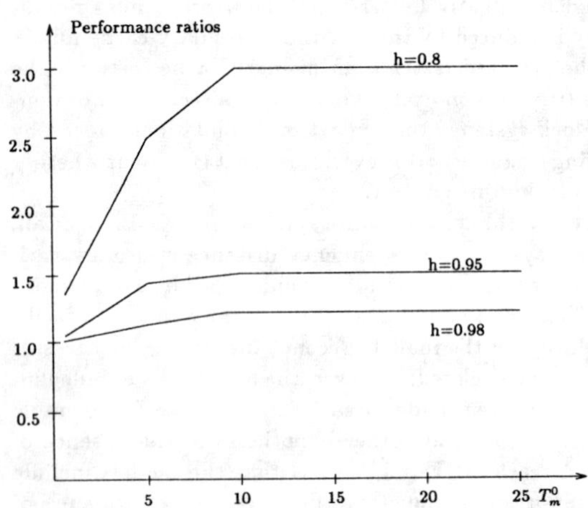

Figure 3: Processor performance ratios of lockup–free cache versus blocking cache as function of T_m^0.

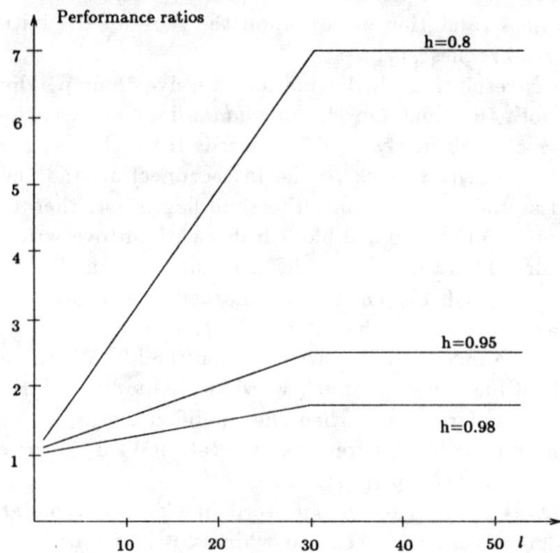

Figure 4: Processor performance ratios of lockup–free cache versus blocking cache as a function of l.

6 Discussion

6.1 Performance and Software

Since the results obtained must be compared not with systems with "perfect" caches, but rather with systems with conventional, blocking caches, Figure 3 shows the ratio of processor utilization of a lockup–free cache versus a blocking cache. Results for different hit rates versus T_m^0 are shown. The improvement of performance is highest for a low hit rate of h=0.8. This is to be expected, since a high miss ratio results in multiple misses in a streak of l consecutive references and these misses can be overlapped. In the ideal case, for example, l misses occur sequentially, until the system blocks due to a dependency with the first miss (we assume $l/d < T_m^0$). The misses are resolved one after another and the total penalty paid for the sequence of l misses is only T_m^0. Hence, the system benefits from frequent misses.

For $l/d > T_m^0$, the system operates at maximum speed, with a processor utilization of 100%. In this case no miss ever causes a penalty, since the system does not block on multiple misses and all misses are always resolved before a dependency can occur. For higher hit rates the probability of overlapping misses decreases and the performance ratio degenerates.

Since the implementation of an infinite number of MSHR buffers is clearly impossible, it is interesting to derive the number of miss buffers used on average. It is possible to estimate the average number of busy buffers in the cache as follows. Let t_i be the average time per instruction. The average time to execute N instructions is Nt_i and a total of $Nd(1-h)$ misses must be processed, requiring a total service time of $Nd(1-h)T_m$ from the miss buffers. Therefore the average number of busy buffers is

$$\frac{d(1-h)T_m}{t_i} = \frac{d(1-h)T_m^0}{1+d(1-h)T_m^0}[1+l(1-h)] \quad (case\ 1)$$

$$or\ = d(1-h)T_m^0 \quad (case\ 2)$$

This value is upper-bounded by $1 + l(1-h)$. For all of the examples of Figure 3, the average number of busy buffers is less than 2.75. Clearly, maximum performance is guaranteed when the system can never "run out of" MSHR buffers. For fixed cache and memory access latencies the required number of buffers is $T_m^0 d$.

A cache with a number of MSHR buffers can be very useful. Such a cache can offer substantial improvement over a locking cache when the hit rate is not very high. Moreover, the performance of the system improves more for lower hit rates. This fact can benefit systems in three particular circumstances.

1. Any system with a low hit rate benefits from lockup-free caches consistently.
2. Context switches always cause very low transitory hit rates. A lockup-free cache can help "smooth" the performance dip in the system behavior after such context switches.
3. A cache which usually exhibits a good hit rate, may be sensitive to particular "pathological" workloads which can lower the hit rate for particular applications, or, especially, for operating system calls. As in the case of context switches, the cache can adapt to such workload changes if it is lockup-free.

Figure 4 shows the ratio between the MIPS rates of the lockup-free cache system with an infinite buffer and of the locking cache system as a function of l. For this case, $T_m^0 = 20$ and $d = 1.5$. As is to be expected the performance ratio increases linearly until $l/d = T_m^0$ up to a point where the lockup-free cache system operates at peak speed and remains constant. In the case of a hit rate $h = 0.8$, the maximum performance improvement over the locking cache system is 700%. Again, it is evident, that the performance improvement is much higher for workloads with low hit rates.

Since the inter-dependency distance l affects the performance of the system greatly, techniques on how to increase l are important. These techniques can be classified into software and hardware techniques. In many cases the software approach must go hand-in-hand with the hardware approach.

1. The compiler can attempt to increase l within the instruction stream by reordering instructions in a more favorable way.

2. All load instructions should be non-blocking; as they are implemented in the IBM RT processor [10].

3. The compiler can generate special instructions which explicitly load data into cache, long before they are needed. Such non-blocking load operations enable the compiler to control selective prefetching of data. These loads should be generated in bursts.

4. For instruction access misses not to cause blocking, several consecutive instructions can be prefetched ahead of instruction decode time. Only `branch` instructions will cause blocking in this case. If branches are delayed as in RISC processors, l can be increased.

5. We believe that even in conventional machines, l can sometimes be very high. For example, in high-level languages, data are frequently moved around in the memory, enbloc, to facilitate such concepts as "scoping". If the compiler generates code for such housekeeping chores efficiently, then l can conceivably be large.

6.2 Implementation

The three lockup-free cache schemes described present three different levels of implementation complexity. Clearly, a one-word block size lockup-free cache is the simplest to implement and probably lends itself best to bus-based systems with only a few processors. In such a system cache operations are not significantly slowed-down by MSHR control activity. The penalty paid for this simplicity is the reduced cache hit rate due to the small block size. Either systematic or compiler-controlled prefetching of words is likely to be necessary in such a system to properly benefit from the cache architecture.

Systems based on exclusive blocks require more complex cache controllers and can suffer from allocation inefficiencies. Depending on the application, data allocation into exclusive blocks can be trivial or near-impossible. Many scientific applications, especially those dealing with linear algebra, exhibit good spatial data locality and orderly data sharing. Traditionally vector processors have been used to attack such problems. Multiprocessors with exclusive block lockup-free caches with large block sizes, may constitute another architectural philosophy to attack these problems. Small systems may be built using shared buses, and larger systems can be constructed using hierarchies of buses.

Systems based on non-exclusive blocks are most difficult to implement. Such systems require the most *miss status space* in each cache. However, little software support is needed for such systems. Compilers must simply differentiate between the three data types defined in Section 2 to guarantee that the system is weakly ordered. Due to the complexity of the cache, this scheme is probably best implemented in large systems with at least several dozens of processors.

7 Conclusion

Three schemes to implement lockup-free caches in multiprocessors have been presented. Each scheme presents a trade-off between cache complexity and performance improvement. While examples are given for a simple bus-based invalidation protocol, we believe that most other cache coherence protocols can work in conjunction with lockup-free caches.

We have shown that the processors of a multiprocessor system may resolve multiple misses concurrently if the system is weakly ordered. Weakly ordered multiprocessors require that shared writable data are modified exclusively from within critical sections. This restriction can be enforced by the compiler. In the case of exclusive cache blocks, the compiler must further ensure that all data allocated to a block are modified only from within a single critical section.

A simple model has been derived to exhibit the usefulness of lockup-free caches. The results are encouraging and show that on average a system need only track a small number of pending misses to experience performance improvements.

8 References

[1] A.J. Smith, "Cache Memories", *ACM Computing Surveys*, Vol. 14, No.3, Sept. 1982, pp.473-530.

[2] L. M. Censier and P. Feautrier, "A New Solution to Coherence Problems in Multicache Systems," *IEEE Transactions on Computers*, Vol. C-27, No.12, December 1978.

[3] D. Kroft, "Lockup-free Instruction Fetch/Prefetch Cache Organization," *Proceedings of the 8th International Symposium on Computer Architecture*, June, 1981.

[4] P.M. Kogge, "The Architecture of Pipelined Computers," *McGraw-Hill Book Company*, 1981.

[5] M. Dubois, C. Scheurich and F. Briggs, "Memory Access Buffering In Multiprocessors," *Proceedings of the 13th International Symposium on Computer Architecture*, June 1986.

[6] M. Dubois, "Effect of Invalidations on the Hit Ratio of Cache-Based Multiprocessors," *Proceedings of the 1987 International Conference on Parallel Processing*, Aug. 1987.

[7] R.L. Lee, P.-C. Yew, and D.H. Lawrie, "Multiprocessor Cache Design Considerations," *Proceedings of the 14th International Symposium on Computer Architecture*, Pittsburgh, June 1987.

[8] C. Scheurich and M. Dubois, "Concurrent Miss Resolution in Multiprocessor Caches," *Proceedings of the 1988 International Conference on Parallel Processing*, Aug. 1988.

[9] J.H. Patel, "Analysis of Multiprocessor with Private Cache Memories," *IEEE Transactions on Computers*, Vol. C-31, No. 4, April 1982.

[10] C.E. Gimarc and V.M. Milutinovic,"A Survey of RISC Processors and Computers of the Mid-1980's," *IEEE Computer*, Sept. 1987.

CRegs: A New Kind of Memory for Referencing Arrays and Pointers

Henry Dietz

School of Electrical Engineering
Purdue University
West Lafayette, IN 47907
hankd@ee.ecn.purdue.edu
(317) 494 3357

Chi-Hung Chi

Phillips Laboratories
345 Scarborough Road
Briarcliff Manor, NY 10510

Often, pointer and subscripted array references touch memory locations for which there are several possible aliases, hence these references cannot be made from registers. Although conventional caches can increase performance somewhat, they do not provide many of the benefits of registers, and do not permit the compiler to perform many optimizations associated with register references. The CReg (pronounced "C-Reg") mechanism combines the hardware structures of cache and registers to create a new kind of memory structure, which can be used either as processor registers or as a replacement for conventional cache memory. By permitting aliased names to be grouped together, CRegs resolve ambiguous alias problems in hardware, resulting in more efficient execution than even the combination of conventional registers and cache can provide.

This paper discusses both the conceptual CReg hardware structure and the compiler analysis and optimization techniques to manage that structure.

Keywords: cache, register, register-allocation, data-aliasing, compiler-optimization.

1. Concepts

To explain how and why CRegs[1] improve performance, it is first necessary to analyze how and why conventional registers and cache can fail to improve performance (as well as how and why they can improve performance).

1.1. Registers

A register array is a relatively small, fast, local memory residing in an address space separated from that of main memory. The structure of a register memory cell is given in Figure 1.

name:	*datum*

Figure 1: Register Memory Cell Structure

By placing a value in a register, one can reap at least four benefits:

[1] The fast access time of values in registers reduces latency.

[2] A reference to a register typically does not interfere with references along the path(s) to main memory, thereby effectively increasing usable bandwidth to main memory.

[3] Typically, the predictability of register references aids in compile-time optimization of code and simplifies hardware. Optimizations are aided in that reference times can be known at compile time; hardware is simplified in that register references in most machines cannot cause pipeline bubbles.

[4] Because register names are typically shorter than memory addresses, referencing values in registers actually decreases the required instruction-fetch bandwidth — even though registers typically cannot hold instructions.

The "catch" is that, for most programs, many values cannot benefit from being kept in registers. Although it is true that sometimes a value cannot be kept in a register because the hardware provided too few registers, even given an infinite number of registers, a large fraction of the values computed within any program should not be kept in registers. To understand why some values should not be kept in registers, one must understand a little bit of compiler flow analysis.[2]

Suppose a particular segment of a program refers to two names, one called α and the other called β. If one of α and β is a pointer, or one is a call-by-address argument to this routine and the other is a variable which was accessible in the caller's scope, or both are elements of the same array (such as `a[i]` and `a[j]`), etc., then it is possible that even though α and β look like different names, they refer to the same object. In other words, changing the value of one might change the value of the other, i.e., α and β might be aliases for the same object.

If compile-time analysis can prove that α and β cannot be aliases for the same object, then α and β can each be assigned to a register and each can be kept there indefinitely. Instead, if the compiler can prove that α and β are always aliases for the same object, then α and β are assigned to share a single regis-

[1] A patent application for the CReg invention is currently in progress.

[2] The description given here of the ambiguous alias problem is a gross oversimplification intended only to give an intuitive introduction to the problem. This issue is currently one of the richest research areas within compiler technology; more detailed discussions of this problem appear in [All83], [Bur84], [BuC86], [All86], [Ste86], and [Die87].

ter, and again the object can be kept in a register indefinitely. However, if the compiler isn't sure if α and β refer to the same object, or if α and β only sometimes refer to the same object, we say that α and β are ambiguously aliased to each other.

At this point, it is useful to point out that compile-time analysis techniques for determining if α and β are aliases for each other are, at best, complex to implement and easy to confuse. Confusion results in the "safe" assumption that α and β are ambiguously aliased to each other. In addition, in many cases it is *theoretically impossible* for the compiler to determine whether α and β are aliased, in which case the compiler must again assume that they are ambiguously aliased. A good example of such a case is determining whether `a[i]` and `a[j]` are aliased in code like Listing 1.

```
readln(i, j);
b := a[i] + a[j];
```

Listing 1: Compile-Time Unresolvable Aliasing Problem

If the compiler's best "guess" is that α and β are ambiguously aliased, then placing either value in a register will require "flushing" that register whenever either α or β is stored into. This "flushing" is usually needed so often that the cost of referencing α and β from registers is actually greater than the cost of referencing them from main memory, hence, placing α and β in registers would degrade, rather than improve, performance.

1.2. Cache

A cache is a "small" memory holding rapidly accessible copies of values addressed associatively by main memory addresses. The conceptual structure of a cache memory cell is shown in Figure 2.

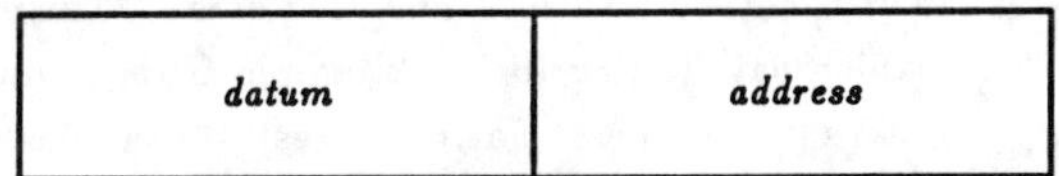

Figure 2: Cache Memory Cell Structure

Of the four benefits listed for placing a value in a register, however, in general, caches only insure [1]: a reduction in access latency. Benefit [2], which is based on the lack of interference between register and main memory data paths, does not hold for a traditional cache, except in that other processors in a multiprocessor system typically would not see interference from cache references on a particular processor's cache.

The predictable reference time for a register reference, benefit [3], is not echoed in cache reference because of the concept of a cache miss. Some would argue that, given a large enough cache, the probability of having a cache miss can be made arbitrarily low; however, we believe this misses the point. One reason we disagree with the very-large cache argument is that the access speed of a memory is related to the size of its address space (e.g., if one can fit the cache on the processor chip, it will probably function much faster than if it is referenced across several chips). Another reason is that the cost of implementing an arbitrarily large cache is also arbitrarily large — it isn't very cost effecitive. In any case, unless the cache is as large as the entire virtual address space of the machine, one will occasionally suffer a cache miss, and this implies that extra hardware/software effort must be made to cope with this situation.

Benefit [4] is based on the reduction of required instruction-fetch bandwidth due to use of short names in referencing values. This cannot be applied to cache because the register correspondence between short names (register numbers) and long names (memory addresses) must be explicitly established by register `Load` and `Store` instructions, whereas the mapping in a cache is unknown to the software. In other words, a compiler cannot tell which cache line of a conventional cache will hold a copy of a particular value it is referencing — hence, it cannot use the cache line number to address the value. The desired value might not even be in the cache, either because it has not yet been placed there or because placing some other entry in cache "bumped" the desired entry out of cache.

The above discussion might lead one to conclude that registers are far better than cache, so why use cache? The answer is simply that while ambiguously aliased values cannot be profitably placed in registers, they can be placed in cache.

1.3. CRegs

Unlike registers, cache-registers (CRegs) may be used to buffer values which may have ambiguous aliases; unlike cache, CRegs provide the ability to use short names for variables instead of addresses (thereby reducing instruction-fetch bandwidth requirements) and also provide for conceptually duplicate entries (many-to-one mapping of short names into addresses). CRegs provide all four advantages of registers; but CRegs provide these advantages for all values, ambiguously aliased or not.

The conceptual structure of a CReg memory cell is a superset of both cache and register cell organizations, as illustrated in Figure 3.

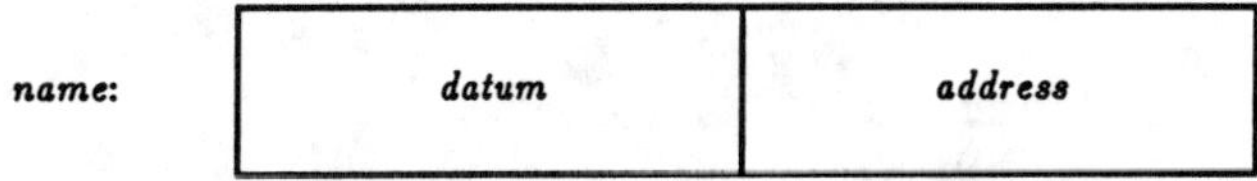

Figure 3: CReg Memory Cell Structure

Each CReg is a register which holds both address and data fields. When a CReg is referenced (by CReg number — a short name), an associative search is made to find neighboring CRegs which have the same value in their address field. Any CRegs found by this association *are* aliases for the CReg directly named, and the CReg hardware simply maintains coherence of these entries. This associative function is implemented by hardware very similar to that implementing the associativity of a cache, however, unlike a cache, CRegs avoid making memory references on an aliased `Load` operation by using *duplicate entries in the CReg array.* (The precise operation of CRegs is described in greater detail in the example of the following section.)

Although the STM (generalized Short Term Memory cell) [Sit79] employs a memory cell structure similar to that of a CReg, STMs did not support CReg-like associative function. Likewise, the "rack" described in [StS85], suggests a similar cell structure, but is not associative. The register-addressed stack cache mechanisms of various processors could be argued to provide benefits similar to that of CRegs; however, they do so only for items in the top few stack cells. Since these items are a subset of the items which could have been kept in registers, stack caches also fail to provide a solution to the aliased-item reference problem.

The implementation, and hence the circuit complexity, of a CReg array is virtually identical to that of a similar-size cache; the CReg array is slightly simpler because the hardware is explicitly told where to make each entry (what CReg number), whereas conventional caches use hardware-implemented policies, such as LRU, to decide which line to replace. However, CRegs can be managed as efficiently as registers, hence, unlike cache, very small CReg arrays are quite useful. For example, simply replacing the registers of a conventional processor with CRegs (and, incidentally, not even changing the instruction set) is typically both feasible and effective to the extent that the number of memory references made by the processor can often be halved.

2. An Example

An example clearly illustrates the advantage of being able to use CRegs for all value references, whether ambiguously aliased or not. Consider the FORTRAN code of Listing 2.

```
C
C     A call-by-address subroutine
C
      SUBROUTINE NASTY(I, J, K)
 10   I = J * K
 20   K = J + K
      RETURN
      END
```

Listing 2: FORTRAN Sample Code

The subroutine `NASTY` operates on three arguments, `I`, `J`, and `K`, which are all passed using call by address. Since FORTRAN permits `I`, `J`, and `K` to reference the same cell of main memory, the values of `J` and `K` cannot be blindly placed in conventional registers in the code for line 10 and simply reused in the code for line 20 — to do so would produce incorrect results if `I` refers to the same main memory cell as either `J` or `K`. To place these variables in conventional registers, the compiler would need to know precisely which of the arguments referenced the same cells — the classic ambiguous alias problem discussed earlier. Hence, unless the compiler is permitted to generate multiple encodings of `NASTY` (one for each possible set of variable aliases), none of `I`, `J`, and `K` can be kept in registers.

However, all of these variables can be placed in CRegs. In fact, if this is done, the references in line 20 will *always* be served within CRegs — main memory will not be accessed. Table 1 shows all possible combinations of aliases for `I`, `J`, and `K`, and, for each alias set, where the values of `J` and `K` are to be found.

Table 1: CReg Place of Reference for `J` and `K`

Aliases	Where `J` is	Where `K` is
`I`, `J`, `K` disjoint	CReg for `J`	CReg for `K`
`I` is `J`	Assoc. `I`,`J`	CReg for `K`
`I` is `K`	CReg for `J`	Assoc. `I`,`K`
`J` is `K`	Assoc. `J`,`K`	Assoc. `J`,`K`
`I` is `J` is `K`	Assoc. `I`,`J`,`K`	Assoc. `I`,`J`,`K`

As indicated earlier, the read requests in line 20 for `J` and `K` are always satisfied within the CReg array. The entries in the table which say "CReg for" are simple CRegs acting as ordinary registers (with no associative access); the entries which say "Assoc." are satisfied by the associative memory function of the CRegs. (Notice that the associative function depends on the existence of *duplicate entries* in the CReg array — which would not be permitted in a conventional cache.) Further, since all three variables can be placed in CRegs, the references in line 20 would simply use the CReg names, rather than memory addresses, because a CReg name *implies* a main memory address. This fact also permits *entire instructions to disappear*: `Store` instructions can be implicit, using a "dirty bit" and a "lazy store" mechanism.

It can be argued that the references in line 20 *might* be satisfied in a more conventional cache, thereby avoiding a main memory reference in the same way that CRegs avoid the reference; however, only CRegs can guarantee that this occurs under all circumstances (as we detailed in the previous section). Even accepting that a conventional cache *might* avert the main memory references as CRegs do, CRegs also reduce the *instruction fetch* bandwidth requirements by permiting short CReg names to be used for `I`, `J`, and `K` rather than long main memory addresses.

The next subsection briefly describes a simple RISC register-based processor design and its adaptation to use CRegs instead of registers. In the subsection following that, the above example is encoded and the execution traced for this RISC machine.

2.1. A RISC Processor using CRegs

There are many possible implementation techniques for CRegs. In this section, we discuss a simple modification of a RISC processor design which replaces a register array with a CReg array[3]. The point here is not to propose a RISC architecture, but rather to show the difference between register-based and CReg-based versions of the same architecture.

The example architecture is a 16-register RISC machine whose register Rf (register 15) is also the PC (program counter). Replacing the registers with CRegs, we obtain the programmer's model given in Figure 4.

R0:	D0	A0	R8:	D8	A8
R1:	D1	A1	R9:	D9	A9
R2:	D2	A2	Ra:	Da	Aa
R3:	D3	A3	Rb:	Db	Ab
R4:	D4	A4	Rc:	Dc	Ac
R5:	D5	A5	Rd:	Dd	Ad
R6:	D6	A6	Re:	De	Ae
R7:	D7	A7	Rf:	Df/IR	Af/PC

Figure 4: CReg RISC Programmer's Model

The first difference one notices is that each CReg has two fields, the data and address fields. Quite naturally, the PC is the address field of Rf, which implies that the data field of Rf is the IR (instruction register); although it is not a major point of this paper, prefetch of instructions beyond a branch is really just another flavor of ambiguous alias reference, and it too is handled using CReg associativity.

The programmer's model also reflects fragmentation of the 16 CRegs into four sets of four CRegs each. Since it may be difficult to construct cache-like hardware which is more than about 4-way associative [Smi78], the 16-CReg array is broken into associative groups of four CRegs each[4]. For example, if CReg R1 holds D1=5, A1=601 and an instruction attempts to load the contents of memory location 601 into R2, an associative load will occur (without a main memory reference) and R2 will hold D2=5, A2=601. If one tried to load the contents of memory location 601 into R4 instead of R2, since R1 and R4 are in different associative sets, a memory reference would be needed to load R4 and the value loaded might not match the value in R1. Obviously, the "trick" is to always place names which are ambiguously aliased together in the same set . . . compiler techniques to accomplish this are discussed in sections 3.2 and 3.3. If CReg hardware can be built without this segmentation, the only results are that compilation becomes easier and the CRegs become more effective.

The instruction sets of the RISC and CReg RISC machines are identical, hence there are no changes to describe.

2.2. Code for the Example

Using the original (conventional register-based) RISC design, the instruction sequence for the lines 10 and 20 of the FORTRAN program in listing 1 would be as given in listing 2. (To simplify the example, no special handling of delayed loads or other compiler optimizations are assumed.)

```
Ld      R0,@argJ        ;R0 <- addr(J)
Ld      R1,@R0          ;R1 <- J
Ld      R2,@argK        ;R2 <- addr(K)
Ld      R3,@R2          ;R3 <- K
Mul     R4,R1,R3        ;R4 <- R1 * R3
Ld      R5,@argI        ;R5 <- addr(I)
St      @R5,R4          ;mem(R5) <- R4
Ld      R1,@R0          ;R1 <- J
Ld      R3,@R2          ;R3 <- K
Add     R4,R1,R3        ;R4 <- R1 + R3
St      @R2,R4          ;mem(R2) <- R4
```

Listing 3: Register RISC Code

Listing 3 should be compared with the CReg RISC instruction sequence given in Listing 4. (As Listing 3, Listing 4 does not reflect the application of any compiler optimizations.)

---

[3] This is not implying, for example, that CRegs could not be implemented in any other way — in fact, CRegs can even be implemented by taking a conventional off-chip cache and simply mapping some portion of the global memory address space into literal cache addresses (cache line addresses rather than associative cache line address labels). A conventional processor could then use short offsets from an index register to reference these CRegs by name.

[4] Unlike caches which are grouped into sets by address-space, the CRegs in this machine are grouped into sets by CReg name-space. Alternatively, CReg sets could be time-space partitioned. For example, associative access to CRegs {R0, R1, R2, R3} may complete in two cycles, for CRegs {R4, R5, R6, R7} in three cycles, etc. Provided the number of cycles (time-multiplexed associative sets) is not greater than the main memory reference time, a compiler can consider this cost function in allocating CRegs so as to maximize probable benefit.

```
Ld      R3,@argJ        ;D3 <- addr(J), A3 <- argJ
Ld      R0,@R3          ;D0 <- J, A0 <- addr(J)
Ld      R4,@argK        ;D4 <- addr(K), A4 <- argK
Ld      R1,@R4          ;D1 <- K, A1 <- addr(K)
Mul     R2,R0,R1        ;D2 <- R0 * R1
Ld      R5,@argI        ;D5 <- addr(I), A5 <- argI
St      @R5,R2          ;A2 <- D5, mem(A2) <- D2
Add     R1,R0,R1        ;D1 <- D0 + D1, mem(A1) <- D1
```

Listing 4: CReg RISC Code

The first seven instructions of both register and CReg code sequences appear to serve the same purpose; however, they do not imply the same memory references. Further, in the rest of the code, a single instruction in the CReg version replaces four instructions in the conventional register code.

To make these differences more visible, we will consider the situation which occurs using CRegs when `I` is an alias of `K` (i.e., addr(`I`) is addr(`K`)). Figure 5 shows the progression of CReg contents as the CReg RISC code of Listing 4 is executed. In each of the diagrams of Figures 5a-5h, CReg associative sets which are not involved in the actions caused by this code sequence are not shown. The additional field on each CReg in Figures 5a-5h is the "dirty" bit — a 1 indicates a dirty value, which may be lazily stored back to main memory, reseting the dirty flag. Notice that dirty bits are also set/reset associatively.

R0:	—	—	-
R1:	—	—	-
R2:	—	—	-
R3:	addr(J)	argJ	0

R4:	—	—	-
R5:	—	—	-
R6:	—	—	-
R7:	—	—	-

Figure 5a: CReg Contents after Executing `Ld R3,@argJ`

R0:	J	addr(J)	0
R1:	—	—	-
R2:	—	—	-
R3:	addr(J)	argJ	0

R4:	—	—	-
R5:	—	—	-
R6:	—	—	-
R7:	—	—	-

Figure 5b: CReg Contents after Executing `Ld R0,@R3`

R0:	J	addr(J)	0
R1:	—	—	-
R2:	—	—	-
R3:	addr(J)	argJ	0

R4:	addr(K)	argK	0
R5:	—	—	-
R6:	—	—	-
R7:	—	—	-

Figure 5c: CReg Contents after Executing `Ld R4,@argK`

R0:	J	addr(J)	0
R1:	K	addr(K)	0
R2:	—	—	-
R3:	addr(J)	argJ	0

R4:	addr(K)	argK	0
R5:	—	—	-
R6:	—	—	-
R7:	—	—	-

Figure 5d: CReg Contents after Executing `Ld R1,@R4`

R0:	J	addr(J)	0
R1:	K	addr(K)	0
R2:	J*K	—	-
R3:	addr(J)	argJ	0

R4:	addr(K)	argK	0
R5:	—	—	-
R6:	—	—	-
R7:	—	—	-

Figure 5e: CReg Contents after Executing `Mul R2,R0,R1`

R0:	J	addr(J)	0
R1:	K	addr(K)	0
R2:	J*K	—	-
R3:	addr(J)	argJ	0

R4:	addr(K)	argK	0
R5:	addr(K)	argI	0
R6:	—	—	-
R7:	—	—	-

Figure 5f: CReg Contents after Executing `Ld R5,@argI`

R0:	J	addr(J)	0
R1:	J*K	addr(K)	1
R2:	J*K	addr(K)	1
R3:	addr(J)	argJ	0

R4:	addr(K)	argK	0
R5:	addr(K)	argI	0
R6:	—	—	-
R7:	—	—	-

Figure 5g: CReg Contents after Executing `St @R5,R2`

R0:	J	addr(J)	0
R1:	J+(J*K)	addr(K)	1
R2:	J+(J*K)	addr(K)	1
R3:	addr(J)	argJ	0

R4:	addr(K)	argK	0
R5:	addr(K)	argI	0
R6:	—	—	-
R7:	—	—	-

Figure 5h: CReg Contents after Executing `Add R1,R0,R1`

It is interesting to note that the lazy store mechanism, in the case traced above, would very likely avoid performing the store to main memory which was implied in Figure 5g (since the store implied in 5h makes 5g a "dead store" because `I` and `K` are actually the same object).

3. Compiler Technology

The basic compiler technology needed to make good use of CRegs is very similar to that needed to perform register allocation, however, there are a few complications. The first complication is that names must be grouped according to which other names they are ambiguously aliased with, henceforth called an **alias set**; this is discussed in the next subsection. The subsection after that discusses the problem of reasonably packing alias sets into CReg associative sets and of allocating registers given such a packing.

Throughout this section, our intent is *not* to provide the best possible CReg management, but rather to demonstrate that reasonably good CReg management is not particularly difficult to implement.

3.1. Alias Sets

As discussed above, the fundamental flaw in static analysis of conventional-language programs is that it is not possible to statically determine, for all variables, which ones *are* aliased to which others at each point in the program. The CReg mechanism does not aid in solving this problem; however, it changes the problem into one which can be solved. The alias problem for CRegs is simply finding which items *can be* aliased to each other. We call this problem the construction of **alias sets**.

The basic tools with which alias sets are constructed are the familiar algorithms of compiler flow analysis (including dependence analysis). These tools have been particularly well-honed in pursuit of efficient automatic parallelization. The presentation here is intended merely to provide a brief overview to the analysis involved in creating alias sets.

3.1.1. Names

The first issue to resolve in grouping names into alias sets is the basic question of what constitutes a name. Each variable could be considered a name, however, this is not the most useful definition. The difficulty is rooted in the fact that a variable α may be an alias for a variable β within one region of a program, while α may be an alias for δ in another section of the code. In such a case, considering α to be a name used for grouping into alias sets, it would be necessary either to make the alias set containing α be $\{\alpha,\beta,\delta\}$ or to make the alias set for α be $\{\alpha,\beta\}$ in one region of code and $\{\alpha,\delta\}$ in another. Ideally, names should be chosen so that each name is a member of an alias set whose contents are independent of position in the program, yet where no names are included unnecessarily.

The solution to this naming problem is simply to incorporate control and data flow information in the names: however, the mapping from user variable names into these **aliased-object names** is surprisingly complex. For example, if the user has declared `i` to be an `int` variable and `p` to be an `int *` which is initially set to point at `i` (e.g., `p=(&i);`), then references to both `i` and `*p` use the same aliased-object name: user names are mapped many-to-one into aliased-object names. This means that if the compiler can detect that two user names are unambiguously aliased to each other, these two user names will share a single aliased-object name. The rule is more precisely expressed as:

Definition 1: User-Name Merging
The user-created names α and β can be merged into a single aliased-object name within some region of code *iff* the values associated with the names α and β are known to be the same throughout that region of code.

which also implies that explicitly made copies of values can all share a single aliased-object name (i.e., the compiler can perform copy propagation).

On the other hand, in a code sequence like `i=j; . . . i=k;`, the user name `i` will be mapped into multiple aliased-object names, one for each different value stored into `i`. This rule is best expressed in terms of **D-U chains** and **U-D chains** [AhS86]:

Definition 2: User-Name Spliting
Let U be the set of uses of (loads from) the user name α. For each use $u_i \in U$, let the U-D chain rooted at u_i be called d_i. If, for any i and j, $d_i \cap d_j \neq \emptyset$, then let $d_i = d_i \cup d_j$ and delete d_j. When no more such merger/deletions can be performed, each of the remaining sets (d_i) can be represented by a separate aliased-object name.

Notice that values which do not have programmer-assigned names, such as intermediate results within an expression, also may be assigned aliased-object names by the above rules.

3.1.2. Formation of Alias Sets

Given the above definitions, it is relatively easy for a compiler to generate a set of names appropriate for grouping into alias sets; but what is an alias set? There are actually several compile-time distinguishable types of aliases:

[1] A name α is a **true alias** of the name β if α is known to always be associated with the same value that is associated with β. (Notice that, if this is so, the two names may be merged by Definition 1 given above.)

[2] A name α is an **intersection alias** of the name β if α and β are known to share some elements of their values, however, perhaps not all elements. For example, if `a` is a `struct` containing members called `b` and `c`, then `a` and `a.b` are intersection aliases. Intersection aliases occur most often in code referring to arrays.

[3] A name α is a **sometimes alias** of the name β if α is known to be a true or intersection alias for β under some circumstances at runtime, however, α is not an alias for β under other circumstances. For example, references to `a[i]` and `a[5]` are sometimes aliases if `i` could be equal to `5`.

[4] A name α is an **ambiguous alias** for β if α is an intersection alias or sometimes alias for β, or if the compiler is unable to determine the relationship between α and β.

[5] A name α is **mutually exclusive** of β if α and β are *not* related by any of the above alias types. If, for all β, α is mutually exclusive of β, then α is **unambiguous.**

For the purpose of CReg assignment, an alias set is a set of names grouped by "closure" of the ambiguous alias relation. In other words, given a name *n*, the alias set for *n* consists of *n* $\cup$ (all names which are ambiguous aliases of *n*) $\cup$ (all names which are ambiguous aliases of those names) $\cup \ldots$. Notice that these alias sets have several useful properties:

Uniqueness

If α is a name in alias set *S*, then α is in no other alias set. This assignment is also independent of the region of code in which α is referenced.

Completeness

If α is a name, it is a member of some alias set; if α is mutually exclusive of all other names, then the alias set which contains α is a singleton set containing α.

Relationship to CReg Assignment

The number of elements in an alias set is the maximum possible number of CRegs which that set could use beneficially (i.e., it is the upper bound on CRegs needed, achieved only if all names are simultaneously live [AhS86]). In fact, the elements of an alias set *are* the items which are assigned to CRegs.

3.2. CReg Allocation

Given that the source program has been analyzed and that the collection of alias sets is known, the next step is to assign values to CRegs and to generate code reflecting that assignment. Since CRegs closely resemble registers, it is not surprizing that the allocation schemes for CRegs closely resemble those for register allocation, except for the need to operate on alias sets. If, for example, all alias sets obtained from a program are singleton sets, CReg allocation *is precisely* register allocation.

Due to limitations of hardware circuit complexity, the (simultaneous) assocativity of a CReg array is constrained to be a small number: typically four (just like the associativity of cache). However, it is quite reasonable to have an array much larger than just four CRegs — breaking the CReg array into associative sets as described in the example CReg RISC processor of section 2.1. Consequently, the first and the most important rule of CReg allocation is to put all elements from each particular alias set into the same CReg associative set. At first, this sounds overly constrained, since an alias set containing more than four elements cannot possibly "fit" into a four-element CReg associative set, however, experience with compiler automatic parallelization technology [Ste86] has shown that the average number of *simultaneously active* ("live") names within an alias set is very rarely more than three[5].

Another key issue in CReg allocation is CReg **spilling.** An item is spilled from a register if a register is needed for some other item, yet no registers are empty. Here, the problem is that if a single name from an alias set is to be referenced from a CReg associative set other than that which contains the other elements of the alias set, *all* elements of the alias set must first be flushed from the CRegs. This makes spilling of alias sets highly undesirable: spills defeat the benefits gained from CReg hardware automatically maintaining consistency across multiple names in an alias set.

As an illustration of the above guidelines, the following subsection presents an easily implementable CReg allocation scheme based on usage counts [Fre74]. Although good enough to demonstrate the advantages of CRegs, this CReg allocation scheme is far from optimal (measuring optimality in terms of minimizing the total execution time for all references). An optimal CReg allocation scheme based on machine state transition modeling [ChD87] is currently under investigation within the Compiler-oriented Architecture Research group at Purdue University (CARP).

3.3. Example CReg Allocation Scheme

The main modification to conventional register allocation based on usage counts [Fre74] is that CReg allocation is effectively heirarchical: one first allocates alias sets to CReg associative sets and then allocates individual CRegs within each set.

To describe the algorithm, it is first necessary to define some measures which will be used to define allocation priorities in the algorithm. The **usage count** of an alias set is defined as the total number of references to names within the alias set which appear in the program segment under consideration. For best results, each reference which appears in the program text should be weighted according to its expected frequency of execution relative to other references. Expected execution frequencies can be estimated by examining the program control flow [Die87]; for example, references in the `then` clause of an `if` statement have about one half the execution frequency of those which precede the branch. References inside a loop are weighted by the expected number of times the loop will iterate. The **cost-savings estimate** of an alias set is therefore:

```
Cost = ((Usage Count) *
         ((Cost of Memory Reference) -
          (Cost of CReg Reference))) -
       ((Size of Alias Set) *
        (Cost of CReg Load))
```

[5] This number makes sense in that code like a[i]=a[j]*a[k] only uses three names — the number three seems to be a side-effect of the dominance of binary operations.

The **size** of an alias set is equal to the maximum number of simultaneously live values in that set within its live range period (as suggested earlier, the upper bound on this number is the number of names in the alias set, and this is an acceptable approximation). The **live range** of an alias set is set of references during which any name within the alias set is live.

Given these definitions, the CReg allocation scheme is:

[1] Compute the alias sets for references within the program. This was described in section 3.1. Size and cost estimates are associated with each alias set, as described above.

[2] Assign alias sets to CReg sets. The assignment procedes to allocate alias sets in the following way:

  [2a] The unallocated alias set with the largest cost-savings estimate is allocated first.

  [2b] If multiple alias sets have the same cost-savings estimate, the one with the largest size is allocated first.

  [2c] If there is more than one CReg set which can fit the current alias set, the CReg set which is the "best fit" is chosen.

  [2d] If there is no CReg set which can fit the current alias set, then the alias set is placed in the CReg set for which the estimated spill cost to make space for the alias set is the lowest. The estimated spill cost for a CReg set to fit a new alias set is computed by summing the costs to remove alias sets (in reverse order of allocation) from that CReg set until the number of free CRegs in the set is $\geq$ the size of the alias set. If an alias set is larger than the number of CRegs in a CReg set, then, for the purpose of allocating CReg sets, the estimated spill cost for a CReg set to fit that alias set is computed by summing the costs to remove all alias sets from that CReg set.

[3] Perform the CReg allocation within each CReg set independently as:

  [3a] Keep all CRegs in use as much as possible.

  [3b] When CRegs must be spilled, the alias set(s) with the minimum total cost-savings estimate should be chosen.

4. Conclusions

In this paper, the CReg, a new architectural concept, is introduced. The first section argued that registers and cache are inherently unable to provide good efficiency in accessing aliased objects because neither structure embodies the concept of an aliased object in such a way as to allow a compiler to manage aliased references. The second section presented a detailed discussion of the operation of CReg hardware in managing aliased references; an outline of the new compilation technology associated with managing CRegs — in particular, operating on alias sets — is given in section 3.

At the writing of this paper, the performance of CRegs has been examined directly for only a few small examples. Performance for these examples has been very encouraging. Table 2 gives a *static* comparison of using registers only, registers plus an arbitrarily large cache, or CRegs only, for the RISC machine mentioned earlier. The FORTRAN benchmark is that given in Listing 2, considering only the code for the assignment statements; the C benchmark is a typical encoding of quicksort in C, using pointers to mark the start and end of the subarray to be sorted.

Table 2: Static Comparison of CRegs with Registers and Cache

Benchmark	Registers Only	Registers + Cache	CRegs Only
FORTRAN assignments			
Total Instruction Words	14	14	11
Total Memory References (Min)	23	20	12
Total Memory References (Max)	23	23	17
C quicksort			
Total Instruction Words	94	94	50
Total Memory References (Min)	157	124	72
Total Memory References (Max)	157	157	80

Ongoing work at Purdue University includes the construction of a simulator and a compiler so that *dynamic* results can be obtained for a much larger set of benchmarks and so that CReg design tradeoffs can be investigated.

References

[AhS86] A. V. Aho, R. Sethi, and J. D. Ullman, *Compilers: Principles, Techniques, and Tools*, Addison Wesley, Reading, Massachusetts, 1986.

[All83] J. R. Allen, *Dependence Analysis for Subscripted Variables and its Application to Program Transformations*, Rice University, Ph.D. Thesis, April 1983.

[All86] F. Allen, "The Parallel Translator Project," NASA / ICASE Parallel Languages and Environments Workshop, November 1986.

[BuC86] M. Burke, R. Cytron, "Interprocedural Dependence Analysis and Parallelization," SIGPLAN Symposium on Compiler Construction, 1986, pages 162-175.

[Bur84] M. Burke, *An Interval Analysis Approach Toward Interprocedural Data Flow,* IBM, Yorktown Heights, New York, Research Report RC 10640 (#47724), July 1984.

[ChD87] C. H. Chi and H. Dietz, *Compiler-Driven Cache Policy (Known Reference String)*, Purdue University Technical Report TR-EE 87-21, June 1987.

[Die87] H. Dietz, *The Refined-Language Approach to Compiling for Parallel Supercomputers*, Polytechnic University, Ph.D. Thesis, June 1987.

[Fre74] R. A. Freurghouse, "Register Allocation Via Usage Counts," *Communications of the ACM*, Vol. 17, No. 11, November 1974, pp. 638-642.

[Sit79] Richard Sites, "How To Use 1000 Registers," Caltech conference on VLSI, January 1979.

[Smi78] A. J. Smith, "A Comparitive Study of Set Associative Memory Mapping Algorithms and Their Use for Cache and Main Memory," *IEEE Transactions on Software Engineering*, Vol. 4, No. 2, March 1978, pp. 121-130.

[Ste86] K. Stein, *Refined C Compiler Status Report*, Internal Report, Stevens Institute of Technology, 1986.

[StS85] G. L. Steele Jr. and G. J. Sussman, "The Dream of a Lifetime: A Lazy Variable Extent Mechanism," ACM SIGPLAN order number 552800, 1985, pp. 163-172.

An Efficient Pipelined Dataflow Processor Architecture

Jack B. Dennis

Laboratory for Computer Science
Massachusetts Institute of Technology
Cambridge, MA 02139

Guang R. Gao

School of Computer Science
McGill University
Montreal, H3A 2K6

Abstract

This paper demonstrates that the principles of pipelined instruction execution can be effectively applied in dataflow computers, yielding an architecture that avoids the main sources of pipeline gaps during program execution in many conventional processor designs. The new processing element design uses an architecture called *argument-fetch dataflow architecture*. It has two parts: a *dataflow instruction scheduling unit* (DISU) and a *pipelined instruction processing unit* (PIPU). The PIPU is an instruction processor that uses many conventional techniques to achieve fast pipelined operation. The DISU holds the dataflow signal graph of the collection of dataflow instructions allocated to the processing element, and maintains a large pool of enabled instructions available for execution by the PIPU. The new architecture provides a basis for achieving high performance for many scientific applications. To show that the realization of an efficient dataflow processing element is feasible, a trial design and fabrication of an *enable memory*–a key component of the DISU–is reported.

1 Introduction

This paper discusses design principles and issues for a pipelined dataflow processor architecture. We wish to show how the principles of pipelind instruction execution can be effectively applied in dataflow computers, yielding an architecture that avoids the main sources of pipeline gaps encountered during program execution in many conventional processor designs. This capability stems from the fine-grain instruction scheduling mechanism derived from the data-driven model of program execution. The dataflow instruction scheduler can be implemented in a processing element design that keeps the instruction execution pipeline filled because all instructions held in the processor are candidates for initiation. This unique program execution power can be effectively exploited in many problems of scientific computation by constructing of software pipelined machine code blocks that correspond to array definitions in the source program.

The new processing element design uses an architecture called the *argument-fetch data flow architecture*. It has two parts: a *dataflow instruction scheduling unit* (DISU) and a *pipelined instruction processing unit* (PIPU). The DISU holds the data-flow signal graph of the collection of dataflow instructions allocated to the processing element, and maintains a record of which instructions are enabled by satisfaction of conditions for execution. This pool of enabled instructions is available for execution by the PIPU.

The PIPU is an instruction processor that uses conventional techniques to achieve fast pipelined operation. The principle of RISC architecture that no instruction is initiated unless it has no data conflict with instructions in the pipeline is honored by this processing element since the dataflow model guarantees that no pair of simultaneously enabled instructions can be in conflict over data. Thus pipeline gaps caused by conditional branch instructions cannot arise. In some RISC architectures, the compiler is expected to ensure that no pair of instructions in the pipeline are in conflict over data. In the dataflow processor, this requirement is satisfied by obeying the dataflow model. In the RISC architecture, only a small window of instructions can

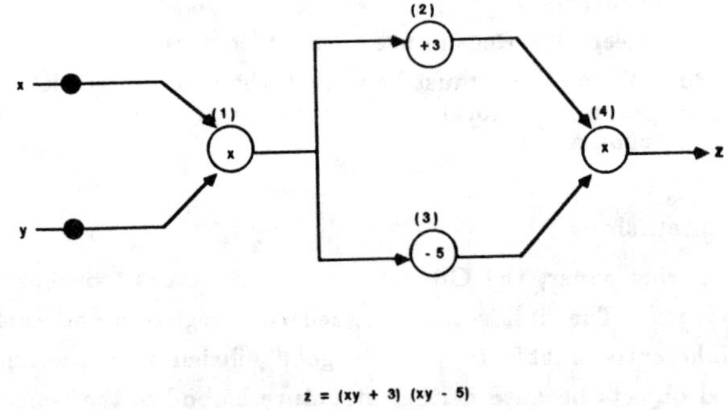

Figure 1: A static data flow graph

be considered for initiation, whereas in the dataflow architecture, thousands of instructions from different code blocks are considered candidates for initiation.

The argument-fetching architecture provides a basis for achieving full performance for many scientific application codes through use of a compiler able to perform global dataflow analysis and identification of array definitions. The architecture has a significant advantage over vector pipelined computers is that it is no longer essential that the array definitions be expressible as vector operations to achieve peak performance.

2 Contrasts in Static Dataflow Architecture

2.1 Efficiency Issues in the Argument-Flow Architecture

In static data flow model, an actor becomes enabled when data tokens become available on its input arcs and its output arcs (the places for holding result tokens) are empty. The *firing rules* for static data flow graphs [6] state that any enabled actor may be chosen to fire. Figure 1 illustrates the operation of a static data flow graph for computing the expression $z = (xy + 3)(xy - 5)$. According to the firing rule, actor 1 is enabled because both of its inputs are available, and each of its result arcs is empty.

In a dataflow processor, instructions loaded into the processor represent, more or less directly, actors of a dataflow program graph. In the argument-flow dataflow architecture, known as a *dataflow circular pipeline*, such an instruction typically has two spaces to receive operand values, and a field that holds a *destination list* indicating the target instructions to which result values or signals are to be sent. The arrival of a result value corresponds to placing a token on the input arc of an actor; the arrival of a signal (an *acknowledge signal*) from a successor instruction means that a result token has been removed from one of an actor's output arcs.

Note that the delivery of a result value to the operand receiver of an instruction template accomplishes two purposes: (1) its signals to the target instruction that an input is available; and (2) it transmits the data value itself from an instruction to one of its successors. Inefficiencies arise from the decision to keep data information (values) and control information (addresses) bound together in packets as they traverse the circular structure of the processor.

In the course of considering a great variety of hardware schemes for realizing the behavior of dataflow graphs, we discovered the advantage of separating the data and signaling roles of the information packets. Once this has been done, it becomes evident that it is better for an instruction to fetch its own arguments from a data memory than for its predecessor instruction(s) to store result value(s) in the operand fields of several target instructions. These considerations have led us to the *argument-fetch architecture.*

Before presenting the architecture, we introduce the *signal graph* model which serves as an abstract model for the *argument-fetch* architecture.

2.2 Data driven signal graphs

The signal graph representation of the data flow graph G in Figure 1 is shown in Figure 2. Formally, this dataflow program is a *program tuple* (P, S) in which the *instruction list*

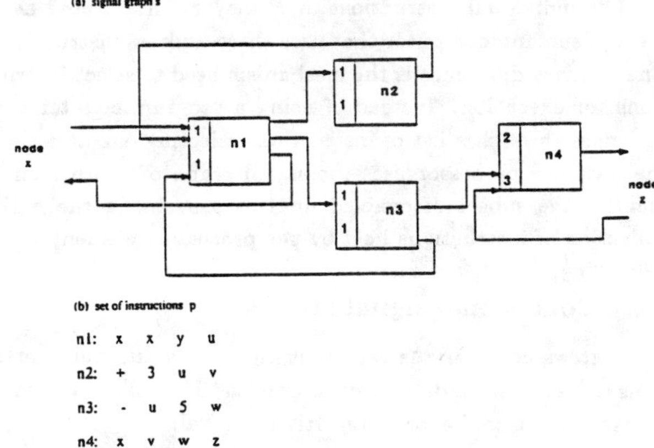

Figure 2: A data flow program tuple (P,S)

P is a list of instructions each corresponding to one actor of G. The instructions in P do not contain information about the sequencing of instruction execution. Instead, the sequencing information is given separately by the *dataflow signal graph* S. Although the signal graph shown in Figure 2 looks similar to the original data flow graph G, the signal graph S has the following features and differences:

1. Each node in S contains a reference to an instruction in P;

2. A node does not contain information about instruction execution; that is specified by reference to the instruction list P;

3. The arcs in S (called *signal arcs*) represent only the sequencing information, i.e. an arc from actor u to actor v specifies that a signal is to be sent to v after actor u is fired; the signal arcs do not specify the treatment of result values;

4. Each node in S holds two fields that are part of the dataflow instruction scheduling mechanism: the *count* field indicates how many signals must yet be received for the node to become enabled; the *reset* field gives the value to be placed in the count field when the node is fired.

In Figure 2, for example, node 1 in S contains a reference n_1 to the instruction (* x y u) in the set P. The figure also gives the count and reset values for each node. The reset value for node 1 is four because it must receive signals from nodes x and y and two from nodes 2 and 3) before it becomes enabled. However, its count field is only two because signals from node 2 and node 3 are not required for the first firing of node 1.

The individual instructions in P may be interpreted as in a von Neumann computer that uses three-address instructions. The primary difference is the mechanism used to select instructions for execution. Instead of using a program counter that advances through a list of instructions selecting one at a time, the dataflow processor uses the signal graph of a program to identify the subset of enabled instructions among the entire collection of instructions held by the processing element.

2.3 Conditional signal graphs

Next we consider the representation of conditional expressions in dataflow models for computation. The following example is a conditional expression written in Val.

z = if i = 1 then i + x else i - x endif

The corresponding program tuple (P, S) for the conditional expression is shown in Figure 3. In this model, ***conditional signaling*** takes the place of the T, F, and merge actors. The test instruction of node 1 produces a boolean result that determines which successor nodes receive signals (T means signal if true; F means signal if false; U means signal unconditionally). When node 1 fires, node i is signaled unconditionally, and node 2 or node 3 is signaled depending on whether or not $i > 1$. The merge is implemented by having instructions n_2 and n_3 use the same result address z. Therefore, the destination node z will see only the "merged" result. Note that node z must send a

(a) signal graph

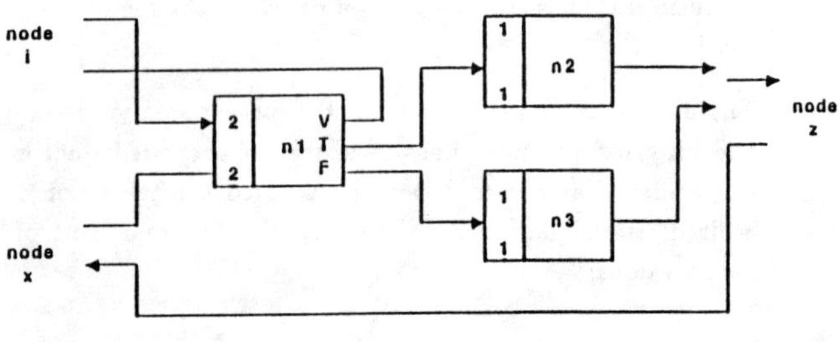

(b) set of instructions

n1: > i 1 j
n2: + j x z
n3: - j x z

Figure 3: A conditional argument-fetching data flow program (P,S)

signal back to node x to indicate that it is safe to generate and store a new value at location x.

Use of the signal graph model appears to provide a considerable saving in the number of dataflow instructions required to carry out typical computations.

3 The Argument-Fetch Dataflow Processor

The argument-fetch dataflow processor consists of two major sections (Figure 4), each designed to perform its separate function efficiently. The Dataflow Instruction Scheduling Unit (DISU) implements the signal graph of the dataflow program and identifies instructions that are available for execution. The Pipelined Instruction Processing Unit (PIPU) executes enabled instructions and informs the DISU when each instruction finishes execution.

The *fire* link in the figure is for transmitting the addresses

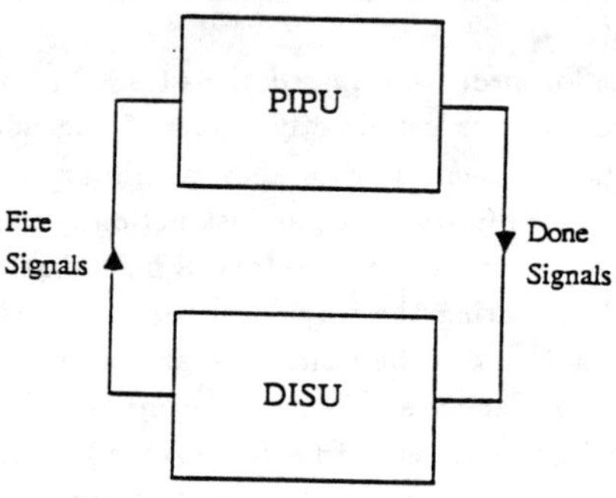

Figure 4: A argument-fetching data flow processor

of enabled instructions from the DISU to the PIPU. The *done* link is for transmitting the done signals, each containing the address of an instruction which has completed execution in the PIPU, together with a ***condition code*** used by the DISU to control the sending of conditional signals.

Since many instructions will be processed concurrently, many fire signals will be sent to the PIPU before the first one is acknowledged by a done signal. In a balanced design, the DISU will be able to supply fire signals to the PIPU just fast enough to keep the instruction execution pipeline operating continuously at full capacity.

3.1 The pipelined instruction processing unit: PIPU

The organization of the PIPU is shown in Figure 5. It consists of four sections that implement the usual functions of instruction fetch, operand fetch, operation execute and, result store. We assume that the readers are familiar with the basic principles of pipelined SISD architecture (for background knowledge see Chapter 6 of [17]). In this design, any effective address calculation is included in the instruction fetch stage, and the scalar operation unit performs the function of selecting and storing elements of arrays.

There can be no pipeline gaps in the PIPU so long as a continuous supply of enabled instructions is maintained in the

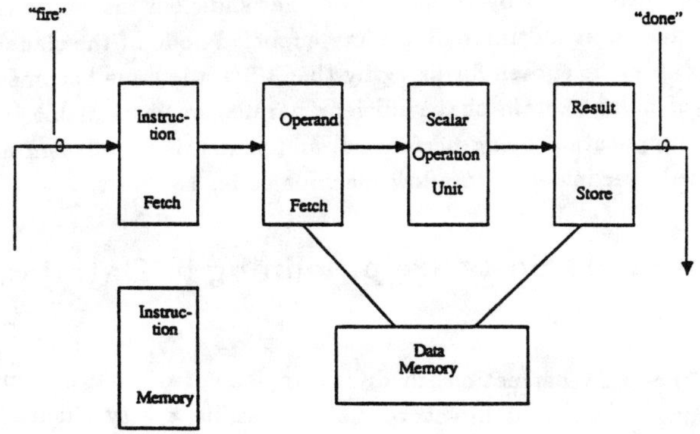

Figure 5: The structure of PIPU

DISU. Once an instruction has been entered into the pipe, it continues advancing through the stages, being held up only when needed resources are engaged by other work units in the pipe.

There are no branch instructions with undetermined outcomes to make the utility of processing subsequent instructions uncertain. Furthermore, since the dataflow origin of the signal graph guarantees the absense of data conflicts in the PIPU, there is no need for any data interlocks in the pipeline.

These same principles characterize the execution pipelines of RISC architectures. However, the pipeline in a RISC can be only a few stages long because the sequential form of the stored program limits the effectiveness of instruction lookahead. Increasing the number of stages soon diminishes the pool of instructions available for initiation. This limitation makes it difficulat for a RISC architecture to effectively overlap the execution of slow memory accesses or floating point arithmetic operations.

Ensuring a continuous supply of enabled instructions is easy because any instruction held in the instruction memory may be entered into the PIPU on any machine cycle. Thus the instructions required to fill the pipeline may be taken from

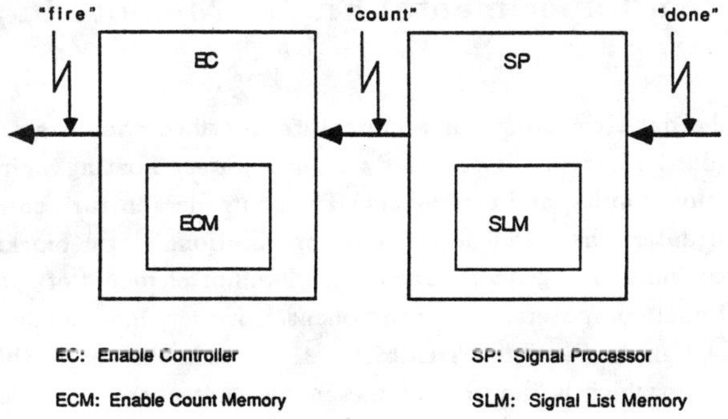

Figure 6: The structure of DISU

many independent code blocks of the program.

Each of the four sections of the PIPU may consist of several pipeline stages to match the timing requirements of memories and operation units. Since successive work units may require different numbers of clock cycles to pass through sections of the PIPU, buffering and leapfrogging of work units will help smooth out the flow of work units and allow simple instructions to be completed as early as possible.

In Section 4, we examine in more detail the sources of pipeline gaps in conventional processing units and show that they arise for reasons that do not apply to the dataflow architecture.

3.2 The dataflow scheduling unit: DISU

The structure of the DISU is shown in Figure 6. It consists of a ***signal processing unit*** (SP) and an ***enable controller unit*** (EC). The signal graph of a program is represented in the DISU by information stored in a ***signal list memory*** (SLM) of the SP unit and the ***enable count memory*** (ECM) of the EC unit. The SLM holds a ***signal list*** for each node of the signal graph, and the ECM holds the count and reset values for each node. A signal list represents the set of signal arcs leaving the associated node of the signal graph.

In response to a done signal for instruction n_i, the SP unit reads the corresponding signal list and sends a ***count command*** to the EC unit for each active entry in the list. (The set of active entries may depend on the condition code that accompanies the done signal.)

The EC unit handles each count command by decrementing the count value for the indicated node and testing for zero. If the count becomes zero, an enable flag for the node is set and the count value is set to the reset value. The EC unit continuously monitors all of the enable flags and issues fire commands for enabled nodes. Since the mechanism used to select enabled instructions for execution is crucial to obtaining full performance of the dataflow processor, further explanation of the EC unit and a discussion of an experimental implementation is provided in Section 6.

4 Eliminating Pipeline Gaps

4.1 Conditional branch

Branch instructions raise significant problems in the design of high performance pipelined computers because they interfere with the steady flow of executable instructions into the pipeline. Conditional branches are especially troublesome because the correct choice of successor instruction may depend on a result yet to be produced by an instruction still in the pipeline. Some studies have shown that if branch instructions appear in only one out of ten instructions, throughput could be reduced by a factor of three. [21], and the dynamic frequency of branch instructions may be very high [2,28].

Computer architects have invented several techniques to reduce the performance impact of conditional branches in conventional pipelined processors. One important technique is the *delayed branch* whereby a branch transfer does not take place until some fixed number k of instructions following the branch instruction have also been executed [18]. The challenge is given to the programmer or compiler designer to find instructions that can make effective use of the k instruction initiation cycles during which the branch outcome is unknown. Although the idea is old, it has only recently been applied in practical machine designs, some recent RISC architectures in particular [16,23].

Another method is using *branch prediction* where the branch outcome is assumed to be true, and the execution is allowed to proceed on that assumption [18]. If the branch outcome turns out to be false, execution is backed up to cancel any effects of the unneeded instructions. The compiler must generate code so the most likely branch outcome is true. If the compiler cannot predict well, the cost of implementing branch prediction may not be justified.

A third idea is to make predictions during program execution based on the branch history of the program. In implementation, a branch history table is needed to record the recent history of branches. An example is the *branch target buffer* in the MU5 computer [21].

Each of these methods reduces the effect of conditional branches on pipeline performance, but none solves the problem completely. The complexity of control required and the hardware cost involved have been a constant source of debate.

4.2 Pipeline gaps from data dependencies

The performance of pipelined processors is limited by data dependencies. Operand fetch for an instruction must not occur until the operand values have been stored. If an operand is the result of a previous instruction, execution of the current instruction must be delayed until the previous instruction completes its execution.

Hardware and software solutions to this problem can be used in conventional pipelined computers: hardware solutions employ *reservation stations* where an instruction waits for its operands while subsequent instructions may proceed [26]. Software solutions use compiler code scheduling techniques to insure that the dependency distance is sufficiently large that hazards are impossible. Code scheduling is done by reordering instructions and inserting dummy instructions [15].

4.3 Pipeline gaps in dataflow architecture

The dataflow architecture eliminates the sources of these problems. In the argument-fetch architecture, the signalling mechanism replaces the use of branch instructions and no instruction is entered into the execution pipeline unless its execution is certain. Moreover, no instruction can be enabled if it uses a result of an instruction that is in execution. This is guaranteed by coding every data dependence the signal graph, and is the responsibility of the compiler.

In the dataflow architecture, the only way for gaps to arise in the execution pipeline is that the DISU runs out of enabled instructions. Keeping the execution pipeline full is accomplished simply by being certain that sufficient instructions are enabled at all times. Since any enabeled node of the signal graph may be chosen for firing by the DISU, the issue becomes one of being certain that sufficient parallelism is available in the computation being performed, and that this parallelism is carried over into the dataflow machine code.

5 Support Software pipelining in Dataflow Programs

The fine-grain instruction scheduling implemented in the argument-fetching dataflow architecture makes possible a very efficient form of software pipelining – the arcs drawn between actors correspond to addresses in stored dataflow machine code and not to wired connections between logic elements. Array operations in large-scale numerical computationscan be organized in large dataflow software pipelines in which hundreds of actors in many stages are executed concurrently. We have found that the major sections of several benchmark codes for solving partial differential equations are readily expressed as pipelined dataflow machine code blocks.

In the Val language, expressions that lead to pipelined dataflow code blocks are conveniently written as *forall expressions*. The automatic translation of such high-level programs into efficient machine code blocks has been studied and a code mapping scheme has been proposed in [12].

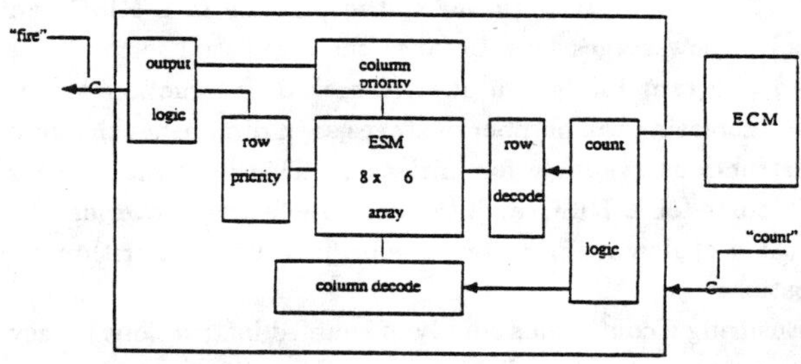

Figure 7: An architecture for the enable controler

6 An Experimental Enable Memory in a VLSI Circuit

In the dataflow processor architecture, most components are standard sorts of digital hardware–memories, floating point functional units, and controllers. The controllers in turn comprise datapaths, sequencers, and combinational logic blocks. These kinds of logic components are familiar elements of conventional computers. One component, however, has no counterpart in conventional architectures. This is the the enable memory which is the part of the enable controller that holds the enable flags for all of the dataflow instructions loaded into the processing element. The enable memory must hold the flags for several thousand dataflow instructions and must be able to select enabled instructions for initiation at a very fast rate. To meet performance demands, both for setting and clearing flags, and for selecting enabled instructions, a very special design is required.

At M.I.T. an experimental enable memory device has been designed to support 128 dataflow instructions. The architecture of the chip is illustrated in Figure 7. It consists of an 8 by 16 array of one-bit cells (the *Enable State Memory* ESM) and specialized control logic for the count updating and selection functions. For each count command, the count logic decrements the corresponding count field in the Count/Reset Memory. If the count becomes zero, the corresponding bit in the Enable State Memory is set, indicating that the instruction is enabled. At this time the reset field is copied into the count field to prepare for the next cycle of enabling of the instruction.

The selection of instructions for execution is done by the row and column priority logic which is carefully designed to ensure fairness. The row logic selects each row in turn, and reads the contents of any non-zero row into the column logic. No row is considered again until all other rows have been examined. The column logic scans the selected row from left to right, issuing a fire command for each bit that is on.

The design of an enable memory device for 128 instructions has been translated into a three micron CMOS layout and was fabricated through the MOSIS service of DARPA. Testing of packaged devices has shown they perform the intended functions and can work at a clock rate of 5 MHz [11].

7 Conclusions

The processing element architecture discussed here is the basis for a multiprocessor computer architecture that offers superior performance to conventional architectures for multiprocessor systems. This is because the pipelined execution units of the dataflow machine can be kept fully utilized even when only scalar parallelism is available in the application being run. The stream of initiated instructions may contain interleaved instructions from all parts of the program that have been loaded into the processing element. This possibility is not supported by any other processor architecture known to us.

A successful compiler for a dataflow computer must perform a global analysis of data dependencies in the source program and identify the array definitions embedded in the program. If the program is written in a functional programming language such as Val ([1,19]), then this analysis is far easier than is the case for a conventional language such as Fortran. Nevertheless, Fortran programs may be successfully analyzed using techniques developed by Kuck, Kennedy and others [22], and rules for good programming in Fortran can be formulated so that all important array definitions can be recognized by a compiler.

The work presented here is a further refinement of dataflow processing element designs developed in research on dataflow computer architecture conducted at the M.I.T. Laboratory for Computer Science under Professor Jack B. Dennis [8]. Many graduate students and others participated in the project and have contributed to the genesis and evolution of the processing element architecture described in this paper.

A general-purpose multiprocessor data flow graph simulator is currently being constructed to study the instruction set design and compiler construction for the argument-fetching dataflow architecture at McGill University.

Acknowledgements

We would like to thank Anna Arcuri for preparation of the final manuscript.

References

[1] Ackerman, W.B. and Dennis, J.B., *Val – A Value-Oriented Algorithmic Language: Preliminary Manual*, Technical Report 218, Laboratory for Computer Science, MIT, Cambridge, MA, June 1979.

[2] Clark, D. W. and Levy, H. M., *Measurement and Analysis of Instruction Use in the Vax-11/780*, The 9-th Annual Symposium on Computer Architecture, 10(3), pp. 9-17, April 1982.

[3] Dennis, J.B., *Data Flow Computer Architecture*, Technical Report, Laboratory for Computer Science, MIT, TR-385 Oct., 1987.

[4] Gao, G.R., *A Pipelined Code Mapping Scheme for Static Data Flow Computers*, Ph.D dissertation, Laboratory for Computer Science, Aug. 1986.

[5] Hennessy, J. L. et al, *Hardware/software Trade-offs for Increased Performance*, in Proceeding ACM SIGARCH/SIGPLAN Symp. Architectural Support for Programming Language and Operating Systems, Palo Alto, CA, March 1982, pp. 2-11.

[6] Hennessy,J. L., *VLSI Processor Architecture*, IEEE Transaction on Computers, Vol. c-33, No. 12, Dec. 1984

[7] Kogge, P. M., *The Architecture of Pipelined Computers*, McGraw-Hill, 1981.

[8] Lee, J. F. K. and Smith, A., *Branch Prediction Strategies and Branch Target Buffer Design*, Computer 17(1), Jan. 1984.

[9] McGraw, J., *The Val Language: Description and Analysis*, ACM Transactions on Programming Language and Systems, Vol. 4, No.1, Jan, 1982.

[10] Morris, D. and Ibbet, R. N., *The MU5 Computer System*, Springer-Verlag, 1979.

[11] Patterson, D. A., *Reduced Instruction Set Computers*, CACM, Vol. 28, No. 1, Jan., 1985.

[12] Tomasulo, R. M., *An Efficient Algorithm for Exploiting Multiple Arithmatic Units*, IBM J. Research and Developments, Vol. 11, 1967, pp. 25-33.

Efficient Vector Processing on a Dataflow Supercomputer SIGMA-1

Kei Hiraki Satoshi Sekiguchi Toshio Shimada

Electrotechnical Laboratory
1-1-4 Umezono, Tsukuba-shi
Ibaraki, 305, Japan

Abstract

Efficiency in vector handling is the key to obtaining high performance in numerical programs. So far, the main defect of dataflow computers is inefficiency in vector processing. We propose structure-flow processing as a new scheme for handling data structures such as vectors in dataflow architecture. The main objective of structure-flow processing is to enhance vector processing performance of a dataflow computer. In this structure-flow processing scheme, the arrival of a data structure unrolls the control structure which processes the data structure itself. A high-level structure is an implementation mechanism of a structure-flow scheme on a practical dataflow computer. Since all the computation is executed by instruction-level dataflow architecture, scalar level parallelism and function level parallelism are also fully utilized by this scheme. The SIGMA-1 architecture that supports high-level structure processing are discussed and the performance is measured. According to the measurement, vector programs can be executed three to four times faster than by unfolding using scalar dataflow processing.

1 Introduction

A structure is a set of element data with a structural relationship between elements. Vectors, matrices, sets, and lists are examples of structures used in computer programs. Since a program can dynamically read and write any data item to a structure, a structure can introduce dynamic behavior to a program. Furthermore, a structure is useful to describe complicated algorithms that are represented as iterative or recursive applications of simple operations to elements of structures.

On the other hand, iterative or recursive application of primitive operations on elements is an important source of parallelism in programs. In fact, it is the main source of parallelism used in vector-pipelined and parallel supercomputers. The method to handle structures must be highly efficient in these aspects. Especially, efficiency in vector handling is the key to obtaining high performance in numerical programs.

So far, a number of researches have been performed on structure handling in dataflow architecture. Misunas [1] and Ackerman [2] have proposed a tree structured implementation of a structure whose elements are strictly evaluated. Their objective is to reduce the overhead due to copy operations caused by the replacement of structure elements. Arvind and Thomas [3] have proposed an I-structure that uses non-strict evaluation of elements. They have suggested that the I-structure can potentially exploit more parallelism from the program than strictly evaluated structures.

The Manchester dataflow machine has a non-strict structure in a matching memory [4] and a separate structure store [5]. In the former case, a special matching function is used for storing and accessing structure elements, and indexing is realized by label exchange instructions. Gaudiot [6] has proposed a token relabeling scheme for structure handling equivalent to the I-structure from a similar point of view. In the token relabeling scheme, the index operation is performed in the special instruction that changes the tag of the element data for reducing the overhead caused by read and write operations.

The structure handling methods listed above are based on element-wise access to the structure. To gain high performance in numerical programs, parallelism in a structure must be fully utilized, and a unified computing scheme within total structure level parallel processing and element-wise scalar level parallel processing is necessary.

This paper proposes a new scheme for vector processing, structure-flow processing, and a high-level structure, a mechanism to implement it on a practical dataflow architecture. The main objective of structure-flow processing scheme is to gain high performance in numerical programs that can be efficiently executed on commercial supercomputers. The main objective of the high-level structure is to store a structure-flow in structure memory and to simplify element-wise structure access operations. Since all the computation is executed by instruction-level dataflow architecture, scalar level parallelism and function level parallelism are also fully utilized by this scheme.

Section 2 describes the structure-flow scheme. Section 3 describes a high-level structure. Section 4 shows programming examples. Section 5 describes the SIGMA-1 ar-

CH2617-9/88/0000/0374$01.00 © 1988 IEEE

chitecture that implements structure-flow processing, and performance measurements are discussed in section 6.

2 Structure-flow Processing

In a von Neumann processor, a data structure is stored in a one-dimensional memory and the logical position of the element is calculated as an indexed address or a pointer address. When a program accesses the whole structure, the iterative or recursive control structure is spread at first. Then addresses for elements are calculated according to the control structure. Finally, elements are accessed to and from memory. In other words, the control structure makes a stream of structure data. This corresponds to the control flow model of computation.

When element-wise structure access is used in a dataflow computation, structure access is processed in the same way except that the instructions are triggered by the arrival of input data. This can be considered as a dataflow programs simulating von Neumann style structure access. However, our experiences in the SIGMA-1, a dataflow supercomputer developed at the Electrotechnical Laboratory [7,8 and 9], shows that there are several problems in element-wise access to a structure:

- The number of executed instructions increases because of dataflow overhead such as control structure unrolling, calculating the logical positions of structure elements and accessing them.
- The number of transferred packets on the interconnection network increases because a read and a write packet are necessary for each structure element.
- The number of packets which occupy the matching memory increases because a lot of packets are necessary to calculate the address and access the structure elements.

These problems result in inferior vector performance to pipelined vector supercomputers.

To handle data structures in the dataflow computing scheme efficiently, a consistent treatment of a whole structure by the dataflow principle is as important as element-wise handling.

Structure-flow processing is a new scheme for structure handling in the dataflow principle.

A **structure-flow** is defined as a set of element data flowing in the form of packets with two kinds of identifiers.

The basic idea of structure-flow processing is that the arrival of a structure-flow invokes the control structure that processes the structure itself.

Structure-flow processing begins when the structure-flow arrives at the template program. The structure-flow can be processed by static or tagged-token dataflow architecture.

Two kinds of identifier are necessary for structure-flow processing. The first is the identifier of the whole structure and the second is the identifier that indicates the logical position of the element data. The first is used for identifying the program template that processes the structure and is represented as a part of the packet identifier attached to the data. The second is used for unrolling the control structure on the template to process the whole structure. When the static dataflow mechanism is used, the second is the order of packets in the structure-flow. In this case, the evaluation of structure elements is restricted to strict evaluation. When the tagged token mechanism is used, the second is also a part of the packet identifier (tag).

When a structure is a vector, the second identifier indicates the index address. A loop construct that processes the vector is invoked when the structure-flow arrives at processing elements. When the structure is a matrix, the identifier indicates encoded two-dimensional indices. A nested loop construct is invoked when the structure-flow arrives. When the structure is a list, the identifier indicates the binary representation of the tree address. The structure-flow invokes a recursive control structure that processes the whole list structure. During structure-flow processing, the logical position in the control structure is indicated by the above identifier. Hence, an iterative or recursive relationship in the control structure can be replaced by the arithmetic operation on the identifier.

In the template program, structure-flow processing is performed using the following instructions.

Normal instructions: They are used for element-wise processing to input structure-flows and intermediate values. Integer and floating point arithmetic instructions, boolean instructions,switch, subroutine call and return are included in normal instructions.

Iterative and recursive relation: This is used for passing value over the control structure. It is realized by arithmetic operations on the identifier. An exchange between an identifier and a data item (EXCHG) for index vector operations is included in this class.

Comparison of the logical structures: This is used for testing the structure of a structure-flow. Comparison is realized by the compare instruction between identifiers and data.

Detection of termination: Termination of structure-flow processing is detected by counting the number of elements or detecting the end of structure packet.

Generating a new structure-flow: An output structure flow is generated by an identifier generating instruction. A new identifier is calculated from the current identifier or passed as an input operand to the instruction.

Element-wise operation: Element-wise operation such as read and write on an element is realized by copying all the structure and conditional operations on the identifier.

3 High-level Structure

Elements in a structure are placed in matching memories and buffers without a high-level structure. Since the cost of matching memories and buffers is higher than that of conventional structure memories, structure-flows must be stored in structure memories in programs that use large-scale structures.

Storing a structure-flow in structure memory is also necessary for efficient element-wise accesses to the structure, because the whole structure must flow through the processing unit when only an element is necessary for the program. Conventional access to the structure memory is much cheaper than the direct structure-flow approach in this case.

A **high-level structure** is an active structure memory with structure-flow generating and terminating primitives. The structure memory is either an asynchronous memory with deferred bits and a waiting queue or a plain memory.

In the following discussion, the architecture is assumed to be based on the SIGMA-1 for the simplicity of description.

A high-level structure consists of a high-level structure (HLS) header and a high-level structure body with primitives listed in Table 1. The HLS header consists of an HLS body descriptor, a counter that counts the number of elements in the HLS body, a skip value that is used in a matrix access and the return address where the HLS informs the occurrence of some event such as the end of HLS creation. Figure 1 shows the construction of the high-level structure. When the HLS body is a scalar variable (SHLS), the place for the descriptor is directly used for the variable.

Since the HLS body is a one-dimensional normal structure, element-wise access to the HLS is easily realized by the conventional READ and WRITE primitives.

Structure-flow processing with an HLS is performed in the following steps:

1. Allocation of the HLS in structure memory(MKHLS).

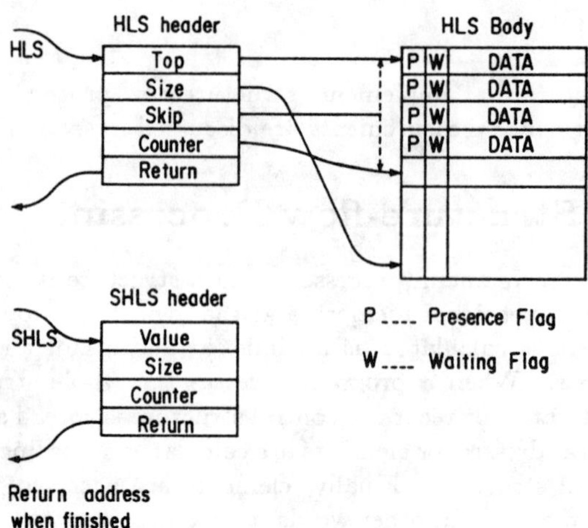

Figure 1: A High Level Structure

2. Structure-flow generation by the structure memory. When a generation instruction (GENSF) is executed in the processing unit, the trigger packet to generate the structure-flow is passed to structure memory. Then the structure memory reads all the elements and sends them to processing units as a structure-flow. The end of the structure flow is indicated by the special tag in the last element data item. An reverse index generating instruction (VSTX) triggers the primitive in structure memory that generates a reverse-index structure-flow. The identifier on a packet of them is come from read data from the HLS body for gather operation described in section 5.5.

3. Processing the structure-flow by processing elements. This is the same as that described in the previous section.

4. Storing the structure-flow in the HLS. When the program generates a structure result, a new structure-flow is generated by the structure-flow generating instructions (VSTORE) and the new structure-flow is sent to the processing element or the structure memories. When it is sent to the processing element, it invokes the new template. When it is sent to the structure memory, it is stored to the high-level structure. When the program generates a scalar result, the intermediate scalar results are sent to the SHLS in the structure memory by the SHLS storing instructions (SSTORE).

5. Detection of the end of structure-flow processing. When the program generates a structure result, detection of the end is performed by counting the number of elements stored in the HLS. When it reaches a predefined value, the HLS returns the packet that

indicates the end of structure-flow processing. When the program generates a scalar result, an SHLS is used instead of an HLS. The counter is used as a reference counter when not all the elements in the structure-flow are used in the program, or when the structure-flow is sparse, the counter is used as a reference counter.

6. Deallocation of the HLS from the structure memory.

4 Vector processing by structure-flow Processing

From the practical point of view, the purpose of structure-flow processing is to add a vector processing facility to a dataflow computer. The importance of a vector processing facility in numerical computations is widely recognized because a high-end vector supercomputer is more than ten times faster than the fastest scalar computer. Without a vector processing facility, the performance of a dataflow processing element is nearly equal to that of a von Neumann scalar computer [9]. Consequently, the application field of those dataflow computers without vector processing facilities are restricted to what cannot be executed in vector supercomputers with high efficiency. This section describes how vectorized primitives are implemented by high-level structure processing.

4.1 Simple Vector Operations

Simple vector operations are the most common vector primitives. The can be written by a user program as:
$for(i = 0; i \leq limit; i = i + 1)\ a[i] = b[i] + c[i];$

The operation is one of integer and floating point arithmetic operations and boolean operations. This program is implemented by high-level structure processing, as shown in figure 2. Since the operation can be an arbitrary dataflow graph, an arbitrary combination of operations written as:
$for(i = 0; i \leq limit; i = i{+}1)\ a[i] = b[i]\ op\ c[i]\ op\ d[i]\ op \cdots;$
can be processed as a software chaining program.

4.2 Vector to Scalar Operations

Inner products, sums, and finding maximum value are included in this class. For example, an inner product is calculated by:
$for(i = 0, s = 0; i \leq limit; i = i + 1)\ s = s + a[i] * b[i];$

This is implemented as shown in figure 3. In figure 3, the end of structure processing is detected by the scalar high-level structure (SHLS). The final result is sent from the SHLS and then the garbage token on the operation nodes is erased.

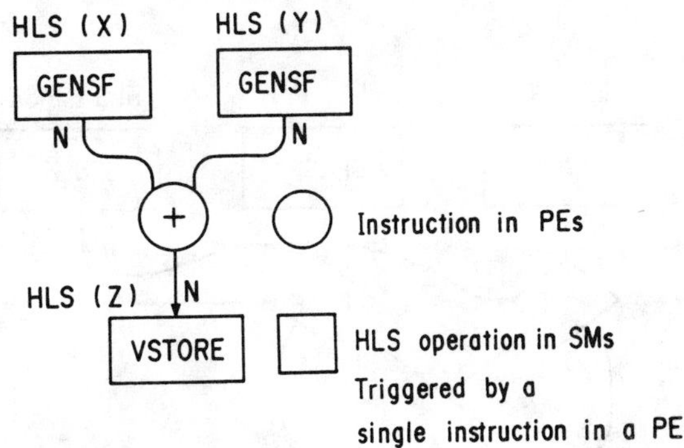

Figure 2: Simple Vector Operation (Vector ADD)

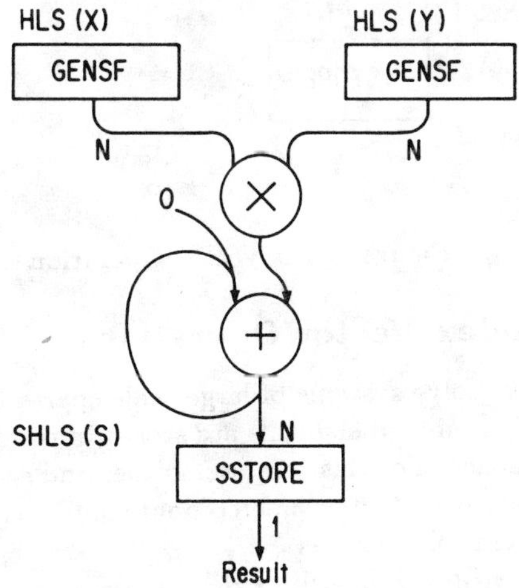

Figure 3: Vector to Scalar Operation (Inner Product)

4.3 Bit Vector Operations

Conditional expressions in a loop construct are realized by the bit vector operation in vector supercomputers. For example,
$for(i = 0; i \leq limit; i = i{+}1)\ a[i] = mask[i]\ ?\ b[i]{+}c[i] : b[i] - c[i];$
is realized by the mask-register operation. By high-level structure processing, the conditional expression is realized by an ordinary dataflow program that includes the SWITCH instruction shown in figure 4. Thus, bit vector operations are implemented in high-level structure processing. Furthermore, complex conditional expressions that cannot be realized by a vector supercomputer are easily implemented by high-level structure processing.

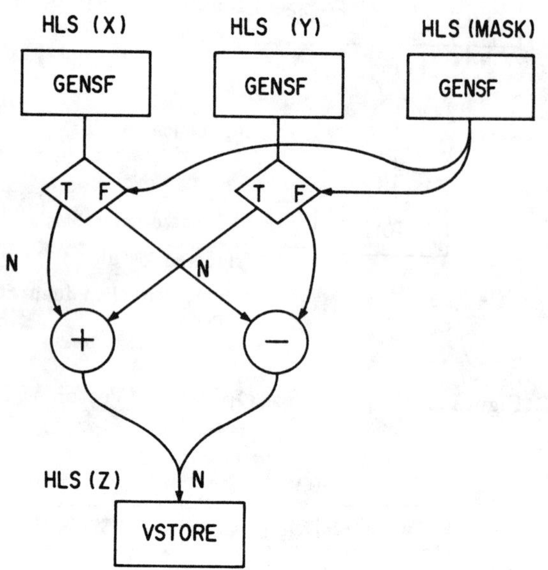

Figure 4: Bit Vector Operation

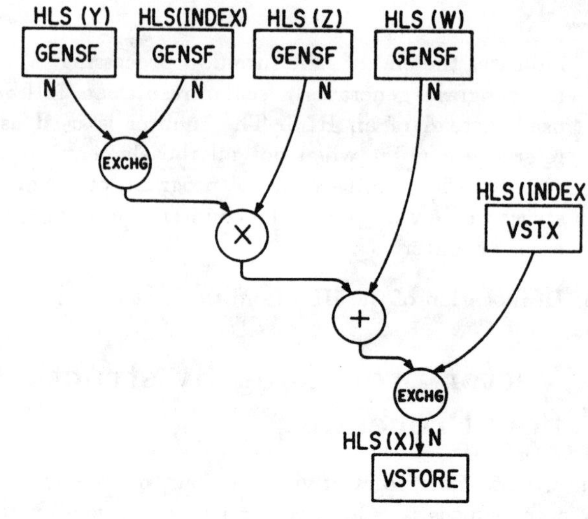

Figure 5: Index Vector Operation

4.4 Index Vector Operations

In order to solve systems of large scale sparse linear equations, only non-zero elements are stored in memory to save memory space. For this purpose, gather and scatter primitives are used in vector supercomputers. Especially, index vector operations such as

$x[index[i]] = y[index[i]] * z[i] + w[i];$

frequently appear in iterative algorithms for large sparse linear systems.

This example is realized by the dataflow program shown in figure 5. In figure 5, a primitive that exchange the data item and the identifier is used for scatter operation and the reverse-index generating primitive is used for gather operation.

4.5 More Complex Operations

When a function call is in the innermost loop construct, or when there is long range data dependency between in the loop and out of the loop, a vector arithmetic unit cannot be used in commercial supercomputers. Structure-flow processing can fully utilize parallelism in these cases because both the template program for the loop construct and the function in the loop or the program out of the loop are based on the same dataflow computing principle.

Thus, vector processing primitives in a vector supercomputer are efficiently realized by the structure-flow processing scheme.

5 SIGMA-1 Architecture

Structure-flow processing is implemented in the SIGMA-1, a dataflow supercomputer developed at Electrotechnical Laboratory. Figure 6 shows the global architecture of the SIGMA-1. The system consists of 128 processing elements (PEs), 128 structure processing elements (SEs), 32 local networks (LNETs), a global network (GNET), 16 maintenance processors, a service processor and a host processor. I/O channels in all the SEs, maintenance processors and service processor form the maintenance architecture. The maintenance architecture is used for I/O operations, system monitoring, performance measurements and maintenance operations [10]. The whole system is synchronous and operates under a single 10 MHz clock.

Figure 7 shows the detailed architecture of a PE and an SE. A PE executes all the instructions except structure operations, and an SE executes structure operations such as high-level structure operations, read, write, allocation, deallocation and I/O operations.

A PE operates in a two-stage pipeline. The *firing stage* is the first stage of the pipeline which consists of an input FIFO buffer, a link register file, an instruction memory and a matching memory. The second stage is the *execution stage* that consists of execution units including a floating point arithmetic unit, an integer arithmetic unit, a multiplier, a structure address generator and an Packet-IDentifier (**PID**) generator.

The matching memory fires the execution of instructions with two input operands. Chained hashing hardware is used to upgrade the performance of the matching memory.

Chained hashing matching memory makes FIFO queues on each key, enabling multiple entries with the same key. This is utilized in static structure-flow processing mentioned in section 2. An instruction is fetched from the instruction memory in the *firing stage*. The instruction address is calculated by the **PID** of the input packet and the contents of the link register. Here, the link register is used as a base register for the instruction address.

In the *execution stage*, the operation of the floating point arithmetic unit, the integer arithmetic unit, the multiplier and the structure address generator is similar to that in a von Neumann processor. The **PID** generator produces the **PID** attached to output packets using input operands and the instructions fetched by the *firing stage*.

An SE consists of an input FIFO buffer, a structure memory, two flag logics that support fast structure managements and SE instruction triggering, a structure controller and an I/O channel.

A structure is allocated on the structure memory on the SE. The buddy system implemented by hardware is used to increase the speed of allocating and deallocating structure.

The local network is a 10 by 10 crossbar packet switching network. Eight ports are used for communicating PEs and SEs within a cluster, and two ports are used for communicating with the global network. The data width of each port is 49 bits. Thus, a local network can transfer at most 50 M packets in a second, or 600 M Bytes per second. The global network is a two-stage omega network that connects 32 local networks. It transfers 2 G Bytes per second maximum. The global network is used for communicating clusters and accessing structures.

In the SIGMA-1, vector processing by high level structures are implemented as follows:

- Allocation and deallocation of a high-level structure is performed in a SE. Since these operation is supported a buddy system hardware, the execution time of them is as fast as shown in Table 2. When the high-level structure is allocated, all the elements in the structure is cleared by the flag-bit hardware in 1 clock cycle.
- GENSF and VSTX is performed in SEs. The structure controller distributes the results in structure-flow processing to the destination PEs and SEs. This unit enables interleaving access to SEs.
- All arithmetic operations, conditional operations and EXCHG are executed in PEs.
- VSTORE and SSTORE are executed in PEs. These instructions produce VSTORE and SSTORE packet respectively and send them to destination SEs. A sticky token mechanism is normally used in these instructions for increasing performance.

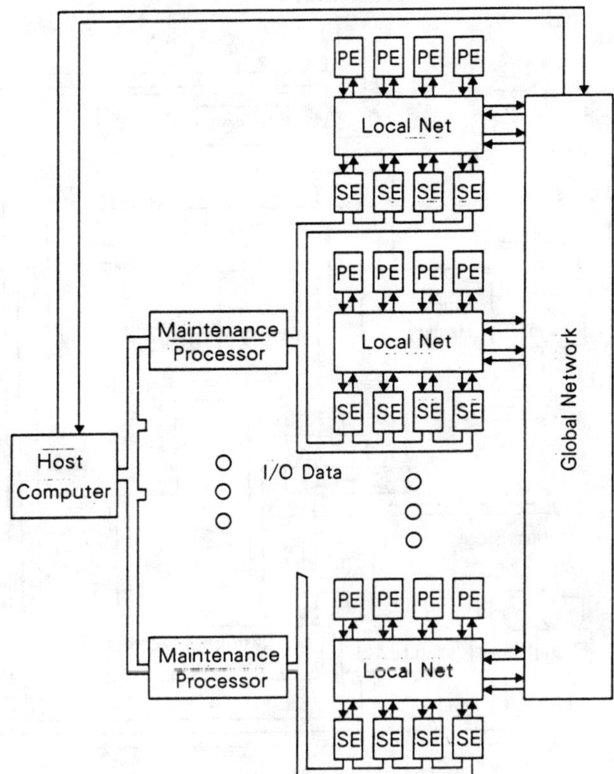

Figure 6: Global Organization

6 Performance Evaluation

The high-level structure processing performance was measured on the SIGMA-1. Table 2 summarizes the execution time for instructions and structural operations. The pipelined execution time indicates effective execution time when all the pipeline stages are occupied. The turn around execution time indicates the interval time of the instruction execution when the program is purely sequential.

When the program is parallel, a PE can execute an instruction every two to three clocks in most of the instructions. However, two packets are necessary for two input instruction, and six clocks are necessary to complete the execution. As the clock period is 100 nanoseconds, the basic performance of the PE is estimated at 1.7 MFLOPS. This maximum performance has been observed in a scalar processing program[9].

The performance has been measured on
(1) an inner products (Q = Q + x(k) * y (k)),
(2) a vector addition (z(K) = x(k) + y(k)), and
(3) a first order difference (x(k) = Y(k+1) - y(k)).

The program has been executed on a processing element

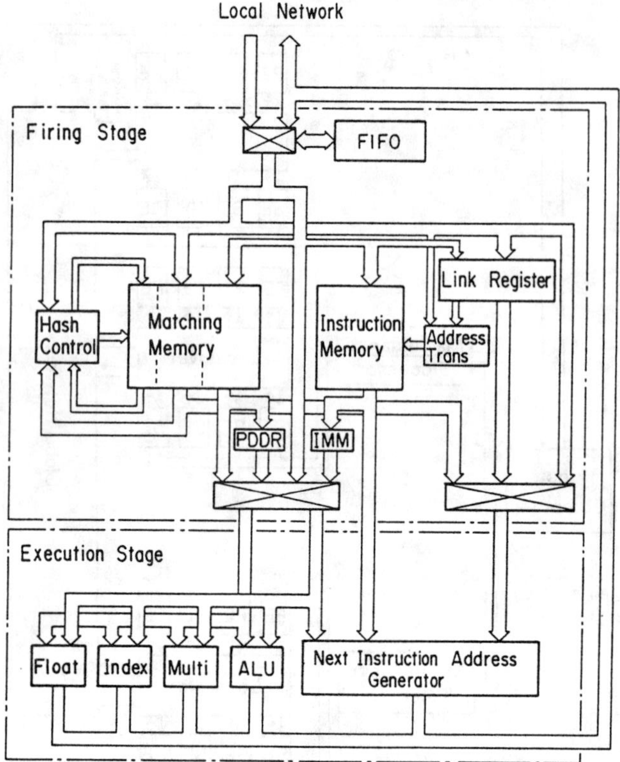

(a) Processing Element

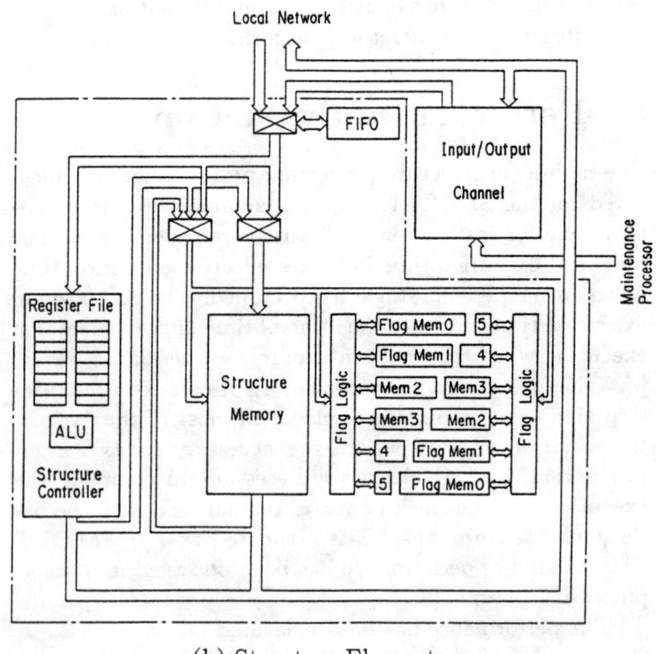

(b) Structure Element

Figure 7: Block Diagrams of a PE and an SE

(PE) and two to three structure memories (SEs). The performance has been plotted in figure 8, where the solid line shows the performance using high-level structure processing and the dotted line shows the performance using loop unfolding by software.

The vector length required to achieve half the maximum performance and the speed-up ratio of vector to scalar operation [10] are commonly used performance indices for vector supercomputers. The former indicates the overhead for beginning and terminating vector operations and the latter indicates the number of structure handling and loop constructing instructions in scalar processing.

As shown in figure 8, the half performance vector length in all the programs is between 4 to 8. Since it is more than 10 in the shortest commercial supercomputer, the overhead for beginning and terminating vector operations in high-level structure processing is less than that in commercial supercomputers. This shows that a short pipelined dataflow computer with high-level structure processing is superior to commercial supercomputers in short vector programs because long pipeline architecture is essential to obtain high performance in commercial supercomputers.

With regard to the speed-up ratio, the tree programs are executed by high-level structure processing 3 to 4.4 times faster than by scalar processing. The speeding up ratios are lowered because the SIGMA-1 cannot have three input instructions, and separate arithmetic and VSTORE instructions are necessary. If the processing element can have three input instructions, these two can be reduced to a single instruction. In this case, the performance of these programs are 1.7,1.7 and 0.8 MFLOPS. The speed-up ratios are then 4.5, 10.5 and 5.0. Thus, high-level structure processing introduces remarkable performance enhancement to the SIGMA-1.

7 Concluding Remarks

This paper proposed structure-flow processing as an efficient structure handling scheme. Then, the high-level structure was the proposed an an implementation mechanism of structure-flow processing on a practical dataflow supercomputer. When this processing mechanism is used for numerical computations that frequently use vectors, the overhead on unfolding loops for vector processing is completely eliminated. As the program is written by dataflow graphs that may have conditional expressions and function calls, vector processing using this scheme is more flexible than that using vector supercomputers.

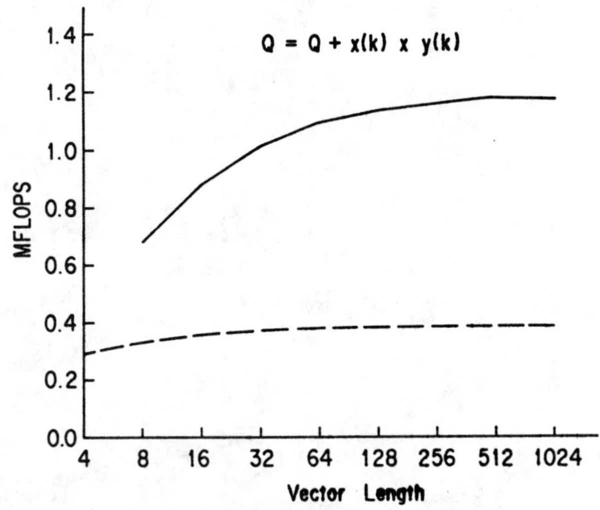

(a) Inner Products

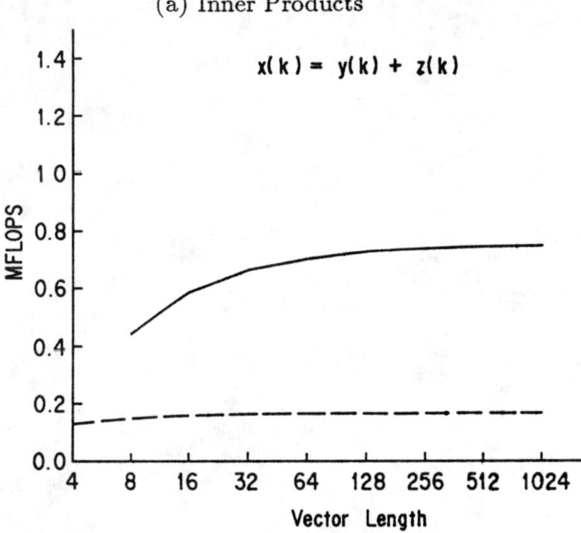

(b) Vector Addition

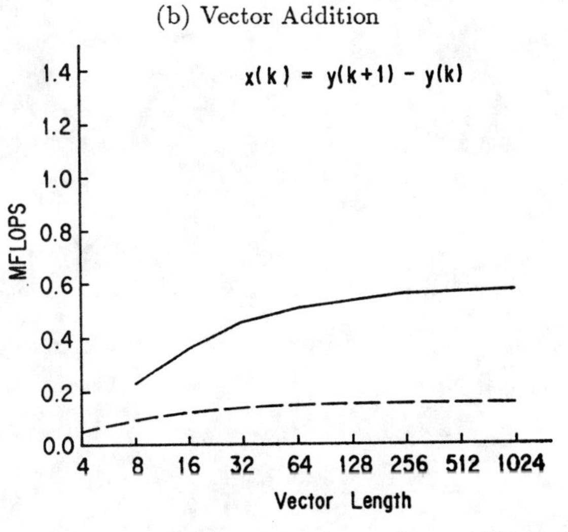

(c) First Order Difference

Figure 8: Performance on the SIGMA-1

Acknowledgements

We greatly appreciate the valuable interaction with Dr. T. Yuba, Chief of Computer Architecture Section and the members of the section. We also thank Dr. H. Kashiwagi, Dupty Director-General, Electrotechnical Laboratory for his support. This study was performed as part of the national project High-speed computation system for scientific computation" of MITI, Japan.

References

[1] Misunas, D.P.,"Structure Processing in a Dataflow Computer," Proc. Sagamore Computer Conference on Parallel Processing, 1975, pp.230-234

[2] Ackerman, W.B.,"A Structure Processing Facility for Dataflow Computers," Proc. Int. Conf. Parallel Processing, 1978, pp.166-172.

[3] Arvind and Thomas, R.E.,"I-Structure: An Effective Data Structure for Functional Languages," MIT,LCS-TM178, Lab. for Computer Science, MIT, 1978.

[4] Gurd, J., Kirkham, C. C. and Watson, I., "The Manchester Prototype Dataflow Computer," Commun. ACM, Vol. 28, No. 1, 1985.

[5] Sergeant, J. and Kirkham, C. C., "Stored Data Structures on the Manchester Dataflow Machine," Proc. Int. Symp. Computer Architecture, 1986, pp.235-242.

[6] Gaudiot, J.L.,"Method for Handling Structures in Data-flow Systems," Proc. Int. Symp. Computer Architecture, 1985, pp.352-358.

[7] Hiraki, K., Nishida, K. and Shimada, T.,"A Hardware Design of the SIGMA-1 - A Data Flow Computer for Scientific Computations," Proc. Int. Conf. Parallel Processing, 1984, pp.851-858.

[8] Hiraki, K., Nishida, K., Sekiguchi, S. and Shimada, T., "Maintenance Architecture and Its LSI Implementation of a Dataflow Computer with a Large Number of Processors," Proc. Int. Conf. Parallel Processing, 1986, pp.584-591.

[9] Hiraki, K., Sekiguchi, S. and Shimada, T.,"System Architecture of a Dataflow Supercomputer," Proc. TENCON87, IEEE,1987, pp.1044- 1049.

[10] Hockney, R.W. and Jesshope, C.R.,"Parallel Computers," Adam Hilger, 1981.

References

Algorithms - I

Chair: Jack Dongarra
Argonne National Laboratory

Vectorized Monte Carlo Molecular Aerodynamics Simulation of the Rayleigh Problem

*Daniel V. Pryor**
Supercomputing Research Center
4380 Forbes Boulevard
Lanham, MD 20706
(301) 731-3731
pryor@super.org

Patrick J. Burns
Department of Mechanical Engineering
Colorado State University
Fort Collins, Colorado 80523
(303) 491-7709
pburns@csugreen.bitnet

ABSTRACT

A fully vectorized version of a 1-dimensional Monte Carlo algorithm applied to molecular aerodynamics is presented. The algorithm is applied to the Rayleigh problem, an impulsively accelerated, heated flat plate, and is implemented on the CYBER 205. Issues relating to the details of vectorization, including the use of bit addressability, the maintaining of long vector lengths, and vector gather/scatter use, are discussed. Speedup factors due to vectorization in the range of 5 to 18 are reported, and depend upon problem parameters. The results indicate that, under certain circumstances, the problem performs well on vector architectures.

Keywords: vectorization, parallel algorithm, coarse/fine grain, branching, sparse operation, gather, scatter.

Introduction

There are presently two numerical approaches to modeling physical problems. The first, and most often used, is the set of classical methods based on continuum analysis, providing a ''macroscopic'' view of problems. These typically require the discretization of appropriate partial differential equations by methods such as finite difference or finite element. Classical methods are thus often associated with large linear systems. When these linear systems are well behaved, as they can be in the case of simple geometries, regular grids, and sparse coupling between nodes, then these methods are quite efficient. For problem situations that depart from these conditions, the difficulty in setting up the problem increases, as does the computational cost to solve it.

The second approach to physical problems involves Monte Carlo methods, which are based upon ''tracing'' microscopic particles such as molecules, electrons, or photons, the motions of which are modeled according to probabilistic estimates known or inferred from experience. The computations associated with individual particles are typically very simple, and are not made more difficult in a geometrically irregular environment. But since Monte Carlo methods rely on statistical assumptions, a numerical model usually requires a large number of simulated trials in order to preserve in the computation the statistical properties assumed in the model. For this reason, Monte Carlo methods have seen limited use. Indeed supercomputers are just now becoming powerful enough to simulate ''real'' problems using Monte Carlo methods.

There has been increasing activity in recent years in mapping Monte Carlo methods to vector and parallel architectures. Late developments include the work of Martin, et al. [1]. in dealing with a vectorized zonal approach for tracing photons in axisymmetric regions. The work by these authors has resulted in speedup factors of approximately 5 over optimized scalar code on Cray 1 and single processor Cray X-MP machines, and twice that amount when compared to current CDC 7600 production code. These speedups are due to the vectorization of the problem (fine-grained parallelism). A parallel processor photon tracing code (coarse-grained parallelism) has been implemented by Sequent Computer Systems [2], and is reported to have achieved nearly linear speedup when applied to a system of 12 processors. In the work of Bobrowicz et al. [3], particles are retained in queues until some optimal number have accumulated. In this way, arithmetic operations are delayed until they can be done at efficient vector lengths. Pryor and Burns [4,5] have achieved speedup factors in the range of 15 to 30, for photon tracing problems, on the Cyber 205.

For the problem considered in this study, several references deserve mention. Boltzmann [6] and Tsien [7], establish a firm theoretical background for understanding the physics of dilute gases. The simulation of molecular dynamics on digital computers became well established in 1956 with the work of Alder and Wainwright [8]. At that time, the capacity of digital computers was taxed with even rudimentary problems. As digital computers have grown in capability, the investigations have become more numerous, as described in the review article by Derzko [9]. Our focus here is on the Direct Simulation Monte Carlo (DSMC) method of Bird, et al. [10-14]. While this method has been implemented in a parallel (but non-vector) coarse-grained algorithm on a Perkin-Elmer system [15], it is our intention to investigate a fine-grained approach on a vector architecture.

Vectorization Considerations

Supercomputers made available after the Cray 1 have become much more powerful in handling Monte Carlo simulations and other problems which can be thought of as irregular or discontinuous in structure, as opposed to the type of models which simulate ''continuous'' processes. The most important development in present-day supercomputer architectures in solving these irregularly structured problems has been the introduction of the vectorized indexed gather/scatter instructions (and their similar derivatives) in the hardware of machines such as the CYBER 205, the Cray X-MP, the Cray 2, and the ETA-10. The algorithm we have implemented depends heavily upon some form of this hardware capability.

The nature of the molecular aerodynamics problem makes it a possible candidate for vectorization, since over a small enough time interval, each molecule can be treated as an independent particle,

* This work was done while Daniel Pryor was an employee of the Institute for Computational Studies, Ft. Collins, CO.

CH2617-9/88/0000/0384$01.00 © 1988 IEEE

thus exhibiting a fine-grained parallelism. Also, the amount of computation involved in tracing the path of a single molecule is small. Additionally, regions of space (referred to as "cells") can be defined to restrict collisions to only molecule pairs within a cell (localization of action). Each cell can then be treated independently, with only a slightly coarsened degree of parallelism, thus providing a further potential for vectorization.

The problem to overcome in this particular setting relates to the character of the individual events, particularly the interactions among the molecules. These interactions force the system to depart from the strict independence condition that proves useful in vectorizing other problems [4]. Thus the problem we consider here is a less perfect match for vector hardware than is the photon transport problem. Within a discrete time step, some molecules may collide a number of times, others a different number of times, others not at all. In a sequential tracing algorithm, these unknowns would normally result in a number of IF-tests in a computer program. But if the algorithm is to be vectorized, such tests must be eliminated. The supercomputers mentioned above allow the branching that is implied by such tests to be "rearranged" in order to permit the vector hardware access to the problem. The major algorithm steps are outlined in the following section, with emphasis on physical understanding of the process.

The problem is the simulation of low density molecular aerodynamics by the Direct Simulation Monte Carlo (DSMC) method as developed by Bird [10]. Due to CPU and memory limitations, the DSMC approach has been applied to only localized regions in space and time. The objective of this study was to investigate the feasibility of applying the vector hardware found in modern supercomputers, to a difficult, and traditionally scalar problem. Since this problem requires a large amount of branching, in the scalar sense, to model the physical situation, it was not known *a priori* whether it would make sense to employ a vector approach to this problem. The amount of overhead associated with data motion, and the management of the accompanying index lists is certainly a nontrivial factor in this coding exercise. Obviously, in any effort of this sort, the goal is to maximize the speedup, relative to the purely scalar algorithm, or to at least identify operating ranges in which a parallel version (in this case, the vector version) will outperform the scalar version. In particular, we wish to investigate the sensitivity of the execution timings to certain parameters, with a view toward understanding how to best scale up the problem while maintaining efficient execution. A successfully vectorized algorithm, provided it exhibits high speedup, should allow the attack of much larger problems.

Algorithm Description

It was decided to experiment with a very simple problem, but with enough "real world" applicability to assess the feasibility of extension to more complex situations. The Rayleigh problem, as described by Yang and Lees [16], and solved by Bird [10], was chosen as the problem of interest because of its simplicity and the published results with which to compare. Further, the scalar algorithm is given in Appendix G of Reference 10. We have implemented this scalar algorithm on the Cyber 205 as a base case. This code was compiled with all scalar optimization options enabled. Automatic vectorization was also enabled, but no loops of any substance could be vectorized. All of the results of the timings of the vector algorithm will be compared with timings of this algorithm.

The Rayleigh problem, as stated by Bird, is transient, and unidimensional. As shown in Figure 1, a uniform initial state exists in a low density gas. At time = 0^+, the infinite plate located at $Y=0$ is impulsively accelerated to the right, and, simultaneously, subjected to instant heating. Energy and momentum diffuse vertically in time via molecule motion and subsequent collisions. The plate moves to the right with a non-dimensional velocity of $U_W=2$, and the non-dimensional temperature of the plate is $T_W=1.6$. The free stream has zero mean velocity and a nondimensional temperature of 1. Full details of the problem can be found in Reference 10.

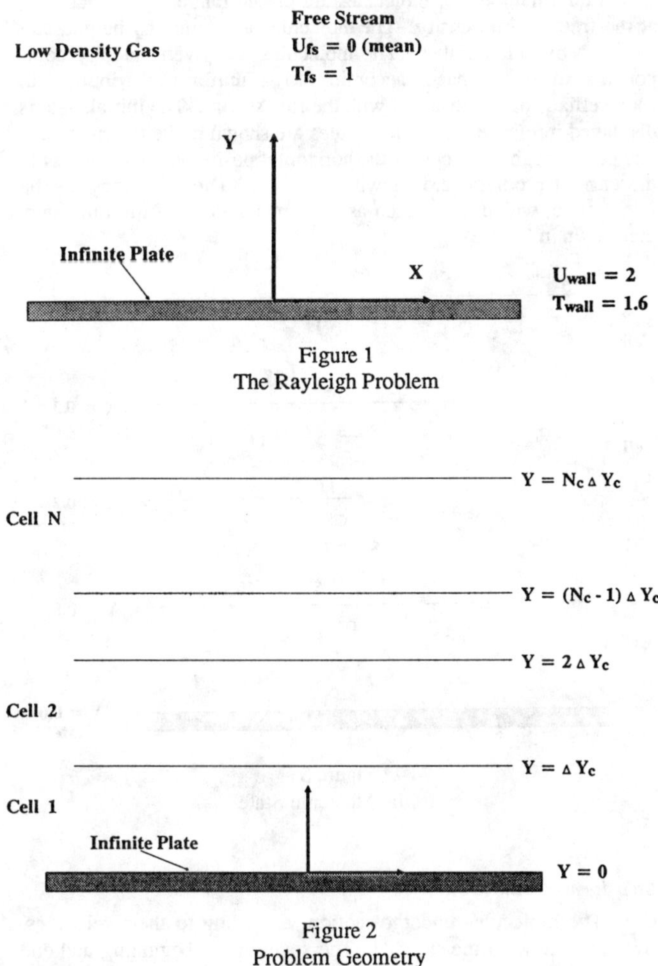

Figure 1
The Rayleigh Problem

Figure 2
Problem Geometry

The geometry is discretized into cells, as shown in Figure 2, where the maximum value of Y, $(N_c \, \Delta Y_c)$, is problem dependent. Time is also discretized into constant intervals. This presents some difficulty, i.e. since density and velocity vary spatially (cell by cell), the collision frequency also varies spatially. Thus, each collision in each cell advances time by a different amount, requiring time to be traced in each cell. A natural consequence is that, to achieve synchronization, the cells where time advances rapidly are left dormant while the others "catch up." When all cell times equal or exceed the time step, collisions are reactivated in all cells. This is a manifestation of even further random branching, beyond that occurring in the collision and reflection processes.

The ultimate basis for vectorization of the algorithm is the physical process. To illustrate the process, a sample problem with only four cells and twenty molecules is presented. The major steps of the algorithm will be discussed, and output from the vectorized algorithm will be shown.

Initialization

Equal numbers of molecules are placed randomly in each cell, at the free stream density. The molecules are sorted by height, and gathered by cell number. The molecules are given velocity components in three space, according to a uniform distribution in Maxwellian space consistent with the free stream. The initial state is displayed in Figure 3. The molecules are shown in their correct vertical positions, but for clarity the horizontal positions (meaningless in the current problem) are shown spread out. The cell times for the initial state, which are chosen as random fractions of the time step, are shown in Figure 4.

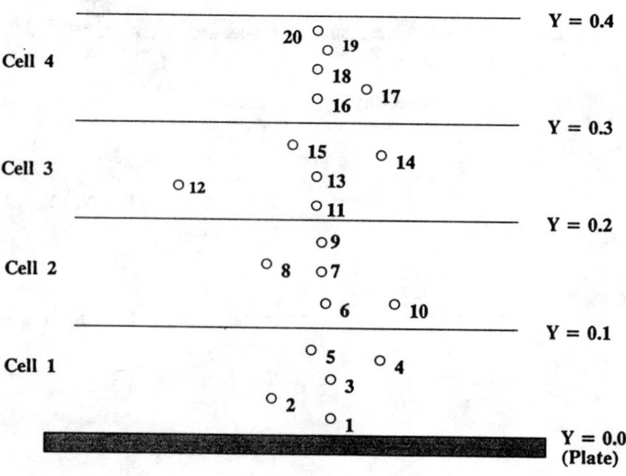

Figure 3
Initial Molecule State

Step 1 - Molecule Motion

The molecules undergo motion, according to their velocities, over the "flow" time step, Δt_f. The states at the beginning and end of the molecule motion are shown in Figure 5. The arrows shown in the figure illustrate the change in vertical position of the molecule (they do not represent velocity). For clarity, only a few typical arrows are included in the figure.

During this step, molecules which pass the top boundary are specularly reflected. For the present example, none reach the top boundary. Molecules also interact with the bottom boundary, a

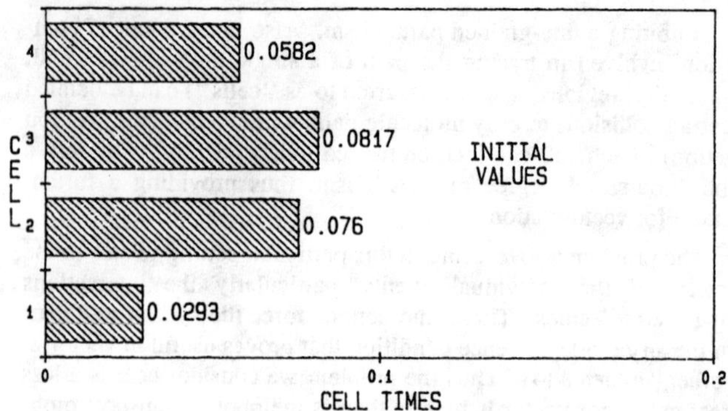

Figure 4
Cell Times for Initial State

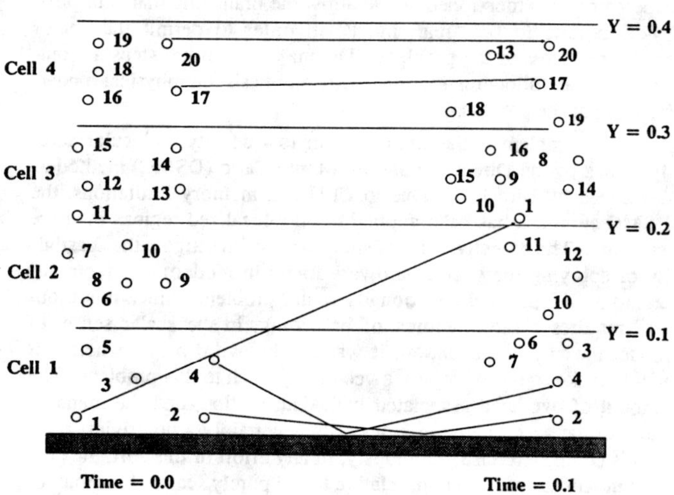

Figure 5
Step 1 - Molecule Motion

heated, moving plate. In this example, molecules 2 and 4 collide with the surface, where energy and momentum are exchanged (an accommodation coefficient of 1 is used), and the molecules are then diffusely reflected from the moving, heated surface. Vector lengths for the motion, specular reflection from the top boundary, and interaction with the plate are: 20, 0, and 2, respectively.

Step 2 - Collisions

Attention is now turned to collisions, where energy and momentum are exchanged between molecule pairs. In the previous step, the point of reference was the molecule; in this step it is the cell, i.e. molecule indices are gathered cell-by-cell. The goal here is to achieve synchronization. That is, a sufficient number of collisions must be allowed to occur in each cell, for all of the cell times, Δt_c, to advance beyond the flow time ($\Delta t_f = 0.1$). Collision pairs are restricted to exist within each cell. Two molecules within each cell, shown highlighted in Figure 6, are randomly chosen as candidates for collision. For the "hard-sphere" molecules under study, the probability of collision is proportional to their relative speed, V_R. To ensure that the maximum relative speed within each cell is used to compute the collision probability, the maximum relative speed in each cell is traced and updated. For every vector computation of relative speed within the active cells, where the computed relative speeds exceed the current maximum relative speeds stored for the cells, the computed relative speeds are "scattered" into the vector of maximum relative speeds, to be used in subsequent computation. Here, all four cells are active, since each cell time is less than the flow time. A vector of four random numbers is generated, and compared with the probabilities for collision in the cells. Where the random numbers are in the range of collision probabilities (cells 1,3, and 4), collisions occur and the time, t_c, advances in these cells according to:

$$\Delta t_c = \frac{2\Delta y_c}{N_c^2 \chi \|V_R\|},$$

where Δy_c is the size of cell c, χ is the collision cross section, and N_c, is the number of molecules in cell c. Figure 7 illustrates the cell times after Event 1. Note that, where a collision does not occur (cell 2), time does not advance.

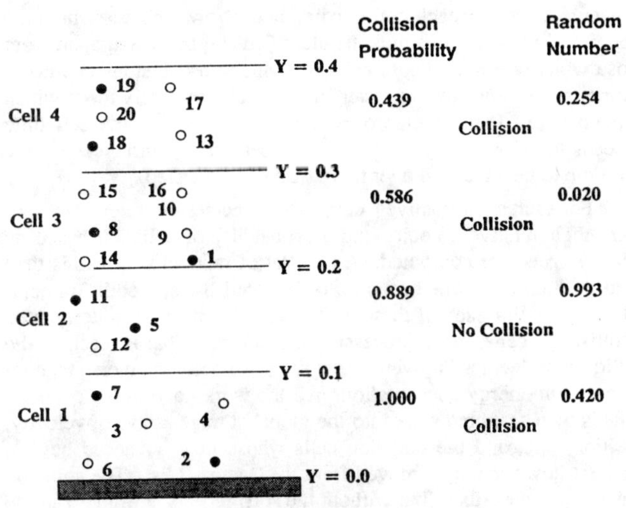

Figure 6
Step 2 - Collisions, Event 1

The process repeats until all cell times advance to exceed the flow time. As the process occurs, individual cell times exceed the flow time, and these cells then become inactive. The initial vector length thus decreases with advancing iteration until all cell times exceed the flow time, at which point the flow time step is complete. For the example problem, only cell 2 remains active. Two new molecules, shown highlighted in Figure 8, are randomly chosen as candidates for collision. (The fact that these are the same two chosen in Event 1 is mere coincidence.) Thus Event 2 begins. A collision occurs, and the time advances in cell 2 to exceed the flow

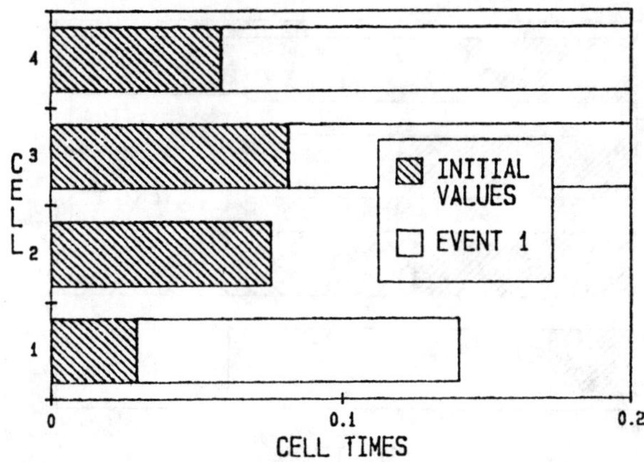

Figure 7
Cell Times After Event 1

time, as shown in Figure 9.

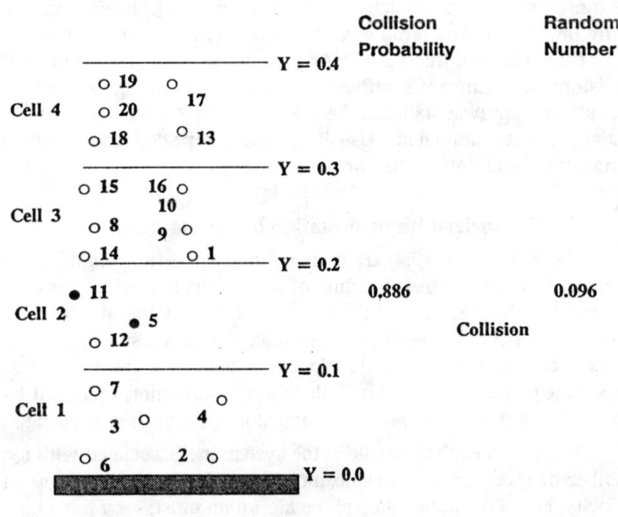

Figure 8
Step 2 - Collisions, Event 2

Normally, a much larger number of collisions occur in each cell during a flow time step. Also, due to the low number density in the sample problem (chosen to simplify the explanation), the cell times advanced very rapidly, sometimes over multiple flow time steps. This is also not typical of the process for larger problems.

Step 3 - Updating

The final algorithmic task during the time step is the collection of statistics within the cells. Each cell is polled to determine physical characteristics of interest, e.g. number density, temperature, mean velocity, etc. For the results reported in this paper, updating occurred every flow time step. Normally, many flow time steps

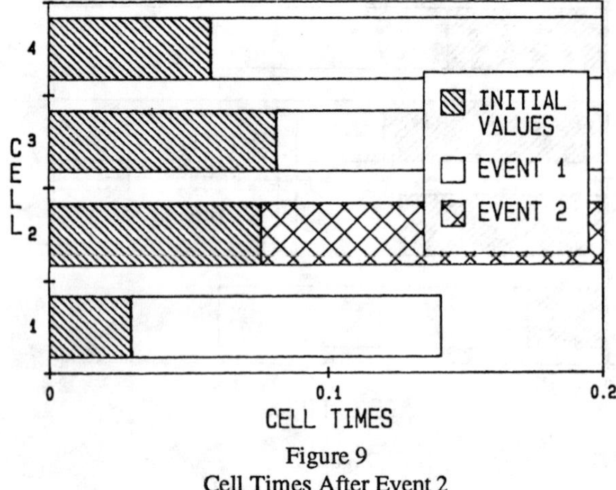

Figure 9
Cell Times After Event 2

occur between statistical updates.

All three of these steps are applied in succession until an amount of time equal to the "run time step" has elapsed. (The completion of all flow time steps is called a "run".) At this time the entire process may be rerun with the system state preserved from the end of the run time interval. During a run time step, the number of collisions occurring are insufficient to be statistically significant. To provide an improved statistical base, multiple runs are performed and statistics are accumulated. Usually runs are repeated until all field variables exhibit good behavior.

Vectorized Implementation of the Algorithm

The algorithm applied to this model has two major components. The first is the modeling of the molecule motion, for each molecule in the system, and the second is the modeling of the collisions which occur between pairs of molecules as a result of the previous increments of molecule motion. There is a third, but less important process that simply collects the information produced by the motion and collision processes, and stores it for postprocessing.

Recall that each molecule in the system has associated with it a number of quantities such as position, energy, three components of velocity, etc. The motion step of the algorithm must, for a fixed time interval, advance all molecules in the direction of motion at the beginning of the time step. If any molecules exit the top of the highest grid cell, they are specularly reflected back into the grid, so that symmetry of the system is preserved at the top boundary. At the bottom boundary is the surface, where for each increment of molecule motion, a number of molecules may strike the surface. These must also be reflected back into the system, but with adjustments in energy and momentum to account for energy exchange with the surface.

All of these calculations (in the motion step) are performed using vector operations, and data are moved with the use of the compress/decompress instructions available in the Cyber 205 hardware. This is certainly a reasonable first choice for the data movement required by the algorithm, but there are two other strategies that may prove to be useful: 1) constructing index lists corresponding to molecules which undergo changes in velocity or direction, and using gather/scatter instructions rather than the compress/decompress (this may help, since in most cases the number of such molecules would be small compared to the total number of molecules, and the gather/scatter instructions are usually faster when used in sparse operations) and 2) using some mix of scalar and vector instructions. This could be most useful when "sparsity" as a fraction of vector length was not the issue, but rather when the absolute number of operations was so small that vector overhead would dominate the computation time in vector units. In any case, the three approaches could be easily integrated using only a single branch to the proper section of code, based on the number of special molecules.

The second of the two major steps models the collisions of molecules. In this section, the position array is sorted with respect to height from the surface. Clearly this adds to the cost of the computation, and can be costly in some operating ranges, as we will show. In others, its execution is of negligible cost. Once the sort is complete, it is a trivial matter to find the first (lowest) molecule in each cell with the use of the specialized Q8VLTI function on the Cyber 205. (Q8VLTI is a Fortran vector-valued intrinsic function that returns the number of elements that precede the first encountered element of the second vector argument which is less than each element of the first vector argument [17].) Along with the first molecule in each cell, the molecule count for each cell is computed. Now the cells which are "eligible" for collisions must be identified and processed apart from those which are not. Those cells for which no collisions can occur during the current flow time step are, initially, precisely those which contain either 0 molecules or 1 molecule, or where the cell time exceeds the flow time (it is possible in certain rare instances for the cell time to be advanced over more than one time step).

For each such "active" cell, two molecules are selected at random, their relative velocity and a probability of collision based on relative speed are computed. A new set of random numbers is then used to determine whether, on a cell-by-cell basis, a collision actually occurs. For each of these active cells that have been designated "collision" cells, more processing is required. That is, each of the colliding molecules is given a new set of velocity components, consistent with energy conservation. All the work done in the collision cells is then scattered back into the global storage arrays of velocity, position, etc., and the collision cells whose time advanced beyond the next flow time are removed from the "active" list. The collision process just described (but without the sort) repeats until there are no cells remaining active.

Wherever possible, arrays are stored in a manner which reduces the number of vector operations that must be performed. For example, there are $2 \times 3 \times (\textit{number of collisions})$ velocity components which must be scattered back to the global velocity arrays, after being recomputed. The new velocities are stored in adjacent arrays, as are the global velocities. Thus the scatter operation from six packed component arrays into three larger arrays can be done in a single instruction. The same sort of technique is used in selecting random indices to represent molecules in active cells. A vector of length $2 \times (\textit{number of active cells})$ (or $2N_a$) of random numbers is generated. The first half of the random array is converted to integers, each scaled to the number of molecules in an active cell. The second half is converted to integers scaled to 1 less than the number of molecules in the active cells. Whenever the jth random number is greater than or equal to the $(j+N_a)^{th}$ random number, the $(j+N_a)^{th}$ number is incremented by 1. Thus with a very small number of vector operations, each active cell is sampled (without replacement) for two random indices, and there results a pair of unique molecules representing each active cell.

Results and Discussion

The vector and scalar codes were exercised by varying certain problem parameters. To assess relative performance, CPU timings were generated by subtracting from the total run time the time for initialization (i.e. time required to load the program into memory, open files, establish a drop file, etc.). Shown in Figure 10 are timings, plotted on a log-log scale, for both versions of the code when the number of cells are varied. The number of molecules per cell and the cell height are held constant at values of 20 and 0.2, respectively. So, for this graph, the problem grows by "stacking" additional, identical cells on the grid, so that the geometry and the number of molecules grow commensurately with the number of cells. The speedup, defined as the ratio of the scalar CPU time to the vector CPU time, is shown in Figure 11, forming an inverted "U" shape versus the number of cells. This behavior was further investigated by establishing the percentage of the time the vector algorithm spends in each of steps 1 through 3: molecule motion, collisions, and updating statistics, respectively - as shown in Figure 12. The drop-off in speedup at low numbers of cells is due to the relatively large startup time for the short vector operations. Also, as the absolute magnitude of the CPU time is very small, there is the effect of a portion, i.e. I/O, subroutine calls, etc., of the algorithm being inherently scalar in nature, and consuming an appreciable percentage of time. Both of these effects are observed to wane (as they should) as the number of cells grows.

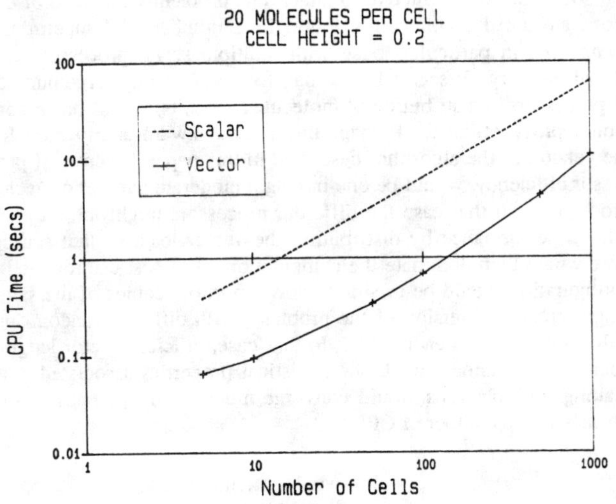

Figure 10
CPU Times vs. Number of Cells;
Cell Height and Number of Molecules per Cell Fixed

At large numbers of cells, the algorithm spends most of its time calculating collisions. The time spent in molecule motion is

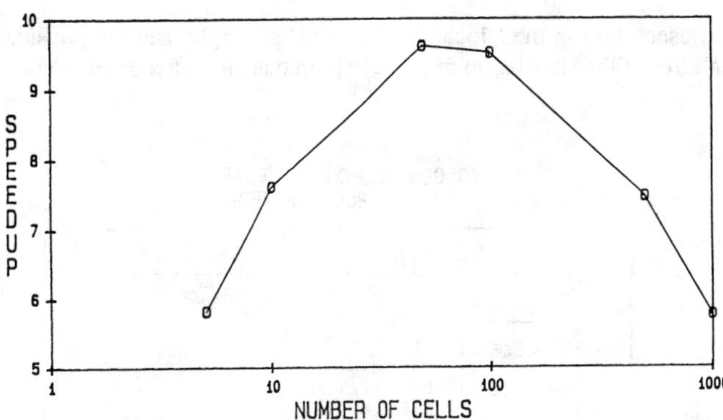

Figure 11
Speedup vs. Number of Cells;
Cell Height and Number of Molecules per Cell Fixed

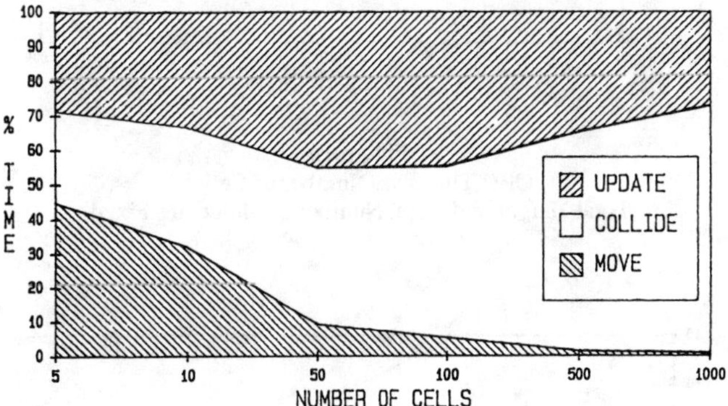

Figure 12
Step Timings vs. Number of Cells;
Cell Height and Number of Molecules per Cell Fixed

minimal. The speedup decreases in this region of the domain due to the increasing load associated with the "stragglers" at the end of the flow time step. This is unfortunate, as larger problems will experience poorer performance in this section of the code. However, as mentioned above, it may be possible to identify a threshold count of active cells below which the algorithm switches into scalar mode. Thus the problem noticed here could be partially alleviated, and we would see a flattening of the curve as the number of cells becomes large.

Figures 13, 14 and 15 show, respectively, CPU time, speedup and percentage of time spent in Steps 1 through 3 for the case where the geometry and the total number of molecules are held constant and the number of cells is varied. As the number of cells decreases from 1000 to 50 (all else held constant), the speedup increases from a factor of 5 to a factor of 18. The results are consistent with the reasoning given above - the last place finishers in a group of 1000 are likely to be slower than those in a group of 50. It is noted, however, that large numbers of molecules in each cell cause a loss of representation in the "locality of action" principle, and the physical validity of the simulation must be held in question after some point.

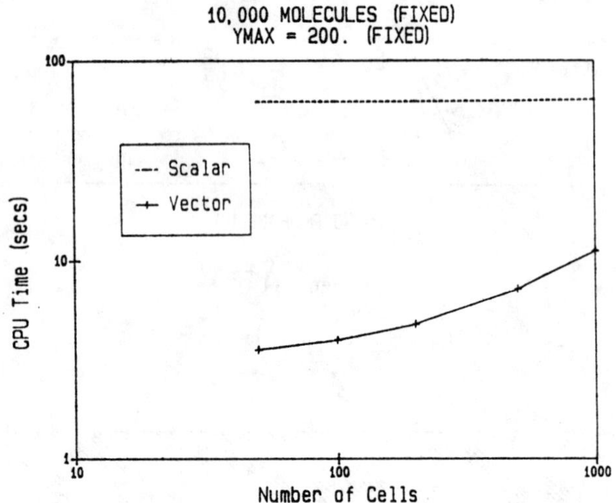

Figure 13
CPU Times vs. Number of Cells;
Total Height and Total Number of Molecules Fixed

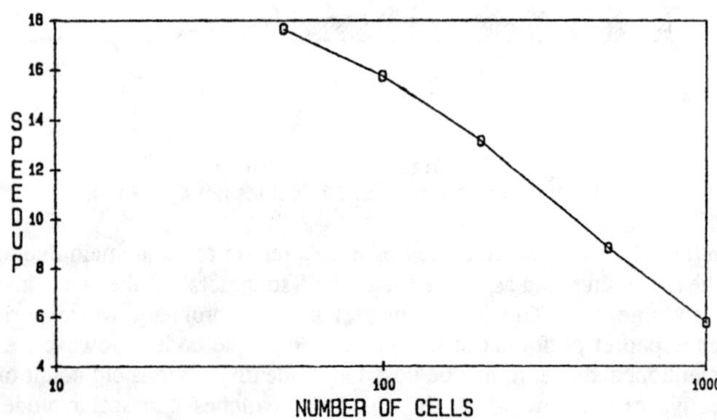

Figure 14
Speedup vs. Number of Cells;
Total Height and Total Number of Molecules Fixed

In conclusion, we found that it does pay to vectorize this algorithm, and that the weaknesses of the vector implementation have been exposed. Furthermore we feel that these weaknesses are correctable by abandoning the vector attack as the algorithm nears the end of the flow time step, or whenever it makes sense to do so.

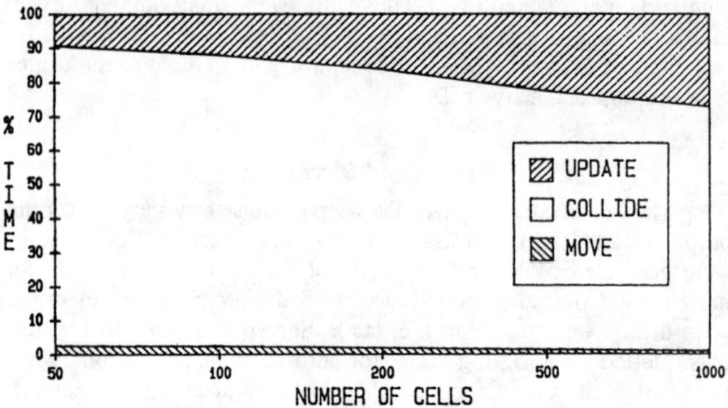

Figure 15
Step Timings vs. Number of Cells;
Total Height and Total Number of Molecules Fixed

Recommendations

The algorithm should be extended to multi-dimensions. This should be a relatively trivial bookkeeping matter, provided a regularly connected grid is employed - standard mapping procedures should aid in this regard. Adaptive re-meshing will probably be necessary, but this is well understood at the present time. With two- and three- dimensional geometries, the sorting of molecules by height would occur in each "cell column," leaving the remainder of the problem identical to that solved herein. Also, more realistic material models need to be employed. We are presently investigating this. Indications are that these will also be amenable to vectorization.

It would be instructive to attack this problem with some of the more advanced architectures found in a number of "supermini" computers, in particular those with multiple scalar processors and global memory. It seems likely that, for a sufficiently large number of processors, a distribution of molecules (or cells) across processors would prove efficient. Perhaps the most awkward architecture for the version of the algorithm described in this paper, in terms of processor efficiency, would be one having a moderate number of vector processors. In that case the different processors might inhibit each other's performance by distributing the vector load, so that startup time would then dominate the computation. The best use for such a configuration would be to simply solve multiple copies of the same single processor version of the problem (with different random initialization), one on each CPU. In that case, efficient vector lengths could be maintained, while the statistical properties associated with making multiple runs would converge much faster, perhaps nearly linearly in the number of CPUs.

Acknowledgements

The authors wish to thank Ms. Diana Rose for typing the manuscript, and Colorado State University for supplying Cyber 205 time. We are grateful to Dr. Jim Moss of NASA Langeley and Dr. Graham Bird for their valuable guidance and discussion. We sincerely thank Mr. Jim Maltby for his assistance with the graphics.

References

[1] W.R. Martin, P.F. Nowak and J.A. Rathkopf, "Monte Carlo Photon Transport on a Vector Supercomputer," *IBM J. Res. Develop.*, Vol. 30, No. 2, (March 1986).

[2] Sequent Computer Systems, "Parallel Ray Tracing Case Study," *TN-85-09 (rvp) Rev 1.0*, (1985).

[3] F.W. Bobrowicz, J.E. Lynch and K.J. Fisher, "Vectorized Monte Carlo Photon Transport," *Parallel Computing*, 1, (1984).

[4] D.V. Pryor and P.J. Burns, "A Parallel Monte Carlo Model for Radiative Heat Transfer," *Proc. SIAM 1986 National Meeting*, (July 21-25, 1986), Boston, MA.

[5] P.J. Burns and D.V. Pryor, "Vectorized Monte Carlo Radiative Heat Transfer Simulation of the Laser Isotope Separation Process," *Proceedings 2nd Annual Conf. on Supercomputing*, Santa Clara, CA (May 3-8, 1987).

[6] L. *Boltzmann, Lectures on the Theory of Gases* (Russian), Gostekhizdat, Moscow (1956).

[7] H. Tsien, "Superaerodynamics, Mechanics of Rarefied Gases," *Journal of Aeronautical Sciences*, pps. 653-664 (1946).

[8] B.J. Alder and T. Wainwright, "Molecular Dynamics by Electronic Computers," *International Symposium on Transport Processes in Statistical Mechanics*, Brussels, pps. 97-131 (1956).

[9] N.A. Derzko, "Review of Monte Carlo Methods in Kinetic Theory," *University of Toronto, Institute for Aerospace Studies Review*, 35, pps. 1-78 (1972).

[10] G.A. Bird, *Molecular Gas Dynamics*, Clarendon Press, Oxford (1976).

[11] D.J. Auld and G.A. Bird, "Monte Carlo Simulation of Regular and Mach Reflection," *AIAA Journal*, 15, pps. 638-641 (1977).

[12] J.E. Hueser, L.T. Melfi, G.A. Bird and F.J. Brock, "Analysis of Large Solid Propellant Rocket Engine Exhaust Plumes Using the Direct Simulation Monte Carlo Method," *AIAA-84-0496*, (1984).

[13] J.N. Moss, V. Cuda, Jr., and A.L. Simmonds, "Nonequilibrium Effects for Hypersonic Transitional Flows," *AIAA-87-0404* (1987).

[14] V.K. Dogra and J.N. Moss, "Direct Simulation of Stagnation Streamline Flow for Hypersonic Reentry," *AIAA-87-0405* (1987).

[15] J.N. Moss, Personal Communication, NASA Langeley Research Center (1987).

[16] H.T. Yang and L. Lees, "Rayleighs Problem at Low Mach Number According to the Kinetic Theory of Gases," *Journal of Mathematics and Physics*, XXXV, pps. 195-235 (1956).

[17] CDC CYBER 200 Fortran Version 2 Reference Manual, Control Data Corporation, 1981.

Adaptation of the ISODATA Clustering Algorithm for Vector Supercomputer Execution

P.H. Schow and G.A. Riccardi

Paper not received in time for publication.

Highly Vectorized Algorithm for Transient Simulation of Space Reactor Systems

B. Nassersharif J. S. Peery M. D. DeHart

Department of Nuclear Engineering
Texas A&M University
College Station, TX 77843-3133

Abstract

Current interest in the application of nuclear reactor driven power systems to space missions has generated a need for an accurate systems model which is capable of handling the nonlinear transient simulation of such systems [1],[2]. A project to develop a code specifically designed to model and analyze space reactor systems is currently ongoing at Texas A&M. This code, named CENTAR (**C**ode for **E**xtended **N**onlinear **T**ransient **A**nalysis of Extraterrestrial **R**eactors [3],[4]), is written especially for space systems and is highly vectorizable and machine-independent. Timing tests of the code have been run on VAX, CRAY, NEC, CONVEX and SUN systems. These tests demonstrate that CENTAR executes approximately seven times faster in vector mode than scalar mode on a CRAY X-MP. A one-loop model of a thermoelectric-based space reactor system (SP-100-like) was developed to demonstrate the code's capabilities. The SP-100-like model consisted of 24 components containing a total of 67 computational cells. Using a constant time step, this model ran two times faster than real time on a CRAY X-MP. A code assessment plan is currently under development.

INTRODUCTION

One of the most viable options for the production of large amounts of electricity in a space environment is nuclear power, using a closed loop, single phase liquid metal coolant with a thermoelectric conversion cycle. However, because of the difficulty of maintenance and repair in space and the cost of lifting a system to Earth orbit and beyond, power plants must be capable of large scale energy production for extended periods while maintaining a high degree of reliability, maintainability, survivability, and safety (RMSS). Based on economic and physical considerations, experimental modeling should be preceded by and accompanied by numerical modeling. This is the standard approach used in the design of earth-based reactors. Thus there is a need for computational models which can handle the special circumstances and considerations found in space reactor systems. Component-specific models will be necessary to gain a detailed understanding of the performance of a particular component. System models will be necessary to understand how components of a system interact and to determine transient behavior of the system under normal and abnormal transients, and to allow simulation of transient and possibly adverse conditions to study reliability, maintainability, survivability, and safety issues.

CURRENT STATUS OF SPACE REACTOR CODES

At present, relatively little research has been performed in the modeling of space-based nuclear power systems. For the most part, attempts have been made to use existing codes written for terrestrial light-water reactor designs to model space reactor designs, by changing material-property and heat transfer packages and setting the gravitational body force to zero. In addition, fast reactor codes which are sometimes used in space reactor modelling efforts are not generally appropriate for space reactor applications because they concentrate on modeling core disruptive accidents and two-phase flow in one-gravity. Moreover, existing codes are not capable of explicitly modeling space-reactor-specific components such as thermoelectric elements (TE's), thermoelectromagnetic (TEM) pumps, heat pipes, or radiator elements. Finally and perhaps most importantly, most existing codes were written seven to fifteen years ago, and are therefore not optimized for supercomputing environments. Thus they are not capable of taking advantage of the potential for speed-up associated with highly vectorized coding. Ishiguro et. al. [7] describe current nuclear reactor system codes as "low performance codes" and suggest that improved performance would only be possible if the codes were carefully designed for vector processing from the beginning. They conclude that rewriting these codes for vector machines would not be economical. Currently, General Electric is developing the ARIES-FS computer code; however, documentation for this code is proprietary and no publications could be found.

CENTAR, **C**ode for **E**xtended **N**onlinear **T**ransient **A**nalysis of Extraterrestrial **R**eactors, is under development. The first version of the code, CENTAR I, was completed in the fall of 1987. CENTAR has been developed with the shortcomings of existing systems codes in mind, and will represent a major advancement in space power systems simulation, design verification, and accident management.

CENTAR DESCRIPTION

Code Overview

CENTAR is composed of several specialized modules, each of which solves mass, momentum and energy for an arbitrary fluids network. A fluids package is used to model fluid behavior throughout the system. A wall heat transfer package models the heat transfer characteristics of all walls, insulation, and structure around the system. A fuel element thermal analysis package is used to predict the temperature behavior and heat transfer characteristics of the reactor fuel rods. A kinetics package uses a six-group point kinetics formulation to model reactivity feedback and control, and the ANS 5.1 decay-heat curve to model shutdown decay-heat production. A pump package models the behavior of thermoelectromagnetic pumps, and a heat exchanger package models not only thermal effects in TE heat exchangers, but also predicts electrical power production for a given configuration. An accumulator package models coolant expansion/contraction accumulators.

CENTAR has been built from the ground up with vectorization in mind. A design requirement of a minimum of 80% vectorization has been set. Currently, CENTAR executes almost seven times faster in vector mode than scalar mode on a CRAY X-MP. CENTAR is being developed in standard FORTRAN-77 [8] on a VAX-8650 computer system. Parallel efforts concentrate on vectorization of the code using the analyzer/optimizer/vectorizer tools on an NEC SX-2 supercomputer [9]. The code is also being implemented on a CRAY X-MP. A SUN/UNIX implementation is also under development. It is important to note that there is only one version of the code that runs on all of the aforementioned computer systems. Some execution speed has been sacrificed for transportability by not implementing system dependent libraries.

Fluid Dynamics Package

The fluids package in CENTAR is designed to solve the coupled mass, momentum and energy equations for an arbitrary liquid metal fluid network in a micro-gravity environment. The fluid is assumed to be single phase and in a liquid state. Lithium is the fluid currently under consideration, however, the code has been written to allow for different liquid metal coolants. The package models a general fluid system by dividing the system into individual components. The components that the fluids package is currently capable of modeling are: generalized piping, plenums, accumulators, heat exchangers, thermoelectromagnetic pumps, pressure boundaries, core channels, tees, and heat pipes.

Several assumptions where made in the development of the conservation equations . First, the fluid is considered to be Newtonian and incompressible, but thermally expandable. This assumption allows the equations of state to be solely a function of temperature. Second, gravity is not considered. It is assumed that only frictional losses due to wall friction (structural friction is modeled by an additive loss coefficient) are important. Lastly, heat transfer is allowed through the walls to the fluid. In addition, axial conduction and internal energy production in the fluid are modeled. A development of the differencing equations is given below.

The conservation equations are given in differential form as:

Mass

$$\frac{\partial \rho}{\partial t} + \frac{\partial(\rho v)}{\partial x} = S_{mass} \; ; \tag{1}$$

Momentum

$$\frac{\partial v}{\partial t} + v\frac{\partial v}{\partial x} = -\frac{1}{\rho}\frac{\partial P}{\partial x} - \frac{C_f v|v|}{2D} \tag{2}$$

Energy

$$\frac{\partial(\rho C_p T)}{\partial t} + \frac{\partial}{\partial x}(\rho C_p v T) = \frac{\partial}{\partial x}\left(k\frac{\partial T}{\partial x}\right) + q'''_{wall} + q'''_{internal} + S_{energy} \; ; \tag{3}$$

Equations of State

$$C_P = C_P(T); \tag{4}$$

$$\rho = \rho(T). \tag{5}$$

The above coupled nonlinear fluid dynamic equations are differenced over a staggered mesh system shown in Figure 1 by employing a semi-implicit method along with a backwards difference approximation to the spatial derivatives.

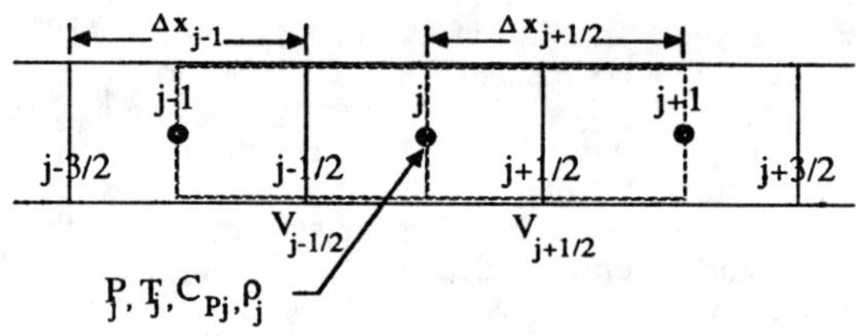

Figure 1: Typical staggered mesh used in CENTAR numerics.

The mass and energy equations are differenced over mesh cells while the momentum equations are staggered at cell interfaces. The resulting equations are given as;

Mass (at j)

$$\frac{\alpha^n \rho_j^{n+1} - \alpha^n \rho_j^n}{\Delta t} + \frac{\left(\alpha^n \rho^n v^{n+1} A\right)_{j+1/2}}{Vol_j} - \frac{\left(\alpha^n \rho^n v^{n+1} A\right)_{j-1/2}}{Vol_j} = \frac{S_{mj}}{Vol_j}, \tag{6}$$

Momentum (at j-1/2)

$$\frac{v_{j-1/2}^{n+1} - v_{j-1/2}^{n}}{\Delta t} + \frac{v_{j-1/2}^{n}\left(v_{j+1/2}^{n} - v_{j-3/2}^{n}\right)}{2\Delta x_{j-1/2}} = -\frac{1}{\left(\alpha^n \rho_{j-1/2}^n\right)}\frac{P_j^{n+1} - P_{j-1}^{n+1}}{\Delta x_{j-1/2}} - \frac{C_f v_{j-1/2}^{n+1}\left|v_{j-1/2}^{n}\right|}{2D}, \text{ and} \tag{7}$$

Energy (at j)

$$\frac{\alpha^n(\rho C_pT)_j^{n+1}-\alpha^n(\rho C_pT)_j^n}{\Delta t}+\frac{\left((\alpha\rho C_pT)^nAv^{n+1}\right)_{j+1/2}}{Vol_j}-\frac{\left((\alpha\rho C_pT)^nAv^{n+1}\right)_{j-1/2}}{Vol_j}=\frac{k_{j+1/2}^n\left(T_{j+1}^{n+1}-T_j^{n+1}\right)}{\Delta x_{j+1/2}\Delta x_j}+\frac{k_{j-1/2}^n\left(T_{j-1}^{n+1}-T_j^{n+1}\right)}{\Delta x_{j-1/2}\Delta x_j}+\frac{h^nA_w}{Vol_j}\left(T_w^n-T_j^{n+1}\right)+\frac{S_{ej}}{Vol_j}. \tag{8}$$

It should be noted that in the development of Equation 8, an implicit formulation was used for the the fluid axial conduction term. It is felt that this formulation is imperative for studying reactor startups in present space reactor designs. To transform the differential equations into difference equations, variational forms are used. These approximations are given for the independent variables as

$$\rho_j^{m+1}=\rho_j^m+\left(\frac{\partial\rho}{\partial T}\right)_j^m\delta T_j^m\ , \tag{9}$$

$$C_{p_j}^{m+1}=C_{p_j}^m+\left(\frac{\partial C_p}{\partial T}\right)_j^m\delta T_j^m\ , \tag{10}$$

$$T_j^{m+1}=T_j^m+\delta T_j^m\ , \tag{11}$$

$$P_j^{m+1}=P_j^m+\delta P_j^m\ , \tag{12}$$

$$v_{j+1/2}^{m+1}=v_{j+1/2}^m+\left(\frac{\partial v_{j+1/2}}{\partial P_j}\right)^m\delta P_j^m+\left(\frac{\partial v_{j+1/2}}{\partial P_{j+1}}\right)^m\delta P_{j+1}^m\ , \text{ and} \tag{13}$$

$$v_{j-1/2}^{m+1}=v_{j-1/2}^m+\left(\frac{\partial v_{j-1/2}}{\partial P_j}\right)^m\delta P_j^m+\left(\frac{\partial v_{j-1/2}}{\partial P_{j-1}}\right)^m\delta P_{j-1}^m \tag{14}$$

where m is the iteration index. Substitution of the variational forms into the mass and energy equations results in algebraic equations of the form [10],

$$A_m\delta T_j+X_m\delta P_j+Y_m\delta P_{j+1}+Z_m\delta P_{j-1}=I_m\text{, and} \tag{6}$$

$$A_e\delta T_j+B_e\delta T_{j+1}+C_e\delta T_{j-1}+X_e\delta P_j+Y_e\delta P_{j+1}+Z_e\delta P_{j-1}=I_e. \tag{7}$$

These equations are developed for every cell in the system and placed in one matrix to be solved, thus coupling the entire system. This method allows for the entire fluid system to be solved for in one pass as opposed to a component by component approach. Solving the entire system in one pass allows for longer vector loops than the component by component approach.

The other components require special formulations because of their boundary conditions. The plenum component is special since it can have multiple inlet and outlet components. Because of the complexity of such a system, the plenum is treated as a mixing cell where momentum is not conserved. The accumulator poses an interesting problem of coupling mechanical forces with fluid forces. The accumulator is modeled as a pipe component with a zero velocity boundary condition at the mechanical-fluid interface.

The pressure of the fluid in the accumulator is determined from the mechanical forces. The heat exchanger and nuclear fuel rod channel components are identical to a general piping component except that multiple wall heat transfer media exist. The thermoelectromagnetic pump component acts as a momentum source to a fluid cell but does not actually occupy a cell. This pump model is a direct-current electromagnetic pump with the added feature of internal thermoelectric (TE) converters [11] providing current. This model incorporates the side currents through the coolant duct walls, the fringe resistance of the pump entrance and exit regions, and the counter-emf developed by the liquid as it moves through the magnetic field. The pump package determines the momentum head developed across the pump from the current produced by the TE converters and passes this information to the fluids package. A set of primary and secondary pipes are assumed in the current pump model; however the code can be easily modified to accommodate one primary and two secondary pipes configuration. The heat pipe component is presently modeled with an effective conductivity model. This model will be replaced with a much more detailed model in a later version of the code.

The reactor core can be modeled with as many channels as the user desires. Each channel may have a different number of fuel pins (or no fuel pins) and axial power distributions. Currently, no cross flow between channels is allowed. Future versions of the code will allow cross flow. The core modeling capability is extremely powerful and flexible. Even though the fluid dynamics is one dimensional, the core network model allows emulation of almost two dimensions (we have called it a 1.5 dimensional model in the core).

The phrases "systems code" and "vectorization" have been regarded as incompatible in the past. This is primarily due to the component by component solution technique used, where most components have very few nodes. This results in very short vector loops. In addition, past system codes contain numerous IF statements to determine component types and boundary conditions. To overcome these deficiencies, CENTAR reorders the components by their type such that the exact memory location for each component type is known. This is the real "heart" of CENTAR's ability to solve very complex reactor systems but still maintain its high degree of vectorization. In addition, CENTAR determines, prior to running the transient, the location of the cell to the right and left of each cell. This information along with a supercomputer's gather-scatter ability allows CENTAR to have vector loops that in most cases have a length equal to the total number of fluid cells. Therefore, the vector length increases as the problem size increases.

An iterative technique is used to solve the nonlinear equations. An initial guess for the velocities is made with an explicit pass over the momentum equation. The mass and energy system is then solved using a Newton-Raphson iteration technique. This method is Courant limited. We are planning to implement a stability-enhancing method similar to the two step (SETS) method developed at Los Alamos National Laboratory [12].

Wall Heat Transfer Package

A wall heat transfer package was developed to calculate heat transfer and storage in the wall of all components. This allows thermal communication between fluid inside the component with the wall and anything external to the wall. This model allows either cylindrical or rectangular geometries, with Stefan (radiative), Robin (convective), and Neumman (conductive) boundary conditions. In addition, multiple material types are allowed at any given axial location. Within each material, a variable number of nodes may be specified.

Conduction through a wall is calculated by solving the one-dimensional nonlinear transient heat conduction equation. Axial wall conduction is neglected, but axial nodes are coupled via the fluid in the component. The differential form of the equation is given by:

$$\rho C_p \frac{\partial T}{\partial t} = q''' + \frac{1}{r^g}\frac{\partial}{\partial r}\left(r^g k \frac{\partial T}{\partial r}\right) + f\tau J \frac{\partial T}{\partial r}. \quad (17)$$

The thermoelectric "switch," f, turns on an additional term in the conduction equation to account for energy production inside the thermoelectric elements. The geometric "switch," g, is set to 0 when rectangular geometry is used, and 1 when cylindrical geometry is used. All material properties are temperature dependent. Writing this equation in finite difference form results in:

$$\frac{\rho_i C_{p_i}}{\Delta t}\left(T_i - T_i'\right) = q_i''' + \frac{2 r^g_{i+1/2} k_{i+1/2}}{r_i^g \left(\Delta r_{i-1} + \Delta r_i\right) \Delta r_i}\left(T_{i+1} - T_i\right)$$

$$- \frac{2 r^g_{i-1/2} k_{i-1/2}}{r_i^g \left(\Delta r_{i-1} + \Delta r_i\right) \Delta r_{i-1}}\left(T_i - T_{i-1}\right) + \frac{f\tau J}{\left(\Delta r_{i-1} + \Delta r_i\right)}\left(T_{i+1} - T_{i-1}\right) \quad (18)$$

where T_i' is the old temperature and all other values of T are new temperatures. A fully implicit scheme is used to solve wall heat transfer.

At a given axial location, for N radial nodes, N equations are written. At n = 1, the node adjacent to the fluid, T_{i-1} is eliminated and a convective boundary condition based on the fluid temperature and a heat transfer coefficient calculated by the fluids package is used. Similarly, at n = N, the outer wall node, T_{i+1} is eliminated and a user specified boundary condition is used to complete the equation. Specification of a radiative boundary condition requires input of the effective temperature to which the outer wall radiates and a material number from which temperature dependent emissivity for wall surface is computed. Similarly, specification of a radiative boundary condition requires input of the bulk temperature of the fluid and the heat transfer coefficient for the fluid-wall interface. The set of N coupled equations results in a tridiagonal matrix which is solved in a single pass using a partially vectorized tridiagonal matrix solving routine. Since heat transfer is only modelled in the radial direction, vectorization is obtain by doing the forward elimination in the axial direction. The back-substitution does not vectorize.

Heat generation in the wall (as a result of internal or surface energy deposition by lasers, neutral particle beams, neutrons, or gamma rays) can be modelled. Shielding or insulation around a pipe can also be modeled. Specification of multiple materials within each wall allows accurate modeling of the internal heat transfer characteristics of thermoelectric devices. Pumped-fluid type of radiators can be modelled using one or several rectangular pipes of appropriate size with fluid inside the pipe.

The wall heat transfer module is an extremely versatile computational model which determines wall temperature for all components in an assembled system in both steady state and transient calculations. It is written in FORTRAN 77 with emphasis placed on numerical techniques which facilitate vectorization; execution speed was a major consideration when writing the code. The entire module has been benchmarked with analytical solutions [13]. These benchmarks have shown excellent agreement for time step sizes up to 0.1 seconds and relatively coarse grid spacings.

PIPWAL is the most thoroughly tested module in CENTAR. Execution-time testing of the code has been performed on several vector and scalar machines. Table 1 below summarizes the time performance of the module when run on various machines. The FORTRAN source was identical in all cases.

Table 1.
Execution Time (sec) and Normalized Time for PIPWAL

Machine	CPU Time (Seconds)	Normalized Time
VAX 8300	11521	501.00
VAX 8800	1123	48.83
CRAY X-MP	24	1.04
NEC SX-2	23	1.00
CONVEX C1	540	3.48

Fuel Element Thermal Analysis Package

The temperature distribution for the average rod in each core channel is computed by the fuel element thermal analysis routine. The average rod is presumed to operate at the channel-averaged power and its cladding temperature is fed back to the fluids routine to compute the channel coolant temperature for the next time step.

A wide range of noding options is available to the user. The user may specify a fraction of the power production to occur in the liner and cladding to model gamma heating. Fuel, cladding and liner melting are not modeled.

In solving the heat conduction equation, azimuthal symmetry is assumed, reducing the heat conduction equation for cylindrical geometry to:

$$\rho C_p \frac{\partial T(r,z)}{\partial t} = q'''(r,z,t) + \frac{1}{r}\frac{\partial}{\partial r}\left(r\, k(T) \frac{\partial T(r,z)}{\partial r}\right) + \frac{\partial}{\partial z}\left(k(T) \frac{\partial T(r,z)}{\partial z}\right). \quad (19)$$

A semi-implicit finite difference technique is used to set up the system of simultaneous equations. Radial temperatures can change rapidly with time and position, and are solved implicitly in a tridiagonal form. Axial temperatures merely provide coupling, and are solved explicitly.

Results: One Loop SP-100-Like [14] Model

An SP-100-like reactor system model was developed to test CENTAR's ability to model space reactor systems. This model involved eight different component types and required a total of 24 components (67 computational cells). A nodalization diagram of the system is shown in Figure 2. The one-loop model was developed by using the best published data available on General Electric's SP-100 reactor design

[14]. The actual SP-100 reactor design consists of twelve loops. The twelve loops were collapsed into one loop by preserving system volume, length, and heat transfer area.

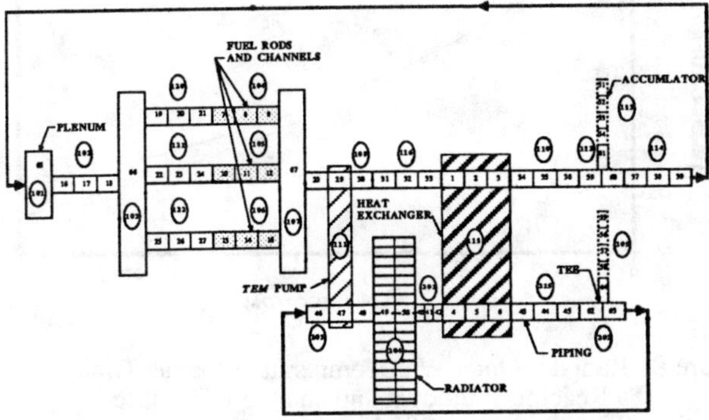

Figure 2: One-loop Representation of the SP-100 Design.

A simulated reactor shutdown transient was run using CENTAR and the one loop model. The primary reason for this transient was to test the coupled fluid and heat transfer packages in CENTAR. This transient is just one of many transients that are currently being run with the one-loop model of the SP-100-like reactor system to test the coupled packages in CENTAR.

The initial conditions were assumed to be the following: the primary temperatures are 900 K, the secondary temperatures are 500 K, the system pressure is 0.12 MPa, and the primary side is completely insulated (all energy transport is forced to go through the heat exchanger). The thermoelectromagnetic elements produced a current which produced a pump head due to the temperature difference between the primary and secondary loops. The initial velocity profile was assumed to be zero, but within several seconds the profile adjusted to produce a pressure drop which matched the pump head. As the transient progresses, the secondary and primary side temperatures approach one another. The reduced temperature difference between the primary and secondary sides results in a smaller pump head. Figure 3 demonstrates the fluid velocity

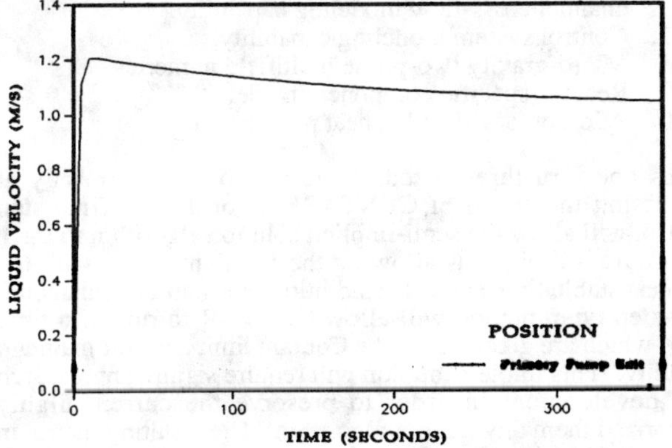

Figure 3: Liquid Velocity at the Pump Exit Versus Time for for a Reactor Shutdown and Initial Velocity of 0.0 m/s.

correction due to the initial guess and decay due to a reduced pump head for the node at the outlet of the pump on the primary side. The effects of the reduced temperature difference on primary and secondary pump head is displayed in Figure 4. Figures 5 and 6 show the transient temperature

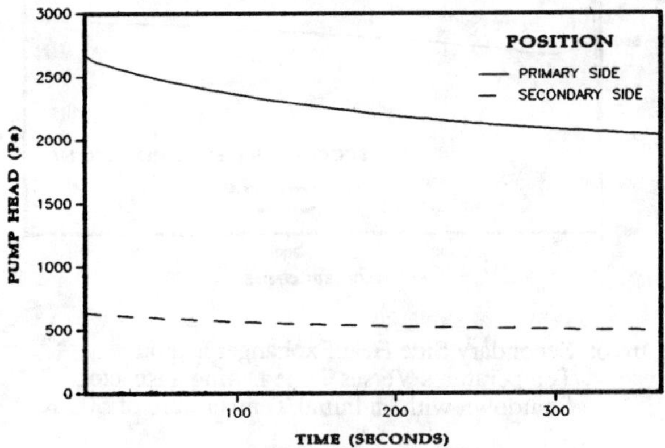

Figure 4: Pump Head Versus Time During Reactor Shutdown.

response in the heat exchanger inlet and outlet nodes on the primary and secondary sides, respectively. The initial rapid drop and increase in primary and secondary heat exchanger fluid temperatures, respectively, demonstrate the axial conduction model in the fluids package and are a result of the initial fluid velocity guess. As the primary side cools off and the secondary side heats up one would expect the fluid to contract on the primary side and expand on the secondary side.

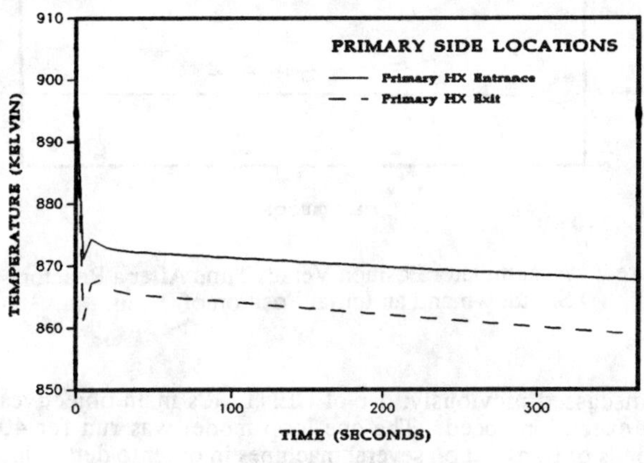

Figure 5: Primary Side Heat Exchanger Liquid Temperatures Versus Time During a Reactor Shutdown with an Initial Temperature of 900 K.

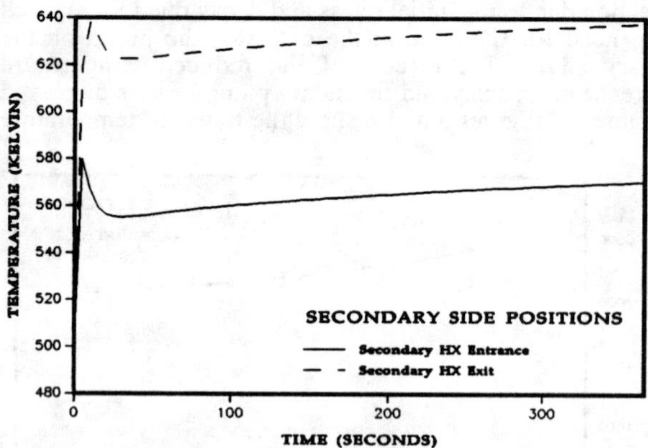

Figure 6: Secondary Side Heat Exchanger Liquid Temperatures Versus Time During a Reactor Shutdown with an Initial Temperature of 500 K.

This phenomena is exhibited through the accumulator displacement in Figure 7. Lastly, a transient profile of the radiator's outside wall temperature is given in Figure 8. This plot depicts the radiators response to reactor shutdown and the assumed space temperature of 300 K.

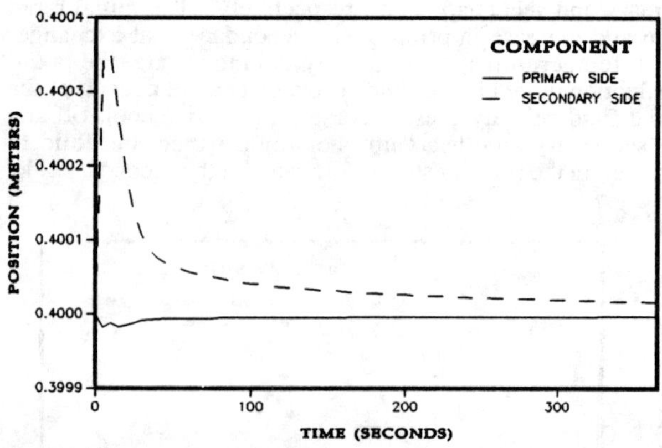

Figure 7: Accumulator Position Versus Time After a Reactor Shutdown and an Initial Position of 0.4 m.

As discussed previously, one of CENTAR's main objectives was execution speed. The one-loop model was run for 40 seconds of transient on several machines in order to determine the performance of the code. Table 2 depicts the results of this study. CENTAR ran this model slightly less than two times real time on a CRAY X-MP. In addition, the code performed almost seven times faster in vector mode than scalar mode on a CRAY X-MP. As a comparison, the code execution speed on a VAX 8650 was more than 50 times larger than that on the CRAY.

Table 2.
Execution Time (sec) and Normalized Time for CENTAR

Machine	CPU Time (Seconds)	Normalized Time
VAX 8650	1091	51.95
CRAY X-MP (scalar)	133	6.33
CRAY X-MP (vector)	21	1.00

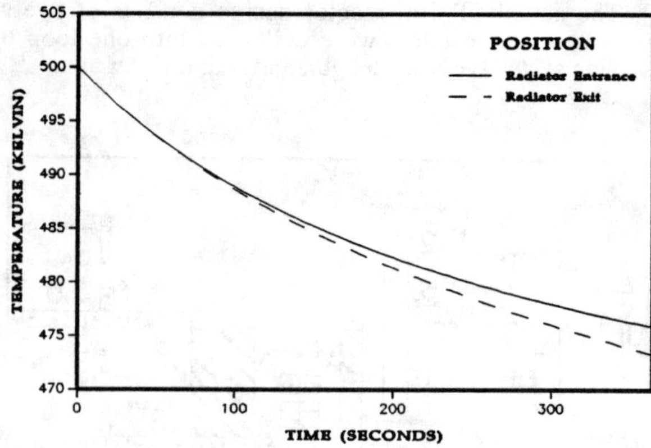

Figure 8: Radiator Outer Wall Temperature Versus Time After a Reactor Shutdown and an assumed Space Temperature of 300 K.

FUTURE PLANS

The first version of CENTAR is a major milestone in the family of CENTAR codes. Although the current version has a high degree of vectorization, significant portions of the code remain to be vectorized. It is expected that the code will be able to run a real time simulation of a 300 node system. In the future versions of the code we will concentrate on addressing specific needs of multimegawatt space reactor systems. The first version of CENTAR was primarily targeted at SP-100 and SP-300 systems with component models specific to those systems. Future versions of the code will include specific models for two-phase thermodynamic cycles. The following is a list of future enhancements currently planned:

1. Implementation of time step control.
2. Enhancement of the semi-implicit numerics to include the stability enhancing two-step [12] method.
3. Optional iterative matrix solvers for the thermal hydraulics module.
4. Addition of plume modeling for external plume impingement and transient change in outside radiative heat transfer boundary conditions.
5. Enhancement of the intelligent pre-processor, post-processor, and interactive user-interface modules.
6. Enhancement of the core model by addition of core channel cross-flow modeling capability.
7. Control system modeling capability.
8. Micro-gravity two-phase multifield numerics.
9. Reactor-specific component models.
10. Addition of a detailed heat pipe model.

Items one thru three listed above are focused primarily at increasing the speed of CENTAR's algorithms. Time step control will allow the semi-implicit solution algorithm to track the Courant limit, thus allowing the transient to run with the greatest stable time step. The addition of a stability enhancing two-step type method will allow CENTAR to run with time steps which are greater than the Courant limit and still maintain stability. This implementation will require significant research and development in order to preserve the current highly vectorized themalhydraulics algorithm. The resulting matrix in the thermal hydraulics module is very sparse and of size 2N by 2N where N is the number of fluid cells. Currently, this matrix is solved with Gaussian Elimination with partially pivoting which can not vectorize the back substitution. It is felt that a vectorized iterative matrix solver such as a "smart" Gauss-Jordon (no operations on the zeros of the matrix) would decrease CENTAR's execution time for most transients.

CONCLUSIONS

A highly-vectorized systems code has been developed at Texas A&M University to model space power systems under transient conditions: CENTAR - Code for Extended Nonlinear Transient Analysis of Extraterrestrial Reactor Systems. CENTAR is a new and powerful tool for space reactor simulation. CENTAR has been written with emphasis placed on vectorizable coding and has been tested on vector machines such as CRAY and NEC supercomputers. Most modules have been run independently, and have been benchmarked against analytical solutions. For example, the fluids package has been benchmarked for transient axial conduction and sinusodial pressure ossilations test cases. In addition, the modules and individual components in CENTAR are currently being benchmarked with SASSYS, a liquid metal systems analysis code [15].

ACKNOWLEDGEMENTS

We thank Cray Research Inc. for the use of their computer resources in experimenting with our vectorized algorithms. This work was performed partially under a Presidential Young Investigator Foundation grant.

REFERENCES

[1] A. D. Alley and et. al., Private Communication on the ARIES-FS Computer Code, GE Astro-Space Division, San Jose, CA, December 1987.

[2] M.S. El-Genk and J.T. Seo, "Parametric Analysis of the SP-100 System Performance,"4th Symposium on Space Nuclear Power Systems, Albuquerque, NM, January 12-16,1987.

[3] B. Nassershari, J.S. Peery, and M.D. DeHart, "CENTAR - Highly Vectorized Code for Analysis of Space Reactor Systems," Third International Symposium on Science and Engineering on Cray Supercomputers, Minneapolis, MN, September 9-11, 1987.

[4] B. Nassersharif, J.S. Peery, and M.D. DeHart, "CENTAR - Code for Extended Nonlinear Transient Analysis of Extraterrestrial Reactor Systems," American Nuclear Society Winter Meeting, Los Angeles, November 1987.

[5] R. Meyer, F. Halfen, and A. Alley, "SP-100 Performance Modeling," 4th Symposium on Space Nuclear Power Systems, CONF-870102-Summs, Albuquerque, NM, January, 1987.

[6] M.S. El-Genk, J.J. Buksa, and J.T. Seo, "A Self-Induced Thermoelectric Electromagnetic Pump Model for SP-100Systems," 3rd Symposium on Space Nuclear Power Systems, Albuquerque, NM, January 13-15, 1986.

[7] M. Ishiguro et. al.,"Performance Analysis of Vectorized Nuclear Codes on a Facom VP-100 at the Japan Atomic Energy Research Institute," The International Journal of Supercomputing, Vol. 1, No. 3, Fall 1987, pp. 45-56,1987.

[8] ANSI, American National Standard Programming Language FORTRAN, American National Standards Institute, New York, 1978.

[9] NEC Corporation, SX Software Release 1.2, Analyzer/SX,Vectorizer/SX, and Optimizer manuals, NEC Corporation, Japan, 1986.

[10] J.H. Mahaffy, D.R. Liles, and T.D. Knight, "Review of Solution Approach, Mehtods, and Recent Results of the TRAC-PF1 System Code," Mathematics and Computation Topical Meeting of the American Nuclear Society, March, 1983.

[11] A.H. Barnes, "Direct-Current Electromagnetic Pumps," Nucleonics, pg. 16, January, 1953.

[12] J.H. Mahaffy, "A Stability-Enhancing Two-Step Method for Fluid Flow Calculations,"J. Comput. Phys., 46, pp. 329-341, 1982.

[13] M.N. Ozisik, Heat Conduction, John Wiley &Sons, New York, 1980.

[14] R. Manvi and T. Fujita, Users Handbook Basic Configurational Tradeoffs for SP-100 Program, NASA Jet Propulsion Laboratory, CA, June 27, 1987

[15] F.E. Dunn, et. al., "The SASSYS-1 LMFBR Systems Analysis Code," ANL/RAS 84-14, March, 1987.

NOMENCLATURE

C_f	=	Darcy friction factor
C_p	=	specific heat
f	=	thermoelectric switch
g	=	geometry switch
k	=	conductivity
k_s	=	spring constant
P	=	pressure
Q	=	volumetric flow rate
q'''	=	volumetric heat source
R	=	resistance
S	=	source
T	=	temperature
t	=	time
v	=	velocity
μ	=	viscosity
ρ	=	density
τ	=	Thompson coefficient

A Parallel QR Factorization Algorithm using Local Pivoting[*†]

Christian H. Bischof

Department of Computer Science
Cornell University
Ithaca, New York 14853

Abstract. This paper presents a new parallel version of the Householder algorithm with column pivoting for computing the QR factorization of a matrix. In contrast to the standard algorithm we employ a local pivoting scheme that allows for efficient implementation of the algorithm on a parallel machine, in particular one with a distributed architecture. An inexpensive but reliable incremental condition estimator is used to control the selection of pivot columns by obtaining cheap estimates for the smallest singular value of the currently created upper triangular matrix R. Numerical experiments show that the local pivoting strategy behaves about as well as the traditional global pivoting strategy. They also show the advantages of incorporating the controlled pivoting strategy into the traditional QR algorithm to guard against the known pathological cases.

1 Introduction

One of the standard problems in numerical linear algebra is the solution of the linear least squares problem

$$\min \|Ax - b\|_2 \tag{1}$$

where A is an $m \times n$ $(m \geq n)$ matrix. The common way to approach this problem [12,17,19] is via a *QR factorization*

$$AP = QR \tag{2}$$

of A. Here P is an $n \times n$ permutation matrix, Q is an $m \times n$ matrix with orthogonal columns (i.e. $Q^TQ = I_n$) and R is an upper triangular $n \times n$ matrix. If A is a dense matrix, Q is usually computed by a sequence of *Householder Transformations*

$$H = I - 2u\,u^T.$$

Choosing

$$u = \frac{x + \text{sign}(x_1)\,\|x\|_2\,e_1}{\|x + \text{sign}(x_1)\,\|x\|_2\,e_1\|_2} \tag{3}$$

we can reduce a given vector x to a multiple of the canonical unit vector e_1 since

$$(I - 2u\,u^T)\,x = -\text{sign}(x_1)\,\|x\|_2\,e_1.$$

If A has full rank, we can avoid exchanging columns when computing the QR factorization, i.e. P in (2) will be the identity. If the rank of A is not known, we can employ column pivoting [3]. The idea is to choose as next column always the one that has the highest residual with respect to the subspace spanned by the columns that were selected before. The hope is that in the resulting QR factorization (2) of A the ill-conditioning of A will reveal itself by a small trailing subblock of R: if $\sigma_1 \geq \sigma_2 \geq \ldots \geq \sigma_n$ are the singular values of A and we partition R into

$$\begin{pmatrix} R_{11} & R_{12} \\ 0 & R_{22} \end{pmatrix} \tag{4}$$

with an $r \times r$ lower right hand block R_{22} then it is easy to show [12, page 19] that

$$\sigma_{n-r+1}(A) \leq \|R_{22}\|_2\,.$$

While there are counterexamples (see section 5) where the column pivoting strategy fails to reveal ill-conditioning of A, it works well in practice.

Another alternative is to compute the *Singular Value Decomposition* (SVD)

$$A = U\Sigma V^T \tag{5}$$

of A. Here U and V are orthogonal matrices whose columns are the left– and right–singular vectors of A, respectively. $\Sigma = \text{diag}(\sigma_i)$ contains the singular values of A. The SVD is at least twice as expensive to compute as the QR factorization and for that reason the QR factorization with column pivoting is usually preferred.

There is also a middle path between QR factorization and SVD. As was pointed out originally in [11] we can use the singular vector corresponding to the smallest singular value to find a permutation P that will guarantee a small r_{nn} if $\sigma_n(A)$ is small. Chan [4] and Foster [9] extend this idea to higher dimensions. Their idea is to first compute any QR factorization of A and then "peel off" the small singular values of R one after the other by computing an

*This work was supported by the U.S. Army Research Office through the Mathematical Science Institute of Cornell University, by the Office of Naval Research under contract N00014-83-K-0640 and by NSF contract CCR 86-02310.

† A preliminary version of this paper was published in the proceedings of the 3rd International Conference on Supercomputing, Steve and Lana Karthashev, Eds.

CH2617-9/88/0000/0400$01.00 © 1988 IEEE

appropriate singular vectors at each step. Let us from now on assume that A has r small singular values and that there is a well-defined gap between σ_{n-r} and σ_{n-r+1}. It is shown in [11] that a well-defined gap is necessary to make a sensible decision on the numerical rank of A. Then Chan proves that if r is not too large his algorithm will compute a "rank-revealing QR factorization" in the sense that R_{22} in (4) is guaranteed to be small.

On a single processor the Householder QR factorization without pivoting requires $O(mn^2)$ flops, column pivoting requires an additional n^2 flops and the rank-revealing QR algorithm requires an additional $3rn^2$ flops on average [4]. So the computational complexity of these algorithms is comparable on a single-processor machine.

The situation is quite different on a multiprocessor machine especially if it is based on a distributed architecture. The Householder QR algorithm without pivoting can be very efficiently parallelized simply by pipelining the computation [1,20]. So one processor can still be busy finishing a previous update while another already computes the next Householder vector. The introduction of column pivoting makes pipelining impossible since all processors have to synchronize to select the next pivot column. Hence the Householder QR algorithm essentially proceeds in a lock-step fashion which results in a serious loss of efficiency on machines that previously could profit from the pipelining.

In Chan's algorithm the steps after the initial QR factorization are hard to parallelize. For each of the r small singular values of A, the algorithm computes an approximate singular vector via inverse iteration. On average this requires two iteration steps [4] and hence the solution of four triangular equation systems per small singular value. Although much progress has been made recently in solving triangular equation systems on distributed architectures [7,14,13,18] this problem can by no means be parallelized as efficiently as the inital QR factorization. In addition the permutation deduced from the singular vector destroys the upper triangular shape of R which then has to be restored by a sequence of Givens rotations. Again that is essentially a sequential process that is hard to parallelize [7]. Apart from their sequential nature, an inherent difficulty in parallelizing the equation solving and QR update steps is that the computational work is of the same order of magnitude as the amount of data it involves. That is we have to perform $O(n^2)$ flops using $O(n^2)$ data. Since R is distributed throughout the system it is hard to mask the communication overhead with the little arithmetic work to be performed. So the post-processing of R can end up being a good part of the overall computation time on a parallel machine.

In this paper we suggest a new QR decomposition algorithm that avoids these penalties and can be efficiently parallelized. By using a *local* pivoting strategy we are able to pipeline the computation and at the same time identify the set of columns of A responsible for its ill-conditioning. In section 2 we outline the pipelined Householder QR algorithm and motivate the local pivoting strategy. Section 3 introduces a condition estimator that allows us to monitor the numerical soundness of the local pivoting strategy and presents numerical results showing its robustness. Section 4 combines these ideas into an effective parallel algorithm for determining the numerical rank of A and thus solving the linear least squares problem. Numerical results obtained by simulating the parallel algorithm are presented in section 5. We summarize our results and outline possible directions of future research in section 6.

2 The Householder QR Algorithm with Local Column Pivoting

The Householder QR algorithm without pivoting processes the columns of A in their natural order from left to right. If we have a parallel machine, it is natural to group the processors into a logical ring and deal out columns in a round-robin fashion. This technique staggers the computation across the processors and guarantees a load balanced computation. It allows simple static assignment of data to processors and is for the most part synchronized by the flow of data between processors. Due to these attractive characteristics, the pipelining technique has been widely used [10,13,16]. If special vector hardware can be exploited, several Householder matrices can be bundled together by using the WY factorization [2,21] to arrive at a block pipelined algorithm [1].

In contrast the QR algorithms with traditional column pivoting at each step chooses the column that has the highest residual with respect to the subspace spanned by the columns already selected. This residual is easy to compute and can be updated cheaply as new columns are selected [8]. But in the parallel setting, the selection of the pivot column introduces a synchronisation point. Each processor can easily choose its local candidate pivot column by considering only the columns that are assigned to it. Choosing the global pivot column on the other hand requires that each processor either makes its local pivot information known to all other processors or that a designated processor collects all the local pivot informations. So global pivoting essentially forces the program into a lockstep mode that may severly curtail performance.

The easiest way out of this dilemma is to forgo global pivoting altogether and content oneself with local pivoting. A simplified version of the resulting algorithm for a ring of processors is given in Figure 1. We distribute columns of A to processors in a round-robin fashion. To be precise, let us assume that we have p processors $proc_0, \dots, proc_{p-1}$ and that a_j is the jth column of A. Then processor $proc_i$ receives columns a_j where

$$i = (j-1) \bmod p.$$

This is commonly referred to as the *column wrap mapping*. The array C is local to each processor and contains the $cols_k$ columns assigned to processor $proc_i$ ($\sum_{i=0}^{p-1} cols_k = n$)

p_{left} and p_{right} designate the left and right neighbour of $proc_k$, respectively.

$$u \leftarrow genhh(x)$$

```
processor proc_k
    lcnt ← 0; {counter for HH vectors generated in proc_k}
    gcnt ← 0; {counter for HH vectors generated globally}
    foreach ∈ {1, ..., cols_k} do
        perm_i ← (k + 1) + (i − 1)p; { wrap mapping}
        res_i ← ||c(:, i)||_2 ;
    end foreach
    if (k = 0) then {determine first pivot column}
        lcnt ← gcnt ← 1 ;
        determine first pivot column, send it it p_right and
        update all other columns as shown in main loop below.
    end if
    while (lcnt < cols_k) do {main loop}
        receive u from p_left ; gcnt ← gcnt + 1;
        if (u not generated by p_right) then send u to p_right end if
        if (k = gcnt mod p) then { my turn to generate next HH vector }
            lcnt← lcnt + 1;
            { complete enough of H(u) update to determine next pivot column }
            z ← c(gcnt:m, lcnt:cols_k)^T u ;
            c(gcnt+1, lcnt:cols_k) ← c(gcnt+1, lcnt:cols_k) − 2u(2:m−gcnt+1) z ;
            res_i ← sqrt(res_i^2 − C(gcnt, i)^2) , i ∈ {lcnt, ..., cols_k}
            Let pvt ∈ {lcnt, ..., cols_k} be such that res_pvt is maximal
                { guarded pivoting strategy will be inserted here }
            c(gcnt:m, pvt) ← c(gcnt:m, pvt) − 2u(1) z^T ;
            û ← genhh(C(gcnt+1 :m, pvt)); gcnt ← gcnt + 1;
            if (gcnt < n) then send û to p_right end if
            c(gcnt:m, lcnt:pvt−1) ← c(gcnt: m, lcnt:pvt−1) − 2u(2:m−gcnt+2)z^T ;
              { complete H(u) update }
            c(gcnt:m, pvt+1: cols_k) ← c(gcnt: m, pvt+1: cols_k) − 2u(2:m−gcnt+2)z^T ;
              { complete H(û) update }
            c(:, pvt) ↔ c(:, lcnt); perm_lcnt ↔ perm_pvt ; res_pvt ← res_lcnt ;
            c(gcnt:m, lcnt+1:cols_k) ← apphh(û, c(gcnt, lcnt+1:cols_k)) ;
        else  { apply H(u) update }
            c(gcnt:m , lcnt+1:cols_k) ← apphh(u, C(gcnt:m , lcnt+1:cols_k));
        end if
        res_i ← sqrt(res_i^2 − c(gcnt, i)^2) , i ∈ {lcnt + 1, ..., cols_k}
    end while
```

Figure 1: The Pipelined QR Algorithm with Local Pivoting

returns u as defined by (3) and

$$A \leftarrow apphh(u, A)$$

returns $H(u)\,A$. The vector *perm* is used to store the permutation matrix. If $perm(i) = l$, then the lth column of A has been permuted into the ith position. The vector *res* contains the residuals that the columns not yet chosen have with respect to the other columns already selected. To save space, "HH" is used as an abbreviation for "Householder".

It is worth pointing out that a processor that has to generate a new pivot column completes only as much of the previous Householder update as is necessary to update *res* and to determine the next pivot column. This is important since we want to avoid that other nodes are idle waiting for a new Householder vector to arrive.

The problem with the strictly local pivoting strategy is obviously numerical stability. As a pathological example, assume that all columns in processor 1 are nearly equal. As a result, processor 1 will make bad choices after it has generated the very first Householder vector. The resulting upper triangular matrix R will be very ill-conditioned but will not necessarily have a small lower right hand block. So in order for the local pivoting strategy to be numerically stable, we have to *guard against choosing nearly dependent pivot columns.*

3 An Incremental Estimator for the Smallest Singular Value of a Triangular Matrix

To guard against choosing "bad" pivot columns, we have to monitor the smallest singular value $\sigma_{min}(R_i)$ where R_i is the leading $i \times i$ upper triangular matrix generated after applying i Householder transformations to A. The exact computation of $\sigma_{min}(R_i)$ by inverse iteration for example is too expensive, especially since a good order-of-magnitude estimate suffices for our purposes.

A common idea underlying condition estimators [5,6] is to exploit the implication

$$Rx = d \implies \frac{1}{\sigma_{min}(R)} = \|R^{-1}\|_2 \geq \frac{\|R^{-1}d\|_2}{\|d\|_2} = \frac{\|x\|_2}{\|d\|_2}$$

by generating a large norm solution x to a moderately sized right hand side d and then to use

$$\hat{\sigma}_{min}(R) := \frac{\|d\|_2}{\|x\|_2}$$

as an estimate for $\sigma_{min}(R)$. The hope is that x will be an approximate singular vector corresponding to the smallest singular value and that as a consequence $\hat{\sigma}_{min}(R)$ will not be too much of an over-estimate of $\sigma_{min}(R)$. Our choice of algorithms for an condition estimator is severely restricted by the fact that it is not feasible to access the previously generated R when we want to decide on the suitability of a new pivot column. To be more precise, given a good estimate $\hat{\sigma}_{min}(R)$ defined by a large norm solution x to $Rx = d$ and a new column $\begin{pmatrix} v \\ \gamma \end{pmatrix}$ of R, we want to obtain a large norm solution y to

$$R'y = \begin{pmatrix} R & v \\ 0 & \gamma \end{pmatrix} y = \hat{d}$$

without accessing R again. None of the condition estimators surveyed by Higham [15] has that property, but the two-norm condition estimator suggested by Cline, Conn and Van Loan [5] can be modified to conform to those restrictions. The idea then is the following:

Given x such that $R^Tx = d$ with $\|d\|_2 = 1$, find $s := \sin\varphi$ and $c := \cos\varphi$ such that $\|y\|_2$ is maximized where $y = \begin{pmatrix} z \\ \delta \end{pmatrix}$ solves

$$\begin{pmatrix} R^T & 0 \\ v^T & \gamma \end{pmatrix} y = \begin{pmatrix} sd \\ c \end{pmatrix}. \tag{6}$$

We here exploit the fact that R' and R'^T have identical singular values. An easy calculation shows that maximizing $\|y\|_2$ is equivalent to maximizing

$$\Phi(\varphi) = s^2\beta - 2\alpha sc \tag{7}$$

where

$$\alpha = v^Tx \text{ and } \beta = \gamma^2x^Tx + \alpha^2 - 1.$$

Taking derivatives in (7) and setting $\eta = \beta/(2\alpha)$ we find two possible solutions:

$$s_{1,2} = \frac{1}{\sqrt{1+\mu_{1,2}}}$$

where

$$\mu_{1,2} = \eta \pm \sqrt{1+\eta^2}.$$

The corresponding cosine values are

$$c_{1,2} = s_{1,2}\,\mu_{1,2}.$$

To choose between the two possibilites, we compute $\Phi(s_1)$ and $\Phi(s_2)$ and choose the sine/cosine pair that results in the greater value for Φ. For the special case $\alpha = 0$ we obtain $c_1 = 1, s_1 = 0$ and $c_2 = 0\, s_2 = 1$. The new approximate singular vector y as defined by (6) is then given by setting

$$z := sx \text{ and } \delta := \frac{c - s\alpha}{\gamma}.$$

The resulting estimate for the smallest singular value $\sigma_{min}(R')$ of R' is

$$\hat{\sigma}_{min}(R') = \frac{1}{\|y\|_2}.$$

From this description it is clear that this condition estimator satisfies our algorithmic constraints. Given a current R_i we only need to save the current solution x and its norm $\|x\|_2$ to arrive at an estimate for $\sigma_{min}(R_{i+1})$. Furthermore the calculation is inexpensive. For a $k \times k$ matrix R_i we only need $2k$ flops to arrive at an estimate for $\sigma_{min}(R_{i+1})$. So altogether it costs only n^2 flops to run this condition estimator alongside the generation of an $n \times n$ triangular matrix.

To assess the accuracy of our condition estimator, we performed the suite of tests suggested by Higham [15]. Three different types of test matrices are employed. In each test, upper triangular matrices R were generated by computing the QR factorization of various $n \times n$ matrices A for $n = 10, 25, 50$ both with and without column pivoting.

Test1 (see Table 1): The elements of A were chosen as random numbers from the uniform distribution on $[-1, 1]$. Fifty matrices were generated for each n. As observed by Higham, this type of matrix usually is well-conditioned. Over the whole test the minimum, maximum and average values of the two-norm condition number $\kappa_2(A) = \sigma_1/\sigma_n$ were $21, 1.4 \cdot 10^4$ and $2.0 \cdot 10^3$ respectively.

Test2 (see Tables 2 and 3) and *Test 3*: In these tests we used random matrices A with preassigned singular value distributions $\{\sigma_i\}$. Random orthogonal matrices U and V were generated using the method of Stewart [22] and then A was formed as in (5). For each value of n and each singular value distribution, fifty matrices were generated by choosing different matrices U and V. For test 2 we chose the exponential distribution

$$\sigma_i = \alpha^i,\ 1 \leq i \leq n$$

where α is determined by $\kappa_2(A)$. For test 3, we chose the sharp-break distribution

$$1 = \sigma_1 = \cdots = \sigma_{n-1} > \sigma_n = \frac{1}{\kappa_2(A)}.$$

The figures given in Tables 1–2 are the ratios

$$\hat{\sigma}_{min}(R)/\sigma_{min}(R) \geq 1$$

The first number in each pair is the maximum ratio over the fifty matrices and the second is the average ratio. All

Table 1: *Results of Test 1*

pivoting	$n=10$	25	50
no	2.2/1.4	6.6/2.4	7.0/3.1
yes	2.3/1.5	3.2/2.0	3.9/2.6

Table 2: *Results of Test 2 without Pivoting*

κ_2	$n=10$	25	50
10	1.8/1.3	1.7/1.4	1.6/1.4
10^3	3.0/1.9	2.5/2.0	3.2/2.2
10^6	8.1/1.9	6.3/2.6	4.2/2.8
10^9	6.1/2.2	5.9/3.0	5.2/3.2

Table 3: *Results of Test 2 with Pivoting*

κ_2	$n=10$	25	50
10	1.6/1.3	1.6/1.4	1.7/1.4
10^3	2.2/1.5	2.3/1.8	2.5/2.0
10^6	2.8/1.5	3.4/2.1	3.4/2.5
10^9	2.4/1.6	3.3/2.2	4.3/2.7

results were rounded to two significant digits. For Test 3 we observed a ratio of 1.0 (i.e. the estimate had at least two correct figures) in all cases. These results show that our conditon estimator produces indeed good estimates. We overestimate $\sigma_{min}(R)$ only by a small factor and the results vary only little with condition number, matrix size and singular value distribution. Pivoting increases the accuracy of the condition estimator and we can confidently expect similar accuracy when applying this estimator to matrices R generated by the local pivoting strategy.

4 The QR Algorithm with Controlled Local Pivoting

With the condition estimator we now have the tool to insure the numerical stability of the local pivoting strategy. Using the same notation as in the algorithm of Figure 1 processor k now can check whether $c(:,j)$ is a reasonable choice for the next pivot column before computing $\hat{u}$. Assuming that processor k knows the current estimate x as well as $\|x\|_2$ for the current upper triangular matrix R_{gcnt}, all that is needed for the next condition estimator step is the last column $\begin{pmatrix} v \\ \gamma \end{pmatrix}$ of R_{gcnt+1}. But

$$v = c(1:gcnt, j)$$

has already been computed and from the definition of u and res it follows immediately that

$$\gamma = -\text{sign}(c(gcnt+1, j))\, res_j.$$

So all the information for the next condition estimator step is readily at hand and we can compute a new approximate singular vector y for R_{gcnt+1}.

With

$$\alpha = \max_{1\le i\le n} \|a_i\|_2$$

being the norm of the largest column of A, we then take

$$\hat{\sigma}_{min}(R_{gcnt+1}) = \frac{1}{\eta_1 \|y\|_2} \qquad (8)$$

as an estimate for the smallest singular value of R_{gcnt+1} and

$$\hat{\kappa}(R_{gcnt+1}) = \eta_2\, \alpha \|y\|_2 \qquad (9)$$

as an estimate for the true condition number of R_{gcnt+1}. The scaling factors η reflect the trust we have in the accuracy of our estimates. A large η will result in too pessimistic estimates, a small η might lead to underestimation. Based on the numerical results of section 3 we recommend $\eta_1 = 3$ and $\eta_2 = 10$. The choice of η_2 reflects the fact that in general the norm of the largest column is a good estimator for the largest singular value of a matrix.

Comparing the estimates (8) or (9) against a chosen threshold we will then accept or reject a candidate pivot column. The exact threshold depends heavily on the application, in particular the accuracy of the initial data. If the data is accurate to machine precision ϵ, a candidate pivot will in general be rejected if $\hat{\sigma}_{min}(R_{gcnt+1}) = O(1/\epsilon)$.

If the candidate pivot column is rejected, processor k has exhausted its supply of "reasonable" columns and from then on it will only apply Householder vectors generated by other processors to its remaining columns. If on the other hand we accept the candidate pivot column, then processor k will actually compute $\hat{u}$, send $(\hat{u}, y, \|y\|_2)$ to its right neighbour and then proceed as in Figure 1. It should be noted that y and $\|y\|_2$ have to be forwarded only to the processor that will generate the next Householder vector, while $\hat{u}$ will eventually be known to all processors. So the propagation of the condition estimator results will result in only a minor increase in data traffic.

This scheme continues until no processor has any acceptable pivot candidate left. Assuming that altogether we generated $\hat{n} = n - \hat{r}$ Householder vectors, we have at this point computed the incomplete QR factorization

$$AP = \begin{pmatrix} Q_1 & Q_2 \end{pmatrix} \begin{pmatrix} R_{11} & R_{12} \\ 0 & \hat{A} \end{pmatrix} \qquad (10)$$

where Q_1 is $m \times \hat{n}$, Q_2 is $m \times (m - \hat{n} + 1)$ and $Q = [Q_1, Q_2]$ is orthogonal. R_{11} is upper triangular of size $\hat{n} \times \hat{n}$ and $\hat{A}$ is of size $(m - \hat{r} + 1) \times \hat{r}$. Our controlled pivoting strategy gives us an estimate for $\sigma_{min}(R_{11})$ and further we know that adding any of the leftover $\hat{r}$ columns of AP would result in a decrease of the smallest singular value below our chosen threshold. So we have good reason to assume that $\hat{r}$ is the dimension of the numerical null space of A. Then we can set $\hat{A}$ in (10) to zero and use the resulting truncated QR factorization to solve the least squares problem (1).

Table 4: min/avg/max Values of the Condition Numbers of R using Local and Global Pivoting

Distribution	break 1	break 9	exponential
$\kappa_{par}(R)$, $p = 8$	2.7 /5.1 /8.0	6.4 /13 /46	7.2e6 /1.1e7 /1.6e7
$\kappa_{par}(R)$, $p = 32$	3.7 /7.7 /23	10 /180 /6.1e3	7.6e6 /1.3e7 /1.9e7
$\kappa_{trad}(R)$	2.8 /3.7 /4.8	4.3 /5.7 /7.8	7.2e6 /1.0e7 /1.9e7
$\kappa_{opt}(R)$	1.0	1.0	8.1e6

5 Numerical Experiments

To assess the numerical behavior of the proposed local pivoting scheme, we simulated the parallel algorithm using PRO-MATLAB and compared it with the traditional QR factorization algorithm with global column pivoting. Various 100×100 matrices were generated and the local pivoting strategy simulated on 8 and 32 processors.

For tests 1 to 3 we generated 50 random matrices for each singular value distribution $\{\sigma_i\}$. For all matrices the largest and smallest singular values were 1 and 10^{-9} respectively.

Break 1 Distribution: $\sigma_1 = \ldots = \sigma_{99} = 1$; $\sigma_{100} = 10^{-9}$.

Break 9 Distribution: $\sigma_1 = \ldots = \sigma_{91} = 1$; $\sigma_{92} = \ldots = \sigma_{100} = 10^{-9}$.

Exponential Distribution: $\sigma_1 = 1; \sigma_i = \alpha^{i-1} (i = 2, \ldots, 99)$; $\alpha = (10^{-9})^{\frac{1}{99}}$.

Setting the rejection threshold for the smallest singular value to 10^{-7} and discounting the estimate for the smallest singular value (8) by a factor of $\eta_1 = 3$ we reject a candidate pivot column in the parallel algorithm if

$$\frac{1}{\|y\|_2} = \hat{\sigma}_{min}(R_{gcnt+1}) \leq 3 \cdot 10^{-7}.$$

For the traditional QR factorization algorithm we use the last diagonal entry of R_{gcnt+1} as estimate and reject a candidate pivot column if

$$| r_{gcnt+1,gcnt+1} | \leq 3 \cdot 10^{-7}.$$

Table 4 shows the condition number $\kappa(R)$ of the upper triangular matrices R generated by controlled local pivoting and by traditional column pivoting on those matrices. Letting σ_{cutoff} be the smallest singular value greater than 10^{-7} then the optimal value we can achieve for $\kappa(R)$ is $\kappa_{opt}(R) = 1/\sigma_{cutoff}$. Furthermore let $\kappa_{par}(R)$ be the condition number resulting from the parallel scheme and $\kappa_{trad}(R)$ the condition number resulting from the traditional column pivoting scheme. For $\kappa_{par}(R)$ and $\kappa_{trad}(R)$ observed minimum, average and maximum values are displayed. These results show that guarded local pivoting is about as effective as full column pivoting in generating a well-conditoned R — especially if there are more than just a few columns in each processor. Except for the break 9 example the transition from 8 to 32 processors had no noticeable effect. The break 9 example shows that the local pivoting strategy will deteriorate if the matrix is highly rank-deficient and the number of columns per processor is small. This is not very surprising in that the pivoting choices of each processor are very limited. Due to the high dimension of the numerical null space a processor may be forced to consider columns that are suboptimal but whose choice results in a matrix R_i where $\sigma_{min}(R_i)$ is still well above the threshold. The average values for the break 9 distribution on 32 processors in Table 4 are somewhat misleading in that they make the local pivoting strategy look worse than it really is. If we ignore the one experiment where R had condition number 6.1e3, we obtain for the other 49 runs the condition number distribution shown in Figure 2. We see that in the vast ma-

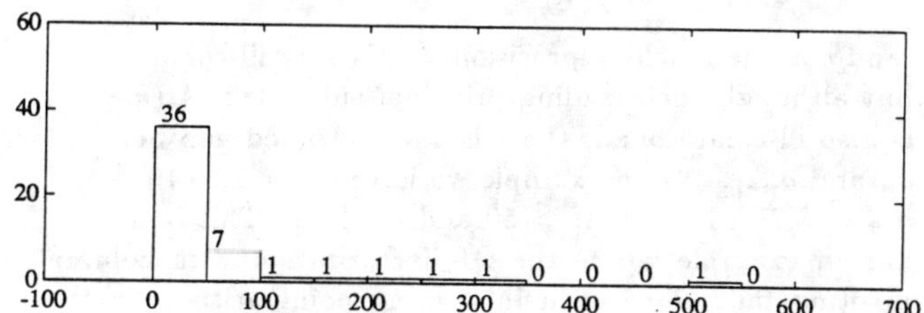

Figure 2: Condition Number Distribution of R for the *break 9* Distribution with $p = 32$

jority of cases the condition numbers of R were less than 100. It should be noted that in the case where we only have 3 columns per processor the computational speed of the pipelined algorithm would in all likelyhood not be good anyhow due to the already mentioned dominance of the startup and final phases of the algorithm.

For the sharp break distributions there is a well-defined gap between the singular values before and after the acceptance threshold and both local and global column pivoting identify the numerical nullspace correctly in all cases. As already pointed out earlier, the determination of numerical rank becomes problematic if there is no well-defined gap between singular values that are considered "large" and "small". The exponential distribution is such a problematic case. There are 77 singular values that are larger than 10^{-7} but there is no well-defined break. To be exact: $\sigma_{75} = 1.8 \cdot 10^{-7}, \sigma_{76} = 1.5 \cdot 10^{-7}, \sigma_{77} = 1.2 \cdot 10^{-7}$ and $\sigma_{78} = 1.0 \cdot 10^{-7}$. The column pivoting strategy reflects this difficulty in accepting less than 77 columns and the observed results are displayed in Table 5. So for example in 24 of the 50 runs we accepted 75 columns in the local pivoting scheme using 8 processors. These results show that even for an ill-defined problem the guarded local pivoting scheme is very reliable

Table 5: Frequency of Accepting Columns for the Exponential Distribution

No. of columns accepted	72	73	74	75	76
local pivoting, $p = 8$	2	3	12	24	9
local pivoting, $p = 32$	5	11	23	9	2
global pivoting	0	2	29	18	1

in that it leans towards a small underestimate of the dimension of the numerical range space of A.

Our last example shows the advantage resulting from integrating the incremental condition estimator with the global pivoting scheme. Let

$$A_n = \mathrm{diag}(1, s, s^2, \ldots, s^{n-1}) \begin{pmatrix} 1 & -c & \cdots & \cdots & -c \\ 0 & 1 & \ddots & & \vdots \\ \vdots & \ddots & \ddots & \ddots & \vdots \\ \vdots & & \ddots & 1 & -c \\ 0 & \cdots & \cdots & 0 & 1 \end{pmatrix} + \Delta$$

where

$$\Delta = \mathrm{diag}(n\epsilon, (n-1)\epsilon, \ldots, \epsilon), c^2 + s^2 = 1$$

and ϵ is the machine precision. A_n is very ill-conditioned, but although each leading principal submatrix $A_k (k \leq n)$ is also ill-conditioned, there is a well-defined gap between σ_n and σ_{n-1}. As an example we have $\sigma_{49} = 1.2 \cdot 10^{-3}$ and $\sigma_{50} = 3.7 \cdot 10^{-12}$ for $n = 50$ and $c = 0.5$. This is a well-known example where the QR factorization with column pivoting fails since even in floating point arithmetic the matrix is its own QR factorization but no trailing block of R is small to reveal its ill-conditioning. In this example both the local and global pivoting schemes select the the columns in their natural order. However the incremental condition estimator integrated into the parallel scheme detects the ill-conditioning of the leading principal submatrices A_k — it never overestimates the smallest singular value by a factor of more than 1.5. So while the column pivoting scheme fails the incremental condition estimator insures that failure will not go unnoticed. Given its negligible extra cost this suggest the usefulness of incorporating the incremental condition estimator into the global column pivoting scheme.

The matrix A_n is also an example where the local pivoting scheme performs better than the global one. Let $\tilde{A}_{50}$ be the same matrix as A_{50} except that the order of columns has been reversed. For the global column pivoting scheme this permutation is without consequences and it fails. The parallel scheme simulated on 8 processors on the other hand correctly identifies the numerical nullspace of $\tilde{A}_{50}$. While this is an exceptional occurence due to the special structure of A_n, it is nonetheless surprising since intuitively one would expect the global pivoting strategy to always perform better than the local one.

6 Conclusions

This paper presented a new variant of the Householder QR algorithm with column pivoting. In that context we introduced a new incremental condition estimator that allowed us to update the estimate for the smallest singular value of the upper triangular matrix R as new columns were added to R. The update required only $O(n)$ flops and the saving of $O(n)$ words between successive steps. Despite its small computational cost, experiments with a variety of matrices demonstrated the reliability of the condition estimation algorithm. This condition estimator made it possible to implement a strictly local pivoting scheme for the QR factorization by guarding against an improper choice of pivot columns. Numerical experiments show that the local pivoting scheme performs by and large as well as global pivoting. There even exist cases where the local pivoting scheme succeeds while the global pivoting scheme fails.

We also gave an example showing the usefulness of integrating the incremental condition estimator with the traditional global column pivoting strategy. The n^2 flops for the condition estimator might be a worthwhile investment to guard against the pathological cases that are not revealed by the traditional QR factorization algorithm with column pivoting.

We are currently investigating the effect of a dynamic threshold for the acceptance or rejection of a pivot column. Starting with a relative conservative threshold and relaxing it as the computation proceeds is likely to result in better conditioned leading submatrices of R. The penalty is a possible loss of effiency as processors might have to reconsider the same column as pivoting candidate at a later stage of the algorithm.

References

[1] Christian Bischof. A pipelined block QR decomposition algorithm. In Garry Rodrigue, editor, *Proceedings of the 3rd SIAM Conference on Parallel Processing for Scientific Computing*. SIAM Press, 1988. *to appear.*

[2] Christian H. Bischof and Charles F. Van Loan. The WY representation for products of Householder matrices. *SIAM Journal on Scientific and Statistical Computing*, 8:s2–s13, 1987.

[3] P. A. Businger and G. H. Golub. Linear least squares solution by Householder transformation. *Numerische Mathematik*, 7:269–276, 1965.

[4] Tony F. Chan. Rank revealing QR factorizations. *Linear Algebra and its Applications*, 88/89:67–82, 1987.

[5] A. K. Cline, A. R. Conn, and C. F. Van Loan. *Generalizing the LINPACK Condition Estimator*, volume 909 of *Lecture Notes in Mathematics*, pages 73–83. Springer Verlag, Berlin, 1982.

[6] A. K. Cline, C. B. Moler, G. W. Stewart, and J. H. Wilkinson. An estimate for the condition number of a matrix. *SIAM Journal on Numerical Analysis*, 16:368–375, 1979.

[7] Thomas F. Coleman and Guangye Li. Solving systems of nonlinear equations on a message-passing multiprocessor. Technical Report CS-87-887, Cornell University, November 1987.

[8] J. J. Dongarra, J. R. Bunch, C. B. Moler, and G. W. Stewart. *LINPACK Users' Guide.* SIAM Press, 1979.

[9] L. V. Foster. Rank and null space calculations using matrix decomposition without column interchanges. *Linear Algebra and its Applications*, 74:47–71, 1986.

[10] George A. Geist and Michael T. Heath. Parallel Cholesky factorization on a hypercube multiprocessor. Technical Report ORNL-6190, Oak Ridge National Laboratory, 1985.

[11] G. H. Golub, V. Klema, and G. W. Stewart. Rank degeneracy and least squares problems. Technical Report TR-456, Dept. of Computer Science, University of Maryland, 1976.

[12] Gene H. Golub and Charles F. Van Loan. *Matrix Computations.* The Johns Hopkins University Press, 1983.

[13] Michael T. Heath and Charles H. Romine. Parallel solution of triangular systems on distributed-memory multiprocessors. Technical Report ORNL/TM-10384, Oak Ridge National Laboratory, 1987.

[14] Michael T. Heath and Charles H. Romine. Parallel solution of triangular systems on distributed-memory multiprocessors. Unpublished Manuscript, 1988.

[15] Nicholas J. Higham. A survey of condition number estimation for triangular matrices. *SIAM Journal on Scientific and Statistical Computing*, 29(4):575–598, 1987.

[16] Ilse Ipsen, Youcef Saad, and Martin Schultz. Dense linear systems on a ring of processors. *Linear Algebra and its Applications*, 77:205–239, 1986.

[17] Charles L. Lawson and Richard J. Hanson. *Solving Least Squares Problems.* Prentice Hall, 1974.

[18] Guangye Li and Thomas F. Coleman. A new method for solving triangular systems on distributed memory message-passing multiprocessors. Technical Report 87-812, Cornell University, 1987.

[19] Åke Björck. *Handbook of Numerical Analysis*, volume 1, chapter Least Squares Methods. North Holland, 1087.

[20] Alex Pothen and Padma Raghavan. Distributed orthogonal factorization: Givens and Householder algorithms. Technical Report CS-87-24, The Pennsylvania State University, 1987.

[21] Robert Schreiber and Charles Van Loan. A storage efficient WY representation for products of Householder transformations. Technical Report CS-87-864, Cornell University, 1987.

[22] G. W. Stewart. The efficient generation of random orthogonal matrices with an application to condition estimators. *SIAM Journal on Numerical Analysis*, 17:403–409, 1980.

Algorithms - II

Chair: Leah Jamieson
Purdue University

VECTORIZATION OF CONJUGATE-GRADIENT METHODS FOR LARGE-SCALE MINIMIZATION

I. M. Navon,
Supercomputer Computations Research Institute
and Dept. of Mathematics
Florida State University
Tallahassee, FL 32306-4052

P. K. H. Phua,
Dept. of Info. Systems and Computer Science
National University of Singapore

and M. Ramamurthy
Dept. of Atmospheric Sciences
University of Illinois
Urbana-Champagne, IL 61801

ABSTRACT

Vectorization techniques are applied here for the vectorization of the non-linear conjugate-gradient method for large-scale unconstrained minimization. Until now the main thrust of vectorization techniques has been directed towards vectorization of linear conjugate-gradient methods designed to solve symmetric linear systems of algebraic equations. Computational results are presented using a robust limited-memory Quasi-Newton-like conjugate-gradient algorithm due to Shanno and Phua [21], applied to large-scale unconstrained minimization problems arising in meteorological applications. The vectorization of the non-linear conjugate-gradient method results in speed-ups up to a factor of 21 compared to the performance of the scalar code, when minimizing non-linear functions of $10^4 - 10^5$ variables. A sizable reduction in the CPU, time required for the minimization of large-scale non-linear functions is obtained-pointing to the advantages of vectorization for large-scale numerical unconstrained minimization problems, where local minima of non-linear functions is to be found using the non-linear conjugate-gradient method.

1. INTRODUCTION

During the last few years conjugate-gradient methods were found to be the best available tool for large-scale non-linear minimization of functions occurring in geophysical applications. We consider here the case when function evaluation is expensive and gradients are evaluated by finite differences. The objective function $F(x)$ is often described by a complex computer code and the derivatives of $F(x)$ are not available analytically. Generally in this case no higher derivatives are used. Therefore for large-scale unconstrained minimization with expensive function evaluations and in the absence of analytical gradients, each gradient evaluation requires N function evaluations.

The cost of solving the optimization problem i.e.

$$\min_{x \in R^n} F : R^n \rightarrow R^n \tag{1}$$

is dominated by the function and finite difference gradient evaluations.

In the present paper we present the results of the vectorization of the memoryless Quasi-Newton conjugate-gradient code due to Shanno and Phua [26] applied for finding the local minimizer of large-scale meteorological problems involving $10^4 - 10^5$ variables. In such cases it is not unusual for each evaluation of $F(x)$ to require up to a minute on a single processor of the CYBER-205. The results point to the vectorization of the function and gradient evaluation code, as well as the vectorization of the conjugate-gradient routine itself to result in a significant speed-up, i.e. in a sizable reduction in the CPU time required for the minimization.

Our approach may be then used in a multiple processor architecture using concurrent evaluations as proposed by Schnabel [20]. It is concluded that vector processors are advantageous for large-scale non-linear unconstrained minimization problems where the local minima of non-linear functionals is found using the conjugate-gradient method.

As for the non-linear conjugate-gradient method which constitutes the topic of the present research paper – a thorough review of the available literature points out to the fact that the absolute totality of the research activity carried by a small number of researchers was directed towards efforts in parallelizing the conjugate-gradient method – and to our best knowledge – no effort was directed towards vectorizing the method.

Parallelization of the non-linear conjugate-gradient method can be introduced by approximating the successive gradients by finite-differences of the function values calculated in parallel – and one can accelerate the linear searches by simultaneous function evaluations at preselected gridpoints along the search direction.

Several authors (Chazan and Miranker [2], Sloboda [22], Sutti [23,24], and Schendel and Schyska [19]) designed parallel versions of Powell's non-gradient method [15] generating conjugate search directions by minimization over geometrically parallel manifolds. This results in simultaneous line searches, but computational experience up to date is too limited (see Lootsma [8]).

The Hatfield Polytechnic Group has investigated conjugate-gradient methods of Nazareth [12] which generate conjugate search directions without exact linear searches (see Dixon, Ducksbury and Sing [4], Dixon and Patel [3], Dixon, Patel, and Ducksbury [5], Patel [13], and Schnabel [18]). Other work on parallel optimization is reported in Straeter and Markos [26]. Housos and Wing [6,7] used pseudo-conjugate directions for the solution of the non-linear unconstrained op-

CH2617-9/88/0000/0410$01.00

timization problem on a parallel computer using the Powell [15] non-gradient method. Other efforts involved Mukai [9], Pierre [14], Van-Laarhoven [25], etc. No report appears to be available of speeding up the non-linear conjugate-gradient method for large-scale optimization on vector computers.

This issue is of crucial importance when we solve problems with expensive function/gradient evaluations which appears to be the case for large-scale meteorological applications.

It is important to develop very efficient unconstrained minimization algorithms not only because the problem occurs in many instances on its own – but even more so because an unconstrained minimization problem must be solved in the inner-loop of the solution of important constrained non-linear problems. As mentioned by Schnabel [18] vector computers may be advantageous in the case of large-scale unconstrained minimization.

These large-scale minimization problems occur in applications in meteorology, computational chemistry and structural optimization to cite but a few of the application fields.

In Section 2 we will describe the relevant large-scale meteorological problems where the constrained non-linear optimization, e.g., the Augmented-Lagrangian formulation was applied. A large-scale unconstrained optimization problem must be invariably solved in the inner-loop of the solution of the Augmented-Lagrangian constrained non-linear minimization. The robust (see Navon and Legler [11]) conjugate-gradient solver, its structure and computational complexity will be described in Section 3. Numerical results concerning the vectorization of the conjugate-gradient code and in particular the vectorization of the function/gradient evaluation part of it will be presented in Section 4.

Results concerning the performance of the conjugate-gradient code under scalar, automatic vectorization and refined manual vectorization will be numerically and graphically presented and discussed in Section 5. The resulting speed-ups of the conjugate-gradient method and the relative improvements in performance will be tabulated and summarized.

Finally, the impact of the number of variables in the non-linear function to be minimized on the speed-up performance of the vectorized non-linear conjugate-gradient code for a particular vector supercomputer, e.g., (the CYBER-205) will be discussed.

Section 6 will include a summary and conclusion remarks where implications for vectorization of different non-linear conjugate-gradient methods applied to large and very large-scale unconstrained minimization.

2. TYPICAL LARGE-SCALE METEOROLOGICAL PROBLEMS

To exemplify the large-scale problems encountered in meteorology we will briefly present two such problems.

A) ENFORCING CONSERVATION OF INTEGRAL INVARIANTS USING THE AUGMENTED-LAGRANGIAN METHOD

An Augmented-Lagrangian method is applied to enforce conservation of total mass, total energy and potential enstrophy for a limited-area model of the two dimensional shallow-water equations. The non-linear equality constrained problem is transformed in a series of unconstrained minimization problems (Bertsekas [1]).

The functional F is defined by:

$$\sum_{j=1}^{N_x}\sum_{k=1}^{N_y} \alpha(U-U_0)^2+\alpha(V-V_0)^2+\beta(H-H_0)^2 \quad (2)$$

where $N_x\Delta x = L$ and $N_y\Delta y = D$, where L and D are the dimensions of the rectangular domain over which the shallow water equations are being solved.

The functional was solved subject to three equality constraints :

$$\begin{aligned} &E_n - E_0 \\ &Z_n - Z_0 \\ &H_n - H_0 \end{aligned} \quad (3)$$

where n and 0 denote the values of the integral invariants at time $t_n = n\Delta t$ and $t_0 = 0$ respectively. Here the vector x has $3N_xN_y$ components where x is given by:

$$x = \left(u_{11},\ldots,u_{N_xN_y},v_{11},\ldots,v_{N_xN_y},h_{11},\ldots,h_{N_xN_y}\right)^T. \quad (4)$$

For a coarse resolution of a grid of 12×15 we had a function with 540 variables, i.e. the unconstrained minimization was carried out on a non-linear function of 540 variables.

A refined mesh test was also carried out for a mesh space increment of:

$$\Delta x = \Delta y = 40 \text{ km and } \Delta t = 360 \text{ sec} \quad (5)$$

whereas the original grid had a mesh spacing of 400km and a time step of numerical integration of 3600 sec.

In the refined mesh test we had $150\times111\times3$ variables, i.e. 50000 variables in the non-linear unconstrained minimization.

2.1. Constrained adjustment to suppress Lamb waves

In meteorological applications one is often interested in suppressing external gravity waves in a 3-D model by modifying the observed wind field in such a way that the vertical motions at the lowest level of a three-dimensional atmospheric model vanish.

An alternative way is to regard this adjustment as a variational adjustment of the horizontal wind fields in a pressure coordinate system (x,y,p) so that the pressure tendency $\frac{dp_s}{dt}$ is zero everywhere and p_s is the surface pressure.

The continuity equation in pressure coordinates is given by

$$\frac{\partial u}{\partial x}+\frac{\partial v}{\partial y}+\frac{\partial w}{\partial p}=0. \quad (6)$$

Integrating this equation from the top to the bottom of the atmosphere and assuming the vertical velocity $w = 0$ at both end points we obtain (see Ramamurthy [16], Ramamurthy and Carr [17]).

$$\int_0^{p_s} \left(\frac{\partial u}{\partial x} + \frac{\partial v}{\partial y} \right) dp = 0. \tag{7}$$

Using this equation as a constraint will ensure that

$$\frac{dp_s}{dt} = 0. \tag{8}$$

In other words, using the continuity equation as a strong constraint will enable us to suppress Lamb waves (Ramamurthy [16]).

The Lamb waves are high speed acoustic-gravity waves which appear as solutions to the primitive equations in numerical weather prediction along with slow, physically relevant meteorological waves. As such, we are interested in suppressing the Lamb waves which can be viewed as noise in a meteorological model and which moreover impose very stringent computational stability conditions on the allowable time step Δt.

The functional for which the stationary value is to be found for this problem is:

$$\begin{aligned} f = & \int_x \int_y \int_p \left[(u - \tilde{u})^2 + (v - \tilde{v}) \right]^2 dx\, dy\, dp \\ & + \int_x \int_y \left[\lambda \int_0^{P_s} \left(\frac{\partial u}{\partial x} + \frac{\partial v}{\partial y} \right) dp \right] dx\, dy, \end{aligned} \tag{9}$$

where $\tilde{u}$ and $\tilde{v}$ are the analyzed horizontal wind components – while u and v are the observed horizontal wind components – and λ is the Lagrange multiplier.

In a discrete Augmented-Lagrangian formulation we obtained

$$\begin{aligned} L = & \sum_i \sum_j \sum_k \Big[(u_{ijk} - \tilde{u}_{ijk})^2 \\ & + (v_{ijk} - v_{ijk})^2 \Big] \Delta x \Delta y \Delta p \\ & + \sum_i \sum_j \lambda_{ij} \left[\sum_k \left(\frac{u_{i+1,j,k} - u_{i-1,j,k}}{2\Delta x} \right.\right. \\ & \left.\left. + \frac{v_{i,j+1,k} - v_{i,j-1,k}}{2\Delta y} \right) \Delta p \right] \Delta x \Delta y \\ & + \frac{1}{2} \sum_i \sum_j C_{ij} \left[\sum_k \left(\frac{u_{i+1,j,k} - u_{i-1,j,k}}{2\Delta x} \right.\right. \\ & \left.\left. + \frac{v_{i,j+1,k} - v_{i,j-1,k}}{2\Delta y} \right) \Delta p \right]^2 \Delta x \Delta y. \end{aligned} \tag{10}$$

where

C_{ij} are the penalty terms.

λ_{ij} are the Lagrange multipliers.

Our model domain is rectangular with a resolution of (46 × 46) grid points while in the vertical we have 10 discrete levels resulting in this application in a function of 46 × 46 × 10 × 2 components *i.e.* ≈ 42320 components. A coarser mesh case where the mesh spacing was increased by a factor of 2 in the horizontal resulted in a function of 23 × 23 × 10 × 2 components ≈ 10000 variables. The gradient of the discrete Augmented-Lagrangian function L with respect to $\underline{x}$ where $\underline{x}$ is given by

$$\underline{x} = \left(u_{111}, \ldots, u_{N_x N_y N_p}, v_{111}, \ldots, v_{N_x N_y N_p} \right)^T \tag{11}$$

for the three dimensional limited-area domain in the x, y and p coordinates ($N_x \Delta x = L$, $N_y \Delta y = D$, $N_p \Delta_p = H$) is given by

$$\begin{aligned} \left. \frac{\partial L}{\partial u} \right|_{ijk} = & 2 \left(u_{ijk} - \tilde{u}_{ijk} \right) \Delta x \Delta y \Delta p \\ & + \sum_k \left(\frac{u_{i+1,j,k} - u_{i-1,j,k}}{2\Delta x} \right. \\ & \left. + \frac{v_{i,j+1,k} - v_{i,j-1,k}}{2\Delta y} \right) \Delta p \\ & \cdot \left(\frac{C_{i-1,j} - C_{i+1,j}}{2\Delta x} \right) \Delta x \Delta y \end{aligned} \tag{12}$$

$$\begin{aligned} \left. \frac{\partial L}{\partial v} \right|_{ijk} = & 2 \left(v_{ijk} - \tilde{v}_{ijk} \right) \Delta x \Delta y \Delta p \\ & + \left(\frac{\lambda_{i,j-1} - \lambda_{i,j+1}}{2\Delta y} \right) \Delta x \Delta y \Delta p \\ & + \sum_k \left(\frac{u_{i+1,j,k} - u_{i_1,j,k}}{2\Delta x} \right. \\ & \left. + \frac{v_{i,j+1,k} - v_{i,j-1,k}}{2\Delta y} \right) \Delta p \\ & \cdot \left(\frac{c_{i,j-1} - C_{i,j+1}}{2\Delta y} \right) \Delta x \Delta y. \end{aligned} \tag{13}$$

The same inexact minimization of the Augmented-Lagrangian of Bertsekas [1] is applied using the same rules for updating the multipliers and penalties.

The same non-linear conjugate-gradient unconstrained minimization method, `CONMIN` [26], is used to minimize the Augmented-Lagrangian discrete functional.

3. THE LIMITED MEMORY QUASI-NEWTON CONJUGATE-GRADIENT METHOD

In our application we used the limited memory Quasi-Newton conjugate-gradient method of Shanno and Phua [26] implementing a restructured version of `CONMIN`, which was found to be robust and performing for a wide series of meteorological and geophysical applications [11]. This routine allows the user to use either a conjugate-gradient method or, if memory is available the Quasi-Newton BFGS algorithm. The Beale restarted memoryless Q.N. conjugate-gradient requires $7N$ single/double precision words of working space.

For solving our large-scale non-linear unconstrained optimization problems, memory considerations mandate using the conjugate-gradient method.

As shown by Le [10] the basic formula for CPU consumption in an optimization code is:

$$T = t_f(n_f + nn_g) + t_i n_i \tag{14}$$

where t_f and t_g are the times required for function and gradient calculation respectively, while t_i is the average overhead execution time per iteration.

Here n_f is the number of function evaluations, n_g is the number of gradient evaluations, where:

$$t_g = nt_g \tag{15}$$

and n_i is the number of iterations.

The computational cost of CONMIN depends on the number of function and gradient evaluations more than on the number of additions and multiplications within CONMIN itself which is about $20N$ additions and $22N$ multiplications for a normal iteration of the conjugate-gradient code.

The frequency of restart iterations in comparison with normal iterations was one to three and it was extremely rare for a given direction to be used for more than 10 iterations.

4. VECTORIZATION TECHNIQUES

In this section we describe the various steps taken to speed up the CONMIN conjugate-gradient algorithm for the CYBER-205 vector processor. Because of its memory to memory architecture the CYBER-205 has a longer vector start-up time than say a register to register supercomputer such as the CRAY X/MP. To achieve top performance it is necessary to increase the vector length on the CYBER-205 to fairly long vectors.Its half performance vector length is about 100. Most of the CPU consumption in the conjugate-gradient algorithm was in two sections :

a) Function and gradient evaluation,

b) actual minimization step.

The actual ratio between the two is problem dependent, depending on the complexity of the objective function, number of variables, etc. As a first step we restructured CONMIN so that all the DO loops could be vectorized, where the bulk of the DO loops perform inner products and summations. We used the Q8 SSUM and Q8 SDOT operations which have an initial vector start-up of 96 and 107 cycles respectively.

Hence the larger the N in the DO loop, the lesser the impact of the start-up time on the final performance of the two operations. Having vectorized the minimization routine, the main task is to vectorize the often heavy compute-intensive FUNCT routine which performs the function and gradient evaluation for subsequent use in CONMIN.

The number of function evaluations depends amongst others on the rate of convergence, the step-size requirements and the number of Beale restarts.

In general vectorization in FUNCT necessitated collapsing two and three dimensional arrays into one dimensional arrays to extract top performance from the CYBER-205.

Use of control bit vectors was also necessary.Such collapsing is done very efficiently on the bit addressable CYBER-205 with the help of WHERE statements that enable us to mask the results along the boundary grid points by pre-initializing those addresses to zero bits with Q8 VMKO calls.

Also the largest loop range was made the innermost loop in those loops where collapsing was not possible due to the iterative nature of the computations.

5. DISCUSSION OF NUMERICAL RESULTS

By timing the runs of the conjugate-gradient large-scale minimization code (using SPY for instance) it became immediately evident that effectively the bulk of the CPU time was spent in the FUNCT routine for function and gradient evaluation.

As such our vectorization effort was mainly directed towards performance improvement of the FUNCT routine. We first applied automatic vectorization (such as VAST-2) for instance.

Further improvement in the speed-up due to vectorization was achieved by using manual vectorization hereby referred to as supervectorization.

In both large-scale problems the improvement due to automatic vectorization was rather marginal-and it was only after performing manual vectorization that impressive speed-ups were achieved. In the first problem (AUGLAG) the speed-up due to vectorization was a factor of almost 65 in the FUNCT routine. The net speed-up for this problem was an impressive factor of 21. For the coarser mesh version of AUGLAG (23×23) the improvement was already reduced since the CYBER-205 has a slower vector start-up time compared to the CRAY computer and the performance efficiency of the CYBER-205 has a strong dependence on the vector length.

On the other hand for the conservation of integral invariants treated in this study only a factor of about 7 speed-up was attained for the fine mesh (111×115). This clearly reflects the problem dependent nature of the computational cost for the gradient and function evaluation routines.

The total speed-up for this problem was also a factor of 7. For a very coarse mesh version of GUSTAF (12×15) the speed-up due to the vectorization was only by a factor of about 2, again reflecting on the longer break-even point for vector computations on the CYBER-205 supercomputer.

A more detailed break-down of the computational cost and the overheads associated with the large-scale minimization using CONMIN are illustrated in the following Tables. The relative percentages of the CPU time spent in the various parts of the minimization code (namely CONMIN itself and the function and gradient evaluation routines) are depicted in the accompanying figures.

These figures display the relative percentages for scalar code, automatic vectorization and super (manual) vectorization given as percentages of the total CPU time spent in the minimization code. For the first problem (AUGLAG), a reversal of the relative percentage of CPU time spent in FUNCT –the function and gradient evaluation routine versus the CPU time spent in CONMIN itself is noticed.

This fact is even more evident in the fine mesh case ($46 \times 46 \times 10$) which involves minimization over a very long vector (40000 variables).

In contrast for the second problem (GUSTAF), the function and gradient evaluation routine dominates by far the bulk of the computational cost, and this trend persists in all three versions of the code (scalar, auto and supervector) for both short and long vectors. However a speed-up factor of 7 was achieved due to manual vectorization for the entire minimization code.

6. SUMMARY AND CONCLUSIONS

Vectorization of the non linear limited memory Q.N. like conjugate-gradient method applied to large-scale minimization problems using the CYBER-205 vector processor has been implemented. For the problems considered the function and gradient evaluation dominate the CPU time spent in minimization. By performing automatic and then hand vectorization we succeeded in achieving a sizable reduction in the CPU time required for finding the local minimum of non-linear functions of $10^4 - 10^5$ variables.

This confirms the Schnabel [20] hypothesis that vector computers are advantageous in the case of large-scale unconstrained optimization. This approach could prove vital in further applications in meteorology, for instance for the adjoint 4-D data assimilation problem where each iteration of the conjugate-gradient method requires 2-3 model integrations for the length of the assimilation period and the application is not easily amenable to concurrent calculations. The speed-up is, however, both problem and also computer dependent and the results are more impressive for large-scale

Problems where the number of variables is of the order of 10^4. Use of multiple vector processors would allow multiple evaluations of $F(x)$ to be performed concurrently with each evaluation performed optimally by a vector processor. This is the case for ETA^{10} and the ALLIANT.

REFERENCES

[1] D. P. Bertsekas, "Constrained Optimization and Lagrange Multiplier Methods," Academic Press, 395pp, 1982.

[2] D. Chazan and W. L. Miranker, "A nongradient and parallel algorithm for unconstrained minimization," *SIAM Jour. on Control*, **8**, 207–217, 1970.

[3] L. C. W. Dixon and K. Patel, "The place of parallel computation in numerical optimization." IV Parallel algorithms for nonlinear optimization, Tech. Rep. 125, Numerical Optimization Centre, Hatfield Polytechnic, 1982.

[4] L. C. W. Dixon, P. G. Ducksbury, and P. Sing, "A parallel version of the conjugate-gradient algorithm for finite-element problems," Tech. Rep. 1132, Numerical Optimization Centre, Hatfield Polytechnic, 1982.

[5] L. C. W. Dixon, K. D. Patel, and P. G. Ducksbury, "Experience running optimization algorithms on parallel processing systems," NOC Tech. Rep. 138, Numerical Optimization Centre, Hatfield Polytechnic, 1983.

[6] E. C. Housos and O. Wing, "Parallel nonlinear minimization by conjugate-gradient " in Proceedings of the International Conference on Parallel Processing, Los Alamitos, IEEE proceedings, 157–158, 1980.

[7] E. C. Housos and O. Wing, "Pseudo-conjugate directions for the solution of the nonlinear unconstrained optimization problem on a parallel computer," *Jour. Optim. Theory and Appls.* **42**, 2, 169–180, 1984.

[8] F. A. Lootsma, "State-of-the-art in parallel unconstrained optimization" in Parallel Computing 85, M. Feilmeir, E. Joubert and V. Schendel (*eds.*), North-Holland, 157–163, 1986.

[9] H. Mukai, "Parallel algorithms for unconstrained optimization" in Proceedings of the 18th IEEE Conference on Decision and Control, **1** 451–454, 1979.

[10] D. Le, "A fast and Robust Unconstrained Minimization Method Requiring Minimum Storage," Math Prog., **32**, 41–68, 1985.

[11] I. M. Navon and D. M. Legler, "Conjugate-gradient methods for large-scale minimization in meteorology," *Monthly Weather Review*, **115**, 1479–1502, 1987.

[12] L. Nazareth, "A conjugate-gradient algorithm without linear searches," JOTA **23**, 373–387, 1977.

[13] K. D. Patel, "Parallel computation and numerical optimization," Tech. Rep. No. 129, Numerical Optimization Centre, Hatfield Polytechnic, 1982.

[14] D. A. Pierre, "A nongradient minimization algorithm having parallel structure with implications for an array processor," *Computers and Electrical Engineering*, **1**, 3–21, 1973.

[15] M. J. D. Powell, "An efficient method for finding the minimum of a function of several variables without calculating derivatives," *Computer Jour.*, **7**, 155–162, 1964.

[16] M. Ramamurthy and F. Carr, "Four-dimensional data assimilation in the monsoon region, Part 1: Experiments with wind data," *Mon. Weath. Rev.*, **115**, 1987.

[17] M. Ramamurthy, "Four-dimensional data assimilation in a limited area model for the Monsoon Region," Ph. D. dissertation, University of Oklahoma, Norman, OK, 308 pp., 1986.

[18] R. B. Schnabel, "Parallel computing in optimization," *Computational Mathematical Programming*, **15**, Nato ASI Series F, K. Schittkowsky (*ed.*), Spring-Verlag, 357–381, 451 pp., 1985.

[19] U. Schendel and M. Schyska, "Parallelle Algorithmen in der Nicht-linearen Optimierung," Preprint 161/84. Fachbereich Mathematik, Freie Universitatät Berlin, 1984.

[20] R. B. Schnabel, "Concurrent Function Evaluations in Local and Global Optimization," *Comp. Methods in Appl Mech. Eng.*, **64**, 537–552, 1987.

[21] D. F. Shanno and K. H. Phua, "Matrix conditioning and nonlinear optimization," *Math. Program*, **14**, 149–160, 1978.

[22] F. Sloboda, "A conjugate direction method and its applications," Proceedings 8th IFIP Conference on Optimization Techniques, Wurtzburg, Springer-Verlag, 1977.

[23] C. Sutti, "Nongradient minimization methods for parallel processing computers, Part 1," JOTA, **39**, 4, 465–474, 1983.

[24] C. Sutti, "Nongradient minimization methods for parallel processing computers, Part 2," JOTA, **39**, 4, 475–488, 1983.

[25] P. J. M. Van Laarhoven, "Parallel variable metric algorithms for unconstrained optimization," *Math. Programming*, **33**, 68–81, 1985.

[26] T. A. Straeter and A. T. Markos, "A parallel Jacobsen-Okwan Optimization Algorithm," *NASA Tech. Note*, **D-8020**, NASA-Langley, VA, 1975.

[27] D. F. Shanno, K. H. Phua, "Remark on Algorithm 500," *ACM Trans. Math. Software*, **6**, 4, 618–622, 1980.

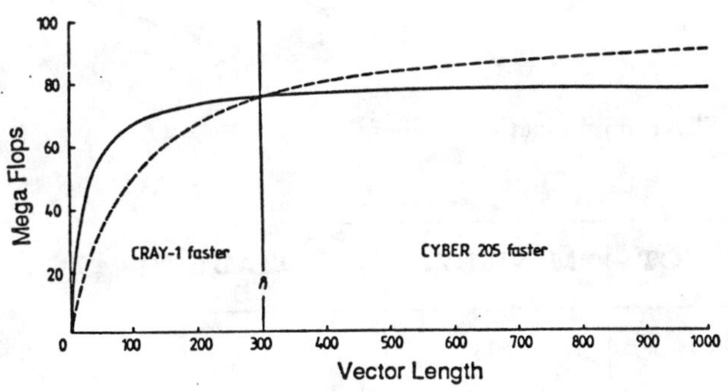

Figure 1. Performance of the 2-pipe CYBER 205 (broken line) and the CRAY-1 (full line) as a function of vector length (Source Hockney and Jesshope, Parallel Computers: Architecture, programming and algorithms, 1981.)

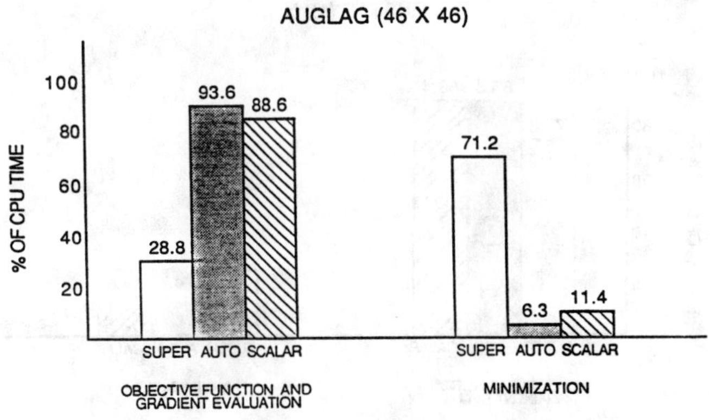

Figure 2. Histograms of the relative percentages of scalar, automatic vectorization and super (manual) vectorization code given as percentages of total CPU time spent in minimization code (AUGLAG (46 × 46).

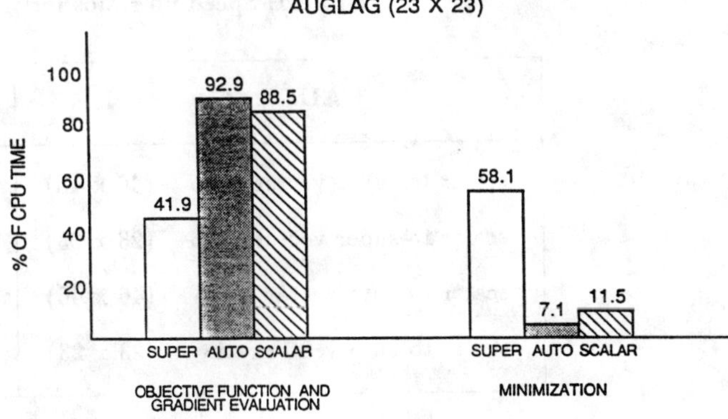

Figure 3. Same as Fig. 2 except for AUGLAG (23 × 23)

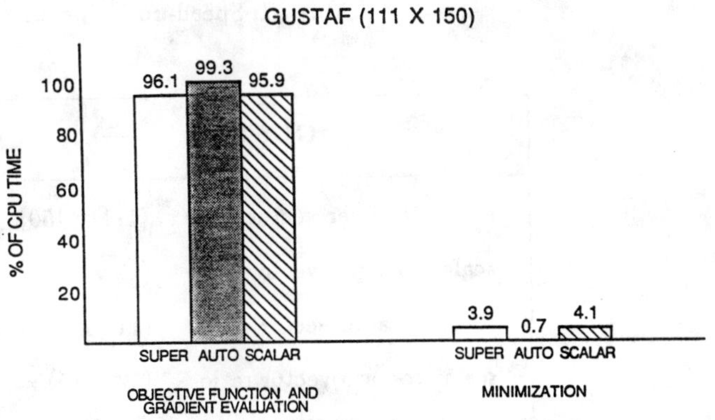

Figure 4. Same as Fig. 2 except for GUSTAF (111 × 150)

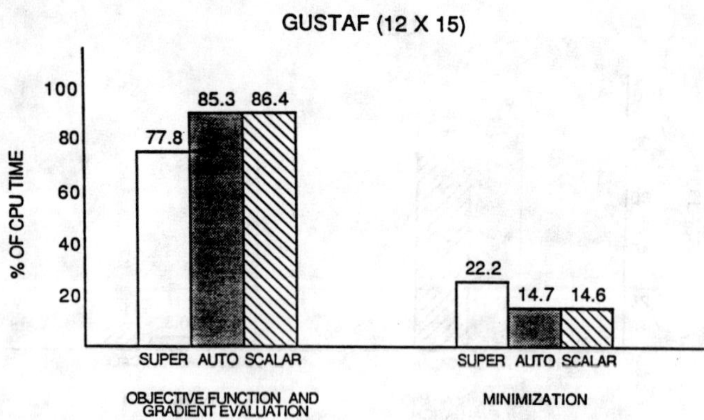

Figure 5. Same as Fig. 2 except for GUSTAF (12 × 15)

Table I: Speed-up ratios for the AUGLAG minimization problem

AUGLAG		FUNCT	MINIMIZ.	TOTAL
scalar to super vector ratio	(46 x 46)	64.8	3.35	21.00
scalar to super vector ratio	(23 x 23)	31.9	2.97	15.03
scalar to auto vector ratio	(46 x 46)	1.76	3.35	1.86
scalar to auto vector ratio	(23 x 23)	1.72	2.91	1.80

Table II: Speed-up ratios for the GUSTAF minimization problem

GUSTAF		FUNCT	MINIMIZ.	TOTAL
scalar to super vector ratio	(111 x 150)	6.71	7.03	6.73
scalar to super vector ratio	(12 x 15)	1.90	1.05	1.71
scalar to auto vector ratio	(111 x 150)	1.20	7.03	1.25
scalar to auto vector ratio	(12 x 15)	1.11	1.00	1.1

Table III: Timing details for the AUGLAG (46 × 46) minimization problem for various levels of vectorization

AUGLAG (46 x 46) - Hand Vectorized	
Time spent in FUNCT	= 0.0334 secs.
Time spent on FUNCT calls	= 0.1003 secs.
Time spent in CONMIN (total)	= 0.3491 secs.
Time spent in minimization	= 0.2487 secs.
AUGLAG (46 x46) - Automatic Vectorization	
Time spent in FUNCT	= 1.2316 secs.
Time spent on FUNCT calls	= 3.6949 secs.
Time spent in CONMIN (total)	= 3.9436 secs.
Time spent in minimization	= 0.2488 secs.
AUGLAG (46 x 46) - Scalar	
Time spent in FUNCT	= 2.1649 secs.
Time spent on FUNCT calls	= 6.4945 secs.
Time spent in CONMIN (total)	= 7.3278 secs.
Time spent in minimization	= 0.8333 secs.

Table IV: Timing details for the AUGLAG (23 × 23) minimization problem for various levels of vectorization

AUGLAG (23 x 23) - Hand Vectorized	
Time spent in FUNCT	= 0.0131 secs.
Time spent on FUNCT calls	= 0.0395 secs.
Time spent in CONMIN (total)	= 0.0942 secs.
Time spent in minimization	= 0.0547 secs.
AUGLAG (23 x 23) - Automatic Vectorization	
Time spent in FUNCT	= 0.2428 secs.
Time spent on FUNCT calls	= 0.7291 secs.
Time spent in CONMIN (total)	= 0.7849 secs.
Time spent in minimization	= 0.0558 secs.
AUGLAG (23 x 23) - Scalar	
Time spent in FUNCT	= 0.4178 secs.
Time spent on FUNCT calls	= 1.2533 secs.
Time spent in CONMIN (total)	= 1.4158 secs.
Time spent in minimization	= 0.1625 secs.

Table V: Timing details for the GUSTAF (111 $\times$ 150) minimization problem for various levels of vectorizatior

GUSTAF (111 x 150) - Hand Vectorized	
Time spent in FUNCT	= 0.08362 secs.
Time spent in CONMIN (total)	= 0.08699 secs.
Time spent in minimization	= 0.00337 secs.
GUSTAF (111 x 150) - Automatic Vectorization	
Time spent in FUNCT	= 0.46648 secs.
Time spent in CONMIN (total)	= 0.46985 secs.
Time spent in minimization	= 0.00337 secs.
GUSTAF (111 x 150) - scalar	
Time spent in FUNCT	= 0.56127 secs.
Time spent in CONMIN (total)	= 0.58508 secs.
Time spent in minimization	= 0.02371 secs.

Table VI: Timing details for the GUSTAF (12 $\times$ 15) minimization problem for various levels of vectorization

GUSTAF (12 x 15) - Hand Vectorized	
Time spent in FUNCT	= 0.00281secs.
Time spent in CONMIN (total)	= 0.00361 secs.
Time spent in minimization	= 0.00080 secs.
GUSTAF (12 x 15) - Automatic Vectorization	
Time spent in FUNCT	= 0.00481 secs.
Time spent in CONMIN (total)	= 0.00564 secs.
Time spent in minimization	= 0.00083 secs.
GUSTAF (12 x 15) - Scalar	
Time spent in FUNCT	= 0.00535 secs.
Time spent in CONMIN (total)	= 0.00619 secs.
Time spent in minimization	= 0.00084 secs.

A Strassen-Newton Algorithm for High-Speed Parallelizable Matrix Inversion

David H. Bailey
NASA Ames Research Center
Moffett Field, CA 94035

Helaman R. P. Ferguson
Supercomputer Research Center
Lanham, MD 20706

Abstract

This paper describes techniques to compute matrix inverses by means of algorithms that are highly suited to massively parallel computation. In contrast, conventional techniques such as pivoted Gaussian elimination and LU decomposition are efficient only on vector computers or fairly low-level parallel systems.

These techniques are based on an algorithm suggested by Strassen in 1969. Variations of this scheme employ matrix Newton iterations and other methods to improve the numerical stability while at the same time preserving a very high level of parallelism. One-processor Cray-2 implementations of these schemes range from one that is up to 55% faster than a conventional library routine to one that, while slower than a library routine, achieves excellent numerical stability.

The problem of computing the solution to a single set of linear equations is discussed, and it is shown that shown that this problem can also be solved efficiently using these techniques.

Introduction

The problem of efficient machine computation of linear equation solutions and matrix inverses for dense systems was recently considered to be solved. One needed only to apply one of the well-known reduction techniques, such as Gauss-Jordan elimination, LU decomposition, or the like (Press 1986, 20–70). The performances of a wide variety of scientific computers performing such operations are available in listings such as Dongarra's LINPACK results (Dongarra 1987).

However, the recent development of very highly parallel systems, with the prospect of massively parallel systems in the near future, is forcing researchers to take a second look at these techniques. The problem is that traditional schemes do not seem to be conducive to highly parallel computing. For instance, a linear equation solution of an $n \times n$ system using a Gauss-Jordan elimination scheme with partial pivoting requires

1. n searches for the maximum entry in the current column.
2. n interchanges of rows to place the pivot element on the diagonal.
3. n divisions of the row containing the pivot by the pivot element.
4. n reductions of the rows by the pivot row.
5. An unscrambling of the columns of the matrix (if a true inverse is desired).

Of these operations, only item 4 admits any parallelism beyond a single row or column vector (i.e., $O(n)$ processors). Further, the row and column operations are often very short vector operations. Item 1 is singularly ill-suited for highly parallel evaluation. It follows that an implementation of this algorithm on a highly parallel system (i.e., $O(n^2)$ processors) would idle large numbers of processors for a significant fraction of the time.

Adaptations of these traditional algorithms suitable for efficient highly parallel evaluation may eventually be found. However, it is at least as likely that these algorithms are hopelessly unsuited for such systems. In any event, it appears that completely different approaches to this problem need to be considered.

Strassen's Algorithm for Matrix Multiplication

The fact that matrix multiplication can be performed with fewer than $2n^3$ arithmetic operations has been known since 1969, when V. Strassen published an algorithm that asymtotically requires only about $4.7n^{2.807}$ operations (Strassen 1969). Since then other such algorithms have been discovered (Kreczmar 1976, Pan 1980 and 1984). Currently the best known result is due to Coppersmith and Winograd (1987), which reduces the

CH2617-9/88/0000/0419$01.00

exponent of n to only 2.38. Until recently, however, such advanced algorithms for matrix multiplication were considered to be academic curiosities with no hope of practical application (see for example Press 1986, 74–76). Indeed, it was estimated at the time Strassen's paper was published that the "crossover point" of his algorithm (i.e., the size of a square matrix for which Strassen's algorithm would run faster than the traditional method) was well over 1,000 (Gentleman 1987).

Strassen's algorithm for matrix multiplication is as follows. Let the matrices A, B, and $C = A \times B$ be divided into half-sized blocks:

$$\begin{bmatrix} A_{11} & A_{12} \\ A_{21} & A_{22} \end{bmatrix} \begin{bmatrix} B_{11} & B_{12} \\ B_{21} & B_{22} \end{bmatrix} = \begin{bmatrix} C_{11} & C_{12} \\ C_{21} & C_{22} \end{bmatrix}$$

Then the result may be calculated as follows:

$$\begin{aligned} P_1 &= (A_{11} + A_{22})(B_{11} + B_{22}) \\ P_2 &= (A_{21} + A_{22})B_{11} \\ P_3 &= A_{11}(B_{12} - B_{22}) \\ P_4 &= A_{22}(B_{21} - B_{11}) \\ P_5 &= (A_{11} + A_{12})B_{22} \\ P_6 &= (A_{21} - A_{11})(B_{11} + B_{12}) \\ P_7 &= (A_{12} - A_{22})(B_{21} + B_{22}) \\ C_{11} &= P_1 + P_4 - P_5 + P_7 \\ C_{12} &= P_3 + P_5 \\ C_{21} &= P_2 + P_4 \\ C_{22} &= P_1 + P_3 - P_2 + P_6 \end{aligned}$$

It should be pointed out that the intermediate matrices $P_1, P_2, \cdots, P_7$ may all be computed concurrently. The last four lines may also be computed concurrently, but their cost is generally insignificant compared to the previous seven lines.

The computational savings of employing Strassen's algorithm derives from the fact that only seven half-sized matrix multiplications need to be performed, whereas eight are required with the standard algorithm. Thus for fairly large matrices, where the cost of performing this algorithm is dominated by the cost of multiplying the half-sized blocks, a savings of approximately 14% can be realized (in theory) over the traditional method.

Strassen's method can of course be recursively employed to multiply the half-sized blocks, and so on down to individual matrix elements if desired. For every level of recursion, an additional 14% savings can be realized. However, in practice this recursion is only performed down to the level at which the losses due to bookkeeping costs and short vector lengths overwhelm any savings due to fewer floating-point operations being performed. On the Cray-2, for example, this crossover point was found to be for matrices of size 128 × 128.

Each level of recursion also multiplies the number of concurrently executable tasks by seven. Thus when even as few as four levels of recursion are employed, thousands of independent tasks are generated. Once tasks are smaller than the crossover point, each individual task still has substantial amounts of parallelism. For example, using the traditional scheme for matrix multiplication, each of the 16,384 result elements of a 128 × 128 operation can be computed concurrently. Therefore this method has almost unlimited parallelism; it is apparently limited only by the capacity of the particular interconnection network to support the necessary data movement (Gentleman 1978).

Other details of practical implementations of Strassen's matrix multiplication algorithm may be found in Bailey (1987).

Strassen's Algorithm for Matrix Inversion

Not nearly as well known as Strassen's algorithm for matrix multiplication is a related algorithm for matrix inversion, which appeared in the same paper. This algorithm can be described as follows. Let the matrices A and $C = A^{-1}$ be divided into half-sized subblocks:

$$\begin{bmatrix} A_{11} & A_{12} \\ A_{21} & A_{22} \end{bmatrix}^{-1} = \begin{bmatrix} C_{11} & C_{12} \\ C_{21} & C_{22} \end{bmatrix}$$

Then the result C may be calculated as follows:

$$\begin{aligned} P_1 &= A_{11}^{-1} \\ P_2 &= A_{21} \times P_1 \\ P_3 &= P_1 \times A_{12} \\ P_4 &= A_{21} \times P_3 \\ P_5 &= P_4 - A_{22} \\ P_6 &= P_5^{-1} \\ C_{12} &= P_3 \times P_6 \\ C_{21} &= P_6 \times P_2 \\ C_{11} &= P_1 - P_3 \times C_{21} \\ C_{22} &= -P_6 \end{aligned}$$

These steps, for the most part, cannot be performed concurrently. However, for a large matrix there is enough work within each step to admit massively parallel computation. In particular, the computation required to perform this algorithm at a certain level is dominated by the cost of the six matrix multiplications, which can of course be performed by Strassen's matrix multiplication algorithm. The two matrix inversion operations in the above can be performed by recursive application of this same method. It can easily be seen that with just a few levels of recursion, almost all real work is square matrix multiplication.

That this technique is faster than conventional techniques even in a one-processor implementation can be seen in Table 1, which contains some Cray-2 performance figures for matrices containing Gaussian pseudorandom data. In this table, the columns headed "Cray Library" contain figures for Cray's MINV routine. MINV is coded in assembly language and is very highly optimized for the Cray-2 — it runs at 300 MFLOPS or more on a single processor. The columns headed "Strassen" contain figures for a recursive implementation of Strassen's algorithm as above, with matrices of sizes 128×128 or smaller performed with MINV. The timings shown are the means of ten runs on a single processor, with a normal background of other jobs on the three remaining processors. The error statistics are the geometric means of the root-mean-square (RMS) errors for the ten runs. The RMS error E for a single trial is computed as

$$E = \frac{1}{n}\sqrt{\sum_{i,j}(B_{ij} - I_{ij})^2}$$

where B is the product of the computed inverse with the original matrix and I is an $n \times n$ identity matrix.

Actually, the results in the Cray Library columns were obtained by using a special version of MINV that does not perform determinant calculations. For these large matrices, even the extremely large dynamic range of the Cray-2 ($10^{\pm 2,465}$) is insufficient, and floating-point overflows result when determinants are calculated. In addition to this modification, a matrix to be inverted by MINV is first copied into an array with an odd first dimension. This avoids the substantial performance loss that otherwise results from bank conflicts when a matrix whose size is divisible by a power of two is accessed by rows.

While the timings listed in Table 1 are very encouraging, the error statistics indicate that the Strassen routine is not as numerically stable as MINV, which employs Gauss-Jordan elimination with partial pivoting. Indeed, for large matrices the Strassen inverse scheme is only accurate to about seven digits (on the average), even when full 14-digit arithmetic is employed. This may be sufficient for some applications known to be highly stable, but for other applications it is unsatisfactory.

A Pivoted Version of the Strassen Matrix Inverse Algorithm

The principal reason for the mediocre accuracy statistics of the Strassen inverse scheme is that the algorithm as described above first attempts to invert the upper left $n/2 \times n/2$ matrix. If this block is well-conditioned, then a fairly accurate full-sized inverse will be produced. If this block is near-singular, then the accuracy of the full-sized inverse will be poor. If this block is singular, the method will fail.

This analysis suggests that a pivoted version of Strassen's scheme would exhibit greater stability. Indeed, if the full-sized matrix is well-conditioned, then either the upper left corner block or the lower left corner block must be well-conditioned. If the lower left corner block is well-conditioned, then the inverse of the full-sized matrix may be computed by a variant of the Strassen matrix inverse algorithm, as follows:

$$\begin{aligned}
P_1 &= A_{21}^{-1} \\
P_2 &= A_{11} \times P_1 \\
P_3 &= P_1 \times A_{22} \\
P_4 &= A_{11} \times P_3 \\
P_5 &= P_4 - A_{12} \\
P_6 &= P_5^{-1} \\
C_{12} &= P_3 \times P_6 \\
C_{21} &= P_6 \times P_2 \\
C_{11} &= P_1 - P_3 \times C_{22} \\
C_{22} &= -P_6
\end{aligned}$$

This suggests the following alternate scheme for matrix inversion: compute the inverse and determinant of both the upper left and lower left blocks, and proceed with the variant of the Strassen algorithm corresponding to the block with the largest determinant. The determinant of a block may be easily computed along with the inverse as a part of either variant of Strassen's inverse algorithm, as follows. First note that

$$\begin{bmatrix} A_{11}^{-1} & 0 \\ -A_{21}A_{11}^{-1} & I \end{bmatrix} \begin{bmatrix} A_{11} & A_{12} \\ A_{21} & A_{22} \end{bmatrix} = \begin{bmatrix} I & -A_{11}^{-1}A_{12} \\ 0 & A_{22} - A_{21}A_{11}^{-1}A_{12} \end{bmatrix}$$

As a result, one can calculate

$$\det(A_{11}^{-1}) \det \begin{bmatrix} A_{11} & A_{12} \\ A_{21} & A_{22} \end{bmatrix} = \det(A_{22} - A_{21}A_{11}^{-1}A_{12})$$

Thus it follows that

$$\det \begin{bmatrix} A_{11} & A_{12} \\ A_{21} & A_{22} \end{bmatrix} = \det(A_{22} - A_{21}A_{11}^{-1}A_{12}) \det(A_{11})$$

By a happy coincidence, the two matrices indicated in the last line are exactly equal (except for sign) to the two matrices whose inverses are computed in the first variant of the Strassen inverse algorithm (see the formulas for P_1 and P_6). A similar result holds for the second variant. The determinant of the $n/2 \times n/2$ block can be calculated by recursive application of this same procedure.

At the bottom level of recursion, Cray's MINV can be used to obtain both the inverse and determinant, since calculation of the determinant of a 128×128 or smaller block does not overwhelm the machine precision. One way to avoid floating-point overflow in the recursive calculation of larger determinants is to take the square root of the product of the determinants before passing the result to a higher level.

While the determinant is for most problems a satisfactory measure of condition, other easily computed statistics can also be used. For example, a simple enhancement of the determinant calculation is to normalize it by the maximum entry of the block, or by the sum of the absolute values of the entires. This prevents such pathologies as a block consisting of a small constant times the identity being rejected because its determinant is small.

Employing Newton Iterations to Enhance Precision

The precision of the results may be further enhanced by employing matrix Newton iterations. A quadratic Newton iteration is defined as

$$X_{k+1} = (2I_n - X_k A)X_k$$

where X_k is an approximation to the inverse of A. It can be easily shown that for suitable choices of a starting matrix X_0, the iterates X_k converge quadratically to A (Pan and Reif 1985). This means that each iteration approximately doubles the number of correct digits in the entries of X_k. Higher order Newton iterations can also be defined that exhibit m-th order convergence (Ferguson 1987). In the following, however, quadratic Newton iterations will be implied.

One very attractive feature of matrix Newton iterations is that they are massively parallelizable, since they involve only matrix multiplications and matrix subtractions. The matrix multiplications can of course be efficiently performed using Strassen's algorithm. However, the total cost of computation is quite high. One Newton iteration applied to a full-sized matrix alone requires twice the number of floating-point operations as is normally required to compute the inverse using a classical technique such as Gauss-Jordan elimination. Nonetheless, its suitability for parallel processing may well overcome this disadvantage on a massively parallel system.

There are several ways that Newton iterations can be employed in conjunction with Strassen's inversion algorithm. One is to simply apply one Newton iteration to the final result of a pivoted Strassen scheme. Another is to apply a Newton iteration to the result at each level of recursion except the highest level. As it turns out, this increases the total computational requirement only fractionally, yet it significantly increases the accuracy of the result. Finally, one can apply a Newton iteration to each level of recursion including the highest level.

Tables 2 and 3 contain detailed results of Cray-2 runs employing the above schemes. The column headed "MINC" contains results for Cray's MINV, with the modifications described above (i.e. no determinant calculation, and the input matrix is copied to an array with an odd first dimension before referencing MINV). MINS is a "no-frills" implementation of Strassen's basic matrix inverse algorithm. MINX is the pivoted version, employing both variants of the Strassen algorithm and determinant calculations. MINY in addition employs one Newton iteration at each level of recursion (except the highest level) to refine the accuracy of the intermediate results. MINZ also employs a Newton iteration at the highest level. As before, the CPU times are the means of the run times (in seconds) of ten trials, and the error statistics are the geometric means of the RMS errors of the ten trials.

It can be seen from the table that both MINS and MINX have faster run times than MINC. Even MINY, which employs Newton iterations at all levels except the highest, still is only slightly slower than MINC. MINZ requires more than twice as much CPU time (on a single processor) as MINC. The accuracy statistics, however, indicate a steady progression of improvement among the four new schemes. MINY is almost as good as MINC, and MINZ appears to be on a par with or slightly better than MINC.

Solution of a Single Set of Linear Equations

One objection often raised in the discussion of matrix inversion is that most applications of matrix techniques only require the solution of a single set of linear equations. For this case standard reduction methods can produce the solution in about one third the time required for a full matrix inversion followed by matrix-vector multiplication.

However, even this problem can be efficiently solved by the application of the above techniques. Let $Ax = b$ denote a set of linear equations. Let $A_{11}, A_{12}, A_{21}, A_{22}$ be the four half-sized sections of A, and let x_1, x_2, b_1, b_2 be corresponding halves of x and b. Then the system

Matrix	Cray Library		Strassen		Time	Error
Size	CPU Time	Error	CPU Time	Error	Ratio	Ratio
128	0.0214	1.50E-13	0.0231	1.50E-13	0.926	1.00E 0
200	0.0796	2.87E-13	0.0652	4.58E-11	1.221	6.26E-3
256	0.1373	1.69E-13	0.1208	6.28E-12	1.137	2.69E-2
400	0.5394	3.37E-13	0.4372	3.95E-10	1.234	8.53E-4
512	1.0498	3.91E-13	0.7866	3.68E-09	1.335	1.06E-4
800	3.8273	9.46E-13	2.9879	6.87E-09	1.281	1.38E-4
1024	8.1224	8.55E-13	5.5440	1.40E-07	1.465	6.10E-6
1600	30.0079	1.67E-12	22.0779	1.53E-07	1.359	1.10E-5
2048	62.0103	1.52E-12	39.9997	3.59E-07	1.550	4.24E-6

Table 1: Cray-2 Strassen Algorithm Performance Results

Size	MINC	MINS	MINX	MINY	MINZ
128	0.0214	0.0231	0.0205	0.0216	0.0223
200	0.0796	0.0652	0.0748	0.0739	0.1709
256	0.1373	0.1208	0.1315	0.1377	0.3159
400	0.5394	0.4372	0.5060	0.6969	1.4261
512	1.0498	0.7866	0.9227	1.3203	2.5881
800	3.8273	2.9879	3.6127	5.7284	10.7166
1024	8.1224	5.5440	6.6607	10.5752	19.6775
1600	30.0079	22.0779	25.9482	43.1163	78.9089
2048	62.0103	39.9997	47.8864	79.4194	146.5576

Table 2: Cray-2 CPU Times for the Five Algorithms

Size	MINC	MINS	MINX	MINY	MINZ
128	1.497E-13	1.497E-13	1.497E-13	1.497E-13	1.497E-13
200	2.869E-13	4.584E-11	8.341E-12	8.341E-12	1.192E-13
256	1.687E-13	6.277E-12	6.503E-12	6.503E-12	6.253E-14
400	3.371E-13	3.952E-10	1.085E-10	1.769E-11	1.944E-13
512	3.914E-13	3.679E-09	1.082E-10	1.217E-11	1.964E-13
800	9.462E-13	6.870E-09	4.315E-09	2.757E-10	7.626E-13
1024	8.551E-13	1.402E-07	4.677E-09	9.911E-11	6.030E-13
1600	1.674E-12	1.529E-07	7.343E-08	8.913E-10	1.937E-12
2048	1.522E-12	3.587E-07	5.280E-08	1.778E-09	1.535E-12

Table 3: Cray-2 Error Statistics for the Five Algorithms

may be solved as follows:

$$\begin{aligned} A_{11}x_1 + A_{12}x_2 &= b_1 \\ A_{21}x_1 + A_{22}x_2 &= b_2 \\ x_1 &= A_{11}^{-1}(b_1 - A_{12}x_2) \\ (A_{22} - A_{21}A_{11}^{-1}A_{12})x_2 &= b_2 - A_{21}A_{11}^{-1}b_1 \end{aligned}$$

and this system may be solved by recursively applying the same algorithm. Once x_2 is obtained, x_1 can be computed from the third line. Note that at a given level of recursion, the only items that have significant cost are the two matrix multiplications and one matrix inversion in the left-hand side of the last line. These operations may be efficiently performed by applying Strassen's matrix multiplication algorithm and one of the matrix inversion algorithms discussed above. The expression on the right hand side of the last line has virtually no cost for large n, since its only operations are one matrix subtraction and one matrix-vector multiplication. Similarly, the cost of computing x_1 once x_2 is obtained is insignificant when n is large. The overall cost of solving a linear system using this method is only slightly more than one third of the cost of inverting the full-sized matrix.

Conclusion

Four variations of Strassen's matrix inversion have been described, each of which is highly suited for massively parallel computation. Each of the four has different CPU time/accuracy characteristics. They range from a routine that is 55% faster than traditional methods, even on a one-processor system, to a routine that achieves excellent numerical stability in addition to retaining its suitability for massively parallel computation. These methods can also be applied to obtain an efficient solution of a single linear system.

There are obviously many more combinations of these techniques, some of which have been suggested in this paper. Higher order Newton iterations could also be explored, although it did not appear that the higher order methods would be cost-effective for the variations tried in this study.

Due to the very high level of parallelism inherent in these algorithms, it is believed that they will be particularly effective on highly parallel systems. Clearly the only way to decide such issues is to try such techniques on highly parallel systems and compare them with conventional matrix techniques. It is hoped that some parallel experiments of this sort can be performed during the next year.

REFERENCES

1. Bailey, David H., "Extra-High Speed Matrix Multiplication on the Cray-2", *SIAM Journal on Scientific and Statistical Computing*, to appear, manuscript dated September 1987.

2. Coppersmith, D., and Winograd, S., "Matrix Multiplication via Arithmetic Theory", *19th ACM Symposium on Theory of Computing*, 1987, p. 1 - 6.

3. Dongarra, Jack J., "Performance of Various Computers Using Standard Linear Equations Software in a Fortran Environment", Argonne Technical Memorandum No. 23, October 27, 1987.

4. Ferguson, H.R.P., Bailey, D.H., and Galway, W.F., "A Numerically Stable, High-Precision, Parallelizable Matrix Inversion Algorithm", manuscript dated January 1987.

5. Gentleman, W. Morven, "Some Complexity Results for Matrix Computations on Parallel Processors", *Journal of the ACM*, Vol. 25 (1978), p. 112-115.

6. Gentleman, W. Morven, private communication, March 1987.

7. Kreczmar, A., "On Memory Requirements of Strassen Algorithms", in *Algorithms and Complexity: New Directions and Recent Results*, J. F. Traub, ed., Academic Press, New York, 1976.

8. Kronsjo, Lydia, *Computational Complexity of Sequential and Parallel Algorithms*, John Wiley, 1985.

9. Pan, V., "New Fast Algorithms for Matrix Operations", *SIAM Journal on Computing*, Vol. 9 (1980), p. 321-342.

10. Pan, V., "How Can We Speed Up Matrix Multiplication?", *SIAM Review*, 26 (1984), p. 393-415.

11. Pan, V., and Reif, J., "Efficient Parallel Solution of Linear Systems", *ACM Symposium on Theory of Computing*, May 1985.

12. Press, W.H., Flannery, B.P., Teukolsky, S.A., and Vetterling, W.T., *Numerical Recipes*, Cambridge University Press, New York, 1986.

13. Strassen, V., "Gaussian Elimination Is Not Optimal", *Numerical Mathematics*, Vol. 13 (1969), p. 354-356.

On High-Speed Computing with a Programmable Linear Array*

PeiZong Lee and Zvi M. Kedem

Computer Science Department
Courant Institute of Mathematical Sciences
New York University
251 Mercer Street
New York, NY 10012-1185

Abstract— It has been observed by many researchers that systolic arrays are very suitable for certain high-speed computations. In this paper, using a formal methodology, a single simple programmable linear systolic array capable of solving large number of problems drawn from a variety of applications is designed. The methodology is applicable to problems solvable by sequential algorithms that can be specified as nested for loops of arbitrary depth. The algorithms of this form that can be computed on the array presented in this paper include 25 algorithms dealing with signal and image processing, algebraic computations, matrix arithmetic, pattern matching, database operations, sorting, and transitive closure. Assuming bounded I/O, for 18 of those algorithms the time and storage complexities are optimal, and therefore no improvement can be expected by utilizing dedicated special purpose linear systolic arrays designed for individual algorithms.

Index Terms— Parallel processing, programmable systolic array, VLSI, signal and image processing, algebraic computations, matrix arithmetic, pattern matching, database operations, sorting, and transitive closure, nested loop algorithms, algorithm transformations.

1 Introduction

It is the goal of this paper to present a single high-speed linear array programmable systolic computer capable of performing a large number of basic scientific computations. Specifically we will deal with algorithms that can be described as nested for loops.

Systolic arrays were used before in order to solve critical problems much faster than that achievable by standard architecture computers. As an example, we refer the reader to the description of the Warp computer [1] designed at CMU. It consisted of ten cells and for its target applications, such as signal processing, it achieved speedups of several hundreds in comparison to a VAX 11/780 class computer.

It is of interest that many of time consuming scientific algorithms are structured as nested loops, which are inherently regularly structured. Lamport [14], Banerjee *et al.* [2], and other researchers have mapped them into general-purpose multiprocessor system. However, such systems required complicated control units and optimized schemes for allocation of machine resources.

Kung [9] [10] [11], Moldovan [19], and others mapped such algorithms onto special-purpose systolic arrays. A systolic array is a special-purpose parallel device, made out of a few simple processing-element (PE) types whose interconnection pattern exhibits regularity and locality and is especially suitable for VLSI implementation. Several array structures have been proposed, including linear arrays, mesh-connected arrays, and hexagonal arrays. In a typical application, such arrays would be attached as peripheral devices to a host computer which inserts input values into them and extracts output values from them [11]. For systolic algorithms, consult H.T. Kung, Guibas, Thompson, Hwang and Chen, Mead and Conway, Ullman, Kuhn, S.Y. Kung, Ramakrishnan *et al.*, and Moldovan: [10] [11] [5] [6] [7] [18] [24] [8] [13] [23] [19] [20].

However, many researchers [6] [22] [15] [21] approached each target application in isolation. The systolic computers they designed were generally very efficient; however, they were limited to a narrow set of applications. Thus the high design and fabrication costs could not be easily amortized. Furthermore, to solve a wide range of problems one may require to connect several systolic devices of different capabilities to the host computer.

It is our goal to present a programmable linear array that can solve many problems as efficiently as previously designed linear arrays that were specifically targeted to a single application only. The problems we will solve using this array on domain from signal and image processing, algebraic and matrix application, database operations and others. A theoretical method used to design linear arrays was developed by the authors in [17]. That paper presents formal necessary and sufficient conditions for correct implementation of nested for loop algorithms on linear systolic arrays. Using those conditions, we present in this paper a design of a PE whose communication capabilities form a superset of those required by each individual application, as those are completely characterized by the conditions stated in [17].

It is important to note that the method allows construction of PEs with constant number of registers and thus the array is modularly extensible. Furthermore, if the problem size is large with respect to the array, the computation can be partitioned.

As we will show later, for many applications the computation of our programmable linear array is of provably optimal complexity. Thus it cannot be surpassed by special purpose devices targeted to a single application only. This makes it especially attractive when high-speed computation is a critical requirement.

Although this paper deals with specific set of problems we choose as a target set of applications, the method can be used to produce linear arrays solving certain other target applications when the original sequential algorithm can be stated as nested for loops. Therefore, we describe, but not in complete detail and formalism, our methodology. The interested reader is referred to our fundamental results as stated in [17].

The rest of this paper is organized as follows. In Section 2 we demonstrate our methodology by synthesizing a longest common subsequence algorithm. In addition, we introduce the classification of data streams which allows us to formulate conditions on the target linear array. In Section 3 we briefly discuss the necessary and sufficient conditions to transform nested loop algorithms onto linear arrays which were introduced by our previous paper [17]. In Section 4 we design a programmable processor element (PE) which can be used to build a programmable linear array. This linear array can evaluate 25 important nested for loop algorithms. We also briefly discuss two other designs. In Section 5 we discuss the partitioning of computations on our linear array. Finally, some concluding remarks are given in Section 6.

2 A running example

To introduce the concepts used by us in designing a general purpose linear array, we will use a specific example, that of computing the length of the longest common subsequence of two sequences. The treatment of this example, based on the theoretical results of [17], will also provide the reader with the intuition helpful in understanding the methodology.

In [17], we considered the problem of synthesizing linear systolic arrays from depth p nested loop algorithms. That approach was based on Lamport's hyperplane method [14]. Banerjee *al.*

*This work was partially supported by the Office of Naval Research under the contract N00014-85-K-0046.

[2] and Moldovan [19] also used hyperplane method. However, Lamport and Banerjee *et al.* transformed p nested loop algorithms onto an MIMD (Multiple Instructions and Multiple Data) machine. Moldovan transformed p nested loop algorithms to 1-D time hyperplane and $(p-1)$-D space hyperplane $(p-1)$-D systolic arrays, which did not result in linear arrays unless $p = 2$. In contrast, we restricted ourselves to using linear arrays only, which are especially attractive in practice. Thus, we transformed p nested loop algorithms to 1-D time hyperplane and 1-D space hyperplane (1-D) (linear) systolic arrays.

In this section, we describe our method, as applied to the example problem. We thus examine the longest common subsequence algorithm [25] that is structured as *2* nested for loops.

```
Input : Arrays A[1..m] and B[1..n].
Output: Matrix C[1..m,1..n], where C[i,j] = the length of
    the longest common subsequence of A[1..i] and B[1..j].
    for i = 1 to m
        for j = 1 to n
            if A[i] = B[j]
            then C[i,j] := C[i-1,j-1] + 1
            else C[i,j] := max{C[i,j-1], C[i-1,j]}
        end_for
    end_for
```

There is one executable statement, which contains six tokens (i.e. $A[i]$, $B[j]$, $C[i-1,j-1]$, $C[i,j-1]$, $C[i-1,j]$, and $C[i,j]$) in the loop body. (We will write "token" for an entry of an array and "variable" for the name of the array, if this does not result in confusion.) The loop index set is $I^2 = \{(i,j)^t | 1 \leq i \leq m, 1 \leq j \leq n\}$.

Our goal is to transform this *2* nested loop algorithm into a 1-D time hyperplane and 1-D space hyperplane linear array algorithm $(\mathbf{H}, \mathbf{S})$, where $\mathbf{H} = (h_1, h_2)$ and $\mathbf{S} = (s_1, s_2)$ are vectors. (The vectors are of length two as the original algorithm consisted of *2* nested loops.) The vectors are used to "distribute" the indices in time and location (space). Given an index $(i,j)^t$, the mapping transforms the indices $\begin{pmatrix} \mathbf{H} \\ \mathbf{S} \end{pmatrix} (i,j)^t = \begin{pmatrix} h_1 i + h_2 j \\ s_1 i + s_2 j \end{pmatrix} = \begin{pmatrix} t \\ l \end{pmatrix}$, where t and l specify the time and the location of index $(i,j)^t$ iteration to be executed.

$h_1 x_1 + h_2 x_2 = d$ for various values of d define a family of hyperplanes. Thus $\mathbf{H}$ partitions indices $(i,j)^t \in I^2$ so that they lie on a family of parallel hyperplanes, and such that all the indices lying on one hyperplane can be executed simultaneously. Similarly, $s_1 x_1 + s_2 x_2 = e$ for various values of e define a family of hyperplanes. $\mathbf{S}$ partitions indices $(i,j)^t \in I^2$ so that they lie on a family of parallel hyperplanes, and such that all indices lying on one hyperplane are mapped to the same PE which will execute the loop body for these indices.

We will frequently write "hyperplane" for a family of parallel hyperplanes, the vector defining them, or an individual hyperplane in the family, if this does not result in confusion. Our method consists of several steps.

2.1 Data-dependence vectors, data streams, and data links

To proceed, we label each token in the loop with an index $(i_1, i_2)^t$. Such labeling was introduced by Lamport [14] and was also used by Banerjee *et al.* [2] and Moldovan [19].

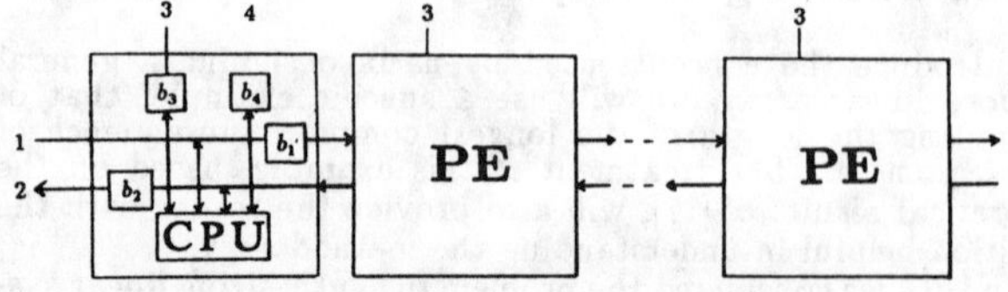

Fig. 1. A linear array comprised of PEs. There are four types of data links. b_1, b_2, b_3, and b_4 are lengths of the buffers.

As the consequence, the longest common subsequence algorithm is:

```
Input : Arrays A[1..m] and B[1..n].
Output: Matrix C[1..m,1..n], where C[i,j] = the length of
    the longest common subsequence of A[1..i] and B[1..j].
    for i = 1 to m
        for j = 1 to n
1.          A^(i,j)[i] := A^(i,j-1)[i];
2.          B^(i,j)[j] := B^(i-1,j)[j];
3.          C^(i,j)[i-1,j-1] := C^(i-1,j-1)[i-1,j-1];
4.          C^(i,j)[i,j-1] := C^(i,j-1)[i,j-1];
5.          C^(i,j)[i-1,j] := C^(i-1,j)[i-1,j];
6.          C^(i,j)[i,j] := C^(i,j)[i,j];
7.          if A^(i,j)[i] = B^(i,j)[j]
            then C^(i,j)[i,j] := C^(i,j)[i-1,j-1] + 1
            else C^(i,j)[i,j] := max{C^(i,j)[i,j-1], C^(i,j)[i-1,j]}
        end_for
    end_for
```

After labeling, the number of statements in the loop body increases. However, all these additional statements are trivial assignment statements as they are used only for defining the data-dependence vectors ("data-dependence vector" was also introduced by Lamport [14] and used by Banerjee *et al.* and Moldovan). A *data-dependence vector* of a variable can be viewed as difference of indices where a token of that variable is used and where that token was generated.

We now examine these "new" assignment statements. If the token is on the left-hand-side of :=, it means that the token is regenerated in index $(i_1, i_2)^t$; if the token is on the right-hand-side of :=, it means that the token was previously generated in index $(i_1, i_2)^t$. In line 1, $A^{(i,j)}[i]$ means that $A[i]$ is regenerated in step $(i,j)^t$ and $A^{(i,j-1)}[i]$ means that $A[i]$ was previously generated in step $(i,j-1)^t$ and is used in step $(i,j)^t$. Similarly, for B and C in lines 2-6. The original loop's body, line 7 can then be executed following these "bookkeeping" operations: **if** $A^{(i,j)}[i] = B^{(i,j)}[j]$ **then** $C^{(i,j)}[i,j] := C^{(i,j)}[i-1,j-1]+1$ **else** $C^{(i,j)}[i,j] := \max\{C^{(i,j)}[i,j-1], C^{(i,j)}[i-1,j]\}$.

From lines 1 to 6, we get six data-dependence vectors,

$d_1 = (0,1)^t$ for $(A^{(i,j)}[i], A^{(i,j-1)}[i])$,
$d_2 = (1,0)^t$ for $(B^{(i,j)}[j], B^{(i-1,j)}[j])$,
$d_3 = (1,1)^t$ for $(C^{(i,j)}[i-1,j-1], C^{(i-1,j-1)}[i-1,j-1])$,
$d_4 = (0,1)^t$ for $(C^{(i,j)}[i,j-1], C^{(i,j-1)}[i,j-1])$,
$d_5 = (1,0)^t$ for $(C^{(i,j)}[i-1,j], C^{(i-1,j)}[i-1,j])$, and
$d_6 = (0,0)^t$ for $(C^{(i,j)}[i,j], C^{(i,j)}[i,j])$.

We will say that d_1 is *with A*, d_2 is with B, d_3, d_4, d_5, and d_6 are with C.

We wish to map this algorithm onto a linear array. We do not provide here a formal definition of a linear array, but refer the reader to a typical array shown in Fig. 1. It will be used to describe important component present in linear arrays we will construct. (It is not supposed to solve the problem we are discussing, but to serve as an informal definition.)

The array consists of a sequence of PEs, which are connected by several data links, which could be of four types. Each of these types is present in Fig. 1. There are four types of data links. A data link of type 1 "flows" from left to right, a data link of type 2 flows from right to left, a data link of type 3 is "fixed" in a PE and needs an I/O port for transferring tokens between the host computer and the PE, a data link of type 4 is also fixed in a PE; however, it does not need an I/O port because it does not need to transfer tokens between host computer as it is used for storage of temporary data. In addition, each data link may or may not have a buffer, which consists of registers. The lengths of the buffers for different data links may be different.

Data streams, which consist of tokens, pass through these data links. Tokens are used and regenerated (modified or not modified) in PEs according to the computation specified. A linear array algorithm manages the data streams so that tokens' results are the same as those in the original sequential algorithm.

We now relate data-dependence vectors of the sequential algorithm to data streams of the systolic array. This is a fundamental step in the development of a correct systolic array implementation. Of course, there are no data streams in the sequential algorithm, because it needs only one processor and the data is stored in random access memory. However, systolic arrays must deal with data streams. This follows from the obvious fact that the loop indices are mapped to PEs, and therefore, different loop indices may be mapped to different PEs.

We now consider how to handle tokens traveling between PEs. The general strategy will be to dedicate a data link to tokens associated with a single specific data-dependence vector.

Consider the six tokens $A[i]$, $B[j]$, $C[i-1,j-1]$, $C[i,j-1]$, $C[i-1,j]$, and $C[i,j]$ in the loop body for loop index $(i,j)^t$. We will consider $A[i]$ as a typical case. $A[i]$ was generated in index $(i,j)^t - d_1 = (i,j-1)^t$. As we mentioned above, indices $(i,j-1)^t$ and $(i,j)^t$ could be assigned to different PEs, say PE_a and PE_b. Therefore, we must arrange so that $A[i]$ can move from PE_a to PE_b. We can assign $A[i]$ which is with d_1 to utilize data link 1 (of type not yet determined), connecting $PE_a, PE_{a+1}, \ldots, PE_b$. In the special case where $PE_a = PE_b$, we assign a local register in PE_a (PE_b) to store $A[i]$. To be able to use the concept of data link in this case too, we will say that if the token is not moving, then data link 1 consists of local registers.

Similarly, $B[j], C[i-1,j-1], C[i,j-1], C[i-1,j]$, and $C[i,j]$ are assigned to use data links 2-6, respectively. Therefore, data link i naturally corresponds to data-dependence vector d_i for $1 \leq i \leq 6$ in our example. It will be convenient to refer to the tokens using data line i as *data stream* i.

We now describe the relation among variables, data dependence vectors, data links, and data streams. If a variable V is with some number $\delta(V)$ data-dependence vectors, we will dedicate $\delta(V)$ links to it. In effect, $\delta(V)$ copies of that variable will be "traveling" through the array, each in a dedicated data link. A variable, in general, is a vector, a matrix, or a higher dimensional array and therefore may consist of many "atomic" entries. In each data link dedicated to the variable, all those entries will appear during the execution of the algorithm. Formally, we will say that several *data streams* (one per data link) are associated with each variable and each data stream consists of all the *tokens* (individual atomic entries) of the variable.

2.2 Zero-One-Infinite

We now need to classify data streams in order to characterize the behavior of the tokens. In [17] we formally classified data-dependence vectors for some restricted cases and then used that classification to prove properties of the corresponding data streams. As in this paper our focus of interest is on the structure of the systolic array, we will consider data streams directly. This will result in slightly less formal, but still precise development, which lends itself to and easier exposition. Furthermore, we are discussing in this paper a wider class of applications, and therefore our treatment here is more general than in [17].

We first present a classification, and then will apply it immediately to our example. Consider some data dependence vector d_i with some variable X. Let x be any token of data stream i corresponding to d_i. Then based on the behavior of tokens of the data stream i, we can classify it as being of one of the following three types:

type 1 : $d_i = \vec{0}$. The token x is either generated only once in data stream i but will not be used in data stream i (but may be used in another data stream) or the token x is used only once in data stream i but is not generated in any data stream (it was read as an input value).

type 2 : $d_i \neq \vec{0}$ and the token x is generated once only in data stream i (say in $\bar{I} - d_i \in I^p$) and is used once only in data stream i (say in $\bar{I} \in I^p$).

type 3 : $d_i \neq \vec{0}$ and the token x is used (and regenerated) in data stream i in all indices of I^p of the form $\bar{I} + md_i$ for some $\bar{I} \in I^p$ and all integers m.

Lemma 1 *(Zero-One-Infinite): The three types are exhaustive, that is, no other case is possible.* □

We will say that d_6 is of type 1, because $C[i,j]$ is generated in index $(i,j)^t$ only. We will say that d_3 is of type 2, because in the original algorithm $C[i-1,j-1]$ is on the right-hand-side of := and its array index entry is not equal to that of the token $C[i,j]$, which is on the left-hand-side of :=. For example, $[i-1,j-1] \neq [i,j]$ for $C[i-1,j-1]$ and $C[i,j]$. Similarly, d_4 and d_5 are of type 2. We will say that d_1 is of type 3, because $A[i]$ is used (and regenerated) in all indices of I^2 of the form $\bar{I} + md_i$ for some $\bar{I} \in I^2$ and all integer m. Similarly, d_2 is of type 3.

Let us elaborate on the above. $A[i]$ (with d_1) is in data stream 1 of type 3. It will be used and regenerated in all indices of I^2 of the form $\bar{I} + md_1$ for some $\bar{I} \in I^2$ and all integer m. Similarly for $B[j]$ in data stream 2.

$C[i-1,j-1]$ (with d_3) is in data stream 3 of type 2. It is generated once only in $(i-1,j-1)^t$ and is used once only in $(i,j)^t$. Thus, $C[i-1,j-1]$ can be destroyed after it was used in index (i,j). If we further examine the execution in index step $(i-1,j-1)$, $C[i-1,j-1]$ was originally not created in data link 3. In fact, $C[i-1,j-1]$ was a copy of another token $C[i-1,j-1]$ generated in data stream 6. (The copying was done in a PE.) Therefore, we treat data stream 3 as a temporary data stream. Similarly, for tokens $C[i,j-1]$ and $C[i-1,j]$ in data links 4 and 5.

The above is related to the behavior of $C[i,j]$ (with d_6) in data stream 6 of type 1. The token is generated in data stream 6 but never used again in that data stream. Its value, however, is not lost but is copied as input value for other data streams. For example, $C[i,j]$ is copied to data links 3, 4, and 5 (corresponding to data streams 3, 4, and 5).

We further elaborate on the importance and usefulness of data streams' classification.

1. It allows us to understand the tokens' behavior in data streams. For example, tokens in data stream of type 3 can not be destroyed during computation. However, tokens in data stream of type 2 can be destroyed after they are used once.

2. It points out that output result will not be in the data stream of type 2.

3. It allows us to determine whether or not two tokens could collide in data links as was formally studied in [17].

4. It determines whether we can use a bounded (constant) I/O linear array to implement a nested loop algorithm or not. For example, if some $d_i = \vec{0}$, in the resulting array each PE will need an I/O port for transferring tokens with the host computer. In that case, the data stream of type 1 corresponding to d_i uses data link of type 3 (see Fig. 1). As the consequence, the total number of I/O ports cannot be constant.

2.3 The example continued

We now continue with our example. We say that index I_2 *depends* on index I_1 if and only if $I_2 = I_1 + m_1d_1 + m_2d_2 + m_3d_3 + m_4d_4 + m_5d_5$ for $m_i \geq 0$ and $1 \leq i \leq 5$ and at least one of m_i is positive. (There is no dependency for $d_6 = \vec{0}$.) These relationships can be described by a data-dependence graph as shown in Fig. 2.

As stated at the beginning of Section 2, we partition indices $(i,j)^t \in I^2$ by a 1-D time hyperplane $\mathbf{H}$ and a 1-D space hyperplane $\mathbf{S}$ so that all the indices lying on one hyperplane of $\mathbf{H}$ can be executed simultaneously and all the indices lying on one hyperplane of $\mathbf{S}$ are mapped to the same PE for execution.

In order to preserve the data-dependence relations, $\mathbf{H}d_i > 0$ must be true for all data-dependence vectors d_i. (This was proved by Lamport [14].) In order to prevent two different indices $I_1, I_2 \in I^2$ from being mapped to the same PE at the same time, $\mathbf{S}I_1 \neq \mathbf{S}I_2$ or $\mathbf{H}I_1 \neq \mathbf{H}I_2$. If $p = 2$ (depth *2* nested for loops), this condition reduces to the linear independence of $\mathbf{H}$ and $\mathbf{S}$. If $p > 2$ this reduction does not hold.

To further exhibit the interaction between the algorithm and candidate target systolic arrays, we will discuss several mappings $(\mathbf{H},\mathbf{S})$ for our example of the longest common subsequence. They will all satisfy the two conditions in the previous paragraph. We will see that additional conditions need to be introduced.

If we let $\mathbf{H} = (1,2)$ and $\mathbf{S} = (1,1)$, the time-location relation is shown in Fig. 3. (The dashed lines labeled with $i + 2j = d$ are the hyperplanes containing indices executed at a single time instance. The dashed lines labeled with $i + j = e$ are the hyperplanes containing indices executed at a single PE. Similar notation will be used in Figs. 4, 5, and 6.) Although this mapping preserves the data-dependence relations and $\mathbf{H}$ and $\mathbf{S}$ are linearly independent, $(\mathbf{H}, \mathbf{S})$ is not a feasible mapping. Let us examine why. Consider the data token $C[2,2]$ in data stream 3. It was generated in index $(2,2)^t$ in PE_4 at time instance 6 and it was used in index $(3,3)^t$ in PE_6 at time instance 9. Therefore, $C[2,2]$ spends $\frac{9-6}{6-4} = 1.5$ time units traveling through each PE. This is not possible, as each token can spend only an integer time units traveling through a PE.

If we let $\mathbf{H} = (1,1)$ and $\mathbf{S} = (1,0)$, the time-location relation is shown in Fig. 4. This mapping also preserves the data-dependence relations and $\mathbf{H}$ and $\mathbf{S}$ are linearly independent. In contrast with the previous mapping, this is a correct mapping (as $\mathbf{H}$ and $\mathbf{S}$ satisfy the necessary and sufficient constraint listed in Theorem 2 in Section 3). We now analyze how many data links of type 3 are needed (the "type" of data links was introduced in Subsection 2.1). We consider the data-dependence vectors d_1 and d_6. $d_1 = (0,1)^t$ is with A (which is an input variable and thus needs to be transferred from the host computer), and $\mathbf{S}d_1 = (1,0)(0,1)^t = 0$. Therefore tokens of A do not move in the array and data stream 1 is fixed in PEs. Thus we need a data link of type 3 (with an I/O port in each PE) for it. $d_6 = (0,0)^t$, and as we discussed in Section 2.2, it will also require a data link of type 3 (with an I/O port in each PE). We try to minimize the number of I/O ports and therefore would like to minimize the number of links of type 3. In fact we will be able to get by with a single link of type 3 for our programmable array which solves many problems in addition to the longest common subsequence problem.

If we let $\mathbf{H} = (1,1)$ and $\mathbf{S} = (1,-1)$ then the time-location relation is shown in Fig. 5. This is a correct mapping (as $\mathbf{H}$ and $\mathbf{S}$ satisfy the necessary and sufficient constraint listed in Theorem 2). However, this mapping requires data links of both type 1 and type 2. For the purpose of partitioning, as explained in Section 5, we prefer to not have data links of both types. This leads us to prefer another mapping, which we specify in the next paragraph.

If we let $\mathbf{H} = (1,3)$ and $\mathbf{S} = (1,1)$, the time-location relation is shown in Fig. 6. This is a correct mapping (as $\mathbf{H}$ and $\mathbf{S}$ satisfy the necessary and sufficient constraint listed in Theorem 2). The resulting linear array is shown in Fig. 7. As this is our preferred implementation, we will describe in greater detail.

The mapping maps index $(i,j)^t$ into $PE_{\mathbf{S}(i,j)^t} = PE_{i+j}$ and executes it at step $\mathbf{H}(i,j)^t = (i + 3j)$. We now describe the behavior of the resulting linear array:

1. Each PE has six data links, data links 1-5 of type 1 flow from left to right. Data link 6 of type 3, is fixed in PEs. The tokens of A are pipelined and enter into the linear array in data link 1. The tokens of B are pipelined and enter into the linear array in data link 2. The tokens of C (only one copy) are pipelined and enter into the linear array in data link 6. The tokens of C in data links 3-5 are intermediate results of data stream 6 in data link 6.

2. We now consider the speed of the data streams. Formal conditions will be given in Theorem 2 in next section. For now, we examine Fig. 7. The tokens of B in data stream 2 (and the tokens of C in data stream 5) flow at full speed, that is, there is no delay for the tokens of B in data link 2 (and of C in data link 5).

   The tokens of C in data stream 3 flow at half speed, that is, there is one unit time delay when a token enters a PE, or say, there is a delay buffer with one shift register for the data link 3 of C.

   The tokens of A in data stream 1 (and the tokens of C in data stream 4) flow at one third speed, that is, there are two units of time delay when a token enters a PE, or say, there is a delay buffer with two shift registers for the data link 1 of A (and for the data link 4 of C).

   The tokens of C in data link 6 are read one by one (at half speed) directly from the host computer into the PEs (initially, $C[i,j] = 0$ and we use a local register to store it), and write back to host computer after one unit time.

3. In each index execution, when the six tokens: $A[i]$ from data link 1, $B[j]$ from data link 2, $C[i-1,j-1]$ from data link 3, $C[i,j-1]$ from data link 4, $C[i-1,j]$ from data link 5, and $C[i,j]$ from data link 6 enter $PE_{\mathbf{S}(i,j)^t} = PE_{i+j}$ at time $\mathbf{H}(i,j)^t = i + 3j$; the PE executes the instruction **if** $A[i] = B[j]$ **then** $C[i,j] := C[i-1,j-1] + 1$ **else** $C[i,j] := \max\{C[i,j-1], C[i-1,j]\}$.

   The resulting token $C[i,j]$ is put on data link 6 and also copied onto data links 3-5.

In this example, we found a time hyperplane $\mathbf{H}$ and a space hyperplane $\mathbf{S}$ so that they map the longest common subsequence algorithm to linear array. In general, as we claimed earlier, the time hyperplane $\mathbf{H}$ and the space hyperplane $\mathbf{S}$ must satisfy certain constraints which we will state next.

3 Necessary and sufficient conditions

A correct linear array mapping $(\mathbf{H}, \mathbf{S})$ from a depth p nested loop algorithm to a linear array implementation must preserve the data-dependence relation, the right tokens must be in the right places at the right times, and no data tokens must collide in data links.

We now state constraints that a correct mapping must satisfy (for more details see [17]). Let I^p be the index set of a p nested loop algorithm. Consider three cases of data stream i, depending on the values of d_i and $\mathbf{S}d_i$.

1. $d_i = \vec{0}$ (data stream of type 1) :
In this case, tokens are stored in local registers; therefore, they will not collide in data links. Since they are stored in local registers, CPUs can get them when they are needed.

As a token in data stream i is used or generated only once in some index $\bar{I} \in I^p$, it will not be used or generated in data stream i again. Therefore, it has no dependency relation in data stream i.

2. $d_i \neq \vec{0}$ and $\mathbf{S}d_i = 0$ (data stream of type 2 or type 3) :
Similar to case 1, tokens are stored in local registers; therefore, they will not collide in data links. Since they are stored in local registers, CPUs can get them when they are needed. Unlike for case 1, a token in data stream i is used or generated more than once in different indices in I^p; therefore, linear array mappings must preserve data-dependence relation. Thus, $\mathbf{H}d_i > 0$ must be true.

3. $d_i \neq \vec{0}$ and $\mathbf{S}d_i \neq 0$ (data stream of type 2 or type 3) :
In [17], we characterized $(\mathbf{H}, \mathbf{S})$ and all d_i's in this case:

Theorem 2 : *A linear-array algorithm* $(\mathbf{H}, \mathbf{S})$ *maps a p nested loop algorithm correctly into a linear array if and only if it satisfies the following five conditions.*

1. $\mathbf{H}d_i > 0$.

2. If I_1 *and* I_2 *are two indices of* I^p *then*

$$\begin{pmatrix} \mathbf{H} \\ \mathbf{S} \end{pmatrix} (I_2 - I_1) \neq \begin{pmatrix} 0 \\ 0 \end{pmatrix}.$$

3. The number of shift registers in each PE for the data link i is $|\frac{\mathbf{H}d_i}{\mathbf{S}d_i}| - 1$.

4. If $\mathbf{S}d_i > 0$, *then data stream i flows from left to right and it will be fed into the linear array at* $PE_{\min\{\mathbf{S}I_1 | I_1 \in I^p\}}$. *If* $\mathbf{S}d_i < 0$, *then data stream flows from right to left and it will be fed into the linear array at* $PE_{\max\{\mathbf{S}I_2 | I_2 \in I^p\}}$.

5. If $(I_2 - I_1) \neq m d_i$ *for all integers m, then* $\mathbf{H}(I_2 - I_1)\mathbf{S}d_i \neq \mathbf{S}(I_2 - I_1)\mathbf{H}d_i$ □

Even though Theorem 2 is relevant only to case 3 above, the following Corollary describes the time and space complexity of the complete linear array implementation.

Corollary 3 :

1. *Total number of PEs is* $M = \max\{|\mathbf{S}(I_2 - I_1)| \mid I_1, I_2 \in I^p\} + 1$.
2. *Total execution time is* $T = O(\max\{|\mathbf{H}(I_2 - I_1)| \mid I_1, I_2 \in I^p\} + N)$, *where* $N = M(\sum_{i=1}^{K}(b_i + 1))$. □

We will say that $(\mathbf{H}, \mathbf{S})$ uses an *N-storage* linear array, where $N = M(\sum_{i=1}^{K}(b_i+1))$, because N is the sum of the total number of the delays in all data links. (That is, the sum of the total number of the local registers plus $M \cdot K$.)

Because of space limitations we had to omit many details, for which we refer the reader to the theoretical paper [17].

4 A programmable linear array

4.1 Application domain

In this section, we design a PE that we will use to build a programmable linear array. This programmable linear array can be used to solve 25 problems. The problems appear in the following applications:

Signal and image processing :
1. discrete Fourier transform (DFT),
2. finite impulse response filter (FIR),
3. convolution [18],
4. deconvolution [15].

Pattern matching :
5. string matching,
6. longest common subsequence,
7. correlation [4].

Algebraic computation :
8. polynomial multiplication,
9. polynomial division [10],
10. long multiplication for integer string,
11. long multiplication for binary number [3].

Sorting and transitive closure :
12. bubble sort [16],
13. transitive closure [5].

Relational database operations :
14. Cartesian product,
15. join operations [9].

Matrix arithmetic :
16. matrix vector multiplication,
17. matrix multiplication [18] [22] [17],
18. L-U decomposition,
19. matrix orthogonal triangularization,
20. inversion of non-singularly triangular matrix,
21. triangular linear system [6],
22. two dimensional tuple comparison [15],
23. matrix inversion,
24. linear system,
25. least square computation [11].

We can use our method as it is possible to specify programs to solve the above problems as *2* or *3* nested for loop algorithms.

4.2 A programmable PE

A programmable PE, which we will use, is illustrated in Fig. 8. As seen there, there are eight data links and one CPU. Links 1 through 6 flow from left to right. In addition, each of them has a pair of I/O ports to connect to the adjacent PEs. Links 1 and 2 have no shift registers, links 3 and 4 have one shift register, links 5 and 6 have two shift registers.

Links 7 and 8 are fixed in PEs. In addition, each link contains only one local register. Link 7 needs to transfer tokens between the host computer and the PE; therefore, it needs an I/O port. Link 8 needs not to transfer tokens with the host computer; therefore, it does not need I/O ports.

The CPU, which has enough computation ability to solve the above problems, can read input data directly from data links, compute some functions, and write computation results directly to data links.

4.3 Utilization of the PE to the problems of interest

In this subsection, we illustrate applications of the programmable linear array according to the implicit structures (data dependence relations) of the original sequential algorithms. For the above 25 problems, we first find their 25 p nested loop algorithms. Then we divide the first 22 algorithms into 7 groups depending on their multisets of data-dependence vectors, D_{Ag}, which we have found. The last three problems can be decomposed to problems in the previous 22 problems. Finally, for each group we devise linear array algorithms $(\mathbf{H}, \mathbf{S})$ that satisfy Theorem 2 in Section 3.

For each original p nested loop algorithm, if there are k data-dependence vectors, then there are k data links corresponding to them. For each group of algorithms, we will first list their data-dependence vectors, second list their corresponding data links of the data-dependence vectors, third list a linear array algorithm we use, fourth list time complexity of the linear array implementation, fifth list storage complexity of the linear array implementation (the "storage" is the total sum of the number of the local registers plus $M \cdot k$), sixth list the number of I/O ports needed for the linear array implementation. Finally, we list the members of the group. For uniform complexity specification, we assume for simplicity that all loop index variables range from 1 to n.

Structure 1 :
$D_{Ag} = ((0,1)^t, (1,0)^t, (0,1)^t, (1,0)^t)$.
Corresponding data links used : 1, 3, 2, 4.
Linear array algorithm : $\mathbf{H} = (2,1)$ and $\mathbf{S} = (1,1)$.
Time complexity : $O(n)$.
Storage complexity : $O(n)$.
Number of I/O ports needed : $O(1)$.
Problem solved :
1. discrete Fourier transformation (DFT).

Structure 2 :
$D_{Ag} = ((0,1)^t, (1,1)^t, (1,0)^t)$.
Corresponding data links used : 1, 3, 5.
Linear array algorithm : $\mathbf{H} = (3,1)$ and $\mathbf{S} = (1,1)$.
Time complexity : $O(n)$.
Storage complexity : $O(n)$.
Number of I/O ports needed : $O(1)$.
Problems solved :
2. finite impulse response (FIR) filters,
3. convolution,
4. deconvolution,
5. string matching,
7. correlation,
8. polynomial multiplication,
9. polynomial division.

Structure 3 :
$D_{Ag} = ((1,0)^t, (1,1)^t, (0,1)^t, (0,1)^t)$.
Corresponding data links used : 5, 3, 1, 2.
Linear array algorithm : $\mathbf{H} = (3,1)$ and $\mathbf{S} = (1,1)$.
Time complexity : $O(n)$.
Storage complexity : $O(n)$.
Number of I/O ports needed : $O(1)$.
Problems solved :
10. long multiplication for integer string,
11. long multiplication for binary number.

Structure 4 :
$D_{Ag} = ((1,0)^t, (0,1)^t)$.
Corresponding data links used : 8, 1.
Linear array algorithm : $\mathbf{H} = (1,1)$ and $\mathbf{S} = (0,1)$.
Time complexity : $O(n)$.
Storage complexity : $O(n)$.
Number of I/O ports needed : $O(1)$.
Problem solved :
12. bubble sort.

Structure 5 :
$D_{Ag} = ((1,0,0)^t, (0,1,0)^t, (0,0,1)^t)$.
Corresponding data links used : 3, 1, 5.
Linear array algorithm : $\mathbf{H} = (2\delta, 1, 3\tau)$ and $\mathbf{S} = (\delta, 1, \tau)$.
If problem size n is even then $\delta = n+1$ and $\tau = n$, otherwise, (n is odd) $\delta = n$ and $\tau = n+1$.
Time complexity : $O(n^2)$.
Storage complexity : $O(n^2)$.
Number of I/O ports needed : $O(1)$.
Problems solved :
13. transitive closure,
17. matrix multiplication,
18. L-U decomposition,
19. matrix orthogonal triangularization,
20. inversion of non-singularly triangular matrix,
22. two dimensional tuple comparison.

Structure 6 :
$D_{Ag} = ((0,1)^t, (1,0)^t, (1,1)^t, (0,1)^t, (1,0)^t, (0,0)^t)$.
Corresponding data links used : 5, 1, 3, 6, 2, 7.
Linear array algorithm : $\mathbf{H} = (1,3)$ and $\mathbf{S} = (1,1)$.
Time complexity : $O(n)$.
Storage complexity : $O(n)$.
Number of I/O ports needed : $O(n)$.
Problem solved :
6. longest common subsequence.

Structure 7 :
$D_{Ag} = ((0,1)^t, (1,0)^t, (0,0)^t)$.
Corresponding data links used : 1, 3, 7.
Linear array algorithm : $\mathbf{H} = (2,1)$ and $\mathbf{S} = (1,1)$.
Time complexity : $O(n)$.
Storage complexity : $O(n)$.
Number of I/O ports needed : $O(n)$.
Problems solved :
14. Cartesian product,
15. join operations,
16. matrix vector multiplication,
21. triangular linear system.

Although we only chose a specific linear array algorithm for each group, other linear array algorithms, which satisfy Theorem 2, can also be implemented on our programmable linear array.

The last three problems (problems 23, 24, and 25) can be decomposed to a sequence of the problems listed above. To solve 23. matrix inversion, $A^{-1} = (LU)^{-1} = U^{-1}L^{-1}$, we first do an L-U decomposition, then do inversions of two triangular matrices, and then do a matrix multiplication. To solve 24. linear system, we first do an L-U decomposition or matrix orthogonal triangularization, then we solve a triangular linear system. Finally, to solve 25. least square computation [11], we first do a matrix orthogonal triangularization, then we solve a triangular linear system.

We now analyze time and storage complexities of the above linear array implementations. Consider a general p nested loop algorithm for the set of problems listed above. The number of loop iterations is $O(n^p)$ ($|I^p| = O(n^p)$) and the execution time is $O(n^{p-1})$. We need $O(n^{p-1})$ storage locations. There are various way of deciding on the appropriate number of PEs. It is possible to use only $O(n)$ PEs, thus obtaining the optimal processor/time product of $O(n^p)$. This, however, requires storage of $O(n^{p-2})$ in each PE. Thus, if we want the array to be *modularly extensible*, that is for each PE to have constant amount of storage, we may actually prefer in practice to use $O(n^{p-1})$ PEs. Therefore, we consider here storage/time product (instead of using traditional processor/time product) to analyze the complexity.

For linear array algorithms of Structure 1-4 and 6-7, storage/time product is optimal, that is, storage $\times$ time $= O$(the number of loop iterations).

It is more complex to analyze the complexity results of linear array algorithms of Structure 5. Ramakrishnan and Varman [22] showed that it needs at least $\Omega(n^2)$ storage for matrix multiplication on any architecture. Therefore, the storage complexity of our linear array implementation for matrix multiplication is optimal. However, we can not show that the time complexity is optimal. Although in [17] we showed that $O(n^2)$ time is optimal in a bounded (constant) I/O linear array implementation, the linear array we propose here has $O(n)$ I/O ports (because each PE has one I/O ports for data link 7). However, we did not find any linear (systolic) array implementations whose time complexity is less than $\Omega(n^2)$.

4.4 Restrictions to bounded I/O

We can also design variants of programmable linear arrays depending on the special-purpose application domains we deal with. We conclude this section by mentioning two of the more interesting of such designs.

1. Consider the case where all the algorithms for the applications of interest fall in Structures 1-5 as listed in Subsection 4.3. This class of algorithms contains the algorithms to solve 18 problems numbered 1-5, 7-13, 17-20, and 22-23 in Subsection 4.1. Then we can design a programmable PE with data links 1-5 and 8 only. That is, data links 6 and 7 are not needed. Thus, we obtain a bounded I/O programmable linear array.

Linear array algorithms of this bounded I/O linear array implementations are the same as that in Subsection 4.3. Therefore, the complexity results are also the same as that in Subsection 4.3. Although it is beyond the scope of this paper, it can be shown that our linear array algorithms in this bounded I/O linear array implementation are both time optimal and storage optimal.

Let us sketch the argument. In [17], we showed that bounded I/O linear array implementations of algorithms in Structure 5 are both time optimal and storage optimal. We now briefly state the method we used. For the class of algorithms in Structure 5, we first proved the general result that time complexity is equal to storage complexity. For matrix multiplication, both time and storage complexity are $O(n^2)$.

As a matrix had n^2 input/output data and there was only a constant number (three) of input ports, the input time required was $\Omega(n^2)$. Thus the algorithm's time complexity was optimal. The storage complexity could not be less than $\Omega(n^2)$, otherwise time complexity could be less than $\Omega(n^2)$ contradicting the fact that time complexity was $\Omega(n^2)$. Therefore, storage complexity was also optimal.

By using that method, we can show that the linear array implementations of Structures 1-4 are also both time optimal and storage optimal. Thus our new bounded I/O programmable linear array implementation has the minimum hardware requirement to get optimal time and storage complexity. Bounded I/O special purpose devices targeted towards a specific application from Problems 1-5, 7-13, 17-20, and 22-25 <u>cannot</u> improve on this linear array implementation.

2. Consider the case where we still have to implement all the algorithms in Structures 1-7; however, we are restricted to designing a programmable linear array with a constant number of I/O ports. That is, I/O ports of data links 7 are prohibited.

In this case, the tokens of variables with data-dependence vectors $d_i = (0,0)^t$ must be preloaded in each PE before execution and downloaded after execution. For example, variables with $d_i = (0,0)^t$ in Structures 6 and 7. Therefore, each PE must have local memory to store these data. This results in the need for additional memory and memory addressing and control hardware as in Warp array [12].

5 Partitioning the computation

In this section, we briefly state how to apply the method of partitioning the computation which we studied in [17] to our programmable linear array implementation. Suppose that $I^p = \{(i_1, i_2, \ldots, i_p)^t \mid l_j \le i_j \le u_j \text{ and } u_j - l_j = O(n) \text{ for } j = 1, 2, \ldots, p\}$. For each value of n, we require a (virtual) linear array of some size. If we are given an array with smaller size, we need to partition the algorithm. We will state how to do that if all the data streams flow in the same direction or are fixed in PEs. In the sequel we will refer to the algorithms considered so far as *unpartitioned*.

Suppose then that for problem size characterized by n as above, we need an $N = N(n)$ storage linear array requiring time T for an unpartitioned algorithm. If we are given only a k-storage linear array for $k < N$, then we will consider feeding the data streams $\lceil N/k \rceil$ times into this k-storage linear array. This approach is illustrated in Fig. 9. In Fig. 9-a, if the data streams need to be fed into the N-storage linear array once only, then in Fig. 9-b, the data streams will be fed into the k-storage linear array $m = \lceil N/k \rceil$ times. Thus, the new algorithm can be naturally divided into m *phases*.

Since T time is required to feed the data streams into the linear array once, the total execution time is $O(TN/k)$. Next, suppose that this k-storage linear array contains q PEs and some index $\bar{I}$ is executed in $PE_{\mathbf{S}\bar{I}}$ in the unpartitioned algorithm. Then, $\bar{I}$ will be executed in $PE_{((\mathbf{S}\bar{I}-\min\{\mathbf{S}I_1|I_1\in I^p\}+1) \bmod q)}$ in the partitioned algorithm ($a \bmod b \in \{1,2,\ldots,b\}$). Furthermore, it is executed at time $\mathbf{H}\bar{I}$ in phase $\lceil(\mathbf{S}\bar{I}-\min\{\mathbf{S}I_1|I_1 \in I^p\}+1)/q\rceil$. We state the above as the following condition:

Condition : *If all the data streams either have the same direction or are fixed in PEs (for all* d_i, $\mathbf{S}d_i \geq 0$*), and* q *is the number of PEs in the available linear array, then for the partitioned algorithm* $(\mathbf{H_q}, \mathbf{S_q})$:

- $\mathbf{H_q}\bar{I} = \mathbf{H}\bar{I}$ in phase $\lceil(\mathbf{S}\bar{I} - \min\{\mathbf{S}I_1|I_1 \in I^p\} + 1)/q\rceil$;
- $\mathbf{S_q}\bar{I} = (\mathbf{S}\bar{I} - \min\{\mathbf{S}I_1|I_1 \in I^p\} + 1) \bmod q$.

Note: This condition applies if we do not utilize any information about special properties of the specific problem and its unpartitioned solution that could hold for some special cases. Thus, it is applicable to general p nested loop algorithms. We are studying some important problems for which advantage can be taken of the problem's structure. They are, however, beyond the scope of this paper.

All linear array algorithms we listed in Subsection 4.3 satisfy the partitioning condition. Therefore, all of them can be modified to partitioned versions. It is straightforward to create the partitioned version of these algorithms, and we omit the details from this presentation.

Finally, as mentioned in Subsection 2.3, $\mathbf{H} = (1,1)$ and $\mathbf{S} = (1,-1)$ is a correct mapping. However, $\mathbf{S}d_1 = \mathbf{S}d_4 = \mathbf{S}(0,1)^t = -1$ and $\mathbf{S}d_2 = \mathbf{S}d_5 = \mathbf{S}(1,0)^t = 1$. That is, data streams 1 and 4 flows from right to left and data streams 2 and 5 flows from left to right. Data streams of this linear array algorithm do not flow at the same direction, and therefore this linear array algorithm does not meet the partitioning condition.

6 Conclusions

A programmable linear systolic array has been derived in this paper. It can evaluate a large class of p nested loop algorithms used in signal and image processing, pattern matching, algebraic and matrix computation, sorting, transitive closure, and database operations. These include algorithms to solve 25 important problems.

The speedups, (processing time in a single processor)/(processing time in the linear array), of the linear array implementation of the above algorithms are linear ($O(n)$) with respect to the problem size n. These speedups are especially attractive when using the linear array to support real-time computation.

When the number of I/O ports is restricted, we designed a new bounded I/O programmable linear array, which also had the same speedups to solve 18 of the above 25 problems. In addition, this linear array implementation can be proved to be both time optimal and storage optimal for those 18 algorithms. Any other bounded I/O device, even special purpose, targeted towards a specific application from the 18 problems *cannot improve* on this linear array implementation.

The method used to design the array was based on the theoretical result of authors' previous report [17]. That report presents formal necessary and sufficient conditions for correct implementation of nested for loop algorithms on linear systolic arrays. The method allowed us to design PEs with constant number of registers and thus the array is modularly extensible. Furthermore, if the problem size is big with respect to the available array, the computation can be partitioned.

In order to find other practical implementations, a software tool has been developed to help in analyzing data-dependence vectors and in selecting specific implementations optimizing additional criteria. It will be described in a forthcoming report.

Due to a systematic transformation method, simple type of PE, local communication, easy design by using VLSI technology, amortization of the high design and fabrication costs over a large application domains, high parallelism, high speedups, and the success of CMU Warp computer, we believe that the concept of designing programmable linear arrays will be of significance in the solution of classes of important problems.

References

[1] M. A. Annaratone, E. Arnould, T. Gross, H. T. Kung, M. Lam, O. Menzilcioglu, and J. A. Webb, "The WARP Computer: Architecture, Implementation, and Performance," *IEEE Trans. Comput.*, vol. C-36, pp. 1523-1538, Dec. 1987.

[2] U. Banerjee, S. C. Chen, D. J. Kuck, R. A. Towle, "Time and Parallel Processor Bounds for FORTRAN Like Loops," *IEEE Trans. Comput.*, vol. C-28, pp. 660-670, Sep. 1979.

[3] M. C. Chen, "The Generation of a Class of Multipliers: Synthesizing Highly Parallel Algorithms in VLSI," *IEEE Trans. Comput.*, vol. C-37, pp. 329-338, Mar. 1988.

[4] M. J. Foster and H. T. Kung, "The Design of Special-Purpose VLSI Chips," *IEEE Computer*, pp. 26-40, Jan. 1980.

[5] L. J. Guibas, H. T. Kung, and C. D Thompson, "Direct VLSI Implementation of Combinatorial Algorithms," *CALTECH Conf. on VLSI*, pp. 509-525, Jan. 1979.

[6] K. Hwang and Y. H. Cheng, "Partitioned Matrix Algorithms for VLSI Arithmetic Systems," *IEEE Trans. Comput.*, vol. C-31, pp. 1215-1224, Dec. 1982.

[7] K. Hwang and F. A. Briggs, *"Computer Architecture and Parallel Processing,"* New York, Mcgraw-Hill, 1984.

[8] R. H. Kuhn, "Transforming Algorithms for Single-Stage and VLSI Architectures," in *Proc. of the workshop on Interconnection Networks for Parallel and Distributed Processing, IEEE CH1560-2*, pp. 11-19, 1980.

[9] H. T. Kung and L. Lehman, "Systolic (VLSI) Arrays for Relational Database Operations," *ACM SIGMOD*, pp. 105-116, 1980.

[10] H. T. Kung, "Use of VLSI in Algebraic Computation: Some Suggestions," in *Proc. of the ACM Symposium on Symbolic and Algebraic Computation*, pp. 218-222, 1981.

[11] H. T. Kung, "Why Systolic Architectures ?" *IEEE Computer*, pp. 37-46, Jan. 1982.

[12] H. T. Kung, "Systolic algorithms for the CMU WARP Processor," in *Proc. Seventh Int. Conf. Pattern Recognition*, pp. 570-577, July 1984.

[13] S. Y. Kung, "On Supercomputing with Systolic/Wavefront Array Processors," in *Proc. IEEE*, vol. 72, pp. 867-884, July 1984.

[14] L. Lamport, "The Parallel Execution of Do Loops," *CACM*, pp. 83-93, Feb. 1974.

[15] G. Li and B. Wah, "The Design of Optimal Systolic Arrays," *IEEE Trans. Comput.*, vol. C-34, pp. 66-77, Jan. 1985.

[16] P.-Z. Lee, "A New VLSI Synthesis Method," M.S. Thesis, National Tsing-Hua University, Taiwan, 1984.

[17] P.-Z. Lee and Z. M. Kedem, "Synthesizing Linear-Array Algorithms from Nested For Loop Algorithms," to appear in the special issue on parallel and distributed algorithms, *IEEE Trans. Comput.*, Dec. 1988, preliminary version also available as NYU Computer Science TR-355, March 1988.

[18] C. Mead and L. Conway, *"Introduction to VLSI Systems,"* Addison-Wesley, 1980.

[19] D. I. Moldovan and J. A. Fortes, "Partitioning and Mapping Algorithms into Fixed Size Systolic Arrays," *IEEE Trans. Comput.*, vol. C-35, pp. 1-12, January 1986.

[20] D. I. Moldovan, "ADVIS: A Software Package for the Design of Systolic Arrays," *IEEE Trans. CAD*, vol. CAD-6, pp. 33-40, Jan. 1987.

[21] P. Quinton, "Automatic synthesis of systolic arrays from uniform recurrent equations," in *Proc. 11th Annu. Symp. Comput. Architecture*, pp. 208-214, 1984.

[22] I. Ramakrishnan and P. Varman, "Modular Matrix Multiplication on a Linear Array," *IEEE Trans. Comput.*, vol. C-33, pp. 952-958, Nov. 1984.

[23] I. Ramakrishnan, D. Fussell, and A. Silberschatz, "Mapping Homogeneous Graphs on Linear Arrays," *IEEE Trans. Comput.*, vol. C-35, pp. 198-209, March 1986.

[24] J. D. Ullman, *"Computational Aspects of VLSI,"* Computer Science Press Inc., 1984.

[25] C. B. Yang and R. C. T. Lee, "Systolic algorithms for the LCS problem," in *Proc. Int. Comput. Symp.*, Taipei, Taiwan, R.O.C., pp. 895-901, 1984.

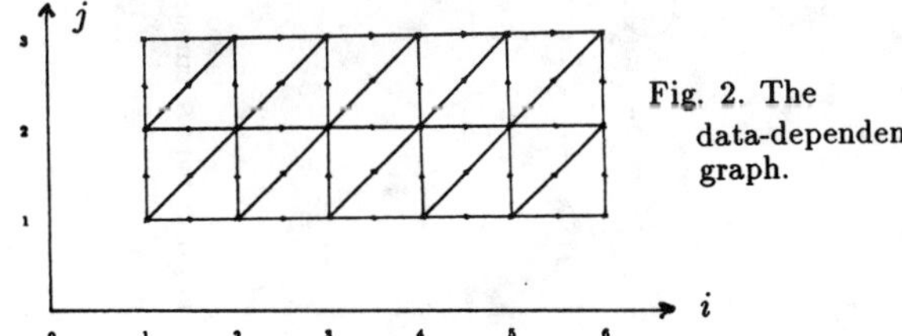

Fig. 2. The data-dependence graph.

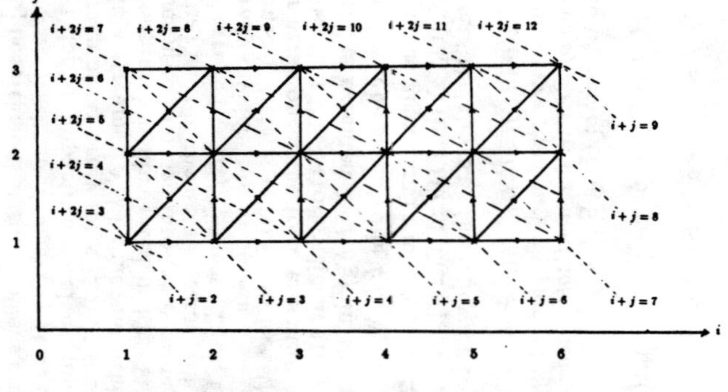

Fig. 3. Time-location relation of $\mathbf{H} = (1,2)$ and $\mathbf{S} = (1,1)$.
The dashed lines labeled with $i + 2j = d$ are the hyperplanes containing indices executed at a single time instance, say d.
The dashed lines labeled with $i + j = e$ are the hyperplanes containing indices executed at a single PE, say PE_e.

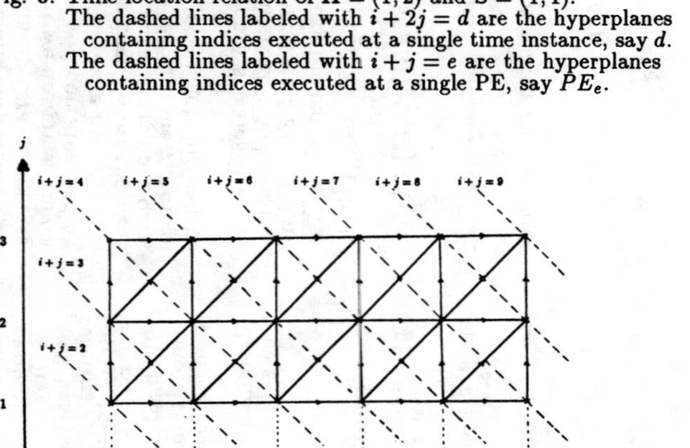

Fig. 4. Time-location relation of $\mathbf{H} = (1,1)$ and $\mathbf{S} = (1,0)$.

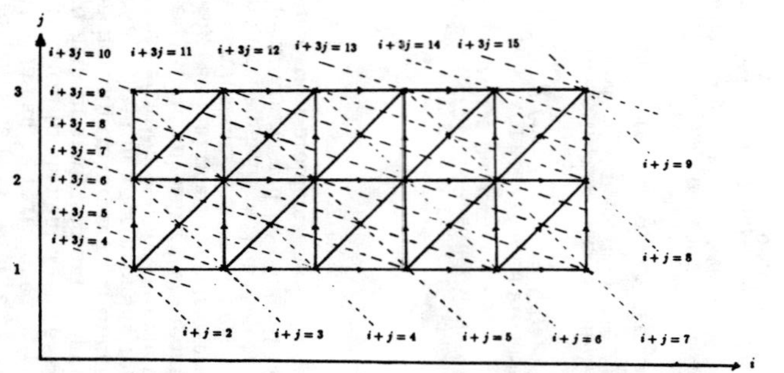

Fig. 6. Time-location relation of $\mathbf{H} = (1,3)$ and $\mathbf{S} = (1,1)$.

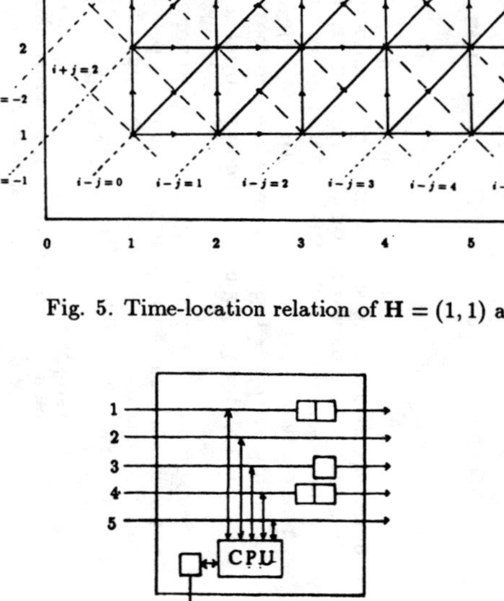

Fig. 5. Time-location relation of $\mathbf{H} = (1,1)$ and $\mathbf{S} = (1,-1)$.

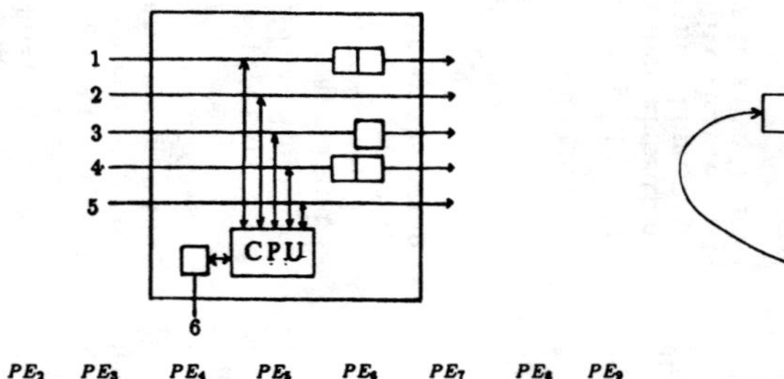

Fig. 7. The PE for computing the longest common subsequence and six steps during the computation by $\mathbf{H} = (1,3)$ and $\mathbf{S} = (1,1)$. $\mathbf{H}(i,j)^t = i + 3j$ and $\mathbf{S}(i,j)^t = i + j$.

Fig. 8. Our programmable PE.

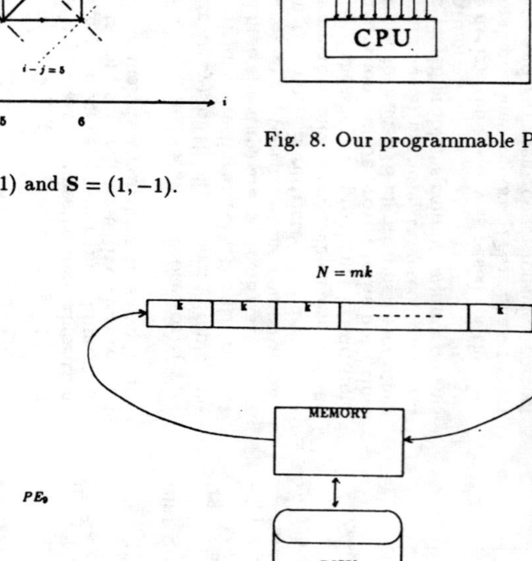

Fig. 9-a. $N = mk$ and data streams are fed into the N-storage array only once.

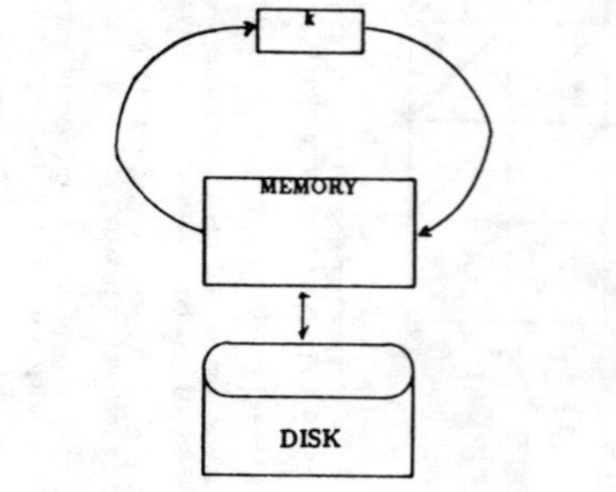

Fig. 9-b. Data streams are fed into the k-storage array m times.

A Transformational Approach to the Derivation of Hardware Algorithms from Recurrence Equations

Norihiko Yoshida

Department of Computer Science and Communication Engineering
Kyushu University
Hakozaki, Fukuoka 812, JAPAN

Abstract

Hardware algorithms have a significant impact on the supercomputing of matrix computation and signal processing. In this paper, we propose a new approach to the derivation of hardware algorithms from recurrence equations, which is based on program transformation, and we also introduce a new representation for hardware algorithms, which we call Relational Representation. In our approach, we transform one relational program corresponding to a given recurrence equation (namely a specification) to another relational program corresponding to a hardware algorithm (namely an implementation). Based on the unfold/fold transformation method of logic programs, we have formalized several transformation tactics. We have succeeded in deriving several implementations of hardware algorithms, such as pipelines, orthogonal grids and trees, from their respective specifications in recurrence equations.

1. Introduction

With the advances in VLSI technology and the increasing demands for higher performance, highly parallel architectures are now pervasively researched and developed. In particular, many computations which were previously implemented in software are going to be implemented in hardware. Such computations in special-purpose hardware are often called hardware algorithms. They have a significant impact on the supercomputing of matrix computation and signal processing. But designing hardware algorithms is still a very hard job. Some systematic methodology is strongly required for designing both a large collection of fine-grained process cells connected to each other and the various operations of each cell.

As for sequential algorithms, several formal techniques have been proposed for designing them systematically. Among them, program transformation in particular is bearing fruitful results. It is, in its essence, a technique to transform one program to another equivalent one. A set of correct transformation rules has been established, and many transformation tactics have been formalized.

For our aim at designing hardware algorithms systematically, we applied a formal technique such as the above. In this paper, we propose a new approach to the derivation of hardware algorithms from recurrence equations, which is based on program transformation.

In order to apply program transformation, we should have a formal representation of hardware algorithms which can express both inner-cell operations and cell configurations in an integrated form. We, therefore, introduce a restricted subset of concurrent logic language, which we call Relational Representation. It also serves as an executable hardware description.

Chapter 2 introduces Relational Representation after briefly reviewing hardware algorithms, and also notes its translations. Chapter 3 describes program transformation applied to relational programs, and formalizes several transformation tactics for deriving hardware algorithms. Chapter 4 gives an example of the transformational derivation of hardware algorithms. Chapter 5 contains concluding remarks.

2. Relational Representation of Hardware Algorithms

2.1 Hardware Algorithms

First, we specify what we call a hardware algorithm here. It is a class of highly parallel processor arrays with the following characteristics :

A) a regular (recursively-defined) configuration ;
B) local connections of cells by channels ;
C) lock-step synchronization of the whole system ;
D) deterministic operations of cells.

For example, we consider a finite impulse response (FIR) filter for signal processing defined by the following recurrence equation :

$$y_i = w_0 x_i + w_1 x_{i+1} + .. + w_{k-1} x_{i+k-1}$$

where w: weight,
x: source sequence, y: drain sequence.

Figure 1 shows its corresponding hardware algorithm in the case where k is 4, in which a box denotes a cell, and an arrow denotes a channel. When receiving data, each cell sends data out after a small duration, which is called a *beat*. This pipeline has streams of x's and y's flowing in the same direction along the channels. Y's stream has one more beat of delay per cell, so as to make it flow at half of x's rate.

A hardware algorithm is usually described in such an informal manner. Understanding its behavior intuitively or formally is difficult, and simulation by hand is often required. Some systematic techniques for designing hardware algorithms, especially systolic arrays, have been proposed [1, 2, 3, 4], but few are widely used.

2.2 Relational Representation

In order to apply program transformation to the derivation of hardware algorithms, we should have their formal representation. It should be able to express both inner-cell operations and cell configurations in an integrated form, and be of an inductive nature [5]. So-called concurrent logic languages such as Guarded Horn Clauses [6] and Concurrent Prolog [7] meet these requirements.

In these languages, a program for a hardware algorithm could be composed of some uniform predicates with different interpretations. A predicate with procedure interpretation would express an inner-cell operation, while a predicate with process interpretation would express a cell configuration with shared variables for channels to connect cells [8].

As mentioned in Chapter 3, a set of correct transformation rules has only been established so far for a restricted class of concurrent logic programs, not for the general class yet. We, therefore, introduce a subset of concurrent logic languages with the following restrictions, and hence call it *Relational Representation* (or *RR* for short) :

A) Specify the input/output mode of arguments ;
B) Allow no nondeterminacy (namely no *guard*).

These restrictions together mean that a clause to execute in a predicate is fixed as soon as all its input arguments are instantiated. They do not spoil the ability of concurrent logic languages to express hardware algorithms.

As for notation, we basically follow a logic language Prolog [9]. A capitalized symbol denotes a variable, and "[A|L]" denotes a list, where A and L are its *car* and *cdr* parts respectively. We only modify a notation of clauses, in order to specify the mode of arguments, as follows :

$$Q :: P_1, P_2, .., P_l.$$
$$\text{where } P_i, Q \equiv (I_1, .., I_m)P(O_1, .., O_n)$$

In this, P_i $(i = 1..l)$ and Q denote terms, P is a predicate symbol, I_j $(j = 1..m)$ are input arguments and O_k $(k = 1..n)$ are output arguments.

As in concurrent logic languages, a cell is expressed by a tail-recursive predicate in RR. For example, a cell p performing an operation f with an input channel XX, an output channel YY and an internal state transition S → T (without delay considered here) is expressed as :

```
(S,[X|XX])p([Y|YY]) :: (S,X)f(T,Y), (T,XX)p(YY).
```

Conversely, a predicate in RR expresses a cell when satisfying the following set of conditions (C1) :

A) It is tail-recursive ;
B) Its every input is a list constructor or a variable ;
C) Its every output is a list constructor.

A configuration of cells is also expressed by a predicate. For example, a pipeline pp of the same cells p (without delay considered here) is recursively expressed as :

```
(XX)pp(ZZ) :: (XX)p(YY), (YY)pp(ZZ).
```

2.3 Delay

A relational program has no concept of delay in its essence, while a hardware algorithm utilizes delay in order to control the flow rates of its streams.

In a hardware algorithm, a cell sends outputs at the next beat after receiving inputs, and the next cell receives them almost immediately. Now, imagine the situation where a cell sends outputs immediately upon receiving inputs, and the next cell receives them at the next beat. As shown in Figure 2, this consideration proves that a delay along a channel would be the equivalent of a delay in a cell. This means that every chan-

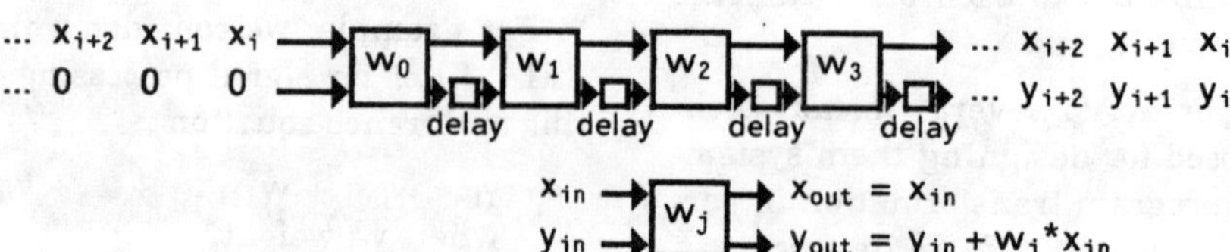

Figure 1. A Hardware Algorithm of an FIR Filter.

nel, instead of every cell, must have one or more beat(s) of delay.

A beat of channel delay can be expressed by a shift of a list. For example, a pipeline of cells p and q connected by a channel YY is expressed, with delay considered, as:

```
(XX)pq(ZZ) :: (XX)p(YY), ([⊥|YY])q(ZZ).
```

where "⊥" denotes the so-called bottom. If any input is the bottom, a cell bypasses all its inputs to outputs with no operation. We introduce an operator " + " to denote this shift of a list:

```
+XX ≡ [⊥|XX]
```

2.4 Translations

We can translate a recurrence equation into a relational program in a straightforward manner, since both are of an inductive nature. For example, the recurrence equation defining an FIR filter shown in Section 2.1 has another form as follows:

$$y_i^{\,0} = 0$$
$$y_i^{\,j+1} = y_i^{\,j} + w_j x_{i+j}$$

A relational program corresponding to it is as follows:

```
(WW,XXi)fir(YYo) :: (WW,XXi)pp(YYo).          (P1)
(WW,[Xi|XXi])pp([Yo|YYo]) ::
      (WW,[Xi|XXi])p(Yo), (WW,XXi)pp(YYo).
([],XXi)p(0).
([W|WW],[Xi|XXi])p(Yo) ::
      (WW,XXi)p(Ya), (W,Xi,Ya)f(Yo).
(W,⊥,Yi)f(Yi).
(W,Xi,⊥)f(⊥).
(W,Xi,Yi)f(Yo) :: (W,Xi)*(Yb), (Yi,Yb) + (Yo).
```

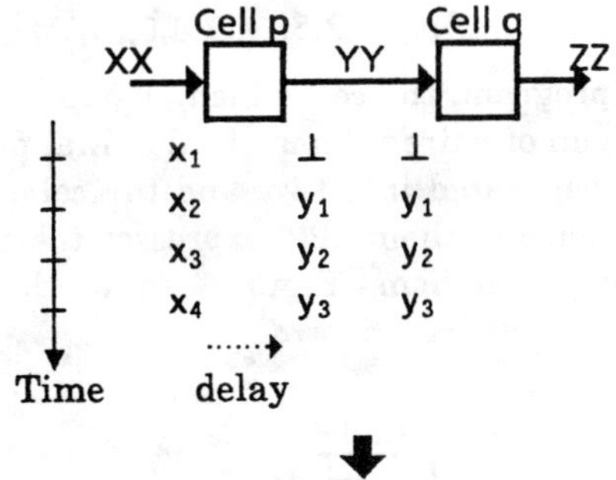

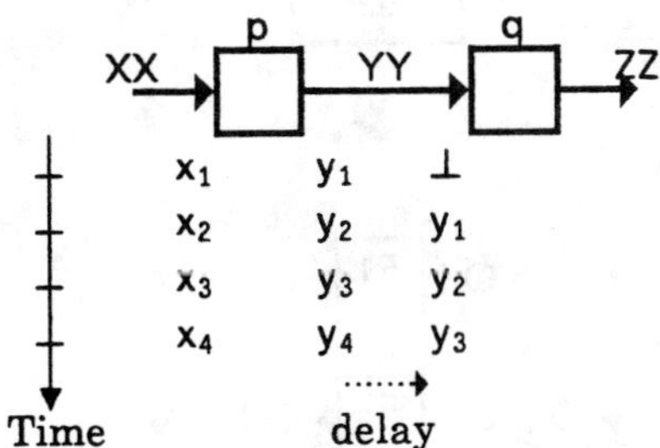

Figure 2. Delay along a Channel instead of in a Cell.

In this, WW, XX and YY express the sequences of w's, x's and y's respectively. P expresses the recurrence equation itself, while pp expresses x's and y's progression according to the suffix i.

We can also translate a hardware algorithm into a relational program in a straightforward manner, as shown in the previous sections. A relational program corresponding to the hardware algorithm of an FIR filter is as follows:

```
(WW,XXi)fir(YYo) ::                              (P2)
      (WW,XXi,[0,0,..])pp(_,YYo).
([],XXi,YYi)pp(XXi,YYi).
([W|WW],XXi,YYi)pp(XXo,YYo) ::
      (W,XXi,YYi)p(XXa,YYa),
      (WW, + XXa, + + YYa)pp(XXo,YYo).
(W,[Xi|XXi],[Yi|YYi])p([Xi|XXo],[Yo|YYo]) ::
      (W,Xi,Yi)f(Yo), (W,XXi,YYi)p(XXo,YYo).
(W,⊥,Yi)f(Yi).
(W,Xi,⊥)f(⊥).
(W,Xi,Yi)f(Yo) :: (W,Xi)*(Yb), (Yi,Yb) + (Yo).
```

In this, p expresses each cell, while pp expresses the cell configuration.

Lastly, we can translate a relational program easily into a concurrent logic program, since RR is a restricted subset of concurrent logic language. By executing a translated program, we could simulate the behavior of a hardware algorithm.

3. Transformation of Relational Programs

3.1 Program Transformation

Program transformation is a technique to transform one program to another equivalent one [10, 11]. For logic programs, the unfold/fold transformation method has been established [12]. It transforms a program by combining very primitive rules including *unfold* and *fold*:

Unfold: A :: B, C, D. C :: E, F. → A :: B, E, F, D.
Fold: A :: B, E, F, D. C :: E, F. → A :: B, C, D.

The unfold/fold transformation is correct (semantics-preserving) for concurrent logic programs which imply well-formed causalities and do not have so-called *don't care* nondeterminacy [13]. RR is a restricted subset of concurrent logic language so as to specify causalities (by the mode of arguments) and not to allow nondeterminacy. We, therefore, can apply the unfold/fold transformation for logic programs to relational programs with no modification, if we are careful with their causalities.

We transform a program with a sequential (stepwise) combination of rules. In order to apply program transformation to practical problems, we should structure transformation sequences. This is done by formalizing transformation tactics [14]. Each tactic is a specific combination of primitive rules like a *macro*. By formalizing tactics, we can transform a program with more specific and abstract tactics, instead of primitive minute rules. In this case, primitive rules serve as axioms for proving the correctness of the tactics.

The assorted tactics for the transformational derivation of hardware algorithms are of three types : for deriving cell configurations, for cascading channels, and for introducing delay. Here, we show some typical tactics, using a form of "initial program schema → final program schema". The outline of their correctness proofs based on the primitive unfold/fold rules are found elsewhere [15].

3.2 Tactics for Deriving Cell Configurations

The essence of a tactic for deriving a cell configuration is mapping an inner-cell operation in the initial program onto a cell configuration in the final program. Practically, this mapping is done by making a more inner (or lower) predicate express a cell, as shown below :

1) Tactics for Deriving Pipelines

The simplest pipeline is composed of two consecutive cells. A tactic for deriving it is as follows :

```
([X|XX])PP([Z|ZZ]) :: (X)FF(Z), (XX)PP(ZZ).
(X)FF(Z) :: (X)F1(Y), (Y)F2(Z).
        ↓                                        (T1)
(XX)PP(ZZ) :: (XX)P1(YY), (YY)P2(ZZ).
([X|XX])P1([Y|YY]) :: (X)F1(Y), (XX)P1(YY).
([Y|YY])P2([Z|ZZ]) :: (Y)F2(Z), (YY)P2(ZZ).
```

In this, XX and ZZ are input and output channels respectively. In the initial program, PP expresses a cell, since it satisfies the condition set C1 shown in Section 2.2. FF expresses an inner-cell operation composed of F1 and F2. In the final program, P1 and P2 express cells, since they satisfy C1. PP expresses a cell configuration as a pipeline of P1 and P2 with an intermediate channel YY. The sequence of F1 and F2 in the initial program is mapped onto the pipeline of P1 and P2 in the final program. Figure 3 shows this transformation. T1 is the converse of the *loop fusion* (or the *combining*) tactic [14] or the *process fusion* [13].

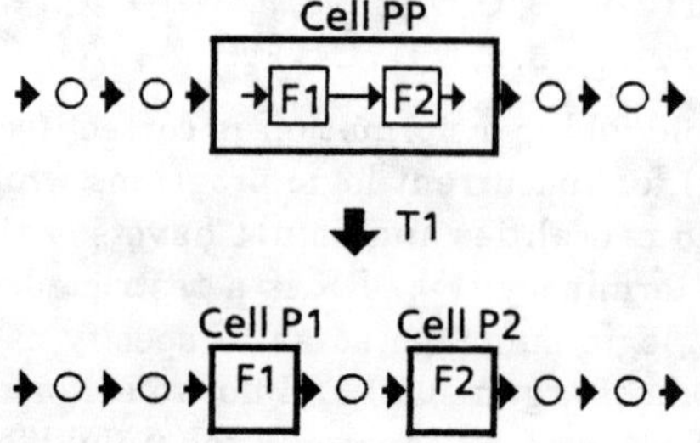

Figure 3. Derivation of a Simple Pipeline.

We can easily generalize T1 to the derivation of pipelines of more than two cells, and moreover recursive pipelines as follows :

```
([X|XX])PP([Z|ZZ]) :: (X)FF(Z), (XX)PP(ZZ).
(X)FF(Z) :: (X)F(Y), (Y)FF(Z).
        ↓                                        (T2)
(XX)PP(ZZ) :: (XX)P(YY), (YY)PP(ZZ).
([X|XX])P([Y|YY]) :: (X)F(Y), (XX)P(YY).
```

2) Tactics for Deriving Parallelisms

The simplest parallelism is composed of two adjacent cells. A tactic for deriving it is as follows :

```
([Xs|XX])PP([Zs|ZZ]) :: (Xs)FF(Zs), (XX)PP(ZZ).
([X1,X2])FF([Z1,Z2]) :: (X1)F1(Z1), (X2)F2(Z2).
        ↓                                        (T3)
(XX)PP(ZZ) ::
      (XX)t(XXs), (XXs)PP'(ZZs), (ZZs)t(ZZ).
([XX1,XX2])PP'([ZZ1,ZZ2]) ::
      (XX1)P1(ZZ1), (XX2)P2(ZZ2).
([X|XX])P1([Z|ZZ]) :: (X)F1(Z), (XX)P1(ZZ).
([X|XX])P2([Z|ZZ]) :: (X)F2(Z), (XX)P2(ZZ).
```

where the predicate t is to transpose a list of lists as :

```
([[1,2],[3,4],[5,6],..])t([[1,3,5,..],[2,4,6,..]])
```

In the initial program, the cell which PP expresses operates on a stream of paired items. In the final program, the stream is separated into two, and the cells P1 and P2 operate on each of them. PP' expresses the configuration as their parallelism. Figure 4 shows this transformation.

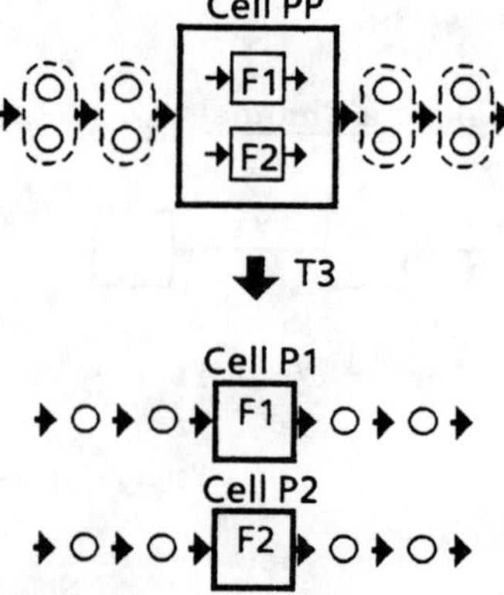

Figure 4. Derivation of a Simple Parallelism.

We can easily generalize T3 to the derivation of parallelisms of more than two cells, and moreover recursive parallelisms as follows :

```
([Xs|XX])PP([Zs|ZZ]) :: (Xs)FF(Zs), (XX)PP(ZZ).
([X|Xs])FF([Z|Zs]) :: (X)F(Z), (Xs)FF(Zs).
        ↓                                              (T4)
(XX)PP(ZZ) ::
      (XX)t(XXs), (XXs)PP'(ZZs), (ZZs)t(ZZ).
([XX|XXs])PP'([ZZ|ZZs]) ::
      (XX)P(ZZ), (XXs)PP'(ZZs).
([X|XX])P([Z|ZZ]) :: (X)F(Z), (XX)P(ZZ).
```

3) Tactics for Deriving Trees

The base method for deriving a tree of cells is called the *recursive doubling* [16, 10], which introduce a bilinear recursion as follows :

```
([Xs|XX])PP([Z|ZZ]) :: (Xs)FF(Z), (XX)PP(ZZ).
([])FF(E).                  % E is the identity of F.
([X|Xs])FF(Z) :: (Xs)FF(Y), (X)G(X'), (X',Y)F(Z).
        ↓                                              (T5)
(XX)PP(ZZ) :: (XX)t(XXs), (XXs)PP'(ZZ).
([XX])PP'(ZZ) :: (XX)P'(ZZ).
([XXs1@XXs2])PP'(ZZ) ::
      (XXs1)PP'(YY1), (XXs2)PP'(YY2),
      (YY1,YY2)P(ZZ).
([X|XX])P'([Z|ZZ]) :: (X)G(Z), (XX)P'(ZZ).
([Y1|YY1],[Y2|YY2])P([Z|ZZ]) ::
      (Y1,Y2)F(Z), (YY1,YY2)P(ZZ).
```

where the operator "[@]" is to divide a list into two as :

[1,2,3,4,5,6] = [[1,2,3]@[4,5,6]]

T5 is applicable only if F is associative. Figure 5 shows this transformation.

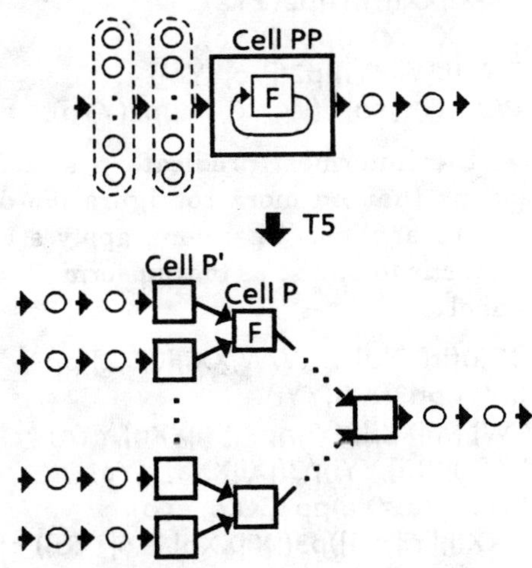

Figure 5. Derivation of a Tree.

3.3 Tactics for Cascading Channels

One of the tactics for cascading channels transforms outflow channels to cascade ones. This is exactly the same as the *recursion removal* [17] for sequential programs. It is as follows :

```
([])P(E).
([X|XX])P(Z) :: (XX)P(Z'), (X,Z')F(Z).
        ↓                                              (T6)
(X)P(Z) :: (X,E)P'(Z).
([],Z)P'(Z).
([X|XX],Z)P'(Z'') :: (X,Z)F(Z'), (XX,Z')P'(Z'').
```

T6 is applicable only if F is associative.

The other transforms branch channels to cascade ones. It is as follows :

```
..., (XX)P1(), (XX)P2(), ...
([X|XX])P1() :: (X)F1(), (XX)P1().
        ↓                                              (T7)
.., (XX)P1'(XX'), (XX')P2'(XX''), ..
([X|XX])P1'([X|XX']) :: (X)F1(), (XX)P1'(XX').
```

Figure 6 shows these two transformations.

3.4 Tactics for Introducing Delay

A cell with the same amount of additional delay along every input and output channel is equivalent to the original cell. Namely, the following transformation is correct :

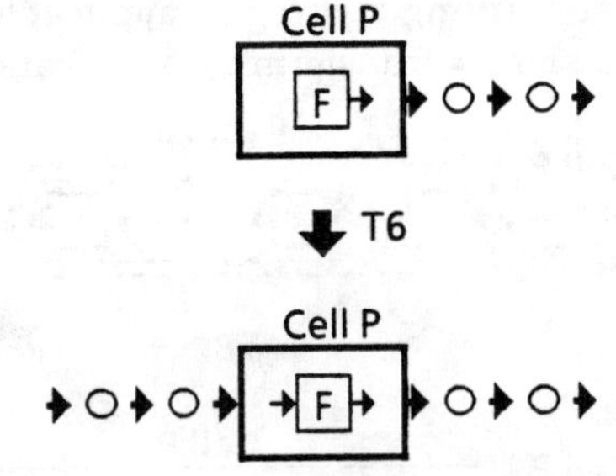

(a) Cascading an Outflow Channel.

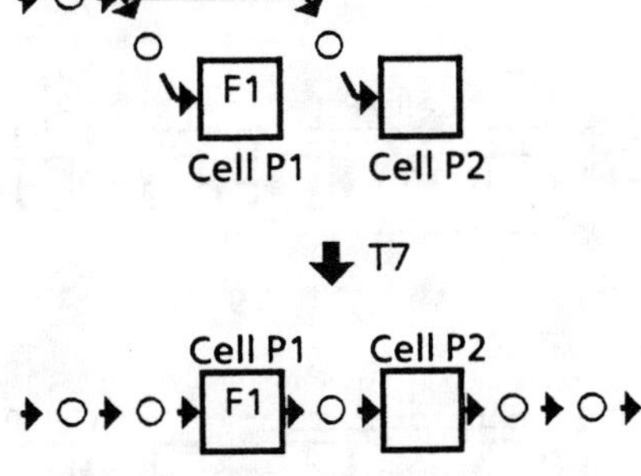

(b) Cascading a Branch Channel.

Figure 6. Tactics for Cascading Channels.

$$(S,I_1,\ldots,I_m)P(O_1,\ldots,O_n)$$
$$\downarrow$$
$$(S,+I_1,\ldots,+I_m)P(+O_1,\ldots,+O_n)$$

We, hereafter, make an assumption that we may ignore delay (or " + " operators) on the last output channel. Then, for example, the following tactics for recursive cell pipelines are correct :

```
(XX)PP(ZZ) :: (XX)P(YY), (YY)PP(ZZ).
        ↓                                   (T8)
(XX)PP(ZZ) :: (XX)P(YY), (+YY)PP(ZZ).

(XX)PP(ZZ) :: (YY)P(ZZ), (XX)PP(YY).
        ↓                                   (T9)
(XX)PP(ZZ) :: (YY)P(ZZ), (+XX)PP(+YY).
```

In these, a beat of additional delay is put along the arguments of PP. A " + " on ZZ, which is the last output channel in T8, is omitted. Figure 7 shows these two transformations, where "–" denotes the inverse of " + ". A transformation sequence should end with these tactics so that every channel is arranged to have one or more beat(s) of delay.

3.5 Transformation Strategy

We should have a transformation strategy to decide how to combine transformation tactics. Some channel-cascading tactics should be applied before configuration-deriving ones, the other channel-cascading ones should be applied afterwards, and delay-introducing ones should be applied last. In the case where several configuration-deriving tactics are applicable to a given program, we should transform its predicates in the order "from outer to inner". In the case where several transformation sequences are applicable to a given program, we should select one following a certain criterion.

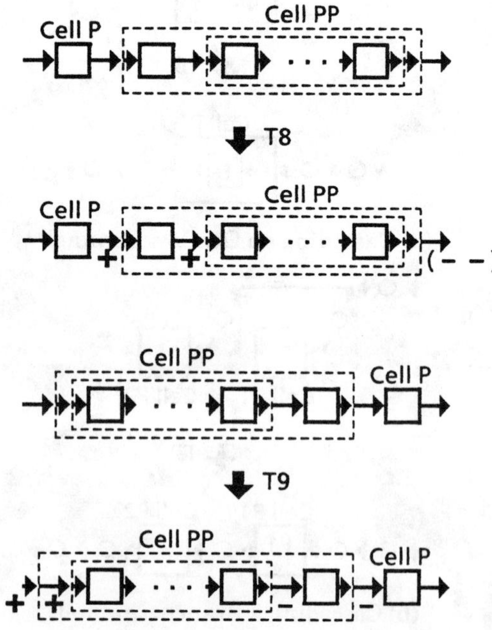

Figure 7. Tactics for Introducing Delay.

4. Derivation Example of Hardware Algorithms

Transformational derivation of a hardware algorithm is to transform one relational program corresponding to a given recurrence equation (namely a specification) to another relational program corresponding to a hardware algorithms (namely an implementation). We describe, using a simple example, the concrete derivation of hardware algorithms, especially to show how transformation sequences are composed of the tactics shown above.

The relational program P1 shown in Section 2.4 is the one translated from the recurrence equation defining an FIR filter. In this, pp satisfies the condition set C1, which means that pp expresses a cell, while p expresses an inner-cell operation. This system is composed of one cell.

① First, apply a channel-cascading tactic to p so as to transform it to a tail-recursive predicate :

```
(WW,XXi)fir(YYo) :: (WW,XXi,[0,0,..])pp1(YYo).
(WW,[Xi|XXi],[Yi|YYi])pp1([Yo|YYo]) ::
    (WW,[Xi|XXi],Yi)p1(Yo),
    (WW,XXi,YYi)pp1(YYo).
([],XXi,Yi)p1(Yi).
([W|WW],[Xi|XXi],Yi)p1(Yo) ::
    (W,Xi,Yi)f(Ya), (WW,XXi,Ya)p1(Yo).
```

② Apply a pipeline-deriving tactic to pp1 and p1 :

```
(WW,XXi)fir(YYo) :: (WW,XXi,[0,0,..])pp2(YYo).
([],XXi,YYi)pp2(YYi).
([W|WW],[Xi|XXi],YYi)pp2(YYo) ::
    (W,[Xi|XXi],YYi)p2(YYa),
    (WW,XXi,YYa)pp2(YYo).
(W,[Xi|XXi],[Yi|YYi])p2([Yo|YYo]) ::
    (W,Xi,Yi)f(Yo), (W,XXi,YYi)p2(YYo).
```

③ Now, the innermost predicate p satisfies C1, which means that no more configuration-deriving tactics can be applied. Therefore, apply a channel-cascading tactic to pp2 so as to transform XX to a cascade channel :

```
(WW,XXi)fir(YYo) :: (WW,XXi,[0,0,..])pp3(__,YYo).
([],XXi,YYi)pp3(XXi,YYi).
([W|WW],[Xi|XXi],YYi)pp3([Xi|XXo],YYo) ::
    (W,[Xi|XXi],YYi)p3([Xi|XXa],YYa),
    (WW,XXa,YYa)pp3(XXo,YYo).
(W,[Xi|XXi],[Yi|YYi])p3([Xi|XXo],[Yo|YYo]) ::
    (W,Xi,Yi)f(Yo), (W,XXi,YYi)p3(XXo,YYo).
```

④ Lastly, apply a delay-introducing tactic to pp3 so as to make channels XX and YY have one or more beat(s) of delay (XXo and YYo are the last output channels, so "+"'s along them are omitted) :

```
(WW,XXi)fir(YYo) :: (WW,XXi,[0,0,..])pp4(_,YYo).
([],XXi,YYi)pp4(XXi,YYi).
([W|WW],XXi,YYi)pp4(XXo,YYo) ::
      (W,XXi,YYi)p4(XXa,YYa),
      (WW,XXa,+YYa)pp4(XXo,YYo).
(W,[Xi|XXi],[Yi|YYi])p4([Xi|XXo],[Yo|YYo]) ::
      (W,Xi,Yi)f(Yo), (W,XXi,YYi)p4(XXo,YYo).
```

Again applying a delay-introducing tactic to pp4, we get exactly the same relational program as P2 shown in Section 2.4. It can be translated into a hardware algorithm of an FIR filter.

Figure 8 shows the transition of the FIR filter system along the transformational derivation shown above.

We show another derivation example only as a schematic diagram. Figure 9 shows the transition of a matrix-vector product system along the transformational derivation. This is a case where some transformation procedures are applicable, in which the former tree is faster than the latter pipeline, while the latter is more compact.

5. Conclusions

In this paper, we proposed a new approach to the derivation of hardware algorithms from recurrence equations, which is based on program transformation. We also introduced a new representation for hardware algorithms, which we call Relational Representation.

Relational Representation is a subset of concurrent logic language, since a set of transformation rules has only been established so far for a restricted class of concurrent logic programs. It has two eminent characteristics. One is that it can express both inner-cell operations and cell configurations in an integrated form. The other is that a program in it can be easily translated into a concurrent logic program, and we could simulate the behavior of a hardware algorithm by executing the translated one on some concurrent logic programming system.

Transformational derivation of a hardware algorithm is to transform one relational program corresponding to a given recurrence equation (namely a specification) to another relational program corresponding to a hardware algorithm (namely an implementation). In our approach, formalizing tactics promotes well-formed organization and easy augmentation of the derivation technique.

We have succeeded in deriving several implementations of hardware algorithms from their respective specifications in recurrence equations. Besides the ones shown as examples, we have derived orthogonal grids, but not hexagonal grids yet. There is one open problem. If an outcome relational program can not correspond to any implementation, either its specification or its transformation sequence is not good. But we can not now say which is the case, since we have not yet completed the transformational derivation technique.

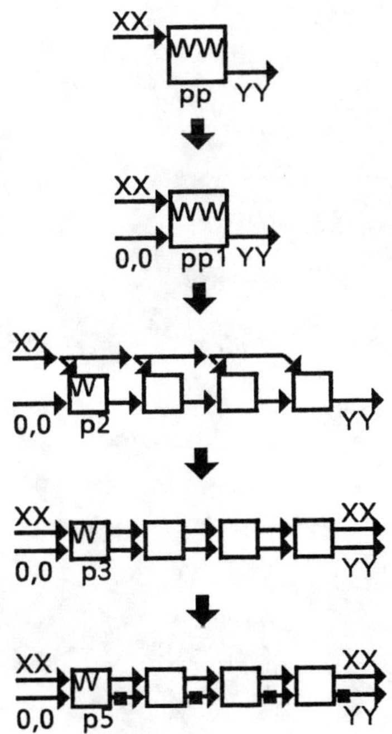

Figure 8. Derivation of an FIR Filter System.

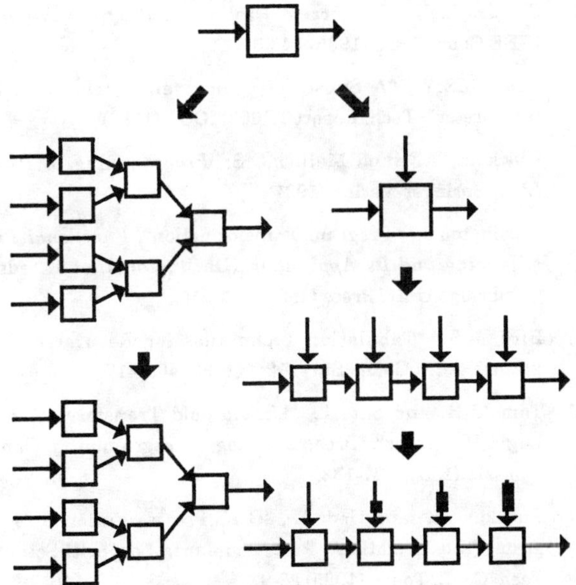

Figure 9. Derivation of a Matrix-Vector Product System.

It is worth to note that this work has a close relationship to stream programming in functional languages [18, 19, 20, 21], since both use, as their bases, stream interpretation of lists with lazy evaluation.

Hardware algorithms have a significant impact on the supercomputing of matrix computation and signal processing. We believe that this work has proved that the transformational derivation of hardware algorithms is indeed promising.

Acknowledgment

The author would like to thank Professor Kazuo Ushijima and Professor Shinji Tomita of Kyushu University for their valuable support and encouragement, and also thank Doctor Jiro Tanaka of Fujitsu Ltd. for his advice concerning stream programming.

References

[1] Moldovan,D.I., "On the Design of Algorithms for VLSI Systolic Arrays", Proc. IEEE 71:1 (1983) 113-120.

[2] Li,G.-J. and Wah,B.W., "The Design of Optimal Systolic Arrays", IEEE Trans. C-34:1 (1985) 66-77.

[3] Lam,M.S. and Mostow,J., "A Transformational Model of VLSI Systolic Design", IEEE Comp. 18:2 (1985) 42-52.

[4] Huang,C.-H. and Lengauer,C., "The Derivation of Systolic Implementations of Programs", Acta Inf. 24 (1987) 595-632.

[5] Hoare,C.A.R., *Communicating Sequential Processes*, Prentice-Hall (1985).

[6] Ueda,K., *Guarded Horn Clauses*, MIT Press (1988).

[7] Shapiro,E.Y., "Concurrent Prolog : A Progress Report", IEEE Comp. 19: 8 (1986) 44-58.

[8] Shapiro,E.Y., "A Subset of Concurrent Prolog and Its Interpreter", Tech. Report TR003, ICOT (1983).

[9] Clocksin,W.F. and Mellish,C.S., *Programming in PROLOG*, Springer-Verlag (1981).

[10] Darlington,J., "Program Transformation", *Functional Programming and Its Application* (Darlington,J. et.al. eds.), Cambridge Univ. Press (1982) 193-215.

[11] Bird, R.S., "Tabulation Techniques for Recursive Programs", ACM Comp. Surv. 12:4 (1980) 403-417.

[12] Tamaki,H. and Sato,T., "Unfold/Fold Transformation of Logic Programs", Proc. 2nd Logic Programming Conf., Uppsala (1984) 127-138.

[13] Furukawa,K. and Ueda,K., "GHC Process Fusion by Program Transformation", Proc. 2nd Japan Soc. Soft. Sci. and Tech. Conf., Tokyo (1985) 89-92.

[14] Feather,M.S., "A System for Assisting Program Transformation", ACM Trans. Prog. Lang. Syst. 4:1 (1982) 1-20.

[15] Yoshida,N., "Transformational Derivation of Highly Parallel Programs", Proc. 3rd Int. Conf. on Supercomputing 3, Boston (1988) 445-454.

[16] Kogge,P.M. and Stone,H.S., "A Parallel Algorithm for the Efficient Solution of a General Class of Recurrence Equations", IEEE Trans. C-22:8 (1973) 786-793.

[17] Huet,G. and Lang,B., "Proving and Applying Program Transformation Expressed with Second-Order Patterns", Acta Inf. 11 (1978) 31-55.

[18] Ida,T. and Tanaka,J., "Functional Programming with Streams", Proc. IFIP '83, Paris (1983) 265-270.

[19] Ida,T. and Tanaka,J., "Functional Programming with Streams – Part II –", New Generation Computing 2:3 (Ohmsha, JAPAN) (1984) 261-275.

[20] Wadler,P., "Applicative Style of Programming, Program transformation and List Operators", Proc. 1981 Conf. on Functional Programming Languages and Computer Architecture, Portsmouth (New Hampshire) (1981) 25-32.

[21] Kieburtz,R.B. and Shultis,J., "Transformation of FP Program Schemes", ibid. 41-48.

Supercomputing Center Management

Chair: Ron Deiss
NASA Ames Research Center

Supercomputer Integration Program at Boeing

Ronald B. Griffin
Janusz S. Kowalik
Melvin R. Scott

Boeing Computer Services
P.O. Box 24346, MS 7M-30
Seattle, Washington 98124

Abstract. In the introduction, we define supercomputers as specialized machines, describe their impact on software and applications, and introduce two major supercomputing issues: visualization and communication.

Section 2 discusses the main subject of the paper which is supercomputer integration programs. Section 3 describes our current experience related to the Alabama Supercomputer Network. Sections 4 and 5 are conclusions and references, respectively.

Keywords: Supercomputer installation, environment, management.

1. INTRODUCTION

There are three basic criteria for evaluating a computer architecture: performance measured in the number of operations per second, memory capacity, and cost. Machines whose primary purpose has been to provide the maximum performance and memory capacity have become known as supercomputers. They are mainly intended for solving large-scale scientific and engineering problems. More specifically, we can distinguish several classes of computational problem areas in science and engineering that require supercomputers [Stone (1987)]:

1. numerical computations such as: computational fluid dynamics, weather forecasting, oceanographic modeling, structural analysis;
2. time critical problems: robotics, control systems, speech recognition, image processing;
3. I/O intensive problems: database systems, transaction system;
4. graphics and design problems: CAD/CAM;
5. artificial intelligence: search and pattern recognition, inferencing.

Each class of applications has associated with it appropriate solution algorithms typically dominated by some operations, such as: floating point arithmetic operations, fixed point arithmetic operations, bit manipulations, string and pattern matching, etc. In order to provide high performance processing for a given class of applications, supercomputer architectures have to be optimized for the related operations. Consequently, supercomputers are specialized machines whose performance peaks for certain kinds of operations. In this paper, our focus will be on supercomputers for numerical applications dominated by floating point operations, commonly known as the number crunchers.

Supercomputers take advantage of specialized advanced architectural features such as: cache and register memories, multibanked main memories, multiple pipelined vector units and parallel CPUs. This specialized architecture impacts optimal choices of the computational algorithms and the code structures. Usually software revisions have to be made to adjust conventional codes to new supercomputer architectures. These revisions may be needed at various levels of the software development cycle:

(a) problem definition,
(b) algorithm selection,
(c) global program design, or
(d) local DO-loop construction.

In some cases, only small portions of the existing codes are affected and vectorizing compilers may be adequate for obtaining substantial improvements in processing performance. In others, it is preferable to use codes implementing modern algorithms which may be vastly superior in comparison with algorithms developed for earlier generations of nonvector machines. Thus, supercomputers significantly enlarge the set of practically solvable problems, but they also influence the optimal choice of solution algorithms, the design of computer programs and the user environments. This influence will be even more profound with the emergence of supercomputer systems composed of a large number of processors such as CRAY-3, CRAY-4, and ETA-10.

Another supercomputing issue that is at least as important as the computational efficiency and the hardware-software fit is the issue of user productivity. One of the elements of user productivity is his ability to access, generate and display data quickly and conveniently. Supercomputers typically require large amounts of input data and produce large amounts of output. Advanced graphics capabilities are required to facilitate the process of data analysis and to enhance the human insights involved in problem solving. The visualization facilities may include high performance workstations, color printers, slide makers, laser printers, movie cameras and other devices that convert spatial data to pictures which are more comprehensible to humans than large tables of numbers. Distributed graphics systems running between a workstation and a supercomputer have been described and successfully used in practical applications [Choi and Levit (1987)]. The use of advanced visualization techniques is an indispensable component of supercomputer systems and significantly increases their capability and user productivity [Frenkel (1988)].

Visualization is only one component of the total user interface environment which must offer to the user many other functionalities. In the current supercomputing environment, the user's primary point of contact with the system is a workstation or a personal computer. The user needs to manage all computing services from the workstation, and although different processors are used to provide these services, the user wants to see these functions as extensions of the workstation function.

Ideally, the user should be able to accomplish the following tasks from the workstation:

(a) compile, debug and execute application programs on the supercomputer,
(b) access the mass storage system, and examine large data files,
(c) edit source code and data files,
(d) use graphics analysis interactively and display data on the workstation or other devices, and
(e) do text processing.

To provide these functionalities, the entire distributed supercomputing system must be properly interconnected at several different levels: local area network (LAN), wide area network (WAN) and gateways. The extensive information flow in the system and the convenient access to this information is as important as is the increasingly impressive computational power of supercomputers.

2. COMPONENTS OF INTEGRATION

A productive supercomputer environment requires significantly more than the presence of a supercomputer and data communications. It must support personal productivity, allow efficient use of computer resources, and encourage effective management and operation of a supercomputer center. To achieve the full benefits of a supercomputer, a total supercomputer environment must be built; an environment in which scientists can increase their productivity, and applications can efficiently exploit the power of the supercomputer.

In a productive environment, scientists and engineers will be able to concentrate on design and analysis rather than the computer system. They will have appropriate training, support, and software tools to allow them to easily use the system. Applications programs will exploit the architecture of the supercomputer. The supercomputer center will tend to the details (e.g., operating systems support, file backups, etc.) and will provide security and integrity protections to deliver a reliable and stable service, essential ingredients for user productivity.

Environment

Up to now, we have been describing an environment in which scientists and engineers are using the supercomputer in a way that increases their productivity. Now let's take a look at that computing environment as it exists today and the way it will be in the future.

Today's supercomputing environment is heterogeneous. There are a number of computers, each with their own special capabilities and features, supplied by multiple vendors which may include multiple operating system options. There are various systems architectures for different uses and there may be several generations of hardware and software that must coexist within each system. A constant stream of innovations are over the horizon and we, in Boeing, are like other advanced engineering/scientific users in that we buy the best technology to solve a given problem regardless of vendor. A successful supercomputer environment must incorporate new generations of hardware and software in an upward-compatible manner, allowing the buyer/user to concentrate on the job to be done – his job. The user must be able to exploit the unique attributes of each system's architecture and move data as well as computations to where they are needed, when they are needed.

The computing environment of today also includes a proliferation of standard networks and protocols. The "alphabet soup" jungle of LANs, WANs, MANs, backbone networks, private networks, and public networks is only the tip of the iceberg. Add to these the standards of ISO, SNA, X.25, TCP/IP, and ISDN, and the user is in a quandary of how to approach his solution for a computing environment that will grow, expand, and not become obsolete. Often there are industry standards, de facto standards, vendor standards, and customer standards to be considered when looking at broadband, baseband, token passing, CSMA/CD, CSMA/CA, 802.3, 802.4, and 802.5 to make effective use of the system.

A basic connectivity must be developed among all machines that provides tight integration for frequently used combinations. There must be a transparency, a seamless hiding of underlying layers of complexity for the users while providing each access to the diversity of network functions and services.

The computing environment has evolved. First, there was the concept of batch; then timesharing – one computer with many users. Personal computing was developed providing one user with one computer.

Finally, today there are many computers and many users all networked together. This, then, is the challenge in today's engineering and scientific computing environments – to form a network of hardware, software, and communications into an effective service to a large, diverse community of users.

The supercomputer is not an island. As with any large mainframe installation, the supercomputer requires many other resources before it can be fully functional. Supercomputers tend to be more dependent on supporting services, and there is usually a much greater level of connectivity. This is required both to make the supporting services available to the supercomputer, and to allow users of pre-existing systems to capitalize on their base of knowledge and access the supercomputer through the systems with which they are familiar.

A productive supercomputer environment does not depend solely upon the installation of a supercomputer. It is an amalgam of the supercomputer, facilities, supporting hardware, maintenance, systems software, applications software, a communication network, user support, production support services, training, and managing the transition to the supercomputing environment (See Figure 1).

It is important to realize that supercomputer vendors produce computational engines, not fully functional systems. The missing elements of the total supercomputer system have to be provided by the purchaser or an independent integrator.

In addition to these individual components, there is one more very important ingredient: Mission Management provided by one organization to ensure that all of the components work well together in a complex, multi-vendor environment.

Facilities

One of the first and most obvious requirements for a supercomputer center will be a proper facility, one that satisfies the physical requirements for a stable operating environment.

Facilities requirements for a supercomputer differ from those of a conventional mainframe only in degree. Whether a supercomputer is to be installed in an existing data center or housed in a new facility, careful attention must be paid to providing adequate floor space, water, power and air-conditioning, continuous power supply, security protection, seismic protection, and operator visibility and control. However, today's supercomputers bring additional concerns. For example, they often create a heavier load per square foot of floor space than conventional mainframes, and special high load "pads" must be built into the machine room floor. Also, they may consume larger amounts of electricity than conventional mainframes, and have accompanying requirements to dissipate larger amounts of heat.

Supporting Hardware

In providing the supercomputer facilities, special attention must be paid to providing convenient access for users, building on to their current mainframe and workstation experience, and providing storage and management tools for the large amounts of data associated with the use of a supercomputer.

While a conventional mainframe might support all of its own communications access and data storage requirements, a functional supercomputer center will need front-end processors to provide user access to the supercomputer; a file server to extend the supercomputer's storage capacity and to provide data shoring within the center; and a local network to connect the constituent parts.

An example is the Boeing supercomputer data center in Bellevue, Washington. The Cray X-MP is dependent upon DEC, CDC, and IBM systems for front-end services, and upon CDC systems for file service. The computers communicate over Network Systems Corporation HYPERchannel networks. The DEC VAX front-end runs Cray Research Station software and acts as a DECNET gateway to the X-MP. The CDC Cyber 875, 750 and 760s serve as front-ends using Boeing-developed network software, and are extensively used for pre-and post- processing of X-MP jobs. The IBM systems are direct front-ends to the X-MP, and provide remote batch, and pre- and post-processing services. The Cyber 825 and 730s host the Boeing File Management System (FMS), providing a uniform interface from all processing services to a multi-level storage hierarchy. In addition, Boeing runs a combination of locally developed and vendor supplied software over the HYPERchannel networks.

Closely coupled to the supercomputer center is the new Boeing Computational Fluid Dynamics Laboratory (CFD Lab). AT the CFD Lab, interactive color graphics workstations provide job preparation and post-processing capabilities. The applications engineer can inspect complex configurations before beginning calculations and can obtain immediate pictorial understanding of the results.

Maintenance

The productivity of scientists and engineers depends upon a stable and reliable system, and effective maintenance of both hardware and software is essential to this stability.

Preventive maintenance on hardware is normally supplied by the vendor on a regular schedule, usually on a weekly basis. Additional maintenance will be required to fix hardware problems as they arise. Maintenance is also required on systems software to test and install vendor updates and local enhancements, and to locate and correct errors. Since supercomputers are an expensive and critical resource, it is important to minimize the time that they are out of service for hardware and software maintenance. Some outages are unavoidable. As specified in the maintenance plan, sufficient time for preventive maintenance must be provided and it will be necessary to remove the system from production use for software maintenance and error corrections.

To facilitate maintenance and minimize supercomputer down-time, quick take-down and start-up procedures for operators should be provided to allow active jobs to be suspended and restarted after maintenance. Also extensive use of vendor supplied operating system simulators for software debugging and a thorough quality assurance and problem management program to detect and correct software errors before they can become part of the system should be offered. These same procedures also help in acceptance testing of new hardware and fosters cooperation among all parties involved.

Systems Software

Systems software for supercomputers (e.g., operating systems, compilers, utilities, etc.) has matured over the last five years, but enhancements or modifications are often necessary to address site specific requirements. These requirements might include accounting and account management, connectivity and sharing of data among disparate hosts, security, resource management, data center operations, and additional utilities for the user community.

The highly interconnected nature of a supercomputer environment creates a greater need than is normally found in conventional mainframe installations for systems software to address the global problems of the computer center (e.g., connectivity, accounting, data sharing). Also, since supercomputer users are migrating from other computer systems, they often request favorite features and utilities to be ported to the supercomputer.

Boeing has developed an extensive set of supercomputer systems software and a number of features have been accepted by Cray Research for incorporation into their standard systems software. Some of the most significant efforts have been in the areas of accounting, validation, and account management. In an environment consisting of a Cray X-MP, with Cyber, IBM and VAX front-ends, all account validation is performed against a single validation file. Users have to deal with only one account rather than one for each processing service, and the account maintenance organization has only one set of accounts and validation information. Similarly, all of the accounting information generated during job execution on the X-MP or the Cybers is processed through a single system.

Supercomputer applications often require large volumes of data. Since it may not be possible to configure enough on-line storage directly on the supercomputer to satisfy demand, Boeing has addressed the problem by building a File Management System that expands the on-line storage capacity of a supercomputer. Additional capabilities such as data sharing between diverse systems (e.g., Cray, CDC, IBM); uniform access to multilevel storage hierarchy (e.g., disk and tape); and a tree-structured directory which contains file attributes such as titles and keywords are also provided.

Application Software

A computing environment must include supporting applications software, such as graphics and mathematical libraries, and application programs used by a diverse community of users. These software tools make efficient use of the supercomputer resources and help to increase productivity by reducing the lead time from problem conception to solution.

Today, many supercomputers are used in an environment where the applications programmer is developing a job file on a workstation. Depending upon the size of the problem, the job is submitted to run on either the supercomputer or a conventional mainframe and output is routed back to the workstation for post-processing. Versions of the applications program must be available on the supercomputer and the conventional mainframe, and they must both communicate with the workstation. As applications are added or modified, care must be taken to ensure that high performance is still achieved on the supercomputer. Stable communications must be maintained between processing tiers, program versions remain under careful version control, and users are provided with necessary documentation updates and timely consultation.

As a result of the complexity of the architectures for a supercomputer system, the requirements for discipline and organization in the acquisition, installation, and consultation for such software are generally more pronounced.

Communication Network

The external communications requirements for a supercomputer system, much like those of a conventional mainframe, are dictated by the geographic dispersion of its user community. Distributing the power of a supecomputer to the user community, which may be centrally located or widely scattered, requires a communications network consisting of lines, modems, and communications processors. Security may be a prime concern as well be the potential problem of bridges and gateways to other networks (e.g., Apollo domain, Digital Equipment DECNET, etc.).

Access to a supercomputer installation may be tightly contained within a building or campus, or it might be best to form a regional supercomputer center with extensive outside communications. Another possibility might be an arrangement of regional supercomputer centers, each with a mini-supercomputer (e.g., SCS, Alliant, Convex, etc.) with attached workstations to service local centers.

User Support

Conversion and optimization services are offered to users of vector computers who need the services of highly qualified analysts, expert in the fields of software conversion and optimization. They will enable the user to take advantage quickly of the capacity of a new supercomputer by simplifying the task of converting programs from conventional mainframes to a supercomputer. The key thing to remember, of course, is that the reduced run time is not an end in itself. What is important is that shorter run times will multiply the productivity of the scientists and engineers and allow them to tackle larger and more difficult problems, thus enabling a technical competitive edge.

Because supercomputer architecture is different from conventional mainframes, some work beyond routine code conversion will usually produce significant gains. This leads to apparently conflicting goals: better performance by exploiting the architecture of a supercomputer (i.e., machine dependence) vs. code portability to adapt to a changing environment.

Boeing has developed a methodology for systematically and efficiently converting applications programs by making use of a variety of productivity tools. This methodology allows optimizing programs for a given architecture while supporting program portability.

Hardware vendor-supplied vectorizing compilers and analysis tools are used for general program conversion and performance enhancement.

Two Boeing-developed building block libraries, BCSLIB and VectorPak, are used to assist in further optimization. BCSLIB is a general set of FORTRAN callable mathematical functions. VectorPak is a library of highly optimized, possibly machine dependent, computational kernels. It is accessed directly or through BCSLIB.

Codes are analyzed using software analysis tools to determine which portions are most computationally intensive. These key portions can often be replaced by calls to BCSLIB or VectorPak. This analyze/optimize procedure is often an iterative process.

Program portability is maintained with the use of BCSLIB and VectorPak because only the VectorPak kernels are machine dependent, and FORTRAN equivalents of VectorPak routines can be employed on nonvector computers. Thus, with these libraries, the user not only attains high performance on supercomputer architectures but also maintains portability.

We have also developed an educational program called the Supercomputer Institute Program which provided three intensive, month long seminars to attendees representing universities throughout the United States and Canada sponsored by the National Science Foundation, the Department of Defense, and the National Institutes of Health. This is not classroom training, but rather an intensive examination of the research perspectives that can be gained by using modern supercomputers. An active program of user training and communication is an integral part of a successful supercomputer environment. Users groups, newsletters, and forums are used to ensure timely forecasting and feedback on changes in the environment and services.

Implementation and Operations

Supercomputer center services necessary for a successful supercomputer installation include operations, on-line storage backup and archiving, performance analysis and tuning, and training and documentation. These services are familiar to any large computer center operation and are essential to the effective management, operation, and protection of system resources.

An item that is often overlooked in the planning of a supercomputer center is the interface with equipment vendors for facility acceptance and installation planning and support. Receiving and testing equipment, operations tools and procedures, and performance analysis and tuning are all elements of the day-to-day operations management of the center. Individuals who will act as a single point of contact must be equipped with updated procedures and techniques for the new environment.

Transition Management

Recent improvements in vector computers consisting of improved performance, increased memory, and additional I/O speed, have created a new opportunity for a large number of users who have not been able to solve their large, compute-intensive problems on traditional mainframe computers. Transition Management recognizes a path for engineering and scientific users to move or transition from the machine environment they are currently using, to an enriched environment containing advanced, vector processing computers.

Transition Management helps the user to gain insights into the new challenges raised by vector computing and assess the impact from an objective perspective. The analysis should be made in systems integration, facilities requirements for hardware, communications and networking, software conversion and optimization, training, current applications, requirements for new applications, user environments, and program planning and control.

Potential users of supercomputers should be offered the ability to achieve rapid utilization of this new resource. Provision must be made for code analysis and benchmarking, conversion services, optimization services, and training. Using advanced software tools and libraries, software conversion and optimization can be performed prior to the arrival of the supercomputer. By performing these services in advance of delivery, the impact on productivity to the user at installation is reduced and the customer achieves a much higher utilization of the supercomputer sooner. Migration to the new system, then, becomes an installation and verification procedure performed by experts, rather than an intense conversion activity on a new system by untrained or newly trained personnel.

End-to-End Accountability

In addition to all of the individual components of a total supercomputing environment, you will need something else: the "glue" to make all of the parts come together, and to keep them working smoothly in concert. The glue is Mission Management provided by one organization to ensure end-to-end accountability in a multi-vendor environment and that the system architecture in place supports change and growth.

The well known difficulties of problem identification and resolution in a multi-vendor environment are compounded with the introduction of new vendors and connectivity in a supercomputer installation. No matter how well intentioned and cooperative the various parties may be (e.g., data center, computer vendors, software vendors, communications suppliers), consistently successful problem resolution will occur only if there is one organization that can be held accountable for making sure that things are working correctly.

One organization should be accountable for the complete startup process from early development and procurement, through installation and acceptance, to production use of the supercomputer. One organization should be accountable for isolating and resolving user problems, for seeing that the supercomputer is successfully integrated into the existing data center, for providing access from existing systems, sharing data among computers, and coordinating conversion and optimization of applications programs.

3. ALABAMA EXPERIENCE

History and Objectives

In January 1987, Boeing was awarded the contract to design, implement, and manage the Alabama Supercomputer Network (ASN) for the State of Alabama. The original idea for the state to obtain a supercomputer was advanced by former Governor George C. Wallace in a meeting in April 1984 with officials from the University of Alabama System and Auburn University. The objectives of the proposal were to install a supercomputer and a high speed communications network which would be used to:

1. Enhance research and graduate programs of Alabama Universities
2. Attract high technology industry to the State of Alabama
3. Provide disaster backup for state data processing facilities

In 1986, the Alabama Supercomputer Network Authority (ASNA) was organized to initiate the plan for a state-of-the-art supercomputer network. The Authority recognized that the design, implementation, and management of such a network should be contracted to a firm specializing in systems integration and facilities management. The plan was to include a supercomputer to be located in a new state facility in Huntsville, with eight nodal sites (located at major universities around the state) connecting to the supercomputer via high speed communication lines. There were several important aspects to the proposal by Boeing which contributed to a very successful installation.

System Design

The centerpiece of the ASN (See Figure 2) is a CRAY X-MP/24 which has two processors and four million words of central memory. In addition, it contains two I/O processors, a 32 million word Solid State Storage Device (SSD) and 13 DD-49 disks. UNICOS was chosen over COS as the operating system. This was not an easy decision. At the time the decision was made (December 1986), UNICOS was still a very immature operating system and there was a very limited amount of applications software available. However, Cray Research, Inc. (CRI) was committed to UNICOS as the operating system of the future for all of CRI's products. Another important factor was that COS is a batch operating system with some interactive capability, whereas UNICOS is an interactive operating system with a batch subsystem. Starting with COS and migrating to UNICOS at some future time would have complicated the design of the front-end machines and the network, as well as would have required extensive conversion for users.

Network Design

The X-MP is connected to a Network Systems Corporation (NSC) HYPERchannel and front-ended with two Digital Equipment (DEC) VAX 8250s. The 8250s are also connected to an Ethernet which contains all of the communication devices for the state-wide network. At each of the nodes, a small Ethernet is employed to logically extend the local network to the central site. Each node employs either a VAX 8250 or an IBM 9370-65 as a nodal computer. TCP/IP was chosen as the protocol on the network because it appears to be the most flexible for future expansion of the network. The versatility of our network design allowed the universities to choose either a DEC or IBM nodal computer as well as the capability of connecting a wide range of workstations.

Facilities

In order to have a stable operating environment, careful attention must be paid to the physical requirements of the facility. The State decided to build a new facility in Huntsville for the supercomputer rather than try to renovate an existing building. Neither the architect nor the builder had ever built a computer center for a supercomputer. Boeing supplied numerous suggestions on modifications and monitored the progress of the building. These suggestions were in the areas of air conditioning, floor layout, floor support, continuous power supply, electrical wiring, mechanical requirements, and security protection.

Bellevue Integration Laboratory

The schedule for the installation of the supercomputer and the network was dictated by the date on which the building could be occupied, which was November 1987. Since Boeing has an X-MP and a HYPERchannel in Bellevue, Washington, we decided to develop a small replica of the Alabama network. This allowed us to learn several important aspects of the design prior to the installation in Alabama. Some of these were the resolution of several errors in vendor supplied documentation and software, the check out of several design considerations, the development of operating procedures, the development of an accounting package for UNICOS, and perhaps most important, the provision of some valuable training for our systems analysts.

Fast Start

The Fast Start program was designed to give potential users of the ASN access to and training on Boeing's X-MP prior to installation of the Alabama equipment. This was accomplished by first giving a series of lectures on state-of-the-art supercomputing, classroom training on how to access the Boeing X-MP and vectorization techniques, development of a complete user manual, and one-on-one consulting. Over 350 attended the introductory lectures and over 75 used the Boeing X-MP. All of the original allocation of the Fast Start program was utilized by the universities. There were a few problems in that the Boeing X-MP runs COS instead of UNICOS and users had low speed (1200 baud) access. Other user support came from the Engineering and Scientific Services (ESS) organization in Bellevue. ESS consists of approximately 180 highly trained staff in numerous mathematical, engineering, chemical and physical disciplines.

Installation

The building was completed as scheduled. This allowed for the X-MP and all of the associated equipment to be installed as scheduled. During December and January, friendly users were allowed to access the network and supercomputer to help resolve any problems. The entire system was put through a 30-day acceptance for the State beginning February 1, 1988. During this period, the CRAY was available 99.9 percent of the time while the network and the nodal machines were available, respectively, 99.7 percent and 99.8 percent of the time.

Application Software and User Support

In order for a supercomputer to be properly utilized, it is vital that high quality applications software be available and for the users to be adequately trained. Boeing has installed a number of commercially available software packages and converted numerous others to the UNICOS operating system. Just as in the Fast Start program, heavy emphasis has been placed on training. Boeing has taught over forty classes around the state on the introduction to the UNICOS operating system, access to the network, and vectorization techniques. This has allowed the utilization of the machine to grow at a much faster pace than was originally planned.

Lessons Learned

The systems integrator must be able to supply expertise in all of these areas if the design, implementation, and ongoing management of the supercomputer facility is to be successful. Boeing's proposal to the State of Alabama had all of these ingredients and they proved to be valuable to the success of the design and implementation phases of the project. The Fast Start program, the Bellevue integration lab, and the access to the Engineering and Scientific Services organization were aspects that the State of Alabama considered as real selling points. The ESS staff consulted with a number of users on special problems. The Bellevue facilities staff made a number of recommendations on the new building which helped to eliminate some potential costly delays. The Bellevue integration lab resolved a number of problems and this contributed significantly to a smooth installation. Through the Fast Start program, we were able to get over 75 users trained on the use of the X-MP prior to the installation in Alabama. Upon Installation, these users, as well as many others, were able to immediately utilize the supercomputer with only a short introduction to UNICOS. Since installation, the utilization of the supercomputer has grown faster than originally planned. The Alabama experience has shown how important it is for the contractor to have experience in all phases of systems integration and facilities management.

4. CONCLUSIONS

The supercomputer is a part – albeit a very big part – of the environment and must work in concert with a series of solution support systems that include:

- Facilities: a fully **operational and reliable** computing environment.
- Supporting Hardware: supporting computer mainframes and integration software to maximize the efficiency of a supercomputer.
- Maintenance: fully operational procedures to facilitate maintenance of hardware and software system.
- Systems Software: an operating system which drives the supercomputer and integration software which links the multiple computers together.
- Applications Software: to provide the discipline and organization in the acquisition, installation, and consultation of application programs.
- Communication Network: to provide the data communication network and to support the total supercomputer systems environment.
- User Support: to provide efficient data center service and to give training and documentation for successful management and operation of a supercomputer center.
- Implementation and Operations: To establish a single point of contact in the day-to-day operational management of the center that is trained and equipped with procedures and techniques to work in the new environment.
- Transition Management: facilities provided by a combination of software tools and skills for analysis and conversion of software, to achieve a higher utilization of the new resource sooner.
- Mission Management: the binding force which an experienced systems integrator provides in the integration of all the components of a successful supercomputer center.

5. REFERENCES

- D. Choi and C. Levit, Implementation of Distributed Interactive Graphics System, the International Journal of Supercomputer Applications, Vol. 1, No. 4, 1987, pp. 82-95.
- K. A. Frenkel, The Art and Science of Visualizing Data, Comm. ACM, Vol. 31, No. 2, 1988, pp. 111-121.
- H. S. Stone, High Performance Computer Architectures, Addison-Wesley Publishing Co., 1987.

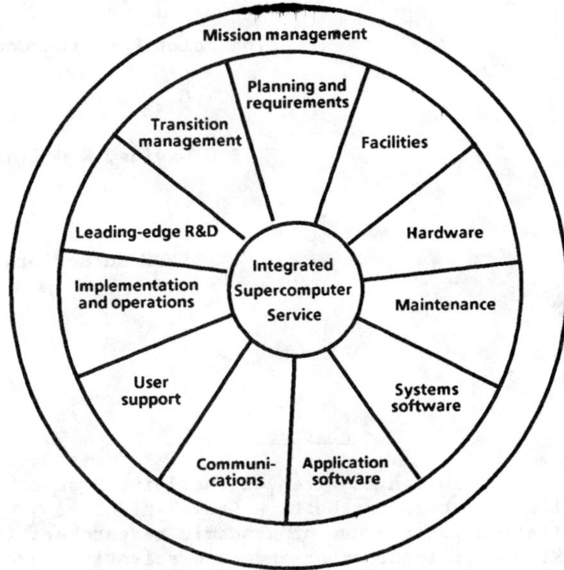

Figure 1

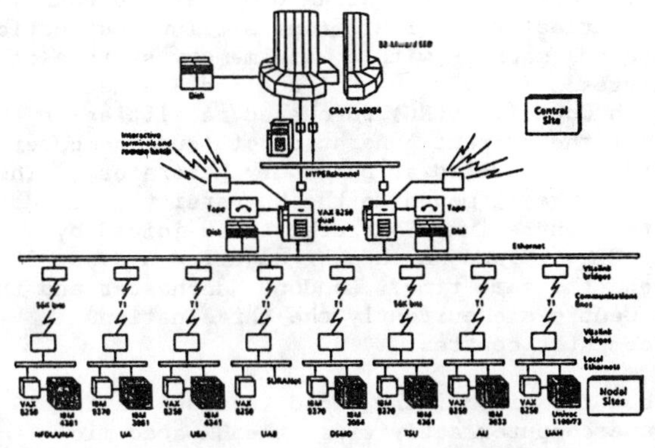

Figure 2

The Joint Research Councils' Supercomputing Unit

B W Davies, R G Evans, T Daniels, D J Rigby

SERC Rutherford Appleton Laboratory

Abstract

A brief description is given of the Joint Research Councils Supercomputer Unit, a Cray X-MP/48 installation for the use of academic researchers in the UK. Operational experience and scientific use of the machine is discussed.

Introduction

The history of academic supercomputing in the UK dates probably from the provision of the original Ferranti 'Atlas' at the Atlas Computer Laboratory in 1964. 'Atlas' was a 1 MIP (one million instruction per second) machine with a main memory storage of 256 Kbytes. In 1979 the Science and Engineering Research Council (SERC) purchased facilities on the first of the current generation of 'supercomputers' the Cray-1, operated at Daresbury Laboratory. The Daresbury Cray-1 moved to the University of London computer Centre in 1983 (later to be joined by a second Cray-1) and Manchester acquired a Cyber 205 at about the same time. London, Manchester and the Atlas Centre are currently the three national supercomputer centres.

At about the time of the rapid increase in the US NSF supercomputer activities, the UK academic funding bodies (ie the Advisory Board for the Research Councils, the University Grants Committee and the Computer Board) set up a working party under Prof John Forty of the University of Warwick (now Vice Chancellor of Stirling University) to investigate the UK requirement. The working party set out to look at the need for supercomputing facilities over the whole of academic research, in the social sciences and humanities, as well as the traditional areas of science and engineering.

The Forty working party looked at a variety of disciplines and concluded that there was a strong scientific case for the central provision of a supercomputer of the most powerful type available. A technical sub- group looked at the technical options including a variety of manufacturers and architectures and concluded that a tried and proven system such as the Cray X-MP/48 was the best option. The potential of highly parallel systems to provide high power at low cost was recognised and the Forty report recommended support to develop more advanced hardware and software on machines of this type, particularly those of UK manufacture.

Since a supercomputer would necessarily be 'remote' for most of its users it was regarded as essential to upgrade the UK academic network 'JANET' and the panel endorsed a £5M programme proposed by the Computer Board.

As a result of the Forty report the ABRC made available the necessary capital for a Cray X-MP/48 to be installed at the Rutherford Appleton Laboratory where it is operated by SERC on behalf of all the Research Councils and the British Academy.

On a futuristic note, the Forty report recommended that in three years the Cray X-MP should be augmented by the new state of the art machine, eg a Cray-3 or Cray Y-MP, and thereafter a new machine should be acquired every three years.

The Cray X-MP/48 was delivered to the Atlas Centre on December 3 1986. Installation and commissioning by Cray engineers were completed on January 12 1987. Acceptance tests were completed on February 1 and a trial service to users started the next day. Peer Review access and control was introduced on April 1, and the computer was formally opened by the Secretary of State for Education and Science, the Right Honourable Kenneth Baker MP, on April 15. From installation stage to the end of this first period the commissioning and operation of the facility has been very successful. As this paper demonstrates, the large number of users attached and the progress to date fully justify the decision to procure a Cray X-MP/48.

CH2617-9/88/0000/0450$01.00 © 1988 IEEE

Hardware Description

The major components of the hardware installation at the Atlas Centre are shown in Figure 1. As its name implies the Cray X-MP/48 has four central processors and 8 Mwords of real memory. Each processor has a 8.5 nsec cycle time and with both vector floating point units active has a peak performance of 235 MFlops. If it is possible to assign all four cpu's to an individual job then the X-MP/48 is almost a 1 GFlop machine. In addition to the 8 Mwords of memory the machine is provided with 32 Mwords of 'solid state disk' (SSD) with a bandwidth of 1000 Mbytes/sec. The system software enables the user to treat the solid state disk exactly as a conventional disk drive.

Twelve DD49 disk drives, each with a capacity of 1.2 Gbytes and a data transfer rate of 40 Mbytes/sec, provide a total of 14 Gbytes of 'conventional' disk storage for the X-MP/48. Past experience has shown that disk storage capacity is one of the major bottlenecks limiting performance of supercomputers, particularly if data is staged out to the front-end in significant quantities. The amount available on the X-MP was judged adequate to support currently executing jobs, but was clearly inadequate to hold more than a small fraction of the permanent filestore. An alternative solution to staging data to the front end was found by exploiting an existing Masstor M860 storage system.

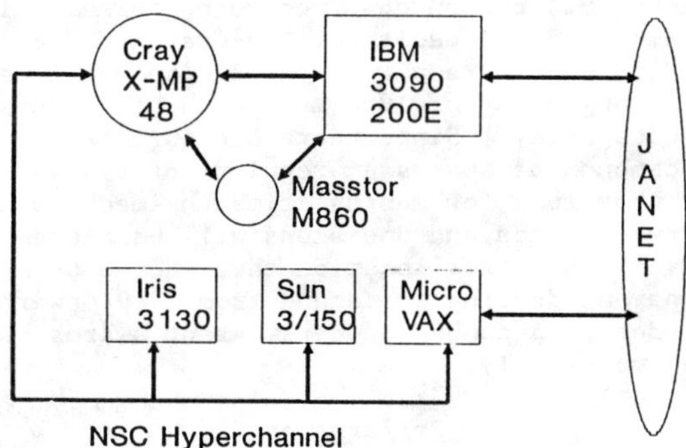

Figure 1

Our model of M860 is capable of storing 110 Gbytes on reusable cartridges containing 66 feet of 2.7 inch tape recorded using a helical scan rotary head. An automatic cartridge retrieval mechanism means the device is able to retrieve data from any part of its store in less than 20 seconds without operator intervention. Soon after installing the X-MP it was established that the M860 could be successfully attached to its IBM channel interface, where it appears as a bank of 3420 tape drives. The problem of driving the control part of the M860 (to instruct it which cartridge to mount) was quickly solved by trapping the mount messages issued by COS to the station software in the IBM front-end, and using the existing driver running under VM to control the M860. Thus control is exercised from the IBM front end, but data flows directly from the M860 to the Cray. (We understand Cray Research are considering a similar technique to support such devices in a general way under UNICOS). With these arrangements the Cray archive product was found to work to the M860 without modification. It provides a means of migrating data from disk to M860 automatically and from M860 to disk on demand. The resulting two level 'disk store' is completely invisible to users and provides the capacity to hold virtually the entire file store on line.

The system was introduced early in 1987 and has provided a reliable and valuable service since then. As a result data staging to the front-ends is completely negligible.

The success of this scheme is limited only by the capacity of our M860, which is shared with the IBM service. At present around 30 Gbytes are used by the Cray, although this is likely to grow. We are currently looking with great interest at automated cartridge stores which use standard IBM 3480 cartridges as an alternative means of providing higher capacity for minimum cost, although models of the M860 with Terabyte capacities are now available. An extremely large filestore is seen as an essential component of a supercomputing service for the 1990's.

System Software

The Cray X-MP/48 runs the standard Cray batch job operating system COS version 1.16. With the relatively small SSD size on this installation the SSD roll-out feature first introduced in COS1.16 has been essential in maintaining good high priority turnaround to jobs requesting large SSD allocations. The intention is at some future date to migrate to UNICOS since it provides the interactive facilities which are increasingly regarded as an essential feature of all advanced computing systems, however until 1989 UNICOS will lack some features such as archive support. It is possible to run 'guest' operating systems on the Cray X-MP but at present with rather inflexible allocations of cpu and memory. For this reason we do not anticipate running concurrent COS and UNICOS user services but we will run UNICOS in this mode as soon as possible for familiarisation.

An unusual feature of our installation is that the Cray job scheduling and accounting is largely controlled by the IBM VM front-end. This has the advantage that changes to the scheduling algorithm are easy to install since they do not involve any changes to COS. This was seen as being particularly valuable during the start-up period when changes to job scheduling were expected to be required frequently.

The scheme adopted relies on manipulating the COS job priority by commands from a locally written scheduler running under VM. The scheduler is notified of the entry and exit of jobs by messages sent via the station from locally written versions of the CHARGES and ACCOUNT programs which are invoked at the start and end of every job. Jobs in the input queue are held at priority zero which ensures they do not begin execution until required. The scheduler then simply sets the priority to suitable non-zero value whenever it wants to place a job into execution. The algorithm which determines the order of execution of work is then totally separate from COS. The dispatching of jobs once they enter execution is controlled by COS in a completely standard way.

The information about a job required by the scheduler is held under VM in an SQL database, and can easily be interrogated by users. Accounting data is held in a similar way, also under VM. These systems are very similar to the scheduling and accounting systems used to control our VM batch and MVS services, permitting much of the code to be common.

Front End Services

For most users the Cray is front-ended by an IBM 3090/200E running VM/CMS which also provides computing services to several hundred SERC and university users. In June 1988 IBM announced that the Atlas Centre was to be its UK centre for supercomputing, and we anticipate installing a 3090/600E with six vector facility processors later this year.

A microVAX running VMS is provided for general Cray use but is limited to about 50 users. Any university user in the UK can submit Cray jobs from his local machine provided that it supports the Job Transfer and Manipulation Protocol (JTMP) or File Transfer Protocol (FTP) defined on the JANET network. Currently about 90% of Cray jobs come from the IBM front end, about 5% via JTMP/FTP and 5% from the VAX.

Sun 3/160 and Silicon Graphics Iris 3130 workstations provide a UNIX front end service but only on the RAL site. The VAX and UNIX machines are connected to the Cray by a NSC hyperchannel.

The Sun 3/160 provides users with access to the FORGE software for analysing and optimising Cray FORTRAN source code. Currently we have a single user licence for FORGE on the Sun, but we are collaborating with Pacific Sierra on a multi user VM/CMS version which will make FORGE more asily useable by our remote users. The Iris 3130 is a high performance colour graphics workstation intended for interactive manipulation and display of data generated on the Cray. Currently the interaction is only at the level of file transfer using the Cray station software, but tighter coupling should be possible when UNICOS is introduced.

The Cray X-MP/48 is operated by staff of the Atlas Centre of the Rutherford Appleton Laboratory on behalf of all the Research Councils. There is a management committee, the Atlas Centre Supercomputer Committee (ACSC), chaired by Professor A J Forty. The interface between the Atlas Centre and its users is via a User Meeting convened by Professor Pert of York who is an ex-officio member of the ACSC. There is also a bi-monthly users' newsletter, ARCLIGHT.

Peer Review and the Computing Workload

Access to the computer, other than for use by industry or other paying customers, is via Peer Reviewed grant application to one of the Research Councils or to the British Academy. There are also arrangements, delegated to the Head of the Atlas Centre, for giving pump-priming access of up to five cpu hours of Cray time to potential grant applicants who wish to run small jobs in order to assess the amount of computing to request in a subsequent application.

Figure 2 shows the demand approved by Peer Review in cpu hours per month over the period April 1987 to March 1991, broken down according to scientific discipline. The capacity of the Cray X-MP/48 is about 2200 cpu hours per month, and so commitment from the beginning of 1988 is approaching the machine capacity. Since there are further announcements of awards at regular intervals it is likely that in a few months' time the machine will be over-committed and decisions will be needed on the levels of over allocation that should be made. The apparent decline in demand from 1989 onwards is simply due to a number of early grant awards being for two years only.

Performance

The Cray X-MP/48 hardware has proved very reliable in service, granted that the amount of preventive maintenance required (6 hours per week) is well above the norm for conventional computers. The Cray operating system software initially failed on average six times per week, but is now running with only one or two failures per week which is about the average for other Cray X-MP installations. Our statistics on machine availability are shown in Figure 3.

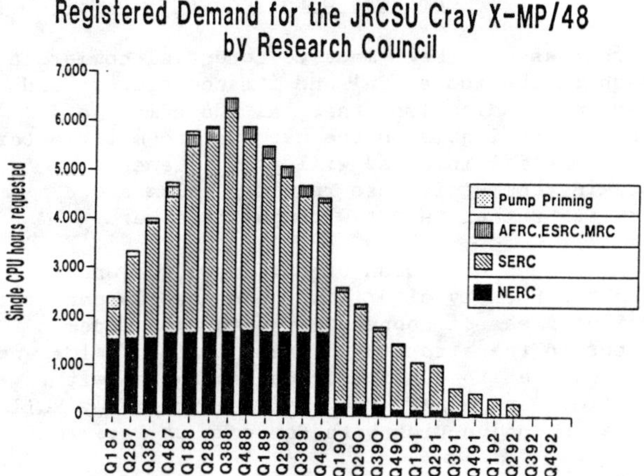

Figure 2

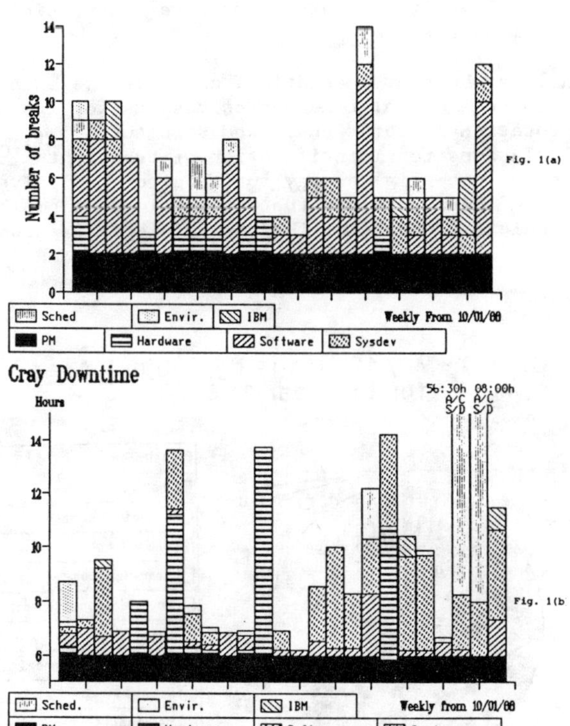

Figure 3

Since August 1987 it has been possible to monitor the performance that users are extracting from the Cray on individual jobs. Figure 4 shows a histogram of the average MFlops (millions of floating point operations) per processor second attained. The average weighted by job time is 39.5 Megaflops, a significant number of jobs are achieving over 100 Megaflops, and a few jobs reach 200 Mflops. Almost all these jobs run on a single processor of the Cray X-MP/48, for which the theoretical maximum performance is about 235 Mflops. The statistics on Mflops are broken down according to scientific discipline, but the only conclusion we would wish to make from this is that users (typically the environmental sciences and some chemists) with large production codes are well optimised.

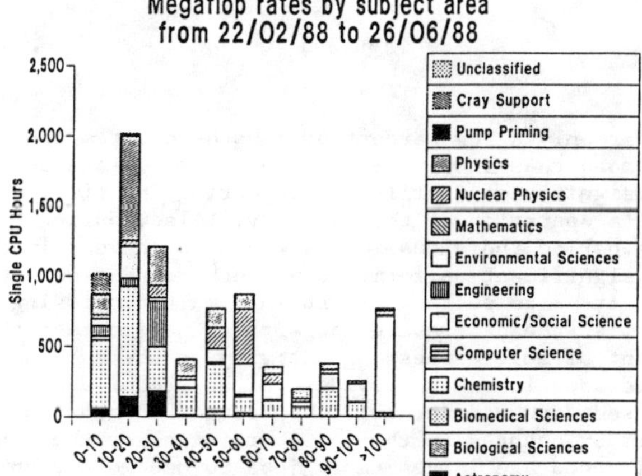

Figure 4

One of the features that distinguishes the Cray X-MP/48 from the supercomputers at ULCC and UMRCC is its larger memory. As is to be expected users are beginning to exploit this, and Figure 5 shows distribution of job memory sizes in the period August-November 1987 which shows substantial activity up to 4 Mwords. The lack of jobs above 4 Mwords causes us some concern that users with the largest jobs may be receiving poor turnaround.

To sustain efficient overall performance of the Cray X-MP/48 as job memory sizes grow, users will have to be encouraged to make their large memory jobs use more than one processor by using 'multi-tasking' and 'micro-tasking' techniques. Otherwise for example it would be possible for the 8 Mword memory to be occupied by a sequence of pairs of 3-4 Mword jobs each of which used only one processor. In such circumstances two of the machine's four processors would be idle and half the overall processing power would be unused.

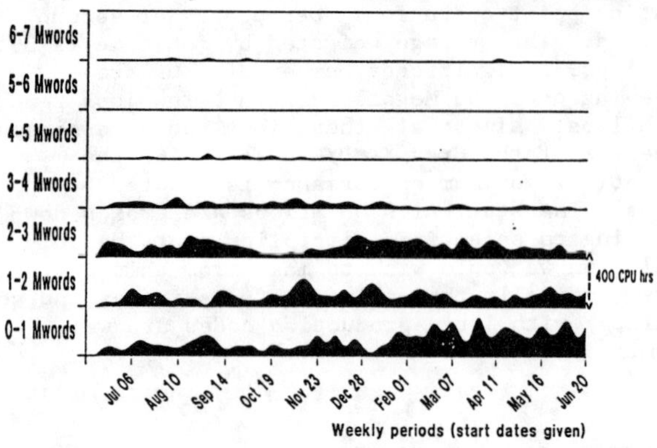

Figure 5

So far only a few percent of jobs have attempted to use more than one processor. This has not caused any significant inefficiencies during the first year's operation of the facility. Also, during this period individual users would not have gained any significant performance or turn-round time benefits from putting effort into multiprocessing. Staff at the centre are now working to increase the amount of multiprocessing activity on the machine. Assistance is being provided in the techniques to be used, and pressure will be brought to bear on users by changes in the job charging algorithm that will encourage large memory jobs to use more than one processor. On the positive side, some of the largest projects have already spontaneously adapted their programs for multiprocessing on the basis that this is a prerequisite for making real progress in the longer term. It is likely that this view will gradually become accepted by other large projects as they complete the first round of advances that the Cray has enabled and they look to their longer term plans.

Prior to release COS 1.16 of the Cray operating jobs using the Solid State Device for file storage were not 'rolled-out' by jobs of higher priority. This has meant that some users have had some difficulties with high priority jobs being blocked by low priority work. Following the introduction of COS 1.16 the scheduling of the SSD as a generic resource has greatly improved and users have responded very favourably.

Scientific Support

A small Advanced Research Computing Unit (ACRU) has been set up at the Atlas Centre to provide skilled computational science support for users of the Cray X-MP/48 and to foster the use of supercomputing in new areas including collaboration with industry. It is hoped to build the unit up to about 12 staff.

Contacts with Industry

Approaches have been made to potential commercial users in the industrial and finance sectors and there are indications that, as the number of packages available on the machine becomes greater, so commercial interest will grow. Generally speaking commercial use requires value added services rather than raw computing power.

Two meetings have been organised in conjunction with the Society of British Aerospace Companies to examine areas of cooperation with the academic sector in the aircraft and aero engine fields and this has led to continuing collaboration with Cranfield and a research position funded by Rolls Royce in conjunction with Pembroke College, Oxford.

The Scientific Programme

Since the JRCSU provides a service to all the UK universities and Research Councils its scientific programme is naturally very diverse and cannot be described comprehensively. The distribution of machine use by scientific discipline, shown in Figure 6 shows an equitable spread over many subject areas. Some of the larger, or more interesting programmes are:

* A large body of theoretical chemists use both ab initio and molecular mechanics methods for instance in rotational/vibrational band structure calculations for identification of transient species, potential energy surfaces for explosives, study of catalysts and the interactions of small molecules and proteins for pharmacological purposes.

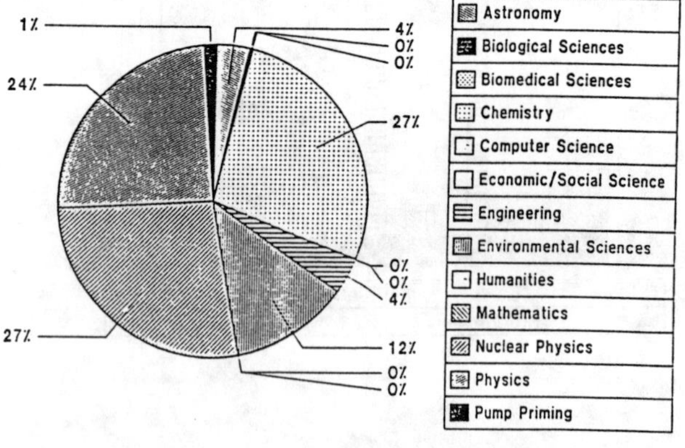

Figure 6

* Protein crystallographers are integrating the X-ray observations with molecular dynamics modelling to give a mutual constraints analysis and structure refinement time down from six months to a few hours of X-MP time.

* Atomic physics calculations now find a variety of applications in other areas of science, for example in astrophysical (stellar) opacities, in thermonuclear fusion plasmas (JET) and in the emerging science of X-ray lasers.

* Band structure calculations of the new high temperature super- conductors are being carried out for a variety of stoichiometries while fluids such as liquid neon and liquid helium where quantum effects dominate are also being studied.

* Astrophysical applications include atomic physics calculations, precision modelling of earth satellite orbits, gravitational many body simulations and pulsar searches involving 32 million point Fourier transforms.

* Environmental modelling is a large user of machine time with three large projects studying the North Sea, the Antarctic Ocean and Global Atmospheric Modelling

* Crack propagation in metals is simulated by high resolution finite element methods with elastic/plastic flow models. This is being applied to such critical structures as PWR pressure vessels.

* From the social sciences area, the Cray X-MP is being used to study the regional statistics on cancer cases, and establishing a bias-free significance for apparent geographical 'clusters'.

Conclusions

1. There is a high level of demand from within the UK universities for a machine of this performance.

2. Users are limited in the speed with which they can take up awards of machine time by outside factors such as recruitment of post-doctoral research workers.

3. The use of the M860 as a filestore is easy, works well, is well liked by users and reduces the load on the front end by a large factor. It also allows the Cray disks to be used mainly for temporary files.

4. Users with large production codes will put a substantial effort into code performance, while others must trade off machine time versus human time.

Author Index

Author Index